COLD-BLOODED

THE TUCSON MURDERS

ALSO BY JOHN GILMORE

On the Run with Bonnie and Clyde

Inside Marilyn Monroe

Crazy Streak

L.A. Despair

Severed: The True Story of the Black Dahlia Murder

Laid Bare: A Memoir of Wrecked Lives and the Hollywood Death Trip

Fetish Blonde

Live Fast - Die Young: Remembering the Short Life of James Dean

The Real James Dean

Manson: The Unholy Trail of Charlie and the Family

Hollywood Boulevard

COLD-BLOODED
THE TUCSON MURDERS

JOHN GILMORE

AMOK
LOS ANGELES

Amok Books edition, 2014

Cover design by Ross Goza and Carson Gilmore
Copy editing by John Tottenham
Book design by Carson Gilmore
Published by Amok Books
Los Angeles, California

First Edition
Bibliographic Information for Library of Congress
Cataloging-in-Publication Data

Gilmore, John, 1935-
Cold-Blooded: The Tucson Murders
by John Gilmore

ISBN-13: 978-1-878923-25-7

1. Schmid, Charles, 1942-1975. 2. True Crime - American History - Southwest Americana - Crime journalism - 1960s. 3. Criminals - Arizona - Tucson. 4. Serial Murder. 5. Criminal court trials

Amok Books are available to bookstores through our primary distributor: SCB Distributors, 15608 South New Century Drive, Los Angeles, CA 90248. Phone: 800-729-6423, 310-532-9400. Fax: 310-532-7001.

UK Distributors: Turnaround Distribution, Unit 3, Olympia Trading Estate, Coburg Road, Wood Green, London N22 6TZ. Phone: (0181) 829 3000. Fax: (0181) 881 5088.

To view the complete Amok Books catalog, please go to www.amokbooks.com.

10 9 8 7 6 5 4 3 2 1

PREFACE by JOHN GILMORE

PERHAPS A THOUSAND or more 'hardline' followers of my work have inquired as to why, "way back," I rarely identified myself in my books, despite the praise of critics and scholars, as with this book, *Cold-Blooded: The Tucson Murders*, described as "an American true crime classic;" a following work, *Severed The Story of the Black Dahlia Murder*, received similar recognition. The answer is diamond-clear for me, the author, stepping aside from the rush of reporters and newsmen. I was too closely involved with the principals—be they killers or victims, or others accused of deeds they played no part in. I was there to understand the truth, and I did not want to shift my focus from the truth that I believed to be undeniable. There was no room in these confused, unhappy, disturbed lives for me to call attention to myself. I did not doubt the validity of the highly-charged subjects I'd connected to—creatures dashing about, blindfolded in the dark—nor did I seek to share a single beam from a searchlight into that cave of pure evil.

The reality of what I dealt with in *The Tucson Murders* was beyond a general task. I was climbing inside the head of the key player, Charles Schmid, nicknamed Smitty in high school.

After entrenching myself in Tucson, in an area that was once known as the "Strip," I'd been handling personal matters for Smitty, who'd appointed me his "Personal Manager" following the end of his murder trial where he'd been found guilty of killing two teenage sisters. Our meetings took place at the Pima County Jail, and our correspondence was between Tucson and Los Angeles. We discussed areas of his impressive amount of musings, all specifically written to me and which he warned me were being copied extensively by the prosecuting attorney's office pending Smitty's upcoming trial for the murder of Alleen Rowe, and his trial would proceed, though the victim's body had never been found.

Smitty was transferred to the old territorial prison at Florence, Arizona, where I was fingerprinted, photographed (front and profile views, both sides), and recorded as Smitty's manager. My background was documented along with notations that I was not an attorney, but represented Schmid in other personal matters. The file was stamped "Approved," and Smitty was processed onto Death Row.

We met several times to talk about areas of written material sent to me, and his mental musings in general now that he could see the "little house," the Death Chamber, less than a hundred feet from his cell window.

Alleen was like an angel, pure innocence, and unknown to Smitty before being selected as his victim. When he could no longer contrain himself, he told his part-time girlfriend, Mary French, "I want to kill a girl. I want to see what it's like, and if I can get away with it."

Years later, Mary would say, "There were no bounds for Smitty. He broke all the bounds, all rules, and had no safety nets below. He became no longer the person I knew. Like he wasn't even human anymore. All he could feel, she said, "was what he experienced in himself. He didn't see us as real people anymore. What was inside him was exploding like a bomb."

AUTHOR'S NOTE (1970 Dial Press New York edition)

THE MURDER CHARGES brought against twenty-three-year-old Charles Schmid, Jr., on November 10, 1965, resulted in one of the Southwest's most sensational murder cases. Its notoriety reached around the world. The desert community of Tucson was flooded with reporters, some from as far away as Paris and Tokyo. The pretrial publicity played so heavily on "the gruesome and sordid" aspects of the crimes that several of the reporters claimed it would be impossible to find an impartial jury in Arizona, or perhaps anywhere in the Southwest.

In early February, shortly before Schmid's first murder trial, I became involved in the case as a freelance journalist. The proceedings against Schmid were at once vague and complex. One reporter said, "The sensationalism has overshadowed something important: Many facts of the case fit together like the pieces of a well-made jigsaw puzzle, while others seem to have come from a different box."

It was upon that concept that I felt a thorough presentation of the case would become necessary. But contradictions more inherent in psychology than in judicial matters focused my attention on the individuals accused and those who had been involved in the history of the murders. I believed that only through them could I perhaps understand enough to attempt to relate the events to a reader.

I became acquainted with Charles Schmid, Jr. on the third day of his first trial, and remained the only writer involved with him during that period of his life and the year to follow. All quotations attributed to him are taken from his diaries, letters, and memoranda transferred to me, and from our conversations over several months at Pima County Jail in Tucson, and on Death Row at the Arizona State Penitentiary in Florence.

I have attempted to follow the threads as a single story and present the picture as completely as possible. This book, then, is a reconstruction of that time in Tucson, and all material not derived from official sources, court proceedings, and actual occurrences is the result of extensive interviews and close contact with principals whose names appear throughout the text.

The names of a few individuals who played but a minor role in the cases have been changed. And to those other persons who have chosen to remain anonymous I wish to extend my appreciation for cooperation in the development of this book.

To two persons I am especially indebted, for without their confidence and generous assistance, this work could not have been undertaken. My most grateful acknowledgements go to Major Lois E. Hudson and Mr. Gary Greenberg, of Tucson, Arizona.

JOHN GILMORE
Tombstone, Arizona, 1969

Asked by a *New York Times* reporter, "Do you feel time is passing too quickly?" I answer: like a speeding locomotive on a non-stop track. She says, "So many places—so many people you've experienced..." Again, "Yes," but memories are not of those dark tunnels, nor the scorching, sun-baked desert highways. Two individuals will always remain in memory for their confidence and generous assistance. Though, yes, time has passed quickly, my most grateful and heartfelt acknowledgements remain with Major Lois E. Hudson, former U.S. Army Intelligence, and Mr. Gary Greenberg, writer and television News Director for Tucson, Arizona.

John Gilmore
Hollywood, CA, 2014

PART ONE

ON THE MORNING of November 10, 1965, a police car carrying five officers and detectives and a nineteen-year-old boy drove along River Road, bordering the city of Tucson, Arizona, turned off on a narrow road called Pontatoc, and headed north into the desert. In the early light the land stretched out in sand-gray slopes, rocky, desolate, thick with catclaw and saguaro cactus. Where the asphalt ended pebbles rattled up in the fenders of the car. Trails rutted by countless car and motorcycle wheels branched away from the road like dried tributaries to disappear in the hills.

The boy said, "There's the radio towers."

Leaving the car parked on a trail, the policemen followed the boy past the radio towers through an area littered with empty beer cans, known to local teenagers as the Drinking Spot. Brush and old newspapers, caught by the wind, rolled against the men's legs as they hiked a short distance north. The area was strewn with cans, car parts, seats with jutting springs, punctured tires, junk, and strands of hair. The further they walked, the more hair they found; long reddish-blond hair, clinging to rocks and cactus. Skirting the junk piles, the boy finally stood on open ground atop a small hill; at his feet were disjointed bones and the upper half of a skull. The odor was heavy. A large black stain had spread over the ground in a rectangular shape and seeped into the sand like oil.

"That's Gretchen," the boy said, and as the policemen spread out he walked away, still staring at the ground.

A detective knelt and examined the skull. Glancing up at Bruns, he said, "This looks to me like it would be more like Wendy, don't you think?" The boy came back and looked down at the bones. He stooped, shrugged, stood up and again walked away, Further west he pointed out other bones, and the jawbone of the skull. Similar stains spotted the area and there were signs of digging, as though someone had attempted to shovel a grave in the hard-packed earth. It seemed apparent to the detective that the ground had proved too hard for digging, and that the corpse had been dumped there like the tin cans and car seats. And then the sun, the elements, and the animals had worked over the remains for months.

"Over here," the boy called. Down in a sandy wash, a second skeleton was lying under a mesquite tree, half-clothed in remnants of a jersey blouse, the knees raised and slightly apart. A pair of pinstriped capri pants were wrapped around one leg.

Richie Bruns, the boy leading the police, told them that the two skeletons were the remains of seventeen-year-old Gretchen Fritz and her thirteen-year-old sister, Wendy, both still on the police blotter as missing juveniles. Richie said, "They won't be reported missing anymore." He'd told the Tucson police that both girls had been murdered by Richie's closest friend, Charles Schmid.

In 1942, a pregnant girl came to the Hillcrest Nursing Home in Tucson. She told the proprietors, Mr. and Mrs. Charles Schmid Sr., that she was going to bear a child out of wedlock and did not want to divulge the name of the father. Arrangements were made for the Schmids to adopt the infant.

At eleven o'clock on the night of July 8, 1942, Charles Schmid Jr. was born. The records of the birth, detailing the mother's identity, were sealed within an envelope and held in a Tucson bank, to be given to the child when he reached the age of twenty-one.

The nursing home around which Charles Schmid spent his childhood had been founded in 1921 by Charles Schmid Sr.'s mother. Schmid Sr. was a native of Tucson, had attended Tucson High, and graduated in 1924. When he went to work for the fire department there was only one firehouse in Tucson, with one "shiny new fire truck." When he married Katharine, a registered nurse from New England who came to work in the nursing home, Charles Schmid Sr.'s mother, "a stern old woman with a will like tempered steel," did not approve of the marriage, "and the way Katharine was, big, determined, sometimes cold as ice, the two didn't exactly hit it off."

A sign outside the nursing home, a long whitish one-story building, reads **OVER 31 YEARS' EXPERIENCE IN TUCSON**. Across the street is a neat stucco house with a steel fence surrounding the property, and here the Schmid's live. Next to it stands a smaller one-bedroom house with weathered siding and a green tarpaper roof. It has been on the property for over sixty-six years, and it became the "personal house" of Charles Schmid Jr.

As a child, Charles Schmid was a trickster. His vivid imagination often overshadowed his abilities. A grammar-school teacher recalled her impressions of Schmid in the second grade: "He was an overly curious boy. He was brighter than most but seemed to be interested only in what he wanted to be interested in. The rest—well, it was like when you draw down a window shade."

Another teacher remembered that during his fifth year in grammar school she had been "at a loss to understand him *well.* His behavior was more than proper and he was one of the most courteous boys, he never caused any actual trouble, yet he was unreachable in a way." She said that often he would give "a below-average account of himself, not because he wasn't able to make more of what he was doing, but as though he just didn't care about it."

Schmid has few recollections of his early childhood. He has told friends that his foster father used to whip him at times, "apparently for no reason. I hate him and he hates me. We can't even sit in the same room and talk about the weather without getting into an argument."

To one friend he confided that Katharine Schmid had told

him that she had been in love "with a man that owned 200 suits." Schmid claimed that Katharine often spoke about the "wonderful man with 200 suits, how much she was in love with him," and he told the friend, "When the guy dies, I'll maybe inherit the suits."

"All I really remember about elementary school," he says, "was that I liked the people, but instead of the challenge of learning something new I'd race through assignments to be the first one done, it didn't matter whether I was right or wrong since I seemed to know the answers anyway. The feeling of this knowledge lying dormant gave me the weirdest sense of hallucinations. I'd shut my eyes and the logical solution would appear...."

Schmid recalls that he "loved to run and run and every time I ran I didn't feel frightened. I was very, *very* frightened of being left alone and never went home from school on time because my parents were working and being so alone was dreadfully frightening.

"It seemed I always ran across busy roads, over walls, and into dangerous places where I was liable to be hurt. I didn't know whether this stemmed from a secret desire to hurt myself for attention, or simply because I just wanted to. When I received a bicycle I ran it off hills and down flights of stairs until we finally made a race track."

Paul Graff was Schmid's closest friend in elementary school. Paul's mother found young Schmid's behavior incredible. "He would tell the tallest tales with such a clear-headed attitude that it made one sit in a trance just listening to him. Then he would laugh and joke about it."

Schmid spent one summer riding bicycles with Paul. "I won most all of those races because something inside me made me win. The times I'd lose was due to my recklessness." Schmid enjoyed getting into mischief with Paul. "Paul was different and it fascinated me to be with him, but at times he frightened me at some of the things he'd want to do."

Paul and a friend named Roger once had an adventure that ended with their being sentenced to Fort Grant Industrial School. He had killed a man. It started with the boys running away from home and taking a .22 rifle. After buying some beans at El Rancho Shopping Center, they rode their bikes out of town and camped under a bridge the first night. The next day they hiked, shooting rabbits, and finally ate the last of the beans. They decided to try a holdup. "There just wasn't anything else to do," Paul recalls.

Roger lay in the road, pretending to be hurt, while Paul flagged down a car. Finally an Air Force captain stopped to help them, and Paul thrust the rifle toward his face. "It had a hair trigger," Paul says. "I tried to lower it but I couldn't and it went off and hit him in the cheekbone."

"The guy started to spurt blood," Roger recalls. They dragged the body behind some bushes and hiked out to hide in the desert. By nightfall the sheriff's deputies found them. On the trip back to Tucson in the patrol car, Paul said, "Boy, this is going to be a big story. The biggest one this year. Wait'll you-know-who hears about this. He'll have to shoot two people to catch up with me."

A San Francisco journalist traveling through Tucson in the late 1880s reported it as "a city of mudboxes, dingy and dilapidated, caked and baked into a composite of dust and filth." Some of those adobe hovels remain but the town has changed. From a population of 7,500 in 1900 (Tucson High's graduating class in 1910 consisted of nine seniors), Tucson today has over 309,000 inhabitants. The population more than doubled during World War II. In 1960 it was estimated that the population had grown at a rate of 368.4% over the previous ten years and since then it has quadrupled with subdivision after subdivision rolling out beyond the old city limits into Pima County, taking with it clusters of supermarkets and shopping centers.

Despite its high rate of growth, a bumper sticker stating: TUCSON WANTS INDUSTRY is a frequent sight. There are jobs in copper mining, agriculture, and a complex of air and missile facilities, but these are not enough to meet the demand for work. Many young people are unemployed and the prevailing wage scale is low.

Tucson's schools have failed to accommodate the city's large teenage population. A few of the high schools have devised a system of split sessions. One shift attends classes from 6:00 A.M. to noon, and another from noon until 6:00 P.M. Especially for those students with scholastic ambition, the broken routine presents problems. Many of the families have not lived in Tucson long enough to be considered residents and many leave within a year. There are large numbers of transients and drifters, families as ever-shifting as the desert surrounding Tucson. Their children have little ambition and show a high dropout rate.

A Southern Pacific folder in the 1890s announced that "Tucson receives the sick and sends them away every whit whole." The city has always been a refuge for the infirm, the sick, the disabled, and the retired. Hospitals, nursing homes, and rest centers form an essential part of Tucson's economy. The asthmatic and arthritic are attracted by the perennial sun and consistently dry air, for Tucson is a city surrounded by desert, an island of some eighteen by twenty miles with an elevation of 2,400 feet, situated in a broad valley bordered by mountains that rise from five to nine thousand feet.

Frequently people go out into the desert to commit suicide, and murderers to dispose of their victims. It is said that a corpse decomposes so swiftly in the desert that after six weeks it is hard to tell how long the body has been there. Old people in rest homes have wandered off, as though summoned from their beds, to be absorbed by the elements. One elderly man parked his car, placed his shoes and folded his jacket by the roadside, and walked into the desert. When found days later his body was already partially decomposed.

"Tucson is dead," the kids complain. Most of them are uninterested in school and are unemployable. The desert takes nothing and offers nothing, but remains an encompassing burden. Life is a drag. "There's nothing to do." Every year over 600 teenagers disappear from Tucson, the majority of them girls.

"Downtown?" says a police sergeant. "Hell, after dark you can roll a bowling ball straight through it and not hit a damn thing. Speedway's where the action is. That's where they go."

East Speedway: a long, broad unzoned road reaching from downtown Tucson east across the city, fading into the foothills and cactus, crowded with drive-ins, hamburger havens, service stations, used-car lots, laundromats, and rock 'n' roll clubs. Female minors are admitted to places serving liquor, and boys can obtain false ID cards for around ten dollars.

"You got to have a hot engine, bitchin' wheels," one boy says. "You cruise Johnnie's Drive-In, go around and come out, in the driveway then head down Speedway and back again. Cruise Johnnie's some more or drive out to the desert. If there's no beer parties in the desert, there's always parties at someone's house."

Charles Schmid, known as 'Smitty' in high school, proved a superb gymnast with strength that made up for his lack in size. "A wonderful athelete," a homeroom teacher says, "but he was an indifferent student. Most of his grades were D's. I believed he had exceptional intelligence, but he did not know what to do with it, or use it constructively. There was no *guiding* line."

In 1960 Schmid led the school to the State Gymnastics Championship, winning the flying rings and still rings, placing in the long horse, and taking fifth on the horizontal bar.

According to Schmid, "I tried as hard as I could and made the tryouts for freshman football, but I couldn't express myself as an individual in football, so I quit. I wanted something that depended on my actions *solely*, and nobody else was needed to depend on. I decided on gymnastics. The weird and marvelous exhibitions fascinated me, so head over heels I plunged. I read books, studied techniques of famous gymnasts, and then worked to build my body to suit the application. In one year the weird and mystic dream descended and made everything believable to me. I could do it, there was no doubt about it."

Repeatedly in Schmid's life, and as far back as he can recall, he has been aware of "seeing events" in his mind before they actually occurred.

He says, "I soon felt engulfed by the strange hallucination of knowing that I could do it, seeing myself doing it before it happened. The things that other gymnasts struggled months to achieve I accomplished in a matter of days.

"The first year I barely made the team, the second, third, and fourth I became city and then state champion. It is difficult for me to explain how I was champion for three years straight with only one semester of practice. All I can say is that whatever trick or event seemed impossible to others, I'd shut my eyes and everything would seem logical, so I'd do it. I wish I could honestly say I worked harder than others, but as I progressed everything seemed easier."

Schmid's foster parents had given up the operation of Hillcrest and opened Katharine's Craycroft Center, a luxurious, red-brick nursing home at a leased location on Craycroft. The old Hillcrest was in use as a boarding house for elderly people. Schmid had his own quarters in a sand-toned territorial house on the same property as the new nursing home, and since his sixteenth birthday he had been receiving an allowance of $300 a month. He had a new car and a motorcycle, and his foster parents were later to admit that they did not interfere in their son's life. Katharine felt that "Charlie had his own life to lead."

As a fifth-year student, Schmid was no longer eligible to compete in gymnastics. Just before graduation, he was caught taking some tools from welding class to work on a roadster he was building, and was temporarily suspended. He could have returned and graduated after a semester but he never asked to be readmitted. Schmid says: "I quit out of boredom." He started hanging around Speedway, drinking and picking up girls.

"Everyone knew who Smitty was," an ex-classmate recalls. "They all called him 'Smitty,' and I really thought his name was Smith or something. He was a little older than the rest of the kids, not much but more mature in ways, and he was a kind of hero to them. But he was a loner, and had a peculiar popularity. The girls went for him, along with those that wanted to act like Smitty. He was strange and probably the most conceited person in Tucson, but it's no lie he had a way of acting that excited people."

There were the rock clubs, the hangouts, the parties. The life along Speedway was important to Schmid and he once tried to describe what it meant to him. He wrote:

"A wild expressive mass jerks spasmodically to the liquid drums and pulsing sounds from the amplifiers. All the yes sirs and no sirs are absent, and an exchange of physical desire obscures the rancid reality around them. The hungry kisses accented by a pill or a few beers is a cheap and easy way to find security, and the quick, too-soon responses and climaxes insure protection from the outside world. The teenager is frightened, beyond belief by the world he is being forced into. What sense is it to wait for sexual intercourse, he reasons, when it's available now? Why not take a pill, or get drunk, at least there is a happy void to fall into. All the doubts are still there but they're pleasantly obscured. All that matters is the good feeling you're getting from speed and intoxication. Granted, there are some kids who try to untangle the incredible mess, but how can they do it alone when the rest would rather sit in the corner smoking pot? But why shouldn't they be disillusioned and find other worlds? All the pretty little tinsel and ribbons society wraps the box with to tantalize them in hopes they'll want it and try harder than ever, is just a fairy tale to conceal the dirty contents inside. The blind faith you try to project to seal the leaks is proving to be more and more fallible. It doesn't matter anymore if a button-happy idiot blows up the world."

Richie Bruns, a tall, gangly youth, was to become Schmid's closest friend and most receptive ear for Smitty's philosophy. Richie's family came to Tucson from Columbus, Ohio, when Richie was in the fourth grade. The family made the trip to the Southwest because both Richie's father and older brother suffered from asthma. "My brother had it so bad," Richie says,"he almost died when he was four." Richie lived with his family in a modest house on Winsett in Tucson, on the east side not far from the Schmids'. His father was an electronics technician and his mother was employed as a manicurist. Richie's brother, working for his master's degree at the university, had never been in trouble, but Richie was well known to the Tucson police by the time he was a freshman at Rincon High. It was around this time that he first saw Smitty. "He'd cruise down in his red convertible along the street between the main building and the cafeteria, and all the kids would come running out and gather around the car. He had his hair dyed black and he sometimes wore a sleeveless poncho or vest to show off his build, and wore engineer boots, the real 'tuff' kind with buckles on the sides. Smitty was bitchin.'"

Richie had been suspended or expelled from high schools four times before his eighteenth birthday. Then, during his second semester at Rincon, Richie quit school and began to spend most of his time around Speedway.

"I was hanging around the Coppa," he recalls, "where they had these pinball machines, and all you had to do to play was pick them up and drop them. It would rack up about ten games. I'd get there early in the morning and drop the machines and play them all day. Al Easton, who lived in back of the Coppa, was going with Carol White. She'd hang around the Coppa and guys were on the make.

"Wasn't long before Carol and Al broke up. I'd been spending days and nights at Al's house and I started to see Carol. I'd sleep with her and use Al's as an excuse, that I was staying over at his place. But I'd sneak out and go to Carol's. Al knew all about it but he didn't care. He said fine. Carol had all kinds of brothers and sisters and no dad. The old lady was drunk and gone most of the time, whoring or getting on welfare, and Carol took care of the kids. She had to be mother at fourteen to all those brothers and sisters through the week with no money."

There was a motorcycle crowd around the Coppa; their bikes lined the front of the building. Richie would see Smitty around the Coppa. "He had a Harley CH," Richie says, "but he was not part of that crowd. Smitty played at being a bike guy, but the real bike guys didn't go for his games." Things were rough at that time, but Richie says "I was just a fifteen-year-old, one of those kids that hang around and look stupid. Even after they put up the **NO LOITERING** signs we'd just hang around."

Eventually, Richie began spending most of his time at Carol's. "Others would come by with booze and money for Carol, and she'd entertain and I would stay there all the time. It went on like that for about three months, the summer.

"At nights we'd lay out on the grass and look at the sky. I didn't care, it was like I didn't have parents. Nobody knew who you were, nobody came around or cared, and it was nice, laying out there and staring up at the sky. Sleep a little. It was paradise for a fifteen-year-old."

This came to an end. "One night I was staying with Carol," he says. "We were having sex on her front porch, it was a closed-in place, with the TV going. Carol had only her panties on. We were lying on the old couch out there and suddenly her old lady comes rushing up, shaking a .45 at my head. She'd been watching us through the screen. She was drunk and that .45 kept shaking in her hand, pointing right at my head.

"Later, Al, Carol, and I broke into a house and we got caught. Al's little sister saw us and told her old lady, who called the cops. I got put on probation then. They said I couldn't hang around Carol or Al ever again. I did anyway. After that they sort of cracked down on Carol and her family. Carol got sent to Good Shepherd up at Phoenix. After that I kept thinking about how I was going to see her—break into Good Shepherd and all that. I kept plotting and writing it all down, how I was going to do it. My old lady gave my writing to the probation officer and there was more trouble.

"I started working at the car wash and took off work one day and went to the Coppa. This faggot comes in and starts flashing this damned money and asks me if I want a beer. I said, 'Yeah, sure,' so I went out with him and he bought a six-pack. I really got wiped out of my mind. He drives out in the desert and starts proposing all this shit and I told him where to go.

"I'd told him I'd run away once and he told me how I could run away because he could pose as my old man. I said, 'Well, fine, let's go.' That was the last thing I remember until I woke up and was looking at some scummy side of town and I said, 'Hey, where the hell are we?' 'We're in Phoenix,' he said. 'Let's turn around and go back,' I told him. On the way back I start driving and the center line starts weaving and then we're in the ditch. He pulls me out and says, 'Cops saw that, cops coming.'"

When the police picked up Richie, he said, "The queer showed me a gun," and the police let him go. But the incident wasn't over. "Next day the cops came and tell me a guy like the queer was found in a ditch on the scummy side of Phoenix, shot. They'd found him dead. They take me down to Mother Higgins juvenile detention, apparently on suspicion of murder. Then I think they found the guy who killed the queer, but I got sent up to Fort Grant for breaking probation."

At Fort Grant, Richie remembers, "Eight people sit at a table, three bowls with main foods. The object is to grab a bowl and hold it up in the air when you are done. Some kitchen help comes around and picks up the bowls. There are so many bowls in the air, chances are you won't get to eat unless you grab fast as soon as grace is said. They can't wait, and just grab as soon as it's said and 'chop down.'"

Schmid's school friend, Paul Graff, had just returned from Fort Grant. Schmid recalls, "Something in my mind clicked when Paul was released. As his best friend, he came to me for help and nothing else seemed to matter." Schmid had broken off with one girlfriend and had been invited to another girl's house for dinner. He asked if he could bring his good friend along.The girl was reluctant, then said, "You better not tell them who he is or anything."

Usually adults were impressed by Schmid. "He was courteous, attentive, especially to his friend's mothers. Full of life and energy," as one parent recalls. "There was something odd about him, the makeup, his hair dyed, but he'd explain that he was performing with a group, playing guitar, and he was every bit a gentleman."

The dinner was not a success. Conditioned by Fort Grant meals, Paul began grabbing and wolfing, as though his life depended on how much he could get into his mouth at once. Schmid says, "Paul was the most sarcastic person I had ever seen. It seemed impossible that Fort Grant had changed him so completely. His manners ruined the dinner and he was so rude to her parents we were asked to leave. That ended my visits to the girl's house."

On the street, Paul said he had nowhere to go. "He was just standing there," Schmid says, "the food still on his mouth, staring at the ground. I asked my parents if he could stay at our house, they said yes, so he moved in. During this time I was involved with several girls, and with cars (the roadster I put together turned 135 inside of three blocks), and with practicing the guitar and taking singing lessons from a woman coach in Tucson. I just really wasn't attracted to the kind of life Paul had been used to. He was just burning with a hate for everything and he was doing some extremely heavy drinking."

They drove down to Nogales. Smitty wanted to order custom-made shoes and also look at some jewelry. "I told him not to buy any booze because we'd get caught smuggling it across the line. But when I'd gone to the bathroom Paul bought three big bottles of tequila, hid one of them in the glove compartment and the others in the rear trunk. When we were questioned at the border, I said we didn't have any liquor. He didn't believe us and made me open the trunk and then another one looked in the glove compartment.

"My car was impounded and it was to cost me $20 to get it out. Paul had $35 but he wouldn't loan me the twenty. I had loaned Paul a hundred dollars while he was with me, given him a roof and free food, and even got him some work at the hospital. We hitchhiked back to Tucson, and as soon as we arrived Paul packed his things and left.

"I was so disappointed I took a quart of Falstaff and drank it.

Intoxication accented my feelings." But a week later Paul returned, offering apologies which were accepted lightly. There were other things on Smitty's mind. He was seeing a girl named Sandy. She was married. He'd also been designing some automotive parts and had progressed to the point where a business venture seemed possible. He decided to go to California to purchase a furnace for an aluminum factory, so, with over $2,000 stuffed into the top of his boot, he went on his "business trip," thereby avoiding a confrontation with Sandy's husband.

He was detained by the Beverly Hills police on suspicion of robbery, but was released when the $2,000 in question was accounted for. For several days he stayed in Los Angeles, and was later to say that he'd spent the time with an "L.A. whore who taught me some tricks." He returned to Tucson, and the business venture, like other enterprising schemes Smitty would hit upon from time to time, failed to materialize.

After six months at Fort Grant, Richie was released. "The first thing I did was go back to the bowling alley. The first hour back I was with Russ and the other guys." At the Coppa or Rollerama he'd see Paul, "a wino who had to have a drinking companion like every other wino, and I'd drink with him." Through Paul he got to know Smitty, and they started going out every Saturday night. "We'd hang around the Coppa, then split with a case of beer in the trunk, and go out to the desert, park, shit around. If Smitty wanted to stay in the Rollerama, it was me and Paul, Paul drunk on wine. We'd drive Smitty's car and I'd bum chugalugs with him."

Other nights, Richie would take a motor scooter he had "acquired" at the time, drive to the Coppa and drink with whoever was there, and then go to Rollerama, "strictly Smitty's crowd," where he'd circulate among the drinking groups or "just hang around." Most of the time he didn't have enough money to go inside, so he and Paul would stay outside with the drinking groups. Richie recalls: "They'd have Chuck Berry, Fats Domino, Bill Black Combo, and draw quite a crowd. But all the juvenile delinquents would be hanging around in the parking lots and I was one of them." There were frequently fights with cops, deputies arresting kids, and every week the Liquor Control would crack down."

Schmid often went into Rollerama to get a girl. "He'd take her out to the desert by the Apache Drive-In," says Richie. "Paul and I would wait. Many nights I waited while Smitty was with some girl in her bedroom." There was a girl named Sue Nemer for a while and, according to Richie, "Her old man never liked Smitty, it was something right off from the beginning. When Smitty broke up with her, Paul started making it with her and Smitty didn't like it. He couldn't go in the pad and found himself in the position of waiting on Paul instead of Paul and I always waiting on him. Many times we'd been there waiting when Smitty'd come running out, 'Get the hell out,' with his clothes in his hand, charging out through some chick's bedroom window screen. He didn't like being in that position, of waiting for Paul, so one night when Paul was in there with Sue, Smitty went to Mr. Nemer's car and disassembled part of the engine on the carport, laid it out in parts. Paul got blamed and Mr. Nemer threatened to shoot Paul if he ever came near the house."

One particular night Smitty seemed "really quiet." He was walking with Richie along Craycroft to Johnnie's on Speedway. Richie was quiet too, he was thinking of running away, of heading north. Maybe west.

They sat for a while on the brick wall by the driveway at Johnnie's. Richie told Smitty that he wanted to get on the move again.

"Smitty didn't say anything right away," Richie recalls, "then he told me about his *real* old lady."

According to Richie, Smitty told him the following:

During a family upset at the Schmids', the grandmother revealed to Smitty that he was an adopted child. He refused to believe her and went immediately to Katharine. "Yes, that's true," his foster mother said. She took him to the bank and asked for the sealed envelope. She handed it to Smitty and said, "You're old enough now to know, I suppose."

Then Smitty made a trip to Phoenix, and later told Richie that he had confronted the woman named in the envelope as being his real mother. Smitty said the woman told him, "I didn't want you when you were born, or even before you were born, and I don't want you now. Get out." Smitty said she slammed the door in his face.

Art Meyers, a mutual acquaintance of Schmid remembers Richie as "kind of weird. The kids in school didn't think much of him, and they thought Smitty was a fruit, a creep. You see, Rincon is a twink school. It's pansy-like, all the guys wearing them wingtip shoes, saddle shoes, big, ugly, fat loafers, sandals, surfer hair style, I mean stuff like that. Forget it! I wouldn't go for that and we just dressed the way we liked to dress. Smitty and Richie, we all dressed alike, ascots and stuff like that, just trying to be different.

"A lot of kids, they didn't see you going along with the crowd, so they thought something different of you. But if they didn't like it? Too damn bad! They can go to hell. We'd put on our go-to-hell ascots and go-to-hell shoes, and if they didn't like it, too damn bad. Richie wore suits and ties and even a topcoat in summer, and always wore shades.

"When Richie was in school, he even wore suspenders. Richie's not dumb at all. His older brother's a real clean-cut guy, goes to the university to be a teacher, and Richie has a complex. He has a pretty good home in a pretty good part of town, his old man was okay, his mom was okay, but Richie's juvenile trouble resulted from a complex. His folks gave his brother all the attention, everything went to his brother. And Richie, he had to do something...."

In January of 1963, Richie was returned to Fort Grant, convicted on two counts of burglary.

While Richie was in Fort Grant ("The first time there I was scared, but the second time you know what the stakes are, when you'll get out, and that's it"), Smitty rented a house near 28th and Woodland with Paul and two other boys, Kenny and David.

There were other friends: Art Meyers, who played drums for a rock group Smitty fronted, and John Saunders. "Saunders started coming around to the house," Smitty says. "He seemed to like my music, and later I got him a job at our hospital, gave him some clothes and a lot of my records. I tried to get girls for him. He dated but they didn't like him. I couldn't understand that because I always thought John was quite good-looking."

Slim, with a sensitive face, John Saunders was a poor student, constantly beaten, bullied, or teased by his classmates. An only child, he'd been afflicted as an infant with allergies producing scabs which encrusted his entire body. To keep him from scratching, his parents used to tie his hands and feet to the sides of his crib at night. Eventually he was cured of the allergy and the scars, but he had become so conditioned by the ropes that he couldn't sleep without being bound hand and foot. He developed asthma.

"Once when he was at the house," Smitty recalls, "something happened and John got into a fight with Paul, who hit him so hard he knocked him out. John didn't regain consciousness and Paul panicked. Finally he did become conscious but went into a catatonic stupor. We quickly invented a story that John fell off the roof. This was to keep Paul out of trouble as John was only seventeen and Paul was twenty-one.

"He (John) stayed at the hospital for a week recuperating. His parents knew he was there but they did not come to see him or offer to pay the medication bill."

One of the girls Smitty frequently went around with was Mary Rae French, sixteen. Mary had been living in Tucson only six months when she met Smitty. Her family came from Texas and occupied a modern beige house in the southeast section of Tucson. One of her teachers at Palo Verde High, where John Saunders was also enrolled, considered Mary "a slow girl, given to lapses of daydreaming or simply staring into space. She couldn't keep herself down on any subject long enough for it to sink in. And before she dropped out of school, she had quite frankly developed a bad reputation for herself."

Schmid met Mary at a desert beer party. "Mary was so wiped out she didn't even know her name," Schmid recalls. "Later she was appealing to me because of thc things she'd been through and I sort of understood. She had a terrible problem about speaking to people and a hypernervousness that made her stutter sometimes. On the first real date she got completely drunk and weeped out the history of her terrible family life.

"But she'd been hurt by so many things I think she hated the world. She had so many problems I don't believe she really knew what was going on around her. If she did she never showed it. Whenever I had friends over or fooled around and played my guitar, she was hostile and silent. I'd try to get her to socialize but her constant fear of people doing her wrong would end it. Yet, except for my never being true to her, we seemed to get along."

Schmid was having relations with a number of girls at the time. "Even though I was 'madly in love' with some particular girl at some particular time, as soon as I'd leave her I'd find another girl. I couldn't stand being without a girl for even a moment, and as hard as I'd try I couldn't be true. Each girl was something new and different. I liked them all."

He would propose marriage to several girls simultaneously, and often took small amounts of money from some of them. Under the impression that he was going to marry her, Mary French accepted a job Smitty had arranged at the hospital, and placed her earnings in a joint account with him.

"I enjoyed being a gigolo," Schmid says. "Since I thought I'd never fall in love anyway, going with those girls and getting paid for it was my idea of fun. I had sex, money, and all I had to do was laugh or tell a few jokes, which came naturally anyway. I also enjoyed taking girls from my buddies. Actually girls were just a plaything at that time. I couldn't believe anyone could take them as seriously as some others did. Life was a funny joke full of phony people and if I couldn't fight them I was damn sure going to join them and be A-Number One phoniest.

"When I made a girl cry by going out with another girl after I'd promised not to, I rationalized it by saying, 'Cry tonight and I'll make you laugh tomorrow.' It sounded crazy but it worked. All the incredible lies I told them. The wilder and more ridiculous the stories, the more they believed it as gospel. To avoid marriage I told one girl I was part Negro and if we had a baby it would be polka-dotted. I did it to get rid of the girl but she really got determined to get married after that.

"The story about my leukemia originated with some girl I was going with when I was seventeen. The purpose was to give her the impression I had a short time to live and would she be so kind as to make me happy by having sex with me. It worked so well eventually everyone believed I had leukemia. I was surprised at the speed the rumors spread. Only a few words assured me of success with sex.

"Other stories ranged from cancer of the heart to ten or twelve foster parents who had disowned me. Some had tried to sell me across the border for white slavery.

"I said that as a child my legs were all twisted and crippled and that was the reason I was so short, not to mention the operations performed on my pitiful limbs, or the elaborate stretching machine that had drained my family into poverty. Then there were sick brothers and sisters demanding money for emergency operations or burying stillborn children.

"One brother was insane and kept locked in a small room somewhere and I was his sole support. Some of the stories were of a more fantastic nature like I'd flown jet planes during the war, and that I was the chairman of a secret organization that met at midnight for perverted sexual pleasures. Later on I was to tell a tale that I'd committed murder, shot a boy and buried him in the desert. I said the boy had been responsible for the death of a girl I loved, an automobile accident.... I said I cut off his hands before I buried him. So the extent I'd go for my girls was frankly unlimited. To me, the fact that I'd actually be believed was the most incredible part of all. I lived in a swirl of confusion but I didn't drown. Instead, the constant confusion gave me fire to want to live more."

It was Smitty's intention to get enough money together to cut a record. Art Meyers thought Schmid had talent. He recalls,

"He was pretty good, pretty fair. We played at his house and over at my house a couple of times. He sings all right, he wanted to impersonate Mr. Elvis Presley. They do look alike, a little bit, the way Smitty combs his hair, his blue eyes, the sideburns. I told him once, 'You look like Elvis,' and he said, 'I can't stand the guy, I can't stand him.' The time we got together at his place, though, I went into his room and the walls were plastered with pictures of Elvis, records, pictures, photos...."

But to Richie, Smitty was more candid. "Some people think I try to be like Elvis Presley," Richie recalls Smitty saying. "But the fact is that Presley's a creep—I don't even *like* the guy. But he's setting the *pace* and in order to *make* it, I'll have to cut a record that'll be better than Presley, except that he's setting the pace, the way I want to go to make it good." And Smitty was studying Presley's songs, manners, singing along with Presley and taping the voice.

Smitty says, "I found I couldn't sing and play lead guitar both so I taped my guitar playing over and over until I had it perfect. Then I recorded about thirty songs on my tape recorder and concealed my recorder in my specially made amplifier. At parties I could sing and play lead guitar the way I wanted it and still joke and cut up without having to worry about making a mistake playing. I faked the playing perfectly. But one party, I remember, the cord came out of my guitar and to this day there is a girl wandering around out there who can't figure out how my electric guitar played without a cord. I told her some idiotic thing I dreamed up.

"The bass, rhythm, and drums could never figure out how I played so perfectly. It was a blast joking everybody. I'd sit around and crack up for hours over it.

"Occasionally for laughs I'd tape some extremely difficult song some guitar player who'd played professionally for fifteen or twenty years had done, and I'd fake playing it at a party and sing also. People couldn't believe it. I practiced for hours in front of a mirror, it was a ticklish delight for me to pull it off so beautifully. I'd never overdo it, so no one caught on.

"Later, after the trial runs, I put controls on the guitar itself to control the starting and stopping of the recorder, also the tone and volume. Was life ever one big happy blast.

"My voice had always sounded all right, at least to me, so I never really gave a damn whether anyone liked it or not. I liked it; so far as anyone else goes, it doesn't really matter."

Schmid's music and half-baked plans for fame revealed the same insincerity as did his romances. He tried to arouse sympathy with his tales of ill luck or shortcomings, to convince others that he was a cripple, incurably sick, or morally debased. Although Schmid passed this off as a tactic which he repeated only because it was successful, he admittedly had little concern for the girls themselves. One of them says, "Some girls went out with him just to see what he was like, he'd win them over and then be on his way. And still they didn't know what he was like."

Mary French, who was so "out of it" that she hardly seemed to know what was happening, was merely an extreme example of Smitty's girls, all of whom tended to be "lost," a group apart, seeking in some way to be different, to challenge.

Smitty was different, they said. It didn't matter that he stuffed his boots with rags and pieces of folded cardboard to make himself appear taller. It didn't matter that he wore makeup, dyed his hair, and was "disliked by most kids." In fact it seemed to make him more important. Everybody talked about him. Everybody thought he was special—or so he thought. And among those that sought his company he was a leader. "Everyone knew Smitty." He had money, wheels, a pad of his own, and most importantly "he did whatever he wanted to do."

There was a band playing at a new shopping center, and Richie, released from Fort Grant, wandering around, saw Smitty "racing around with John Saunders," then saw him later at the bowling alley. Richie says, "The old Coppa group had completely split up. The real bad guys were either married or in prison." The juvenile problem at Rollerama had resulted in its being temporarily closed down.

One afternoon Richie was walking to the bowling alley when Smitty drove by and stopped and picked him up. Smitty had a new bronze Ford Falcon, but he complained that Katharine had cut off his allowance temporarily, due to financial troubles at Craycroft. "Things were rough," Richie says. "He didn't have any money and was restless as hell. We got to talking about some of the people we knew, like Paul laying some girl and thought she was pregnant, and we talked about Saunders."

In order to get money from his foster mother, Smitty obtained enrollment papers from the university and convinced her that he would be attending classes, "although he bought no books, no texts, nothing," according to Richie. Smitty would occasionally wake Richie up at 6 A.M. "First thing in the morning I'd hear his car outside and then his boots crunching the gravel, then bang-bang-bang on my bedroom window. Sometimes the goddamn sun wasn't even shining yet."

They'd talk. Smitty kept a toothpick in his mouth and would work it around casually as he spoke. At times he sat with a clothespin fastened to his lower lip. Both lips were often so heavily covered with Chapstick that they appeared whitish and wet. He began wearing darker makeup on his face, or Man-Tan. A slight mole on one cheek was accented with a black pencil.

Richie says, "The makeup got progressively worse as time went on. And the mole, it started out a little teeny thing, it kept getting bigger and bigger. I think eventually it would have covered the whole side of his head.

"He went out and got these boots he'd had made down in Nogales. These things were something else, black, laces all the way up the back, real long things with all kinds of knots, big knots tied all the way down. They had a cowboy heel that comes way in and out, they looked just like the old shoes that you see these old women used to wear years and years ago with the laces coming up the back. And the pointed fronts, and then he'd put the rags in them and his feet were real wide, coming way out on the sides.

Paul looked at them one day and said, 'What's happened to him? He looks like a clown.'

"I was embarrassed. He had straps coming across the instep, square straps with more laces, then big long cowboy heels that came in too much at an angle, and the things came out real boxy to points on the toes."

Smitty often stared at his transformation in the rearview mirror of his car. Richie says, "He was constantly admiring himself in the mirror, pursing his lips, checking his eyes, touching his face here and there like a girl. The rearview mirror was so twisted around in that position that it wouldn't work in any other position. It just kept falling down."

With nothing else to do, Richie spent most of his time with Smitty, once in a while with Art Meyers, who remembers, "We played pool a lot, we were pretty close. Not too many people got along with Richie, he's a little off his cord, I know that, but he's a real comical guy. And Smitty is like that too, a real comical guy. So their characters were sort of combined. That's why they got along so good, once upon a time."

Richie recalls, "Smitty never liked to go on a date alone. One thing about him, he hated to go on a date by himself. He always had to double with somebody. He had to make an affair out of everything. He just *couldn't* go out with a girl alone. That's why I doubted all his bullshit about who he'd fucked; with practically every girl's name mentioned, he'd say, 'Oh, I fucked her. Yeah, I fucked her.'

"He especially liked to double-date if he knew the other guy was with a girl Smitty knew and could have control over. If he had two girls along that dug him, he'd be the center of attention, plus he talked a lot, and made with all the jokes. He talks and talks and is the center, doesn't shut up for a moment from the minute he meets a girl's parents."

Except Mary French. Richie says, "She wasn't like all the other schoolgirls. Anytime he wanted to, Smitty could just go around to Mary's, knock on the window at three in the morning or so, and she'd let him in."

Although Richie would double-date with Smitty, he says, "Me, when I go out alone, I mean, I got along better by myself. I can't do anything in a crowd. As soon as I'm in a crowd I completely shut up. That's why I never got along in school. I become somebody in the corner. I can't go into a strange crowd and make friends, like Smitty does. He had the ability to go around strangers and start talking, joking, making friends. I never was that way."

In fact it was Smitty's easy manners that Richie felt so drawn toward. Plagued by tensions and constant dissatisfactions, ashamed of his thinness, Richie was in many ways Smitty's antithesis. "Nothing bugged Smitty," Richie would say with envy. His success with girls was nothing like Smitty's.

Schmid remembers: "Richie once asked me how I turned on a girl to interest her in having sexual relations. He was having such rotten luck.

"I told him my routine with this girl named Beverly, my getting her into the bedroom, telling her a few jokes, making her a vodka cocktail and getting her in a laughing mood. Then I laughed with her and started tickling her. We fell back on the bed and I kissed her hair, forehead, cheeks, lips, and nibbled her ear lobes. I frenched her ear and the roof of her mouth with my tongue. I kissed her feverishly and with heated passion. She started to come back with her tongue and that's when I went into act two.

"I got up very quickly and sat on the edge of the bed. She said, very excitedly, 'What's wrong?' I looked at her and pretended to be very sad and hurt. 'Are you sick?' she asked.

"I looked even more sad and hurt and turned my head from her. She was shocked out of her mind. While my head was turned I conveniently dabbed some salt in my eyes. I had some in my shirt pocket. This caused a release of water which simulated tears and then I looked at her. She was taken off balance when she thought I was crying, and asked why. It was then that I'd tenderly take her hand and rattle off some tender garbage that would always come to me at such times. It went something like this:

"She'd say, 'What's wrong? Why are you crying?'

"I'd say, 'Oh, darling, the tears I cry aren't tears of pain, they're tears of happiness. Never, no, never, have I seen someone as beautiful as you are right now. How could I be so fortunate as to kiss you tonight?'

"Then I'd kiss her hand," Smitty said, "very softly and tenderly and say, 'As I kissed you this moment I must certainly have kissed an angel because never before have I felt so... so clean inside.'

"Then another kiss, further up the arm, more garbage, more kisses, more poetic crap, more kisses, finally a kiss on the lips and then I'd promise never to leave her and I'd fight dragons all for her. All this bull took about an hour.... Oh, the crap I'd go through to set this up was very precise. Proper music, gobs of flowers, a wine bottle.

"This wine bottle was a special item. I spent twenty-five dollars for a vintage 1900 wine bottle, empty of course, and then I'd fill it with anything available—cheap wine or champagne, even beer once, then seal it with wax. Then when she arrived at my house for dinner I'd break open the bottle and she was very impressed at the expense to make her happy.

"Damn, were they gullible. My worst problem was to keep from laughing. When I'd get caught laughing I'd simply say I laughed because being with her made me so happy.

"From there I'd go to the bedroom, usually to dance. My stereo was in the bedroom and it was more convenient to dance in the bedroom so records could be changed. One thing would lead to another.

"The dinner and dancing would often come after a wild, exhausting night of dancing or running through the rain—very romantic, that rain. This would make them tired and set the mood. After the poetic garbage, tears, and pledges of devotion, about an hour or two of preliminaries would occur until I was positive the height of passion had occurred. Then I'd very discreetly disrobe her.

"I learned a very good technique to undo buttons and brassiere straps from a whore in California. Very seldom would the girl know her blouse and brassiere were disconnected until soft kisses sent her the message. Then my mouth, tongue, and kisses would probe other areas. This, combined with more intimate caresses, would virtually assure the completion of sexual intercourse.

"Well, after Richie heard about this with Beverly he decided to give it a whirl. But he drank too much and the girl slapped him—not once, but twice."

After a night of drinking and driving around, Bruns and Smitty would often park in the nursing home driveway, and Smitty would talk. Richie remembers it as "talk about God and stuff like that. About society, about what goes on in a girl's head. What does a girl want? He kept telling me, 'What are you going to offer a girl? You going to say I offer you my love?' What is love? He'd say, 'Nobody loves anyone. They want security.'

"And he'd say, 'God must be up there enjoying Himself because this all has to be nothing but a game, and we have to be little puppets and I resent having to be a puppet. And I'm supposed to love Him more than I love anybody, more than anything else, and He hasn't got the guts to show me His face. If I loved somebody, I wouldn't send him to hell for all eternity, whereas God would, so God isn't a kind God, but a cruel God, and all the Christians are the ones that have the plague thrown down on them. You say you love God, so He throws a plague down to test your so-called love. It's just a big game to Him, look what He did to His own son. God must be a hypocrite, He's a jealous God, and jealousy is a fault. God made me, and if I'm imperfect it's because He made me imperfect, so therefore God can't blame me for anything I do wrong; it's His fault.'"

Smitty had an abiding interest in this pseudo-theologizing. He says, "I had an incredible urge to read everything I could about philosophies and religion. When I was younger my parents took me to church every Sunday, but everything the preacher said about God sounded so much like the Easter Bunny. I distinctly recall thinking to myself, 'What will happen when all the grown-ups find out the preacher is lying just like they lied to me about the Good Fairy and Santa Claus?

"After I'd read something and it would conflict with what I'd been taught, I began to have doubts about everything. The booze and the girls had a numbing effect on these doubts."

Schmid read Epicurus and also "the various agnostic doctrines, esthetes and hedonists. The ones that seemed to me the most logical were the agnostics, even though the hedonists made the most sense. The stoics suffered too much but I thought their concepts were good. I'd learned that most people would rather exist in a fairy tale. I thought I wanted truth, if not that, then at least I wanted happiness. If everything was based on a pleasure-pain cycle, then I chose to receive more pleasure than pain. I gave my mind to seeking answers on its own. Involvement with pleasure seemed far more sensible than fighting a losing battle with rules and regulations. All the people I knew just sat back and said, 'Wow, it's happening,' but I had to know how and why, and I read everything I could.

"But I knew I was cynical about it. It appeared to me that I was sometimes adrift on an ocean of uncertainties and my anchor permanently entangled in a seaweed of frustration. Then suddenly, before the drowning waves of accusations destroyed me, a lifeboat of cynicism preserved in laughter would rescue me. Somewhere in the depths of me this bubble of mockery prevails under the most excruciating circumstances."

Smitty could not take things as seriously as Richie did. Smitty was searching for pleasure, and it was not that rules and regulations were in opposition to that search, more that they were at times an interference. The "rules and regulations" did not really exist for Smitty. His life was being lived one segment at a time, while Richie, worrying over Smitty's soliloquies, began to notice things:

"Smitty and I were on the outside looking in. We'd walk into a restaurant and everybody looks at us like we're something from Mars. But they're actually afraid of us because we represent a threat to them. Actually, they're nothing but puppets themselves, and they know it, and they haven't got any self-respect. It's an imitation world. Everybody's phony, full of phony ideas and phony attitudes, phony principles."

Smitty, determined to be different, to be *himself,* stood out from the crowd. "I wasn't made to go through life at twenty-five miles an hour. I've got an awful lot of living to do before I'm too old to run upstairs without getting winded. Something, man, something too powerful inside me drives me and makes me different. I have to wear different clothes, I have to wear different shoes that I've designed, I've got to make my car different and I have to be different and I want to be....

"I can't be a puppet or do what everybody else does. I don't have any cause or rebellion—most people want to be alike. I don't. I want to be an individualist.

"I might be one of the last to do and express what I feel. I'm going to have doubts about life and the existence of God until someone proves different. I can't accept all the crap and hypocrisy I hear about Jesus and God. My basic logic tears apart the contradictions of today's religions."

What seems to have been Schmid's alone, made Charles Schmid into Smitty, and what led him to do what he had to do, was his vast insecurity. He felt that he would never shake it. Already an immense gulf separated him from his foster parents. Although he spoke of "an incredible raw wildness that refuses to lie dormant," as having broken his life into a series of freewheeling moments designed "to receive more pleasure than pain," he knew that his style of life was derived from insecurity. And this was driving him toward destruction, the "duels with Death and his disciples," toward some final liberating act which he supposed would somehow end the chaos he could not understand.

He wrote later, "I tried to cram as much experience into my life as possible. The basic wild and uninhibited attitudes have always originated from a fear of insecurity. Long ago it became accepted to my reasoning that everything in the world exists on a temporary basis only. I resented it and it accounts for the constant frustrations I endure. Without something to tax my brain of its currents of anxiety I was not happy. I hated ruts and the constant monotony of life. I grasped and challenged head-on. Experience has complemented my originality and forced it to project itself in countless channels, those set patterns and formalities I violate in search of this originality, constantly I searched and devised original plans of action."

One of Schmid's earliest memories was of trying to gain attention by recklessness, something that would hurt him, that he would later link to preoccupation with God's punishing him. He preferred a God who punished to a God who wasn't there. The great fear was of being abandoned in a world that was indifferent to him. It was better to arouse hostility than indifference.

Schmid wrote of the feeling of being alone and the fright it awakened in him. "The uncertainties of tomorrow and the lost yesterdays add tangible fuel to my inner rebellion. I honestly feel I was cast into the wrong period of time by some quirk of fate. My deepest recollection is that of actual vagueness to time. My earliest memory is of surging over a deep pool of water when I was five. The experience is strikingly clear, even today. That was the first taste of fright and it became thrilling and compelling. Perhaps this cast the mold for future events.

"I honestly wish I could channel the furies of my mind and body into a constructive field, but boredom of everything I try causes loss of appeal. On a motorcycle or in my roadster at 120 miles per hour the world seems so damn appealing. The ecstasy of wind, noise, and the possibility of some unknown element casting disaster in my path, to test my physical and mental dexterity and the speeding-up of events causes a tremendous release similar to sexual orgasm. With any reduction of speed life becomes a reality and catches me, to subdue me in its boredoms, frustrations, and other complexities. The extreme speed and dangers frighten me but paradoxically stimulate me as well.

"I truly wish I could be a great surgeon, or philosopher, or author, or anything constructive, but in all honesty I'd rather turn my amplifier full-blast and listen to the noise until I'm enveloped. Lovemaking combined with animal passions and a hint of cruelty as I reach sexual fulfillment is far more basic and sensible than the involvement with some theoretical manifestation that later proves itself not so absolute after all."

Themes of self-destruction were repeated throughout Schmid's life. Of his gymnastic ability, he wrote, "The thing that kept me fascinated with gymnastics was that it frightened me. If I slipped or fell that could very well be the last time. Each trick I did became more and more daring and I was tempted to let go just to know if I really would let go.

"It was a paradox, all my life I'd hated and feared to be alone and what occurred to me was that in gymnastics I was tempting injury or death which was surely solitude. I think I wanted to find out if anyone really cared, if it really mattered one way or the other. I enjoyed gymnastics because I was afraid. But during my last year of high school I quit gymnastics completely. I knew if I continued my recklessness would hurt me.

"Once, at Sabino Canyon, I almost drowned. There was a storm and the creekbed rose with the oncoming rush of water. For an unknown reason I accepted a dare to jump across the torrent." (Richie and some others were there at the time.) "I missed by at least ten feet, but instead of screaming for help this incredible laughter prevailed. I was swept downstream and this maniacal laughter continued. I found myself actually enjoying the predicament and the feeling that I was completely helpless, that my fate depended on nature, was extremely exciting. Fast speed and music provide an excitement similar to that incident. Pleasure, laughter, and excitement emanated from most every situation I undertook. Then came skydiving.

"Before my motorcycle accident, one summer I saw a hurricane that seemed to have great meaning. From the murky sky there came a flash of lightning, white with heat as it greedily devoured a whirlpool of liquid turbulence to combine in a cyclopean monster. Hungrily it ripped everything from the face of the earth.

"I stopped the engine in horrid fascination as I tried to overpower the temptation of joining in the raw power. Sometimes I get so close and I can grab the surprise package and rip the covering to view the contents, it goes a little higher or farther away and I'm lost again. But I go a little faster, just a little faster, and there it is again and I'm close, real close. So I edge over that point of no return and I can't come back again, so I make a last grab and life jumps back and away and laughs as I plunge into darkness. The skydiving frightened me to such an extent that I knew I had to try it."

North of Tucson, Smitty made the required five static jumps, but on the sixth one, a free fall, he recalls, "As I was waiting to jump the wind blasted by and soaked me in its freedom. The approach zone came nearer and I had the desire to shed my clothes completely and spring off the perch naked of any guilt or inhibition. It was tempting. I jumped prematurely from the plane's ladder and laughed as they screamed for me to wait.

"After I waited the allotted five seconds to pass, I no longer wanted the parachute to open. It was one of the strangest feelings of my life. I was enraptured and kept falling, wondering if they were screaming down there, or what. The air rushed by and filled my lungs with crystals of fright, yet the fright acted as an explosive fury to rack my body with a thousand sensations. Each heartbeat increased the sensation. I was attaining an incredible orgasm, almost totally sexual, falling helplessly. All my mind could register was that no one could go faster and I was quickly leaving the whole God-damned phony, rotten insecurity behind me, the fairy-tale world of stupidity, and since they created it, I wasn't really part of it anyway, nor did I really want to be.

"I imagined I heard the spectators' screams, pleading, and that made absolutely no sense. Why should they care, why did they want me in their world at that precise moment; I tried to accept and believe what they believed, it was just that this driving fury dominated me.

"There was no sensible reasoning behind their motives. Was it the conscience inside straining too hard that merited their actions? Isn't conscience a learned reaction based on environment, man from his most primitive surroundings had to find something to worship. Is it because all the uncertainties horrify him to such an extent he's in constant fear of loneliness and despair? Something kept pounding inside me to wait, I was going faster than anyone could and the whole rot—the mixed-up world was left behind. I was gone, I was like drunk and could decide my own fate. I'd been tempted not to open the chute but I did.

"Many, many nights after that I lay awake wondering if I jumped alone would I open the chute in time, if I sensed no begging, pleading eyes around to penetrate my mind and cause me to rescue their consciences. And I knew I couldn't go back, that the temptation not to pull the parachute open would eventually win."

In this parachuting incident, Schmid ran through all the themes relating to his "duels with Death and his disciples." Again tempting somebody or something, other people, nature, perhaps God, to see if they cared enough to stop him from killing himself. Schmid was convinced that ordinarily they didn't. Reality, day-to-day living, is that "God-damned phony, rotten insecurity," the world the other people or God created that "I wasn't really a part of...." And again, the danger drew attention to Smitty; there was constant exhibitionism in all of Smitty's bizarre acts. In the free fall, since he was falling through the sky, he had to imagine what other people were doing, but he was fairly certain they were pleading with him, screaming for him to pull the ripcord.

All the escapades were shadowed by death, the only real certainty to end the "constant fear of loneliness and despair." He sought to drive himself beyond the ordinary, to some final confrontation which would end his isolation.

He never quite reached the point of suicide. "From the chambers of complexities in my soul, I called upon a strength to omit the thought of suicide. But the emptiness within my heart was too resurgent. I meditated on the decision of my death when suddenly an icy blackness paralyzed my actions."

But if he was not finally ready to kill himself he found ways to make the world pay attention. If they wouldn't love him, they might hate him. If he couldn't kill himself, he might kill others.

In a tight corner, Smitty described how he felt. He wrote: "I feel so alone and abandoned as if I were cast somewhere in the midst of my childhood again. I feel as if I were a mountain among mountains, only my mountain stood alone and frightened, ever attacked by the wind and the elements. On one side there is a steep perpendicular wall of black wet rock, streaked by ice and snow. No neighboring peaks protect this wall which stands exposed, ever covered with snow, attacked by the wind, oppressed by the overbearing weight of blue ice and boulders made heavier by the glistening shells of white crust, attacked by the leverages and pressures greater than any mountain can resist forever.

"My mountain bore the oppressive weight and resisted the leverages of the normal rhythm and tension of earth, rock, snow, and ice, until in one second of one hour of some day there could be added the one snowflake, drop of water, or mote of dust, and because of this infinitesimal disturbance the precise measure of a balance and rhythm would be torn free, and an avalanche of snow, ice, boulders, and valley-rending sounds would be torn loose from the mountain wall and take with it, in its plunge toward destruction, the bowels torn from the body of the sheer wall, to make more dreadful the blind engulfment, destruction, and burial of the good and the bad, the evil and innocent, no matter who or what lay in the path of the avalanche."

There came a time in the spring when the avalanche at last began to move.

PART TWO

ONE NIGHT IN MAY, 1964, a young girl disappeared. Her name was Alleen Rowe, she was fifteen years old, a sophomore at Palo Verde. She lived on Calle Cuernavaca, four doors away from Mary French. She was friendly with Mary but they were different: Alleen was a sensitive, above-average student who spoke seriously of college, was fascinated with oceanography, reincarnation, Russian novels. She took long walks in the desert to gather unusual stones, and told a friend, "I love the desert, it makes me feel alive." Even when the rest of Tucson kept their windows up to escape the heat, Alleen liked to feel the sun and know that she was part of the desert. "Everything becomes alive," she said. Yet at other times, infected with an adolescent melancholy, she'd dwell on thoughts of death, often discussing mortality with her mother, a registered nurse on night shift at the Tucson Medical Center.

Mrs. Norma Rowe had brought her two sons, Alleen, and a small brown dog to Tucson less than a year before. Although her house was somewhat older and not as large as the project houses on Calle Cuernavaca, Norma thought it had more personality. There was cactus and small cuttings arranged in flowerpots along the east wall. The seashells, some spindly shrubs, and odd-shaped stones distinguished it from the project houses.

As a divorced, single mother, Norma faced a number of difficulties and life was "not an easy chore." She had few friends in Tucson, but was close to her daughter, Alleen, and mother and daughter considered themselves "friends." Norma didn't want any walls between them, but recently a certain distance had developed. Alleen had been seeing a boy from the university and he had given her his ring. Norma approved of the student, but was less sure about some of the others Alleen knew, like Mary French.

At fifteen, Alleen had soft blond hair, made more yellow by the sun, framing the pleasant oval of her face. Her sea-blue eyes were bright and alert. Notwithstanding her age, she was more a woman than a child, and she told her mother all about her conversations with Mary, talks that dwelt heavily on sex. Mrs. Rowe didn't approve but Alleen defended Mary. "Alleen used to come giggling to me about all the things Mary French had told her that day. 'You should hear her talk,' she used to say. And when I asked her why she listened, Alleen said she thought Mary was a nice girl. Alleen was so full of mercy that it never occurred to her that anyone would harm her."

The temperature on Sunday, May 31, 1964, stayed near ninety throughout the day. After dinner, wearing a black bathing suit and rubber sandals, Alleen watched the Beatles on television. It was still too warm in the house. She had planned to study for exams the following morning. She had to be at school by 6 o'clock, but she grew sleepy as the balmy night closed in.

Shortly before nine o'clock, while Norma prepared to leave for work, Alleen took a bath, set her hair in curlers, then climbed into bed.

Norma announced she was leaving for work and entered Alleen's room. She saw Alleen's school books laid out on the table by the bed, along with her purse. Alleen was lying on her left side the way she usually slept, her left arm partially over her right shoulder. In the dim light, Norma saw the metal curlers in her daughter's hair. She said good night and closed the door slightly. It was a few minutes after nine when Norma left for work.

Earlier that afternoon, Alleen had been talking to Mary in front of the French house. Both girls were standing near the curb when a bronze Ford Falcon approached on Calle Cuernavaca. Smitty brought the car to a stop at the curb. John Saunders was with him and there was another boy in the rear seat.

When Mary came to the car, Smitty said, "Get Alleen to go out with John tonight." While Smitty waited, Mary talked to Alleen. After a few minutes, Mary returned to the car and told Smitty Alleen couldn't go. Alleen started home and Smitty drove off. Mary went inside. "Smitty called a little later," Mary recalls. "He told me to call Alleen and get her to go out with John. He called four or five times more." Mary called Alleen three times, asking her to go out, suggesting that they double date. But Alleen said she couldn't go.

Before dinner, Alleen was at a house nearby with a friend who was babysitting, and Mary went over and talked to her again about the plans for that night. Then Mary returned home. It was about eight o'clock when Smitty arrived with John Saunders.

Mary knew that Smitty had more on his mind than a double date. Sometime before that night, Smitty had talked about "killing someone." He'd told Mary, "I want to kill someone. I want to kill a girl." He wanted to see what it would be like and if he "could get away with it." He had prepared a list of names, candidates for killing. One was Alleen Rowe.

It was almost eight o'clock. Smitty had John in the car when he came to Mary's house. Mary says that Smitty then told her that "He wanted to kill someone and that he wanted to do it tonight and asked me if I would try to talk Alleen into going out with John. He said that he would hit her with a rock and bury her in the desert." When Mary complained that she had tried repeatedly to get Alleen to go with John and failed, Smitty said, "If you can't get Alleen, get someone else."

Mary called a few other girls but none of them would go out with John. Smitty left and Mary returned to the house where Alleen's friend was babysitting, and she again spoke to Alleen about going out with John.

Finally, Mary says, "Alleen went home and she called me from her house and told me that she would go out with him, but she couldn't leave until her mother went to work."

Smitty returned to the French house, alone, and Mary told him Alleen would go with them. They'd have to wait until after her mother left. Then Mary accompanied Smitty to John's house.

"John and Smitty got a shovel," Mary says, "and put it in the trunk of the car. I saw them take it out later." They drove around for a while and "drove by Alleen's house but her mother's car was still there. We just drove around. We kept driving by until the car was gone." Then they parked by the alley at the Rowe house.

"I got out," Mary recalls, "walked up through the alley, and tapped on her bedroom window." A few moments later, "She came out the back door. She had on a bathing suit and shift. Her hair was in curlers."

Alleen was barefoot and carrying a pair of sneakers. Mary got into the front seat alongside Smitty. "John and Alleen were in the back seat." They drove east along 22nd Street and turned off at Harrison Road, at the edge of the desert, barren, bleak. Mary had visited that wedge of sand near Golf Links Road many times in the past with Smitty, when they "got drinking." She says, "The four of us got out of the car. We walked down into the wash."

After walking for a while they found a place where they could be comfortable and sat down. They started talking. Mary says, "Someone mentioned the radio and Smitty asked me if I would go up to the car and get one. It was pretty far away. He said he would go with me, and we went up to the car. We had just got to about the top of the wash when we heard Alleen scream. 'She needs help,' Smitty said. He told me to get in the car and stay there and he ran back down. I went and got into the car."

According to Saunders, when Smitty returned to the wash, Alleen was pulling away from John. Smitty said, "What's happening?" but before either could reply, Smitty grabbed Alleen. He told John, "Put your hand over her mouth."

John attempted to keep her quiet while Smitty bound her arms behind her back. John recalls that Smitty was using a guitar cord and that Alleen was asking, "Why are you doing this? What's wrong?"

"Mary wants us to do it," Smitty said. "She hates you, Alleen."

"Why? I don't believe you," Alleen said, then John reports that Smitty led her further down into the wash. They stopped. John says, "Smitty told me, 'Take her bathing suit off.' But I couldn't get it all the way down. 'Her hands are tied—here,' I said, 'I can't get it down.'" Smitty then untied her and removed her bathing suit. He spread her shift on the ground and told her to "lay down."

Alleen was lying naked and Smitty told John, "Go ahead." John knelt down and tried to kiss her but Alleen was crying, so he got back up and said, "It's no good, I can't, Smitty, not the way she's acting now." Then Smitty told John, "Go take a walk."

John remained standing for a moment and Smitty said, "What are you waiting for? I said take a walk." Off by himself, John smoked a cigarette until he heard Smitty calling, "John, hey, John!"

When Saunders returned to the wash, Alleen had her bathing suit back on and was adjusting the straps. When she saw John, Alleen turned away and walked further down into the wash. Smitty indicated for them to follow her, and both walked a few feet behind her. "Smitty picked up a rock and handed it to me," John says, "meaning for me to hit her with it. 'I can't,' I said to him and handed the rock back to him. Smitty said, 'Go tell Mary to come down here.'"

Mary had stayed in the car. She recalls: "About thirty or forty-five minutes passed, until John came back to the car and said that Smitty wanted me to come back down." John remembers that "Mary was crying. I said, 'Smitty wants you to come back down there.' Mary said, 'No, I don't want to go. If he wants me he'll have to come and get me himself.'"

"John left," Mary says, "and I stayed in the car. I was in the front seat, not the driver's seat, but the other."

Back down in the wash, John found Alleen lying on the ground, on her back. "Her face and head were covered with blood," John says. "Smitty's hands were bloody—so was the front of his shirt. He said, 'Where's Mary?' I said, 'She said for you to come and get her.'"

Mary was still waiting at the car. "Smitty came up to the car," she says. "He was talking but I never said anything. He was breathing real hard and seemed excited. He got in the car and said, 'We killed her.' He said, 'I love you very much,' and he kissed me and he went to the back of the car and got the shovel. The next morning there was blood on my blouse where he touched me, on my shoulder."

At the car, Mary says Smitty told her that John had struck Alleen with a rock. "And he said, 'She took off running,' and John chased her and hit her again. He said John tried to have relations with her but he couldn't."

Mary got out of the car and walked back down to the wash with Smitty. Alleen was on the ground, "a couple of yards from where John was just standing there. She just had the bathing suit on. The curlers were off and she was all messed up—blood on her face and her head." Mary noticed no signs of movement or breathing from Alleen that might indicate she was still alive.

Smitty told John to start digging, and handed him the shovel.

John started digging. Smitty said, "Come on, we've got to bury her." Smitty began to dig with his hands. He said to John, "Give Mary the shovel."

Mary says, "They told me to start digging, so I dug." John and Smitty continued digging with their hands. "Smitty told me to take her feet and he took her arms and put her in the hole. John was holding her somewhere on the side."

The three placed the body into the hole. John remembers that he took the shift from the ground and put it in the hole while Smitty started shoveling dirt in over the body. Mary then relieved Smitty with the shoveling while he and John gathered up the hair-curlers from around the area. "We put them in a pile," Mary says, "and took and threw some sand over them."

John helped Mary fill up the hole. "Better leave the shovel," Smitty said. He then took off his bloodstained shirt and buried that along with the shovel. "We went back up the slope to the car," Mary says. "They wiped the car of fingerprints, the front and the back seat. Then they took me home."

On the way, Mary remembers, "Smitty wanted us to stick to the same story that John had a date with her that night and when we went over to pick her up she wasn't home, so we took John home and then the two of us went out."

When Norma Rowe returned from work early that morning, she went to bed thinking all her children were in school and didn't wake up until her two boys returned that afternoon. It occurred to her then that Alleen should have been home from school before her brothers, since her classes at Palo Verde let out earlier. Clint, Norma's oldest son, said that he hadn't seen Alleen but suggested she'd remained after school for something.

Norma went about her household chores and began to notice that things were not as they usually were. Alleen had left her bed unmade–that was unusual. Norma saw the school books on the table where she remembered seeing them the night before. Alleen's purse was still there. Sitting on the edge of the bed, Norma checked the money and personal things Alleen always took with her. Looking around uneasily, Norma saw that the room had not changed since she'd left for work. Something seemed wrong to Norma.

She examined her daughter's closet and found nothing missing except the black bathing suit Alleen had been wearing. Then Norma telephoned Palo Verde. The administrative office informed her that Alleen had not attended any of her classes.

Hanging up, Norma sat stunned for several moments, wondering what she should do. She placed calls to a number of people who might possibly know where Alleen was. No one had any idea where she might have gone or if anything had happened to her. Then Norma remembered that the night before Alleen had phoned the university student she had been going with, but had been unable to reach him. Norma spoke to the boy at length but he had no knowledge of Alleen's whereabouts.

By now it was dark. Norma Rowe faced the fact that her

daughter was really missing. Reluctantly, she telephoned the police department.

The evening before, six criminals had escaped from the Pima County Jail felony tank. During the night sheriff's officers and police search parties had apprehended five, but the sixth and most desperate criminal had eluded the patrols until late that morning. The urgency had slackened at police headquarters by the time an officer received Norma's call.

"Girls disappear for a while after disagreements with their parents," he told Mrs. Rowe. "Some have a boyfriend the parents don't take a liking to and there's other reasons why juveniles take off, but usually they return home as soon as they're hungry." The officer said, "This happens more often than—"

"You're wrong," Norma said. "This is not the case with my daughter, Alleen." She reported the reasons for her apprehension: the unmade bed, the purse and books untouched, an above-average student absent from an entire day of school. None of Alleen's clothes were missing, she told the officer, she'd taken no money, and all she'd been wearing was a bathing suit.

"Only a bathing suit?" the officer said, interested, but he repeated his reassurances. Mrs. Rowe was quick to deny that this particular case had anything to do with boyfriends, elopements, disagreements with parents.

She said her daughter had never left home before and she knew something terrible had happened to her. She reported that Alleen's boyfriend at the university said that he hadn't seen her. Then she mentioned the names of other friends of her daughter, people she didn't approve of.

Fears for her daughter's safety had been building in her all day. After a pause she revealed to the officer what he later told a fellow policeman was one of the most ridiculous and weird stories he'd ever heard from a mother.

She said Alleen had reported to her that some kind of sex club, involving young boys and girls from Palo Verde and other schools, was in operation, engaging in perverse sexual conduct, drugs, liquor, and organized prostitution. Alleen had told her, Norma said, that the leaders of the group had tried to get her into the club but her daughter had repeatedly refused to have anything to do with them. Now, Norma feared, this group had tried to force Alleen into their terrible activities, Alleen had again refused, and the leaders had done something to keep Alleen quiet.

The police would investigate, the officer said, and he asked Norma to contact them immediately as soon as she received any word from her daughter. Mrs. Rowe replied that she was afraid she would never hear from her daughter again.

Discussing the situation with his fellow officer, the policeman who had taken the call wondered whether such a thing could actually exist at one of Tucson's better high schools.

"It might just be," the fellow officer said, "that some of these women might not know their daughters' ways like they might think they do."

An investigation failed to disclose any evidence to support Norma Rowe's suspicions. It failed, in fact, to reveal anything in the Rowe neighborhood that was out of the ordinary except the girl's disappearance. Norma rechecked her daughter's wardrobe and only one other piece of clothing was missing, a yellow-checked shift with a lace hem. Nothing in the house suggested that Alleen had been removed from the premises by force; her two brothers, asleep at the time of her disappearance, would have heard something had the girl been forced from the house. No indication of a struggle of any kind existed. But where could she have gone, they wondered, in nothing but a bathing suit and a yellow shift?

During the days that followed, Norma kept after the police. She carefully drafted a list of people she suspected. With nothing else to go on, the police questioned those on the list, but none of them provided any information regarding Alleen. The names included Mary French, who was questioned eight or nine times the first day, and John Saunders and Charles Schmid.

On that first day, Mary recalls that Smitty called her about every half hour, "maybe ten times or more. He wanted to know if the police had been over to question me and he said that they would ask him to take a lie-detector test." At 5:30 that evening, "Smitty came over to my house. He stayed a short time and then went home. He returned about eight o'clock with John Saunders." Mary says they drove out to River Road and "up some dirt path and parked there."

Then, she said, "Smitty made us both repeat the story that we were going to tell the police so that we would all have it straight." It was about ten or ten-thirty when he drove Mary home.

A week after Alleen's disappearance, Norma Rowe's ex-husband telephoned from Texas to relate a dream he'd had, "a nightmare," in which his daughter was murdered in the desert.

Norma was convinced that the dream was in fact what had happened. She repeated it to the police, who said they were interested in more factual evidence. Despite Norma's constant suggestions, the police had nothing to go on, no starting point from which a proper investigation could proceed.

Detective Sergeant Robert Wilhelm, in charge of Juvenile Detail, conferred with Tucson Police Chief Bernard Garmire, but had little to tell him. Working under Wilhelm, several other detectives questioned and requestioned a number of people who knew Alleen, but none of the leads checked out.

Then, on July 1, one month after Alleen's disappearance, the police made a public announcement that the investigation had intensified and would continue. Actually, however, very little had happened aside from routine procedure.

Meanwhile, Mrs. Rowe conferred with reporters, private detectives, and anyone who expressed even a remote interest in the search for her daughter. A salesman calling on her would be informed of the facts, of the indifference of the police, and would be enlisted as a source of possible information.

Alleen's school acquaintances were re-questioned, as were Mary French, John Saunders, and Charles Schmid. Nobody gave any information. The adolescents were called in again and again until their parents and later their family lawyers began to complain. Injunctions were obtained prohibiting the police from further interrogations of the children. One lawyer stated, "These kids have no information and are being badgered by the police to cover up for their own lack of information about the missing girl."

Of course, there were a number of unconfirmed reports. Alleen had been seen down in Nogales, across the street on Stone Avenue, and in a number of southwestern cities. The police kept trying, but after a while they began to lose interest. Alleen's Palo Verde class moved into its junior year; there was still some gossip at school as to what had happened to her, but there were a lot of other things to talk about.

In March 1965, Norma Rowe went to Phoenix to discuss the case with the state's attorney general and demand results. She said the Tucson police were apathetic and that *something* had to be done. Dissatisfied with the reassurances of the attorney general's office, she then went to the head of the Federal Bureau of Investigation in Arizona. He didn't know very much about the case. Calling in reporters, she told them she was meeting with the U.S. Attorney's office in Tucson and that she had hired her own lawyer and would continue to pursue the issue "until they find my daughter one way or the other."

In the first week in March, Norma met again with the press. Her spirits sagging, she told them, "The police think she is simply a runaway. I'm sure she is dead. She's lost forever."

A week later Clint Rowe, age fourteen, answered the telephone and heard the voice of an anonymous caller who sounded like an old woman. The caller said she was bothered by what appeared to be "a grave near the end of the greens." She went on to tell Clint that "in the past there has been some really rough groups of kids out there, drinking and having wild parties."

The same anonymous caller talked to police and was more specific. She told them of seeing a grave near the golf course at Rolling Hills Estates and suggested that it could very well conceal the body of a young girl.

On Saturday morning the police, led by Sergeant Wilhelm,

walked through the area the caller had indicated. They could not find the grave in question or anything even resembling a grave, although they searched not only "the end of the greens" but the entire course and surrounding area. Later, Mrs. Rowe conducted her own search of the golf course, without obtaining any results. But the news of the search stirred up more calls, leads, and contradictory hints as to the girl's whereabouts, none of them useful. More missing-persons bulletins were mimeographed and sent to law-enforcement agencies, where they were piled on top of fliers in similar cases, all of them describing girls who seemed to have vanished into the air.

Looking anywhere for an answer, Norma Rowe consulted a New Jersey psychic. The oracle proved cryptic, and at her request Norma sent the woman an item belonging to Alleen, to be used as an inductor; the idea was for the woman to hold the inductor in her hands and through it receive vibrations which would clarify the mental picture. Nothing happened.

Alleen's former classmates finished their junior year and left Palo Verde for summer vacations. Nothing had come of the official inquiry. The missing-persons bulletin on Alleen Rowe was buried under a pile of more recent cases.

During the month of May, 1964 (the month Alleen Rowe vanished), Paul Graff married the girl he had been living with and moved away from Smitty and his friends. A few weeks later Mary French left Tucson temporarily and Smitty drove his motorcycle to Phoenix to take a physical for the army.

Smitty wanted no part of the service. "I resisted for two basic reasons," he says, "one being the regimentation and conformity, and the other that I didn't particularly relish the idea of shooting somebody to satisfy the whim of some idiot." When he filled out the forms, he listed himself as a conscientious objector, but the army didn't accept this as reason for deferment since Smitty had stated no religious preference. "Fortunately," he says, "my heart had an irregular beat, probably rock 'n' roll and my blood pressure was so low I was listed officially as 1-Y. I burned up the highway on the way back from Phoenix."

Although Smitty was once again receiving an allowance of $300 a month, Katharine and Charles Schmid Sr.'s luxurious new hospital had gone into receivership, and the Schmids were entering litigation.

Lawyer John Price, acting on the Schmids' behalf, had obtained an injunction prohibiting the police from requestioning Smitty in the Alleen Rowe disappearance. Following that, John Saunders left Tucson to join the navy, and now Richie Bruns was seeing Smitty almost every day. "It was like we were brothers," Richie says.

According to Smitty, "It was like Richie wanted to tell me everything, and I couldn't figure it out. I told him I wasn't his father confessor and didn't have to hear the sordid details of his life story. He'd say, 'Yes, I have to tell you. You've got to know. We're friends, aren't we?' But confessing things to me didn't seem to stop him from continuing to do them, the things he did, that he couldn't stop doing."

But it didn't matter to Smitty as he had stories of his own to tell Richie. Smitty habitually told him "stories about what a terrible man he was," and, encouraged by Smitty's confidence, Richie in turn would divulge his secrets, many of them fictional. Once he told Smitty that he'd hitched a ride on a freight train and found an old hobo in a boxcar.

"I pushed this old bum out of the door," Richie said. "I watched him fall and I think he broke his back or something. He made a weird noise hitting the ground."

Smitty wanted to know if, in Richie's opinion, the hobo had turned to a skeleton. Richie said, "Yeah, if he's dead. If no one found him, then I really believe I killed him."

During the early summer, Richie recalls, Smitty had wanted to order a pair of piranha fish from South America. They could be bred in a big jar, kept warm, then dumped into Sabino Lake. "All the kids with skinned knees," Richie said, "like those Band-Aid commercials on television."

One night after cruising the teenage hangout, they wound up at Johnnie's Drive-In on Stone Avenue with "nowhere to go and nothing to do." Smitty suggested they drive to San Diego.

Richie agreed and took over the driving. "I was speeding," Richie says, "and drunk too. I kept banging against the sides of the hills and every time I'd hit a dip in the road, Smitty would bounce around in the back seat where he was sleeping. Once I hit a bend so hard it tossed him off the seat and on the floor. He just got back up and tried to make himself comfortable, using my jacket as a pillow."

They checked into a cheap hotel in San Diego and cruised the beaches the following day. "There were all these sailors running around the place and Smitty said we might run into John Saunders. Later, Smitty suggested we catch a couple of girls, rape them, and murder them."

That night in San Diego, "we prowled around the beaches, even underneath the piers and along those waterfront hot dog stands, hunting for victims. He said he wanted young-looking girls. I thought he was drunk—having illusions.

"I thought, 'fuck it,' it was cold and getting colder. My jacket was back at the hotel. Smitty kept on walking around the beaches and I walked back to the hotel. When I got back in the room I jacked off. It relieved the tension and then I got my jacket."

Richie wanted to return to Tucson. He says, "Smitty was still prowling the beach like a wolf. He looked weird. I said, 'Come on, man, come on.'"

In July, 1964, Smitty noticed a sixteen-year-old blonde at Himmel Park Swimming Pool off Speedway. She was wearing a polka-dot bathing suit, sandals, and her shoulder-length yellow hair waved from side to side as she ran along the edge of the pool. Her name was Gretchen Fritz. She seemed a little nervous, jumpy, and there was something about her, a stray-cat look in her eyes that made

Smitty think of her as being "like a wreck looking for it to happen."

He pointed the "skinny blonde" out to Richie, who then found out the names of the boys Gretchen had been going with. Smitty saw that she was driving a new red-and-white Le Mans and he flirted with her at the pool. When she left, he followed her home, staying well behind so that she wouldn't notice him.

From what he could see of her house behind the adobe wall that enclosed the property, it seemed almost like a mansion. She lived on East Elm, one of the most fashionable streets in Tucson.

Gretchen's father, Dr. James Fritz, was one of the leading heart and chest specialists in the Southwest, a board member of the Union Bank, and his wife, Nancy, was socially prominent. They attended all the best parties in Tucson. Gretchen had two older sisters, both married, one younger brother, and a younger sister, Wendy, still in junior high school.

But Gretchen was different from the other members of her family. She didn't fit in at the exclusive private school her parents sent her to; she was a nonconformist with eccentric ideas: she told a classmate she scorned boys and admired prostitutes "who get money for what most boys expect to get free." One teacher regarded Gretchen as a "troublemaker, and the child is a psychopathic liar."

Her contemporaries considered her spoiled: "I guess beyond repair," one girl said, and added that she was almost "psychotically jealous." Gretchen had a bad reputation among teenagers as an "easy put-out," and when asked about such matters Gretchen seemed pleased and offered a wry smile. "They're just jealous," she'd say.

Gretchen was constantly cutting classes to cruise Speedway and was suspected of various juvenile crimes. In the summer of her senior year she was in serious trouble over the attempted holdup of a liquor store. The headmaster of the school requested that she not return and recommended psychiatric treatment.

"Gretchen was all right with the girls," a friend recalls, "but the minute a boy was there she'd change—like 'bang,' a Jekyll-Hyde sort of thing."

Several days after he had noticed Gretchen at the pool, Smitty went into the kitchen at Craycroft Center and loaded an assortment of pots and pans into a cardboard box. Then he set out for East Elm.

The box was clumsy but he juggled it up to Gretchen's house. Gretchen answered the door and Smitty told her he was selling pots and pans. She seemed reluctant to let him in. But when she recognized him from the swimming pool she said it would be okay. Smitty immediately launched into a spiel on pots and pans and unloaded the cardboard box.

"But they all look like they've been used," Gretchen said. Smitty then explained that these were samples, and tried to get them back into the box. Gretchen watched him curiously and said she would buy them all.

"These particular ones are not for sale," Smitty said. "They're my samples."

"But I want these," Gretchen insisted. Smitty was just as insistent that he couldn't sell his samples. If he did, he'd get fired, he told her. Gretchen didn't believe him; then Smitty confessed that he wasn't a salesman at all.

"I dreamed it all up to meet you," he said. "I couldn't just come here and knock on your door; I really and truly didn't want to be that brash. It would be like I was trying to pick you up."

Gretchen started to laugh, and then suddenly she was crying. Smitty didn't understand it. She hurried from the room, only to return moments later and ask if he cared for a cocktail. Her mercurial moods aroused a different interest in him. He felt foolish about the pots and pans, and accepted.

Gretchen brought two drinks to the sofa and she and Smitty sat and talked. She said no one had ever cared enough before to dream up something that stupid, and added that he'd be surprised at some of the "lines" she'd heard. "If you want," she said, "we can meet at Sabino tomorrow."

Richie went with Smitty to Sabino Canyon the following day. "Gretchen had two of her scummy girlfriends with her," he said. "This one fat pig kept trying to nestle up close to me. Smitty kept telling her about 'Richie,' he wanted her to go with me so we could double on the way back.

"I had my quart of beer and was content to sit on the rock and enjoy my beer, watch the water, you know. This pig, you could just see oil and grime all over her. And she was sweating."

Richie insulted the girl and Gretchen "blew her mind. She sort of fell in the water, then Smitty pushed her the rest of the way in with all her clothes on."

Recalling that day, Richie says, "I believe my insulting her pig friend is the reason Gretchen and I disliked one another from the start. It only got progressively worse."

On his first date with Gretchen, Smitty remembers, "She had too much to drink, although she handled it as though it was an everyday occurrence with her. She began to tell me she was pregnant, the guy had left her and she said her parents didn't love her. She said she hated her family and had tried to run away several times. Last time she'd been sent to a private school. Once she'd tried to rob the liquor store with some friends (the ones that had been at Sabino with her).

"She told me she was afraid of her parents and her brother-in-law had something to do with the Mafia. The more she spoke about her problems, guys leaving her, family disagreements, the more I felt something for her. It was like, 'Here we go again.'"

Richie says, "Smitty screwed her in short order, but she cried when he took off her bra, because nothing was there."

When it was over, Smitty recalls, "...she jerked back and said, 'Now that you've got what you want you'll leave just like the rest, because I know you're no different than them.' I said, 'What do you know about me?' I couldn't hurt her, not then, and I said I wasn't like the rest. 'I probably love you,' I told her.

"As soon as some time had passed and we were going around together, being seen at Johnnie's almost every night for a while, the word got around and I started to receive various stories about Gretchen. I didn't believe them, but..."

Richie had talked to a number of boys Gretchen had gone with, and their advice to Smitty was to keep away from her. Even one of Gretchen's friends warned him: "She'll get you in one hell of a mess and she won't care. She does things like the world belongs to her."

Once she ran out of gas on Speedway and, with the help of a girlfriend, siphoned gas from a car at the curb. The police caught them and she was in trouble again.

One boy told Smitty, "Gretchen is *dangerous*, just like it says on a box of dynamite."

But Smitty became increasingly involved with Gretchen Fritz. "Gretchen's father caught me naked at her house once but he didn't make me stop seeing her. I used to slip in through her window at night; we'd make love while her parents were asleep in another part of the house. Her mother saw footprints outside Gretchen's window and discovered what was happening. She didn't know I was having sex with Gretchen but she suspected."

A friend sums up Gretchen's relationship with Smitty: "She was always lonely and looking for someone to love her. At times she didn't even care who it was. Smitty gave her what she wanted but she was afraid of losing him. She knew he was going out with other girls, like Mary French for one, and when she'd find out they would quarrel. I remember one night they were at a show and started arguing about something. Smitty had to hit her several times to stop her hysterics. She cried a lot but never told me what they'd fought about. Then, five minutes later, they were holding each other. It wasn't easy to get to know Gretchen."

After a while, Smitty considered breaking off with her. He didn't want to leave her but his friends told him it would be the best thing.

One of them suggested an "out" for Smitty by putting her in the wrong. The idea, according to Smitty, was "for me to catch her with another guy, thus giving me an excuse. So Richie, Johnny, and I got this kid, Charles Stenz, to have her meet him at the park, the plan being that I'd come out of the bushes, act angry, then break up with her. Richie would be hiding in the bushes and be there as a witness. Everything went according to plan. Gretchen turned up . . ."

The way Richie remembers what followed: "Smitty slapped her. But then Gretchen told him that Charles Stenz, to bait her into coming, had told her that he had something he wanted to tell her about Smitty, and so she had come not just for the sake of going out, and Smitty made up with her."

Smitty says, "I tried to break up with her but couldn't manage it, and once before when I'd tried to break up with her she'd gotten drunk and was arrested for reckless driving, going on the wrong side of Speedway against the traffic. They put her on probation."

Complicating Smitty's relation with Gretchen was an apparent rivalry between Gretchen and Richie. "I never really understood why," Smitty says, "but she made life miserable for him in general." Gretchen said the reason she didn't care for Richie was that she feared he would involve Smitty in some serious trouble. Richie had been to a reformatory and thus represented a bad influence on Smitty. Richie also had the habit of confessing some actual and fictional misdeeds to Smitty, which alarmed Gretchen.

Smitty says, "I told her that Richie kept telling me about his activities, saying he had to even though it was none of my business, and Gretchen said, 'He wants you to know as much as he does, so you'll both be the same.' I'd say she was wrong."

Art Meyers had a more dispassionate view of the situation. "Bruns and Smitty were always together. They were inseparable. But Richie didn't like Gretchen at all. He told me he despised her. He had no specific reason. I didn't like her either. Gretchen thought she was pretty cool. She thought she was too hot, if you know what I mean."

Smitty felt that Richie had trouble dating girls. "From the time I knew him he went out with only four girls on his own and they all eventually dropped him. Some of them told me he was either on pills, drunk, or would try to rape them in some way. He used to bring some slob to the house on Woodland and once some girls we picked up at the drive-in. I had a hard time with Gretchen because she found out all about the ones we picked up at the A-1 Drive-In, and she seemed to know all the details."

Smitty says that he tried to arrange dates for Richie. "But they all disliked him or wouldn't go out with him. I wasn't really aware of it at the time but Gretchen was blackballing him at school with all the other girls. At one party he and Gretchen got into a serious fight. I didn't exactly understand what he was talking about until I learned that he'd been blackballed."

One night Richie was drunk and got into trouble on his own. Smitty recalls, "Gretchen really enjoyed finding out about it. She made it seem as though it was a lesson, and I should learn from it. I couldn't appreciate her view, as Richie and I had parties, booze, and girls and a lot of kicks. I pretended to take it seriously, only trying to keep Gretchen in place and thinking that I was totally true to her and had nothing to do with anyone else.

"It required ingenuity on my part; Gretchen was hardly a fool. I thought that being engaged to her, Mary French, and Darlene Kirk would satisfy me but even then I wanted more. I even seriously thought of bigamy, like if somewhere along the line I could meet two relatively wealthy girls, I'd marry them both under aliases and live off them comfortably. I'd use the guitar playing as an excuse to be gone for long periods of time, while I lived with one, then the other. I used to laugh when I thought of the predicaments I'd be in if the record I planned to cut turned out successfully.

"Now how could I sensibly explain that I did go with three girls at once and I did give them rings and it was necessary for me to fabricate certain stories so as not to be discovered?

"Gretchen demanded my fidelity, or fidelity on the part of anyone she went with, but as soon as my back was turned she was running around herself. The only thing I had in my favor was that she wasn't as cool about it as I was."

Darlene Kirk, a thin, brown-haired sixteen-year-old daughter of a Tucson postman, was one of Smitty's steadies at the time, one of the girls he proposed marriage to. Smitty had asked Darlene to babysit and give him the money she earned so he could further his rock 'n' roll career. Darlene was a Presley fan. Richie says, "She had Elvis pictures stuck to her mirror and life-sized ones all over the windows." Although she could appreciate Smitty's emulation of her idol, she wasn't enthusiastic about investing in his career.

According to Richie, Smitty hoped to get money by becoming engaged to her. "He bought her a $3 engagement ring and told her, 'Cutting a record will cost money,' as he slipped the ring on her finger. 'Before we can get married,' Smitty told her, 'I'll need a lot of money.'" When Darlene didn't contribute, Smitty told her he had other things to do.

"Darlene was moping around the school," Richie recalls, "and asking, 'Why won't Smitty call me?'" She used to give Richie messages to pass on to Smitty, and "whenever she did see Smitty, she always wore black stockings because Smitty had told her to." Finally, after some tearful scenes, she gave Richie the engagement ring to return to Smitty. Richie said he couldn't do that, and then considered dating her himself. "Smitty," he rationalized, "couldn't care less about her or the other girls."

After a couple of dates, Richie felt that Darlene could hold her liquor. He prized himself on being a seasoned drinker, and especially detested Gretchen's "inability at holding liquor. She was notorious for it. She would get totally out of her head on one can of beer, and at a party for El Rancho stores, where Paul was working, Gretchen barfed all over the tables. It was disgusting."

Later, Bruns and Gretchen were involved in an incident that confirmed their mutual dislike. Richie had acquired a white 1950 Cadillac convertible, and one night he says, "I was with a girl named Mimi and we were pulling out of Johnnie's on Speedway and Craycroft and Smitty was coming down the street on the other side and had Gretchen with him and he saw me going out and he honked.

"I pulled over and he went through Johnnie's and came back over. He asked me who the girl was, what her name was, and Gretchen whispered in his ear that she looked like a whore, and Mimi heard it, so, after we left and were driving around, Mimi decided she wanted to fight Gretchen or make her take it back.

"I took Mimi over to Smitty's and I told Smitty that she wanted to fight Gretchen. And Smitty said, 'That sounds like a pretty good idea.' He said to me, 'This is what she needs.' We decided to get a double date and go out to the show and give Mimi a chance to fight Gretchen. So I went home and later that night he called me up and said he talked to Gretchen, but Gretchen was expecting trouble and she made him promise that when any trouble started Smitty would make both of us get out and walk home. He said, 'What we'll do is go get the BB gun over at Paul's, take the BBs out and everything, and when she makes me leave the car you pull the gun on me and in that way it won't make me look so bad and I won't have to make you walk home.'"

Richie got the BB gun from Paul and later that night at a drive-in movie, Richie says, "Mimi asked Gretchen why she called her a whore. Gretchen denied that she called her a whore and Mimi said, 'Why, I heard you.' Gretchen said, 'You are imagining things, seeing something.' Mimi kept taking her cigarette and flicking it on Gretchen's hair and so kept giving her a hard time. But Gretchen wouldn't get out of the car and fight, and finally she turned to Smitty and said, 'All right, make him get out.'

"Smitty turned around and winked at me and I pulled the gun on him and I said, 'Uh-uh, I ain't going nowhere.'" Mimi and Gretchen continued to bicker and they decided to leave the drive-in. Richie told Smitty to keep driving and at one point left the car and ditched the gun in the desert. "Finally, I went home and Smitty came over and picked me up and we got the gun and took it back to Paul's."

Days later, everyone was talking about how Richie pulled a gun at the drive-in.

According to Richie, Smitty was jealous of anyone even mildly interested in Gretchen. He developed several interesting ploys to keep her out of the reach of prospective rivals. He involved Richie in a campaign of writing anonymous letters to Gretchen's parents, containing such questions as: "Where was your darling daughter when you were having dinner last night? She was down at Johnnie's seeing Smitty." Smitty had Richie write these on his typewriter, because, he claimed, Gretchen's mother knew his handwriting. The idea was to have Gretchen's parents keep a closer eye on her so that she'd have less chance to see other boys. Smitty then dictated letters concerning Gretchen and VD to the health department, letters Richie would type and mail for Smitty.

Then Smitty told Gretchen that Richie was behind the letters, and knew everything about her. According to Richie, Smitty said to Gretchen, "Richie has all this stuff over your head and he's blackmailing me with you. He says if I stop hanging around with him, stop loaning him money and that, he's going to the police with all he knows about you and you'll be sent to Good Shepherd."

At this time, Richie and Smitty were still competing with each other in the stories they told about themselves. They had carried it a step further, according to Richie, by planning crimes, assaults, mayhem, and even murder together.

One night at Smitty's they were talking about Gretchen, about Darlene, and then about how they hated a girl named Mary Tyler. Richie recalls, "Smitty suggested, 'Let's go get her.' He said, 'I'll take care of the old man and old lady, and you take care of Mary and her brother.'" Another boy actually drove them over to the house, and while Smitty waited in the car, Richie scaled a wall and made his way to the rear of the house. The plan was for Richie to gain entrance for Smitty. Richie attempted to open the rear door but it was dead-bolted.

"I stood there for a minute," Richie remembers, "and thought about the time we went to San Diego. Then I just faked the rest of it." When he returned to the car he told Smitty, "There's someone walking around in there. Let's get out of here."

It was not long thereafter that Smitty related to Richie what had actually happened to Alleen Rowe. John Saunders had been discharged from the navy and was accompanying Richie, Smitty, and another boy named Rick on a hunting trip through the Golf Links area. "Smitty and John went down into the wash to scare up some rabbits," Richie recalls, "and they were gone approximately half an hour."

Later, "at the golf place, parked at the corner of Desert and 15th, Smitty referred back to our previous conversations, when he told me that he had been questioned in the case after the girl disappeared, and his lawyer had got an injunction against the police and they couldn't talk to him about it. He was bragging about that, but he told me at this time that he did kill Alleen Rowe, and that when they'd left the car on the hunting trip they didn't go down to scare up jackrabbits but went down to the grave and that he stuck a stick in the ground to see how she smelled after she had been there so long.

"He said an animal had burrowed itself into where the grave was and had been eating the body."

Bruns did not give much further thought to Smitty's story. The following week, however, while waiting in Smitty's car which he was using to pick up Darlene Kirk at Rincon, Richie mentioned to a couple of kids that Smitty was supposed to have murdered the Rowe girl. Richie says, "It was just conversation, like what's new."

One night Richie was drinking beer with Smitty and Saunders at the Hi-Ho. "John had been caught shoplifting," Richie recalls, "and there was something about an assault charge against him." John and Smitty were talking and Richie was concentrating on his beer when the subject of the Rowe girl came up.

Richie remembers John asking Smitty, "Did you ever burn those clothes?"

"What clothes?" Smitty asked.

John said, "You know, oh–*hers*."

Smitty looked at him and shook his head and said, "Wow, what's the matter with you? She wasn't even wearing any clothes."

The next afternoon, sitting in Johnnie's Drive-In, Smitty told Richie the details of the Rowe killing. Richie says, "He told me that Mary French had gotten Alleen out of the house and that they drove out there and Smitty and Saunders took Alleen down into the wash there and they made her take off her bathing suit, and that both of them had sexual relations with her and then they made her put back on her bathing suit.

"First of all he tried to strangle her, but she wouldn't strangle because she kept doing something with her chin, so he picked up a rock and bashed it over her head. Then he went back to the car and got a shovel and buried her on the side of the hill underneath a tree and he said that if Mary French ever knew he had relations with her she would probably kill him."

In September, while Paul was staying at Smitty's house for a week, Smitty also told Paul about the murder. Paul didn't believe Smitty. "He told me they buried her in the desert," Paul says. "He asked me to go out there and see the grave, almost in a joking manner. I didn't go."

Several days after Paul left, Richie tried without success to call Smitty. He found him at the Ranch Restaurant after spotting the Falcon in the parking lot.

Richie said to Smitty, "I called you all day yesterday and there was no answer. What's the deal?"

Smitty replied, "I fixed the phone so it won't ring. I can turn it back on and it'll ring when I want it to."

"What did you do that for?" Richie asked.

"Gretchen's been calling night and day," Smitty said. "I know if the damn thing rings I'll pick it up."

Richie began to think. "Nobody bugged the Smitty I knew." He says, "Nobody bothered the Smitty I knew, so I asked him why he was doing all this stuff for Gretchen. He was acting like a little kid.

"He told me he'd taken her out there and showed her where he'd buried Alleen Rowe, and she was holding that over his head, if he didn't do exactly what she said.

"He took her out there to show her what sort of guy he was, to see if she still loved him. He's that way, he wants to find out if people care, if anyone cares. He couldn't be normal. But girls ate on him."

Gretchen was "blackmailing" Smitty and it was beginning to "get under his skin." He discussed with Richie ways of hurting Gretchen. "He knew when her parents would go out, which was quite often. She would be home alone at night. What he wanted me to do was call to Gretchen when her parents were gone, he would get on the phone, and Gretchen would naturally ask if I was there and he would say, 'Yeah,' and he would want people to verify it at his folks' hospital there that were watching. While he was talking on the phone, I was to go and ring Gretchen's doorbell and when she would open the door I was to throw acid in her face."

But Smitty's feelings about Gretchen were still ambivalent. Richie says, "If he fucked up Gretchen, nobody would want her, but he said, 'If I really fucked her up, then maybe I wouldn't want her either.' It was good logic."

In October 1964, Katharine and Charles Schmid Sr. declared bankruptcy. Katharine's luxurious Craycroft Center had gone into receivership and the Schmids estimated their loss at over $300,000. They returned to Hillcrest on East Adams, where Smitty took over the small one-bedroom house next door to the Schmids' home.

Smitty painted the bedroom, windows and two glass doors that opened to the backyard flat black. He laid a green satin spread over the bed, installed his stereo next to it, and began to entertain his friends. But Richie felt that he was losing contact with Smitty.

"We were known on the east side," Richie says, "especially after that incident with the gun at the drive-in.

"After Smitty moved on Adams, he began hanging around with some southside people." Richie resented Smitty having left the "eastside bunch," for Richie didn't know anyone from the south side. "Smitty uses people, except me and Paul.

"I used Smitty's car, his credit cards, I even used Smitty's credit cards to put gas in my car. Outside of Paul and myself he used everyone, especially on East Adams, and all they did was sit around and listen on some old rusty record player."

One of Smitty's friends from the south side was a sixteen-year-old girl named Irma Jean Kolt. She'd dropped out of Pueblo High School after being absent twenty-seven days the first three months of her sophomore year. Irma Jean was also the mother of an infant whose father had fled Tucson on receiving news of his coming paternity. In the summer of 1965 she was unemployed and living with her parents.

According to Smitty, "Irma Jean was a pretty screwed-up kid; her father had one arm missing and was always out of work while her mother, an alcoholic, had been in and out of mental hygiene clinics for years, but fun at times if she was loaded.

"I'd lost my license over a traffic ticket and my car had been impounded. So, in Irma Jean's mom's car, with Mrs. Kolt driving, somewhere about July 15th, we headed down to Nogales along with Shirley and Kitty Bates, two teenage sisters that didn't do much except goof around Speedway."

They had lunch across the border, a few drinks, and did some shopping. Returning to Tucson they came across a stalled car whose driver was waving to the passing cars. His name was Bill Morgen and he was out of gas. His wife was slumped in the front seat.

"Our car is so damn crowded we can hardly move," Smitty recalls, "so the girls say, 'Sorry, with all the packages we don't have room to take you into town for gas.' So we leave. Except that I started spouting off how rotten it is just to leave them there. We go back and give them a ride twenty-five miles into town for gas and then return them.

"When they tell me their hard-luck story, down and out, no place to go, broke flat, I offer them my house and food, free, until they can get on their feet." Gassed up, the Bates' car followed Smitty back to Tucson. "We drop them off at my house, then go to the Kolts' house, where Irma Jean leaves her mom, and the three girls take me home.

"They came in for a while, while the Morgens were there and then, on their way out, Irma Jean was adjusting her blouse when Gretchen pulls up and sees Irma Jean doing this; naturally, she gets the wrong idea. Furious, Gretchen chased me around the house and I climbed a tree in the backyard. She tried to climb up after me but she couldn't, so she threw rocks instead, then raced off to find Irma Jean and the other girls somewhere up Speedway. They all stopped, I learned later, and one thing led to another. After the insults they talked, Irma Jean and Shirley told Gretchen about me messing around with other girls, and told her the name of one that I was engaged to. Gretchen blew her mind."

Smitty had to do something immediately to cool things with Gretchen. "I quickly told them (the girls) a fantastic story to the effect that Gretchen had a diary that said I'd killed some guy because he had run over my girlfriend and left, that I'd taken him out to the desert, shot him, and then buried him. I decided on something drastic because it would tie in with part two of my plan, what I called the Blackmail Bit. I fabricated a story that Gretchen knew I was messing around and she would have me arrested by turning the diary over to the police. Irma Jean and Shirley agreed to help, to get me back on good terms with Gretchen. I told them to tell Gretchen I wasn't messing around and that they had just tried to make her jealous, which they knew they could.

"The plan got more involved when I even told Irma Jean's mother that Gretchen had something on me, because I knew that Gretchen would believe *her* if she confirmed that I wasn't messing around with other girls. I laughed to myself at the cleverness, the way I'd smoothed things over.

"Bill Morgen and his wife, Doris, were there in my house and didn't seem to have any intentions of leaving." It occurred to Smitty that the Morgens might talk to Gretchen "and unknowingly tell her, if she asked, what I did with other girls." So Smitty told the Morgens the same story he'd told the Kolts and the Bates sisters. "In fact, I hinted to several people that Gretchen was blackmailing me; this of course allowed me greater freedom in my choice of girls and enabled me to keep Gretchen cool at the same time. All I did was simply insert a few key words and they took the blackmail bit from there. I naturally figured if it worked so good before, it would again and it did, at the time."

While all this was going on, Smitty was becoming more involved with his house guests. "Bill Morgen showed no concern or enthusiasm about looking for work. I wondered exactly what sort of trade Bill might have. He told me he was an upholsterer and that he'd lost his business.

"It was another hard-luck story, but the prospect of an upholstery business sounded interesting to me. My mom was having trouble at the time with the bankruptcy, so I couldn't get the extra money from her. It was sort of up to me. I offered to hock all my guitars and equipment and use whatever money I had on the side to set us up in business.

"One night the Morgens had a big fight and Doris called the police and had her husband arrested for being drunk. She kept screaming out in the street even after the cops had taken him to jail. And she blamed me for his drinking. My mother asked them to leave, but the next day it was discussed and I hocked the rest of my equipment to start again.

"No sooner had we managed to establish the upholstery shop at my house than Irma Jean's father arrived looking for work, so we took him in as a partner. I felt sorry for him, having only one arm, and the other Kolts in the shape they were. But as soon as we started some actual upholstering, the license people informed us we were zoned wrong to operate such a business. Mr. Kolt suggested we move the business to his house in South Tucson. I considered Irma Jean a friend and I liked her family, though I saw that there wasn't even enough food in their house to feed Irma Jean's baby.

"Operating out of the Kolts', very soon I came to the realization that Bill Morgen could not upholster, that he frankly knew nothing about it. After talking it over with Mr. Kolt, we decided to hire in an actual upholsterer. The man who answered the ad was named Arizona Mechanic; it was his authentic name, although it made the whole thing sound like a fairy tale."

Smitty's business venture, like his previous spurts of productivity, eventually ended in chaos. He says, "The upholstery shop was in full gear with Arizona Mechanic doing the upholstery. Then, behind my back, Bill asked Arizona Mechanic to go into partnership with him and drop me and Mr. Kolt. He was disgusted anyway with Bill's drinking, so Arizona Mechanic said no and told us about it.

"I decided I'd had enough of the Morgens. I'd given them a house rent-free, food which they never paid for nor were asked to, paid off the balance on their car, hocked all my musical equipment, and in turn, he tried to betray me.

"I then told him it was best to dissolve the partnership, but they could remain in my house until they made other arrangements. I stayed at the Kolts', working day and night, and for a couple of days Bill dropped in occasionally, and the last time he told me he was leaving for Phoenix."

Richie, with his feelings about the southside crowd, had not been seeing Smitty regularly. He describes Smitty's house on Adams at that time as "a stopping-off place. If someone on the south side wanted to go dick around on Speedway, they'd stop off at Smitty's and get a beer or something. Smitty used them and they used him. He didn't like anybody and was trying to escape from Gretchen. They were creeps, he even told me.

"After a period of time after Gretchen had been hounding him on the phone, keeping track of him every second, every day he told me that she had told him that he had fun all his life and everything he ever wanted he got and she had never had any fun. And now it was her turn and she was going to make him miserable. It kept building up from there and one minute he said that he would kill her and the next he'd dream up stories of throwing acid into her face, and things like that, work out little plans like that."

Richie had also talked to Paul. Both believed that Gretchen was "ruining Smitty," and both wanted to help. Paul had access to a quart of sulfuric acid, and Richie was willing, but Smitty would change his mind.

"No," Smitty would say, "it's no good."

During this time, Richie too had problems, but of a different nature. Darlene Kirk, the postman's daughter, was not seriously in love with Richie, and gave no indication that she would be. Art Meyers, a classmate of Darlene's, remembers their relationship as "kind of one-sided. After Smitty dropped Darlene, Richie was meeting her at Sunset Rollerama. He'd always liked her, he said, and after Smitty was through with her he said he'd like to take a chance at it. Richie invited her out and then several dates followed, but Darlene, more or less recovering from the falling-out with Smitty, didn't really seem to care. Richie was 'weird' she said. 'He's too excited about things, and he doesn't make a lot of sense. But he's sort of fun to be with at times.'

"He got to her," Art recalls, "and they started going around together," after Smitty had moved away from the east-side crowd. "They looked pretty good. It came to the point where he bought her pretty good rings and wrote all kinds of love poetry to her. Then Darlene told me she asked Richie if she ever broke up with him what would he do. He said, 'Baby, I'll make you sorry.'

"Darlene didn't like being threatened, if you know what I mean, like she was being forced to go with him, so she broke it up. She sent the rings back by some other guy."

Richie asked Smitty for advice. He dictated a message which Smitty wrote down on a strip of cardboard with a grease pencil. The message was supposed to be from someone asking for a meeting with Richie "behind the Enco station to tell you what a whore Darlene is."

In full accord with one another, Smitty then punched Richie several times about the face. Richie says, "My nose was bleeding, my lip was bleeding and my eye was getting black and blue when Smitty dropped me off at Malvern, the corner where Darlene's house was." Richie told Smitty, "I'll need about five minutes before you come in." Then Richie forced his way into Darlene's house in order to "spill blood on her carpet and her bedspread and the furniture there, and I held up the piece of cardboard and said, 'I got the bastard for this.'"

When Smitty arrived he said he'd heard that "Richie damn near killed a guy behind the Enco station," and as he helped Richie out of the Kirk house, he told Darlene, "Richie must really love you, Darlene."

"Just get him out of here!" was Darlene's reply.

For Smitty there came a break in the pressure. Gretchen went to California with her parents on vacation. After the collapse of the upholstery business, Smitty says, "I felt drained and disgusted with people. Gretchen was gone, so I decided to invite all my friends over for parties. For a couple of days Bobby Garcia stayed at my house and he invited his friends as well. I'm not sure how long the parties went on, but the idea lasted for a couple of weeks.

"I'd managed to forget about the Morgens and suddenly Gretchen returns, learns of the parties, and is furious with me. As soon as she storms out, Mary French arrives (she had been in Texas) and demands that I marry her because, she claims, she's expecting my baby. Mary called my mother and demanded a large sum of money to take off and have the baby quietly, but my mom doesn't have the money."

The day after Mary left, a disgruntled Richie asked to borrow Smitty's car. He said he was following Darlene Kirk. While Richie was in the house, Smitty received a phone call from Gretchen. When it was finished, Richie says, "He just put the phone down gently and walked into the bathroom. We were all there talking and all of a sudden the door of the bathroom was flying against the heater. It was like the house was going to fall apart and he ran out the back door."

Richie stayed where he was. He says, "Somebody went out back after him and came back in and then I went out and he was out there walking, pacing up and down by his car. I said, 'What's up?' He said she just told him on the phone that when she was over in California and she had some relations with a guy over there. Then Smitty went over and sat down on the car and started crying and saying, 'I really loved that,' then I just walked back in. The phone rang again and I picked it up. It was Gretchen and Smitty yelled through the screen door to give him the phone outside. He sat down and was talking and I didn't hear nothing he said."

For the next few days, Smitty says, "Everything was fine, until Gretchen then decided that *she* was pregnant and wanted to know what I intended to do about it. I said, 'At the moment, nothing.' We got into an argument at her house and she was screaming senselessly so I left. A week passed and on Monday afternoon of August 16th she came to my place and asked me to run away with her, she said we'd elope. I told her no, that I couldn't do that, so she got into her car and slammed the door. She turned around once and yelled, 'Smitty, you rat!' and drove away."

That night of Monday, August 16, *Tickle Me,* starring Elvis Presley and Julie Adams, was playing at the Cactus Drive-In Theatre at 22nd Street and Alvernon. At approximately seven-thirty, Gretchen, driving a Pontiac Le Mans, left for the movie with Wendy, her thirteen-year-old sister. Gretchen's mother, Nancy Fritz, had noticed Gretchen's increased restlessness since their return from San Diego, and was especially aware of it that evening while she dressed to attend the theater with her husband, Dr. Fritz. But Gretchen and Wendy left the house before Mrs. Fritz had a chance to talk to her.

During an intermission at the Cactus Drive-in, while Wendy went to buy refreshments, Shirley Bates came to Gretchen's car. Shirley says, "We talked about Smitty, and I told her someone said he was giving a party but I didn't know who was there. Gretchen got mad about it and didn't say anything else."

The following morning Nancy Fritz discovered that neither Gretchen nor Wendy had returned home. There would have been no real cause for alarm if Gretchen had been alone, but because Wendy had been with her, Mrs. Fritz was worried. She telephoned Gretchen's friends, who said they hadn't seen her, then Mrs. Fritz called Katharine Schmid at Hillcrest.

Mrs. Schmid replied, "I have no idea where she could be. Smitty said he didn't know anything either, but volunteered to check around and ask some of the others.

"You mean she didn't come home at all?" Smitty asked. He placed several phone calls. One was to a sixteen-year-old girl named Gloria Andrews, and he told her that both Fritz girls were missing. Gloria recalls, "He said now he could go out with anyone he wanted to."

Finally Mrs. Fritz called the police. They made a routine check of the neighborhood, then the Cactus Drive-In where Gretchen had said she was going. Nothing turned up and an all-points bulletin was issued on the car. The police also visited the houses of friends of both girls, but received no concrete information.

Because of Dr. Fritz's community standing, the police thought that perhaps the girls had been kidnapped. But after several days had passed and no one asked for ransom they dismissed the idea. "They wouldn't wait this long," a detective said. "There'd be no point to it. More than likely they've run away."

Smitty was questioned by the police. He had no information to offer, but suggested that Gretchen had made new friends while she was in San Diego and could have returned there to visit them.

Since the police were familiar with Gretchen as a headstrong, willful girl, they soon thought she had just driven off somewhere, and proceeded with a routine missing-persons investigation, not bothering to check out Smitty's San Diego lead. When they failed to get results, Nancy Fritz hired a private detective, William Heilig, who ran a security patrol in Tucson. Supplied with photographs, descriptions, and names of the girls' friends, Heilig launched an inquiry. That night, shortly before midnight, four days after the sisters had disappeared, Gretchen's red-and-white Pontiac was found in an annex parking lot of the Flamingo Hotel on Stone Avenue near Speedway.

The speedometer had sixty additional miles on it, but someone had disconnected it. There were traces of gravel and mud on the floor of the front and back seats. The driver's seat had been pushed all the way back. Gretchen's purse containing $20 and change, two ticket stubs from the Cactus Drive-in. Gretchen's keys, and a business card from Smitty's upholstery venture with Bill Morgen were also found. This alarmed Nancy Fritz who said, "She would never leave these things." Heilig and city detectives examined the car and made an investigation of the neighborhood around the Flamingo Motel. No one had seen the car being parked.

The next day Range Deputy John Gammons, patrolling the area south of Tucson, received a report that two girls fitting the descriptions of Gretchen and Wendy Fritz had been seen hitchhiking along the Nogales highway. It was reported that the girls were picked up by a car heading toward the Mexican border, some sixty miles south.

With news of the deputy's report, Nancy Fritz was hopeful and asked that Pima County Sheriff Waldon Burr send Gammons across the border to find the girls. Sheriff Burr said he did not have the authority to send a deputy into Mexico, that such an expedition would incur unjustified expense. Dr. Fritz then volunteered expenses and Gammons went to Mexico.

In Nogales, the deputy questioned some of the local inhabitants, showing them pictures of the girls, and more than ten people swore they'd seen them boarding a southbound bus for Hermosillo and Guaymas. Gammons went further into Mexico and westward along the Gulf of California. He met numerous persons who had seen two girls similar to those in question, and the deputy obtained "almost positive identification" in two other tourist towns. He consulted with the Mexican immigration authorities but they had no record of the missing girls' having obtained tourist permits.

Then a Mexican policeman reported he had issued a traffic citation to two girls answering the descriptions who were driving a Volkswagen the wrong way on a one-way street. The policeman said there was a *turista* sticker on the windshield. This too was checked out by Gammons but with no results.

Some 460 miles further into Mexico, in a resort at Mazatlán, two girls similar to the Fritz sisters had been cited for wearing bikinis around the beach club. Girls of their approximate description had been seen "around some of the teenage places in the tourist section." Then a report came that they had checked into a motel in another town. Gammons pursued these leads, but found nothing. He was then ordered to return to Tucson by Sheriff Burr, who felt that the deputy could not be spared any longer.

The sheriff's department printed hundreds of handbills in Spanish, with pictures and descriptions of the girls, for distribution south, and arrangements were made with a Mexican newspaper to carry similar notices in hopes of turning up further leads.

Back in Tucson, private detective Heilig kept talking to Smitty, who was annoyed by the repeated questioning.

"I even talked to some of the others," Smitty told the detective, "but they haven't any ideas about it. I just don't know what I can tell you further."

"But surely," Heilig persisted, "two girls like that wouldn't vanish without someone knowing something about it. You were going steady with her for several months, and she gave you no idea, not even an inclination that she wanted to leave, or was planning to go somewhere?"

"Oh, sure, she was always ready to leave," Smitty said. "She talked about it often, but there was nothing definite, no plans. I said she might have gone back to San Diego, that's really the best I can do."

The day after Gretchen disappeared, Smitty had called Richie. He asked him if the police had been to see him, then told him, according to Richie, that "Gretchen had run away last night and she took Wendy with her and left in the car."

Richie recalls that "Sergeant Wilhelm had been over and left his card. I called Wilhelm, and the only thing I told him was that Gretchen's car drove by my house about twelve o'clock that night, the night they were supposed to have disappeared."

About a week later Richie was sitting in Smitty's living room, drinking beer. Richie says, "He told me that he supposed that I knew what had happened to Gretchen, and I said 'No, I don't,' and then he told me that he had killed Gretchen and Wendy, and that he had done it right there in the living room of the house where we were at, and that he just didn't care anymore.

"After he killed Gretchen, Wendy was still going 'Ah, ah, ah,' gasping, and then he said it just stopped. He said that he took the bodies and carried them out and put them in the trunk of Gretchen's car and put them in the most obvious place where he could get caught, he just didn't care.

"I wasn't totally convinced that he'd killed Alleen Rowe, but I was fairly certain of it because of that conversation between him and John, and the fact that Alleen had disappeared. I knew she couldn't possibly run away and make it, at her age. After Smitty told me, 'I guess you know what happened to Gretchen,' then I was convinced of Alleen Rowe." Richie says, "Smitty told me, 'That's three, counting Alleen. Each time it gets easier.'"

A few days after this conversation, Richie says, "Paul came to my house and asked, 'Is there anything Smitty told you that he did to Gretchen?' Smitty had just gone crazy, things like that. The phone rang and I answered it. It was Smitty, and Paul was still on the porch. Smitty told me the reason he kicked Paul out was because Paul was talking about me, and Smitty told him that he, Paul, wasn't going to run Smitty's life, and he'd pick his own friends. I didn't say anything to Paul about Smitty calling."

The official investigation proceeded without results. Nancy Fritz consulted an astrologer who told her the girls were dead. Heilig, the private detective, thought "This Charles Schmid knows more than he's telling." And then a group known as the "Tucson Mafia" entered the case. Arrangements had been made for these underworld figures to put pressure on Schmid in the hope of bringing forth specific information. Schmid had told Heilig he believed the girls had gone back to San Diego. If this were true, the Mafia was prepared to deliver Schmid to San Diego to search for the girls.

Smitty received a telephone call and was told that two men would pick him up and bring him to a meeting. They advised him to be ready when they called. Earlier, Smitty had called Richie and others, telling them there was to be a party. But shortly after seven o'clock, before the party was to begin, an automobile with New Jersey plates stopped in front of Smitty's house. One neatly dressed young man came to the door and escorted Smitty to the car. "Since I didn't seem to have much choice anyway," Smitty says, "I went with them."

Sometime later, Richie arrived at Smitty's. "The damn house was deserted, so I sat on the curb and after a while Gerry Wells and Frank came by and said, 'Smitty said there's supposed to be a party.' I said, 'He called me up too.' Frank said, 'Well, let's go in.'"

Smitty was driven south of Speedway to an apartment on Alvernon. "They took me upstairs," Smitty says, "and introduced me to some jolly old fat man named Charles "Batts" Battaglia. The Bonanno brothers were there and some others who didn't do anything but sit and sneer at everything that went on.

"At first I thought I was dreaming and had wandered into a movie set at Metro-Goldwyn-Mayer, but no, I was actually in the middle of what everybody referred to as the Mafia and the underworld. Even though I expected to be beaten with a rubber hose or something like that, nothing like that even remotely occurred." Smitty recalls that the eldest Bonanno did most of the talking. "So you're the famous Smitty," the man said.

"Yes, sir."

"Understand you used to be the big champion in high school sports."

"Gymnastics," Smitty said.

"What happened to you?"

"Sir?"

"You look like a punk," the man replied, in a friendly way. "Whatta you say for yourself?"

"About what in particular?" Smitty replied.

They wanted to locate Gretchen and her sister, and Smitty recalls, "They asked me go to find them. When I said they were probably in San Diego and to ask a certain boy there, and he would know if anyone would. This Bonanno said 'No, you go find them.'

He smiled, and said see if I could find them.

"Next thing they said was that they wanted to talk to Richie Bruns." Then the two men drove Smitty back to East Adams.

By then a few others Smitty had invited to the party had arrived, Jimmy Scott, some girls. Richie says, "They were all sitting around. Smitty comes with two men, both smoking cigars. Smitty started mingling and just shooting the shit, then he came over and said, 'I want to talk to you outside a minute.' We walked outside and the other two guys came out. They got in the car. Smitty and I were talking on the step, and he told me the guys from the Mafia wanted to talk to us, that they wouldn't hurt us. I said, 'What do they want to talk to us about?'"

Smitty relates: "When I told Richie they wanted to talk to him about Gretchen, he turned white as a sheet and asked me if they had found them and why did they want to talk to him? I told him they seemed decent enough. He asked me again if I was sure they hadn't found them, I just laughed and said, 'If they found them why would they want me to go to California?'"

According to Richie, Smitty told him, "Somebody's hired them to find out where she is. They want me to go to San Diego to look for them, as I suggested they might be there." Then, Richie says, "Smitty looked worried. He said, 'What the hell am *I* going to do in San Diego? What the hell am I supposed to do there?'"

Richie got in the car with Smitty and when they arrived at the apartment on Alvernon, Richie was no longer impressed. "This Bonanno sitting there talking like he's so smart, saying, 'Gee, we didn't have a hard time finding you.' Why should they have a hard time? All they had to do was look in the phone book, that ain't no detective work."

There were others there but Richie didn't know their names, only that he had seen their pictures in the newspapers in connection with the Mafia. "This one man that did most of the talking," Richie recalls, "said they had been asked by a friend to locate the Fritz girls and that of all the names that came up of people that should know what happened, they had picked me and Smitty." The conversation,

Richie says, concerned Smitty going to California to find the girls. "Some old man was sitting there about eighty in his arthritis. They didn't impress me and I wasn't scared of them. They asked me if I knew where Gretchen was and I said, 'I couldn't care less.' Then the two people that picked us up at Smitty's house drove us to Johnnie's on Craycroft and Speedway. Left us off on the Craycroft side and we were walking over to where we used to sit. I asked Smitty what he was going to do when he got to California. Smitty said, 'I guess I'll just have to fake it out as best I can.' Then he said, 'If they turn up we're in pretty bad trouble. I think we ought to talk to Paul.'

"Smitty was shook by the Mafia, believe me. He was worried about the fact that people were looking for the girls.

"We bummed a ride, stopped off at Pine Crest Liquors, got some booze, hitched another ride over to Paul's. We woke him up and were sitting around talking out front. We told him what had happened with the Mafia, and he didn't believe us. Paul thought we were both having delusions, and did not even believe that the Mafia had even contacted us. He said we ought to go home and sleep it off. Then Paul said, 'But if they did, then you better call the FBI, if you're so worried about it.'"

Paul drove them back to Smitty's house, where Smitty called the FBI. Smitty says, "I was unable to reach anyone in the local office. Then I called all the way to Washington, D.C., to get J. Edgar Hoover on the phone but there were complications and he couldn't get through. I left Richie back at my house, went next door to my parents' house and told them what had happened, then called the FBI from their house. Again I couldn't reach them, but Richie had called again too and left a message with somebody at their office."

Richie said, "Washington called back and woke the jokers up here in Tucson." About forty-five minutes later Smitty came back to his house. Richie had been thinking.

"We went out," Richie says. "I told him that my neck was in this because the Mafia guys that picked us up said we were lucky that these big-wheel guys didn't just talk. When the other guys come in *they* will do more than talk. And I said to Smitty, 'My neck is in this too now. *I* am supposed to be the one that hates her so much and everybody knows this and if the bodies are found it will be my neck as much as yours, if not more. I suggest we go up there and bury them, if they're laying out there.'"

But, Richie admitted later, "I wasn't really *that* concerned that my neck was in it too, along with Smitty. I wanted to see the bodies. If there's a body laying out in the desert, later on they'd rush out there like vultures. I wasn't so much a vulture, I wanted to find out. It was either a put-up or shut-up deal. If he killed the girls and they're laying out there dead and he knows where they are, he can take me to them. If not, it's just a bunch of crap.

"I said, 'If you see those bodies out there, we better bury them.' He agreed. So I said, 'Let's go.' He said, 'Fine.' That kind of shocked me right there."

Smitty went to his parents' house and got the keys to their station wagon. They went around behind the nursing home to the tool shed. Richie says, "We went into the shed looking for a shovel but couldn't find one and so we came back over and went to his father's station wagon and there was a shovel, a flat shovel, in the back of the station wagon. It didn't have a point on it, it was the type of shovel you shovel coal with, stuff like that."

Using the station wagon, they drove to Johnnie's on Stone Avenue and stopped for hamburgers to go. Ten minutes or so later, Richie was driving north on River Road, then east to Pontatoc, eating the hamburgers.

Richie recalls, "I completely doubted it when he told me to drive to the old drinking spot. The place was nothing but a spot for making out and drinking booze. He told me to stop the car, we got out, took the shovel out, and he started walking west from where the drinking spot is and walked down a ways and he said he couldn't find her, and then he said, 'Wait a minute, I smell her,' and I walked one way and he walked the other. When I smelled the smell, I knew. In a way I was a little bit afraid, but it was a creepy feeling more than afraid. A creepy feeling, not fear."

They walked down along the wash and, Richie says, "A couple

of seconds later he said, 'Come here,' and I walked over to where he was and he was kneeling down, and he just nodded and said, 'That's Gretchen.' I looked down and there was just a sort of black form down there, and all the ground around it was turned black.

"You couldn't see it when looking over it, because of the black. Looking down on it, at first when I was standing over it, I felt part of the same feeling that someone would feel if they read an obituary of somebody they disliked intensely dying, a type of satisfaction, really. Not pity, not anything of that nature."

Richie examined the body. "I could feel the top, and I felt the hair. It was all like wiry, and that smell was on me all the time. But I couldn't really see it, distinguish it. Looking down over it, being right on top of it, you could strain but you couldn't tell anything. You couldn't distinguish eyes, nose, mouth, teeth; it was just black, looked like something down there.

"And the hair. You could see the bra. The whole blouse was open, and you could see this white of the bra, and see this rag tied around the legs. An old rag, knotted in the center, both legs tied.

"He said, 'Wendy should be up further on the hill,' so he started walking up the hill and a minute later he said, 'Come here,' and I walked up and he said, 'That's Wendy.' It was just a pile of black dirt, looked thrown over something like, it looked like it was bulging up, couldn't make out anything, it was black like somebody had spilled oil there. I could see part of a leg sticking up out of the ground.

"I said, 'We better bury the bodies,' so we walked down past Gretchen to the wash further down the hill where the ground looked the softest and tried to dig a grave with the shovel, but I couldn't dig with it because the ground was too hard and the shovel didn't have a point. He told me to shovel for a while and he went looking for a softer place.

"I was still trying to shovel. He then came back over and he said we had better move Gretchen because she was lying out in the open on the side of the hill there. He walked back up to where Gretchen was and he grabbed hold of her by a rag tied around the calf of her legs, both legs, and he grabbed ahold of her by that and dragged her down the hill.

"I could see the form, one arm was sticking up, the hand out. It was stiff. It just dragged like that, like a hollow shell, it didn't even look like there was any weight to it. That was grotesque, seeing that. That was like seeing a horror movie.

"He drug her down into the wash part there, under this mesquite tree, dropped it there. We just left Wendy where she was. We started walking back up and he told me that I better go down and wipe her shoes off and wipe some prints off, and he stood there and I walked down and I took out my handkerchief and wiped it over real quick. Then I walked back up to where he was and he told me to take the shoe off and throw it. At the side of the mound, there was apparently one leg sticking out with a shoe still on her foot. I did what he said. I took off the shoe and threw it."

Walking back to the car, Richie recalls, "Smitty told me, 'You are in it as deep as I am now.' I don't know what we talked about back at the car, except the car. We were going to say we had decided to go to Phoenix because we were scared of the Mafia, but had decided to come back."

Richie stayed over at Smitty's house that night, haunted by what he had seen and experienced. The next day Smitty left early to get a haircut and Richie got up and went through Smitty's record collection. He says, "I took a few records I wanted to borrow, called the old man, and went home."

When Smitty returned from the barber shop he found that the FBI had contacted his parents, had come to the house and left just before he arrived. Smitty says, "The following evening the Mafia called and asked if my suitcase was packed. They said they were coming to pick me up for the trip to California. They seemed nice and polite about everything and on the trip they even gave me $20 for cigarette money. The plan was to check into a motel in San Diego, I'd call the boy that Gretchen knew, we'd find the girls and then return home with us. The Mafia assured me that nothing would happen to Gretchen as far as the law was concerned and everything would be all right.

"As soon as we checked into the motel, I tried to telephone the boy, to get a hold of him, but I was told he wouldn't be home that night. We remained there at the motel and decided that I should show pictures of her around the beach places and try to find anyone that had seen her. I spent the afternoon doing this, spent the $20, and walked around the beach places showing the pictures and asking if anyone had seen them or knew their whereabouts. The two Mafia guys remained at the motel.

"Along about three or four o'clock in the afternoon a bunch of policemen pulled up and said that I was under arrest for impersonating an FBI agent, and while they were taking me to the police station they informed me that I was to be charged with murdering Gretchen and Wendy Fritz.

"I really couldn't believe it, but the cops scared me and at the station I managed to call Tucson and asked my mother for help. The police did not book me though, and I was kept in a holding cell for over an hour until a man came in and asked me if I wanted to take a lie-detector test.

"I said yes, and he took me from the holding cell and into another room. There he left me. Soon another man came in and asked me a few questions and then unexpectedly he released me to go home.

"By then I was really confused. I wanted to take off immediately but I didn't have enough money left, at least not enough for fare back to Tucson, and I didn't know what I was supposed to do about the Mafia men. So I headed back to the motel in hopes of getting some money from them. There didn't seem to be any reason why they'd detain me any longer.

"But they were not at the motel and the manager came to me and said the police had been there moments before, and that they'd removed them from the motel in handcuffs. I quickly went to the nearest phone booth and called my mother collect. I asked her what I should do. She said she'd wire me some money in care of the ticket office at the Greyhound Bus depot, and said I should call her back at seven o'clock if anything went wrong, and if she didn't hear from me that would mean that I was on my way home. If I did call her back it would mean that I'd been arrested again.

"I really felt mixed up and waited around the bus depot. As soon as the wire finally came I bought a ticket to Tucson and waited some more for the bus. I had a hamburger and some coffee in the diner, then headed for home."

When Smitty was taken to San Diego, his parents went to Richie's house to see whether Richie had also been taken on the ride. They told Richie what had happened and, Richie recalls, "I was surprised he'd gone, since I never thought anything would come of it."

Back in Tucson, Smitty told Richie the Mafia had chased him along the beach, shooting guns after him, and that he had been arrested and held on murder charges. "Smitty said he couldn't find the guy that laid Gretchen over there. He said he was walking around beaches, showing her picture like an ass, playing the role."

For some time, Richie had been going through his "own personal hell," watching Malvern Street and Darlene Kirk's house in an attempt to stop her from going out with other boys. Richie says, "We broke up because of her parents finding out about a so-called *suicide* attempt of mine, but we went together in secret until the stress became too great." They were saying that Richie broke into Rincon High and jimmied Darlene's locker to get at any notes she'd received from other boys.

Art Meyers recalls, "One night there was holes cut through her screen door and it looked like burglars to Darlene, but her old man was pretty sure it was Richie.

"What happened was that from that day on Richie watched the street twenty-four hours. He had an old '50 Cadillac, and up and down, up and down her street. Without stopping. He climbed trees to watch her, he'd hide behind garbage cans, he even hid inside one and he'd use binoculars. He terrorized the whole neighborhood, and everyone was scared of him. Little kids saw the car coming and would run to their yards.

"He's pretty smart about laws and stuff like that," Art says. "He knows what he's doing and he said he could walk the streets without getting in any trouble. He borrowed Smitty's parents' dog and used that a few times in case anyone showed up to take Darlene out or anywhere. He was carrying a baseball bat and told the police he was just protecting the neighborhood from burglars or that he'd just come from the park where he was playing ball."

Richie says, "It wasn't so bad when I was on the block, but when I was away from it, like I was really hurting. Many times I was running around that block like a nut. I'd see a car, something would happen. I'd take off and I'd get to the point where I couldn't hardly breathe sometimes. I'd get so excited, everywhere at once."

Smitty had given an account of his San Diego trip to the Tucson police and the FBI. They listened with interest and questioned him some more about Gretchen.

By now the city was filled with wild rumors and lurid stories of what had happened to the Fritz girls. Private detective William Heilig still thought there was more information to be obtained from Smitty. His interest had been rearoused by having listened to a tape recording made by Norma Rowe in which she named John Saunders, Mary French, Schmid, and others as having some connection with her daughter's disappearance. Checking further, Heilig got hold of Saunders' police record: disorderly conduct, shoplifting, and simple assault. Also, a court summons to answer charges had been sent to Saunders on April 9, 1965, which Saunders had failed to acknowledge. The police found no trace of Saunders, which meant that he'd been out of Tucson at least since April 9th. Heilig requestioned everybody, trying to crowd them into making some sort of move that would lead to more concrete information. He and the police questioned teenagers over and over, and one of them commented, "Like they can't find anything on their own and are going to pull anything out of somebody like some crazy tooth-happy dentist." Finally, as had happened after the Alleen Rowe disappearance, parents obtained court injunctions barring further harassment of those "being subjected to interrogation."

Earlier, around September 1, Paul Graff had moved back into Smitty's house. He needed $180 to get a divorce from his wife, and Smitty sold an insurance policy to get him the money. Smitty's Falcon was still impounded so Paul came along as chauffeur on Smitty's first date with a girl named Diane Lynch.

She was fifteen and lived with her family in a rundown Quonset hut on a dirt street in South Tucson. They had come to Arizona from Iowa seven years before. Her father, Buck, had tried to find work as an unskilled laborer. He abandoned his family in Tucson after hearing that Mexicans worked there for 12¢ an hour—when they were able to get work.

Diane's eldest sister, Thelma, married a gas-station attendant at sixteen, leaving Diane the oldest child remaining at home. She had five sisters and two small brothers. It had been the hope of Diane's mother that her daughters would be married by the age of fifteen. Diane attended Amphitheater High School where she knew Gloria Andrews. Gloria knew Smitty.

"One day in the school cafeteria," Diane recalls, "Gloria came up to me and said she wanted to go someplace that night but she didn't have a date. I was going steady with a boy named Mike Delson, so he got her a date and we all doubled to the Hi-Ho to hear some rock 'n' roll.

"Mike and I were not getting along too well and Gloria could see it. She said she'd return the favor for me sometime by getting me a date and she asked me if I knew Smitty, that everybody knew Smitty. I didn't and then she said that I *had* to go out with him. Later she told me, 'If you don't go out with him he'll blackmail me.' 'Blackmail you how?" I asked. She said she didn't know but he just would. Gloria showed me a picture of Smitty and I thought he was really cute, so I said I'd go out with him, and Gloria was so insistent about it." Diane was a slight girl, weighing only eighty-seven pounds, with delicate features and extremely long eyelashes.

When Smitty saw her for the first time she seemed to him to be "just my size."

With Paul as chauffeur, they went to a Mexican taco café in South Tucson. Smitty thought the tacos were great and Paul drank a lot of beer. Paul made Diane uncomfortable; all his comments seemed to have an edge to them. Smitty concentrated on Diane. The discussion centered on Gloria. Smitty laughed and said she'd called him up and offered him ten dollars if he'd take Diane out for a few nights. "Get to her, make her think you're in love with her, then drop her like a ton of bricks and hurt her real bad," Gloria had said.

It occurred to Diane that Gloria was interested in Mike, and that the date with Smitty was a scheme to make Mike jealous. But Diane liked being with Smitty; though she'd been with him for less than an hour, she thought she'd already fallen in love with him. Paul dropped them off at Johnnie's on Stone and said he'd come back later. Smitty and Diane sat by the window and shared coffee and cigarettes. When Paul didn't return they walked hand in hand to Sambo's, another restaurant a few blocks north.

"Are you really playing the game Gloria put you up to?" Diane asked.

Smitty said, "Of course not," and grinned.

They were eating pancakes when they were approached in Sambo's by an elderly woman wearing Indian jewelry who had been staring at them from the counter. She came to their table and introduced herself as an astrologer, the representative of Universalism and Fortune. Smitty said he was "absolutely fascinated," and the woman sat down and told them, "You two must never see one another again. And under no circumstances must you marry one another, or for that matter any relatives of your families marry one another." The woman said she had been watching them carefully and could easily see their fortune "as though it's smoke coming off your bodies." If her injunctions were disobeyed, she said, "hard trouble will come of a serious nature." The woman's forebodings spread gloom as the pancake syrup hardened.

They left Sambo's, walked south to Speedway and past the

Flamingo Hotel. Smitty stopped Diane and with a smile asked her if she'd care to become his "permanent wife."

Diane says, "I didn't even think it over when he said that. I just said, 'Okay.'"

Smitty recalls, "I was so disgusted with everything and everyone, I was madder than hell. Life was spinning a hundred miles a second and hurtling all my possessions away from me. I'd sat and figured that in one summer I'd lost what amounted to everything, even the damned cat I had. I can't explain what happened when I met Diane, I only know it did happen and so fast I couldn't really believe it, and it wasn't that I just wanted sex with her. In fact I pushed it back."

They played blackjack and Monopoly at Smitty's house while they were waiting for Paul to come and drive her back to South Tucson. When Paul arrived, according to Smitty, he'd had too much to drink and didn't say a word.

While Paul had been staying at the house, from September 1 until Smitty's first date with Diane, there had been parties. Gloria Andrews, Shirley and Kitty Bates, and others had attended. Paul "made home brew from potatoes and cactus juice," and there was beer from the supermarket. All this ended when Smitty started seeing Diane. He took her to school in the morning and met her in the cafeteria for lunch.

"Before I dropped out," Diane says, "I'd leave during the afternoons with Smitty. He would stay at our house in the evening, watching television, playing with my two smaller brothers. He once ate eleven tacos at one sitting, but usually averaged about seven. I got so I could eat six and we drank Pepsis while we ate.

"Then we'd go to the movies on the weekends at the drive-in where they played five monster pictures, and when the last picture is over the sun is already shining on the screen. They'd let carloads of kids in for one dollar a car. "Or we'd go over to Smitty's house. Paul had left his home brew stocked in Smitty's refrigerator but nobody liked it except Richie Bruns. He was there one day walking back and forth in Smitty's house and drinking the home brew Paul had there. Richie asked me questions about my family and walked back out of the house.

"Smitty and Paul had a pretty bad fight after Smitty and I were going out. Paul said, 'How can you marry a whore like that?' and Smitty was so mad he smashed his fist through a wall. Paul's divorce came through and he moved out and went to New Orleans.

"Anybody who needed money, Smitty would give it to them. He gave it to them until he didn't have any left and then they'd get mad. He's a soft touch. If he had ten dollars and you went up to him and said you needed $10, said you had to have it real bad, he'd give it to you. Three-fourths of the $300 a month from Katharine went to his friends, like Richie and Paul."

During this time, Smitty took to wearing a bandage that covered the bridge of his nose. He told his friends, "It happened in a bike accident." Diane rather liked it. Richie says, "That patch on his nose, originally he did a real good job. He looked like he really broke his nose, with that type of splint on it." With heavy makeup, the fake mole enlarged, "that patch on his nose," and wearing a white dinner jacket and high-collar shirt, Smitty married Diane on October 24, 1965.

Diane says, "We got married in Nogales. I wore a white satin dress with fur cuffs and a wedding veil. That night, back in Tucson, we had a reception at Katharine's. Jimmy Scott was there, Gerry Wells, and so was Richie Bruns.

"Richie seemed in a daze and just sat there staring at Smitty and me. He said he didn't believe we were married. Katharine and my mother tried to prove it to him, showing him the certificate, but he just refused to accept the facts and wouldn't believe we were married."

Smitty walked outside with Gerry, Jimmy, and Richie, who wanted him to go with them to celebrate the wedding, to leave Diane at home with "the others."

Smitty said to Richie, "I just got married, man. I'd like to spend tonight with my wife."

Richie motioned Smitty to the side and asked, "How can you do this? You know what's happening?"

"What's happening?" Smitty asked.

Richie said, "I mean... the dead girls."

"What 'dead girls,' Richie? What're you talking about?" Smitty said, smiling.

Diane says, "Then Smitty and I drove to Johnnie's. We'd gotten his car out of impoundment and that night we put over 300 miles on it, just driving all around Tucson. Smitty was having fun driving and there just wasn't anything else to do. When we returned to the house we found empty glasses and it was obvious Richie had brought Gerry over and they'd been drinking. But they must not have finished because they took the bottle with them.

"After that we'd invite friends over for dinner, Ronald Baines and Jack Spiers; we used to go on picnics at Sabino with Jimmy Scott and his girl. We'd have spaghetti quite a bit and Smitty wanted French toast for breakfast every morning. Then he'd turn on his stereo and play Elvis Presley records. Morning, noon, and night it was Elvis. Smitty would sing along with the records and then record his own voice singing the Elvis songs.

"Sometimes we would help out at the nursing home, serving food, washing clothes, but not very often, and the rest of the time there wasn't much to do. At nights we would sit home playing cards, Monopoly, or dominoes, or driving around to Johnnie's. He said he'd teach me to play cards real good and we'd take a trip to Las Vegas.

"I loved Smitty very much and we were happy. We'd gotten a charge account at Montgomery Ward's and decided to refurnish the house. Smitty wanted to get the yard in shape. He began by laying a new winter lawn and then setting in bulbs along the walk to the house."

PART THREE

RICHIE'S SURVEILLANCE OF the Kirks on Malvern Street had intensified. (If he'd looked into himself at what he was doing around the clock, he'd have said, *forget it.*) He rarely slept. He couldn't eat. At six feet tall, he weighed only 102 pounds. Then he smashed up his old Cadillac. Art Meyers recalls that "one night when he was racing around her house because he thought some guy was showing up to take her out, he smashed his car into an ice cream truck, and the driver almost died he was so broken up."

The accident occurred at a T-intersection. Richie, circling the block, approached Malvern on Desert Avenue, when the ice-cream truck turned left suddenly off Malvern. Richie smashed the truck broadside.

The driver settled back in the seat, his head raised, and began to moan in an odd way. It looked to Richie "like he was putting on a weird act," and Richie began to laugh. "It was so damn funny," he says, "and I guess I was shocked or something. I began to laugh at the funny way the guy was moaning, and when the cops were coming, I got out and saw blood all over the guy's seat, and his arms all twisted up."

Richie lost his license for three years because of the accident, but he didn't give up his patrol of Darlene's house. He borrowed Art Meyers's car and continued to circle the block, but when Art heard that Richie nearly had another accident, he refused to lend him thc car again.

Aware of the Lynch family's indigence, Richie suggested that they rent a vacant house across the street from the Kirks'. The rent was too high for them, but Richie said he'd pay half the rent and furnish the place if they would do him a little favor.

Diane says, "He wanted my folks to move in there and he wanted to sit in the front yard for a while every night, and said that if we didn't want him to sit in the yard then he could sit up on the roof for a while." But the Lynch family didn't take the house and Richie was left to his own devices.

"People were beginning to talk about it," Diane recalls. "When he was on the sidewalk he'd tell them he was a free citizen on a public street (he'd even tell this to people who were just passing by and didn't care what he was doing). Smitty had given him more money to keep watching Darlene because he couldn't watch her and look for work too."

Darlene's father talked to the police and was told he'd have to file a complaint. But Mr. Kirk said he would wait a while. "Maybe Bruns will burn himself out." But there was no slackening in Richie's patrols as the weeks progressed. Many times Mr. Kirk wasn't able to see Richie, but he *knew* he was nearby, "hiding behind something."

Richie's vigil had an unnerving effect on his victims. Mr. Kirk says, "One night after about a couple months of it, I got this air pistol (that looked real) and went out there, confronted him on the sidewalk, and said, 'Get the hell away from here or I'll shoot you.' But he said, 'Go ahead, go ahead and shoot, you'd be doing me a favor.' I didn't know what else to do except run back in the house and lock the door."

On another occasion, Mr. Kirk tried to talk Richie out of his mania, "to reason with him." He says, "Only once did I get to talk to him. I guess we talked for about forty-five minutes. I wanted to know just what was going on with him, I wanted to know *why* he was doing what he was doing—spying on others. I listened to Richie and he said a lot of things, but when it was over I didn't know any more than before we'd talked about it.

"You stand there and listen to him and look into those eyes, and damn, it gives you the strangest feeling." Kirk sighed and shook his head. "I don't know. I'm just a common man. How did I get involved in all this?"

Richie never gave up. "Even without a car," he said, "I was actually keeping track of them. Her brother had a car, and his friends had cars. They would come over and drive her someplace, hide her down on the floorboards, plus all those friends of theirs trying to give me a hard time.

"It really gave me a feeling of satisfaction, having that whole neighborhood terrorized.

"A real thin guy like me, and all those big men over two hundred pounds, with families and all, all scared of me. It was a real feeling of having power, being able to terrorize that whole block of all those people."

But he was beginning to attract too much attention.

Richie says, "When you see cops on every street corner, you could always look around and see a cop, and you know you're being tailed. They started watching my house. Every time I looked out through the window I could always see a cop, and if I couldn't see one, I'd leave and then I'd see one before I got two or three blocks."

One policeman, Donald Hill, began "to pass the time of day" with Richie, going to and from his vigil at Malvern. During one of these brief conversations, Richie made the mistake of voicing some threats to Hill, concerning the Kirks. Officer Hill jotted them down. They had a case.

On November 3, 1965, Richie appeared in city court, charged with disorderly conduct after harassment of the Kirk family. The dean from Rincon High, Art Meyers, and other witnesses were called to testify against him. Richie's attorney was John Price, suggested by the Schmids. According to Richie, Price "looked around and saw all the prosecution witnesses, they were all over the place, and Price figured he'd better make a deal. There was even a uniformed cop waiting there to take me to jail."

Price talked to the judge before the trial and entered a plea of guilty. The lawyer said, "He's been infatuated with the girl to the point of not being able to control himself. All he needs is to get out of town for a while to get over this." The judge agreed.

According to Richie, "The judge talked for about twenty minutes, a big pep talk about when he was a kid, and from there it was arranged that I'd get out of town on the first plane."

Richie was placed on probation for six months, and under the terms of the arrangement he was to leave Tucson for "at least ninety days." The court ordered the records to show that it was the court's understanding that Richie would go to Ohio to live with his grandparents.

Earlier that same day an article appeared in the *Arizona Daily Star:*

> "...TEENAGE GIRLS HAVE DISAPPEARED INTO THIN AIR ... detectives frankly admit they have no ideas where they have gone. The mothers ... fear foul play and ... insisted from the beginning that their daughters were dead."

Regarding Alleen Rowe:

> "Intensive investigation has failed to give police even a hint as to her whereabouts. While city detectives were doggedly pursuing that case two more girls disappeared."

Gretchen and Wendy Fritz:

> "Police still have no leads to their disappearance."

The *Daily Star* went on to report that:

> "City detectives had several times questioned a Tucson boy who was known to have been an

acquaintance of Alleen Rowe and the oldest Fritz girl, seventeen-year-old Gretchen. Confidential police sources say they believe the underworld was contacted by the parents of one of the missing girls in an effort to find her. They say the mutual acquaintance of the three girls was the person approached and that the youth went to California to find the missing girl but without success. Police have kicked around dozens of theories Detective Wilhelm admits that it is possible that one or all of the girls could be victims of foul play. But he is generally inclined to believe they are alive."

"'There are thousands of reasons why teenage girls run away,' Wilhelm said, 'or leave home, and we have absolutely nothing to indicate that these girls' lives were in danger.' He pointed to the fact that it would be quite easy for a girl to fix herself up to look older. 'She could cut her hair, dye it, use more makeup; a girl can make herself look years older,' he said. 'We have checked out every tip as fast as we get it, but so far we have drawn a blank.'"

That afternoon Richie was driving around Tucson with Art Meyers. Richie says, "Smitty was coming off a side street there and he saw us driving by. I was sitting shotgun, and saw Smitty. He yelled, 'Richie!' and we pulled over. Smitty pulled up behind. He knew I was going out of town.

Smitty looked dirty and unkempt to Richie. It wasn't the Smitty that Richie had known. "Smitty got out of his car," Richie says. "He looked taller but he was hobbling like a crippled person. He smelled bad. The makeup was caked all over his face and the splint thing that had looked good had got to be just a dirty old bandage, and snot was on his nose."

"Man, you look bad," Richie told him.

Smitty grinned and said, "That's the advantage of being a married man. You don't have to worry about that."

Art drove Richie home in time for supper and Richie packed his clothes for the trip. He says, "Here was a court order saying I couldn't walk down the street anymore, and the first thing Darlene does is get in a car with some friends and comes by my house, and laughs 'Hahahahahaha!' I was very pissed, and I couldn't even eat."

His mother drove Richie to Tucson International Airport and he got on a plane for Chicago. He says, "I was kind of sick when I saw Tucson leaving behind me. But I was really pissed off."

The flight from Tucson to O'Hare Field in Chicago took about two hours, and Richie waited there a few hours for a plane to Columbus, Ohio. He drank coffee, and 7-Up, smoked cigarettes, and wandered around the Chicago terminal.

When he got to Columbus, where his grandmother met him at the airport, Richie says, "I felt out of place. What am I doing here? It wasn't right."

Richie didn't think about Darlene "too much" the first night. He spent most of his first day in town looking for a job. "The rest of the time I was just checking the town around there. The second night I started thinking about Darlene. I was feeling kind of pissed."

The second day he wandered around downtown Columbus, "checking the places," but he felt anxious and out of place, "sort of sick the rest of the day." That night, his third in town, facing eighty-seven more similar nights (according to the court order), he began drinking beer and then went to bed. After lying in bed for what seemed like hours, Richie suddenly "sat straight up and said out loud, 'I can't take it anymore!'"

Richie recalls, "I went bopping out the door and down the steps, and I said to my grandmother, 'I gotta call my old man.'"

His grandmother replied, "It's way late in the morning. What you got to call out there for? What's the matter?"

Richie said, "I can't wait," and then tried to explain to her everything that had happened in Tucson since he became involved with Smitty. It seemed odd to him when he finally put it in words for another person. His grandmother listened but scarcely believed what she was hearing. She said, "Well, wait until morning. You've been drinking."

Richie cried, "He could be out killing someone else!" and called his father in Tucson. Richie says, "I told the old man I was scared I might be blamed for whatever Smitty had done. The old man wasn't a bit surprised. He said, 'Now a lot of things make sense. It'll be all right. I'll call.'"

His father said he would go down and explain it to the police in Tucson. Within an hour a Tucson detective called back and Richie told him, "Well, there's this guy, this friend of mine, I mean he *was* a friend, and it's about the Fritz sisters, and this friend told me he'd killed Alleen Rowe, him and a couple of other people that helped him do it, you know—"

It sounded awkward and unconvincing over the phone, but he went on, "No, he *murdered* these girls. Who? His name's Smitty. I mean Schmid. That's right, Charles Schmid."

The detective said, "Would you be willing to come back here to Tucson and show us the bodies?"

"Yes, I would," Richie replied. "Just get me back to Tucson."

Richie then went to bed and slept for a few hours. He said he hadn't slept that well for a long time. The next morning Detective Wilhelm of Tucson and a detective from the Columbus Police Department arrived at the house. His grandmother woke Richie, saying, "The men are here. They're downstairs."

Richie says, "After about fifteen minutes, after I packed, we left and went in a cop car to the police station in downtown Columbus, and I made some short statements promising to go back to Tucson, that it was of my own volition, and show the Tucson police where the bodies were. I filled out one paper for Alleen Rowe, and one for Gretchen and Wendy." Richie told the police that he was doing it because he was the only one who could stop Smitty.

Then they went to a café in Columbus for breakfast. Richie asked, "Where am I going to stay when you get me back?"

Wilhelm replied, "Oh, we have a special place for you."

"Which jail is that?" Richie asked.

"No, we've got a room for you," Wilhelm said.

There was a pause, then Richie asked the question he had been leading up to: "Will I be more or less prosecuted for waiting this long, I mean, for not sort of talking about it before this?"

Wilhelm said, "I'll see to it that you won't be prosecuted. The guy I want is Smitty."

That day, November 9, 1965, a major electrical blackout occurred throughout the east, and Richie and Wilhelm were delayed most of the day at the Columbus airport before they could get a plane for Chicago. At Chicago, there was another wait until Wilhelm was able to get a jet nonstop to Tucson. While Richie slumped, trying to grab some sleep on a seat in the airport, he could only think that he didn't want to say anything that might incriminate him, or to indicate that he was afraid he might be blamed for anything Smitty had done. He would make it clear he wasn't an accomplice.

"The guy was really cranking time on the plane to Tucson," Richie says. "We made the flight in a little over an hour and a half. It was about one-thirty in the morning when we arrived in Tucson. There were all kinds of detectives waiting there for us.

"We drove to El Rancho Shopping Center and I got a pack of cigarettes. Then they took me to a motel on Alvernon. Detective Hill, who had handled the case against Richie for harassing Darlene Kirk, "was in a room next to me and another one was in the other room, and there was one sat up with me in my room. I couldn't sleep. I lay there and bullshitted."

They came for Richie between six and seven the next morning and drove to Johnnie's on 22nd for breakfast. Richie had bacon and eggs. As they sat there, more and more detectives kept coming in. "The numbers grew," he said. "All the bigwigs were there. The head of the detectives and the guy that takes all the crime pictures." Then the whole group left as a body and drove north on Craycroft to River Road. "Five cops, me, the guy that takes pictures, at first, six in the car, the other guy followed. They drove straight up to Pontatoc... that lonely, empty road.

"On the way up there I was convinced there weren't any bodies. I was scared. They parked and we all got out, and at first I couldn't find them. I almost walked on Wendy, where she was, I didn't even see her.

"At night things had looked different. It had looked to me like Wendy was planted underneath a big bush, and I was looking for a big bush with a big mountain of dirt beside it.

"All of a sudden, I was standing on open ground, and here was skeletons and bones and everything scattered all over the place. And the hole she'd been dug up in was only a couple of inches deep. So actually what happened was that dirt was thrown over her, and this big mound I was looking for was actually just a little hole, nothing at all.

"'That's Gretchen,' I said. I didn't see the mountain of dirt, and I thought this must be Gretchen. The detectives were walking around the desert and I started walking away, because if that had been Gretchen, Wendy would have been up the other way."

A detective knelt and examined the skull. He said, "This looks to me like it would be more like Wendy, don't you think?" He looked up at Richie, who walked back and looked down at the bones. The skull was small. Richie knelt down and happened to raise his eyes past the detective's shoulder. He sensed something familiar. He was facing the wash.

"I looked down and there was the wash down there," Richie says. He got up and started walking. Wilhelm was walking along the other side of the slope, and when he saw where Richie was headed, he started diagonally across the slope, both approaching a mesquite tree from different angles.

Richie called out, "Over here."

"Yes, I see the hair," Wilhelm replied.

Richie says, "They all sort of walked over and stood around and looked for a while. Then they got in a little conference," and Richie was not allowed to hear what they said.

As Detective Hill approached the group, Richie asked, "Would you pick up Darlene now?" Richie then claimed that he had been watching Darlene because he was afraid Smitty would kill her. He said he had informed on Smitty because he couldn't protect her after he'd been exiled from Tucson.

Hill said, "Talk to them, I'm sure they'll pick her up."

Richie recalls, "They said they'd pick her up if I'd confront Smitty. I said I didn't think it would do any good. I knew Smitty and he wouldn't confess."

The police then drove Richie to the southeast desert area off Golf Links Road, to see if he could find Alleen Rowe's grave. Smitty had told him where it was, but Richie had never visited the grave. He was unable to find it, and a detective said, "We'll get Saunders and French back here."

The hair surrounding the "old drinking spot" was gathered and put in plastic containers. Fragments of blouses were found, undergarments, and a pair of blue-and-black shorts along with a white shoe.

Bones from the first skeleton were collected into plastic sacks by an ambulance attendant, and the second skeleton was placed in a single large plastic bag, then delivered to the Arizona Mortuary. Dr. Louis Hirsch, the coroner's pathologist, had studied the remains in the desert. He continued his examination at the mortuary, noting that the hands, feet, and several other bones from the skeletons were missing. His conclusion was that the bones were the remains of two young girls, approximate age and height of the Fritz sisters. But he was not able to determine the cause of death.

Detective Lieutenant George Robles, forty-two, a soft-spoken, mild-mannered man, one of the few Tucson policemen to have "dropped a man with a bullet," was assigned to arrest Charles Schmid. To avoid spreading the case "throughout the police force and sheriff's offices," Lieutenant Robles, his partner Clarence Dupnik, and Sergeant Wilhelm were given complete charge of the case. They would make all the arrests and control the suspects. Robles says, "I was asked to study the entire case in what seemed like a matter of minutes." County Attorney Norman Green specifically instructed the detectives to "write up no reports in connection with the arrests of Schmid, Saunders, and Mary French."

Robles says, "I went through the files beginning with the disappearance of Alleen Rowe and repenciled Schmid's name, underlining it on page after page, even before the disappearance of the Fritz sisters. I said, what the hell, why wasn't this guy brought in *long* before this?"

Other detectives told him of the injunctions which had prevented them from questioning Schmid further and Robles said, "To hell with injunctions, this guy should've been picked up and held. He was nailed right *here*," he said, underlining Schmid's name again. Robles says, "It made me sick to see the guy's name again and again and again and to realize he'd never been booked even on *suspicion*–it's like a person's hands are tied and you have to sit back and watch it happen. Injunctions, like hell."

It was Robles's belief that if Schmid had been picked up and held following the disappearance of Alleen Rowe the police might have prevented the murders of the Fritz sisters.

That morning, Wednesday, November 10, the twenty-second day of his marriage, Smitty was working in the yard before breakfast, but didn't have the right shoes to be digging. Diane said, "My Dad's got a pair of cowboy boots that are pretty beat up, and maybe too big for you."

"I can fix that," he said. He crushed a couple beer cans and fitted them into the boots. Diane gave him a couple rags, old towels that Smitty padded over the beer cans. "Presto!" he said, and pulled on the boots. He had planted some bulbs along the walk and started to rake weeds.

Diane was hanging new drapes in the house, which had previously gained a sofa and a modern easy chair from Montgomery Ward's. The past few days Smitty and his father had laid new linoleum in the kitchen. Smitty was planning to paint the house and do something about the loose shingles on the roof. While he was raking weeds and leaves into a pile, Diane took the washing across to the hospital laundry.

Smitty noticed a car on Second pull past the house and head

south toward Speedway. A few minutes later he saw the same car come around the other side of the block, turn into an alley and drive behind his parents' house, then slow momentarily at the rear of Smitty's house. Then it went to Second Avenue, came around the corner, and stopped at the curb with the motor idling. Two men were in the front seat.

Smitty thought the Mafia were after him again. As he worked in the yard he continued to notice the car poking around the neighborhood.

From inside her house, Katharine Schmid saw the car and watched it suspiciously. Raising a pair of binoculars she focused on the windshield of the car: the man in the passenger seat was holding a pair of binoculars to his eyes. Katharine stepped back from the window.

Diane loaded the washer and returned to the house. She was taking the garbage out when she saw Smitty pacing back and forth in the alley, looking both ways.

"What's the matter?" she asked him.

"Nothing."

"What are you looking for, Smitty?"

"That car," he said, brushing some dirt from his pants. "Didn't you see that car around here?"

"No."

Smitty went around to the front, saying, "Never mind." Diane followed and asked if he was hungry. "I guess I am," he said. "How about French toast?"

About three hours passed. The car with the two men had kept a steady watch on Smitty's house from various places in the neighborhood. It was shortly after twelve o'clock when the telephone rang and Diane went to answer it. "It's Jimmy," she said. Smitty took the phone in the bedroom and Diane heard him laughing as she entered the living room. Then she jumped, startled, as three men came quickly across the front yard and onto the porch. She hurried to the door as one of the men thrust it open and said, "Hi, is Smitty here?"

The three pushed themselves into the house. "Where's Smitty?" one of them asked.

Robles recalls, "When I walked through that front door he was talking on the phone and dragged it into the bedroom. I've arrested most of the murderers in Tucson but seeing this guy, the way he looked, the way his face was with all that stuff, makeup, that smudged black mole or whatever it was, I have to admit I was shocked for a moment. Seeing him face to face sort of set me back. Dupnik said, 'He's a nut.'"

The police grabbed the phone from Smitty and asked who he was talking to. Smitty said, "Jimmy," but when the detectives demanded to know who was speaking on the other end, the phone went dead. They seized Smitty and said, "You're under arrest."

"What am I under arrest for?"

"Murder," Dupnik said, "Come on, let's go."

Smitty swung his arm free. "Hey, wait a minute, what the hell is this?"

"No, let's go," Dupnik insisted.

"Who the hell am I supposed to have murdered?"

"You tell us," Robles said as the other detectives jerked Smitty's arms behind his back and locked his wrists in handcuffs. They were hustling him out through the living room when Smitty asked to see his mother.

"No, you're coming now," Robles answered.

Diane yelled, "Smitty!" as they pushed him through the front door and across the yard.

"Get my mom!" Smitty yelled.

They took Smitty out to the car and Robles started back into the house, but Katharine, Robles says, "threw that big body of hers up in the doorway, her arms raised up like this and started with that search warrant stuff, and brackety-brackety-brack, and I said to myself, 'Oh, no, she means business.'

"Smitty was out there hollering, 'Call John Price,' so we left. Schmid kept saying, 'Are you guys for real? Prove to me you're city cops. I could be being kidnapped again. Are you city cops?'"

Robles said, "Forget it, Charlie."

When they got Smitty to police headquarters, Robles says, "We were walking him through this room, and it's the polygraph room, but we were only going through there to get to another room, and he starts with this, 'Oh, no, I'm not taking anything like that,' and 'You're not getting me to take a polygraph,' and brackety-brack, so I said, 'Forget it, Charlie, we're not giving you any lie-detector.'"

Schmid kept protesting the polygraph, making a speech on the effects and shortcomings of the polygraph test, even as Robles led him into another room and closed the door. Robles said to him, "Forget it, Charlie."

In the small room with a two-way mirror on one wall, the detectives played tapes which Richie had made implicating Smitty in the murders and also accusing Mary French and John Saunders. Smitty made faces and kept saying, "What is this? Are you guys for real? Who is that? What is this?"

Robles says, "We wanted a confession, although I didn't think he'd give it. I took off the tape and said, 'Which side you want to hear–one or three?' He said, 'How about five?' Real smart.

"Then Dupnik said to him, 'You know what you are? You're a psycho.' You ought to have seen old Charlie, he just froze up and his eyes narrowed, mean, he was burning."

Outside in the corridor, Richie was watching through the two-way mirror. Police Chief Garmire came down the hall and took Richie into another room and asked him if he was feeling tired. Richie said no. Then Dupnik came in, and according to Richie, "He asked me if I'd go in and confront Smitty. They felt that if I confronted him that possibly he'd confess. Another detective asked, 'Does this guy have anything on you?' I said, 'No.'"

Richie was led into the room with Smitty, "who was sitting in a chair in one corner of the room." Richie says, "One detective was sitting behind a desk and Robles was standing near the door. Smitty and I were looking at each other."

Robles recalls, "They were both glaring at one another. Charlie said to him, 'I know why you're doing this, I know why you're doing all this.'"

Richie remembers, "Dupnik and another detective came in, and this detective said to Smitty, 'Man, if you don't confess this you're going to go out of your mind. You can't keep something like this on your mind.'"

Smitty glanced again at Richie and said, "I know why you did it."

"Did what?" Richie asked.

"Fingered me."

Richie said, "You would have to have done something for me to finger you."

Smitty made insinuations about Richie, and Dupnik said, "I thought you said this guy doesn't have anything on you?"

"Man, he's just trying to sit there and tell you that *I* did it," Richie said.

"I'll prove my innocence in the trial," Smitty announced. "I'll get a trial and prove it."

A detective said, "Yeah? You might just have to stand trial three times."

Richie looked at Smitty and said, "You're sick, man. You need help."

A uniformed policeman entered the room quickly and said, "Tinney's coming." Richie was hustled from the room and as he went up the steps attorney William Tinney, "carrying his briefcase and looking straight ahead," according to Richie, was on his way down into police headquarters, followed by John Price.

Smitty was booked on two open murder charges at approximately 1:10 that afternoon. The press had gathered but the police kept the photographers back while the booking took place. Then Smitty was asked to remove his boots. He seemed reluctant to do so, as if intimidated by the request. When he took them off he appeared several inches shorter. The photographers crowded around and started snapping pictures. Smitty sat down on the floor and refused to stand up for them.

The contents of his boots filled half a shoe box. There were folded-up rags cushioning flattened beer cans, which were covered over with a wadding of more rags and pieces of cardboard.

At the same time, Chief Garmire called together a hurried press conference and released details of the investigation.

One hour after the booking, Charles Schmid Jr. was arraigned before Justice of the Peace Toby LaVetter. His attorney, William Tinney, asked him for the court how long he had lived in Tucson. "Twenty-three years," Smitty replied, and that was all he said.

The arraignment lasted half an hour. Tinney tried to invoke a rule banning all but the principals and court officials from the courtroom, but LaVetter denied the motion, saying he believed the rule applied only to a hearing, not an arraignment.

Tinney said, "I think we owe a duty to try for once to have a trial without all the flame and fury we've had in the last twenty-five." He said he wanted to avoid publicity. "I'm only trying to be fair. I'm merely trying to avoid prejudice to the defendant's right."

His motion to set a reasonable bond was also denied and Schmid was ordered held without bail until the hearing scheduled for 10 AM on December 13, 1965.

Back at Smitty's house, the police had obtained a warrant and started ransacking the place. They dumped the contents of drawers onto the bedroom floor and pulled clothes from the closet. They asked Diane to identify them and she said, "Mine and Smitty's—why? Why?"

The detectives took the cushions off of sofas and chairs, reached behind the water heater, picked through laundry. They took Smitty's tapes and a few other odds and ends out to their car.

Finally, Diane asked what they were looking for. "If it's a gun," she said, "I'll give it to you." She quickly found Smitty's .22 and gave it to one of the detectives. The man looked at it impassively.

"A guitar string," he said.

"A what?" Diane asked.

"A guitar string. You know. You seen one around here?"

Diane shook her head. "Were there any strings missing from his guitar?" the detective asked.

"He doesn't have his guitar," she replied.

The detectives kept on looking. Next door two other detectives asked Katharine Schmid about the same item. "There's no guitar strings in this house," she replied. "He never kept his things here, and he doesn't have his guitar at the moment."

"Tell me," one detective said, "were all the strings on his guitar the last time you saw it?"

"I don't know if there were strings on it or not," Katharine said. "What's the difference?"

The search turned up no guitar strings, and a disgruntled crew of detectives left the premises.

Meanwhile, Richie had been taken to the Alameda Building Detective's Office where he sat and waited. He smoked cigarettes and chewed his fingernails. Some articles found near the spot where the skeletons had been uncovered were presented to him for identification. He was shown a pair of wrap-around sunglasses, resembling a pair Richie had owned, and Richie said, "The last time I saw them was one night in Smitty's car."

Soon a policeman informed him that "Chief Garmire has just gone on the radio to announce the news." The policeman added, "Darlene's been picked up, just to let you know we kept our side of the bargain." Richie sat for another hour. Then Norman Green and Chief Assistant County Attorney William Schafer came in to talk to him.

Richie says, "Schafer was curious, like why were the bodies black, as I'd described about that night. 'What was the black?' he wanted to know. A cop told him it was a natural reaction, it was the chemicals. Schafer was wondering, perhaps it meant they were poisoned or something, and he was particularly curious that the legs were tied which showed premeditation. A secretary was brought in and I started giving statements. This continued until late and then a cop drove me home.

"He took me to the door and my old lady asked if they were supposed to keep me there, and he said, 'No, he's free to come and go as he pleases.'"

It was evening now. At the Arizona Mortuary, Dr. Hirsch

compared the teeth in the skeletons to charts by a dentist who had done some work on the Fritz sisters. The fillings and surgery performed on Gretchen and Wendy, the dentist reported, matched the fillings and surgery observed in the skeletons. Dr. Fritz had been summoned to identify the clothing found in the desert. That evening he came to the mortuary and looked at the articles. He said it was similar to the clothing owned by his daughters but he did not know what the girls had been wearing on the night they disappeared.

Meanwhile, Charles Sr. and Katharine Schmid left their home on East Adams to meet with Tinney in his offices a few miles east on Broadway. It was about eight in the evening when he told them the outcome of a conference he'd had earlier that afternoon with Chief Garmire and County Attorney Norman Green. Katharine Schmid remembers that Tinney told them: "They are determined to do all in their power to put Charles in the gas chamber. They will settle for nothing short of the death sentence."

"What are we going to do?" Katharine asked.

Tinney said he planned to prepare for a long, hard case and that "it might become necessary for me at some point to bring in additional counsel." He also advised them the case would be expensive and that a substantial sum of money was required for the defense.

Within three days of Schmid's arrest, Sheriff Burr had as many as thirty men searching the east desert area for the grave of Alleen Rowe, and the police had traced the whereabouts of John Saunders and Mary French.

While Detective Dupnik flew to Connecticut with a fugitive warrant for Saunders, Lieutenant Robles left for Texas to arrest Mary French. Robles landed in Temple, Texas, and went by taxi to Belton. He didn't have a warrant with him and made arrangements to have one wired to Belton.

"The police department in Belton," Robles recalls, "was in one room, and the fire department across the hall in another room." He asked to speak to the chief of police, but was told, "Gus isn't here right now. What's the problem?"

Robles didn't want to discuss his business without a warrant, and only asked for the address of the French family. The man at the desk insisted on knowing what business Robles had in Belton. Finally, Robles located Gus, the police chief, and told him that he was there to talk to Mary French concerning a runaway girl from Tucson. The chief said, "You come all the way down here about a runaway?"

The chief said he'd "send Lou up the road to see if the Frenches lived there." Robles wanted to accompany Lou.

"He'll just see if she's there and come on back and tell us," the chief said. "You don't have to go up there with him."

Robles said, "I'd prefer to. I'll go with him."

The French house looked like part of a project, similar to the place they had occupied in Tucson. Robles thought they'd recently moved in because there wasn't any furniture in the front room. Mary's mother answered the door and appeared unconcerned, even though she asked, "You come all the way from Tucson just to ask about her? Haven't they found that girl yet? Isn't that something?Well, Mary's taking a shower."

Mrs. French went into another room and Robles heard her call, "There's a detective here from Tucson, Mary, wants to talk about that missing Rowe girl or whatever her name is."

Robles waited for a long while. He says, "It seemed like I waited and waited, and all the while I was thinking that Mary might have snuck out the bathroom window." Finally, Mary came out of the bathroom with a towel wrapped around her wet hair. She appeared indifferent.

"I'd like to ask you a couple of things about Alleen Rowe, Mary," Robles said.

"Oh," Mary replied.

"Maybe it would be better if you got something on and we could go over to the sheriff's and talk a little better over there."

"Oh." Mary shrugged and went back into the bathroom. She closed the door and Robles heard the water running.

Robles waited again. He says, "All the mother had to do was say, 'Like hell you're taking her anywhere,' or, 'She's not talking about anything without a lawyer here.' So I had to play it very cool. The last thing I was about to do was even breathe a word of murder or arrest or anything like that."

Mary came out of the bathroom slowly, wearing a dress. "Where are we going?" she asked.

"I thought we could probably talk better out of the house, you know," Robles replied.

Mary shrugged and told her mother she was going out. The mother walked to the door, wiping her hands on a kitchen towel. "They haven't found that girl yet?" she asked.

"I don't even know an Alleen Rowe," Mary said. "I don't know what I can say to you."

"We'll just talk a little," Robles said.

At the sheriff's office, Robles left Mary in one room and told the sheriff the real story. He said he was expecting a warrant to be wired and that the girl was to be charged as an accomplice in a homicide.

Back in the room with Mary, Robles talked to her for a while, "just nonsense," he recalls, "talking about nothing. She kept saying she didn't know Alleen Rowe or anything about her disappearance. She'd answer questions but would volunteer nothing on her own."

Meanwhile, the sheriff sent for the justice of the peace, a small man who was also the town's barber, so that he could prepare for the extradition proceedings. The warrant finally arrived, and the judge asked, out of curiosity, if he could sit in on the questioning. Robles agreed, realizing that the judge would be the best possible witness to a statement. He returned to Mary, who was getting bored, and talked to her for "a few more minutes before laying it on the line."

"Okay, Mary," Robles said. "Let's knock off the nonsense. I'm here to talk about Alleen Rowe and you've been implicated in her death. You, Charlie, and John Saunders."

Mary didn't cooperate. Robles recalls, "Out of all the people I've questioned on the Schmid case, out of all those people, Mary is just about the coldest person I've ever talked to. Like ice."

Finally, Robles said to Mary, "You know Smitty got married, you know that?"

Robles says, "It was the only reaction I got out of her. She just changed for a split second. I could see it really got to her. Then she told the whole story, once again answering questions, everything, but volunteering nothing. The statement was five pages, single-spaced. Mary was sitting to my right side, I was sitting and punching the typewriter and the judge was back in the chair near the door.

"Mary's story was pretty close to what Bruns had said Charlie told him," Robles said, "but Mary got into all the details. Smitty had wanted to kill someone, a girl, Mary told Robles, just to see what it felt like and to see if he could get away with it. He used Mary to lure Alleen Rowe from the house and into the car with Smitty and John. Smitty drove to the desert where he and John killed Alleen." Mary said that she had not been present when Alleen was killed, but that Smitty told her how they'd done it, with a rock, and then Mary helped them bury the body.

Robles later said, "Naturally, I had to pry the details out of Mary, not that she wasn't willing to talk, but you just have to pry everything out of her."

Mary was put in jail at the sheriff's office and her father came down with Mary's suitcase. "It was a big suitcase," Robles says, "and packed full of everything the girl owned, it seemed."

Mary's father was worried and kept asking, "What's going to happen to her?" Robles told him only that she'd be taken back to Tucson "to talk some more there."

Mrs. French did not come to see her daughter in jail, but she commented, "If she played the game, she'll have to pay the piper."

Later, at the airport in Temple, Texas, Mary went into the toilet and Robles waited for twenty minutes before rapping on the restroom door. He recalls, "The thought that she'd taken off out a rear window scared the hell out of me." But Mary was still there, smoking a cigarette. "We gotta go," Robles called to her.

He had trouble catching a flight out of Dallas, and Mary kept dragging her feet, falling behind. Every few minutes Robles had to say, "Come on, Mary, we gotta go. Come on, Mary, we gotta go."

"Oh," was all Mary ever said.

John Saunders was located at his sister's home in Northford, Connecticut, where he was working as a carpenter's helper. He was arrested there by Dupnik and returned to Tucson on a fugitive warrant. He confessed to being an accomplice in the murder of Alleen Rowe, but maintained that Smitty had done the actual killing.

While a crowd of officials and newsmen were waiting at the Tucson airport for the detective's arrival with Saunders, Dupnik left the plane as it made its stop in Phoenix. There, a single car was waiting for them.

They drove from Phoenix to Tucson and went directly to the desert, where Saunders was led out to the wash to show police the grave of Alleen Rowe. But he could not find it.

Detective Wilhelm met Mary and Robles as they stepped off the American Airlines Astrojet. One newsman asked the girl, "Are you Mary French?" but she turned away and settled with Robles in the rear seat of Wilhelm's car.

Soon they arrived at the desert where Saunders had been unable to find the grave. Detectives carrying shovels trailed Mary as she wandered through the cactus. She walked down the sloping bank of the wash then turned west and started hunting for landmarks. Flashbulbs splashed her pale face at almost every step. The earth in the area had already been turned up where Saunders had indicated several possible sites for the grave. Mary appeared uncertain. She marked one site and, when nothing was found, looked again and came up with another two hundred yards away. After hours of digging and finding only some rusty beer cans and two rusted hair curlers, one officer shrugged off the search and said they had "been led on a wild-goose chase." Another referred hopefully to the hair curlers and said, "We'll ask Norma Rowe if these belonged to her daughter."

A confusion of flashbulbs and reporters with tape recorders greeted Smitty, Saunders, and Mary French when they entered the courtroom building for their arraignment for the murder of Alleen Rowe. None of the defendants said anything in court. Saunders looked frightened, barely moving a muscle, and Mary French cried, turning from reporters to hide behind Detective Robles.

Saunders was represented by a court-appointed attorney, Edward Morgan. Mary had no counsel, but a motion that the proceedings be postponed until she could be represented was denied, along with Tinney's motion that the courtroom be cleared of reporters and spectators.

Morgan said he wouldn't allow his client, Saunders, to continue looking for the remains of Alleen Rowe. He and Tinney both asked that separate hearings be set for the defendants and this motion was also denied. The same day Superior Court Judge Roylston denied a petition by Tinney for a temporary restraining order against the Tucson newspapers to black out further coverage of the charges against Schmid.

Norma Rowe's suspicions had been confirmed. During an interview she granted on the day of arraignment, she said, "After all, I knew what happened eighteen months ago when my daughter Alleen was murdered by thrill-seeking teenagers, but I couldn't convince anybody else. Nobody wanted to hear the truth.

"Alleen had been invited, coaxed, and finally ordered to join the sex club," Mrs. Rowe went on. "And this wasn't just something Alleen dreamed up. 'The club's the thing,' she said. 'You've got to belong to be in.' But Alleen had apparently made up her mind that she wanted nothing to do with the 'in' group, and I think she was trying to either get back out or stay out when she was murdered. And this club is still in operation. A lot of kids are out of town, but there is still a club. I think the murderers either took her out to the desert to get her into the group and she refused or she already knew too much and they decided to kill her when she wouldn't go along with them."

Mrs. Rowe spoke with no visible emotion. She named a boy in a southern state and a girl living in the Midwest as additional suspects in the murder of Alleen. "I have given both these names to the police and one of the detectives even told me that he thought the boy was in on Alleen's disappearance. But I don't think they have tried to track them down. Alleen was trying to avoid this bunch of creeps, she had been seeing a fellow from the university, a concert violinist. She died wearing his ring."

Norma Rowe's charges shocked many people into believing that an elaborate conspiracy existed, and daily stories on the case kept public interest at a high pitch.

Newspapers and broadcasts following the arrests of the suspects gave detailed approximations as to how and why the murders were committed. Chief Garmire had released stories that "Schmid met the girls on the night they disappeared and drove with them in the family car, the vehicle they had left home in to attend a drive-in movie. In a quiet part of the city, the source said, the car was stopped and while Gretchen was out of the auto her sister was strangled inside. When Gretchen returned, she too was strangled."

A television broadcast reported, "Police Chief Garmire says the motive for the slaying of the three young girls was jealousy stemming from a conspiracy among a teenage clique. Detectives are investigating the possibility that the Fritz sisters were killed because they knew about the slaying of Miss Rowe."

Publicity became a major issue in the case. Public interest was fed by the further stories on the search for Alleen Rowe's body. The sheriff's deputies continued to dig. Every possible place near the wash was unearthed and for days dozens of police and newsmen tramped through the desert with shovels and metal detectors, finding nothing.

Then a legion of high-school students aided in the search. They seemed on a party treasure hunt, digging with their hands, children's shovels, and broken motorcycle fenders. They kept their strength up with hamburgers, Cokes, and trips to drive-ins for french fries and malts. One girl showed up with soup spoons from

Johnnie's Drive-In, explaining: "We're looking for a body that's been buried for a long time, I guess, and it's probably fallen all apart and things."

They found objects and brought them to the sheriff: old shotgun shells, a soleless shoe, some reddish rocks with a bit of animal bone embedded in them. The search spread under overcast skies to several hundred yards of desert; bulldozers and other heavy equipment of the Burris-White Machinery Company were employed and soon the wash was pocked with gouges so that it resembled a field that had been worked over by a battery of mortars.

The sheriff told reporters that he was beginning to think the grave had been moved, and Mrs. Rowe thought so too. Nevertheless, she said, the rusty hair curlers originally found were Alleen's. "I'm sure they were hers," she told the press. "There is no doubt in my mind. She and I used the same long bobby pins. There is one girl in a million who uses those long pins like that."

The police began to develop their case, and kept the press informed of everything they found. Irma Jean Kolt was reported missing, then telephoned from California to say that she was staying there with Shirley Bates. Irma Jean discussed the diary Smitty had told her about, and Sheriff Burr said that he had received numerous phone calls about a diary belonging to Gretchen. "Those callers told us that if we got Gretchen's diary, we would get considerable information on these murder cases."

Mrs. Kolt told reporters, "Irma Jean knew a few more things than she should have. There are too many people involved and this thing is really spreading out. Irma Jean and her friends knew about these parties and that is why I forbade her to run around with Smitty.

"Charlie sat in my living room and said that some day he was going to kill Gretchen because she was holding something over his head ,and when the Fritz girls disappeared my daughter said to me, you want to bet they'll never find Gretchen alive?"

The news media stressed the importance of the diary as a motive for the murders. "Where is the missing link?" they asked.

Again, police came to Smitty's house looking for the diary, turning everything upside down, even taking his television set apart. They didn't find it.

There was no diary.

By now the murder was one of Tucson's better-known tourist attractions and there was a steady stream of cars past Smitty's house, the supposed grave site of Alleen Rowe, and among the rubble where the Fritz sisters' skeletons had been found.

Sheriff Burr now held to the theory that tropical storm Tillie had carried away the Rowe girl's remains in September 1964. County Attorney Norman Green made it clear that he would proceed with his case with or without a body, citing a ruling in a similar case that made this possible.

The Schmid case received national attention. Reporters from both coasts were visiting Tucson. A *Time* magazine article under the title "Secrets in the Sand," appeared with all the details. Other national publications were interested, and Tucson began to complain about this blemish on its image as a healthy place, "full of sunshine and dry air."

Then, on November 23, 1965, in an action perhaps unprecedented in U.S. courts, Superior Court Judge Richard Roylston approved an injunction requested by William Tinney that prohibited police and sheriff's officers, the county attorney, and his deputies, from any further discussion of the Schmid case with the news media. Judge Roylston declined, at the same time, to issue an injunction forbidding the press from discussing the murders at all. "In effect," the *Tucson Citizen* reported, Roylston "put news media on probation."

Roylston said he feared that continued news reports of recent "quantity and quality" would prejudice Schmid's case. He could only guess what higher courts would do when faced squarely with the issue of the "conflict between free press and fair trial," but said that he felt the courts would eventually be compelled to set forth new guideposts as to how much the press could be told in advance of a trial.

Commenting on Tinney's request for a news blackout, Judge Roylston said, "If I grant it, silencing both press and law authorities, I'll be infringing on the rights of the press. If I don't, I'll be infringing on the rights of this defendant to an impartial trial by jury. If news coverage is continued as it has been, the defendant's right to a fair trial will be impaired. It is conceivable that the high courts would say that the defendant is unable to get a fair trial in any county of a state due to pretrial publicity, and free the defendant, just because his rights have been violated to such an extent as to make an impartial trial impossible."

The public and press were not admitted to the pretrial hearing.

The small glass window on the courtroom door was covered with black paper and taped from within. A window at the rear of the courtroom, left open for ventilation, was guarded by a deputy who shook his head at the few newsmen below, then closed the blinds.

In the room, the defendants and their witnesses were sworn in and ordered not to discuss the case with anyone. The prosecutor did not present his witnesses at the opening of the hearing.

As Smitty stood before the bench in a baggy double-breasted suit, he was still nursing a hope that the charges against him would be dropped. This collapsed when Norman Green announced on November 24th that Saunders would plead guilty to first-degree murder and Mary French would plead guilty to reduced charges. Attorneys for both defendants told the court that their clients would testify for the state against Schmid. "It's obvious that somebody made a deal," Tinney said. "This has been going on since November 10th."

Saunders's attorney, Morgan, was asked why he let his client plead guilty to first instead of second degree murder. He said, "If a person is sentenced to life in Arizona, he could be eligible for parole in about seven years. Second-degree murder carries a sentence ranging from a ten-year minimum to life imprisonment."

The preliminary hearing on the two murder charges against Schmid lasted three and one-half days. On November 30th he was bound over for trial in Superior Court.

At the close of the hearing Justice of the Peace LaVetter commented, “I didn’t learn anything new from the hearing that I hadn’t already read in the newspapers. I’ve been asked why I bound Schmid over, but all the state has to do at a preliminary hearing is produce probable cause to believe that a crime was committed.” He said the state had done this, but added, “It’s certainly not one of the best cases in the world. In fact it’s one of the worst.”

One week later John Saunders was sentenced in Superior Court by Judge Collins. He received life imprisonment and would be eligible for parole in seven years.

Judge Roylston sentenced Mary French on two charges, of being an accessory to murder and concealing and compounding a felony, but let her serve them concurrently. She would be eligible for parole in four to five years.

Schmid was scheduled to be tried in Superior Court on February 15, 1966, for the murders of Gretchen and Wendy Fritz.

Norman Green made it clear that the state would settle for nothing short of the death penalty.

PART FOUR

MY DEAREST DIANE, Oh, honey, I miss you so much, I want to hold you and make love to you and have a Christmas tree and a snowball fight. I want to go on all the rides at an amusement park and go back east to see your friends and grandparents, and start a band, and especially go see Country & Western stars, and go to Hawaii and California, and play in the ocean with you. I want to play cards and miniature golf with you, and race cars, and laugh and cry, and do what we want and even have a couple of kids.

Believe it or not I really want some kids some day after we've done everything we want. It will make our love even stronger, if that's even possible. Just think, the kids will be ours, all ours. Damn will they be dolls. I hope you want kids someday because I really and truly do. A kid will be the greatest gift besides your love you could ever give me. I want to get your dad a farm and see them happy and take your sisters out and have parties once in a while and go walking in the rain with you, some hot summer day and get soaked and not give a damn and laugh

> and smile and make you happy & just do what we want with no one telling us what to do.

> I want to send you flowers every day and eat French toast and listen to records and cut our own songs and records and make my parents and yours happy. I want to take you to Mardi Gras in New Orleans and get lost with you in all the fun and excitement. I want to do everything we had planned for us and even more because that's the way I am. I've got to have fun and have a blast whenever we can because life is short and we deserve to be happy. I want to dance with you and tell you jokes, and do silly stupid things just for fun. I want to run down the street at 12 midnight and wake people up just to tell them I love you. Just when we got a car and enough money to do these things *this* crap has to happen. Why, we'll never know.

Enclosed by a steel Cyclone fence, the windowless one-story Pima County Jail building sits on the desert west of Tucson like a cement box. From Cell 14, Tank E, Charles Schmid wrote a letter to his wife almost every day while awaiting trial. He repeatedly insisted on his innocence to Diane, who had no way of knowing the facts. It seemed at times as if he was trying to convince himself, like most confined men cut off from their ways of life.

Smitty continued in his letter:

> Maybe it happened so when I get out we'll have even more fun and appreciate everything more. We just started to have fun and the real blast was just beginning. Fate slipped up on me and took it away, but someday I know I'll be found innocent. Even if it's after they kill me at least you'll know I loved

> you, and what I wanted, and more of what I'm like. For better or worse, darling, this is what I'm like. If nothing else at least I gave you all I had. I just know I'll be out soon and in your arms and we'll be doing a hundred million more things than what I've said we'd do. When I get out I don't want to waste a minute.

All Smitty's past outlets for expressing himself, except for Diane and his parents, had been silenced at the advice of his attorney, William Tinney.

On a Thursday he wrote:

> What do you do everyday? I get up, eat, then vomit, go to sleep, then go to mail call, go back to sleep or play cards till lunch, throw up some more, go back to sleep and pray some miracle will happen so I can see you for a little while, then go to garbage, I mean supper, then play cards and hope I'll see you or somebody, then I go to my cell and crawl under my cot. I won't sleep on that damn steel bed because the light hurts my eyes. I usually stay up all night and draw pictures or write you letters. Write and tell me what you do everyday and what you think about kids. It wouldn't be till we're both ready though, after we have our fun. Oh, damn, honey, I'm not an animal to be caged up like I am. I have to be free. I'm going crazy. Please write everyday and say you love me and dream about me. You can't imagine what this lonely hell is like in here. I'm made to love and be with you. Every day I wonder if I'll ever see you again. I've told them I'll take a lie-detector or truth serum but they don't care. I can't say anything more except if I live or die at least you know I love you. Maybe they have guitars in

> heaven. All my love forever given, *Smitty.*

> Blue Monday Dec 13, you can't imagine how I miss you this close to Christmas. They lied terribly in court today, but I still believe they'll believe *me.* You thought you were sneaky coming down to court today but I saw you going into the girls' rest room.

> NO more! I mean it. They're not going to find out who you are...

> Since you couldn't kiss me good night last night, Homer did! Don't believe me? I've got a big hickey to prove it, right on my neck. Did you get the drawing of Homer? He comes up out of the plumbing at night, the pipes are so clogged with crap he stinks like hell sometimes. The preliminary hearing is over [for Rowe]. Friday I go to see when I go to trial. Are your Christmas lights turned on yet? Do you think it'll snow? What should we get Homer for a present? I'm hip, a girl friend. Maybe Homer should be called Homerette–he's pregnant. Not by me, honest. What do you give baby rats to eat? Do they eat people? If they do I'll probably be first! I hope you have a happy birthday.... Don't worry, everything is going OK, I mean it. Your handsome, skinny, adorable proud god-father of seven baby rats, *Smitty.*

Schmid would stand trial for the murder of Alleen Rowe on March 15, 1966, thirty days following the trial scheduled for the Fritz murders. Again Norman Green made it clear that the state would ask for the death penalty.

Smitty wrote in early January:

> I feel real weird, I really don't know why though. I saw Bill [Tinney] today, he even looked worried. I've got the awfulest feeling something's up. I don't know what tho. I sure hope everything works out. I feel so empty and mixed up, I guess it's just one of those times. Tension is building again. I miss you. Bill says the lie detector and sodium pentathol [sic] wouldn't be admissible in court. I guess that's taken care of. Sometimes I wonder if he knows what the hell he's talking about. He sure does lie to me. I really don't like him worth a damn. I'll keep him though. I'll bet money he'll screw everything up in court. Since he's so determined to keep everything from me I've lost all my respect for him. Why should he care anyway–he's already got all the publicity he needs, and he's already paid so naturally he'll lose interest. Maybe I'm wrong. I hope so. Anyway there's not much I can do. I'll just continue to be his little tinker toy. I sure love and miss you. I'm afraid all this crap has changed me inside. Lately I've lost respect for everything, except you. I feel so damn mad at everything. I'll probably go to sleep tonight and everything will be back to normal tomorrow. All I can think of to say is that I love you and miss you more than ever right now. Every night when we get together again we're going to lie in bed and smoke cigarettes and tell each other what the happiest moments of our lives were that day.
>
> 3 or 4 A.M. Oh honey I can't sleep worth a damn. You're the only one who can understand anything about me. I can't get the thought out of my head that I'll be found innocent. I know I will. I want to

be happy with you but this hate I've got might ruin it. I'm just sick and tired of accepting all their crap without fighting back. You're the one decent thing I've got left out of this mess. If you love me as much as you say you do, and I know you do, then help me forget them or this hate will ruin our chance for happiness. Maybe if I'm with you and away from all these cruddy people I'll feel different, but right now I feel different than I *ever* have in my life.

Unbelievable Thursday. Oh, honey, you'll never believe what I'm going to tell you, not even in your wildest dreams. You had just left yesterday when I got a message from this lady I know.

She is a singing instructor and her name is Helen, and she lives on Drexel. I think I showed you the house, a purple one. Well, a long time ago I'd taken a couple of singing lessons from her and she taped my voice. She lives in Los Angeles now and she saw my name and pictures in the paper. I got to know her real well and sent her a Xmas card and flowers for her birthday last year. She's fifty-seven years old. She always thought I was polite and a doll and that I had a real tuff voice. When she saw I was in trouble and she thought I might need money for help, so she took my tapes to a friend of hers who works at RCA recording studios in Hollywood. He listened to them and looked at my pictures in the paper and told her if I could get out of this mess he will arrange an audition. He also said the publicity I had gotten would be great, because if I'm found not guilty people will think I've gotten a rotten deal and want to give me a chance. Won't that be great! All my life I've waited for this chance.

> He really thinks I've got a tuff voice. Can you believe it! I've got to get out of this mess!
>
> Baby just think, maybe everyone will love me instead of hate me and I'd be so proud telling everyone you're my wife and they can eat shit!
>
> Maybe this is the answer to our prayers, we'll have money, fame, clothes, cars, houses–for your parents and mine, and most of all we'll have each other. I just can't believe it!
>
> I sure miss decking out in my Continentals and vest and high-collar shirts like I used to, Baby. People will think we're the tuffest couple anywhere. Soon we'll be together and on our way to a fairyland life.
>
> I can't especially wait to tell every girl who wants me to get lost because I've got the cutest, sexiest, and best wife in the whole world. ALL MY LOVE forever given to the most wonderful wife in the world, who, without her letters and courage I'd never make it. Your soon to be the next Elvis Presley, except I'll be better, *Smitty.*

He advised Diane to start saving $25 a week.

> We'll need a little to go to California for the audition. We're still going back east first, tho, for a couple of weeks just to meet your friends & grandparents and have a little fun because we'll be pretty busy after I start cutting the songs. Damn I can't wait to get out!
>
> You sure looked sharp Thursday. How did you

> know I dig sexy, sheer black stockings. I really eat up on the way you dress, from your hair to your pointed-toe black high heels and ALL that's bitchin in between. If you see any shoes or high-collar shirts I might dig, pick up on them. Your soon to be famous husband.

Smitty continued to proclaim his love for Diane. Since his marriage had been a desperate attempt to create some stability at the center of his life, he meant much of what he was saying. But again this was one isolated part of his life, and he forgot the times he had repeated the same words on more cynical occasions.

In the middle of January he wrote:

> I'm so damn glad you don't want kids. I've got to do so, so many things first. Don't expect me to be a model husband and be meek and mousy and quiet all the time. I'm just not that way. But you already know that. Don't expect me to settle down in one place too long. I'm MAD and ANGRY with people but I'll laugh at them. I've *got* to have a really tuff car again! and a cycle. I've got to have my band and sing again. If this RCA audition falls through, I'll try again and again and again until I prove I'm good enough to cut my songs. I know I can. And I think the audition will prove it. I'll make it big or I won't make it at all. We'll either be rich or poor, I won't settle for middle road anymore. It's not worth it.
>
> All my life I was either a big success or a big failure. Everything's got messed up when I compromised and took the middle road to sacrifice everything for my rotten friends. I hope you understand because I need you badly (I haven't got anybody else).

> Well, doll, it seems to be getting a little bit worse than before, but don't worry, there's always a rainbow after every storm.
>
> It's about 10 or eleven P.M. and it sounds like rain out. You know, it's funny but we've never been together in the rain yet. Someday or even night we'll lay in bed and the rain will patter down on the roof and I'll look at you and tell you how much I love you in a thousand different ways, and be so glad I married you. It seems like we've been married for a long time to me right now. The rain sort of makes me sad but most of all it makes me wish I was in your arms and telling you a hundred different things.
>
> I'm here listening to the radio and all they play is shitty opera, and you know how I hate that. I hope you won't forget to call those people (at the Tucson *American)* but of course you won't.
>
> Do you know I've been locked up almost three months now? I feel like I'm all drained out inside. It's like I'm dead inside. I really want to GO GO GO! when I'm finally freed. It seems funny how all my friends are really helping right now. It's about time. Maybe everyone will find out what a rotten rat ding-dong Richie really is.
>
> I sure did like that tuff outfit you had on. That necklace was just the crowning touch to make you look great. At least I sure as hell won't be ashamed to take you anywhere, especially to the recording audition! Ha ha!

On the night of February 14, Schmid wrote:

> Well, tomorrow kangaroo court begins. I wonder if they'll sell tickets? Just imagine, 'Ladies and Gentlemen, we now present the biggest farce in history.' Oh, well, maybe they have guitars and bitchin cars in heaven. All I'd have to do then is wait for you and everything would be great.
>
> Did you dye your wig yet? I'll bet it looks great. Did you know everyone thought you looked like Mary French? I didn't think so.
>
> Come down Wed night if you want. Don't ever forget that if something goes wrong and some idiot tries to shoot me on the way to court and kills me, that I love you and at least I *was* true to you, even though I wasn't to anyone else and you made me happier than I've ever been in my life.

Smitty looked like a new man when he entered the Pima County Courthouse on Tuesday morning, February 15, 1966. He wore a white shirt, a conservative black-and-brown tie, charcoal herringbone jacket, tan trousers, and new loafers. Some of the black hair dye had grown out, and his natural reddish-brown hair could be seen at the nape of his neck. Newsmen and reporters lined the second-floor corridors as Smitty, smiling tensely, came through the stairwell door from a basement holding cell. Casual, as though Deputy Henry Booth was not at his back, Smitty paused briefly before Art Meyers, a defense witness. "Good luck," Art said, reaching out his hand. The courtroom was spacious and new, with bronze reliefs of Lincoln and Washington framing the judge's bench. Schmid sat at the wide glass-topped defense table of light oak, holding twenty blue-bound volumes with gold lettering: *Arizona Revised Statutes Annotated.* Tinney's motions to exclude

Charles Schmid, Jr., a successful and athletic student, nicknamed "Smitty" by his peers.

Smitty's strength and power as a gymnast, on display.

The Schmid family lived (in house, left) on East Adams, in Tucson, Arizona, across the street from the Hillcrest Nursing Home, which they owned and operated, and where Smitty worked after school. In short order, Smitty's foster parents gave him a gold-colored Ford Falcon, and the small house adjacent to his family (house right).

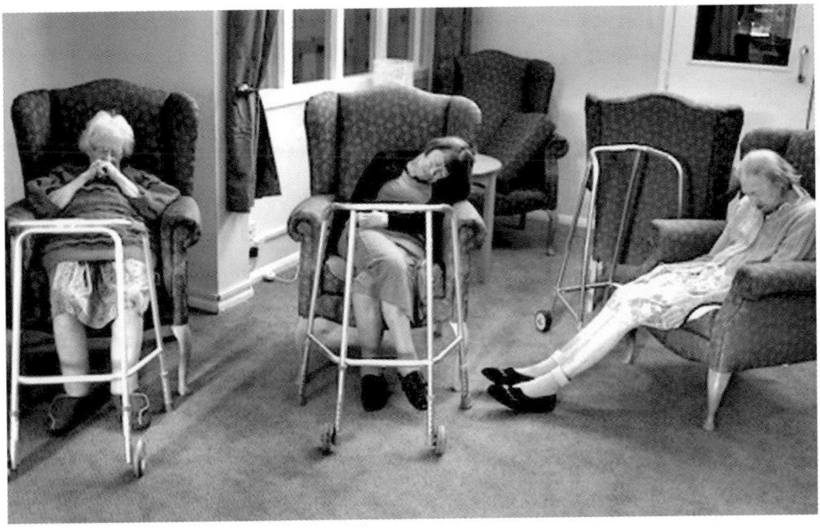

In the mid-1960s, the Schmids' Hillcrest Nursing Home began to experience financial problems, and eventually went into receivership.

Speedway Boulevard became a haven for Tucson's restless teenagers.
The many clubs and hangouts catered to the fast-moving clientele.

Many teenage girls on Tucson's restless scene
became single mothers.

SPECIAL

Police Bulletin

P. O. BOX 1071
TUCSON POLICE DEPARTMENT
TUCSON, ARIZONA

Tucson

Bernard L. Garmire
CHIEF OF POLICE

NORMA ALLEEN ROWE, WAF, DOB 27 October 1948, Dallas, Texas, 120# blonde hair, brown eyes, fair tanned complexion, white blemish center of back, small scar right eyebrow, very faint. Missing since 31 May 1964 at 2230 hours from 7342 Calle Cuernavaca, Tucson, Arizona. The only clothes at time she left home is a one piece black bathing suit, blouse with yellow flowers and orange rubber thongs. Destination unknown.

Any information - Tucson Police Department, Tucson, Arizona, phone 791-4404 or 791-4411.

Juvenile Detail, Case #276330.

Though Tucson suffered a problem with runaways, Alleen Rowe was not one of them. Above, her missing persons bulletin issued by the Tucson police.

Gretchen Fritz (at right), was one of Smitty's last girlfriends—a wilful daughter of wealthy Tucson parents.

Gretchen, the summer before her death.

Nogales, Mexico: Charles Schmid marries Diane Lynch, angering many of his girlfriends...

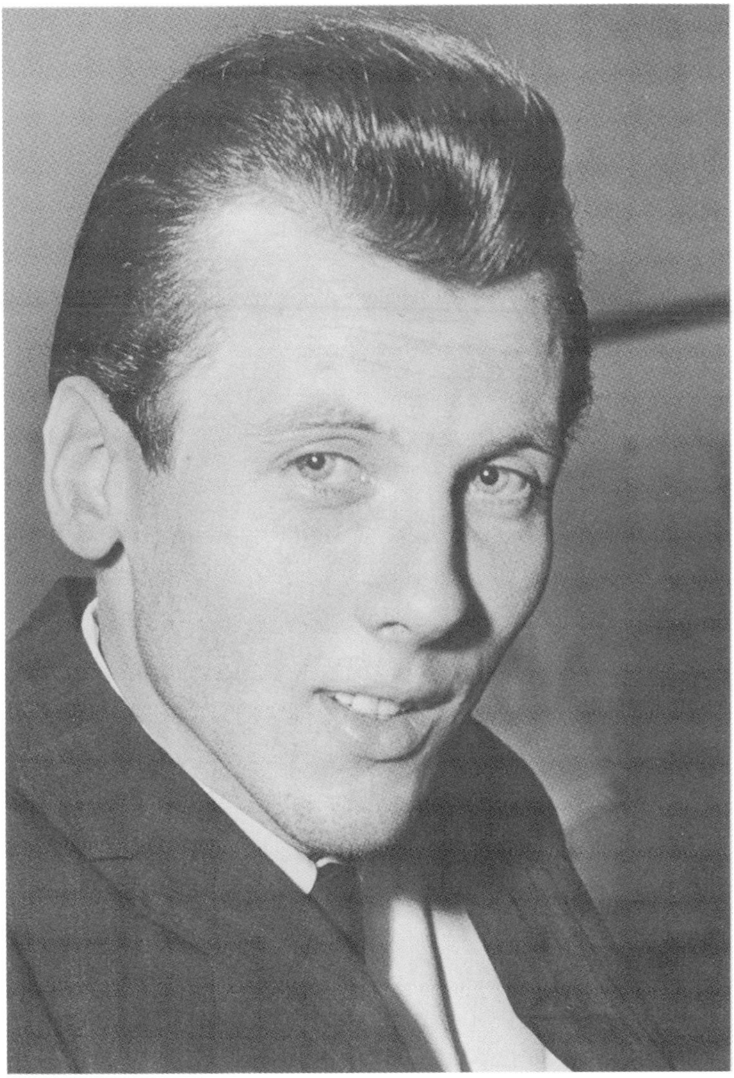

... also angering his once-best friend and sidekick, Richie Bruns.

Smitty was arrested following Richie's admission that he helped Smitty bury the bodies of the Fritz sisters.

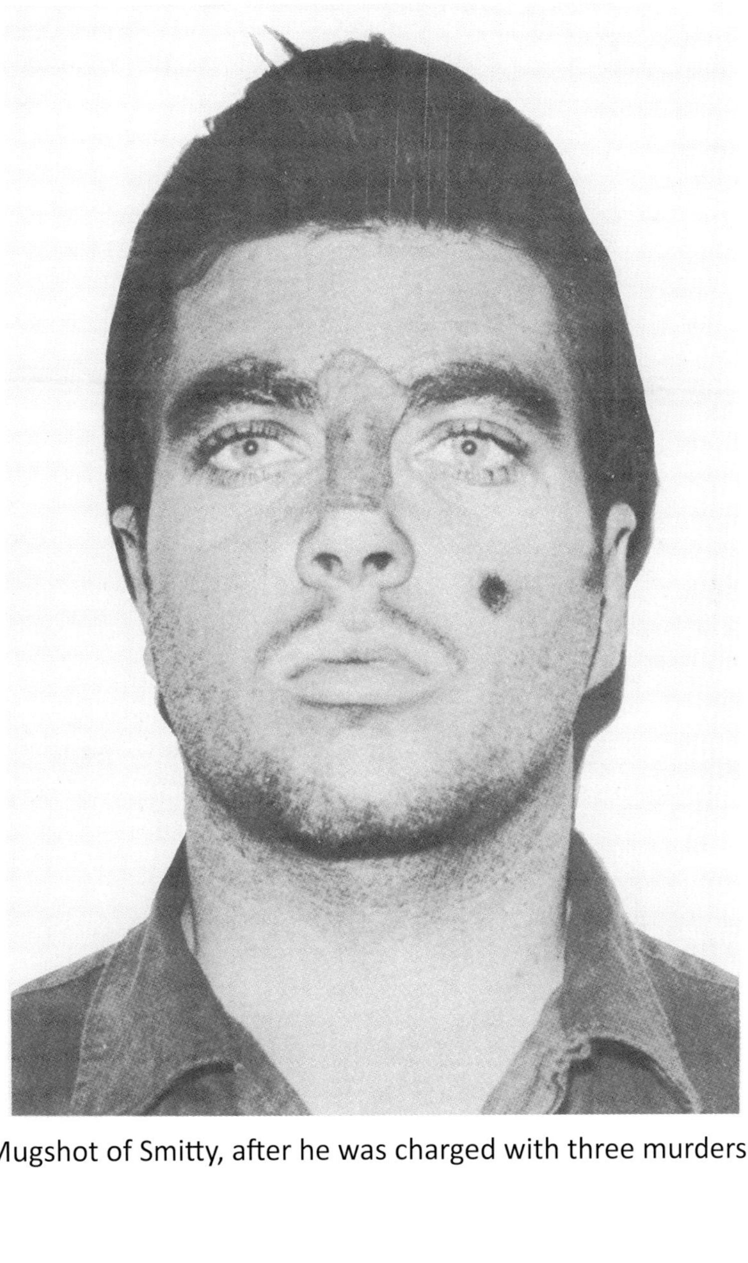

Mugshot of Smitty, after he was charged with three murders.

Richie Bruns leads Tucson police
to the remains of Gretchen Fritz
and her sister, Wendy.

Mary French, Schmid's girlfriend before his marriage, was arrested as a participant in the death of Alleen Rowe.

Mary French is led to find Alleen's shallow grave—which they did not find.

John Saunders, (above) after being sentenced to life imprisonment for his part in the death of Alleen Rowe.

Mary French is also convicted.

Mask of confidence—Smitty is sure that Alleen's body will not be found, thus eliminating a third trial.

The legal strategy engineered by defense attorney William Tinney and Smitty was intended to convince the jury that Richie Bruns actually killed the Fritz sisters.

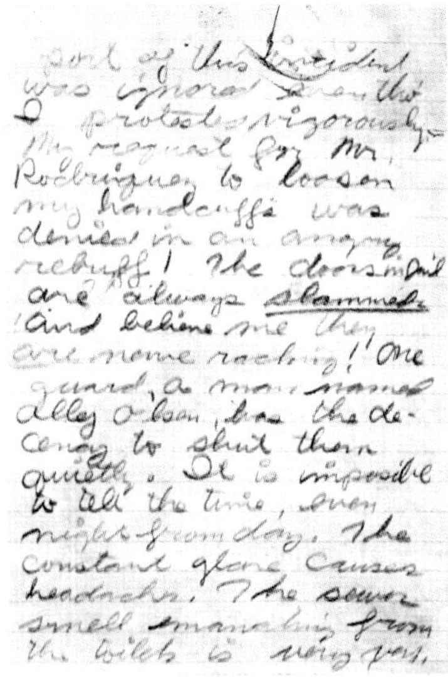

part of this incident was ignored. When I protested vigorously, my request for Mr. Rodriguez to loosen my handcuffs was denied in an angry rebuff! The doors in jail are always slammed. And believe me they are nerve racking! One guard, a man named [illegible], has the decency to shut them quietly. It is impossible to tell the time, even night from day. The constant glare causes headaches. The sewer smell emanating from the toilets is [illegible].

Smitty's cartoon of Homer the Rat (above), and a sample of Smitty's journal, (right), both composed at Pima County Jail.

Smitty being handcuffed to be returned to jail, following his conviction for the Fritz murders, for which he receieved two death sentences.

Even though Alleen Rowe's body remained undiscovered, the Tucson District Attorney was preparing a trial for her murder. Smitty fired his attorney for the Fritz case, and asked the author to secure representation from Percy Foreman (above), the most famous and expensive defense attorney in the country. Foreman viewed the psychitric testimony on Smitty, which he felt would "scare the pants off any attorney." He said, "The lawyer should be made to take half the juice."

Percy Foreman, unable to take the case, recommened F. Lee Bailey. (above, right). Bailey took the defense of Schmid for Alleen Rowe's murder, for which he was going to to be tried despite the missing body. Author John Gilmore (above, left) is pictured on the way to introduce Bailey to Schmid at Arizona State Prison.

Bailey (above, right), decided to keep attorney William Tinney as a consultant on the Alleen Rowe case.

Smitty had been transported to Arizona State Prison, in Florence, where he awaited execution for the Fritz murders. He languished on Death Row writing further letters to his wife and "philosophical ruminatons" on death in the gas chamber—which was visible less than 100 feet from his cell.

On Bailey's instructions, Smitty eventually pleaded guilty to Alleen's murder. The girl's body remained missing. Smitty was then convinced by a probation officer and Pima County Sheriff Waldon Burr to show them where he'd buried the girl. John Gilmore was present when Smitty revealed Alleen's shallow grave.

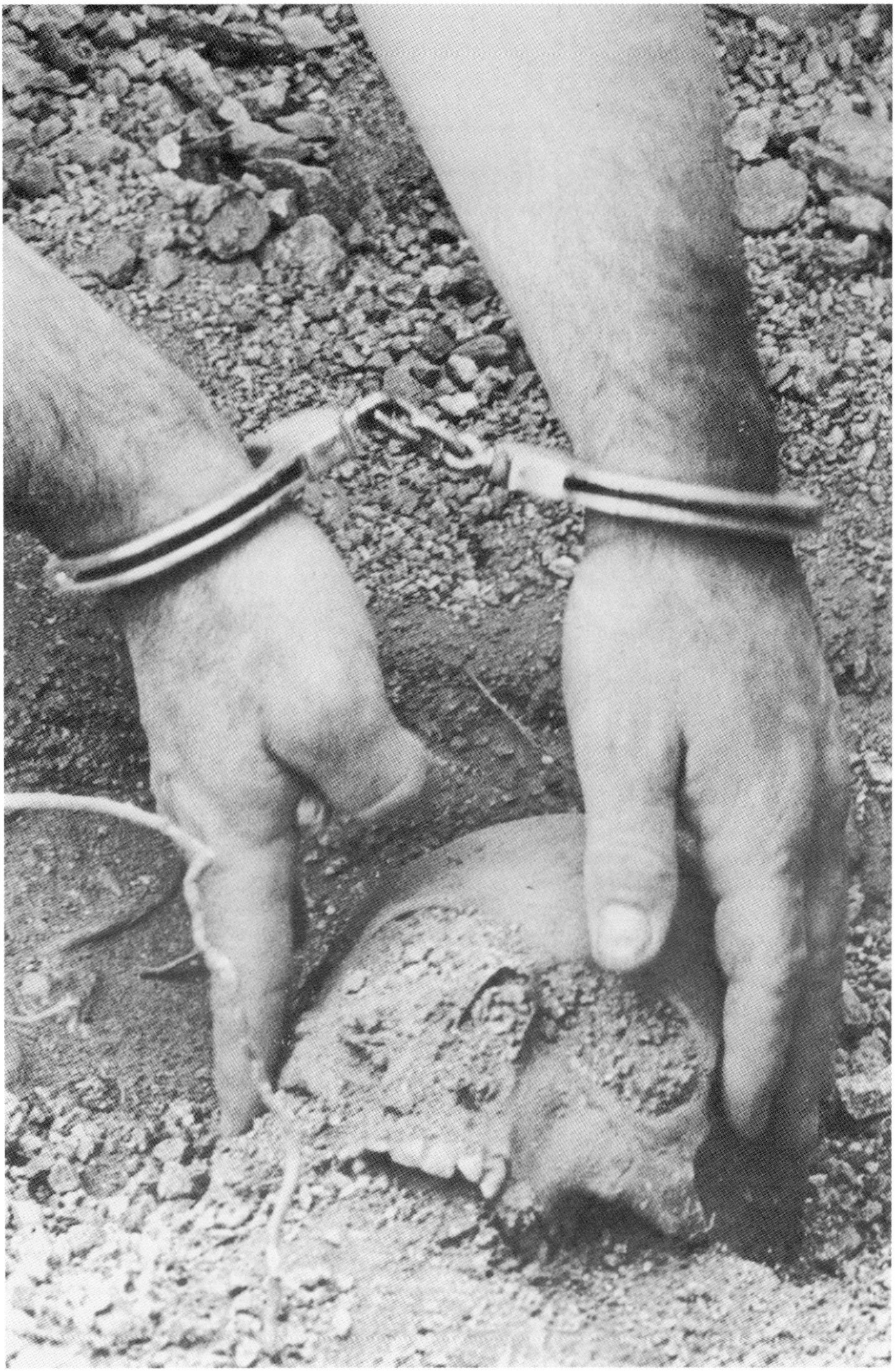

An attempt to reveal that Alleen's skull would show no fractures, would prove the opposite. A manacled Smitty lifting the skull from the shallow grave (above).

Smitty's personal party house (the scene of a double murder), remained empty, deserted and abandoned, until it would eventually be demolished.

the press had been denied, and reporters filled seats flanking both sides of a drinking fountain within the railing and to Schmid's right. One newsman's elbow rested on the clerk's desk.

After a few minutes the room slowly started to fill with prospective jurors. Smitty heard a woman whisper: "I thought he was bigger than that. He's really very small, isn't he? Huh, I thought he'd be a lot bigger than that." She sounded disappointed.

"Look at his hands," a man said, leaning toward a heavy-set woman in a flowered dress. "They're small but powerful. You can tell." Smitty took his hands from the table and folded them in his lap. His attorney had advised him to sit quietly and listen attentively.

Tinney, a deliberate speaker with a slight stutter (which some colleagues insisted won him sympathy), came into the court and sat next to his client. Later Tinney was to tell a friend, "Way back in law school Edward Bennett Williams thought up the rules for practicing criminal law. The four necessary rules are 1–get paid, 2–get a continuance, 3–get another continuance, and 4–never plead guilty."

Then William Schafer III, chosen by the county attorney to prosecute, entered the room through a door to the clerk's office carrying two big manila folders containing the state's case against Charles Schmid.

Finally, the wood panels behind the bench opened and the presiding judge, the Honorable Lee Garrett, an elderly man with slight, birdlike features, his eyes a frosty blue behind rimless glasses, took his seat on the bench.

While the clerk read the roll of ninety-eight prospective jurors, Smitty glanced frequently at the clock. Extra chairs had been brought in to accommodate the overflow of reporters.

It took almost an hour for the last juror to answer, "Here." Judge Garrett then read the formal charges against Schmid.

"The defendant has entered a plea of guilty," the judge said. Smitty seemed dazed, Tinney half-rose from his chair and Schafer blinked curiously at the judge, who sensed the trouble and went on, "Oh, did I say guilty? I meant the defendant is pleading not guilty."

At a recess one reporter discussed the case with several newsmen, and was overheard by some prospective jurors. "The thing about the diary," he said, "sticking that in there as a motive, they're missing the entire point. The thing about *why* he did it. The question here, which seems to be overlooked, is *why* all these kids knew about the murders and no one said a goddamn word."

In the selection of the jurors, the prosecution sought men and women unopposed to the death penalty. Only a few seemed to object to it, and some of these expressed a willingness to allow for it when dealing with "this sort of case." Jurors with any reservations were asked by Schafer: "Even when it deals with the death of a *child*?" Each time Tinney objected to that line of questioning. Jurors with substantial reservations about the death penalty were finally disqualified by the prosecution.

The jury selection moved along slowly. The next day Tinney made a motion for a mistrial when one prospective juror said he could not be impartial in the case because he had two daughters and "the youngest one's name is Wendy." Tinney claimed the answer showed a "hostile attitude and answers to questions that prejudiced Schmid." The motion was denied.

To nearly all the jurors, Tinney's final question was: "Can you promise me that you will base your verdict only on the evidence you hear in court and not on the stuff you have seen or read in the press?"

After exhausting almost the entire ninety-eight-man panel in nearly three full days of examination, a jury was decided upon. Most of those excused said they either couldn't invoke the death penalty or couldn't be locked up for the two or three weeks Judge Garrett had informed them the trial would take. The jurors included a hardware merchant, a janitor, a copper miner with ten children, the widow of a gas-station operator, a welder's wife, an ex-airline stewardess married to a soft-drink bottling company sales manager, a retired mining engineer, a carpenter's wife, a tavern-owner's wife, the wife of a trailer court manager, and the wife of a loan-company operator.

Only one, a woman, was a lifelong resident of Tucson. Three others had lived in the city approximately twenty years. Some were recent arrivals, having moved from California, Washington, Illinois, Indiana, Iowa, New York, Ohio, West Virginia, and Wisconsin. Most of the twelve were over fifty, three over sixty, and only one was below forty. Four men, a widow, and seven middle-aged housewives had testified that they were in favor of the death penalty and "would not hesitate to recommend it."

With the jury dismissed from the courtroom, Tinney submitted a motion to bring in a clinical psychologist to testify that the jurors selected had been subconsciously affected by the pretrial news coverage concerning the case. Glancing at a sheet of yellow legal-pad paper, Tinney said, "Twelve of the jurors have read about the case. Ten have seen it on TV, and six have discussed the case with other people. Seven have heard about it on the radio and one has read about it in *Time* magazine. Now don't get me wrong. I'm not saying the jurors were lying. I know they were telling the truth to the best of their ability. They were not evasive, but I propose to show that subconsciously they had absorbed much of this information. Because of this I am asking the Court to permit me to call Dr. Roland Tharp, a clinical psychologist at the University of Arizona, and let him testify. "He will say that even though a person may try to put much information behind him, he cannot really do so because of the subconscious level cranked into the mind at the unconscious level. A person may be as honest as the day is long, but he cannot control what remains in his subconscious mind." Judge Garrett said he would hear the psychologist's testimony the next day in the absence of the jury.

At 8:30 the next morning Tinney produced a large cardboard box filled with newspaper clippings, TV and radio tapes, and a bulky roll of posters covered with clippings on the Schmid case. He also submitted tear sheets from the last few editions of the Tucson newspapers, with red and blue marks indicating stories, articles, and photographs relating to the trial.

"These exhibits," Tinney said, "are intended to support my contention that even though the jurors have been honest and upright, they may have erred in saying they had not actually made up their minds about Schmid's guilt or innocence."

When Dr. Tharp took the witness stand he looked over the exhibits, thought over each question carefully, and testified "it would be impossible for a juror who has read or seen accounts of the Schmid case to disregard this in reaching a verdict.

After this testimony, Judge Garrett said that psychiatry was a recent and hardly exact science. He spoke of the "study of the mind" as on a par with hypnotism and witchcraft. What Dr. Tharp might say today, Judge Garrett said, he would deny tomorrow on the basis of further discoveries made in the interim. Therefore, he denied the motion for a one-year postponement of the trial, concluding, "All of the jurors have stated they will be fair and just in their deliberation."

The bailiff left the room to summon the jury and Smitty wrote on a sheet of yellow paper:

> My trial actually begins. It's been such a long time just waiting, I can't believe it's really happening. It's hard to believe what I'm really doing here, but here I am. It was sure nice outside, the air was cold and sort of like crystals but the sun was very bright, for the minute or two I got to see it. I sure wanted to be with Diane. I wonder if she went to the movies the other night and what she saw. I hope I can be with her before Easter anyway. I guess we're about ready to begin.

The jury was seated and William Schafer stood up, consulted a sheet of paper on the table, laid his pencil aside, and turned to the jury. It was nine thirty.

"Ladies and gentlemen of the jury," Schafer began. "Now is the time that is set aside in each trial for the state, or the prosecution, and the defense, if it so desires, to give you an outline of what our evidence will show.

"The story of this case, the murders of Gretchen and Wendy Fritz, Number 15028, will be told by about thirty witnesses, more or less. These will be doctors, police officers, anthropologists, and teenagers; teenagers who knew both Wendy and Gretchen Fritz, and who knew the defendant. And when these stories are told, when all this evidence is pieced together, you will see that the state has proved to you two first-degree murders ...with deliberation, with premeditation; two murders with a motive, two murders to cover up a prior murder. The story of—"

"If it please the Court," Tinney said, interrupting the prosecutor. "If counsel could approach the bench."

"You may," Judge Garrett replied.

Out of the jury's hearing, Schafer and Tinney stood before the bench. Tinney said, "If the Court please, on the basis of the county attorney's opening statement and his comment that he would prove that the motive for the alleged homicide was to cover up for a prior murder, I move for a mistrial and ask at this time to be heard on my argument in support of that. It is highly prejudicial."

"There will be other references to the same thing I will make in the next few minutes," Schafer said.

The judge ruled that Tinney could argue his objection to the motive of a prior murder at the conclusion of Schafer's opening statement without prejudicing his objection. "Is that agreeable?" Judge Garrett asked.

"It is not agreeable," Tinney replied. "No, if that is the Court's decision, that is the Court's decision. I perhaps can reserve my right now to argue any further comments along this line."

Then Schafer resumed his address to the jury: "Case number 15028 begins in the very early morning hours on November 10, 1965. It was on that morning a number of police officers and one boy got into a car and drove off into the desert off Pontatoc Road." He told how the skeletons had been found, and how they were identified as Gretchen and Wendy Fritz, "two girls who had disappeared from home on the night of August 16, 1965, when they did not return home from a movie at the Cactus Drive-In." Schafer said, "Now that really is the end of the story of Gretchen and Wendy Fritz.

"The beginning of that story goes back some months before that, actually before they even knew the defendant, Charles Schmid. They met him, at least Gretchen did, sometime in the fall of 1964. But before that you will see the facts that gave rise to this, the circumstances that were mentioned occurred before that, months before that, May 31, 1964.

"You will hear that Gretchen knew, because the defendant told her, that on that night he and John Saunders and Mary French killed a young woman named Alleen Rowe and that he had taken Gretchen Fritz out to where that body was buried east of town in the desert, which was a secret. She kept this secret all during the time she dated Charles Schmid, and she went with Charles Schmid, and this continued for a number of months from the fall when they first met in 1964, through that fall, the winter and into the spring of 1965.

"Shortly after that, however, that relationship began to change. The relationship began to wane. What was once there apparently was not there anymore. It was considerably lessened. It was about this time that Gretchen started to pester and bother the defendant. She called him any number of times, sometimes as much as five or six times a day. She was greatly annoyed that he was seen with other girls; that there were gatherings and parties at his house, of the defendant, where other girls attended. Gretchen did not attend any of these parties. She called for him at his house. This pestering and bothering did upset the defendant. He expressed this to a number of his friends. He told that he was tired of it. That he did not like it and that he didn't want to take any more of it, that he did not like the bothering and the pestering. But he told a number of people that he could not stop what was going on because there was something Gretchen Fritz had over him, something that she had that made him do what he did.

"You will hear that he told one of his closest friends, Richard Bruns, that he had killed the Rowe girl, and he had told Gretchen about it, and that Gretchen is holding this against him, and that he cannot do what he wants because of this.

"Then you will hear that in July 1965, shortly before the girls disappeared, the defendant took in two boarders, a William Morgen and his wife Doris who is a cripple, confined to a wheelchair. She spent a lot of time, and she lived with the defendant at home. Most of her time was spent there.

"From the beginning of July, that time on to the end of July, they lived at Charles Schmid's home. You will hear that during this time a number of friends came over to the house on various occasions and during this time Mr. Schmid expressed to Mr. Morgen that he did not like the pestering and bothering. Mr. Morgen will tell you that every day Gretchen would call the house, but he did not see Gretchen very often, but he talked to her a number of times on the phone. A number of times she would come over to the house and meet the defendant behind the house, back in the alley, and a number of times he would go out and apparently meet her.

"And then you will hear that one night when Mr. Morgen was sitting with the defendant in the car in front of the house, the defendant told him that Gretchen had stolen a diary of his and that it contained something that would put him in jail for a long time. He told this to Mr. Morgen as well as to a few other friends that there was a diary that Gretchen had had that he could not get it back, and that whatever was in it would get him into an awful lot of trouble with the police. To one person he said that whatever was in it would put him in the electric chair.

"On this occasion he tells Mr. Morgen the story that is in the diary. He told him and he also told this, I believe, to two young teenagers, who you will see here, that in the diary is the story of his killing a young boy, a sixteen-year-old boy he killed. That this young boy was in an automobile accident with a prior girlfriend of Schmid's. The girl was killed, but the boy was unharmed. That after this Mr. Schmid took the boy out to the desert, shot him, killed him, cut off his hands, and buried him. This is what he told Mr. Morgen. He also told him this is what Gretchen had against him. And this is why she does what she does.

"Mrs. Morgen also answered the phone a number of times. She will tell you that Gretchen called five or six times a day, every day, practically, and that many times they had arguments on the phone, many arguments about the diary that Mrs. Morgen had heard. That the defendant expressed to them a desire to kill Gretchen. He said a couple of times, 'I am going to kill her.' Mr. Morgen will describe to you that he used some kind of action with his hands. He told both of them on one occasion that he was going to strangle her, would like to get her neck and strangle her. On another occasion he told Mr. Morgen that 'What is in that diary will get me into a whole lot of trouble with the police, and I am going to get that diary. I know there is a way.'

"They moved away at the end of July and they can tell you that shortly before they moved away, Mr. Schmid, the defendant here, told them that sooner or later, within a few days, Gretchen is going to go away—she is going to go to Ohio with an aunt, or some statement like that. She is going to live with an aunt. While the Morgens are there with the defendant, Gretchen never does leave. Mrs. Morgen will tell you that all of a sudden there came a day there were no more phone calls from Gretchen, she was no longer aware of her calls. But Gretchen actually did go away in the month of August, but she went west to California on a vacation with her family, and then she came back from California, which was about August 10th or 11th.

"A day or so after that the defendant comes over to Gretchen's house at night, sometime around nine. Her brother, Robert Fritz, who is sixteen years old, lets him in the back door and once in the door he goes straight to Gretchen's bedroom. The brother listens. He hears them argue. The defendant comes out after a few minutes, and is followed by Gretchen, who is crying. They go out to the backyard and they argue some more and the brother can't make out the argument. The defendant hits Gretchen and knocks her against the wall. He leaves and he says, 'That's it,' or 'that's the end.'

"This is just one or two days before the girls disappear. You will hear that on the afternoon of the 16th of August, a Monday, the defendant and Gretchen argue again. This time on the phone. And this was a good argument. We will then hear that that evening the Fritz family decide they were going to go to a drive-in. Mr. and Mrs. Fritz went to one drive-in and so far as they knew Gretchen and her sister, Wendy, were going to go to another drive-in, the Cactus Drive-In. They did leave the house. That is the night the girls disappeared.

"The next day you will hear that there were a number of phone calls which were exchanged between the defendant and some of his teenage friends, and between Mrs. Fritz and the defendant.

"You will hear that within a number of days after the disappearance of the girls, the defendant told a number of people that the girls were in California, that they were with somebody but he didn't say who, somebody he knew how to contact, only he could do it. He told other people that he had taken the girls to Mexico for a day, and then to California. He told some that he did not know where they were. You will hear one teenager say that she called Charles Schmid and talked to him and he had told her that he had seen Wendy and Gretchen just five hours before they disappeared. That he told this girl that Gretchen and Wendy came to him and Gretchen wanted the defendant to marry her. He refused. They argued and they left, and that was the last he saw of them. You will hear that within a week or two weeks after the girls disappeared he took his closest friend, Richard Bruns, to the place where he had hidden the bodies. You will hear at that time that shortly before that he told Richard Bruns that he had killed the girls. He told him that he had killed Gretchen first and then Wendy, and he made a motion with his hands—then he took them up to Pontatoc and dumped them there, and within that period of two weeks he takes Mr. Bruns out to where the bodies are located and within two months after that, Mr. Bruns, as you have heard, tells the police and initiated the search that I have described to you.

"When you hear all these things and see these witnesses, it will be the only conclusion that this defendant committed murder in the first degree on Gretchen and Wendy Fritz and there is one penalty. Thank you."

Schafer, head bowed slightly, returned to his table and sat down. The judge looked at Tinney.

"Do you have any legal matters you want to take up now?"

Tinney rose. "I have a legal matter but I would like to make the opening statement, and take that up first."

"You may."

Tinney stood at the end of the defense table, his hands resting on the statute books, and he did not move during his statement, but spoke directly to the body of jurors.

"I think first, we better say, so it is clear right now, that anything that the prosecutor has said or anything that I am going to say is not evidence. It is only what we think the evidence is going to be and what we think we can prove to you.

"You aren't going to hear any evidence in this case until a witness is sworn by that clerk and that witness walks over and gets in that chair and talks to you. All that our comments are for is to orient you in outline form about the case that we are going to prove to you. It is going to become apparent in a minute that each of us thinks we are going to prove something different to you. A whole lot of small pieces are going to come out in this case. The evidence is going to show a whole lot of small pieces, however, all of the case is not going to be given to you by thirty witnesses, because I have a few witnesses that you will hear from. And all of the case is not in until after you have heard those thirty witnesses. In fact, as the Court will instruct you, you are not to even begin talking about this case between yourselves until after *all* of the evidence is in, or even to decide anything until all of the evidence is in.

"Our case is that Smitty did not kill Gretchen and the child. They argued like kids do. They argued hot and heavy and then ten minutes later they loved. And Gretchen was never afraid of Smitty.

And Smitty never threatened Gretchen's life. But somebody did kill Gretchen and the child. Somebody hated Gretchen, and Gretchen was afraid of somebody. And somebody threatened Gretchen's life and somebody knows too much about how the girls died. And somebody fingered Smitty for it. And somebody was Bruns."

The prosecution's first witness was Mrs. Nancy Fritz. She answered Schafer's questions calmly but when asked to identify articles of clothing, she crumpled. "Yes, yes, those are theirs," she said, her breath magnified through the microphone at her throat. Then with a sudden move she turned her face from the shoe boxes containing the articles. Tinney objected to the prosecutor's insistence on the identification, and stipulated he would agree that "those particular clothing were the kind of clothing worn by the two sisters." Mrs. Fritz regained her composure and told the Court of the last time she had seen her daughters.

She said of Schmid, "He always acted courteous toward Gretchen in my presence. Gretchen never expressed any fear of Schmid, and she never told me about him saying he murdered someone."

In cross-examination, Tinney questioned her about Bruns, and related the incident of Bruns threatening Gretchen with a gun. "Was Gretchen afraid of Bruns?" Tinney asked.

Mrs. Fritz replied, "I wouldn't say she was afraid of him, but she disliked him."

Following Mrs. Fritz on the stand were a number of witnesses called by Schafer to establish the discovery and identity of the remains found in the desert and the possible cause of death. On the stand, Dr. Louis Hirsch was asked by Schafer about possible neck injuries, and the pathologist said that the remains were "too mummified" to make such a determination.

It was the prosecution's theory that the girls had been strangled with a cord from Schmid's guitar, and a number of witnesses were presented to try to establish this point. Detectives testified that they found a guitar cord in the desert near the jawbone of one skull, but could not support this finding with a police photograph. A Sears,

Roebuck employee said that the cord "fit" Smitty's guitar, and added, "It's a very popular model." A man from a pawnshop said that the guitar had been pawned there on July 20 by the defendant, but he didn't know if the cord was with the guitar on that date. The detective who retrieved the guitar from the pawnshop testified that he turned the guitar and a guitar cord over to the City County Crime Lab, but they had been unable to determine if the cord "found at the scene" had been the cord used on Schmid's guitar. Under cross-examination, the captain acknowledged that the cord could have fit a number of guitars, including Schmid's.

Despite the ambiguity over the guitar cord, the Tucson newspapers summed up the testimony in headlines: "Guitar Cord Murder Weapon," and "Strangled By Guitar Cord."

The next day the prosecution called Irma Jean Kolt's mother, who testified that during the period her husband had worked with Smitty in the upholstery business she had overheard a telephone conversation between Smitty and Gretchen. "When he hung up," Mrs. Kolt said, "he said, 'I'm going to kill that bitch.'"

Mrs. Kolt said Gretchen called Smitty two or three times a day and that "he told me, 'I wish she'd get off my back, that she'd disappear, get lost, quit hounding me.'" She said the defendant told her Gretchen was holding something over his head, but that she didn't know what it was.

Tinney was able to bring out that Mrs. Kolt did not think Smitty was making a real threat. "You didn't think about calling up the police," Tinney asked, "to say there was going to be a homicide?"

"No, sir," Mrs. Kolt replied.

Her daughter Irma Jean took the stand, her hair combed so it practically covered one eye. About the diary, she testified: "I asked him why he did everything Gretchen said, why he jumped every time she asked for something. Smitty said Gretchen had stolen a diary from his house and that the diary contained information about a guy he had killed, cut off his hands, and buried him in the east." She said that Smitty had further told her he hated Gretchen and wished she'd stop bothering him."

Tinney asked her if she'd considered telling the police about the diary. Irma Jean replied, "I just didn't think it was true. I just let it slide by." Then she smiled at Smitty from the witness stand and as she passed the defense table she whispered to Smitty, "How are you?"

Shirley and Kitty Bates both testified that they had heard Smitty tell Irma Jean about the diary. Her eyes darting nervously about the courtroom, Shirley said she had visited Smitty's house a number of times during the summer and had heard Smitty express dislike for Gretchen.

Kitty burst into tears when her eyes met Smitty's. "I can't look at him," she sobbed.

Robert Fritz testified to the argument between Gretchen and Smitty outside the Fritz home a few days before Gretchen disappeared. He said Schmid pushed her against a wall and "Gretchen fell down crying and he said, 'That's it!' and she said, 'Don't,' or something like that."

The jury was told how Schmid had asked Charles Stenz to arrange to meet Gretchen in the park, so that Schmid would have an excuse to break off their relationship. Stenz said Schmid was hiding in the bushes. "He came out and slapped her down. She got up and started crying." Stenz also recalled that Smitty had said, "Sooner or later I am going to kill that bitch," and added that he did not think this was uttered "in a joking manner."

On Monday morning, February 21, the prosecution called John Saunders to the witness stand. When Schafer asked John his name, he replied, "I refuse to answer the question on the ground that it may tend to incriminate me under the laws of Arizona and the United States."

Saunders gave the same reply to two more questions until Tinney objected to further questions, "on the ground that these kinds of answers are prejudicial in front of the jury." Judge Garrett had the jury removed from the courtroom and Tinney moved for a mistrial, arguing that "Saunders should not have been placed on the stand if it was known that he would answer in the manner he did.

The answers could cast a question in the mind of the jury about as to what he might say, and cause the jury to begin speculating." The prosecution withdrew Saunders, and Tinney's motion was denied.

After a short recess, the next witness called was Mary French. She entered the courtroom apprehensively, shoulders slumped. Her hair was fluffed out in a bouffant style but there was little color in her face. She wore a camel sweater and a tan skirt. After a few routine questions, Tinney objected to her testifying, because she could not have knowledge of the murder of the Fritz sisters, since she was not in Tucson at the time of their death and was appearing solely to testify to another crime, for which there was no *corpus delicti*, "because it might prove a motive in this case." Tinney's objection was overruled.

Mary spoke without a break in her deadpan composure, although she was asked several times to "speak up." Her account of the murder of Alleen Rowe, delivered in an amplified monotone, seemed to hypnotize the crowd of spectators filling the extra chairs and standing within the courtroom.

After Schafer's direct examination, in which there was no mention of Gretchen or Wendy Fritz, Tinney, in his cross-examination, made it plain that Mary had not seen the actual murder of Alleen Rowe, and that she had not tried to warn Alleen that she was in danger, even though Schmid had told her he intended to kill Alleen. Tinney also tried to discredit Mary's motive for testifying by asking her about the child she told Smitty she was going to have. She admitted that she had not given birth.

"After your staying with Charlie as husband and wife for that period of time, did you get angry with him?" Tinney asked.

"Yes," Mary replied.

"Over another girl?"

"Yes."

"And was that other girl Gretchen or some other girl?"

"Gretchen."

Paul Graff was called, as a hostile witness. He had been brought from New Orleans to testify for the prosecution, although the police there had told him he did not have to return to Tucson as a witness. Outside the courtroom, Paul said that Chief Garmire had warned him that if he did not testify for the state, there would be a warrant issued for his arrest. "I was told this," Paul says, "and if I didn't say exactly what they wanted me to say, I'd be held and questioned in regards to *my* part in the thing."

On the stand, Paul said he had lived at Schmid's house for a couple of weeks the preceding September. Smitty had told him about killing a girl in the desert, and that Saunders and Mary French were with him at the time of the killing. Paul said he discounted the story. "He asked me to go out and see the grave, almost in a joking manner. I didn't go."

Asked by Schafer if Schmid told him where the girl was buried, Paul said, "He just made a vague reference to an old drinking spot."

Schmid's affair with Gretchen was "a stormy one," Paul admitted. "One time he would tell me he was madly in love with her, then that they had an argument, and again that he was in love with her." Paul said he moved out of Smitty's house following a disagreement. "Smitty got very emotional, I hadn't seen him get that way before. He smashed his fist into a wall and said God was punishing him."

Tinney brought out in cross-examination, over Schafer's objections, the bad feelings between Gretchen and Bruns. Paul said that Bruns told him he "detested, hated, that he'd wanted to throttle," Gretchen because she had "blackballed him at high school socially."

Paul said he had never heard of a diary until a few weeks before when he was questioned by the police. He said that Dupnik, having come to New Orleans, told him the police had pages of this diary. But Paul said, "I never saw the pages or had heard of a diary up to that time."

After he left the witness stand, Paul was approached by newsmen in the corridor who barraged him with questions. He stared at them blandly for a moment, then said, "I utterly despise Tucson, its police, the Tucson newspapers and you. I hope I never come here again. All I want to do is get out of this town. You had your say in

1957." He left Tucson on a Greyhound bus the following morning.

Bill Morgen, summoned by the prosecution, entered the courtroom in rumpled pants and soiled checkered shirt. His wife, Doris, slumped in her wheelchair, hair untidy, waited in the hallway to testify after her husband.

"Schmid said he'd been in love with this girl," Bill Morgen recalled from the witness stand, "and this girl and this guy got involved in an auto accident and the girl was killed, so he took this guy out in the desert, the guy begged for his life, but he said he shot him anyway and cut off his hands." Morgen said Schmid had told him Gretchen had stolen the diary, and now had enough on Schmid to send him to the electric chair. "I didn't believe Schmid was capable of a murder," but he quoted Schmid as saying, "I'd like to kill that bitch. I'd like to twist her pretty little neck."

Mrs. Morgen, testifying from her wheelchair, said when Schmid told her about the diary, she said, "Oh, no, Smitty, you're kidding," and he said, "No, I'm serious." Later he told her, "There has got to be a way to get it back. I'm making plans now."

About a week before they left his house, she said, "Smitty rushed into the house and closed windows and pulled down the blinds. He was shaking all over, looked real pale. I asked him what was wrong and he said, 'The cops are coming to get me. Gretchen has turned me in.'" On another occasion he told her Gretchen was returning the diary and giving him some money. "He had just talked to her on the phone and seemed real happy." One night, Smitty came home dirty and said Gretchen had left him out in the desert and he'd had to walk back. That was when he said, "I'm going to kill her when I get my hands on her." Like the other witnesses, Mrs. Morgen had not taken Schmid's threats seriously.

Wednesday morning, February 23, Richie Bruns arrived at Superior Court. He wore tight black Continental slacks, high-heeled Beatle boots, and his hair was heaped up in a pompadour and combed straight back on the sides. He walked casually into the courtroom wearing a pair of purple wrap-around sunglasses, which he removed as he took the witness stand. During the lengthy testimony that followed, he looked at Smitty frequently, evenly. Richie could recall nothing by calendar dates, only by incidents surrounding the dates in question.

He said that Smitty had told him about the killing of Alleen Rowe, and recounted some of the details of that conversation, such as the hunting trip with Saunders when Smitty had "stuck a stick in the ground to see how she smelled after she had been there so long."

Richie testified as to the off-again, on-again relationship between Smitty and Gretchen. He told of Smitty's increasing anger, of his actions shortly before Gretchen disappeared, and of Smitty's confessing the murder to him. He talked about the incident with the Tucson Mafia and then of accompanying Smitty to try and bury the bodies of the Fritz girls. As they went back to the car that night Smitty told him, "You are in it as deep as I am now."

Under extensive cross-examination, Tinney brought out Bruns's ill-feelings toward Gretchen, despite Schafer's repeated objections. But he was unable to show that Bruns had done more than talk against Gretchen. And Tinney was unable to shake Richie's basic story, that Smitty had told him he had killed the Fritz sisters and had taken him to the graves.

Tinney asked, "After you got up in Ohio did it concern you that your handkerchief was back at the grave site?"

"No," Richie replied.

"Did it concern you that perhaps your prints might be on Gretchen's shoes?"

Richie said, "No."

"Did it concern you that perhaps your prints were on the tennis shoe?"

"No."

"Did it concern you that your prints might be on Gretchen's shoe?"

"No."

Asked if he'd ever discussed putting the bodies on Darlene Kirk's front door, Richie replied that he had. "I came over and Smitty asked me how I was getting along with Darlene. I said I wasn't getting along too good. He said maybe we ought to get Gretchen and put a noose around her neck and put her on the front porch, and ring the doorbell and that would bring her around."

"And Smitty said that?" Tinney asked.

"Yes."

Gloria Andrews was among the remaining teenagers waiting to testify for the prosecution. Oddly, testimony that was basically confusing became, according to the press, the "most damning evidence."

Wearing a furry white sweater, with her bleached hair framing her colorless face, Gloria testified that she had gone to Smitty's house for a party on the night of August 16, and that "not long after I got to the house there was a phone call and Smitty told Paul to answer it. Paul told Smitty it was Gretchen, and that she wanted to meet him and if he didn't come, that she'd tell her father."

According to Gloria, Smitty "started walking into the bedroom and called Paul to come with him, and I heard Smitty say, 'I'm going to get that bitch if it's the last thing I do.' Then Smitty said he was going to see Gretchen."

Gloria testified that Smitty and Paul left the house, Smitty carrying an old black briefcase. They returned between one and one thirty in the morning.

"I was the only one there," Gloria said. "As they approached, I heard Smitty say 'You'd better shut up, Mike and the rest might still be there.'" As they came into the house Paul said that he "wasn't in it and wasn't going to get in it."

Schafer asked Gloria to describe Schmid's appearance at that time. She said, "He was pretty messed up. His hair was down all over his face, he was dusty and raggedy-looking, he looked scared, he looked like something was wrong with him." Paul left the house minutes later, Gloria said, and took two large butcher knives with him. The next day she received a call from Schmid and he said the Fritz girls were missing and, "He said now he could go out with anyone he wanted to."

Tinney's cross-examination established that Gloria had trouble remembering things. Asked when she first attended one of Smitty's parties, she said around the first of August, but admitted she was uncertain who was there. Tinney pressed for this information, and Gloria replied, "I don't know who all was there because I got drunk."

"Because you were drunk?" Tinney echoed.

"Yes, and I don't know who all was there," Gloria repeated. The calm she had sustained through Schafer's questioning was starting to wear thin under Tinney's probing. He asked for further details on the party. Gloria said she had been brought to the party early, between five and seven, by a boy named Gerry Wells. When Tinney asked her what time she left, Gloria replied, "Oh, that night we stayed all night."

Tinney continued to ask about this party and found that Gloria, her sister Martha, then fifteen, and another girl stayed all night, but Gloria wasn't sure whether Gerry stayed. Then Tinney asked about another party, two weeks after the Fritz girls disappeared. This time Gloria said Jimmy Scott had brought her to the party and she supplied the names of others who had been there.

"What time did you get to that party?" Tinney asked.

After a pause, Gloria replied, "I don't remember."

"Did you have anything to drink that night?"

"I don't know."

"Did you get drunk that night?"

"No."

"Did you stay all night?"

"No."

"What time did you go home that night?"

Gloria sat staring blankly at Tinney. He said, "Was your answer that you don't know again?"

She didn't reply. Her shoulders started to shake and she began to cry. "Who took you home?" Tinney repeated.

"I guess it was Jimmy."

"I don't want a guess," Tinney demanded. "Who?"

Gloria started to sob. She tried to speak but couldn't. Judge Garrett interrupted the proceedings as Gloria mumbled something that sounded as if she said Jimmy Scott had "promised" to take her home.

Finally, she gained control of herself and Tinney again asked whether Jimmy had indeed taken her home from Smitty's. "I don't remember," Gloria replied.

Tinney moved his line of questioning to the night of August 16, but the only admission he could gain from Gloria was that she had been in Smitty's house during the time the Fritz girls were killed and had not seen or heard any violence. This contradicted the story Bruns claimed he had heard from Smitty, that the girls had been murdered in the living room.

Gloria Andrews left the courtroom in tears. She stood trembling in the corridor; there was no one to meet her. A photographer aimed his camera and she covered her face with her sweater, then ran downstairs and outside into the crowd that lined the street to watch the annual Fiesta de los Vaqueros parade.

Martha, Gloria's younger sister, nervously gripping the arms of the witness chair, testified that she had attended several parties at Schmid's house that summer. But she didn't go to the house on the night of August 16.

Several other witnesses added a few minor details and then the prosecution closed its case. Tinney made a series of motions for a direct acquittal, for a reduction of charges, for striking certain testimony, and a motion for mistrial based on the testimony concerning the deaths of Alleen Rowe and the unnamed boy buried in the desert, "the boy with his hands cut off." He argued that the state had not proven a *corpus delicti* in either case. "I don't think testimony about these things was necessary, and obviously it was prejudicial," Tinney said. He also argued that the state produced no evidence by any coroner, pathologist, or eyewitness, and no confession as to how the girls actually died. In denying Tinney's motions, Judge Garrett said the evidence "is not weak from a legal standpoint at this time," and he would leave the degree of murder to be determined by the jury.

The defense started by calling a series of witnesses testifying to the "stream of hostility" between Bruns and Gretchen. Jimmy Scott, sixteen, confirmed the threats made by Bruns and the hostility Bruns had displayed toward Gretchen. But under cross-examination by Schafer, Scott disclosed that he had discussed plans to "get Bruns for telling the police that Smitty had murdered Gretchen and Wendy."

Schafer asked, "Did you talk of shooting him?"

"Yes," Scott replied.

Referring to Ronald Baines, the next witness scheduled to be called by the defense, Schafer asked Scott, "Was mention made of using the guns Baines had?"

"Yes."

"One of the shotguns could be used to get Bruns?"

"Yes," Scott answered. When Schafer asked whether he had been present at a party in August, when Smitty received a phone call from Gretchen, Scott said that he had, and the call had enraged Smitty. "He was shouting," Scott testified, "said he would kill her."

On the witness stand, Ronald Baines claimed he had heard Bruns say that he'd "like to kill Gretchen and was going to kill her. Bruns said that he didn't think Gretchen was good enough for Smitty." That same evening, he said he'd seen Bruns "waving around a chrome-plated pistol."

Under cross-examination, Baines admitted he disliked Bruns intensely. "Isn't it true that Bruns idolized the defendant?" Schafer asked.

"Yes, sir," Baines replied.

"And isn't it true that Bruns dressed like him?"

"Yes, sir."

"And you did too, dress like the defendant?"

"Sometimes," Baines said, red-faced, nervous, uncertain of what he was saying. Schafer had weakened the point of Bruns's threats to kill Gretchen by disclosing the plans the group had made to kill Bruns. A shotgun, to the jury, seemed a more deadly weapon than a chrome-plated pistol. The defense had established through the testimony of Scott and Jack Spiers, sixteen, that Paul Graff had not been present at the party in August that Gloria Andrews had attended. The party Gloria had attended, Spiers testified, had occurred in September. He added that Gloria was "quite drunk" that night, and that he did not see Paul at any of Schmid's parties in August.

A number of young girls also testified to Bruns's feelings against Gretchen. One was Darlene Kirk. But when Tinney tried to bring out the threats Bruns had made against Darlene and her family, Schafer objected and Judge Garrett ruled that "Bruns is not on trial here. Whether Miss [Kirk] was afraid of Bruns is not material."

When Schmid heard this ruling he threw down a ballpoint pen in disgust. "Stop that," Tinney told him, and Schmid folded his hands in his lap.

Tinney called Charles Schmid Sr.

Middle-aged, slightly stoop-shouldered, wearing a loose-fitting green suit and horn-rimmed glasses, Mr. Schmid took the stand. He avoided Smitty's intent gaze and addressed his answers to the jury.

He said his son, Charlie, sometimes helped out at the nursing home and played his guitar at local nightclubs. Charlie received an allowance of approximately $300 per month, he said, and he and his wife let Charlie move into the little house next door and knew about the parties but never interfered.

Mr. Schmid had not seen his son on the night of August 16, but said his wife telephoned there around ten thirty to get them to quiet down. At that time, he recalled, Charlie was in his house.

Charles Sr. answered in a straightforward manner but in one way his testimony virtually abolished the alibi entered earlier in the trial by Tinney, who said he had obtained information that Schmid was with another couple, or his parents, on the night of August 16.

Court was adjourned until Monday morning. That night, Friday, February 25, from his cell in Pima County Jail, Smitty wrote to Diane:

> It's strange but for the first time I've actually come to the realization that I'm being framed and that in a few weeks time I'll be dead. I don't really think we'll win anymore. The witnesses we have all did their best to tell the truth, but I guess it's not enough. Gloria and Martha lied as did Richie, but I guess you know that by now. If it wasn't for all the bad publicity, maybe I'd of had a chance, but I was convicted before the case was ever tried. I guess everyone had their revenge for me being nice to them. The press *never gave me* a chance. I guess they were paid off. Ronnie Baines told how the cops coerced him, but I doubt if anyone believed him. They won't allow any of the evidence against Richie in. Some of my witnesses won't testify. I guess there is nothing else to do but let them finish what they started. It would be too late to do anything without causing a lot of red faces.
>
> Face it, honey, they're big wheels and they can't afford to admit to defeats. It shouldn't bother them to kill me because I'm nobody to them. They've twisted and distorted the truth *so* bad I'm even mixed up. I'm not really scared to die, but I wish we could of had more time together. We could have been so happy. I guess that's fate tho! Well, maybe they have guitars in heaven.

During the trial, no witness was to reveal as much composure or self-assurance as Mrs. Katharine Schmid. On Monday, February 28, she took the stand to try to provide an alibi for Smitty on the night of August 16. She appeared calm, a stout, well-built woman, wearing glasses, a black round-neck silk dress, a six-strand pearl necklace, little pearl earrings, and a close-fitting hairdo.

She repeated what her husband had already said, that she had called her son on the phone the night of August 16 "and told him to turn down the music so as not to create a disturbance." About ten minutes later, she said, "Charlie came over to the house and said he'd be more quiet. He sat down on the floor, ate pizza with us, and watched television for a while. And then he went home."

Paul had not been at Smitty's house during the entire month of August 1965, Mrs. Schmid testified. She was sure because a boy named Bobby Garcia had been staying there at the time. She said she had carried three meals over to the little house for them. (Tinney had planned to call Bobby Garcia as a witness. Garcia was in the courtroom on Monday morning, but when his name was called he could not be found.)

The guitar cord the state had introduced in evidence as being found near the Fritz girls' bodies was black. Mrs. Schmid testified that "all of Charlie's guitar cords were gray."

Even under strong cross-examination, Katharine Schmid had a sharp answer for practically every question. Smitty hunched forward in his seat when Schafer asked Mrs. Schmid, "Is he your son?"

She said, "He has been my son since he was one day old. He is my son by choice." Mrs. Schmid had never questioned him about what he did with his $300 allowance, and she paid his bills for him. She also served him meals in the little house and kept it clean for him.

"Did he have a regular job?" Schafer asked.

"Well, he mowed the lawn sometimes and was always available to do anything I wanted," Mrs. Schmid replied. "He would do anything I asked." But she admitted he had no regular duties.

"How many parties were held in your son's house in July and August of last year?" Schafer inquired.

"Four or five."

"Were you aware of the parties?"

"Yes."

"Were you aware of the ages of the girls who attended them?"

"Some of them."

"But you never asked your son about them?"

"I did not."

Schafer also asked Mrs. Schmid about Gretchen Fritz. Did Mrs. Schmid like her?

"Personally, no," she replied. "I did not like Gretchen because of the reputation she had."

"Did you ever talk to your son about her reputation?"

"I did not. I never discussed Gretchen with anybody."

"Was Smitty's relationship with Gretchen good?" Schafer asked.

"The same as any other so-called romance."

"Did you ever see Gretchen?"

"I did not."

Schafer also inquired about Smitty's habits of dress. "How tall are you?" he asked Mrs. Schmid.

"About five foot five inches."

"How tall is Charlie?"

"About the same height."

"Did you know he wore lifts in his boots and practiced walking in them?"

"He wore lifts in his boots to make himself three inches taller."

"Did he practice walking with these things in his boots?"

After a pause, she replied, "Yes."

Tinney called only two further witnesses. One, Honey Prince, seventeen, stated that the party Gloria Andrews had testified about as occurring on August 16 had actually taken place on September 8. Honey knew because she kept a diary about such activities. The second witness, Art Meyers, said that he'd been with Bruns until six-thirty on August 16, but not after that. Bruns had testified he'd spent most of that evening with Meyers.

The following day, March 1, both the prosecution and defense made their final arguments and gave the case to the jury. Schafer explained to the jurors that under Arizona law first-degree murder was "the unlawful killing of a human being with malice aforethought." He summarized all the occasions on which Schmid had threatened to do away with Gretchen. "You will remember," Schafer said, "that from Charles Stenz on to all the other witnesses, we showed you, time and time again, statements by the defendant, not in jest, not in a joking manner, [but] serious, when he was mad, when he was hot mad." Schafer defined the threats to kill Gretchen as "express malice aforethought, a deliberate intention to take away a human life." After defining "implied malice aforethought," Schafer said, "What else but an abandoned and malignant heart dumped the bodies unceremoniously out on the desert ground, what else but an abandoned and malignant heart would brag about what happened? What else but an abandoned and malignant heart would kill these girls to cover up a prior murder, the prior murder being that of Alleen Rowe of which you have any number of references to?"

Reviewing the testimony, Schafer admitted how heavily the state's case rested on Bruns's testimony. He said, "If you believe Mr. Bruns, there has been a confession in this case. This is all the state 'need prove to' you. We have proved the crime, the unlawful killing. There is a complete and absolute confession by the defendant to Mr. Bruns. If you believe this, the state needs go no further."

Schafer said that if Bruns had been lying he would have made up a much tighter story, one "that would have left you with no doubt in your minds whatever. He could have made up a story as to exactly how it was done." But Bruns's story, Schafer said, had enough small inconsistencies to bear the mark of truth.

After a lengthy review of the testimony, Schafer concluded with a plea for the jury to do its duty. He said they had a decision to make which "no one enjoys making."

"Capital punishment is the most powerful deterrent known to the law," Schafer said, "and in some cases it is the only just result. The punishment must fit the crime. When it does not, the punishment is of no use." In some cases, he said, the jury might find there were circumstances which would militate against the imposition of the death penalty. But, he continued, "There is nothing in this case that we, as human beings, can sympathize with or understand, There is callousness, indifference, inhumanity. A killing because of a prior killing does not identify it with anyone. There is no mercy in this case whatsoever. Whatever mercy existed, died in that far-off plot of ground on Pontatoc Road on August 16th."

In concluding his summation, Schafer said, "This man has forfeited any rights that he would have. This man has forfeited his right to walk among us. Your verdict and judgment is death. Thank you."

Tinney, speaking slowly, denied that the state had proved anything. In his closing remarks, he said the prosecution's case left "many whys, wheres, mistakes, and exaggerations," the trial was only an approximation and "the fragile web of circumstantial evidence is only a theory."

Tinney said, "I have a theory too, and that is that Bruns did it and not Schmid." Everyone knew Bruns hated Gretchen, he reminded the jury. "Where was Bruns on the night of August 16?"

Gloria Andrews's testimony he disputed, not by saying she lied but merely by the fact that she was mistaken about the date. The party she thought had taken place in mid-August actually was sometime in September.

Calling for logic and fairness from the jurors, Tinney stood by Schmid's side and said, "I do not deny that there were fights between the defendant and Gretchen and stupid acts. But we do deny murder. Our plea to murder is not guilty."

After a rebuttal by Schafer, Judge Garrett's charge was brief, saying that they could either find Schmid guilty of murder and recommend the death sentence, find him guilty with a sentence of life imprisonment, or find him innocent. He told them they could convict on circumstantial evidence, but that "if you have a reasonable doubt whether or not the defendant was present at the time the crime was committed, he is entitled to an acquittal."

At 2:15 that afternoon, the jurors walked single file from the courtroom and into the jury room. Tinney gathered his papers, shook Schmid's hand, and said, "Charlie, good luck."

In the clerk's office, Judge Garrett told a newsman, "The

evidence is circumstantial, but it is for the jury to decide."

The dozens of newsmen and writers for national publications left the court, expecting a long vigil, and except for the clerk gathering exhibits to be taken to the jury room if necessary, the courtroom had emptied by two thirty. In the corridor, a TV news director said, "It'll be one, maybe two days, they'll bring in an acquittal." The other reporters were waiting near the jury room, discussing which one would remain after midnight when the jury would be taken to the hotel and locked up for the night.

The secretary in Judge Garrett's office said, "The possibility of an early verdict in such a complex case seems remote."

Sitting together on one long Naugahyde sofa, Mr. and Mrs. Schmid, Diane, and her mother remained in the hallway. "We're going to stick around here," Mr. Schmid told a reporter, "at least for a little while."

At 3:15 the jurors asked for refreshments: Coke, some coffee. It was supplied by one of the bailiffs. Another hour and ten minutes passed. The buzzer from the jury room was sounded again and the bailiff stuck his head into the opened door, then, retreating quickly and closing the door, he said, "They've got a verdict!"

Schafer could not be located. Deputy County Attorney Healy said, "He's on his way home. No one expected a verdict so soon. I'll take it for him."

"Better have them bring Smitty back up here," the bailiff said, "before they take him to jail for the night."

Quickly the courtroom began to fill. There were more spectators now, more newsmen, more than the court could contain. They pushed together in front of the courtroom door. Katharine Schmid waited in the corridor, deciding not to enter the courtroom with Charles Sr. and Diane.

Tinney walked into the courtroom with a grim, set expression. Smitty was escorted in by Deputy Booth and sat at the defense table, his arms folded, breathing hard. The jury had deliberated two hours and ten minutes when they filed back into the jury box. Finally, Judge Garrett took his seat on the bench.

"Members of the jury, have you reached a verdict?" he intoned.

"We have, Your Honor," answered the foreman, handing two slips of paper to the bailiff. The clerk of the court then read them in a quavering voice.

"In the case of the state of Arizona versus Charles Howard Schmid Jr., we find the defendant guilty and set the penalty at death."

Diane let out a cry and started sobbing uncontrollably. Smitty did not move. Tinney leaned back and blinked several times. Deputy Attorney Healy smiled to himself. The jurors were staring ahead blankly. Smitty waved for his wife to be quiet, but everyone else in the courtroom seemed to be buzzing, blotting out the clerk's reading of the second verdict, that in the murder of Wendy Fritz: guilty, penalty of death. But no one heard it.

Tinney rose and asked that the jury be polled individually, and as they were polled Smitty rocked back and forth, looked at the reporters, the court officials, and the clerk, who was reading the roll. Each juror confirmed his verdict, then Tinney requested permission to question the jurors about whether they had been influenced by information they had received outside the courtroom. Garrett denied this, saying, "I've never heard of such a motion before."

The judge thanked the jury and dismissed the jurors, having forgotten to set the time for sentencing. Court was not officially adjourned. Then Diane jumped up in a burst of sobs, climbed the railing separating the spectators from the court, and used a chair as a rung to reach her convicted husband. A newsman grabbed up his camera before she could step on it.

"Smitty! Oh, Smitty!" she cried in his arms.

"It's okay, honey," he said in a half-whisper, "It's okay." At that a cameraman aimed his camera to snap a picture. While Diane was being ushered behind the railing, Judge Garrett's voice rose sharply above the excitement.

"This hasn't been a show!" he said. "You people here would like to make it a show!" Then he snapped to the nearest newsman, pointing threateningly, "Did you take a picture?"

"No, Your Honor," the reporter said.

"Well, you be careful or one of you may wind up in jail. It's not been easy to be lenient with the press in this case. I'll put the first man in jail that takes a picture!"

Tinney then reminded the judge that he had not set the time for sentencing. Judge Garrett restored order to the chaotic courtroom and set the time at March 11, 1966, at 9 in the morning.

"To avoid another outburst like that," Tinney said, "I ask that Schmid be removed from the court while it is still in session, Your Honor."

"Granted," the judge said and as Deputy Booth led young Schmid away from the defense table, Diane reached out her hand and Smitty squeezed it for a moment before Booth handcuffed his hands behind his back.

"Well, Henry," Smitty said to the deputy, "that's the way it goes." He was escorted out into the hall, past his weeping mother and through the stairwell door to be taken to a car waiting downstairs.

The courtroom cleared, with Diane following Schmid Sr. through the spectators. Mrs. Lynch was behind her, grasping the girl's arms. Flashbulbs popped, and Schmid Sr. covered his face with a newspaper.

"Any comment? Any comment?" the reporters entreated. Smitty's father muttered, "We will stand by our son." Diane's mother, trying to protect her, screamed, "Go away, you vultures! You've seen it all, got what you wanted, now go away!"

Outside, Tinney was asked if he planned to appeal. He replied, "I'm going home to dinner. I don't know about you but I'm going home to my wife and family."

The jury foreman was more cooperative. He said, "No particular piece of evidence stood out in our minds. We considered the case as a whole picture. After I was elected foreman we waited about five minutes in silence before we began discussing anything. Then anyone who had anything to say said it, and we let the few members who hadn't spoken think it over for themselves." All the jurors, he continued, "especially the women, were very deliberate when they expressed their views. I personally was a bit surprised to find so much agreement. On the death penalty, on the first and second ballot, two jurors withheld their votes. But there was no argument against the death penalty and after discussion we voted again and reached a decision." It took only one ballot to convict Schmid. But a second was taken to verify, he added. Three ballots were passed before the jury voted unanimously for the death penalty, and this, the foreman said, was accomplished within the first thirty minutes of the time the jury entered the jury room.

Schafer said the verdict was "the quickest ever that I can recall involving the death penalty."

PART FIVE

THAT EVENING OF March 1st, sitting on the edge of his cot in Cell 14, one leg crossed and the blue-lined writing pad on his knee, Smitty wrote:

> The mockery of justice finally completed its cycle and the distortion of truth riddled reality to form a clause of *guilty*. But I expected to lose, any of the fanatical contributions that led to my conviction were deeply embedded in the jurors' minds before any presentation of evidence, and the news media groveled in squeamish delight over the anticipation of the verdict.
>
> The hungry cyclopean vultures forever aiming their one eye in my direction. Ultimately and undoubtedly the decision will be reversed and the final revenge will be mine. But alas, revenge is sickening. As I contemplate the future, my mind probes the depths of this solitude in search of a rationalization for this incredible insanity that constantly haunts me, taunting me with thoughts of destruction and the ultimate death they hope to deliver me.

> The disappointment was not too harsh as I was rather pessimistic of the outcome. My companionship with Death which will surely be my companion and enemy for a multitude of days, will not conquer me. I will occasionally enjoy the duels with Death and his Associates, and hope my instinctive intrepidness will name me as the victor.
>
> I've considered the remote possibility that my appeal will be rejected and death would be the next progression. At this time, as I shut my eyes and visualize the process of dying, I anticipate a new adventure instead of fear. Naturally, I hate to relinquish my physical existence at this time, but destiny pursues other channels and rivers and I am merely the life-blood of their existence to flow in endless pursuit of its whim.

Schmid continued making entries in his notebook while Tinney began the complicated series of legal maneuvers to appeal the verdict. Tinney contacted the law offices of attorney F. Lee Bailey in Boston, requesting an outline of Bailey's appeal for Dr. Sam Sheppard based on "pretrial publicity," upon which Tinney would base the appeal for Schmid. Schmid wrote:

> Today's events poisoned my soul with such fury and insurgent uprisings I actually felt nausea. As the fires of hell burn perpetually so does the wildness and uninhibited thoughts of my mind. Eternally the primitiveness of my anger roars within the depths of my subconscious to devour my reasoning power. The words and thoughts I transpire come in a rapid staccato from some unknown source below the thoughts of my subconscious. Each conformation

> of thought that flows from my untapped reservoir is not premeditated, but a hereditary response prompted by the same fury that serves as a guidepost for my actions.

> Will life completely banish me, and my identity become so left behind no amount of speed will ever let me surpass it again? I'm so afraid this incredible raw wildness that refuses to lie dormant has driven me down a one-way road of recklessness, completely devoid of detours.

During this time, a writer who had closely followed the trial gained an interview with a nineteen-year-old boy who claimed to have been a friend of Smitty's, and who had attended some parties on East Adams following the disappearance of the Fritz girls. The boy, at the time of the interview, was staying in New Mexico as a fugitive from a stolen-car incident in Arizona. He said that on one occasion Smitty had told him how he killed the sisters.

"I don't know why Smitty did it exactly except he said he choked them with his hands. Gretchen's sister was watching TV and he killed Gretchen in the bedroom, then came out and choked the sister. He said Gretchen was making noises and he went back and put her in the living room, and choked her again. He said he choked the sister twice too, even though he knew she was dead the first time. He said he pissed a little in his pants and then sat on the front on those concrete steps there for a while until he got to thinking that he would take the bodies out of the house. He said he dropped them off up in the desert and didn't think about covering them over or hiding them."

The boy also said he had read about the trial and believed Schmid could have "beaten it" with a better lawyer.

In Tucson, Tinney had already made a number of motions for delay of the Rowe trial, because of the unfavorable publicity Schmid had received. Appearing before Judge Mary Anne Richey, Tinney requested a delay of at least five months, saying, "We need time for the public to read about other crimes and headlines. We just got through with a trial which had as much publicity as a trial could have. Is it fair to have a trial of this man starting next Tuesday?"

Opposing the motion, Schafer said, "The more time that elapses, the more difficult it will be to find witnesses."

Judge Richey granted a delay, saying: "What bothers me is that in the Fritz murder trial much testimony pertaining to the Rowe case was admitted into evidence and this testimony received about as much coverage as the Fritz case. I think it would be impossible to get a fair and impartial jury at this time. For these two reasons: publicity and the sworn testimony of the Rowe case already made public in the Fritz trial, I am ordering the trial continued to October 4, 1966."

Tinney also attempted to have sentencing postponed in the Fritz conviction, but after one delay Schmid was brought before Judge Garrett in Division II on March 25, 1966. Additional motions to postpone the sentencing were submitted by Tinney, but were rejected by Judge Garrett, who then asked if there were any reason why he should not then pronounce sentence.

Schmid, standing before the bench, stunned the entire courtroom, including his attorney, by bursting out: "I have a reason, Your Honor, and I demand that I have a sodium pentothal test to prove that I am innocent of these crimes." He continued in an excited voice, saying that his conviction resulted from "the perpetration of a fraud by the police and the county attorney's office. My conviction was a mockery of justice. The pretrial publicity did nothing but condemn me, condemn me, condemn me!"

Judge Garrett replied, "The Court doesn't have the jurisdiction or authority to grant your request," but indicated that Schmid's request might be considered by a higher court. Then, looking at the papers before him, he said, "This is a moment I'd rather not face. This is only the second time in twenty years on the bench that I've had to pronounce the death penalty. But it is my duty." After a pause, he then directed that Schmid be taken to the Arizona State Penitentiary in Florence and executed on the morning of June 17, 1966, by the administration of lethal gas.

Judge Garrett's secretary recalled that "the Judge was so shaken by the dual pronouncements of death sentences, that I asked a newsman to go into his chambers and say hello. He needed someone to say something to him."

As soon as Schmid returned to his jail cell, he wrote:

> The only part of today's events that caused any preponderant anxiety was the fact that my deliverance wasn't more eloquent. I had the usual pretrial trembles and in my opinion my elocution was below par, though I did enter my demand for pentothal. Originally I'd planned to include a manifold of statements, but the remembrance of Plato's 4 cardinal virtues of prudence, fortitude, temperance, and justice, overruled the decision. Plus the undue embarrassment of my erstwhile attorney caused me to withhold any further disclosure of evidence obtained.

On the last Sunday in March, Schmid spoke to the writer he'd confided in previously, to do with the boy from New Mexico. Schmid told the sheriff that the writer had now become Schmid's confidant. With the writer on the opposite side of the greenish, steel-barred bulletproof window of the visiting room, Schmid held the prisoner's phone hard against his ear and as he spoke he tapped on the thick glass with one finger for emphasis. "I want to take the stand under a sodium pentothal injection and challenge all their witnesses to do the same."

A nervous rash had reddened one side of his neck, and a long lock of the freshly black-dyed hair shadowed one eye. The gray T-shirt had a hole in the chest and his baggy blue dungarees stamped PIMA COUNTY JAIL sagged below his waist.

He had decided that he needed a new lawyer. "I've been seriously thinking of contacting another attorney," he told the writer, "not one around here. The one I've had in mind is this Percy Foreman. He appears to be very aggressive and that's what I need. Perhaps he might be interested if you told him about all the lawsuits providing I win."

Percy Foreman was widely known throughout the country for never losing a client. Contacted, Foreman said, "I've at least twenty-six other murder cases pending which the judges had to reset over the last eighteen months and as a result it is highly unlikely that I would be able to accept any additional cases. I don't think it would be fair to the courts to which I'm committed." He went on to say, "It would have been a most interesting case, but the boy has already been tried and convicted. I don't imagine he'll be tried on the other one until the others have been determined on appeal. If it were a new case, if I had the maneuvering ability, the right to make the record, it's the type of case I would accept for whatever the boy would be able to pay."

Foreman said he didn't know the prosecutor in the case nor the Arizona laws but that he sometimes thought "the power of the news media have greater weight than the criminal code or code of criminal procedure. If you put it big enough in ink, why there are politicians, ambitious for advancement, who will continue to act.

"I'm not a headline hunter and I've lots of rules about my practice. I'm not sure there are lawyers in Arizona who can render better service to Charlie Schmid than I can. I didn't read the testimony but it seemed a classic case for some psychiatrist with all the bizarre painting of the face and lips and the putting of tin cans in his boots." Foreman asked whether "competent psychiatrists" had testified, and was told that no psychiatric testimony had been submitted during the trial. "It's not my policy, as I said before, to criticize lawyers but the lawyer for this boy ought to have to take half the juice. This was a classic case for a psychiatrist from all that bizarre testimony."

Schmid was transferred from Pima County Jail to the penitentiary sixty miles north at Florence. There, from his cell on Death Row, in a cluster of new green cells at half-basement level, he could view the death house less than one hundred feet away.

Separate from the other buildings, the "Little House" was a small adobe building, with a slanted roof like a narrow garage and a metal smokestack reaching skyward. No doors on the north side of the building; just a worn brick wall. On the west end was a low door like an iron slab closely fitted into the wall, which was opened by a large flat-headed key. The floor of the witness room was old concrete. A large display case extended along the brown wall, containing rows of photographs of those executed by hanging.

The actual rope noose used surrounded each individual photograph. Twenty-eight nooses nailed around twenty-eight photographs. On June 22, 1928, four Chinese were hanged between 5:16 and 6:33 that morning, one rope used for all four men.

One photograph was of a woman, Eva Dugan, framed by the rope used for her execution on February 21, 1930.

In 1933, Arizona changed from hanging to execution by lethal gas. There were thirty-five more photographs in the display case of those put to death in the gas chamber. Three soldiers were executed on January 8, 1943, and the last execution had occurred on March 14, 1963.

Opposite the display case, three narrow windows revealed the rear of an octagonal metal chamber, like a one-man sea-diving bell. In the center stood a perforated steel chair with thick worn leather straps attached through the back. More straps and buckles rested on the arms of the chair, and two hung down from the front legs. The chair faced an oval-shaped steel door. A narrow aluminum-painted pipe extended from the wall behind the chair, up through the ceiling of the chamber. Another pipe, old and rusted in places, extended from the right wall to empty over a concrete pit sunken into the floor beneath the chair.

On the south wall of the Little House were three doors: one to a closet-like preparation room, one opening onto the gas-chamber door, and another, at the east end of the building, shoulder-wide with an enameled metal sign CONDEMNED CELL in the type of block letters used on industrial washrooms. Beyond the door in the center of the dim, gray room, were two smaller cells. Moss-colored stains encrusted the toilet bowl in each cell. The bars were a thatch of square steel rods, painted but peeling and rusted in places. The cell doors were thick metal slabs with slots punched through at eye level. The deathwatch room and condemned cells had not been cleaned since the previous execution. On the crossbar in one cell, above a striped dusty mattress, sat a sardine can stuffed with crushed-out cigarette butts.

In the room were an old card table, a cane chair with a dusty seat, an old boxy television set, and some wrinkled and dog-eared magazines. One wall was a wide sliding door, made of mismatched and dented parts of welded iron, with holes, cracks, and two-inch gaps at the hinges, this the door through which the condemned was led from the waiting cell to the gas chamber. No sounds of the preparations escaped the condemned waiting for the door to open.

Five days after being admitted to Death Row, Charles Schmid wrote in his journal:

> I sit on my bunk and look out the window and there is a little house out there and I know inside the little house may lay my fate. The reality of death had been obscured by hope, but the last hour before the final decree, it finally became a reality. What would death be like? The last breath, the last light and color, the last movement and touch, the last flickering of consciousness, the last dream, the lost and fading face of love–and then nothing, the dreamless, unsleeping, unawakening night of death.
>
> The image is so real you try to tell yourself it doesn't matter, that death will be a fascinating experience,

> an adventure, a terminal point at the end of all our roads, but even that isn't sufficient to enable the rationalization. The evolvement [sic] of being born and dying, perhaps a similar chain that forms a perpetual circle. From nothing at birth into nothing at death. No more is death just a concept or idea or a conundrum. It is tapping you on the shoulder and whispering in your ear, and the vacant haunting eyes mock you, ever patient, ever waiting. All your life you stack the blocks carefully, precisely, only to have them kicked everywhere and taken from you. The horrible feeling of knowing you'll die, that it is all prearranged, decays you. It's a feeling of dying before the execution, because you *are* dying every day more and more. All plans and dreams, the living from day to day is gone, and you know it. You shut your eyes and hope when you awake it will be gone, but it is not. You look to the window and there it is....You had thought that life had meaning, a reason. Death takes it away, one cold clean sweep and it is gone. That one tangible thing, the reason for life, the one sensible thing that made it endurable, is gone.
>
> Everything's a farce, a dirty cruel joke, a hoax. Dead. Dead. That's all, just dead.

Through the writer that Schmid had contracted as his exclusive, personal manger, Schmid began negotiations with Percy Foreman. At this same time, he began drawing up a proposal for sodium pentothal to be introduced as evidence in court. Contesting the guilty verdict, he seemed obsessed with the idea that a pentothal test would clear him. Schmid submitted the proposal, in which he stated: "Should the action of Sodium Pentathol [sic] produce evidence contrary to the jury's verdict, a retrial must be declared immediately." But he also stated, "Any negative result to the test should in no way alter, change, or hamper the defendant's right for appeal, etc." In conclusion, Schmid said, "No device or drug yet known to man is proven 100 percent accurate in determining truth or error. Any state of mental illness, whether it be neurotic, psychotic, or psychopathic in nature, can produce results other than the truth."

But Schmid concluded by stating, "Sodium Pentothal could and should be admissible as real and tangible evidence."

Focusing on the value of publicity, Schmid tried another tactic, having the writer make arrangements for an exclusive interview with George Scott of Tucson's station KCUB. On April 14, 1966, the interview was taped on Death Row, and aired the following day.

During the interview Scott asked about Bruns's testimony during the trial. Schmid said, "That is a highly controversial subject, but there was definite proof that he did misquote and lie under oath, and there was nothing I could do about it, because I could not take the stand. It was my lawyer's advice that I shouldn't take the stand because it wasn't needed."

Scott asked about Schmid's proposal concerning sodium pentothal. "I have a letter pending right now," Schmid replied. "I have already sent it off. I have sent several out to the county attorney, and in the letter I have asked Mr. Schafer or Mr. Green to contact Mr. Fritz and Mrs. Rowe and anybody else he wants to, and to come up here directly, because he does have the power, I am sure he does, and give me sodium pentothal. I would be more than willing to have Mr. Fritz administer the sodium pentothal." But Schmid said he had not received an answer from that letter yet.

Later in the interview he told Scott, "I realize that the press has to keep the public informed of various events, but I believe they should take an objective stand, or an impartial stand, and I do not believe they did this in this case, and it did very much prejudice my trial, anything I would have had to say. When I was in the courtroom and before they picked the jurors, I overheard some of the comments like, 'I hope they pick me because I'd be more than happy to give him the pill.' I mean it was things like that that made me feel, well, I don't have a chance no matter what I said, I really wouldn't. And then when we asked for a change of venue and denied, how could I expect to have a trial? They should at least have given me that much of the benefit of a doubt. But it was denied me."

Scott said, "Charles, many of us in the news media would glance over at you during the trial and wonder what feelings were going through you at the time, what feelings you were experiencing. Would you care to comment on that at this moment?"

"Well," Schmid replied, "to be perfectly honest with you, when I first went into trial, even though I did hear the comments by the prospective jurors, I really felt that I was going to get some kind of trial, or at least be able to present my case and prove that I didn't kill Gretchen or Wendy, and that Richard did, but as soon as the judge ruled that I wouldn't be able to admit any evidence against Richie in our trial it just–it just deflated me completely."

"Did you get a chance to see *Life* magazine?" Scott asked.

Schmid laughed, "Oh did I ever! I couldn't believe it, I really couldn't. I read the magazine and I looked at the pictures and in all honesty I thought they were talking about somebody else. I said, 'This couldn't be me, really it couldn't be. How could anybody be like that, really?' And then I read it from an objective view, and I thought, if I was reading it, and I was somebody else I would think the guy was guilty, and a rotten guy, and a monster too. I really couldn't believe it."

"Charles, you have been in Death Row for now approximately three weeks. What are your feelings now that you do have this much time on your hands?"

"The guards and other inmates have been pretty nice to me and let me see all the magazines and all the pretrial publicity that was denied me before this time, and I can get somewhat of an idea of what really happened, and what they said, and try and figure out a reason why they did it, although I really haven't found it. I read a little bit, like *Time* magazine that came out before the trial, then I glance up and look out the window and I see the gas chamber out there and the Little House, and it really makes me wonder and sometimes I just pray to anything or anybody, or anything I can, and ask why does it have to happen to me."

"Charles, you have been portrayed as wearing makeup, and also dyeing your hair—"

"Irregardless of whether I do or don't," Schmid said, "I would like to know what difference does it make if I did or didn't do such things as they claim I did, considering makeup, etcetera? I really thought this was America, and if I felt like doing something like that, I could. If I wanted to dye my hair green, what difference would it make? But no, the newspapers and magazines, they have to say it was really a terrible crime that this perverted little animal wore makeup and dyed his hair. Everything I read–it seems like it is a crime to be short, you know. They say, 'Well, this short, little teenage Lothario!' And Lothario, of course, is some man portrayed in somebody's play, I can't recall right now, maybe I don't know what it was, but he was very unscrupulous, and a sex maniac, and things like that. They incorrectly called me 'a teenage Lothario.' Well, I would like to say, where is the evidence to prove all of this, their obvious contentions that I do this and do that?"

"Almost all the press media, Charles, portrayed you as wearing cowboy boots with rags or tin cans stuffed in the shoes."

"It was just to add to their fictional character of the monster that they made up. It helped the image so why shouldn't they put it in?"

Scott asked about Schmid's guitar playing, and if he ever performed professionally.

"Yes, I have," Schmid replied, "on several occasions I have played for different bands, and I have had my own band. That is just something that I really enjoy, that's all. The one thing that I really can't understand, it really amazes me no end, is that by the law in our land in America and democracy, a person is completely innocent until proven guilty, but yet everything that was said about me, prior to my trial, was guilty, guilty, guilty, guilty. There was nothing else involved but guilt."

"How did you feel the very first day of court?" Scott asked.

"At that time I wasn't aware of the pretrial publicity or anything that had happened, and I felt very confident that I would go in there, and I would present my case as it actually happened and I'd be perfectly able to convince everybody that I was completely innocent, and had nothing to do with it. So I sat down and the judge started to read the charges against me, and then instead of saying, 'The defendant pleads not guilty,' he said, 'The defendant pleads guilty.' And I felt like somebody had dropped a bomb on me, and I couldn't believe it, and I said, 'Huh? What's happening, what's wrong?' and he said, 'Oh, excuse me, I mean the defendant pleads not guilty,' and then everybody kind of chuckled like that, and I said 'What's wrong, I mean, this doesn't sound quite right?' Of course, you know, it probably doesn't mean anything, but it was just–it was just–gave me a brief example of what was yet to come, and it made me aware of what to expect. And then as it progressed and further and further, I saw he wasn't going to allow my case to be presented, and so anything I obviously had to say wouldn't do any good."

"Charles, as you sit here day after day in Death Row, what feelings do you have?"

"The things that really bother me most is that I am going to be literally murdered for something I didn't do, and sooner or later there is going to be another crime committed, and it is going to be proven without any doubt whatsoever that I am completely innocent, and then it is going to be too late and everybody is going to say, 'Gee, we are really sorry, Smitty, but it's too late now because you are dead. But here is a dollar for your wife, or two dollars, but we are really sorry we made a mistake, but that is just the way life is.' And it's hard for me to believe that life or people would be so cruel."

A few days after the interview was broadcast, Percy Foreman

decided against entering the Schmid case, telling the writer, "I just can't leave these other people in the lurch. But I've thought it over and I believe the best contribution I could make to the boy there would be to get him a lawyer that could make the most of the situation. Do you know Lee Bailey?"

At the time, F. Lee Bailey of Boston was awaiting the Supreme Court's decision on the appeal for Dr. Sam Sheppard. Foreman said, "This whole Schmid case sounds like the sort of case Bailey could really get himself into. He's a young man, probably the second best attorney in the country, very aggressive."

The writer contacted Bailey who expressed interest in the case. He had heard of Arizona lawyers showing a willingness to accept a case at the onset of a trial, but losing their commitment in the courtroom. Bailey told the writer, "They're local lawyers and they can't afford to stick their necks out. That's why there's renegade lawyers like me. You can't blame local attorneys, especially when there's gruesome murders involved." He said he would be in Tucson in two days.

When he arrived, the writer showed Bailey the bulging file of pretrial publicity on Schmid's case, and scanning through the material while en route to the prison, Bailey said, "This is what you need to crack a case like this apart. There's just about as much here as Sam Sheppard's."

At the prison, waiting for Schmid to be brought from Death Row, Bailey stared at the walls and gun turrets, the corroded spikes of the high iron gates, and a large rectangular mirror above the gate, which a prison guard was watching. Finally, Schmid was brought to the gate before the visiting room. The cuffs on the sleeves of his old army jacket were folded back several times. "He's very small, isn't he," Bailey said to the writer. Then, inside the visiting room moments later, Bailey said to Schmid, "Looks like you've got yourself a lot of trouble."

Schmid grinned. "I guess I have, sir." He then insisted on his innocence to the Boston lawyer, saying that all he wanted was a fair trial. He told of his efforts to obtain an examination under sodium pentothal. Bailey recommended instead a lie-detector test which he said was "infallible, if administered the right way by a qualified expert."

Schmid seemed uncertain. "If something went wrong, mechanically, say that the county attorney could find something there to use against me, I mean it's what they've done with every single thing."

"The test I'd have administered would be a sure bet," Bailey said, "and the best thing to throw right back at a conviction like this Fritz trial. By that I don't mean it would necessarily change anything, but it would be putting your best foot forward. I'd bring the most qualified man in to give you the test, and if everything you've said is true, the results of the test would be the first direct move." He said there would have to be a retrial, but he couldn't see how it could be brought to court in Arizona.

Bailey asked Schmid about funds needed to finance another trial and appeals. Schmid's answers didn't impress him. After an hour and a half Bailey was returned to Tucson, where he discussed the case first with Schmid's parents and later at dinner with Tinney. Bailey inquired as to why Schmid had not testified in his own defense and Tinney told him that he had been trying to protect the trial record for the appeal. If Schmid had taken the stand, Schafer might have antagonized him and then Schmid might have incriminated himself beyond repair.

The lawyer also mentioned the lack of psychiatric testimony in a case that seemed to call for it, which had concerned Foreman. Bailey was concerned as well and had telephoned Tinney to ask about the testimony. After his meeting with Schmid, and heading back to Tucson, Bailey told the writer that Tinney said, "if there had been psychiatric examinations, the results would scare the pants off any lawyer."

Before leaving town the following morning, Bailey met briefly with Schmid's parents who were impressd with the lawyer's notoriety but said they were very short on funds and were seriously in debt. Outside the courtroom, he asked the writer if there was another source of financing for the second trial or appeals. The writer said, "I can't think of any."

"So there isn't a nickel," Bailey said.

Before he took off solo in his Learjet, he told the press he didn't see any necessity for becoming involved in Schmid's defense, adding, "He has perfectly competent counsel in Mr. Tinney, whom I hold in great respect." He also said, "This case involves pretrial publicity and so of course I was interested in it. The decision of the Supreme Court in the Sheppard case will be very important to defendants in future sensational cases. The Charlie Schmid case is a bad case of trial by newspaper. If the Sheppard decision comes down right, you can forget about the Schmid conviction."

Two weeks later, Bailey wrote to the writer who was then in Los Angeles, saying he believed Schmid's parents were committed to Tinney and that arranging a defense would necessarily involve "some coordinated thought between Charlie and his folks." But he went on say that, "although I am satisfied that Bill Tinney is very able, I am sure that he has no desire to defend a man who questions his ability. I will be happy to defend Charlie if that is his wish. However, I would be reluctant to do so unless Bill is retained as co-counsel because as a result of our conference I am impressed with his understanding of the case."

Bailey stated that while he would like to defend Schmid on a cost-free basis, he was unable to do so, and requested some formal fee arrangement. Attempts were made to set up a defense fund, but with a notable lack of success. After three weeks, the total sum accumulated to $36, and no one would volunteer to hold the fund in trust.

In the meantime, Schmid's wife, Diane, and her mother announced at a news conference that she was suing for divorce. "We'll get his car and she should have that house, too," Diane's mother said. "He owes her that much."

Diane was asked if she still loved her husband, but her mother cut her reply short, saying, "That doesn't matter. *His* mother's trying to break them up. She wants to keep Diane over there away from her own family. When we went over to get her clothes she wouldn't even let Diane have the wedding pictures just because Smitty hadn't seen them. I'll get even with her for the way she talked to me."

That evening, in a televised interview, mother and daughter stated that the grounds for divorce would be mental cruelty, the result of Schmid's "anger, his uncontrollable temper, and because he's capable of violence and probably guilty of the charges against him."

When Schmid got the news he said, "It was like a blow in the stomach. I just couldn't believe it. When I saw her the week before she told me everything had been straightened out and she was going to live with my mother who would take care of her. I've been afraid for her and I thought she'd be safer living with my family. I know she's young and I know it's hard for her, but I didn't expect she'd do this."

He speculated that "some movie people came to town and offered Diane a contract if she would divorce me so that it would agree with a fictionalized version of a movie being made on the story in *Life* magazine." Sighing, Schmid continued, "I've hit the very bottom now and there's only one way left and that's up."

Schmid continued to hope that F. Lee Bailey would represent him at the second trial set for October 4th. Bailey had said, "It is difficult for me to believe that Arizona will actually bring Charlie to trial for the Rowe murder in October. It would be obviously impossible to assemble two, let alone twelve, citizens who are ignorant of the fact that Schmid was judged guilty of a double murder earlier this year."

Then on June 20 Bailey wrote, saying that he was accepting the retainer and was entering the case. Shortly thereafter, the Supreme Court ruled in an 8-1 decision, that Samuel Sheppard had not received a fair trial because of the "massive, pervasive, and prejudicial publicity that attended his prosecution."

Bailey brought his own polygraph expert in from Florida, stating, "I'm sending for the only man I trust to give Charlie the lie-detector test he has asked for. If he's lied to me, I'll just turn the results over to his mother and forget it."

On Thursday night, August 11, after seeing the results of ten hours of exhaustive tests with Schmid, Bailey announced publicly and with confidence that he would take the case of Charles Schmid.

Back in Tucson, the writer and "personal manager" for Schmid said, "Unknown to most, what this was on Bailey's part was a try at swaying public opinion, and also a demonstration on his part to show a 'refusing to back down' position that he believed could intimidate his opposition. Bailey then told Schmid, 'Charlie, I don't know whether you'll be out of here next summer or eleven years from now, but you'll be out.'"

PART SIX

"AN ARTICLE A day keeps justice away," Tinney told Judge Garrett on September 16 at a continuance hearing for Schmid. "The newspapers keep hitting over and over again on Schmid. I don't see how a jury can be impaneled now. We're having a contest between the court and the press. The Tucson press has put on a spirited campaign to cover anything in order to bring in the name of Charles Schmid. I complain of this because he has another trial awaiting him." Tinney asserted that the "daily doses of Schmid" would affect even the judges. "All but two Superior Court judges are seeking reelection. In such a campaign by a judge, no matter how honorable he is, he can't help but be swayed by public opinion. And the opinion of this community is adverse to my client."

Tinney argued for more than an hour, and then Judge Garrett denied his motions. The Rowe trial remained set for October 4th.

Five days later Tinney and Bailey filed a petition asking the U.S. District Court to take over jurisdiction of the case and have it removed out of the state of Arizona. They argued that with all the pretrial publicity, Schmid could not be assured his constitutional rights. After some legal maneuvers, the U.S. Circuit Court agreed to hear arguments on the petition, and meanwhile postponed the Rowe trial.

On Death Row, Schmid continued to write:

> Nights are no different than days. Sleep is a friend sometimes but one I cannot trust completely. I sense it as a tempting seductress I welcome when my limbs grow partially paralytic. There is a semidarkness now within my cell. The heat is unbearable but I know the pleasures of sleep will overcome me shortly. The only pleasure outside of sexual fantasies that remains is the fantasies of my dream world when I lapse into an unconsciousness from sleep.
>
> The dreams are so similar to actual reality, I'm unable to distinguish any particular difference. Perhaps my dreams are actually reality and what I assume to be real, my supposedly conscious hours, is merely a horrible nightmare. It's strange but I can only recall three dreams where I've distinguished colors. The depths were accented with an irrevocable beauty. Each day now as I try to remember the sequences, the clarity becomes sharper and more focused.
>
> If death is simply a continuance of this dreamworld, it would be rather pleasant and I would find it acceptable. I would very much enjoy sleeping twenty-four hours a day provided the dreams were included. Perhaps they are real, perhaps it is an escape. I simply cannot comprehend.

He was allowed his guitar and amplifier in his cell but had to decline an invitation to join the prison band. Time was passing. The District Court postponement of the Rowe trial had "suspended it in limbo," Schmid wrote. He had enrolled in some correspondence courses on business and economics, and his parents sent him textbooks and a daily copy of the *Wall Street Journal.* He was permitted to spend one hour a day outside.

The Federal court ruled against Tinney and Bailey's request for a change of venue. Schmid's trial was set for April 3, but Bailey, at this time, would be in Sarasota, Florida, defending Dr. Carl Coppolino. Tinney claimed that he himself was unprepared to defend Schmid without Bailey, and sought a further postponement of the trial. While Schmid was being brought from State prison, news was released that four subpoenas had been issued by Schmid's attorneys, calling on Schafer, County Attorney Norman Green, and the attorneys for Saunders and Mary French to testify to "deals made."

As soon as Schmid arrived at Pima County Jail, he granted another interview to George Scott of station KCUB, whose first question was about Schmid's continuance hearing.

Schmid said, "I believe the whole purpose of Mr. Schafer's rebuttal in court concerning my continuance is for actually one reason only, and that's because he's really afraid to face Mr. Bailey in the courtroom–because Mr. Bailey has a reputation for uncovering fraud and discovering truth. Personally I believe that the newspapers and a lot of other people have been unfair to Mr. Tinney. He has received no money whatsoever from the taxpayers or anyone else as reimbursement for acting as co-counsel for Mr. Bailey. As far as his integrity goes, let me tell you this much: if we were refused a continuance in order that Mr. Bailey would be able to be present, Mr. Tinney would have laid his license on the line and we would have refused to put up a defense at all and just sat there in court.

"It seems justice is a very expensive thing when you're on the side of the fence where poor people live, and I'm on that side now. If I hadn't been fortunate enough to have Mr. Bailey, I'd be a lot more frightened though. I can't help but wonder what would happen if a person was in a similar situation that I was, and wasn't fortunate enough to have Mr. Bailey and his team of investigators to investigate and uncover the truth, as Mr. Schafer has his police force, police-women, and his team of investigators to do what they want twenty-four hours a day."

Schmid then told Scott, "When Mr. Bailey and one of the most qualified polygraph experts administered me a polygraph examination, they telephoned Mr. Schafer and asked him to be present before they gave me any knowledge I was to have a test, and he flatly refused. And he also flatly refused to accept the results of that test."

"How do you expect to come out?" Scott asked.

"I can only guarantee you one thing, and one thing only, and that's that I'll never give up, not now, not ever, no matter what. Not until the truth is firmly established once and for all. And sooner or later it's going to be, I know this."

At the hearing before Judge Roylston, Tinney stated that he himself had not been in recent contact with the defendant, that Bailey had conferred with Schmid, starting with an interview in July. In protesting Tinney's motion for continuance, Schafer said that Tinney's statement that he had not communicated with his client since last July was "shocking."

Tinney said that Bailey "has had his private investigators in Tucson," and added that recent defense efforts had been conducted "all to the exclusion generally of myself. Our position," Tinney told the judge, "is that the defendant has contracted with Bailey to appear and defend him in his trial. The taxpayers aren't paying a penny for the attorneys who are defending Mr. Schmid."

Schafer asserted that the prosecution was not aware of any extensive efforts to have the Coppolino trial postponed, and charged that Tinney had told him last October, "You won't get Charlie to trial for two years."

Despite further protests by the county attorney, Judge Roylston granted a continuance and reset the trial date for May 10, 1967.

The sensational nature of the case and the addition of F. Lee Bailey to the cast of characters assured massive coverage by the news media. Judge Roylston therefore established an extensive set of regulations to try to prevent Schmid's case being prejudiced before the trial had even begun.

Bailey lost his defense of Dr. Coppolino and flew to Tucson on

May 9 in his private eight-seater Learjet. The white aircraft touched down at 7:03 that evening, and moments later Bailey climbed down to face the group of reporters. One newsman asked, "You going to be set to go tomorrow?"

"Oh, yes," Bailey said confidently. "Oh, yes." Overlooked by the reporters, Tinney, who had arrived to meet Bailey, walked quietly around the Learjet, examining the plane admiringly.

"Do you think losing the Coppolino case will have any effect on this trial?" Bailey was asked.

"I hope not. It shouldn't," he replied.

"How many times have you seen Charles Schmid?"

"Oh, I'd say four or five times, I haven't kept count."

"Where do you draw the line in fighting for a client?"

Bailey said, "Oh, it's a very clear line. We don't suborn any perjury, manufacture any evidence, or represent something to a jury which we know is not true."

The newsman asked: "Would you go on representing a client who pleaded innocent to a crime even though you knew he was guilty of the crime?"

"I might," Bailey said after a moment. "I might if he insisted on it."

"If you win this case with Charles Schmid," the newsman asked, "will you be working on the Fritz appeal?"

"I'm not going to discuss this case until a jury is impaneled and locked up." Bailey left the airport in Tinney's air-conditioned Volkswagen.

On the morning of May 10, the Tucson *American* reported:

> One of the strangest trials in the history of U.S. jurisprudence will open today when Boston trial lawyer F. Lee Bailey begins the defense of Charles Schmid for a murder already used by the state to convict and sentence him to death for two other murders.

The second trial was taking place in Division 7 of Superior Court, containing only thirty seats, and attendance was limited to the defense and prosecution staff, Schmid's parents, and a selected number of newsmen.

Questioning prospective jury members, Bailey emphasized what he termed a "holocaust of pretrial publicity," and objected to the prosecution's excluding jurors opposed to the death penalty. He made it clear that he would base Schmid's defense on the absence of a *corpus delecti*, and repeatedly asked whether the jurors would be prejudiced against Schmid if he didn't testify in his own behalf. Bailey also challenged jurors displaying knowledge of Schmid's previous conviction.

Judge Roylston called a panel of 125 jurors, considerably more than is usual in a murder trial. From these a panel of forty-one would be chosen, of which the prosecution and defense would each be allowed to challenge thirteen without cause. The remaining fifteen would make up the twelve-member jury, with three alternates.

"Do you think Charlie Schmid is innocent until proven guilty?" Bailey asked one prospective juror.

"Yes, sir."

"Do you think he might be innocent even though I'm here to defend him?"

"Oh, yes, sir."

To another juror he asked bluntly, "To put it simply, do you believe he did it?"

The jurors were not sure, and were challenged for cause.

Bailey did everything he could to disqualify jurors. He seemed to think that if a panel could not be chosen from the original 125 he would have made his point about undue pretrial publicity and a mistrial might be declared. Judge Roylston gave Bailey some hope when he said that if a panel was not chosen from the first 125, any additional jurors summoned might have read or heard reports of the proceedings and thus be eligible to challenge.

After emphasizing the absence of the body, Bailey's questions would stress that the state had to prove that a murder occurred in the county before it could begin to prove that Schmid committed it.

Yet if the remaining evidence was strong enough, Schafer would ask, would the absence of the corpse keep the jurors from returning a guilty verdict?

"We don't use probabilities," Bailey told a woman juror, "so long as there is a *possibility* that the alleged victim might turn up somewhere, would you be inclined to vote for the death penalty or hold up?"

At noon recess, Katharine Schmid talked to the writer. "I don't know why Mr. Bailey keeps avoiding me," she said. "We've tried for two days to speak to him, but every time we get close to him he just keeps his face straight ahead and just brushes past us as though he doesn't even know who we are. I don't understand that. Charlie said that Mr. Bailey hasn't talked to *him* at all, and he's wondering what's going on."

The following day, Bailey asked the court to forbid the jury to sentence Schmid to death if he was convicted. "We will maintain that the power to execute should be withheld," Bailey said, "since there is no body and because death is an irrevocable sentence if she should turn up." He indicated sternly that defense would appeal any conviction, and that Schmid was indigent. "We're just making a record here in this case," he said. The selection of the panel moved slowly. The tape recorder and court stenographer's machine silently recorded the words and technicalities, questions, answers, objections, instructions, recesses. The procedure was numbing. Schmid sat impassively with his arms folded, alongside Tinney, who said nothing throughout. At the end of the day, a reporter said in the corridor, "No jury's going to be selected, not in this trial."

Before court reconvened on the fifth day of jury selection, according to an informed source, Tinney and Bailey saw Schafer alone in Judge Roylston's chambers and Tinney said with a grin, "How about second-degree? Have you given that any thought? It would save the state the expense of a long trial and appeal and retrial, and it would knock down one of our grounds for appeal in the Fritz case."

Schafer replied in the negative, and Bailey laughed and commented, "You know what Charlie would say to pleading guilty, don't you?" and he thrust up the middle finger of one hand.

When Judge Roylston was seated in the courtroom and the session began, Bailey moved for another mistrial, charging that the *Arizona Star* was "making a deliberate effort to keep the defendant from getting a fair trial." He accused the paper of publicizing information which Roylston had asked reporters not to mention on three occasions. "If this keeps up," Bailey said, "the defense might as well throw in the towel."

During the long six days, Judge Roylston, the prosecutor, and Bailey had individually examined 130 jurors, 97 had been excused, and Bailey had objected to the calling of a new group. The judge still had under advisement Bailey's mistrial motion, based on the grounds that the *Star* had repeatedly printed prejudicial information. On its own part, the *Star* was convinced that Bailey's only motive for appearing in Arizona was to muster personal publicity. The newspaper decided not to print the lawyer's name and referred to him as "one of Schmid's attorneys."

On Thursday, May 18, the jury selection began for the first time without some sort of motion from Bailey. He sat quietly most of the morning, questioning only two prospective jurors. Many had been disqualified before Bailey had interviewed them. Only thirty-five panel members had been chosen and the outlook for a jury was dim until Judge Roylston discovered that Arizona law required only thirty-two members, so the original juror panel was reduced to thirty-five with one alternate instead of three. Under these rules the panel was completed.

The judge told the nine men and three women that he would allow them to return home that night, but that they would be sequestered the next morning at which time the testimony would begin. Court was adjourned until 10 A.M. Friday.

That Thursday evening, in answer to an urgent request, Charles Schmid Sr. climbed into Smitty's dusty Falcon and drove to County Jail. He entered the visitor's aisle and nodded to his son on the other side of the bulletproof glass. Then he picked up the telephone.

"I'm preparing a writ to dismiss both Mr. Bailey and Bill," Smitty said. "I'll defend myself in this trial."

"You can't fire them!" Mr. Schmid said and asked for an explanation.

"The county attorney's offered a deal and Mr. Bailey told me he's taking it, he wants me to plead guilty to second-degree murder." Schmid spoke rapidly: the jury was impossible, and Bailey had informed him before the afternoon session that Schafer had proposed that Schmid plead to reduced charges. "Mr. Bailey told me it was the only way to save my life. He said if he went ahead I'd be convicted and sentenced to death." Schmid went on to explain that Bailey had informed him that Schafer was bringing in the Fritz case, even though it was after the fact, and having it admitted as suppression of evidence. "They're going to use it the same way they used this one in the last trial, just the other way around. Bailey said it'll destroy the appeal on the Fritz case and I'd be dead within ninety days."

Charles Sr. didn't understand. "If the county attorney's so damn sure they'll get the death sentence, then why's he offering deals?"

"To save the state the cost of the trial and appeals, and Mr. Bailey's made it clear we'll appeal. He told me the jury's completely prejudiced and dying to give me the gas." Schmid told his father that he had been "caught off guard" by his lawyer's information and that he had said, "Hell no! We'll win! No deal, there's no body!" Then, Schmid told his father, Tinney had said, "You haven't a prayer and because of the Fritz stuff being admitted you'll be dead in ninety days."

Schmid's father advised him to "hold off on the writ business until we can get this settled with Bill."

At 9:15 that night, Katharine Schmid contacted Tinney. He told her it was true, Schafer had proposed the deal. According to Mrs. Schmid, Tinney told her, "But we're not accepting it. Whenever a prosecutor makes a deal we have to present it to the defendant, so I told [Charlie] today. But we're not taking it."

Friday morning, before the trial began, Judge Roylston ruled that he would allow testimony on the Fritz murders to be admitted as evidence. Bailey sought a last-ditch motion asking for a mistrial, change of venue, and continuance on the grounds that members of the jury knew of Schmid's prior convictions. He said, "The defendant is already two strikes down," and indicated that because of this the jury perhaps would be "more willing to convict him" for the alleged Rowe murder.

A fair trial in some other city in Arizona might be possible, Bailey said, but the trial should be moved out of the state. He criticized the makeup of the jury also; persons well-informed of the convictions of Saunders and French should be disqualified from service. His final attempt to halt the trial was to question Judge Roylston's jurisdiction over the case; unless Schmid's conviction for the Fritz killings was reversed by an appellate court, he would be executed, and Bailey questioned whether the judge could "try a carcass for the crime."

Bailey's motions were denied and the prosecution began its opening statements. In August of 1965, Schafer told the jury, Charles Schmid murdered Gretchen Fritz because he had told her of the Rowe murder, and she was holding it over his head.

"The defendant wanted to kill a girl in 1964 to see if he could do it and see how it felt. He asked Mary French to get him a girl. Schmid gave her a list of prospective victims and Alleen Rowe was one of them."

Schafer then briefly told of the murder of Alleen Rowe as described by Mary French and said that Schmid had confessed the murder to two friends, and later to Gretchen Fritz. He described Schmid's relationship to Gretchen and told of that murder. Schafer concluded that Mary French's testimony and other evidence would prove that Schmid was guilty of "premeditated murder" and should receive the death sentence.

Bailey declined to make an opening statement, and then Schafer called Norma Rowe as the first witness for the state. Mrs. Rowe burst into tears when the prosecutor showed her a picture of Alleen. When asked about her daughter's relationship with the three who allegedly killed her, Mrs. Rowe said that on one occasion Alleen told her, "Some people you go along with. You don't cross them. They could run you down with a car."

Norma Rowe was followed on the stand by Mary French who repeated much of the testimony offered in the Fritz trial, with a few additional details. She now said that Saunders first hit Alleen with a rock and she started running, but Schmid caught up with her and struck the fatal blow with a stone.

Bailey tried to discredit Mary, implying that she hated Alleen Rowe and was lying about Schmid's part in the crime because he refused to marry her when she was pregnant with his child.

Bailey asked, "Did you hate Alleen Rowe?"

"No."

"Did you go to her assistance?"

"No."

Bailey asked Mary why she had gone to such lengths to lure Alleen from the house.

Mary replied, "I didn't really believe they would do it." She sighed listlessly.

Schafer had intended on calling John Saunders as his third witness, but Saunders had changed his mind about a lot of things: he now contended he was railroaded by his previous attorneys into making his guilty plea, and his present counsel informed Schafer that Saunders would take the Fifth Amendment if summoned.

Roylston announced that unless the defense could produce law to the contrary, Saunders's sealed preliminary hearing transcript could be admitted and read to the jury. Bailey asked for time to study the legality of the matter, since he and Tinney had not considered the possibility of such a move by Schafer.

"Mr. Bailey," Judge Roylston said, "we have about a fifteen-minute recess coming up. If you can find any cases on this matter in that time, I'll be happy to look at them."

"Your Honor," Bailey countered, "my law professors would shudder to think that such an important point would be allotted only fifteen minutes for research."

"Mr. Bailey," the judge replied, "that's why you had law professors, to teach you how to look up things you needed in a hurry."

The day ended with attorneys arguing about whether the Saunders's transcript could be admitted. As the jury was being kept sequestered, Judge Roylston scheduled a court session for the next day, Saturday.

But at 9:15 the following morning, no one was in court but the newsmen and Schmid's parents. As minutes ticked by, everyone began to surmise that something was up. Schmid's parents finally reached Tinney in the hallway who told them Bailey was "sick," that he wouldn't be coming to court today. More to the point, he told them that they had decided to accept Schafer's deal. "Charlie will escape the gas chamber," Mrs. Schmid was told, and that Mr. Bailey was having it arranged for Charlie to be placed in a mental institution.

"I want to talk to Charlie," Katharine said, "and you better get Mr. Bailey here."

"He's sick today."

Mr. and Mrs. Schmid were allowed to consult with Charlie in a jury room not in use. They said their son was saying, "I don't want any part of this! I said I'm *not* accepting it and I'm not pleading guilty."

Tinney disappeared temporarily while Katharine listened to her husband protest the county attorney's proposal. Minutes later, Tinney again entered the jury room, accompanied by Bailey.

"He looked in the pink of health," Katharine recalls. "And the only reason he went and got Mr. Bailey was to force the issue about changing Charlie's mind."

Bailey insisted, "This jury is set to hang him even before we started this trial," and that the only realistic choice facing Schmid was death in the gas chamber or life in prison. Schmid seemed uncertain.

"What should I do, Mom?" he asked.

Katharine Schmid was bewildered. "I can't answer that for you, I just can't, Charlie. You'll have to make that decision."

Tinney confirmed Bailey's gloomy prognosis of their chances in court. Finally, when Schmid appeared to understand that the Fritz appeal was at stake, he seemed to weaken, and at that moment Bailey informed the family it was time to enter the courtroom. Schmid muttered a barely audible, "Okay."

After a brief meeting in the judge's chambers, the court convened at 11:30. Bailey arose and stated that Schmid would enter a plea of guilty to second-degree murder. The defendant, he said, had made a "certain admission" to him the previous summer during the lie detector test. "The defendant is in dire need of psychiatric help, although under the law as it now stands, he is not legally insane," Bailey said. "When it became apparent that the state's evidence was overwhelming, counsel advised the defendant to plead guilty to a noncapital charge. The defendant is guilty of the crime and believes it is in his best interest to so plead."

Tinney concurred with Bailey's statements and Judge Roylston asked Schafer if he would consent to a guilty plea to the reduced charge. Schafer answered with a quiet "Yes." The judge then asked Schmid to rise.

"Do you desire to enter this plea?" Roylston asked.

After a brief pause, Schmid said, "Yes."

"Have any promises been made to you?"

Schmid shook his head. "None."

"Have any threats been made to you?"

"None."

"Is this a voluntary plea?"

"Yes."

"Are you pleading because you are guilty or for some other reason?"

Schmid stared at the floor, then looked up at the bench.

"Because I am guilty," he said.

The judge tentatively set the date for sentencing for June 2, 1967. But Bailey asked that Schmid be given psychiatric examinations. "My position," Bailey said, "is that the defendant is in need of such help."

Tinney also asked for "a few days to contemplate the issue and talk with the experts whom we plan to consult."

The jurors were excused. Court was adjourned; Schmid was handcuffed and led from the courtroom.

Immediately following the session, Bailey gave an interview at the Tucson Press Club, one block from the courthouse. Tinney was at his side but remained silent. When asked what effect Schmid's plea would have on his career, Bailey replied, "What the hell has this got to do with my career? I can't see where this has anything to do with my win-loss record. It just doesn't apply. An attorney's first concern is adequately defending his client, you fellows can't see beyond a win-loss record to the defense of a client. Justice means guilty people should plead or be convicted and the innocent should be acquitted. That's what we've done in this case. My career has nothing to do with it."

He suspected that Schmid was guilty, Bailey said, despite a lie-detector test that Bailey had administered which showed Schmid was telling the truth when he said he was innocent, contradicting what he had said in court.

Bailey was asked whether they had difficulty in convincing Schmid to plead guilty.

"I wouldn't say we had to argue with him," Bailey said with a smile. "Pleading guilty was not a decision of mine to make. He had to decide." As the trial date approached, Bailey said, he became more convinced that Schmid was guilty. "Yes," he said confidently, "I knew he was guilty before the trial started. I let the state present its evidence to show the defendant what he was up against." He told the newsmen he first mentioned a change in plea Friday at the close of court. "I just mentioned it in passing. This morning I put it to him as a serious proposal. He took it without an argument. He had been giving it a lot of thought." Bailey continued, "We had to *let* him see the state's evidence before he would decide, though. As long as he could sit in his cell and think that counsel could magically make the witnesses go away, he was reluctant to plead. I wouldn't say we had to argue with him, though."

"Mr. Bailey," a reporter asked, "most if not all the facts printed about the case were eventually admitted in the trials, surely Schmid was well aware of the state's evidence long before your arrival here in Tucson?"

Bailey shrugged. He stressed that he had received no pay for his services, and had found the trial "financially disastrous, but pleasant in most other respects." He said Schmid was sick and needed psychiatric help, adding that anyone who committed an irrational crime was mentally unsound.

"Miss French's testimony would have been corroborated, and furthermore, I felt that the jury was behind her," Bailey said. "What I'm worried about now is the corrosive effect this might have on him in regard to the Fritz case."

Several hours later at the Tucson airport, Bailey gave a last-minute interview with a reporter before he took off in his Lear jet. He said he knew Schmid was guilty about the third time he talked to him, and that it was Schmid's decision to plead guilty "based on the advice of his counsel under the circumstances of the case at the moment."

The reporter asked, "How did you get a second-degree from Schafer?"

"Oh, I think he felt it was the wisest course in the best interest of the county. If I'd been the prosecutor I would certainly agree. The trial was costing a lot of money, the appeal, it would cost several hundred thousand dollars and probably would have gone to another retrial."

"Do you consider this case a loss?"

"A guilty man pleads guilty, he can't be considered a loss to anyone." Then, minutes later, F. Lee Bailey flew away.

The writer was discussing the case with County Attorney Schafer while both were attending a small party. "The first time they offered me the deal," he said to a friend, "I turned it down because I wasn't sure what they were up to." Then, he said, two days later on the last day of jury selection, Tinney again mentioned Schmid pleading guilty. Schafer had said, "Yeah, okay," but nothing came of it until Saturday. "The reason I accepted their deal," Schafer said, "was because I really doubted that the jury would vote for the death penalty when there wasn't a body." Second-degree meant keeping Schmid in prison that much longer. "And just to hear him say it in a public arena was worth it. But I just can't figure out how in the world they got him to plead guilty."

Schafer said that Mary French was still in love with Schmid and he, Schafer, was never sure if she'd testify, right up to the moment when she was seated on the witness stand. But the most important reason for accepting the deal was, Schafer said, "If the Fritz case conviction is reversed and we have to retry it, we couldn't have referred to the Rowe murder." One of the points on Schmid's appeal was that the evidence concerning the Rowe case was wrongly introduced as evidence in the Fritz case. "The defense argued at the Fritz trial that the Rowe case should not have been admitted because Schmid hadn't been tried and he hadn't been convicted of it. Without Schmid's guilt being established in the Rowe matter, there would be very little if any evidence in a Fritz case retrial because there would be no motive."

No sooner had Schmid returned to County Jail on Saturday than he seized upon a new strategy which he would confide only to Sheriff Burr. He started talking about a "sellout" by Tinney and Bailey. He trusted no one, not even his parents, because "they went along with Tinney and Bailey's sellout."

Dan Sakall, the adult probation officer assigned to Schmid's presentencing report, listened to Schmid along with the sheriff, who had "little use for Bailey." Sheriff Burr thought the lawyer was "looking for an easy way out when he saw his shiny armor getting dented."

For several days the sheriff talked with Schmid. He said candidly that Schmid had told him "the whole story," except where Alleen Rowe was buried.

"Schmid's story makes some sense," Sheriff Burr said, "he's got some facts on his side. He's real friendly and talkative, except when the talk gets around to the body. He clams up, gives a blank look, or says, 'I'd like to help but I don't know.'"

Schafer said he was not sure if Schmid even knew where the body was. He said he would ask Tinney for Schmid's cooperation in finding the remains. "Bailey said to me on Saturday that he thinks Schmid knows where the body is, but wasn't sure."

Tinney replied that he didn't know if Schmid "knows where it is. However, I will do anything that is reasonable."

On Saturday, Tinney spent a few minutes with Schmid at the jail. He then told the sheriff of Schmid's confession to Bailey. Sheriff Burr recalled that "when I lightly called the lawyer on the contradiction [of who suggested the plea], Tinney just gave a grin and I dropped the subject."

Schmid sent handwritten letters to both Bailey and Tinney, dismissing them as his attorneys, then sent a thirty-eight page writ to Judge Roylston, asking for a new trial. Schmid cited, "The use of extreme mental coercing instigated by Mr. Bailey and followed through by co-counsel Mr. Tinney, in highly persuasive and misleading tactics utilized to direct a plea of guilty on the defendant." He stated that on various occasions both attorneys had said to him, "We'll do just enough to protect the record for an appeal and nothing else. You haven't a chance, Smitty, give it up. You know you're guilty, you can't hold on much longer, you're a sick man. Do you want to kill your mother?"

Pleading guilty to second degree was not done by free choice, Schmid said, and Bailey had expressed a desire to "get the damned thing over with." Schmid noted the denial for change of venue and that after denying him reassurance of an effective, adequate defense, his attorneys "set about to demolish his resistance to the guilty plea," and that he agreed with them finally "out of fear, fear of an attorney possessing godlike powers of destruction," and fears of "mentally murdering my beloved parents by the ensuing litigation." Schmid said he now fully expected both Bailey and Tinney to pull out of the appeal on the Fritz case.

Then, in outlining a plan for a final move to prove his innocence, Schmid said: "By the recovery of said corpse, evidence will become apparent that death did not occur by cranium mutilation, bashing, stoning, or any other direct process in which a heavy blunt object was utilized to crush the skull, but in fact occurred when Mr. Schmid heard Miss Rowe scream and returned to find her lying prone on the ground, partially stripped of clothing, and dead from the strangling effects of Mr. Saunders's hands."

Schmid said that he was aware that "Mr. Saunders suffered a severe sexual repression that resulted in his actions," but for which Schmid felt that "Saunders does not deserve to die."

Further, "The defendant gladly risks his life for an attempt to remove the fog enveloping and distorting the truth," he said. "The defendant does not ask for reappointment of counsel and will gladly accept the responsibility of defense in solitude, if necessary, thus saving the taxpayers added burden. But in the interest of truth, intrinsic to justice, grant him this opportunity to fight."

Charging that Bailey told him his case was "hopeless under sagebrush justice," Schmid accused him of a "breach of confidentiality, an irresponsible attitude and general disinterest, deceivement [sic], and the deliberate coercing of the defendant for purposes valuable to Mr. Bailey, and detrimental to the defendant during a time in which the defendant was unable to resist."

Schmid sent a copy of the writ to the *Citizen*, waiving publication rights. "Publicity," said a reporter, "is a two-edged sword."

Tinney declined to comment on Schmid's allegations, and Bailey could not be reached.

Upon receipt of the document, Roylston said he would treat Schmid's "accusations that he was coerced into pleading guilty as a motion to withdraw his plea." He said he would hear Schmid's request for a new trial and "all other pending matters" at nine o'clock Monday morning, June 12, the time for sentencing.

Schmid contacted former Deputy County Attorney William Healy and asked him to take over his defense. Healy refused, saying it would constitute a conflict of interest since he represented the county at the time the Fritz case began. Another attorney also refused the case. Saunders's new lawyer had requested that his hearing transcript against Schmid be kept secret. Appearing before Judge Roylston, Schafer opposed this motion and also asked that Schmid's request to withdraw his guilty plea be denied, citing in his memorandum that: "Apparently the sole basis for the defendant's request is the allegation that his lawyers coerced him into such a plea. Aside from a personal denouncement of Mr. Bailey, the defendant in no way shows that anyone forced him to plead guilty. Schmid not only told the court that he had not been coerced or promised anything, but that he had killed Alleen Rowe and that he pleaded 'because I'm guilty.'" Schafer felt that Schmid's motion to withdraw his plea "seems more an outgrowth of the realization that now he will have to pay for his own confessed acts."

In private, Schafer was still uncertain as to what had happened. He believed that Schmid would not have received the death sentence, and said, "I really can't figure out why Charlie entered that plea. Without the body, I wouldn't have done it if I was in his place."

A man who "grew airsick at the thought of flight," Schafer kept thinking of Kansas City, where he had flown to twice to interview a witness during his preparation for the Rowe trial. With an astonished look, Schafer said, "Neither Bailey nor Tinney seemed interested in what my witnesses were going to say. They didn't even question them. Bailey asked me to write up what my witnesses were going to say and he'd stipulate to all of it. 'All of it?' I asked him. He said, 'Sure, just write it up.' It took me about three hours to type it up and he stipulated to it."

Sometime before the trial began, Schafer had telephoned county attorneys in other states to consult with them concerning the Boston attorney. "Now," Schafer said, "he seemed to have other things on his mind. He was tricky but it was all surface." According to Schafer, he felt that if he had put up a fight, he would only have camouflaged Bailey's inadequacy. "Here I was planning for a war, and I didn't even get an argument," Schafer said. "So I let him play it out on his own." But the prosecutor had not counted on such an abrupt halt to the activity. "When they asked me if I'd take second degree, I thought 'Holy Cow, do they realize what they're doing?' I didn't believe them, and I didn't let on that I was shocked. So I sort of sat back and waited for whatever was going to happen."

Since the trial, Tinney had publicly praised Schafer's handling of the case, saying that each time a defense motion was made Schafer had one or more legal citations to support the state's position.

The court finally appointed attorney William Scanland to represent Schmid's interests, and he appeared with Schmid on June 19, for sentencing.

Judge Roylston first questioned two psychiatrists, Dr. Cutts and Dr. Abbuhl. Both testified that in their opinion the defendant knew "right from wrong," knew the nature and quality of his acts, and was mentally able to assist counsel in his own behalf.

When asked whether Schmid knew the nature of the proceedings against him when he made his plea, Dr. Cutts replied that he had no definite opinion and "could only make an educated guess."

Replying to the same question, Dr. Abbuhl said that Schmid "probably did understand the nature of the proceedings against him on May 20." He said that he had talked to Schmid twice, "for about forty-five minutes the first time on May 29, and for about an hour the second time on June 5." Answering a question from Scanland, Dr. Abbuhl said that Schmid had refused to submit to psychological tests. Judge Roylston interjected that Schmid had also refused to submit to tests from court-appointed psychologists on two occasions.

After the two psychiatrists had finished testifying, Judge Roylston said that he was prepared to hear Schmid's motion to withdraw his guilty plea. Scanland promptly announced that the defendant "asks that his motion be abandoned and withdrawn."

Roylston asked Schmid if there had been any promises or threats made in connection with his decision to withdraw his motion.

Schmid paused for a few seconds, shook his head and murmured, "No." Asked if his decision was voluntary, he wiped his nose with the back of his sleeve and said, "Yes." Then Scanland asked that Schmid's "writ to withdraw his plea be stricken from the record and destroyed."

The judge denied the request to destroy the document and ordered it sealed, "not to be opened except by order of the court."

Referring to the psychiatric hearing, that Schmid was legally sane, the judge ruled that the defendant was eligible for sentence. "Is there anything you wish to advise the court of before sentencing, Mr. Scanland?"

The attorney asked for court appointment of other psychiatrists for further examinations, but the request was denied. Judge Roylston then asked if there was any legal reason why Schmid should not be sentenced. Scanland said the only other reason would be "for a pre-sentence hearing for mitigation."

"I will consider any matters for mitigation at this time," the judge said, but Scanland replied that he had "nothing at this time." Judge Roylston then asked Schmid if he had anything to say before sentence was passed upon him.

Schmid stood up so abruptly it started Scanland. His face twitching slightly, Schmid said, "No."

Roylston then pronounced the sentence. Fifty years to life imprisonment at the Arizona State Penitentiary.

Tears in his eyes, in a barely audible voice, Schmid asked the judge if he could reject the sentence. "I would prefer death."

There was no statutory provision for rejecting the sentence. Schmid was handcuffed and led from the courtroom.

Under this sentence, Schafer said, Schmid would be eligible for parole in about thirty years, and with the Rowe case concluded (minus the body), the prosecution moved ahead to oppose anticipated litigation in the appeal of Schmid's death sentences in the Fritz case. Schafer asserted that Schmid's withdrawal of the coercion claim might hurt his appeal in the Fritz case. "The next step for us," Schafer said, "is the Fritz appeal. We will now await the filing of the defense's initial brief. We don't know exactly what we will have to respond to until we see their brief. But we do know from the first trial that one of the main contentions was the connection between the Fritz and Rowe cases. The defendant claimed at that time [during the Fritz trial], that he had not killed the Rowe girl, thus making no reason for killing Gretchen." The county attorney then emphasized: "He has not only pleaded guilty and been sentenced for killing Miss Rowe, but there is no doubt whatsoever that he did kill the Rowe girl. The withdrawal of the motion that he was coerced into pleading guilty removed all doubt from the matter."

But Schafer still wondered about the development of Schmid's guilty plea. He asked a confidant of Schmid's, and was told: "It wasn't difficult. Schmid was convinced that *you* had offered the deal in hopes of ending a costly trial, that you were being fair as it would be his only way to escape the gas. If he didn't accept your deal, he'd be dead in ninety days."

"How would he be dead?" Schafer asked.

"Because of the introduction of the Fritz case into the Rowe trial. He was led to understand that such evidence would automatically kill his appeal in the Fritz case, and as a result he'd be dead in ninety days—the death sentence carried out."

Schafer looked bewildered. "I've never heard of such a thing. My god! I don't even know how something like that could *work* legally!"

Attorney Scanland, after filing notice of appeal as his last official act for Schmid, requested that he be allowed to withdraw from the case.

At the County Jail, Schmid now refused to see any visitors except Sheriff Burr and Dan Sakall. On Friday morning, June 23,

1967, Schmid told Sakall, "I want to lead the authorities to the grave of Alleen Rowe."

Sheriff Burr got in touch with Judge Roylston and received court approval to have Schmid search for the body. Two lawyers present at the jail were asked to accompany the search party as impartial witnesses. Both consented. Smitty's past personal manager was, at Smitty's request, accompanied, but chose to remain at a distance.

Wearing a white shirt, dark trousers, hands manacled in front, Schmid climbed into the back seat of a deputy's car and smoked casually as they drove to the desert area off Harrison Road.

In the blinding sunlight, Schmid walked out into the desert to an arroyo about 300 yards south of Golf Links Road and a quarter of a mile east of Harrison, accompanied by Dan Sakall and the sheriff.

Schmid indicated two sites as the possible grave, but subsequent quick digging with his hands uncovered nothing. Then, appearing to recall something, he scrambled up the slope of the wash, glanced around, and pointed to a gnarled Palo Verde tree.

"That's the spot," he said. "I'm sure now."

The spot he pointed to was only fifty yards from the area John Saunders and Mary French had led police to, which had precipitated twenty months of amateur digging, earth moving equipment and teams of professional archeologists.

Schmid hurried across the rocky wash, carrying the shovel, and dug as well as he could with his wrists handcuffed, moving away a layer of sandy earth, then a few more shovelfuls and suddenly one knee joint was uncovered, then the pelvis of the skeleton, approximately six inches below the top layer of a shallow grave, seemed to rise to the surface

Pathologist Edward Brucker arrived and he, Schmid, and Sakall probed the area until they uncovered the skull, the jaws parted wide and the cavity packed with sand. Three years and twenty-three days since the night of her disappearance, Alleen Rowe was finally found.

Sheriff Burr brushed the bones with a whiskbroom. Spectators were gathering to view the half-clad skeleton. "We came as fast as we could," a woman said, "as soon as we heard the news."

"Daddy, there's the head," a small boy said. "Where's the rest of it?"

"Don't worry," his father replied. "They'll dig it up, you'll see it," and he hoisted the kid onto his shoulders so he could see the grave.

On his knees, Schmid, his wrists manacled, cradled the skull in his hands and said excitedly to Brucker, "You see? There's no cranium damage, no contusions to the skull."

The rubber soles of the tennis shoes on the feet of the skeleton had rotted, but her black bathing suit was well preserved. Reporters and newsmen started to arrive and television cameramen shot close-ups of the skull. Burr held the skull in his hand for the cameras, then passed it to Walter Birkby, an anthropologist from the university, who said he couldn't tell immediately if the skull had been fractured.

"There's no fractures," Schmid insisted, squatting alongside Burr and the pathologist. Schmid stood up and stared at a man holding a child and said pointedly, "I think it's shameful that people bring kids to see a thing like this."

Brucker disjoined the lower jaw from the skull, then placed all the bones into three cardboard boxes.

The professionals and the condemned hiked back to their parked cars. Smitty's *confidant* had been sitting next to the grave; a photographer took his picture, and the *confidant* abruptly got up and headed to his car.

By Saturday morning, an autopsy and detailed X-rays revealed fractures at the base of the skull. There was no evidence of damage to the cervical vertebrae. The area around the fractures was coated with dried blood, indicating that the fractures were induced while Alleen Rowe was still alive. A rock found near the skull was also examined and blood specks were found on its sharp end. The rock was included in the closetful of papers and accumulated objects that made up the closed Alleen Rowe file.

Back at Pima County Jail, Sheriff Burr told the *confidant*,

"Charlie doesn't have any regrets about anything he's done. He doesn't feel sorrow, not even remorse. I don't even think he feels pain. He doesn't like anybody, and says that he has no close ties with anybody. He says he never, never has been close to anyone."

EPILOGUE

THE DAY SCHMID uncovered the body, I received a phone call late at night from a television newsman I knew. The films of Schmid showing the grave and Burr holding up the skull had appeared on the evening news. "So Burr and Sakall wooed old Charlie," the newsman said. "I figured they'd convince him that only *he* could set the record straight. They must have worked pretty skillfully on him."

It had come to an end, all but the appeals and the waiting, perhaps the years of reviewing the volumes of transcripts that included some twenty-odd books of pretrial publicity. But it was over.

A few days later I saw Schmid at the penitentiary. He was playing badminton with three other Death Row inmates. I spoke to him through the high wire fence. He looked different. Smaller, perhaps, older.

"I'm not stupid," he said. "If I had known her head was broken like that I would never have taken them out there." The difference I'd noticed was especially true of his eyes. They were clearer, but they still betrayed nothing of whatever he felt—if, in fact, he felt anything. As he absently thrust the handle of his racket through the mesh of the fence, he smiled slightly and said, "If I did it, I'd like to find out why. The answer might help somebody else." He winked.

The two death sentences and fifty-to-life term had anchored

him firmly behind those old territorial walls outside Florence. He was a *dead man*, condemned to the gas chamber. But even there, bunched in with the others also awaiting the gas, Smitty was the the stranger. He moved in his own path, revealing little of the churning—the pending confrontation with his own extinction. Those that he sidled up to when he thought they might prove useful in some way, saw only the articulate shell that was Smitty, the "mask," as it were.

He wrote about the life-mask he'd made of himself, shortly before he'd been arrested at his house on Adams. He'd poured a five-pound bag of plaster of Paris into a big bowl borrowed from Hillcrest, mixed in water, and then poured this into a large cookie tin with about a two-inch rim. He'd let this harden slightly, just soft enough to push a finger into it. Then, having coated his face with Vaseline, he bent over the tin and pressed his features into the plaster. Holding his breath for several moments, he then brought his face up slowly and backwards from the hardening plaster. There it was—the impression of his face. He let it harden more, then picked it up and tipped it one way and then the other. It took on a three-dimensional quality.

Smitty wrote:

> I saw it, the instructions to do this in a book one time on making puppets. How you could fashion your own puppet. I'd been thinking of making some Elvis puppets. You had to first make the head and then the body was something else. You had to make it out of material—cloth, and wires. Maybe just being so bothered with the Morgens and the upholstery business got me thinking back on things, like when I'd been a kid. I had a sort of puppet, one of those hand puppets you stick your hand in and make them wiggle their hands and their arms. I don't remember the head of it. Maybe it was an animal. It might've been a lion,

> some kind of lion, and it had a grey rag body. I used to put it on my hand and growl.

When the plaster impression of Smitty's face had dried, he wadded the concave impression with wood putty. "Plastic wood putty," he'd noted. He had to push it in hard and make sure it was embedded into every indentation. He wanted the duplication of his face to be perfect.

Finally, when the putty was hard and dry, Smitty used a "ball-headed hammer" to break apart the plaster mold.

"What I had in mind was a joke," he wrote. "Like fixing it up on a dummy's body and hanging it in the closet, like I'd hanged myself. Calling Gretchen over and saying I'm going to kill myself, and by the time she'd get there I'd be dead." Leaving the closet door open enough to arouse anyone to look further, they'd open the door, he said, and find him *hanged.* First, he'd had to put the finishing touches to the mask—sanding lightly, painting eyebrows, lips, the eyelashes. "I became so disturbed in doing this, I had to stop it. I looked at what I'd done and said, 'This is a mask of death.' I'd fashioned my own death mask. I'd created the mask of the death of myself."

It came to Smitty that if in fact he had managed such a mystical action—"lf someone could transpose their spirits to a mask-like a totem—then one's death takes in everything they are and they are no longer bothered by the implications of their actions. Something like that is what struck me like a white lightening [sic] bolt and I thought, 'Then this must be protected,' and it wasn't for a joke anymore—no more of Gretchen and Richie or anyone. Instead it was a joke on the Universe."

For a month he'd kept the mask hidden in the little bedroom, on Adams, underneath a bunch of old clothes he never wore anymore. "And then," Smitty said, "it was like something was taken away from me. Sort of lifted off of me. I can't explain what it was but I never thought about it again because I knew I had accomplished something in the same way a medicine man accomplishes something."

Inmate Robert Gleason was one of those few that Smitty "sniffed out," as Gleason puts it. No stranger to prison walls, and a few years older than Schmid, Gleason had been in and out of Arizona State Prison, "like I was on a revolving, rubber platform." Gleason was serving ten-to-twenty on a murder conviction, stemming from an attempted robbery. He claimed to know his way around, knew more than most, was an avid reader and ran a floating library, exchanging for cigarettes and favors. "I loaned books to Schmid," he says. "He wanted to read Dostoevsky's book, *Crime and Punishment.* Or so he claimed he read it, and maybe the parts he did read intrigued him very much. While I don't think he had an overall or concrete picture of the story from a literary sense, he said he couldn't identify with the killer who was driven by the guilt of his crime."

Not having an overall picture of anything, Gleason felt, was a clear reflection of Schmid's personality. "I got to see that pretty quick," he says, "because of my experience with people in prison." Schmid didn't have the discipline to go very far. Lots of discipline when it came to self-figured or self-assigned physical things. He worked so hard at the physical side of himself that he was almost like a person with superhuman strength. He did one-arm push-ups and stunts like that. Few could do them, but there was only like a little part of his thinking that dealt with his surroundings. What I'm saying is Schmid adjusted to prison life only on the physical side. The rest of him was somewheres else—that part that had never surrendered, like someone with a fever that never leaves them, never lets them get back into any situation with their normal surroundings."

One couldn't get at that part of Smitty, and the penitentiary couldn't take it away from him. "It's something that has to be surrendered," Gleason says.

"What happens is you fall apart," he says. "You erode with the very thing you won't surrender. It turns into a poison that spreads through you—slowly, but turns you black like you've been burned."

Smitty didn't worry about the gas chamber or his own death. "I don't think there are many others who talked about it or saw it the same as Smitty." For him it was something of a burden, an inconvenience, like it was an interruption of that world he carried privately. "He wasn't afraid of it," Gleason says, but maybe he should've been. Smitty told the older inmate he'd take the gas if the execution could be televised.

"He felt that his trials had been unfair, and his sentences had been unfair. He'd go on about the unfairness with all these three-buck words he used that made his speeches bloom up like a chef's salad. A lot of others didn't want to listen to him. He had reasons worked out for everything, and it seemed to all boil down, as Schmid put it, to his being a perfect guy in an imperfect society populating an imperfect world. He said, 'look to the universe—to the heavens, not the hells.'

"The thing about the killer in *Crime and Punishment,* was that Smitty wasn't driven by any guilt complexes. He experienced no guilt about anything he'd ever done—only the mistakes he'd made personally that caused him inconveniences. If you were to open up his head like cutting a melon in half, you'd see why he told me he didn't think about sex so much as he thought about killing. He'd been joking, he said, but you'd see in there that he hadn't been joking at all. He *thought* about the killings he'd done. Ran them back in his head like you'd play a tape over and over. Personally, I feel that was at the root of his ideas of busting out. Just talked about it like you'd talk about anything—passing time. Nobody knew what Schmid had in mind when he badgered the warden about getting an exercise horse so Schmid could stay in shape. Maybe the warden figured Schmid'd get in such good shape that they'd hold some gymnastic competition," Gleason says. "It was a pretty big concession by the prison."

But the exercise horse was only a step in Schmid's plan to escape. He hollowed out the horse and rigged a door at one end so he could slip himself into it, then close the door. "No one knew anything about it before it happened," Gleason says. "Smitty rigged up his own Trojan horse. The guys didn't know he was hiding inside it when they came to take the horse back to the warehouse where it was stored when not in use."

Schmid's plan had been to hide in the warehouse until he could manage getting out of the warehouse. But he was missed sooner than expected and a search was made, ending with Schmid being found, hiding in a warehouse closet.

Though trouble fell hard on Schmid for the attempted escape, his efforts were enthusiastically admired by another young death row inmate, Robert Benjamin Smith, convicted of multiple murder.

A thin, pretty-faced, effete boy, Smith had made a name for himself the summer following Schmid's trial for the Fritz murders. Smith had been a high school senior in Mesa, Arizona, and later said he decided to kill people because he wanted to "get known, just wanted to make a name for myself."

Obsessed with Schmid's trial, and with killers Charles Whitman and Richard Speck, Smith left his house one day in November carrying nylon rope, plastic sandwich bags, two knives, and a .22 pistol which his parents had given him. Less than two miles from his home, he entered the Rose-Mar College of Beauty, brandished the gun but was ignored. He fired a shot which shattered a mirror, then ordered five women and two children into a back room.

One woman, trying to dissuade him, said, "There'll be forty people here in five minutes!"

Smith said, "I'm sorry, but I didn't bring enough ammunition for them."

His plan had been to bind the women, tie the plastic bags over their heads and watch them suffocate. But when the sandwich bags wouldn't fit over their heads, he forced them to lie on the floor in a circle, their heads toward the middle. He then shot them, stabbing one woman who tried to get away. When the police arrived, Smith was there—standing over the bodies. Two were dead and three died later, including a three-year-old girl.

Smith laughingly confessed to the killings. He was "smart," one officer said, "but jittery, girl-shy, and he supports germ warfare." It was reported that at the funeral for the victims, a preacher standing over the coffins said, "It was God's will."

While waiting to be executed, Smith and Schmid became friendly, the two claiming ownership of a "real life Homer the rat"—a jailhouse mouse that Smith kept in a cardboard box.

"That Smith character," Gleason says, "gave one the feeling that he was a punk—a faggot, and he was disliked strongly, maybe only a little more than Smitty who was disliked in a different way. Schmid threatened people because of his ideas of superiority, and a lot of the political—penitentiary politics—advantages he'd exercise like he'd taken them on for himself." Smitty still couldn't shake the idea of breaking out of prison. He confided that it obsessed him, *drove* him, and he formed a "suicide pact" with Robert Smith.

"That followed the situation with the mouse—or rat," Gleason says. "Some others got it and cut its legs off and sent it back in on string," a message to Smitty he failed to heed in his try for a "suicide" with Smith. While he later confided that it "hardly mattered if he (Smith) bled to death, I knew that once in the hospital I'd manage a break successfully. " While they attempted to pare at themselves with blades, neither Smith nor Smitty suffered more than superficial wounds that were bandaged in the hospital. Without Smitty's being bedded on a ward, the escape plan failed to materialize.

"Schmid would talk about the girls he'd had—a real lover boy," says Stanley Wess, another Death Row resident, recalling Schmid. "He'd talk about the crowd he'd ran with and the parties they'd had, like he was still that same guy, and a bunch of bum breaks separated him from the life he'd been living on the outside—back along East Speedway, a guitar and some chick in a sharp car. " Wess claims that Schmid hated prison. "Not that anybody *likes* it here, but Smitty had the color of a guy who hates it. It shows on you—turns you a color. You learn to live or you learn to die. Most guys learn not to hate it but to live out the hand you've been dealt. Very few guys die."

But Schmid was a *dead man,* says Gleason, "dead through to

his bones and you knew it by walking around with him and what he gave off with the others. He was a sort of leper."

"Even after he beat the gas by the moratorium on death sentences—like Charles Manson and every other guy on death row. Everybody was commuted from death to, life, but Schmid was still the *dead man* walking through it, like they say, 'Dead man coming through...'

"It didn't mean anything that he was going to live instead of die. The fact of getting the gas never played much of a part in his *real* scheme of thinking. Schmid lived out 'there' and in that place inside of himself that no one could get at. You were supposed to shrink your circumferences," Gleason says. "I'd tell him that. But the reason he couldn't was because he never took the medicine they dished out. A lot of guys feel they got what was coming—they know the score, even if they don't admit it right out. They have to get it worked out like the guy in *Crime and Punishment,* and they don't make any bones about it once it's been dished out."

Smitty felt he *owed* nothing. He'd talk any line if it suited his purposes, and he "ran over others," as Gleason puts it, without feeling he owed anyone anything.

"What he'd done, the crimes he'd committed, were okay with him but what was happening to *him* was a rotten shame—an inconvenience of the worst kind.

"He couldn't see that he was paying a price, and that the price asked of him was more than he'd ever have in *his* pocket, for what *he'd* done. The killings cost him more than he could afford at the time that he did them, but he *bought* it and did them. The law says you have to pay. You play the game, you pay the piper like it says. But Smitty didn't see it that way."

By 1972, Smitty figured he'd paid enough. Six years for three murders was enough. After all, he wrote, he was still not claiming responsibility for Alleen Rowe's murder. He blamed John Saunders for the killing, and claimed that he himself had only made the decision to bury the body. As concerned the girls—Gretchen and Wendy—Schmid said he had blacked out. He didn't know what had happened, but when he “came to consciousness,” there were the bodies in his house. He knew he’d have to haul them out to the desert.

Gleason says, “We talked a couple of times in private conversation, and I’d say to myself, ‘How do such guys get into this world?’ He was saying how it was a gross miscarriage of justice, a ‘travesty on fairness.’ He’d take the blame for having made the mistake, he’d say, and he didn’t condone what he’d done exactly, but he clearly believed that his system of dues-to-be-paid was different from mine, from the rest of us behind bars.

“He’d go before the parole board, put on the old Smitty charm that all the gals had gone for, and he’d present himself as deserving another chance. He liked talking about it that way, putting it that way—*another chance*.”

But there was no way for Schmid to see that he’d used up his chance. His big break had been with the moratorium and beating ‘the little house’. He got *life*. But he wasn’t interested in getting a break—he wanted reedom.

“‘Haven’t I paid enough?’ he’d cry to the board, trying to get across to them his ‘intellectual accomplishments,’ as he’d call them. But they’d want to hear about the murders.

“‘They wanted to hear horror stories,’ Smitty told me,” Gleason says. “They didn’t want to hear about what he’d done in stir to improve himself or how smart he was or how clever he thought he was. They wanted to hear about the blood and the guts.

“They’d say no, he hadn’t paid enough. He’d put on the suffering act and wink with one of those well-lubricated eyes—kidding, he’d be kidding. Putting them on. And he still wouldn’t let loose of the idea of busting out.”

It seemed to Gleason and Smith, and to others, that Schmid wasn’t bothered by talk of the killings. He enjoyed the sense that he’d had life or death at the tips of his fingers. In his hands. He only wanted the parole board to believe that rehashing such matters was more than painful to him.

He’d talked to Gleason about the mask he’d made of himself,

explaining that he'd "killed" himself years ago—"inside of myself," he'd said. He laughed once, saying he'd had a death mask of himself so he could "view" himself in death. Confessing that he'd made it as a joke, he said he stuffed pants and a shirt with dirty laundry and rigged the "scarecrow" on a broom, with the wood putty face mounted at the top, "rigged through the head of the broom."

Gleason says, "I asked him if he'd told the parole board about the dummy and he gave me one of those looks. He said the girl he'd married not long before he was busted had found the face in a drawer one night and thought for a second it was a dead person's face he'd carved off someone's body and had it hidden. Even though there wasn't any blood in the drawer, the girl *saw* red, saw what she thought was rotten blood and screamed blue murder. Smitty said he thought that scare was one of the reasons she divorced him while he was in the jug." Another reason he didn't mention such things to the parole board, he said, was "because somebody'd get the idea I haven't got sufficient guilt feelings about the past." He told Gleason he replied to the board with what he believed they wanted to hear—"just like I've told everybody." His performance with the parole board demanded that Arizona give him his freedom. The fact was simply that he had no freedom. He confided to killer Smith that if his demands were not met, he'd simply have to take it upon himself to "change the course of events."

On November 11, 1972, Smitty tried another escape. This time he made it, along with another inmate. Gleason remembers "the other guy he busted out with split up from Smitty near Phoenix. Practically everyone in the state had been alerted to the breakout. In fact, the cops down in Tucson had police protection at the homes of those people who'd testified against Smitty at the trials."

It was a Monday afternoon, and Schmid was sneaking through the Phoenix train yards, trying to catch a freight heading south to Tucson. He ran into a drifter who at first failed to recognize Schmid, and together they slept in a ditch waiting to hop the morning freight train.

Schmid had found a blonde wig, a garish yellow bouffant style that clashed starkly with his darker skin and quickly-sprouting, black beard stubble. With the wig on his head and the drifter at his side, Schmid spent the day and a half tracking a ride to Tucson. He had hoped to find some of his old friends in Tucson who might help him get to California.

Though the drifter later claimed he did not know it was Schmid he was running with, he would have future stories to tell about Smitty's complaints to do with prison—and with his escape attempts. Schmid had an option, he told the drifter. If he couldn't get help from his old Tucson chums, he'd hop a train to Yuma and from there make it across into Mexico where he could hide "and take it easy."

A Southern Pacific employee named Bill Lanier was working the switching yards the following morning when he noticed "two guys standing between two diesel engines. It was that weird yellow wig," Lanier says. "Maybe I would've just went on and not paid attention, but it was so grotesque I had to look at the guy, and I just looked at him *because* of that fruitcake wig. And getting a look, my knees went weak. It was Charles Schmid. I'd gone to school with the guy— everybody knew he'd escaped from prison."

Pretending that he hadn't noticed the pair, Lanier turned away, "like I hadn't seen them—like I didn't care who they were—just a couple of bums, but I went back to the line telephone and called the cops. It was just a little after six in the morning."

Responding to the call from the railroad yards, Tactical Operations Officer Barry Headricks told another policeman, Wayne Inman, that he couldn't believe it was Smitty. "I competed against the guy in gymnastics back in high school. He was so good," Headricks says, "he was a powerhouse. He could've been one of the best gymnasts in the United States."

At the freight yards, the officers spotted Schmid and the drifter beside a shack near the field at Aviation and Country Club Roads. As the officers approached the two, Smitty was the first to speak. "How you doing?" he asked.

"Well," Headricks said, "where you heading?"

Smitty said, "Just trying to hop a freight to Yuma. Is it all right if we do that?"

"Yeah..." Headricks said. "It's okay," and he talked for a minute more, turning sideways enough to free his revolver without Smitty noticing. "Then I stuck the gun in their faces," Headricks says, and shouted, "Freeze!"

"Don't shoot!" Smitty yelled, throwing up his hands. "Don't shoot us!"

The police wanted to know about the other prisoner that had escaped and broke off in Phoenix, but Smitty said, "I'm a convict. I don't say anything. I don't talk."

By that afternoon, Schmid was back in Florence behind the prison walls. This time placed in maximum security. "Then," says Gleason, "from that point on he seemed to do a turnaround—became two kinds of guys, pushing himself further while walking on others to do it. He said in solitary he made the decision to play it by their game, work things from the inside. He was going to be a smart guy, and this means going political. In a prison that makes you someone dangerous. You can't be trusted by those around you. It means that someone's going to kill you. "

He changed his name to Paul David Ashley and wore his hair shoulder-length for a while. He wrote music, essays—complaints and predictions. He envisioned proving that God did not exist, and by mastering himself, man therefore *became* the master. A power above law and order. Schmid claimed to some that he could "legislate" law and order. What some began to sense or suspect was that Schmid now fancied himself "wielding an ultimate power over others."

He remembered every detail of the murders—how he'd killed Alleen Rowe and then the other two. Every moment of the killings was "right there in his head," says Robert Gleason. "It was like this was his secret, even though the world didn't care about the details he thought he knew, and he kept it with him like a secret weapon.

"He felt he'd paid already, but the parole board said he hadn't paid enough." Schmid raged against their "blindness," and against their "stupidity." Though he raged in a methodical, controlled manner, some inmates were saying Smitty's mouth was bigger than his brain. "He'd buttered his way from solitary to the Honor Dormitory," Gleason says. "He believed he was a big man. A lot of people didn't share his ideas about himself. He was small to them, small not only in the size of him which he made up for in muscular development."

Two inmates, Dennis Roy Eversole, and Jimmy Ferra, thought it might not be a bad idea to bring Smitty down a couple of notches.

It was Thursday afternoon shortly before 3:30 when Chief of Security Captain Dale Davis was notified to go to Dormitory One, of the Outside Trusty Area, where Schmid had been found badly cut up. Warden Harold Cardwell, Assistant Warden Dwight Carey, and another security guard found Schmid in a pool of blood on the cell floor. He had been stabbed a number of times in the face and body.

Within minutes, the prison doctor, the driver, and Assistant Warden Carey left with Schmid in the Arizona State Prison ambulance. The first stop was the Pinal County Hospital, where Schmid was admitted in shock and heavy bleeding from "sunk-in knife wounds to the chest," and knife wounds to the stomach and face. Following initial treatment and temporary closing of some of the wounds, Schmid was transferred to the emergency room of the Maricopa County General Hospital in Phoenix.

By nine thirty that night, Katharine and Charles Schmid Sr. were at the hospital, and a social worker had talked to Schmid to determine his emotional status and to "relieve any anxiety he may have had at that time."

Schmid underwent surgery that night and the following day, continuing to bleed profusely from what the doctors called "a sucking wound of the right chest." Drains were placed in the stomach wounds and transfusions continued while surgery was performed on his right eye, which had been penetrated by a knife blade. The severely damaged eyeball was removed from the socket and extensive surgery was performed to close the wound.

After the "crime scene" at the prison had been secured, Captain Davis was called back to the area. Bloody clothing and two shank knives had been found in a trash bunker. The clothes and weapons were placed in a box and locked in Warden Cardwell's car trunk.

Captain Davis reported "numbers on some of the articles of clothing, and these had what appeared to be blood on them."

Inmates Dennis Eversole and James Ferra were handcuffed and taken to the Warden's office, and at about 5:00 PM Davis read the Miranda warning to the inmates. "They stated they understood their rights and did not wish to talk to us," says Davis. Eversole and Ferra were then placed in Investigative Detention.

While an investigation was being conducted within the prison, Warden Cardwell received a report the following day from Maricopa County Hospital on Schmid's condition—"very critical."

Dwight Carey made a report on the "dying declaration" by Schmid, and Captain Davis took a statement from the prison staff physician, who referenced the dying declaration on tape to be transcribed and signed.

While the Pinal County Attorney and Deputy County Attorney inspected the evidence and crime scene at the prison, and were advised of the investigation to that point, Schmid's condition worsened. One of the surgeons said, "Any of the wounds suffered [by Schmid] could have caused the death of most individuals under these same set of circumstances. The amount of wounds and force of the attack might've appeared lethal at the moment, but the patient's general physical condition has been such that he's been able to pull through this far."

But despite Smitty's "built like a brick shithouse" strength, he began to fail quickly on the tenth day following the attack.

He was pronounced dead on March 30, 1975.

Convicted of Schmid's murder, Dennis Eversole was sentenced to ten to ten and one-half years, but was murdered in the same prison by another inmate the day after Christmas, three years after Schmid's murder.

James Ferra was sentenced to ten to twenty years, to be served concurrently with the life sentence he had received for another murder conviction. He was released on Parole for Life in 1982.

At the request of his parents, Schmid's body was returned to the prison and buried at the prison cemetery on April 2, 1975.

Graveside services were conducted by both Protestant and Catholic chaplains, again at the request of his parents. "I was there when they put him into the ground," Gleason says. "There'd been betting pools to see how long he'd last—how long it'd take him to die. A couple of others from the New Dorm were there as the diggers filled up the hole. It was Wendy Fritz, the little girl Smitty'd killed along with her sister, that I was thinking about that day. And it occurred to me that some magic circle had been formed—made something a whole, continuous thing. And it was over with. I thought, '*Now—now* Smitty's paid the price. It was all paid up."

ABOUT THE AUTHOR

Described by the *Sydney Morning Herald* as the "quintessential L.A. noir writer," John Gilmore has been acclaimed internationally for his true crime work, his literary fiction and Hollywood memoirs. As one of today's most controversial American writers, Gilmore boasts a following that spans the globe, from Hong Kong to his native Hollywood. He has traveled the road to fame in many guises: kid actor, stage and motion picture player, beatnik painter, poet, screenwriter, low-budget movie director, and novelist. His work has been translated into numerous languages. After heading the writing program at Antioch University in San Francisco, Gilmore taught and lectured extensively while producing an indelible mark in crime literature with *Severed: The True Story of the Black Dahlia Murder*, and *L.A. Despair: A Landscape of Crimes & Bad Times.* Gilmore lives in the Hollywood Hills, where he is at work on a major novel.

Also by John Gilmore from Amok Books

ON THE RUN WITH BONNIE AND CLYDE

Decades in the making, *On the Run With Bonnie & Clyde* is a fast moving and gut-wrenching, highly original exploration into the personalities of the star-crossed lovers and "public enemies" Bonnie Parker and Clyde Barrow. A thoroughly researched, in-depth study of the true natures of these notorious outlaws, *On the Run* breaks away from the usual police-blotter procedurals on these outlaw lovers.

Delving deep into their characters in his unique and uncompromising style, Gilmore places the reader squarely inside a stolen 1932 V-8 with the desperadoes on a dusty, two-year, devil-take-the-high-road spree of robberies, shoot-outs and murder. Through the dark windshield of legend, the short lives of these outlaw icons on a relentless ride to an infamous end—in a torrent of blood and bullets—emerge as unforgettably real. *On the Run* includes a controversial critical perspective of the unlawful ambush murder of Bonnie Parker, who was never officially accused of a violent crime.

"If you're going to read one book on Bonnie and Clyde, this is it - the most definitive work that brings the reader to the gritty reality of the era." - *Marshall Terrill*

ISBN: 1-878923-22-6 (trade paper)

$19.95, 368 pp., illustrated

Also by John Gilmore from Amok Books

L.A. DESPAIR

A Landscape of Crimes and Bad Times

John Gilmore delivers his ultimate, relentless panorama of sex, violence and death in five raw chronicles of SoCal sickness:

—Porn legend John Holmes and untouchable Hollywood crime lord and drug impresario Eddie Nash — the unvarnished story of the sex-and-coke laced Wonderland murders.

—"King of Western Swing" and early L.A. TV's singing cowbow phenomenon Spade Cooley walking the line of nightmare, depravity and murder.

—Hollywood's fallen angel Barbara Payton —seemingly hell-bent to descend from Movie Star Sexpot to the gutters and dumpsters of real-life Tinseltown.

—From gorgeous Hollywood hooker to San Quentin's gas chamber, the infamous Ice Blonde murderess Barbara Graham.

—Highway Hitchhike-Killer Billy Cook unleashing his cold-blooded hate for the human race.

"John Gilmore is the best non-fiction writer of our time, the type of writer that grabs by the throat and by the heart." - *Maximum Rock 'n' Roll*

ISBN: 1-878923-16-1 (trade paper)

$19.95, 344 pp., illustrated

www.amokbooks.com

Also by John Gilmore from Amok Books

LAID BARE

A Memoir of Wrecked Lives and the Hollywood Death Trip

Acclaimed as a powerful chronicler of the American Nightmare through his gripping examinations of the near-mythic Southern California murders (the Black Dahlia, Tate-LaBianca), author John Gilmore draws upon his own resevoir of personal experiences as he turns his sights on our morbid obsession with Celebrity and the ruinous price it exacts from those who would pursue it. With caustic clarity and 20-20 hindsight, John Gilmore recounts his relationships with James Dean, Janis Joplin, Lenny Bruce and many other denizens of the twentieth century's dubious pantheon both on the way up and at the peaks of their notoriety.

"Beautifully written in a style somewhere between Jack Kerouac and Charles Bukowski... This is an an astonishing book." - *Sight and Sound*

"John Gilmore deals with mythically familiar subjects, but not to turn them inside out. Instead he boils off the myth and shows you how things really were, and what things felt like to the people living what later became a myth. You will encounter no receieved ideas, no clichés, no deference to popular myths and opinions, and best of all, no lies. He's an amazing writer, and *Laid Bare* is his most astonishing book." - *Gary Indiana*

ISBN: 1-878923-08-0 (trade paper)

$16.95, 250 pp., illustrated

www.amokbooks.com

Also by John Gilmore from Amok Books

MANSON

The Unholy Trail of Charlie and the Family

Random murder and savage overkill, mind control and trips, Satanism and witchcraft, cursed glamour, Haight Ashbury, rock 'n' roll, biker gangs, sexual rebellion and dune buggies tearing across Death Valley in search of the "hole in the earth..."

The persona of Charles Manson and his bizarre sway over the Family remain riveting a quarter of a century down the line. At the time of the killings, Charles Manson was instantly demonized by the media. Today he has become an icon of rebellion — "the spirit of annihilation." *Manson* is a gripping and chilling account of one of the most fascinating crime sagas of our time, now available in a revised and updated edition containing 36 pages of previously unpublished photos. New vectors into the kaleidoscopic tale which spins inexorably out the slayings emerge in this updated edition with new material on killer Bobby Beausoleil and his occult alliance with experimental filmmaker Kenneth Anger.

"Fascinating!" - *Library Journal*

"A well-researched ethnography of the Manson Family more than an investigation of their crimes." - *Chicago Reader*

"A psychogeographical history of Manson and his family... Charlie considered him [Gilmore] a suitable medium for his messianic message." - *Dazed and Confused*

ISBN: 1-878923-13-7 (trade paper)

$15.95, 208 pp., illustrated

Also by John Gilmore from Amok Books

SEVERED

The True Story of the Black Dahlia

The Black Dahlia murder hit post-war Los Angeles like a bombshell... An impenetrable mystery—the crown jewel of LAPD's unsolved murders. Even before her savage death, beautiful 22-year-old Elizabeth Short, an aspiring starlet and nightclub habitué, was known as the Black Dahlia—now a magnetic icon in American pop culture, an almost mythical symbol of Hollywood noir. In this expanded edition John Gilmore plumbs the depths of the dark core of this terrifying story that, he argues, can never be truly solved. Here's the real Elizabeth Short—the enigmatic Black Dahlia.

"The most satisfying and disturbing conclusion to the Black Dahlia case. After reading *Severed*, I feel as if I truly know Elizabeth Short *and* her killer." - *David Lynch*

"The best book on the Black Dahlia—in fact, the only reliable book." - *Colin Wilson*

"This project stands as the only authentic true-crime book written on America's most bizarre and haunting murder case." - *Charles Higham*

ISBN: 1-878923-17-X (trade paper)

$17.95, 238 pp., illustrated

Human Dignity and Fundamental Rights

Human Dignity and Fundamental Rights

Maddox Clooney

STATES
ACADEMIC PRESS
www.statesacademicpress.com

Published by States Academic Press,
109 South 5th Street,
Brooklyn, NY 11249, USA

ISBN: 978-1-63989-274-7

Cataloging-in-Publication Data

Human dignity and fundamental rights / Maddox Clooney.
p. cm.
Includes bibliographical references and index.
ISBN 978-1-63989-274-7
1. Respect for persons--Law and legislation. 2. Civil rights. 3. Human rights.
I. Clooney, Maddox.

K3249 .H86 2022
342.085--dc23

For information on all States Academic Press publications
visit our website at www.statesacademicpress.com

STATES
ACADEMIC PRESS

Contents

Preface

The right of a person to be respected and valued, and to be treated ethnically for their own sake is termed as human dignity. Violations of human dignity takes place when an individual is humiliated, instrumentalized or objectified, degraded, and dehumanized. Absolute poverty and relative poverty are two of the major causes which result in the violation of human dignity. The rights of individuals which are necessary for their moral, spiritual, and intellectual development, and for their existence and all-round development are defined as fundamental rights. Some of the rights included in fundamental rights are equality before the law, freedom of speech, and freedom of expression, religious and cultural freedom. The topics included in this book on this area of study are of utmost significance and bound to provide incredible insights to readers. It explores all the important aspects of human dignity and fundamental rights in the present day scenario. Those in search of information to further their knowledge will be greatly assisted by this book.

The information contained in this book is the result of intensive hard work done by researchers in this field. All due efforts have been made to make this book serve as a complete guiding source for students and researchers. The topics in this book have been comprehensively explained to help readers understand the growing trends in the field.

I would like to thank the entire group of writers who made sincere efforts in this book and my family who supported me in my efforts of working on this book. I take this opportunity to thank all those who have been a guiding force throughout my life.

Maddox Clooney

1

Introduction

1.1 Introduction

Human dignity is the core philosophical notion that has inspired international human rights for over half a century and has driven constitutional analysis in the areas of social justice[1] and respect for human personality and freedom.[2] It features in the text of many contemporary constitutions and has been found to exist as an unexpressed value in others.[3] Yet its effects on constitutional analysis have not been constant. The same, or similar, language in particular constitutional texts has yielded widely differing outcomes.[4]

This book seeks to examine the constitutional jurisprudence on dignity in South Africa and Ireland. It analyses the rich case-law of the Constitutional Court in South Africa, contrasting it to the slender pickings among the judgments of the Irish courts.[5] It attempts to explain why such a profound difference in outcome has occurred and it proposes a way forward for the Irish courts, consistent with Irish constitutional norms, in the light of the lessons that may be learnt from South Africa.

1 G Whyte *Social inclusion and the legal system: Public interest law in Ireland* (2002) 46.

2 W Binchy 'Dignity as a constitutional concept' in O Doyle & E Carolan (eds) *The Irish Constitution: Governance and values* (2008) 307.

3 As above.

4 Binchy (n 2 above) 308; W Binchy 'The role of comparative and public international law in domestic legal systems' (2010) 23(3) *Advocate (South Africa)* 58 at 61.

5 Binchy (n 2 above) 318 - 319; G Hogan & G Whyte *JM Kelly: The Irish Constitution* (2004) [2.1.32]-[2.1.34], [7.3.222]-[7.3.223].

Why should there be such a profound difference in the jurisprudence of the two countries? The book points out the following answers. The South African Constitution[6] is manifestly transformative in character, replacing the harsh positivism and lack of respect for the equal and inherent worth of the person which characterised the apartheid regime.[7] This Constitution, in embracing the values of equal respect and inherent dignity, has transformed the judicial resolution, not merely of issues relating to race and ethnicity, but of matters completely removed from that context. The new constitutional understanding of the individual and society, and so the place of dignity in the constitutional order, has resulted in the refashioning of the law in areas of social justice, such as housing, health provision and education, but also in relation to personal conduct and personal relationships. It is, in retrospect, no surprise that a dignity-based new constitutional order should have led the courts to the conclusion that same-sex marriage is a constitutional necessity.

The experience in Ireland has been quite different. The Constitution of 1937 can be regarded in some respects as a cuckoo in a common law nest, imported from outside to a radically hostile culture of legal practice and judicial analysis.[8] It contains a reasonably clearly identifiable philosophy and value system – largely that of Thomism,[9] tempered by Enlightenment-inspired civil liberties.[10] This philosophy was no doubt consistent with the broad attitudes of Irish society in 1937 but not at all easy to harmonise with a system based on common law, case-by-case determinations, eschewing grand theory, where rights were not stated but emerged inferentially from the absence of legal constraints.[11]

6 Constitution of the Republic of South Africa 1996.

7 A Chaskalson 'Human dignity as a constitutional value' in D Kretzmer & E Klein (eds) *The concept of human dignity in human rights discourse* (2002) 133, 138.

8 R Keane 'Judges as lawmakers: The Irish experience' (2004) 4(2) *Judicial Studies Institute Journal* 1 at 9.

9 GF Whyte 'Natural law and the Constitution' (1996) 14 *Irish Law Times* 8 at 8 - 9; GF Whyte 'Some reflections on the role of religion in the constitutional order' in T Murphy & P Twomey (eds) *Ireland's evolving constitution, 1937 - 1997: Collected essays* (1998) 60.

10 W Binchy 'The Supreme Court of Ireland' in B Dickson (ed) *Judicial activism in common law supreme courts* (2007) 171; Hogan & Whyte (n 5 above) [1.1.55], [7.1.08]-[7.1.18], [7.1.22] fn 42; Keane (n 8 above) 10, 13 - 14, fn 17; Whyte (n 1 above) 46 - 51.

11 The common law's theory of personal liberty was based on the principle that no legal sanction could be imposed for what was not expressly forbidden by law: AV Dicey *Introduction to the study of the law of the constitution* (1915) xxxvii, 203 - 204.

Moreover, the strong tradition of deference to parliamentary sovereignty[12] was slow to fade. It is true that for a period of a couple of decades, from the mid-1960s to the mid-1980s, the Irish constitutional jurisprudence on fundamental rights developed exponentially, under the inspiration of Ó Dálaigh CJ and more particularly Walsh J.[13] These two judges can now be seen as faithful exponents of the philosophy of the Constitution, who grasped its radically transformative effects on the traditional common law model, based on deference to parliamentary sovereignty, and the strongly positivist philosophy which had been in the ascendancy. Walsh and Ó Dálaigh opened up the possibility of a judicial understanding of constitutional rights as being based on a human rights philosophy.[14] The implications for the doctrine of the separation of powers were equally radical. Yet, other judges, while acquiescing in the Walsh/Ó Dálaigh approach, had no great enthusiasm for it. Their training and background generally gave them no particular expertise in philosophical reflection. With the departure of Ó Dálaigh CJ and, later, Walsh J, and perhaps more importantly, with changes in Irish society in which the standing of the Catholic Church and, consequently, respect for its social philosophy, has weakened greatly, the present disposition of Irish judges to uphold and develop a natural law understanding of human dignity has become almost imperceptible.[15]

The book argues that, consistent with the notion that there is a discernible philosophy and value-system within the Constitution, including respect for human dignity, the Constitution permits – indeed requires – courts to develop a rich jurisprudence which, while not necessarily going as far as judges in South Africa have done, nevertheless involves a far greater judicial commitment to giving substance to these values.

With human dignity as their constant lodestar, the South African courts play their constitutionally-mandated part in the national mission to transform relationships in society by moving them from their morally indefensible apartheid roots of inequality, humiliation and enforced vulnerability on the

12 See Dicey (n 11 above) xviii-xix, 37 - 38; B Walsh 'The Constitution and constitutional rights' in F Litton (ed) *The Constitution of Ireland 1937 - 1987* (1988) 91.

13 Binchy (n 10 above) 169, 171 - 172; Keane (n 8 above) 9 - 10; JM Kelly *A short history of Western legal theory* (1992) 425.

14 B Walsh 'Constitutional adjudication' (1995 - 1996) 17 *Holdsworth Law Review* 153 at 159.

15 Binchy (n 10 above) 214 - 215.

particularly odious ground of race to a foundation of reciprocity in a humane community exhibiting respect for the inherent dignity, equality and freedom of each of its members. The person is positioned in society, where human rights – linked with correlative duties – are harmonised to the greatest extent possible. This well-developed communitarian understanding of dignity supported by constitutional norms clearly reasoned and articulated by the judiciary contrasts with the Irish courts' sporadic acknowledgment of the dignity of the atomised individual without taking into account the emphasis in the Constitution on social justice which also requires human dignity to be located in a group setting. Because of the dramatic switch from the exclusivity embedded in the previous regime to a polity committed to embracing all citizens, it is not surprising that the transformative process was based on the value of human dignity, which recognises the inherent worth of each person. What is startling is that the Irish judges (unlike their South African counterparts) have shown great reluctance to examine the foundational norms and value systems of the Constitution. Their failure, combined with an unnecessarily stringent application of the separation of powers, has inhibited the development of a jurisprudence laying strong emphasis on human dignity.

As South Africa has shown, a communitarian application of human dignity can be the foundation of a humanist philosophy that promotes equality in many spheres and combats discrimination on the grounds of, *inter alia*, race, gender, civil status and cultural background, as well as extending the ambit of the right to life from mere survival to the leading of a dignified healthy meaningful life with sufficient nourishment and shelter to enable the development of fulfilling relationships and participation in society with the enjoyment of civil and political rights. Its ethos requires that prisoners, children, nomadic people, the disabled and other marginalised or vulnerable groups be treated with equal respect. It protects against degradation and humiliation in the punishment meted out for crimes and in the sanctions for civil law breaches. The all-pervasive influence of human dignity is evident in these examples of the diverse areas where it has been successfully invoked: bodily and mental integrity, fair procedures in the justice system, freedom to express oneself and to form publically-recognised relationships, upholding of reputation, and preservation of a private sphere with the autonomy to take an informed decision on how best to lead one's life and to decide on what private information to reveal. Its reciprocal nature is evident in its curtailment of self-degradation and its limiting effect on the exercise of rights to accommodate the rights of others or the common good.

Why has a comparison between the Irish and South African case-law revealed such a marked divergence between the reliance on and understanding of human dignity in each jurisdiction? One explanation is that the South African Constitution has unequivocally espoused human dignity as a foundational value and contains multiple textual references to it. Its Bill of Rights also includes a non-derogable individual right to respect for human dignity. When interpreting or developing the law, the courts are explicitly directed to promote the Bill of Rights' underlying values, spirit, purport and objects. Contrast the Irish Constitution, containing just one reference to dignity – and that is not embodied in it, but in the Preamble. At first glance on a literal reading of the Constitution, it might be thought that the Preamble is superfluous to its interpretation. But a deeper study reveals that the Irish Constitution is also values-based and I propose that, in the absence of an interpretation clause, reliance should be placed on the reference to dignity in the Preamble as a factor when interpreting the document. The Preamble refers to the common good and social order, which is evidence of a communitarian understanding of dignity with its emphasis on mutual interdependence.[16] The values of human dignity and social inclusion could mandate judicial enforcement of socio-economic rights.[17]

A purposive approach is an appropriate method of interpretation in certain circumstances – particularly when concepts such as equality, personal rights and values are deliberately left vague to enable them to be applied in changing circumstances. So in the quest for the meaning of the Constitution, a purposive interpretation reflecting its values is apt. As an objection might be made to the relevance of human dignity and a study of the South African Constitution to the Irish situation, before embarking on the comparative review this introductory chapter will examine interpretative methods more closely and establish the veracity of the method proposed in this book.

16 A O'Sullivan & PCW Chan 'Judicial review in Ireland and the relationship between the Irish Constitution and natural law' (2006) 15(2) *Nottingham Law Journal* 18 at 21. See also C McHugh 'Socio-economic rights in Ireland: Lessons to be learned from South Africa and India' (2003) 4 *Hibernian Law Journal* 109 at 113.

17 McHugh (n 16 above) 118, 126, 128.

1.2 Framework of study and relevance to proposition

The purpose of this chapter is to outline the proposition, sketch the main lessons which the Irish courts may learn from South Africa, defend the interpretative method proposed for the Irish Constitution and describe the research methodology.

Chapter II examines the role of dignity in contemporary jurisprudence, its meaning in philosophy, and its history, sources, roles and impact. Rationales from the human being's nature, spirituality, reasoning capacity and status in the community have amalgamated to provide a coherent perception of human dignity, which merits mutual love in relationships and a common commitment to respect for each other in order to experience the full breadth of humanity in social solidarity – a modern appreciation of human dignity that supports a communitarian understanding of the concept in law. Noted in the jurisprudence are dignity's association with other rights, its close relationship with equality, its relevance to groups, its pivotal place in human rights and its implications for democracy.

Chapter III describes the historical background to the South African Constitution and reviews its provisions on fundamental rights. Its values are shaped by the traditional concept of *ubuntu*, which promotes harmonious communal living while recognising each participant's right to respect.

In Chapters IV to VI the case-law in South Africa on dignity is evaluated. Chapter IV focuses on the *right* to dignity and the idea of equal respect, which underpinned the case-law condemning discrimination on the grounds of sexual orientation. This right has had a significant impact on the types of punishment that are available as a legal sanction, protection of family life, defamation laws, the handling of crimes of sexual violence and children's rights. These diverse areas where the right to dignity has had an effect show that, in the hands of judges committed to the constitutional transformative ideal, it has a far-reaching potential to improve society for the benefit of the community as a whole and for individuals in it.

Chapter V shows the association of the *value* of dignity with other rights, in particular freedom and security, fair trial, privacy and autonomy, freedom of expression and equality.

Again, it is evident that a judiciary willing to engage the constitutional value of dignity to interpret the purpose of the provisions in the Constitution will find that this yields a better insight into all fundamental rights whose true nature will consequently be more readily understood by the public – an added bonus on top of the recognition in law of the position of the individuals concerned.

Chapter VI deals with economic and social rights. Although certain socio-economic rights are set out in the Bill of Rights, the courts read the Constitution as a whole and utilise an objective notion of human dignity to discern the scope of these rights. In the reconciliation of scarce resources with protection of human dignity, collective rights have ensured judicial scrutiny of government programmes to meet urgent social needs. While the executive is held accountable, the courts have adopted a collaborative approach insisting on consultation between the parties and engagement to seek a reasonable solution. The judiciary has not usurped the policy roles of the other arms of state and has given the government and legislature an opportunity to rectify deficiencies that have come to light, but the courts have not hesitated to intervene when they have detected *mala fides* or prevarication in delivering results. A review of the justiciability and judicial enforcement of socio-economic rights in a number of countries reveals that even where there is no explicit recognition in a constitution of these rights, there is a solid foundation on which they can be claimed and adjudicated. Respect for the human dignity of all members of society has ensured at least the minimum protection for the vulnerable. Therefore, even though the Irish Constitution does not contain as many specific socio-economic rights as its South African counterpart, the judicial approach to them in South Africa can be adapted for Ireland.

Chapter VII examines the Irish case-law and compares it with the South African jurisprudence. The historical development of dignity is traced and its philosophy sought in Irish decisions. Some startling comparisons (and a few stark contrasts) emerge between South Africa and Ireland in substantive law. Although dignity can best be understood as an aspect of the natural law philosophy on which the Irish Constitution is largely, though not exclusively based, there has been little judicial effort to substantiate a natural law understanding of dignity in key areas of equality and personal rights. The chapter reviews relevant case-law thematically. What emerges is a jurisprudence in stark contrast to that of South Africa, with an impoverished judicial understanding of the implications of dignity for developing, if not transforming, key areas of the law.

Remedies and the scope of fundamental rights are covered in Chapter VIII. The horizontal application in Ireland of constitutional rights might be considered to have resulted in a reshaping of the common law corpus of remedies in the light of constitutional values. Yet little has emerged. Some traces may be found in the area of defamation, for example,[18] but Irish courts have achieved less than their South African counterparts, who have worked with the conceptually weaker constitutional model of indirect horizontally.[19]

Finally, the conclusions from this comparative review are stated in Chapter IX. There are similarities in the normative framework of the Constitutions of both countries, and some useful guidelines can be extracted to reinvigorate Irish jurisprudence. There are significant lessons to be learnt which will be summarised briefly at the end of this chapter.

1.3 Purposive interpretation

Courts have adopted two opposing interpretative approaches in relation to constitutions, namely the literal and the purposive. Each one has its rightful place provided it is applied in the context to which it is suited. Gerard Hogan and Gerry Whyte pointed out that the literal approach focusing on the language in the text is most appropriate in relation to technical provisions.[20] But its shortcomings are evident when there is an apparent conflict within the document.[21] The broad purposeful method is a better tool to discover the meaning of fundamental rights and public policy, because it discerns the people's intentions as embodied in the Constitution and identifies the purpose and objective in protecting human rights while using the textual language as a guide.[22] The literal theory is a product of parliamentary supremacy and, as George Devenish put it, is associated in South Africa with 'primitive legal positivism of the by-gone era, of imperialism,

18 *Hunter v Gerald Duckworth & Co Ltd* [2003] IEHC 81 (see n 236 in Ch VIII).

19 The Bill of Rights has direct horizontal application, but the Constitutional Court has preferred to have recourse to indirect horizontality, which is also facilitated by the Constitution: D Moseneke 'Transformative constitutionalism: Its implications for the law of contract' (2009) 20 *Stellenbosch Law Review* 3 at 8. See Ch III, 3.2.3.2; G Devenish *A commentary on the South African Bill of Rights* (1999) 19 - 20, 24 - 25, 31 - 32.

20 Hogan & Whyte (n 5 above) [1.1.03].

21 R Byrne & JP McCutcheon *The Irish legal system* (2009) [15.130].

22 Hogan & Whyte (n 5 above) [1.1.05].

colonialism and white minority rule'.[23] He rejects a mere technical exercise in constitutional interpretation and notes that a purposive approach involving values is required.[24] Constitutions are now regarded as *sui generis* and require a generous purposive construction, so the ordinary rules of statutory construction are not applied rigidly.[25] Etienne Mureinik argues for an interpretation where text, purpose and values are weighed to produce a value-coherent interpretation by which 'the judge is charged with the duty of finding the construction most consonant with the morality that affords the best explanation of the legal system.'[26]

A canon of interpretation first expressed in Ireland in 1980 was that of harmonious interpretation, which regards the Constitution as having a single scale of values that should be read without internal discord.[27] It may require a literal interpretation to yield to a purposive one.[28] Similarities can be seen

23 G Devenish 'The evolution and development of a value-based and teleological interpretation of statute and common law in South Africa as a result of the 1996 Constitution' in E Quansah & W Binchy (eds) *The judicial protection of human rights in Botswana* (2009) 116.

24 Devenish (n 23 above) 117. On values-based interpretation, see Devenish (n 19 above) 606 - 608.

25 CM Fombad 'The constitutional protection against discrimination in Botswana' (2004) 53 *International and Comparative Law Quarterly* 139 at 145.

26 E Mureinik 'Administrative law in South Africa' (1986) 103 *South African Law Journal* 615 at 623.

27 Hogan & Whyte (n 5 above) [1.1.12]-[1.1.13], citing *Dillane v AG* [1980] ILRM 167 (SC).

28 Hogan & Whyte (n 5 above) [1.1.16]. This did not happen in *People (DPP) v O'Shea*, where the majority diverged from Henchy J's vision of the Constitution as 'an ensemble of interconnected and interacting provisions which must be brought into play as part of a larger composition, and which must be given such an integrated interpretation as will fit it harmoniously into the general constitutional order and modulation': [1982] IR 384 (SC) 426. Henchy J noted that in a constitution 'the letter killeth, but the spirit giveth life': as above. In 1985 a differently composed Supreme Court effectively repudiated the majority reasoning in *O'Shea*, and adopted Henchy J's harmonious approach in which the scheme of the entire constitution is regarded to prevent a literal construction defeating the Constitution's fundamental purpose, thus resolving conflicts between two provisions: *Tormey v Ireland* [1985] IR 289. Henchy J rejected a hierarchy of rights, *Tormey* above, 295 - 296:

> The rule of literal interpretation, which is generally applied in the absence of ambiguity or absurdity in the text, must here give way to the more fundamental rule of constitutional interpretation that the Constitution must be read as a whole and that its several provisions must not be looked at in isolation, but be treated as interlocking parts of the general constitutional scheme. This means that where two constructions of a provision are open in the light of the Constitution as a whole, despite the apparent unambiguity of the provision itself, the court should adopt the construction which will achieve the smooth and harmonious operation of the Constitution. A judicial attitude of strict construction should be avoided

in the South African jurisprudence where the harmonious reading of the Constitution as a whole is favoured, as exemplified by Sachs J in *Prince II*,[29] *Van Heerden*[30] and *NM v Smith*.[31] Harmony is useful when it results in the constitutional purposes being achieved. As Rory O'Connell stated, 'courts must not simply harmonise those provisions, they must aim to realise their purpose, and more particularly the central purposes of the Constitution.'[32]

When values are being considered, the question arises as to whether they are to be ascertained by gauging what they meant in 1937 when the people adopted the Constitution or whether they have a current meaning.[33] Although the historical approach sometimes has a role to play, John Kelly thought it was not the correct viewpoint here and proposed that the 'present-tense' approach was appropriate for standards and values, such as 'personal rights', 'common good', 'social justice', 'equality' and – in the context of private property guarantees – for concepts like 'injustice'.[34] This accords with Walsh J's dictum in *McGee* that as 'the prevailing ideas' of the virtues in the Preamble 'may be conditioned by the passage of time', the Constitution is interpreted 'in the light of prevailing ideas and concepts.'[35]

It has to be recognised that applying a purposive interpretation to a constitutional text whose values are capable of assuming a different content or scope over a period of time can present formidable intellectual challenges.[36] A purposive interpretation based on an originalist perspective is a far simpler endeavour. Here the task is to identify the original purpose of those who

> when it would allow the imperfection or inadequacy of the words used to defeat or pervert any of the fundamental purposes of the Constitution.

Henchy J's dissenting views in *O'Shea* were cited frequently in later cases and were approved by Keane CJ in *People (DPP) v MS*: [2003] IESC 24, [2003] 1 IR 606 at 619. See Byrne & McCutcheon (n 21 above) [15.144]-[15.147]; G Hogan 'Constitutional interpretation' in Litton (n 12 above) 184; Hogan & Whyte (n 5 above) [1.1.03], [1.1.15]-[1.1.16], [1.1.19]-[1.1.20], [1.1.50], [7.1.49]; J Kelly 'The Constitution: Law and manifesto' in Litton (n 12 above) 214 - 215.

29 *Prince v President of the Law Society of the Cape of Good Hope* 2002 2 SA 794 (CC) [155].

30 *Minister of Finance v Van Heerden* 2004 6 SA 121 (CC) [136].

31 2007 5 SA 250 (CC) [204].

32 R O'Connell 'Guardians of the constitution: Unconstitutional constitutional norms' (1999) 4 *Journal of Civil Liberties* 48 at 51 (footnote omitted).

33 Whyte (n 1 above) 24, 27.

34 Kelly (n 28 above) 215.

35 *McGee v AG* [1974] IR 284 (SC) 319. On *McGee*, see FX Beytagh, Jr 'Privacy in perspective: The experience under foreign constitutions' (1984) 15 *University of Toledo Law Review* 449 at 493 - 504.

36 See Binchy (n 2 above) 312 - 313.

created the Constitution and construe the language of the text accordingly. But if key concepts can change their meaning over time in the light of 'prevailing ideas', then the historical purpose loses its centrality and the courts must construct an artificial purpose based on the changed corpus and shape of the new values. In describing this as an artificial purpose, the intent is not to stigmatise the process as involving falsity or disingenuousness, but rather to identify the fact that the courts are no longer engaging exclusively in a process of historical detection of actual purpose – instead they are involved in a more complex process of seeking to draw from an indentified cluster of values (including newly developed or reshaped values) a coherent normative philosophy. Undoubtedly there is purpose in the interpretative process, but it relates more to the purpose of achieving philosophical coherence rather than to identifying the purpose of those who created the Constitution.

So far as the reference to dignity contained in the Preamble is concerned, it seems entirely reasonable to apply an originalist interpretation to it (in the first place at least) in order to appreciate its significance as part of the philosophical system embraced by the Constitution in 1937. It may be appropriate for the court thereafter to examine whether dignity has acquired a different meaning in the light of 'prevailing ideas'. One must concede such a theoretical possibility of change, but, so far as dignity is concerned, it may be argued that the philosophical understanding of the concept, rooted in the inherent equal value of every human being, integrated in social relationships whose purpose should be to enhance human flourishing, has not been replaced by a Lockean concept of dignity, which is contingent on personal circumstances and facts external to each human being.[37] The 'prevailing ideas' would reasonably include those reflected in all the great international human rights instruments, beginning with the Universal Declaration of Human Rights (Universal Declaration) of 1948,[38] which includes references to dignity that clearly envisage that it is shared, equally and inherently, by everyone.

37 John Locke's understanding of dignity was that its actualisation is vulnerable, dependent on wilful actions of society and is to be safeguarded by political and social institutions grounded on a social contract: D Ritschl 'Can ethical maxims be derived from theological concepts of human dignity?' in Kretzmer & Klein (n 7 above) 96.

38 Universal Declaration of Human Rights (adopted 10 December 1948) UNGA Res 217 A(III).

It must be acknowledged that two decisions of the Supreme Court – *Re a Ward of Court (withholding medical* treatment*) (No 2)*[39] and *Roche v Roche*[40] – are difficult to reconcile with a natural law understanding of dignity; yet neither decision sought to invoke changing 'prevailing ideas' on dignity as a reason for adopting a different interpretation of the concept and both professed broad loyalty to the interlinked constitutional understanding of human rights.

Frank Michelman's suggestion for interpretation captures the multi-faceted holistic nature of the task which must give effect to the underlying values:[41]

> On the constitutional level, legal interpretation succeeds by construing legal words, intentions, and purposes, yes, but by construing them decidedly in the light of consequences, and by appraising consequences decidedly in the light of an emergent national sense of justice to which the interpretations are themselves, recursively, contributing.

1.3.1 Review of interpretative methods in the case-law

A review of the Irish case-law shows judicial support for the purposive values-focused interpretation. In *AG v Paperlink* in 1983 Costello J noted that the Constitution was 'a political instrument as well as a legal document' and that a purposive, rather than a strictly literal, approach to its interpretation was appropriate.[42] He expanded on this view in *Murray v Ireland*:[43]

> [W]hilst not ignoring the express text of the Constitution, a purposive approach to interpretation which would look at the whole text of the Constitution and identify its purpose and objectives in protecting human rights, is frequently a desirable one.

Hardiman J in *Sinnott v Minister for Education* viewed the terms 'historical', 'harmonious' and 'purposive' as disparate aspects of interpretation which

39 [1996] 2 IR 79. See GF Whyte 'The right to die and the Irish Constitution' (1997) 3 *European Public Law* 235.

40 [2009] IESC 82, [2010] 2 IR 321. Murray CJ expressly linked the moral status of embryos with human dignity, but he declined 'to pronounce on the truth of when human life begins' on the grounds that when a broad consensus did not exist on such a complex multi-faceted issue, it was a policy choice to be exercised by the legislature: *Roche v Roche* above, [44]-[45], [49]-[50]. See R Byrne & W Binchy *Annual review of Irish law 2009* (2010) 246 - 251, 469 - 480.

41 FI Michelman 'A constitutional conversation with Professor Frank Michelman' (1995) 11 *South African Journal on Human Rights* 477 at 485.

42 [1984] ILRM 373 (HC) 385.

43 [1985] IR 532 (HC) 539.

form part of every constitutional construction.[44] The established interpretative approach of the Supreme Court was described by Murray CJ in *A v Governor of Arbour Hill Prison* as 'the teleological approach – a universally recognised method of interpreting constitutional and other legal norms', which meant that (even though the Constitution did not expressly say so) the ambit and effect of a particular constitutional provision fell to be considered 'within the rubric and scheme of the Constitution as a whole' and involved taking into account the Constitution's 'objectives, principles and provisions' as a whole.[45]

As MacMenamin J indicated in *Health Service Executive v X*, it is beyond doubt that statutes for the protection of vulnerable people are to be construed in a broad purposive manner reflecting constitutional values and compatible with the Constitution itself.[46]

The purposive approach infused with constitutional values can be seen in operation in South Africa. All the judges in *S v Mhlungu* agreed that a purposive interpretation was appropriate,[47] but there was a difference of opinion between them on how it applied to the particular provisions under scrutiny. Devenish described the majority judgment of Mahomed J as '[t]he high water mark of a values-based interpretation'.[48] Kriegler J, dissenting in *Du Plessis v De Klerk* because he would have applied the interim Constitution[49] horizontally, stated, '[i]t is ... trite that the Constitution is to be interpreted purposively and as a whole, bearing in mind its manifest objectives.'[50]

Chaskalson P in *Makwanyane* approved of the purposive interpretation of fundamental rights taking into account the context, including the history and background to the adoption of the Constitution, aimed at securing for 'individuals the full measure' of its protection.[51] O'Regan J agreed that the

44 [2001] 2 IR 545 (SC) 688. In *Sinnott*, he used the purposive approach as outlined by Costello J in *AG v Paperlink*: as above.

45 [2006] IESC 45, [2006] 4 IR 88 [71]-[72].

46 [2011] IEHC 326 [63]-[64], [67].

47 [1995] ZACC 4, 1995 3 SA 867 (CC) [8] (Mahomed J), [63] (Kentridge AJ dissenting), [97] (Kriegler J), [129] (Sachs J). See J Church *et al*, *Human rights from a comparative and international law perspective* (2007) 203.

48 Devenish (n 23 above) 97.

49 Interim Constitution of the Republic of South Africa 1993.

50 1996 3 SA 850 (CC) [123].

51 *S v Makwanyane* 1995 6 BCLR 665 (CC) [9]-[10], citing *Minister of Home Affairs v Fisher* [1980] AC 319 (PC) 328.

courts' responsibility was to develop fully constitutional rights and in that quest to seek the purpose for which a right was included in the Constitution.[52] She clarified that the purposive or teleological approach did not invariably result in a generous meaning – at times it required a narrower or specific definition.[53] In delving for the purpose, the common South African values could form a basis on which to develop a South African human rights jurisprudence and Mokgoro J, relying on the reference to it in the epilogue to the Constitution[54] and 'the underlying idea and its accompanying values ... expressed in the preamble', identified the value of *ubuntu* (humaneness) as the unifying thread.[55] She equated its spirit with the internationally recognised human dignity from which human rights derive.[56]

Guided by 'the broad and ample style' of the chapter in the Constitution of Bermuda providing for the protection of fundamental rights and freedoms[57] as well as by the influence on the drafters of the European Convention on Human Rights[58] and the Universal Declaration, Lord Wilberforce in *Minister of Home Affairs v Fisher* backed a 'generous interpretation avoiding what has been called "the austerity of tabulated legalism," suitable to give to individuals the full measure of the fundamental rights and freedoms referred to.'[59] The Privy Council rejected simply interpreting the Constitution 'with less rigidity, and greater generosity, than other Acts' and chose a broader perspective where it was treated as a *sui generis* instrument with its own principles of interpretation that recognised its character and origin.[60]

52 n 51 above, [325].

53 As above.

54 n 49 above, Epilogue, 3rd para.

55 n 51 above, [307 - 308].

56 n 51 above, [309].

57 Constitution of Bermuda 1968, Ch I.

58 Convention for the Protection of Human Rights and Fundamental Freedoms, 213 UNTS 222 (ECHR).

59 [1980] AC 319 (PC) 328.

60 *Fisher* (n 59 above) 329. Lord Wilberforce explained, as above:

> Respect must be paid to the language which has been used and to the traditions and usages which have given meaning to that language. It is quite consistent with this, and with the recognition that rules of interpretation may apply, to take as a point of departure for the process of interpretation a recognition of the character and origin of the instrument, and to be guided by the principle of giving full recognition and effect to those fundamental rights and freedoms with a statement of which the Constitution commences.

The Supreme Court of Canada has endorsed the purposive approach to definition of the fundamental rights and freedoms in the Canadian Charter. In *R v Big M Drug Mart Ltd* Dickson J considered the values underlying Canadian 'political and philosophic traditions' when he interpreted the purpose of freedom of conscience and religion[61] and concluded that the Charter gave equal protection to manifestation of religious non-belief and refusal to participate in religious practice as it did to the expression and practice of religion.[62]

1.3.2 A preamble as an indicator of values

In jurisdictions where the constitution has a normative thrust it has been accepted widely that it is legitimate to look to its preamble to discern the underlying values to be applied to interpretation of the substantive provisions. A preamble usually sets out *basic values* supported by the community and spells out common *aspirations* and *goals* for the future.[63] Although generally the preamble to a constitution does not contain directly enforceable rules of law, it can play a substantial role in interpreting and applying the constitution.[64] It does not have the limited importance traditionally attached to the preambles of statutes, as it contains considerably more information on the history of the constitution and the purposes for enacting it.[65] IM Rautenbach describes its significance:[66]

> A constitutional preamble is therefore an important source whenever a provision of the constitution is interpreted by applying the principles that the history and origin of the provision, the constitution as a whole, and the purpose of the provision must be taken into account.

The South African Constitution differs from the Irish one in that specific values on which the democratic State is founded are listed in Section 1. Human dignity,[67] equality, human rights and freedom are mentioned first[68] –

61 Canadian Charter of Rights and Freedoms 1982, Sec 2(a).

62 [1985] 1 SCR 295 [123]. See PW Hogg *Constitutional law of Canada* (2007) *Vol 1* at 552 - 553, *Vol 2* at 49, 51, 135 - 136, 252, 255.

63 IM Rautenbach *Rautenbach-Malherbe constitutional law* (2012) 73.

64 Rautenbach (n 63 above) 74.

65 Rautenbach (n 63 above) 75.

66 n 63 above, 75.

67 On human dignity as a value, see S Woolman 'Dignity' in S Woolman *et al* (eds) *Constitutional law of South Africa* (2006) [36-22]–[36-25].

these values are repeated in other provisions of the Constitution.[69] Constitutional supremacy is also a founding value[70] and, as recited in the Preamble, the Constitution was adopted by the people as the supreme law. A perusal of the preambular text shows that the first goal is to establish a society with democratic values and social justice.[71] Another aim is an improved quality of life and personal freedom to achieve one's full potential. All the values are designed to ensure human dignity and freedom in an accountable, responsive and open political system.[72] The Preamble indicates that the Constitution gives a central place to the dignity of the individual and also endeavours to restore the collective dignity of the state and of the people.[73] These universal values are expressed in *ubuntu.*[74]

The values in the Preamble to the Irish Constitution are prudence, justice and charity. The aims relevant to human rights are to assure the dignity and freedom of the members of an orderly society while promoting the common good. The Constitution was adopted by the people, who are sovereign and the source of all State powers.[75] It is remarkable that, despite the different circumstances and eras in which they were adopted, there are such striking similarities between the values and aspirations in the South African and Irish documents – the South African Constitution echoes the common commitment to a just society where human dignity and individual liberty are respected. Furthermore, both documents with supremacy in law were adopted by the people.

The next subsection will examine the role of the preamble in divining the meaning of the constitution in South Africa, Ireland and other jurisdictions.

68 Sec 1(a).

69 Secs 7(1) (rights), 36(1) (limitation of rights), 39(1)(a) (interpretation of Bill of Rights).

70 Sec 1(c).

71 C Roederer 'Founding provisions' in Woolman *et al* (n 67 above) [13-4]. See also H Klug *The Constitution of South Africa: A contextual analysis* (2010) 110.

72 Devenish (n 19 above) 11 - 12.

73 LM du Plessis 'The evolution of constitutionalism and the emergence of a constitutional jurisprudence in South Africa: An evaluation of the South African Constitutional Court's approach to constitutional interpretation' (1999) 62 *Saskatchewan Law Review* 299 at 315.

74 Devenish (n 19 above) 12.

75 Constitution of Ireland 1937, Art 6.1.

1.3.3 The preamble in the courts

The South African courts have invoked the Preamble to the Constitution to discern its goals and to amplify its values.[76] Some examples will illustrate this point. We have already seen that Mokgoro J referred to the values in the Preamble in *Makwanyane*.[77] Her colleagues in that case did likewise. Chaskalson P,[78] Ackermann[79] and Mahomed[80] JJ mentioned the new order envisaged by the Preamble where all would enjoy fundamental rights and freedoms in a constitutional state. Sachs J deduced from, *inter alia*, the Preamble the requirement for 'an amplitude of vision' where the Constitution speaks for all of society and not just one section of it (as previously).[81] In *Ferreira v Levin* he read the Constitution as a whole (including the Preamble) as establishing a setting allowing for a more expansive role for the word 'freedom' than a narrow reading of the text in isolation would admit.[82] That the Preamble is a marker for constitutional values and cannot be ignored when interpreting the Constitution is evident from his following remarks in *Mhlungu*:[83]

> The Preamble in particular should not be dismissed as a mere aspirational and throat-clearing exercise of little interpretive value. It connects up, reinforces and underlies all of the text that follows. It helps to establish the basic design of the Constitution and indicate its fundamental purposes.

The provisions in the Constitution are meant to give effect to the values and goals encompassed in the Preamble, so the literal meaning is circumscribed.[84] Rautenbach confidently asserts the principle:[85]

76 S Levinson 'Do constitutions have a point? Reflections on "parchment barriers" and Preambles' in EF Paul *et al* (eds) *What should constitutions do?* (2011) 162 - 164. See also T Roux 'Democracy' in Woolman *et al* (n 67 above) [10-22].

77 Text to n 55 above.

78 n 51 above, [130] fn 159.

79 n 51 above, [155]-[156].

80 n 51 above, [262].

81 n 51 above, [362]-[363].

82 1996 1 SA 984 (CC) [255].

83 n 47 above, [112] (footnote omitted).

84 Rautenbach (n 63 above) 75.

85 n 63 above, 75 (footnote omitted).

> [P]rovisions of the Constitution *must* therefore *always* be interpreted and applied within the context of the preamble and not only in the case of vague and ambiguous concepts. In a particular case, this could mean that the literal, clear meaning of a constitutional provision will not be followed, because it must be interpreted and applied *as qualified by the values and goals set out in the preamble and in other provisions of the Constitution.*

Liav Orgad has categorised the Preambles to the Irish and South African Constitutions as 'interpretive', the role of interpretive preambles being rooted in the common law tradition as an aid to the construction of statutes.[86] He observed invocations of the Preamble to interpret the Constitution and as a tool to guide in understanding its spirit in both jurisdictions.[87] It is true that the Irish Preamble has been used by the judiciary on occasion as an interpretative aid.[88] Although not asserted as confidently as Sachs J did in *Mhlungu*, the Supreme Court affirmed in *Buckley (Sinn Féin) v AG* that the Constitution should be construed to give effect to the objectives of promoting the common good to assure the individual's dignity and freedom as set out in the Preamble.[89] Within two years of adoption of the Constitution ('with its most impressive Preamble ... the Charter of the Irish People'), Gavan Duffy J in *State (Burke) v Lennon*, being determined not to 'whittle it away', had viewed the dignity and freedom of the individual as one of the 'cardinal principles' proclaimed in the Preamble.[90] Disallowing an appeal from Gavan Duffy J's decision, Geoghegan J considered it possible that the implication of a limitation of the personal right of freedom was negatived more strongly by this 'solemn reference' in the Preamble.[91]

86 L Orgad 'The preamble in constitutional interpretation' (2010) 8 *International Journal of Constitutional Law* 714 at 723 - 724.

87 n 86 above, 724.

88 See Hogan & Whyte (n 5 above) [2.1.07]-[2.1.18]; text to n 33-n 35, n 38-n 41 in Ch VII.

89 [1950] IR 67 at 80 - 81 (O'Byrne J):

> In the enacting portion of the Constitution, contained in the Preamble, the people of Ireland, seeking, amongst other things, 'to promote the common good, with due observance of Prudence, Justice and Charity, so that the dignity and freedom of the individual may be assured ... adopt, enact and give' to themselves the Constitution. These most laudable objects seem to us to inform the various Articles of the Constitution, and we are of opinion that, so far as possible, the Constitution should be so construed as to give to them life and reality.

90 [1940] IR 136 (HC) 143, 155.

91 *Burke v Lennon* (n 90 above) 178.

Since the people's purpose in adopting the Constitution could be discerned from it, thereby helping to determine 'the meaning of and the effect to be given to particular provisions', the Supreme Court endorsed the use of the Preamble as an interpretative aid in *AG v Southern Industrial Trust Ltd*.[92] In *McGee* Walsh J adopted the same stance as O'Byrne J in *Buckley* and placed the onus on the judiciary to apply the values in the Preamble to interpret the Constitution.[93] Budd J followed suit.[94] Citing Walsh J's dictum, O'Higgins CJ in *State (Healy) v Donoghue* found that justice in the courts must import regard to the individual's dignity (not only fairness and fair procedures).[95] He agreed with the judge at first instance (Gannon J) that fair procedures apply in criminal trials; however, in serious cases justice also required the provision of legal assistance and means-related aid.[96] Gannon J had highlighted the judiciary's primary role in protection from injustice, its part in furthering the constitutional aims articulated in the Preamble being equal to that of the other arms of state:[97]

> The promotion of the common good so that the dignity and freedom of the individual may be assured, being the objective stated in the preamble to the Constitution, is as much a function and responsibility of the judicial organ of the State as of the legislature or the executive.

The 'broad motivating and purposive considerations' in the Preamble set the scene for Henchy J in *Garvey v Ireland*, where he underlined the importance of a livelihood and an honourable retirement to a person's dignity and

92 [1960] 94 ILTR 161 (SC) 175 (Lavery J).

93 n 35 above, 319:

> According to the preamble, the people gave themselves the Constitution to promote the common good with due observance of prudence, justice and charity so that the dignity and freedom of the individual might be assured. The judges must, therefore, as best they can from their training and their experience interpret these rights in accordance with their ideas of prudence, justice and charity.

94 n 35 above, 322:

> When the preamble to the Constitution speaks of seeking to promote the common good by the observance of prudence, justice and charity so that the dignity and freedom of the individual may be assured, it must surely inform those charged with its construction as to the mode of application of its Articles.

Henchy J referred to the Preamble in a rhetorical, but forceful, way: Hogan & Whyte (n 5 above) [2.1.17]; see text to n430 in Ch VII.

95 [1976] IR 325 (SC) 347 - 348.

96 n 95 above, 348 - 350.

97 n 95 above, (HC) 335.

freedom.[98] By the late 1980s the courts had adopted a purposive interpretation relying on the goals and values in the Preamble, as Murphy J recognised in an *obiter dictum* in *Lawlor v Minister for Agriculture*.[99]

Following Henchy J's view in *O'Shea*,[100] O'Flaherty J in *AG v X* agreed that the Constitution should be read harmoniously – the spirit could prevail over the letter.[101] He held that an injunction restraining a woman from travelling abroad to have an abortion would interfere to an unwarranted degree with her freedom of movement, the authority of the family and the aspiration in the Preamble to assure the dignity and freedom of the individual.[102] Finlay CJ also adopted a harmonious values-based interpretation of the right to life in accordance with the concepts of prudence, justice and charity in the Preamble, as explained by Walsh J in *McGee*.[103]

In 2011 Hogan J in *Aslam v Minister for Justice and Equality* granted a pregnant asylum seeker an injunction restraining her transfer out of the country by air or sea, because the State had constitutional obligations to protect her and her unborn child's life and health.[104] Guided by the Preamble, he was required to interpret these obligations in a fashion that assured her dignity.[105] When considering an asylum seeker's application for judicial review of a decision denying her claim in *E v Minister for Justice Equality and Law Reform*, he continued the same theme and, echoing Henchy J's comments in *Garvey*, he pointed out that the obligation to respect fair procedures assured the dignity of the individual as set out in the Preamble – it was not 'an

98 [1981] IR 75 (SC) 99. The Supreme Court held that the guarantee of fair procedures in Article 40.3 of the Constitution applied to the Government's exercise of its power of removal from office of the Garda Commissioner.

99 [1987] IEHC 4, [1990] 1 IR 356 at 375 - 376:

> [I]t does seem to me that the teleological and schematic approach has for many years been adopted in this country – though not necessarily under that description – in the interpretation of the Constitution. The innumerable occasions in which the preamble to the Constitution has been invoked and in particular the desire therein expressed 'to promote the common good, with due observance of Prudence, Justice and Charity, so that the dignity and freedom of the individual may be assured, true social order attained, the unity of our country restored and concord established with other nations' in seeking to 'fill the gaps' in the Constitution is itself an obvious example of the teleological approach.

100 See n 28 above.

101 [1992] IESC 1, [1992] 1 IR 1 at 87.

102 n 101 above, 88.

103 n 101 above, 52 - 53, citing n 35 above, 318 - 319.

104 [2011] IEHC 512 [33], [36].

105 n 104 above, [34].

exercise in pure formalism, but ... rather an opportunity to enable the person affected to fairly put his or her case.'[106]

Denham CJ in *MD v Ireland* associated the equal treatment of all human persons with 'the principles of freedom, justice and human dignity, which, *inter alia*, the preamble of the Constitution aims to safeguard.'[107] Finnegan J recognised human dignity as a key constitutional objective protected by the Preamble in *People (DPP) v Murray*.[108]

Murphy J (partially dissenting) in *DPP v Best* construed the right and duty of parents to educate their children in Articles 42 teleologically in the light of the purpose for adopting the Constitution as explained in the Preamble:[109]

> Article 42.1 and 42.2 recognise that it is for parents to educate their children. This provision is not based on any proprietary right of the parents or functional analysis of the educational process. It is grounded on the acceptance of the belief that it is the moral right and duty of parents to educate children and that by exercising that and the other fundamental rights referred to in the Constitution the goals identified in the Preamble may be achieved.

This review of Irish case-law from the earliest days of the Constitution up to 2012 has shown that the courts have consistently returned to the Preamble as an indicator of constitutional values to be used to discern the people's purpose in enacting the Constitution and the meaning of specific provisions. The Preamble with its reference to human dignity has been invoked in diverse areas such as fair criminal trial, punishment for crime, equality, privacy, autonomy, expression, education, admission of refugees and freedom of movement. It can be a guide to the unenumerated rights springing from specific provisions in the Constitution to cope with changing circumstances.[110]

There are other examples of national courts enlightening the meaning of their constitutions by reference to the preamble. When it considered a

106 [2012] IEHC 3 [13].

107 [2012] IESC 10 [38].

108 [2012] IECCA 60.

109 [1999] IESC 90, [2000] 2 IR 17 at 65 - 66.

110 R Cannon 'Matters of Irish Constitutional debate: Originalism, democracy and natural law' (1995) 5 *Irish Student Law Review* 22 at 32.

challenge to the procedure for ratification of the Lisbon Treaty,[111] the German Federal Constitutional Court relied, *inter alia*, on the resolution contained in the Preamble to the Basic Law[112] to serve world peace as an equal partner in a united Europe in order to show that the principle of openness towards European law applied.[113] Hence, there was a constitutional mandate to realise a united Europe.[114] The French Constitutional Council gave binding legal force to the Preamble to the 1946 Constitution[115] as an independent source of human rights in 1971, when it struck down a law for breaching freedom of association.[116] The Preamble has also supported socio-economic rights in France.[117]

The Indian Supreme Court decisions are littered with references to the constitutional preamble and its association with human dignity.[118] The Preamble and human dignity have underpinned rights in various spheres including the right to travel as part of personal liberty;[119] health and safety at work imposing obligations on the employer and on the state to protect current and retired employees;[120] and equality, where social justice is aimed at achieving substantial social, economic and political equality,[121] and the reservation of government jobs for the historically deprived has been upheld.[122] Construing fundamental rights in the light of the Preamble, the Court in *Randhir Singh* deduced that the principle of 'equal pay for equal work' could be applied to employees receiving different scales of pay based on no classification or irrational classification for identical work under the

111 Treaty of Lisbon amending the Treaty on European Union and the Treaty establishing the European Community [2007] OJ C306/1.

112 Basic Law for the Federal Republic of Germany 1949.

113 *Treaty of Lisbon* case, BVerfG, 2 BvE 2/08, Absatz-Nr (1-421) (30 June 2009) 222, 225. See Orgad (n 86 above) 725.

114 n 113 above, 225.

115 Constitution of the French Republic 1946.

116 Decision No 71-44 (16 July 1971). See Orgad (n 86 above) 726 - 727.

117 See text to n 69-n72 in Ch VI.

118 See text to n 250 -n 254, n 275 -n 285 and n 289 -n 295 in Ch III; Orgad (n 86 above) 727 - 728.

119 *Maneka Gandhi v Union of India* [1978] INSC 16, 1978 SCR (2) 621.

120 *Consumer Education & Research Centre v Union of India* [1995] INSC 91, JT 1995 (1) 636. See text to n445 in Ch V.

121 *Air India Statutory Corp v United Labour Union* [1996] INSC 1400.

122 *Indra Sawhney v Union of India* 1992 Supp (3) SCC 217.

same employer.[123] Referring to the Preamble as an aid to interpretation in *Minerva Mills*, Chandrachud CJ captured the far-reaching nature of democracy embodied in the Constitution as securing the dignity of the individual in the community:[124]

> Democracy is not an empty dream. It is a meaningful concept whose essential attributes are recited in the preamble itself: Justice, social, economic and political; Liberty of thought, expression, belief, faith and worship, and Equality of status and opportunity. Its aim, again as set out in the preamble, is to promote among the people an abiding sense of 'Fraternity assuring the dignity of the individual and the unity of the Nation'.

This has remarkable resonances of the Irish constitutional vision of the person placed in society.

Judges in Australia and Canada have occasionally resorted to the Preamble. Three of the High Court judges in *Leeth* referred to it – Brennan J considered that the constitutional unity of the Australian people 'in one indissoluble Federal Commonwealth' recited in the Preamble to the Commonwealth of Australia Constitution Act 1900 meant that offenders against the same law could not be exposed to different maximum penalties depending on the locality of the sentencing court.[125] Taking an even stronger line, Deane and Toohey JJ used the Preamble to help ascertain the 'conceptual basis' of the Constitution from which emanated an implied guarantee of legal equality.[126]

The majority in the Canadian Supreme Court decision on the *Provincial Judges' Salaries* case adjudged that although the Preamble to the Canadian Constitution Act[127] was not a source of positive law, it had important legal

123 *Randhir Singh v Union of India* [1982] INSC 24, 1982 (3) SCR 298. See text to n 442 -n 443 in Ch V.

124 *Minerva Mills Ltd v Union of India* [1980] INSC 141, 1981 SCR (1) 206 at 240.

125 *Leeth v Commonwealth* [1992] HCA 29, (1992) 174 CLR 455 [7]. See M McKenna *et al* 'First words: The Preamble to the *Australian Constitution*' (2001) 24 *University of New South Wales Law Journal* 382 at 391 - 392; A Winckel 'A 21st century constitutional Preamble – An opportunity for unity rather than partisan politics' (2001) 24 *University of New South Wales Law Journal* 636 at 645 - 646.

126 *Leeth* (n 125 above) [9].

127 Constitution Act 1867.

effects – it recognised and affirmed judicial independence as an unwritten norm.[128] It went further than ordinary statutory preambles, which could identify the purpose of a statute and aid in the construction of ambiguous statutory language, as the Preamble to the Act embodying the Constitution articulated political theory by recognising and affirming the basic principles at the source of its substantive provisions.[129] The Court saw that the Preamble was more than the key to construing express provisions of the Act, but also invited the use of those principles to fill out gaps in the constitutional scheme.[130] Lamer CJ, delivering the majority judgment, eloquently portrayed the Preamble as 'the grand entrance hall to the castle of the Constitution'.[131]

The United States Supreme Court has used the Preamble as a tool of constitutional interpretation.[132] Justice Brennan in *Goldberg v Kelly* observed that the purpose of public assistance was to promote welfare and liberty – aims listed in the Preamble.[133] Although the issue of whether and in what manner it should be used has been debated,[134] the judicial references to it still

128 *Reference re Remuneration of Judges of the Provincial Court (PEI)* [1997] 3 SCR 3 [94]-[95], [109]. See Hogg (n 62 above) *Vol 1* at 204 - 205; McKenna *et al* (n 125 above) 397; JW Penney & RJ Danay 'The embarrassing Preamble? Understanding the 'supremacy of God' and the *Charter*' (2006) 39 *University of British Columbia Law Review* 287 at 297. For a critical review of this case, see J Goldsworthy 'The Preamble, judicial independence and judicial integrity' (2000) 11 *Constitutional Forum* 60.

129 n128 above, [95].

130 As above.

131 n128 above, [109].

132 D Himmelfarb 'The Preamble in constitutional interpretation' (1991) 2 *Seton Hall Constitutional Law Journal* 127 at 145. On the use of the Preamble in the courts, see M Handler *et al* 'A reconsideration of the relevance and materiality of the Preamble in constitutional interpretation' (1990) 12 *Cardozo Law Review* 117 at 119 - 123. On the Preamble to the Constitution of the United States generally, see JM Beck 'The Preamble of the Constitution' (1926) 14 *Georgetown Law Journal* 217. For a comparison between the Preambles to the Irish and the US Constitutions, see B Walsh '200 years of American constitutionalism – A foreign perspective' (1987) 48 *Ohio State Law Journal* 757 at 760.

133 397 US 254 (1970) 265. See text to n414-n415 in Ch V.

134 For arguments in favour of the Preamble having a role in discerning the values supporting unenumerated rights, see GP Carrasco & PW Rodino, Jr '"Unalienable rights," the Preamble, and the Ninth Amendment: The spirit of the Constitution' (1990) 20 *Seton Hall Law Review* 498.

135 Orgad (n 86 above) 720.

provide the Preamble with some constitutional weight.[135]

In many jurisdictions (including, as illustrated, South Africa and Ireland) the judiciary resorts to a constitution's preamble to identity the values shared by the community and the common objectives. The courts then use those identified values to interpret and apply the provisions in the constitution. The preamble can reinforce deep norms embodied in a constitution. It should be read by the judges, not in isolation, but as one key to the philosophy endorsed, which, in turn, will elucidate the purpose of rights, their meaning and the most appropriate harmonious interpretation to give effect to constitutional values in a modern changing society.

1.3.4 Philosophies supporting a values-based interpretation

A values-based interpretation requires articulation of a cogent moral foundation for decisions in compliance with the constitutional role assigned to the judges.[136] Invoked should be those shared principles explicitly or implicitly encompassed within the constitution and applied as mandated by the constitution interpreted in a purposive manner.

Fortunately since World War II there are many international and regional human rights instruments expressing universally agreed norms across diverse cultures available to support the judiciary in divining the meaning of values in national constitutions. In modern multi-cultural societies there is no need to resort to personal or widely-held (but not universally-shared) moral, religious or political convictions – nor, indeed, could this potentially-partisan view be justified.[137] The task is to adhere to the common values enshrined in the constitution and to apply those principles in cases arising for adjudication.

A review of the South African case-law shows that overall the judges have adhered to the universal constitutional values without imposing their own personal morality or the morality of any section of society in the adjudication process. They have not avoided grappling with difficult moral issues as can be seen in the litigation concerning sexual orientation[138] and

136 Devenish (n 19 above) 608.

137 Although there is a view that the idea of human rights is ineliminably religious, this does not deny that those who are not religious can take human rights seriously: MJ Perry 'Is the idea of human rights ineliminably religious?' in A Sarat & TR Kearns (eds) *Legal rights: Historical and philosophical perspectives* (1997) 252. See text to n 30 -n 33 in Ch II.

138 See Ch V, 5.5.3.

religious freedom.[139] Despite their usual objectivity, on occasion the influence of their personal moral and religious beliefs has become apparent.[140]

The South African Preamble refers to God[141] and the Irish Preamble has an even more conspicuous religious ethos resonant of its time.[142] The jurisprudence of Roman-Dutch law was natural law,[143] but the judiciary has not relied on it to interpret the Constitution – there have been occasional references to *ubuntu*. The judgments reflect constitutional values from a secular universally accepted perspective.[144] This is as it should be, since the Constitution recognises the right to freedom of conscience and religion.[145]

In addition to guaranteeing similar freedoms,[146] the Irish Constitution guarantees not to endow any religion.[147] Therefore, as in South Africa, a secular approach to interpreting the Constitution and the common values it encompasses is appropriate.[148] However, this does not mean that natural law[149] cannot be an *aid* to interpretation. 'Natural law' has been equated with

139 *Eg*, *S v Lawrence* 1997 4 SA 1176 (CC), *Christian Education South Africa v Minister of Education* 2000 4 SA 757 (CC), *Prince II*) (n 29 above), *MEC for Education: KwaZulu-Natal v Pillay* 2008 1 SA 474 (CC).

140 *Eg*, *Le Roux v Dey* where Mogoeng J did not agree with his nine colleagues that the choice to lead a heterosexual lifestyle, and to be known as heterosexual, should not be protected by legal action: [2011] ZACC 4, 2011 3 SA 274 (CC) [9].

141 'May God protect our people.' See Levinson (n 76 above) 168.

142 'In the Name of the Most Holy Trinity, from Whom is all authority and to Whom, as our final end, all actions both of men and States must be referred, We, the People of Éire, Humbly acknowledging all our obligations to our Divine Lord, Jesus Christ, Who sustained our fathers through centuries of trial... .' See Levinson (n 76 above) 170, 171; MJ Perry 'What do the free exercise and nonestablishment norms forbid? Reflections on the constitutional law of religious freedom' (2003) 1 *University of St Thomas Law Journal* 549 at fn 66; MJ Perry 'A right to religious freedom? The universality of human rights, the relativity of culture' (2005) 10 *Roger Williams University Law Review* 385 at fn 36.

143 Devenish (n 19 above) 630.

144 See Devenish (n 19 above) 639.

145 Sec 15(1).

146 Art 44.2.1°.

147 Art 44.2.2°.

148 On secular and religious approaches to constitutional interpretation, see Whyte 'Some reflections on the role of religion in the constitutional order' (n 9 above) 54 - 59.

149 On natural law, see n204 and text thereto in Ch VIII. See also Hogan & Whyte (n 5 above) [7.1.08]-[7.1.20], [7.8.14]; MJ Horwitz 'Natural law and natural rights' in Sarat & Kearns (n 137 above) 39 - 51; G Whyte 'Religion and the Irish Constitution' (1997) 30 *John Marshall Law Review* 725 at 739 - 744; Whyte (n 1 above) 27 fn 76.

the neutral term 'justice'.[150] Walsh J made the connection in *McGee*:[151]

> Articles 41, 42 and 43 emphatically reject the theory that there are no rights without laws, no rights contrary to the law and no rights anterior to the law. They indicate that justice is placed above the law and acknowledge that natural rights, or human rights, are not created by law but that the Constitution confirms their existence and gives them protection.

Explicit reliance on natural law has waned in recent decades – Murphy J's acknowledgment of the influence of Thomist natural law in *DPP v Best*[152] is an exception.[153]

In *Re Article 26 and the Regulation of Information (Services outside the State for Termination of Pregnancies) Bill 1995*, the Supreme Court held that the Constitution was the fundamental supreme law of the State representing the will of the people – hence, it ruled out natural law as being superior to specific provisions in the Constitution and it could not be called on to invalidate an amendment passed by the people in a referendum.[154] When Hamilton CJ, who delivered the judgment, went on to consider the right to life of the unborn he made a sweeping statement that the Court had already rejected the argument 'that the natural law was superior to the Constitution and that no provision of the Constitution or of any Act enacted by the Oireachtas or any judicial interpretation thereof can be contrary to natural law'.[155] Although a plausible reasoned defence might be made of his conclusion insofar as it concerns the *Constitution*, his immunisation of *statutes* and *judicial decisions* was undoubtedly too broad – he went further than was necessary to decide the issues in the case and ignored the wording of the Constitution itself, which refers to 'inalienable' rights and rights 'antecedent to positive law'.[156] The Supreme Court's reasoning has been described as

150 O'Connell (n 32 above) 54, 60, 61.

151 n 35 above, 310; see also n 35 above, 317 - 318.

152 n 109 above, 65.

153 Hogan & Whyte (n 5 above) [1.1.55].

154 [1995] IESC 9, [1995] 1 IR 1 at 43. See Byrne & McCutcheon (n 21 above) [15.183]-[15.186]; Hogan & Whyte (n5) [7.1.23]-[7.1.29]; GJ Jacobsohn 'An unconstitutional constitution? A comparative perspective' (2006) 4 *International Journal of Constitutional Law* 460 at 467 - 470; O'Connell (n 32 above) 64 - 66; O'Sullivan & Chan (n 16 above) 30 - 32, 35 - 36; AF Twomey 'The death of the natural law?' (1995) 13 *Irish Law Times* 270.

155 n 154 above, 50.

156 See text to n 205 -n 207 in Ch VIII.

'somewhat simplistic and lacking in sophistication'[157] and 'instructively deficient'.[158] No attempt was made to resolve the conflict between two provisions in the Constitution – both of which were the result of amendments to the Constitution. Indeed, the conflict was not even acknowledged. Neither was the issue of natural law addressed thoroughly.

That Hamilton CJ himself did not intend to wipe out natural law entirely from constitutional jurisprudence is evident in his judgment in the *Ward of Court* case less than three months later, where he referred to unenumerated natural rights ancillary to the right to life.[159] Indeed, when he was a High Court judge in *Northampton County Council v ABF* he had enthusiastically accepted the legal legitimacy of natural law and stated, '[t]he natural law is of universal application and applies to all human persons'.[160] He asserted that natural law rights were 'recognised by Bunreacht na hÉireann and the courts created under it as antecedent and superior to all positive law'.[161]

Since it is of universal application, it can be deduced that natural law is not confined to the religious tradition – as Roderick O'Hanlon said, it is 'in essence immutable' and 'is not contingent on contemporary *mores* or any particular culture, because it resides in the innermost common denominator of all humankind through all generations, that is, human reason.'[162] The origins of natural law can be traced back to the pre-Christian days of Aristotle, whose philosophical ideas influenced the adoption of the doctrine by scholars of various religions centuries later.[163] It formed a strong vein in the jurisprudence of the courts of the United States of America.[164] The dignity of

157 Whyte 'Natural Law and the Constitution' (n 9 above) 11. See also, as above, (footnote omitted):

> Essential premises are not properly established; judicial precedents and constitutional provisions which appear to endorse natural law theory are not properly engaged (and, indeed, in the case of Mr Justice Walsh's remarks, are perversely cited in support of a positivist understanding of the Constitution which he would never endorse); and there is a failure to address obvious questions raised by the judgment, such as whether there is any residual role for natural law theory under the Constitution and, if so, for which variants of that theory.

158 Jacobsohn (n 154 above) 469.

159 n 39 above, 123 - 124. See Byrne & McCutcheon (n 21 above) [15.187]-[15.194].

160 [1982] ILRM 164 (HC) 166.

161 As above.

162 RJ O'Hanlon 'Natural rights and the Irish Constitution' (1993) 11 *Irish Law Times* 8 at 8.

163 See Kelly (n 13 above) 57 - 58; T Murphy 'The cat amongst the pigeons: Garrett Barden and Irish natural law jurisprudence' in Doyle & Carolan (n 2 above) 128, 133 - 134.

164 Devenish (n 19 above) 630.

man recognised in natural law was the unifying theme behind adoption of the Universal Declaration – it was universally acceptable to all cultures and to those of all religions and of none.[165] Its appeal is secular (as well as undoubtedly religious). A non-sectarian view of human dignity was taken by Henchy J in *McGee*[166] and *Norris*,[167] where his application of respect for dignity would require the State to preserve as great a range of authentic moral choice based on the personal make-up of the individual as is consistent with the common good[168] – it did not mean that the law could impose a particular institutional religious view on the conscientious individual.

The common good (a prime constitutional aim), like human dignity, is rooted in natural law philosophy.[169] As William Binchy said, 'it envisages a social scaffolding capable of supporting the individual fulfilment of human potential.'[170]

1.3.5 Judicial practice

Unlike the South African judiciary, Irish judges in recent decades have avoided engagement with the philosophical and moral dimensions to contentious disputes.[171] They have not leveraged the strong value system in the Constitution. The result has been a failure to vindicate personal rights, to assure the human dignity of the individual in the community and to promote the constitutional aim of social justice. Reliance on the other arms of government to comply with the State's constitutional duties has been misplaced. The power structure in Ireland has continued with very little challenge. By failing to intervene to redress social exclusion in the socio-economic sphere, the judges are not fulfilling their constitutional duty to

165 See 2.2.1.1 in Ch II.

166 n 35 above.

167 *Norris v AG* [1984] IR 36 (SC).

168 Binchy (n 2 above) 315; S Henchy 'Precedent in the Irish Supreme Court' (1962) 25 *Modern Law Review* 544 at 550.

169 Binchy (n 2 above) 315 - 316; Kelly (n 13 above) 423 - 424.

170 Binchy (n 2 above) 316.

171 *Eg*, *Roche v Roche* [2006] IEHC 359, [2009] IESC 82, [2010] 2 IR 321 (see text to n 387 -n 389 in Ch VII). See 7.2 in Ch VII. The European Court of Human Rights allows the states a margin of appreciation when there is not a European consensus on the moral issue arising and when the appropriate legal protection has not been resolved in the majority of states: *Vo v France* (App no 53924/00) (2005) 40 EHRR 12 [82]. However, a dissenting view was that there could be no margin of appreciation in application of an absolute right: as above, [O-III8] (Ress J).

uphold the Constitution, and are not defending and vindicating personal rights.[172] Accordingly, Irish democracy is falling short of realising the constitutional value of a just social order, in which the freedom and dignity of the individual is assured.[173]

The trend in recent years to revert to the positivist view of the Constitution is regrettable, as it runs contrary to its spirit and purpose garnered from a reading of the document as a whole – the Preamble in addition to the fundamental rights and other substantive provisions contained within it. It runs contrary to Seamus Henchy's conviction that the Constitution broke 'with the positivist character of the common law', a conclusion which he attributed to the fact that the Preamble 'makes clear that the Constitution and the laws which owe their force to the Constitution derive, under God, from the people and are directed to the promotion of the common good.'[174]

The Irish Preamble approved by the people in 1937 was prophetic in anticipating the Universal Declaration with its emphasis on human dignity by more than a decade.[175] It was the first national constitution to specifically refer to dignity in the sense of being inherent in all people. Although Christopher McCrudden has named four countries (Mexico, Germany, Finland and Portugal) as incorporating the concept of dignity in their constitutions before Ireland in 1937,[176] a closer examination of those constitutions shows that this is not correct – the references to dignity were either to dignity as status,[177] adopted by subsequent amendment[178] or implied by the use of an analogous term.[179]

The Supreme Court's virtual closing off of identifying more unenumerated rights (in the socio-economic area at least)[180] has inhibited the

172 McHugh (n 16 above) 126, 129.

173 McHugh (n 16 above) 129.

174 Henchy (n 168 above) 550.

175 Walsh (n 12 above) 92.

176 C McCrudden 'Human dignity and judicial interpretation of human rights' (2008) 19 *European Journal of International Law* 655 at 664. See text to n 104 -n 108 in Ch II.

177 The original constitution adopted by Finland in 1919 mentioned 'hereditary dignity'.

178 The original constitutions adopted by Mexico in 1917 and by Portugal in 1933 contained no reference to dignity.

179 The German Reich Constitution of 1919 stated that the principles of justice were aimed at the attainment of 'humane conditions of existence' for all.

180 G Whyte 'Rights and judicial activism' in B Fanning *et al* (eds) *Theorising Irish social policy* (2004) 172 - 174.

courts from keeping pace with the legal problems presented by the changes in modern life and advancing technology.[181] The judges need to overcome their reluctance to grasp the philosophies underlying the Constitution. Instead they could expose its values, interpret its provisions in accordance with those values and apply them to cases coming before them for adjudication. Novel legal issues arising in the increasing complexity of modern life where people are more mobile than in the past and there is much diversity in Irish society will ensure a continuing demand for the judiciary to take this step. As Brian Walsh expressed it, the Constitution has given the judiciary a position of special responsibility as 'the ultimate interpreters of the law and of the Constitution itself', and this requires that the fundamental human rights of minorities be guaranteed so that they can 'permanently withstand the assaults tolerated or even initiated by occasional despotic majorities.'[182]

One area where the values will have an impact is in enforcement of the Hague Convention on Child Abduction, which allows a state to refuse to return a child to the requesting jurisdiction if it would not be permitted by the 'fundamental principles of the requested State relating to the protection of human rights and fundamental freedoms.'[183] The correct application of this provision requires clarity on the content and boundaries of the fundamental human rights principles in the Irish Constitution. So far there has been a dearth of considered judicial analysis of these principles – the

181 *TD v Minister for Education* [2001] IESC 101, [2001] 4 IR 259. Keane CJ pointed out that the Supreme Court had not specifically endorsed the view that unenumerated rights flowed from the Christian and democratic nature of the State and neither had it decided whether the declaration of unenumerated rights should be the courts' function rather than that of the Oireachtas: above, 281. He had first expressed these doubts three years earlier: *IO'T v B* [1998] 2 IR 321 (SC) 369 - 370. See Byrne & McCutcheon (n 21 above) [15.60]. In *IO'T v B* Keane J relied (wrongly in my view) on remarks of Walsh J in *McGee* and on the judgment in *Regulation of Information Bill* to deduce that 'no identifiable and superior *corpus* of law' existed to which judges might have recourse: above, 372.

182 B Walsh 'The judicial power, justice and the Constitution of Ireland' in D Curtin & D O'Keeffe (eds) *Constitutional adjudication in European Community and national law: Essays for the Hon. Mr. Justice T.F. O'Higgins* (1992) 157.

183 Convention on the Civil Aspects of International Child Abduction (adopted 25 October 1980, entered into force 1 December 1983) 19 ILM 1501 (1980) (Hague Convention on Child Abduction), Art 20.

courts have preferred to take the easier option of deciding the cases before them on narrow points of law or fact.[184]

If a conflict emerged between rights under European law and the fundamental rights protected by the Irish Constitution, a thorough analysis of the values enshrined in the Constitution would strengthen the judicial evaluation.[185]

184 *Eg*, *Nottinghamshire County Council v B* where the parents of two children challenged an application by the English local authority to have them returned to England: [2011] IESC 48. The parents claimed that they and their children constituted a family under Articles 41 and 42 of the Constitution and that return of the children would be in breach of those rights because the law of the United Kingdom permitted adoption of the children of married couples in circumstances where it would not be permitted in Ireland: above, [4]. The Supreme Court upheld the decision of Finlay Geoghegan J to return the children because their adoption was no more than a 'possibility'; furthermore, O'Donnell J, who delivered the Court's judgment, considered that the UK adoption regime was 'not so fundamentally at odds' with the forms of adoption permitted under the Irish Constitution: above, [67], [89]. He did not explore the human rights norms underlying the Irish Constitution, but concentrated more on the value of international co-operation: above, [60], [64]-[65], citing Constitution of Ireland 1937, Art 29. His terminology dismissed resistance to international co-operation on human rights grounds as 'isolationism' and 'fundamentalist': above, [45], [63]. He raised (but did not decide) the question of the level of constitutional protection afforded to non-citizens travelling to Ireland and suggested that Article 40.1 of the Constitution (the equality provision) could be relevant: above, [84]. By focusing on the Irish court's order of *return* of the children rather than on what might happen to them (*eg*, adoption) if they were *returned* to England, O'Donnell J narrowed the level of protection under the Convention: above, [54], [61]. The test he applied was not whether there was a constitutional difference between the two regimes, but whether what was proposed or contemplated in the requesting state departed 'so markedly from the essential scheme and order envisaged by the Constitution' and was such a direct consequence of the court's order that return was not permitted by the Constitution: above, [54]. A difference in the law relating to the care of children between the jurisdictions (even if the foreign law would be unconstitutional if enacted in Ireland) was not the issue – that difference could be ignored if the laws in both jurisdictions were 'recognisably part of the same spectrum' of views; to justify a refusal to return it was necessary to show that the manner in which the children would be dealt with by the courts on their return 'must necessarily offend against the provisions of the Irish Constitution if administered in an Irish court': above, [52]. O'Donnell J focused on the compatibility of the legal *systems* rather than compliance of the requesting jurisdiction with the *constitutional standards* of the requested state: above, [45], [63]-[64], [66]. Although he referred to case-law concerning natural law, he did not deliberate on this aspect: above, [30], citing *Northampton County Council v ABF* (Hamilton J, relying on Walsh J in *McGee*). See R Byrne & W Binchy *Annual review of Irish law 2011* (2012) 153 - 154, 223 - 229.

185 See M Cahill 'Constitutional exclusion clauses, Article 29.4.6° and the constitutional reception of European law' (2011) 34 *Dublin University Law Journal* 74 at 96.

1.4 Research methodology

As this is a comparative study, I engaged in substantial doctrinal research. My literature review started with fundamental rights concentrating on the South African and Irish Constitutions and international human rights. It broadened out to other African and European countries (particularly Germany), and to Canada, India, Israel, the US, Australia, and New Zealand. Some of these countries were chosen for comparison because they are in geographical proximity to South Africa or Ireland, being in the continents of Africa or Europe, or have similar legal backgrounds to them. The review of the literature and case-law had revealed that the fundamental rights jurisprudence in Germany, Canada, India and Israel had a particular emphasis on dignity. The South African Constitutional Court has mainly referred to Canada, Germany, India and the US in its judgments.[186] The regional systems in Europe, Africa and America had interesting comparisons.

Relevant case-law and legislation were noted. Tracking of new developments was necessary. The content and impact of various human rights instruments and systems were taken into account. The conclusions were drawn from engaging in deductive and inductive reasoning. The application of sub-conscious reasoning to the doctrine elicited preliminary findings, which were refined by critical evaluations. The study culminated in the writing of a report that combined an understanding of the relevant theory and its practical application with the results of comparative research.

1.5 Summary of major lessons

The examination of constitutional interpretation has substantiated the proposition that the Irish courts should adopt a purposive values-based approach taking the reference to human dignity in the Preamble as a serious factor. Apart from reliance on the Preamble, human dignity is germane to the debate on human rights because of its universal acceptance in international

186 Church *et al* (n 47 above) 80.

instruments.[187] The Universal Declaration, with its several references to human dignity regarded as inherent, has grown in importance since it was first signed and is now widely considered to be part of customary international law.[188]

Another reason for taking human dignity seriously is because it is intrinsically linked with specific fundamental rights in the Constitution as supported by the text and case-law. The Irish courts have found that there is an unenumerated right to dignity.[189] In the equality context Article 40.1 was defined as referring to our dignity as human beings.[190] The values of privacy and dignity have been associated with a prisoner's personal rights under Art 40.3.1.[191] Justice in the courts implies regard for the dignity of the individual as well as fairness and fair procedures.[192] Hardiman J noted that the dignity of the individual requires fair procedures in public administration.[193] The higher level of constitutional protection afforded to a person's dwellinghouse under Article 40.5 is because secure occupation of it is necessary for human dignity.[194]

187 Costello P referred to the concepts in the Preamble and in Article 40.1 (the common good, dignity, freedom and equality) as being recognised in the Universal Declaration: *Molyneux v Ireland* [1997] 2 ILRM 241 (HC) 243. Murray J mentioned the recognition in the Universal Declaration 'of the inherent dignity and of the equal and inalienable rights of all members of the human family': *North Western Health Board v HW* [2001] IESC 90, [2001] 3 IR 622 at 736. In the same case, Hardiman J stated, '[a]mple scope must be given to the fundamental values of human dignity': above, 747.

188 J van Aggelen 'The Preamble of the United Nations Declaration of Human Rights' (2000) 28 *Denver Journal of International Law and Policy* 129 at 131.

189 See text to n 46-n50 in Ch VII.

190 See text to n 14 in Ch VII.

191 See text to n 232 -n 241 in Ch VII. Hardiman J identified values based on respect for human rights and dignity as underlying the necessity to treat prisoners properly: see text to n 55 in Ch VII.

192 *Healy v Donoghue* (n95) 348. McGuinness J relied on the same principles to constrain the DPP from reversing a decision not to prosecute after that decision had been communicated to a suspect without any caveat: *Eviston v DPP* [2002] IESC 62, [2002] 3 IR 260 at 318 - 319. The entitlement of unconvicted prisoners not to be made to stand trial in prison garb (based on the presumption of innocence) is in order to avoid stigmatisation and to maintain the dignity of the individual: *People (DPP) v Davis* [2001] 1 IR 146 (CCA) 152, citing *Estelle v Williams* 425 US 501 (1976) 518 (Justice Brennan dissenting).

193 *Dellway Investments Ltd v National Asset Management Agency* [2011] IESC 14, citing DG Morgan & G Hogan *Administrative law in Ireland* (2010). See Byrne & Binchy (n 184 above) 170 - 172.

194 See text to n 23 in Ch VII. There is statutory immunity from criminal and civil liability for injury or damage caused by the use of reasonable force in defending one's dwelling: Criminal Law (Defence and the Dwelling) Act 2011 secs 2 & 5.

The part played by human dignity in the Preamble as a fundamental constitutional value, its role as the basis of international human rights instruments, the fact that it has been recognised as an unenumerated right, and the connections between dignity and constitutional rights merit the Irish judges giving it greater prominence in their decisions. There is no convincing argument in favour of ignoring or overlooking it. On the contrary, if it were analysed in depth and applied by the judiciary, it could lead to a coherent articulation of the impact of the Constitution on individuals in a shared society in the context of their everyday lives. People would then have a clearer picture of the implications for them of the Constitution in practice and would have confidence that they could rely on the judiciary to uphold constitutional values and rights.

The main messages are in the areas of equality, socio-economic rights, the legal status of unmarried fathers, punishment of children, prison conditions, the extent of state responsibility to protect human rights, and civil liability for failures of the police and state-endorsed agents. There are helpful pointers relating to publication of private information, the parameters of informed consent, regulation of research and aids to human reproduction, prohibition of hate speech, development of the laws of defamation and contract, quantum of damages and effective remedies.[195]

Examined against a standard of accountability, Irish law could follow on the lines of South African jurisprudence a remoulding of tort law in the light of constitutional values. Since some constitutional rights do not depend on the state for their existence, they are enforceable against all those with whom the individual has relationships to the extent that they are capable of being applied. The Irish courts' incoherent explanations and haphazard approach to the enforcement of rights in private law could be put on a structured basis by applying the constitutional norms of human dignity and the common good to discern the nature and extent of each right. Adoption of the indirect horizontal effect doctrine as in South Africa would be beneficial.

195 The damage to a defamed person's dignity and standing in the community could be repaired by a public apology, a judicial finding of defamation and a modest sum in compensation. Similarly where a severely impaired person is unaware of the impact of the injuries received, their human dignity could be reconciled with society's values by a smaller award than that merited by a fully-conscious plaintiff.

2

Human Dignity and its Role in Contemporary Jurisprudence

2.1 The philosophical dimension

The dignity of the person refers to the special status given to all individuals by virtue of being human.[1] The first occurrence of the 'dignity of man' was a philosophical expression invented by a Greek aristocrat, Panaetius of Rhodes, and translated into Latin by a Roman nobleman.[2] It was eventually connected with Stoic theology.[3] As it could be understood as pure ethics, it could be combined with Judaeo-Christian beliefs.[4]

1 The term 'dignity' in literature or conversation has different meanings depending on the context. Its many definitions include 'the state of being worthy of honour or respect', 'a high or honourable rank or position' and 'high regard or estimation': *The concise Oxford dictionary of current English* (1991) 326. When applied to states, royalty or diplomats, it can be associated with status and signify that an entity, office or person is deserving of exceptional honour. A dignitary is 'a person holding high rank or office' and is superior to others in certain respects: as above. The adjective 'dignified' indicates that a person or event conducts themselves in a respectful way. One definition is 'noble or stately in appearance or manner': as above. A dignified person is someone with self-esteem, who is conscious of their own worth without being boastful or over-endowed with pride.

2 H Cancik '"Dignity of man"' and "*persona*" in Stoic anthropology: Some remarks on Cicero, *De officiis I* 105-107' in D Kretzmer & E Klein (eds) *The concept of human dignity in human rights discourse* (2002) 27.

3 In the philosophy of the Stoics and in Roman humanism, there was a *collective* notion of *dignitas humana* that did not have the modern egalitarian meaning: J Habermas 'The concept of human dignity and the realistic utopia of human rights' (2010) 41 *Metaphilosophy* 464 at 473. Humans were of superior rank to 'lower' forms of life because of faculties such as reason and reflection: as above.

4 Cancik (n 2 above) 27. Cf L Sossin 'The "supremacy of God", human dignity and the *Charter of Rights and Freedoms*' (2003) 52 *University of New Brunswick Law Journal* 227 at 229 - 230.

Yair Lorberbaum remarked that the concept of human dignity and the sanctity of human life are historically bound up (at least in Jewish tradition and to a great extent in early Christianity, which draws from it) with the biblical notion of humankind created in the divine image.[5] The idea of *Imago Dei* is to be found in Mesopotamia and perhaps in ancient Egypt as well.[6] Lorberbaum acknowledges it is arguable that the modern content of human dignity has nothing in common with these ancient thought structures, but has its origins in modern anthropology, metaphysics and the ethics of Immanuel Kant and other Enlightenment thinkers.[7] He has recourse to Paul Ricoeur's view that 'the symbol gives rise to thought' as a counter-argument.[8] In ancient times, dignity was more often a symbol of social status and therefore of superiority rather than of equality. But Cicero and some other classical Roman writers also used the concept of *dignitas hominis* to refer to the dignity of human beings as such without being dependent on any additional status.[9]

In philosophical terms, 'human dignity' has been recognised since ancient times. It and the term 'human being' are synonymous. Each person is unique. Humanity has always been regarded as superior to animals and other species.

5 Y Lorberbaum 'Blood and the image of God: On the sanctity of life in biblical and early rabbinic law, myth, and ritual' in Kretzmer & Klein (n 2 above) 55. See also L Ackermann *Human dignity: Lodestar for equality in South Africa* (2012) 35 - 37; YM Barilan 'From *imago dei* in the Jewish-Christian traditions to human dignity in contemporary Jewish law' (2009) 19 *Kennedy Institute Ethics Journal* 231; JJ Coughlin 'Pope John Paul II and the dignity of the human being' (2003) 27 *Harvard Journal of Law and Public Policy* 65 at 71 - 73, 79; I Englard 'Human dignity: From antiquity to modern Israel's constitutional framework' (2000) 21 *Cardozo Law Review* 1903 at 1904, 1906 - 1917; GP Fletcher 'In God's image: The religious imperative of equality under law' (1999) 99 *Columbia Law Review* 1608 at 1615 - 1618, 1620; M Freeman 'The problem of secularism in human rights theory' (2004) 26 *Human Rights Quarterly* 375 at 387 - 389; KJ Hasson 'Religious liberty and human dignity: A tale of two declarations' (2003) 27 *Harvard Journal of Law and Public Policy* 81 at 85 - 88; E Venckiene 'The importance of historical discourse for the legal protection of human dignity at present' (2010) 119 *Jurisprudence* 147 at 152 - 154, 157; WJ Wagner 'Universal human rights, the United Nations, and the *telos* of human dignity' (2005) 3 *Ave Maria Law Review* 197 at 221 - 222, 225. On *Imago Dei* and human rights, see G Butler 'The essence of human rights: A religious critique' (2009) 43 *University of Richmond Law Review* 1255 at 1263, 1272; JB Elshtain 'The dignity of the human person and *The idea of human rights: Four inquiries*' (1999) 14 *Journal of Law and Religion* 53 at 63 - 64; E Regan *Theology and the boundary discourse of human rights* (2010) 70, 85.

6 Lorberbaum (n 5 above) 55.

7 n 5 above, 84.

8 n 5 above, 84, citing P Ricoeur *Symbolism of evil* trans E Buchanan (1967) 348.

9 C McCrudden 'Human dignity and judicial interpretation of human rights' (2008) 19 *European Journal of International Law* 655 at 657.

Cicero contrasted man with animals.[10] Philosophers saw that the capacity for rational thought and free will distinguished human beings.[11] According to Christian Starck, classical and Christian concepts of human dignity and freedom recognised an important social aspect, where human beings were interdependent, as evidenced by the enshrinement of fraternity and solidarity in the early political structures.[12] In sub-Saharan Africa, the mutually supportive relationship between human dignity and equality has spawned the social concept of *ubuntu.*[13] Langa CJ of South Africa, having translated it from Zulu as 'a person is a person through another person', said it described the essence of humanity and what it means to be a human being.[14]

The equality of all human beings was a conclusion of the Christian view that all are equally the image of God. Thus, human beings have a metaphysical anchor as the basis for their freedom, equality and fraternity.[15] Human dignity does not signify simply autonomy. Starck describes it as 'self-determination which is exercised on the basis that everyone – not simply the person claiming the right to self-determination – is of value in his or her own right.'[16] Equal consideration is to be given to the other.

The inherent dignity of the individual demands respect from others on a reciprocal basis. The rationale for designating the human person as special has metamorphosed or extended over the centuries. The enigmatic question is – what is the meaning of life and what is our purpose in it?

An individual's inner worth is at the core of their being. Their personality is unique to them and they are entitled to forge their own identity. Identity

10 He focused on the difference in mental capacities, as in this extract, '[i]t is vitally necessary for us to remember always how vastly superior is man's nature to that of cattle and other animals; their only thought is for bodily satisfactions… . Man's mind, on the contrary, is developed by study and reflection': McCrudden (n 9 above) 657, citing Cicero, *De officiis I* at 30. On Cicero's idea of human dignity, see K Saastamoinen 'Pufendorf on natural equality, human dignity, and self-esteem' (2010) 71 *Journal of the History of Ideas* 39 at 49 - 51.

11 C Starck 'The religious and philosophical background of human dignity and its place in modern constitutions' in Kretzmer & Klein (n 2 above) 180.

12 As above.

13 On *ubuntu*, see Ackermann (n 5 above) 77 - 81; T Metz 'Human dignity, capital punishment, and an African moral theory: Toward a new philosophy of human rights' (2010) 9 *Journal of Human Rights* 81 at 82 - 85.

14 Langa CJ 'A reply to Professor William Binchy on "Constitutionality, the rule of law and socio-economic development"' (Lecture at Southern African Chief Justices Forum in Botswana 2009) 7 http://www.venice.coe.int//SACJF/2009_08_BTW_Kasane/default.htm (accessed 24 September 2013).

15 Starck (n 11 above) 181.

16 As above.

and personality are deeply significant for each individual in the passage through life.[17] The assurance of the scope to all people in society to achieve their full potential to lead meaningful lives in accordance with their unique identity and to express their own personality requires respect for each other from all members of society.

Dignity is the opposite of shame.[18] It is equated with honour, particularly with the aim of redressing a humiliating assault on dignity, and is the entitlement of all human beings irrespective of status.[19]

Because of our mutual dependence in society, dignity invokes duties and responsibilities towards others as well as respect for oneself and others. There is a common interest in protecting or enhancing the dignity of all members of society provided that all reciprocate.

Mette Lebech profers four distinct rationales that have developed and amalgamated to provide a more coherent understanding of human dignity.[20] The first rationale to gain credence was in the time of Cicero and antiquity when the physical superiority of humans gave them the right to dominion over animals and other creatures. The second rationale emerged in the Middle Ages when Thomas Aquinas identified the discerning feature of humans as being their likeness to God. Each individual was deserving of respect because of their spirituality. In modern times after the Reformation, the spiritual dimension was thought wanting and Kant developed a third rationale which

17 Cardinal Manning viewed dignity as the achievement of the individual's potential in life. Each life has value in its own right irrespective of comparisons with others. In 1874 Cardinal Manning described the dignity in physical labour aimed at helping others as well as oneself, HE Manning *The dignity and rights of labour, and other writings on social questions* (1934) 6:

> [I]n the mere labour of the body there is a true dignity. The man who puts forth the powers of the body, and that honestly, for his own good and the good of his neighbour, is living a high and worthy life, and that because it is his state in the world. It is the lot in which we are placed, and any man who fulfils the lot of his existence is in a state of dignity.

Humility, being the absence of jealousy and envy, is a feature of dignity. Cardinal Manning expressed it as follows, 'I know nothing that is more undignified than for a man to think there is nobody of higher stature, morally or intellectually, than himself. The smallest man on earth is the man who thinks there is nobody greater than himself.': above, 15. He considered that the four cardinal virtues of prudence (guiding the intellect), justice (guiding the will), temperance (governing the passions) and fortitude (sustaining the whole person) 'underlie all the dignity of man, and they justify all his rights': above, 33 - 34.

18 C Safrai 'Human dignity in a rabbinical perspective' in Kretzmer & Klein (n 2 above) 105.

19 On the generalisation of the concept of dignity, see Habermas (n 3 above) 472 - 475. See also M Dan-Cohen 'A concept of dignity' (2011) 44 *Israel Law Review* 9.

20 M Lebech 'What is human dignity?' (2004) 2 *Maynooth Philosophical Papers* 59 at 60.

imputed superiority to human beings by virtue of their reasoning capacity and free will. Mary Wollstonecraft saw that politics significantly affected the lives of people in society and the fourth rationale attributed to her was based on the status of each individual in the community.

These four rationales combine to explain why human beings have human dignity. A further step is necessary in order to experience what it really means to be human. Relationships between individuals open up the various aspects of humanity. The relationships in question can be based on love, family ties or friendship.[21] They can be between spouses or life partners, within families and extend to neighbours, the local community, wider society, the state and internationally. Love of all other individuals as well as love of oneself gives the full experience of humanity. It reveals the essential attributes of what it means to be human and the depth of the individual's identity beneath one's nature, spirituality, reason and social integration.[22] Lebech deduces that it is only in love that we adequately identify the other. We have to rely on love in practice to give content to the idea of human dignity.[23]

Richard Stith endorsed the preference expressed by John Finnis for respecting human beings rather than simply valuing them.[24] But Stith considers that love for one another based on God's love for us might be a better foundation for relationships than respect. Being made in the image of God, we, in turn, should love each other because of God's love for us and our likeness to God. A loving person cares for the individual because of his or her unique existence and not because of their achievements.[25] Love responds and gives the other freedom. It does not seek to control the other. The sanctity of each individual requires reverential treatment.

As the ideal religious base of love does not have universal appeal, Stith settles for the secularly-acceptable respect for others as a more widely

21 n20 above, 67.

22 n20 above, 68.

23 Lebech concludes, 'we learn to respond out of our own depth to the equally fundamental value of the other. Hence, as an expression, "human dignity", refers beyond criteria to the fundamental value of the existence of individual human beings.': as above. See also M Lebech 'On the problem of human dignity' (2010) 21(4) *Bioethics Outlook* 3 at 5, 8.

24 Stith quoted Finnis, '[h]uman beings are not just "values" ... rather, they are persons each incommunicably, non-fungibly individual in [a] peculiar, deep way, and so entitled, one by one, to be respected.': R Stith 'The priority of respect: How our common hu-manity can ground our individual dignity' (2004) 44 *International Philosophical Quarterly* 165 at 169, citing J Finnis 'Public reason, abortion and cloning' (1998) 32 *Valparaiso University Law Review* 361 at 377.

25 n24 above, 174.

embraced starting point. He sees human beings as beginnings, not ends.[26] They should be given the opportunity to develop their personality in order to achieve their full potential. Respond to others, but be prepared to release them rather than holding them.[27] Eschew control.[28] Acknowledge their wishes and defer to them. A retreat, not a charge, is often required.

The common commitment to respect for each other is a source of solidarity and the foundation of society. There is mutual interest in respecting each other, so that all can develop and grow. The quest in life is to find and be true to one's identity. Respect for the identity and inviolability of each person is a better foundation for society than a value judgement of the individual.[29]

Michael J Perry is an adherent of the 'love' doctrine.[30] God loves us; therefore, we must all love each other. In the absence of love, Perry paints the gloomy spectre of Nietzsche's nihilism.[31] He is convinced that morality founded on the claim that every human being has inherent dignity and is therefore inviolable has solely a religious basis. This is the cornerstone of human rights.[32] Having analysed the works of various philosophers (including Ronald Dworkin, Martha Nussbaum, Richard Rorty, Leo Tolstoy, Richard Posner, Raimond Gaita and Finnis), he discounts a non-religious footing for the morality of human rights.[33]

Dworkin perceives that human beings can be sacred or inviolable from a secular perspective as well as from a religious point of view.[34] The secular proponent sees each individual as 'a creative masterpiece' attributable to a combination of natural and human intervention.[35] Sacredness or inviolability arises through history or association.[36] A person is the highest product of

26 n 24 above, 166.

27 n 24 above, 178.

28 n 24 above, 180.

29 Stith sums up, '[w]e can find solidarity more safely in a common respect than in a common goal.': n 24 above, 184.

30 MJ Perry *Toward a theory of human rights: Religion, law, courts* (2007).

31 n 30 above, 29.

32 On Perry and the religious basis for human rights, see Butler (n 5 above) 1263 - 1267.

33 MJ Perry 'The morality of human rights: A nonreligious ground?' (2005) 54 *Emory Law Journal* 97 at 150.

34 R Dworkin *Life's dominion: An argument about abortion and euthanasia* (1993) 25, 82. See SC Rockefeller 'Comment' in C Taylor *et al*, *Multiculturalism: Examining the politics of recognition* (1994) 95.

35 n 34 above, 82 - 83.

36 n 34 above, 74.

natural creation and of deliberative human creative force.[37] Because of the intrinsic importance of these two elements, no-one should violate anyone else and everyone commands respect and protection from everyone else.[38] Human life can have instrumental and subjective value as well as intrinsic value.[39]

Autonomy is necessary in order to develop one's personality. Adults have the right to make decisions defining their own lives. Dworkin explains the importance of respect for autonomy thus:[40]

> Recognizing an individual right of autonomy makes self-creation possible. It allows each of us to be responsible for shaping our lives according to our own coherent or incoherent – but, in any case, distinctive – personality. It allows us to lead our own lives rather than be led along them, so that each of us can be, to the extent a scheme of rights can make this possible, what we have made of ourselves.

Democracy provides an environment where people have the freedom to make rational choices for themselves. Dworkin links dignity to freedom,[41] and makes a further link from dignity through freedom to democracy:[42]

> Because we cherish dignity, we insist on freedom, and we place the right of conscience at its center... Because we honor dignity, we demand democracy.

Each individual has experiential and critical interests in life.[43] It is essential for individuals and for their integrity that their lives as a whole make sense

37 n 34 above, 82.

38 n 34 above, 84.

39 n 34 above, 72. On dignity as intrinsic human worth, see N Rao 'Three concepts of dignity in constitutional law' (2011) 86 *Notre Dame Law Review* 183 at 196 - 202.

40 n 34 above, 224.

41 The connection is evident in the following passage, n34 above, 239:

> ... a true appreciation of dignity argues ... for individual freedom, not coercion, for a régime of law and attitude that encourages each of us to make mortal decisions for himself. Freedom is the cardinal, absolute requirement of self-respect: no one treats his life as having any intrinsic, objective importance unless he insists on leading that life himself, not being ushered along it by others, no matter how much he loves or respects or fears them.

Law regards self-application as important and looks wherever possible to voluntary compliance: J Waldron *Dignity, rank, and rights* (2012) 52, 63. It only resorts to coercion as a last resort and – when coercion is necessary – dignity is respected in the manner of enforcement: Waldron above, 63 - 64 (footnotes omitted).

42 n 34 above, 239.

43 n 34 above, 201.

and that they have lived a good life according to their own convictions. Integrity is closely connected to dignity and is important in people having the freedom to live their lives in a responsible fashion as they see fit.[44] Self-respect is a necessary ingredient in acting with integrity and in nurturing one's own dignity. Dworkin alludes to our antipathy towards the attempted waiver of dignity when he highlights the lack of self-respect in a person acting without integrity.[45] As bad, or even worse, are those who do not recognise that they have compromised their own dignity.[46]

Dworkin defines a person's right to be treated with dignity as 'the right that others acknowledge his genuine critical interests: that they acknowledge that he is the kind of creature, and has the moral standing, such that it is intrinsically, objectively important how his life goes.'[47] Human dignity is based on the intrinsic value of life, which merits the regard in which one is held by oneself and by others.

Irrespective of their conduct, everyone should be treated with respect, or at least, should not be treated with disrespect or suffer indignity. The community disapproves of those who do not have self-esteem and do not appreciate their own dignity. However, there is not necessarily a duty on others to advance an individual's critical interests. Rather, the obligation is to recognise and respect those interests no matter what the circumstances. Dworkin endorses Kant's principle that people should be treated as ends, not means.[48] Only the individuals themselves are entitled to define what is important to them in the passage through life.

Another secular supporter is Nussbaum, who considers that the good of other human beings is worth pursuing in its own right.[49] She attributes this caring characteristic to the basic social emotion of compassion.[50] One feels

44 n 34 above, 205.

45 '[W]e think that someone who acts out of character, for gain or to avoid trouble, has insufficient respect for himself.': as above. The right to be treated as a person cannot be waived: H Morris *On guilt and innocence: Essays in legal philosophy and moral psychology* (1976) 53.

46 n 34 above, 235.

47 n 34 above, 236.

48 Dworkin explains that principle as not requiring 'that people never be put at a disadvantage for the advantage of others, but rather that people never be treated in a way that denies the distinct importance of their own lives': as above.

49 MC Nussbaum 'Skepticism about practical reason in literature and the law' (1994) 107 *Harvard Law Review* 714 at 718.

50 n 49 above, 719.

disturbed when bad things happen to others. Pity or compassion arises because of the seriousness of the disturbing situation, which is not attributable to any fault on the sufferer's part, and an empathy with the other's dilemma because it could happen to oneself.[51] Compassion can co-exist with human dignity.[52]

Denise Réaume identifies dignity as the good in virtue of which we are owed respect, which she considers a more basic concept than Peter Birks' notion of equal respect, although implicit in his account.[53] It has a dual operation, the corollary of respect from others being self-esteem.[54] Dignity is violated by *treating* a person with dishonour or worthless as a moral personality (irrespective of whether they *feel* demeaned or worthless).[55] A social aspect arises because of our common association as members of the human race.[56] Dignity is not just autonomy.[57] Our commonality demands that we respect each other simply for being human.[58]

Kant's philosophy of life is premised on the absolute inner worth of the individual, which gives rise not only to duties to others but also to a 'necessary

51 MC Nussbaum 'Compassion: The basic social emotion' (1996) 13(1) *Social Philosophy and Policy* 27 at 31.

52 n 51 above, 45.

53 DG Réaume 'Indignities: Making a place for dignity in modern legal thought' (2002) 28 *Queen's Law Journal* 61 at 64, citing P Birks 'Harassment and hubris: The right to an equality of respect' (1997) 32 *Irish Jurist* 1.

54 n 53 above, 85.

55 n 53 above, 91.

56 n 53 above, 87.

57 According to L'Heureux-Dubé J in the Supreme Court of Canada, while some mentally ill patients may have 'a low level of awareness of their environment because of their mental condition', which may influence their own conception of dignity, 'an objective appreciation of dignity' prevailed and there could be 'interference with the safeguard of their dignity' despite the fact that the patients might have 'no sense of modesty': *Quebec (Public Curator) v Syndicat national des employés de l'hôpital St-Ferdinand* [1996] 3 SCR 211 [108]. In another Canadian case, Robins JA highlighted the equal dignity of the mentally ill and the importance of their autonomy: *Fleming v Reid* (1991) 82 DLR (4th) 298 (Ont CA) 311.
Jeremy Waldron suggests that the issue of how human dignity applies to infants and to the profoundly disabled can be addressed by applying the rank of equality to all humans by virtue of their unrealised potential rationality (albeit that the subject's rationality is evolving or may even be impossible to achieve by virtue of his or her condition): n 41 above, 29.

58 Réaume puts it thus, '[a]s human beings we are called upon to treat others "as fellow members of a common association," to be honoured not particularly for our accomplishments but simply because of our membership in the human race.': n 53 above, 85, citing TE Hill, Jr 'Social snobbery and human dignity' in *Autonomy and self-respect* (1991) 170.

duty to oneself'.[59] Inner worth is different from moral worth. Thomas E Hill, Jr, explains:[60]

> Kant ascribes to human personality a worth which is not diminished or increased by what a person does. It depends not on his actions but upon his capacities. This is a man's 'inner worth' as a person, based on the fact that he is a moral agent rather than upon his moral achievements.

The duty of each person to oneself and towards other human beings flows from the dignity of the person. Dignity is above value and is irreplaceable. An individual is entitled to respect from all other rational beings. Humanity's uniqueness is derived from the distinguishing feature of being able to reason and exercise free will. Autonomy is the ground of dignity and, is 'a property of the will of every rational being, namely, the property of legislating to oneself universal (moral) laws without the sensuous motives of fear, hope for reward, and the like.'[61]

According to Hill, Kant saw that the capacity to be rational and self-governing set us apart from the lower animals and gave us dignity. Moral conduct is the practical exercise of this 'noble capacity'.[62] Because all individuals have the ability to rationalise, all are equal and should be treated as equals. People are ends in themselves and must not be used solely as a means to an end. They are not to be regarded as objects. Each human being has inherent dignity and an unparalleled personality. Kant's practical imperative in simplistic terms was: act so that you treat humanity (whether yourself or another) always as an end (not as a means).[63] Hill points out the distinction between 'humanity in a person' and the entire person, leading to the deduction that Kant recognised that human beings have characteristics,

59 I Kant *The moral law: Groundwork of the metaphysic of morals* trans HJ Paton (2005) 107. On Kant's theory of inherent dignity, see Ackermann (n 5 above) 56 - 62; SRS Bedi *The development of human rights law by the judges of the International Court of Justice* (2007) 52 - 54; D Hicks *Dignity: The essential role it plays in resolving conflict* (2011) 4 - 5; M Rosen *Dignity: Its history and meaning* (2012) 10, 19 - 31, 55, 80, 143, 153 - 154; Saastamoinen (n 10 above) 48 - 49; D von der Pfordten 'On the dignity of man in Kant' (2009) 84 *Philosophy* 371.

60 TE Hill, Jr *Dignity and practical reason in Kant's moral theory* (1992) 166 - 167.

61 n 60 above, 47, citing Kant (n 59 above) 115, 120.

62 n 60 above, 36 - 37.

63 The precise version is: 'Act in such a way that you always treat humanity, whether in your own person or in the person of any other, never simply as a means but always at the same time as an end': Kant (n 59 above) 106 - 107.

such as animal instincts and talents, apart from their humanity.[64] The dignity of humanity arises from man's rational nature, which should direct his will.[65] The element of duty is apparent here. While Kant conceded that people are imperfect and do not always act rationally or fulfil their duties to themselves or to others, he steadfastly adhered to the precept that even the most heinous individual should not be abused.[66] Irrespective of his situation, he retains the capacity to act rationally, although he may not be disposed to do so. Kant had faith in humanity and the inextinguishable spark of goodness in each of us because of our capacity to rationalise.[67]

There is a dual aspect to Kant's imperative. The negative aspect inhibits treating another solely as a means. The positive angle enjoins us to treat humanity as an end.[68] One conclusion to be drawn from this is that there is not an outright embargo on treating people as means, provided they are also treated as ends. Kant urged us not to value a person's individuality, but his humanity, which he holds in common with others.[69]

Dignity is an 'incalculable' value.[70] Kant characterised it as 'an unconditional and incomparable worth'.[71] Unconditional worth means that a perfectly rational person would value dignity.[72] To understand its incomparable worth, it is necessary to distinguish between price and value. Dignity has value and worth, but is priceless. There can be no trade off between dignity and something with mere price.[73]

Our relationships with others should be moulded to accord with the requirements of dignity. Clearly we have a primary duty not to destroy the other person or ourselves by degradation or suicide; this duty arises, not because a person is irreplaceable, but because it degrades humanity.[74] Each

64 n 60 above, 39. Kant considered that the basis of human worth commands respect; Waldron pointed out that this is not exactly respect for persons – what commands respect is the capacity for morality; this involves respecting something within a person, not a person him- or herself: n 41 above, 24 - 25.

65 n 60 above, 39 - 40.

66 n 60 above, 41.

67 As above.

68 As above. See also P Capps *Human dignity and the foundations of international law* (2009) 108.

69 n 60 above, 43 fn 2.

70 n 60 above, 10.

71 n 60 above, 47, citing Kant (n 59 above) 115.

72 n 60 above, 48.

73 As above.

74 n 60 above, 51.

one has a duty to develop his rational capacities and to strive to exercise reason in moral contexts.[75] Try to reason with others, not to manipulate them, and do not treat anyone as worthless.[76] Allow individuals the freedom to form and pursue their own life plans, subject to the constraint that others be allowed a similar freedom.[77] Individual liberty is limited by a concern for the liberty and rational development of all.[78] Help others to set their own ends and to pursue them rationally.[79] Honour human rationality in ourselves and in others in our words, symbols and deeds.[80]

The concept of dignity has a long tradition in non-Western societies. However, there the emphasis is on duties owed to others. The focus is frequently on the community rather than on the individual.

Human dignity is the foundation of society and civilisation in Islam and originated in the creation of man, when, according to the Koran, God 'bestowed dignity on the progeny of Adam' by breathing His Own Spirit into him.[81] Stressing our interdependence, Abdullah al-Ahsan has defined human dignity as 'the recognition and respect of human need, desire and expectation one individual by another'.[82] Since all human beings are descended from Adam and his spouse, every person possesses dignity.[83] It is not earned by meritorious conduct and is the right of everyone regardless of colour, race and religion.[84] There is a prohibition on violating the personal dignity of all, whether a Muslim or non-Muslim, pious or of ill-repute, law-

75 n 60 above, 52 - 53.

76 n 60 above, 53.

77 n 60 above, 54. Dignity can be used negatively as a constraint on infringement of another's rights or it can have a positive slant in support of the assertion of rights. 'Human dignity as empowerment' can be distinguished from 'human dignity as constraint': D Beyleveld & R Brownsword *Human dignity in bioethics and biolaw* (2001) 11. The judiciary is more inclined to use it as a constraint when the legislature has democratically considered the various rights involved and has made a choice as to which route to adopt: A Clapham *Human rights obligations of non-state actors* (2006) 558. Human dignity is a basis for extending existing human rights to new situations or for devising new rights.

78 n 60 above, 56.

79 n 60 above, 54.

80 n 60 above, 55.

81 A al-Ahsan 'Law, religion and human dignity in the Muslim world today: An examination of OIC's Cairo Declaration of Human Rights' 24 (2008 - 2009) *Journal of Law and Religion* 569 at 569, citing Koran 17:70, 15:29, 32:9, 38:72.

82 n 81 above, 569.

83 n 81 above, 569, citing Koran 4:1.

84 MH Kamali *The dignity of man: An Islamic perspective* (2002) 1.

abiding or a criminal.[85] Human dignity in Islamic texts is affirmed in a variety of contexts, including the unity and equality of mankind.[86] According to Linda Hogan and John D'Arcy May, dignity is an absolute value in Islam (an Abrahamic faith based on the doctrine of creation), but it is in danger of being eclipsed by the overwhelming presence of the utterly transcendent God.[87] The primary responsibility of the Muslim is submission to God and the practice of religious duties rather than insisting on one's entitlements because of one's dignity as a human being, which in any case is a gift from God.[88]

In traditional societies, the tendency is to base human relations on the exchange of gifts instead of expressions of respect and gratitude.[89] The correlative to recompense for good is retribution for evil.[90] The ancestral and natural spirits are an integral part of the community and what it means to be human.[91] For the indigenous people in the Pacific Islands, the primary source of human dignity is a relationship to land through participation in the kinship group.[92] The social aspect of this human relationship may provide a nexus with other societies' understanding of dignity.[93]

Hindu society is founded on the ideas of duty (*dharma*) and deeds (*kharma*), which determine our existence and rebirths.[94] The *Bhagavadgîta* (the Hindu equivalent of the New Testament) regards caste duty and disinterested action as the highest moral ideal.[95] This socially structured inequality is compounded by gender inequality.[96] Hierarchy is the natural norm in India.[97] The traditional caste system is a blatant denial of human dignity.[98] But,

85 Kamali (n 84 above) 2.

86 Kamali (n 84 above) 3.

87 L Hogan & J D'Arcy May 'Constructing the human: Dignity in interreligious dialogue' in R Ammicht-Quinn *et al* (eds) *The discourse of human dignity* (2003) 79.

88 As above.

89 Hogan & D'Arcy May (n87) 80.

90 As above.

91 As above. See also T Metz 'African conceptions of human dignity: Vitality and community as the ground of human rights' (2012) 13 *Human Rights Review* 19 at 24.

92 Hogan & D'Arcy May (n87) 81, citing JD May 'Human rights as land rights in the Pacific' (1993) 6 *Pacifica* 61 - 80.

93 Hogan & D'Arcy May (n 87 above) 82.

94 Hogan & D'Arcy May (n 87 above) 84.

95 As above.

96 Hogan & D'Arcy May (n 87 above) 83.

97 As above.

98 Hogan & D'Arcy May (n 87 above) 82.

within the boundaries of each caste, there is egalitarianism.[99] Gandhi believed that the caste method could remain as a means of ordering society, if it rid itself of the pattern of defining lower castes as morally and spiritually inferior.[100]

The absence of self is the foundation of Buddhism.[101] Liberation is achieved through wisdom and compassion.[102] Morality is based on duties and priority is given to the communal.[103] While compassion is compatible with dignity, the lack of emphasis on the human personality removes a rationale for dignity in religions originating in the West and in the Enlightenment philosophy.

2.2 Law

2.2.1 History

Dignity is not endowed by states or by the international order. It is innate in each human being. The role of dignity in law developed during the course of the twentieth century.[104] It began appearing as a concept in constitutions in the first half of the century, including those adopted in Mexico,[105] Weimar Germany,[106] Finland,[107] Portugal,[108] Ireland,[109] Cuba,[110] Spain[111] and Costa

99 Hogan & D'Arcy May (n 87 above) 84.

100 As above.

101 Hogan & D'Arcy May (n 87 above) 85.

102 Hogan & D'Arcy May (n 87 above) 86.

103 As above.

104 McCrudden (n 9 above) 664. See also C Dupré 'Human dignity in Europe: A foundational constitutional principle' (2013) 19 *European Public Law* 319 at 319 - 325.

105 Political Constitution of the United Mexican States 1917 (amended 1946), Art 3(II)(c).

106 Constitution of the German Reich 1919, Art 151. See Habermas (n 3 above) 468.

107 The initial reference was to 'hereditary dignity': Constitution of Finland 1919, Art 15. It was amended in 1995 to guarantee the 'inviolability of human dignity' (Sec 1) and to refer to 'the security required for a dignified life' (Sec 15a).

108 Political Constitution of the Portuguese Republic 1933, Art 45.

109 Constitution of Ireland 1937, Preamble, 5th para:

> And seeking to promote the common good, with due observance of Prudence, Justice and Charity, so that the dignity and freedom of the individual may be assured, true social order attained, the unity of our country restored, and concord established with other nations.

110 Constitution of the Republic of Cuba 1940, Art 20.

111 Charter of the Spanish People 1945, Arts 1 & 25.

Rica.[112] This can be attributed to a variety of influences such as the emphasis on dignity in the Catholic religion,[113] the Enlightenment[114] and socialism.[115]

2.2.1.1 UN Charter and Universal Declaration

After the atrocities and wholesale assault on dignity during the Second World War, dignity was incorporated in international agreements attempting to prevent a recurrence of such appalling treatment of human beings. It was mentioned in the United Nations Charter[116] and in the Universal Declaration of Human Rights (Universal Declaration).[117] One of the main aims of the UN Charter as set out in its Preamble was 'to reaffirm faith in fundamental human rights, in the dignity and worth of the human person, in the equal rights of men and women and of nations large and small.'[118] The reference to dignity was inserted at the suggestion of Field Marshal Jan Smuts from South Africa at the San Francisco conference where the UN Charter was adopted in 1945.[119] The Preamble to the Universal Declaration placed the recognition of the fundamental dignity and equal and inalienable rights[120] of people as 'the foundation of freedom, justice and peace in the world'.[121] There is a second reference to dignity in the Preamble when it refers back to

112 Political Constitution of the Republic of Costa Rica 1949, Art 56.

113 Catholic Church *Catechism of the Catholic Church* (1999) [27], [225], [306], [308], [356]-[357], [364], [369], [872], [1004], [1468], [1487], [1645], [1691]-[1692], [1698], [1700]-[1876], [1934]-[1935], [1938], [1956], [2203], [2261], [2275], [2284]-[2301], [2324], [2334]-[2335], [2418], [2424], [2436], [2524]. See McCrudden (n 9 above) 658.
The Catholic religion imbued a sense of responsibility for one's decisions by asserting that man had to take some action to secure forgiveness for sins rather than adopting the fatalistic doctrine of predestination: Butler (n 5 above) 1307.

114 On the Enlightenment and human rights, see Butler (n 5 above) 1262, 1267, 1269, 1305.

115 McCrudden (n 9 above) 664. The Catholic influence was evident in Portugal, Ireland and Spain, the socialist in Finland, and both Catholic and social democratic/socialist in Central and South American countries: as above.

116 Charter of the United Nations (signed 26 June 1945, entered into force 24 October 1945) 59 Stat 1031, UNTS 993, 3 Bevans 1153 (UN Charter) Preamble.

117 Universal Declaration of Human Rights (adopted 10 December 1948) UN General Assembly (UNGA) Res 217 A(III) Preamble, arts 1, 22 & 23.

118 n 116 above, Preamble, 1st para, 2nd point.

119 JP Humphrey *Human rights and the United Nations: A great adventure* (1984) 67.

120 The foundation of the concept of inalienable rights that pertain to the individual had crystallised by the end of the 17th century: G Peirce *Dispatches from the dark side: On torture and the death of justice* (2010) vii.

121 n 117 above, Preamble, 1st para.

dignity, equality and social progress mentioned in the UN Charter:[122]

> Whereas the peoples of the United Nations have in the Charter reaffirmed their faith in fundamental human rights, in the dignity and worth of the human person and in the equal rights of men and women and have determined to promote social progress and better standards of life in larger freedom.

Article 1 Universal Declaration declares:

> All human beings are born free and equal in dignity and rights. They are endowed with reason and conscience and should act towards one another in a spirit of brotherhood.

Here the Kantian influence is evident. It embraces the individual and community aspects, as well as engaging the intellect and moral conscience of the person. In the course of the drafting of the Universal Declaration, the South African representative CT Te Water objected to the inclusion of the words 'dignity and rights'.[123] His initial objection was because he did not agree to the extension of equality to all rights, personal, social, economic and political, irrespective of whether or not they were fundamental.[124] He also insisted there was no universal standard of dignity.[125] He backtracked subsequently and supported a Guatemalan proposal to move draft article 1 to the Preamble on the basis that it was a statement of fact, not a right.[126] In the South African delegation's view, the dignity of the individual was a broader and deeper concept than a right.[127] If fundamental human rights were respected, the dignity of the individual person would be automatically recognised.[128] Eleanor Roosevelt (Chairperson of the Human Rights Commission and of the Drafting Committee established by it) said that the word 'dignity' had been considered at great length and the Human Rights

122 n 117 above, 5th para.

123 MA Glendon *A world made new: Eleanor Roosevelt and the Universal Declaration of Human Rights* (2001) 144.

124 UNGA 3rd Session Third Committee 95th Meeting (6 October 1948) UN Doc A/C.3/SR.95 at 91 - 92.

125 UNGA 3rd Session Third Committee 95th Meeting (n 124 above) 92.

126 UNGA 3rd Session Third Committee 96th Meeting (7 October 1948) UN Doc A/C.3/SR.96 at 96.

127 As above.

128 As above.

Commission had decided to include it to emphasise the inherent dignity of all mankind.[129]

Economic and social rights were incorporated in the Universal Declaration at Articles 22 to 27 at the insistence of Latin American and Communist countries, who battled with the North Atlantic countries and their allies over the emphasis to be accorded to them as compared with the hitherto more important civil and political rights.[130] Eleanor Roosevelt was committed to Franklin D Roosevelt's 'four freedoms', which included freedom from want and this, according to Mary Ann Glendon, ensured that they 'would be a constant touchstone for all members of the Commission.'[131] Article 22, introducing this set of rights, refers to dignity and development of the personality.[132] The right to work in Article 23 also mentions dignity.[133]

These international texts were concluded after much deliberation and with a lot of effort to obtain a common platform between various nations with widely different cultures and backgrounds. The agreed basis for human rights in the Universal Declaration is secular humanist.[134] Reference to a divine origin or a basis in nature was avoided. Jacques Maritain has noted that in the course of negotiations on the text of the Universal Declaration there was a divergence of views between those who accepted and those who rejected natural law as the cornerstone of human rights.[135] The drafters adopted a practical approach and contented themselves with a statement and

129 UNGA 3rd Session Third Committee 98th Meeting (9 October 1948) UN Doc A/C.3/SR.98 at 110. See G Hughes 'The concept of dignity in the Universal Declaration of Human Rights' (2011) 39 *Journal of Religious Ethics* 1 at 3; J Reinbold 'Political myth and the sacred center of human rights: The Universal Declaration and the narrative of "inherent human dignity"' (2011) 12 *Human Rights Review* 147 at 161.

130 J Morsink 'The philosophy of the Universal Declaration' (1984) 6 *Human Rights Quarterly* 309 at 334.

131 n 123 above, 42.

132 It reads:

> Everyone, as a member of society, has the right to social security and is entitled to realization, through national effort and international co-operation and in accordance with the organization and resources of each State, of the economic, social and cultural rights indispensable for his dignity and the free development of his personality.

133 Art 23(3): 'Everyone who works has the right to just and favourable remuneration ensuring for himself and his family an existence worthy of human dignity, and supplemented, if necessary, by other means of social protection.'

134 Morsink, (n 130 above) 334.

135 J Maritain 'Introduction' in UNESCO (ed) *Human rights: Comments and interpretations: A symposium* (1949) 13.

enumeration of human rights without any reference to their foundation.[136]

Rights are subject to limitation. Maritain differentiated between the possession and the exercise of rights and said that, even in the case of inalienable rights, their exercise can be modified and limited in the interests of justice.[137] Economic, social and cultural rights cannot be implemented without some restrictions on the freedom and rights of the individual.[138] There are conflicting views on the values determining the application of rights. Human dignity means different things to different groups. According to Maritain, for some 'the mark of human dignity lies firstly and chiefly in the power to appropriate individually the gifts of nature so that each may be in a position to do freely what pleases him'; some see dignity 'in the power to place those gifts under the collective control of the social body'; and others see dignity 'in the power of bringing the gifts of nature into service for the joint attainment of an immaterial good and of the free self-determination of the person'.[139] Because of diverse deeply held values, these issues could not be resolved in the Universal Declaration.

Glendon rightly said that the Universal Declaration 'heralded a new moment in the history of human rights.'[140] It emphasised dignity and insisted on the link between freedom and solidarity.[141] Her overview neatly captures the interdependence between the individual and society, and the intermingling of rights:[142]

> When read as it was meant to be, namely as a whole, it is an integrated document that rests on a concept of the dignity of the human person within the human family. In substance, as well as in form, it is a declaration of interdependence – interdependence of people, nations, and rights.

UNESCO's 1947 enquiry into the theoretical basis of human rights concluded that human dignity underlies the philosophy of freedom and democracy in

136 n 135 above, 14.
137 n 135 above, 15.
138 As above.
139 n 135 above, 16.
140 n 123 above, 173.
141 As above.
142 n 123 above, 174.

human rights.[143] It emphasised the necessity of continually fostering dignity.[144] Mahatma Gandhi in a letter to UNESCO in 1947 pointed out that all rights 'came from duty well done.'[145] Even the right to live 'accrues to us only when we do the duty of citizenship of the world.'[146] He advocated correlating 'every right to some corresponding duty to be first performed.'[147]

Susan Waltz's research into the drafting of the Universal Declaration shows that the small states played a significant part in the procedure. She concludes that without their presence and active participation, the Universal Declaration might have been shorter and more inspirational (as the United States wanted).[148] It probably would not have included 'socioeconomic rights or consistent condemnation of discrimination. The rights of women might also have been downplayed.'[149] Quite often the proponents of human rights were small states (particularly those in Latin America) and non-governmental organisations. In contrast, the United Kingdom and France were somewhat opposed to the Universal Declaration.[150] The US was an enthusiastic advocate for human rights during World War II when it was seeking the support of other states for the war effort. After the end of the conflict, it lost interest, but was forced by the smaller states to fulfil its commitment to human rights.[151] It is incorrect to think that the views of the US dominated the content of the Universal Declaration. Waltz highlights the subsequent effect of the Cold War, which politicised human rights.[152]

In order to prevent the resurgence of totalitarianism, which was interpreted as a reaction to extreme individualism, there is an emphasis in the Universal Declaration on the community rather than solely on the

143 'The grounds of an international declaration of human rights' in UNESCO (n135) Appendix II at 259.

144 'The United Nations cannot succeed in the great purposes to which it is committed unless it so acts that this dignity is given increasing recognition, and unless steps are taken to create the conditions under which this dignity may be achieved more fully and at constantly higher levels.': as above.

145 In UNESCO (n 135 above) 18.

146 As above.

147 As above.

148 S Waltz 'Universalising human rights: The role of small states in the construction of the Universal Declaration of Human Rights' (2001) 23 *Human Rights Quarterly* 44 at 70.

149 n148 above, 71.

150 n148 above, 70.

151 n148 above, 69 - 70.

152 n148 above, 69.

individual.[153] This can be seen from the insertion of the word 'alone' in Article 29(1), which locates people necessarily in the community for development of their full potential.[154]

The value of dignity had universal appeal, but for a variety of reasons.[155] It was not simply a Western ideal, but was attractive to South American, Latin American, African and Eastern countries. The basis of the appeal was not solely Christianity, but those with the Kantian view and followers of Eastern philosophy were equally sympathetic to the concept.

In a look back more than 50 years after adoption of the Universal Declaration, William Joseph Wagner indicated that interest groups and states have used human rights for their own political purposes.[156] As a result, some are sceptical of Western human rights.[157] However, Wagner considers that human rights can be moulded by adding social content and that the Universal Declaration was a worthwhile endeavour, as it tried to replace force with human dignity.[158]

2.2.1.2 ECHR and EU Charter

The term dignity is not used explicitly in the European Convention on Human Rights (ECHR).[159] As it is expressly based on the Universal Declaration, it is implicitly based on the latter's assertion of human dignity.[160]

153 Morsink (n 130 above) 329.

154 Morsink (n 130 above) 334. Art 29(1) reads: 'Everyone has duties to the community in which alone the free and full development of his personality is possible.'

155 The Kenyan High Court explained that the universality of the Universal Declaration was based on 'a common heritage of humankind which is the oneness of the human family and the essential dignity of the individual': *RM v AG* [2006] AHRLR 256 (KeHC 2006) [69].
For legal reasons in support of the claim that human dignity is the moral source from which all of the basic rights derive their meaning, see Habermas (n 3 above) 466 - 470.

156 n 5 above, 214, 216 - 217.

157 Wagner (n 5 above) 199. See W Osiatynski 'On the universality of the Universal Declaration of Human Rights' in A Sajó (ed) *Human rights with modesty: The problem of universalism* (2004) 33 - 50.

158 n 5 above, 223, 225.

159 Convention for the Protection of Human Rights and Fundamental Freedoms, 213 UNTS 222 (ECHR).

160 G Moon & R Allen 'Dignity discourse in discrimination law: a better route to equality?' [2006] *European Human Rights Law Review* 610 at 621.

In any event, the European Court of Human Rights has made it clear in its jurisprudence that dignity is a foundation value of democracy.[161]

The European Union Charter of Fundamental Rights signed in Nice in 2000 placed the individual at the heart of the Union's activities and declared human dignity, freedom, equality and solidarity its foundational values.[162] The entire of Chapter I is devoted to dignity rights directed towards the physical and mental aspects of personal security.[163] There is an unequivocal demand that dignity be protected in Article 1, which reads: 'Human dignity is inviolable. It must be respected and protected.' Unsurprisingly, the right to life is proclaimed[164] and torture, inhuman or degrading treatment or punishment,[165] slavery[166] and forced labour[167] are proscribed.

Article 2 (dealing with the right to life) contains an explicit prohibition on the death penalty.[168] The right to integrity is set out in Article 3. Modern scientific developments have necessitated the inclusion of a ban on eugenics, the sale of body parts and cloning, and informed consent is required for participation in scientific experiments and medical treatment.[169] In another sign of the times and increased mobility, human trafficking is forbidden.[170]

Individual dignity is central to workers' rights. Under the umbrella of solidarity, Article 31 of the EU Charter acclaims workers' rights to conditions respecting their dignity along with their health and safety.[171] Article 25 asserts the rights of the elderly in the context of equality: 'The Union recognises and respects the rights of the elderly to lead a life of dignity and independence and to participate in social and cultural life.'

161 As above. See *Gündüz v Turkey* (App no 35071/97) (2005) 41 EHRR 5 [40]: 'the Court would emphasise, in particular, that tolerance and respect for the equal dignity of all human beings constitute the foundations of a democratic, pluralistic society.'

162 Charter of Fundamental Rights of the European Union (2000/C 364/01) [2000] OJ C364/1 (EU Charter) Preamble. See Dupré (n 104 above) 332 - 333.

163 n 162 above, Arts 1 - 5. See P Craig & G de Búrca *EU law: Text, cases, and materials* (2011) 395 - 396.

164 n 162 above, Art 2.1.

165 n 162 above, Art 4.

166 n 162 above, Art 5.1.

167 n 162 above, Art 5.2.

168 n 162 above, Art 2.2.

169 n 162 above, Art 3.2.

170 n 162 above, Art 5.3.

171 n 162 above, Art 31.1.

2.2.1.3 Popularity of dignity

In the second half of the twentieth century, the concept of dignity gained widespread acceptance. It is routinely mentioned in international treaties. Some European Directives have focused on it and a growing number of nations have included it in their constitutions. The reference to dignity in the Universal Declaration has frequently been the impetus for incorporation of dignity in national constitutions.

2.2.1.4 International humanitarian texts

The initial stimulus for the inclusion of dignity in humanitarian texts was war. In 1863 the US required that prisoners be treated with dignity.[172] After the Second World War the International Committee of the Red Cross proposed that the Geneva Conventions protecting prisoners of war should include preambles incorporating: '[r]espect for the personality and dignity of human beings constitutes a universal principle which is binding even in the absence of any contractual undertaking.'[173] The Conventions, as adopted, included Common Article 3 prohibiting, *inter alia*, 'outrages upon personal dignity, in particular humiliating and degrading treatment.'[174] The statutes of international criminal tribunals and the Rome Statute establishing the International Criminal Court have referred to 'outrages upon personal dignity'.[175]

Dignity played a role in abolitionist policies, so it is not surprising that the Slavery Convention 1956 echoes back to the UN Charter in affirming

172 McCrudden (n 9 above) 667, fn 82, citing 'Instructions for the Government of Armies of the United States in the Field' (Lieber Code), 24 Apr 1863, Art 75.

173 McCrudden (n 9 above) 667, fn 84, citing 'Remarks and Proposals submitted by the International Committee of the Red Cross', Document for the consideration of Governments invited by the Swiss Federal Council to attend the Diplomatic Conference of Geneva (21 Apr 1949) (Feb 1949) 8.

174 McCrudden (n 9 above) 668, fn 85, citing Geneva Convention (III) Relative to the Treatment of Prisoners of War (adopted 12 August 1949, entered into force 21 October 1950) 75 UNTS 135, Art 3.

175 Statute of the International Criminal Tribunal for Rwanda, UNSC Res 955 (8 November 1994) UN Doc S/RES/955, Art 4(e); Agreement between the United Nations and the Government of Sierra Leone on the Establishment of a Special Court for Sierra Leone (with Statute) (signed 16 January 2002, entered into force 12 April 2002) 2178 UNTS 138, Art 3(e); Rome Statute of the International Criminal Court (signed 17 July 1998, entered into force 1 July 2002) 2187 UNTS 90, Art 8.2(b)(xxi). See McCrudden (n 9 above) 668.
On genocide, see T Meron *Human rights and humanitarian norms as customary law* (1989) 11 - 12, 110 - 111; A Vincent *The politics of human rights* (2010) 106 - 118.

'faith in the dignity and worth of the human person'.[176] Likewise, given the prominence of the principle of the 'dignity of labour' in the growth of the trade union movement, there is an emphasis on dignity in International Labour Organisation Conventions.[177]

2.2.1.5 UN human rights instruments since the 1960s

Following up on the aspirations in the Universal Declaration, in 1966 the International Covenants on Civil and Political Rights (ICCPR)[178] and on Economic, Social and Cultural Rights (CESCR),[179] which comprise the International Bill of Rights, fleshed out states' obligations. They highlight the importance of dignity and acknowledge it as the foundational value.[180] The Preambles to ICCPR and CESCR set the scene in identical terms:

> Considering that, in accordance with the principles proclaimed in the Charter of the United Nations, recognition of the inherent dignity and of the equal and inalienable rights of all members of the human family is the foundation of freedom, justice and peace in the world,
>
> Recognizing that these rights derive from the inherent dignity of the human person …

176 McCrudden (n 9 above) 668; Supplementary Convention on the Abolition of Slavery, the Slave Trade, and Institutions and Practices Similar to Slavery (adopted 7 September 1956, entered into force 30 April 1957) 226 UNTS 3, Preamble.

177 McCrudden (n 9 above) 669. See International Labour Organisation (ILO) Indigenous and Tribal Populations Convention C107 (adopted 26 June 1957, entered into force 2 June 1959) (40th Session) (Geneva) Preamble, Art 2.3; ILO Discrimination (Employment and Occupation) Convention C111 (adopted 25 June 1958, entered into force 15 June 1960) (42nd Session) (Geneva) Preamble; ILO Employment Policy Convention C122 (adopted 9 July 1964, entered into force 15 July 1966) (48th Session) (Geneva) Preamble; ILO Workers with Family Responsibilities Convention C156 (adopted 23 June 1981, entered into force 11 August 1983) (67th Session) (Geneva) Preamble.

178 International Covenant on Civil and Political Rights (adopted 16 December 1966, entered into force 23 March 1976) 999 UNTS 171 (ICCPR).

179 International Covenant on Economic, Social and Cultural Rights (adopted 16 December 1966, entered into force 3 January 1976) 993 UNTS 3 (CESCR).

180 John McGinnis has criticised international human rights treaties and customary law as inadequate protectors of human dignity: JO McGinnis 'The limits of international law in protecting dignity' (2003) 27 *Harvard Journal of Law and Public Policy* 137 at 137. He considers that the dignity of the poor would be better served by focusing on the tangible benefits and increased standards of living and education obtained by World Trade Agreements: above, 138. Vested interests stand to gain by implementation of rights.

Dignity is mentioned in Article 10 of ICCPR: 'All persons deprived of their liberty shall be treated with humanity and with respect for the inherent dignity of the human person.'[181]

Article 13 of CESCR, having recognised the right of everyone to education, continues:[182]

> [The State Parties] agree that education shall be directed to the full development of the human personality and the sense of its dignity, and shall strengthen the respect for human rights and fundamental freedoms.

Conventions banning discrimination on the grounds of race and gender are among the many that have referred to dignity. The Convention on the Elimination of Racial Discrimination refers three times to dignity in its Preamble.[183] It takes into consideration that the UN Charter 'is based on the principles of the dignity and equality inherent in all human beings', that the Universal Declaration 'proclaims that all human beings are born free and equal in dignity and rights' and that the 1963 UN Declaration on the Elimination of All Forms of Racial Discrimination:

> ... solemnly affirms the necessity of speedily eliminating racial discrimination throughout the world in all its forms and manifestations and of securing understanding of and respect for the dignity of the human person.[184]

The Preamble to the Convention on Discrimination against Women in 1979 also mentions dignity three times.[185] Having noted the focus on dignity in the UN Charter and in the Universal Declaration, it goes on:

181 n 178 above, art 10.1. This right is violated by the enforced disappearance of people (*ie,* their arrest, detention or abduction with the authorisation, support or acquiescence of a state or a political organisation, followed by a refusal to acknowledge that deprivation of freedom or to give information on their fate or whereabouts, with the intention of removing them from the protection of the law for a prolonged period of time): *Bousroual (Saker) v Algeria* UNHR Committee (24 April 2006) 86th Session UN Doc CCPR/C/86/992/2001 [9.2]. See also *Mulezi v Democratic Republic of the Congo* UNHR Committee (23 July 2004) 81st Session UN Doc CCPR/C/81/D/962/2001 [5.3].

182 n 179 above, art 13.1.

183 International Convention on the Elimination of All Forms of Racial Discrimination (adopted 7 March 1966, entered into force 4 January 1969) 660 UNTS 195.

184 UNGA Res 1904 (XVIII) (20 November 1963) UN Doc A/RES/1904 (XVIII).

185 Convention on the Elimination of All Forms of Discrimination against Women (adopted 18 December 1979, entered into force 3 September 1981) 1249 UNTS 13.

> Recalling that discrimination against women violates the principles of equality of rights and respect for human dignity, is an obstacle to the participation of women, on equal terms with men, in the political, social, economic and cultural life of their countries, hampers the growth of the prosperity of society and the family and makes more difficult the full development of the potentialities of women in the service of their countries and of humanity.

In 1986 the UN gave formal recognition to the central importance of dignity in standards it adopted for new human rights instruments which should be 'of fundamental character and derive from the inherent dignity and worth of the human person'.[186] International instruments since then have referred to dignity in mainstream human rights areas and also in topics not traditional human rights territory. In the mainstream category are conventions on the Rights of Children in 1989,[187] Migrant Workers in 1990[188] and the Disabled in 2007.[189] An example in the non-traditional class is an agreement on funding for agricultural development adopted at a conference in Rome in 1976, in which the first paragraph of the Preamble recognised that a continuing world food problem was afflicting many people in the developing countries and was jeopardising 'the most fundamental principles and values associated with the right to life and human dignity'.[190]

Dignity was the central organising principle of the Vienna World Conference on Human Rights in 1993.[191] The Declaration and Programme of Action adopted dignity as foundational to human rights generally[192] and in particular areas like the prohibition of gender-based violence and

186 UNGA Res 41/120 (4 December 1986) UN Doc A/Res/41/120, para 4(b).

187 Convention on the Rights of the Child (adopted 20 November 1989, entered into force 2 September 1990) 1577 UNTS 3, Preamble, arts 23, 28, 37, 39 & 40.

188 International Convention on the Protection of the Rights of All Migrant Workers and Members of their Families (adopted 18 December 1990, entered into force 1 July 2003) 2220 UNTS 93, arts 17 & 70.

189 International Convention on the Protection and Promotion of the Rights and Dignity of Persons with Disabilities (adopted 13 December 2006, entered into force 3 May 2008) (2007) 46 ILM 443, Preamble, arts 1, 3, 8, 16, 24 & 25.

190 Agreement Establishing the International Fund for Agricultural Development (adopted 13 June 1976, entered into force 30 November 1977) 1059 UNTS 191.

191 McCrudden (n 9 above) 670. This Second World Conference on Human Rights was attended by over 170 governments.

192 World Conference on Human Rights 'Vienna Declaration and Programme of Action' (25 June 1993) UN Doc A/CONF.157/23, Preamble.

harassment,[193] the abolition of extreme poverty[194] and biomedical ethics.[195] Conventions since then have contained specific provisions protecting dignity in relation to diverse matters such as the criminal justice process in relation to children,[196] minimum welfare of migrant workers and their families,[197] health of the disabled[198] and their treatment as autonomous individuals,[199] reintegration of abused children and disabled people,[200] reputation,[201] and control of personal data.[202] UNESCO gave a central role to dignity in the Universal Declaration on the Human Genome and Human Rights in 1997.[203]

2.2.1.6 Regional treaties

Apart from UN instruments, regional treaties have embodied references to dignity illustrating the widespread acceptance of dignity as a fundamental value. There are examples in Inter-American, African and Arab texts, as well as those in Europe. The Preamble to the American Declaration of the Rights of Man of 1948 agreed in the same era as the Universal Declaration refers twice to dignity and connects duties with the dignity of liberty.[204] The right to property in the Declaration acknowledges the importance to a person's

193 n 192 above, pt I, art 18.

194 n 192 above, pt I, art 25.

195 n 192 above, pt I, art 11.

196 Convention on the Rights of the Child (n 187 above) arts 37 & 40. These provisions were reference points for the Supreme Court of Appeal when it upheld an appeal against the leniency of a sentence on a girl for the murder of her grandmother and theft, as the trial judge failed to give sufficient weight to the gravity of the offence and the interests of society: *DPP Kwazulu-Natal v P* [2006] 1 All SA 446 (SCA) [15], [22], [26].

197 Convention on the Rights of Migrant Workers (n 188 above) art 70.

198 Convention on the Rights of Persons with Disabilities (n 189 above) art 25.

199 Convention on the Rights of Persons with Disabilities (n 189 above) art 3.

200 Convention on the Rights of the Child (n187) art 39; Convention on the Rights of Persons with Disabilities (n 189 above) art 16.

201 International Convention for the Protection of All Persons from Enforced Disappearance (adopted 20 December 2006, opened for signature 6 February 2007) UNGA Res 61/177, UN Doc A/RES/61/177, art 24.

202 Convention for Protection from Enforced Disappearance (n 201 above) art 19.

203 McCrudden (n 9 above) 671 fn 120; UNESCO 'Universal Declaration on the Human Genome and Human Rights' (11 November 1997) Gen Conf 29 C/Res 16, Preamble, arts 1, 2, 6, 10 - 12, 15, 21 & 24.

204 American Declaration of the Rights and Duties of Man, OAS Res XXX adopted by the Ninth International Conference of American States (1948) reprinted in Basic Documents Pertaining to Human Rights in the Inter-American System OEA/Ser L V/II.82 Doc 6 Rev 1 at 17 (1992) Preamble, 1st and 2nd paras:

dignity of basic needs such as a home.[205] The American Convention on Human Rights mentions dignity in relation to humane treatment[206] and the prohibition on forced labour.[207] It provides a privacy right to have one's honour respected and dignity recognised.[208] The Inter-American Convention on the Prevention, Punishment and Eradication of Violence against Women refers to dignity several times.[209]

Having referenced dignity twice in its Preamble, Article 5 of the African Charter on Human and Peoples' Rights commences with the right of every individual 'to the respect of the dignity inherent in a human being and to the recognition of his legal status' and continues to ban all 'forms of exploitation and degradation of man' including slavery, torture,[210] and inhuman or degrading treatment.[211] Article 3 of the Protocol to the African Charter on Women's Rights asserts a woman's right to dignity and development of her

All men are born free and equal, in dignity and in rights, and, being endowed by nature with reason and conscience, they should conduct themselves as brothers one to another.

The fulfillment of duty by each individual is a prerequisite to the rights of all. Rights and duties are interrelated in every social and political activity of man. While rights exalt individual liberty, duties express the dignity of that liberty.

See VB Monsalve & JA Román 'Tensions of human dignity: Conceptualization and application to international human rights law' (2009) 11 *SUR - International Journal on Human Rights* 39 at 44 - 45.

205 American Declaration of the Rights and Duties of Man (n 204 above) Art XXIII: 'Every person has a right to own such private property as meets the essential needs of decent living and helps to maintain the dignity of the individual and of the home.'

206 American Convention on Human Rights (adopted 22 November 1969, entered into force 18 July 1978) 1144 UNTS 123, Art 5. On dignity in the American Convention on Human Rights, see Monsalve & Román (n 204 above) 46 - 47.

207 n 206 above, Art 6.2.

208 n 206 above, Art 11.1.

209 Inter-American Convention on the Prevention, Punishment and Eradication of Violence against Women (adopted 9 June 1994, entered into force 5 March 1995) (1994) 33 ILM 1534, Preamble, Arts 4 & 8. See Monsalve & Román (n 204 above) 47 - 48.

210 The African Commission found that the government of Sudan was responsible for torture, because – even though it had punished some torturers – it had not taken preventive measures such as halting of incommunicado detention, effective remedies, and ongoing investigations into allegations: *Amnesty International v Sudan* [2000] AHRLR 297 (ACHPR 1999) [56]-[57]. It also stated that holding an individual without permitting him or her to have any contact with his or her family, and refusing to inform the family if and where the individual was being held, was inhuman treatment of both the detainee and the family concerned: above, [54].

The security forces in Cameroon tortured a journalist and human rights activist physically and mentally in violation of ICCPR: *Njaru v Cameroon* UNHR Committee (14 May 2007) 89th Session UN Doc CCPR/C/89/D/1353/2005 [6.1].

211 African Charter on Human and Peoples' Rights (adopted 27 June 1981, entered into force 21 October 1986) (1982) 21 ILM 58 (African Charter).

personality.[212] The Protocol upholds the right of elderly,[213] disabled[214] and imprisoned pregnant or nursing women[215] to be treated with dignity.

Dignity in the Arab Charter on Human Rights of 2004 has a religious basis.[216] Article 3 affirms the equality of men and women within a religious framework.[217] In Article 17 there is protection for the dignity of children embroiled in the criminal legal process. States are obliged to take 'measures to guarantee the protection, survival, development and well-being of the child in an atmosphere of freedom and dignity.'[218] People deprived of their liberty should 'be treated with humanity and with respect for the inherent dignity of the human person.'[219] States are tasked with safeguarding the dignity, self-reliance and social participation of the disabled.[220]

The government of Nigeria was found to have violated this provision by sending armed gangs to attack human rights activists and to destroy their homes: *Constitutional Rights Project v Nigeria* [2000] AHRLR 227 (ACHPR 1999) [45], [48]. Rapes and physical searches of refugees by Guinean soldiers after a speech by the President incited them to act against the refugees constituted inhuman treatment: *African Institute for Human Rights and Development (Sierra Leonean refugees in Guinea) v Guinea* [2004] AHRLR 57 (ACHPR 2004) [57], [62], [72].

212 Protocol to the African Charter on Human and Peoples' Rights on the Rights of Women in Africa (adopted 13 September 2000, entered into force 25 November 2005) CAB/LEG/66.6; reprinted in 1 *Afr Hum Rts LJ* 40:
(1) Every woman shall have the right to dignity inherent in a human being and to the recognition and protection of her human and legal rights;
(2) Every woman shall have the right to respect as a person and to the free development of her personality.

213 n 212 above, Art 22(b).

214 n 212 above, Art 23(b).

215 n 212 above, Art 24(b).

216 League of Arab States, Arab Charter on Human Rights (adopted 22 May 2004, entered into force 15 March 2008) reprinted in (2005) 12 IHRR 893, Preamble, 1st para:
Based on the faith of the Arab nation in the dignity of the human person whom God has exalted ever since the beginning of creation and in the fact that the Arab homeland is the cradle of religions and civilizations whose lofty human values affirm the human right to a decent life based on freedom, justice and equality.

217 n 216 above, Art 3.3: 'Men and women are equal in respect of human dignity, rights and obligations within the framework of the positive discrimination established in favour of women by the Islamic Shariah, other divine laws and by applicable laws and legal instruments.'
See J Rehman *International human rights law* (2010) 380.

218 n 216 above, Art 33.3.

219 n 216 above, Art 20.1.

220 n216 above, Art 40.1. Unjustified segregation of the mentally retarded is discrimination: *Olmstead v LC* 527 US 581 (1999). On *Olmstead*, see SB Caley & SD Caley 'The *Olmstead* decision: The road to dignity and freedom' (2010) 26 *Georgia State University Law Review* 651 at 654 - 662.

2.2.1.7 National constitutions

It is interesting to note that countries where there has been wholesale abuse of people have protected human dignity in post-atrocity laws.[221] These include Germany and South Africa. Germany's Basic Law adopted in 1949 gave dignity the most predominant place.[222] Article 1 is devoted to the protection of human dignity, which is the foundation for directly enforceable human rights.[223] The foundational values in the South African Constitution are dignity, equality and freedom;[224] it also recognises dignity as a self-standing right.[225] Israel is another country that has highlighted human dignity in its basic laws.[226]

Christopher McCrudden points out that the incorporation of dignity into national constitutions in Europe was popular in the 1970s following the collapse of dictatorships in Greece, Spain and Portugal, and in the 1990s after the fall of the Berlin Wall, which signalled the turn to democracy in Central and Eastern Europe.[227] The German Constitution and its interpretation by the German Constitutional Court was influential, not just in Europe, but also in South Africa and Israel.[228]

There are significant differences in the use of dignity in the various texts reflecting cultural relativism and pluralism.[229]

According to McCrudden, some countries, particularly those with Catholic or Islamic outlooks, 'use dignity as the basis for (or another way of expressing) a comprehensive moral viewpoint, "a whole moral world view",

221 See H Botha 'Human dignity in comparative perspective' (2009) 20 *Stellenbosch Law Review* 171 at 175 - 177.

222 McCrudden (n 9 above) 665; Basic Law for the Federal Republic of Germany 1949. On dignity in German constitutional law, see Botha (n 221 above) 178 - 196; J Church *et al, Human rights from a comparative and international law perspective* (2007) 100 - 102.

223 It reads:

(1) The dignity of man inviolable. To respect and protect it is the duty of all state authority.
(2) The German people therefore acknowledge inviolable and inalienable human rights as the basis of every community, of peace and of justice in the world.
(3) The following basic rights bind the legislature, the executive and the judiciary as directly enforceable law.

224 Constitution of the Republic of South Africa 1996, Sec 1(a).

225 Sec 10.

226 Israel - Basic Law: Human Dignity and Liberty 1992 (amended 1994), Secs 1a, 2 & 4; Basic Law: Government 2001, Sec 39(d).

227 n 9 above, 673.

228 As above.

229 As above.

which seems distinctly different from region to region.'[230] He instances Ireland's 1937 Constitution and Arab human rights texts as examples of this trend.

2.2.2 Sources

Dignity was a right of personality and status in legal systems based on Roman law.[231] Many European jurisdictions have had a long-standing right to personality, which has a community aspect and is not solely concerned with autonomy and the right to self-determination. It acknowledges the person as a social being, who communicates and interacts with other members of society. The moral integrity of the individual is recognised, as is the need of security for each person's own ethical standards. The dignity of everyone in the community is protected. The aim is harmony between society and the individual's expression of his or her unique personality in accordance with their own priorities without the imposition of uniform standards in deeply personal issues.

In Germany and France, rights of personality are protected.[232] James Whitman has tracked their origin in Germany to the Roman law concept of insult, which in ancient Rome protected certain damage to possessions, and evolved to protect against public insult.[233] It was based on honour and matured to safeguard non-economic interests and various kinds of disrespect.[234] Whitman points out that the dignity of the '*ancien régime*' was not *human* dignity, but was 'intended to guarantee that high-status persons would be treated better than low-status persons'.[235] In twentieth century Continental Europe, 'human dignity' in a reaction against the *status quo* was extended by a pattern of levelling up to all sectors of the population.[236]

230 n 9 above, 675. Dignity does not provide an agreed content to human rights. McCrudden considers that it has a more limited institutional benefit in 'providing a language in which judges can appear to justify how they deal with issues such as the weight of rights, the domestication and contextualization of rights, and the generation of new or more extensive rights': n 9 above, 724.

231 McCrudden (n 9 above) 657.

232 On personality rights in Germany, see Church *et al* (n 222 above) 108 - 109.

233 JQ Whitman 'The two Western cultures of privacy: Dignity versus liberty' (2004) 113 *Yale Law Journal* 1151 at 1183.

234 Whitman (n 233 above) 1184.

235 JQ Whitman 'Human dignity in Europe and the United States: The social foundations' (2004) 25 *Human Rights Law Journal* 17 at 17.

236 Whitman (n 235 above) 18.

South Africa, with a Roman-Dutch basis for its law, recognised a tort of injury to dignity. Infringement of a person's *dignitas* constituted a delict and compensation could be claimed with the *actio iniuriarum*, which applied between private individuals and did not lie against the state.[237] Mokgoro J explained it in *Dikoko v Mokhatla*:[238]

> The law of defamation is based on the *actio injuriarum*, a flexible Roman law remedy which afforded the right to claim damages to a person whose personality rights had been impaired by another. The action is designed to afford personal satisfaction for an impairment of a personality right and became a general remedy for any vexatious violation of a person's right to his dignity and reputation.

The South African constitutional concept of dignity is much broader than the pre-existing personality right. Nelson Mandela in his speech in Trafalgar Square in 2005 viewed overcoming poverty as an act of justice rather than charity; it protected fundamental human rights, the right to dignity and a decent life.[239]

Many states worldwide with different value systems, cultures and legal backgrounds have given prominence to dignity in their constitutions or case-law. Its ambit stretches across continents to countries such as India,[240] where dignity is mentioned in the Preamble to its Constitution (similar to Ireland), Japan,[241] Hong Kong[242] and Malaysia[243] in Asia, to Peru[244] and Argentina[245]

237 IJ Kroeze 'Human dignity in constitutional law in South Africa' in European Commission for Democracy through Law, *The Principle of Respect for Human Dignity* (Proceedings of the UniDem Seminar, Montpellier, 2 - 6 July 1998) http://www.venice.coe.int/webforms/documents/CDL-STD%281998%29026-e.aspx#P1070_198886 (accessed 24 September 2013).

238 2006 6 SA 235 (CC) [62].

239 McCrudden (n 9 above) 663.

240 Constitution of India 1950.

241 Constitution of Japan 1946.

242 Hong Kong Bill of Rights Ordinance 1991.

243 The High Court of Malaysia has held 'it is the fundamental right of every person within the shores of Malaysia to live with common human dignity': E Daly 'Constitutional dignity: Lessons from home and abroad' Widener Law School Legal Studies Research Paper Series no 08-07 http://ssrn.com/abstract=991608 (accessed 16 January 2009), citing *Kanawagi A/l Seperumaniam v Dato' Abdul Hamid Bin Mohamad* [2004] 5 MLJ 495, 506 (High Court Malaysia - Kuala Lumpur) (Fiaza Tamby Chik J).

244 Constitution of Peru 1993.

245 The Argentine Supreme Court has held that 'the right of reply is a natural fundamental right that is essential to the legitimate defense of one's dignity, honor and privacy':

in South America, to Poland,[246] Macedonia[247] and Hungary[248] in Eastern Europe, and to Belgium[249] and Portugal[250] in Western Europe.

2.2.3 Roles and impact

Dignity is not merely an ethical cornerstone of the international legal order, but its use in multiple international instruments has led to it becoming a substantive guarantee in its own right to-day assuring respect for each individual and giving protection against humiliating and degrading treatment.[251]

Human dignity has a variety of roles in law. It can be a value, a principle or a right. Gay Moon and Robin Allen explain:[252]

> The appeal to respect for human dignity can be made to assert a value that ought to be shared by all; to invoke a principle to stand alongside other fundamental principles (including in particular the principle of equal treatment) to help determine how that other principle should be applied; and to claim a remedy for the violation of a self-standing right.

Sometimes it can be a fundamental value, being the bedrock of a constitution. Dignity has featured in jurisprudence in its various guises and has been interpreted by the courts in different ways. Frequently this has caused confusion, as the judges have not made clear the context in which it is being used and how the concept works.[253]

Daly (n 243 above), citing Corte Suprema de Justicia [CSJN] [Supreme Court of Justice], 7/7/1992 *Ekmedjian v Sofovich* Fallos (1992-315-1492) (Arg), *reprinted in* Angel R Oquendo, *Latin American Law* (Foundation Press, New York 2006) 245.

246 Constitution of the Republic of Poland 1997.

247 Constitution of the Republic of Macedonia 1991.

248 Constitution of the Republic of Hungary 1949, as amended.

249 Constitution of Belgium 1970, as amended.

250 Constitution of the Portuguese Republic 1976.

251 N Petersen 'Human dignity, international protection' in R Wolfrum (ed) *The Max Planck encyclopedia of public international law* (2008) 10 http://www.mpepil.com (accessed 10 October 2008). The Ugandan High Court held the state vicariously liable and made an award of damages against it for the humiliating and degrading actions of the police in sexually harassing a woman, contrary to the constitutional provision requiring respect for human dignity and protection from inhuman treatment: *Mukasa v AG* [2008] AHRLR 248 (UgHC 2008) [41], [43], citing Constitution of the Republic of Uganda 1995, Art 24.

252 n 160 above, 615.

253 As above; R O'Connell 'The role of dignity in equality law: Lessons from Canada and South Africa' (2008) 6 *International Journal of Constitutional Law* 267 at 284.

Some commentators have been enthusiastic supporters of the use of dignity in law, while others have been less enamoured with it or have criticised it as a vague concept which has detracted from other legal principles or values.[254] It has played a growingly significant role in Canadian jurisprudence, particularly in the area of equality law; however, it has drawn adverse reaction from some quarters.[255]

There is no reference to dignity in the US Constitution, but it has related concepts including a ban on cruel and unusual punishment and a due process clause.[256] The US Supreme Court has invoked the concept of dignity sporadically. Vicki Jackson sees scope for its development:[257]

> Although some members of the U.S. Supreme Court in the postwar period have embraced dignity as a motivating principle for the U.S. Bill of Rights, the role of the concept of 'human dignity' in the Court's jurisprudence is episodic and underdeveloped.

She explains that the difference between the European notion of human dignity and that prevailing in much of the US is due partly to 'the interactions among newer and older legal ideas and the varying capacities of existing legal systems to assimilate newer legal norms to existing traditions.'[258]

The concept of dignity played an important role in the US Supreme Court decision in *Lawrence v Texas* holding that the state ban on sodomy violated the Due Process clause.[259] Delivering the Opinion of the Court,

254 Supporters include E Grant 'Dignity and equality' (2007) 7 *Human Rights Law Review* 299; MD Goodman 'Human dignity in Supreme Court constitutional jurisprudence' (2006) 84 *Nebraska Law Review* 740. For criticisms, see A Foster 'The role of dignity in Canadian and South African gender equality jurisprudence' (2008) 17 *Dalhousie Journal of Legal Studies* 73; RJ Fyfe 'Dignity as theory: Competing conceptions of human dignity at the Supreme Court of Canada' (2007) 70 *Saskatchewan Law Review* 1. The strengths and weaknesses of using dignity are pointed out by D Feldman 'Human dignity as a legal value' Part 1 *Public Law* [1999] 682, Part 2 *Public Law* [2000] 61; T Khaitan 'Dignity as an expressive norm: Neither vacuous nor a panacea' (2012) 32 *Oxford Journal of Legal Studies* 1.

255 Moon and Allen said that some Canadian jurists regard the dignity discourse as unhelpful, and, even detrimental, in the development of human rights (in Canada principally concerned with equality rights): n 160 above, 617.

256 VC Jackson 'Constitutional dialogue and human dignity: States and transnational constitutional discourse' (2004) 65 *Montana Law Review* 15 at 16.

257 n 256 above, 17 (footnotes omitted).

258 n 256 above, 20.

259 539 US 558 (2003); Jackson (n 256 above) fn 9.

Justice Kennedy considered that the State should not interfere in private relationships and that adults' liberty to choose did not detract from their dignity.[260] He referred back to the Court's decision in *Planned Parenthood of Southeastern Pa v Casey* to explain the respect the Constitution demands for liberty in making personal choices.[261]

US jurisprudence has primarily emphasised the importance of privacy. This is compatible with the ethos in a nation where the liberty of the individual is supreme and there is abhorrence of government interference. Individual states have references to dignity in their constitutions. Montana is unique among the states in the US in having an explicit and wide guarantee of individual dignity in its 1972 Constitution.[262] Section 4 in its Declaration of Rights is devoted to individual dignity.[263] Montana was inspired to focus on dignity in its Constitution by the Puerto Rican Constitution adopted in 1951 and which, in turn, had been influenced by the Universal Declaration.[264] The Constitutions of Illinois and Louisiana, adopted in 1970 and 1974

260 n 259 above, 567:

> The statutes do seek to control a personal relationship that, whether or not entitled to formal recognition in the law, is within the liberty of persons to choose without being punished as criminals.
>
> This, as a general rule, should counsel against attempts by the State, or a court, to define the meaning of the relationship or to set its boundaries absent injury to a person or abuse of an institution the law protects. It suffices for us to acknowledge that adults may choose to enter upon this relationship in the confines of their homes and their own private lives and still retain their dignity as free persons. When sexuality finds overt expression in intimate conduct with another person, the conduct can be but one element in a personal bond that is more enduring. The liberty protected by the Constitution allows homosexual persons the right to make this choice.

261 n 259 above, 574, citing *Planned Parenthood of Southeastern Pa v Casey* 505 US 833 (1992) 851:

> These matters, involving the most intimate and personal choices a person may make in a lifetime, choices central to personal dignity and autonomy, are central to the liberty protected by the Fourteenth Amendment. At the heart of liberty is the right to define one's own concept of existence, of meaning, of the universe, and of the mystery of human life. Beliefs about these matters could not define the attributes of personhood were they formed under compulsion of the State.

262 Jackson (n 256 above) 21.

263 Constitution of Montana 1972, Art II Sec 4:

> The dignity of the human being is inviolable. No person shall be denied the equal protection of the laws. Neither the state nor any person, firm, corporation, or institution shall discriminate against any person in the exercise of his civil or political rights on account of race, color, sex, culture, social origin or condition, or political or religious ideas.

264 Jackson (n 256 above) 22 - 25.

respectively, refer to dignity, but not as comprehensively as that of Montana.[265]

The dignity clause may have played a role in the occasional assertions by the Montana Supreme Court that the state constitution provides different more expansive rights than in the federal Constitution.[266] In *Armstrong v State* the court held that a legislative ban on certified physician assistants from performing abortions violated the right to privacy and invoked the dignity clause to support its conclusions.[267] As Jackson says, the court appeared to attribute both some independent value to the 'dignity' clause and a coherent connectedness between the right to dignity and other rights.[268]

The dignity clause in the Puerto Rican Constitution has been significant in the case-law of its Supreme Court, which has asserted that the inviolability of human dignity is the foundational concept at the base of the Commonwealth's commitments to democracy and human rights.[269] In contrast to other states where the legislature led the way in introducing no-fault divorce, the abandonment of the fault system came through the Supreme Court in Puerto Rico in *Figueroa Ferrer v Commonwealth* where it held that the requirement for fault to obtain a divorce violated Puerto Rico's constitution;

265 Jackson (n 256 above) fn 21. On dignity in the Constitution of Illinois, see E Gertz 'Hortatory language in the Preamble and Bill of Rights of the 1970 Constitution' (1973) 6 *John Marshall Journal of Practice and Procedure* 217 at 227 - 231, 234.

266 Jackson (n 256 above) 29.

267 1999 MT 261, 296 Mont 361, 989 P2d 364; Jackson (n 256 above) 30. The European Court of Human Rights found that Ireland had a positive obligation to secure to a pregnant woman whose life was at risk effective respect for her private life by legislation or the provision of a regulatory regime giving an accessible and effective procedure by which she could establish whether she qualified for a lawful abortion in Ireland in accordance with Article 40.3.3° of the Constitution: *A v Ireland* (App no 25579/05) (2011) 53 EHRR 13 [267]. For reviews of the *A* case, see S Krishnan 'What's the consensus? The Grand Chamber's decision on abortion in *A, B and C v Ireland*' [2011] *European Human Rights Law Review* 200; J Mortimer 'Failing to legislate for lawful abortion – The impact of *C*' (2011) 105(2) *Gazette of the Law Society of Ireland* 16; E Wicks '*A, B, C v Ireland*: Abortion law under the European Convention on Human Rights' (2011) 11 *Human Rights Law Review* 556.

268 n 256 above, 30, citing *Armstrong* (n 267 above) [72]:

> Respect for the dignity of each individual – a fundamental right, protected by Article II Section 4 of the Montana Constitution – demands that people have for themselves the moral right and moral responsibility to confront the most fundamental questions about the meaning and value of their own lives and the intrinsic value of life in general, answering to their own consciences and convictions. Equal protection ... requires that people have an equal right to form and to follow their own values in profoundly spiritual matters. ... Finally the right of individual privacy ... requires the government to leave us alone in all these most personal and private matters.

269 Jackson (n 256 above) 33.

the court criticised the fault regime in divorce for requiring married couples either to mislead the court or to surrender aspects of their private lives to public scrutiny.[270] The constitutional principles of dignity and privacy 'are based on principles which aspire to universality,' and 'protect … dignity and private life in divorce proceedings through the expression of the mutual decision to obtain a divorce.'[271]

In the US, priority is given to individual rights in contrast to the socialist outlook in the continental European tradition, where dignity is central to the common good as well as being an attribute of the individual. Glendon has called for a return to the founding values of the US with more emphasis on responsibility and sociality.[272] She criticised the legal fraternity's emphasis on achieving individual civil rights and the heavy stress in American legal education on the distinction between law and morality.[273] The rights culture had jettisoned the values of dignity and freedom and embraced instead the fulfilment of 'insistent unending desires'.[274] The balance should be redressed by focusing on duties and the individual's responsibility towards the community.

Neomi Rao supports the precedence given in the US to the enforcement of individual rights over community interests.[275] She is a critic of the European use of dignity to promote socialist ideologies at the expense of the freedom of the individual.[276] Rao accepts that she is out of touch with the times in not endorsing human dignity as a constitutional value.[277] For her, dignity is a noble-sounding abstraction, which some see as providing 'an irreducible minimum of recognition for all individuals.'[278] She denounces the proportionality review in modern constitutionalism as diluting rights and trading them off against other political and social needs.[279] While the US Supreme Court balances rights, it does so infrequently, and gives more scope

270 107 PR Dec (1978); Jackson (n 256 above) 34, fn 71. Most couples obtained divorce by mutual consent, but through a judicial charade: Jackson (n 256 above) 34.

271 Jackson (n 256 above) 34, citing *Figueroa Ferrer* (n 270 above) 301.

272 MA Glendon *Rights talk: The impoverishment of political discourse* (1991) 143.

273 n 272 above, 85.

274 Glendon (n 272 above) 171.

275 N Rao 'On the use and abuse of dignity in constitutional law' (2008) 14 *Columbia Journal of European Law* 201 at 256.

276 n 275 above, 221 - 222, 255.

277 n 275 above, 255.

278 As above.

279 n 275 above, 256.

for argument about individual rights.[280] She advocates a new take on dignity based on the American Constitution and legal traditions, which would emphasise individual liberty and self-determination rather than the newer communitarian view found elsewhere.[281]

Mahatma Gandhi, who comported himself in a highly dignified manner, articulated a non-Western philosophy and promoted the community aspect of living rather than individual rights.[282] He advocated *dharma*, which is based on duty arising out of communal responsibility.[283]

The Universal Declaration of Human Responsibilities adopted by the InterAction Council of former world leaders in 1997 affirmed human dignity and equality as the basis of freedom, justice and peace in the world.[284] This assertion implies obligations. All people have the responsibility to strive for the human dignity and self-esteem of others.[285]

African culture is less individualistic and the common good has been emphasised more. The African concept of *ubuntu* marries the individual and the community. It binds the interests of the individual with those of the society within which the individual lives. While the dignity of the individual is recognised, the common good is the primary target. It may be that this was essential in order to ensure survival in a difficult natural environment and in an even more challenging social and political arena when the European settlers arrived. Social solidarity has been the principal aim of traditional communities. *Ubuntu* recognises the dignity of the individual in the context of the common good. The idea is that it is in the interests of each individual to look after their neighbours and to work for the welfare of other members of the community. A giver can turn into a beneficiary if circumstances change. It has resonances of the Christian ethos of doing unto others as you would want done unto you.

Dignity played a primary role in the South African case *Makwanyane* where the death penalty was held to be unconstitutional.[286] Langa J

280 As above.

281 As above.

282 NMI Goolam 'Human dignity – Our supreme constitutional value' (2001) 4 *Potchefstroom Electronic Law Journal* 1 at 5.

283 As above.

284 Universal Declaration of Human Responsibilities (adopted 1 September 1997) InterAction Council, Preamble.

285 Declaration of Human Responsibilities (n 284 above) art 2.

286 *S v Makwanyane* 1995 6 BCLR 665 (CC); McCrudden (n 9 above) 688.

considered that *ubuntu* was relevant and brought out its community aspect with mutual duties in addition to respect for the individual's dignity.[287] The element of reciprocal love in *ubuntu* was significant for Mahomed J.[288] Mokgoro J linked dignity with *ubuntu* while highlighting group co-existence in harmony.[289]

Other African countries also place a value in their constitutions and jurisprudence on the dignity of the individual. Zimbabwe invoked the concept of dignity when it too declared the death penalty unconstitutional.[290]

287 n 286 above, [224]:

> The concept [*ubuntu*] is of some relevance to the values we need to uphold. It is a culture which places some emphasis on communality and on the interdependence of the members of a community. It recognises a person's status as a human being, entitled to unconditional respect, dignity, value and acceptance from the members of the community such person happens to be part of. It also entails the converse, however. The person has a corresponding duty to give the same respect, dignity, value and acceptance to each member of that community. More importantly, it regulates the exercise of rights by the emphasis it lays on sharing and co-responsibility and the mutual enjoyment of rights by all.

For a critique of the explanations the Constitutional Court gave for thinking that an *ubuntu* ethic entailed that the death penalty was an unconstitutional violation of human dignity, see Metz (n 13 above) 85 - 91.

288 n 286 above, [263]:

> 'The need for *ubuntu*' [in the postamble to the Constitution] expresses the ethos of an instinctive capacity for and enjoyment of love towards our fellow men and women; the joy and the fulfilment involved in recognizing their innate humanity; the reciprocity this generates in interaction within the collective community; the richness of the creative emotions which it engenders and the moral energies which it releases both in the givers and the society which they serve and are served by.

289 n 286 above, [308]:

> Generally, *ubuntu* translates as humaneness. In its most fundamental sense, it translates as personhood and morality. Metaphorically, it expresses itself in *umuntu ngumuntu ngabantu*, describing the significance of group solidarity on survival issues so central to the survival of communities. While it envelops the key values of group solidarity, compassion, respect, human dignity, conformity to basic norms and collective unity, in its fundamental sense it denotes humanity and morality. Its spirit emphasises respect for human dignity, marking a shift from confrontation to conciliation.

See Church *et al* (n 222 above) 207 - 208.

290 *Catholic Commission for Justice and Peace in Zimbabwe v AG* [1993] 2 LRC 279 (SC of Zimbabwe) [23], [37], [49], [87], [122]. The prolonged delays in executing the death penalty and the harsh incarceration conditions were held to be serious enough to amount to inhuman treatment contrary to Section 15(1) of the Constitution of the Republic of Zimbabwe 1979: *Catholic Commission* above, [120]. The legislature responded by amending the Constitution to provide that delay in executing the death sentence would not contravene that subsection: Constitution of Zimbabwe Amendment (No 13) Act 1993 sec 2. See AR Gubbay 'The protection and enforcement of fundamental human rights: The Zimbabwean experience' (1997) 19 *Human Rights Quarterly* 227 at 232, 240 - 242; J Small & E Grant 'Dignity, discrimination, and context: New directions in South African and Canadian human rights law' (2005) 6(2) *Human Rights Review* 25 at fn 70.

In *Jumbe v AG* the High Court of Malawi struck down legislation reversing the onus of proof in corruption charges, as it breached the constitutional right to a fair trial, which included the presumption of innocence and the right to silence, and was not justified under the limitation clause in the Constitution; Katsala J invoked democratic principles when he stressed that the accused should be treated with dignity as fellow human beings, notwithstanding the odious and contemptible nature of corruption.[291]

While accepting that there are different philosophies of life and various cultures throughout the world, it is worthwhile striving to find common ground for co-existence, where the interests of the community, states and international world order will be protected while respecting the dignity of the individual. Chandra Muzaffar asks that our rights and responsibilities be guided by universal moral and spiritual values.[292] He sees human dignity as the common starting point.[293]

Jack Donnelly pointed out the historical difference between the Western alliance of human dignity and human rights, on the one hand, and the traditional place of human dignity in non-Western societies, on the other.[294]

291 [2005] MWHC 15 at 47:

> Admittedly corruption is bad. It is evil and it has to be rooted out of our society. It is counter productive and it seriously retards development. Those that engage in corruption in a way violate the citizens' right to development as enshrined in section 30 of the Constitution. They, among other things, divert for their own use public resources thereby depriving the general public the benefit from such resources. Such people are selfish and greedy at the expense of everyone else. Surely, if caught, they must be dealt with firmly.
>
> However, inasmuch as we may harbour hatred for such people, we can only show and prove to the whole world and indeed to ourselves that we are an open and democratic society and that we cherish and promote the values that underlie such a society if we treat those we suspect of committing heinous crimes with dignity as fellow human beings and afford them all the protection that accused persons enjoy under the Constitution. I do not see any justification for limiting their right to be presumed innocent bearing in mind that they are mere suspects and have not been convicted of the alleged crimes.

292 C Muzaffar 'From human rights to human dignity' (1995) 29(4) *Bulletin of Concerned Asian Scholars* 6 at 8.

293 As above: 'The great challenge before us is to develop this vision of human dignity culled from our religious and spiritual philosophies into a comprehensive charter of values and principles, responsibilities and rights, and roles and relationships acceptable to human beings everywhere.' See also C Muzaffar *Rights, religion and reform: Enhancing human dignity through spiritual and moral transformation* (2002) 34 - 35.

294 J Donnelly 'Human rights and human dignity: An analytic critique of non-Western conceptions of human rights' (1982) 76 *American Political Science Review* 303 at 303. See also W Binchy 'The role of comparative and public international law in domestic legal systems' (2010) 23(3) *Advocate (South Africa)* 58 at 61.

Islamic, African, Chinese and Indian societies have valued dignity, but have not historically embraced universal human rights. Instead these societies have given precedence to the common good. He considers that in an era when there is a focus on the individual, universal human rights are appropriate for all societies. Independent evidence for this trend can be gauged from the fact that international gatherings have endorsed human rights and, indeed, have selected human dignity as a, if not the, foundational value grounding human rights.[295]

In contrast to Donnelly's focus on individual rights at the expense of social justice, Guy Haarscher looks at the relationships between each individual and society.[296] The dignity of each member should be considered and the norm should be respect for the other.[297]

In the final debate in the UN General Assembly on the Universal Declaration in 1949, the Indian delegate's view was that the basis of rights is neither the state nor the individual human being, but the human person participating in social life and working towards national and international co-operation.[298] The emphasis is on the individual in society rather than on the individual *per se* or the state.

Dignity as a value can be an excellent interpretative guide to constitutions. In some, it is the primary value overtly expressed or the judiciary has identified it as such. In other states, it is one of the basic values and takes its place on an equal footing with values such as freedom and equality.

2.2.4 Association with other rights

2.2.4.1 Equality

The dignity of the individual is inextricably linked with equality. Because each person has inherent worth, all are regarded as equal. Therefore it is not a surprise to find that dignity and equality are closely associated. According to Jo Pasqualucci, the Inter-American Court of Human Rights relies on natural law to hold that equality arises directly from the unity of the human

295 J Donnelly *Universal human rights in theory and practice* (2003) 41.

296 MB Dembour *Who believes in human rights? Reflections on the European Convention* (2006) 236.

297 As above.

298 UN Secretariat *Our rights as human beings: A discussion guide on the Universal Declaration of Human Rights* (1949) 24.

family and is inextricably linked to the dignity of the individual.[299] The Court explained that the principle of non-discrimination

> cannot be reconciled with the notion that a given group has the right to privileged treatment because of its perceived superiority. It is equally irreconcilable with that notion to characterize a group as inferior and treat it with hostility or otherwise subject it to discrimination in the enjoyment of rights which are accorded to others not so classified.[300]

In South Africa dignity is the springboard for substantive equality. Sachs J explained the effect of a dignity analysis in *National Coalition for Gay and Lesbian Equality v Minister of Justice* (*Sodomy* case):[301]

> The focus on dignity results in emphasis being placed simultaneously on context, impact and the point of view of the affected persons. Such focus is in fact the guarantor of substantive as opposed to formal equality.

The treatment of some groups in society as inferior to others is prohibited as being contrary to the equality of all human beings. In the *Sodomy* case, where legislation criminalising sexual intimacy between gay men was found unconstitutional, Sachs J condemned as inequality the criminalisation of people because of their humanity.[302] The South African judiciary does not have unfettered discretion to find a lack of equality based on the judges' own views, but has a structured method for assessing the merits and legal import of each situation.

299 JM Pasqualucci 'The evolution of international indigenous rights in the Inter-American human rights system' (2006) 6 *Human Rights Law Review* 281, citing OC-4/1984, *Proposed Amendments of the Naturalization Provisions of the Constitution of Costa Rica* IACtHR Series A 4 (1984) [55].

300 As above.

301 1998 12 BCLR 1517 (CC) [126].

302 n301 above, [129]:

> At the heart of equality jurisprudence is the rescuing of people from a caste-like status and putting an end to their being treated as lesser human beings because they belong to a particular group. The indignity and subordinate status may flow from institutionally imposed exclusion from the mainstream of society or else from powerlessness within the mainstream; they may also be derived from the location of difference as a problematic form of deviance in the disadvantaged group itself, as happens in the case of the disabled. In the case of gays it comes from compulsion to deny a closely held per-sonal characteristic. To penalise people for being what they are is profoundly disrespectful of the human personality and violatory of equality.

Moon and Allen promote dignity as an element that can help achieve substantive equality.[303] They consider that the Aristotelian concept of equality is insufficient to address historical disadvantage.[304] Dignity attacks discrimination based on class or social status.[305] The use of dignity by the judiciary as an aid to achieve equality can entrench social solidarity.[306]

Dignity requires that people be treated well, whereas equality simply puts all in the same (not necessarily good) position. In this context dignity is a contested concept. For some, as in South Africa, it is a powerful basis for substantive equality. But for others, as for a coterie in Canada, it can limit the range of anti-discrimination laws.[307]

2.2.4.2 Freedom and security

In legal terms dignity has been important frequently in trying to ensure that no-one suffers indignity at the hand of the state. It protects personal safety and demands humane treatment. Hence there is a clear ban on torture and on cruel treatment even of those who have violated others. Accused people and convicted prisoners are entitled to be treated with dignity. In South Africa prisoners established the right to vote while incarcerated in *August v Electoral Commission*, where Sachs J described the vote as 'a badge of dignity and of personhood', signifying 'everybody counts'.[308]

The imprisonment of judgment debtors in South Africa without a criminal trial was found to be an infringement of their constitutional rights to freedom and security.[309] The court invoked the constitutional right to dignity as an interpretative aid. While the goal of the legislation to provide a mechanism

303 n 160 above, 645:

> [R]espect for human dignity operates in a number of important ways in giving greater meaning to the desire to secure equality. As a cornerstone of human rights, it requires that individuals be respected for their innate humanity, and that they should not be used as objects, as means to an end, but as ends in themselves. This imperative has very important consequences for enriching the equality discourse. In particular it counters stigma, stereotyping, prejudice and the exclusion from benefits or opportunities which are some of the minimum conditions for a life with dignity.

304 n 160 above, 643.

305 As above.

306 Moon & Allen (n 160 above) 649.

307 Andrew Foster analysed the focus on dignity to define equality in Canada and South Africa and concluded, 'the use of dignity as a normative standard for determining violations of equality has itself reinforced the formalism it was intended to overcome': Foster (n 254 above) 74.

308 1999 3 SA 1 (CC) [17].

309 *Coetzee v Government of the Republic of South Africa* 1995 4 SA 631 (CC).

for the enforcement of judgment debts was a legitimate and reasonable government objective, the means were not justified since it resulted in the unjustifiable imprisonment of those who were impecunious and could not pay, as well as those who had sufficient resources but refused to discharge their legal obligations.

Those involved in armed conflict have the right not to be tortured and must be dealt with in a decent fashion.

2.2.4.3 Fair trial

The right to a fair trial is based on the dignity of the person. The elements of rationality and free will in dignity have led to a ban on serious criminal responsibility without *mens rea*. It offends the inner worth of the individual to impose guilt in the absence of intention to commit a crime or knowledge of the transgression. Hardiman J quoted from Canadian jurisprudence in *CC v Ireland*, when the Supreme Court found unconstitutional legislation criminalising sexual relations with a girl under 15 years because it exposed a person without mental guilt to a maximum sentence of life imprisonment and failed to respect the accused's liberty and dignity.[310]

Respect for dignity, in particular the freedom and security of the person, has resulted in an amelioration of harsh or precipitative civil procedures for collection of debts. The defaulting debtor is entitled to a fair hearing with advance notice of the possibility of punitive measures being imposed.[311] As support for her decision to this effect in *McCann v Judge of Monaghan District Court*, Laffoy J referred to *Coetzee* as finding:

> ... the sanction of imprisonment is ostensibly aimed at the debtor who will not pay, but it also strikes at those who cannot pay and simply fail to

310 [2006] IESC 33, [2006] 4 IR 1 [21]:

> Wilson J [in *R v Hess; R v Nguyen* [1990] 2 SCR 906] went on to review the academic authorities. She concluded:
>
> > 'Our commitment to the principle that those who did not intend to commit harm and who took all reasonable precautions to ensure that they did not commit an offence should not be imprisoned stems from an acute awareness that to imprison a mentally innocent person is to inflict a grave injury on that person's dignity and sense of worth. Where that person's beliefs and his actions leading up to the commission of the prohibited act are treated as completely irrelevant in the face of the state's pronouncement that he must automatically be incarcerated for having done the prohibited act, that person is treated as little more than a means to an end.'

On *Hess*, see PW Hogg *Constitutional law of Canada Vol 2* (2007) 395 - 397.

311 *McCann v Judge of Monaghan District Court* [2009] IEHC 276.

> prove this at the hearing due to negative circumstances created by the provisions themselves.[312]

The dignity of those accused of war crimes must be respected, as Sachs J made clear in *S v Basson*.[313]

2.2.4.4 Privacy and autonomy

Dignity has been inextricably linked with the rights to privacy and autonomy. The Victorian Law Reform Commission in Australia's research into workplace privacy revealed a social aspect to the intermingling of these three elements.[314] Privacy can have connotations of territory, confidentiality or the freedom to make intimate personal decisions. The inherent worth of the individual demands that each person be allowed to exercise free will responsibly; every individual must be given the space to choose the course of action which makes life meaningful for him or her. This may not coincide with what the majority considers correct behaviour. Respect for dignity usually requires that society support them in their decision. Tolerance is not enough, but a more active level of endorsement is required.

The right to self-determination is limited by the bounds of dignity. A person is not permitted to violate their own dignity. In France a man of low stature claimed that he wished to earn a livelihood by taking part in dwarf-throwing competitions, which were banned. His challenge to this law failed. The UN Human Rights Committee accepted the State's argument that dwarf-throwing was an affront to dignity, which threatened public order; France

312 n 311 above, citing n 309 above, [13].

313 2005 1 SA 171 (CC) [126]:

> The effective prosecution of war crimes and the rights of the accused to a fair trial are not antagonistic concepts. On the contrary, both stem from the same constitutional and humanitarian foundation, namely the need to uphold the rule of law and the basic principles of human dignity, equality and freedom.

314 Victorian Law Reform Commission 'Workplace Privacy: Issues Paper' (2002) [2.38]:

> Privacy always includes and refers to autonomy and dignity. This means that the protection of privacy will always encompass the following rights:
> - not to be turned into an object or thing, that is, not to be treated as anything other than an autonomous human being; and
> - not to be deprived of the capacity to form and develop relationships.
>
> This right of privacy is aimed not just at the protection of the individual's privacy, but at protecting privacy as a social value.

On privacy as a social value, see H Delany *et al*, *The right to privacy: A doctrinal and comparative analysis* (2008) 18 - 20.

had authority to ban dwarf-throwing to prevent public disorder. The claimant's right to self-determination did not prevail.[315]

In common law systems privacy first became established as a central legal value in the US and had its origins in 1880 when Thomas Cooley argued that there was a 'right to be let alone'.[316] The earliest manifestation of dignity in the autonomy context was in allowing the fulfilment of decisions about procreation and in allowing access to contraceptives. A constitutional right to privacy was established by the US Supreme Court in *Griswold v Connecticut* when it struck down a state statute which made it an offence for married couples to use contraceptives.[317] Famously, in *Roe v Wade* the right to privacy protected women's autonomy in respect of their bodies.[318] The majority of the Supreme Court held that the right was not absolute, so the grounds on which the state was entitled to prevent abortions were restricted.[319]

The dignity of the person has been intertwined with the autonomy of adults in obtaining legal recognition for the right of homosexuals to have sexual relations in private without fear of prosecution and is prominent in their quest to obtain the right to marry same-sex partners. The US Supreme Court resiled from its earlier enthusiasm to protect privacy in *Bowers v Hardwick* when a narrow majority refused to uphold the right of adult homosexuals to engage in consensual sexual relationships.[320] This contrasts with the European Court of Human Rights' decision in *Dudgeon v UK*, where the states were found to have a restricted margin of appreciation in view of the degree of personal intimacy.[321]

315 *Wackenheim v France* UNHR Committee (26 July 2002) 75th Session UN Doc CCPR/C/75/D/854/1999. See Rao (n 39 above) 226 - 227. See J Waldron 'Dignity, rights, and responsibilities' (2011) 43 *Arizona State Law Journal* 1107 at 1130 - 1131.
France, South Africa and Germany are inclined to separate dignity from autonomy to give the legal conception of dignity an expanded more positive, community-based meaning: Rao (n 39 above) 220.

316 TM Cooley *A treatise on the law of torts* (1880) 29. See D Feldman *Civil liberties and human rights in England and Wales* (2002) 516.

317 381 US 479 (1965).

318 410 US 113 (1973).

319 Feldman (n 316 above) 519.

320 478 US 186 (1986).

321 (App no 7525/76) (1982) 4 EHRR 149 [52]:

> [N]ot only the nature of the aim of the restriction but also the nature of the activities involved will affect the scope of the margin of appreciation. The present case concerns a most intimate aspect of private life. Accordingly, there must exist particularly serious reasons before interferences on the part of the public authorities can be legitimate for the purposes of Article 8 (2).

The limits to the bounds of privacy when one enters into relationships were explained by Ackermann J in *Bernstein v Bester*:[322]

> A very high level of protection is given to the individual's intimate personal sphere of life and the maintenance of its basic preconditions and there is a final untouchable sphere of human freedom that is beyond interference from any public authority. So much so that, in regard to this most intimate core of privacy, no justifiable limitation thereof can take place. But this most intimate core is narrowly construed. This inviolable core is left behind once an individual enters into relationships with persons outside this closest intimate sphere; the individual's activities then acquire a social dimension and the right of privacy in this context becomes subject to limitation.

O'Regan J amplified this conception of privacy in referring to our interdependence in society and the supportive role to be played by each other and by the state.[323]

Transsexuals also base their claims to legal recognition on privacy and autonomy. In *Goodwin v UK* the European Court of Human Rights found that the UK breached the right to private life by refusing to record Ms Goodwin's altered gender and considered that the margin of appreciation diminished as social attitudes changed over time.[324] Society must be tolerant

322 1996 2 SA 751 (CC) [77].

323 *Bernstein* (n 322 above) [150]:

> In my view, the democratic society contemplated by the Constitution is not one in which freedom would be interpreted as licence, in the sense that any invasion of the capacity of an individual to act is necessarily and inevitably a breach of that person's constitutionally entrenched freedom. Such a conception of freedom fails to recognise that human beings live within a society and are dependent upon one another. The conception of freedom underlying the Constitution must embrace that interdependence without denying the value of individual autonomy. It must recognise the important role that the state, and others, will play in seeking to enhance individual autonomy and dignity and the enjoyment of rights and freedoms.

324 (App no 28957/95) (2002) 35 EHRR 18 [90]:

> [T]he very essence of the Convention is respect for human dignity and human freedom. Under Article 8 of the Convention in particular, where the notion of personal autonomy is an important principle underlying the interpretation of its guarantees, protection is given to the personal sphere of each individual, including the right to establish details of their identity as individual human beings. In the twenty first century the right of transsexuals to personal development and to physical and moral security in the full sense enjoyed by others in society cannot be regarded as a matter of controversy requiring the lapse of time to cast clearer light on the issues involved. In short, the unsatisfactory situation in which post-operative transsexuals live in an intermediate zone as not quite one gender or the other is no longer sustainable.

of different identities.[325]

Dignity is central in decisions on medical treatment and its continuation or withdrawal.[326] The controversial areas of abortion and the right to die raise issues of dignity, privacy and autonomy. *Re Quinlan* in the US established the right to refuse medical treatment.[327] The common law right to informed consent and constitutional privacy right are relevant. *Cruzan v Director, Missouri Department of Health* upheld the state's right to insist on clear evidence of the person's wishes before agreeing to the withdrawal of medical treatment.[328] Justice Brennan, dissenting, prioritised dignity in death.[329]

Jeremy Miller, having reviewed US case-law, considered that dignity should replace privacy as the prime constitutional value.[330] The liberty to determine one's path without intrusion by the state creates individuality and promotes dignity in the form of self-respect, self-worth and value.[331] According to Miller, '[p]rivacy can promote crime, but dignity promotes only goodness.'[332]

2.2.4.5 Freedom of expression

Communication is an aspect of dignity. Because of this, freedom of expression is an important right. Dickson CJ of the Canadian Supreme Court in *R v Keegstra*, a prosecution for hate speech, considered that freedom of expression was essential in a participative democratic society based on dignity

325 *Goodwin* (n 324 above) [91]:

> No concrete or substantial hardship or detriment to the public interest has indeed been demonstrated as likely to flow from any change to the status of transsexuals and, as regards other possible consequences, the Court considers that society may reasonably be expected to tolerate a certain inconvenience to enable individuals to live in dignity and worth in accordance with the sexual identity chosen by them at great personal cost.

326 On dignity in the area of bioethics, see Rao (n 39 above) 232 - 234.

327 355 A.2d 647 (1976) (SC of New Jersey).

328 497 US 261 (1990).

329 'Dying is personal. And it is profound. For many, the thought of an ignoble end, steeped in decay, is abhorrent. A quiet, proud death, bodily integrity intact, is a matter of extreme consequence.': *Cruzan* (n328) II A.

330 JM Miller 'Dignity as a new framework, replacing the right to privacy' (2007) 30 *Thomas Jefferson Law Review* 1 at 50:

> Courts must recognize that privacy is a mere shell of dignity that will continue to be cracked and chipped until it disappears. Dignity, in contrast, will survive because it is intrinsic and fundamental to human beings, the minimization of which is much more suspect than making public one's secret behavior.

331 As above.

332 n 330 above, 51.

and equality.[333] It often comes into conflict with other values. In *Keegstra* Dickson CJ found that the dignity of the targets of the speech took precedence over free speech.[334]

Guy Carmi has pointed out the difference between the values underlying free speech in the US and other Western democracies. In the US the guiding value is liberty, whereas in Germany and many other Western democracies the value of human dignity is supreme.[335] The characteristics of dignity 'include a communitarian approach to human rights, the promotion of positive rights, paternalism, and the protection of audience rights.'[336] The use of the proportionality analysis by European courts is another distinguishing feature leading 'to speech restrictive results when free speech is balanced with other rights – predominantly human dignity.'[337]

Notwithstanding the emphasis on freedom of expression in the US, even there hate speech has been curtailed.[338] Alexander Tsesis has called for extension of the protection against hate speech to prohibit speech that is not intimidating but which incites an audience to commit discrimination at work or in public places.[339] Tsesis sums up the benefits of this step, '[s]uch an extension of current American jurisprudence would indicate a greater respect

333 [1990] 3 SCR 697 at 70:

> Freedom of expression is a crucial aspect of the democratic commitment, not merely because it permits the best policies to be chosen from among a wide array of proffered options, but additionally because it helps to ensure that participation in the political process is open to all persons. Such open participation must involve to a substantial degree the notion that all persons are equally deserving of respect and dignity. The state therefore cannot act to hinder or condemn a political view without to some extent harming the openness of Canadian democracy and its associated tenet of equality for all.

See Hogg (n 310 above) 61, 276, 294 - 295.

334 n 333 above, 72:

> [G]iven the unparalleled vigour with which hate propaganda repudiates and undermines democratic values, and in particular its condemnation of the view that all citizens need be treated with equal respect and dignity so as to make participation in the political process meaningful, I am unable to see the protection of such expression as integral to the democratic ideal ...

335 GE Carmi 'Dignity versus liberty: The two western cultures of free speech' (2008) 26 *Boston University International Law Journal* 277 at 323.

336 n 335 above, 371.

337 n 335 above, 374.

338 In *Virginia v Black* the Supreme Court held that a state may ban cross burning carried out with the intent to intimidate: 538 US 343 (2003).

339 A Tsesis 'Dignity and speech: The regulation of hate speech in a democracy' (2009) 44 *Wake Forest Law Review* 497 at 532.

for human dignity than for degrading expression.'[340] He instances France as a country which has banned hate speech while holding freedom of expression in high regard. There the emphasis is on the promotion of democracy rather than on 'the naive libertarian belief' common in the US that 'truth will emerge even when inflammatory statements are made about vulnerable groups.'[341] Another example is Sweden where the free expression of ideas is regarded as central to a democracy, but the Swedish Supreme Court has restricted free speech on occasion including incitement to hatred against a protected group.[342]

Dignity can be used by both sides in a dispute to promote their own viewpoint.[343] In these types of conflict, the best approach is not to look at a hierarchy of rights to establish precedence, but to have regard to the context in which the conflict arises and to see where the best interests of dignity lie. It is not always a matter of trading one person's dignity off against another's or against the common good. The integrity of the individual has to be made central and respect shown for the core identity of the human personality.

2.2.4.6 Social, economic and cultural rights

Individuals cannot realise their full potential, if they do not have the basic resources to enable them to achieve it and to respect their dignity. Dignity could be the foundation for requiring states to provide social, economic and cultural support to individuals and groups. In an appeal for global assistance to relieve poverty in Africa and the enforcement of socio-economic rights, Nsongurua Udombana described the effect of poverty, '[e]xtreme or abject poverty – the "poverty that kills" – violates the sacred right to life, and the supreme value of human dignity.'[344]

There is a minimum core of subsistence needed for the realisation of human dignity. There has been criticism from some quarters of this proposition for not going beyond the minimum necessary for survival. McCrudden sees three elements in the minimum core of human dignity:

340 As above.

341 n 339 above, 525.

342 n 339 above, 531. According to Tsesis, '[t]he Court thereby acknowledged that hate speech stifles victims from participating in democracy while it increases bigoted individuals' right to self-determination.': as above.

343 *Eg, Independent Newspapers (Pty) Ltd v Minister for Intelligence Services* [2008] ZACC 6, 2008 5 SA 31 (CC).

344 NJ Udombana 'Life, dignity, and the pursuit of happiness: Human rights and living standards in Africa' (2008) 27 *University of Tasmania Law Review* 47 at 81.

first, the ontological aspect focused inward on the individual; second, the relational perspective looking outwards towards society; and third, the limited-state claim, which is the principle that the state exists for the individual and not *vice versa*.[345] His analysis has not detected any norm in law requiring the provision of more than the minimum needed to preserve dignity.

Oscar Schachter as far back as 1983 evoked Kant in finding that the dignity of the person required at least the recognition of a minimal concept of distributive justice to satisfy the essential needs of everyone.[346] A person cannot foster dignity if in abject poverty. Schachter concedes that the minimum may not be enough.[347]

The right to life has been interpreted as meaning more than simply existence.[348] The Indian Supreme Court has held that the constitutional right to life and personal liberty includes

> the right to live with human dignity and all that goes along with it, namely, the bare necessities of life such as adequate nutrition, clothing and shelter over the head and facilities for reading, writing and expressing oneself in diverse forms, freely moving about and mixing and commingling with fellow human beings.[349]

Living clearly extends beyond survival to basic needs and freedom to interact with others.

The Inter-American Court of Human Rights has stated that the fundamental right to life is broader than freedom from the arbitrary deprivation of life.[350] It includes the right to live a '*vida digna*' or a dignified

345 n 9 above, 679.

346 O Schachter 'Human dignity as a normative concept' (1983) 77 *American Journal of International Law* 848 at 851. As the idea of a just society is connected with the promise of emancipation and human dignity, the norm underlying distributive justice is autonomy: J Habermas *Between facts and norms: Contributions to a discourse theory of law and democracy* trans W Rehg (1998) 418.

347 'Some would probably go beyond this and contend that substantial equality is a necessary condition of respect for the intrinsic worth of the human person. "Each person is as good as every other" may be inferred as a plausible maxim.': n 346 above, 851.

348 The African Commission stated that the inviolability of human beings and respect for the life and dignity of the person give a broad interpretation of the right to life, which was not protected by living in a state of constant fear and/or threats: *Aminu v Nigeria* [2000] AHRLR 258 (ACHPR 2000) [18].

349 McCrudden (n 9 above) 693, citing *Mullin v Administrator, Union Territory of Delhi,* AIR 1981 SCR (2) 516 at 518.

350 *Indigenous Community of Yakye Axa v Paraguay* Series C 125 [2005] IACHR 6 [161]. See Pasqualucci (n 299 above) 310.

existence.[351] The Inter-American Court held that the state, pursuant to its duty to guarantee life, has the obligation to generate living conditions that are at least 'minimally compatible with the dignity of the human person'.[352] The state 'has the duty to adopt positive concrete measures oriented to satisfy the right to a "*vida digna*," especially when dealing with persons in a situation of vulnerability and risk', including indigenous communities.[353]

The issue of housing for destitute people was addressed by the South African Constitutional Court in *Government of the Republic of South Africa v Grootboom* when it found that the State was obliged to devise and implement a programme to progressively realise the right of access to adequate housing and that it must provide for relief to those living in crisis situations.[354] In 1990 the UN Committee on Economic, Social and Cultural Rights monitoring implementation of CESCR had found that socio-economic rights contain a minimum core.[355] The Court declined to use this as a yardstick because it did not have enough information to assess what would be the appropriate level in the conditions pertaining in South Africa.[356] It found that the obligation on the State was to have a reasonable programme reasonably implemented and kept under continuous review.[357] The State could not ignore a significant segment of society.[358] Yacoob J adverted to the importance of assessing the situation in the light of the fundamental value of dignity.[359]

The interaction of constitutional rights and foundational values such as dignity can form the basis of socio-economic and cultural rights. The tension between the judiciary and the other arms of government in an effort to

351 *Yakye Axa* (n 350 above) [161]-[162], citing *Children's Rehabilitation v Paraguay* Series C 112 [2004] IACHR 8 [156].

352 *Yakye Axa* (n350) [162]. See Pasqualucci (n 299 above) 310.

353 *Yakye Axa* (n350) [162]. See Pasqualucci (n 299 above) 310.

354 2001 1 SA 46.

355 *Grootboom* (n354) [29].

356 n 354 above, [33].

357 n 354 above, [42]-[43].

358 n 354 above, [43].

359 n 354 above, [83]:

> The proposition that rights are interrelated and are all equally important is not merely a theoretical postulate. The concept has immense human and practical significance in a society founded on human dignity, equality and freedom. It is fundamental to an evaluation of the reasonableness of state action that account be taken of the inherent dignity of human beings. The Constitution will be worth infinitely less than its paper if the reasonableness of state action concerned with housing is determined without regard to the fundamental constitutional value of human dignity.

preserve the separation of powers is evident worldwide.[360] Yacoob J in *Grootboom* said the question of how to enforce socio-economic rights was 'a very difficult issue which must be carefully explored on a case-by-case basis.'[361] Bearing this in mind, Chaskalson CJ (now retired) described the challenge:[362]

> A balance must be struck between the role of the court as interpreter and upholder of the Constitution, and the role of government in a democratic society as policymaker and lawmaker. That is not easily done. Inevitably, claims for the enforcement of socio-economic rights are hard cases. They are hard, not only because they draw courts into policy matters, including possibly the budget itself, but because of the abject living conditions of many people in our country and their legitimate demands that this be addressed now that apartheid is over.

2.2.5 Groups

Dignity applies in relationships and in the wider community. The dignity of groups is protected. It has a collective aspect and seeps into the national psyche and into the international realm.

David Feldman identified three levels on which human dignity operates: 'the dignity attaching to the whole human species; the dignity of groups within the human species; and the dignity of individuals.'[363] He commented that the second level

> ... excludes discrimination between groups on irrelevant grounds, and allows them to assert rights to exist and to continue their traditions. Rules against genocide, apartheid, and incitement to racial hatred fall in this category, as do arrangements for giving remedies for group libels. Treating a person with respect for their dignity is incompatible with

360 On the legitimacy of court adjudication, see Habermas (n 346 above) 279.

361 n 354 above, [20].

362 A Chaskalson 'Dignity and justice for all' (2009) 24 *Maryland Journal of International Law* 24 at 32.

363 n 316 above, 125.

> discrimination on grounds which are morally irrelevant, providing a link between the values of dignity and equality.[364]

There are subjective and objective aspects to human dignity. Feldman explains how those who lack individual capacity, such as young children or patients in a persistent vegetative state, can have intrinsic human dignity in an objective sense:[365]

> The subjective aspect is concerned with one's sense of self-worth, which is usually associated with forms of behaviour which communicate that sense to others. The objective aspect is concerned with the state's and other people's attitudes to the individual or group, usually in the light of social norms or expectations. It is in this sense that people who lack the capacity to cultivate the subjective aspect of dignity can nevertheless be said to have a type of dignity which demands respect.

Iacobucci J of the Canadian Supreme Court in *Law v Canada* described human dignity of individuals and groups and how it is harmed by marginalisation.[366]

South Africa goes beyond the mere prohibition of discrimination against members of disadvantaged groups to a more positive recognition of the value of all in society, as expressed by Goldstone J in *President of the Republic of South Africa v Hugo*:[367]

> [T]he purpose of our new constitutional and democratic order is the establishment of a society in which all human beings will be accorded equal dignity and respect regardless of their membership of particular groups.

364 n 316 above, 126.

365 n 316 above, 127.

366 *Law v Canada (Minister of Employment and Immigration)* [1999] 1 SCR 497 [53]:

> Human dignity means that an individual or group feels self-respect and self-worth. It is concerned with physical and psychological integrity and empowerment. Human dignity is harmed by unfair treatment premised upon personal traits or circumstances which do not relate to individual needs, capacities, or merits. It is enhanced by laws which are sensitive to the needs, capacities, and merits of different individuals, taking into account the context underlying their differences. Human dignity is harmed when individuals and groups are marginalized, ignored, or devalued, and is enhanced when laws recognize the full place of all individuals and groups within Canadian society.

367 1997 4 SA 1 (CC) [41].

German constitutional law firmly places the individual in the community. Grant's study led to her to the following conclusion:[368]

> The invocation of human dignity thus requires arguments about freedom and autonomy to be considered within the context of the needs of the community as a whole, rather than being concerned with the individual in isolation.

The Federal Constitutional Court envisaged the individual encircled by the community in the *Life Imprisonment* case.[369]

2.3 Horizontal application

There is much academic debate over whether human rights can be enforced horizontally between private parties or whether the onus is solely on the state to respect and protect human rights. Andrew Clapham considers that it is not possible to confine protection to the public sphere.[370] An individual's dignity should not be violated from any source, whether public or private. Clapham concludes:[371]

> This examination of contemporary applications of the values of dignity and democracy points to their evolving nature and new considerations which demand that human beings can enjoy dignity and democracy even where the threats to these values come from non-state actors.

368 n 254 above, 309.

369 Grant (n 254 above) 309, citing 45 BVerfGE 187 (1977) (Fed CC of Germany) translated in Kommers, *The Constitutional Jurisprudence of the Federal Republic of* Germany (2nd edn Duke University Press, London 1997) 307 - 308:

> The free human person and his dignity are the highest values of the constitutional order. The state in all of its forms is obliged to respect and defend it. This is based on the conception of man as a spiritual-moral being endowed with the freedom to determine and develop himself. This freedom within the meaning of the Basic Law is not that of an isolated and selfregarding individual, but rather [that] of a person relating to and bound by the community. In the light of this community-boundedness it cannot 'in principle be unlimited'. The individual must allow those limits on his freedom of action that the legislature deems necessary in the interest of the community's social life; yet the autonomy of the individual has to be protected. This means that [the state] must regard every individual within society with equal worth.

370 n 77 above, 553.

371 As above.

Prudent judicial intervention is necessary when those in power baulk at protecting dignity because of self-interest or a fear of antagonising a section of the electorate. The judiciary is entrusted with upholding dignity, while not usurping the legislature's role entirely. Clapham has faith in the capacity of the judiciary to do this even when the violator of dignity is from the private sphere.[372] He instances Ireland[373] and South Africa[374] as countries that have applied human rights obligations in the private sector.

Murray Hunt found Kriegler J's approach persuasive in his dissenting judgment in *Du Plessis v De Klerk*,[375] as he focused on fundamental rights as 'all pervasive and superior legal norms'.[376] Hunt interprets Kriegler J's views as meaning:[377]

> [P]rivate relationships are left undisturbed insofar as they are not regulated by law, but once law becomes involved in regulating those relationships, they have lost their truly private nature and the State, as the maker, the administrator, the interpreter and the applier of the law which governs those relationships, is bound to act in all those roles in a way which upholds and protects the rights made fundamental by the Constitution.

Kriegler J explained graphically the impact of the fundamental rights in Chapter 3 of the interim Constitution[378] on private relationships and on the State.[379]

372 n 77 above, 558:

> [W]e have to trust the judges to juggle commitments to dignity and democracy in the context of individual complaints. Where the legislature has failed to address the best way to properly protect either dignity or democracy from assaults by private actors, human rights law may demand judicial intervention. Judges will usually be careful not to cause a constitutional crisis by usurping the legislature. Judges can ... usually find interpretative devices to ensure that the enjoyment of human rights is protected from the actions of non-state actors.

373 n 77 above, 554, fn 74, citing *Rodgers v ITGWU* [1978] ILRM 51, which held that a trade union cannot deny a right to disassociate and must comply with fair procedures.

374 n 77 above, 555 - 558, citing *Christian Education South Africa v Minister for Education* 2000 10 BCLR 1051 (CC), where the issue was essentially the human rights of children versus the human rights of parents.

375 1996 3 SA 850 (CC) [135].

376 M Hunt 'The "horizontal effect" of the Human Rights Act' [1998] *Public Law* 423 at 434.

377 n 376 above, 434 - 435 (footnote omitted).

378 Interim Constitution of the Republic of South Africa 1993.

379 n 375 above, [135]:

> Unless and until there is a resort to law, private individuals are at liberty to conduct their private affairs exactly as they please as far as the fundamental rights and freedoms

Hunt favours the Irish *sui generis* constitutional tort over the restrictive American approach:[380]

> In marked contrast to the American requirement of 'state action', the Irish constitutional jurisprudence allows individuals to sue other private parties by directly invoking their constitutional rights as the source of their claim.

William Wade also supports the Irish approach:[381]

> Since human rights are general principles of justice, of the kind enshrined and entrenched in written constitutions, they have a universal and fundamental character which ought, one might think, to be operative *erga omnes*.

Thus, the obligation to respect dignity has an effect on relationships between individuals in certain circumstance.

As society evolves, so does the ambit of human dignity. The accepted wisdom changes in each generation. There are mind-boggling scientific developments that require ethical and legal standards to be applied to ensure they continue for the benefit of society as a whole while respecting the individual's integrity, equality and autonomy. Human dignity is an excellent yardstick for assessing what is acceptable to the individual and what is best for the community at large.

More often than not, there is a mélange of values, principles and rights involved in assessing human rights. Frequently equality, dignity, freedom, privacy and the common good are issues in contention. It is usually not possible to isolate one value on which to base a decision. A multi-faceted

> are concerned. As far as the Chapter is concerned a landlord is free to refuse to let a flat to someone because of race, gender or whatever; a white bigot may refuse to sell property to a person of colour; a social club may black-ball Jews, Catholics or Afrikaners if it so wishes. An employer is at liberty to discriminate on racial grounds in the engagement of staff; a hotelier may refuse to let a room to a homosexual; a church may close its doors to mourners of a particular colour or class. But none of them can invoke the law to enforce or protect their bigotry. One cannot claim rescission of a contract or specific performance thereof if such claim, albeit well-founded at common law, infringes a Chapter 3 right. One cannot raise a defence to a claim in law if such defence is in conflict with a protected right or freedom. The whole gamut of private relationships is left undisturbed. But the state, as the maker of the laws, the administrator of laws and the interpreter and applier of the law, is bound to stay within the four corners of Chapter 3.

380 n 376 above, 429.

381 W Wade 'Horizons of horizontality' (2000) 116 *Law Quarterly Review* 217 at 224.

approach is required. It can be a balancing exercise by the legislature and, in default, by the judiciary, to decide what the right answer is at the present time. The principle of proportionality has assumed importance in recent decades in adjudication of personal rights.

2.4 Democracy

Respect for dignity is not enough. Democracy requires active protection, and even promotion, of dignity. Participation by individuals in the democratic process enhances the dignity of all in society. It also is an overt manifestation of the equality of all individuals. In *Doctors for Life International v Speaker of the National Assembly* Sachs J highlighted the benefit of participation in democracy for marginalised groups.[382] He returned to the theme of the importance of being heard for dignity and self-respect, when he dissented in *Merafong Demarcation Forum v President of the Republic of South Africa*:[383]

> [I]t is important to remember that the value of participation in governmental decision-making is derived not only from the belief that we improve the accuracy of decisions when we allow people to present their side of the story, but also from our sense that participation is necessary to preserve human dignity and self-respect.

Susan Marks considers that democracy invokes social and economic rights in addition to the commonly accepted civil and political rights.[384] She sees risks to democracy by ignoring some categories of human rights and points out the

> tension between the proclaimed indivisibility of civil, political, economic, social, and cultural rights and the priority accorded to some of those

382 2006 12 BCLR 1399 (CC) [234]:

> Minority groups should feel that even if their concerns are not strongly represented, they continue to be part of the body politic with the full civic dignity that goes with citizenship in a constitutional democracy. Public involvement will also be of particular significance for members of groups that have been the victims of processes of historical silencing. It is constitutive of their dignity as citizens today that they not only have a chance to speak, but also enjoy the assurance they will be listened to.

383 2008 5 SA 171 (CC) 298.

384 S Marks *The riddle of all constitutions: International law, democracy and the critique of ideology* (2000) 107.

> rights. This affects the prospects for deepening democracy within nation-states, for, if equality is to be secured in the opportunities for political participation, all categories of human rights need protection.[385]

Humane governance, as defined by Richard Falk is 'the effective realization of human rights, including economic and social rights, and the extension of participatory mechanisms and accountability procedures'.[386]

Political marginalisation reinforces subordinate socio-economic status. Clapham points out that the protection of dignity can have an impact on other values such as freedom.[387] The equality necessary to protect an individual's dignity may curtail another's freedom. Participation in democracy by acceptance of the democratic will[388] in the common interest might dilute an individual's autonomy. He advocates resolving conflicts, not by establishing a hierarchy of rights, but by examining the context in each case.

2.5 Assessment

Feldman warned against relying on dignity as a right or value because it was 'culturally dependent and eminently malleable'.[389] Using dignity as a yardstick could give rise to complications on account of the lack of clarity on its central core because of disagreement on what makes life good for individuals and societies.[390] The various ways in which dignity operates can give rise to confusion. He also feared that the indeterminate nature of dignity gives too much scope to the judiciary and could weaken the legislature in a democracy.[391] Protection of dignity can be paternalistic and undermine respect for autonomy.[392] This could arise when the individual does not

385 As above.

386 RA Falk *On humane governance: Toward a new global politics* (1995) 125.

387 n 77 above, 533.

388 The source of the legitimacy of democratic will-formation includes, on the one hand, the communicative presuppositions that allow the better arguments to come into play in various forms of deliberation and, on the other, procedures that secure fair bargaining conditions: Habermas (n 346 above) 278 - 279.

389 'Human Dignity as a Legal Value' Part I (n 254 above) 698.

390 Feldman 'Human Dignity as a Legal Value' Part II (n 254 above) 75.

391 'Human Dignity as a Legal Value' Part II (n 254 above) 76.

392 As above.

recognise their own dignity and is prohibited from exercising their free will to attempt to destroy it. The autonomy of another member of society might also be inhibited in the interests of protecting an individual's dignity. Feldman noted that dignity has been used in some jurisdictions to advance social rights.[393] Because of the importance of dignity in the case-law of the European Court of Human Rights, he considered that the value was likely to become increasingly significant in the UK with the enforcement of the Human Rights Act 1998.[394] Feldman's prediction proved correct. According to Moon and Allen the dignity discourse has pervaded equality jurisprudence in the UK and has also been included in legislation.[395]

Susie Cowen acknowledges the multi-factorial nature of the dignity concept.[396] However, she considers it useful because of its concern with the collective as well as the individual: 'It makes little sense to speak of the worth of human beings in isolation. Human beings are social creatures. This idea is found in the concept *ubuntu*.'[397] The value of equality is insufficient on its own to give meaning to the equality right, but supported by dignity it can deliver substantive equality and can serve transformative and distributive justice roles.[398]

Social and economic rights may be pursued by relying on the dignity of the person. While the primary instigator is the legislature, the judiciary needs to step in when the legislator has failed to protect dignity. In some societies, those in power can become the new elite to the exclusion of the poor and uneducated. In a democracy, the best solution is a dialogue between the judiciary and the legislature. This preserves the separation of powers doctrine, while ensuring that the constitution is a living instrument of practical benefit to individuals.

Joan Small and Evadné Grant support the use of dignity by the South African and Canadian courts to further substantive equality.[399] In South Africa, the courts define dignity by looking at the individual in association

393 'Human Dignity as a Legal Value' Part II (n 254 above) 61.

394 'Human Dignity as a Legal Value' Part II (n 254 above) 75.

395 n 160 above, 625 - 626.

396 S Cowen 'Can "dignity" guide South Africa's equality jurisprudence?' (2001) 17 *South African Journal on Human Rights* 34 at 58.

397 n 396 above, 50.

398 n 396 above, 55.

399 n 290 above, 54.

with group membership.[400] The contextual enquiry in Canada and South Africa leads to flexible jurisprudence adapted to each case, but backed by a structure and not reliant on the judiciary's own unilateral opinion.[401]

Dignity is drawn on by judges in a wide range of jurisdictions from dissenting or concurring opinions in the International Court of Justice, to the European Court of Human Rights and in domestic courts, including the French *Conseil Constitutionnel* and Canadian, German, South African and Irish courts.[402]

400 n 290 above, 42.

401 n 290 above, 51.

402 McCrudden (n 9 above) 682 - 685.

3

South African Constitution: Fundamental Rights

3.1 Historical background

3.1.1 Politics

Following the abolition of apartheid[1] and the formation of a democratic

1 The apartheid era had commenced in 1948 when the National Party formed the first government consisting of Afrikaners only: TRH Davenport & C Saunders *South Africa: A modern history* (2000) 377. The concept originated in the mid-1930s, among Afrikaner intellectuals, who wanted some 'vertical' separation of the races: Davenport & Saunders above, 373. The government applied apartheid in a plethora of laws and executive actions with four ideas at heart of the system; first, the population comprised four racial groups – white, coloured, Indian and African – each with its own inherent culture; second, whites, as the civilised race, were entitled to have absolute control over the state; third, white interests should prevail over black interests and the state was not obliged to provide equal facilities for the subordinate races; fourth, the white racial group formed a single nation, with Afrikaans- and English-speaking components, while Africans belonged to several (eventually ten) distinct nations or potential nations – a formula that made the white nation the largest in the country: L Thompson *A history of South Africa* (2001) 190.

Apartheid is an Afrikaans term meaning 'apartness' or 'segregation': LW Potts 'Law as a tool of social engineering: The case of the Republic of South Africa' (1982) 5 *Boston College International and Comparative Law Review* 1 at fn 2. Racial segregation and white domination of South African social, political and economic life were firmly established prior to 1948: Potts above, 1 - 2. Longstanding official governmental policy had been to confine Africans to special locations in the urban areas; one of the first projects undertaken at the Cape settlement of 1652 was to plant a hedge of bitter almonds to separate the Dutch garrison from the coloured population: Potts above, 24. In the Orange Free State, whites excluded Asians from residence and real property ownership: Potts above, 24 - 25. Using the Natives Land Act 1913 and the Native Trust and Land Act 1936, the Union Parliament set aside 14% of the land in South Africa for exclusive ownership by Africans: Potts above, 25.

Preceded by the prohibition of sexual intercourse between white women and African

government,[2] a new constitution was adopted in South Africa in 1996.[3] The drafting process absorbed much time,[4] lots of effort and the talents of a multitude of legal intellectuals.[5] Emerging from a background of a racially divided[6] unequal society based on an inhumane[7] premise of white supremacy entrenched in a plethora of complicated petty laws,[8] the framers of the

men, the Immorality Act 1927 made it illegal between unmarried Europeans and Africans: Potts above, 34.

Almost without interruption from 1809, South African law required African males to have passes from their home jurisdictions while in white areas: Potts above, 37.

2 Following the first non-racial election held in April 1994, Nelson Mandela was elected president and formed the Government of National Unity consisting of the African National Congress (ANC), the National Party and the Inkatha Freedom Party: Davenport & Saunders (n 1 above) 568 - 569; Thompson (n 1 above) 263 - 264. On democratisation in South Africa, see IM Rautenbach *Rautenbach-Malherbe constitutional law* (2012) 16 - 18.

3 Constitution of the Republic of South Africa 1996.

4 The process was initiated at the Convention for a Democratic South Africa (CODESA) held on 20 and 21 December 1991, where one of the working groups established was tasked with drafting a constitution for a democratic non-racial South Africa; CODESA was opened by Chief Justice Corbett and presided over by Judges Mahomed and Schabort; CODESA subsequently broke down; following violence, the government and the ANC signed a Record of Understanding on 26 September 1992; negotiations resumed and the negotiators agreed a draft interim constitution in November 1993 providing for the new parliament to act as a constitutional assembly to draw up the first fully democratic constitution: Davenport & Saunders (n 1 above) 560, 563 - 566, 571. See also I Currie & J de Waal *The Bill of Rights handbook* (2005) 4 - 6; Thompson (n 1 above) 252 - 258.

5 Cyril Ramaphosa (ANC) chaired the Constitutional Assembly and the Constitutional Committee, which was the main negotiating and co-ordinating structure reporting directly to the Constitutional Assembly; Kader Asmal was a member of the Constitutional Committee: H Ebrahim *The soul of a nation: Constitution-making in South Africa* (1998) 180, 198, 334 fn 17. The Theme Committee dealing with fundamental rights (of which Asmal was also a member) was supported by a Technical Committee of specialists and experts, namely, Prof H Cheadle, Prof J Dugard, Ms S Liebenberg, and Prof I Rautenbach: Ebrahim above, 182 - 183, 184, 339 fn 29. A workshop on human rights and international law was held in April 1995, organised jointly by the Constitutional Assembly, Parliament, and the Raoul Wallenberg Institute from Sweden: Ebrahim above, 184 - 185.

6 The population in 1996 was almost 44 million comprising 77% Africans, 12% whites, 8.5% coloureds and 2.5% Asians: Davenport & Saunders (n 1 above) 428.

7 The United Nations General Assembly (UNGA) declared that the practice of apartheid constituted 'a crime against humanity': UNGA Res 3151 (XXVIII) (14 December 1973) UN Doc A/RES/3151(XXVIII) G, Preamble.

8 Legislation covered a broad sweep of segregationist policies to keep state control on a racist basis over people covering (with examples in brackets) where they lived (Bantu Land Act 1913, Asiatic Land Tenure and Indian Representation Act 1946, Group Areas Acts 1950, 1957 and 1966), their education (Bantu Education Act 1953), work (Apprenticeship Act 1922 making skilled trades more accessible to white youths), marriage and sexual relations (Prohibition of Mixed Marriages Act

Constitution aimed to build a legal model for an inclusive democratic nation. The new regime recognised that to achieve meaningful change it was not enough simply to give all citizens the franchise,[9] but it was necessary to remove the inequities that had characterised South African society and to improve the living conditions of the majority who had struggled in poverty for generations. Another crucial factor was the polarised and diverse

1949, Immorality Act 1957), facilities (Reservation of Separate Amenities Act 1953), movement (Bantu (Abolition of Passes and Coordination of Documents) Act 1952 – a misleading title, as this legislation coordinated the pass laws rather than repealing them), and culture (State-Aided Institutions Act 1957 enforcing segregation in public libraries and places of entertainment): J Dugard *Human rights and the South African legal order* (1978) 65, 68 - 70, 75, 78 - 82; Davenport & Saunders (n 1 above) 271, 389, 390 - 391, 397. See also Potts (n 1 above) 20 - 41.

The Group Areas Act was the core of apartheid, having as its aim the segregation of the different races into their own groupings and limitation of their land rights in South Africa to the bare minimum; DP Malan, the Prime Minister when it was first introduced, described the Bill as 'the essence of the apartheid policy': F Meer *The ghetto people: a study of the effects of uprooting the Indian people of South Africa* (1975) 4.

HF Verwoerd replaced the static term of apartheid with separate development in government parlance; he saw the total separation of white and black as the ideal aim; he viewed apartheid as more than territorial separation of the races; it comprised religion and the political, social, economic and every other sphere of life; maintenance of the colour bar was the most important issue: Davenport & Saunders (n 1 above) 391 - 392.

9 Although whites, coloureds and Indians had voting rights to elect representatives to three uniracial chambers based on separate ethnic rolls under the Tricameral Con-stitution (Constitution of the Republic of South Africa 1983), African leaders had rejected a proposal for a Council for Blacks: Davenport & Saunders (n 1 above) 502; Thomp-son (n 1 above) 225 - 226. The government had transformed the ad-ministration of Africans by abolishing the Natives Representative Council in 1951 and grouping the reserves into territories destined to become homelands administered under white tutelage by a set of Bantu authorities, consisting mainly of hereditary chiefs; in 1971 the Bantu Homelands Constitution Act empowered the government to grant the homelands independence and the Transkei became the first to become independent in South Africa's terms in 1976, having been made self-governing in 1963: Thompson (n 1 above) 191. Verwoerd's government commencing in 1959 had given the first firm commit-ment to some kind of independence for the African areas: Davenport & Saunders (n 1 above) 407. See *Mabaso v Law Society of the Northern Provinces* [2004] ZACC 8, 2005 2 SA 117 (CC) [38]; *Mashavha v President of the Republic of South Africa* [2004] ZACC 6, 2005 2 SA 476 (CC) [51].

Historically, there were divergent franchise policies with the vote being enjoyed by all races in the Cape from 1853, but denied to Africans and Indians in Natal from 1865 and 1896 respectively: Davenport & Saunders (n 1 above) 123. As had happened in the Transvaal in 1885, the Franchise Act 1896 in Natal meant effective disen-franchisement of Indians without the appearance of discrimination on racial grounds; the vote was denied to those whose countries of origin did not have representative institutions founded on the Parliamentary franchise: Davenport & Saunders (n 1 above) 121. Jan Smuts' token enfranchisement of Indians in 1946 – rejected as inadequate by the Indians themselves – was reversed by the new government in 1948: Davenport & Saunders (n 1 above) 379. Hertzog's legislation in 1936 giving Africans three white representatives in the Assembly was opposed by a small number of white parliamentarians with conflicting liberal and segregationist attitudes: Davenport & Saunders (n 1 above) 328 - 329. After a skirmish between the courts and the other

backgrounds of people in South Africa. They ranged from the various indigenous tribes with the oldest heritage in the country,[10] through the Indians whose ancestors were brought to South Africa as slave-like[11] indentured labourers[12] or came as traders[13] starting in the nineteenth century, to the descendents of the settlers of European origin[14] and the 'coloureds', being

two branches of government, legislation was eventually passed in dubious circumstances in 1956 removing coloured voters from the common electoral roll: Thompson (n 1 above) 190 - 191.

10 The Africans were descendants of the San hunter-gatherers, the Khoikhoi pastoralists and the Bantu-speaking mixed farmers, who formed various tribal chiefdoms such as the Zulu and Xhosa: Thompson (n 1 above) 10, 16. On the Khoisan peoples and the emergence of Bantu-speaking chiefdoms, see Davenport & Saunders (n 1 above) 6 - 13.

11 Other forms of servitude could resemble slavery in substance, although different in legal form; the House of Commons in Britain recognised this in 1828 when it passed a unanimous resolution securing to all natives of South Africa the same freedom as enjoyed by other free people there; this arose following denunciation by missionaries of the holding by the Afrikaners of their Cape Coloured servants in a semi-service status under a system akin to indenture recognised by Roman-Dutch law: H Tinker *A new system of slavery: The export of Indian labour overseas 1830 - 1920* (1993) 15. The British government banned the slave trade throughout the Empire in 1807; the British parliament emancipated slaves in the Empire to take effect after a four-year apprenticeship in 1838: Davenport & Saunders (n 1 above) 47. Fatima Meer deduced that the indentured workers' 'state of unfreedom was little different from that of the slaves'; they were on the lowest rung of the hierarchy: Meer (n 8 above) 2.

12 The first batch of 340 indentured Indian labourers arrived in Durban aboard the *Truro* ship on 16 November 1860: JB Brain *Christian Indians in Natal 1860 - 1911: An historical and statistical study* (1983) 246; Tinker (n 11 above) 97. The indentured labourer system was introduced to South Africa to meet the demand of white settlers for workers in the sugar and cotton industries, as the required interests and skills were not present in traditional African society; laws were passed by the Natal Legislative Council in 1859 and by the Indian Government in 1860 extending to Natal the existing system for emigration of Indian workers to tropical and subtropical British and French colonies; colonists who wanted to employ indentured Indians applied to the Natal Government, which would arrange and pay for the recruitment, transport and assignment of the Indians, the employers being liable to repay these costs in instalments: L Thompson 'Co-operation and conflict: The Zulu Kingdom and Natal' in M Wilson & L Thompson (eds) *The Oxford history of South Africa* (1969) 387 - 388. The indentured labour system in South Africa came to an end when India banned emigration to South Africa from 1 July 1911: Tinker (n 11 above) 313. For further information on Indian indentured labourers in South Africa, see RA Huttenback *Gandhi in South Africa: British imperialism and the Indian question, 1860 - 1914* (1971) 2 - 26; Tinker (n 11 above) 96 - 97, 272 - 273, 283 - 285, 287 - 291, 293 - 306, 312 - 314. There were also indentured Chinese labourers in South Africa; they were introduced from 1904 to meet a labour shortage in the gold mines: Davenport & Saunders (n 1 above) 237.

13 From the late 1870s, Gujerati traders (commonly Muslims) came to South Africa under their own initiative and set up shops in competition with whites in Natal, the Transvaal and the Orange Free State: Davenport & Saunders (n 1 above) 121.

14 Two English captains annexed the Cape without authority on behalf of King James I in 1620: Davenport & Saunders (n 1 above) 8. The Dutch East India Company established a base in Table Bay in 1652 and subsequently brought in European

the mixed race mainly the progeny of whites and other races.[15] Within these groupings there was also divisiveness with a history of tensions among the native tribes[16] and a well-publicised antipathy between the Europeans of English and Dutch origin against the backdrop of the Boer War almost 100 years earlier.[17] Deaths and detentions during the apartheid era left their scars.

settlers, including Huguenot refugees fleeing from France in 1689 and many German-speakers during the 18th century: Davenport & Saunders (n 1 above) 21 - 22. Having seized the Cape in 1806, Britain legally acquired it under a treaty with the Netherlands in 1815: Davenport & Saunders (n 1 above) 42 - 43. British emigrants settled in the new district of Albany in the eastern Cape in 1820: Davenport & Saunders (n 1 above) 44. A small settlement of British traders and hunters established itself at Port Natal in 1824: Davenport & Saunders (n 1 above) 113. The Voortrekkers migrated from the Cape in the Great Trek in the 1830s and formed the Republic of Natalia (the first Boer state) in 1839: Davenport & Saun-ders (n 1 above) 80. It was short-lived, as it submitted to British control in 1842: Davenport & Saunders (n 1 above) 113. A new Voortrekker republic was established north of the Vaal in 1844: Davenport & Saunders (n 1 above) 81. The Orange Free State Republic of 1854 adop-ted a constitution based on Cape Dutch and Voortrekker experience and also on American and European precedents: Davenport & Saunders (n 1 above) 84.

15 The coloureds were concentrated mainly in the western part of South Africa, particularly in the Cape; their ancestors included indigenous Khoisan people and slaves from Indonesia, Madagascar and tropical Africa: Thompson (n 1 above) 113. See also Davenport & Saunders (n 1 above) 33; A Hepple *South Africa: A political and economic history* (1966) 11 - 12.

16 Tribal conflict was particularly marked during the Mfecane wars from about 1817 until the murder of the Zulu chief, Shaka, in 1828: Davenport & Saunders (n 1 above) 17 - 18; Thompson (n 1 above) 113. Violence among black South Africans was prevalent from the mid-1980s, particularly between Inkatha gangs and Zulu-supporters of the United Democratic Front in what is now KwaZulu-Natal: Davenport & Saunders (n 1 above) 486 - 487; Thompson (n 1 above) 229 - 230.

17 The South African War (the Boer War to the British, the Second War of Freedom to Afrikaners) was from 1899 to 1902: Thompson (n 1 above) 141 - 143. Against a background of the discovery of gold and a perceived threat of Africans uniting to throw off white rule, the British had annexed the Transvaal in 1877: Hepple (n 15 above) 85. The First Boer War (called the First Freedom War by the Boers) started when the Transvaal Boers rose up against the British in December 1880 and ended a few months later with the Transvaal regaining its independence; there was an agreement on self-government, subject to British suzerainty: Hepple (n 15 above) 86. The realisation that the gold mines were extensive attracted many foreigners (mainly British) to Johannesburg: Hepple (n 15 above) 89. They campaigned unsuccessfully for full citizenship rights and ultimately petitioned the British government for protection: Hepple (n 15 above) 89, 91. Following unproductive negotiations between the British and President Kruger of the Transvaal, the (Second) Boer War broke out between Britain and the Transvaal in October 1899; because of its defensive alliance with the Transvaal, the Orange Free State was also at war with Britain: Hepple (n 15 above) 91. At the end of the war during which many were interned and died in concentration camps established by the British, the Boers surrendered, and the Transvaal and the Orange Free State became British colonies: Hepple (n 15 above) 91 - 92.

On the Boer War 1899 - 1902, see also Davenport & Saunders (n 1 above) 223 - 232.

Many in the previously privileged class resented the change.[18] Reconciliation between the various strata in society and redress of the injustices suffered were primary aims in the new South Africa.

The first step was to draft an interim Constitution, which was adopted in 1993 and came into effect on 27 April 1994.[19] It was the result of protracted negotiations between the representatives of the apartheid state and its opponents.[20] While not procedurally a revolt because it was adopted by a statute of the old constitutional order, Laurie Ackermann has categorised the change as 'a substantive constitutional revolution' which 'imploded the apartheid constitution and structures'.[21] The interim Constitution established a formula for drafting another constitutional document and for its adoption by the Constitutional Assembly in a democratic fashion to ensure public ownership and acceptance.[22] Following an initial rejection of some provisions,[23] the new Constitution was approved by the Constitutional Court on 4 December 1996[24] and took effect on 4 February 1997.[25]

18 The resentment manifested itself in drastic action resulting in death and destruction on some occasions. On 10 April 1993, Chris Hani (a communist and previously the leader of MK, the militant ANC wing *Umkhonto we Sizwe*) was murdered allegedly with the encouragement of white political leaders: Davenport & Saunders (n 1 above) 565. On 25 June 1993 the Afrikaner Weerstands Beweging (AWB), led by Eugene Terre'blanche, drove an armoured vehicle through the doors of the World Trade Centre near Johannesburg and trashed the chamber where the negotiations on the draft constitution were taking place: Davenport & Saunders (n 1 above) 566.

19 Interim Constitution of the Republic of South Africa 1993. It was a liberal democratic constitution, including ideas borrowed from western Europe and the US, modified by South African experience; it contained an elaborate Bill of Rights with economic rights as well as the classic civil and political rights; several sections (including those dealing with human rights) were ambiguous and would need to be fleshed out by political action or resolved by the Constitutional Court: Thompson (n 1 above) 257 - 258.

20 Currie & de Waal (n 4 above) 4.

21 LWH Ackermann 'Equality and the South African Constitution: The role of dignity' (2000) 60 *Heidelberg Journal of International Law* 537 at 538. See also L Ackermann *Human dignity: Lodestar for equality in South Africa* (2012) 5 - 6, 14 - 15. Currie & de Waal (n 4 above) 2, have also described it as 'a constitutional revolution'.

22 The National Assembly doubled as a Constitutional Assembly, which set up its own structures; submissions from the public were encouraged and all meetings of the Constitutional Assembly and its committees were open to the public: Davenport & Saunders (n 1 above) 571 - 572.

23 Certification of the Constitution of the Republic of South Africa, 1996 1996 4 SA 744 (CC) (First Certification case).

24 Certification of the Amended Text of the Constitution of the Republic of South Africa, 1996 1997 2 SA 97.

25 President Mandela signed the definitive text at Sharpeville on 10 December 1996: Davenport & Saunders (n 1 above) 572.

3.1.2 Legal system

The local legal backdrop was Roman-Dutch law.[26] It became the common law as a result of Dutch and British colonisation from 1652 to the end of the nineteenth century.[27] Indigenous African law was applied in certain circumstances.[28] Pius Langa has described indigenous systems of law and custom as having been 'tolerated to the extent that their principles were not repugnant to the dominant system of law.'[29] English law had considerable influence, particularly on procedure, and reached its high point at the creation of the Union of South Africa in 1910.[30] This can be attributed partly to the fact that English was the official language of the courts for a substantial period.[31] The right of appeal to the Privy Council was abolished in 1950.[32] South Africa left the Commonwealth in 1961,[33] the year in which it became a republic,[34] and did not rejoin it until 1 June 1994 after the abolition of

26 See J Church *et al*, *Human rights from a comparative and international law perspective* (2007) 55 - 56; CN Okeke 'African law in comparative law: Does comparativism have worth?' (2011) 16 *Roger Williams University Law Review* 1 at 34 - 35.

27 W de Vos 'Roman-Dutch law in South Africa at the end of the century – and thereafter' in A Anghie & G Sturgess (eds) *Legal visions of the 21st century: Essays in honour of Judge Christopher Weeramantry* (1998) 73. On the development of South African common law, see Ackermann *Human dignity: Lodestar for equality in South Africa* (n 21 above) 87 - 95; F du Bois 'The past and present of South African law' (2004) 32 *International Journal of Legal Information* 217 at 221 - 227.

28 De Vos (n 27 above) 74. On the features of the indigenous system, see Church *et al* (n 26 above) 63 - 65.

29 P Langa 'Legal visions – South Africa in the 21st century' in Anghie & Sturgess (n 27 above) 102.

30 n 29 above, 83.

31 n 29 above, 81.

32 n 29 above, 78.

33 The government had intended to follow the precedent whereby India remained a member of the British Commonwealth when it became a republic; however, at a conference of Commonwealth countries, the African members, supported by Canada and India, sharply criticised apartheid, and South Africa then withdrew from that loose association: Thompson (n 1 above) 188.

34 Prime Minister Smuts' efforts to douse the republican propaganda of the opposition during the election campaign in 1948 had failed: Davenport & Saunders (n 1 above) 370. The National Party had earnestly wanted a republic since forming a government after that election; there was an initial disagreement between Malan and JG Strijdom's wing of the National Party which advocated separatist republicanism until they were persuaded in 1951 that the issues of republican status and Commonwealth membership were separable: Davenport & Saunders (n 1 above) 378. With Verwoerd's succession as Prime Minister in 1958, the government made a major change in the political orientation of South Africa by deciding to go for a republic: Davenport & Saunders (n 1 above) 407. The National Party achieved a major Afrikaner ethnic objective in 1961 when, after obtaining a narrow majority in a referendum of the white electorate,

apartheid. From the 1960s the South African courts tended to apply pure Roman-Dutch law.[35] Despite the infiltration of English law, Roman-Dutch law was the substantive private common law.[36]

3.1.3 International isolation

On the international front South Africa had isolated itself from the human rights treaties originating from the United Nations and had not participated in the formation of the African Charter in 1981.[37] Its representatives had taken an active part in the drafting of the United Nations Charter[38] and the Universal Declaration of Human Rights (Universal Declaration).[39] However, South Africa fell foul of the UN in 1946 when the General Assembly criticised the treatment of people of Indian origin and passed a resolution saying that Indians in South Africa should be treated in conformity with agreements

the government transformed South Africa into a republic: Thompson (n 1 above) 188. The government had excluded all non-whites from any share in the making of the Republic: Davenport & Saunders (n 1 above) 418. The inauguration of the Republic in May 1961 was marked by a general strike called by the newly-established National Action Council led by Mandela: Davenport & Saunders (n 1 above) 420. Indian South Africans were recognised as citizens of the Republic for the first time in 1963: Davenport & Saunders (n 1 above) 418.

35 n 29 above, 85.

36 n 29 above, 91.

37 African Charter on Human and Peoples' Rights (adopted 27 June 1981, entered into force 21 October 1986) (1982) 21 ILM 58 (African Charter).

38 Charter of the United Nations (signed 26 June 1945, entered into force 24 October 1945) 59 Stat 1031, UNTS 993, 3 Bevans 1153 (UN Charter). CH Heyns & F Viljoen 'Country study – South Africa' in CH Heyns & F Viljoen (eds) *The impact of the United Nations human rights treaties on the domestic level* (2002) 539. Field Marshal Jan Smuts submitted a draft Preamble, a shortened slightly modified version of which was accepted at the San Francisco Conference: WG Grewe & DE Khan 'Drafting history' in B Simma (ed) *The Charter of the United Nations: A commentary Vol 1* (2002) 11. See also Davenport & Saunders (n 1 above) 516.

39 Universal Declaration of Human Rights (adopted 10 December 1948) UNGA Res 217 A(III). South Africa abstained from voting on the Universal Declaration ostensibly because it went far beyond the rights and freedoms contemplated in the Charter; it objected to the inclusion of social, cultural and economic rights, freedom of movement and universal participation in government; its delegate observed that there was no universality in the concept of equality nor any universal standard in the different concepts of dignity; South Africa's position lacked integrity and was erected not because of its philosophical merits, but for the protection of the system of apartheid: J Morsink *The Universal Declaration of Human Rights: Origins, drafting, and intent* (1999) 26 - 28, fn 52. See also T Lindholm 'Article 1: A new beginning' in A Eide *et al* (eds) *The Universal Declaration of Human Rights: A commentary* (1992) 39, 43, 49; MA Glendon *A world made new: Eleanor Roosevelt and the Universal Declaration of Human Rights* (2001) 144, 146.

between the two countries and the UN Charter.[40] As a result of the elections by whites in 1948 the National Party came to power and set about institutionalising apartheid, which was based on the false assumption that blacks were an inferior race.[41] It passed a plethora of statutes and regulations based on racial discrimination, which favoured the already powerful and dominant whites at the expense of the black majority.[42] Ackermann described it thus:[43]

> The state did its best to deny to blacks that which is definitional to being human, namely the ability to understand or at least define oneself through one's own powers and to act freely as a moral agent pursuant to such understanding or self-definition. Blacks were treated as means to an end and hardly ever as an end in themselves; an almost complete reversal of the Kantian imperative and concept of priceless inner worth and dignity.

Mainly at the instigation of Asian and African states, the question of apartheid was raised in the General Assembly in 1952 and on many occasions before the General Assembly and the Security Council in subsequent years.[44] A group of experts appointed by the Secretary-General of the UN recommended in 1964 that South Africa should incorporate into its constitution a

40 JP Humphrey *Human rights and the United Nations: A great adventure* (1984) 15; UNGA Res 44(I) (8 December 1946) UN Doc A/RES/44(I). In December 1946, Mrs Pandit of India made a scorching attack on South Africa's Indian policy at the second session of the GA, while Dr AB Xuma (ANC) lobbied Assembly delegates in New York: Davenport & Saunders (n 1 above) 517. The Indian government's support for South African Indians in the international arena goes back to 1917 when it first gave a clear warning that it intended to press for fair treatment for Indians in Commonwealth countries: Davenport & Saunders (n 1 above) 279. When Malan introduced legislation in 1925 to make repatriation of Indians easier to effect, the South African government agreed to receive a fact-finding commission from India; a round-table conference eventually took place between the South African and Indian governments over four weeks from 17 December 1926: Davenport & Saunders (n 1 above) 306 - 307.

41 A Chaskalson 'Dignity and justice for all' (2009) 24 *Maryland Journal of International Law* 24 at 26.

42 A Chaskalson 'Human dignity as a constitutional value' in D Kretzmer & E Klein (eds) *The concept of human dignity in human rights discourse* (2002) 138.

43 Ackermann 'Equality and the South African Constitution: The role of dignity' (n 21 above) 540 (footnote omitted).

44 SD Bailey 'The Security Council' in P Alston (ed) *The United Nations and human rights: A critical appraisal* (1992) 312 - 313. The League of Nations had never subjected South Africa to the intensity of moral pressure which bore down it at the UN, apparently because the political values of the League were intrinsically European and harboured colonialist assumptions: Davenport & Saunders (n 1 above) 341. See also Thompson (n 1 above) 214.

bill of rights based on the Universal Declaration.[45] The Security Council had described apartheid as incompatible with the Universal Declaration in 1963,[46] and went on in 1976 to reaffirm it as 'a crime against the conscience and dignity of mankind'.[47] In 1972 it endorsed the struggle of the oppressed people in South Africa as being in compliance with the Universal Declaration.[48] It reaffirmed in a resolution in 1980 that apartheid was a severe violation of dignity, '... the policy of apartheid is a crime against the conscience and dignity of mankind and is incompatible with the rights and dignity of man...'[49]

In 1955 the ANC adopted the Freedom Charter.[50] Many of its principles were incorporated in the South African Constitution when it was drafted by the ANC-led government 40 years later.[51]

45 Bailey (n 44 above) 312.

46 UN Security Council (UNSC) Res 182 (4 December 1963) UN Doc S/Res/182(1963) para 2.

47 UNSC Res 392 (19 June 1976) UN Doc S/Res/392(1976) para 3. See Bailey (n 44 above) 312.

48 UNSC Res 311 (4 February 1972) UN Doc S/Res/311(1972) para 3.

49 UNSC Res 473 (13 June 1980) UN Doc S/Res/473(1980) para 3. For a comparison between the meaning of dignity in human rights theory and the way dignity was discussed in anti-apartheid literature, see E Coundouriotis 'The dignity of the "unfittest": Victims' stories in South Africa' (2006) 28 *Human Rights Quarterly* 842.

50 The Freedom Charter was an expression of collective human dignity in its promise and claim for the recognition of specific human rights in a future South Africa: H Klug 'The dignity clause of the Montana Constitution: May foreign jurisprudence lead the way to an expanded interpretation?' (2003) 64 *Montana Law Review* 133 at 144. At a Congress of the People attended by 3 000 people of all races at Kliptown, south of Johannesburg, on 26 and 27 June 1955, sections of the Charter were voted on by show of hands; it demanded a non-racial, democratic system of government, and equal protection for all before the law; it urged nationalisation of the banks, mines and heavy industry, as well as land redistribution; it sought equal work and educational opportunities, and the removal of restrictions on family life: Davenport & Saunders (n 1 above) 404. See also Thompson (n 1 above) 208 - 209.

The ANC had earlier Bills of Rights; one in 1923 asked for equal rights for all civilised men; another dating from 1943 – couched in the moderate language of western liberal thinking – demanded the 'freedom of the African people from all discriminatory laws whatsoever': Davenport & Saunders (n 1 above) 362.

51 RF Haigh 'South Africa's criminalization of "hurtful" comments: When the protection of human dignity and equality transforms into the destruction of freedom of expression' (2006) 5 *Washington University Global Studies Law Review* 187 at 193.

3.1.4 Apartheid jurisprudence

The judiciary faced a dilemma during the apartheid era. Parliament was supreme[52] and judicial review of the validity of legislation was

52 Following the Statute of Westminster 1931, the supremacy of Parliament was confirmed by the Appellate Division of the South African Supreme Court in 1937 when in *Ndlwana v Hofmeyr NO* 1937 AD 229 it dismissed a challenge by a disen-franchised African to the Representation of Natives Act 1936 on the grounds that the wrong procedure had been used to enact it. The Court ruled that the Union Parliament, being fully sovereign, could adopt any legislative procedure it thought fit: Davenport & Saunders (n 1 above) 331; Dugard (n 8 above) 29.

The supremacy issue caused a constitutional crisis in the 1950s stemming from the government's attempt to remove the coloured voters from the common electoral rolls, which was an entrenched provision in the Constitution adopted on formation of the Union in 1910 (Constitution of the Union of South Africa 1909) and was only amen-dable by special procedure. The Separate Representation of Voters Act 1951 purported to place coloured voters on a separate roll with power to elect four members to the Assembly, one to the Senate and two to the Cape Provincial Council (whites only to the Assembly and Senate, but not explicitly so to the Council). It was passed by ordinary legislation and not by the special procedure for entrenched provisions. In *Harris v Minister of the Interior* (the *Vote* case) 1952 2 SA 428 (AD), the Appellate Division declared the Act invalid because the special procedure had not been used. Parliament then passed the High Court of Parliament Act 1952 purporting to transform Parliament into a High Court with power to review all cases in which the Appellate Division declared legislation invalid. The Appellate Division ruled in *Minister of the Interior v Harris* (the *High Court of Parliament* case) 1952 4 SA 769 (AD) that this legislation was also invalid on the ground that the 'High Court of Parliament' was Parliament under another name: Davenport & Saunders (n 1 above) 379 - 380; Dugard (n 8 above) 30 - 31; Thompson (n 1 above) 190 - 191.

In 1955 two acts were passed by ordinary procedure – the Senate Act 1955 enlarging the Senate and altering the method of election of senators to give the government the majority required under the entrenched clause amendment procedure, and the Appellate Division Quorum Act 1955 increasing the number of appellate judges to 11. The South Africa Act Amendment Act 1956 (revalidating the Separate Representation of Voters Act 1951 and removing the coloured voters from the common electoral rolls) received the required majority under the entrenched clause amendment procedure (thanks to a packed Senate): Dugard (n 8 above) 31; Thompson (n 1 above) 191. The enlarged Appellate Division in *Collins v Minister of the Interior* 1957 1 SA 552 (AD) agreed by a majority of 10 to one that the South Africa Act Amendment Act was valid; Schreiner J (the sole dissentient) considered it was not correct to view the two statutes separately and that the new Senate, created for purpose of circumventing the entrenched clauses, was not the type of Senate contemplated by the South Africa Act in the entrenched provisions: Dugard (n 8 above) 32. Schreiner J was the senior judge of appeal, but – contrary to tradition – was overlooked for the role of Chief Justice in 1957; the government was unable to forgive his persistent opposition to their legislative scheme to remove coloured voters from the common role and his steadfast dedication to the notion of equality before the law: Dugard (n 8 above) 286.

For a full review of the judgments in the four cases mentioned, see J Davidson 'The history of judicial oversight of legislative and executive action in South Africa' (1985) 8 *Harvard Journal of Law and Public Policy* 687 at 710 - 720; I Loveland *By due process of law? Racial discrimination and the right to vote in South Africa, 1855 - 1960* (1999) 205 - 208, 285 - 290, 309 - 313, 366 - 371.

prohibited.[53] There was a conflict between the positive law and moral right. Apartheid was a denial of common humanity.[54] The establishment's view was that it was the judges' role to enforce apartheid laws based on an immoral system. The judiciary itself showed deference to the legislature and the executive as far back as 1934 when it accepted that if the Minister had an unfettered discretion by statute, it was not the court's function 'to curtail its scope in the least degree'; it adopted the principle that Parliament 'may make any encroachment it chooses upon the life, liberty or property of any individual subject to its sway' and it was 'the function of courts of law to enforce its will'.[55]

The same attitude was apparent in 1960 when a court held that the condition for the exercise of emergency powers of arrest and detention was not the factual state of danger to public order or safety, but the *opinion* of the Minister, magistrate or commissioned officer; it stated, '[t]he Court cannot substitute its own opinion'.[56]

Although the British notion of parliamentary sovereignty was originally designed and actually served to protect the basic freedoms of the citizenry against abridgement by the executive, the South African adaptation of the concept differed in that the restraints on the British parliament (representative government and faithful adherence to the historical objectives of equal protection of citizens' rights) were absent: JD van der Vyver 'Depriving Westminster of its moral constraints: A survey of constitutional development in South Africa' (1985) 20 *Harvard Civil Rights-Civil Liberties Law Review* 291 at 291 - 292, 306 - 307. On the development of parliamentary supremacy in South Africa prior to the Union, see Dugard (n 8 above) 16 - 24.

53 A Chaskalson 'From wickedness to equality: The moral transformation of South African Law' (2003) 1 *International Journal of Constitutional Law* 590 at 592, citing Republic of South Africa Constitution Act 1961 sec 59.
Judicial review was not unknown in the Dutch colonies of South Africa; the Orange Free State Constitution of 1854 enshrined it; but judges used it sparingly and often met with opposition when they did: Davidson (n 52 above) 688. On judicial review in the Orange Free State and Transvaal colonies, see Davidson (n 52 above) 691 - 697.

54 TH Madala 'The principle of respect for human dignity' in European Commission for Democracy through Law, *The principle of respect for human dignity* (Proceedings of the UniDem Seminar, Montpellier, 2 - 6 July 1998) http://www.venice.coe.int/webforms/documents/CDL-STD%281998%29026-e.aspx#P927_185139 (accessed 24 September 2013).

55 Dugard (n 8 above) 327, citing *Sachs v Minister of Justice* 1934 AD 11 at 36 - 37.

56 Dugard (n 8 above) 111, citing *Stanton v Minister of Justice* 1960 3 SA 354 (T).

However, as John Dugard pointed out, the Roman-Dutch legal heritage embodied principles advancing equality[57] and liberty,[58] which judges could

57 South African common law is colour-blind: n 8 above, 71. In 1882 Kotzé CJ declared that the court was bound to do equal justice to every individual without regard to colour or degree except where the law expressly provided to the contrary: n 8 above, 72 fn 97, citing *Re Marechane* [1882] 1 SAR 27 at 31. In *R v Plaatjies* 1910 EDL 63 it was held that a municipality might not set aside a separate part of a stream for exclusive white swimming even though it provided for a separate (and apparently equal) part for black swimming, and in *Williams v Johannesburg Municipality* 1915 TPD 106 the decision was that a municipality authorised to work trams for public use might not set aside certain trams for the use of coloured persons: n 8 above, 312. Although some lower court decisions had inclined to the view that separate facilities for different racial groups could never be reasonable, in 1934 the Appellate Division of the Supreme Court in a majority decision upheld the validity of regulations establishing separate post office counters for white and black on the ground that discrimination coupled with equality was not unreasonable: n 8 above, 64, citing *Minister of Posts and Telegraphs v Rasool* 1934 AD 167. Gardiner AJA (in dissent), invoking the 'fundamental principle that in the eyes of the law all men are equal', viewed the relegation of Indians to a non-European counter as humiliating treatment impairing the *dignitas* of the person affected: n 8 above, 315 - 316, citing *Rasool* at 185, 187, 190 - 191. After *Rasool* the courts struck down discriminatory subordinate legislation where there were unequal facilities, but refused to regard 'mere technical inequality of treatment' as sufficient to set aside subordinate legislation and insisted on substantial inequality: n 8 above, 64, citing *R v Carelse* 1943 CPD 242 at 253; *R v Abdurahman* 1950 3 SA 136 (AD) 145.

Lee Potts pointed out that the South African version of European law rejected the concept of equity and significantly limited the concept of equality before the law by confining it to white South Africans only: n 1 above, 17. In addition to the courts not sitting as courts of equity, other principles of the South African legal culture that facilitated the implementation of apartheid were, first, the courts would not interfere in discriminatory practices sanctioned by Parliament; second, the courts would decide *ultra vires* questions on the side of the executive; third, white popular opinion on race questions would inform judicial interpretations of ambiguous race legislation: n 1 above, 49.

58 In 1912 the Appellate Division ordered the government to pay damages to strikers for their illegal treatment as awaiting trial prisoners and castigated the authorities for their conduct: n 8 above, 326, citing *Whittaker v Roos* 1912 AD 92. In 1916 when the Transvaal Provincial Division overturned the conviction of a socialist politician under wartime legislation for 'exciting public feeling' in what was – as recounted by John Dugard – 'a vicious attack on the war effort', Wessels J warned that if liberty were to be suppressed, it was to be suppressed by the legislature and not by the court: n 8 above, 326 - 327, citing *R v Bunting* 1916 TPD 578 at 583 - 584. 30 years later Price J pronounced that the right to personal liberty was 'always guarded by courts of law as one of the most cherished possessions of our society': n 8 above, 108, citing *Mpanza v Minister of Native Affairs* 1946 WLD 225 at 229.

choose in resolving conflicts in laws affecting race[59] and security.[60] In 1954 the Appellate Division interpreted a provision allowing banning orders restricting freedoms of movement and expression in the Suppression of Communism Act 1950 as obliging the Minister to comply with the *audi alteram partem* rule, but the Act was amended after the adverse court decision.[61] A similar decision in 1956 relating to the banishment provision of the Black Administration Act 1927 upheld the right of a banished person to be heard in his defence *before* the issue of a banishment order; it received like treatment, as amending legislation was introduced to exclude its operation.[62] The Appellate Division widened the scope of the writ of *habeas corpus* in 1975 when it held that individuals concerned about corporal punishment being inflicted on suspected members of political organisations in South West Africa had *locus standi* to institute proceedings on their behalf; Rumpff CJ considered that there should be a wide construction because illegal deprivation of liberty was 'a threat to the very foundation of a society based on law & order'.[63]

Sir James Rose Innes (Chief Justice 1914 – 1927) was a notable defender of individual rights and expressed critical views of the other branches of government when he found himself opposed to legislation.[64] His philosophy of strict construction of statutes denying equality of treatment prevailed in

59 The Appellate Division of the Supreme Court overruled the decision of a trans-portation board withholding a taxi-cab licence from an Asian on the grounds of his race: n 8 above, 318, citing *Tayob v Ermelo Local Road Transportation Board* 1951 (4) AD 440. It also promoted equality and liberty in *R v Lusu* 1953 2 SA 484 (AD), when it set aside a conviction imposed on a black man during the defiance campaign of the early 1950s for entering a 'European waiting room' in a railway station on the ground that the administration had failed to provide substantially equal facilities for blacks: n 8 above, 318; however, the government retorted by enacting the Reservation of Separate Amenities Act 1953, which invalidated this construction: n 8 above, 65; Davenport & Saunders (n 1 above) 387. On the interpretation of race legislation, see Davidson (n 52 above) 728 - 734.

60 J Dugard 'Should judges resign – A reply to Professor Wacks' (1984) 101 *South African Law Journal* 286 at 286. This article was in response to R Wacks 'Judges and injustice' (1984) 101 *South African Law Journal* 266. See also R Wacks 'Judging judges: A brief rejoinder to Professor Dugard' (1984) 101 *South African Law Journal* 295.
On the interpretation of security legislation, see Davidson (n 52 above) 734 - 741.

61 Dugard (n 8 above) 138 - 139, citing *R v Ngwevela* 1954 1 SA 123 (AD).

62 Dugard (n 8 above) 331, citing *Saliwa v Minister of Native Affairs* 1956 2 SA 310 (AD).

63 Dugard (n 8 above) 351 - 352, citing *Wood v Ondangwa Tribal Authority* 1975 2 SA 294 (AD) 310 - 311.

64 Dugard (n 8 above) 287, 385.

Dadoo Ltd v Krugersdorp Municipal Council (upholding acquisition of land by Asians through a company)[65] and in *R v Detody* (preventing the pass laws from being extended to African women).[66] He and Kotzé JA dissented in *R v Padsha* where the majority upheld the validity of regulations prohibiting non-white Asian immigrants, but the dissentients refused to accept the popular meaning of 'Asiatic' in South Africa and insisted that if the regulations were valid they must extend to all Asians, whether white or coloured in appearance.[67]

Although English common law and the Roman-Dutch law provided the procedural and substantive bases for the South African legal system, the spirit of these laws had not penetrated deeply enough into basic values of the South African society to prevent the establishment of the apartheid legal system.[68] The South African common law strives, in accordance with Roman-Dutch principles, to maintain a stable equilibrium between all rights of legal subjects.[69] The judiciary had scope to make moral decisions in some circumstances.[70] There were some notable decisions upholding freedom of association, but frequently the legislature amended the law in their aftermath to support the oppressive regime. For instance, following a decision restraining the police from attending a political meeting on private premises, the Criminal Procedure Act was amended to permit *any* policeman to enter *any* premises at *any* time without a warrant where he suspected on reasonable grounds that *any* crime had been or was likely to be committed or that preparations for the commission of *any* offence were likely to be made on the premises.[71] Another example was the amendment of the Suppression of Communism Act in 1962 after the Appellate Division had ruled that a ministerial prohibition under the Act on any gathering of any number of persons having a common lawful or unlawful purpose could not apply to social gatherings.[72] Van Zijl J of the Cape Provincial Division in a case arising out of a student protest emphasised the important role of public protest in a democracy and

65 1920 AD 530.

66 1926 AD 198. Dugard (n 8 above) 310 - 311.

67 1923 AD 281. Dugard (n 8 above) 308 - 310.

68 Potts (n 1 above) 11 - 12.

69 Van der Vyver (n 52 above) 325.

70 Chaskalson (n 53 above) 594.

71 Dugard (n 8 above) 144 - 145, citing *Wolpe v Officer Commanding SA Police, Johannesburg* 1955 2 SA 87 (W).

72 Dugard (n 8 above) 162 - 163, citing *R v Kahn* 1955 3 SA 177 (AD).

stated that freedom of speech and freedom of assembly were 'part of the democratic right of every citizen'.[73]

According to Arthur Chaskalson, the common law requirement to interpret statutes in accordance with the principles of liberty and equality gave

> ... room for moral decisions in the development and application of the common law, in the interpretation and application of statutes not directly affected by apartheid, and even, though to a limited extent, in the interpretation and application of apartheid laws.[74]

Didcott J described a chasm between laws as passed by parliament and justice:[75]

> Parliament has the powers to pass the statutes it likes and there is nothing the Courts can do about that. The result is law. But it is not always the same as justice.

Faced with a plethora of racially discriminatory laws, although some members of the judiciary did not show independence of spirit in politically-charged conflicts, Dugard's view is that in this they behaved no differently from judges in the United States and Britain in times of crisis.[76] The best traditions of South African law compared favourably with those of Anglo-American and Western European legal systems and those traditions were upheld on a daily basis by South African judges in less divisive cases.[77] An exceptional political case was where the Appellate Division rejected an allegation that the Dean of Johannesburg had committed an offence under the Terrorism Act, *inter alia*, by paying money to dependants of political

73 Dugard (n 8 above) 186, citing *S v Turrell* 1973 1 SA 248 (C) 256.

74 n 53 above, 594.

75 Chaskalson (n 53 above) 593, citing *Re Dube* 1979 (3) SALR 820 (N) 821. In 1976 Didcott J (then of the Natal court) departed from restrictive decisions in *Rossouw v Sachs* 1964 2 SA 551 (AD) and *Schermbrucker v Klindt NO* 1965 4 SA 606 (AD) when he approved an interpretation of the Terrorism Act which provided some minimal relief and comfort to the family of a detainee: Dugard (n 8 above) 359, citing *Nxasana v Minister of Justice* 1976 3 SA 745 (DCLD).

76 n 8 above, 387.

77 As above. The Innes tradition of critical judicial comment was followed by South African judges in respect of legislation which judges considered politically colourless; some of these acts of judicial censure resulted in benevolent reforms by the legislature, including the abolition of compulsory whipping for certain offences and modification of mandatory minimum sentences for recidivists: Dugard (n 8 above) 385.

prisoners; Ogilvie Thompson CJ interpreted the Act with strict regard to the context to which it related, namely, participation in terrorist activities.[78]

The assessment of Rodney Davenport and Christopher Saunders is that the Supreme Court had not generally disgraced itself except, frequently, in political cases. They cite high profile cases in defence of the courts: a very sharp interdict on the use of third-degree methods by the security police against a political detainee in *Gosschalk v Rossouw* (March 1966);[79] a ten-year prison sentence imposed on a security policeman for carelessly shooting and killing a detainee, whom he was merely attempting to intimidate, in *S v Van As* (1984); the setting aside of a conviction by the Supreme Court of Bophuthatswana under the South African Terrorism Act by the Appeal Court, because the Act, though it extended to the Territory, was repugnant to Bophuthatswana's Declaration of Fundamental Rights, which placed the onus of proof on the State (May 1982); the finding by the Cape Supreme Court that it was unreasonable to expect ordinary readers of books to be aware in every case of whether a book was on the banned list (1981); and the judgment of the Supreme Court of South West Africa laying down that South West African People's Organisation (SWAPO) infiltrators captured while bearing arms were entitled to be tried as prisoners of war (1983).[80]

While recognising that there were some exceptions, the Truth and Reconciliation Commission (TRC) condemned the judiciary in general for its willingness to uphold unjust laws without comment and for readily accepting police evidence over that of the accused.[81] Leaders of the judiciary had made a written submission to the TRC acknowledging the failure of the judiciary as an institution to protect basic rights during the apartheid era.[82]

78 Dugard (n 8 above) 348 - 349, citing *S v ffrench-Beytagh* 1972 3 SA 430 (AD) 457.

79 Dugard has a less benign view of *Gosschalk v Rossouw* 1966 2 SA 476 (C): n 8 above, 132, 135.

80 n 1 above, 582.

81 Chaskalson (n 53 above) 597.

82 A Sachs *The strange alchemy of life and law* (2009) 76. The submission was made in October 1997 by the five senior judges who presided over the courts after 1994 (Chief Justices Corbett and Mohamed, Deputy Chief Justice van Heerden, and Constitutional Court President Chaskalson and Deputy President Langa); they acknowledged the role of the courts in upholding apartheid, and the effect of apartheid in causing poverty and suffering on a massive scale, and dragging down the morale of law-enforcement agencies; they recognised the prevalence of torture and the cruelty of detention without trial; they criticised the overwhelming whiteness of judicial appointees, and the positivist attitudes of some judges who accepted that a law properly enacted was by definition just, regardless of its content; on the favourable side, they attached importance to the rearguard action of some judges in standing up for the rule of law: Davenport & Saunders (n 1 above) 582 - 583.

The TRC was an attempt to make South Africans come to terms with their past by addressing the crimes of apartheid. It had power to grant amnesties to individuals, on condition that they revealed the truth and could prove their actions were politically motivated. After looking at precedents in eastern European and Latin American states that had recently rejected authoritarian regimes, parliament created the TRC with a mandate to deal with gross human rights violations since 1 March 1960. It was comprised of 17 commissioners of balanced gender and diverse racial backgrounds, and was chaired by Archbishop Desmond Tutu. The TRC was divided into three committees dealing with gross human rights violations, amnesty, and reparations for victim. It had a large budget, much of it from foreign donors, and set up an elaborate organisation with regional offices and a large number of employees who took more than 20 000 statements from victims of political violence. Starting in December 1995, it worked for more than two years and held over 50 public hearings around the country. More than 7 000 individuals applied for amnesty. The TRC was criticised by both sides of the divide, and its report was the subject of court challenges by former President FW de Klerk and the ANC. It revealed information about the heinous behaviour of agents of the apartheid regime and showed that some ANC operatives had committed serious crimes. Leonard Thompson regards the TRC as neither advancing the cause of racial reconciliation nor of bringing justice to the victims of political violence.[83] Tutu and Judges Goldstone and Sachs argued that the truth was a necessary part of the healing process.[84] Strengthened by the testimony of victims and the often corroborative evidence of amnesty applicants, some people felt that justice should be allowed to run its full course.[85]

83 n 1 above, 274 - 278.

84 Davenport & Saunders (n 1 above) 701.

85 Davenport & Saunders (n 1 above) 702. For a detailed review and assessment of the TRC, see Davenport & Saunders (n 1 above) 690 - 703.

In South African law there has been a long-standing remedy for violation of dignity and reputation under the umbrella of protection of a personality right.[86] Mokgoro J described it in *Dikoko v Mokhatla*:[87]

> The law of defamation is based on the *actio injuriarum*, a flexible Roman law remedy which afforded the right to claim damages to a person whose personality rights had been impaired by another. The action is designed to afford personal satisfaction for an impairment of a personality right and became a general remedy for any vexatious violation of a person's right to his dignity and reputation.

Jonathan Burchell distinguished between the historical divisions of impairments of reputation, dignity and person in the *actio iniurarum*.[88] The Roman-Dutch legal tradition in South Africa prevailed over the English stream of law to give a higher protection to reputation.[89] Impairments of dignity included invasions of privacy, unlawful arrest and malicious prosecution.[90] The significance of the remedy for infringement of dignity is evident from Burchell's assessment:[91]

86 Steven Heyman segregated personality rights in the US into three categories (with the corresponding wrongs in brackets): first, the right to personality, which is subdivided into the substantive right to mental and emotional well-being (intentional infliction of emotional distress) and the formal right to 'an inviolate personality' comprising privacy (unreasonable intrusion or exposure) and personal dignity (insulting words); second, the right to self-expression through speech and conduct (improper regulation); and third, the right to image or reputation (defamation and related torts): SJ Heyman *Free speech and human dignity* (2008) 55. On the development of the tort of intentional infliction of emotional distress, see DP Duffy 'Intentional infliction of emotional distress and employment at will: The case against tortification of labor and employment law' (1994) 74 *Boston University Law Review* 387 at 392 - 395; D Givelber 'The right to minimum social decency and the limits of evenhandedness: Intentional infliction of emotional distress by outrageous conduct' (1982) 82 *Columbia Law Review* 42 at 43 - 45; H Harrington 'Alabama Supreme Court recognizes intentional infliction of severe emotional distress as an independent cause of action: *American Road Service Co v Inmon*, 394 So. 2d 361 (Ala. 1980)' (1982) 12 *Cumberland Law Review* 525. For a definition of the tort and its interpretation in practice, see Givelber above, 45 - 75.

87 2006 6 SA 235 (CC) [62] (footnotes omitted).

88 JM Burchell 'The protection of personality rights' in R Zimmermann & D Visser (eds) *Southern cross: Civil law and common law in South Africa* (1996) 640.

89 Truth *per se* is not a defence to a defamation action – it is only a defence when publication of the truth is for the public benefit: Burchell (n 88 above) 644.

90 Burchell (n 88 above) 640.

91 n 88 above, 650. On the influence of apartheid on private law, see C Roederer 'The transformation of South African private law after ten years of democracy: The role of torts (delict) in the consolidation of democracy' (2006) 37 *Columbia Human Rights Law Review* 447 at 453 - 468.

> The protection of human dignity under the *actio iniuriarum* is undoubtedly one of the most impressive and enduring legacies of Roman law, and a feature which places the South African law of delict in the forefront of the protection of what is arguably the most fundamental of all human rights.

As well as the more usual usages to defend privacy and to prevent unwarranted arrest and prosecution, the remedy came to be used to safeguard an individual from insulting words or conduct, interference with parental authority, breach of promise to marry, and adultery.[92] The *actio iniurarum* is not confined to insult, even though insulting behaviour and the expression of arrogance played a formative function in the development of the idea of *animus iniuriandi.*[93] The case-law up to the middle of the twentieth century did not give any substance to the concept of privacy, but from the 1950s a right to be free from encroachments into one's private realm began to develop in South Africa and gave protection against unreasonable intrusions into the private sphere, public disclosure of private facts, appropriation of name or likeness, and portrayal in a false light.[94]

3.2 Fundamental rights in the South African Constitution

3.2.1 Transitional phase

The interim Constitution marked the boundary between the old regime based on discrimination with a privileged white minority and the new democracy where all are equal and the human dignity of each individual is respected.[95]

92 n 88 above, 650. See J Campbell 'Litigating human dignity: the Roman-Dutch common law' [2011] *European Human Rights Law Review* 375.

93 n 88 above, 651 - 652. Burchell interpreted the Supreme Court's decision in 1993 extending a remedy for invasion of privacy to an artificial or juristic person – which obviously cannot experience insult in the strict sense – as a rejection of a limiting requirement of insult: n 88 above, 652, citing Corbett CJ in *Financial Mail (Pty) Ltd v Sage Holdings Ltd* 1993 2 SA 451 (AD) 460-3, esp 462A-E.

94 n 88 above, 652.

95 Respect for dignity is an affirmation of fundamental human equality; by resisting the temptation to humiliate the white minority, Mandela and the other black African leaders gave all groups the chance to escape the cycle of revenge: J Glover *Humanity: A moral history of the twentieth century* (2012) 150.

Langa described the fact that agreement was reached at all on an interim Constitution as 'a remarkable feat' and 'one of the miracles of the century': n 29 above, 109.

It took two years to negotiate its terms between a myriad of different political groups with diverse interests. New structures to support democracy included the Constitutional Court[96] and the Human Rights Commission.[97] An elected Constitutional Assembly, modelled on the Indian experience,[98] comprising the National Assembly and the Senate was established to draft a new Constitution based on 34 Constitutional Principles.[99] The agreed draft was to be proofed by the Constitutional Court and certified by it as complying with the Principles before becoming operative.[100]

The Preamble set the scene for a complete break with the old order by signalling the need to create a state where there would be 'equality between men and women of all races so that all citizens shall be able to enjoy and exercise their fundamental rights and freedoms'.[101] The Principles crystallised that theme by stating clearly that the new democratic government's aim was to achieve a society where there was gender and racial equality.[102] This was an acknowledgment that the starting point was inequality in a society deliberately divided along racial lines and therefore there were many inequities to be gradually removed. Not only was past discrimination to be eliminated, but there was an edict to take positive steps to promote equality and national unity.[103] The new document should provide for entrenched justiciable 'universal fundamental rights, freedoms and civil liberties' drafted after considering, *inter alia*, the fundamental rights listed in Chapter 3 of the interim Constitution.[104] The justiciability of rights broke with the past supremacy of positive law and parliament's complete autonomy to enact binding laws supporting an immoral apartheid system. The recognition that equality could not be achieved without the improvement of living conditions and the existence of socio-economic rights was evident from the edict in Principle V that the legal system should ensure an equitable legal process

96 n 19 above, Sec 98.

97 n 19 above, Sec 115. CESCR plays a significant role in the Commission's special mandate to monitor socio-economic rights: CH Heyns & F Viljoen 'Overview of study results' in Heyns & Viljoen (n 38 above) 19.

98 Sachs (n 82 above) 69.

99 n 19 above, Secs 68, 71(1) & Sch 4.

100 n 19 above, Sec 71(2).

101 n 19 above, Preamble, 1st para.

102 n 19 above, Sch 4, Principles I, III & V.

103 n 19 above, Principle III.

104 n 19 above, Principle II.

and equality before the law to include programmes to relieve the plight of the disadvantaged – particularly those disadvantaged on the grounds of race, colour or gender. While the separation of powers was expressed in Principle VI, the judiciary was specifically singled out as the organ of state with power 'to safeguard and enforce the Constitution and all fundamental rights.'[105]

The interim Constitution was not merely a transitional measure, but was supreme,[106] binding and justiciable.[107] Section 7(4) provided for the courts to adjudicate on alleged breaches of the fundamental rights in Chapter 3 and for relief to be sought in a representative capacity.[108]

The first enumerated fundamental right was equality in Section 8. It gave protection against direct and indirect[109] unfair discrimination in general and particularly singled out discrimination on the grounds of race, gender, sex, ethnic or social origin, colour, sexual orientation,[110] age, disability, religion, conscience, belief, culture or language.[111] Measures to redress past discrimination,[112] whether against individuals or groups,[113] were allowed.[114]

105 n 19 above, Principle VII.

106 *Pharmaceutical Manufacturers Association of South Africa, ex p President of the Republic of South Africa* [2000] ZACC 1, 2000 2 SA 674 [19]-[20], [44]-[45], [49].

107 Currie & de Waal (n 4 above) 5; n 19 above, Sec 4.

108 Class actions and public interest litigation were allowed: n 19 above, Sec 7(4)(b)(iv) & (v) respectively.

109 The explicit prohibition on indirect discrimination was inserted because the South Africans wanted to avoid the American interpretation of the Fourteenth Amendment only to forbid intentional discrimination: AK Wing 'The South African Constitution as a role model for the United States' (2008) 24 *Harvard BlackLetter Law Journal* 73 at 76.

110 The South African Constitution was the first one to include sexual orientation in its protections: Wing (n 109 above) 75.

111 n 19 above, Sec 8(2).

112 Aware of the American debate on reverse discrimination and wanting to avoid a rash of reverse discrimination cases, the drafters made it clear that affirmative action is part of the notion of equality, rather than an exception to it: Wing (n 109 above) 76.

113 In embracing group-based remedies, even though they may disadvantage individuals from a privileged group, the South Africans go beyond the individualistic approach of US jurisprudence: Wing (n 109 above) 76. It is naïve to think that prejudices can be combated without an insistent affirmative emphasis on the equal worth and dignity of groups; if a dignitary slur on an individual is based wholly or partly on contempt for the group to which that individual belongs as a collective entity, then assertion of the equal dignity of the group as an entity may be necessary to rebut prejudice: J Waldron 'The dignity of groups' (2008) New York University School of Law Public Law Research Paper No 08-53 http://ssrn.com/abstract= 1287174 (accessed 26 September 2013) 19.

114 n 19 above, Sec 8(3)(a).

Restoration of land rights where people had been dispossessed on a discriminatory basis during the apartheid regime was an entitlement.[115] *Prima facie* evidence of unfair discrimination was sufficient, subject to rebuttal by the defence.[116]

The right to life was set out in Section 9. There was a specific right to dignity in Section 10, '[e]very person shall have the right to respect for and protection of his or her dignity.' Broadly accepted civil and political rights were incorporated based on physical security, justice and democratic norms.[117] Interestingly, there was a specific right to privacy concentrating on the physical aspect, possessions and communications.[118]

Freedom of religion, belief and opinion in Section 14 extended beyond established religions to conscience.[119] Freedom of expression, association and peaceful assembly[120] were guaranteed.[121] Personal property rights were subject to expropriation for public purposes on payment of compensation.[122] There was a right to basic education and equal access to educational institutions.[123] Again, taking account of pluralism, the right to be educated in the language of one's choice within reason was granted,[124] private segregated schools could be established on cultural, language or religious grounds provided there was no racial discrimination,[125] and there was a general right

115 n 19 above, Sec 8(3)(b).

116 n 19 above, Sec 8(4).

117 n 19 above, Secs 11, 12, 18 - 22, 24 & 25.

118 'Every person shall have the right to his or her personal privacy, which shall include the right not to be subject to searches of his or her person, home or property, the seizure of private possessions or the violation of private communications': n 19 above, Sec 13.

119 State-endowed religious observances were allowed provided they were equitable, free and voluntary: n 19 above, Sec 14(2). Taking cognisance of the multi-cultural nature of South African society, personal, family and marriage laws could be tailored to different religions: n 19 above, Sec 14(3).

120 The Supreme Court of Ghana found that the prohibition on holding a public rally without a police permit constituted a serious abridgment of responsible human and civil rights inherent in a democracy and intended to secure the freedom and dignity of man: *New Patriotic Party v Inspector-General of Police* [2001] AHRLR 138 (GhSC 1993) [53], [55]. See also *Inspector-General of Police v All Nigeria Peoples Party* [2007] AHRLR 179 (NgCA 2007).

121 n 19 above, Secs 15, 17 & 16 respectively.

122 n 19 above, Sec 28(3).

123 n 19 above, Sec 32(a).

124 n 19 above, Sec 32(b).

125 n 19 above, Sec 32(c).

to choose one's language and culture.[126]

Free enterprise was the basis of the economy, but intervention was allowed to protect workers, foster human development and to improve the quality of life and working conditions, provided the measures were compatible with a democracy based on equality and freedom.[127] Workers' rights were given constitutional status.[128]

Unusually in comparison with traditional constitutions and with a nod to posterity from solidarity rights, which had the potential to endow societal benefits in the future as well as in the present, protection extended beyond the purely personal to the environment.[129] Another modern feature was Section 30 relating to children's rights, which was an acceptance of the temporal changes in people's enjoyment of rights. The justiciability of socio-economic rights was recognition of the need to make human rights a reality for people deprived by state action of physical and monetary benefits. Certain standards of living were necessary to enjoy fully civil and political rights.

None of the fundamental rights was absolute. The entrenched rights in Chapter 3 were subject to limitation by law to the extent that it was reasonable and compatible with a free and equal democracy.[130] The essential content of the right could not be negated and the limit on certain entrenched rights (including the right to human dignity) must also have been necessary.[131] Fundamental rights were all-pervasive. Courts were obliged to have regard to them, their spirit and aims when interpreting laws, and in applying and developing the common and customary law.[132]

126 n 19 above, Sec 31. On the development and meaning of the right to culture, see J Amoah & T Bennett 'The freedoms of religion and culture under the South African Constitution: Do traditional African religions enjoy equal treatment?' (2008) 8 *African Human Rights Law Journal* 357 at 367 - 368, 371 - 372.

127 n 19 above, Sec 26.

128 n 19 above, Sec 27.

129 'Every person shall have the right to an environment which is not detrimental to his or her health or well-being': n 19 above, Sec 29.

130 n 19 above, Sec 33(1)(a).

131 n 19 above, Sec 33(1)(b). Its role in the limitation of rights is the key, in practice, to the idea of human dignity serving as a foundational principle: Klug (n 50 above) 148.

132 n 19 above, Sec 35(3).

3.2.2 Constitution of 1996

3.2.2.1 Drafting and adoption

The new Constitution drafted by the Constitutional Assembly did not differ markedly from the interim document.[133] Most judicial decisions under the interim Constitution remain authoritative.[134] The Constitutional Assembly adopted a constitutional text on 8 May 1996.[135] The Constitutional Court approved many of its provisions, but rejected, *inter alia*, the failure to entrench the right of individual employers to bargain collectively.[136] Judicial scrutiny of a constitution before becoming effective was unique. Iain Currie and Johan de Waal describe it as 'an unprecedented and extraordinary exercise of judicial review.'[137] Despite the fact that the Constitutional Assembly was the pinnacle of the country's democratic institutions, the certification process empowered an unelected Constitutional Court to pronounce on its efforts with reference to a set of principles formulated by unelected negotiators.[138]

There was an objection to the inclusion of socio-economic rights on the basis that they were not universal, and should not be justiciable because of the separation of powers and budgetary implications arising from their enforcement.[139] The Court overruled the first objection, since the Constitutional Assembly was not confined to including only universal rights, but was entitled to add additional rights. The second objection was dismissed, as it considered that these rights are justiciable at least to some extent; the Court pointed out that upholding civil and political rights also has budgetary implications at times.

Objection was taken to the omission of family rights and the right to marry.[140] The Court found that the values of dignity, equality and freedom as well as the right to dignity in Section 10 would protect the right to marry and freedom of choice in relation to one's spouse.[141] They also provide negative

133 It received 86% support – well in excess of the two-thirds majority required: Currie & de Waal (n 4 above) 6, fn 21; n 19 above, Sec 73(2).

134 Currie & de Waal (n 4 above) 6.

135 The draft text was adopted with only two negative votes and a small number of abstentions: Davenport & Saunders (n 1 above) 572.

136 *First Certification* case (n 23 above) [69].

137 n 4 above, 6.

138 As above.

139 *First Certification* case (n 23 above) [76]-[78].

140 *First Certification* case (n 23 above) [96].

141 n 23 above, [100].

protection for family life. The drafters of the Constitution steered a middle course in relation to the family in order to cater for a multi-cultural society with varying views on these issues and also to take account of different individual lifestyle choices.[142] Many of the constitutional provisions provided direct and indirect support for marriage and the family. The Court did not enter into the abortion debate raised in the context of the rights to bodily integrity.[143]

The phrase 'fundamental rights, freedoms and civil liberties' in Constitutional Principle II of the interim Constitution should not be broken down into separate words and examined in isolation.[144] The Court said that as a whole it conveyed a composite idea firmly established in human rights jurisprudence. These rights vary from country to country.

With regard to the limitation of rights, the new text omitted the reference to the limitation being 'necessary' and required it only to be reasonable and justifiable. The Court said that the qualification 'necessary' was not universally accepted in national constitutions as the norm for limiting rights.[145] Section 36 of the new Constitution dealing with the limitation of rights embodied the requirement of proportionality and was in conformity with the interpretation given to that term in *Makwanyane*, where the death sentence was held to be unconstitutional.[146] There Chaskalson P had found that the task of adjudicating on the validity of limitations on rights involved weighing up competing values and an assessment based on proportionality, and continued:[147]

> The fact that different rights have different implications for democracy, and in the case of our Constitution, for 'an open and democratic society based on freedom and equality', means that there is no absolute standard which can be laid down for determining reasonableness and necessity. Principles can be established, but the application of those principles to particular circumstances can only be done on a case by case basis. This is inherent in the requirement of proportionality, which calls for the balancing

142 n 23 above, [103].

143 n 23 above, [59]-[60].

144 n 23 above, [50].

145 n 23 above, [90].

146 *S v Makwanyane* 1995 6 BCLR 665 (CC). On the proportionality analysis in South Africa, see A Stone Sweet & J Mathews 'Proportionality balancing and global constitutionalism' (2008) 47 *Columbia Journal of Transnational Law* 72 at 124 - 131.

147 n 146 above, [104].

> of different interests. In the balancing process, the relevant considerations will include the nature of the right that is limited, and its importance to an open and democratic society based on freedom and equality; the purpose for which the right is limited and the importance of that purpose to such a society; the extent of the limitation, its efficacy, and particularly where the limitation has to be necessary, whether the desired ends could reasonably be achieved through other means less damaging to the right in question.

He alluded to the different roles of the organs of state and the delicate balance to be struck by the judiciary in respecting the separation of powers.[148] Writing extrajudicially, Albie Sachs described *Makwanyane* as having treated proportionality as 'the vertebral support of the whole legal analysis'.[149] Jeremy Waldron considers it more compatible with dignity to have standards such as 'reasonable care' in order to facilitate thoughtfulness about situations than to lay down a rule; this permits ordinary people to recognise a norm, apply it to their conduct, make a determination and act on it.[150] The South African courts have unequivocally adopted proportionality as a central principle.

Among other objections dismissed in the *First Certification* case were to provisions relating to horizontality of rights,[151] and access to information.[152]

The Indian freedom struggle and the processes used to accommodate diversity in a democratic national framework influenced Nelson Mandela's generation and are reflected in the Constitution, which owes much to the spirit of Gandhi with his focus on compassion and self-denial[153] as well as to

148 He quoted Lamer J of the Supreme Court of Canada who had said in the *Prostitution Reference*, 'the role of the Court is not to second-guess the wisdom of policy choices made by legislators.': n 146 above, [104], citing *Reference re ss 193 and 195(1)(c) of the Criminal Code of Manitoba* (1990) 48 CRR 1 at 62.

149 n 82 above, 206.

150 J Waldron *Dignity, rank, and rights* (2012) 53.

151 n 23 above, [53]-[56], [200]-[202].

152 n 23 above, [82]-[87].

153 Gandhi (like Martin Luther King) exemplified the virtue of dignity by claiming his rights publically, forcefully and without exaggerating or underestimating how his rights should be seen by others: MJ Meyer 'Dignity as a (modern) virtue' in Kretzmer & Klein (n 42 above) 198, 205 - 207. For an account of Gandhi in South Africa, see B Chandra *India's struggle for independence 1857 - 1947* (1989) 170 - 176; Davenport & Saunders (n 1 above) 121 - 122, 244 - 245, 276 - 278; Huttenback (n 12 above) 46 - 331; S Mehra *Human rights: A Gandhian perspective* (2006) 14, 21 - 25; Tinker (n 11 above) 283 - 284, 288 - 289, 300, 314.

the institutionalisation of democracy in the philosophy of Nehru.[154] Other influences come from the rest of Africa, Europe, North and South America.[155] Sachs has observed that the notion of universal human rights permits their adoption to many cultural contexts and does not equate to the globalised imposition of one set of values on all humanity.[156]

3.2.2.2 Supremacy and values

The Preamble leaves no doubt that the Constitution is supreme and transformative.[157] The purposes in adopting it as 'the supreme law of the Republic' recognise that socio-economic benefits are necessary to achieve social justice and for full personal development.[158] The Constitution aims to change the unjust ethos of the past to a society where all are cherished equally.

The founding values in Section 1 include human dignity and the achievement of equality irrespective of race or sex.[159] It is more difficult to amend Section 1 than other parts of the Constitution.[160] Chapter 2 contains a

154 Sachs (n 82 above) 91 - 92. India's nationalist leaders (including Nehru and Gandhi) viewed human rights as indivisible and interconnected; they were imbued with socialist philosophy: V Sripati 'Constitutionalism in India and South Africa: A comparative study from a human rights perspective' (2007) 16 *Tulane Journal of International and Comparative Law* 49 at 66.

155 Sachs (n 82 above) 92.

156 As above.

157 For a definition of transformative constitutionalism, see KE Klare 'Legal culture and transformative constitutionalism' (1998) 14 *South African Journal on Human Rights* 146 at 150. On the Constitutional Court's procedural authority and interpretative mandate as a transformative court, see EC Christiansen 'Transformative constitutionalism in South Africa: Creative uses of Constitutional Court authority to advance substantive justice' (2010) 13 *Journal of Gender, Race & Justice* 575 at 578 - 594.

158 Preamble, 5th para, points 1 - 3: The Constitution was adopted, *inter alia*, to
- Heal the divisions of the past and establish a society based on democratic values, social justice and fundamental human rights;
- Lay the foundations for a democratic and open society in which government is based on the will of the people and every citizen is equally protected by law;
- Improve the quality of life of all citizens and free the potential of each person.

159 Sec 1(a), (b).

160 A Bill amending it has to receive the support of three-quarters of the National Assembly instead of the two-thirds majority required to change other provisions (except for the amending provision itself, which is subject to the higher threshold): Sec 74(1). The entrenchment of founding values seems partly attributable to the influence of the German Basic Law: Ackermann 'Equality and the South African Constitution: The role of dignity' (n 21 above) 543.

On amendments made, see H Corder 'The Republic of South Africa' in D Oliver & C Fusaro (eds) *How constitutions change: A comparative study* (2011) 274 - 276.

Bill of Rights.[161] Dignity has been given a more prominent and recognised place than in the interim Constitution. As well as including it in the founding values, the definition of the right to dignity in Section 10 has been extended to read, '[e]veryone has inherent dignity and the right to have their dignity respected and protected.' The additional text underscores the recognition that human dignity is not merely a protected and entrenched right, but that the concept of human dignity is definitional to what it means to be a human – that all humans have inherent dignity as an attribute independent of and antecedent to any constitutional protection thereof; Ackermann argues that human dignity has been accepted as a categorical constitutional imperative.[162] An understanding of what it means to be human involves a belief that human beings are self-aware in ways that add dimensions to matters such as experiencing abuse or facing death; our understandings of human capacity and human desire are relevant.[163] Chaskalson described the affirmation of human dignity as one of the founding values of the Constitution as significant,[164] because although human dignity was immanent in the values and rights of democracy, freedom and equality emphasised in the interim Constitution, it was not recognised as a foundational value.[165] The right to dignity in Section 10 is stronger, as it refers to 'the "inherent dignity" of all people, thus asserting that respect for human dignity, and all that flows from it, is an attribute of life itself, and not a privilege granted by the state'.[166]

In *Hyundai* Langa DP pointed out the focus on the dignity of all in the new transformative Constitution:[167]

> The Constitution is located in a history which involves a transition from a society based on division, injustice and exclusion from the democratic

161 Secs 7 - 39.

162 LWH Ackermann 'The legal nature of the South African constitutional revolution' [2004] *New Zealand Law Review* 633 at 647.

163 PC Davis 'Responsive constitutionalism and the idea of dignity' (2009) 11 *University of Pennsylvania Journal of Constitutional Law* 1373 at 1374.

164 Kriegler J also stated, 'the right to life, to human dignity and to bodily integrity are individually essential and collectively foundational to the value system prescribed by the Constitution': *Ex p Minister of Safety and Security: Re S v Walters* 2002 4 SA 613 (CC) [28].

165 A Chaskalson 'Human dignity as a foundational value of our constitutional order' (2000) 16 *South African Journal on Human Rights* 193 at 196.

166 n 165 above, 196 (footnote omitted).

167 *Investigating Directorate: Serious Economic Offences v Hyundai Motor Distributors (Pty) Ltd* 2001 1 SA 545 (CC) [21].

> process to one which respects the dignity of all citizens, and includes all in the process of governance. As such, the process of interpreting the Constitution must recognise the context in which we find ourselves and the Constitution's goal of a society based on democratic values, social justice and fundamental human rights. This spirit of transition and transformation characterises the constitutional enterprise as a whole.

Writing extrajudicially, Langa suggested that the Epilogue to the interim Constitution, which identified the need to change by healing the wounds caused by the divisions of the past and embracing a future founded on 'human rights, democracy and peaceful co-existence and development opportunities for all', provided a basis for understanding transformative constitutionalism.[168] Peggy Cooper Davis considers that the South African Constitutional Court's decisions concerning issues such as the death penalty, procedural due process, consensual sodomy and gay marriage show that responsive constitutionalism can yield a respect for human dignity that commits one to much more than saying 'never again' to apartheid.[169] Dikgang Moseneke (also writing extrajudicially) indicated that in order to achieve substantive equality (the primary purpose of the Constitution), transformative adjudication must aim for social redistributive justice by looking at violations of human rights in the context of the socio-economic conditions of groups and by having regard to the historical context.[170] He pointed out that as the Constitution's transformative mission is altruistic rather than individualistic, the change being sought was not only freedom, but also the achievement of equal worth and social justice, which was allied, *inter alia*, to substantive equality.[171] Ngcobo J in *Daniels* also pinpointed dignity as the focal point.[172]

The central position given to dignity as a value brought the South African legal order in line with post-World War II constitutionalism and closer in

168 P Langa 'Transformative constitutionalism' (2006) 17 *Stellenbosch Law Review* 351 at 352.

169 n 163 above, 1375.

170 D Moseneke 'Transformative adjudication' (2002) 18 *South African Journal on Human Rights* 309 at 318 - 319.

171 D Moseneke 'Transformative constitutionalism: Its implications for the law of contract' (2009) 20 *Stellenbosch Law Review* 3 at 12.

172 'The new constitutional order ... affirms the equal worth and equality of all South Africans. The recognition and protection of human dignity is the touchstone of this new constitutional order.': *Daniels v Campbell* 2004 5 SA 331 (CC) [54].

language to the Charter of the Organisation of African Unity[173] and the African Charter,[174] both of which record 'the fact that freedom, equality, justice and dignity are essential objectives for the achievement of the legitimate aspirations of the African peoples'.[175] It is in accord with the foundational role attributed to dignity in the UN Charter and human rights instruments.

The Constitution marks a radical shift to democracy and is not just a tweaking of the old constitutional order.[176] The South African Constitution (like the German one) embodies a normative value system.[177] The Constitutional Court drew an analogy between the South African and the German Constitutions, and cited the German Federal Constitutional Court as saying:[178]

> The jurisprudence of the Federal Constitutional Court is consistently to the effect that the basic right norms contain not only defensive subjective rights for the individual but embody at the same time an objective value system which, as a fundamental constitutional value for all areas of the law, acts as a guiding principle and stimulus for the legislature, executive and judiciary.

The Court in *Carmichele* contrasted the South African Constitution with the US Constitution, which distinguishes between government action and in-

173 Charter of the Organisation of African Unity (adopted at Addis Ababa 25 May 1963) (OAU Charter) Preamble.

174 n 37 above, Preamble.

175 Chaskalson (n 165 above) 196.

176 The Constitution has a transformative role 'from a grossly unequal society' to one based on equality between all: *Bato Star Fishing (Pty) Ltd v Minister of Environmental Affairs and Tourism* 2004 4 SA 490 (CC) [74] (Ngcobo J). Ngcobo J differentiated it from other constitutions where it is assumed that all are equal, and mentioned the US as an example where the equal protection clause in its Constitution has limited application to the government's programme to remedy race discrimination: above, [74], fn 10, citing *Fullilove v Klutznick* 448 US 448 (1980), *City of Richmond v JA Croson Co* 488 US 469 (1989).

177 See Roederer (n 91 above) 497 - 499; CJ Roederer 'Working the common law pure: De-veloping the law of delict (torts) in light of the spirit, purport and objects of South Africa's Bill of Rights' (2009) 26 *Arizona Journal of International and Comparative Law* 427 at 484 - 501.

178 *Carmichele v Minister of Safety and Security* 2001 4 SA 938 (CC) [54], and *Du Plessis v De Klerk* 1996 3 SA 850 (CC) [94], citing *First Abortion* case, BVerfGE 39, 1 (1975) [41].

See H Botha 'Human dignity in comparative perspective' (2009) 20 *Stellenbosch Law Review* 171 at 200.

action resulting in the state not being liable for not preventing harm.[179] Similar to the European Convention on Human Rights (ECHR),[180] positive obligations are imposed by the South African Constitution.[181] As Chaskalson said, '[t]he Constitution demands a moral reading of its provisions'.[182] The common law must be developed to conform with the Constitution's value system.

3.2.3 The Bill of Rights

3.2.3.1 Scope

The Bill of Rights is the cornerstone of democracy in South Africa.[183] Section 7 reaffirms 'the democratic values of human dignity, equality and freedom.'[184] Rights are not absolute, but can be limited as in Section 36 or elsewhere in the Bill.[185] Section 36 denotes carefully the boundaries of the limitation by reference to the underlying values.[186] Balancing of individual rights against community interests is necessary at times, but Chaskalson pointed out that rights can be interpreted in ways that avoid conflict.[187]

179 n 178 above [45], citing *DeShaney v Winnebago County Department of Social Services* 489 US 189 (1989).

180 Convention for the Protection of Human Rights and Fundamental Freedoms, 213 UNTS 222 (ECHR).

181 *Carmichele* (n 178 above) [45]. Pierre de Vos observed that the obligation on the state in Section 7(2) of the Constitution to respect, protect, promote and fulfil the rights in the Bill of Rights entailed a combination of negative and positive duties, and applied to all rights whether classified as civil and political or social and economic: P de Vos 'Pious wishes or directly enforceable human rights? Social and economic rights in South Africa's 1996 Constitution' (1997) 13 *South African Journal on Human Rights* 67 at 78 - 79.

182 n 53 above, 608 (footnote omitted).

183 Constitution of the Republic of South Africa 1996, Sec 7(1).

184 As above.

185 Sec 7(3).

186 Sec 36(1):

> The rights in the Bill of Rights may be limited only in terms of law of general application to the extent that the limitation is reasonable and justifiable in an open and democratic society based on human dignity, equality and freedom, taking into account all relevant factors, including
> (a) the nature of the right;
> (b) the importance of the purpose of the limitation;
> (c) the nature and extent of the limitation;
> (d) the relation between the limitation and its purpose; and
> (e) less restrictive means to achieve the purpose.

See Rautenbach (n 2 above) 306 - 314.

187 n 165 above, 201.

There is a broad approach to *locus standi* in constitutional issues in contrast with the restrictive common law requirements.[188] In addition to those directly affected, access to the court is granted to their representatives when they are unable to act themselves.[189] Class actions,[190] public interest litigation[191] and proceedings by associations[192] are permitted. Section 39 of the Constitution obliges the courts to 'promote the spirit, purport and objects of the Bill of Rights'[193] and makes it clear that other common or customary law or statutory rights only exist to the extent that they are consistent with the Bill.[194] When interpreting the Bill, a court, tribunal or forum must 'promote the values that underlie an open and democratic society based on human dignity, equality and freedom'.[195] The spirit of the foundational values is to be observed.

The supremacy of the Bill of Rights is evident. But it is not simply a domestic measure. There is a clear instruction to courts to consider international law when interpreting the Bill of Rights.[196] They may also consider foreign law.[197] South African courts have used foreign decisions in order to fill

188 Currie & de Waal (n 4 above) 80.

189 Sec 38(b).

190 Sec 38(c).

191 Sec 38(d).

192 Sec 38(e).

193 Sec 39(2). See Rautenbach (n 2 above) 260 - 264.

194 Sec 39(3).

195 Sec 39(1)(a).

196 Sec 39(1)(b). South Africa has the first Constitution setting out an explicit mandate for the courts to use comparative and international law in their human rights reasoning: E Örücü 'Comparative law in practice: The courts and the legislator' in E Örücü & D Nelken (eds) *Comparative law: A handbook* (2007) 427. Having reviewed cases from many jurisdictions, Paolo Carozza concluded that the centre of gravity of the global jurisprudence he observed regarding the death penalty was in the affirmation of the dignity of the human person and the principle that human rights law exists to protect that dignity; some weight was also given to foreign sources by the transnational character of the dialogue: PG Carozza 'My friend is a stranger: The death penalty and the global *ius commune* of human rights' (2003) 81 *Texas Law Review* 1031 at 1079. He discerned an emerging global *ius commune* of human rights in which the concept of human dignity, with its universal appeal, served as a common currency of transnational judicial dialogue and borrowing in matters of human rights: PG Carozza 'Human dignity and judicial interpretation of human rights: A reply' (2008) 19 *European Journal of International Law* 931 at 932. The new *ius commune* embodied the value of subsidiarity, with its attendant pluralism, rather than uniformity: above, 934.

On the courts' use of international law, see Church *et al* (n 26 above) 194 - 196; D Moseneke 'The role of comparative and public international law in domestic legal systems: A South African perspective' (2010) 23(3) *Advocate (South Africa)* 63 at 65 - 66; Okeke (n 26 above) 36 - 37.

197 Sec 39(1)(c).

a vacuum left by the temporary absence of indigenous jurisprudence. When the national jurisprudence is sufficiently plentiful and sophisticated, the use of foreign law could be expected to decline significantly. Where there is a transformative constitution, it is more likely that foreign experience will be drawn on to exemplify how transformation is possible on particular issues.[198] The Constitutional Court's use of foreign law shifted from embracing it initially for guidance, then to regarding it with circumspection, and most recently to dialogue by taking account of foreign jurisprudence without apology.[199]

Most of the rights are conferred on persons as such, but citizens' and political rights can be invoked by citizens, and children's rights are granted to minors.[200] Workers and employers have rights,[201] and juristic persons may have rights in certain circumstances.[202]

3.2.3.2 Horizontal application

The fundamental rights in the interim Constitution were held in *Du Plessis v De Klerk*[203] not to bind individuals directly so as to have horizontal application in disputes between private individuals.[204] This was principally on account of the omission of the judiciary from Section 7(1), which read, '[t]his Chapter shall bind all legislative and executive organs of state at all levels of government.' The Constitutional Assembly was concerned not to tolerate private violations of rights and created a different application scheme in the 1996 Constitution.[205] It included the judiciary in the application provision

198 C McCrudden 'Human rights and judicial use of comparative law' in E Örücü (ed) *Judicial comparativism in human rights cases* (2003) 14 - 15.

199 Langa CJ 'A reply to Professor William Binchy on "Constitutionality, the rule of law and socio-economic development"' (Lecture at Southern African Chief Justices Forum in Botswana 2009) 3 - 5 http://www.venice.coe.int//SACJF/2009_08_BTW_Kasane/default.htm (accessed 24 September 2013).

200 G Devenish *A commentary on the South African Bill of Rights* (1999) 20.

201 Sec 23.

202 Devenish (n 200 above) 20, 22 - 24.

203 n 178 above. For analyses and criticism of *Du Plessis*, see Ackermann *Human dignity: Lodestar for equality in South Africa* (n 21 above) 255, 262 - 264; J Fedtke 'From indirect to direct effect in South Africa: A system in transition' in D Oliver & J Fedtke (eds) *Human rights and the private sphere: A comparative study* (2007) 364 - 371; Klare (n 157 above) 179 - 187; Moseneke 'Transformative constitutionalism: Its implications for the law of contract' (n 171 above) 6 - 7.

204 Currie & de Waal (n 4 above) 33.

205 Currie & de Waal (n 4 above) 34. Sections 8 and 9(4) of the 1996 South African Constitution have effectively reversed the holdings in *Du Plessis* that the interim Constitution did not apply directly in relations between private persons, nor did it directly apply to private common-law litigation: AS Butler 'Private litigation and

in Section 8(1), '[t]he Bill of Rights applies to all law, and binds the legislature, the executive, the judiciary and all organs of state.' It also imposed an obligation on individuals to uphold the rights of other individuals in certain circumstances.[206]

According to Currie and de Waal, questions concerning the horizontal application of the Bill of Rights cannot be determined in the abstract, but require a contextual enquiry – provided that the circumstances of a particular case should not be used to frustrate the clear intention of the drafters to extend the direct operation of the provisions of the Bill of Rights to private conduct.[207] The purpose of a provision and the nature of the duty imposed by the right are important considerations.[208] The same duties may not be imposed on an individual as on the state where financial outlay is required. Currie and de Waal give an example of a privately-funded hospital, which would not be subject to the same obligations under the Bill of Rights as a public hospital.

3.2.3.3 Socio-economic rights

In contrast with earlier constitutions which tentatively recognised socio-economic rights[209] or contained a single, all-encompassing guarantee,[210] the South African Constitution includes specific guarantees relating to housing,[211] healthcare,[212] welfare,[213] and other socio-economic rights recognised as

constitutional rights under sections 8 and 9 of the 1996 Constitution – Assistance from Ireland' (1999) 116 *South African Law Journal* 77 at 77. Very few countries have similar constitutional provisions; those that do include Brazil, Malawi, Namibia and Zambia: Butler above, 78, fn 8.

206 'A provision of the Bill of Rights binds a natural or a juristic person if, and to the extent that, it is applicable, taking into account the nature of the right and the nature of any duty imposed by the right.': Sec 8(2). See Rautenbach (n 2 above) 295 - 298.

207 n 4 above, 53. More often than not, the Constitutional Court has avoided the direct application of a provision in the Bill of Rights to a common law rule, but has resorted to indirect horizontality facilitated by Section 39(2) of the Constitution, which obliges courts to promote the spirit, purport and objects of the Bill of Rights when developing the common law; although legal academics have criticised or praised this method of adjudication, a third group has argued that indirect horizontality is better suited to produce an incremental and cohesive body of constitutionalised common law: Mose-neke 'Transformative constitutionalism: Its implications for the law of contract' (n 171 above) 8.

208 n 4 above, 54.

209 DM Beatty *The ultimate rule of law* (2004) 119 - 120, fn 3, citing Constitution of India, Part IV, and Constitution of Ireland, Art 45.

210 Beatty (n 209 above) 120, citing Constitution of Japan, Art 25.

211 Sec 26.

212 Sec 27.

213 As above.

separate justiciable rights.[214] Although from a different background, after the fall of the Berlin Wall in 1989 countries of central and eastern Europe also favoured this approach.[215] In Hungary the Constitutional Court has drawn on dignity in its decisions on socio-economic rights.[216] The Basic Law in Israel has been interpreted as generating a right to the minimal material conditions necessary to exist.[217] Other examples of constitutions with justiciable socio-economic rights are those of Lithuania,[218] Finland,[219] and Portugal.[220]

While socio-economic rights are not explicitly recognised in the United Kingdom, they have been implicated through the right not to be subjected to inhuman or degrading treatment. The House of Lords in *Limbuela* held that there had been a breach of Article 3 ECHR[221] when asylum seekers denied support were faced with starvation and homelessness.[222] Baroness Hale stated

214 See Rautenbach (n 2 above) 413 - 418. On the different generations of rights and the options concerning socio-economic rights considered when the Bill of Rights was being drafted, see Sachs (n 82 above) 166 - 168. Human dignity is foundational to all types of rights, drawing them together and acting as a reminder of their principled indivisibility: C Dupré 'Unlocking human dignity: towards a theory for the 21st century' [2009] *European Human Rights Law Review* 190 at 202. Dupré explains that human dignity's historical focus on autonomy makes it the queen of civil and political rights; its fundamental material and humane dimension also makes it the queen of economic and social rights; it may be the archetype of the third generation solidarity rights (the right to peace or to a healthy environment): above, 199, 202.

215 Beatty (n 209 above) 120, citing Constitution of Hungary.

216 C McCrudden 'Human dignity and judicial interpretation of human rights' (2008) 19 *European Journal of International Law* 655 at 693. Combined with the right to life, the framework of social institutions supporting the right to social security has been interpreted as requiring the minimum necessary to guarantee the right to human dignity, thus imposing an obligation on the state to provide shelter for the homeless in dire circumstances: above, 693, fns 271 - 273, citing Decision 42/2000 (XI 8) AB, Constitutional Court file number: 5/G/1998, published in the Official Gazette (Magyar Közlöny) MK 2000/109.

217 McCrudden (n 216 above) 701.

218 Constitution of Lithuania 1992.

219 Constitution of Finland 1999.

220 Constitution of Portugal 2005.

221 'No one shall be subjected to torture or to inhuman or degrading treatment or punishment.'

222 *R (Limbuela) v Secretary of State for the Home Dept* [2005] UKHL 66, [2006] 1 AC 396. The state was culpable for inaction in the face of unacceptable conditions, which the claimants alleged required 'a person to sleep rough, thus exposing him to risks to health and safety and depriving him of dignity': above, 400. The fact that the primary intention was not to degrade or humiliate was not an exculpatory factor.

Limbuela was significant, first, for finding that 'inhuman and degrading' covered denial of the most basic needs to a seriously detrimental extent and, second, for

that Article 3, along with the right to life, was the most important of the ECHR rights and reflected 'the fundamental values of a decent society, which respects the dignity of each individual human being, no matter how unpopular or unworthy she may be.'[223]

The right to respect for private and family life, and for a person's home in Article 8 ECHR also has socio-economic implications. In *Connors v UK*, where Article 8 was the basis for the right not to be evicted summarily, the European Court of Human Rights recognised that it imposed a positive obligation on states to facilitate the lifestyle of vulnerable minorities – in this case, the nomadic traditions of gypsies.[224]

The Inter-American Court of Human Rights has adopted a broad approach to the right to life and considers its exercise as essential for the exercise of all other human rights.[225] In the *Street Children* case against Guatemala it held that a person's right to life[226] included 'the right that he will not be prevented from having access to the conditions that guarantee a dignified existence'.[227] The Court upheld the complaints against the state, which had violated the children's rights by breaching the negative obligation not to deprive them of their lives arbitrarily and also the positive obligation to protect street children by investigating, prosecuting and punishing crimes against them.[228] In its examination of the rights of the child to protection by society and the state,[229]

recognising that the state was responsible for the destitution because the legal structure rendered the individuals destitute by prohibiting them from obtaining paid work while simultaneously withdrawing social support: S Fredman *Human rights transformed: Positive rights and positive duties* (2008) 236 - 237.

223 n 222 above, [76].

224 (App no 66746/01) (2005) 40 EHRR 9 [84].

225 *Villagrán Morales* case (the '*Street Children*' case) Series C 63 [1999] IACHR 17 [144].

226 American Convention on Human Rights (adopted 22 November 1969, entered into force 18 July 1978) 1144 UNTS 123, Art 4.

227 n 225 above, [144]. The case concerned the torture and murder of street children by the police, who were attempting to deal with juvenile delinquency and vagrancy. The state's lax attitude meant that the crimes against street children continued in the knowledge that the authorities at the very least condoned the extreme actions of the security forces.

On the *Street Children* case, see VB Monsalve & JA Román 'Tensions of human dignity: Conceptualization and application to international human rights law' (2009) 11 *SUR - International Journal on Human Rights* 39 at 52 - 53.

228 The Court expanded the conception of the right to life to meet basic needs: McCrudden (n 216 above) 693.

229 American Convention on Human Rights (n 226 above) Art 19.

it reiterated its view of the dual nature of the state's default. It criticised the violation of the children's physical, mental and moral integrity and their lives, and also the failure to prevent at-risk children from

> living in misery, thus depriving them of the minimum conditions for a dignified life and preventing them from the 'full and harmonious development of their personality', even though every child has the right to harbor a project of life that should be tended and encouraged by the public authorities so that it may develop this project for its personal benefit and that of the society to which it belongs.[230]

The protection afforded to prisoners has evolved from the prohibition of intentional torture and physical maltreatment through its extension to precluding impairment of their mental and intellectual well-being to a requirement to provide reasonable living conditions for them.[231] The intermingling of civil and political rights with socio-economic rights is consonant with the ethos of the Vienna Declaration, which placed them on the same platform and demanded that they be promoted equally.[232]

It is noteworthy that the Vienna Declaration pre-dated agreement on the interim Constitution in South Africa. The international human rights model was one of the influences on the drafters.[233] Although they sought precedent constitutions mentioning socio-economic rights, the only ones the drafters could find incorporated them merely as non-justiciable directives of state policy.[234] They adverted to the Irish and the Indian[235] Constitutions, both of which were in this category.[236]

230 n 225 above, [191].

231 In Canada and the US two distinct bases – residual liberty and intolerable conditions – have justified intervention when an otherwise proper detention has been rendered unlawful because the custodial conditions are excessive or interfere with the fundamental rights of prisoners: A Hoel 'What rights do you take to prison? *Habeas corpus* and prison conditions' (2009) 83 *Australian Law Journal* 395 at 397.

232 World Conference on Human Rights 'Vienna Declaration and Programme of Action' (25 June 1993) UN Doc A/CONF.157/23, pt I, art 5:

> All human rights are universal, indivisible and interdependent and interrelated. … While the significance of national and regional particularities and various historical, cultural and religious backgrounds must be borne in mind, it is the duty of States, regardless of their political, economic and cultural systems, to promote and protect all human rights and fundamental freedoms.

233 Sripati (n 154 above) 108.

234 Sachs (n 82 above) 168.

235 Constitution of India 1950.

236 Sachs (n 82 above) 168.

In view of the crucial influence of Indian constitutional jurisprudence on the formation and development of the Bill of Rights in South Africa, it is worth examining some central aspects of that jurisprudence. Unlike its Irish counterpart, the Indian Supreme Court construed the fundamental rights combined with the directives to give practical effect to social and economic rights. For over a quarter of a century after gaining independence in 1947, the Indian judiciary had a somewhat fraught relationship with the other two branches of government. Initially there were skirmishes over the power of the government to amend the Constitution to pare back property rights in order to achieve social justice and a more equal society. Vijayashri Sripati described the battle between the Parliament and the Court during the first two decades as being over land reform, compensation for expropriation of private property and the abolition of the privy purses (compensation payable to former princes); her view was that the Court aligned itself with the propertied classes and repeatedly blocked Parliament's attempts to water down the right to property through constitutional amendments to implement the directive principles.[237] Venkat Iyer has a different perspective and regards the Court's actions up to 1973 as constitution-reinforcing entirely consistent with the role of the courts in a liberal democracy; the Court saw the naked power of an encroaching state as the biggest threat to freedom and the rule of law.[238]

The integrity of the judiciary was tested – and some would say, found wanting – by the declaration of an emergency in 1971 and the abrogation of safeguards on detention with the suspension of *habeas corpus* applications to enforce fundamental rights to equality, life and liberty in 1975. Indira Gandhi, as Prime Minister after the 1971 elections, enacted a series of constitutional amendments that made any law implementing any or all of the directive principles immune from judicial review; Sripati described as 'historic' the constitutional bench's judgment in *Keshavananda* conceding that although Parliament had unlimited powers to amend any part of the Constitution (including the right to property), such sweeping away of judicial review was destructive to the 'basic features' or 'basic structure' of the Con-

237 n 154 above, fn 298.

238 V Iyer 'The Supreme Court of India' in B Dickson (ed) *Judicial activism in common law supreme courts* (2007) 131.

stitution and therefore unconstitutional.[239] Sripati was critical of the Supreme Court's deference to the government during the emergency.[240] *Keshavananda* is seen as the high-water mark of judicial activism in the entire history of independent India; the Supreme Court did not list the elements of the 'basic structure' of the Constitution, leaving them to be decided on a case-by-case basis.[241] The 'basic structure' doctrine was imported to India from the West and reinterpreted there.[242]

Tensions between the judiciary and the government boiled over because of *Keshavananda*; within a day of the judgment, the government announced it was passing over three senior judges, who were in the majority in that case, for the office of Chief Justice and appointed Ray J, who had supported the government's position; the three judges and the incumbent Chief Justice, who had only one day left in office, tendered their resignation amidst strong protests from the public, media and legal community over their treatment.[243] Iyer described the period 1973 - 1977 as 'easily the least glorious in the annals of the Supreme Court', when it became highly politicised and significantly marginalised.[244]

In the *Habeas Corpus* case the Supreme Court in a majority decision upheld the government's actions.[245] Iyer labelled the majority judgments 'remarkable' for their summary rejection of arguments based on natural law and on the importance of judicial scrutiny of executive action where basic freedoms were involved, and for the enthusiasm with which the judges endorsed the positions advocated by the emergency regime; remarks by Beg J and Ray CJ were seen by many as insulting to detainees; in view of credible reports about widespread abuse and torture of detainees, this raised serious questions about the objectivity and impartiality of the Court; Ray CJ even

239 n 154 above, fn 298, citing *Keshavananda Bharati v State of Kerala* AIR 1973 SC 1461. For analyses of *Keshavananda*, see B Neuborne 'The Supreme Court of India' (2003) 1 *International Journal of Constitutional Law* 476 at 491 - 492; GJ Jacobsohn 'An unconstitutional constitution? A comparative perspective' (2006) 4 *International Journal of Constitutional Law* 460 at 471, 472, 473 - 475, 479, 480 - 481, 483, 486; M Dalal 'India's new constitutionalism: Two cases that have reshaped Indian law' (2008) 31 *Boston College International and Comparative Law Review* 257 at 262 - 263.

240 n 154 above, 97, fn 300.

241 Iyer (n 238 above) 130.

242 A Buss 'Dual legal systems and the basic structure doctrine of constitutions: The case of India' (2004) 19(2) *Canadian Journal of Law and Society* 23 at 23.

243 Iyer (n 238 above) 133.

244 n 238 above, 137 - 138.

245 *Additional District Magistrate, Jabalpur v Shukla* [1976] INSC 129, 1976 SCR 172.

questioned the patriotism of the detainees' counsel by suggesting they had wilfully and grossly exaggerated the emergency regime's actions.[246] The judges' observations and the Court's visible determination to shut out any possibility of judicial review for human rights infringements represented an unmistakable capitulation by the Court in the face of executive pressure.[247] Khanna J dissenting (finding that the rule of law did not permit the revocation of fundamental rights) based his decision on natural law pre-dating the Constitution and was adamant that procedural and substantive safeguards could not be extinguished. Prime Minister Indira Gandhi passed over Khanna J for the position of Chief Justice in 1977 in favour of Beg J (one of the majority judges in the *Habeas Corpus* case); Iyer described her move as 'a further display of contempt for judicial independence'.[248]

Sachs described the Indian Court's interpretation as 'creative', by using the directives 'to give texture and substance to fundamental civil and political rights that were directly enforceable in the courts.'[249] A more detailed look at the Indian case-law at this juncture will be instructive.

Having survived onslaughts as an institution (albeit with a rather tarnished reputation as a defender of fundamental rights), the Supreme Court redeemed itself in 1978 in *Maneka Gandhi* and held that the Constitution should be read as an integrated document encompassing due process.[250] The Court gave an integrated reading to the rights to personal liberty and life in Article 21, the various freedoms in Article 19 (including freedom of expression and of movement) and equality in Article 14.[251] The goal of fundamental rights, as identified by Beg CJ, was to secure political and social justice in a free and

246 n 238 above, 135.

247 Iyer (n 238 above) 136.

248 n 238 above, 137.

249 n 82 above, 168.

250 *Maneka Gandhi v Union of India* [1978] INSC 16, 1978 SCR (2) 621. It overruled its earlier decision in *Gopalan v State of Madras* [1950] INSC 14, 1950 SCR 88. The government had impounded Maneka Gandhi's passport ostensibly in the public interest without prior notice. As she had not been given the opportunity to contest its cancellation or to put forward her reasons for going abroad for consideration, she had been denied a fair hearing and the government's arbitrary action infringed her right to equality before the law. Bhagwati J categorised equality as 'a dynamic concept with many aspects and dimensions' and it could not 'be imprisoned within traditional and doctrinaire limits.': above, 674.
See Church *et al* (n 26 above) 126 - 128.

251 The Supreme Court reads these three Articles as the 'golden triangle' forming the touchstone of the essential features of Part III of the Constitution: S Baer 'Dignity, liberty, equality: A fundamental rights triangle of constitutionalism' (2009) 59 *University of Toronto Law Journal* 417 at fn 10.

equal society thereby assuring the dignity of the individual.[252] The right to personal liberty included the unenumerated right to travel as a method of self-expression and freedom as a moral agent, which Bhagwati J based in human dignity.[253] A restrictive constitutional interpretation was eschewed by Krishna Iyer J, who recognised the dynamic nature of a state's fundamental law:[254]

> [T]o look at the little letters of the text of Part III *de hors* the Discovery of India and the Destiny of Bharat or the divinity of the soul and the dignity of the person highlighted in the Preamble unduly obsessed with individual aberrations of yesteryears or vague hunches leading to current fears, is a parsimonious exercise in constitutional perception.

An expansive interpretation has continued to be the hallmark of Indian jurisprudence. It can be seen in *Mullin*, where Bhagwati J was influenced by the 'luminous guideline' of the US Supreme Court to follow a wide liberal approach flexible enough to deal with changes in society and various circumstances.[255] Applying this method, the right to life was not confined to 'mere animal existence' and meant 'something much more than just physical

252 n 250 above, 648:

> Articles dealing with different fundamental rights contained in Part III of the Constitution do not represent entirely separate streams of rights which do not mingle at many points. ... Their waters must mix to constitute that grand flow of unimpeded and impartial Justice (social, economic and political), Freedom (not only of thought, expression, belief, faith and worship, but also of association, movement, vacation or occupation as well as of acquisition and possession of reasonable property), of Equality (of status and of opportunity, which imply absence of unreasonable or unfair discrimination between individuals, groups and classes), and of Fraternity (assuring dignity of the individual and the unity of the nation), which our Constitution visualises.

253 'It cannot be disputed that there must exist a basically free sphere for man, resulting from the nature and dignity of the human being as the bearer of the highest spiritual and moral values.': n 250 above, 695.

Freedom of movement does not exist in all circumstances, but depends on the context. Bhagwati J outlined the test to be applied based on the nature and depth of integration of the claimed right with an enumerated right (n 250 above, 697):

> What is necessary to be seen is, and that is the test which must be applied, whether the right claimed by the petitioner is an integral part of a named fundamental right or partakes of the same basic nature and character as the named fundamental right so that the exercise of such right is in reality and substance nothing but an instance of the exercise of the named fundamental right.

254 n 250 above, 718.

255 *Mullin v Administrator, Union Territory of Delhi* [1981] INSC 12, 1981 SCR (2) 516 at 527. In *Mullin* the Court upheld the right of a detainee to receive family visits and to consult with her lawyer.

survival'.[256] It should be dignity-supporting.[257] Remarks by Bhagwati J on the extent of the right to life[258] combined with other fundamental rights, including equality, opened the door to the practical enforcement of socio-economic rights in future cases.[259]

In *Bandhua Mukti Morcha* Bhagwati J declared that the right to live with human dignity enshrined in Article 21 of the Constitution derived its 'life breath' from the directive principles.[260] In this case brought on behalf of bonded labourers[261] working in stone quarries, the state was required to invest 'their right to live with basic human dignity, with concrete reality and content' by ensuring observance of social welfare and labour laws enacted to protect workers.[262] Bhagwati J stated that 'inaction' on the part of the state in securing implementation of the legislation would amount to 'denial of the right to live with human dignity'.[263]

The right to live with human dignity was a central theme in the Supreme Court's judgment in 1982 in *People's Union for Democratic Rights*, where it

256 n 255 above, 528.

257 As above:

> The fundamental right to life which is the most precious human right and which forms the ark of all other rights must therefore be interpreted in a broad and expansive spirit so as to invest it with significance and vitality which may endure for years to come and enhance the dignity of the individual and the worth of the human person.

258 The Indian Supreme Court's interpretation of the right to life is at the forefront of an approach which infuses the values of positive freedom, solidarity, and equality into fundamental rights, thereby opening up the possibility of recognising positive duties even in relation to civil and political rights; the positive duties flow directly from the Court's affirmation of the central values for which the right to life stands; Sandra Fredman mentions in particular the value of positive freedom: Fredman (n 222 above) 206.

259 n 255 above, 529:

> [T]he magnitude and content of the components of this right [to live with human dignity] would depend upon the extent of the economic development of the country, but it must ... include the right to the basic necessities of life and also the right to carry on such functions and activities as constitute the bare minimum expression of the human-self.

260 *Bandhua Mukti Morcha v Union of India* [1983] INSC 206, 1984 (2) SCR 67 at 103. He acknowledged that the terms of the Constitution meant that the directive principles were not enforceable in court, but where legislation already existed the state could be obliged by the courts to enforce it: as above.

261 The bonded labour system had been abolished by the Bonded Labour System (Abolition) Act 1976.

262 n 260 above, 103 - 104.

263 n 260 above, 103. The state's duty extended to rehabilitation of the released individuals with support to avoid them living a free life in penury. As Bhagwati J discerned, '[t]he bonded labourer who is released would prefer slavery to hunger, a world of "bondage and (illusory) security" as against a world of freedom and starvation.': n 260 above, 133.

held that the state had a constitutional obligation to enforce the rights of workers, who were weak and had been treated unequally, against private entities.[264] The Court transformed the policy directive to secure equal pay for equal work in Article 39(d) of the Constitution into a fundamental right by using this directive principle to enhance the rights to equality before the law in Article 14 and to equality of opportunity in public employment in Article 16 in *Randhir Singh*.[265] Reddy J interpreted equality rights as directed to all in society, including the majority who were workers, and he pointed out that the 'equality clauses of the Constitution must mean some thing to everyone.'[266]

The right to life includes the right to a livelihood in the sense of a means of living, but does not entail a right to carry on a trade or business of one's choice.[267] The livelihood right was established in *Olga Tellis* through the medium of the right to life.[268] Sandra Fredman pointed out that the Court, although using the vocabulary of a right to livelihood, only imposed a duty to consult those facing eviction and did not insist that alternative pitches with proper infrastructure be provided as a condition precedent to removals.[269] There was a negative obligation on the state not to deprive people of their livelihood without giving them the opportunity to be heard

264 *People's Union for Democratic Rights v Union of India* [1982] INSC 67, 1983 SCR (1) 456. The Court also promoted the right to equality of the vulnerable and historically disadvantaged in a hierarchical society. Equal bargaining power is often absent in relationships between powerful employers and workers keen for a job at any price: see above, 490 (Bhagwati J). The prohibition of discrimination against specified historically disadvantaged groups in Article 15 of the Constitution could be another basis for a substantive equality doctrine: CA MacKinnon 'Sex equality under the Constitution of India: Problems, prospects, and "personal laws"' (2006) 4 *International Journal of Constitutional Law* 181 at 190. Equality should be understood as non-subordination instead of uniformity: above, 200.

This was a significant decision and, according to JN Pandey 'heralded a new legal revolution'; his assessment is that it 'clothed millions of workers in factories, fields, mines and projects sites with human dignity' giving them rights to wages, sustenance, shelter, medical aid and safety: JN Pandey *The constitutional law of India* (2008) 231.

265 *Randhir Singh v Union of India* [1982] INSC 24, 1982 (3) SCR 298 (SC). The Court held that the same pay scales should apply to drivers in the police force as to drivers of heavy vehicles in other departments.

266 n 265 above, 305.

267 *Sodan Singh v New Delhi Municipal Committee* [1989] INSC 258, 1989 (3) SCR 1038 (SC).

268 *Olga Tellis v Bombay Municipal Corporation* [1985] INSC 155, 1985 SCR Supl (2) 51. For a succinct view of *Olga Tellis*, see CB Raju *Social justice and the Constitution of India: With reference to SC's/ST's* (2007) 72.

269 n 222 above, 143.

in a fair, just and reasonable procedure. The Court did not impose an affirmative duty on the state to provide work, so the pavement dwellers could be evicted in the public interest, provided that they had been allowed a fair hearing. It acknowledged that to evict them from their homes on the pavement was equivalent to depriving them of their right to work, since they were unable to survive in their rural villages and needed to live near their workplaces in the cities where work was available. Chandrachud CJ drew on the US experience of due process to prevent arbitrary action by the public authorities.[270] He found that there were two purposes to the right to be heard: first, an instrumental one to try to change the outcome and, second, an intrinsic value consisting of

> the opportunity which it gives to individuals or groups, against whom decisions taken by public authorities operate, to participate in the processes by which those decisions are made, an opportunity that expresses their dignity as persons.[271]

Participation was evidenced by dialogue comprising the giving and receiving of explanations, articulating and listening to reasons for and against the measure, thereby expressing and respecting dignity as persons irrespective of the outcome.

In contrast to *Olga Tellis*, Gauntlett JA held that the right to life in the Constitution of Lesotho did not encompass a right to a livelihood, as the Constitution imposed limitations on the right to life.[272] Furthermore, Lesotho dealt with socio-economic rights (including the opportunity to secure a livelihood) as principles of state policy and not as fundamental rights.[273] Also in contrast was Ghana, when Ofari Atta J held that the right to life of those who had built houses in a flood plain could be justifiably interfered with by being evicted in the public interest to allow the construction of

270 The outcome appeared puzzling to some commentators in view of the ringing rhetoric in earlier passages of the judgment and critics suggested that the Court failed to invalidate the enabling legislation because it did not have the courage to take such a politically risky step; Pierre de Vos has countered critics with his explanation that the Court insisted that the pavement dwellers could only be removed on certain stringent conditions: n 181 above, 82.

271 n 268 above, 91.

272 *Baitsokoli v Maseru City Council* [2005] LSCA 13 (CA of Lesotho) [17], [28].

273 *Baitsokoli* (n 272 above) [18]-[19].

drains to prevent flooding in future, thus protecting the right to life of others.[274]

In *Consumer Education and Research Centre*, the Indian Supreme Court found that the right to live with dignity imposed obligations on the employer and on the state to safeguard the health of workers during work and in retirement.[275] The Court integrated the right to life in Article 21 of the Constitution with the Preamble and directive principles,[276] which amplify that right. The ethos of social justice was imbued in the Preamble and in the directive principles.[277] The Constitution envisioned social justice as 'its arch to ensure life to be meaningful and liveable with human dignity.'[278] Ramaswamy J gave a comprehensive exposé of social justice in *Air India* describing it as 'a dynamic device to mitigate the sufferings of the poor, weak, dalits, tribals and deprived sections of the society and to elevate them to the level of equality to live a life with dignity of person.'[279]

The Supreme Court was consistent in its approach in *LIC of India*, a case concerning the right to life insurance on reasonable conditions, when it reiterated that the Preamble, the fundamental rights and the directive principles combined to give a right to livelihood as a meaningful life, which required the provision of social security and benefits on equal terms.[280] With resonances of previous *dicta* concerning employers and employees in

274 *Asare v Ga West District Assembly* (Suit No 36/2007) (Ghana High Court) 2 May 2008.

275 *Consumer Education & Research Centre v Union of India* [1995] INSC 91, JT 1995 (1) 636. This case concerned those employed in the asbestos industry. See Raju (n 268 above) 74 - 75.

276 The novel feature of including directive principles in the Constitution was borrowed from the Irish Constitution: Pandey (n 264 above) 385; Jacobsohn (n 239 above) 471.

277 Particularly those in Article 38, which enjoins the state to strive to secure a social order to promote the welfare of the people, and in Article 39(e) requiring state policy to prevent abuse of the health of workers.

278 n 275 above, 657 [20]. The manifestation of the goal of social justice was the opportunity for self-expression and enjoyment of life supported by a basic level of healthcare and income in a communal setting. See as above:

> Social security, just and humane conditions of work and leisure to workman are part of his meaningful right to life and to achieve self-expression of his personality and to enjoy the life with dignity, the State should provide facilities and opportunities to them to reach at least minimum standard of health, economic security and civilised living while sharing according to the capacity, social and cultural heritage.

Social justice uses the rule of law to achieve equality in results: n 275 above, 658 [21].

279 *Air India Statutory Corp v United Labour Union* [1996] INSC 1400 (SC). He positioned the rule of law as 'a potent instrument of social justice to bring about equality in results.'

280 *LIC of India v Consumer Education & Research Centre* [1995] INSC 272, 1995 SCC (5) 482.

People's Union for Democratic Rights,[281] Ramaswamy J was prepared to dismantle unequal negotiation terms. The right to life in a welfare state obliged the state and doctors employed in state hospitals to provide timely medical assistance in the case of emergencies and, in default, the Supreme Court held that the injured person was entitled to compensation.[282]

The Constitution of India in not merely a legal document, but also a social document providing for a social contract, whose goals are achieved through the fundamental rights and directive principles; the essence of the social contract, as a political theory (in its most common form as proposed by Jean-Jacques Rousseau) is that in order to live in society, human beings agree to an implicit social contract, which gives them certain rights in return for giving up certain freedoms they would have in a state of nature.[283]

The range of fundamental rights has been expanded in many areas by an interpretation taking a broad inclusive view of the Constitution and invoking the Preamble and directive principles to enrich the interpretation of equality and the right to life. By interpreting the right to life in Article 21 of the Constitution in the light of the directive principles, the majority of the Supreme Court in *Unni Krishnan* held that every child has a right to free education up to the age of 14 years.[284] Reddy J for the majority was clear that the Constitution was an integrated document, the fundamental rights in Part III being fleshed out by the directive principles in Part IV.[285] The Constitution was amended in 2002 to add a new fundamental right in Article 21A requiring the state to provide free compulsory education to children from six to 14 years old. The fact that as a result of *Unni Krishnan* a child denied education could approach the courts for an order compelling the government to provide facilities was used as a strategic tool by activists seeking improvements in primary education.[286] The Supreme Court played a crucial role in bringing education to the forefront of the national agenda.[287]

281 n 264 above.

282 *Paschim Banga Khet Mazdoorsamity v State of West Bengal* [1996] INSC 659, 1996 (4) SCC 37.

283 P Sharma *Welfare state, right to life and capital punishment in India* (2005) 84. On Rousseau's concept of law, see P Capps *Human dignity and the foundations of international law* (2009) 182 - 183.

284 *Unni Krishnan v State of Andhra Pradesh* [1993] INSC 60, 1993 (1) SCR 594.

285 n 284 above, 649.

286 V Sripati & AK Thiruvengadam 'India: Constitutional amendment making the right to education a Fundamental Right' (2004) 2 *International Journal of Constitutional Law* 148 at 153.

287 Sripati & Thiruvengadam (n 286 above) 157.

The affirmative action provisions in the Constitution have been given an expansive interpretation by the Supreme Court.[288] In *Sawhney*,[289] the Court upheld reservation by the government of jobs in the public sector[290] for the dalits (formerly called the 'untouchables' and formally referred to as the 'Scheduled Castes'),[291] Scheduled Tribes[292] and other socially and educationally backward classes. However, in relation to the other backward classes, it ordered the government to exclude the creamy layer.[293] Sawant J emphasised the importance of socio-economic benefits to enable an individual to be fulfilled as a person, to participate in society and to enjoy civil and political rights to the full.[294] Reddy J (delivering a separate judgment in

288 The affirmative action provisions have been enhanced by constitutional amendments to equip them to address social and economic deprivation – particularly in the areas of education and public employment.

289 *Indra Sawhney v Union of India* 1992 Supp (3) SCC 217. On the judgment and the background to it, see K Nagarajan 'Compensatory discrimination in India sixty years after independence: A vehicle of progress or a tool of partisan politics' (2009) 15 *Washington and Lee Journal of Civil Rights and Social Justice* 483 at 499 - 505.

290 The reservation was made in accordance with the provision in the Constitution allowing affirmative action in favour of backward classes inadequately represented in employment in the public sector: Art 16(4).

291 Nagarajan (n 289 above) 485. On the socio-economic condition of dalits, see A Anderson 'On dignity and whether the Universal Declaration of Human Rights remains a place of refuge after 60 years' (2009) 25 *American University International Law Review* 115 at 139.

292 Scheduled Tribes are tribal communities who live in isolated pockets of India: Nagarajan (n 289 above) 487. They are specified by the President and may be altered by Parliament: Constitution of India 1950, Art 342.

293 n 289 above, [810], [882]. The 'creamy layer' is the term applied to the privileged section of the other backward classes: Nagarajan (n 289 above) 504. The Supreme Court's determination of 'Scheduled Caste' status recognises that membership of a dalit caste *per se* subjects individuals to a particularly egregious form of discrimination ('untouchability') regardless of socio-economic status, and merits positive action; in contrast, the determination of 'other backward classes' takes into account the socio-economic gains achieved by many members of backward castes in India – who are not subject to untouchability practices – and confines constitutional protections more strictly to those in greatest need by using empirical evidence of economic status: S Narula 'Equal by law, unequal by caste: The "untouchable" condition in critical race perspective' (2008) 26 *Wisconsin International Law Journal* 255 at 325. The definition of the creamy layer to be excluded should not necessarily be determined solely on income or economic grounds, but social capacity (which could include educational achievements) was relevant also: n 289 above, [809].

294 n 289 above, [414]:

> [T]he social and political justice pledged by the Preamble of the Constitution to be secured to all citizens, will remain a myth unless first economic justice is guaranteed to all. The liberty of thought and expression also will remain on paper in the face of economic deprivations. A remunerative occupation is a means not only of economic upliftment but also of instilling in the individual self-assurance, self-esteem and self-

Sawhney) pointed out the modern addition of social justice in the economic and political spheres to the original revolutionary demands of liberty, equality and fraternity, and, as he stated, '[f]raternity assuring the dignity of the individual has a special relevance in the Indian context.'[295]

In *Thakur* the Supreme Court confirmed the *ratio decidendi* in *Sawhney* when it upheld legislation reserving educational places in public institutions for members of castes, tribes and other backward classes.[296] The legislation had been enacted to progress the directive principle in Article 46 of the Constitution promoting the educational and economic interests of the weaker sections of society.[297] The Constitution permits special provision to be made for admission of members of castes, tribes and other backward classes to educational institutions.[298] Balakrishnan CJ regarded the directive principles and the fundamental rights as equally important and significant, since the rationale for categorising directive principles as non-justiciable was simply a desire not to make an infant state accountable immediately for not fulfilling the obligations arising under them.[299] He found that the application of the creamy layer principle to identification of the socially and educationally backward class was necessary, because one of the main criteria for determining that class was poverty.[300]

The identification of those communities that constitute the socially and educationally backward classes, and the extension of quotas to them, has caused much controversy and violence in India – unlike the reservation

> worthiness. It also accords him a status and a dignity as an independent and useful member of the society. It enables him to participate in the affairs of the society without dependence on, or domination by, others, and on an equal plane ... The employment under the State, by itself, may, many times help achieve the triple goal of social, economic and political justice.

Equality required that affirmative action be confined to those who were actually socially and economically backward, as its object was 'not to uplift a few individuals and families in the backward classes but to ensure the advancement of the backward classes as a whole.'; the aim was to develop the social capacities of individuals until they were able to compete with others on equal terms: n 289 above, [521].

295 n 289 above, [637].

296 *Thakur v Union of India* [2008] INSC 613. On *Thakur* and its background, see Nagarajan (n 289 above) 505 - 507; MP Singh '*Ashoka Thakur v Union of India*: A divided verdict on an undivided social justice measure' (2008) 1 *National University of Juridical Sciences Law Review* 193 at 193 - 197.

297 *Thakur* (n 296 above) [22], citing the Statement of Objects and Reasons for Central Educational Institutions (Reservation in Admission) Act 2006 (Act 5 of 2007).

298 Art 15(5).

299 n 296 above, [173].

300 n 296 above, [150].

system for dalits and Scheduled Tribes, which has aroused less controversy.[301] In implementing the reservation policy, the state has to strike a balance between the competing claims of the individual under Article 16(1) guaranteeing equality of opportunity in relation to employment and the reserved categories falling within Article 16(4).[302]

The Supreme Court of India's broadening of the *locus standi* rules and other innovations to facilitate public interest litigation[303] have enhanced greatly the practical implementation of socio-economic rights.[304] The initial impetus was to deal with grievances by prisoners and gross human rights abuses. It started in the late 1970s when the Court relaxed the formalism of traditional litigation to allow disadvantaged groups increased access to justice.[305] As a result, the Supreme Court has obtained a highly controversial transformative role in the protection and promotion of the actual enjoyment of human rights.[306] Public interest litigation has covered a wide range of issues such as vulnerable children, environmental protection, public health, consumer protection, maintenance of state-run hospitals, distribution of

301 Nagarajan (n 289 above) 487.

302 *Jitendra Kumar Singh v State of Uttar Pradesh* [2010] INSC 20 [33].

303 Bhagwati and Sen JJ both pointed out that adversary litigation differs from public interest litigation and exhorted the state to embrace it instead of resisting petitions brought on behalf of the poor and vulnerable: *Bandhua Mukti Morcha* (n 260 above) 102, 174. Bhagwati J stated that public interest litigation was rather 'a challenge and an opportunity to the government and its officers to make basic human rights meaningful to the deprived and vulnerable sections of the community and to assure them social and economic justice': n 260 above, 102. See Church *et al* (n 26 above) 122, 129 - 131.

304 Iyer (n 238 above) 143.

305 Iyer (n 238 above) 141. There were hints that the Supreme Court was on the verge of a new era in 1976: Neuborne (n 239 above) fn 111. Iyer has outlined the procedural and substantive innovations comprised in the process as including: first, widening of the rules of *locus standi* to permit someone else to approach the court on behalf of a victim too poor or otherwise unable to do so personally; second, a greater investigative role for the court with the court perhaps appointing commissioners or committees to gather facts and materials; third, closer collaboration between the parties and the judges – and occasionally even third parties; fourth, creative moulding of reliefs; and, fifth, post-litigation monitoring by the court of its orders: n 238 above, 141 - 142. See also Fredman (n 222 above) 124; Neuborne (n 239 above) at 502 - 503.

306 Fredman (n 222 above) 124. This raises questions about the proper function of the courts in a democracy, but Fredman considers that courts can act as a catalyst for democratic pressures which ultimately make recalcitrant or incompetent governments act; according to her, the ideal behind public interest litigation is to construct the court as a vehicle for social conversation between co-equal citizens; instead of interest-bargaining, where success depends on economic or political power, judicial process requires decision making based on a dynamic interplay between the different perspectives brought together in the social conversation; the courts can enhance accountability, facilitate deliberative democracy, and promote equality: n 222 above, 125.

government largesse, investigation of corruption by state agencies, maintenance of standards in public education, and affirmative action in favour of backward classes.[307] By a combination of finding unenumerated constitutional rights from an expansive reading of the fundamental rights (particularly the rights to life, equality and the various freedoms) invigorated by the directive principles and the use of public interest litigation to allow friends of the vulnerable access to the courts, the Indian Supreme Court has given concrete recognition to socio-economic rights with practical benefits for the marginalised.[308]

Iyer considers that public interest litigation has not always succeeded in making distributive justice a reality for the weak and oppressed because of the inability of the courts to enforce its orders on the massive scale required and lack of resources and/or will on the part of the politicians and bureaucrats to carry out the necessary reforms.[309] He also criticised public interest litigation, first, for allowing scope for 'judge-shopping' particularly in the early years by having an unstructured manner of dealing with individual petitions to named judges; second, by creating a two-tier system discriminating against ordinary litigants; third, for being misused by those with private axes to grind or opportunistic publicity-seekers; fourth, for needlessly

307 Iyer (n 238 above) 143. In a case dealing with child prostitution, the Court correctly categorised prostitution as not only a social ill but also a socio-economic problem and, therefore, considered that preventive rather than punitive measures should be taken to combat it: *Vishal Jeet v Union of India* [1990] INSC 176, 1990 (2) SCR 861. A public health issue was taken up as public interest litigation after receipt by the Chief Justice of a letter indicating that insecticides, colour additives and food additives banned as carcinogenic elsewhere were in widespread use in India: *Ashok v Union of India* [1997] INSC 491.

Common Cause (a registered society dedicated to public causes) has been successful in promoting practical solutions and holding people accountable by resorting to the courts. In one case initiated by it, the Supreme Court issued detailed directions with time lines requiring the authorities to put properly structured arrangements in place for hearing consumer complaints in lieu of the ad hoc solutions devised by the courts: *Common Cause v Union of India* [1993] INSC 7, 1993 (1) SCR 10. In its challenge to a government minister, who had been biased in the allotment of petrol pumps and retail dealerships and had favoured relations of staff, government colleagues and business contacts, the Court took a decisive stance and as well as ordering the quashing of ministerial orders, cancellation of allotments, and the sale by public auction of petrol pumps re-possessed by the authorities, it gave the minister two weeks to show to the Court why he should not be prosecuted and pay damages: *Common Cause v Union of India* [1996] INSC 1199.

308 India understands that there is no contradiction between economic and social rights and political and civil rights, knowing that economic and social rights make access to rights of citizenship meaningful; it realises that equality and freedom are not opposed but work together: MacKinnon (n 264 above) 202.

309 n 238 above, 150 - 151.

delaying developmental projects.[310] Pathak J redressed abuses of public interest litigation by requiring in future verification of the allegations in a petition save in exceptional circumstances such as *habeas corpus* applications; he also stipulated that petitions should be addressed to the entire Court and not to a particular judge.[311]

India is not alone in using directive principles to bring about socio-economic improvements. The Supreme Court of Ghana, using the modern interpretative approach of treating a constitution as a living organism rather than adhering to the original intent, held in *Ghana Lotto Operators* that there was a rebuttable presumption that all constitutional provisions (including the directive principles) were justiciable and that any ambiguity concerning the legal enforceability of the directive principles should be decided in favour of fundamental rights.[312] The Court found that it had jurisdiction to strike down legislation incompatible with a sound healthy economy, whose underlying objectives – as set out in the directive principles – included affording ample opportunity for individual initiative and creativity, and fostering an enabling environment for a pronounced role for the private sector.[313] The economic objectives in the directive principles were legally binding and not simply a matter of conscience for government.

In an action brought in Ghana in 2008 by a lawyer, respect for dignity was the foundation for gaining acceptance for improvement in living and working conditions. There was a successful outcome to the litigation after the Supreme Court found that he had *locus standi*.[314] Prior to taking proceedings, he had sought on numerous occasions to have the government change the practice of employing workers to carry human faeces in pans on their heads from residences in Accra.[315] He claimed it was an affront to their dignity and to the dignity of Ghanaians as a whole contrary to Article 15(1) of the Constitution, which provides that the dignity of all shall be inviolable. He also maintained it contravened Article 15(2)(a) as it was cruel, inhuman and degrading, and Article 15(2)(b) because it detracted from their dignity and worth as human beings. An amicable settlement was reached and it was

310 n 238 above, 151 - 152.

311 *Bandhua Mukti Morcha* (n 260 above) 158.

312 *Ghana Lotto Operators v National Lottery* [2009] 3 LRC 235.

313 Constitution of the Republic of Ghana 1992, Art 36(2)(b).

314 *Adjei-Ampofo (No 1) v Accra Metropolitan Assembly* [2007-2008] SCGLR 611.

315 n 314 above, 612.

agreed that the practice would be phased out.[316] Under the terms of settlement Accra Metropolitan Assembly committed itself to construct public toilet facilities, to ensure that planning and development permits were only granted for plans that made adequate provision for proper facilities and to prosecute those who failed to comply with the ban on pan latrines.[317]

From the comparative analysis I have undertaken, it is clear that there has been a shift in favour of the justiciability of socio-economic rights. The rift between civil and political rights and socio-economic rights has been sealed internationally and domestically in many countries either by specific constitutional recognition or by a dynamic judicial interpretation of stated fundamental rights – sometimes enlivened by directive principles – to develop unenumerated rights. There has also been a change in outlook in academic circles. Two legal scholars mentioned by David Beatty as having moved from a position of favouring the omission of socio-economic rights from constitutions to embracing the idea wholeheartedly were Cass Sunstein, one of America's most prolific scholars, and Dennis Davis, 'a legal giant in South Africa', who became a judge.[318] They were both inspired by the South African Constitutional Court's decision in *Grootboom* ruling that national, provincial and municipal governments had a collective responsibility to develop programmes that would provide emergency shelter and relief for squatters living in 'crisis conditions'.[319] Sunstein was impressed by the decision's carving out a middle ground between making social and economic rights fully enforceable individual entitlements and denying them any recognition in law.[320] Davis was the judge in the court at first instance to whom Irene Grootboom and her co-squatters prayed for relief; he saw things in a new light when confronted with the squalor and deprivation of those before his court.[321] While the Court recognised that foundational values of human dignity, freedom and equality are denied those without food, clothes or shelter, it was sensitive to the fact that government could respond in many ways that would meet the requirements of the Constitution.[322]

316 *Adjei-Ampofo (No 2) v Accra Metropolitan Assembly* [2007-2008] SCGLR 663 at 663.

317 n 316 above, 663 - 664.

318 n 209 above, 126 - 127.

319 n 209 above, 127, citing *Government of the Republic of South Africa v Grootboom* 2001 (1) SA 46.

320 n 209 above, 128.

321 n 209 above, 128.

322 n 209 above, 128 - 129.

The rigid political and economic rule bordering on dictatorship during the apartheid era did not regard all people as human beings and rode roughshod over their dignity, not just by deprivation of the majority of civil and political rights to vote, freedom of movement and free speech, but also by favouring economically the minority – but politically dominant – whites at the expense of the black population regarded as servile, cheap labour and dispensable. This led to an enormous gulf between the two sectors, with most blacks being left with inferior education and housing. Sachs perceived that there was a link amounting to interdependence between the absence of civil and political rights and the lack of socio-economic benefits, so that restoration of dignity in South Africa necessitated both 'the development of increased respect for the personality rights and freedom' of every individual and 'the creation of material conditions for a dignified life for all.'[323] Without education, the poor were ill-equipped to demand political rights. Without the vote, they lacked the democratic clout to canvass for improved social conditions. The interrelatedness of civil and political rights and socio-economic rights helps resolve the tensions that inevitably arise in the enforcement of the latter because of lack of adequate resources to completely satisfy the needs of all. There can be reconciliation between the libertarian whose emphasis is on the individual, autonomy and choice, and the communitarian, who sees our social setting as dictating choices.[324] Sachs labels the reconciliation of the liberty and community views in the South African Constitution the 'dignitarian' approach, which 'united the right to be autonomous with the need to recognise that we all live in communities.'[325] He summarised this development, '[i]t was the fundamental right of all human beings to have their basic human dignity respected, that linked the right to

323 n 82 above, 172. Venitia Govender asserted that economic, social and cultural rights are more than mere policy goals, and are entitlements and guarantees without which the realisation of civil and political rights would be superficial and severely constrained: V Govender 'Economic, social and cultural rights in South Africa: Entitlements, not mere policy options' in B Klein Goldewijk *et al* (eds) *Dignity and human rights: The imple-mentation of economic, social and cultural rights* (2002) 75. See also J Sarkin 'The role of national human rights institutions in post-apartheid South Africa' in J Sarkin & W Binchy (eds) *Human rights, the citizen and the state: South African and Irish approaches* (2001) 48.

324 For an assessment of the link between the foundational values and material circum-stances in South African jurisprudence and in human rights literature, see S Cowen 'Can "dignity" guide South Africa's equality jurisprudence?' (2001) 17 *South African Journal on Human Rights* 34 at 52 - 54.

325 n 82 above, 173. See S Hennette-Vauchez 'A human *dignitas*? Remnants of the ancient legal concept in contemporary dignity jurisprudence' (2011) 9 *International Journal of Constitutional Law* 32.

freedom with the right to bread.'[326] It was not only the poor whose dignity was undermined by apartheid, but the dignity of the privileged whites and of society in general was assailed by the intentional institutionalised non-recognition of the humanity of all, irrespective of race or colour.[327]

The ANC's constitutional guidelines published in 1988 mentioned socio-economic rights.[328] In 1992 the ANC produced a draft Bill of Rights that encompassed rights for workers and in the social, welfare, health and educational areas.[329] There was political opposition from the apartheid government represented by the National Party, which viewed the social welfare rights as a threat to the system of white and Afrikaner privilege that existed under apartheid.[330] The strength of the ruling party's position prior to elections in 1994 explains why the interim Constitution contained fewer

326 n 82 above, 173.

327 Ackermann 'Equality and the South African Constitution: The role of dignity' (n 21 above) 540. Gandhi realised that the supposed benefactors in a traditional hierarchy are themselves humiliated by the belittling of fellow human beings: Meyer (n 153 above) 199 - 200.

328 H Corder & D Davis 'The constitutional guidelines of the African National Congress: A preliminary assessment' (1989) 106 *South African Law Journal* 633 at 633, 641. Starting with the Freedom Charter in 1955, the ANC had inextricably linked social welfare with post-apartheid liberation: EC Christiansen 'Using constitutional adjudication to remedy socio-economic injustice: Comparative lesson from South Africa' (2008) 13 *University of California at Los Angeles Journal of International Law and Foreign Affairs* 369 at 378.

The first significant comprehensive contribution dealing with the broader considerations of constitutional rights was authored by Sachs who, during the second half of the 1980s, published a number of papers arguing for redistribution of wealth through a transformative constitution: DM Davis 'Socioeconomic rights: Do they deliver the goods?' (2008) 6 *International Journal of Constitutional Law* 687 at 687 - 688. Sachs proposed that an orderly and fair redistribution of wealth be achieved by establishing a minimum floor of rights to a series of carefully defined social and economic goods: above, 688. See also MS Kende *Constitutional rights in two worlds: South Africa and the United States* (2009) 29.

In keeping with the universal principle of the interrelatedness of all human rights, Moseneke has also supported the substantive fulfilment of socio-economic rights through transformative adjudication: 'Transformative adjudication' (n 170 above) 318.

329 Davis (n 328 above) 688. Ideologically opposed to this proposal were first, neoliberals, who regarded the market as the effective agent for the distribution of social capital; they were wary of increasing the state's power of interference in the private sphere, thereby minimising individual liberty and hindering the operation of the market: above, 688 - 689. Second, social democrats opposed it as a threat to democracy by giving the unelected judiciary broad capacity for judicial review and scope for interfering with legislation passed by a democratically elected parliament and with implementation of the executive's policies; they also feared the creation of a new judicial elite: above, 689.

330 Christiansen (n 328 above) 379.

socio-economic rights than the final Constitution negotiated after the ANC had received overwhelming electoral support.[331]

The range of protection that the Constitution affords to basic needs is wide. The housing and healthcare, food, water and social security rights in Sections 26[332] and 27[333] of the 1996 Constitution were completely new with no parallel rights in the interim Constitution.[334] Starting from the negative obligation perspective, first, there is at the very least a prohibition on the State and others from preventing or interfering with the individual's right of access to housing.[335] Second, there is a positive obligation on the State to provide housing on a progressive basis. The extent of the State's duties differs according to the economic resources available to different sectors of the population.[336] Some may be able to rent or buy their own accommodation. The State's resources can be concentrated on those without means or access.[337] Third, framed in negative terms, arbitrary evictions are banned, and there is the protection of court scrutiny before eviction from a home or before a home is demolished.[338]

331 Christiansen (n 328 above) 379 - 380. In the Constitutional Assembly debates ANC negotiator Asmal stressed the need for material benefits and security in order to be liberated: Christiansen (n 328 above) 378, fn 66, citing Rep of South Africa, Debates of the Constitutional Assembly 24 Jan to 20 Feb 1995 at 122 - 23 (1994-96) and 3 Debates of the Constitu-tional Assembly, 122 - 23 (1996).

332 It reads:

(1) Everyone has the right to have access to adequate housing.
(2) The state must take reasonable legislative and other measures, within its available resources, to achieve the progressive realisation of this right.
(3) No one may be evicted from their home, or have their home demolished, without an order of court made after considering all the relevant circumstances. No legislation may permit arbitrary evictions.

333 The text is:

(1) Everyone has the right to have access to
  (a) health care services, including reproductive health care;
  (b) sufficient food and water; and
  (c) social security, including, if they are unable to support themselves and their dependants, appropriate social assistance.
(2) The state must take reasonable legislative and other measures, within its available resources, to achieve the progressive realisation of each of these rights.
(3) No one may be refused emergency medical treatment.

334 Devenish (n 200 above) 357.

335 L Chenwi 'Putting flesh on the skeleton: South African judicial enforcement of the right to adequate housing of those subject to evictions' (2008) 8 *Human Rights Law Review* 105 at 116, citing *Grootboom* (n 319 above) [34].

336 Currie & de Waal (n 4 above) 586.

337 Currie & de Waal (n 4 above) 587.

338 Chenwi (n 335 above) 116.

Mirroring the nature of the rights relating to housing,[339] the right to healthcare, nutrition and welfare[340] may not be directly infringed by retrogressive provisions, while reasonable legislative and implementation measures to achieve progressive realisation of the right are required.[341] The right to emergency medical treatment is a negative one not to be arbitrarily excluded from that which already exists, in that no-one requiring medical assistance urgently can be turned away from a hospital which is able and available to provide the service.[342] It does not extend to routine medical treatment and is not necessarily free.[343] Under Section 35(2)(e) detained people have an unqualified right to adequate medical treatment, as well as to adequate accommodation, nutrition and reading material.[344]

Children have an unconstrained right in Section 28(1)(c) to 'basic nutrition, shelter, basic health care services and social services'. Basic education is the right of children and adults.[345] The State's obligation in relation to further education is to make it progressively available and accessible through reasonable measures.[346]

As we have already seen, when the Constitution was being drafted, there was considerable debate over whether socio-economic rights should be justiciable.[347] Sachs, who was involved in drafting the Constitution, thought that the equal protection clause and affirmative action, although they would have helped the black middle classes, were not enough to lift the standards of living of the desperately poor.[348] The problem was not just to prevent

339 Currie & de Waal (n 4 above) 591.

340 The difference between the welfare provisions is that social security refers to insurance schemes to which workers and employers contribute for the purposes of financial old-age pensions, medical and unemployment insurance, whereas social assistance financed from public funds is based on need, entitlement to it and the extent of that entitlement being assessed on a case-by-case basis: Currie & de Waal (n 4 above) 591 - 592. The availability of social security and social assistance depends on schemes having been established by the State or privately based on legislation requiring their establishment: Currie & de Waal (n 4 above) 592.

341 Currie & de Waal (n 4 above) 591.

342 Currie & de Waal (n 4 above) 592.

343 Currie & de Waal (n 4 above) 593.

344 As above.

345 Sec 29(1)(a).

346 Sec 29(1)(b).

347 Sachs (n 82 above) 167. See also S Liebenberg 'South Africa: Adjudicating social rights under a transformative constitution' in M Langford (ed) *Social rights jurisprudence: Emerging trends in international and comparative law* (2008) 75 - 77.

348 n 82 above, 169.

continuing or new discrimination, but to ensure that everyone was entitled to at least the minimum decencies of life.[349] Davis described the Constitution that emerged as representing an alternative vision to the neoliberal framework with its focus on globalisation.[350] It moved beyond the conception of rights as a shield against a sovereign espoused by Hobbes to rights involving significant claims on state and community resources.[351]

3.2.3.4 Environmental rights

The environmental rights were strengthened in the 1996 Constitution in Section 24.[352] The word 'harmful' replaced 'detrimental' in the interim Constitution, which was a considerable improvement in the standard of protection. However, it is still enshrined in negative terms and is not a positive right to a healthy environment.[353] Protection was improved by extending the duty (albeit a negative one) from the State to the private sector; this is done by reading Section 24(a) in conjunction with Section 8 allowing for direct horizontal application of the 1996 Constitution against privately-owned enterprises, which often cause massive environment degradation.[354]

349 As above.

350 n 328 above, 690. A transformative constitution (as in South Africa) can protect and promote social citizenship by offsetting some of the corrosive effects of neoliberalism: DM Davis *et al* 'Social rights, social citizenship, and transformative constitutionalism: A comparative assessment' in J Conaghan *et al* (eds) *Labour law in an era of globalization: Transformative practices and possibilities* (2002) 511, 534.

351 Davis (n 328 above) 690 - 691. It is of the social democratic genre: Davis (n 328 above) 690.

352 It provides:

> Everyone has the right
> (a) to an environment that is not harmful to their health or well-being; and
> (b) to have the environment protected, for the benefit of present and future generations, through reasonable legislative and other measures that
> (i) prevent pollution and ecological degradation;
> (ii) promote conservation; and
> (iii) secure ecologically sustainable development and use of natural resources while promoting justifiable economic and social development.

See LJ Kotzé 'A critical survey of domestic constitutional provisions relating to environmental protection in South Africa' (2008) 14 *Tilburg Law Review* 298 at 303 - 309; Rautenbach (n 2 above) 396 - 397.

353 Currie & de Waal (n 4 above) 525.

354 Currie & de Waal (n 4 above) 524.

Protection of the environment for posterity in Section 24(b) is a positive obligation on the State to take the initiative to achieve this by reasonable legislative and other measures.[355]

It is unlikely to have direct horizontal application.[356]

3.2.4 Dignity

Dignity and equality are inextricably linked in the Constitution. They are the foundational values mentioned in Section 1[357] and, together with freedom, are the basic democratic values which restrict the limitation of rights[358] and govern the interpretation of the Bill of Rights.[359] In times of emergency, the rights to equality and dignity are non-derogable – equality to the extent that unfair discrimination is based solely on the grounds of race, colour, ethnic or social origin, sex, religion or language, and dignity in its entirety.[360]

355 Currie & de Waal (n 4 above) 527. See *BP Southern Africa (Pty) Ltd v MEC for Agriculture, Conservation, Environment & Land Affairs* [2004] ZAGPHC 18 (High Court, Witwatersrand Local Division). The elevation of environmental rights to a fundamental justiciable human right sets the goal of attaining a protected environment 'by an integrated approach, which takes into consideration *inter alia* socio-economic concerns and principles': above, 25 (Claassen J). The Constitution 'envisages that environmental considerations will be balanced with socio-economic considerations through the ideal of sustainable development': *Fuel Retailers Association of Southern Africa v Director-General Environmental Management, Department of Agriculture, Conservation and Environment, Mpumalanga Province* [2007] ZACC 13, 2007 6 SA 4 (CC) [45]. See also *MEC: Department of Agriculture, Conservation and Environment v HTF Developers (Pty) Ltd* [2007] ZACC 25, 2008 2 SA 319 (CC) [60]-[61]. Environmental considerations have to be accorded appropriate recognition and respect in administrative processes: *Director: Mineral Development, Gauteng Region v Save the Vaal Environment* [1999] ZASCA 9, [1999] 2 All SA 381 (A) [20]. The courts must ensure that adequate and effective mechanisms are provided to the State for the proper enforcement of environmental obligations: *Minister of Water Affairs and Forestry v Stilfontein Gold Mining Co Ltd* [2006] ZAGPHC 47 (High Court, Witwatersrand Local Division) [17.3].

On *BP Southern Africa*, see W Du Plessis & L Britz 'The filling station saga: Environmental or economic concerns?' [2007] *Journal of South African Law* 263 at 265, 271; J Glazewski & E Witbooi 'Environmental law' [2004] *Annual Survey of South African Law* 397 at 404 - 408. On *Fuel Retailers*, see T Murombo 'From crude environmentalism to sustainable development: *Fuel Retailers*' (2008) 125 *South African Law Journal* 488. Cf *Minister of Public Works v Kyalami Ridge Environmental Association* [2001] ZACC 19, 2001 3 SA 1151 (CC), criticised in M Kidd 'Greening the judiciary' (2006) 9 *Potchefstroom Electronic Law Journal* 1 at 2 - 3.

356 Currie & de Waal (n 4 above) 524 - 525.

357 Sec 1(a).

358 Sec 36(1).

359 Sec 39(1)(a).

360 Sec 37(5)(c).

Equality rights are set out in some detail in Section 9.[361] Section 9(1) embodies two concepts: first, the right to equality before the law, which is inherent in the rule of law, and, second, equal protection and benefit of the law.[362] 'Equal protection' comes from the American idea of constitutional equality and 'equal benefit', taken from the Canadian Charter of Rights, broadens the equality guarantee from procedure to the substance of the law.[363]

The commitment to substantive equality is endorsed again in Section 9(2) by the reference to 'full and equal enjoyment of all rights and freedoms'.[364] Legislative and other measures may safeguard or assist previously disadvantaged individuals or groups in the interests of achieving substantive equality. Affirmative action was explicitly allowed to avoid disputes as in the US and to avoid merely formal equality.[365] In Lesotho there was an unsuccessful challenge by a man who was unable to stand as a local government election candidate in his home electoral division because that division had been reserved for women.[366] The Court of Appeal rejected his argument that the court *a quo* had been unduly deferential to the legislature and found that the measures (designed to achieve important objectives) were not arbitrary, unfair or irrational; they impaired rights as little as possible; and there was a proportionality between the effects of the measures and the objective.[367]

361 It reads:

(1) Everyone is equal before the law and has the right to equal protection and benefit of the law.

(2) Equality includes the full and equal enjoyment of all rights and freedoms. To promote the achievement of equality, legislative and other measures designed to protect or advance persons, or categories of persons, disadvantaged by unfair discrimination may be taken.

(3) The state may not unfairly discriminate directly or indirectly against anyone on one or more grounds, including race, gender, sex, pregnancy, marital status, ethnic or social origin, colour, sexual orientation, age, disability, religion, conscience, belief, culture, language and birth.

(4) No person may unfairly discriminate directly or indirectly against anyone on one or more grounds in terms of subsection (3). National legislation must be enacted to prevent or prohibit unfair discrimination.

(5) Discrimination on one or more of the grounds listed in subsection (3) is unfair unless it is established that the discrimination is fair.

362 Devenish (n 200 above) 40, fn 40.

363 Devenish (n 200 above) 40, citing H Cheadle & D Davis 'Equality' in D Davis *et al* (eds) *Fundamental rights in the Constitution* (1997) 61. On equal protection, see Church *et al* (n 26 above) 148 - 149.

364 Devenish (n 200 above) 41; *National Coalition for Gay and Lesbian Equality v Minister of Justice* 1998 12 BCLR 1517 (CC) (*Sodomy* case) [62].

365 Chaskalson (n 41 above) 36. On affirmative action, see Rautenbach (n 2 above) 326 - 327.

366 *Ts'epe v Independent Electoral Commission* [2005] AHRLR 136 (LeCA 2005).

367 n 366 above, [38]-[40].

Unfair discrimination, whether direct or indirect, by the State is prohibited by Section 9(3). Grounds additional to those particularised in the interim Constitution are pregnancy, marital status and birth. Protection from discrimination on the grounds of birth promotes personal dignity (a key aspect of which is individual autonomy) by ensuring that each person can create her own identity, free from the constraints of ascriptive status, and is treated on the basis of individual merit.[368] A corollary of autonomy-linked personal dignity is that an individual achieves and fulfils this dignity through her own capabilities and conduct; this is an illustration of the transition from status-based dignity to conduct-based dignity.[369]

Section 9(4) was another innovation, which gave the anti-discrimination provision horizontal effect backed by legislation to be introduced within three years.[370] Subsections 9(2)-(4) make it clear that discriminatory or disparate impact as well as intent is actionable under the Constitution.[371] It can be deduced from other parts of Constitution that the right in Section 9(4) is not dependent on legislation.[372] Section 9(5) carries forward a presumption that discrimination on one of the listed grounds is unfair unless it is proven to be fair.

In contrast, the right to dignity is succinct.[373]

3.2.4.1 The values dimension in South African jurisprudence

The case-law from South Africa exudes a values perspective. Recognising that dignity is the inviolable central essential gravity at the soul and heart of each individual,[374] Sachs J articulated an inviolable core beyond the realm of the state:[375]

> ... there is a core to the individual conscience so intrinsic to the dignity of the human personality that it is difficult to imagine any factors whatsoever that could justify its being penetrated by the state.

368 SD Shadowen 'Personal dignity, equal opportunity, and the elimination of legacy preferences' (2010) 21 *George Mason University Civil Rights Law Journal* 31 at 40, 81.

369 Shadowen (n 368 above) 44.

370 Sch 6, Sec 23(1).

371 Wing (n 109 above) 76.

372 Devenish (n 200 above) 41.

373 Sec 10.

374 On the universality and individuality of human dignity, see J Habermas 'The concept of human dignity and the realistic utopia of human rights' (2010) 41 *Metaphilosophy* 464 at 473 - 475. On the philosophical foundations of human dignity in South African constitutional law, see Botha (n 178 above) 207 - 209.

375 *S v Lawrence* 1997 4 SA 1176 (CC) [168]. On *Lawrence*, see Kende (n 328 above) 223 - 226.

The inviolability of the private sphere from unreasonable searches and seizures was mentioned by van der Westhuizen J, quoting Jackson J (dissenting) in a US case: [376]

> [O]ne need only briefly to have dwelt and worked among a people possessed of many admirable qualities but deprived of these rights to know that the human personality deteriorates and dignity and self-reliance disappear where homes, persons and possessions are subject at any hour to unheralded search and seizure by the police.

While these remarks are valid insofar as they protect the privacy of the person's physical presence and tangible environment, they do not give any recognition to the inviolable nature of dignity, which cannot 'disappear' or be lost or waived by its holder. Richard Stith has said, '[w]e cannot forfeit or waive our humanity nor change its status as a principle' nor can we 'legally consent to be enslaved (to be reduced from person to property) nor to be killed'.[377] In German law, a waiver of dignity is not acceptable; it has absolute effect and cannot be balanced against other legal interests.[378] The *Daschner* case held that because of the absolute ban on torture, which infringes dignity, the pleas of self-defence (of oneself or of another) or necessity were unreasonable and did not apply.[379]

The German Constitutional Court held that a statute passed in the wake of the 9/11 terrorist attacks, permitting the German air force to shoot down airliners that had been taken over by terrorists was not compatible with the protection of dignity in Article 1 of the Basic Law; the Court stated it was 'absolutely inconceivable' to intentionally kill the crew and the passengers of a hijacked plane, even when they were 'doomed anyway'; human dignity

376 *Magajane v Chairperson, North West Gambling Board* 2006 5 SA 250 (CC) [64], citing *Brinegar v US* 338 US 160 (1949) 180 - 81.

377 R Stith 'The priority of respect: How our common humanity can ground our individual dignity' (2004) 44 *International Philosophical Quarterly* 165 at 182.

378 E Klein 'Human dignity in German law' in Kretzmer & Klein (n 42 above) 148 - 149, 157 - 159.

379 F Jessberger 'Bad torture – good torture? What international criminal lawyers may learn from the recent trial of police officers in Germany' (2005) 3 *Journal of International Criminal Justice* 1059 at 1065, 1073; see also Ackermann *Human dignity: Lodestar for equality in South Africa* (n 21 above) 119 - 120; A Cassese tr 'Respect for human dignity in today's Germany: Regional Court (*Landgericht*) of Frankfurt am Main, decision of 20 December 2004, *Daschner Wolfgang and E.* case' (2006) 4 *Journal of International Criminal Justice* 862; *Gäfgen v Germany* (App no 22978/05) (2011) 52 EHRR 1.

enjoys 'the same constitutional protection regardless of the duration of the physical existence of the individual human being.'[380]

Naming dignity as an absolute value may have a useful symbolic effect in a society such as Germany with its traumatic history of human rights violations, but David Weisstub suggests that proportionality may be more appropriate for balancing collective and individual interests in liberal democratic societies without such a history.[381] There is a distinction between autonomy, which can be waived, and dignity, which is inviolable; therefore consent may not be a defence to criminal physical harm.[382]

In *Mohamed* the Court – casting doubt on whether a suspected criminal could validly consent to his removal to the US to face a criminal charge involving the death penalty thereby endangering his life – noted the statement in the German *Peep Show* decision that '[h]uman dignity is an objective, indisposable value, the respect of which the individual cannot waive validly.'[383]

Ackermann J linked dignity and freedom with respect for the individual's unique humanity:[384]

> Human dignity cannot be fully valued or respected unless individuals are able to develop their humanity, their 'humanness' to the full extent of its potential. Each human being is uniquely talented. Part of the dignity of every human being is the fact and awareness of this uniqueness. An individual's human dignity cannot be fully respected or valued unless the individual is permitted to develop his or her unique talents optimally. Human dignity has little value without freedom; for without freedom personal development and fulfilment are not possible.

380 Waldron (n 150 above) 27, citing 115 BVerfGE 118 (15 Feb 2006) (Federal Constitutional Court of Germany). See also Ackermann *Human dignity: Lodestar for equality in South Africa* (n 21 above) 120 - 122; Botha (n 178 above) 195.

381 DN Weisstub 'Honor, dignity, and the framing of multiculturalist values' in Kretzmer & Klein (n 42 above) 276 - 277.

382 V Bergelson 'Autonomy, dignity, and consent to harm' (2008) 60 *Rutgers Law Review* 723 at 729 - 730.

383 *Mohamed v President of the Republic of South Africa* 2001 3 SA 893 (CC) [62], fn 55, citing German Federal Administrative Tribunal's *Peep Show* decision BVerwGe 64, 274 (1981) [English translation by Michalowski & Woods, *German Constitutional Law – The Protection of Civil Liberties* (Ashgate/Dartmouth, Aldershot, 1999) at 105]. On the *Peep Show* case, see Botha (n 178 above) 182, 185.

384 *Ferreira v Levin* 1996 1 SA 984 (CC) [49].

These views on the freedom to develop one's unique potential are correct, but Ackermann J erred in saying that self-awareness is necessary for human dignity.[385]

385 The concept of dignity does not reflect the subjective state of mind of the perpetrator or the victim, but instead has an 'objective,' normative meaning; Vera Bergelson gave as an example voluntary cannibalism which *by its very terms* denies people equal moral worth and, thus, assaults the victim's dignity – even that of a willing participant; she described what was at stake as people's moral dignity, or dignity of personhood, as opposed to social dignity, or dignity of rank: n 382 above, 730 - 731.

In a different context, Denise Réaume has proposed replacing the tort of intentional infliction of nervous shock with a dignity-based tort of intentional outrage to dignity, which would substitute the legally protected interest of dignity for the weak concept of emotional tranquillity as a foundation for expansion of tort law; her rationale is that it is the desire to inflict distress or humiliation that constitutes the assault on dignity rather than the causing of that precise effect; to *treat* a person as worthless as a moral personality offends dignity irrespective of whether one succeeds in making that person *feel* worthless: DG Réaume 'Indignities: Making a place for dignity in modern legal thought' (2002) 28 *Queen's Law Journal* 61 at 86, 90 - 91.

There are various views on whether awareness on the part of the victim is a necessary element in the tort of false imprisonment. Fawsitt J of the Irish Circuit Court considered it was not and stated, '[t]he fact that a person is not actually aware that he is being imprisoned does not amount to evidence that he is not imprisoned, it being possible for a person to be imprisoned in law, without his being conscious of the fact and appreciating the position in which he is placed': *Dullaghan v Hillen* [1957] Ir Jur Rep 10 (CC) 15. In the UK, the House of Lords ruled in *Murray v Ministry of Defence* [1988] 2 All ER 521 that false imprisonment was actionable without proof of special damage, and it was not necessary for a person unlawfully detained to prove knowledge of the detention or harm. Because the law attached 'supreme importance to the liberty of the individual', Lord Griffiths refused to follow the US route, which required that the person confined be conscious of the confinement or be harmed by it: above, 529, citing Restatement of the Law, Second, Torts 2d (1965) § 35, p 52. He doubted *Herring v Boyle* (1834) 1 Cr M & R 377, 149 ER 1126, and approved instead the dictum in *Meering v Grahame-White Aviation Co Ltd* of Atkin LJ, who thought 'a person can be imprisoned while he is asleep, while he is in a state of drunkenness, while he is unconscious, and while he is a lunatic' or while unknowingly being confined in a locked room, or while being restrained (without being locked in) within defined bounds, although damages would be affected by whether the imprisoned person was conscious of it or not: above, 528 - 529, citing (1919) 122 LT (CA) 53 - 54. In the US, since the interest protected is regarded as a mental one, resembling apprehension of contact in the assault cases, the Restatement of Torts has taken the position that there can be no imprisonment unless the plaintiff is aware of it at the time – the mere dignitary interest in freedom from unconscious confinement is not worthy of redress; this position is opposed by three American decisions in cases of children and an incompetent: WP Keeton (ed) & WL Prosser *Prosser and Keeton on the law of torts* (1984) 47 - 48, citing *Robalina v Armstrong* NY 1852, 15 Barb 247; *Commonwealth v Nickerson* 1861, 87 Mass (5 Allen) 518; *Barker v Washburn* 1911, 200 NY 280, 93 NE 958. For criticism of the requirement of consciousness of confinement, see S Reed 'Is knowledge of the fact of imprisonment by the plaintiff a necessary element in false imprisonment?' (1944) 32 *Kentucky Law Journal* 212; WL Prosser 'False imprisonment: Consciousness of confinement' (1955) 55 *Columbia Law Review* 847; DS Cohen 'False imprisonment: A reexamination of the necessity for awareness of confinement' (1975) 43 *Tennessee Law Review* 109; SH Nahmod 'Awareness of confinement for false imprisonment: A brief critical comment' (1976)

Sachs J in the *Sodomy* case pinpointed dignity as the underlying value in the Bill of Rights and related it to self-worth and equality:[386]

> It will be noted that the motif which links and unites equality and privacy, and which, indeed, runs right through the protections offered by the Bill of Rights, is dignity. This Court has on a number of occasions emphasised the centrality of the concept of dignity and self-worth to the idea of equality.

In *Soobramoney v Minister of Health (Kwazulu-Natal)* the same judge endorsed Ronald Dworkin's view of the composition of the sanctity of life and stressed the importance of the law in supporting the freedom of society to make choices.[387] Sachs J explained the religious-based philosophy of life in *Minister of Home Affairs v Fourie*:[388]

> For many believers, their relationship with God or creation is central to all their activities. It concerns their capacity to relate in an intensely meaningful fashion to their sense of themselves, their community and

15 *Duquesne Law Review* 31. See also L Vold 'The legal allocation of risk in assault, battery, and imprisonment – The *prima facie* case' (1938) 17 *Nebraska Law Bulletin* 149 at 193.

In an action for battery, it is not essential that the plaintiff should be conscious of the contact at the time it occurs; interest in personal integrity still is entitled to protection, although the plaintiff is asleep or under an anaesthetic or otherwise unaware of what is going on; a technical infringement attracts nominal damages; more serious events can confer an entitlement to compensation for the resulting mental disturbance, *eg*, fright, revulsion or humiliation: Keeton & Prosser above, 40.

Assault is essentially a mental rather than a physical invasion; since the interest involved is the mental one of apprehension of contact, the plaintiff must be aware of the threat of contact: Keeton & Prosser above, 43 - 44. See also Vold above, 177 - 178.

386 n 364 above, [120] (footnotes omitted).

387 1998 1 SA 765 (CC) [55], citing Dworkin *Life's dominion: An argument about abortion and euthanasia* (1993) 240, 241:

> [The present case] does point to the need to establish what Dworkin has in his book *Life's Dominion*, called the 'relative importance of the natural and human contributions to the sanctity of life'. He concludes his study with the eloquent reminder that if people are to
>
> > 'retain the self consciousness and self respect that is the greatest achievement of our species, they will let neither science nor nature simply take its course, but will struggle to express, in the laws they make as citizens and the choices they make as people, the best understanding they can reach of why human life is sacred, and of the proper place of freedom in its dominion.'

Whatever the moral and ethical arguments, the courts are clear that the principle of sanctity of life in the medical context is not absolute: D McQuoid-Mason 'Pacemakers and "living wills": Does turning down a pacemaker to allow death with dignity constitute murder?' (2005) 18 *South African Journal of Criminal Justice* 24 at 26.

388 2006 1 SA 524 (CC) [89] (footnote omitted).

> their universe. For millions in all walks of life, religion provides support and nurture and a framework for individual and social stability and growth. Religious belief has the capacity to awaken concepts of self-worth and human dignity which form the cornerstone of human rights. Such belief affects the believer's view of society and founds a distinction between right and wrong. It expresses itself in the affirmation and continuity of powerful traditions that frequently have an ancient character transcending historical epochs and national boundaries. For believers, then, what is at stake is not merely a question of convenience or comfort, but an intensely held sense about what constitutes the good and proper life and their place in creation.

When describing the death penalty in *Makwanyane*, Chaskalson P used Kantian terminology:[389]

> [Death] is ... an inhuman punishment for it '... involves, by its very nature, a denial of the executed person's humanity', and it is degrading because it strips the convicted person of all dignity and treats him or her as an object to be eliminated by the state.

Although they came to opposite conclusions in a dispute over the validity of a limitation clause in an insurance contract, two judges in *Barkhuizen v Napier* connected freedom and autonomy with dignity.[390] Undoubtedly, the freedom of the competent to regulate their affairs unhindered is critical. However, the converse is not true, as even the incompetent retain their objective dignity, which is deserving of respect.[391] Sachs J (dissenting) in *Barkhuizen v Napier*

389 n 146 above, [26], citing *Furman v Georgia* 408 US 238 (1972) 290 (Brennan J, concurring).

390 2007 5 SA 323 (CC). For Ngcobo J in the majority, '[s]elf-autonomy, or the ability to regulate one's own affairs, even to one's own detriment, is the very essence of freedom and a vital part of dignity.': above, [57]. Jonathan Lewis criticised the Constitutional Court in this case for not awarding costs against the losing party because an important constitutional issue was in dispute; the state was not involved, as it concerned a contractual dispute between two private parties: J Lewis 'The Constitutional Court of South Africa' (2009) 125 *Law Quarterly Review* 440 at 446 - 447.

391 The concept of dignity can be developed to require respect for all sentient beings with the capacity to flourish; the theory recognises the variable nature of the good for diverse beings, requiring that their fundamental interests be protected through fundamental rights: D Bilchitz 'Moving beyond arbitrariness: The legal personhood and dignity of non-human animals' (2009) 25 *South African Journal on Human Rights* 38 at 40. David Bilchitz expanded a theory of value known as the capabilities ap-proach expounded by Amartya Sen and Martha Nussbaum; value in an individual

saw strict contract rules as impeding free will.[392] He cited Davis J, who raised the issue of reciprocal respect for each other:[393]

> '... Parties to a contract must adhere to a minimum threshold of mutual respect in which the "unreasonable and one-sided promotion of one's own interest at the expense of the other infringes the principle of good faith to such a degree as to outweigh the public interest in the sanctity of contracts".'

As Sachs J expounded in *Harksen v Lane*, even in marriage each partner preserves their own identity and personal dignity.[394] O'Regan J advocated harmonious interaction between the individual and society in *Bernstein v Bester*.[395] General assumptions about people's roles in society deny the

life is to be understood in terms of functionings and capabilities: above, 62. It requires respect for those without full autonomy, such as children, the senile and the mentally incompetent, the value of particular functionings and capabilities being determined according to what enables each individual to flourish as the kind of being that it is: above, 63. Bilchitz examines and dismisses as inadequate theories based on personhood, or on human dignity viewed from the perspective of category or the capacity for rational thought and autonomy promoted by Kant: above, 41 - 43, 52 - 56. He rejects rationales from marginal cases such as general capacity, partial autonomy, or social obligation: above, 58 - 60.

On Sen and Nussbaum's capabilities approach, see Ackermann *Human dignity: Lodestar for equality in South Africa* (n 21 above) 70 - 74.

392 'Freedom of contract has been said to lie at the heart of constitutionally prized values of dignity and autonomy. Yet the evolution of contract law suggests that the notion of sanctity of contract has been used to undermine rather than reinforce true volition.': n 390 above, [150] (footnote omitted).

Lewis criticised Sachs J for encroaching on the separation of powers by, in effect, drafting legislation without sufficient evidence on which to assess the facts and develop the law: n 390 above, 451, 458.

393 n 390 above, [140], citing *Mort NO v Henry Shields-Chiat* 2001 1 SA 464 (C) 474J - 475F (references omitted).

394 1998 1 SA 300 (CC) [124]:

> Being trapped in a stereotyped and outdated view of marriage inhibits the capacity for self-realisation of the spouses, affects the quality of their relationship with each other as free and equal persons within the union, and encourages society to look at them not as 'a couple' made up of two persons with independent personalities and shared lives, but as 'a couple' in which each loses his or her individual existence. If this is not a direct invasion of fundamental dignity it is clearly of comparable impact and seriousness.

Dignity can be opened up inwards (relating to the inner mental and emotional world of the person) and outwards (relating to the person's social and relational identity and being): Dupré (n 214 above) 194.

395 1996 2 SA 751 (CC) [150]:

> [H]uman beings live within a society and are dependent upon one another. The conception of freedom underlying the Constitution must embrace that interdependence without denying the value of individual autonomy. It must recognise the important role that the state, and others, will play in seeking to enhance individual autonomy and dignity and the enjoyment of rights and freedoms.

individual's identity. Kriegler J (dissenting) warned about assuming that women are closer than men to their children.[396]

Langa J in *Makwanyane* saw the dual constituents of rights and duties arising out of living in a community:[397]

> [*Ubuntu*] is a culture which places some emphasis on communality and on the interdependence of the members of a community. It recognises a person's status as a human being, entitled to unconditional respect, dignity, value and acceptance from the members of the community such person happens to be part of. It also entails the converse, however. The person has a corresponding duty to give the same respect, dignity, value and acceptance to each member of that community. More importantly, it regulates the exercise of rights by the emphasis it lays on sharing and co-responsibility and the mutual enjoyment of rights by all.

Ackermann J quoted from Kant to illustrate the primacy accorded to freedom, but even Kant accepted that it is limited by the freedom of others.[398]

396 *President of the Republic of South Africa v Hugo* 1997 4 SA 1 (CC) [80] (footnote omitted):

> One of the ways in which one accords equal dignity and respect to persons is by seeking to protect the basic choices they make about their own identities. Reliance on the generalisation that women are the primary care givers is harmful in its tendency to cramp and stunt the efforts of both men and women to form their identities freely.

397 n 146 above, [224]. The Confucian conception of 'human dignity' centres on individual consciousness and respect for every person; with its egalitarian content and recognition of common humanity, it – like *ubuntu* – also gives rise to a corresponding duty to show respect for others: MYK Lee 'Universal human dignity: Some reflections in the Asian context' (2008) 3(1) *Asian Journal of Comparative Law* http://www.bepress.com/asjcl/vol3/iss1/art10/ (accessed 13 April 2010) 19.

Non-Western philosophies – African, Asian and indigenous traditions – lay great emphasis on the obligations/responsibilities of an individual as compared with his or her rights: NMI Goolam 'Human dignity – Our supreme constitutional value' (2001) 4 *Potchefstroom Electronic Law Journal* 1 at 5. Nazeem Goolam considers that since every human being has a responsibility to treat every other human being in a dignified and humane manner, human dignity is a universal human duty: above, 4.

398 *Ferreira* (n 384 above) [52], citing Kant *The metaphysical elements of justice* trans J Ladd (1985) 43:

> Kant conceptualises freedom as the 'only one innate right' in the following terms:
>
> 'Freedom (independence from the constraint of another's will), insofar as it is compatible with the freedom of everyone else in accordance with a universal law, is the one sole and original right that belongs to every human being by virtue of his humanity.'

On the Constitutional Court's understanding of dignity in Kantian terms, see Ackermann *Human dignity: Lodestar for equality in South Africa* (n 21 above) 99 - 102.

As Mahomed J expressed eloquently in *Makwanyane*, reciprocal love for each other enriches not just the lover and the beloved, but wider society as well:[399]

> 'The need for *ubuntu*' [in the postamble to the interim Constitution] expresses the ethos of an instinctive capacity for and enjoyment of love towards our fellow men and women; the joy and the fulfilment involved in recognizing their innate humanity; the reciprocity this generates in interaction within the collective community; the richness of the creative emotions which it engenders and the moral energies which it releases both in the givers and the society which they serve and are served by.

Mokgoro J encapsulated the multi-factorial nature of communication and its importance for dignity:[400]

> ... freedom of speech is a *sine qua non* for every person's right to realise her or his full potential as a human being, free of the imposition of heteronomous power. Viewed in that light, the right to receive others' expressions has more than merely instrumental utility, as a predicate for the addressee's meaningful exercise of her or his own rights of free expression. It is also foundational to each individual's empowerment to autonomous self-development.

O'Regan J illustrated a broad embrace of cultural diversity:[401]

> With human dignity as the lodestar, it becomes clear that treating people as worthy of equal respect in relation to their cultural practices requires more than mere tolerance of sincerely held beliefs with regard to cultural practices.

She understood that 'an approach to cultural rights in our Constitution must be based on the value of human dignity which means that we value cultural

399 n 146 above, [263]. Tabaro J of the Ugandan Constitutional Court stated that *ubuntu* is a concept embraced by all the communities of Uganda; he agreed with Madala J's view of it in *Makwanyane* as being associated with humaneness, social justice and fairness, and permeating fundamental human rights; he also referred with approval to Langa J's conclusion in *Makwanyane* that the concept carries with it the idea of human dignity and true humanity: *Abuki v AG* [1997] UGCC 5 at 9.

400 *Case v Minister of Safety and Security* 1996 3 SA 617 (CC) [26] (footnote omitted).

401 *MEC for Education: KwaZulu-Natal v Pillay* 2008 1 SA 474 (CC) [156].

practices because they afford individuals the possibility and choice to live a meaningful life.'[402]

One's religion is a central aspect of dignity, according to Ngcobo J in dissent in *Prince II*:[403]

> There can be no doubt that the existence of the law which effectively punishes the practice of the Rastafari religion degrades and devalues the followers of the Rastafari religion in our society. It is a palpable invasion of their dignity. It strikes at the very core of their human dignity. It says that their religion is not worthy of protection. The impact of the limitation is profound indeed.

Therefore respect for the beliefs of others and facilitation of the practice of their beliefs is necessary.[404] The majority in *Prince II* approved of Sachs J's contextual approach in *Christian Education* instead of the use of different levels of scrutiny.[405] All the judges in *Prince II* applied the balancing test, but ended up giving different weights to the relevant factors.[406] They all accepted that freedom of religion was infringed, but there was disagreement over whether a workable exception could be framed and policed. Sachs J (dissenting) expanded on the meaning of a contextual balancing exercise and focused on the effect on people:[407]

> The balancing has always to be done in the context of a lived and experienced historical, sociological and imaginative reality. Even if for purposes of making its judgment the Court is obliged to classify issues in

402 *Pillay* (n 401 above) [157]. Steven Rockefeller advocated expanding the politics and ethics of equal dignity so that respect for the individual was understood to involve not only respect for the universal human potential in every person, but also respect for the intrinsic value of the different cultural forms in and through which individuals actualise their humanity and express their unique personalities: SC Rockefeller 'Comment' in C Taylor *et al*, *Multiculturalism: Examining the politics of recognition* (1994) 87.

403 *Prince v President of the Law Society of the Cape of Good Hope* 2002 2 SA 794 (CC) [51] (footnote omitted). On the *Prince* litigation, see L du Plessis 'Affirmation and celebration of the "religious Other" in South Africa's constitutional jurisprudence on religious and related rights: Memorial constitutionalism in action?' (2008) 8 *African Human Rights Law Journal* 376 at 388 - 390; Kende (n 328 above) 229 - 236.

404 On dignity and freedom-of-religion litigation, see C McCrudden 'Multiculturalism, freedom of religion, equality, and the British constitution: The *JFS* case considered' (2011) 9 *International Journal of Constitutional Law* 200 at 221 - 226.

405 n 403 above, [128], citing *Christian Education South Africa v Minister of Education* 2000 4 SA 757 (CC) [30].

406 Sachs (n 82 above) 209.

407 n 403 above, [151].

> conceptual terms and abstract itself from such reality, it functions with materials drawn from that reality and has to take account of the impact of its judgments on persons living within that reality. Moreover, the Court itself is part of that reality and must engage in a complex process of simultaneously detaching itself from and engaging with it. I believe that in the present matter, history, imagination and mind-set play a particularly significant role, especially with regard to the weight to be given to the various factors in the scales.

The balancing of freedom of religion against the public interest in curbing drug use was a particularly difficult task in *Prince II*, where the majority held that the banning of cannabis was justified even though Rastafarians wished to use it for religious purposes. The dilemma for society where religion collides with other community goals is evident in another passage from Sachs J's minority judgment in which he strived to show how reconciliation between apparently conflicting interests could satisfy religious beliefs while benefiting all living in a receptive tolerant community:[408]

> [N]o amount of formal constitutional analysis can in itself resolve the problem of balancing matters of faith against matters of public interest. Yet faith and public interest overlap and intertwine in the need to protect tolerance as a constitutional virtue and respect for diversity and openness as a constitutional principle. Religious tolerance is accordingly not only important to those individuals who are saved from having to make excruciating choices between their beliefs and the law. It is deeply meaningful to all of us because religion and belief matter, and because living in an open society matters.

There can also be a dilemma for the judiciary to ensure respect for the separation of powers while upholding constitutional values, as mentioned by Sachs J after he distinguished the South African accommodation of minority religions from the position in the US:[409]

> [L]imitations analysis under section 36 is antithetical to extreme positions which end up setting the irresistible force of democracy and general law enforcement, against the immovable object of constitutionalism and protection of fundamental rights. What it requires is the maximum

408 n 403 above, [170]
409 n 403 above, [155]

> harmonisation of all the competing considerations, on a principled yet nuanced and flexible case-by-case basis, located in South African reality yet guided by international experience, articulated with appropriate candour and accomplished without losing sight of the ultimate values highlighted by our Constitution. In achieving this balance, this Court may frequently find itself faced with complex problems as to what properly belongs to the discretionary sphere which the Constitution allocates to the legislature and the executive, and what falls squarely to be determined by the judiciary.

The Court used less restrictive means arguments in its reasoning.[410] The UN Human Rights Committee found that there was no breach of the International Covenant on Civil and Political Rights.[411]

Understanding that dignity can be infringed by dehumanising behaviour, treating people as objects or instruments, stigmatising them and stereotyping individuals, Chaskalson P invoked US case-law on the dehumanising effect of capital punishment:[412]

> It degrades and dehumanizes all who participate in its processes. It is unnecessary to any legitimate goal of the state and is incompatible with the dignity of man and the judicial process.

Excessive punishment as a deterrent offends dignity, according to Sachs J in *Mohunram v National DPP*.[413] Kentridge AJ, quoting Dickson CJC, upheld the presumption of innocence as essential to dignity in order to avoid the stigma of being prematurely branded a criminal.[414]

410 E Brems 'Human rights: Minimum and maximum perspectives' (2009) 9 *Human Rights Law Review* 349 at 361.

411 *Prince v South Africa* UNHR Committee (14 November 2007) 91st Session UN Doc CCPR/C/91/D/1474/2006; International Covenant on Civil and Political Rights (adopted 16 December 1966, entered into force 23 March 1976) 999 UNTS 171.

412 *Makwanyane* (n 146 above) above, [91], citing *People v Anderson*, 493 P2d 880 (Cal 1972) 899.

413 2007 4 SA 222 (CC) [146]:

> Deterrence as a law enforcement objective is constrained by the principle that individuals may not be used in an instrumental manner as examples to others if the deterrence is set at levels beyond what is fair and just to those individuals. To do otherwise would be to breach the constitutional principle of dignity.

414 *S v Zuma* 1995 2 SA 642 (CC) [22], citing *R v Oakes* (1986) 26 DLR (4th) 200 at 212 - 213 (Supreme Court of Canada):

> 'The presumption of innocence protects the fundamental liberty and human dignity of any and every person accused by the State of criminal conduct. An individual

The traditional South African concept of *ubuntu* promotes the goal of harmonious communal living, while at the same time recognising each participant's right to respect.[415] We find here the notion and expression of interdependence with benefits accruing to the individual from the community spirit.[416] The intrinsic worth of an individual, and the freedom to develop and maintain an identity, lead to a person having an interest in their reputation in the community.[417] O'Regan J captured the dual interest in reputation:[418]

> The value of human dignity in our Constitution is not only concerned with an individual's sense of self-worth, but constitutes an affirmation of the worth of human beings in our society. It includes the intrinsic worth of human beings shared by all people as well as the individual reputation of each person built upon his or her own individual achievements. The

charged with a criminal offence faces grave social and personal consequences, including potential loss of physical liberty, subjection to social stigma and ostracism from the community, as well as other social, psychological and economic harms. In light of the gravity of these consequences, the presumption of innocence is crucial. ...'

415 *Ubuntu* has resonances of Confucianism, where harmony involves physical and psychological balance, and also a balanced, mutual connectedness among all things in the cosmos; harmony is not uniformity, but means recognising an organic inter-connectedness based in our complementary differences rather than seeing all as equivalent in value: SC Angle 'Human rights and harmony' (2008) 30 *Human Rights Quarterly* 76 at 79. On the concept of *ubuntu*, see Ackermann *Human dignity: Lodestar for equality in South Africa* (n 21 above) 111 - 115; JD Bessler 'In the spirit of *ubuntu*: Enforcing the rights of orphans and vulnerable children affected by HIV/AIDS in South Africa' (2008) 31 *Hastings International and Comparative Law Review* 33 at 41 - 46; Botha (n 178 above) 204 - 205.

416 As Langa CJ amplified in *Pillay* (n 401 above) [53] (footnotes omitted):

> The notion that 'we are not islands unto ourselves' is central to the understanding of the individual in African thought. It is often expressed in the phrase *umuntu ngumuntu ngabantu* which emphasises 'communality and the inter-dependence of the members of a community' and that every individual is an extension of others. According to Gyekye, 'an individual human person cannot develop and achieve the fullness of his/her potential without the concrete act of relating to other individual persons'. This thinking emphasises the importance of community to individual identity and hence to human dignity. Dignity and identity are inseparably linked as one's sense of self-worth is defined by one's identity. Cultural identity is one of the most important parts of a person's identity precisely because it flows from belonging to a community and not from personal choice or achievement.

A similar situation exists in Germany where the individual is not seen as a lone rights-bearer, but is a free person in a social federal state in which people are in-terdependent without encroaching on each other's intrinsic value: LAA Pagán 'Human dignity, privacy and personality rights in the constitutional jurisprudence of Germany, the United States and the Commonwealth of Puerto Rico' (1998) 67 *Revista Juridica de la Universidad de Puerto Rico* 343 at 348.

417 See *Masetlha v President of the Republic of South Africa* [2007] ZACC 20, 2008 1 SA 566 (CC) [98].

418 *Khumalo v Holomisa* 2002 5 SA 401 (CC) [27].

> value of human dignity in our Constitution therefore values both the personal sense of self-worth as well as the public's estimation of the worth or value of an individual.

According to Sachs J, the apartheid system itself clearly debased the oppressed, but it also infringed the dignity of the oppressors.[419] O'Regan J pointed out that tolerance is inexorably associated with free speech,[420] thus allowing room for dissenters as society develops an associative culture.

These examples from South African jurisprudence illustrate the abundance of philosophical analysis underpinning decisions. The judges consistently display an acute awareness of the constitutional values that have a transformative aim rooted in an abhorrence of the previous inhumane apartheid system. They know it is their duty to analyse and translate the Constitution into legally enforceable concepts, and base their judgments on normatively sound rationalised principles.

3.2.4.2 Human dignity and substantive rights

As well as being a unique right in Section 10, dignity has a pre-eminent place in the Bill of Rights, as one of the three democratic values affirmed by the Bill, the other two being equality and freedom.[421] These same values govern the limitation of rights[422] and must be promoted in the interpretation of the

419 *Minister of Finance v Van Heerden* 2004 6 SA 121 (CC) [145]:

> [T]he system of state-sponsored racial domination not only imposed injustice and indignity on those oppressed by it, it tainted the whole of society and dishonoured those who benefited from it. Correcting the resultant injustices, though potentially disconcerting for those who might be dislodged from the established expectations and relative comfort of built-in advantage, is integral to restoring dignity to our country as a whole.

420 *South African National Defence Union v Minister of Defence* 1999 4 SA 469 (CC) *(SANDU)* [8]:

> [Freedom of expression] is closely related to freedom of religion, belief and opinion (section 15), the right to dignity (section 10), as well as the right to freedom of association (section 18), the right to vote and to stand for public office (section 19) and the right to assembly (section 17). These rights taken together protect the rights of individuals not only individually to form and express opinions, of whatever nature, but to establish associations and groups of like-minded people to foster and propagate such opinions. The rights implicitly recognise the importance, both for a democratic society and for individuals personally, of the ability to form and express opinions, whether individually or collectively, even where those views are con-troversial. The corollary of the freedom of expression and its related rights is tolerance by society of different views.

421 Sec 7(1).

422 Sec 36(1).

Bill.[423] By Section 35(2)(e) every detained person has the right to conditions compatible with dignity while in custody.

The right of everyone to have their inherent dignity respected and protected in Section 10 is broadly framed and, as George Devenish says, covers a wide range of circumstances which could constitute a violation of dignity involving not just the liberal democratic rights, but conceivably 'freedom from poverty and disease and a clean and healthy environment in which life is tolerable.'[424] Accordingly it has a significant socio-economic aspect.[425] It may be limited, although in a circuitous fashion – in common with all other rights – the extent of the limitation is itself restricted by the foundational values including human dignity.[426] The rights to dignity and to life[427] are the only rights that are completely immune from derogation in times of emergency.[428] Chaskalson P described their pre-eminent position in *Makwanyane*:[429]

423 Sec 39(1).

424 n 200 above, 83. According to the Kenyan High Court, which interpreted the right to life as including the activity of living in some environment, '[t]he right to a clean environment is primary to all creatures including man, it is inherent from the act of creation': *Waweru v Republic* [2006] eKLR (High Court of Kenya, 2 March 2006) 7. The Court referred to the link in the UN Stockholm Declaration between freedom, equality, and a life of dignity and well-being: above, 11, citing UN Conference on the Human Environment 'Stockholm Declaration' (16 June 1972) UN Doc A/Conf.48/ 14/Rev 1(1973), Principle 1. It took into account the rights of all in society to a clean environment, thus evoking the issue of enviromental justice, and, even though the state authorities had failed to provide safe sewerage treatment works, the Court emphasised the continuous need for traders to accept responsibility and not to commit environmental crimes, which ought to be severely punished: *Waweru v Republic* [2006] eKLR (High Court of Kenya, 2 March 2006) 7, 11 - 12, 14. Sustainable development had a cost element to be met by the developers: above, 6.

In a later majority judgment, the Court confirmed the derivation from the right to life of 'a right to a clean and healthy environment free from pollution of any kind that is detrimental to human health, wealth and/or socio-economic well being and ultimately the human life': *Nabori v AG* [2007] eKLR (High Court of Kenya, 11 December 2007) 126. Having stated that the right to life included the right to live with human dignity, Rawal J continued, '[t]aking any lesser interpretation will be an affront to the dignity of human life and any hindrance or limitation to enjoy the right to live would be derogation of the most fundamental right of any human being': above, 114.

425 n 200 above, 83. The Nigerian High Court held that gas flaring in the course of oil extraction was a gross violation of the fundamental right to life (including healthy environment) and dignity, and that legislation allowing it was unconstitutional: *Gbemre v Shell Petroleum Development Co Nigeria Ltd* [2005] AHRLR 151 (NgHC 2005) [5], citing Constitution of the Federal Republic of Nigeria 1999, Secs 33(1) & 34(1).

426 Sec 36(1). See Rautenbach (n 2 above) 338 - 340.

427 Sec 11.

428 Sec 37(5)(c).

429 n 146 above, [144].

> The rights to life and dignity are the most important of all human rights, and the source of all other personal rights.... By committing ourselves to a society founded on the recognition of human rights we are required to value these two rights above all others.

The reference to 'inherent dignity' in Section 10 acknowledges that it is an innate quality in everyone not dependent on being endowed by the state. The content of human dignity is not set out in the Constitution. Its essence is wider than the more technical meaning in Roman-Dutch law, where it was equated with the conceptually limited term of 'self-esteem' and its infraction invariably involved insult.[430] In any event the tort action for breach of *dignitas* was recognised only in the private law sphere and did not affect the state.[431]

Ackermann J set out the minimum import of dignity in the *Sodomy* case:[432]

> Dignity is a difficult concept to capture in precise terms. At its least, it is clear that the constitutional protection of dignity requires us to acknowledge the value and worth of all individuals as members of our society.

Currie and de Waal describe it as 'the source of a person's innate rights to freedom and to physical integrity, from which a number of other rights flow.'[433] As a value, it 'provides the basis for the right to equality – inasmuch as every person possesses human dignity in equal measure everyone must be treated as equally worthy of respect.'[434] Currie and de Waal explain its place as a right thus:[435]

> As a fundamental right, it has a residual function. It applies where many of the more specific rights that give effect to the value of human dignity,

430 Devenish (n 200 above) 84.

431 IJ Kroeze 'Human dignity in constitutional law in South Africa' in European Commission for Democracy through Law, *The Principle of Respect for Human Dignity* (Proceedings of the UniDem Seminar, Montpellier, 2 - 6 July 1998) http://www.venice.coe.int/webforms/documents/CDL-STD%281998%29026-e.aspx#P1070_198886 (accessed 24 September 2013).

432 n 364 above, [28] (footnote omitted).

433 n 4 above, 273 (footnote omitted).

434 As above.

435 n 4 above, 275 (footnotes omitted).

> do not. In addition, since the rights in the Bill of Rights stem from dignity and are more detailed elaborations of aspects of the concept, the core right to dignity has decisive application only relatively infrequently.

Dignity is referred to in the Constitution in other contexts apart from as an underlying value and in connection with substantive rights.[436]

436 Organs of state are obliged to assist and protect the dignity, first, of the courts: Sec 165(4); second, of the institutions of Public Protector, the South African Human Rights Commission, the Commission for the Promotion and Protection of the Rights of Cultural, Religious and Linguistic Communities, the Commission for Gender Equality, the Auditor-General, the Electoral Commission: Sec 181(3); and, third, the Public Service Commission: Sec 196(3).

Ministers, Deputy Ministers, Premiers, Acting Premiers and members of provincial Executive Councils swear or affirm to uphold their office with honour and dignity: Sch 2, Secs 3 & 5.

4

Right to Dignity and Idea of Equal Respect

As the value of human dignity supports many constitutional rights,[1] the Constitutional Court frequently bases its decisions on a right other than that to dignity in Section 10. In those circumstances, there is no need to consider the right to dignity as the *ratio decidendi*. O'Regan J in *Dawood* revealed the multiple significant roles of dignity resulting in the right to dignity itself often playing a secondary part.[2]

Even though constitutional rights overlap to a great extent, each right is considered individually. In a minority judgment in *S v Jordan*, Sachs and O'Regan JJ refused to recognise a right to autonomy not specifically mentioned in the Constitution, remarked that it was not useful to amalgamate

1 See *Alexander v Minister of Justice* [2010] NASC 2 (SC of Namibia) [99]-[101].

2 *Dawood v Minister of Home Affairs* 2000 3 SA 936 (CC) [35] (footnotes omitted):

> The value of dignity in our Constitutional framework cannot therefore be doubted. The Constitution asserts dignity to contradict our past in which human dignity for black South Africans was routinely and cruelly denied. It asserts it too to inform the future, to invest in our democracy respect for the intrinsic worth of all human beings. Human dignity therefore informs constitutional adjudication and interpretation at a range of levels. It is a value that informs the interpretation of many, possibly all, other rights. This Court has already acknowledged the importance of the constitutional value of dignity in interpreting rights such as the right to equality, the right not to be punished in a cruel, inhuman or degrading way, and the right to life. Human dignity is also a constitutional value that is of central significance in the limitations analysis. Section 10, however, makes it plain that dignity is not only a *value* fundamental to our Constitution, it is a justiciable and enforceable *right* that must be respected and protected. In many cases, however, where the value of human dignity is offended, the primary constitutional breach occasioned may be of a more specific right such as the right to bodily integrity, the right to equality or the right not to be subjected to slavery, servitude or forced labour.

rights to create a new right and went on to consider in turn each right allegedly breached.[3] The right to dignity has a pre-eminent place on a par with the right to life. O'Regan J in *Makwanyane* noted their interlinked nature.[4] She founded the right to dignity and to be treated with respect on the intrinsic worth of the individual.[5]

The Constitutional Court made it clear in *Mohamed v President of the Republic of South Africa* that the right to dignity is one of three rights not subject to being curtailed even when there are weighty countervailing demands.[6] While the Court did not decide on the issue, it raised the notion of non-waiver of the right to dignity.[7]

3 2002 6 SA 642 [53]:

> While we accept that there is manifest overlap between the rights to dignity, freedom and privacy, and each reinforces the other, we do not believe that it is useful for the purposes of constitutional analysis to posit an independent right to autonomy. There can be no doubt that the ambit of each of the protected rights is to be determined in part by the underlying purport and values of the Bill of Rights as a whole and that the rights intersect and overlap one another. It does not follow from this however that it is appropriate to base our constitutional analysis on a right not expressly included within the Constitution.

4 *S v Makwanyane* 1995 6 BCLR 665 (CC) [326]-[327]:

> [T]he right to life was included in the Constitution not simply to enshrine the right to existence. It is not life as mere organic matter that the Constitution cherishes, but the right to human life: the right to live as a human being, to be part of a broader community, to share in the experience of humanity. This concept of human life is at the centre of our constitutional values. The constitution seeks to establish a society where the individual value of each member of the community is recognised and treasured. The right to life is central to such a society.
>
> The right to life, thus understood, incorporates the right to dignity. So the rights to human dignity and life are entwined. The right to life is more than existence, it is a right to be treated as a human being with dignity: without dignity, human life is substantially diminished. Without life, there cannot be dignity.

Likewise the Inter-American Court has interpreted the right to life as including the right to live a dignified existence: *Indigenous Community of Yakye Axa v Paraguay* Series C 125 [2005] IACHR 6 [161], citing *Children's Rehabilitation v Paraguay* Series C 112 [2004] IACHR 8 [156]. See JM Pasqualucci 'The evolution of international indigenous rights in the Inter-American human rights system' (2006) 6 *Human Rights Law Review* 281 at 310.

5 'Recognising a right to dignity is an acknowledgement of the intrinsic worth of human beings: human beings are entitled to be treated as worthy of respect and concern.': n 4 above, [328] (footnote omitted). See IM Rautenbach *Rautenbach-Malherbe constitutional law* (2012) 333 - 337.

6 '[O]ur Constitution sets different standards for protecting the right to life, to human dignity and the right not to be treated or punished in a cruel, inhuman or degrading way. Under our Constitution these rights are not qualified by other principles of justice.': 2001 3 SA 893 (CC) [53].

7 *Mohamed* (n 6 above) fn 55. Erasmus J in the Western Cape High Court, Cape Town, found that a collective agreement cannot amount to a waiver of individual fundamental

4.1 Equal respect

The idea of equal respect was the basis of the decision in the *Sodomy* case, where the Constitutional Court found that the criminalisation of sodomy violated the right to dignity.[8] Having identified the offence as punishment of a form of sexual conduct associated with homosexuals, Ackermann J focused on the law's degradation and devaluation of gay men.[9] Sachs J distinguished breach of the right to dignity from violation of dignity and self-worth under the equality provisions.[10] The right to dignity has a broader brush than

rights to dignity and privacy: *Beja v Premier of the Western Cape* [2011] ZAWCHC 97 [101]. He held that the City of Cape Town in providing unenclosed toilets violated Sections 10 (human dignity), 12 (bodily and psychological integrity), 14 (privacy), 24 (environment), 26 (housing) and 27 (healthcare) of the Constitution: above, [150]. He ordered that the toilets be enclosed: above, [192].

8 I Currie & J de Waal *The Bill of Rights handbook* (2005) 274. The idea of equal re-spect could be said to have originated with Rousseau, who deemed it indispensible for freedom; he considered that the balanced reciprocity that underpins equality is the ideal in a republic; thus the age of dignity was born: C Taylor 'The politics of recognition' in C Taylor *et al*, *Multiculturalism: Examining the politics of recognition* (1994) 45 - 49. On human dignity and equal respect, see J Habermas 'The concept of human dignity and the realistic utopia of human rights' (2010) 41 *Metaphilosophy* 464 at 469 - 470, 472.

9 *National Coalition for Gay and Lesbian Equality v Minister of Justice* 1998 12 BCLR 1517 (*Sodomy* case) [28]:

> Its symbolic effect is to state that in the eyes of our legal system all gay men are criminals. The stigma thus attached to a significant proportion of our population is manifest. But the harm imposed by the criminal law is far more than symbolic. As a result of the criminal offence, gay men are at risk of arrest, prosecution and conviction of the offence of sodomy simply because they seek to engage in sexual conduct which is part of their experience of being human. Just as apartheid legislation rendered the lives of couples of different racial groups perpetually at risk, the sodomy offence builds insecurity and vulnerability into the daily lives of gay men. There can be no doubt that the existence of a law which punishes a form of sexual expression for gay men degrades and devalues gay men in our broader society. As such it is a palpable invasion of their dignity… .

10 n 9 above, [124]:

> The violation of dignity under section 10, on the other hand, contemplates a much wider range of situations. It offers protection to persons in their multiple identities and capacities. This could be to individuals being disrespectfully treated, such as somebody being stopped at a roadblock. It also could be to members of groups subject to systemic disadvantage, such as farm workers in certain areas, or prisoners in certain prisons, such groups not being identified because of closely held characteristics, but because of the situation they find themselves in. These would be cases of indignity of treatment leading to inequality, rather than of inequality relating to closely held group characteristics producing indignity.

equality and protects individuals in circumstances where they are not respected.[11]

Equal respect was also lacking in *Nyathi* and led to a finding of infringement of the equality and dignity guarantees.[12] Mr Nyathi had been awarded compensation against the State for medical negligence, but the State failed to pay the amount due. He was precluded by statute from enforcing the debt against the State and, unfortunately, he died before his challenge to the constitutionality of the legislation could be heard. In a majority decision, the Constitutional Court held that his rights to equal protection of the law in Section 9(1) of the Constitution, to protection of dignity under Section 10, and to access to courts in Section 34 had been breached. Madala J considered that his worth as a person had not been recognised.[13] The State had a particular duty to respect people and there was added insult because of its involvement.[14]

4.2 Punishment

In *S v Williams* juvenile whipping was held to be a contravention of the right to dignity in Section 10 and of the prohibition on cruel, inhuman or degrading

11 Disadvantage is relevant to the equality enquiry because of its connection with dignity – not for its own sake: E Grant 'Dignity and equality' (2007) 7 *Human Rights Law Review* 299 at 321.

12 *Nyathi v MEC for the Department of Health, Gauteng* 2008 5 SA 94 (CC).

13 n 12 above, [45] (footnote omitted):

> The right to dignity entails the right to have one's dignity respected and protected. The circumstances of this case show the potential that section 3 [State Liability Act 1957] has for the limitation of the right to dignity. The applicant was made to wait for an extremely long time for money required to pay for his treatment. Without the rehabilitative treatment, he stood a very slim chance of survival. The state was made fully aware of this very desperate situation but provided no relief. He was then unable to attach state assets due to the operation of section 3. It certainly cannot be said, in these circumstances, that the applicant was treated in a manner that showed recognition for his worth and importance as a human being.

14 n 12 above, [89]:

> In a state that has pledged itself to redeem the dignity of its citizens, it should not be the state itself that tramples on the rights of its citizens. On the contrary, everyone should be working tirelessly to protect and promote that dignity, it being accepted that we are dealing with a majority of previously disadvantaged persons.

treatment or punishment in Section 11(2) of the interim Constitution.[15] Apart from the physical aspect, the treatment of an individual – no matter how despicable – as an object violated dignity.[16] Langa J invoked foreign case-law[17] to this effect:[18]

> In *Furman v Georgia,* Brennan J postulated criteria in the assessment of what amounts to cruel and unusual punishment. He pointed out that punishment does not become 'cruel and unusual' merely because of the pain inflicted. The true significance lay in the fact that members of the human race are treated:

15 1995 3 SA 632 (CC). Over the previous 30 years at least, South African jurisprudence had experienced a growing unanimity in judicial condemnation of corporal punishment for adults, with consistent and emphatic criticism of the practice, it being characterised as 'punishment of a particularly severe kind … brutal in its nature … a severe assault upon not only the person of the recipient but upon his dignity as a human being': above, [11], citing Fannin J in *S v Kumalo* 1965 4 SA 565 (N) 574F. It was also called 'a very severe and humiliating form of punishment': above, [11], citing De Wet CJ in *S v Myute* 1985 2 SA 61 (Ck) 62H.

16 As Richard Stith said '[w]e do not entirely lose our active potential for virtue even by habituation to vice': R Stith 'The priority of respect: How our common humanity can ground our individual dignity' (2004) 44 *International Philosophical Quarterly* 165 at 182.

17 He mentioned a case from Lesotho, where the court imposed restrictions on the whipping of people aged over 30 years: n 15 above, [40], citing *R v Tsehlana* Rev Case 157/77 (HC), cited in SC Neff 'Human rights in Africa: Thoughts on the African Charter on Human and Peoples' Rights in the light of case law from Botswana, Lesotho and Swaziland' (1984) 33 *International and Comparative Law Quarterly* 331 at 339. Aguda JA in Botswana had recognised that certain types of punishment or treatment were 'by their very nature cruel, inhuman or degrading' and also that a punishment not inherently inhuman or degrading might become so 'by the very nature or mode of execution' notwithstanding the fact that popular demand might favour it: *Williams* (n 15 above) [40], citing *S v Petrus* [1985] LRC (Const) 699 at 725G - 726A. See W Binchy 'Dignity as a core constitutional concept' in E Quansah & W Binchy (eds) *The judicial protection of human rights in Botswana* (2009) 181 - 183. On *Petrus*, see: Hon Justice K Dingake 'Expanding the frontiers of fundamental human rights: Judicial protection of human rights in Botswana' in Quansah & Binchy above, 47 - 50; Hon Justice O Tshosa 'Judicial protection of human rights in Botswana and the role of international human rights law' in Quansah & Binchy above, 84 - 85.

Stephen Neff's research showed that the Swaziland courts had been particularly active in imposing restrictions on the use of corporal punishment; in 1978 the High Court there had noted the prevailing opinion among criminologists around the world that the punishment of whipping very rarely, if ever, had any beneficial result and that consequently it should be used only in very exceptional circumstances: Neff above, 339, citing *Kunene v R* CRI Case No 112/78 (HC). In another case it was held that the number of strokes given for an offence should not ordinarily exceed six: Neff above, 339, citing *R v Zwane* CRI Case No 8/73 (HC). A third case held that strokes are never an appropriate punishment for a minor traffic offence: Neff above, 339, citing *R v Nkambule* CRI Case No 21/81 (HC).

18 n 15 above, [28], citing 408 US 238 (1972) 273. The latter case held that capital punishment in Georgia was unconstitutional.

> '... as nonhumans, as objects to be toyed with and discarded ... [and that this is] ... thus inconsistent with the fundamental premise of the Clause that even the vilest criminal remains a human being possessed of common human dignity.'

'The dignity of man' is the basic concept underlying the prohibition in the United States on cruel and unusual punishment.[19] In *Trop v Dulles* Chief Justice Warren pointed out that the policy underlying the prohibition was firmly based in the Anglo-American tradition as far back as the Magna Carta and the phraseology was taken from the English Declaration of Rights 1688.[20] The purpose of the prohibition was to ensure that the State exercised its power to punish within the limits of civilised standards.[21] As identified by Justice Brennan in *Furman v Georgia*, the four fundamental principles to be applied cumulatively to assess whether a sanction is precluded as uncivilised and inhuman, are primarily that the punishment is severe enough to be degrading to dignity, and that it is arbitrary, unacceptable to contemporary society and excessive.[22] When referring to the struggle in the US to balance the desire for retribution[23] against the belief in the equal value of individuals, Justice Brennan described 'the dignity of the individual' as society's 'supreme value'.[24]

The disagreement in US society over whether retribution is an acceptable objective in imposing punishment was reflected by the judges in *Gregg v*

19 *Trop v Dulles* 356 US 86 (1958) 100; *Gregg v Georgia* 428 US 153 (1976) 173. Although law punishes, we deploy modes of punishment that do not destroy the dignity of those on whom it is being administered; respect for the individual's dignity requires that any punishment inflicted should be bearable: J Waldron *Dignity, rank, and rights* (2012) 64. Jeremy Waldron pointed out that punishment should be 'something that a person can endure, without abandoning his or her elementary human functioning' and as he said '[o]ne ought to be able to do one's time, take one's licks, while remaining upright and self-possessed.': as above.

20 n 19 above, 100.

21 As above.

22 n 18 above, 281. For a review of *Furman*, see G Kateb *Human dignity* (2011) 14 - 16; MS Kende *Constitutional rights in two worlds: South Africa and the United States* (2009) 75 - 77.

23 Tabaro J of the Ugandan Constitutional Court considered retribution 'base and sordid' and 'only a euphemism for a primitive instinct in men to revenge whenever wronged', while revenge even in the form of the cruellest of punishments had no demonstrable deterrent effect: *Abuki v AG* [1997] UGCC 5 at 9.

24 n 18 above, 296. See also LM Henry 'The jurisprudence of dignity' (2011) 160 *University of Pennsylvania Law Review* 169 at 171.

Georgia,[25] where the Supreme Court in a majority decision upheld the constitutionality of death penalty legislation introduced in Georgia containing safeguards on the lines outlined in *Furman v Georgia*.[26] Justice Stewart accepted that retribution was no longer the dominant objective in punishment, but neither was it forbidden nor inconsistent with dignity.[27] His endorsement of retention of the death penalty brought into the equation the dignity of the victim and society's interest in deterrence, which could prevail in extenuating circumstances over the dignity of the offender.[28] Justice Brennan in dissent adhered to his stance against the death penalty *per se* and emphasised that foremost among the 'moral concepts' recognised in the US was 'the primary moral principle that the State, even as it punishes, must treat its citizens in a manner consistent with their intrinsic worth as human beings – a punishment must not be so severe as to be degrading to human dignity.'[29]

Retribution as a punitive objective was held by the majority of the US Supreme Court to be inappropriate for the mentally retarded in *Atkins v Virginia* and it held that executions of mentally retarded criminals was a

25 n 19 above. See Kende (n 22 above) 77 - 78.

26 While in the US the death penalty is under dispute but is not considered *per se* to be an offence against human dignity, in Germany the Basic Law abolished it in the light of the Nazi experience; Ernst Benda noted that historical developments, cultural diversity and a society's principal values help to define the content and borderlines of human dignity; this applies even to societies which share a common cultural and religious heritage, as in the US and Germany: E Benda 'The protection of human dignity (Article 1 of the Basic Law)' (2000) 53 *Southern Methodist University Law Review* 443 at 448 - 449.

27 n 19 above, 183. Helen Knowles identified three main categories of dignity in US Supreme Court death penalty opinions, *viz*, human dignity requiring abolition of the death penalty (dignity without death), human dignity coexisting with a heavily regulated death penalty (dignified coexistence), and state dignity emphasising respect for the dignity of the institutional apparatuses of the state that employs the death penalty (institutionalised dignity): HJ Knowles 'A dialogue on death penalty dignity' (2011) 11 *Criminology and Criminal Justice* 115 at 116 - 117.

28 '[T]he decision that capital punishment may be the appropriate sanction in extreme cases is an expression of the community's belief that certain crimes are themselves so grievous an affront to humanity that the only adequate response may be the penalty of death.': n 19 above, 184.

29 n 19 above, 229. See Justice Brennan's extrajudicial comments on the death penalty: WJ Brennan, Jr 'The Constitution of the United States: Contemporary ratification' (1986) 27 *South Texas Law Review* 433 at 443 - 444. For an assessment of Justice Brennan's stance on the death penalty, see: SJ Wermiel 'Law and human dignity: The judicial soul of Justice Brennan' (1998) 7 *William and Mary Bill of Rights Journal* 223 at 233 - 234.

cruel and unusual punishment.[30] Its focus was on the excessiveness of the punishment which should be graduated and proportionate to the offence judged by the prevailing standards of decency informed by objective factors as far as possible.[31]

Similar to South Africa, the prohibition in the European Convention on Human Rights (ECHR)[32] on degrading punishment is designed to protect dignity and physical and psychological integrity, as enunciated in *Tyrer v UK*, where the European Court of Human Rights condemned judicially-authorised birching of a minor.[33] The majority considered that the absence of publicity was not the central issue, as the victim could be 'humiliated in his own eyes, even if not in the eyes of others'.[34] Fitzmaurice J (dissenting

30 536 US 304 (2002). Justice Stevens cited Chief Justice Warren's explanation in *Trop* of the basic concept underlying the Eighth Amendment's ban on cruel and unusual punishments as being 'nothing less than the dignity of man': above, 311, citing n 19 above, 100. Steven Heyman pointed out that notwithstanding the contrast between the crucial importance accorded to the value of dignity in international human rights law and the tendency to conceive of rights in terms of liberty in American law, dignity is an important theme in US Supreme Court jurisprudence: SJ Heyman *Free speech and human dignity* (2008) 40.

31 Lori Church has criticised the decision on the grounds that the Court 'disregarded precedent, dramatically lowered the bar in determining what constitutes a national consensus, misapplied the objective standards used to determine a national consensus, and caused further non-uniformity in an already complex area of the law': LM Church 'Mandating dignity: The United States Supreme Court's extreme departure from precedent regarding the Eighth Amendment and the death penalty [*Atkins v. Virginia*, 122 S. Court. 2242 (2002)]' (2003) 42 *Washburn Law Journal* 305 at 306.

32 Convention for the Protection of Human Rights and Fundamental Freedoms, 213 UNTS 222 (ECHR).

33 (App no 5856/72) (1979-80) 2 EHRR 1 at 11 [33]:

> [A]lthough the applicant did not suffer any severe or long-lasting physical effects, his punishment – whereby he was treated as an object in the power of the authorities – constituted an assault on precisely that which is the main purpose of Article 3 to protect, namely a person's dignity and physical integrity. Neither can it be excluded that the punishment may have had adverse psychological effects.
>
> The institutionalised character of this violence is further compounded by the whole aura of official procedure attending the punishment and by the fact that those inflicting it were total strangers to the offender.

For reviews of *Tyrer*, see MB Dembour *Who believes in human rights? Reflections on the European Convention* (2006) 170 - 176; JA Frowein 'Human dignity in international law' in D Kretzmer & E Klein (eds) *The concept of human dignity in human rights discourse* (2002) 124.

The African Commission described the application of physical violence for offences as 'tantamount to sanctioning state sponsored torture' when it held that the penalty of lashes breached the African Charter: *Doebbler v Sudan* [2003] AHRLR 153 (ACHPR 2003) [42], citing African Charter on Human and Peoples' Rights (adopted 27 June 1981, entered into force 21 October 1986) (1982) 21 ILM 58 (African Charter) Art 5.

34 n 33 above, 10 [32].

on the main issue) distinguished punishment of a juvenile from that of an adult.[35]

The Supreme Court of Zimbabwe held in *Juvenile v S* that a sentence of corporal punishment on a juvenile was an inhuman and degrading punishment contrary to Section 15(1) of the Constitution.[36] The judges disagreed on the constitutional issue and had various views on whether juvenile corporal punishment was equivalent to adult whipping, whether corporal punishment was inherently degrading, and whether corporal punishment in schools or by parents was degrading. Dumbutshena CJ held that the same considerations should apply to physical chastisement of children by schoolteachers and that even a parent's common law right to spank a child was limited; he cited South African cases where judges showed their abhorence towards judicial corporal punishment – in *S v V en 'n Ander*[37] the Appellate Division had highlighted the increasingly popular view 'that it was undesirable and even ill-advised to couple corporal punishment to a long term of imprisonment because it served no acceptable end' and in *S v November en 'n Ander*,[38] Terbutt J had described corporal punishment as 'a drastic punishment', which was also 'humiliating and demoralising'.[39] Gubbay JA disagreed with Fitzmaurice J's dissenting view in *Tyrer*[40] that there was no difference between 'the caning of errant schoolboys and a judicial caning' and considered instead that the concern was 'not with the gradation of the number of cuts', but 'with the essential nature of the punishment itself'.[41] He went further than the European Court of Human Rights and held that 'judicial whipping, no matter the nature of the instrument used and the manner of execution,' was 'inherently brutal and cruel'; furthermore, it was subject to abuse by those

35 n 33 above, 16 [2]. He thought that most punishment involves a loss of dignity, so an effect on dignity was not coterminous with a finding of degrading punishment: n 33 above, 19 [8]. He disagreed with the majority's reasoning in many respects, including the distinction between institutionalised violence and non-institutionalised violence, the differentiation between being beaten by a stranger and by a person known to the offender, and the attribution of a possible psychological consequence to degrading punishment: n 33 above, 20 - 21 [9]. In his view, a distasteful, undesirable, or morally wrong practice did not necessarily amount to a breach of the prohibition on degrading punishment: n 33 above, 24 [14].

36 [1989] LRC (Const) 774; Constitution of the Republic of Zimbabwe 1979.

37 1989 1 SA 532 (A).

38 1988 1 SA 661 (O) 664 C-D.

39 n 36 above, 784.

40 n 33 above.

41 n 36 above, 794 - 795.

administering it and was 'antiquated' and 'counter-productive'.[42] McNally JA (dissenting on the constitutional issue) thought there was 'a very clear distinction between the corporal punishment of adults and the corporal punishment of juveniles' and associated himself with the minority judgment of Fitzmaurice J in *Tyrer*, being of the view that all punishment, including imprisonment, involves an element of degradation.[43]

Corporal punishment infringes the dignity of the perpetrator as well as that of the offender.[44] State-sanctioned degrading punishment is particularly odious and is likely to lead to a general disregard for dignity.[45]

4.2.1 Corporal punishment of children

Corporal punishment in schools is a contentious issue with different attitudes being taken to it in – and frequently within – various countries. In adjudicating on it, judges have given varying weight to dignity, some regarding it as an absolute value and others being prepared to balance it against other interests.

In Namibia the Supreme Court in *Ex p AG, Re Corporal Punishment by Organs of State*[46] unanimously held that the infliction of corporal punishment in government schools pursuant to a ministerial code or state direction

42 n 36 above, 796.

43 n 36 above, 798, 800.

44 'There is no dignity in the act itself; the recipient might struggle against himself to maintain a semblance of dignified suffering or even unconcern; there is no dignity even in the person delivering the punishment. It is a practice which debases everyone involved in it.': *Williams* (n 15 above) [89].

45 *Williams* (n 15 above) [47]:

> If the State, as role model *par excellence,* treats the weakest and the most vulnerable among us in a manner which diminishes rather than enhances their self-esteem and human dignity, the danger increases that their regard for a culture of decency and respect for the rights of others will be diminished.

46 [1991] NASC 2; 1991 3 SA 76 (NmS). The Court in the same case also struck down a sentence of corporal punishment by any judicial or quasi-judicial authority.

Mahomed AJA assessed whether a punishment was inhuman or degrading by looking at domestic and international values. He explained that in exercising an objective value judgment, regard should be had 'to the contemporary norms, aspirations, expectations and sensitivities of the Namibian people as expressed in its national institutions and its Constitution and ... to the emerging consensus of values in the civilised international community': above, 20. His use of national institutions as sources of identification of norms and values added another dimension to judicial interpretation: SK Amoo 'The constitutional jurisprudential development in Namibia since 1985' in N Horn & A Bösl (eds) *Human rights and the rule of law in Namibia* (2008) 50.

This ruling established the liberal credentials of the Namibian Supreme Court and its adherence to international human rights norms: GJ Naldi *Constitutional rights in Namibia: A comparative analysis with international human rights* (1995) 50.

infringed the prohibition on inhuman or degrading treatment or punishment in Article 8(2)(b) of the Namibian Constitution, which falls under the umbrella of respect for human dignity.[47] Mahomed AJA in his lead judgment gave pre-eminence to dignity, which he stated was inherent in juveniles as well as in adults.[48] Therefore the physical pain or the speedy recovery from the punishment was not determinative.[49]

Sachs J referred to this Namibian case in his judgment for a unanimous Constitutional Court in the challenge by Christian Education of South Africa (representing independent Christian schools) to the prohibition by the South African Schools Act of 1996 of corporal punishment in schools.[50] It was alleged that the prohibition interfered with the right of the parents of the pupils to religious freedom, as they had consented to corporal punishment in school since it was part of their religious convictions. The Minister for Education in defence relied, *inter alia*, on the children's constitutional rights

47 Constitution of the Republic of Namibia 1990, Art 8.

48 'Juveniles also have an inherent dignity by virtue of their status as human beings and that dignity is also violated by corporal punishment inflicted in consequence of judicial or quasi-judical authority.': n 46 above, 29.

49 The very fact of state-sanctioned punishment was inherently demeaning, n 46 above, 34:

> A deliberate and systematic assault with a cane on the buttocks of an individual inflicted by a stranger as a form of punishment authorised by a judicial or quasi-judicial tribunal, is inherently a demeaning invasion on the dignity of the person punished. It must, in these circumstances be degrading or inhuman. It does not become less so because a juvenile might conceivably recover from such a basic in-fliction on his dignity sooner than an adult might in comparable circumstances.

Berker CJ (concurring) took the same view and could be taken as favouring the condemnation of all corporal punishment from whatever source no matter how moderate or controlled, n 46 above, 4:

> It seems to me that once one has arrived at the conclusion that corporal punishment *per se* is impairing the dignity of the recipient or subjects him to degrading treatment or even to, cruel or inhuman treatment or punishment, it does not on principle matter to what extent such corporal punishment is made subject to restrictions and limiting parameters, even of a substantial kind – even if very moderately applied and subject to very strict controls, the fact remains that *any* type of corporal punishment results in some impairment of dignity and degrading treatment.

Mahomed AJA left open whether punishment inflicted by a teacher pursuant to a parent's actual delegation of the powers of chastisement would be a violation: n 46 above, 38.

50 *Christian Education South Africa v Minister of Education* 2000 4 SA 757 [46]. On *Christian Education*, see J Church *et al*, *Human rights from a comparative and international law perspective* (2007) 211 - 213; L du Plessis 'Affirmation and celebration of the "religious Other" in South Africa's constitutional jurisprudence on religious and related rights: Memorial constitutionalism in action?' (2008) 8 *African Human Rights Law Journal* 376 at 387 - 388; Kende (n 22 above) 227 - 228.

to equality,[51] dignity,[52] personal freedom and security,[53] and to be protected from maltreatment, neglect, abuse or degradation.[54] The Constitutional Court dismissed the appeal against the finding of the High Court that the ban on corporal punishment in schools did not interfere unduly with the parents' right to religious freedom. The High Court judge had concluded that the legislative prohibition did not constitute a substantial burden on religious freedom and that corporal punishment in schools infringed the children's right to dignity and security of the person. Sachs J did not rule on the constitutionality of parental correction by physical punishment, but assumed that the legislation infringed the parents' rights.[55] The approach in the Constitutional Court was not to portray the problem as the right to bodily integrity versus the right to freedom of conscience, but, as Sachs J described it, to deliver a judgment giving 'a carefully thought-through balancing of the way these two rights inter-connected in the concrete circumstances of the case.'[56] The ruling was that, subject to common law principles governing reasonable chastisement, the Christian Education community could maintain the integrity of their faith at home but not impose corporal correction in the more public environ of the schools.[57] Religious belief is one of the key ingredients in a person's dignity.[58] But it is not the only aspect of dignity that was relevant, as the trend in Southern Africa had been strongly in favour of regarding corporal punishment in schools as in itself violatory of the dignity of the child.[59]

51 Constitution of the Republic of South Africa 1996, Sec 9(1).

52 Sec 10.

53 Sec 12(1)(c), (d) & (e).

54 Sec 28(1)(d).

55 n 50 above, [27].

56 A Sachs *The strange alchemy of life and law* (2009) 272. As Sachs J stated in *Christian Education* '[o]ur Bill of Rights, through its limitations clause, expressly contemplates the use of a nuanced and context-sensitive form of balancing': n 50 above, [30].

57 Sachs *The strange alchemy of life and law* (n 56 above) 272.

58 *Christian Education* (n 50 above) [36].

59 *Christian Education* (n 50 above) [47]. See Grant (n 11 above) 313 - 314. Cf *Canadian Foundation for Children, Youth and the Law v Canada (AG)* 2004 SCC 4, [2004] 1 SCR 76, where the Supreme Court of Canada in a majority decision upheld the constitutionality of the use of reasonable corrective force by parents and teachers. Binnie J (dissenting in part in *Canadian Foundation*) found a violation of the equality provision, but it could be justified in relation to parents. He criticised the Chief Justice for concluding that children's equality rights were not infringed because their dignity was not offended by depriving them of the protection of their physical integrity against the use of unlawful force: above, [72]. He agreed with the conclusion in a report that the child's dignity was breached by the humiliation of corporal punishment, but

The South African Constitutional Court has hesitated to condemn corporal punishment unambiguously and has clearly not found that it violates children's rights in all circumstances, leaving scope for tipping the balance in favour of the parents' rights to exert control by physical means. Langa J in *S v Williams*, which did not deal with corporal punishment in schools, mentioned that it was a controversial topic[60] and stated, '[i]t is not necessary to comment on the suggestion that judicial corporal punishment is in reality no worse than cuts imposed at school'.[61] He referred to the requirement of the European Court of Human Rights that for punishment to be degrading, it had to reach a minimum level of severity, attaching importance to 'the difference between strokes inflicted by a policeman as a result of a court order' and 'corporal punishment administered by a headmaster in terms of disciplinary rules' in a boarding school.[62] The attitudes to the significance of punishment in the school environment differed – the European Court of Human Rights 'seemed to attach some importance to the difference between strokes inflicted by a policeman as a result of a court order ... and corporal punishment administered by a headmaster in terms of disciplinary rules in force within the school in which the youth was a boarder', whereas Justice White in a dissenting opinion in the US Supreme Court considered that when corporal punishment became so severe as to be unacceptable in a civilised society the fact that it was inflicted in public schools did not make it any more acceptable.[63]

mainly by the inherent lack of respect: above, [107], citing C Bernard 'Corporal Punishment as a Means of Correcting Children' Quebec Commission des droits de la personne et des droits de la jeunesse (November 1998) 8. Deschamps J (dissenting) considered that the equality breach was not justified, as the legislation did not meet the proportionality test. Arbour J (also dissenting) thought the legislation infringed the child's security interest, and the deprivation was not in accordance with the principles of fundamental justice, since its wording was vague. For reviews of *Canadian Foundation*, see: PW Hogg *Constitutional law of Canada Vol 2* (2007) 196 - 197, 376, 392, 420, 427 - 428, 632, 669 - 670; G Shannon *Child law* (2010) [2-31], [11-191]; B Shmueli 'Corporal punish-ment in the educational system versus corporal punishment by parents: A comparative view' (2010) 73(2) *Law and Contemporary Problems* 281 at 285 - 286, 314 - 315.

60 n 15 above, [48].

61 n 15 above, [49].

62 n 15 above, [48], citing *Costello-Roberts v UK* (App no 13134/87) (1995) 19 EHRR 112 and *Tyrer* (n 33 above). On *Costello-Roberts* and *Tyrer*, see N O'Neal 'Corporal punishment in public schools: A call for legal reform' (2008) 8 *African Human Rights Law Journal* 60 at 74 - 75.

63 n 15 above, [49], citing *Costello-Roberts* (n 62 above) and *Ingraham v Wright* 430 US 651 (1977) 692.

In *Christian Education*, Sachs J avoided ruling on the extent of children's rights by dealing with the issue of punishment in schools by a proportionality analysis under the limitations clause.[64] He concluded that the legislation prohibiting corporal punishment in all schools – private as well as public – was reasonable and was justified in restricting the parents' rights to religious freedom on the assumption that this freedom included a right to chastise their children.[65] He made a clear distinction between the school and the home, when he stated, 'corporal punishment administered by a teacher in the institutional environment of a school is quite different from corporal punishment in the home environment.'[66]

The Namibian Supreme Court's decision on corporal punishment is wider in scope than that of the South African Constitutional Court, the Namibian Court finding that state-sanctioned corporal punishment in schools infringed children's inherent dignity. Unlike the South African Constitutional Court, it was less open to arguments attempting to justify corporal punishment of young people in a learning environment. In contrast to the Namibian and South African courts, the European Court of Human Rights in a narrow majority of five votes to four found in *Costello-Roberts v UK* that the use of reasonable corporal punishment in schools did not breach the prohibition on inhuman or degrading treatment or punishment in Article 3 ECHR.[67] By requiring a minimum level of severity, the Court accepted that human dignity is not absolute.[68] The US Supreme Court held by a narrow majority in *Ingraham v Wright* that the prohibition against cruel and unusual punishment

64 n 50 above, [32].

65 n 50 above, [50]-[52].

66 n 50 above, [49]. He distinguished conduct in 'the intimate and spontaneous atmosphere of the home' from 'the detached and institutional environment of the school': n 50 above, [49].

67 n 62 above. The Court took into account the context in which the punishment was imposed and its nature, duration, and physical and mental effects on the pupil, whose age, sex and state of health were relevant in certain circumstances: n 62 above, [30]. The approach of the European Court of Human Rights was quite different from that of the Supreme Court of Namibia which emphasised the *inherently* demeaning character of such punishment rather than its relative nature: Naldi (n 46 above) 51.

68 The seven-year old boy in a private school had shown no evidence of 'any severe or long-lasting effects as a result of the treatment complained of', but even if such effects were not shown, the Court indicated that there could be particular circumstances where it could be said that the punishment reached the minimum threshold of severity required; the Court made it clear that it was not endorsing corporal punishment and it had 'certain misgivings about the automatic nature of the punishment and the three-day wait before its imposition': n 62 above, [32].

in the Eighth Amendment was designed to protect those convicted of crime and did not apply to disciplinary corporal punishment in public schools.[69]

At the international level, the United Nations has progressively narrowed any scope for corporal punishment of children by the state, in school and at home. The Convention on the Rights of the Child (CRC) adopted in 1989 has a strong emphasis on the equal dignity of all – children as well as adults.[70] It contains several provisions impacting on corporal punishment of children. There is an obligation on states to legislate and educate to defend children from violence or ill-treatment in article 19(1),[71] which embraces control over all those in charge of children, whether at home, in school or elsewhere. Article 37(a) contains a general ban on torture or other cruel, inhuman or

The four judges dissenting on the Art 3 issue were struck by 'the ritualised character of the corporal punishment' and also mentioned the three-day gap before the headmaster of the school '"whacked" a lonely and insecure seven-year-old boy': n 62 above, 137. They considered that a spanking on the spur of the moment might have been permissible, but viewed as degrading 'the official and formalised nature of the punishment meted out, without adequate consent of the mother': n 62 above, 137 - 138. They adverted to the trend in Europe (and in the UK since the corporal punishment the subject of the complaint) to render unlawful corporal punishment in state and certain independent schools, and felt that the discrepancy caused by the progressive outlawing elsewhere must have added to the degradation of the remaining pupils in independent schools whose disciplinary regimes persisted in corporal punishment: n 62 above, 138.

69 n 63 above. This finding has given the states wide latitude regarding the treatment of the parental privilege to use physical force to discipline children: KL Willis '*Willis v State*: Condoning child abuse as discipline' (2010) 14 *University of California Davis Journal of Juvenile Law and Policy* 59 at 73. In 2008 the Indiana Supreme Court overturned the conviction of a single mother for battery of her son, as parents had a fundamental liberty interest to direct the upbringing of children, which included using 'reasonable or moderate physical force' to control behaviour: Willis above, 89, citing *Willis v State* 888 NE.2d 177 (Ind 2008) 180. Indiana's interest in protecting the welfare of children lost out in the balance against the mother's liberty, and her plea of the parental privilege defence succeeded: Willis above, 89 - 90.

70 Convention on the Rights of the Child (adopted 20 November 1989, entered into force 2 September 1990) 1577 UNTS 3. Although the US and Somalia are the only countries which have not ratified the CRC, the US courts have already begun using it as persuasive authority under the doctrine of 'customary international law': JM Fuller 'The science and statistics behind spanking suggest that laws allowing corporal punishment are in the best interests of the child' (2009) 42 *Akron Law Review* 243 at 256, 258 - 259. On CRC, see S Coetzee 'Discipline in Nigerian schools within a human rights framework' (2010) 10 *African Human Rights Law Journal* 478 at 484 - 487.

71 It reads:

> State parties shall take all appropriate legislative, administrative, social and educational measures to protect the child from all forms of physical or mental violence, injury or abuse, neglect or negligent treatment, maltreatment or exploitation, including sexual abuse, while in the care of parent(s), legal guardian(s) or any other person who has the care of the child.

degrading treatment or punishment of children, but there is no explicit prohibition of corporal punishment. Included in the educational provisions is a duty on states to take measures to ensure that school discipline is administered in a manner 'consistent with the child's human dignity' and in conformity with the CRC.[72]

Recognising the development of norms in society across the globe over time, the UN Committee on the Rights of the Child through its general comments has essentially outlawed all corporal punishment of children in all environments.[73] Its General Comment No 8 dealing with corporal punishment contains reminders of the significance of the dignity of children[74] as a precursor to an adamant statement that the CRC bans all corporal punishment with a consequent obligation on states to enforce the ban.[75] In 1996 Italy's highest Court, the Supreme Court of Cassation, invoking the CRC, effectively prohibited all parental use of corporal punishment, basing its decision, first, on the dignity of the individual – meaning that children were not the objects of their parents – and, second, on the fostering of the child's personality.[76]

72 CRC (n 70 above) art 28(2).

73 There is disagreement among scholars on whether the CRC bans the use of light, educational corporal punishment: Shmueli (n 59 above) 306 - 307. Benjamin Shmueli proposes a reading of the CRC which would interpret it as not barring educational corporal punishment but only violence committed for extraneous purposes: n 59 above, 312 - 313.

74 UN Committee on the Rights of the Child 'General Comment No 8' (2 March 2007) UN Doc CRC/C/GC/8 [2], [5], [7], [16], [17].

75 n 74 above, [18]:

> There is no ambiguity: 'all forms of physical or mental violence' does not leave room for any level of legalized violence against children. Corporal punishment and other cruel or degrading forms of punishment are forms of violence and States must take all appropriate legislative, administrative, social and educational measures to eliminate them.

Courts in many countries have issued decisions, usually quoting the CRC 'condemning corporal punishment of children in some or all settings': n 74 above, [25].

76 UN Committee on the Rights of the Child 'General Comment No 8' (n 74 above) fn 15, citing Cambria, Cass, sez VI, 18 Marzo 1996 [Supreme Court of Cassation, 6th Penal Section, 18 March 1996], Foro It II 1996, 407 (Italy). The Italian Court's own de-scription as cited was:

> The use of violence for educational purposes can no longer be considered lawful. There are two reasons for this: the first is the overriding importance which the [Italian] legal system attributes to protecting the dignity of the individual. This includes 'minors' who now hold rights and are no longer simply objects to be protected by their parents or, worse still, objects at the disposal of their parents. The second reason is that, as an educational aim, the harmonious development of a child's personality, which ensures that he/she embraces the values of peace, tolerance and co-existence, cannot be achieved by using violent means which contradict these goals.

The General Comment requires that states take action against corporal punishment even in the traditional sanctity of the home.[77] Freedom of religion is not accepted as a rationale for corporal punishment.[78] The state has a multiple role in upholding children's rights to be free from corporal punishment. In addition to the requirement to make it 'explicitly clear that the criminal law provisions on assault also cover all corporal punishment, including in the family', it may be possible to have civil and family law measures 'prohibiting the use of all forms of violence, including all corporal punishment.'[79]

4.2.2 Punishment of adults

African countries have varied in their attitude to corporal punishment of adults and in the rate of progress in banning it. In 1987 the Supreme Court of Zimbabwe had held unanimously in *Ncube v S* that adult whipping was unconstitutional, being inhuman or degrading punishments contrary to Section 15(1) of the Constitution.[80] The Ugandan Supreme Court considered

77 Other UN bodies have also recommended 'prohibition and other measures against corporal punishment in schools, penal systems and, in some cases, the family': n 74 above, [22]. The CRC, like all human rights instruments, is 'a living instrument, whose interpretation develops over time'; since the CRC was adopted, the prevalence of corporal punishment of children in their homes, schools and other institutions has become more visible: n 74 above, [20].

78 'Some raise faith-based justifications for corporal punishment, suggesting that certain interpretations of religious texts not only justify its use, but provide a duty to use it. ...but practice of a religion or belief must be consistent with respect for others' human dignity and physical integrity.': n 74 above, [29].

79 n 74 above, [39]. Awareness-raising, public education and the state's monitoring of the progress being made are part of the process of eliminating corporal punishment: n 74 above, [45], [46], [51]. States are expected to insert in their periodic reports under the CRC information on 'the measures taken to prohibit and prevent all corporal punishment and other cruel or degrading forms of punishment in the family and all other settings, including on ... progress towards achieving full respect for children's rights to protection from all forms of violence': n 74 above, [53].

80 [1988] LRC (Const) 442. Gubbay JA delivering the Court's judgment invoked US jurisprudence to describe how he perceived the basic concept against which the protection from inhuman or degrading punishment should be construed, and made a clear link between unacceptable punishment and violation of human dignity: above, 460:

> The *raison d'être* underlying section 15(1) is nothing less than the dignity of man. It is a provision that embodies broad and idealistic notions of dignity, humanity and decency... . It guarantees that the power of the State to punish is exercised within the limits of civilised standards. Punishments which are incompatible with the evolving standards of decency that mark the progress of a maturing society or which involve unnecessary and wanton infliction of pain are repugnant.

corporal punishment in *Oryem v Uganda* and confirmed the Constitutional Court's finding in *Kyamanywa* that corporal punishment – in that case six strokes of the cane – contravened the prohibition in Article 24 of the Constitution on torture, cruel, inhuman or degrading treatment or punishment.[81] In *A v UK*, where the European Court of Human Rights held that the state had a duty to protect individuals against injury from private parties, the stepfather of a child had beaten him severely with a garden cane on more than one occasion, but a jury acquitted him of assault occasioning actual bodily harm and accepted his defence of 'reasonable chastisement'.[82]

The rights to dignity, life and not to be subject to cruel, inhuman or degrading punishment were all breached when South African immigration officers handed over to the FBI a Tanzanian national suspected of having been involved in the bombing of the US embassy in Dar es Salaam.[83] He was put on trial for conspiracy in New York. The Constitutional Court held that the South Africans should have obtained a prior undertaking from the US that the death penalty would not be executed if he were found guilty. In

He was of the opinion that whipping in its very nature was 'both inhuman and degrading' and relied on four adverse features inherent in the infliction of whipping, namely, first, the manner in which it was administered, which rendered it 'not only inherently brutal and cruel, ... but which stripped the recipient of all dignity and self-respect'; second, by its very nature, it treated 'members of the human race as non-humans'; third, it was easily subject to abuse; and fourth, it was degrading to both the punished and the punisher, it caused the executioner and society to stoop to the level of the criminal, and it was likely to generate hatred against the prison regime and the system of justice: above, 466.

See J Rehman *International human rights law* (2010) 316 - 317.

81 [2003] UGSC 30 at 10 - 12 confirming *Kyamanywa v Uganda* (No 10/2000) (Uganda Constitutional Court) 14 December 2001. In Zambia, Chulu J had held in the High Court in 1999 that corporal punishment was 'inhuman, degrading and barbaric' and breached the absolute prohibition on torture, inhuman and degrading punishment in the Constitution: *Banda v The People* [2002] AHRLR 260 (ZaHC 1999) [12], [22].

82 (App no 25599/94) (1999) 27 EHRR 611. The Court approved of the approach in *Costello-Roberts* requiring ill-treatment to attain a minimum level of severity if it is to fall within the scope of Art 3 and confirmed that the assessment of this minimum was relative: above, [20]. The obligation on states under Art 1 ECHR to secure to everyone within their jurisdiction the rights and freedoms defined in the ECHR, taken together with Art 3, required states to take measures designed to ensure that individuals were not subjected to ill-treatment by private individuals; there was a particular obligation to provide effective deterrence to protect children and other vulnerable individuals against serious breaches of personal integrity: above, [22].

In *Z v UK* the European Court of Human Rights found that the local authority had failed to take adequate measures to protect children known to be suffering abuse and neglect at the hands of their parents: (App no 29392/95) (2002) 34 EHRR 3.

See L Hoyano & C Keenan *Child abuse: Law and policy across boundaries* (2010) 185 - 186; Shannon (n 59 above) [2-30], [11-191], [14-05].

83 *Mohamed* (n 6 above).

Soering v UK the European Court of Human Rights had taken a similar view when a West German national alleged that the decision by the United Kingdom Secretary of State for the Home Department to extradite him to the US to face trial in Virginia on a charge of capital murder would, if implemented, breach Article 3 ECHR.[84] Changing views on capital punishment were central to the Canadian decision in *US v Burns*,[85] where extradition to the US without assurances concerning the death penalty or life imprisonment without parole was held to violate the right not to be deprived of life, liberty or security other than in accordance with the principles of fundamental justice in Section 7 of the Canadian Charter[86] and was not justified under the limitations clause.[87]

While all eleven judges in *Makwanyane* agreed that the death penalty was unconstitutional, they based their decisions on varying provisions in the interim Constitution including the right to dignity.[88] Mahomed J referred to

84 (App no 14038/88) (1989) 11 EHRR 439. Although the death sentence *per se* was not contrary to the ECHR, the Court held that extradition to the US with the risk of a death sentence being imposed and exposure to 'death row phenomenon' would violate the prohibition on inhuman or degrading treatment or punishment in Art 3. The Court considered that the manner of imposition and execution of the sentence, the offender's personal circumstances, the proportionality of the sentence to the crime and the conditions of detention could amount to unacceptable punishment: above, [104]. Society's changing views were a factor for the Court, which stated, 'Present-day attitudes in the Contracting States to capital punishment are relevant for the assessment whether the acceptable threshold of suffering or degradation has been exceeded.': as above.

See RKM Smith *Textbook on international human rights* (2012) [14.3.2].

85 2001 SCC 7, [2001] 1 SCR 283 (SC of Canada). See Hogg (n 59 above) 107 - 108, 591.

86 Canadian Charter of Rights and Freedoms 1982.

87 Sec 1. This was contrary to the majority view in *Kindler* 10 years earlier: *Kindler v Canada (Minister of Justice)* [1991] 2 SCR 779 (SC of Canada). But Cory J in dissent then had categorised capital punishment as 'the annihilation of the very essence of human dignity' and explained, '[t]he death penalty not only deprives the prisoner of all vestiges of human dignity, it is the ultimate desecration of the individual as a human being.': above, 53.

88 n 4 above. See analyses by Church *et al* (n 50 above) 67 - 68, 204, 207 - 209, 214 - 215; Kende (n 22 above) 53 - 54, 58 - 73; KE Klare 'Legal culture and transformative con-stitutionalism' (1998) 14 *South African Journal on Human Rights* 146 at 172 - 175; H Klug 'The dignity clause of the Montana Constitution: May foreign juris-prudence lead the way to an expanded interpretation?' (2003) 64 *Montana Law Review* 133 at 150. *Makwanyane* is an example of how a constitutional court in a new democracy may be able to ignore public opinion as a limit on principle: T Roux 'Principle and prag-matism on the Constitutional Court of South Africa' (2009) 7 *International Journal of Constitutional Law* 106 at 118 - 120.

On international and comparative sources referenced in *Makwanyane* and the way they were linked to the local context, see PG Carozza 'My friend is a stranger: The death penalty and the global *ius commune* of human rights' (2003) 81 *Texas Law Review* 1031 at 1056 - 1061.

the effect of the death penalty on the dignity of society as a whole.[89] Ackermann J considered that the individual's right not be put to death gave rise to a corresponding state obligation to defend society from dangerous criminals.[90] He referred to the German *Life Imprisonment* case upholding the constitutionality of life imprisonment provided it gave some hope to the offender, whose right to dignity was not abrogated while in prison:[91]

> The [German Federal Constitutional] Court upheld the law on the basis that it was not shown that the serving of a sentence of life imprisonment leads to irreparable physical or psychological damage to the prisoner's health. The Court did however find that the right to human dignity demands a humane execution of the sentence. This meant that the existing law, which made provision for executive pardon, had to be replaced by a law laying down objective criteria for the release of prisoners serving life sentences. In the course of its judgment, the Court made clear that there is nothing constitutionally objectionable to executing a life sentence in full in cases where the prisoner does not meet the criteria ... [T]he Court said:
>
> > ... 'Human dignity is not infringed when the execution of the sentence remains necessary due to the continuing danger posed by the prisoner and clemency is for this reason precluded. The state is not prevented from protecting the community from dangerous criminals by keeping them incarcerated'.

The German Federal Constitutional Court would not countenance crime deterrence as the sole objective of the criminal justice system, so in Kantian style it required the state to retain respect for the inmate's dignity and to uphold social justice by not turning the offender into an object of crime prevention to the detriment of his constitutionally protected right to social worth and respect.[92]

89 n 4 above, [272]:

> It is not necessarily only the dignity of the person to be executed which is invaded. Very arguably the dignity of all of us, in a caring civilization, must be compromised, by the act of repeating, systematically and deliberately, albeit for a wholly different objective, what we find to be so repugnant in the conduct of the offender in the first place (see *Furman v Georgia* 408 US 238 at 273 (1972) (Brennan J, concurring).

90 '[T]here is a correlative obligation on the state, through the criminal justice system, to protect society from once again being harmed by the unreformed recidivist killer or rapist.': n 4 above, [171].

91 n 4 above, [172], citing 45 BVerfGE 187 (1977) 242. On the *Life Imprisonment* case, see L Ackermann *Human dignity: Lodestar for equality in South Africa* (2012) 126, 128.

92 LAA Pagán 'Human dignity, privacy and personality rights in the constitutional jurisprudence of Germany, the United States and the Commonwealth of Puerto Rico' (1998) 67 *Revista Juridica de la Universidad de Puerto Rico* 343 at 353.

In *S v Dodo* the Constitutional Court dealt with the constitutionality of the Criminal Law Amendment Act 1997 imposing a mandatory life sentence and was satisfied that the statutory provisions were neither disproportionate nor did they interfere unduly with the court's role in sentencing.[93] The court retained the capacity to consider the circumstances and to decline to impose a life sentence should there be substantial and compelling reasons to impose a more lenient punishment. The Constitutional Court reviewed the impact of dignity in its many guises in the South African Constitution.[94] It noted its place as a foundational value as well as a distinct right and that dignity underpins the Bill of Rights. Dignity's association with freedom was significant. Ackermann J invoked the Kantian principle of individuals being deserving of respect because of their inherent worth which required that their dignity be not attacked by treating them as objects on account of the imposition of a disproportionate punishment, whether that be merely disproportionate or disproportionate with a deterrent or reformative purpose.[95]

Comparable sentiments and rationales can be seen in *Tcoeib* when the Namibian Supreme Court dealt with a similar challenge and held that life

93 2001 3 SA 382 (CC). Cf *Niemand v S* [2001] ZACC 11, 2002 1 SA 21 (CC), where legislation imposing an indeterminate sentence on a habitual criminal was found unconstitutional.

94 *Dodo* (n 93 above) [35].

95 *Dodo* (n 93 above) [38], citing *Prinsloo v Van der Linde* 1997 3 SA 1012 (CC) [31]:

> To attempt to justify any period of penal incarceration, let alone imprisonment for life as in the present case, without inquiring into the proportionality between the offence and the period of imprisonment, is to ignore, if not to deny, that which lies at the very heart of human dignity. Human beings are not commodities to which a price can be attached; they are creatures with inherent and infinite worth; they ought to be treated as ends in themselves, never merely as means to an end. Where the length of a sentence, which has been imposed because of its general deterrent effect on others, bears no relation to the gravity of the offence ... the offender is being used essentially as a means to another end and the offender's dignity assailed. So too where the reformative effect of the punishment is predominant and the offender sentenced to lengthy imprisonment, principally because he cannot be reformed in a shorter period, but the length of imprisonment bears no relationship to what the committed offence merits. Even in the absence of such features, mere disproportionality between the offence and the period of imprisonment would also tend to treat the offender as a means to an end, thereby denying the offender's humanity.

See R O'Connell 'The role of dignity in equality law: Lessons from Canada and South Africa' (2008) 6 *International Journal of Constitutional Law* 267 at 273, fn 50. As is evident from the following passage from his judgment in *Dodo* (n 93 above) [37], Ackermann J placed proportionality at the centre of the investigation into whether life imprisonment was constitutional:

> The concept of proportionality goes to the heart of the inquiry as to whether punishment is cruel, inhuman or degrading, particularly where, as here, it is almost

imprisonment was not unconstitutional, regard being had to the fact that the relevant legislation permitted release on parole in appropriate circumstances.[96] Mahomed CJ was mindful of the possibility that, even if the sentence of life imprisonment was not *per se* unconstitutional, its imposition in a particular case might be unconstitutional 'if the circumstances of that case justify the conclusion that it is so grossly disproportionate to the severity of the crime committed that it constitutes cruel, inhuman or degrading punishment in the circumstances or impermissibly invades the dignity of the accused'; he found resonances of this approach in US jurisprudence where grossly excessive sentences had been held to be contrary to the prohibition on cruel and unusual punishment in the Eighth Amendment.[97] He distinguished between unacceptable infringements of dignity and the unavoidable effect on the individual of guilt and sentence:[98]

> The obligation to undergo imprisonment would undoubtedly have some impact on the appellant's dignity but some impact on the dignity of a prisoner is inherent in all imprisonment. What the Constitution seeks to protect are impermissible invasions of dignity not inherent in the very fact of imprisonment or indeed in the conviction of a person *per se*.

He also cited the German *Life Imprisonment* case[99] and used Kantian language to describe the requirement to treat everyone (even convicted criminals) decently:[100]

> It seems to me that the sentence of life imprisonment in Namibia can therefore not be constitutionally sustainable if it effectively amounts to an order throwing the prisoner into a cell for the rest of the prisoner's natural life as if he was a 'thing' instead of a person without any continuing duty to respect his dignity (which would include his right not to live in

> ex-clusively the length of time for which an offender is sentenced that is in issue. … In order to justify the deprivation of an offender's freedom it must be shown that it is reasonably necessary to curb the offence and punish the offender. Thus the length of punishment must be proportionate to the offence.

The sentences imposed for criminal offences must be proportionate to the crime and show respect for the dignity of the offender, irrespective of the public interest in curbing crime by making an example of the individual as a deterrent to others.

96 *S v Tcoeib* [1996] NASC 1; 1996 (1) SACR 390 (NmS).

97 n 96 above, 19.

98 n 96 above, 20.

99 n 91 above.

100 n 96 above, 13.

despair and helplessness and without any hope of release, regardless of the circumstances).

Rehabilitation with the aim of restoring a sense of humanity in those incarcerated was worthy of support, as constitutional values mandated society 'continuously and consistently to care for the condition of its prisoners, to seek to manifest concern for, to reform and rehabilitate those prisoners during incarceration and concomitantly to induce in them a consciousness of their dignity, a belief in their worthiness and hope in their future'.[101]

There was a divergence of views among the judges of the Canadian Supreme Court in *R v Smith* when a majority found that legislation imposing a minimum sentence for importing narcotics breached the ban on cruel and unusual punishment in Section 12 of the Canadian Charter.[102] In Tanzania the Court of Appeal found that capital punishment was an inherently cruel, inhuman and degrading punishment and infringed the right to dignity, but that the death penalty was saved under the limitations clause.[103] It disagreed with the High Court's view that the legislation imposing the death penalty for murder failed the limitations test as it was arbitrary and disproportionate. On the question of whether the death penalty was reasonably necessary to protect the right to life, Ramadhani JA (delivering the Court of Appeal's judgment) considered this was for society to decide and the trial judge had acknowledged that society at that time had so deemed it.[104] The Tanzanian Constitution contains a prohibition on inhuman or degrading punishment or

101 n 96 above, 12.

102 [1987] 1 SCR 1045. McIntyre J (dissenting) set out three characteristics of punishment – any one of which would suffice to render the punishment cruel and unusual – first, its character or duration might outrage the public conscience or be degrading to human dignity; second, it could go beyond what was necessary to achieve a valid social aim, bearing in mind the legitimate purposes of punishment and adequate alternatives; third, it might be arbitrarily imposed by not being applied rationally in accordance with ascertained or ascertainable standards: above, [94]. As there was a possibility of parole in this case, he adjudged the minimum sentence for importing narcotics not to be outrageous or degrading to dignity: above, [96]. See Hogg (n 59 above) 579 - 581.

103 *Mbushuu v R* [1995] 1 LRC 216. On the death penalty debate in Tanzania, see A Gaitan & B Kuschnik 'Tanzania's death penalty debate: An epilogue on *Republic v Mbu-shuu*' (2009) 9 *African Human Rights Law Journal* 459.

104 n 103 above, 232.

treatment.[105] It also protects human dignity in the criminal process and in the execution of a sentence.[106] Basic rights may be limited in the public interest.[107] The Nigerian Supreme Court held that the death penalty is not inconsistent with the constitutional guarantee of the right to life.[108]

The Privy Council in *Reyes v R* was not convinced that the possibility of a pardon was sufficient to save the mandatory death penalty in Belize.[109] Notwithstanding the fact that the right to life was not absolute[110] since the Belize Constitution allowed capital punishment,[111] Lord Bingham found that the mandatory nature of the death penalty infringed the prohibition on inhuman and degrading punishment and treatment.[112]

By a narrow majority in *Kigula v AG* the Ugandan Constitutional Court in 2005 also found that mandatory capital punishment was unconstitutional, as was an inordinate delay in executing the death penalty.[113] Like in Belize,

105 Constitution of the United Republic of Tanzania 1977, Art 13(6)(e).

106 Art 13(6)(d).

107 Art 30(2).

108 *Kalu v S* (1998) 3 NWLR (Pt 509) 531, *Okoro v S* (1998) 2 SCNJ 84, both cited in Nigerian Bar Association, *Training Manual on African Regional Mechanisms for the Promotion and Enforcement of Human Rights: A Toolkit for Lawyers* (Lagos 2010) 20 - 21.

109 *Reyes v R (Belize)* [2002] UKPC 11, [2002] 2 AC 235. Lord Bingham pointed out that mercy came too late in the process after the judicial decision and was distinct from justice: above, [44]. International bodies interpreting human rights instruments had generally accepted the need for 'proportionality and individualised sentencing': above, [40]. Lord Bingham effectively framed the issue in transnational terms and relied on much foreign jurisprudence: Carozza (n 88 above) 1075 - 1077.

110 International instruments (like many national legal systems) do not accord any formal primacy to the right to life itself, as they contain qualifications rendering it less than absolute; in contrast, other rights such as freedom from torture and other ill-treatment, and freedom from slavery and servitude are absolute, and subject to no exceptions of any kind; therefore international human rights law assigns a higher value to the quality of living as a process, than to the existence of life as a state; from the viewpoint of the person concerned, the law tends to regard acute or prolonged suffering (at all events where it is inflicted by others, and so potentially avoidable) as a greater evil than death (ultimately unavoidable for everyone): P Sieghart *The international law of human rights* (1983) 130.

The prohibition on torture, and inhuman or degrading treatment and punishment in Art 3 ECHR is absolute: *Gäfgen v Germany* (App no 22978/05) (2011) 52 EHRR 1 [87], [107], [120], [176].

111 Constitution of Belize 1981, Sec 4(1).

112 Sec 7.

113 [2005] UGCC 8. Okello JA associated the rights to a fair hearing and to equality before the law in his condemnation of the obligatory death penalty; he found that the intrusion on the judicial discretion to determine an appropriate sanction violated the separation of powers, as the legislature had prescribed 'the *only* sentence which the court must impose on conviction': above, 28.

the right to life is not absolute in Uganda,[114] so the Court upheld the death penalty *per se.* Death by hanging passed constitutional muster. Twinomujuni JA stated that one of the general principles of constitutional construction is that fundamental rights and freedoms are to be interpreted having general regard to evolving standards of human dignity.[115] He referred to the minority decision in the US case of *Campbell v Wood*, which concluded:[116]

> Even aside from the risks of decapitation and lingering painful death, hanging is simply inconsistent with 'the dignity of man' ... Hanging is without the slightest doubt, 'cruel and unusual' – in layman's terms and in the constitutional sense.

However, he distinguished the situation in Uganda from this and other international comparisons because of the terms of its Constitution, which expressly authorised the death penalty 'clearly in the knowledge that it would be carried out by hanging', as the practice of hanging criminals in serious crimes had been in vogue for almost 60 years prior to adoption of the Constitution and the people's opinion that it was a suitable method of carrying out the death sentence was a relevant consideration.[117]

Another issue on which Twinomujini JA expressed a view was the fettering of judicial discretion by legislation decreeing that life imprisonment meant a maximum of 20 years, which he interpreted as prohibiting a sentence longer than that period. He considered that the judiciary should be able to tailor the sanction to the circumstances of each case, that the entire sentence should be served (subject to remission for good behaviour or other just cause), and that when a 'life imprisonment' sentence is pronounced, the convict should serve imprisonment for life, describing the legislation as 'another attempt by the legislature to pre-determined sentences without hearing the parties in order to determine an appropriate sentence'.[118] Jamil Mujuzi criticised the wish for life imprisonment to mean the whole of a person's life,

For a review of this Constitutional Court decision, see A Novak 'The decline of the mandatory death penalty in common law Africa: Constitutional challenges and comparative jurisprudence in Malawi and Uganda' (2009) 11 *Loyola Journal of Public Interest Law* 19 at 70 - 74.

114 Constitution of the Republic of Uganda 1995, Art 22(1).

115 n 113 above, 55.

116 n 113 above, 84 - 85, citing *Campbell v Wood* 18 F.3d 662 (1994) (US Court of Appeals 9th Circuit).

117 n 113 above, 86 - 87.

118 n 113 above, 105.

which – as observed by courts in South Africa and Namibia – would be an infringement of the right to human dignity at the time of sentencing, since it deprived the prisoner of any real hope of release from prison.[119]

On appeal in 2009, the Supreme Court unanimously upheld the findings that the mandatory death penalty and a delay of more than three years in carrying it out were unconstitutional.[120] As Okello JA had done in the court below, the Supreme Court highlighted the inequality in the legislation refusing a person convicted of a serious crime an opportunity to plead in mitigation and to have the judge assess their character:[121]

> [A] person accused of stealing a chicken may not only be heard in mitigation, but may actually request the court to inquire into his character and antecedents for purposes of assessing appropriate sentence for him, while on the other hand, a person accused of murder and whose very life is at stake, may not do likewise. We think this is inconsistent with the principle of equality before and under the law.

The Court reiterated that the separation of powers had to be respected and unhindered by removal of its discretion in sentencing:[122]

> The Court has power to confirm both conviction and sentence. This implies a power NOT to confirm, implying that court has been given discretion in the matter. Any law that fetters that discretion is inconsistent with this clear provision of the Constitution.

On the issue of delay, it evoked the inherent dignity of all when it described the legal status of a convict, '[a] condemned person does not lose all his other rights as a human being' and continued, '[h]e is still entitled to his dignity within the confines of the law until his sentence is carried out'.[123] Hanging

119 JD Mujuzi 'Why the Supreme Court of Uganda should reject the Constitutional Court's understanding of imprisonment for life' (2008) 8 *African Human Rights Law Journal* 163 at 177.

120 *AG v Kigula* (No 3/2006) (Uganda Supreme Court) 21 January 2009. For a review of the Supreme Court judgment, see JD Mujuzi 'International human rights law and foreign case law in interpreting constitutional rights: The Supreme Court of Uganda and the death penalty question' (2009) 9 *African Human Rights Law Journal* 576 at 577 - 578, 581 - 588; Novak (n 113 above) 74 - 78.

121 n 120 above, 43.

122 n 120 above, 45.

123 n 120 above, 47. On condemned persons retaining the right to be treated with dignity, see also *Peter Nemi v AG Lagos State* (1996) 6 NWLR 587, cited in Nigerian Bar Association (n 108 above) 23.

was confirmed as constitutional by the majority, the sole dissentient being Egonda-Ntende Ag JSC, who considered hanging as a method of execution as carried out in Uganda to be 'a process that is cruel, inhuman and degrading treatment and punishment', which failed to meet the test of 'the least possible physical and mental suffering' set by the Human Rights Committee under the International Covenant on Civil and Political Rights (ICCPR).[124] Unlike the majority, he read all the provisions of the Constitution together 'to provide a harmonious interpretation that does not do violence to the meaning of any one provision'.[125] He found that hanging as practised in Uganda was 'definitely beyond the pain, suffering or humiliation that should be associated with the death penalty' and that unnecessary continual reminders by a prison warder in the three days beforehand of the impending violent death must cause 'the same amount of mental suffering as that experienced under the death row phenomenon'.[126]

The psychological impact of contradictory notifications about the outcome of an appeal leading to a belief that the death sentence had been commuted, when it was not, and of inexplicably being returned to death row after two years in a different section breached the prohibition on cruel and inhuman treatment in ICCPR.[127]

The High Court in Malawi had a wider range of support for its decision than the Ugandan courts when it unanimously struck down the mandatory death penalty for murder in *Kafantayeni* in 2007.[128] The Court held that the mandatory death sentence infringed the prohibition on inhuman or degrading treatment or punishment and the right to dignity in Section 19 of the

124 n 120 above, 78 - 80, 90, 96 - 97, citing UN Human Rights Committee, *Chitat Ng v Canada* 'Communication No 469 of 1991' (7 January 1994) [16.2], [16.4], and International Covenant on Civil and Political Rights (adopted 16 December 1966, entered into force 23 March 1976) 999 UNTS 171 (ICCPR). On *Ng v Canada*, see Smith (n 84 above) [14.3.2].

125 n 120 above, 85.

126 n 120 above, 96 - 97.

127 *Chisanga v Zambia* UNHR Committee (18 November 2005) 85th Session UN Doc CCPR/C/85/D/1132/2002 [7.3].

128 *Kafantayeni v AG* [2007] MWHC 1, [2007] 5 LRC 353. It was a more focused attack, as the death penalty *per se*, hanging or delay in execution were not raised in the challenge.
This case was not appealed to the Supreme Court of Appeal, but it affirmed the High Court's decision several months later in *Jacob*: Novak (n 113 above) 62, citing *Jacob v Republic* (MSCA Crim App No 16/2006) 19 July 2007 (Malawi Sup Ct App). For reviews of *Kafantayeni* and *Jacob*, see Novak (n 113 above) 63 - 70.

Constitution.[129] It linked the protection against inhuman or degrading treatment in Section 19(3) of the Constitution with the guarantee of respect for human dignity in judicial proceedings contained in Section 19(2), and commented that the latter was 'often overlooked even in the case authorities that we have examined from comparable jurisdictions'.[130] The death penalty itself, expressly preserved by Section 16 of the Constitution, remained available as the maximum punishment for murder. The Court did not deal with the allegations of arbitrary deprivation of the right to life or of breach of the separation of powers, which had been relied on by the accused. It invoked foreign precedents to support its decision, including *Makwanyane*[131] and *Reyes*.[132] Because the mandatory death penalty required a sentence of death to be passed without any opportunity for the defendant to show factors in mitigation, sentencing was not individualised and a sentence could be disproportionate to the defendant's criminal culpability. The Court also found that the mandatory death penalty breached the right to a fair trial, which required fairness of the trial at all stages including sentencing. Although it was not relied on by the accused, the Court of its own motion raised the right of access to justice, and held that it too had been breached, as sentencing was a legal issue for judicial determination within the purview of Section 41(2) of the Constitution effectively granting the right of appeal.

The African Commission accepted that the right to respect for dignity required that the death sentence should not be a disproportionate penalty and explained that it should only be imposed after consideration of whether there were any extenuating circumstances (facts bearing on the commission of the crime, which reduce the accused's moral blameworthiness taking into account the state of mind of the offender at the time of the commission of the offence).[133]

By the time the Kenyan Court of Appeal considered the constitutionality of the mandatory death penalty for murder in *Mutiso* in 2010, the opposition to it had dissipated and the State – obviously recognising the growing trend in Africa[134] and the Commonwealth to strike it down – conceded that it was

129 Constitution of the Republic of Malawi 1994.

130 n 128 above, 358.

131 n 4 above.

132 n 109 above.

133 *Interights (Bosch) v Botswana* [2003] AHRLR 55 (ACHPR 2003) [31]-[33].

134 See J Biegon & M Killander 'Human rights developments in the African Union during 2009' (2010) 10 *African Human Rights Law Journal* 212 at 222 - 223.

unconstitutional and that the trial judge should retain a discretion not to impose the death sentence.[135] The law should evolve in tandem with a civilised society.[136]

This review of challenges to the death penalty in various jurisdictions shows that its complete abolition was easier to achieve in South Africa because of its comprehensive constitutional ban on cruel, inhuman and degrading punishment, the unrestricted articulation of the right to life, the specific right to dignity and the foundational value of human dignity. Unsurprisingly the challenge in countries where the death penalty was specifically permitted by the terms of the constitution failed. However, even there the mandatory death penalty did not withstand scrutiny, as it failed to allow an assessment of individual culpability and responsibility for one's actions.

135 *Godfrey Ngotho Mutiso v Republic* [2010] eKLR [10], [31]. The Court was critical of the State for not taking action earlier to abolish the mandatory death penalty – particularly as only a handful of the those condemned to death in Kenya had been executed leaving the prisons inundated with a huge number of death row inmates: above, [13]-[14]. Notwithstanding the State's concession, the Court considered the case on its merits: above, [12]. It took cognisance of the array of offenders with a wide range of culpability that could be found guilty of murder, and the fact that the mandatory death penalty had been declared to constitute inhuman treatment or punishment in other countries in violation of constitutional provisions similar to those in Kenya: above, [32]-[34]. The judge should consider any mitigating factors relating to the offence and the offender before imposing the death sentence: above, [34]. The Court in *Mutiso* referred to many Commonwealth decisions with approval including *Reyes* and cited extensively from *Kigula* in Uganda, where the death row syndrome was highlighted because of the long delay in carrying out the sentence: above, [23], [29], [32]-[34] (*Reyes*) and [17]-[18], [24]-[25], [35] (*Kigula*).

136 'A law that is caught up in a time warp would soon find itself irrelevant and would be swept into the dustbins of history.': *Mutiso* (n 135 above) [14]. The individual must have a chance to mitigate – otherwise the dignity of humanity would be ignored: n 135 above, [34]. Similar to the challenge in Malawi, *Mutiso* was confined to the narrow issue of the mandatory death penalty and raised neither the constitutionality of the death penalty *per se* (specifically permitted by Constitution of the Republic of Kenya 1963, Sec 71(1)) nor the prescription by law of the death penalty for murder, both of which were within the realm of parliament or the people in a referendum: n 135 above, [22]. The Court found that the mandatory death sentence for murder contained in the Penal Code (sec 204) violated the constitutional protection against inhuman or degrading punishment or treatment (Sec 74(1)) and also breached the right to a fair trial (Sec 77): n 135 above, [36].

A new Constitution approved in Kenya in 2010 recognises everyone's inherent dignity and 'the right to have that dignity respected and protected': Constitution of the Republic of Kenya 2010, Art 28. The Bill of Rights contained in it at Ch Four has been described by Ouko J as 'arguably the most progressive and probably the most liberal in the region and perhaps beyond': *Mbiyu v Commissioner of Police* [2011] eKLR (High Court of Kenya, 5 January 2011).

On the 'civilised standards' rationale, see W Binchy 'The role of comparative and public international law in domestic legal systems' (2010) 23(3) *Advocate (South Africa)* 58 at 61.

The conditions of detention by placing a prisoner in leg-irons or chains were found to be degrading treatment in Namibia in *Namunjepo*.[137] Strydom CJ regarded the degrading treatment as disrespecting dignity.[138]

4.3 Family

Unlike many other constitutions and international human rights instruments, there is no specific provision in the South African Constitution protecting family life.[139] Its absence was challenged unsuccessfully in the *First Certification* case, where the Court held that the foundational values and the

137 *Namunjepo v Commanding Officer, Windhoek Prison* [1999] NASC 3; 2000 6 BCLR 671 (NmS) (SC of Namibia). It was 'a humiliating experience which reduces the person placed in irons to the level of a hobbled animal whose mobility is limited so that it cannot stray': above, 23.

Respect for dignity and the prohibition on cruel, inhuman or degrading treatment in the African Charter precludes not only actions which cause serious physical or psychological suffering, but also those which humiliate the individual or force him or her to act against his will or conscience: *International Pen (Saro-Wiwa) v Nigeria* [2000] AHRLR 212 (ACHPR 1998) [79]. The deplorable conditions in which women, children and aged detainees were held in Rwanda violated their physical and psychological integrity: *Organisation Mondiale Contre la Torture v Rwanda* [2000] AHRLR 282 (ACHPR 1996) [26]. The African Commission held that the denial to detainees of medical attention under health-threatening conditions and access to the outside world does not respect their dignity: *Huri-Laws v Nigeria* [2000] AHRLR 273 (ACHPR 2000) [41]. It noted that the term 'cruel, inhuman or degrading treatment or punishment' is to be interpreted so as to extend to 'the widest possible protection against abuses, whether physical or mental': *Media Rights Agenda v Nigeria* [2000] AHRLR 262 (ACHPR 2000) [71]. See also *M'Boissona (Bozize) v Central African Republic* UNHR Committee (26 April 1994) 50th Session UN Doc CCPR/C/50/D/428/1990 [5.2]; *Civil Liberties Organisation v Nigeria* [2000] AHRLR 243 (ACHPR 1999) [26]-[27]; *Article 19 v Eritrea* [2007] AHRLR 73 (ACHPR 2007) [102]; *Titiahonjo v Cameroon* UNHR Committee (13 November 2007) 91st Session UN Doc CCPR/C/91/D/1186/2003) [6.3]-[6.4].

138 'To be continuously in chains or leg-irons and not to be able to properly clean oneself and the clothes one is wearing sets one apart from other fellow beings and is in itself a humiliating and undignified experience.': n 137 above, 23.

Cf *Engelbrecht v Minister of Prisons and Correctional Services* 2000 NR 230 (High Court of Namibia).

139 *Dawood* (n 2 above) [36].

right to dignity safeguarded the right to marry the person of one's choice, to bring up a family and to live together.[140]

When the non-South African spouses of South African citizens complained that their family life could be disrupted because they had no guarantee that they would be allowed to stay in South Africa while their application for immigration was being processed, the right to dignity was key.[141] The Constitutional Court in *Dawood* held that the legislation was invalid because it breached their right to family life, which covered the right to marry and to sustain a married relationship by living together.[142] Other provisions in the Aliens Control Act governing the issue of work permits to foreign spouses of South African citizens or permanent residents were declared unconstitutional in *Booysen*.[143] Sachs J in the Constitutional Court agreed with the High Court judge's finding that the restrictions could infringe the right to dignity of the South African spouse as well as the foreign one, as alleged by the applicants.[144]

140 *Certification of the Constitution of the Republic of South Africa, 1996* 1996 4 SA 744 (CC) [100]:

> [T]he provisions of the NT [new constitutional text] would clearly prohibit any arbitrary State interference with the right to marry or to establish and raise a family. NT 7(1) enshrines the values of human dignity, equality and freedom, while NT 10 states that everyone has the right to have their dignity respected and protected. However these words may come to be interpreted in future, it is evident that laws or executive action resulting in enforced marriages, or oppressive prohibitions on marriage or the choice of spouses, would not survive constitutional challenge.

141 *Dawood* (n 2 above). The Aliens Control Act 1991 required applicants for immigration permits to be outside South Africa when their permits were granted but exempted spouses and children, who could remain in the country pending the outcome of their applications provided they had valid temporary residence permits: above, [2]-[3].

142 The UN Human Rights Committee found that legislation under which foreign husbands of Mauritian women lost their residence status constituted discrimination on the grounds of sex under ICCPR: *Aumeeruddy-Cziffra v Mauritius* UNHR Committee (9 April 1981) 12th Session UN Doc CCPR/C/12/D/35/1978. In Botswana legislation denying citizenship to children with a Botswanan mother and a foreign father (but not where the father was a citizen of Botswana and the mother was not) was unconstitutional because it breached the Botswanan mother's freedom of movement and constituted sex-discrimination: *AG v Dow* [2001] AHRLR 99 (BwCA 1992) 663 (Amissah JP), 678 (Aguda JA), 683 (Bizos JA).

143 *Booysen v Minister of Home Affairs* 2001 4 SA 485 (CC). The legislation required the foreign spouse to make the application for a work permit from outside the country and not to enter South Africa until the permit had been issued. Furthermore work permits would only be issued to foreign spouses if there were not enough people of their occupation in South Africa.

144 'In many cases the foreign spouse was the sole or main provider for the family and this highly restrictive provision prevented them from fulfilling their duty to support, thereby violating the right to human dignity of both spouses.': n 143 above, [7].

O'Regan J in *Dawood* saw marriage as the pinnacle of carving one's identify and self-fulfilment essential to dignity for a lot of people.[145] She highlighted the social importance of marriage with its associative, community and public elements in addition to the individual and relationship aspects.[146] Family life is not confined to the traditionally recognised unit and other arrangements also deserve respect.[147] Marriage encompasses duties and responsibilities as well as rights, as illustrated in various marriage regimes.[148] O'Regan J viewed marriage with its public and private nature as connoting rights and obligations in inter-personal relationships.

145 n 2 above, [37] (footnotes omitted):

> The decision to enter into a marriage relationship and to sustain such a relationship is a matter of defining significance for many if not most people and to prohibit the establishment of such a relationship impairs the ability of the individual to achieve personal fulfilment in an aspect of life that is of central significance. In my view, such legislation would clearly constitute an infringement of the right to dignity. It is not only legislation that prohibits the right to form a marriage relationship that will constitute an infringement of the right to dignity, but any legislation that significantly impairs the ability of spouses to honour their obligations to one another would also limit that right. A central aspect of marriage is cohabitation, the right (and duty) to live together, and legislation that significantly impairs the ability of spouses to honour that obligation would also constitute a limitation of the right to dignity.

Cf comments by the Court of Appeal for Ontario on marriage in *Halpern v Canada (AG)* (2003) 225 DLR (4th) 529 [5], [107].

146 n 2 above, [30] (footnotes omitted):

> Marriage and the family are social institutions of vital importance. Entering into and sustaining a marriage is a matter of intense private significance to the parties to that marriage for they make a promise to one another to establish and maintain an intimate relationship for the rest of their lives which they acknowledge obliges them to support one another, to live together and to be faithful to one another. Such relationships are of profound significance to the individuals concerned. But such relationships have more than personal significance at least in part because human beings are social beings whose humanity is expressed through their relationships with others. Entering into marriage therefore is to enter into a relationship that has public significance as well.

147 '[F]amilies come in many shapes and sizes. The definition of the family also changes as social practices and traditions change. In recognising the importance of the family, we must take care not to entrench particular forms of family at the expense of other forms.': *Dawood* (n 2 above) [31] (footnote omitted).

148 *Dawood* (n 2 above) [33] (footnotes omitted):

> In terms of common law, marriage creates a physical, moral and spiritual community of life. This community of life includes reciprocal obligations of cohabitation, fidelity and sexual intercourse, though these obligations are for the most part not enforceable between the spouses. Importantly, the community of life establishes a reciprocal and enforceable duty of financial support between the spouses and a joint responsibility for the guardianship and custody of children born of the marriage. An obligation of support flows from marriage under African customary law as well. In terms of Muslim personal law, the husband bears an enforceable duty of support of the wife during the subsistence of the marriage.

The idea that dignity is sustained by fulfilling the duties that arise from the commitment to an intimate relationship with another entered into autonomously as a core expression of one's autonomy brings a moral dimension to the exercise of choice. The question of whether a person should be entitled to resile from a commitment because of a subsequent change of mind is a further moral dimension with legal implications for consideration. Is one obliged to accept the consequences of choices made? It has resonances of the idea that punishment is required because of respect for the dignity of the offender. This was relied on unsuccessfully in the challenge to the ban on corporal punishment in schools, when those seeking freedom to punish pleaded that for believers, including the children involved 'the indignity and degradation lay not in the punishment, but in the defiance of the scriptures represented by leaving the misdeeds unpunished' and that subjectively, for those who shared that religious outlook, no indignity was involved in the punishment.[149] The retributive justice view of punishment is that respect for the humanity of offenders demands that they accept the consequences of their actions in choosing to break the law.[150] Patrick Smith presses for restorative justice, which regards the offender as an essential part of the repairing process for the victim and at the same time aids the offender in his own healing, thus recognising the dignity of both parties.[151] Stephen Garvey has argued for a secular penance in the interests of the offender as part of the process of atonement after a finding and acceptance of guilt.[152] William Binchy made a case for the option to marry without the choice of divorce in order to recognise in law people's mutual lifelong commitments if they so choose as an aspect of their human dignity and in the autonomous exercise of their free will.[153]

O'Regan J's views in *Dawood* were cited by all judges with varying interpretations of the scope of the maintenance rights of a surviving spouse in *Volks v Robinson*, where a woman in a permanent life partnership claimed an entitlement from the estate of her deceased partner on the same basis as a

149 *Christian Education* (n 50 above) [43].

150 PJ Smith 'A method for the madness: Restorative justice as a valid mode of punishment and an advancement of Catholic social thought' (2005) 44 *Journal of Catholic Legal Studies* 433 at 444.

151 Smith (n 150 above) above, 453 - 454.

152 SP Garvey 'Restorative justice, punishment, and atonement' [2003] *Utah Law Review* 303 at 313 - 314.

153 W Binchy 'Autonomy, commitment and marriage' in O Doyle & W Binchy (eds) *Committed relationships and the law* (2007) 174.

wife.[154] Sachs J's dissenting judgment in *Volks* has extensive philosophical analysis of the nature of marriage, which is deserving of societal support in law based on respect for autonomy and the common good. This does not mean that the law should disregard the choice made – voluntarily or because of circumstances – by lifetime partners not to marry.[155] The substantive relationship between the parties was the central issue, showing 'the serious content of the mutual commitment' and not 'the particular form' in which it was expressed.[156] He resisted viewing the issue 'exclusively as one of the sanctity of marriage, or simply of the important social purpose that marriage serves,' but saw it in terms of 'the integrity of the family relationship.'[157] Sachs J recognised the societal importance of marriage, describing also its benefits of self-esteem, equality and freedom for members of the family.[158] But also to be borne in mind were the rights of life partners without the benefit of having formalised their relationship and perhaps with a more enduring quality than a formal, but empty, marriage.[159] There was

154 2005 5 BCLR 446 (CC) [52], [81], [93], [106], [206], [210]. See OC Okafor *The African human rights system, activist forces and international institutions* (2007) 165 - 166, 207.

155 n 154 above, [156] (Sachs J):

> Respecting autonomy means giving legal credence not only to a decision to marry but to choices that people make about alternative lifestyles. Such choices may be freely undertaken, either expressly or tacitly. Alternatively, they might be imposed by the unwillingness of one of the parties to marry the other. Yet if the resulting relationships involve clearly acknowledged commitments to provide mutual support and to promote respect for stable family life, then the law should not be astute to penalise or ignore them because they are unconventional.

156 n 154 above, [215].

157 n 154 above, [217].

158 n 154 above, [223]:

> There is a great social need to promote marriage as an institution which provides stability, security and predictability for intimate family relations. By so doing our society stresses the importance of people taking responsibility for their lives, and showing respect for the fact that they are members of a law-governed and interdependent community. It encourages self-reliance and self-empowerment; helps people escape from a world made up of victimisers and victims into one consisting of free and equal people; and induces the previously disadvantaged and subordinated to advance in life by calling on their inner strengths rather than allowing themselves to fall into dependence on external support.

159 n 154 above, [230]:

> It needs to be remembered, however, that the claim for maintenance stems from the social regard to be given to commitment, intimacy, interdependency and stability in the family. In the case of a married survivor these will be presumed to have existed as a matter of law. However brief, unstable and non-intimate the marriage might have been, the certificate alone would suffice to grant a claim. In the case of the unmarried survivor, on the other hand, the partnership relationship would have to be proved as a matter of fact.

disagreement between Skweyiya J (for the majority) and Sachs J on the nature of marriage. He criticised Sachs J for having over-simplified the matter by saying that the only difference between the surviving life partner and a spouse was a marriage certificate.[160] Ngcobo J (concurring with the majority) regarded the formal aspect and choice of marriage as decisive.[161] Mokgoro and O'Regan JJ in a joint dissenting judgment saw that commitment to a relationship was not the preserve of married couples.[162]

In *Daniels* the Constitutional Court held that 'spouse' for the purpose of intestacy included those married according to the Muslim rites, who, as Moseneke J stated, had been denied recognition in the past because of prejudice (including judicial bigotry) based on a one-sided view of people judged worthy of respect.[163]

The need for change in the definition of the family in accordance with societal advances is clear.

160 n 154 above, [58], [220].

161 n 154 above, [92]:

> The law expects those heterosexual couples who desire the consequences ascribed to this type of relationship to signify their acceptance of those consequences by entering into a marriage relationship. Those who do not wish such consequences to flow from their relationship remain free to enter into some other form of relationship and decide what consequences should flow from their relationships.

162 n 154 above, [106]:

> The celebration of a marriage thus confers extensive legal duties and rights upon the parties to the marriage as a matter of law. As a matter of social relations, it often results in the founding of a family which provides essential human companionship, mutual support and security to the members of that family. However, not every family is founded on a marriage recognised as such in law. Yet members of such families often play the same roles as in families which are founded on marriage and provide companionship, support and security to one another.

163 *Daniels v Campbell* 2004 5 SA 331 (CC) [74]-[75]:

> [The] 'persisting invalidity of Muslim marriages' is, of course, a constitutional anachronism. It belongs to our dim past. It originates from deep-rooted prejudice on matters of race, religion and culture. True to their worldview, Judges of the past displayed remarkable ethnocentric bias and arrogance at the expense of those they perceived different. They exalted their own and demeaned and excluded everything else. Inherent in this disposition, says Mahomed CJ, is 'inequality, arbitrariness, intolerance and inequity'.
>
> These stereotypical and stunted notions of marriage and family must now succumb to the newfound and restored values of our society, its institutions and diverse people. They must yield to societal and constitutional recognition of expanding frontiers of family life and intimate relationships. Our Constitution guarantees not only dignity and equality, but also freedom of religion and belief.

4.4 Defamation

The right to a good name and reputation form part of the right to human dignity.[164] Hefer JA's view in the Supreme Court of Appeal in *National Media Ltd v Bogoshi* was that the recognition of the right to respect for and protection of dignity in Section 10 of the Constitution 'must encompass ... the right to a good name and reputation.'[165] In balancing the right to protect one's reputation against the freedom of the press, he re-interpreted the common law by holding that strict liability of the media was incompatible with the benefit of public debate.[166] The reasonable publication defence in *Bogoshi* was approved by the Constitutional Court in *Khumalo v Holomisa*, where O'Regan J balanced the dignity in reputation against freedom of expression, which are frequently in conflict in defamation actions.[167]

164 Currie & de Waal (n 8 above) 392.

165 1998 4 SA 1196 (SCA) 41, citing *Holomisa v Argus Newspapers Ltd* 1996 2 SA 588 (W) 607E-G.

166 n 165 above, 25:

> If we recognise, as we must, the democratic imperative that the common good is best served by the free flow of information and the task of the media in the process, it must be clear that strict liability cannot be defended... Much has been written about the 'chilling' effect of defamation actions, but nothing can be more chilling than the prospect of being mulcted in damages for even the slightest error.

The decision was correct, but the SCA had been criticised, *inter alia*, for not acknowledging that its development of the common law principles of defamation was required by the new constitutional values or provisions. Instead, it attributed it to the ordinary dynamic development of the common law: Currie & de Waal (n 8 above) 388 (foot-note omitted). See also HL MacQueen 'Delict, contract, and the Bill of Rights: A perspective from the United Kingdom' (2004) 121 *South African Law Journal* 359 at 373 - 374.

167 2002 5 SA 401 (CC) [43]:

> Were the Supreme Court of Appeal not to have developed the defence of reasonable publication in *Bogoshi*'s case, a proper application of constitutional principle would have indeed required the development of our common law to avoid this result. ... In determining whether publication was reasonable, a court will have regard to the individual's interest in protecting his or her reputation in the context of the constitutional commitment to human dignity. It will also have regard to the individual's interest in privacy. In that regard, there can be no doubt that persons in public office have a diminished right to privacy, though of course their right to dignity persists.

See analyses by Klug (n 88 above) 153 - 154; C Roederer 'The transformation of South African private law after ten years of democracy: The role of torts (delict) in the consolidation of democracy' (2006) 37 *Columbia Human Rights Law Review* 447 at 502 - 504, 512 - 513. Cf *Grant v Torstar Corp* 2009 SCC 61 (SC of Canada), which modified the Canadian law of defamation by recognising a defence of responsible communication on matters of public interest; this would require the media to act proportionately and reasonably when deciding whether or not to publish.

The test for defamation of politicians varies depending on whether the contentious comments relate to their political activities or to their private lives. They are given equal protection in non-political activities, but frank critiques can be lawful in the public arena. Free speech is vital to democracy, so that people are informed, open to debate and can be motivated to participate in society's governing structures. In *Mthembi-Mahanyele* the Supreme Court of Appeal accepted that in some circumstances defamatory political information could be justified under the reasonable publication defence.[168] Lewis JA indicated that there were boundaries:[169]

> That does not mean that there should be a licence to publish untrue statements about politicians. They too have the right to protect their dignity and their reputations. As Burchell puts it:
>
> > 'There are limits to freedom of political comment, especially in regard to aspects of the private lives of politicians that do not impinge on political competence. Politicians or public figures do not simply have to endure every infringement of their personality rights as a price for entering the political or public arena, although they do have to be more resilient to slings and arrows than non-political, private mortals.'

She indicated that the circumstances to be considered in assessing whether a publication about politicians is justifiable included:

> ... the interest of the public in being informed; the manner of publication; the tone of the material published; the extent of public concern in the information; the reliability of the source; the steps taken to verify the truth of the information ...; and whether the person defamed has been given the opportunity to comment on the statement before publication.[170]

In her view, in the case of urgent information crucial to the public, the absence of the opportunity to comment might not be decisive.[171] Mthiyane JA (dissenting) did not agree that there should be a separate or nuanced

168 *Mthembi-Mahanyele v Mail & Guardian Ltd* [2004] 3 All SA 511 (SCA) [64].

169 n 168 above, [67] citing J Burchell *Personality rights and freedom of expression: The modern actio injuriarum* (1998) 229. Jonathan Burchell also said (n 168 above, fn 61, citing Burchell above, 229): 'It has for many years been accepted that greater latitude must be given to freedom of expression on political matters. However, although politicians may, in one sense, be fair game for criticism, it is not completely open season in the political veld.'

170 n 168 above, [68].

171 As above.

reasonable publication defence in relation to politicians.[172] He would prefer harmonisation of the right to freedom of expression with the right to dignity, giving both equal protection, and therefore took the view that barring cabinet ministers from suing 'would undermine the protection of an individual's right to dignity, which includes reputation, and elevate the right to freedom of expression above the right to reputation.'[173]

According to George Devenish, '[t]he operation of the law of defamation has a wider ambit than the mere protection of dignity' as evidenced by the fact that juristic persons can sue for defamation to vindicate their reputations, but the courts have not determined that corporations are the recipients of dignity.[174]

Mayor Dikoko defamed Thupi Mokhatla (the Chief Executive Officer of a municipal authority) when he blamed Mokhatla for deliberately giving his political opponents a basis for an attack on his integrity by changing accounting procedures thereby causing him to run up a debt to the Council for his mobile phone. Dikoko appealed to the Constitutional Court against the successful High Court defamation action brought by Mokhatla.[175] His appeal failed and the Constitutional Court did not interfere with the quantum. A minority would have reduced the quantum including Mokgoro J who felt that the Court should have ordered an apology, as restoration of the plaintiff's dignity would benefit both parties.[176]

Sachs J favoured reparatory remedies and considered it undesirable to have high awards in defamation cases because the main outcome that should

172 n 168 above, [117].

173 n 168 above, [98].

174 G Devenish *A commentary on the South African Bill of Rights* (1999) 87.

175 *Dikoko v Mokhatla* 2006 6 SA 235 (CC).

176 n 175 above, [69]:

> The focus on monetary compensation diverts attention from two considerations that should be basic to defamation law. The first is that the reparation sought is essentially for injury to one's honour, dignity and reputation, and not to one's pocket. The second is that courts should attempt, wherever feasible, to re-establish a dignified and respectful relationship between the parties. Because an apology serves to recognize the human dignity of the plaintiff, thus acknowledging, in the true sense of *ubuntu*, his or her inner humanity, the resultant harmony would serve the good of both the plaintiff and the defendant.

The interest served in many defamation cases in the US embodies a spiritual quality rather than an interest in property or reputation: RR Kwall 'A perspective on human dignity, the First Amendment, and the right of publicity' (2009) 50 *Boston College Law Review* 1345 at 1353.

be sought was an apology to restore dignity and worth in society.[177] A reparatory remedy is more compatible with the public interest than a high award, as it fosters accountability and debate. The defamation in *Dikoko v Mokhatla* had occurred in the course of the mayor being called to account by a governmental committee. In those circumstances, it is important that fear of a high award would not stifle comment, since the chilling effect would be felt by those motivated to speak out in the public interest as well as by those defending their own actions. The remedy advocated by the minority would strike a reasonable balance by encouraging freedom of expression, while ensuring that the dignity of the offended be respected should the boundaries of defamation be crossed. Sachs J captured the adverse effect of high awards well:[178]

> Witnesses before such investigative committees should feel free to speak their mind. As a matter of general principle they should not be made to fear heavy damages suits if they either overstep the mark in the telling, or do not have iron-clad proof to substantiate their testimony. The chilling effect of punitive awards would not only be felt by officials caught with their metaphorical pants down, but by honest whistleblowers and by newspapers simply carrying testimonial exposures.

The constitutional value of *ubuntu-botho* with its solidarity element was 'highly consonant with rapidly evolving international notions of restorative justice.'[179]

The question must be asked whether, and if so to what extent, the constitutional value of dignity is driving the analysis and development of defamation law in South Africa. The trend in common law and civil law jurisdictions had been to promote the free dissemination of information in the public interest by abolishing strict liability for publishing false state-

177 n 175 above, [109]:

> There is a … problem with damages awards in defamation cases. They measure something so intrinsic to human dignity as a person's reputation and honour as if these were market-place commodities. Unlike businesses, honour is not quoted on the Stock Exchange. The true and lasting solace for the person wrongly injured is the vindication by the Court of his or her reputation in the community. The greatest prize is to walk away with head high, knowing that even the traducer has acknowledged the injustice of the slur.

178 n 175 above, [108].

179 n 175 above, [114]. It recognises that to rehabilitate a sentenced offender is 'to recognise the inherent human dignity of the individual offender': *Van Vuren v Minister of Correctional Services* [2010] ZACC 17, 2010 12 BCLR 1233 (CC) [51].

ments. These judgments were not necessarily rooted in protection of dignity, but may have had a different rationale. Indeed, *Bogoshi* itself had developed the common law without overtly relying on the constitutional value of dignity. In his judgment in the Supreme Court of Appeal, Hefer JA referred to the reasonable publication defence enunciated with various local variations in the US, Germany, the European Court of Human Rights, the Netherlands, England, Australia and New Zealand.[180] In balancing the right to freedom of expression with the individual's interest in reputation, the social utility of strict liability in prohibiting the dissemination of false information of no benefit to the public was not as worthy as the good effects in society of encouraging the free flow of useful information.[181] He acknowledged that the Constitution 'rated personal dignity much higher than before', but he did not need to resort to the Constitution to impose the reasonableness requirement.[182]

The constitutional value of human dignity extends beyond the common law notion of self-worth to incorporate the individual's value in the eyes of others, as O'Regan J stated in the Constitutional Court in *Khumalo*:[183]

> *Dignitas* concerns the individual's own sense of self worth, but included in the concept are a variety of personal rights including, for example, privacy. In our new constitutional order, no sharp line can be drawn between these injuries to personality rights. The value of human dignity in our Constitution is not only concerned with an individual's sense of self-worth, but constitutes an affirmation of the worth of human beings in our society. It includes the intrinsic worth of human beings shared by all people as well as the individual reputation of each person built upon his or her own individual achievements. The value of human dignity in our Constitution therefore values both the personal sense of self-worth as well as the public's estimation of the worth or value of an individual.

It must be remembered that freedom of expression itself also invokes dignity and autonomy.

I now propose to undertake a comparative review of the rationale underlying the protection of reputation and the solutions adopted for infringements in other jurisdictions in order to assist in ascertaining whether

180 n 165 above, 26.
181 n 165 above, 22.
182 n 165 above, 43.
183 n 167 above, [27].

respect for dignity is widespread as a guide in defamation actions and whether it is in fact the basis of South African jurisprudence in this area.

In the US, freedom of speech and liberty are prime constitutional values, and there is much tolerance and encouragement of debate and expression of views – particularly of politically-motivated speech.[184] But even there, in the bastion of free speech, Justice Stewart in *Rosenblatt v Baer* – emphasising society's interest in protecting and providing redress for attacks on reputation – based it on human dignity, which he placed at the foundation of a free civilisation.[185]

When Justice Powell in *Gertz* restricted the *New York Times*[186] standard of knowledge or reckless falsity to criticism of public figures in the public or general interest, he reiterated Justice Stewart's focus on the dignity of the individual.[187] The Supreme Court in its majority decision in *Gertz* based its additional protection for private individuals on the fact that, as they had less opportunity for rebuttal, they were more vulnerable and therefore were entitled to recover damages more readily – they had not voluntarily exposed themselves to increased risk of injury from defamatory falsehoods.[188] The Court allowed the states scope for defining for themselves the appropriate standard for defamation of private individuals who were in substantial danger of damage to reputation by the substance of the publication of broadcast, subject only to not imposing liability without fault.[189] Damages were restricted to compensation for actual injury when liability was imposed under a less demanding standard than the *New York Times* test.[190]

184 In recent years, many nations have expanded the protection afforded to defamatory speech on public matters, but few go so far as the US: Heyman (n 30 above) 245 fn 24. See N Rao 'Three concepts of dignity in constitutional law' (2011) 86 *Notre Dame Law Review* 183 at 212 - 214.

185 'The right of a man to the protection of his own reputation from unjustified invasion and wrongful hurt reflects no more than our basic concept of the essential dignity and worth of every human being – a concept at the root of any decent system of ordered liberty.': 383 US 75 (1966) 92.

186 *New York Times v Sullivan* 376 US 254 (1964).

187 *Gertz v Robert Welch, Inc* 418 US 323 (1974) 341.

188 n 187 above, 344 - 345.

189 n 187 above, 347. Steven Heyman agrees with the analysis in *Gertz*, since reputation, being the social aspect of personality, is central to individual dignity and self-realisation: n 30 above, 75. Because free speech confers no general right to violate private reputation, and as these rights are of the same order and value, Heyman concludes that it was appropriate for the Court in *Gertz* to impose liability for injury to reputation based on fault – failure to use reasonable care to determine whether the defamatory statements were actually true: n 30 above, 77.

190 n 187 above, 348 - 349.

Even though reputation is more highly valued on this side of the Atlantic, the European Court of Human Rights allowed more leeway in the expression of opinions on political matters. In *Lingens v Austria* it understood the charged atmosphere that can prevail in the aftermath of elections, when articles were written using the expressions 'basest opportunism', 'immoral' and 'undignified' about the Austrian Chancellor.[191] The magazine publisher, who had been found guilty of criminal libel for accusing the Austrian Chancellor of protecting former Nazis for political reasons and of facilitating their participation in politics, succeeded in his action for violation of his freedom of expression. The Court accepted that the words used appeared likely to harm the politician's reputation, but it had regard to the political background against which the offensive articles had been written and held unanimously that the interference with the freedom of expression in Article 10 ECHR was not necessary in a democratic society and was disproportionate to the legitimate aim pursued.[192]

In Canada considerably more analysis was done of the nature of reputation in *Hill* – an action brought by the Crown attorney – where the Supreme Court found that the common law struck an appropriate balance between the twin values of reputation and freedom of expression.[193] Although not specifically mentioned in the Canadian Charter, Cory J stated that a good reputation was closely related to 'the innate worthiness and dignity of the individual.'[194] The concept of '[t]he innate dignity of the individual' underlay all the Charter rights.[195] Furthermore, reputation was intimately related to the

191 (App no 9815/82) (1986) 8 EHRR 407 at 419 [43].

192 There was disagreement among the judges on whether the right to respect for private life in Art 8 ECHR was engaged, the majority finding that it was not since the comments were made in the context of a public debate in the political arena: n 191 above, 417 [38]. Thór Vilhjálmsson J disagreed, as the comments were made about the Chancellor both as a political leader and as a private individual; therefore he was of opinion that the right to respect for private life in Art 8 was one of the factors relevant to the question whether or not in this case the freedom of expression was subjected to restrictions and penalties that were necessary in a democratic society for the protection of the reputation of others: n 191 above, 423. However, he concluded that this right had in fact been taken into account by the majority when weighing the relevant considerations: n 191 above, 423 - 424.

193 *Hill v Church of Scientology of Toronto* [1995] 2 SCR 1130. See Hogg (n 59 above) 99 - 100, 298 - 300; A Stone & G Williams 'Freedom of speech and defamation: Developments in the common law world' (2000) 26 *Monash University Law Review* 362 at 369 - 371.

194 n 193 above, [107].

195 n 193 above, [120].

196 n 193 above, [121].

constitutionally protected right to privacy.[196] Cory J extolled the benefits to individuals of their reputation in society and regarded its protection as mutually beneficial to all in a democracy.[197] He declined to adopt the *New York Times* standard and was satisfied that the defences of fair comment and qualified privilege were sufficient protection for freedom of expression, saying, '[s]urely it is not requiring too much of individuals that they ascertain the truth of the allegations they publish' and continuing, '[t]hose who publish statements should assume a reasonable level of responsibility.'[198]

Strict liability of the media in England was removed in *Reynolds*, when the English courts broadened the classical test of the duty to impart information the public has an interest in receiving to require a contemporaneous close look at the context and circumstances of publication with a list of factors to be taken into consideration as guidelines in order to establish the reasonableness of the publication.[199] Lord Nicholls gave precedence to reputation founded on the individual's dignity, the preservation of which had societal benefits as well as being of importance to the individual.[200] He

197 n 193 above, [108]:

> Democracy has always recognized and cherished the fundamental importance of an individual. That importance must, in turn, be based upon the good repute of a person. It is that good repute which enhances an individual's sense of worth and value. False allegations can so very quickly and completely destroy a good reputation. A reputation tarnished by libel can seldom regain its former lustre. A democratic society, therefore, has an interest in ensuring that its members can enjoy and protect their good reputation so long as it is merited.

198 n 193 above, [137].

199 *Reynolds v Times Newspapers Ltd* [2001] 2 AC 127 (HL). See W Binchy 'Some unanswered questions in Irish defamation law' in J Sarkin & W Binchy (eds) *Human rights, the citizen and the state: South African and Irish approaches* (2001) 246 - 250; Stone & Williams (n 193 above) 371 - 374.

In Ireland in the absence of legislative reform, Ó Caoimh J endorsed the flexible approach in *Reynolds* as the best way of protecting constitutional rights when reputation and freedom of expression collide, and favoured expansion of the law on qualified privilege to something close to a public interest defence: *Hunter v Gerald Duckworth & Co Ltd* [2003] IEHC 81. Subsequently legislation provided for a defence of fair and reasonable publication on a matter of public interest: Defamation Act 2009 sec 26.

There was a reformulation of *Reynolds* in *Jameel v Wall Street Journal Europe Sprl* [2006] UKHL 44, [2007] 1 AC 359 with clarity emerging that the *Reynolds* defence did not rely on the traditional duty and interest privilege, but was a new public interest defence: K Beattie 'New life for the *Reynolds* "public interest defence"? *Jameel v Wall Street Journal Europe*' [2007] *European Human Rights Law Review* 81 at 83 - 84. The practical message for journalists from *Jameel* was the importance of editorial judgment and contextual accuracy rather than the meaning of words in isolation: Beattie above, 86.

200 n 199 above, 201:

> Reputation is an integral and important part of the dignity of the individual. It also forms the basis of many decisions in a democratic society which are fundamental to

was keen to conform with international human rights norms to arrive at the right balance between freedom of expression and reputation.[201] This was a theme that Lord Steyn also adopted when he referred to the European Court of Human Rights for guidance in drawing the line between permissible and impermissible political speech.[202]

In Australia the High Court held in a majority decision in *Theophanous* that there was implied in the Constitution a freedom to publish material discussing government and political matters, or concerning the performance and suitability for office of politicians.[203] However, the defence of qualified privilege applied if the defendant was unaware of the falsity of the material, which was not published recklessly, and the publication was reasonable in the circumstances. More heed was paid to the politician's reputation than in *New York Times*. In a joint judgment, Mason CJ, Toohey and Gaudron JJ weighed up the advantages of the *New York Times* test, which substantially eliminated the 'chilling effect' of a threatened action for defamation, against the principal criticism that it set 'too little store by the reputation of the person defamed.'[204] They opted to give higher protection to reputation than to freedom of political speech. Restrictions were justified to enable people to live with dignity in society.[205]

> its well-being: whom to employ or work for, whom to promote, whom to do business with or to vote for. Once besmirched by an unfounded allegation in a national newspaper, a reputation can be damaged for ever, especially if there is no opportunity to vindicate one's reputation. When this happens, society as well as the individual is the loser. For it should not be supposed that protection of reputation is a matter of importance only to the affected individual and his family. Protection of reputation is conducive to the public good. It is in the public interest that the reputation of public figures should not be debased falsely. In the political field, in order to make an informed, choice, the electorate needs to be able to identify the good as well as the bad.

201 As above.

202 n 199 above, 215.

203 *Theophanous v Herald & Weekly Times Ltd* (1994) 182 CLR 104. In fashioning a new constitutional defence to override the common law of defamation, the Court owed 'a clear intellectual debt' to *New York Times*: Stone & Williams (n 193 above) 365.

204 n 203 above, 134.

205 n 203 above, 178 - 179 (footnotes omitted) (Deane J, concurring):

> [C]urtailment of the freedom of political communication and discussion is consistent with the [Constitution's] implication [of freedom of political communication and discussion] only to the extent to which it can, according to the standards of our society, be justified in the public interest either for the reason that it is conducive to the overall availability of the effective means of political communication and discussion in a democratic society or it does not go beyond what is necessary either for the preservation of an ordered society or for the protection or vindication of the legitimate claims of individuals to live peacefully and with dignity in such a society.

The High Court was not satisfied with the *Theophanous* finding that there was a constitutional defence to defamation based on freedom of expression, so it reformulated it in *Lange v Australian Broadcasting Corporation*.[206] In this libel action brought by the former Prime Minister of New Zealand, the Court developed the common law defence and held that a publisher relying on qualified privilege for a communication made to the public on a government or political matter must establish that its conduct in making the publication was reasonable in all the circumstances.[207] The Court placed a high value on the implied constitutional principle of freedom of communication concerning political or government matters.[208] It examined the common law right to reputation and stated that the protection of the reputations of those who take part in public life was conducive to the public good.[209] There was no reference to human dignity.

Mr Lange features again in litigation in his own country over articles critical of his performance as Prime Minister.[210] Following a complicated series of appeals, the New Zealand Court of Appeal in *Lange v Atkinson* in 2000 took cultural differences into account and was more inclined to trust the media than in other common law jurisdictions.[211] The outcome was that it protected false statements on political matters, provided the publishers were properly motivated and not seeking unfair advantage.[212] Reasonable

206 (1997) 189 CLR 520. See JG Fleming *The law of torts* (1998) 630 - 631, 642 - 643; Stone & Williams (n 193 above) 366 - 367.

207 As a general rule a defendant's conduct would not be reasonable unless the defendant had reasonable grounds for believing the defamatory imputation was true, took proper steps so far as they were reasonably open to verify the accuracy of the material, and did not believe the imputation to be untrue; the privilege would be defeated if the plaintiff proved that the publication was actuated by ill will or other improper motive: n 206 above, 574.

The *Lange* privilege is narrower than the relatively broad defence that applies in England, where it is not limited to institutional conceptions of politics; the Australian cases have not provided a public interest defence and the privilege there rarely encompasses speech about commercial issues: AT Kenyon '*Lange* and *Reynolds* qualified privilege: Australian and English defamation law and practice' (2004) 28 *Melbourne University Law Review* 406 at 419.

208 n 206 above, 560.

209 n 206 above, 568.

210 Stone & Williams (n 193 above) fn 71.

211 [2000] NZCA 95. It had considered the matter previously in 1998: *Lange v Atkinson* [1998] 3 NZLR 424. The Privy Council then decided in 1999 that the New Zealand court was not bound to apply *Reynolds* nor, indeed, to adopt the Australian solution: *Lange v Atkinson* [1999] UKPC 46, [2000] 1 NZLR 257 [25]. Hence in 2000 it re-visited its 1998 judgment. See Stone & Williams (n 193 above) 377.

212 Binchy (n 199 above) 246.

care was not a necessary criterion.[213] It adopted an extended form of qualified privilege that was context-dependent, retaining the duty and interest test.[214]

In *Trustco Group International Ltd v Shikongo* in 2010,[215] the Supreme Court of Namibia in an appeal from the High Court – which had found *Bogoshi* persuasive[216] – upheld development of the common law to provide a reasonable publication defence to give effect to the constitutional provisions on freedom of expression[217] and the inviolability of dignity.[218] The issues on appeal went to the merits[219] and quantum – the award in the High Court was thought to be the highest ever in Namibia for defamation.[220] O'Regan AJA, delivering the judgment on behalf of a unanimous Supreme Court, placed the onus of proof of responsible journalism and the importance of publication on the publisher.[221] As many other jurisdictions had done, she rejected the balance adopted in the US in *New York Times v Sullivan*, which gave much leeway to the press by finding that actual malice by a publisher was required before liability for defamation of a public official would be imposed.[222] The development of a reasonable publication defence would 'provide greater protection to the right of freedom of speech and the media protected in

213 As above.

214 Stone & Williams (n 193 above) 376. Adrienne Stone and George Williams have concluded that the Court of Appeal seemed to be open to the prospect that competing interests should prevail over freedom of speech, and that, like other courts, it was especially concerned with the competing interest of reputation which it regarded as related to human dignity and privacy: above, 375.

215 [2010] NASC 6. The action was brought by the Mayor of Windhoek against a newspaper that published an article accusing him of being involved in an irregular deal relating to the sale of city land: above, [5]-[6]. He maintained that the allegations were wrong and that the article defamed him by portraying him as dishonest, abusive of his mayoral position and neglectful of his duties to the public: above, [6].

216 n 215 above, [20].

217 Constitution of the Republic of Namibia 1990, Sec 21(1)(a). It is subject to reasonable restriction: Sec 21(2).

218 Sec 8.

219 Neither party defended strict liability as being a reasonable restriction on freedom of expression in a democratic society: n 215 above, [48]. The newspaper proposed that the common law be developed by putting the onus on the plaintiff to prove the falsity of the defamatory statement, whereas the respondent considered that the defence of reasonable publication as set out in *Bogoshi* was appropriate: n 215 above, [35], [48].

220 n 215 above, [21].

221 'The effect of the defence is to require publishers of statements to be able to establish not that a particular fact is true, but that it is important and in the public interest that it be published, and that in all the circumstances it was reasonable and responsible to publish it.': n 215 above, [53].

222 n 215 above, [36]-[37].

section 21 without placing the constitutional precept of human dignity at risk.'[223]

On quantum, the primary question was whether the award of damages was grossly disproportionate to the injury suffered.[224] O'Regan AJA reviewed awards in other cases[225] and referred to Sachs J's views in *Dikoko* on the incongruity of trying to establish a proportionate relationship between vindication of reputation and determining the amount of compensation, since reputation was restored – not by money – but by a judicial finding in favour of the integrity of the individual.[226] But she also referred to Sachs J's opinion that damages were still important in a world that remained so money-oriented.[227] While taking account of the aggravating circumstances of the publication, she reduced the quantum of damages by more than 40%.[228]

To summarise my findings in the comparative analysis I have just undertaken of defamation actions involving the media and public figures, there are some trends evident in the philosophical bases for protection of freedom of speech and reputation. The individual's reputation is universally regarded as deserving of respect, albeit not specifically recognised as a separate right in many jurisdictions. Society has an interest in protecting the reputations of individuals, so it is not solely the concern of the isolated person. It matters to individuals how society views them, as well as how they regard their own dignity and self-worth. Freedom of expression – particularly in the political context in a participative democracy – is an important value to society and its members.[229] Therefore, there is some tolerance of publication errors being made in haste. The proportionality analysis is central to deciding the balance between the competing rights and the answers to the queries raised varies in different jurisdictions according to their cultural values.

Reverting to South Africa, it is quite possible that the common law would have been developed to provide a reasonable care defence in defamation in any event on the basis of the Roman-law *dignitas* concept even without the elevation of human dignity in the Constitution. This happened in other

223 n 215 above, [53]. She did not decide the issue of whether the defence of reasonable publication was confined to media defendants: n 215 above, [56].

224 n 215 above, [90].

225 n 215 above, [92]-[94].

226 n 215 above, [90], citing n 175 above, [110].

227 n 215 above, [91], citing n 175 above, [120].

228 n 215 above, [95]-[96].

229 See *Thint Holdings (Southern Africa) (Pty) Ltd v National DPP* [2008] ZACC 14, 2009 1 SA 141 (CC) [52].

common law countries where *dignitas* was unknown and dignity was not a constitutional right or expressed value.

4.5 Sexual violence

The right to dignity is clearly breached by sexual violence. The Supreme Court of Appeal mentioned its humiliating and degrading effect in *S v Chapman*.[230] Notwithstanding the vile nature of sexual violence and society's laudable desire to deter sexual crimes, the alleged perpetrator's dignity also has to be respected in the criminal process.[231] Imprisonment without culpability or in the absence of the exercise of free will to make a rational choice is contrary to constitutional values. The legislature has some scope to balance the dignity interests of the offender and the victim, but there is a limit.[232] O'Regan J described the boundaries to the imposition of strict liability in *S v Coetzee*.[233]

230 1997 3 SA 341 (SCA) 3:

> Rape is a very serious offence, constituting as it does a humiliating, degrading and brutal invasion of the privacy, the dignity and the person of the victim.
> The rights to dignity, to privacy and the integrity of every person are basic to the ethos of the Constitution and to any defensible civilisation.
> Women in this country are entitled to the protection of these rights. They have a legitimate claim to walk peacefully on the streets, to enjoy their shopping and their entertainment, to go and come from work, and to enjoy the peace and tranquillity of their homes without the fear, the apprehension and the insecurity which constantly diminishes the quality and enjoyment of their lives.

Cf *People (DPP) v Tiernan* [1988] IR 250 (SC) 253. Violence against women is a manifestation of the exercise of male power over them: *Masiya v DPP (Pretoria)* [2007] ZACC 9, 2007 5 SA 30 [28], [77]-[78]. The global institution of male dominance remains despite having been exposed, analysed and organised against for decades: CA MacKinnon 'Gender – The future' (2010) 17 *Constellations* 504 at 504.

231 See *Bothma v Els* [2009] ZACC 27, 2010 2 SA 622 (CC) [33]. The Court of Appeal in Botswana held that a law that mandatorily denied bail to anyone accused of rape was not in the public interest and breached the constitutional right to personal liberty: *S v Marapo* [2002] AHRLR 58 (BwCA 2002) [25], citing Constitution of the Republic of Botswana 1966, Sec 5(3)(b).

232 The restriction on the right and the means used must be proportionate to the public interest to be served: Sachs *The strange alchemy of life and law* (n 56 above) 206.

233 1997 3 SA 527 (CC) [177]:

> [S]ignificant leeway ought to be afforded to the legislature to determine the appropriate level of culpability that should attach to any particular unlawful conduct to render it criminal. It is only when the legislature has clearly abandoned any requirement of culpability, or when it has established a level of culpability manifestly inappropriate to the unlawful conduct or potential sentence in question, that a provision may be subject to successful constitutional challenge.

In Ireland strict liability is also regarded with suspicion by the courts where imprisonment is a sanction. The Supreme Court in *CC v Ireland* asserted that imprisonment without proof of *mens rea* for a serious crime would be incompatible with liberty and dignity and therefore it found unconstitutional legislation imposing strict liability for unlawful carnal knowledge of a minor.[234] Hardiman J expressed the Court's belief that *mens rea* was necessary because 'to criminalise in a serious way a person who is mentally innocent is indeed "to inflict a grave injury on that person's dignity and sense of worth" and to treat him as "little more than a means to an end"'.[235]

The link between inequality and lack of respect for dignity was noted by the Constitutional Court in *Carmichele*, when it endorsed the importance to one's dignity of freedom from the threat of sexual violence.[236] Because of the entrenchment of the rights to life, dignity and freedom and security of the person in the Constitution and because the Bill of Rights bound all state authorities, the Court not only indicated that there was a negative duty on the state not to infringe those rights, but found that that in some circumstances there would also be a positive duty on the state 'to provide appropriate protection to everyone through laws and structures designed to afford such protection.'[237] The Court then went on to set in motion what has turned out to be what Iain Currie and Johan de Waal described as 'considerable development of the law of delict' under the common law in the light of the Constitution.[238] It has led to the state's vicarious liability for failure to prevent

The public interest was on both sides of the equation in *S v Coetzee*, where the issue was whether the reverse onus in two provisions of the Criminal Procedure Act 1977 breached the presumption of innocence and, if so, whether they were justifiable limitations. Madala J posed the dilemma '[i]n any democratic criminal justice system there is a tension between, on the one hand, the public interest in bringing law breakers to book, and, on the other hand, the equally great public interest of ensuring that justice is manifestly done to all': above, [126].

234 [2006] IESC 33, [2006] 4 IR 1.

235 n 234 above, [44], citing Wilson J in *R v Hess* [1990] 2 SCR 906 (SC of Canada).

236 *Carmichele v Minister of Safety and Security* 2001 4 SA 938 (CC) [62] (footnote omitted):

> In addressing these obligations [of the police force] in relation to dignity and the freedom and security of the person, few things can be more important to women than freedom from the threat of sexual violence. As it was put by counsel on behalf of the *amicus curiae*:
>
> > 'Sexual violence and the threat of sexual violence goes to the core of women's subordination in society. It is the single greatest threat to the self-determination of South African women.'

237 n 236 above, [44].

238 n 8 above, 304.

injury. The Constitutional Court in *Carmichele* contrasted the system in the US – differentiating between action and inaction in holding the state not liable for not preventing harm – with the positive obligations imposed by the South African Constitution and the ECHR.[239] It pointed out that the South African Constitution, like the German Constitution, embodies 'an objective, normative value system.'[240] The Constitutional Court did not develop the common law itself, but referred the case back to the lower court for reconsideration. Currie and de Waal explained that on reappraisal, the law of delict was developed

> to encompass state liability in circumstances where state authorities knew or ought to have known at the time of the existence of a real and immediate risk to the life or physical security of an identified individual or individuals from the criminal acts of a third party and … they failed to take measures within the scope of their powers, which, judged reasonably, might have been expected to avoid that risk.[241]

In *Carmichele*[242] the Constitutional Court adopted the approach of the European Court of Human Rights in *Osman v UK* where it had been found that the right to life in Article 2 ECHR obliged the state in some circumstances to take pre-emptive action to prevent harm.[243]

239 n 236 above, [45].

240 n 236 above, [54]. See A Chaskalson 'Dignity as a constitutional value: A South African perspective' (2011) 26 *American University International Law Review* 1377 at 1385; CJ Roederer 'Working the common law pure: Developing the law of delict (torts) in light of the spirit, purport and objects of South Africa's Bill of Rights' (2009) 26 *Arizona Journal of International and Comparative Law* 427 at 495 - 498.

241 n 8 above, 305.

242 n 236 above, [45]. See G Devenish 'The evolution and development of a value-based and teleological interpretation of statute and common law in South Africa as a result of the 1996 Constitution' in Quansah & Binchy (n 17 above) 113 - 114; F du Bois 'State liability in South Africa: A constitutional remix' (2010) 25 *Tulane European and Civil Law Forum* 139 at 142 - 143, 145 - 146, 166, 171; MacQueen (n 166 above) 368 - 369, 386.

243 (App no 23452/94) (2000) 29 EHRR 245. The European Court sketched the parameters of the positive obligation under the ECHR, above, 305 [115]:

> It is common ground that the State's obligation in this respect extends beyond its primary duty to secure the right to life by putting in place effective criminal law provisions to deter the commission of offences against the person backed up by law-enforcement machinery for the prevention, suppression and sanctioning of breaches of such provisions. It is thus accepted by those appearing before the Court that Article 2 of the Convention may also imply in certain well-defined circumstances a positive obligation on the authorities to take preventive operational measures to protect an individual whose life is at risk from the criminal acts of another individual.

It recognised the 'difficulties involved in policing modern societies, the unpredictability

In *Van Eeden* the Supreme Court of Appeal considered the obligations of the police to a woman who was sexually assaulted, raped and robbed by a serial rapist who had escaped from police custody.[244] It held that the police owed the public a legal duty to act positively to prevent the escape from custody of a known dangerous criminal likely to commit further sexual offences where measures to prevent his escape could reasonably and practically have been taken by the police. The state was vicariously liable for the actions of the police and she was entitled to damages. The existence of the duty of the police in these circumstances accorded with the legal convictions of the community and there were no considerations of public policy militating against its imposition.[245] The finding was based on the state's constitutional imperatives to protect human dignity, equality and freedom and security of the person.[246] Vivier ADP judged the state's liability by the yardstick of reasonableness taking into account policy and the community's legal convictions.[247] There are no pre-defined limits to the state's liability, but, as stated by Vivier ADP, each case is individually assessed using the criteria for negligence.[248]

Ms K, who had had an argument with a boyfriend with whom she had been out for the evening, was looking for a telephone to call home when she met three police officers. They offered her a lift home which she accepted. However, they took her to a deserted place, raped and abandoned her. The Court in *K v Minister of Safety and Security* unanimously held that the Minister was vicariously liable.[249] Although the policemen's conduct was a clear

of human conduct and the operational choices which must be made in terms of priorities and resources' and held that the duty on the state 'must be interpreted in a way which does not impose an impossible or disproportionate burden on the authorities': above, 305 [116].

244 *Van Eeden v Minister of Safety and Security* [2002] 4 All SA 346 (SCA).

245 n 244 above, [24].

246 n 244 above, [13], [24].

247 n 244 above, [9]:

> A defendant is under a legal duty to act positively to prevent harm to the plaintiff if it is reasonable to expect of the defendant to have taken positive measures to prevent the harm. The court determines whether it is reasonable to have expected of the defendant to have done so by making a value judgment, based *inter alia* upon its perception of the legal convictions of the community and on considerations of policy.

248 n 244 above, [22]:

> [O]ur courts do not confine liability for an omission to certain stereotypes but adopt an open-ended and flexible approach to the question whether a particular omission to act should be held unlawful or not. In deciding that question the requirements for establishing negligence and causation provide sufficient practical scope for limiting liability.

249 2005 6 SA 419 (CC).

deviation from their duty, there existed a sufficiently close relationship between their employment and the wrongful conduct. O'Regan J unsurprisingly held that the police officers had breached K's rights to dignity and security of the person in Sections 10 and 12 of the Constitution, and went on to explain why the state as employer should be liable in tort for their actions:[250]

> In committing the crime, the policemen not only did not protect the applicant, they infringed her rights to dignity and security of the person. In so doing, their employer's obligation (and theirs) to prevent crime was not met. There is an intimate connection between the delict committed by the policemen and the purposes of their employer. This close connection renders the respondent liable vicariously to the applicant for the wrongful conduct of the policemen.

The finding of vicarious liability was possible because the state and the police had constitutional obligations to prevent crime in general under Section 205(3) of the Constitution.[251] The policemen also had a statutory obligation as part of their work to ensure the safety and security of all South Africans and to prevent crime.[252] Their duty extended to protect the public from crime within the police force as well as from the more usual source in the wider community. The existing common law had a test for establishing vicarious liability similar to that in other jurisdictions focusing both on 'the subjective state of mind of the employees' and the objective question, whether the deviant conduct was 'nevertheless sufficiently connected to the employer's enterprise'.[253]

The Court developed the common law on vicarious liability, as O'Regan J considered that the objective element of the test relating to 'the connection between the deviant conduct and the employment' was sufficiently flexible to incorporate constitutional and other norms.[254] When a court utilised the test, there was a requirement 'to articulate its reasoning for its conclusions as to whether there is a sufficient connection between the wrongful conduct

250 n 249 above, [57].

251 It reads: 'The objects of the police service are to prevent, combat and investigate crime, to maintain public order, to protect and secure the inhabitants of the Republic and their property, and to uphold and enforce the law.'

252 n 249 above, [18], citing Preamble to the South African Police Service Act 1995.

253 n 249 above, [44].

254 As above.

and the employment or not.'[255] In applying the test to the facts in K's situation, O'Regan J held that the objective test had been satisfied as, first, the policemen and their employer all bore a statutory and constitutional duty to prevent crime and protect the members of the public.[256] Second, in addition to the general duty to protect the public, the uniformed policemen had offered to assist K and she had accepted their offer.[257] Third, the conduct of the policemen constituted the commission of the rape and the simultaneous omission of failing while on duty to protect her from harm.[258] These three inter-related factors make it plain that viewed against the background of K's constitutional rights and the constitutional obligations of the policemen and the state, the connection between the conduct of the policemen and their employment was sufficiently close to render the state vicariously liable.[259]

This decision was a fair development of the common law. There was a sufficient nexus between the wrong perpetrated and the employment responsibilities of the police officers to justify a finding of vicarious liability.[260] It has implications for the accountability of the state where employees commit wrongs while deviating from the normal performance of their duties. It also could have application in jurisdictions outside South Africa, as O'Regan J cited foreign jurisprudence to support her reasoning.[261] So it could involve the state in making reparation for abuse by employees with a duty to protect the public, such as those working in institutions caring for children or others in state care, members of the fire brigade, hospital staff or air traffic controllers involved in transgressions.

255 As above.

256 n 249 above, [51].

257 As above.

258 n 249 above, [53].

259 As above.

260 Contrast *Phoebus Apollo Aviation CC v Minister of Safety and Security* [2002] ZACC 26, 2003 2 SA 34 (CC).

261 She cited case-law from England, Canada and the US: n 249 above, [36]-[37], [38]-[40], [41]-[42].

4.6 Children

A child has a right to dignity of its own. Sachs J described the independent personality of the child in *S v M*.[262] The implications of independence for children are personal and associative.[263]

The dignity rights of children range across a broad spectrum and engage freedom to express themselves, communicate, and to know and form their own identities. To enable them to make lifestyle and moral choices when they grow up, education in the broad sense is indispensable. They are entitled to experience and enjoy their childhood in secure surroundings.

Specific children's rights are contained in Section 28 of the Constitution. There is constitutional recognition that, in all matters concerning them, children's 'best interests are of paramount importance'.[264] This rule has some practical difficulties in application, the most serious of which is the absence of guidelines to ascertain its scope.[265] The express recognition of children's rights in the Constitution has had an effect beyond the provision's immediate reach and has given an impetus to children's access to equality and other constitutional rights, as Langa DCJ stated in *Bhe*:[266]

> Section 28 of the Constitution provides specific protection for the rights of children. Our constitutional obligations in relation to children are particularly important for we vest in our children our hopes for a better life for all. The inclusion of this provision in the Constitution marks the

262 2008 3 SA 232 (CC) [18]:

> Every child has his or her own dignity. If a child is to be constitutionally imagined as an individual with a distinctive personality, and not merely as a miniature adult waiting to reach full size, he or she cannot be treated as a mere extension of his or her parents, umbilically destined to sink or swim with them.

263 *S v M* (n 262 above) [19] (Sachs J):

> Individually and collectively all children have the right to express themselves as independent social beings, to have their own laughter as well as sorrow, to play, imagine and explore in their own way, to themselves get to understand their bodies, minds and emotions, and above all to learn as they grow how they should conduct themselves and make choices in the wide social and moral world of adulthood. And foundational to the enjoyment of the right to childhood is the promotion of the right as far as possible to live in a secure and nurturing environment free from violence, fear, want and avoidable trauma.

264 Sec 28(2). See Rautenbach (n 5 above) 422 - 426.

265 B Bekink & D Brand 'Constitutional protection of children' in CJ Davel (ed) *Introduction to child law in South Africa* (2000) 194 - 195. There are varying views on whether it is defective because it is broad and vague, or whether its flexibility is beneficial: above, 194.

266 *Bhe v Khayelitsha Magistrate* 2005 1 SA 580 (CC) [52] (footnotes omitted).

> constitutional importance of protecting the rights of children, not only those rights expressly conferred by section 28 but also all the other rights in the Constitution which, appropriately construed, are also conferred upon children. Children, therefore, may not be subjected to unfair discrimination in breach of section 9(3) just as adults may not be.

In that case the Court found that the African customary law rule of male primogeniture, in the form that it had come to be applied in relation to the inheritance of property, discriminated unfairly against women and extra-marital children, who still suffered from 'social stigma and impairment of dignity'.[267] Ngcobo J partially dissented and considered that the principle of primogeniture did not unfairly discriminate on the basis of age and birth against younger children in the family, as the limitation on their rights imposed by entrusting the responsibilities of a deceased family head to the eldest child was reasonable and justifiable, bearing in mind that the African culture cherished respect for elders, who were required to mentor the young.[268] Statutory provisions governing succession and intestacy also breached the constitutional rights to equality in Section 9(3) and to dignity in Section 10.

The best interests of the child have been given some judicial consideration. In *Fitzpatrick* where legislation prohibiting intercountry adoption was held to be contrary to the rights of the child in Section 28 to the extent that it absolutely proscribed adoption of a South African born child by non-South Africans, Goldstone J did not impose a rigid meaning on the child's best interests.[269] One of the objects of the Hague Convention is to establish safeguards to ensure that adoptions take place in the best interests of the

267 n 266 above, [59]. In Tanzania the prohibition on the sale of inherited clan land by females (but not by males) was held to constitute discrimination on the grounds of sex: *Ephrahim v Pastory* [1990] LRC (Const) 757 (High Court of Tanzania). In adjudicating on a dispute over the distribution of the estate of an intestate polygamous man, the Court of Appeal in Kenya found that it would be unfair discrimination on the grounds of sex to allocate daughters minimal shares on the basis that they would marry: *Rono v Rono* [2005] AHRLR 107 (KeCA 2005).

268 n 266 above, [181], [183].

269 *Minister for Welfare and Population Development v Fitzpatrick* 2000 3 SA 422 (CC). See Shannon (n 59 above) [1-66].

child.[270] Goldstone J pointed out the need for flexibility to ensure the child's welfare.[271]

The Court found in *Du* Toit that the statutory exclusion of an otherwise suitable lesbian couple from adopting a child infringed not only the rights of the proposed adoptive parents, but also breached the principle that the child's best interests were paramount and infringed the child's right to care in Section 28(1)(b) of the Constitution.[272] Skweyiya AJ criticised the Child Care Act for thus depriving children 'of the possibility of a loving and stable family life', which was 'a matter of particular concern given the social reality of the vast number of parentless children' in South Africa.[273]

270 Convention on Protection of Children and Cooperation in Respect of Intercountry Adoption (adopted 29 May 1993, entered into force 1 May 1995) 32 ILM 1139 (1993) (Hague Convention on Intercountry Adoption), Art 1(a). The state had cited the Hague Convention to highlight the international concern given to child trafficking: n 269 above, [25]. South Africa had not signed or ratified the Convention: n 269 above, [26].

271 n 269 above, [18] (footnotes omitted):

> [T]he 'best interests' standard appropriately has never been given exhaustive content in either South African law or in comparative international or foreign law. It is necessary that the standard should be flexible as individual circumstances will determine which factors secure the best interests of a particular child.

272 *Du Toit v Minister of Welfare and Population Development* 2003 2 SA 198 (CC).

273 n 272 above, [22].

5

Value of Human Dignity with other Rights

The value of dignity is frequently used as an aid to interpret other rights and to give them substance. Human dignity's foundational status[1] has meant that it serves as a background principle in the interpretation and development of other rights.[2] Heinz Klug pointed out the similarity between South African and German jurisprudence in this respect – both regard human dignity as a foundational value and both have specific rights to dignity.[3] Reva Siegel has discerned at least three distinct usages of dignity in the substantive due process and equal protection cases in the United States: dignity as life, dignity as liberty, and dignity as equality.[4] Dignity as 'liberty' can be seen when dignity resembles Kantian autonomy, described by Siegel as 'the right of individuals to be self-governing and self-defining, and their commensurate right not to be treated as mere objects or instruments of another's will.'[5] When dignity

1 Human rights emerged because of human dignity serving as 'a conceptual hinge' to connect the internalised rationally justified morality anchored in the individual conscience with coercive positive enacted law: J Habermas 'The concept of human dignity and the realistic utopia of human rights' (2010) 41 *Metaphilosophy* 464 at 470.

2 H Klug 'The dignity clause of the Montana Constitution: May foreign jurisprudence lead the way to an expanded interpretation?' (2003) 64 *Montana Law Review* 133 at 149.

3 As above.

4 RB Siegel 'Dignity and the politics of protection: Abortion restrictions under *Casey/Carhart*' (2008) 117 *Yale Law Journal* 1694 at 1737.

5 n 4 above, 1738 (footnotes omitted). Justice Brennan called the American Constitution 'a sublime oration on the dignity of man, a bold commitment by a people to the ideal of libertarian dignity protected through law': WJ Brennan, Jr 'The Constitution of the United States: Contemporary ratification' (1986) 27 *South Texas Law Review* 433 at 438.

'is concerned with respect, honor, and social standing, and concerns the right of persons to be respected as an equal member of the polity rather than denigrated, subordinated, or excluded', it is dignity as 'equality'.[6]

5.1 Freedom and security

Specific safeguards for the freedom and security of the person are contained in Section 12 of the Constitution.[7] Section 12(1) is devoted to personal freedom,[8] while Section 12(2) relates to bodily and psychological integrity.[9]

5.1.1 Personal freedom

Freedom and security of the person at substantive and procedural levels are in issue when the liberty of the individual is at stake.[10] They can arise in civil

David Bilchitz has criticised the Kantian view on dignity, describing it as 'perhaps one of the least justifiable elements of his moral system'; he questions Kant's view that worth or dignity lies in rational agency alone and that rational nature is the only thing that exists as an end in itself: D Bilchitz 'Moving beyond arbitrariness: The legal personhood and dignity of non-human animals' (2009) 25 *South African Journal on Human Rights* 38 at 54. Even if it is accepted that rational agency is of value, the concept seems to embrace a wide range of mental phenomena not within the capacity of all human beings, *eg*, young children, the senile and persons with mental incapacities: above, 55 - 56.

Jürgen Habermas finds fault with Kant's view of human rights, which obtain their moral content from a universal individual conception of human dignity, because he assimilates human dignity to intelligible freedom thereby losing the connotations of self-respect and social recognition deriving from the status of democratic citizenship: n 1 above, 475.

6 n 4 above, 1739 (footnote omitted).

7 See IM Rautenbach *Rautenbach-Malherbe constitutional law* (2012) 343 - 354.

8 Constitution of the Republic of South Africa 1996, Sec 12(1):

Everyone has the right to freedom and security of the person, which includes the right

a) not to be deprived of freedom arbitrarily or without just cause;
b) not to be detained without trial;
c) to be free from all forms of violence from either public or private sources;
d) not to be tortured in any way; and
e) not to be treated or punished in a cruel, inhuman or degrading way.

9 Sec 12(2):

Everyone has the right to bodily and psychological integrity, which includes the right

a) to make decisions concerning reproduction;
b) to security in and control over their body; and
c) not to be subjected to medical or scientific experiments without their informed consent.

10 See *Lawyers for Human Rights v Minister of Home Affairs* [2004] ZACC 12, 2004 4 SA 125 (CC).

matters as well as in relation to crime. Legitimate deprivation of liberty normally follows a fair trial and conviction. The length of detention must be reasonable, equally applied to all in similar circumstances and give an incentive to improve by a promise of early release for good behaviour.[11] A fair trial respects the dignity of the accused, of the justice system and of society as a whole. The democratic principle of equality demands that all be treated fairly. Section 12(1) of the Constitution contains detailed provisions protecting the individual's freedom and security, while the right to a fair trial is in Section 35(3). There is a case-by-case analysis of whether there has been an infringement of the constitutional right to personal freedom. Dignity and equality as foundational values are relevant in the assessment of the factual situation.

The judges in the Constitutional Court in *Ferreira v Levin* held conflicting views as to the breadth of freedom protected by Section 11 of the interim Constitution.[12] Ackermann J felt that a broad interpretation of freedom was warranted, as in its absence dignity had no practical meaning since people would be unable to achieve self-fulfilment and realise the full extent of their dignity.[13] Chaskalson P considered that dignity was not dependent on that wide a reading of freedom.[14] Sachs J also disagreed with Ackermann J's rendition of Section 11, but thought that the overall constitutional setting, the foundational values and the rights to dignity and privacy would give

11 Parole has a restorative justice aim: *Van Vuren v Minister of Correctional Services* [2010] ZACC 17, 2010 12 BCLR 1233 (CC) [51]. Retrospective deprivation of credits to advance the date of consideration for parole deprived an offender of liberty and did not conform with the rule of law: *Van Wyk v Minister of Correctional Services* [2011] ZAGPPHC 125 (North Gauteng High Court, Pretoria) [22].

12 1996 1 SA 984 (CC). See Klug (n 2 above) 152.

13 'Without freedom, human dignity is little more than an abstraction. Freedom and dignity are inseparably linked. To deny people their freedom is to deny them their dignity.': n 12 above, [49].

14 n 12 above, [173]:

> [N]or do I consider it necessary, as Ackermann J has suggested that it may be, to adopt such a construction in order to give substance to the right to human dignity. In the context of the multiplicity of rights with which it is associated in Chapter 3, human dignity can and will flourish without such an extensive interpretation being given to section 11(1).

In the *Prostitution Reference* in Canada Lamer J cautioned against defining liberty or security of the person in the Canadian Charter in terms of attributes such as dignity, self-worth and emotional well-being, as liberty would then be all inclusive and would give rise to questions about the independent existence in the Charter of other rights and freedoms such as freedom of religion and conscience or freedom of expression: *Reference re ss 193 and 195.1(1)(c) of the Criminal Code (Man)* [1990] 1 SCR 1123 (SC of Canada) 52.

more substance to freedom.[15] Modern society requires state intervention and the inevitable curtailment of individual liberty to some extent in order to provide an environment conducive to the enjoyment of freedom by all. Sachs J rightly said it was unrealistic nowadays to 'equate freedom simply with autonomy or the right to be left alone'.[16] The effective exercise of individual choice depends not just on the state refraining from interference, but taking positive interventionist steps to ensure that people can choose. Mutual compatibility in society is necessary for realisation of freedom, as Sachs J explained:[17]

> Freedom and personal security are thus achieved both by protecting human autonomy on the one hand, and by acknowledging human interdependence on the other. The interdependence is not a limitation on freedom, but an element of it.

The right to freedom in Section 11 of the interim Constitution arose also in *Bernstein v Bester* where O'Regan J considered that the foundational value of dignity would aid interpretation of freedom, security and other rights.[18] In *S v Thebus* the doctrine of common purpose was held to be constitutional and did not violate the rights to dignity or to freedom.[19] Moseneke J did not

15 n 12 above, [255]:

> The text of section 11, which includes a prohibition against detention without trial, as well as the exclusion of torture and other forms of physical and emotional ill-treatment, indicates a narrow concern with the theme of bodily restraint or abuse, rather than a sweeping repudiation of any impediment whatsoever to the orderly pursuit of happiness. On the other hand, the express acknowledgement of the rights to dignity and privacy in sections 10 and 13 respectively, read together with the preamble and the afterword, establish a setting which allows for a more expansive role for the word freedom.

16 n 12 above, [250] (footnote omitted).

17 n 12 above, [251] (footnote omitted).

18 1996 2 SA 751 (CC) [148]:

> [S]ection 11(1) needs to be understood in the context of the fundamental commitment to dignity expressed in our Constitution in section 10. Our Constitution represents an emphatic rejection of a past in which human dignity was denied repeatedly by an authoritarian and racist government. ... The recognition of the value of human beings is a cardinal principle of the Constitution and one which will inform the interpretation of many of the specific rights in the Constitution.

Ackermann J in *De Lange v Smuts* (a challenge to committal to prison for failure to produce documents and to provide information in insolvency proceedings), considered it significant that the use of committal to prison as a means to enforce the disclosure of information in insolvency proceedings was not constitutionally or otherwise objectionable in other open and democratic societies based on dignity, equality and freedom: 1998 3 SA 785 (CC) [39].

19 2003 6 SA 505 (CC).

accept the defence argument that the legal rule dehumanised the perpetrators, because they had chosen voluntarily to participate in the criminal escapade.[20] Deprivation of liberty in South Africa must be in accordance with the basic tenets of the legal system.[21]

The legislation allowing for imprisonment of judgment debtors was found to be a violation of Section 11(1) of the interim Constitution in *Coetzee v Government of the Republic of South Africa*, when Sachs J treated the right to dignity as 'intertwined with' the freedom and security rights, and an aid to interpreting them.[22] The Constitutional Court held in *Malachi v Cape Dance Academy International (Pty) Ltd* that the arrest and detention of an alleged debtor intending to flee the country breached the right to freedom and security in Section 12 of the Constitution and was not a justifiable limitation.[23] The procedural device of civil imprisonment came to the Cape through Roman-Dutch law and was retained with some modification after the English administration replaced the Dutch authority in the Cape in the early 18th century; later, other territories in South Africa legislated for civil imprisonment based on the Cape model; after the establishment of the Union of South Africa in 1910 it was consolidated and modified by successive

20 '[A] person who knowingly, and bearing the requisite intention, participates in the achievement of a criminal outcome cannot, upon conviction in a fair trial, validly claim that his or her rights to dignity and freedom have been invaded.': n 19 above, [41].

21 This approach corresponds loosely with that of the Canadian courts in dealing with the standard of 'fundamental justice' in Section 7 of the Canadian Charter of Rights and Freedoms: I Currie & J de Waal *The Bill of Rights handbook* (2005) 296.

22 1995 4 SA 631 (CC) [43]. In assessing whether the limitation of rights was reasonable and necessary, Sachs J did not establish 'an impossibly high threshold' which would rule out 'genuine weighing by Parliament of reasonable alternatives within the broad bracket of what would not be unduly oppressive' and indicated that what mattered in 'finding "the least onerous solution"' was that 'the means adopted by Parliament fell within the category of options which were clearly not unduly burdensome, overbroad or excessive, considering all the reasonable alternatives': above, [60]. Eva Brems commented that although the maximisation criterion was being applied in principle here, it was interpreted in a way that significantly lowered the standard; instead of looking for the least onerous solution, the Court looked for a not unduly onerous solution: E Brems 'Human rights: Minimum and maximum perspectives' (2009) 9 *Human Rights Law Review* 349 at 364 - 365.

Cf *Julius v Commanding Officer, Windhoek Prison* 1996 NR 390 (High Court of Namibia).

23 [2010] ZACC 13, 2010 6 SA 1 (CC) [34], [41]. Legislation permitting lenders to seize and sell the property of defaulting debtors breached the right of access to court in Section 34 of the Constitution and was not a permitted limitation: *Lesapo v North West Agricultural Bank* [1999] ZACC 16, 2000 1 SA 409 (CC). Contrast *Road Accident Fund v Mdeyide* [2010] ZACC 18, 2011 2 SA 26 (CC).

legislation, which ultimately abolished civil imprisonment as such, but effectively neutralised the abolition by retaining imprisonment of a judgment debtor who had failed to satisfy a judgment debt for contempt of court.[24] In 1986 the South African Law Commission recommended abolition of this procedure; at the request of the Minister of Justice, a further investigation was launched by the Commission and it recommended provisionally that the mechanism of civil imprisonment be retained with modifications.[25]

From a comparative law perspective, there is no universal approach to imprisonment for civil debt. Some countries have prohibited it entirely;[26] others have forbidden imprisonment for non-payment of a contractual obligation, but have allowed imprisonment for civil contempt of court of a recalcitrant debtor with ability to pay. The remedy of imprisonment for the failure to pay a judgment debt can be traced to ancient legal systems such as the Mosaic legislation and the Twelve Tables of early Roman law.[27] The origins of the ban on civil imprisonment date back to 1606 in English law, when nobles were not liable to be arrested for debt because – as explained by the Star Chamber – of their dignity and the presumption of sufficient wealth that could be seized.[28] Eventually in 1970 the ban on imprisonment for debt in England was extended to all.[29] Several international and regional human right instruments adopted since the Second World War prohibit imprisonment for failure to comply with an order for payment of a contractual debt.[30] They include the International Covenant on Civil and Political Rights (ICCPR), article 11 of which reads: 'No one shall be imprisoned merely on the ground of inability to fulfil a contractual obligation.'[31] There is a very similar provision in the Fourth Protocol to the European Convention on

24 W le R de Vos 'Civil imprisonment: The impact of the new Constitution' (1994) 5 *Stellenbosch Law Review* 133 at 135.

25 De Vos (n 24 above) 136.

26 *Eg*, France and the Netherlands: de Vos (n 24 above) 139.

27 De Vos (n 24 above) 134 - 135.

28 J Waldron *Dignity, rank, and rights* (2012) 56 - 57, citing *Isabel, Countess of Rutland's Case* (1606) 6 Co Rep 52 b, 77 ER 332 at 333.

29 De Vos (n 24 above) 138 - 139, citing Administration of Justice Act 1970.

30 De Vos (n 24 above) 141.

31 International Covenant on Civil and Political Rights (adopted 16 December 1966, entered into force 23 March 1976) 999 UNTS 171 (ICCPR). Art 11 is excluded from the provisions in ICCPR which may be derogated from in times of public emergency: art 4(2).

Human Rights (ECHR).[32] The American Declaration of the Rights and Duties of Man does not confine the prevention of imprisonment to debt, but covers other civil obligations with the following wording: 'No person may be deprived of liberty for nonfulfillment of obligations of a purely civil character.'[33]

In *Chinamora v Angwa Furnishers (Private) Ltd* the Supreme Court of Zimbabwe found that there were sufficient legal safeguards to prevent the jailing of an impecunious debtor.[34] The Constitution of Zimbabwe contained a specific recognition that a person could be deprived of personal liberty as authorised by law 'in execution of the order of a court made in order to secure the fulfilment of an obligation imposed on him by law'.[35] The Court held that the legislative provisions and the court rules did not violate the inhibition on deprivation of personal liberty in Section 13(1) of the Constitution.[36] Gubbay CJ distinguished *Coetzee*, as in Zimbabwe there was adequate protection for the debtor since the law differentiated between debtors who could not pay and those who refused to pay.[37] The reformative

32 'No one shall be deprived of his liberty merely on the ground of inability to fulfil a contractual obligation': ECHR Protocol No 4 securing certain rights and freedoms other than those already included in the Convention and in the first Protocol thereto, Art 1.

33 American Declaration of the Rights and Duties of Man, OAS Res XXX adopted by the Ninth International Conference of American States (1948) reprinted in Basic Documents Pertaining to Human Rights in the Inter-American System OEA/Ser L V/II.82 Doc 6 Rev 1 at 17 (1992), Art XXV, 2nd para.

34 [1997] 1 LRC 149. Cf *Noor v Botswana Co-operative Bank Ltd* 1999 (1) BLR 443 (CA) (Botswana).

35 Constitution of the Republic of Zimbabwe 1979, Sec 13(2)(c).

36 Neither was the constitutional protection of the law for every person in Section 18(1) violated, since it was specifically subject to other constitutional provisions, including Section 13(2)(c) allowing deprivation of liberty to ensure fulfilment of a legal obligation: n 34 above, 169 - 170. Because of the avoidable nature of punishment in imprisonment for civil debt, the Court also held that it did not amount to degrading treatment under Section 15(1) of the Constitution: n 34 above, 169. The Court pointed out that a sentence of imprisonment could not be adjudged unconstitutional unless it was blatantly disproportionate to the quality of the offence – the humiliation and degradation felt by a person sentenced to a term of imprisonment did not of itself constitute degrading treatment: n 34 above, 168.

37 n 34 above, 167. The onus was on the creditor to establish the debtor's ability to pay: n 34 above, 166. The procedure required the debtor to produce evidence of his financial position, warned him of the possibility of imprisonment and, by enjoining the court to conduct a meticulous inquiry into his ability to pay, ensured that that issue was properly addressed and examined: n 34 above, 166 - 167. Where the debtor did not attend the hearing, the court would not order imprisonment unless satisfied that there had been personal service of the summons, and, in practice, the court only entertained an application for imprisonment when other enforcement methods had been considered or tried and were inappropriate or unsuccessful: n 34 above, 167.

and autonomous elements necessary to render constitutional imprisonment for non-payment of civil debt are evident in Gubbay CJ's judgment, as he considered it essential that the debtor should have the choice to avoid prison by having access to funds to pay the amount due.[38] He recognised that imprisonment of an impecunious debtor was contrary to international human rights instruments, which were not concerned with the debtor who had the means to pay but obdurately declined to do so.[39] They were aimed at protection of the individual from imprisonment where there was a genuine inability to pay.[40] The international code was not breached in Zimbabwe, which also only targeted those who refused to pay.

In a somewhat analogous situation in *Hicks v Feiock* concerning the burden of proof in punishment for contempt of court of a father for failure to make child support payments, the US Supreme Court focused on the difference between criminal contempt and civil contempt, due process being required only for the former.[41] Justice White pointed out the choice to avoid the conditional penalty available in civil contempt, where it was specifically

When the Irish High Court found that the legislation permitting imprisonment for debt was unconstitutional on the grounds that it breached the guarantee of fair procedure and that it was a disproportionate interference with the debtor's right to liberty, Laffoy J referred to the Supreme Court of Zimbabwe's distinction of *Coetzee*: *McCann v Judge of Monaghan District Court* [2009] IEHC 276.

38 n 34 above, 163:

> Thus the only real effect of imprisonment of an impoverished debtor is that of punishment. It is a punishment that can be avoided by a debtor who is able but unwilling to pay; for satisfaction of the judgment remains within his power. But it becomes mandatory against one without the means to pay. It discriminates between one and the other.

39 n 34 above, 162.

40 n 34 above, 162 - 163.

41 485 US 624 (1988). The case was referred back to the state court for further consideration, as the majority considered it was unclear whether civil or criminal contempt was involved. Justice O'Connor for the dissentients in *Hicks* looked at the beneficiary of the proceedings to assist in ascertaining the nature of the punishment, as she stated, '[t]he most important indication is whether the judgment inures to the benefit of another party to the proceeding.': above, 646. Having considered the objective features of the proceeding and the sanction in order to infer whether it was criminal or civil, the minority concluded it was civil contempt, since the penalty was intended to enforce maintenance payments and not simply to punish for non-compliance with a court order: above, 646, 650 - 651.

Sachs J in *Coetzee* referring to the imprisonment of a judgment debtor and the different objectives of a criminal trial, cited *Hicks* as re-affirming 'the distinction between imprisonment for a fixed period as a punishment for doing something forbidden, and imprisonment as a flexible remedial instrument for failure to fulfil an obligation': n 22 above, [43], fn 34.

designed to compel the doing of some act, in contrast to an unconditional penalty which was criminal in nature because it was 'solely and exclusively punitive in character.'[42] The theme of free choice has resonances in Gubbay CJ's judgment in *Chinamora*.

The Supreme Court of India in *Jolly George Verghese v Bank of Cochin* invoked the value of dignity when it held that a simple default to discharge a judgment debt did not merit imprisonment, as enjoined by article 11 of ICCPR.[43] The Court construed the constitutional rights to equality before the law and equal protection of the laws,[44] to freedom[45] and to fair procedure before deprivation of liberty[46] in the light of the value of dignity. Krishna Iyer J affirmed that the 'high value of human dignity and the worth of the human person'[47] obligated the state not to incarcerate except under law which was 'fair, just and reasonable in its procedural essence.'[48] The legislation was unconstitutional because it implied that a sanction could be imposed if a debtor had the ability to pay at any time since the judgment, even though he later became penniless.[49] The Court required that there be a comprehensive view of the person's situation. Imprisonment of a person to recover a debt required 'proof of the minimal fairness of his wilful failure to pay in spite of his sufficient means and absence of more terribly pressing claims on his means such as medical bills to treat cancer or other grave illness.'[50] An element of dishonesty could also justify imprisonment, as Krishna Iyer J indicated when he set out the parameters:[51]

> The simple default to discharge is not enough. There must be some element of bad faith beyond mere indifference to pay, some deliberate or recusant disposition in the past or, alternatively, current means to pay the

42 n 41 above, 633, citing *Penfield Co v SEC* 330 US 585 (1947) 593.

43 [1980] INSC 19, 1980 SCR (2) 913.

44 Constitution of India 1950, Art 14.

45 Art 19.

46 Art 21.

47 n 43 above, 921.

48 n 43 above, 922. Krishna Iyer J adverted to the change in the legal approach over time, as he stated, '[a] modern Shylock is shacked by law's humane hand-cuffs.': n 43 above, 916. He expanded on the equal worth of the poor, '[i]t is too obvious to need elaboration that to cast a person in prison because of his poverty and consequent inability to meet his contractual liability is appalling. To be poor, in this land of daridra Narayana, is no crime…': n 43 above, 922.

49 n 43 above, 922.

50 As above.

51 As above.

> decree or a substantial part of it. ... [C]onsiderations of the debtor's other pressing needs and straitened circumstances will play prominently.

Imprisonment for crimes of strict liability infringes the right to freedom because the will to commit a crime is absent. South African criminal law, founded on liberal philosophy, as Shannon Hoctor wrote, holds humans morally autonomous and assumes the individual can distinguish right from wrong, has the competency to decide how to act and the capability to realise that decision.[52] Because of human dignity and autonomy, the individual must not be treated as an object or instrument.[53] These moral principles find expression in the necessity for there to be *mens rea* before deprivation of liberty for a crime.[54] O'Regan J in *S v Coetzee* said it had been acknowledged by the courts 'on countless occasions' that 'the state's right to punish criminal conduct rests on the notion that culpable criminal conduct is blameworthy and merits punishment.'[55] Strict liability uses the offender as an instrument of deterrence and can only be allowed for regulatory or minor infringements of the law with correspondingly limited sanctions. Similar principles were applied in Irish law in *CC v Ireland*, where the Supreme Court held that a provision which criminalised and exposed a person without mental guilt to a maximum sentence of life imprisonment failed to respect the liberty or dignity of the individual.[56]

As criminal liability without fault is not consonant with basic tenets of the legal system, Iain Currie and Johan de Waal have deduced that its constitutionality in South Africa depends on it being justified under the general limitation clause.[57]

52 S Hoctor 'Dignity, criminal law, and the Bill of Rights' (2004) 121 *South African Law Journal* 304 at 306.

53 As above.

54 n 52 above, 309. Markus Dubber urges that levels of *mens rea* (*eg*, purpose, knowledge, recklessness, and negligence) should represent degrees to which the offender's act can be conceptualised, first, as a manifestation of her capacity for autonomy and, second, as a manifestation of her view of the victim as a non-person, *ie*, as lacking the capacity for autonomy: MD Dubber 'Dignity in penal law and penal police' (2009) Working Paper http://ssrn.com/abstract=1530545 (accessed 28 September 2013) 5.

55 1997 3 SA 527 (CC) [162].

56 [2006] IESC 33, [2006] 4 IR 1. Subsequently the Criminal Law (Sexual Offences) Act 2006 criminalised defilement of a child, but provided for a defence of 'honest belief' that the child was over age in section 2(3) and section 3(5). The question of the burden of proof of 'honest belief' was considered in *People (DPP) v Egan* [2010] IECCA 28.

57 n 21 above, 297.

The criminal law also incorporates the communitarian aspect *ubuntu*, which is closely aligned to dignity.[58] Langa J described the link between dignity and *ubuntu*, and the mutuality of respect in society in *Makwanyane*:[59]

> [*Ubuntu*] recognises a person's status as a human being, entitled to unconditional respect, dignity, value and acceptance from the members of the community such person happens to be part of. It also entails the converse, however. The person has a corresponding duty to give the same respect, dignity, value and acceptance to each member of that community. More importantly, it regulates the exercise of rights by the emphasis it lays on sharing and co-responsibility and the mutual enjoyment of rights by all.

The interrelationship in communities and the equality in dignity between individuals curtail the freedom to act without regard for the other.

Section 12(1)(c) of the Constitution providing for the right to be free from public or private violence,[60] together with the rights to life and human dignity, impose a positive duty on the state to protect individuals in some circumstances.[61] Because of the constitutional imperative to protect dignity and personal freedom and security, the Court held in *Baloyi* that the state is obliged to deal with domestic violence.[62] Sachs J referred to the positive and negative aspects to the right not to be physically abused.[63]

58 Hoctor (n 52 above) 315.

59 *S v Makwanyane* 1995 6 BCLR 665 (CC) [224]. Habermas emphasised the need to anchor human dignity in equal social status as members of an organised community, where citizens derive their self-respect from the fact that they are recognised by all other citizens as subjects of equal actionable rights: n 1 above, 472.

60 The formulation of the right to freedom from public and private violence as an aspect of the right to freedom and security justifies state intervention in domestic violence; the fact that the right to freedom from violence is a discrete right dispels any argument that the right to freedom and security only provides a guarantee against arbitrary arrest and detention: H Combrinck 'The right to freedom from violence and the reform of sexual assault law in South Africa' in J Sarkin & W Binchy (eds) *Human rights, the citizen and the state: South African and Irish approaches* (2001) 185.

61 *Carmichele v Minister of Safety and Security* 2001 4 SA 938 (CC) [44]. The South African Constitution, like the ECHR, by on occasion requiring operational intervention by the state to prevent harm, points in the opposite direction to the absence of positive rights in the US Constitution: above, [45].

62 *S v Baloyi* 2000 2 SA 425 (CC). This was significant, as there had been a perception that domestic violence was solely a private dispute: W Amien 'Recent developments in the area of women's rights in South Africa: Focusing on domestic violence and femicide' in Sarkin & Binchy (n 60 above) 171 - 172.

63 n 62 above, [11] (footnotes omitted):

> Read with section 7(2), section 12(1) has to be understood as obliging the state directly to protect the right of everyone to be free from private or domestic violence.

The courts have developed the common law incrementally in accordance with constitutional principles to impose vicarious liability in delict on the state, where negligent omissions by the police allowed members of the public to be killed or injured. The Supreme Court of Appeal in *Minister of Safety and Security v Van Duivenboden* held that the negligent conduct of police officers in possession of information reflecting on the fitness of a person to possess firearms gave rise to a duty to take reasonable steps to act on that information in order to avoid harm occurring, such that individuals injured as a result were entitled to compensation from the state.[64] Nugent JA for the majority based his assessment of the circumstances when it should be unlawful to culpably cause loss on the prevailing norms in South Africa.[65] He approached this task in a structured manner and ruled out intuition as a guide.[66] He considered that the norm of accountability had an important role in determining whether a legal duty ought to be recognised.[67] Where accountability could be secured without delictual liability through the political process or by another judicial remedy,[68] compensation would not necessarily be payable by the state.[69] In the absence of an alternative method of accountability, an action would lie provided there were no countervailing

Indeed, the state is under a series of constitutional mandates which include the obligation to deal with domestic violence: to protect both the rights of everyone to enjoy freedom and security of the person and to bodily and psychological integrity, and the right to have their dignity respected and protected, as well as the defensive rights of everyone not to be subjected to torture in any way and not to be treated or punished in a cruel, inhuman or degrading way.

64 [2002] 3 All SA 741 (SCA). On the limits of state liability, see *Brooks v Minister of Safety and Security* [2008] ZASCA 141, 2009 2 SA 94 (SCA); F du Bois 'State liability in South Africa: A constitutional remix' (2010) 25 *Tulane European and Civil Law Forum* 139 at 168 - 169.

65 n 64 above, [16].

66 'When determining whether the law should recognize the existence of a legal duty in any particular circumstances what is called for is not an intuitive reaction to a collection of arbitrary factors but rather a balancing against one another of identifiable norms.': n 64 above, [21].

67 As above.

68 The African Commission requires that a remedy be available, effective and sufficient: *Jawara v The Gambia* [2000] AHRLR 107 (ACHPR 2000) [31]. A remedy is considered available if the petitioner can pursue it without impediment; it is deemed effective if it offers a prospect of success, and it is found sufficient if it is capable of redressing the complaint: above, [32].

69 n 64 above, [21]. Cf *Steenkamp NO v Provincial Tender Board of the Eastern Cape* 2007 3 SA 121 (CC).

policy issues.[70] The state had a constitutional duty to protect an individual's constitutional rights to human dignity, life and security of the person, and, as there was no offsetting public interest, liability attached to the state.[71] The issue was not the general duty of the police to investigate crime.[72]

The Constitutional Court in *Rail Commuters Action Group v Transnet Ltd t/a Metrorail* approved of taking into consideration accountability, as well as other constitutional norms such as 'the principle of effectiveness and the need to be responsive to people's needs', in a contextual enquiry to determine whether a legal duty exists.[73]

In *Minister of Safety and Security v Hamilton* the Supreme Court of Appeal held that the police had a legal duty to exercise reasonable care in considering, investigating, recommending and granting an application for a firearm licence and that the state was liable in damages to a person injured by the licence holder.[74] The police were obliged to take reasonable steps to investigate whether the applicant was competent and fit to possess a firearm. The identifiable norms that Van Heerden AJA balanced were the individual's right to life, bodily integrity and security of the person against 'policy considerations such as the efficient functioning of the police, the availability of resources and the undoubted public importance of the effective control of firearms.'[75] He based his decision, not directly on the Constitution, but on the common law and statutory provisions.[76] However, he was satisfied that the existence of the legal duty on the police in the circumstances was consistent with society's norms and values as reflected in the Constitution.[77]

70 '[W]here the state's failure occurs in circumstances that offer no effective remedy other than an action for damages the norm of accountability will, in my view, ordinarily demand the recognition of a legal duty unless there are other considerations affecting the public interest that outweigh that norm.': n 64 above, [21].

71 n 64 above, [22]. Marais J concurred in the outcome, but for different reasons. He did not base his decision on constitutional grounds.

72 As above.

73 2005 2 SA 359 (CC) [78]. See DM Davis 'Socioeconomic rights: Do they deliver the goods?' (2008) 6 *International Journal of Constitutional Law* 687 at 704 - 705, 707, 708.

74 [2003] 4 All SA 117 (SCA).

75 n 74 above, [35].

76 n 74 above, [36].

77 As above.

5.1.2 Damages for breach of fundamental rights

The question of whether damages over and above those under the normal delictual headings should be awarded for breach of fundamental rights was raised in *Fose*.[78] Fose claimed damages from the State for a series of assaults by members of the police force. In addition to common law damages for pain and suffering, insult, shock, past and future medical expenses and loss of enjoyment of the amenities of life, he claimed 'constitutional damages' including an element of punitive damages[79] for the infringement of his constitutional rights mainly not to be tortured nor subjected to cruel, inhuman or degrading treatment.[80] He also relied on violation of his rights to dignity[81] and privacy.[82] The legal issue that came before the Constitutional Court was whether constitutional damages could and ought to be awarded as appropriate relief under Section 7(4)(a) of the interim Constitution for breach of constitutional rights.[83]

According to Ackermann J, the fact that litigation was a costly venture in a country with many poor people made it even more imperative to secure an effective remedy in the event of a claim being successful.[84] He accepted that it might be necessary for the courts 'to "forge new tools" and shape innovative remedies' in order to do so.[85] In the case at hand involving claims for assault, however, the Constitutional Court found that an award of constitutional damages against the state on top of damages at common law would not be appropriate.[86] Ackermann J considered that the civil and criminal laws should

78 *Fose v Minister of Safety and Security* 1997 3 SA 786 (CC). See C Roederer 'The transformation of South African private law after ten years of democracy: The role of torts (delict) in the consolidation of democracy' (2006) 37 *Columbia Human Rights Law Review* 447 at 491 - 493. Cf *Chituku v Minister of Home Affairs* [2004] ZWHHC 6 (Harare High Court).

79 n 78 above, [12].

80 Interim Constitution of the Republic of South Africa 1993, Sec 11(2).

81 Sec 10.

82 Sec 13.

83 n 78 above, [1].

84 n 78 above, [69]:

> [A]n appropriate remedy must mean an effective remedy, for without effective remedies for breach, the values underlying and the rights entrenched in the Constitution cannot properly be upheld or enhanced. Particularly in a country where so few have the means to enforce their rights through the courts, it is essential that on those occasions when the legal process does establish that an infringement of an entrenched right has occurred, it be effectively vindicated.

85 As above.

86 n 78 above, [73], [75], [88], [104], [106].

be kept separate and that penalties should only be imposed following a criminal prosecution with the attendant procedural safeguards.[87] From his wide-ranging comparative review of damages in foreign jurisdictions and under the ECHR,[88] he ascertained that in some countries (including Ireland) constitutional damages are awarded.[89] He was averse to requiring the state to pay excessive damages for the wrongdoing of the police, as the deterrent effect on individual police officers was doubtful[90] and public monies could be put to better use to prevent assaults by the police in future.[91]

87 n 78 above, [70].

88 Convention for the Protection of Human Rights and Fundamental Freedoms, 213 UNTS 222 (ECHR).

89 n 78 above, [25]-[57]. He distinguished the foreign jurisprudence, as differences in law and procedure existed between the jurisdictions reviewed and South Africa: n 78 above, [58]. The statutory relief and the award of constitutional damages based directly on the Constitution in the US were legislative and judicial responses to the perceived inadequacy of the common law tort remedies: n 78 above, [55]. The recognition of constitutional torts in the US established the right of citizens to hold government accountable for individual harms, which departs from the more traditional democratic approach of holding the government accountable collectively by exercising the will of the majority in elections: SJ Wermiel 'Law and human dignity: The judicial soul of Justice Brennan' (1998) 7 *William and Mary Bill of Rights Journal* 223 at 235.

90 The Irish Supreme Court has held that in an appropriate case exemplary or punitive damages for breach of constitutional rights might be awarded as an effective deterrent: *Conway v Irish National Teachers Organisation* [1991] 2 IR 305 (HC, SC). After this case it was clear that punitive damages might be awarded for breach of a constitutional right in Ireland, but it was less easy to identify the criteria for granting them: W Binchy 'Constitutional remedies and the law of torts' in J O'Reilly (ed) *Human rights and constitutional law: Essays in honour of Brian Walsh* (1992) 217. The circumstances in which exemplary damages would be awarded was clarified subsequently: *Shortt v Commissioner of An Garda Síochána* [2007] IESC 9, [2007] 4 IR 587. The Supreme Court indicated that exemplary damages served several potential purposes including to mark the court's disapproval of a defendant's outrageous conduct: above, [108], [253]. They were also punitive and they might financially punish a defendant as a deterrent to that defendant as well as a deterrent generally to the arrogant use or abuse of power: above, [109], [253]. Although in the form of a financial penalty, an award of exemplary damages was also 'a moral sanction, a mirror to "the proper indignation of the public"': above, [110] (Murray CJ).

91 n 78 above, [72] (footnote omitted):

> In a country where there is a great demand generally on scarce resources, where the government has various constitutionally prescribed commitments which have substantial economic implications and where there are 'multifarious demands on the public purse and the machinery of government that flow from the urgent need for economic and social reform', it seems to me to be inappropriate to use these scarce resources to pay punitive constitutional damages to plaintiffs who are already fully compensated for the injuries done to them with no real assurance that such payment will have any deterrent or preventative effect. It would seem that funds of this nature could be better employed in structural and systemic ways to eliminate or substantially reduce the causes of infringement.

The same attitude is apparent in Didcott J's judgment where he elaborated on the downside of punitive damages against the state.[92] Unlike Ackermann J, he was completely opposed to the introduction by the judiciary of punitive or exemplary damages against the state in any circumstances and was unambiguously of the view that it was a matter for the legislature to decide after investigation by the Law Reform Commission, consultation with experts in the area and perhaps even a judicial enquiry.[93] He was open to the possibility of punitive or exemplary damages against non-state parties because the funds would not come from the public coffers and would be a deterrent, but even if that were thought appropriate it should be the product of legislative action and not of judicial innovation.[94] Kriegler J also viewed an award of punitive damages against the state for assault as futile, but he did not rule out punitive damages in all circumstances.[95]

It is clear that none of the judges favoured punitive damages against the state in assault cases.[96] The taxpayer would end up paying for excessive enrichment of the person assaulted, who took the initiative to sue. The evidence in *Fose* seemed to indicate that assaults and torture by police officers were widespread.[97] The remedy should not be to make excessive awards of damages against the state. To stamp out corruption in the police force would

92 n 78 above, [84]:

> [P]ayment [of punitive or exemplary damages] would come from the public purse and go to the plaintiff alone. Few potential torturers would be scared greatly by such a sequel, one not affecting their own pockets. Nor could it strengthen the cause of vindication for an individual claimant, or even a series of them, to be enriched at the expense of the taxpayer.

93 n 78 above, [85]-[86].

94 n 78 above, [87]. Contrast *Shortt* (n 90 above) [229] (Hardiman J).

95 n 78 above, [103]:

> The relief in this case would come from the public coffers and be directed towards the appellant. The policemen implicated in the appellant's claim could not possibly be deterred by a payment of damages bearing no relation to their own finances. Nor do we vindicate the Constitution by enriching a particular claimant at the cost of the taxpayer – particularly when the problem is far larger than the claimant concerned. In other words, we do not adequately defend the Constitution by merely granting punitive damages in this case, or even in several cases. ... I should stress that punitive damages is not 'appropriate relief' on these facts because it is inefficacious for dealing with the kind of problem that the appellant posits.

96 Contrast the decision of Mwaungulu J in the High Court of Malawi when his award of damages for false imprisonment for 19 years compensated the plaintiff and punished the state for the way it treated him: *Munthali v AG* [2002] AHRLR 102 (MwHC 1993) [27]. His award took into account the injury to feelings (indignity, mental suffering, distress and humiliation): above, [22].

97 n 78 above, [22], [81], [89].

require a practical solution such as better training, supervision and disciplining of the police.

The decision in *Fose* is a narrow one and it did not decide whether punitive damages for breach of constitutional rights generally would be appropriate. Currie and de Waal's assessment is that *Fose* established two general principles – first, where the violation of constitutional rights entails the commission of a delict, an award of damages *in addition* to those available under the common law will seldom be available and, second, even where delictual damages are not available, constitutional damages will not necessarily be awarded for a violation of human rights.[98]

5.1.3 Bodily and psychological integrity

Any doubts that might have existed over whether and to what extent personal freedom allowed control over one's body, mind and thoughts, were removed by Section 12(2) of the Constitution. Abortion is permitted by the right to make decisions concerning reproduction, so this controversial issue does not get as much public debate in South Africa as elsewhere.[99] In acknowledgment of medical and scientific developments, experiments cannot be carried out without informed consent.[100] Currie and de Waal have formulated the following universal question concerning dignity and freedom to find out if the experiments proposed are justified, '[w]hen and to what extent can the benefits which accrue to society for medical and scientific experimentation outweigh considerations of individual dignity and autonomy?'[101]

The essence of the right to freedom and security of the person is a right to be left alone, which creates a sphere of individual bodily inviolability.[102] Section 12(2)(b) distinguishes between 'security in' one's body, which protects bodily integrity against intrusions by the state or others, and 'control over' the body, which is the protection of bodily autonomy or self-determination against interference. Currie and de Waal have described them as different components of the right to be left alone – the former in the sense of 'being left unmolested by others' and the latter in the sense of 'being allowed to live the life one chooses.'[103]

98 n 21 above, 221.
99 Sec 12(2)(a).
100 Sec 12(2)(c).
101 n 21 above, 311.
102 Currie & de Waal (n 21 above) 308.
103 n 21 above, 309.

5.2 Fair trial and imprisonment

Detailed rights for those arrested, detained and accused are set out in Section 35 of the Constitution.[104] Detainees and sentenced prisoners have the right to 'conditions of detention that are consistent with human dignity, including at least exercise and the provision, at state expense, of adequate accommodation, nutrition, reading material and medical treatment'.[105] Fair trial rights are enumerated at length – 15 specific rights being listed in Section 35(3) and providing for matters such as a public trial,[106] the presumption of innocence and not to be compelled to speak or to testify[107] or to give self-incriminating evidence.[108]

5.2.1 Criminal trials

Unlike the apartheid-era rigid system of law enforcement in accordance with the dictates of Parliament, the new South African constitutional legal system was a complete turnaround. It created an upheaval in the assessment of substantive and procedural issues arising in criminal trials. The contrast was apparent to Kentridge AJ in *S v Zuma* when he pointed out that henceforth criminal trials were required to be conducted in accordance with 'notions of basic fairness and justice' and that the right to a fair trial embraced 'a concept of substantive fairness which is not to be equated with what might have passed muster in our criminal courts before the Constitution came into force.'[109] Moseneke J adverted to the comprehensive nature of the constitutional guarantees in criminal trials in *Thebus*, 'the Bill of Rights authorises and anticipates prosecution, conviction and punishment of individuals

104 The arrested person has the right to remain silent, to be informed of that fact, not to be compelled to make a confession, to be brought to court within 48 hours and then either charged, released or informed of the reason for continuing the detention, and to be released on reasonable conditions should the interests of justice so permit: Sec 35(1)(a)-(f).

105 Sec 35(2)(e). They also have rights to be informed of the reason for detention, to consult a lawyer, (at state expense, if substantial injustice would otherwise result), to bring a *habeas corpus* application, and to communicate with and be visited by close family and religious and medical advisers: Sec 35(2)(a)-(d), (f). Dingake J in Botswana High Court held that criminal proceedings were unconstitutional when an accused had been detained without trial for over 16 months and was only informed of the charge just before the start of the trial: *Sekwati v DPP* [2008] BWHC 263.

106 Sec 35(3)(c).

107 Sec 35(3)(h).

108 Sec 35(3)(j).

109 1995 2 SA 642 (CC) [16].

provided it occurs within the context of a procedurally and substantively fair trial and a permissible level of criminal culpability.'[110]

The right to a fair trial and the presumption of innocence are key elements in safeguarding the liberty and dignity of the accused.[111] Avoiding a wrongful conviction is not the only reason for the constitutional provisions to ensure a fair trial, but they are also necessary to uphold dignity and equality, as Ackermann J discerned in *S v Dzukuda*, having pointed out that dignity, equality and freedom lie 'at the heart of a fair trial in the field of criminal justice'.[112]

The consequences of a conviction have severe social implications and cause the community to shun the offender. The rationale behind a fair trial takes into account the associative aspects of the individual and not simply the isolated subjective effects of incarceration on the convicted person. A guilty verdict is the official imprimatur on publicly blaming a person for breaching standards set by society and, as Otto Lagodny said, 'is meant to stigmatize and dishonour the violator', thus encroaching on the offender's

110 n 19 above, [36] (footnote omitted).

111 *Zuma* (n 109 above) [22]; *S v Manamela* 2000 3 SA 1 (CC) [40]. Cf *R v Oakes* [1986] 1 SCR 103, where the Canadian Supreme Court stated that the presumption of innocence protects liberty and dignity; it held that a reverse onus on an accused to disprove on the balance of probabilities that drugs in his possession were for the purpose of trafficking violated the presumption of innocence and was not a justifiable limitation; there was no rational connection with the objective. On *Oakes*, see J Church *et al*, *Human rights from a comparative and international law perspective* (2007) 90 - 91.

112 2000 4 SA 1078 (CC) [11] (footnote omitted):

> There are ... elements of the right to a fair trial such as, for example, the presumption of innocence, the right to free legal representation in given circumstances, a trial in public which is not unreasonably delayed, which cannot be explained exclusively on the basis of averting a wrong conviction, but which arise primarily from considerations of dignity and equality.

On the right of an indigent accused to legal aid to ensure a fair trial, see *Government of the Republic of Namibia v Mwilima* [2002] NASC 8 (SC of Namibia).

Jeremy Waldron described the right to a hearing, where both sides can probe and respond to evidence before a tribunal, which listens to them and gives the response to their arguments in the reasons for its decision, as embodying a crucial dignitarian idea – respecting the dignity of people as beings capable of explaining themselves: n 28 above, 54. By allowing arguments to be put forward to explain how their position fits into a coherent conception of the law, law conceives of people as bearers of reason and intelligence – also a tribute to human dignity: n 28 above, 54 - 55. The right to legal representation follows from people's right to a hearing to express their own view, as they may be unable to do so perhaps because they are poor public speakers or ignorant of the law: D Luban 'Lawyers as upholders of human dignity (when they aren't busy assaulting it)' [2005] *University of Illinois Law Review* 815 at 819. David Luban reasons that our own subjectivity lies at the very core of our concern for human dignity: above, 821.

human dignity.[113] The justification for the guilty verdict is the offender's misuse of responsibility, which Lagodny has portrayed as 'one of the core aspects of human personality'.[114] In *S v Manamela* in a joint judgment dissenting on the application of the limitation clause to the presumption of innocence on the facts, but concurring with the majority that the legislation relating to receiving stolen goods infringed both the constitutional right to silence and the presumption of innocence, O'Regan J and Cameron AJ highlighted the benefits for society and the individual of holding people responsible for their actions.[115]

In order to avoid an unwarranted violation of dignity, which society can only tolerate in regulatory or minor offences with insignificant consequences, the necessity for constitutional safeguards grows with the seriousness of the offence and the public interest in securing a conviction, which Sachs J in *S v Coetzee* labelled the 'paradox at the heart of all criminal procedure.'[116]

An agent of the apartheid regime accused of war crimes abroad retained the right to a fair trial despite the heinous and devastating nature of his activities.[117] It was alleged that Dr Basson (an employee of the South African National Defence Force) had conspired to murder members of SWAPO in Namibia by injecting them with drugs and had provided cholera bacteria to poison the water supply of a SWAPO refugee camp in order to manipulate the outcome of elections in Namibia. Sachs J in the Constitutional Court based Dr Basson's right to a fair trial and the state's interest in the prosecution of war crimes on the same humanitarian principles of dignity, equality and

113 O Lagodny 'Human dignity and its impact on German substantive criminal law and criminal procedure' (1999) 33 *Israel Law Review* 575 at 578 (footnote omitted). In *Oakes* Dickson CJ referred to the accused being subjected 'to social stigma and ostracism from the community': n 111 above, [29].

114 n 113 above, 578.

115 n 111 above, [100], citing T Honoré *Responsibility and fault* (1999) 125:

> Our society asserts individual moral agency and it does not flinch from recognising the responsibilities that flow from it. It is upon this principle that democracy and respect for human rights are built. As Honoré has recently observed:
>
> > '[W]e do well, indeed we are impelled ... to treat ourselves and others as responsible agents. But the argument for welcoming this conclusion is not that our behaviour is uncaused – something that we cannot know and which, if true, would be a surprise – but that to treat people as responsible promotes individual and social well-being. It does this in two ways. It helps to preserve social order by encouraging good and discouraging bad behaviour. At the same time, it makes possible a sense of personal character and identity that is valuable for its own sake.'

116 n 55 above, [220].

117 *S v Basson* 2005 1 SA 171 (CC).

freedom.[118] According to Sachs J, 'the clandestine use of state power to murder and dispose of opponents' showed the ultimate disrespect for these new constitutional values.[119] Endorsement by the established authorities of activities violating fundamental human rights is a betrayal of society's trust in the state to lead by example and the perpetrators should be held accountable.

The benefits of a fair trial extend beyond the interests of the accused and the effect on convicts of societal disapproval of them to upholding the dignity of the judicial system and society's entrusting of the administration of justice to the courts.[120]

In *Kaunda v President of the Republic of South Africa* the families of South African citizens, security workers who feared they would be tried as mercenaries, sought an order directing the South African government to intervene to ensure protection of their rights abroad.[121] The Constitutional Court refused to order the government to intervene. Sachs J's opinion was that the government's obligations did not stop at the borders of the country; while it had 'an extremely wide discretion as to how best to provide what diplomatic protection it can offer', it had 'a clear and unambiguous duty to do whatever is reasonably within its power to prevent South Africans abroad, however grave their alleged offences, from being subjected to torture, grossly unfair trials and capital punishment.'[122]

Currie and de Waal have identified the three prongs to the rationale underlying the right to silence as first, reliability to ensure the truth, second, 'a belief that individuals have a right to privacy and dignity which, whilst not absolute, may not be lightly eroded' and, third, 'to give effect to the privilege against self-incrimination and the presumption of innocence.'[123] This rationale has multiple connections with respect for dignity. Ackermann

118 n 117 above, [126].

119 n 117 above, [112].

120 Sachs J described the presumption of innocence as protecting not only the individual on trial, but maintaining 'public confidence in the enduring integrity and security of the legal system': *S v Coetzee* (n 55 above) [220].

121 2005 4 SA 235 (CC).

122 n 121 above, [275].

123 n 21 above, 751 (footnotes omitted).

J in *Ferreira* explained the right against self-incrimination as based on dignity and the rights to privacy and autonomy intermingled with it.[124]

5.2.2 Humane detention conditions

Detainees awaiting trial and sentenced prisoners are entitled to have their dignity respected.[125] This has been copper-fastened by the Constitutional rights to dignity in Sections 10 and 35(2)(e) and by the foundational

124 n 12 above, [98], citing *Thomson Newspapers Ltd v Director of Investigation and Research* [1990] 67 DLR (4th) 161 at 200 a - c (SC of Canada) (Wilson J, dissenting): 'Having reviewed the historical origins of the rights against compellability and self-incrimination and the policy justifications advanced in favour of their retention in more modern times, I conclude that their preservation is prompted by a concern that the privacy and personal autonomy and dignity of the individual be respected by the state. The state must have some justification for interfering with the individual and cannot rely on the individual to produce the justification out of his own mouth. Were it otherwise, our justice system would be on a slippery slope towards the creation of a police state.'

Luban's view is that compulsory self-incrimination is humiliating, because it enlists a person's own will in the process of punishing her thereby splitting her against herself and causing self-alienation, which the law must never override on pain of violating human dignity: n 112 above, 833 - 835.

Ferreira was cited by Kearns J for the propositions of law, first, that legislation compelling examinees to answer questions put to them (even when the answers might incriminate them) should be necessary (*ie*, no other method existed which could achieve the desired object, but which was less intrusive of the examinee's right against self-incrimination); second, that the privilege against self-incrimination application depends on time, place and context (being a more powerful principle closer to a trial situation and providing greater protection when self-incrimination takes the form of oral communication rather than when the incriminating material has an objective reality): *Dunnes Stores Ireland Co v Ryan* [2002] IEHC 61, [2002] 2 IR 60 at 110, 116, 117.

125 The Nigerian Court of Appeal held that the state has a responsibility to ensure that a person held in custody is not put in undue danger of his health and safety: *Fawehinmi v Abacha* (1998) 1 HRLRA 543, cited in Nigerian Bar Association, *Training Manual on African Regional Mechanisms for the Promotion and Enforcement of Human Rights: A Toolkit for Lawyers* (Lagos 2010) 21. Assaulting a detainee with horse whip, inflicting blows on him with clenched fist and putting him in handcuffs overnight was held to amount to torture and degrading treatment: *Ifeanyi Anyanor v Commissioner of Police, Delta State* (2007) CHR 185, cited in Nigerian Bar Association, above, 21.

The conditions in which a detainee without trial was kept contravened Kenya's obligation to guarantee his right to respect for his dignity and freedom from inhuman and degrading treatment: *Ouko v Kenya* [2000] AHRLR 135 (ACHPR 2000) [23]. Cf *Mao v AG of Uganda* [2003] UGCC 3 (Constitutional Court of Uganda). There was widespread utilisation of torture and of cruel, inhuman and degrading forms of treatment of prisoners held in detention in Mauritania in violation of their right to dignity in the African Charter: *Malawi African Association v Mauritania* [2000] AHRLR 149 (ACHPR 2000) [115]-[118]. The African Commission found that the inhumane conditions in which Gambian detainees were kept in detention centres in Angola breached the same provision: *Institute for Human Rights and Development in Africa v Angola* [2008] AHRLR 43 (ACHPR 2008) [49]-[53].

constitutional values. Because each person has their own identity, each case should be considered individually. According to van Zyl J in *Stanfield v Minister of Correctional Services*, '[w]hat will be "consistent with human dignity" in any particular case will, of course, depend on the facts and circumstances of each such case.'[126]

Although electricity is not regarded as a necessity in South Africa given the conditions of impoverishment in which many people live, the High Court in *Strydom v Minister of Correctional Services* considered that for maximum security prisoners in solitary confinement for 18½ hours a day for all or a substantial portion of the remainder of their lives access to electricity was an indispensable requirement that could not be characterised as 'no more than a comfort or a diversion' and 'could be an amenity of life that makes the difference between mental stability and derangement'.[127] Indefinite deprivation of electricity to enjoy at least some recreational privileges could also affect their prospects of rehabilitation and could amount to cruel or degrading treatment or punishment or detention in conditions inconsistent with human dignity.[128]

At common law in South Africa there was a long-standing recognition of the right of prisoners to be treated with dignity.[129] In 1912 the Appellate Division of the Supreme Court in *Whittaker v Roos* held in favour of two awaiting-trial prisoners, who had been unable to raise bail and had been

126 2003 12 BCLR 1384 (C) (High Court, Cape of Good Hope Division) [89]. Van Zylj J was critical of the prison authorities 'lumping together' all prisoners suffering from terminal diseases when they refused to grant parole to a terminally ill prisoner suffering from lung cancer because of the effect of his release on the penal system and on other terminally ill prisoners: above, [127]. He held that Mr Stanfield should have been released on parole to die with dignity in the company of his family and he placed the prisoner in a societal setting when there was an unavoidable limit on his time to enjoy his dignity on earth, stating: 'The applicant is fully entitled to spend the remaining portion of his life ensconced in his own home in the consolatory embrace of his family. When the time comes for him to pass on, he must be able to do so peacefully and in accordance with his inherent right to human dignity.': above, [132]. Cf *Mnguni v Minister of Correctional Services* [2005] ZACC 13, 2005 12 BCLR 1187 (CC).

127 1999 3 BCLR 342 (W) (High Court, Witwatersrand Local Division) [15], referring to *Minister of Justice v Hofmeyr* 1993 3 SA 131 (A) 141H - 142A.

128 n 127 above, [15]. In *Strydom* high security prisoners wished to have electricity for recreational purposes to enable them to watch television and to listen to radio and music.

129 This protection was developed to extend to all prisoners – whether awaiting trial, in detention without trial, or sentenced.

placed in solitary confinement.[130] In what later become known as 'the Innes *dictum*', Innes J was clear that prisoners retained their personal rights and personal dignity except to the extent defined by law or necessitated by their imprisonment.[131]

Hoexter JA in *Minister of Justice v Hofmeyr* approved of the Innes *dictum*, which meant 'that the extent and content of a prisoner's rights are to be determined by reference not only to the relevant legislation but also by reference to his inviolable common law rights.'[132] The conditions of detention

130 1912 AD 92. Prisoners awaiting trial were entitled to the special protection of the Court, since they were 'in a position of peculiar difficulty and helplessness': above, 125. The segregation order was illegal, as the differentiation it made between them and other awaiting-trial prisoners was neither warranted by the prison regulations nor necessitated by the requirements of prison discipline; the exceptional rigour which the segregation involved amounted to a substantial punishment: above, 121.

131 n 130 above, 122 - 123:

> True, the plaintiffs' freedom had been greatly impaired by the legal process of imprisonment; but they were entitled to demand respect for what remained. The fact that their liberty had been legally curtailed could afford no excuse for a further illegal encroachment upon it. ... They were entitled to all their personal rights and personal dignity not temporarily taken away by law, or necessarily inconsistent with the circumstances in which they had been placed.

The action of the prison authorities in confining the two men in punishment cells and subjecting them to consequential disabilities and discomfort – such as being prohibited from smoking, restricted in exercising, deprived of their boots in the cells, and handcuffed when being moved within the jail – was a wrongful and intentional interference with the 'absolute natural rights relating to personality,' to which everyone was entitled: n 130 above, 122. This constituted an *injuria*, which is a delict dependent on intent, and, in addition to the actual pecuniary loss, it attracted compensation for 'the insult, indignity and suffering' caused: n 130 above, 123. Their ill-treatment was a serious issue, as Innes J stated, '[a] deliberate aggression upon personal dignity and personal liberty is not a trivial matter'; he disagreed with the trial Court's conclusion that the case was not one for heavy damages, and remarked, 'however reprehensible a man's views may be he is entitled to have his personal liberty adequately protected.': n 130 above, 125.

132 n 127 above, 141. The extent to which 'necessary inroads' would be made on a prisoner's personal rights would depend on 'the reason for his detention and the legislation applicable to him'; while making full allowance for this, Hoexter JA considered that the Innes *dictum* was not confined to awaiting-trial prisoners, but was of general application: as above. The Supreme Court unanimously upheld the award of damages to William Hofmeyr, a law student, who – although lawfully arrested and detained under emergency powers – had been held unjustifiably in isolation. His effective solitary confinement was underscored and exacerbated by 'the deprivations suffered ... in regard to lack of indoor exercise, the ban on books and magazines, and the absence of a portable radio in his cell': n 127 above, 152.

When reviewing the quantum of damages, Hoexter JA took a serious view of the effect of solitary confinement on a detainee and agreed with Diemont J's following remarks in *Hassim v Officer Commanding, Prison Command, Robben Island*, 'I can think of few greater hardships than for an active man to be locked up in a small cell day and night, week after week and month after month, in enforced idleness.': n 127 above, 157, citing 1973 3 SA 462 (C) (SC Cape Provincial Division) 480 B-C.

open to scrutiny are not confined to the physical environment, but, as found by Hoexter JA, extend to the psychological sphere.[133] He endorsed the general approach reflected in 'the residuum principle' enunciated by Corbett JA (dissenting) in *Goldberg v Minister of Prisons*.[134] The respect owed to every individual in view of each person's inherent dignity and worth applied regardless of their situation as a prisoner or otherwise.[135] Brand J in the High Court reiterated the position at common law in *Van Biljon*, when he held that two prisoners should be provided with anti-viral therapy which had been prescribed for them on medical grounds.[136] The Supreme Court of Appeal insisted that the humane treatment of prisoners based on constitutional values have a practical effect, when in *Minister of Correctional Services v Kwakwa* it set aside a new privilege system that withdrew advantages given to unsentenced prisoners, and Navsa JA stated:[137]

133 n 127 above, 145:

> One of an individual's absolute rights of personality is his right to bodily integrity. The interest concerned is sometimes described as being one in corpus, but it has several facets. It embraces not merely the right of protection against direct or indirect physical aggression or the right against false imprisonment. It comprehends also a mental element.

See also L Ackermann *Human dignity: Lodestar for equality in South Africa* (2012) 93.

134 n 127 above, 141, citing *Goldberg v Minister of Prisons* 1979 1 SA 14 (A). Corbett JA's recognition that prisoners have residual rights and liberties, which are inviolable, is evident, above, 39:

> It seems to me that fundamentally a convicted and sentenced prisoner retains all the basic rights and liberties (using the word in its Hohfeldian sense) of an ordinary citizen except those taken away from him by law, expressly or by implication, or those necessarily inconsistent with the circumstances in which he, as a prisoner, is placed. Of course, the inroads which incarceration necessarily make upon a person's personal rights and liberties ... are very considerable. ... Nevertheless, there is a substantial residuum of basic rights which he cannot be denied.

Corbett JA's rejection of a rigid approach to distinguishing between 'comforts' (privileges) and 'necessities' (rights) was also approved by Hoexter JA, who had regard to the context in which the prisoners found themselves: n 127 above, 141, referring to *Goldberg* above, 41. What is regarded as a comfort in some cases can be essential to physical or mental survival in others: *Hofmeyr* (n 127 above) 141.

135 'The plain and fundamental rule is that every individual's person is inviolable.': *Hofmeyr* (n 127 above) 153 (Hoexter JA). Cf *Kruger v Minister of Correctional Services* [2005] ZAGPHC 24 (High Court, Transvaal Division) [28], [33], [36]; *Denton v Director-General, National Intelligence Agency* [2006] AHRLR 241 (GaHC 2006) (High Court of Gambia) [33].

136 *Van Biljon v Minister of Correctional Services* 1997 4 SA 441 (C), sub nom *B v Minister of Correctional Services* 1997 6 BCLR 789 (High Court, Cape of Good Hope Division) [42], [61]. See PA McDermott *Prison law* (2000) [9-24]; M Pieterse 'The potential of socio-economic rights litigation for the achievement of social justice: Considering the example of access to medical care in South African Prisons' (2006) 50 *Journal of African Law* 118 at 124 - 126. Cf *Woods v Commissioner of Prisons* [2003] ZWSC 74.

137 [2002] ZASCA 17, [2002] 3 All SA 242 (A) [32].

> The manner in which we treat our prisoners should not be out of line with the values on which the Constitution is based. Human dignity and the advancement of human rights and freedoms and respect for the rule of law are not just hollow phrases. They must be made real.

The promotion of transparency, accountability and good governance, and the constitutional right to information[138] ensured access to a report into the death of a prisoner from AIDS.[139]

However, it would be wrong to think that the courts over the years had upheld invariably the rights of all categories of prisoners to humane detention conditions – particularly those relating to their psychological well-being. Ogilvie Thompson JA delivering the judgment of the Appellate Division of the Supreme Court in *Rossouw v Sachs* distinguished between those detained without trial and unconvicted prisoners awaiting trial.[140] He overruled a lower court ruling which had held that a prisoner detained without trial was entitled to receive reading matter and writing materials.[141] The encouragement of prisoners to study – even though specifically mentioned in the prison regulations – received no practical judicial support in *Hassim v Officer*

138 Sec 32.

139 *Treatment Action Campaign v Minister of Correctional Services* [2009] ZAGPHC 10 (High Court, Transvaal Division) [23], [35]-[36], [38], [40].

140 1964 2 SA 551 (AD) 560, 564. Unlike an awaiting-trial prisoner, a detainee could be detained in custody pursuant to legislation 'at any place', was not entitled to bail, and could be interrogated: above, 559. Although he called the legislation permitting the detention of suspects or reluctant witnesses 'novel and drastic' because it ran counter to the general principles of criminal law against self-incrimination and also precluded a detainee from having access to a legal adviser, Ogilvie Thompson JA accepted the doctrine of parliamentary supremacy and went on the determine that the true purpose of the continued detention authorised by the statute was to induce the detainee to speak and not to 'alleviate the lot of a detainee': above, 558 - 561, 564. Parliament could not be presumed to have intended to authorise maltreatment, such as impairing the detainee's physical or mental health by assaults or inadequate food or living conditions: above, 561, 564. But neither was the detainee to be encouraged to study nor to have library facilities like convicted prisoners: above, 562. Drawing on the analogy of the public interest in disregarding safeguards to liberty in times of extreme emergency, such as war, the legislature could combat subversive activities against public order and the safety of the state: above, 562 - 563. Ogilvie Thompson JA also accepted the validity of the distinction between necessities and comforts, a detainee being entitled to the former as 'a matter of right' but to the latter 'only as a matter of grace': above, 564 - 565.

141 John Dugard criticised this decision because the court exercised 'a series of choices' favouring the executive and failed to disapprove of the detention law which departed from accepted principles of justice: J Dugard *Human rights and the South African legal order* (1978) 336. The court did not simply declare the law, nor was it 'mechanically guided to the legislative intent by fixed rules of precedent and principle': as above.

Commanding, Prison Command, Robben Island, where Diemont J in the Cape Provincial Division of the Supreme Court considered that prison officers had the 'widest discretion' to strike a balance between rehabilitation and enforcing discipline, which in effect gave them control over whether, when and what a prisoner could study.[142] Contrary to the majority in *Goldberg*, Corbett JA's view in relation to the censorship of books and periodicals sent to prisoners detained under security laws was that the prison rules or policy could not deprive them of all access to news.[143]

Grosskopf J of the Cape Provincial Division of the Supreme Court found in *Cassiem v Commanding Officer, Victor Verster Prison* that detainees had pre-existing rights not dependent on statute and that these rights were merely controlled – not taken away –by legislation.[144] In contrast, the Appellate

142 n 132 above, 476 - 477. Notwithstanding that the reasons given for withdrawing permission to study were 'most unconvincing' and that Diemont J found the authorities' ban on legal studies 'quite extraordinary', he was not prepared to interfere with their decisions; while he accepted that deprivation of books was a hardship for an intellectual, he drew an analogy with the hardship for some people to go without cigarettes and held that the right to use the prison library was a privilege that could be withdrawn: n 132 above, 477.

When it came to considering segregation of prisoners, Diemont J discerned a difference between segregation and solitary confinement in the statutory code: n 132 above, 479. The legislation did not provide for complete segregation without work; Hassim was prevented from doing any work, his exercise was severely curtailed, and he was confined to the same type of single cell as was used for solitary confinement for punishment purposes: n 132 above, 480. However, he had not been given a fair hearing prior to being 'marched straight off to the isolation cell' for failing to hand over library books; Diemont J ordered that Hassim be removed from the isolation cell, as he concluded that he had not been merely segregated, but had been placed in solitary confinement as a punishment with the probable intention that it should continue for six months, and this was invalid because he had not been given a hearing and, in any event, the period of confinement exceeded the maximum period of 30 days permitted by legislation: n 132 above, 481.

143 n 134 above, 50. He considered that a prisoner's rights extended beyond the physical to 'his mental and psychological well-being', which was also 'of basic importance': n 134 above, 41.

144 1982 2 SA 547 (C) 552. A notice issued by the Minister of Justice equated detainees with awaiting-trial prisoners: above, 550 - 551. As the correctness of the Innes *dictum* in respect of awaiting-trial prisoners had never been questioned, by extension it also applied to detainees: above, 551. Grosskopf J respected the terms of the legislation, but he interpreted the executive's actions in accordance with the principles of justice, requiring that authority be exercised reasonably for the purpose for which it was given: above, 552. The regulations only permitted a privilege to be withdrawn when that particular privilege had been abused and not as a means of punishment for unrelated misconduct: above, 553. He upheld the entitlement of two Cape Malay detainees to seek redress from the Court when their rights to regular outdoor exercise, letters and visits, and to procure food and reading material were curtailed following an altercation between them and a prison officer because they greeted black detainees, with whom they were prohibited from having any contact: above, 549, 554.

Division of the Supreme Court in *Mandela v Minister of Prisons* took a less sympathetic attitude to a convicted prisoner's challenge to confiscation of privileged documents by the prison authorities.[145] The Court accepted that, for the maintenance of good order, discipline and security, legislation could make inroads into the fundamental right of a prisoner to a legal adviser.[146]

Deliberate neglect of those imprisoned is unacceptable, but there is also a positive obligation to provide adequate sustenance and reasonable facilities for existing with dignity – even when resources are scarce. The condemnation of torture and of cruel and inhumane treatment and punishment has been the foundation for the recognition of the right of prisoners to live in conditions where they have sufficient space, food, bedding, and washing and toilet facilities. I will now take a closer look at the development of this jurisprudence, which has attempted to address the appalling overcrowded and pathetic conditions in which prisoners have been kept in some countries.[147]

De Swardt AJ of the South African High Court held in *Lee v Minister of Correctional Services* that the State was liable to pay damages in delict to a prisoner, who contracted tuberculosis while incarcerated in an overcrowded maximum security prison.[148] The prison authorities had not taken reasonable steps to prevent the spread of the disease and had failed to preserve the prisoner's rights to dignity and to treatment that was not inhuman or degrading.[149]

In Malawi,[150] a prisoner in *Masangano v AG*[151] claimed on behalf of himself and his fellow prisoners that the insufficient and poor quality diet, food, clothing and bedding, and the overcrowding and other conditions in prison

145 1983 1 SA 938 (A).

146 Jansen JA noted that fundamental rights continue after imprisonment, but might be curtailed: n 145 above, 957.

147 Overcrowding is perhaps the single most pressing concern facing African prisons: J Sarkin 'Prisons in Africa: An evaluation from a human rights perspective' (2008) 9 *SUR - International Journal on Human Rights* 23 at 26.

148 [2011] ZAWCHC 13 (Western Cape High Court, Cape Town) [270]. Cf *Mukunto v AG* [1988] ZMSC 22, (1988 - 1989) ZR 31 (SC of Zambia).

149 n 148 above, [263], [268]-[269].

150 Malawi had a history of overcrowded conditions aggravated by poor ventilation contributing to the deaths of prisoners. 259 inmates died in a space of about 18 months: *Masangano v AG* [2009] MWHC 31 at 52 - 53, 55, citing Malawi Prison Inspectorate Report 2004. See also *Achuthan (Banda) v Malawi* [2000] AHRLR 144 (ACHPR 1995) [4], [7].

151 n 150 above.

amounted to torture and cruel, inhuman and degrading treatment or punishment.[152] They also argued that their right to human dignity[153] was violated by the provision of only one meal a day.[154] The High Court found that the overcrowding and poor ventilation amounted to inhuman and degrading treatment of the inmates contrary to Section 19 of the Constitution.[155]

There have been similar findings in Zimbabwe, where lack of resources was not entertained as an excuse for failure to have decent prison conditions. In *Kachingwe v Minister of Home Affairs* the Supreme Court declared in 2005 that police holding cells were degrading and inhumane in violation of the prohibition in the Constitution[156] and were unfit for holding criminal suspects.[157] It made an order with extensive directions to the State to ensure that cells be of reasonable size for the number they were used to accommodate

152 This was prohibited by the Constitution: Constitution of the Republic of Malawi 1994, Sec 19(3).

153 Sec 19(1).

154 n 150 above, 12. The State defended the case on the basis that the issues were non-justiciable, being outside the judiciary's area of competence, and concerned matters of national policy and security: n 150 above, 18. It maintained that the allocation of resources was beyond the purview of the judges, as it involved value judgments having regard to economic and policy considerations: n 150 above, 19. The High Court dismissed these arguments, which were not applicable when the rights of prisoners were involved: n 150 above, 28 - 29. It pointed out that the doctrine of non-justiciability had been criticised because it sought to protect the executive and undermined private rights while weakening the doctrine of separation of powers; in addition it had been argued that it had 'the potential of obstructing confidence and certainty in the expectation of access to the courts for private litigants.': n 150 above, 27. Having noted that the application of the doctrine of non-justiciability was in decline in the United Kingdom and that the human rights culture was now fully fledged, the Court did not think 'that a court should adopt a hands-off approach' where there was a complaint of violation of prisoners' rights or human rights: n 150 above, 28 - 29.

155 n 150 above, 56. The Court asserted the judiciary's duty to protect the human rights retained by prisoners despite their imprisonment, and made an analogy between the modern view that socio-economic rights were justiciable and the justiciability of prisoners' rights: n 150 above, 28 - 29, 32. It directed the State within 18 months to take concrete steps to reduce prison overcrowding by half, and thereafter by periodic reductions to eliminate overcrowding, and also to improve the ventilation in prisons and prison conditions generally: n 150 above, 60. Although one of the specified constitutional rights of prisoners is to be detained under conditions consistent with human dignity, including 'at least the provision of reading and writing materials, adequate nutrition and medical treatment at the expense of the State' (Sec 42(1)(b)), the Court based its decision on the general inviolability of dignity and the prohibition on inhuman and degrading treatment in Section 19.

156 Constitution of the Republic of Zimbabwe 1979, Sec 15(1).

157 [2005] ZWSC 134.

and that the conditions in which suspects were held be improved.[158] There was an obligation on the state to shield everyone from violations of the wide-ranging ban on degrading and inhumane treatment – not to infringe it itself.[159]

In Namibia the High Court found in *McNab v Minister of Home Affairs*[160] that the conditions in a police holding cell were degrading and inhuman and violated an arrested man's constitutional right to dignity.[161] The European

158 In 1999 the Court had made detailed orders directed to the prison authorities in a case concerning the severe conditions in which three US citizens awaiting-trial on terrorism and weapons charges were held in small individual cells in a maximum security prison: *Blanchard v Minister of Justice, Legal and Parliamentary Affairs* [2000] 1 LRC 671. Even though these awaiting-trial prisoners were entitled to the presumption of innocence, they had not been allowed to communicate with each other, to wear their own clothes nor to receive food from outside the prison. For several weeks they had been stripped naked and shackled in leg-irons overnight: above, 676, 682. The prison authorities maintained that their treatment was justified by the seriousness of the charges and the danger that they might escape, but the Supreme Court disagreed with this rationale and held that the prolonged duration of the ill-treatment and its physical and mental effects attained the minimum level of severity necessary to constitute a violation of Section 15(1) of the Constitution, which guaranteed protection from inhuman or degrading punishment or treatment: above, 679, 681.

Gubbay CJ delivering the unanimous judgment of the Court had recognised the need for wide-ranging deference to be accorded to the prison administrators in the adoption and execution of policies and practices they adjudged necessary to preserve order and security, but – notwithstanding this – the courts had a continuing responsibility to enforce constitutional rights: above, 677, citing *Conjwayo v Minister of Justice, Legal and Parliamentary Affairs* [1991] 1 ZLR 105 (S) (SC of Zimbabwe) and *Woods v Minister of Justice, Legal and Parliamentary Affairs* [1994] 1 LRC 359 (SC of Zimbabwe). Gubbay CJ condemned the use of leg-irons and handcuffs except for the prevention of escape during transportation or to restrain violent behaviour: above, 676.

159 Gubbay CJ stated, *Blanchard* (n 158 above) 680:

> [T]he aim ... is to protect both the dignity and the physical and mental integrity of the individual. The prohibition relates not only to acts that cause physical pain but also to those that cause mental suffering to the victim. It is the duty of the state to afford protection against such acts by legislative and other measures, as may be necessary; not, through its officials, to be responsible for their perpetuation.

The provision in the Constitution was akin to art 7 of ICCPR ('No one shall be subjected to torture or to cruel, inhuman or degrading treatment or punishment'): *Blanchard* (n 158 above) 680, referring to ICCPR (n 31 above).

160 2007] NAHC 50.

161 Constitution of the Republic of Namibia 1990, Art 8. The small, overcrowded, poorly-ventilated cell in which he was held was filthy, and infested with cockroaches and lice; toilet facilities were not private; food was served in rubbish bins: n 160 above, [50]. Angula AJ considered that the police officers were not responsible for the notorious horrendous conditions, but liability rested with the State: n 160 above, [49]. Cf *Mothobi v Director of Prisons* [1996] LSCA 92 (CA of Lesotho).

Court of Human Rights has also found that overcrowding[162] and poor prison conditions are a violation of the prohibition on degrading treatment in Article 3 ECHR. In *Orchowski v Poland* respect for dignity required that the state be responsible for assuring the health and welfare of prisoners.[163] An intention to debase or humiliate is not a necessary ingredient in a violation of Article 3.[164]

In Scotland in *Napier v Scottish Ministers* Lord Bonomy had no hesitation in condemning systematic slopping out, '[i]t is clear beyond doubt that, by imposing the regime of slopping out upon prisoners, the respondents failed to accord respect to their dignity.'[165] He rebutted the defence argument that only serious ill-treatment attaining a minimum level of severity fell within the scope of Article 3 of the ECHR[166] and asserted that it could be infringed by exacerbation of suffering flowing from various measures for which the authorities were responsible.[167]

162 Sharon Dolovich considers that in the US the prohibition on cruel and unusual punishment in the Eighth Amendment would be breached if an incarcerated person suffered physical or psychological harm from living under conditions of extreme overcrowding and its attendant effects: S Dolovich 'Cruelty, prison conditions, and the Eighth Amendment' (2009) 84 *New York University Law Review* 881 at 908.

163 (App No 17885/04) ECHR 22 October 2009 [120]:

> Under Article 3 the State must ensure that a person is detained in conditions which are compatible with respect for his human dignity, that the manner and method of the execution of the measure do not subject him to distress or hardship of an intensity exceeding the unavoidable level of suffering inherent in detention and that, given the practical demands of imprisonment, his health and well-being are adequately secured.

Constraints on resources were not an exculpatory factor, above, [153]:

> The Court is aware of the fact that solving the systemic problem of overcrowding in Poland may necessitate the mobilisation of significant financial resources. However, it must be observed that lack of resources cannot in principle justify prison conditions which are so poor as to reach the threshold of treatment contrary to Article 3 of the Convention … and that it is incumbent on the respondent Government to organise its penitentiary system in such a way that ensures respect for the dignity of detainees, regardless of financial or logistical difficulties.

Should the state be unable to reach the threshold, 'it must abandon its strict penal policy in order to reduce the number of incarcerated persons or put in place a system of alternative means of punishment': above, [153].

164 *Kalashnikov v Russia* (App no 47095/99) (2003) 36 EHRR 34 [95].

165 2005 SC 229 (Court of Session Outer House) [51]. For a review and assessment of *Napier*, see S Foster 'Prison conditions, human rights and article 3 ECHR' [2005] *Public Law* 35 at 35 - 37, 39, 43.

166 n 165 above, [64].

167 n 165 above, [73], citing *Pretty v UK* (App no 2346/02) (2002) 35 EHRR 1 [52]. The conditions of detention, taken together, were found to have diminished Robert Napier's human dignity and aroused in him feelings of anxiety, anguish, inferiority and humiliation, thereby subjecting him to degrading treatment: n 165 above, [78].

5.3 Privacy and autonomy

There is a general right to privacy in the South African Constitution, a subset of which – couched in negative terms – are specific rights to be free from interference by the state and others in a tangible physical sense.[168] There is no separate right to autonomy in the South African Constitution. According to Currie and de Waal, the South African Constitution is unusual in combining protection against illegal searches and seizures with the general right to privacy and in making the former a component of the latter.[169] The general right to privacy extends beyond territorial and physical integrity and control over correspondence with others to the freedom to develop one's personality by making and implementing personal decisions of an intimate self-defining nature and by forming relationships.[170] As with all rights, the right to privacy is not absolute and can be limited by societal considerations and the entitlements of other members of the community.

5.3.1 Common law *dignitas*

A common law right to privacy based on *dignitas* pre-dated the Constitution. It coincided with the US model of non-interference with the individual and diminished the more a person exposed himself to society, as explained by Ackermann J in *Bernstein*:[171]

Napier is an indication that the UK courts, applying Art 3 ECHR, may not stick rigidly to the European Court of Human Rights standard designed to apply throughout Europe, but will seek to evolve a sense of 'minimum standards' which is more exacting: S Livingstone *et al*, *Prison law* (2008) 255.

168 Sec 14:

Everyone has the right to privacy, which includes the right not to have
(a) their person or home searched;
(b) their property searched;
(c) their possessions seized; or
(d) the privacy of their communications infringed.

169 n 21 above, 315.

170 In Germany the right to develop one's personality is a necessary and implicit corollary to the guarantee to respect human dignity; since it can be limited by the rights of others, the German Federal Constitutional Court has had to scrutinise complex situations to shape its contours and zealously guards the integrity of the intimate core of privacy against intrusions by others and by the state; it has distinguished between a private sphere of action in which the person's personality develops from actions taken as a consequence of interaction with society: LAA Pagán 'Human dignity, privacy and personality rights in the constitutional jurisprudence of Germany, the United States and the Commonwealth of Puerto Rico' (1998) 67 *Revista Juridica de la Universidad de Puerto Rico* 343 at 354 - 355.

171 n 18 above, [68] (footnotes omitted).

> In South African common law the 'right to privacy is recognised as an independent personality right which the courts have included within the concept of *dignitas*'. 'Privacy is an individual condition of life characterised by seclusion from the public and publicity. This implies an absence of acquaintance with the individual or his personal affairs in this state'. In *Financial Mail (Pty) Ltd v Sage Holdings Ltd* it was held that breach of privacy could occur either by way of an unlawful intrusion upon the personal privacy of another, or by way of unlawful disclosure of private facts about a person. The unlawfulness of a (factual) infringement of privacy is adjudged 'in the light of contemporary *boni mores* and the general sense of justice of the community as perceived by the Court'.

He gave the following examples of wrongful intrusion and disclosure under common law which breached confidence and invaded personal space:[172]

> entry into a private residence, the reading of private documents, listening in to private conversations, the shadowing of a person, the disclosure of private facts which have been acquired by a wrongful act of intrusion, and the disclosure of private facts contrary to the existence of a confidential relationship.

The *actio iniuriarum* protects the right to privacy under *dignitas*. To succeed in this cause of action in the law of delict, it is necessary to prove impairment of privacy, wrongfulness and intention (*animus iniuriandi*) – therefore negligence is insufficient to render the wrongdoer liable.[173] The degree of protection afforded privacy at common law is quite restricted. The plaintiffs in *NM v Smith*[174] sought its development along the lines in which the law of defamation, also protected by the *action iniurarum*, had been expanded by the Supreme Court of Appeal in *Bogoshi*.[175] The Constitutional Court in a majority decision in *NM v Smith* held in favour of the plaintiffs and awarded them damages for the revelation of private information about them without their consent on the basis that the revelations had been intentional.[176]

172 n 18 above, [69] (footnotes omitted).

173 *NM v Smith* 2007 5 SA 250 (CC) [55].

174 n 173 above.

175 *National Media Ltd v Bogoshi* 1998 4 SA 1196.

176 n 173 above, [65]. See CJ Roederer 'Working the common law pure: Developing the law of delict (torts) in light of the spirit, purport and objects of South Africa's Bill of Rights' (2009) 26 *Arizona Journal of International and Comparative Law* 427 at 479 - 481.

Therefore it was not necessary to develop the common law of privacy, as they succeeded under the existing *actio iniuriarum* requiring intention. Madala J for the majority did not rule out the development of the common law in an appropriate case.[177] O'Regan J dissenting on the facts, considered that the common law of privacy should be developed by requiring the media not to negligently or unreasonably reveal private information without consent.[178] She imposed greater delictual liability on the media than on ordinary citizens because of the power of the media and their potential to cause widespread harm to individuals on account of the ease and speed of transmission of information to a large audience.[179] She pointed to the dual factors governing the media's conduct, when she explained why they had a greater obligation to respect privacy than ordinary individuals, 'the media are not only bearers of rights under our constitutional order, but also bearers of obligations.'[180] The right to freedom of expression was put in the balance with the duty to respect people's rights to privacy and dignity.

Sachs J in *NM v Smith*, supporting Madala J's majority judgment, also made some observations favourable to development of the common law. He approved of the development of the law of defamation in *Bogoshi* 'in a way that was sensitive to contemporary concerns and realities, a well-weighted means of balancing respect for individual personality rights with concern for freedom of the press.'[181] The principles developed in it were 'eminently transportable to the law of privacy.'[182] He praised *Bogoshi* for harmonising rights and looking at the context.[183] Langa CJ dissenting in part, agreed with O'Regan J that the common law must be developed in accordance with the spirit, purport and objects of the Bill of Rights, as required by Section 39(2) of the Constitution. The change should be made with regard to media defendants and he thought it 'constitutionally appropriate that the media

177 n 173 above, [57].

178 n 173 above, [179].

179 n 173 above, [177].

180 n 173 above, [177] (footnote omitted).

181 n 173 above, [203].

182 As above.

183 n 173 above, [204]:

> [I]t seeks to harmonise as much as possible respect for human dignity and freedom of the press, rather than to rank them in terms of precedence. The emphasis is placed on context, balance and proportionality, and not on formal and arid classifications accompanied by mantras that favour either human dignity or press freedom.

should be held to a higher standard than the average person.'[184] He did not approve of negligent disclosures of private facts by individuals not in the media, but it was not something that was appropriate for the law to regulate, as 'to extend that standard to ordinary people, and thus to everyday relationships, would be to extend the law too far into intensely personal space.'[185]

5.3.2 Scope of constitutional privacy

The constitutional right to privacy is more extensive than that at common law. Ackermann J, in a wide-ranging and deep analysis in *Bernstein*, pointed out that the scope of privacy was closely related to the concept of identity and that privacy was based on 'what is necessary to have one's own autonomous identity', not on a libertarian 'unencumbered self'.[186] He referred to Rainer Forst's multi-level approach to identity – first, from the abstract individual; second, to the concrete communal; third, to societal membership; and fourth, to the community of humanity itself.[187] At the third level of political discourse, concrete difference and common equality are reconciled, and membership of society requires an acceptance of the individual's obligations towards the right of every member not to be excluded.[188] The community of humanity 'demands mutual respect as a universal moral duty towards persons *as moral persons*'.[189]

Privacy is respect for identity and autonomy, which are aspects of individual dignity.[190] Ackermann J's review of German law led him to conclude, '[p]rivacy is also protected out of respect for dignity'.[191] Dignity

184 n 173 above, [94].

185 As above.

186 n 18 above, [65] (footnote omitted).

187 n 18 above, [66] (footnotes omitted).

188 n 18 above, fn 92, citing R Forst 'How not to speak about identity: the concept of the person in a theory of justice' (1992) 18 *Philosophy & Social Criticism* 293.

189 n 18 above, fn 93, citing Forst (n 188 above).

190 Dignity is at the heart of the approach to privacy: A Chaskalson 'Human dignity as a constitutional value' in D Kretzmer & E Klein (eds) *The concept of human dignity in human rights discourse* (2002) 140.

191 *Bernstein* (n 18 above) [77] (footnote omitted).

embraces privacy, but is more far-reaching than it.[192] O'Regan J in *Khumalo v Holomisa* saw privacy as supportive of dignity.[193]

In *Hyundai* it emerged that the right to privacy is broader than the reach of dignity, as juristic persons – who are not the bearers of human dignity – have privacy rights, albeit not as intense as those of individuals.[194] In *Thint* it was reiterated that a corporate entity does not bear human dignity and therefore 'its rights of privacy are much attenuated compared with those of human beings.'[195]

Langa DP in *Hyundai* adopted Ackermann J's view of privacy as deriving from dignity and described the contraction of the sphere where privacy can be expected as one moves further into community: [196]

> [P]rivacy is a right which becomes more intense the closer it moves to the intimate personal sphere of the life of human beings, and less intense as it moves away from that core. This understanding of the right flows … from the value placed on human dignity by the Constitution.

Currie and de Waal deduce from this that a value (perhaps the principal value) served by privacy is human dignity.[197]

192 Personality – closely linked to privacy and dignity – has a broader reach than privacy, as it extends to relationships and moral integrity giving a more holistic view of the ethical individual: C Dupré 'Human dignity and the withdrawal of medical treatment: a missed opportunity?' [2006] *European Human Rights Law Review* 678 at 688 - 690. Catherine Dupré proposes a more comprehensive understanding of dignity comprising the relationship aspect in addition to the autonomy focus giving a holistic approach and providing positive protection to human rights: C Dupré 'Unlocking human dignity: towards a theory for the 21st century' [2009] *European Human Rights Law Review* 190 at 194, 198.

193 2002 5 SA 401 (CC) [27] (footnotes omitted):

> It should also be noted that there is a close link between human dignity and privacy in our constitutional order. The right to privacy, entrenched in section 14 of the Constitution, recognises that human beings have a right to a sphere of intimacy and autonomy that should be protected from invasion. This right serves to foster human dignity.

194 *Investigating Directorate: Serious Economic Offences v Hyundai Motor Distributors (Pty) Ltd* 2001 1 SA 545 (CC) [18].

195 *Thint (Pty) Ltd v National DPP* [2008] ZACC 13, 2009 1 SA 1 (CC) [77] (footnote omitted).

196 n 194 above, [18], citing *Bernstein* (n 18 above) [77].

197 n 21 above, 320.

5.3.3 Rationale for privacy protection

O'Regan J in *NM v Smith* identified at least two inter-related reasons for the constitutional protection of privacy, the first flowing from the constitutional conception of what it means to be a human being, implicit in which was

> the right to choose what personal information of ours is released into the public space. The more intimate that information, the more important it is in fostering privacy, dignity and autonomy that an individual makes the primary decision whether to release the information.[198]

The second reason for protecting privacy flowed from the democratic need to curb the power of the state and to prevent it from denying liberty and dignity by interfering with our private space.[199] She explained the mutually supportive nature of dignity, freedom and privacy, which are central to human existence:[200]

> The right to privacy recognises the importance of protecting the sphere of our personal daily lives from the public. In so doing, it highlights the inter-relationship between privacy, liberty and dignity as the key constitutional rights which construct our understanding of what it means to be a human being. All these rights are therefore inter-dependent and mutually reinforcing.

The Constitutional Court in *NM v Smith* upheld the individual's right to choose what personal information to reveal to others and to prohibit or put boundaries on further dissemination of the information. Madala J, having referred to the nature and scope of the right of privacy in many jurisdictions as envisaging a concept of the right to be left alone, described it as encompassing 'the right of a person to live his or her life as he or she pleases.'[201] In that case three HIV-positive women claimed that their rights to privacy and dignity had been violated by publication of their names and HIV status in a biography. The Court made it clear that it was not an impairment of dignity to be HIV positive, but that the women's dignity could be infringed by publishing intimate medical facts about them without their consent.[202] In

198 n 173 above, [129], [132].

199 n 173 above, [133].

200 n 173 above, [131] (footnote omitted).

201 n 173 above, [32]-[33].

202 n 173 above, [48], [92], [139].

making the distinction, O'Regan J put control over disclosure of personal information within the realm of privacy, breach of which infringed dignity.[203] She had no doubt that the right to privacy protects people from the publication of private medical information without their consent and that an appropriate balance had to be struck between this right and freedom of expression.[204] O'Regan J found on the facts that publication of the applicants' names and HIV status was neither intentional nor negligent, so she dissented.[205]

The US and German concepts of human dignity are close to each other in the field of privacy, particularly informational privacy and data protection, which act as a buffer against the state's tendency to invade into its citizens' personal affairs.[206] The German Federal Constitutional Court has held that under Article 1 of the Basic Law everyone has the right to informational self-determination.[207] The American term 'privacy' expresses the right to protection of the individual private sphere.[208] Roberta Kwall has also pointed out that the interest served in many privacy and publicity cases in the US embodies a spiritual quality rather than an interest in property or reputation.[209] Because of the high level of attention the German Federal Constitutional Court pays to dignity, the range of social interactions where privacy is protected is wider than that accorded privacy in American jurisprudence.[210]

203 n 173 above, [139]:

> It needs to be said clearly that the stigma attached to those living with HIV/AIDS is inconsistent with the constitutional value of human dignity. Disclosing that a person is living with HIV/AIDS cannot therefore be an infringement of dignity on the grounds that members of the community may improperly think less of them because they are suffering from this frightening illness. It does undermine their dignity to the extent that it denies those living with HIV/AIDS the right to determine to whom and when their illness should be disclosed, which is itself an aspect of the right to privacy ...

204 n 173 above, [136], [147].

205 n 173 above, [168], [189].

206 E Benda 'The protection of human dignity (Article 1 of the Basic Law)' (2000) 53 *Southern Methodist University Law Review* 443 at 450. On the rights to data protection and informational self-determination, see K Möller 'Two conceptions of positive liberty: Towards an autonomy-based theory of constitutional rights' (2009) 29 *Oxford Journal of Legal Studies* 757 at 781 - 782.

207 Benda (n 206 above) 450. On the German right to informational self-control, see SA Kamei 'Partitioning paternity: The German approach to a disjuncture between genetic and legal paternity with implications for American courts' (2010) 11 *San Diego International Law Journal* 509 at 530 - 532.

208 Benda (n 206 above) 450.

209 RR Kwall 'A perspective on human dignity, the First Amendment, and the right of publicity' (2009) 50 *Boston College Law Review* 1345 at 1353.

210 Pagán (n 170 above) 359.

In the US the privacy right represents the constitutional recognition of a liberty interest to make fundamental personal decisions and can be curtailed by a compelling state interest.[211]

The different understandings of the notions of liberty and privacy in the US and Continental Europe lead to differing views on human dignity – Europeans tend to build their sense of dignity upon personal integrity and honour, being reluctant to divulge personal information, while Americans' sense of personal dignity is focused on liberty from intrusion by the state.[212]

5.3.4 Contextual extent of privacy

The right to privacy extends beyond the confines of the home, as is evident from *Magajane* where legislation permitting searches to detect illegal gambling was found to be too broad.[213] Van der Westhuizen J indicated that one of the considerations in assessing whether privacy had been breached or was justified was the individual's 'expectation of privacy', which is 'more attenuated the more the business is public, closely regulated and potentially hazardous to the public.'[214] The purpose of the statutory provision is relevant. Generally there is a low expectation of privacy in business premises, but here the aim to collect evidence for a criminal prosecution was significantly intrusive.[215] Dignity and personality are adversely affected by unauthorised searches and seizures, as they invade the individual's private sphere.[216]

5.3.5 Conflicting interests

Even though they are closely connected and mutually supportive, at times there can be a conflict between autonomy, freedom and privacy on the one hand and dignity on the other. Waiver of dignity is not wholly within the

211 Pagán (n 170 above) 361 - 362.

212 MYK Lee 'Universal human dignity: Some reflections in the Asian context' (2008) 3(1) *Asian Journal of Comparative Law* http://www.bepress.com/asjcl/vol3/iss1/art10/ (accessed 13 April 2010) 15.

213 *Magajane v Chairperson, North West Gambling Board* 2006 5 SA 250 (CC).

214 n 213 above, [50].

215 n 213 above, [94].

216 n 213 above, [64].

power of the beholder.[217] Society and humanity at an overarching level have an interest in preserving dignity – even against the wishes of members of society who may not want to uphold their own dignity whether because they have a different idea of what dignity means, are willing to forego dignity as understood by others, their self-esteem is so low that they do not recognise their own dignity, or for some other reason.[218]

The conflict was analysed when the statutory ban on prostitution survived a challenge by a narrow majority in *S v Jordan*.[219] All the judges concluded that the prostitution provision did not infringe the rights to human dignity and economic activity, and that if it did limit the right to privacy, such limitation was justifiable. They differed on the question of whether the law criminalising prostitution constituted unfair gender discrimination. O'Regan and Sachs JJ, who dissented on the equality issue, pointed out in a joint judgment that the dignity of the prostitute is infringed by her own actions and choices rather than by the law.[220] They assessed the extent of the right to

217 Certain degrading behaviour may be wrongful even if the victim consents, as society has an interest in preserving human dignity: V Bergelson 'Autonomy, dignity, and consent to harm' (2008) 60 *Rutgers Law Review* 723 at 730. The concept of dignity does not reflect the subjective state of mind of the perpetrator or the victim, but instead has an 'objective,' normative meaning: above, 730 - 731.

Consent does not override all deontological rights and duties: KW Simons 'Dworkin's two principles of dignity: An unsatisfactory nonconsequentialist account of interpersonal moral duties' (2010) 90 *Boston University Law Review* 715 at 733.

218 A preference for any one individual's rights when in conflict with those of another must be guided by respect for the equal and inherent dignity of both: BB Lockwood, Jr *et al* 'Working paper for the Committee of Experts on limitation provisions' (1985) 7 *Human Rights Quarterly* 35 at 77.

219 2002 6 SA 642 (CC). Cf the Canadian Supreme Court's majority decision to uphold the constitutionality of legislation making it illegal to solicit in public for the purposes of prostitution and to keep a bawdy house: *Prostitution Reference* (n 14 above). On dignity and prostitution, see N Rao 'Three concepts of dignity in constitutional law' (2011) 86 *Notre Dame Law Review* 183 at 228 - 229.

220 n 219 above, [74]:

> To the extent that the dignity of prostitutes is diminished, the diminution arises from the character of prostitution itself. The very nature of prostitution is the commodification of one's body. Even though we accept that prostitutes may have few alternatives to prostitution, the dignity of prostitutes is diminished not by section 20(1)(aA) [Sexual Offences Act 1957] but by their engaging in commercial sex work. The very character of the work they undertake devalues the respect that the Constitution regards as inherent in the human body.

Christopher McCrudden contrasts this justification by O'Regan and Sachs JJ with their earlier strongly autonomy-based approach in the gay rights cases: C McCrudden 'Human dignity and judicial interpretation of human rights' (2008) 19 *European Journal of International Law* 655 at 706. See also H Botha 'Human dignity in comparative perspective' (2009) 20 *Stellenbosch Law Review* 171 at 203; MS Kende *Constitutional rights in two worlds: South Africa and the United States* (2009) 117 - 120, 126 - 128.

privacy based on the relationships between the parties. The scope of privacy was determined by the nature of the relationship concerned.[221] It was pertinent in 'core' intimate personal relationships, but not in cold commercial transactions – even those involving the sale of sex in the 'penumbra' of privacy.[222] O'Regan and Sachs JJ explained:[223]

> [C]entral to the character of prostitution is that it is indiscriminate and loveless. It is accordingly not the form of intimate sexual expression that is penalised, nor the fact that the parties possess a certain identity. It is that the sex is both indiscriminate and for reward. The privacy element falls far short of 'deep attachment and commitments to the necessarily few other individuals with whom one shares not only a special community of thoughts, experiences and beliefs but also distinctly personal aspects of one's life'. By making her sexual services available for hire to strangers in the marketplace, the sex worker empties the sex act of much of its private and intimate character. She is not nurturing relationships or taking life-affirming decisions about birth, marriage or family; she is making money.

Although the prostitute's privacy is reduced, she still retains the right to have her dignity respected by the police and her customers.[224] While 'her expectations of privacy are relatively attenuated' and she is placed 'far away from the inner sanctum of protected privacy rights', the prostitute is not stripped 'of her right to be treated with dignity as a human being and to have respect shown to her as a person'.[225]

The judgment of Ngcobo J for the majority in *Jordan* is a defensive one in response to the minority judgment of Sachs and O'Regan JJ. The minority took a broader view and looked at the social setting rather than solely at the legislation. In their dissent finding that the prostitution provision constituted unfair indirect discrimination, they pinpointed the vulnerable position of

221 n 219 above, [80].

222 As above.

223 n 219 above, [83], citing Justice Brennan in *Roberts v United States Jaycees* 468 US 609 (1984) 620.

224 n 219 above, [74].

225 n 219 above, [83].

prostitutes in society.[226] There is an ambiguous attitude to prostitutes and their clients, where the former are stigmatised and the latter forgiven.

In *De Reuck* legislation banning possession of child pornography was held to be a justifiable infringement of privacy and freedom of expression of a film producer charged with importing and possessing it.[227] The film producer's rights to privacy and expression had to give way to the dignity rights of the child. It was not just the dignity of the child the subject of the pornography that was infringed, but, as Langa DCJ stated, the humanity of all children was impaired.[228]

5.4 Freedom of expression

Many battles over constitutional rights are between those seeking to assert freedom of expression and those who perceive the ideas sought to be communicated as a threat to their dignity.[229] Frequently free speech has to yield to other constitutional rights or its curtailment is justified under the

226 Andrew Foster criticised the majority and minority decisions in *Jordan*, and concluded that the Constitutional Court was applying dignity selectively and contrary to women's interests: A Foster 'The role of dignity in Canadian and South African gender equality jurisprudence' (2008) 17 *Dalhousie Journal of Legal Studies* 73 at 90 - 92.

227 *De Reuck v DPP (Witwatersrand Local Division)* 2004 1 SA 406 (CC).

228 n 227 above, [63]:

> Children's dignity rights are of special importance. The degradation of children through child pornography is a serious harm which impairs their dignity and contributes to a culture which devalues their worth. ... There is obvious physical harm suffered by the victims of sexual abuse and by those children forced to yield to the demands of the paedophile and pornographer, but there is also harm to the dignity and perception of all children when a society allows sexualised images of children to be available. The chief purpose of the statutory prohibitions against child pornography is to protect the dignity, humanity and integrity of children.

229 Democracy and dignity are both simultaneously empowering and legitimate forms of constraint. Sometimes the protection of democracy demands constraints on individuals' human rights to ensure that the fullest possible deliberation takes place. Those in power may be least interested in ensuring a debate on constraints and may baulk at the idea of legislating such constraints; therefore judges have to be trusted to juggle commitments to dignity and democracy in the context of individual complaints, and in the process they are usually careful not to cause a constitutional crisis by usurping the legislature: A Clapham *Human rights obligations of non-state actors* (2006) 558 - 559.

limitations clause.[230] Section 16(1) of the South African Constitution, contains a general guarantee to all of freedom of expression and lists several specific inclusions in the overall right.[231] The interim Constitution contained no specific exclusions, so Section 16(2) is a novelty barring from protection war propaganda,[232] incitement of imminent violence,[233] and hate speech inciting harm based on race, ethnicity, gender or religion.[234] The hate speech provision was inserted in response to representation by interest groups.[235]

5.4.1 Rationale for freedom of expression

Ronald Dworkin has grouped the justification for free speech into the *instrumental*, which protects democracy and produces good effects for the rest of us, and the *constitutive*, which supposes that free speech is valuable, not just on account of its consequences, but because it is an essential feature of a just political society that government treat all its adult members (except the incompetent) as responsible moral agents.[236] The instrumental view

230 The principle on which freedom of expression is founded (respect for the autonomy and dignity of human beings) also gives rise to other fundamental rights, ranging from personal security and privacy to citizenship and equality; since speakers should be required to respect the fundamental rights of others, the same ideals that justify freedom of speech can determine the limits of that freedom: SJ Heyman *Free speech and human dignity* (2008) 2.

231 Sec 16(1):

Everyone has the right to freedom of expression, which includes
a) freedom of the press and other media;
b) freedom to receive or impart information or ideas;
c) freedom of artistic creativity; and
d) academic freedom and freedom of scientific research.

232 Sec 16(2)(a).

233 Sec 16(2)(b).

234 Sec 16(2)(c). Many democratic countries restrict hate speech, having weighed orators' interests to the right of free expression against both the dignitary harm to individuals and the collective harm to pluralism: A Tsesis 'Dignity and speech: The regulation of hate speech in a democracy' (2009) 44 *Wake Forest Law Review* 497 at 521. Alexander Tsesis considers that the international trend to regulate hate speech is grounded in what is meant to 'secure for all citizens the prerequisites of a life worthy of human dignity': as above, citing MC Nussbaum 'Constitutions and capabilities: "Perception" against lofty formalism' (2007) 121 *Harvard Law Review* 4 at 7. See Rao (n 219 above) 251 - 253.

235 G Marcus *Incitement to hatred: A Southern African perspective* (1998) 14.

236 R Dworkin *Freedom's law: The moral reading of the American Constitution* (1996) 200. Justice Brennan's view was that rights of expression and of conscience reaffirmed 'the vision of human dignity in many ways'; he mentioned, first, self-governance by demanding robust public debate on issues of public importance, which was vital to the development and dissemination of political ideas, and, as importantly, by forging personal political convictions; and, second, the freeing up of private space for intellectual and spiritual development: n 5 above, 442 - 443.

considers that politics is more likely to discover truth, if political discussion is free,[237] or that government is more likely to be less corrupt if it lacks power to punish criticism.[238] The constitutive angle has two dimensions, the first being that morally responsible people insist on making up their own minds about what is good or bad in life or politics, or true or false in matters of justice or faith, so the government insults citizens when it denies them the right to hear contrary opinions that might persuade them to dangerous or offensive convictions.[239] Dworkin describes the free reception of ideas as central to dignity, '[w]e retain our dignity, as individuals, only by insisting that no one – no official and no majority – has the right to withhold an opinion from us on the ground that we are not fit to hear and consider it.'[240] Many regard moral responsibility as also having another, more active, aspect leading to the second constitutive dimension of expressing our convictions to others out of respect and concern for them and so that truth be known, justice served, and the good secured.[241] The articulation of all types of views is posed by Dworkin as dually beneficial by upholding the dignity of both the giver and the recipient. The worth of each individual is accepted by acknowledging the equality of everyone to communicate their ideas.[242]

John Mubangizi has mentioned a third reason why freedom of expression should be given constitutional protection, which is that free speech encourages debate and improves the chances that the truth will surface.[243]

In response to critics of Justice Brennan's stance on free speech, Stephen Wermiel observed that for him it was the ability of the speaker to speak that was at the core of the ideal of human dignity, which he sought to protect in the face of the countervailing interests of the majority who found the speech unwanted or offensive: n 89 above, 236 - 237.

237 n 236 above, 200, citing Justice Holmes in his dissent in *Abrams v US* 250 US 616 (1919).

238 n 236 above, 200.

239 As above.

240 As above.

241 As above.

242 Dworkin also developed his theory of citizens' obligation to comply with the laws of a legitimate state from the principles of dignity and equality: S Sreedhar & C Delmas 'State legitimacy and political obligation in *Justice for hedgehogs*: The radical potential of Dworkinian dignity' (2010) 90 *Boston University Law Review* 737 at 745.

243 JC Mubangizi *The protection of human rights in South Africa: A legal and practical guide* (2004) 87. Steven Heyman considers that the elements of liberty correspond to the major justifications for freedom of expression, *ie*, that freedom of expression is an aspect of external freedom, essential for individual self-realisation, indispensable to democratic self-government, and promotes the search for truth: n 230 above, 2.

This could be regarded as embraced by both of Dworkin's groupings, which overlap.[244] Eric Barendt traced the truth argument back to Milton, although it is especially associated with John Stuart Mill.[245] The three underlying reasons identified were mentioned by O'Regan J in *SANDU*.[246]

Laurence Tribe's analysis of the various rationales for free speech led him to assert that any adequate conception of it must draw on several strands of theory to protect a rich variety of expressional modes.[247] No adequate conception of free speech can be developed in purely instrumental or 'purposive' terms.[248] Free speech is not only a means to some further end, such as successful self-government, social stability or the less instrumental discovery and dissemination of truth, but, as Tribe suggests, it is in part also

244 n 236 above, 201.

245 EM Barendt *Freedom of speech* (2005) 7. McLachlin J (dissenting) in *R v Keegstra*, having referred to the truth rationale for freedom of expression as dating back to Milton, acknowledged that it had been criticised as there was no guarantee that the free expression of ideas would in fact lead to the truth: [1990] 3 SCR 697 (SC of Canada) 110 - 111. However, she considered it could still be argued that it assisted in promoting the truth in ways which would be impossible without freedom of expression: above, 111. Dickson CJ (for the majority) also had doubts about the universal application of the truth rationale and cautioned against overplaying 'the view that rationality will overcome all falsehoods in the unregulated marketplace of ideas': above, 69 - 70. Jacob Weinrib found it surprising that the Supreme Court of Canada had not engaged in an analysis of whether the traditional purposes of freedom of expression cohere with the values in the Canadian Charter, given the transformative implications of the Charter and the Court's indications in *Keegstra* that the purposes taken as underlying freedom of expression might be inadequate: J Weinrib 'What is the purpose of freedom of expression?' (2009) 67 *University of Toronto Faculty of Law Review* 165 at 167.

246 *South African National Defence Union v Minister of Defence* 1999 4 SA 469 (CC) [7] (footnotes omitted):

> Freedom of expression lies at the heart of a democracy. It is valuable for many reasons, including its instrumental function as a guarantor of democracy, its implicit recognition and protection of the moral agency of individuals in our society and its facilitation of the search for truth by individuals and society generally. The Constitution recognises that individuals in our society need to be able to hear, form and express opinions and views freely on a wide range of matters.

As Ryan Haigh has noted, in this passage O'Regan J demonstrated that freedom of speech is fundamental: RF Haigh 'South Africa's criminalization of "hurtful" comments: When the protection of human dignity and equality transforms into the destruction of freedom of expression' (2006) 5 *Washington University Global Studies Law Review* 187 at 208, fn 138.

Cf the view of Dumbutshena AJA of the Namibian Supreme Court that in a democracy 'the citizens must be free to speak, criticise and praise where praise is due'; he continued, '[m]uted silence is not an ingredient of democracy because the exchange of ideas is essential to the development of democracy': *Kauesa v Minister of Home Affairs* [1995] NASC 3; 1995 11 BCLR 1540 (NmS) 28.

247 LH Tribe *American constitutional law* (1988) 789.

248 n 247 above, 785.

an end in itself, 'an expression of the sort of society we wish to become and the sort of persons we wish to be'.[249] Much of our commitment to free speech is because it enhances personal growth and self-realisation.[250] Intellect and rationality cannot accommodate what Tribe described as 'the emotive role of free expression – its place in the evolution, definition, and proclamation of individual and group identity.'[251]

Dworkin's constitutive rationale corresponds with the theory of free speech as an integral aspect of self-fulfilment described by Barendt, who expanded on its benefits for the individual:[252]

> Restrictions on what we are allowed to say and write, or (on some formulations of the theory) to hear and read, inhibit our personality and its growth. A right to express beliefs and political attitudes instantiates or reflects what it is to be human. ...
>
> There is perhaps something uniquely valuable in intellectual self-development. The reflective mind, conscious of options and the possibilities for growth, distinguishes human beings from animals.

While the self-fulfilment argument may justify giving constitutional protection to free speech, this rationale is closely linked to general liberty or moral autonomy.[253] Barendt points out that unlimited speech justified on the basis of self-fulfilment, dignity and equality may be contrary to respect for human dignity.[254]

Currie and de Waal have noted traces of Dworkin's instrumental and constitutive arguments in the South African jurisprudence interpreting the right to freedom of expression.[255] His instrumental strand can be seen in Kriegler J's judgment in *S v Mamabolo* when he indicated that freedom of expression as the communication of ideas is essential for democracy.[256]

249 As above.

250 n 247 above, 787.

251 As above.

252 n 245 above, 13.

253 n 245 above, 14.

254 n 245 above, 15.

255 n 21 above, 361.

256 2001 3 SA 409 (CC) [37]:

> Freedom of expression, especially when gauged in conjunction with its accompanying fundamental freedoms, is of the utmost importance in the kind of open and democratic society the Constitution has set as our aspirational norm. Having regard to our recent past of thought control, censorship and enforced conformity to go-

O'Regan J articulated the constitutive strand – and, indeed, the instrumental one also – in *Khumalo*.[257] Both strands are also evident in Mokgoro J's judgment in *Case*, where she considered that the statutory prohibition on pornography breached freedom of expression in the interim Constitution because it was overbroad.[258] Apart from seeing the dual purpose of freedom of expression, she rightly understood constitutional rights as interrelated and uniting to sustain societal interplay that is of benefit to the giver and receiver of information, which also accords with Dworkin's views. In addition to the advantage to the speaker of broadcasting ideas to another and being listened to, there is a boomerang effect in being able to refine thoughts as a result of the listener's feedback.[259]

> vernmental theories, freedom of expression – the free and open exchange of ideas – is no less important than it is in the United States of America. It could actually be contended with much force that the public interest in the open market-place of ideas is all the more important to us in this country because our democracy is not yet firmly established and must feel its way. Therefore we should be particularly astute to outlaw any form of thought-control, however respectably dressed.

Haigh cited this passage as a demonstration by the Constitutional Court that freedom of speech is fundamental: n 246 above, 208, fn 138. See A Sparks *Beyond the miracle: Inside the new South Africa* (2003) 78 - 82.

257 'Freedom of expression is integral to a democratic society for many reasons. It is constitutive of the dignity and autonomy of human beings. Moreover, without it, the ability of citizens to make responsible political decisions and to participate effectively in public life would be stifled.': n 193 above, [21].

258 *Case v Minister of Safety and Security* 1996 3 SA 617 (CC) [27] (footnotes omitted):

> We must understand the right embodied in section 15 not in isolation, but as part of a web of mutually supporting rights enumerated in the Constitution, including the right to 'freedom of conscience, religion, thought, belief and opinion', the right to privacy, and the right to dignity. Ultimately, all of these rights together may be conceived as underpinning an entitlement to participate in an ongoing process of communicative interaction that is of both instrumental and intrinsic value.

Cf the Supreme Court of Canada's finding that the Criminal Code's prohibition on possession of child pornography infringing freedom of expression was justified under the limitations clause, except for two aspects which were overbroad: *R v Sharpe* 2001 SCC 2, [2001] 1 SCR 45. The reverse onus putting the onus of disproving obscenity on the importer was held unconstitutional in a challenge to the seizure of erotica by customs authorities, although the remainder of the legislation was justified: *Little Sisters Book and Art Emporium v Canada (Minister of Justice)* 2000 SCC 69, [2000] 2 SCR 1120 (SC of Canada).

On *Case*, see Kende (n 220 above) 193 - 197. On *Sharpe*, see PW Hogg *Constitutional law of Canada* (2007) *Vol 2* at 273 - 274, 307; A Slane 'From scanning to sexting: The scope of protection of dignity-based privacy in Canadian child pornography law' (2010) 48 *Osgoode Hall Law Journal* 543 at 560 - 562, 567 - 569, 579 - 580, 584, 586. On *Little Sisters Book and Art Emporium*, see Hogg above, 122, 279, 305 - 306, 540 fn 75, 680.

259 *Case* (n 258 above) [25] (footnote omitted):

> But my freedom of expression is impoverished indeed if it does not embrace also my right to receive, hold and consume expressions transmitted by others. Firstly,

Freedom of expression's importance for good government and for humanity was recognised by Yacoob J in *Phillips* when he said it was 'integral to democracy, to human development and to human life itself.'[260] O'Regan J in *NM v Smith,* where she dissented on the facts, stressed the interrelationship between rights and also the weight to be given to freedom of expression in personal development by exchanging ideas resulting in motivation to action.[261] The outward manifestation of religion and culture are protected by the right to freedom of expression.[262] The banning of Hindu students from wearing nose studs in school limited their right to express their religion and culture which Langa DCJ said was 'central to the right to freedom of expression'.[263] Religious and cultural practices are 'central to human identity and hence to human dignity which is in turn central to equality.'[264]

> my right to express myself is severely impaired if others' rights to hear my speech are not protected. And secondly, my own right to freedom of expression includes as a necessary corollary the right to be exposed to inputs from others that will inform, condition and ultimately shape my own expression. Thus, a law which deprives willing persons of the right to be exposed to the expression of others gravely offends constitutionally protected freedoms both of the speaker and of the would-be recipients.

260 *Phillips v DPP (Witwatersrand Local Division)* 2003 3 SA 345 (CC) [23].

261 n 173 above [145]:

> Freedom of expression is important because it is an indispensable element of a democratic society. But it is indispensable not only because it makes democracy possible, but also because of its importance to the development of individuals, for it enables them to form and share opinions and thus enhances human dignity and autonomy. Recognising the role of freedom of expression in asserting the moral autonomy of individuals demonstrates the close links between freedom of expression and other constitutional rights such as human dignity, privacy and freedom. Underlying all these constitutional rights is the constitutional celebration of the possibility of morally autonomous human beings independently able to form opinions and act on them.

262 In liberal rights discourse, freedom of thought and conscience are each considered to be *absolutely* protected from interference by the law, but the right to *manifest* one's thought or conscience in the form of speech or other action is subject to reasonable limitation by the state on certain specified grounds: PG Danchin 'Defaming Muhammad: Dignity, harm, and incitement to religious hatred' (2010) 2 *Duke Forum for Law & Social Change* 5 at 20 - 21.

263 *MEC for Education: KwaZulu-Natal v Pillay* 2008 1 SA 474 (CC) [94]. See L du Plessis 'Affirmation and celebration of the "religious Other" in South Africa's constitutional jurisprudence on religious and related rights: Memorial constitutionalism in action?' (2008) 8 *African Human Rights Law Journal* 376 at 396 - 401; Kende (n 220 above) 236 - 238. The Supreme Court of Zimbabwe held that expulsion of a Rastafarian from school because of the expression of his religious belief through his hairstyle violated his right to religious expression and was discriminatory: *Dzvova v Minister of Education Sports and Culture* [2007] ZWSC 26.

264 *Pillay* (n 263 above) [62]. See Botha (n 220 above) 206 - 207.

5.4.2 Exclusions from protection

The South African Constitution is read as a whole. Doing so enabled Langa DCJ to indicate in *Islamic Unity Convention* that the reason for the qualifications to freedom of expression in Section 16(2) was the threat to the foundational values including dignity.[265] He found that any restriction on freedom of expression beyond the terms allowed in Section 16(2) 'encroaches on the terrain of protected expression and can do so only if such regulation meets the justification criteria in section 36(1) of the Constitution.'[266] The *Islamic Unity Convention* litigation resulted from a complaint by the South African Jewish Board of Deputies to the Independent Broadcasting Authority that an interview broadcast by a community station owned by the Islamic Unity Convention breached the IBA's Code of Conduct which prohibited the broadcasting of material 'likely to prejudice relations between sections of the population, i.e. Jews and other communities.'[267] In a challenge by the Islamic Unity Convention to the constitutionality of the Code, the Court held that the Code limited the right to freedom of expression and went on to consider whether the limitation was justifiable. It noted that the regulation of broadcasting was a legitimate objective and was mandated by the Constitution because of its importance to national unity and the founding values of dignity, equality and freedom. Langa DCJ considered that the labelling of people by virtue of their innate identity – particularly in view of South Africa's history of institutionalised discrimination – undermined these values.[268] The Court held that the Code went too far and was not sufficiently

265 *Islamic Unity Convention v Independent Broadcasting Authority* 2002 4 SA 294 (CC) [32]:

> Implicit in its provisions [Section 16(2)] is an acknowledgment that certain expression does not deserve constitutional protection because, among other things, it has the potential to impinge adversely on the dignity of others and cause harm. Our Constitution is founded on the principles of dignity, equal worth and freedom, and these objectives should be given effect to.

See Kende (n 220 above) 198 - 200.

266 n 265 above, [34].

267 n 265 above, [2]. The interview dealt with Israel and Zionism as a political ideology; it was asserted that Jewish people were not gassed in concentration camps: n 265 above, [1].

268 n 265 above, [45] (footnote omitted):

> South African society is diverse and has for many centuries been sorely divided, not least through laws and practices which encouraged hatred and fear. Expression that advocates hatred and stereotyping of people on the basis of immutable characteristics is particularly harmful to the achievement of these values as it reinforces and perpetuates patterns of discrimination and inequality.

focused to guide broadcasters in what they might or might not broadcast. While the prohibition in the Code was declared unconstitutional and invalid, the Court's declaration of invalidity was made subject to the proviso that no protection was given to the broadcasting of material that contravened the specific exclusions in Section 16(2).

The hate speech excluded from protection is limited to that which amounts to incitement to cause harm. There are contrary views as to whether the exclusion extends to hurtful comments.[269] Ryan Haigh has pointed out that the right to express one's thoughts and to communicate freely with others 'affirms the dignity and worth of every member of society, and allows each individual to determine what is true and to realize his or her full human potential.'[270] He argues that dignity should not be used to prevent free speech not amounting to the urging of violence.[271] Control over speech during the apartheid era led to oppression and the stripping of people of their dignity.[272] Dissenters should be able to express their views. Prohibiting criticism or the airing of contrary views does not change the attitudes of racists or bigots, but, as Haigh thought, may push them underground, where they may become more dangerous.[273] Encouragement of diverse and dissenting voices is healthy in a democracy. This is in the interests of all, as the principle of suppression of views, once established, could affect oneself in another capacity or a different situation in future. Tolerance – even of one's opponents' views – is necessary for the security of all in society, as Thomas Paine stated, '[h]e that would make his own liberty secure, must guard even his enemy from

269 In *Keegstra* where a teacher had been convicted of wilfully promoting hatred against an identifiable group by communicating anti-semitic statements to his students, the Supreme Court of Canada found that legislation prohibiting hate speech infringed freedom of expression, but was justified under the limitations clause; *mens rea* meant that the offence required intent to promote hatred or knowledge of substantial certainty of it as a consequence; Dickson CJ for the majority stated that freedom of expression in Canada protected all content of expression attempting to convey a meaning (except when communicated in a physically violent form): n 245 above, 37.

There is a distinction between expressive activity that is inconsistent with the dignity of all persons (dignity being a public value which requires that persons not be subject to hatred), on the one hand, and expressive activity which is merely offensive (offence being a subjective reaction rooted in the beliefs of private persons and associations), on the other: Weinrib (n 245 above) 184.

270 n 246 above, 208 (footnote omitted).

271 Weinrib has criticised Ronald Dworkin's analysis of autonomy (a right to moral independence) as permitting hate speech, because he overlooks the capacity of hate speech to undermine the autonomy of others: n 245 above, 178 - 179.

272 Haigh (n 246 above) 209.

273 As above.

oppression; for if he violates this duty, he establishes a precedent that will reach to himself.'[274] Haigh concluded, '[dignity] should not be used as a means to restrict essential freedoms, such as speech, thereby stripping individuals of the very qualities that they are trying to instill into society.'[275]

On the other hand, Currie and de Waal submit that the hate-speech exception includes harm to dignity interests on the basis that it is the speech itself that causes the social and psychological harm, and not the audience 'who may or may not be sufficiently fired up to translate the message into violent action'.[276] They define hate speech as 'advocacy of hatred on a listed ground, intended to cause harm to dignity.'[277]

5.4.3 Limits to protection

Restrictions on freedom of expression have often been justified under the limitations clause. One of the factors to be taken into account in the limitations analysis is the nature of the right and in South Africa freedom of expression in itself is not a foundational value. It plays a vital role in democracy, but there are more significant values to be borne in mind. O'Regan J explained in *Khumalo*:[278]

> [A]lthough freedom of expression is fundamental to our democratic society, it is not a paramount value. It must be construed in the context of the other values enshrined in our Constitution. In particular, the values of human dignity, freedom and equality.

Because of its nature, it has been curtailed when there are more pressing values in play.

Any type of expression not specifically excluded under Section 16(2) is protected to some extent, but may be limited by the application of the foundational values. The South African courts have adopted the broad

274 T Paine 'Dissertation on first principles of government' in *The writings of Thomas Paine Vol III* (1996) 277.

275 n 246 above, 210.

276 n 21 above, 377. Weinrib considers that hate speech may be limited because it seeks to use rights that are founded in the value of human dignity in a manner that denies the dignity of others, and the capacity of others to hold rights, including the right to free expression: n 245 above, 187.

277 n 21 above, 377.

278 n 193 above, [25] (footnote omitted). In Germany the right to dignity has also interacted dramatically with rights to information and freedom of expression providing in the case of Germany a right to control personal information: Klug (n 2 above) 153.

European standard of protection instead of the US position where certain categories of expression are unprotected forms of speech.[279] In *De Reuck* Langa DCJ confirmed approval of the European Court of Human Rights' approach in finding that the Section 16(1)(b) right 'to receive or impart information or ideas' applied '... not only to "information" or "ideas" that are favourably received or regarded as inoffensive or as a matter of indifference, but also to those that offend, shock or disturb...'.[280] Hence child pornography was protected and restrictions on it were subject to justification under a limitation analysis, but it stands on the fringe of expression deserving slight protection because it is of minor benefit to the individuals in question. In view of the underlying reasons for freedom of expression, Langa DCJ did not see the statutory restrictions on child pornography as attacking 'the core values of the right.'[281]

In defamation actions dignity is balanced against freedom of expression, as O'Regan J made plain in *Khumalo*:[282]

> The law of defamation seeks to protect the legitimate interest individuals have in their reputation. To this end, therefore, it is one of the aspects of our law which supports the protection of the value of human dignity. When considering the constitutionality of the law of defamation, therefore, we need to ask whether an appropriate balance is struck between the protection of freedom of expression on the one hand, and the value of human dignity on the other.

The chilling effect of defamation laws and high awards on freedom of the press is regularly criticised – more often than not by journalists. However, in

279 *De Reuck* (n 227 above) [48]-[49]. Heyman advocates the adoption in the US of a liberal humanist approach and understanding freedom of expression within a broader conception of rights based on human dignity and autonomy; this would recognise a strong, liberal right to freedom of expression, while affording protection against the most serious forms of 'assaultive speech'; his rights-based theory of the First Amendment would replace the modern conception of First Amendment issues as conflicts between the individual right to free speech and 'social interests' such as dignity and equality: n 230 above, 2, 4.

280 n 227 above, [49], citing *Islamic Unity Convention* (n 265 above) [29], quoting *Handyside v UK* (1976) 1 EHRR 737 at 754.

281 n 227 above, [59]. He continued: 'Expression that is restricted is, for the most part, expression of little value which is found on the periphery of the right and is a form of expression that is not protected as part of the freedom of expression in many democratic societies.': n 227 above, [59] (footnote omitted).

282 n 193 above, [28].

Dikoko v Mokhatla Swkeyiya J thought it a good thing supportive of dignity that people would desist from saying something potentially defamatory resulting in curbing free speech.[283]

The existence or extent of freedom of commercial speech was an unresolved issue in the *Laugh It Off* case, where Moseneke J described freedom of expression as 'a vital incidence of dignity, equal worth and freedom' carrying 'its own inherent worth' and serving 'a collection of other intertwined constitutional ends in an open and democratic society.'[284] The case involved a conflict between Laugh It Off Promotions CC, a small South African corporation that made social commentary by altering well-known trade marks and printing them on T-shirts for sale, and an international corporation trading as Sabmark International, whose trade mark it had altered. The Constitutional Court decided the case on the basis that Sabmark had failed to prove Laugh It Off's infringement of its trade mark, as it did not show that it was likely to suffer economic harm.[285] Sachs J, in a concurring judgment, would have upheld the decision on more substantial grounds, giving more weight to expression rights and 'the uniquely expressive weight of the parodic form used.'[286] He rightly regarded criticism of the *status quo* and branding as healthy in a democracy and supportive of human dignity.[287] Although the issue of commercial speech was not ruled on in *Laugh It Off*, the Constitutional Court had recognised the individual and collective sides to expression in *SANDU* when O'Regan J indicated 'the importance, both for a democratic society and for individuals personally, of the ability to form and express

283 2006 6 SA 235 (CC) [141]:

> A person who suspects that they may possibly be about to defame someone else is cognisant of the fact that if they do, there may be legal consequences. As a result, they either refrain from making the utterance or do some background checking first. So the kinds of utterances which are chilled are those which an ordinary person may suspect to be defamatory in nature. The chilling of this kind of expression is by no means an undesirable result and is in line with the framework of intersecting rights outlined above in which freedom of expression may well have to take a back seat to dignity in certain circumstances.

284 *Laugh It Off Promotions CC v South African Breweries International (Finance) BV t/a Sabmark International* 2006 1 SA 144 (CC) [45].

285 It was not necessary to make a finding on freedom of expression relied on by Laugh It Off.

286 n 284 above, [74].

287 n 284 above, [108]:

> Laughter too has its context. It can be derisory and punitive, imposing indignity on the weak at the hands of the powerful. On the other hand, it can be consolatory, even subversive in the service of the marginalised social critics. What has been

opinions, whether individually or collectively, even where those views are controversial.'[288]

The US Supreme Court took the view initially that commercial advertising was not encompassed in the right to free speech. In 1942 in *Valentine v Chrestensen* it upheld a ban on commercial advertising – even when combined with political protest, which had constitutional protection.[289] More than 20 years later in *New York Times v Sullivan* it found that paid advertising for political purposes was protected.[290] The change of direction was complete in *Bigelow* in 1975, when the Court struck down a statute in Virginia prohibiting a commercial advertisement for legal abortion services in another state.[291] The information was of interest to the women wishing to have an abortion and to the general public, who could be concerned with law reform and with legal developments in other states. Justice Blackmun distinguished *Chrestensen*, which he said was limited to upholding the ban on commercial advertising as 'a reasonable regulation of the manner in which commercial advertising could be distributed.'[292] It was not authority for the proposition that all statutes regulating commercial advertising were immune from constitutional challenge.[293]

To revert to South Africa, in *Phillips* the Constitutional Court in a majority decision held that freedom to receive and impart information or ideas and freedom of artistic creativity protected in Section 16(1)(b) and (c) were infringed by overbroad restrictions on places of entertainment selling

relevant in the present matter is that the context was one of laughter being used as a means of challenging economic power, resisting ideological hegemony and advancing human dignity.

Free speech as a motivator for change was also referenced by McLachlin CJ and LeBel J of the Canadian Supreme Court in a joint judgment, when they stated, '[free speech] allows a person to speak not only for the sake of expression itself, but also to advocate change attempting to persuade others in the hope of improving one's life and perhaps the wider social, political, and economic environment': *Retail, Wholesale and Department Store Union, Local 558 v Pepsi-Cola Canada Beverages (West) Ltd* 2002 SCC 8, [2002] 1 SCR 156 [32].

288 n 246 above, [8].

289 316 US 52 (1942). *Chrestensen* prevailed until the 1960s when signs of erosion of the commercial-speech doctrine began to appear: TL Tedford & DA Herbeck *Freedom of speech in the United States* (2005) 200.

290 376 US 254 (1964).

291 *Bigelow v Virginia* 421 US 809 (1975).

292 n 291 above, 819.

293 n 291 above, 819 - 820.

liquor.[294] Less restrictive measures could have secured the state's interest in controlling the negative effects of the over-consumption of liquor in public places.

By a majority in *South African Broadcasting Corporation v National DPP* the Constitutional Court held that as reconciliation of rights was not possible, in the situation that arose the right to a fair trial should prevail over the right of the media to broadcast court proceedings.[295] In the interests of justice, the court should 'seek to reconcile the fundamental rights at issue with its obligation to ensure that the proceedings before it are fair.'[296] Although there is no hierarchy of rights in the Constitution, the Court considered that there are circumstances in which one right will take precedence.[297] The tendency is towards fair trial rather than in favour of freedom of expression and open publication of court proceedings.[298] Mokgoro J (dissenting), having said that she considered the public broadcaster had the right and freedom to disseminate information correlating with its duty to inform the public, which, in turn, had the right to receive information,[299] continued, '[i]n an open democracy based on the values of equality, freedom and human dignity, the

294 n 260 above. The challenge was brought by a licensed premises where there was striptease dancing, but the legislation was wide enough to apply to plays and concerts irrespective of whether they represented 'serious works of art or the communication of thoughts and ideas essential for positive social development': n 260 above, [15].

295 2007 1 SA 523 (CC). There were political overtones, as the accused was appealing against his conviction for corruption for bribing Jacob Zuma (now President of South Africa) in order to protect a French armaments company.

Daniel Erskine analysed this case and summarised the Constitutional Court's approach, '[t]he Court recognizes the frustration in granting all rights coequal status because in such a situation none of the rights may receive full expression.': DH Erskine 'Judgments of the United States Supreme Court and the South African Constitutional Court as a basis for a universal method to resolve conflicts between fundamental rights' (2008) 22 *St John's Journal of Legal Commentary* 595 at 604.

296 n 295 above, [53].

297 n 295 above, [55].

298 According to the majority, '[g]iven that a court has a primary obligation to ensure that the proceedings before it are fair, that obligation will always figure large in the exercise of discretion': as above.

299 The legal relations described by Mokgoro J are as conceived by Wesley Hohfeld, who devised a scheme of opposites and correlatives in which a right and a duty are correlatives, the opposite of rights being 'no-rights' and a duty being the opposite of a privilege: WN Hohfeld 'Some fundamental legal conceptions as applied in judicial reasoning' (1913) *23 Yale Law Journal* 16 at 30. See also WN Hohfeld 'Fundamental legal conceptions as applied in judicial reasoning' (1917) 26 *Yale Law Journal* 710 at 710. On the relevance of Hohfeld's theory of jural relations to human rights, see SRS Bedi *The development of human rights law by the judges of the International Court of Justice* (2007) 58 - 59.

right of the public to be informed is one of the rights underpinned by the value of human dignity.'[300]

5.5 Equality

There are tests to be applied by the court in sequence in order to decide if the constitutional guarantees concerning equality have been breached under the framework elaborated in *Harksen v Lane*.[301] As described by Evadné Grant, Section 9(1) plays a 'gate-keeping role'.[302] A measure that does not fall foul of Section 9(1) because the differentiation has a rational connection with a legitimate purpose may still constitute unfair discrimination.[303] Allowing for the fact that to legislate is to discriminate in some fashion, the Court in *Prinsloo* distinguished between 'differentiation which does not involve unfair discrimination and differentiation which does involve unfair discrimination.'[304] It may be justified as corrective action under Section 9(2).[305] In *Van Heerden* Moseneke J disagreed with previous interpretations of Section 9(2) as an exception to the equality code.[306] He underlined the transformative purpose of the entire of Section 9 and an integrated interpretation of the Constitution – with substantive equality (including remedial measures) reaching out its tentacles.[307]

300 n 295 above, [120].

301 E Grant 'Dignity and equality' (2007) 7 *Human Rights Law Review* 299 at 315 - 316. See also Ackermann (n 133 above) 184 - 186.

302 n 301 above, 316. See *Harksen v Lane* 1998 1 SA 300 (CC) [42] (Goldstone J). A provision in the Matrimonial Property Act 1984 unjustifiably denied spouses equal protection and benefit of the law: *Van der Merwe v Road Accident Fund* 2006 4 SA 230 (CC) [58], [63].

303 Van der Westhuizen J explained the difference between the two provisions in *Weare v Ndebele* [2008] ZACC 20, 2009 1 SA 600 (CC) [72] (footnotes omitted):

> Whereas the core of section 9(1) is the idea that no-one is above or beneath the law and that all persons are subject to law impartially applied and administered, the core of the right against discrimination in section 9(3) is dignity. Differentiation becomes unfair discrimination when it is based on grounds that have the potential to impact upon the fundamental dignity of human beings.

304 *Prinsloo v Van der Linde* 1997 3 SA 1012 (CC) [23].

305 Grant (n 301 above) 316.

306 *Minister of Finance v Van Heerden* 2004 6 SA 121 (CC) [32].

307 n 306 above, [31]. See Ackermann (n 133 above) 354 - 356, 361 - 363, 388 - 389; Kende (n 220 above) 166 - 169. Since corrective action is an issue which impacts on the determination of discrimination under Section 9(3), there is a potential overlap between the application of Section 9(2) and (3); this can be seen in *Van Heerden*

Apart from those enumerated in Section 9(3), there are other grounds of unfair discrimination in respect of which there is no presumption of unfairness.[308] The Constitutional Court in *Prinsloo*, relying on South Africa's historical reliance on institutionalised discrimination, identified violation of human dignity as the discerning feature of discrimination, whether on listed or unlisted grounds.[309] The Court made a distinction between the guaranteed right to equality and the right to equal treatment, which does not invariably apply, '[i]n Dworkin's words, the right to equality means the right to be treated as equals, which does not always mean the right to receive equal treatment.'[310] In *Harksen* Goldstone J amplified the features of discrimination on an unlisted ground, relying on the potential to impair dignity or an analogous effect.[311] He cautioned against trying to be too definitive about the grounds of discrimination and illustrated their wide-

where the majority of the Court held that the measure was aimed at ameliorating past disadvantage, and therefore fell within the ambit of Section 9(2), while the minority held that the matter should be resolved under the non-discrimination clause, and Sachs J in a separate concurring opinion took a holistic approach focusing on substance rather than technicalities: Grant (n 301 above) 322 - 323.

Transformation involves not only the fulfilment of socio-economic rights, but also the provision of greater access to education and opportunities through various mechanisms, including affirmative action measures: P Langa 'Transformative constitutionalism' (2006) 17 *Stellenbosch Law Review* 351 at 352.

308 *Prinsloo* (n 304 above) above, [28].

309 n 304 above, [31] (footnote omitted):

> Given the history of this country we are of the view that discrimination has acquired a particular pejorative meaning relating to the unequal treatment of people based on attributes and characteristics attaching to them. We are emerging from a period of our history during which the humanity of the majority of the inhabitants of this country was denied. They were treated as not having inherent worth; as objects whose identities could be arbitrarily defined by those in power rather than as persons of infinite worth. In short, they were denied recognition of their inherent dignity. ... In our view unfair discrimination, when used in this second form in section 8(2), in the context of section 8 as a whole, principally means treating persons differently in a way which impairs their fundamental dignity as human beings, who are inherently equal in dignity.

Recognition of human dignity understood here as the antithesis of the exclusion of humanity under apartheid is concerned with the denial of dignity and does not provide a positive definition: J Small & E Grant 'Dignity, discrimination, and context: New directions in South African and Canadian human rights law' (2005) 6(2) *Human Rights Review* 25 at 37.

310 n 304 above, [32], citing *Taking rights seriously* (1977) 227.

311 'There will be discrimination on an unspecified ground if it is based on attributes or characteristics which have the potential to impair the fundamental dignity of persons as human beings, or to affect them adversely in a comparably serious manner.': n 302 above, [46].

ranging nature.[312] Because it determines the burden of proof, the distinction between the listed and unlisted grounds is important procedurally, but, as Grant says, 'from the point of view of principle, the underlying conception that unites them is the "potential to impair dignity".'[313]

Citizenship was held to be an unlisted ground in *Larbi-Odam* where temporarily-employed foreign teachers with residence permits claimed their dismissal as part of a redundancy programme constituted unfair discrimination, since – unlike citizens – they were not entitled to apply for permanent positions.[314] Mokgoro J in the Constitutional Court found that foreign citizens were a vulnerable group because they were a minority with little political muscle, citizenship was a personal attribute which was difficult to change, and foreign citizens were vulnerable to threats and intimidation.[315] She used the potential to impair dignity as the yardstick for unfair discrimination.[316]

The determining factor in ascertaining whether discrimination is unfair is the impact it has on its victims.[317] Currie and de Waal have emphasised the central importance of dignity to understanding unfair discrimination, which is hurtful or demeaning differential treatment and occurs 'when law or conduct, for no good reason, treats some people as inferior or incapable of less deserving of respect than others' or 'when law or conduct perpetuates or does nothing to remedy existing disadvantage and marginalisation.'[318]

312 n 302 above, [49]:

> These grounds have the potential, when manipulated, to demean persons in their inherent humanity and dignity. There is often a complex relationship between these grounds. In some cases they relate to immutable biological attributes or characteristics, in some to the associational life of humans, in some to the intellectual, expressive and religious dimensions of humanity and in some cases to a combination of one or more of these features. The temptation to force them into neatly self-contained categories should be resisted.

313 n 301 above, 318.

314 *Larbi-Odam v MEC for Education (North-West Province)* 1998 1 SA 745 (CC).

315 n 314 above, [19]-[20]. This provides some insight into the kinds of factors that might be taken into account in determining discrimination, but is not a comprehensive approach: Grant (n 301 above) 318.

In a challenge to legislation regulating the private security industry, the majority and minority both identified refugees as a vulnerable group: *Union of Refugee Women v Director, Private Security Industry Regulatory Authority* 2007 4 BCLR 339 (CC) [24], [28]-[31], [82], [113], [117], [122]-[123], [127].

316 n 314 above, [20].

317 Currie & de Waal (n 21 above) 244, citing *Harksen* (n 302 above) [50]-[51].

318 n 21 above, 244, referring to C Albertyn 'Equality' in H Cheadle *et al* (eds) *South African constitutional law: The Bill of Rights* (2002) 105.

In *Van Heerden* (n 306 above) [116] (footnote omitted), Ngcobo J explained the effect on dignity of being regarded as a second-class citizen:

Goldstone J in *Harksen* set out the factors to be considered when determining whether the impact is unfair, one of which is 'the extent to which the discrimination has affected the rights or interests of complainants and whether it has led to an impairment of their fundamental human dignity or constitutes an impairment of a comparably serious nature.'[319] The contextual factors can be summarised as past systematic disadvantage, the nature and purpose of the challenged measure, and its effect on dignity or, as Grant has labelled them, historical disadvantage, corrective action and impact.[320] They, and others which may emerge, are assessed objectively and cumulatively to determine whether discrimination is unfair.[321]

The impact of a city council's policy of selective recovery of debts on residents of white neighbourhoods was held by the majority of the Constitutional Court in *City Council of Pretoria v Walker* to be 'at least comparably serious to an invasion of their dignity.'[322] Even if the discriminatory measures have some benefits for the disadvantaged, they can be unfair if the basis of the distinction is insulting to dignity. In *Moseneke v Master of the High Court*

> Human dignity is harmed by unfair treatment that is premised upon personal traits or circumstances that do not relate to the needs, capacities and merits of different individuals. Often such discrimination is premised on the assumption that the disfavoured group is not worthy of dignity. At times, as our history amply demonstrates, such discrimination proceeds on the assumption that the disfavoured group is inferior to other groups. And this is an assault on the human dignity of the disfavoured group.

Treating people as inferior is invidious discrimination: Waldron (n 28 above) 48.

319 n 302 above, [51].

320 n 301 above, 320, 321, 323. Foster pointed out similarities between the *Harksen* test to analyse equality issues and the test in Canada derived from *Law v Canada (Minister of Employment and Immigration)* [1999] 1 SCR 497 (SC of Canada): n 226 above, 78 - 79. He considered that the focus on dignity may be particularly problematic in the area of economic and social rights, as courts are less inclined to equate unequal divisions of economic rights with dignity and self-worth, although – in contrast with *Harksen* – he was heartened by the Constitutional Court's association of dignity with socio-economic issues in *Bhe v Khayelitsha Magistrate* 2005 1 SA 580 (CC): n 226 above, 88, 96.

321 *Harksen* (n 302 above) [51].

322 1998 2 SA 363 [81]. Sachs J disagreed on the facts, but gave his view on what could constitute a serious impact analogous to infringement of dignity, above, [129] (footnote omitted):

> It might well be that even in the absence of concrete disadvantage, the symbolic effect of a measure (or the absence of a measure that should have been taken) could impair dignity in a way which constitutes unfair discrimination. This could arise if the selective enforcement involved deliberate targeting whether direct or disguised, or was so related in impact to patterns of disadvantage as to leave the persons concerned with the understandable feeling that once more they were being given the short end of the stick.

See comments of Kende (n 220 above) 163 - 166; Small & Grant (n 309 above) 33, 44; LA Williams 'The justiciability of water rights: *Mazibuko v. City of Johannesburg*' (2009) 36 *Forum for Development Studies* 5 at 17 - 21, 44.

a separate system of administration of estates of deceased people depending on their colour rather than on their economic needs or geographic location was held to be unfair discrimination and also a breach of the right to dignity in Section 10 of the Constitution.[323]

If the discrimination is unfair under Section 9(3), it may still survive as a limitation permitted by law in accordance with Section 36.[324] The limitation clause requires an examination of whether less restrictive means are available to achieve the purpose of the legislation.[325]

323 2001 2 SA 18 (CC). Sachs J pointed out the legislation's faulty foundation notwithstanding the fact that it provided a cheap system for administering estates for black people, above, [22] (footnotes omitted):

> The Minister and the Master suggested that the administration of deceased estates by magistrates was often convenient and inexpensive. However, even if there are practical advantages for many people in the system, it is rooted in racial discrimination which severely assails the dignity of those concerned and undermines attempts to establish a fair and equitable system of public administration. Any benefits need not be linked to this form of racial discrimination but could be made equally available to all people of limited means or to all those who live far from the urban centres where the offices of the Master are located. Given our history of racial discrimination, I find that the indignity occasioned by treating people differently as 'blacks', as both section 23(7) and the regulations do, is not rendered fair by the factors identified by the Minister and the Master.

324 An excellent insight into the judicial decision-making process and the role of proportionality in assessing the constitutionality of the limitation of rights can be seen in the writings of Albie Sachs, who said that the Constitutional Court (of which he was a member) was required to make value judgments, to establish the context, analyse the public objectives sought to be realised and the extent to which the law protected rights: A Sachs *The strange alchemy of life and law* (2009) 208. In determining whether the extent of the limitation was proportionate, the Court gave considerable weight to governmental discretion in the choice of means to achieve a legitimate purpose and granted a margin of appreciation to the government's capacity to make factual evaluations of social priorities and areas requiring legislative intervention: above, 208 - 209. The Court gauged the measure concerned with the constitutional measuring-rod of what would be permissible in an open democratic society based on human dignity, equality and freedom, which involved comparisons with other jurisdictions and checking international legal reasoning and practice: above, 209.

Goldstone J in *Harksen* summarised the process to limit a right: 'This will involve a weighing of the purpose and effect of the provision in question and a determination as to the proportionality thereof in relation to the extent of its infringement of equality.': n 302 above, [52]. O'Regan J disagreed with the majority finding that there was no unfair discrimination against an insolvent man's solvent wife, who maintained that her property had been expropriated by the trustees of her husband's estate under the Insolvency Act 1936 – she had no doubt that the extent of the impairment of the interests of the solvent spouse was 'substantial and sufficient to constitute unfair discrimination': n 302 above, [100]. She went on to carry out a limitations analysis and concluded that the limitation on the wife's right was not justifiable, as the interests of creditors seemed to be favoured disproportionately and there were no similar provisions in other legal systems: n 302 above, [111].

325 Sec 36(1)(e). The Constitutional Court regularly uses less restrictive means arguments in its reasoning: Brems (n 22 above) 361. Several other jurisdictions (*eg*, Germany

5.5.1 Gender

In *President of the Republic of South Africa v Hugo* a prisoner, who was a single father of a child under 12, challenged the constitutionality of the pardon granted by President Mandela to mothers of children under that age.[326] He claimed it unfairly discriminated against him and his son on the ground of sex or gender in violation of Section 8 of the interim Constitution. The Court below held that the pardon was unconstitutional. The appeal succeeded, the majority finding that the pardon amounted to discrimination, but that it was not unfair.[327] The history of past discrimination against women entitled the President to redress past disadvantage. Male prisoners who felt they should be pardoned for family circumstances were entitled to petition the President individually for release. The Court recognised that equality commits to recognising each person's individual worth as a human being. It is not confined to redressing past disadvantage, but is also a positive obligation to accord equal dignity to all.[328]

Goldstone J linked closely dignity and equality:[329]

> At the heart of the prohibition of unfair discrimination lies a recognition that the purpose of our new constitutional and democratic order is the

and Switzerland) use the 'least restrictive alternative' criterion in their constitutional human rights doctrine: Brems (n 22 above) 360.

326 1997 4 SA 1 (CC).

327 Cf *Miller v Albright* 523 US 420 (1998).

328 Goldstone J cited L'Heureux-Dubé J's analysis of equality, n 326 above, [41], citing *Egan v Canada* (1995) 29 CRR (2d) 79 at 104-5:

> 'Equality ... means nothing if it does not represent a commitment to recognizing each person's equal worth as a human being, regardless of individual differences. Equality means that our society cannot tolerate legislative distinctions that treat certain people as second-class citizens, that demean them, that treat them as less capable for no good reason, or that otherwise offend fundamental human dignity.'

The Court relied strongly on Canadian jurisprudence for its definition of equality and the placing of dignity at the forefront of individual rights.

The property system in customary marriage was found to constitute gender-discrimination, as it rendered women 'extremely vulnerable by not only denuding them of their dignity but also rendering them poor and dependent': *Gumede (born Shange) v President of the Republic of South Africa* [2008] ZACC 23, 2009 3 SA 152 (CC) [36]. The exclusion of widows in potentially polygynous Muslim marriages from the statutory provisions for spouses in intestate succession constituted unfair discrimination on the grounds of religion, marital status and gender, and was not a justifiable limitation: *Hassam v Jacobs* [2009] ZACC 19, 2009 5 SA 572 (CC).

329 n 326 above, [41]. See Arthur Chaskalson on the difference between equality in the US and South Africa: A Chaskalson 'From wickedness to equality: The moral transformation of South African Law' (2003) 1 *International Journal of Constitutional Law* 590 at 600. Laurie Ackermann refers to the additional impact of equality because of its association with dignity and discusses *Hugo*: LWH Ackermann 'Equality and

> establishment of a society in which all human beings will be accorded equal dignity and respect regardless of their membership of particular groups.

David Beatty cites *Hugo* as an example of a case holding that there is nothing wrong with singling out one gender for special treatment to promote greater equality between the two.[330]

Goldstone J, who wrote the majority opinion, found the pardon did not fundamentally impair fathers' 'rights of dignity or sense of equal worth.'[331] His views reveal an outdated attitude stereotyping the role of women in the home. However, O'Regan J (concurring) had an interesting alternative perspective to offer. She identified the disadvantage suffered by mothers in society on account of their traditional childminding role as a social fact

the South African Constitution: The role of dignity' (2000) 60 *Heidelberg Journal of International Law* 537 at 547 - 548. Foster reviewed *Hugo* to demonstrate problems with a dignity-centred approach: n 226 above, 75, 77, 88 - 90, 94 - 96.

Jeremy Waldron considers that dignity as applied in *Hugo* is mainly a negative idea, being primarily a way of blocking the impact of group characterisations on individual dignity, rather than a way of talking affirmatively about the dignity of groups: J Waldron 'The dignity of groups' (2008) New York University School of Law Public Law Research Paper No 08-53 http://ssrn.com/abstract=1287174 (accessed 26 September 2013) 18. He concluded, '[i]n the last analysis, *Hugo*-dignity, even when applied to groups is still an individualist idea': as above.

See also Grant (n 301 above) 300; Kende (n 220 above) 92 - 101, 110 - 116; McCrudden (n 220 above) 691; Small & Grant, (n 309 above) 33 - 34.

330 DM Beatty *The ultimate rule of law* (2004) 82, fn 24. Beatty criticised *Hugo* because the majority 'made no serious effort to evaluate the significance of the discriminatory character of the pardon from the perspective of either of the parties to the dispute': above, 96.

331 n 326 above, [47]. O'Regan J displayed the same attitude in describing the impact of the discrimination as 'far from severe': n 326 above, [114]. Beatty considers that even worse than this light partisan assessment of the impact on fathers was the fact that no weight at all was given to the interests of those children whose only parent was an incarcerated father – despite Mandela's primary goal in granting the pardon being to help young children: n 330 above, 97.

Mokgoro J upheld the partial pardon, *inter alia*, because of political and administrative difficulties – politically it would have been impossible to release all men and women with young children 'because of the sheer numbers involved' and 'there would have been great administrative inconvenience in engaging in a case-by-case evaluation for each mother and father as to whether they were the primary care giver for their child': n 326 above, [106].

Beatty's criticism of these three opinions was for the judges' failure to exercise the power of judicial review 'in a detached and impartial way. ... they claimed a sovereignty over John Hugo, and other fathers like him, to interpret such acts of discrimination for themselves that they had no authority to make. They dismissed Hugo's own self-understanding as not worthy of the Court's respect.': n 330 above, 97.

resulting in inequality in work.[332] This view of women's inferior place in the work force attributable to the traditional role accorded to them is correct, but is not relevant in the context of imprisonment. Women were not jailed simply because of their gender, but because they had breached the criminal law. The President's remission reinforced the disadvantage under which women in general laboured, as it confirmed their primary role in society as childminders rather than attempting to reverse that stereotypical attitude.[333] There was no recognition that men also had parental responsibilities – indeed, some of the male fathers imprisoned could have been the primary carers.[334]

Mokgoro J, who agreed that the pardon was unfair discrimination, but considered it justified under Section 33 of the interim Constitution, categorised the stereotyping of fathers as an affront to their dignity and equality.[335] The judgments of Kriegler J (dissenting) and Mokgoro J accord better with the concept of dignity as applying to all equally than does that of Goldstone J. The Presidential pardon did not take into account the individual circumstances of mothers who might not be the primary carers, nor of imprisoned fathers who had childminding duties. All of the judges in *Hugo*

332 '[T]he responsibility for child rearing is also one of the factors that renders women less competitive and less successful in the labour market. The unequal division of labour between fathers and mothers is therefore a primary source of women's disadvantage in our society.': n 326 above, [110].

333 Kriegler J (dissenting from the finding that the pardon was constitutional) pointed out that the advantage given by the pardon to women prisoners was not for the purpose of redressing any discriminatory treatment accorded to them compared with men in the penal setting: n 326 above, [84]. He considered that the pardon's '[r]eliance on the generalisation that women are the primary care givers' was harmful as it tended 'to cramp and stunt the efforts of both men and women to form their identities freely': n 326 above, [80].

Cf Justice Ginsburg's dissent in *Miller* (n 327 above). Her dissent reflected concerns of individual fairness, as there was not a persuasive fit between the government's means and ends in the legislation in question; she opposed the 'preference' for women because she considered that unequal treatment of mothers and fathers legally reinforced gender stereotypes: N Rao 'Gender, race, and individual dignity: Evaluating Justice Ginsburg's equality jurisprudence' (2009) 70 *Ohio State Law Journal* 1053 at 1065.

334 The generalisation perpetuated the attitude that men 'can have only a secondary/ surrogate role in the care of their children' and the pardon reinforced a view that was 'a root cause of women's inequality' in society: n 326 above, [83].

335 n 326 above, [92] (footnote omitted):

> [D]enying men the opportunity to be released from prison in order to resume rearing their children, entirely on the basis of stereotypical assumptions concerning men's aptitude at child rearing, is an infringement upon their equality and dignity. The Presidential Act does not recognize the equal worth of fathers who are actively involved in nurturing and caring for their young children, treating them as less capable parents on the mere basis that they are fathers and not mothers.

accepted the relevance of respect for dignity, but came to differing conclusions through varying routes.[336]

5.5.2 Marital status

In common with many other countries, the issue of whether distinctions made on the grounds of marital status – whether between married and unmarried individuals, between married and unmarried couples, or between a husband and wife within marriage – are legally acceptable has been divisive.[337]

In *Harksen* the solvent spouse of an insolvent man was unsuccessful in her challenge to insolvency legislation, which she alleged discriminated against her because of her marriage thereby infringing her property rights.[338] The Constitutional Court in a majority decision found that she had been treated differently from other people who might have had dealings with the insolvent on the grounds of her marital status, but that the discrimination was not unfair. The legislation inconvenienced her by burdening her with resisting the claim of the trustees of her husband's estate; however, this did not violate her dignity. O'Regan J (dissenting on this aspect) regarded the legislation as adversely affecting the solvent spouse's interests and amounting to unfair discrimination, which was not justifiable under the limitations clause since the interests of creditors were favoured disproportionately. Relying on *Brink v Kitshoff*[339] and *Prinsloo*,[340] she pointed out that the anti-discrimination provision had been interpreted primarily as 'a buffer against the construction of further patterns of discrimination and disadvantage' and that the desire to avoid discrimination was underpinned by the Constitution's commitment to human dignity.[341]

336 It may be that the majority was reluctant to risk political and public ire by finding that the iconic President Mandela, although well-intentioned, had erred by unwittingly perpetuating inequality.

Rory O'Connell analysed *Hugo*, as well as other cases, and concluded that the concept of dignity is 'sufficiently broad so as to allow judges to invoke unarticulated norms to decide difficult issues' and might 'reinforce stereotypes and prejudices rather than combat them': R O'Connell 'The role of dignity in equality law: Lessons from Canada and South Africa' (2008) 6 *International Journal of Constitutional Law* 267 at 284.

337 In South Africa the series of successful sexual-oriented challenges to legislation according benefits only to 'spouses' gave considerable impetus to arguments that denying these benefits to opposite-sex life partners was also unfair discrimination: Currie & de Waal (n 21 above) 254.

338 n 302 above.

339 1996 4 SA 197 (CC).

340 n 304 above.

341 n 302 above, [91].

Sachs J – also dissenting – cconsidered that the unfair discrimination arose because the legislation did not treat the spouses as independent entities and breached their rights to human dignity and privacy. In contrast to the majority, he viewed the legislation as representing 'more than an inconvenience to or burden upon the solvent spouse', as it affronted 'his or her personal dignity as an independent person within the spousal relationship' and perpetuated an archaic vision of marriage viewed in the light of constitutional values.[342] The views of O'Regan and Sachs JJ were more insightful than those of the majority. They detected that the dignity of the spouses had been compromised by treating them as a unit.

The divisiveness in equality cases, where the Constitutional Court was required to take what Albie Sachs described as 'constitutionally-guided value judgments'[343] emerged again in *Volks v Robinson* – a challenge to legislation providing for maintenance for the surviving spouse from the estate of a deceased husband or wife on the grounds that it should also have applied to heterosexual unmarried couples.[344] Mrs Robinson had been in a permanent life partnership with a man for 16 years up to the time of his death, but they did not marry although there was no legal obstacle to marriage. She claimed that the legislation was discriminatory on the grounds of marital status and that it also breached her right to dignity. The Court in a majority verdict rejected the claim of unconstitutionality on the basis that it would be invidious to impose an obligation to maintain a partner after death, but not during their joint lifetimes. Skweyiya J did not regard the differentiation based on

342 n 302 above, [118]. He discerned accurately the insidious, subtle and sometimes disguised nature of discrimination, n 302 above, [123] (footnotes omitted):

> [W]hat is most relevant to the question of unfairness is the assumption which puts together what constitutional respect for human dignity and privacy requires be kept asunder. This is one of those areas where to homogenise is not to equalise, but to reinforce social patterns that deny the achievement of equality … The intrusion might indeed seem relatively slight. Yet an oppressive hegemony associated with the grounds contemplated by section 8(2) may be constructed not only, or even mainly, by the grand exercise of naked power. It can also be established by the accumulation of a multiplicity of detailed, but interconnected, impositions, each of which, de-contextualised and on its own, might be so minor as to risk escaping immediate attention, especially by those not disadvantaged by them.

Barrington J in the Irish High Court in similar fashion pointed out that treatment as an inferior can manifest itself in a superficially trivial regulation: *Brennan v AG* [1983] ILRM 449 (HC) 481.

343 n 324 above, 210.

344 2005 5 BCLR 446 (CC).

marriage as anathema to dignity.[345] A stance influenced by constitutional values and that was more discerning than that of the majority was taken by Sachs J in a dissenting judgment[346] where he regarded the issue from the viewpoint of the family relationship rather than parsing the strict rules of matrimonial law.[347]

Like *Volks* in South Africa, *Nova Scotia (AG) v Walsh* was a divisive case in Canada with the same outcome and, again, differing judicial interpretations.[348] There was disagreement between the judges on the application of choice and liberty to the facts and the impact on dignity. The majority felt that the dignity of those who chose not to marry and to avail themselves of that status should be respected by not imposing the benefits of marriage on heterosexual cohabiting couples. Bastarache J took the view that the dignity of common law spouses was not affected adversely and rationalised it by relying on

345 n 344 above, [62]:

> Mrs Robinson is not being told that her dignity is worth less than that of someone who is married. She is simply told that there is a fundamental difference between her relationship and a marriage relationship in relation to maintenance. It is that people in a marriage are obliged to maintain each other by operation of law and without further agreement or formalities. People in the class of relationships to which she belongs are not in that position. In the circumstances, it is not appropriate that an obligation that did not exist before death be posthumously imposed.

Ngcobo J concurring in the majority decision focused on the importance of marriage as an institution, the obligation imposed on the state by international instruments to respect and protect marriage, and the right freely to marry: n 344 above, [81]-[85]. In their joint dissenting judgment Mokgoro and O'Regan JJ emphasised that the Constitution prohibits unfair discrimination on the ground of marital status: n 344 above, [107]-[108].

346 Embarrassingly for him, his judgment was over twice as long as that of the majority: Sachs (n 324 above) 211.

347 n 344 above, [222]:

> I should add that while it is true that caring for one's family is one of life's great joys, and as such calls for no extra reward, fairness does not inevitably translate into sacrifice. ... It would indeed be a perverse interpretation of family law that obliged one to disregard the fact that the circumstances of need in which a typical survivor might find herself, were produced precisely by her selfless devotion to the deceased and their family during his lifetime. I believe it is socially unrealistic, unduly moralistic and hence constitutionally unfair, for the Act to discriminate against the powerless and economically dependent party, now threatened with destitution, on the basis that she should either have insisted on marriage or else withdrawn from the relationship.

Evadné Grant discerned a structured approach underlying the equality cases by the focus on group membership and the need to build a new society that valued diversity and difference, as mentioned by Sachs J in this case: n 301 above, 327, fn 162. As she stated, while individual affront played an important role in some cases, such as in the sexual orientation cases, the context in which this was considered was that of group membership: n 301 above, 327.

348 2002 SCC 83, [2002] 4 SCR 325 (SC of Canada). See Hogg (n 258 above) *Vol 2* at 625, 632, 643, 678 - 679.

autonomy.[349] In contrast L'Heureux-Dubé J in dissent recognised a threat to dignity.[350] She saw choice as a more complex issue and did not accept the argument that the legislation was enacted to respect choice and therefore did not violate the claimant's dignity.[351]

The divergence between the judges in these cases relating to different treatment of married and unmarried couples is a symptom of the changing attitude towards marriage emerging in society worldwide. Rory O'Connell observed in the case-law a dilemma over the colliding roles of autonomy and welfare in the meaning of dignity.[352]

5.5.3 Sexual orientation

Complaints of discrimination on the grounds of sexual orientation have been less favourably received in the courts than those based on gender differences. Beatty has found that South Africa is among the countries where gays and lesbians have had a higher level of success in challenging traditional laws than elsewhere.[353] He instances South Africa's Constitutional Court, the European Court of Human Rights and the UN Human Rights Committee as being sympathetic to decriminalising sexual behaviour of homosexuals in

349 'There is no deprivation of a benefit based on stereotype or presumed characteristics perpetuating the idea that unmarried couples are less worthy of respect or valued as members of Canadian society. All cohabitants are deemed to have the liberty to make fundamental choices in their lives.': n 348 above, [62].

350 n 348 above, [118]:

> Failing to recognize the contribution made by heterosexual unmarried cohabitants is a failure to accord them the respect they deserve. This failure diminishes their status in their own eyes and in those of society as a whole by suggesting that they are less worthy of respect and consideration. Their dignity is thereby assaulted: they are the victims of discrimination.

351 '[I]t is incorrect to paint each unmarried cohabitant with the same brush as regards the "choice" to cohabit. For many, choice is not an option. For those where choice is in fact an option, few structure their lives by marrying or not marrying to take advantage or avoid particular legal obligations.': n 348 above, [157].

352 'The tension that these cases highlight – between an interpretation of dignity that mandates a protection of a person's autonomy, or free choice, and one that mandates consideration for a person's needs and welfare – reflects a significant divergence in the understanding of the concept of dignity.': n 336 above, 280 (footnote omitted).

353 n 330 above, 99.

contrast with the Supreme Courts of Ireland, the US,[354] Zimbabwe,[355] and Germany's Constitutional Court (at least initially).[356]

In the *Sodomy* case, Ackermann J had no hesitation in finding that the impact intended and caused by the legislation was 'flagrant, intense, demeaning and destructive of self-realisation, sexual expression and sexual orientation' and went on to robustly condemn it.[357] South Africa overturned legislation making it impossible for same-sex partners to adopt children

354 The US Supreme Court decriminalised sodomy as it violated the Due Process Clause of the Fourteenth Amendment in *Lawrence v Texas*, when Justice Kennedy acknowledged that 'adults may choose to enter upon this relationship in the confines of their homes and their own private lives and still retain their dignity as free persons': 539 US 558 (2003) 567. It overruled *Bowers v Hardwick* 478 US 186 (1986). Neomi Rao regarded *Lawrence* as suggesting a substantial opening for the development of a European conception of human dignity, as the Supreme Court conceived of dignity as liberty to engage in sexual acts without criminal sanction and also in the broader sense of being free from demeaning condemnation by the state: N Rao 'On the use and abuse of dignity in constitutional law' (2008) 14 *Columbia Journal of European Law* 201 at 240 - 241. Rao pointed out that *Lawrence* was significant as well in the adoption by the Supreme Court of European juridicial methodology, avoiding the traditional strict scrutiny or rational basis review and coming close to proportionality by examining the state's justifications for its statute, in addition to using European conceptions of dignity: above, 242. Maxine Goodman described *Lawrence* as marking a substantial shift by advancing human dignity as part of affording liberty and not simply as shifting from a privacy to a liberty interest: MD Goodman 'Human dignity in Supreme Court constitutional jurisprudence' (2006) 84 *Nebraska Law Review* 740 at 762. Goodman stated that the novelty in *Lawrence* was the Court's explicit reference to human dignity as a guiding precept: above, 793. Jeremy Miller remarked that the Court's focus on the demeaning impact of the statute reflected awareness that what was being protected was not the individuals' right to do what they like behind closed doors, but protection of the right to be an individual (even if a personal decision is regarded as 'wrong' by others): JM Miller 'Dignity as a new framework, replacing the right to privacy' (2007) 30 *Thomas Jefferson Law Review* 1 at 41. Reva Siegel deduced that *Lawrence* was based on entangled rationales protecting dignity as equality in addition to dignity as liberty; the case raised questions of autonomy and self-definition and of social standing and respect: n 4 above, 1741 - 1742. See further comments on *Lawrence*: J Goehring '*Lawrence v. Texas*: Dignity, a new standard for substantive rational basis review?' (2004) 13 *Tulane Journal of Law & Sexuality: A Review of Lesbian, Gay, Bisexual and Transgender Legal Issues* 727; N Levit 'Theorizing and litigating the rights of sexual minorities' (2010) 19 *Columbia Journal of Gender and Law* 21 at 29 - 31, 36; Rao (n 219 above) 212, 257, 267, 270; JQ Whitman 'The two Western cultures of privacy: Dignity versus liberty' (2004) 113 *Yale Law Journal* 1151 at 1162, 1214.

355 See *Banana v S* [2000] 4 LRC 621 (SC of Zimbabwe).

356 n 330 above, 99, citing *National Coalition for Gay and Lesbian Equality v Minister of Justice* 1998 12 BCLR 1517 (CC) (*Sodomy* case).

357 'There is nothing before us to show that the provision was motivated by anything other than rank prejudice and had as its purpose the stamping out of these forms of gay erotic self-expression.': n 356 above, [76]. Heinz Klug referred to the *Sodomy* case to illustrate the enrichment of the right to equality by its interaction with the right to dignity: n 2 above, 152 - 153.

jointly and held that restricting joint adoption to married persons discriminated on the grounds of sexual orientation and marital status.[358] In addition to breaching the right to equality, it infringed dignity rights and the principle of the paramountcy of a child's best interests.[359] Guardianship and custody rights had been granted to only one of the lesbian partners, thus violating the dignity rights of the other partner by denying her due recognition as a parent, which Skweyiya AJ described as 'demeaning'.[360]

Goldstone J, delivering the unanimous decision of the Constitutional Court in *J v Director General, Department of Home Affairs*, found there was an analogous differentiation in the legislation confining recognition as parents and guardians of children conceived by artificial insemination to heterosexual couples.[361] Kathleen Satchwell was a South African judge, who had lived in a committed relationship with her same-sex partner for many years. She challenged the employment benefits given to judges, as some were restricted to judges' spouses. The Constitutional Court unanimously found

Ackermann J was influenced by South African academic writing and also looked at a wide variety of foreign case-law: n 356 above, [20], [39]-[57]. He probably used the foreign material as backing for his decision rather than seeking guidance from it, relying more on academic writing in coming to his conclusion: DL Carey Miller 'The great trek to human rights: The role of comparative law in the development of human rights in post-reform South Africa' in E Örücü (ed) *Judicial comparativism in human rights cases* (2003) 223 - 224.

The Court looked at the impact on those affected not from a position of power, but responding with empathy to those who were subordinated: PC Davis 'Responsive constitutionalism and the idea of dignity' (2009) 11 *University of Pennsylvania Journal of Constitutional Law* 1373 at 1377. It spoke not in terms of naked absolutes, but in terms unhesitatingly informed by conscientious analysis of South Africa's history and that of other nations, appealing to both logic and experience: Davis, as above. Peggy Cooper Davis contrasted the US Supreme Court unfavourably with the Constitutional Court's judgment in the *Sodomy* case and called the US opinions on homosexual sodomy 'acontextual, ahistoric and lacking in empathy': as above. She stated that the South African Court had committed itself to constructing constitutional rights, liberties, and obligations in a way that reflected the lessons of apartheid and the principles embodied in the struggle against it: above, 1376.

On the *Sodomy* case, see also Kende (n 220 above) 136 - 138; EK Quansah 'Same-sex relationships in Botswana: Current perspectives and future prospects' (2004) 4 *African Human Rights Law Journal* 201 at 210 - 211.

358 *Du Toit v Minister of Welfare and Population Development* 2003 2 SA 198 (CC). See Kende (n 220 above) 141 - 142.

359 n 358 above, [37].

360 n 358 above, [29].

361 2003 5 SA 621 (CC) [14].

that the legislation and regulations concerning judges were unconstitutional, because they discriminated on the grounds of sexual orientation.[362]

The Intestate Succession Act 1987 was unconstitutional to the extent that it conferred rights of intestate succession on heterosexual spouses but not on permanent same-sex life partners. In her judgment on behalf of a unanimous Constitutional Court, van Heerden AJ confirmed the High Court finding that the legislation breached the equality and dignity rights under Sections 9 and 10 of the Constitution of the surviving partner to a permanent same-sex life partnership in which the partners had undertaken reciprocal duties of support.[363]

The Aliens Control Act 1991 facilitated the immigration into South Africa of foreign national spouses of permanent South African residents, but did not extend the same benefits to South African gays and lesbians in permanent same-sex life partnerships with foreign nationals. The Constitutional Court held that it discriminated unfairly on the intersecting and overlapping grounds of sexual orientation and marital status, and seriously limited the equality rights and the right to dignity of permanent same-sex life partners thereby breaching Sections 9(3) and 10 of the Constitution.[364] The statute discriminated in a way which was not reasonable and justifiable in an open and democratic society based on human dignity, equality and freedom. Ackermann J cited Canadian jurisprudence in his judgment for the unanimous Court, thereby evidencing that substantive equality is achieved in Canada and in South Africa through the focus on dignity.[365] He pinpointed the deep effect of discrimination on individual homosexuals touching their very

362 *Satchwell v President of Republic of South Africa* 2002 6 SA 1 (CC). The Court referred to women-to-women marriages in African traditional societies: above, [12]. This is a rare instance of African perspective in South African jurisprudence: Carey Miller (n 357 above) 226. See Kende (n 220 above) 139 - 140.

363 *Gory v Kolver* 2007 4 SA 97 (CC) [19].

364 *National Coalition for Gay and Lesbian Equality v Minister of Home Affairs* 2000 2 SA 1 (CC). See Kende (n 220 above) 138 - 139; Quansah (n 357 above) 211 - 212.

365 The Court used Canadian case-law to support pivotal aspects of its decision, particularly on overlapping categories of discrimination, the notion of equality and its application to the definition of the concept of family: Carey Miller (n 357 above) 225. It brought foreign jurisprudence to bear on the issue of the appropriate remedy and used it to support its decision to 'read in' words to correct the legislation: as above.

existence and rocking the twin values of equality and dignity.[366] He was conscious of the benefits – not just for the individuals involved, but for society – of equal treatment and respect for dignity of all. '[T]he bell tolls for everyone', because, as L'Heureux Dubé J of Canada said, the social costs of discrimination are high and damage the fabric of society.[367] In *Quilter v AG* Thomas J of the Court of Appeal in New Zealand had a similar view, '[i]f [the basic human rights of minority groups are being denied], it is important to spell that denial out if the basic dignity of everyone in a more enlightened age is to be secured.'[368]

South Africa introduced legislation allowing same-sex marriages[369] as a result of the Constitutional Court's judgment in *Fourie* holding that the common law and the Marriage Act 1961 were inconsistent with the equality rights in Sections 9(1) and 9(3) and the right to respect for dignity in Section 10 of the Constitution to the extent that they made no provision for same-sex couples to enjoy the status, entitlements and responsibilities accorded to

366 n 364 above, [42]:

> The sting of past and continuing discrimination against both gays and lesbians is the clear message that it conveys, namely, that they, whether viewed as individuals or in their same-sex relationships, do not have the inherent dignity and are not worthy of the human respect possessed by and accorded to heterosexuals and their relationships. This discrimination occurs at a deeply intimate level of human existence and relationality. It denies to gays and lesbians that which is foundational to our Constitution and the concepts of equality and dignity, which at this point are closely intertwined, namely that all persons have the same inherent worth and dignity as human beings, whatever their other differences may be. The denial of equal dignity and worth all too quickly and insidiously degenerates into a denial of humanity and leads to inhuman treatment by the rest of society in many other ways. This is deeply demeaning and frequently has the cruel effect of undermining the confidence and sense of self-worth and self-respect of lesbians and gays.

367 n 364 above, [82], citing *Canada (AG) v Mossop* (1993) 100 DLR (4th) 658 at 698 b. See the efforts by the Supreme Court of Canada to support equality in *Chamberlain v Surrey School District No 36* 2002 SCC 86, [2002] 4 SCR 710, where there were colliding dignities in claims to freedom of religion and expression on the one hand and equality on the grounds of sexual orientation on the other; the majority held that a school board's decision not to approve books depicting same-sex parented families was unreasonable in the context of a legislative educational scheme whereby approval of books was to be considered according to the broad principles of tolerance and non-sectarianism.

368 n 364 above, fn 110, citing [1998] 1 NZLR 523 (CA) 550.

369 Civil Union Act 2006. South Africa was only the fifth country in the world to legalise gay unions: AK Wing 'The South African Constitution as a role model for the United States' (2008) 24 *Harvard BlackLetter Law Journal* 73 at 76.

heterosexual couples.[370] The issue was not privacy, but enhancement of dignity and of the equality of same-sex couples by public acknowledgment of their status, as Sachs J noted, 'what the applicants in this matter seek is not the right to be left alone, but the right to be acknowledged as equals and to be embraced with dignity by the law.'[371] He adverted to the change in societal attitudes over time, '[t]heir love that was once forced to be clandestine, may

370 *Minister of Home Affairs v Fourie* 2006 1 SA 524 (CC). Sachs J made it clear that an examination of context is imperative to ascertain the impact that an apparently neutral distinction could have on the dignity and sense of self-worth of the persons affected: above, [151]. He pointed out that differential treatment in itself does not necessarily violate the dignity of those affected, but when separation 'implies repudiation, connotes distaste or inferiority and perpetuates a caste-like status', it becomes constitutionally invidious: above, [152]. See also EC Christiansen 'Transformative constitutionalism in South Africa: Creative uses of Constitutional Court authority to advance substantive justice' (2010) 13 *Journal of Gender, Race & Justice* 575 at 595, 597 - 600, 609 - 611; McCrudden (n 220 above) 720.

The Massachusetts Supreme Court, in its decision on same-sex marriage, also referred to dignity and equality as affirmed in the Massachusetts Constitution and stated that it forbade 'the creation of second class citizens': S Baer 'Dignity, liberty, equality: A fundamental rights triangle of constitutionalism' (2009) 59 *University of Toronto Law Journal* 417 at 428 - 429, citing *Goodridge v Massachusetts (Department of Public Health)* 440 Mass 309, 798 NE.2d 941 (2003). See also *Re Marriage Cases* 43 Cal.4th 757 (2008) (SC of California); *Kerrigan v Commissioner of Public Health* 957 A.2d 407 (2008) (SC of Connecticut); *US v Windsor* 133 S Ct 2675 (2013); Kende (n 220 above) 142 - 146, 156 - 157; JA Redding 'Dignity, legal pluralism, and same-sex marriage' (2010) 75 *Brooklyn Law Review* 791 at 800 - 808.

371 n 370 above, [78]. Justice Kennedy took a similar stance in *Lawrence* (n 354 above), which Nancy Levit said had a centrally communitarian thrust requiring the state to affirmatively promote behaviours it wants to support instead of simply imposing the negative onus of not intruding on people's privacy; as Levit stated, '[t]he move that Justice Kennedy makes in *Lawrence* is not just that people are free to pursue certain types of sexual relationships that they want, it is a recognition that those *relationships* are important and something the state should support': n 354 above, 30. In *Lawrence*, the US Supreme Court for the first time recognised 'autonomy of self' as a concept of constitutional significance: Dubber (n 54 above) 8. Having stated that freedom extends beyond spatial bounds, Justice Kennedy continued, '[l]iberty presumes an autonomy of self that includes freedom of thought, belief, expression, and certain intimate conduct'; he then indicated that the case involved personal liberty 'both in its spatial and more transcendent dimensions': n 354 above, 562.

In its decision decriminalising consensual homosexual practices, Delhi High Court relied on the South African *Sodomy* case, Justice Blackmun's dissent in *Bowers v Hardwick* and *Paris Adult Theatre I v Slaton* 413 US 49 (1973) to demonstrate that the right to be left alone was not merely a negative right but implied the more substantive right to private intimacy and autonomy: P Baruah 'Logic and coherence in *Naz Foundation*: The arguments of non-discrimination, privacy, and dignity' (2009) 2 *National University of Juridical Sciences Law Review* 505 at 515, citing *Naz Foundation v Government of NCT of Delhi* WP (C) No 7455/2001, 160 (2009) DLT 277.

now dare openly to speak its name'.[372] The acceptance of the reality and integrity of the intimate life of homosexuals led to a change in the law.[373]

5.5.4 Group identity

South African jurisprudence highlights the dignity of groups and community.[374] It looks at the individual not as an isolated entity, but in association with family and wider society. The value of *ubuntu* in practice paints a picture of an inclusive grouping where the individual's identity is respected in the pursuit of the common good. The aim is that all members be committed to the interests of the group as a whole, or at least accept and understand restrictions necessary to benefit the community.[375] Sonja Grover rightly indicated that a person has dignity as part of a collective and as an individual.[376] In *Merafong Demarcation Forum*, van der Westhuizen J categorised the struggle against colonialism and the apartheid regime's

372 n 370 above, [78]. The fight for lesbian and gay equality was a gradual process beginning with the decriminalisation of sodomy, then various partnership rights were recognised by the courts and finally, after ten years, marriage rights were granted by the legislature after the intervention of the Constitutional Court: Bilchitz (n 5 above) 69. Bilchitz used this progression to illustrate that law is evolutionary and that the great social justice movements have taken time to achieve just laws: as above.

373 The recognition of equal respect for the sexuality of others is a theme that is only beginning to percolate successfully in lesbian, gay, bisexual, and transgendered rights cases: Levit (n 354 above) 36.

O'Regan J differed in the remedy and she would have given immediate relief by developing the common law and reading words in to the statute: n 370 above, [169]. Although the formal difference between the remedies proposed by Sachs and O'Regan JJ related to the requirements of the separation-of-powers doctrine, Theunis Roux considers that what separates the judgments is a difference of opinion concerning the way in which the Constitutional Court should build public support for decisions of constitutional principle: T Roux 'Principle and pragmatism on the Constitutional Court of South Africa' (2009) 7 *International Journal of Constitutional Law* 106 at 122. Cf remedy granted by the Court of Appeal for Ontario in *Halpern v Canada (AG)* (2003) 225 DLR (4th) 529 [156].

374 The South African Constitution provides for recognition of the right of communities to self-determination: Sec 235. See Waldron (n 329 above) 11 - 12.

375 Human dignity determines the essence of a democratic legal order, *ie*, those rights citizens of a political community must grant themselves if they are to respect one another as members of a voluntary association of free and equal persons: Habermas (n 1 above) 469.

376 S Grover 'A response to Bagaric and Allan's "The vacuous concept of dignity"' (2009) 13 *International Journal of Human Rights* 615 at 617. Dignity may mean respect for individual autonomy – for the capacity of each person to choose how to live – or it may require social recognition of one's lifestyle or group: Rao (n 333 above) 1080 - 1081. See also Rao (n 219 above) 187 - 189.

Bantustan policy as a struggle 'for the recognition of the dignity of individuals and communities' as well as for one united country.[377]

According to Ziyad Motala and Cyril Ramaphosa, traditional African societies showed a great respect for human dignity, conceptualised in modern times as African humanism.[378] Decisions in the community were taken by consensus for the benefit of the overall group, where economic benefits were shared and 'individualism was discouraged'.[379] When the person is seen in the first instance as a member of a community rather than as an individual, rights only have relevance if derived from relations with others.[380]

South Africa is a rainbow nation with people of many different cultures and origins living there. It tries to accommodate the interests of each group within a framework of equal treatment of all. In *Gauteng School Bill* the Constitutional Court was asked to resolve a dispute over the constitutionality of certain provisions of an education Bill in Gauteng.[381] The task was to find the correct balance between the importance of overcoming systemic inequality inherited from the past, on the one hand, and preventing legally enforced or *de facto* assimilation of groups wishing to preserve and develop a distinctive identity, on the other.[382] An understanding of the other as well

377 *Merafong Demarcation Forum v President of the Republic of South Africa* 2008 5 SA 171 (CC) [23].

378 Z Motala & C Ramaphosa *Constitutional law: Analysis and cases* (2002) 48.

379 n 378 above, 45 - 46, citing President Kaunda of Zambia (footnote omitted).

380 n 378 above, 46. Ziyad Motala and Cyril Ramaphosa describe the South African Constitution as moving 'beyond the common law and its concept of *atomistic* individuals, towards a consideration of the interests of the majority' resulting in individuals being required on occasion to make sacrifices for the common good: n 378 above, 409. When an individual claims rights against the community, this has implications for the person's autonomy, self-worth and right to privacy: Baruah (n 371 above) 521.

381 *Gauteng Provincial Legislature: Re Gauteng School Education Bill of 1995* 1996 3 SA 165. The petitioners maintained that the legislation did not protect the minority rights of the Afrikaans-speaking community and relied on the education rights in Article 32 of the interim Constitution: above, [5].

See GN Barrie '*Ubuntu ungamntu ngabanye abantu*: The recognition of minority rights in the South African Constitution' [2000] *Journal of South African Law* 271 at 275 - 276; MA Burnham 'Cultivating a seedling charter: South Africa's Court grows its Constitution' (1997) 3 *Michigan Journal of Race & Law* 29 at 35 - 36, 58, fn 108; RR Kriel 'On how to deal with textual ambiguity, *Ex parte Gauteng Provincial Legislature: In re dispute concerning the constitutionality of certain provisions of the Gauteng School Education Bill of 1995*' (1997) 13 *South African Journal on Human Rights* 311; J Sarkin 'The political role of the South African Constitutional Court' (1997) 114 *South African Law Journal* 134 at 145 - 146.

382 According to Sachs J, this task was primarily a matter for democratic resolution by the legislatures, and not for adjudication by the courts in the first instance: n 381 above, [91].

as respect for others' dignity and freedom are essential for the smooth running of a multi-cultural society, as sketched by Prof Carel Boshoff and Carel Boshoff IV, who advocated not closing our eyes to

> the existential reality, intensity and meaning of this intercultural encounter, to the confrontation with those other worlds outside one's own, worlds in which human lives exist with no less legitimacy and no less right to be. ... We should... try to find ways in which this encounter could proceed to an active communication, mutually recognising the others' autonomy and dignity; entering into communion, aiming at a reciprocal revelation and understanding of each other.[383]

Discrimination against defined types of people is an attack on the dignity of the group. It is countered by implementing substantive equality resulting from an investigation of the effect on the dignity of the members of the group.[384]

5.5.5 Comparative equality jurisprudence

This subsection will review developments in equality jurisprudence in other countries in order to enlighten the assessment of the South African case-law.[385] The focus will be particularly on Canada, India and the US. South Africa, in common with Canada,[386] uses human dignity in law not only as a

383 C Boshoff (IV) & C Boshoff 'The sociopolitical conditions for democratic nation-building: an Afrikaner point of view' in N Rhoodie & I Liebenberg (eds) *Democratic nation-building in South Africa* (1994) 164, cited in n 381 above, fn 18.

384 Sachs J explained in the *Sodomy* case (n 356 above) [126]:

> One of the great gains achieved by following a situation-sensitive human rights approach is that analysis focuses not on abstract categories, but on the lives as lived and the injuries as experienced by different groups in our society. The manner in which discrimination is experienced on grounds of race or sex or religion or disability varies considerably – there is difference in difference. The commonality that unites them all is the injury to dignity imposed upon people as a consequence of their belonging to certain groups. Dignity in the context of equality has to be understood in this light. The focus on dignity results in emphasis being placed simultaneously on context, impact and the point of view of the affected persons. Such focus is in fact the guarantor of substantive as opposed to formal equality.

385 Comparative law is being used increasingly by courts on a regular basis as persuasive authority. Human rights advocates see the role of comparison as that of persuasion to an essentially moral position: C McCrudden 'Judicial comparativism and human rights' in E Örücü & D Nelken (eds) *Comparative law: A handbook* (2007) 376. The use of comparative methods by judges in human rights adjudication varies immensely between jurisdictions, within jurisdictions across time, and between the types of human rights claims: above, 376 - 377.

386 On dignity in Canadian equality law, see J Bates 'Human dignity – an empty phrase in search of meaning?' (2005) 10 *Judicial Review* 165; Hogg (n 258 above) *Vol 2* at 628 - 633.

right or as an interpretative or underlying value, but as an anchor in defining inequality.[387] Dignity can assist in reaching 'a transformed society in which quality of life is improved and people's potential is freed.'[388] Unlike other systems of formal equality, which have a comparative base, the South African Constitution focuses on historically disadvantaged and vulnerable people. Assessment of inequality is not a rules-bound formal procedure, but is adapted to the individual without being subjective either from the claimant's or from the judge's perspective. The individual's social relations, membership of a group and place in the wider community are taken into account by 'application of the identified contextual factors, which focus attention on the effect of such discrimination on the dignity of the applicant.'[389] As in German jurisprudence, the community dimension is recognised in South Africa.[390]

The Canadian Supreme Court has defined dignity in more subjective terms than the South African Constitutional Court.[391] The emphasis on feelings in Canada adds more to the concept of dignity than simply looking

387 In South Africa, dignity and equality are interdependent, inequality being established through group-based differential treatment or through differentiation perpetuating disadvantage leading to scarring of the sense of dignity and self-worth: Chaskalson (n 190 above) 140. In Canadian and South African equality law, human dignity functions as a determining factor of the discrimination test: Small & Grant (n 309 above) 35. See also McCrudden (n 220 above) 690.

388 S Cowen 'Can "dignity" guide South Africa's equality jurisprudence?' (2001) 17 *South African Journal on Human Rights* 34 at 42. Susie Cowen agrees with the assumption in the Constitutional Court's jurisprudence that equality 'should be informed by another value, that it does not stand alone as a value': above, 40.

389 Small & Grant (n 309 above) 38. On the impact on a member of the group, see *Sodomy* case (n 356 above) [125]. The inequality of treatment 'leads to and is proved by the indignity': n 356 above, [124].

390 Grant (n 301 above) 312 - 313. This is clear from Sachs J's rejection of autonomy as the sole attribute of dignity in the *Sodomy* case, where he placed the individual in a social setting: (n 356 above) above, [117]. The South African approach contrasts with that in Canada, which relies on individual merit or capacity: Small & Grant (n 309 above) 41.

391 Grant (n 301 above) fn 150.

at dignity as status.[392] After three cases in 1995 (all with strong dissents)[393] revealing diverse approaches to equality, the Canadian Supreme Court resolved the internal conflict when it adopted a united front in *Law* affirming that the purpose of the equality provision in Section 15(1) of the Canadian Charter[394] was to prevent a violation of dignity.[395] Some confusion arose over the application of the dignity test in equality cases after *Law*. Different interpretations of equality and dissenting opinions continued to be seen, as in *Gosselin v Quebec (AG)* where a welfare recipient brought a class action challenging a social assistance scheme on behalf of all welfare recipients under 30, who had been subject to a differential regime.[396] The majority of five judges, in a deeply divided Supreme Court with four dissenters, held against the class action, as an examination of the contextual factors set out in *Law* did not support a finding of discrimination and denial of human dignity. The view of Arbour J in dissent supports fulfilment of basic needs in furtherance of socio-economic rights and full enjoyment of civil and political

392 'Human dignity within the meaning of the equality guarantee does not relate to the status or position of an individual in society *per se*, but rather concerns the manner in which a person legitimately feels when confronted with a particular law.': *Law* (n 320 above) [53] (Iacobucci J).

Scholars criticised the focus in *Law* on dignity, as the decision's doctrinal effects were regarded as weakening the Supreme Court's equality standard: Baer (n 370 above) 462. Susanne Baer saw two problems with *Law*, *ie*, first, contrary to the idea of equality, it used dignity as the placeholder for a particular morality = but equality was directed precisely at forestalling the introduction of particular moralistic values into legislation; second, it employed dignity as a vehicle for paternalism: n 370 above, 463 - 464. She suggested reconsidering dignity in the light of liberty and equality in order to avoid the reintroduction of problematic paternalism into constitutional law: n 370 above, 462. As she explained, '...if dignity is read as one component in the triangle of dignity, equality, and liberty, it is not about being dignified, or about "legitimately feeling" a certain way, but about recognizing human dignity in all its diversity': n 370 above, 465. Ackermann disagrees with Baer on a few points: n 133 above, 339 - 340.

393 *Miron v Trudel* [1995] 2 SCR 418; *Egan v Canada* [1995] 2 SCR 513; *Thibaudeau v Canada* [1995] 2 SCR 627.

394 Canadian Charter of Rights and Freedoms 1982.

395 n 320 above, [51], [88]. The Court endorsed a contextual approach based on what was reasonable rather than accepting without question the claimant's own perspective of his or her feelings: n 320 above, [88]. On *Law*, see Ackermann (n 133 above) 163 - 164, 234 - 238.

396 2002 SCC 84, [2002] 4 SCR 429. For discussions on *Gosselin* see: Bates (n 386 above) 167 - 168; Foster (n 226 above) 88; Grover (n 376 above) 620 - 621; Hogg (n 258 above) *Vol 1* at 916, *Vol 2* at 380 - 381, 632, 669; McCrudden (n 220 above) 701, 707, 719; Rao (n 219 above) 218; RJ Sharpe & K Roach *The Charter of Rights and Freedoms* (2005) 298, 308 - 309; Small & Grant (n 309 above) 48 - 49, 53.

rights.[397] All judges in *Gosselin* accepted dignity as the indicator for equality, but differed in their application of it to the facts.

Individual circumstances are scrutinised closely to see if dignity has been impaired. In *Nova Scotia (Workers' Compensation Board) v Martin* the Canadian Supreme Court unanimously condemned as unjustified discrimination workers' compensation legislation excluding chronic pain sufferers from the regular workers' compensation system and providing instead benefits for just four weeks.[398] Gonthier J found that the dignity of those with chronic pain was affected by society's refusal to accept that their pain was real and on a par with other disabled people.[399]

There was considerable criticism of the use of dignity following *Law*.[400] In *R v Kapp* in 2008, the Canadian Supreme Court – having acknowledged that substantive (not formal) equality was incorporated in the Charter – referred to the criticism of using dignity as a legal test rather than as an underlying value.[401] The Court's new interpretation in *Kapp* of *Law* restored the earlier priority given to the perpetuation of disadvantage and stereotyping as the primary indicators of discrimination. In Canada and South Africa the focus on the context to ascertain if there is inequality resulting in infringement of dignity means 'the judge is less concerned with precedent – although still concerned with certainty and continuity – and more concerned with ensuring that for the case at hand – human dignity is protected' and there are 'continual reminders in the cases that the equality analysis is a guideline for

397 n 396 above, [392]. Dennis Davis cited Arbour J's judgment as an illustration of the potential for a positive rights approach; she interpreted the right to life in the Canadian Charter as including a positive duty to provide a means of livelihood and supported her conclusion that a right to life can impose a positive obligation on the state by reference to other rights, where questions of resources were not at issue: n 73 above, 707 - 708.

398 2003 SCC 54, [2003] 2 SCR 504. See Hogg (n 258 above) *Vol 2* at 632 - 633, 675 - 676. Canadian legislation discriminating on the grounds of disability is subject to harsher analysis than on other grounds.

399 n 398 above, [5].

400 One of the critics argued that, for Section 15 claims, dignity should be replaced with a reformulated grounds analysis focusing on individual and group vulnerability on the basis that the primary purpose of the equality provision was to protect the vulnerable from state-imposed burdens or disadvantages, recognising the potential for the majority to marginalise minority interests understood as social and economic resources, or opportunities to access resources: RJ Fyfe 'Dignity as theory: Competing conceptions of human dignity at the Supreme Court of Canada' (2007) 70 *Saskatchewan Law Review* 1 at 17.

401 2008 SCC 41, [2008] 2 SCR 483 [22]-[23]. See Ackermann (n 133 above) 165 - 166, 241 - 245.

courts to follow, not a set of new rules to be mechanically applied without critical analysis of the ultimate purpose.'[402]

As in South Africa and Canada, judicial interpretation of the Namibian Constitution has accorded a prominent role to the underlying value of dignity.[403] Noting that similar weight was given to it in the South African Constitution,[404] the Namibian Supreme Court affirmed its pervasive nature in *Africa Personnel Services (Pty)*.[405]

Some critics objected to the prominent role played by personal feelings of affront in the analysis of unfair discrimination in South Africa and had misgivings about the suitability of the dignity-based approach with its risk of excessive individualism.[406] Grant has answered these critics and concluded that the South African approach was better than any other because it provided a coherent approach to achieving substantive equality.[407] The protection of rights formed part of an integrated scheme aimed at ensuring protection for and promotion of the inherent dignity of all.[408]

Ronald Dworkin distinguished between the right to equal treatment and the right to treatment as an equal.[409] Human dignity is an implied value

402 Small & Grant (n 309 above) 53. See also C Albertyn & B Goldblatt 'Facing the challenge of transformation: Difficulties in the development of an indigenous jurisprudence of equality' (1998) 14 *South African Journal on Human Rights* 248.

403 Constitution of the Republic of Namibia 1990.

404 *Africa Personnel Services (Pty) Ltd v Government of Republic of Namibia* [2009] NASC 17 fn 89.

405 n 404 above, [33] (footnote omitted).
However, in Namibia infringement of dignity is not a pre-requisite in all cases for success in proving breach of a fundamental right. The Court in *Africa Personnel Services (Pty)* rejected the State's attempt to narrow the ambit of the right to engage in economic activity to individuals on the basis that it protected only the dignity interest of human persons, which the State argued would not extend to juristic persons. Adopting a purposive approach, it broadened its scope to corporations and put equality on the same footing as dignity: n 404 above, [40].

406 Grant (n 301 above) 325. See Botha (n 220 above) 212 - 214.

407 n 301 above, 326 - 328.

408 n 301 above, 328.

409 R Dworkin *Taking rights seriously* (1978) 227. The right to equal treatment is the right to an equal distribution of some opportunity or resource or burden, whereas the right to treatment as an equal is the right, not to receive the same distribution of some burden or benefit, but to be treated with the same respect and concern as anyone else. Charles Taylor categorised Dworkin's distinctions as a liberal society adopting no particular substantive view about the ends of life, but uniting around a strong procedural commitment to treat people with equal respect: C Taylor 'The politics of recognition' in C Taylor *et al*, *Multiculturalism: Examining the politics of recognition* (1994) 56. Foster has stated that for Dworkin it was the right to be treated with equal respect and concern that was fundamental, a view of dignity and equality reminiscent of the language of judges in both Canada and South Africa: n 226 above, 81.

underlying the US equality jurisprudence, although not highlighted – or, indeed, in some politically contentious cases not even named – as such. As early as 1944 Justice Murphy dissenting in *Korematsu* clearly had regard to the dignity of the individual when he castigated treating all those in a group as inferior on the basis of the behaviour of some of its members.[410] Ten years later the value of human dignity – although not overtly stated – was to the fore in the unanimous decision of the US Supreme Court in *Brown v Board of Education* where Chief Justice Warren described the effect of racial segregation in public schools as denigrating to the feelings of black children.[411]

The primary purpose of eliminating discrimination has been to protect the dignity of the victims. The Supreme Court recognised this in *Heart of Atlanta Motel* when it refused to accept that a hotel owner could restrict its clientele to white people.[412] Justice Brennan saw the common thread of

410 *Korematsu v US* 323 US 214 (1944). Referring to the exclusion of all those of Japanese descent from a military area in California during World War II, Justice Murphy was conscious of the need to hold each individual accountable for their own actions and not to stigmatise minorities: above, 240.

411 347 US 483 (1954) 494. In *Brown* Thurgood Marshall (subsequently appointed to the Supreme Court) argued and demonstrated that state-enforced segregation violated the Fourteenth Amendment; his achievement as an advocate in that case has been described as embodying 'his consummate victory' amidst all his triumphs: LC Moore & T Wyatt Cummings 'Justice Thurgood Marshall and his legacy: A living legend's unceasing commitment to justice and equality' (1991) 35 *Howard Law Journal* 37 at 41. While Chief Justice Warren's opinion dealt squarely with education, its outgrowth rendered 'separate but equal' untenable in any sphere: Moore & Wyatt Cummings above, 41.

Goodman is correct in her assessment that in this decision – often described as motivated by the Court's interest in protecting the human dignity of black school children – the Court sought not just to protect black children's public image and reputation, but to protect them from feeling inferior and discouraged: n 354 above, 753. *Brown* was not simply a proportionality exercise to balance the adverse effect on black children of segregated education against the possible loss of self-esteem of white children by integrated schooling: S Tsakyrakis 'Proportionality: An assault on human rights?' (2009) 7 *International Journal of Constitutional Law* 468 at 487 - 488.

412 *Heart of Atlanta Motel, Inc v US* 379 US 241 (1964). While the main focus of the case was on the division of power between Congress and the states, the Court discerned that the aim of the Civil Rights Act 1964 was to uphold personal dignity. Justice Clark, delivering the opinion of the Court, referred to the fact that the Senate Committee had made it clear that its fundamental object was 'to vindicate "the deprivation of personal dignity that surely accompanies denials of equal access to public establishments"': above, 250, citing S1732 S Rep No 872, 88th Cong 2d Sess (10 February 1964) 16. Justice Goldberg, in a concurring opinion, quoted more extensively from the Senate Committee, which had stressed the personal humiliating effect of discrimination and not simply the commercial or social aspect: above, 291 - 292, citing S Rep No 872 above, 16.

The Supreme Court has addressed race and gender discrimination in a robust well-reasoned methodical fashion and has not been waylaid by attributing undue deference to claims of intrusion on freedoms of expression and association.

humiliation and affront to dignity running through discrimination whether on the grounds of race or gender when he confronted a clash between men's freedom of association and women's exclusion from full membership of a non-profit national organisation in *Roberts v United States Jaycees*.[413]

Despite the dissenting view of Justice Black that the Due Process Clause of the Fourteenth Amendment was designed to protect against racial discrimination and his reluctance to extend it to a welfare payment,[414] the majority in *Goldberg v Kelly* insisted that a welfare recipient should be afforded a fair hearing prior to termination of benefit. Public assistance was influenced by a recognition that external forces contributed to poverty and a tradition of protecting people's dignity in the US.[415] After *Goldberg* the Court's willingness to advance human dignity in welfare rights faltered.[416] However, there have been some notable dissenting opinions including that of Justice Marshall[417] in *Dandridge v Williams*, where by a narrow majority the Court held that Maryland was entitled to impose a monetary cap on the amount of aid paid to families with dependent children regardless of the size of the

413 n 223 above, 625. In delivering the opinion of the Court, Justice Brennan referred to the dual damage caused by discrimination – to the individual's dignity and to society by depriving it of the benefit of every member's full participation: as above. The Court used a proportionality analysis to assist it in coming to its conclusions and in order to justify publicly its decision. Extrajudicially, Justice Brennan pointed out that recognition of full equality for women – equal protection of the laws – ensured that gender had no bearing on claims to human dignity: n 5 above, 442.

Having analysed *Brown*, *Heart of Atlanta Motel* and *Roberts* in her review of decisions on access to education and accommodations, Goodman concluded that human dignity retained its strength as a constitutional value, despite competing public opinion: n 354 above, 765.

414 Justice Black described a welfare payment as payment of 'a promised charitable instalment' by the government: *Goldberg v Kelly* 397 US 254 (1970) 275. While he conceded that some of the language of the Fourteenth Amendment can protect others, he described its main aim thus, 'all know that the chief purpose behind it was to protect ex-slaves': as above. In common with the attitude taken by judges internationally, the US Supreme Court allows considerable latitude to the states to decide on social welfare issues and in dispensing available funds: *King v Smith* 392 US 309 (1968) 318 - 319.

415 'From its founding, the Nation's basic commitment has been to foster the dignity and wellbeing of all persons within its borders.': *Goldberg* (n 414 above) 264 - 265 (Justice Brennan). The *Goldberg* holding moved the Supreme Court's human dignity focus to a realm beyond the criminal justice system: Wermiel (n 89 above) 232. See also Church *et al* (n 111 above) 144 - 145; Rao (n 219 above) 236 - 237.

416 Goodman (n 354 above) 784. See also Church *et al* (n 111 above) 146 - 147.

417 As the last Justice appointed by a Democratic President, Justice Marshall found himself in the role of 'perennial dissenter' amid conservative Republican appointees: Moore & Wyatt Cummings (n 411 above) 47.

family and its actual need.[418] In his judgment in which he was joined by Justice Brennan, Justice Marshall's view was that the basis for discrimination was inalterable by the children affected in the same manner as birth within or outside marriage was outside their control.[419]

The jurisprudence over the right to withdraw medical treatment has focused primarily on the liberty and best interests of the patient, rather than on the equality right.[420] The liberty interest is also central to the abortion litigation. Justice Stevens dissenting in part in *Planned Parenthood of Southeastern Pennsylvania v Casey* took a holistic view of human rights when he consolidated liberty, equality and dignity.[421]

418 397 US 471 (1970).

419 n 418 above, 523, citing *Levy* 391 US 68 (1968):

> [G]overnmental discrimination between children on the basis of a factor over which they have no control – the number of their brothers and sisters – bears some resemblance to the classification between legitimate and illegitimate children which we condemned as a violation of the Equal Protection Clause in *Levy v Louisiana*.

Lisa Crooms described Justice Marshall's contribution to our understanding of fundamental rights and constitutional equality as relying on the basic premise that personhood, citizenship and humanity, as matters of constitutional law, require a vigilant court intent on achieving lofty constitutional objectives outstripping outdated notions of liberty, justice and equality: LA Crooms 'A stone's throw to justice: Liberty, equality, and women's rights in the Supreme Court opinions of Justice Thurgood Marshall' (2009) 52 *Howard Law Journal* 559 at 582. Baer has called a move to substantive equality 'the move from an understanding of discrimination as difference, and from an understanding of equality as a group right, to an understanding of discrimination as disadvantage', which 'turns equality into a right to respect and recognition, enabling people to exercise their right to self-determination and to lead a dignified life': n 370 above, 455.

Because people's identities develop within the social world, respect for human dignity also entails a state commitment to meeting dependency needs through supporting caretaking and human development so that people can lead dignified lives: M Eichner 'Families, human dignity, and state support for caretaking: Why the United States' failure to ameliorate the work-family conflict is a dereliction of the government's basic responsibilities' (2010) 88 *North Carolina Law Review* 1593 at 1617.

420 The equality dimension received scant attention in *Cruzan*, where Chief Justice Rehnquist, who delivered the Court's majority opinion, dismissed it in a footnote contending that dissimilar treatment of those capable of making decisions for themselves and those lacking that capacity was justified: *Cruzan v Director, Missouri Department of Health* 497 US 261 (1990) 287 fn 12. See Rao (n 219 above) 233 - 234.

421 'Part of the constitutional liberty to choose is the equal dignity to which each of us is entitled. A woman who decides to terminate her pregnancy is entitled to the same respect as a woman who decides to carry the fetus to term. The mandatory waiting period denies women that equal respect.': 505 US 833 (1992) 920. *Planned Parenthood* differs from earlier abortion decisions in that the Court's decision making was expressly informed by human dignity as part of a woman's liberty interest: Goodman (n 354 above) 761. See also Rao (n 219 above) 211, 231.

In *Rice v Cayetano*, where the issue was the right to vote for trustees of a state agency in Hawaii, Justice Kennedy pointed out that the same suspect rationale – diminution of dignity in disregard of each person's individuality – was behind classification by ancestry and categorisation by race.[422] The Supreme Court in *Bush v Gore* identified one source of the fundamental nature of the right to vote as lying 'in the equal weight accorded to each vote and the equal dignity owed to each voter.'[423] The requirement of due process necessitating a fair hearing was asserted by the Supreme Court in a majority decision in *Hamdi v Rumsfeld*.[424] Maxine Goodman's view is that while Justice O'Connor, writing for the plurality, did not refer to human dignity, the outcome that citizen-detainees should receive fair notice of the reasons for their being classified as enemy-combatants and a right to a hearing before a neutral decision-maker showed that human dignity partially shaped the Court's decision.[425]

Due process, liberty, privacy and dignity were invoked by the Court in *Lawrence v Texas*[426] when by a majority of six to three it overturned *Bowers v Hardwick*[427] and decriminalised intimate sexual conduct between homosexuals. Justice Kennedy encompassed succinctly the elements of freedom, privacy and dignity involved in opting for a personal relationship without fear of being branded a criminal, when he stated, 'adults may choose to enter upon this relationship in the confines of their homes and their own private lives and still retain their dignity as free persons.'[428]

422 528 US 495 (2000) 517. See Rao (n 219 above) 215 - 216.

423 531 US 98 (2000) 104. In a majority decision, the Court held in *Bush* that the manual recounts in the Florida vote for President violated the Equal Protection Clause of the Fourteenth Amendment, as they did not satisfy the minimum standards required for the non-arbitrary treatment of voters. See JA Gardner 'The dignity of voters – A dissent' (2010) 64 *University of Miami Law Review* 435 at 453 - 454. For criticism of reliance on the concept of the human dignity of individual voters rather than on the dignity in their civic role of performing a public service, see Gardner above, 254 - 258.

424 542 US 507 (2004). In *Hamdi* a US citizen captured in Afghanistan, who was categorised as an enemy combatant for allegedly fighting with the Taliban, was considered to have an entitlement to be given a meaningful opportunity to contest the factual basis for his detention before a neutral decision-maker.

425 n 354 above, 793.

426 n 354 above.

427 n 354 above.

428 n 354 above. He interpreted liberty as extending beyond spatial bounds to a more transcendent dimension, explaining that it 'presumes an autonomy of self that includes freedom of thought, belief, expression, and certain intimate conduct': n 354 above, 562.

My review of US jurisprudence shows a clear concern for protection of human dignity as a long-standing basic value in society underlying the Constitution.[429] The Supreme Court judges have not given as deep a philosophical or legal analysis of dignity as in other jurisdictions such as South Africa and Canada. Sometimes, indeed, they have avoided crediting dignity overtly as the rationale behind their decisions, but it can be implied that protection of human dignity was the motivating force of at least some of the judges. There can be no doubt that human dignity was the foundation for the equality decisions on race and gender. It also gave an initial impetus to substantive equality in the welfare area by grounding the due process right to a fair hearing before termination of a benefit, but it has not developed into providing substantive equality or socio-economic rights. Notwithstanding the threat to US security from international sources in the twenty-first century, the value of human dignity has survived in the jurisprudence to provide due process rights for those suspected terrorists who manage to challenge their detention in the Supreme Court.

The constitutional concept of equality in India has been given a wide reach because of the insistence by the courts that its interpretation should be deep and its application meaningful. Zafar Khan sees an extensive role for equality – reaching to the social and economic spheres, promoting fraternity among human beings, and protecting the status and dignity of all.[430] Gurkirat Kaur called the task of the framers of the Indian Constitution 'stupendous',

The Court viewed the Equal Protection Clause as guaranteeing formal equality, so it declined to invalidate the offending statute on that basis and instead held that it violated the substantive right to liberty under the Due Process Clause, which gave homosexuals 'the full right to engage in their conduct without intervention of the government': n 354 above, 578. Catharine MacKinnon has lamented the Court's focus on the privacy right to liberty instead of addressing sex equality, as she considered that the decision extended heterosexuality's substantively sex-unequal rules rather than challenging and changing them: CA MacKinnon 'The road not taken: Sex equality in *Lawrence v. Texas*' (2004) 65 *Ohio State Law Journal* 1081 at 1089.

429 See E Daly 'Human dignity in the Roberts Court: A story of inchoate institutions, autonomous individuals, and the reluctant recognition of a right' (2011) 37 *Ohio Northern University Law Review* 381.

430 ZA Khan 'Equality through legislative measures: The law in book versus the law in action' in M Shabbir (ed) *Quest for human rights* (2005) 250. The caste-ridden Indian society was ripe for equality measures, as it had resulted in the development of unequal social groups who monopolised benefits and privileges for themselves at the expense of the underprivileged, the deprived and the exploited: above, 249.

as '[a] people suffering oppression under a feudal system were grimly struggling to be reborn into a life of dignity and hope.'[431]

The traditional idea of equality based on reasonable classification was adopted and developed by the Supreme Court initially.[432] The equality right in Article 14 of the Indian Constitution[433] forbids class legislation, but it does not forbid reasonable classification to achieve specific ends.[434] The concept of equality based on reasonable classification was challenged[435] by Bhagwati J in a judgment on behalf of himself and two of the other five judges in *Royappa*, where he laid down a new more expansive idea of equality opposed to the dictatorial notion of arbitrary action.[436] Returning to the same theme of equality as being contrary to arbitrary action in *Maneka*

431 G Kaur *Fundamental rights* (2006) 60. Gurkirat Kaur's assessment is that the framers showed an uncompromising respect for human dignity, an unquestioning commitment to equality and non-discrimination, and an abiding concern for the poor and the weak: above, 61.

432 JN Pandey *The constitutional law of India* (2008) 77.

433 'The State shall not deny to any person equality before the law or the equal protection of the laws within the territory of India.' The English concept of 'equality before the law' has the negative implication of the absence of any special privilege for individuals and of all classes being subject to the ordinary law, whereas the American concept of 'equal protection of the law' has the positive implication of equality of treatment in equal circumstances: Pandey (n 432 above) 73.

In *Dalmia*, Das CJ set out the scope of the equal protection clause as enunciated in earlier cases, which made clear that the anti-discrimination provisions extend to laws governing procedure as well as applying to substantive law: *Dalmia v Justice Tendolkar* [1958] INSC 30, 1959 SCR 279 (SC of India) 296 - 298.

434 Pandey (n 432 above) 77. The classification must not be arbitrary, artificial or evasive, and must always rest on some real and substantial distinction bearing a just and reasonable relation to the object sought to be achieved: as above. It has to fulfil two conditions: first, it must be founded on an intelligible *differentia*, which distinguishes persons or things that are grouped together from others left out of the group; second, the *differentia* must have a rational relation to the object sought to be achieved by the legislation: *Choudhry v State of Bihar* [1954] INSC 114, 1955 (1) SCR 1045 (SC of India) 1049.

Group members who are similarly situated in the given set of facts must be treated similarly, but legislation can distinguish between members belonging to different, *ie*, non-homogenous classes: Justice AS Anand 'The constitutional model of equality and fraternity: The Indian experience' in Shabbir (n 430 above) 20 - 21, citing *Dalmia* (n 433 above).

435 Pandey (n 432 above) 78.

436 *Royappa v State of Tamil Nadu* [1973] INSC 214, 1974 (2) SCR 348 (SC of India) 386. Bhagwati J perceived the limits of formal equality, which can be intransigent: CA MacKinnon 'Sex equality under the Constitution of India: Problems, prospects, and "personal laws"' (2006) 4 *International Journal of Constitutional Law* 181 at 188. Article 14 has been invoked in a wide range of cases including litigation relating to service matters, challenging executive action, dealing with the grant of contracts by government, and concerning the rules of admission to educational institutions, the imposition of tax and exemptions from taxation: Anand (n 434 above) 22.

Gandhi, Bhagwati J rejected 'a narrow, pedantic or lexicographic approach' to the equality clause.[437] He described the central normative importance of the rights to equality, life and liberty as supportive of human dignity.[438] After this case, there was a definite change in the construction of Article 14 by the courts, as they responded to society's hopes and aspirations, and it was clear that Article 14 went much beyond the principle of classification.[439] A unanimous Supreme Court in *Nakara* assimilated the doctrines of classification and arbitrariness.[440] Equality before the law combined with the right to live with human dignity ensured that detainees could not be deprived of their rights without fair, just and reasonable procedures in *Mullin*.[441]

The equality provisions in the Constitution in India have not been confined to inalterable categories like race or gender, nor to static conditions. In *Randhir Singh*, where police drivers succeeded in achieving pay parity with other government drivers, the Court gave substance to the fundamental rights to equality before the law and to equal opportunities in public employment by enlivening them through the use of a directive principle providing for equal pay for equal work for men and women.[442] Reddy J did not interpret the directive principle as applying only to equivalence between

437 *Maneka Gandhi v Union of India* [1978] INSC 16, 1978 SCR (2) 621 (SC of India) 674. He continued, '[n]o attempt should be made to truncate its all embracing scope and meaning for, to do so would be to violate its activist magnitude': as above.

438 'These fundamental rights represent the basic values cherished by the people of this country since the Vedic times and they are calculated to protect the dignity of the individual and create conditions in which every human being can develop his personality to the fullest extent.': n 437 above, 667. 'The entire world is a family' was the motto of Vedic civilisation; all had equal opportunity in all walks of life in ancient India; the Vedic age was more liberal in providing equal status to the people: Kaur (n 431 above) 65.

439 Anand (n 434 above) 24.

440 In *Nakara* the Court allowed a challenge to the liberalisation of the formula for calculation of state pensions applicable only to those retiring after a stipulated date: Pandey (n 432 above) 80. Desai J, delivering the Court's judgment, referred to development of equality to help the weaker sections of society or others in need of assistance, and continued, '[l]egislative and executive action may accordingly be sustained if it satisfies the twin tests of reasonable classification and the rational principle correlated to the object sought to be achieved.': *Nakara v Union of India* [1982] INSC 103, 1983 (2) SCR 165 at 179 - 180.

441 In *Mullin* the Supreme Court held that a detainee should be allowed interviews with her family and legal adviser: *Mullin v Administrator, Union Territory of Delhi* [1981] INSC 12, 1981 SCR (2) 516.

442 *Randhir Singh v Union of India* [1982] INSC 24, 1982 (3) SCR 298 (SC of India).

men and women.[443] Affirmative action was seen by Bhagwati J on behalf of the majority in *Jain* as part and parcel of equality, and not an aberration.[444]

The constitutional aims of social justice, equality and dignity reach out to draw in the marginalised to a position of equality with other members of society, as the Court demonstrated in 1995 when it protected vulnerable workers who had been exposed to asbestos in *Consumer Education and Research*.[445] Gender equality in India includes protection from sexual harassment and the universally recognised human right to work with dignity.[446]

Article 16 of the Indian Constitution provides for equality of opportunity in public employment. Reservation of positions for any backward class which the state considers is inadequately represented is allowed by Article 16(4).[447] The temporary exemption of certain castes[448] and tribes[449] from

443 He was insistent that the fundamental rights should be meaningful to 'the vast majority of the people' and stated, '[q]uestions concerning wages and the like, mundane they may be, are yet matters of vital concern to them and it is there, if at all that the equality clauses of the Constitution have any significance to them.': n 442 above, 305.

444 *Jain v Union of India* [1984] INSC 115, 1984 (3) SCR 942 (SC of India). Wholesale reservation of places in colleges for deprived sectors was not permitted, but partial reservation could sometimes be allowed to the extent necessary to fulfil the requirements of the equality provision in Article 14 of the Constitution: Pandey (n 432 above) 85. Equality should be real for the historically deprived: *Jain* above, 968.

445 'Social justice is a dynamic device to mitigate the sufferings of the poor, weak, Dalits, Tribals and deprived sections of the society and to elevate them to the level of equality to live a life with dignity of person.': *Consumer Education & Research Centre v Union of India* [1995] INSC 91, JT 1995 (1) 636 (SC of India) 657 [20].

In another case it was held that life insurance cover should be offered to all on equal terms and could not be confined to employees of the state and of other reputable firms, as to do otherwise would be to breach the equality clause when applied to the right to livelihood as an extension of the right to life: *LIC of India v Consumer Education & Research Centre* [1995] INSC 272, 1995 SCC (5) 482 (SC of India).

446 Pandey (n 432 above) 101. Even though there was no legislation in place to provide safeguards, the Supreme Court stepped in to fill the vacuum and laid down extensive guidelines for employers and for those running institutions to ensure the prevention of sexual harassment of working women: *Vishaka v State of Rajasthan* [1997] INSC 665.

447 The so-called 'Downtrodden' group in India is not homogenous; its three major divisions (Scheduled Castes, Scheduled Tribes and the Other Backward Classes), each having its own characteristic features, distinctive backgrounds and particular problems, comprised 30% of the population in 2006: Kaur (n 431 above) 74.

448 The Indian Constitution allows for affirmative action in favour of 'Scheduled Castes', which is an official euphemism for 'untouchables': Khan (n 430 above) 251. Groups have been isolated and disadvantaged by their 'untouchability' because of their low status in the traditional Hindu caste hierarchy, which exposed them to ill-treatment, severe disabilities, and deprivation of economic, social, cultural and political opportunities: Khan (n 430 above) 252.

449 Affirmative action is permitted under the Constitution for 'Scheduled Tribes', who have 'an astoundingly marginal share' in Indian politics and, hence, large development

passing a test for promotion was challenged unsuccessfully in *State of Kerala v Thomas*, where the Supreme Court was divided on the issue.[450] The Supreme Court in *Thakur* – a challenge to affirmative action to reserve places in schools for members of castes[451] and other backward classes – approved of Bhagwati J's views in *Minerva Mills* linking equality with dignity and liberty and effectively according socio-economic rights the same status as civil and political rights.[452] Balakrishnan CJ in *Thakur* cited a passage from Bhagwati J's partially dissenting judgment in which he regarded the Directive Principles of State Policy[453] as imposing a duty on the State to act to achieve equality for the poor.[454]

From my review of the jurisprudence of the Indian Supreme Court, it is evident that the equality rights in the Constitution have been developed over the years from the confines of the relatively narrow focus of a rigid classification test to encompass the prevention of arbitrary differentiation and even

projects have displaced millions of them, without any compensation: K Sibal 'Law, the Constitution, weaker sections, women, minorities, scheduled castes and their development' in Shabbir (n 430 above) 2.

450 [1975] INSC 224, 1976 (1) SCR 906. One of the majority, Mathew J, analysed the nature of equality of opportunity in depth and distinguished it from formal equality, focusing instead on the need for true equality divorced from life's hazards and irrespective of one's position in society: above, 948.

451 The caste system in India is a glaring example of the systematic denial of human dignity. Compounded by gender inequality, this socially structured inequality would seem to amount to an institutionalised assault on human dignity: L Hogan & J D'Arcy May 'Constructing the human: Dignity in interreligious dialogue' in R Ammicht-Quinn *et al* (eds) *The discourse of human dignity* (2003) 82 - 83.

452 *Thakur v Union of India* [2008] INSC 613 [174]. The Indian Supreme Court has derived socio-economic rights from a constitutional text written as a guarantee of non-interference: Beatty (n 330 above) 155.

For a review of *Thakur*, see MP Singh '*Ashoka Thakur v Union of India*: A divided verdict on an undivided social justice measure' (2008) 1 *National University of Juridical Sciences Law Review* 193 at 193 - 195.

453 Constitution of India 1950, Part IV.

454 *Minerva Mills Ltd v Union of India* [1980] INSC 141, 1981 SCR (1) 206 (SC of India) 324:

> The Directive Principles therefore, impose an obligation on the State to take positive action for creating socio-economic conditions in which there will be an egalitarian social order with social and economic justice to all, so that individual liberty will become a cherished value and the dignity of the individual a living reality, not only for a few privileged persons but for the entire people of the country. It will thus be seen that the Directive Principles enjoy a very high place in the constitutional scheme and it is only in the framework of the socio-economic structure envisaged in the Directive Principles that the Fundamental Rights are intended to operate, for it is only then they can become meaningful and significant for the millions of our poor and deprived people who do not have even the bare necessities of life and who are living below the poverty level.

more ambitiously to the attempt to realise practical equality in a wide socio-economic sphere for a substantial minority suffering from historical deprivation attributable to a variety of sources. The concept of dignity has been used by the Inter-American Court of Human Rights to adjudge whether differentiation was legitimate. Treatment of a group as inferior crossed the boundary.[455]

An approach to equality giving a prominent role to the value of dignity is best placed to achieve substantive equality. The serious comprehensive attempts to give effect to substantive equality by the judiciary in both South Africa and Canada are credited by Joan Small and Evadné Grant to the legal realisation of human dignity being at the conceptual centre of the development of their equality jurisprudence.[456] Apart from the impact of court decisions on the litigants directly concerned, the methodology of human rights litigation in countries like Canada and South Africa supports a dialogue between court and legislature, which could provoke legislative changes.[457] To inhibit frivolous claims and to avoid subjective decisions – both from the judges' and the claimants' perspectives – it is important that a recognised structure be put on the use of the concept of dignity in relation to equality. Equality may be undermined by focusing primarily on dignity and losing sight of group discrimination.[458]

By requiring a claimant to show historical group prejudice, the Namibian Supreme Court has restricted the application of the anti-discrimination clause

455 *Proposed Amendments to the Naturalization Provisions of the Constitution of Costa Rica*, Advisory Opinion OC-4/84, Inter-American Court of Human Rts Series A No 4 (19 January 1984) [55].

456 n 309 above, 54. This is 'not an abstract, individualistic notion, but a concept about the relation between the individual and state, and individual and group, which is circumscribed by concern, respect and consideration': as above.

457 n 309 above, 54 - 55. An example of where a legislative change resulted from a judgment was the passing of the Abolition of Corporal Punishment Act 1997 following *S v Williams* 1995 3 SA 632 (CC): JD Bessler 'In the spirit of *ubuntu*: Enforcing the rights of orphans and vulnerable children affected by HIV/AIDS in South Africa' (2008) 31 *Hastings International and Comparative Law Review* 33 at 88.

458 O'Connell has urged that attention be given to the forms of hierarchy and disadvantage (in the sense of systematic exclusion from community benefits) in society in order to redress them; his conclusion contains a salutary warning of the misuse of the dignity concept by the judiciary not making clear its underlying contextual norms and using it to limit anti-discrimination measures: n 336 above, 285.

in its Constitution. In *Müller* the Court confined claims for redress to situations of past discrimination where the dignity of all was not recognised.[459]

The Namibian Constitution does not include sexual orientation as one of the prohibited grounds of discrimination in Article 10(2). Although the majority decision in *Frank* was decided on the grounds of the right to a fair hearing, O'Linn AJA for the majority was not prepared to find that a same-sex couple was entitled to be treated on an equal basis as heterosexual couples.[460] The Namibian Supreme Court's stance on sexual orientation has reflected the attitude of a conservative society, which apparently wishes to impose the views and moral standards attributed to the majority on all and to enforce those standards on the homosexual community by fear of criminal sanctions for breaching traditional values.[461] O'Linn AJA accepted that the guideline for the judiciary was to give the Constitution a broad liberal pur-

459 *Müller v President of the Republic of Namibia* [1999] NASC 2; 2000 6 BCLR 655 (NmS) 18. Herr Müller, a German citizen, married a Namibian and wanted to take her surname on marriage, but he could not do so without complying with more formalities than a woman who wished to adopt her husband's surname. He challenged the legislation relying, *inter alia*, on his rights to equality before the law and freedom from discrimination on the grounds of sex. The State successfully defended the claim on the basis that the legislation did not breach substantive equality. The Court accepted that the differentiation created by the legislation was grounded on one of the specified grounds in Article 10(2) of the Namibian Constitution, but the differentiation did not in any way impair Herr Müller's dignity. Strydom CJ explained why this was the case, above, 20: 'The Appellant, being a white male, who immigrated to Namibia after Independence, cannot claim to have been part of a prior disadvantaged group. It can furthermore not be said that the purpose of the section was to impair the dignity of males individually or as a group or to disadvantage males.'

The UN Human Rights Committee subsequently found that the gender-based approach of the legislation violated the prohibition on discrimination in ICCPR: *Müller v Namibia* UNHR Committee (28 June 2002) 74th Session UN Doc CCPR/C/74/D/919/2000) [6.8], citing ICCPR (n 31 above) art 26.

460 *Chairperson of the Immigration Selection Board v Frank* [2001] NASC 1 (SC of Namibia). Apart from the fact that sexual orientation was not one of the listed grounds on which discrimination was prohibited, there was no legislative trend in favour of it – in fact the trend was in the opposite direction: above, 132 - 133. The lesbian applicant had not pleaded that her right to dignity was violated, but his view would not have been different if she had done so: above, 142. Article 14 of the Constitution gave the right to marry to men and women (Constitution of the Republic of Namibia 1990, Art 14(1)), so O'Linn AJA declined to take over the legislature's role in extending the provisions of immigration control legislation to same-sex life partnerships; he considered that the legislature's failure to include in the legislation 'an undefined, informal and unrecognized lesbian relationship with obligations different from that of marriage' might amount to 'differentiation', but was not 'discrimination': above, 143. He also declined to regard a homosexual couple as a family, described in Article 14(3) of the Constitution as the 'natural' and 'fundamental' group unit of society: above, 119.

461 O'Linn AJA stated that the value judgment to be made must take cognisance in the first place of 'the traditions, values, aspirations, expectations and sensitivities' of the Namibian people and should be objectively derived from various sources including

posive interpretation,[462] but he confined it unnecessarily to conform with the majority viewpoint at the expense of the equality, dignity, freedom and privacy of those with non-conformist traits in intimate personal preferences. In my view, he retracted from the judiciary's democratic duty to uphold the rights of minorities to equality in the formation and expression of their identities. O'Linn AJA pointed out that the provisions relating to equality and non-discrimination in the Namibian Constitution corresponded to those in the Constitution of Zimbabwe.[463] The case of *Banana v S* in the Supreme Court of Zimbabwe,[464] where the majority upheld the constitutionality of the common law crime of sodomy, was cited liberally in the judgment of the Namibian Court.[465] There was a notable conflict between the views of McNally JA for the majority and of Gubbay CJ in dissent in *Banana*.[466]

Although the Botswana Court of Appeal held in *Kanane*[467] that a provision in its Penal Code targeting indecent behaviour in public or private was unconstitutional on the grounds of gender discrimination because it did not extend to women, it did not strike it down as it had been amended by the legislature to be gender neutral since the date of the offence.[468] Mwaikasu J

the Constitution and the institutions of Namibia as expressed in parliamentary debates and legislation, judicial or other commissions, public opinion as established in properly conducted opinion polls, evidence, court judgments, referenda and expert publications: n 460 above, 106 - 107, 114. This extensive list can hardly be described as containing objective sources by which to gauge the import of constitutional values. See SK Amoo 'The constitutional jurisprudential development in Namibia since 1985' in N Horn & A Bösl (eds) *Human rights and the rule of law in Namibia* (2008) 55 - 56.

462 n 460 above, 101.

463 n 460 above, 133.

464 n 355 above.

465 n 460 above, 115, 133 - 138.

466 See Quansah (n 357 above) 213 - 215. McNally JA was guided by public opinion and relied heavily on the US Supreme Court decision in *Bowers* in finding that the criminalisation of sodomy between men was not unconstitutional, as discrimination on the grounds of sexual orientation was permissible – the law did not discriminate on the basis of gender: n 355 above, 670, 673, citing n 354 above. The Constitution of Zimbabwe included gender – but not sexual orientation – among the listed grounds of prohibited discrimination: Constitution of the Republic of Zimbabwe 1979, Sec 23(2).
Gubbay CJ distinguished the much criticised US decision and found that the common law crime amounted to gender discrimination, which was not justified under the limitations clause in the Constitution: n 355 above, 643, referring to Constitution of the Republic of Zimbabwe 1979, Sec 23(5)(b).

467 *Kanane v S* 2003(2) BLR 64 (CA).

468 Quansah (n 357 above) 206. Public opinion led the Court, which put the onus on the appellant to show that the public demanded decriminalisation – a hurdle he was unable to surmount: KN Bojosi 'An opportunity missed for gay rights in Botswana: *Utjiwa Kanane v The State*' (2004) 20 *South African Journal on Human Rights* 466 at 473.

in the High Court[469] (approving of Lord Devlin's view) had completely subordinated the individual to society leaving little room for deviation from the moral norms of the majority and ignoring any call to respect human dignity.[470] The same conservative attitude in sexual matters prevails in Malawi, where two men – living together as husband and wife (one of whom a psychiatrist assessed as having gender disorientation) – went through an engagement ceremony and were convicted by the Blantyre Chief Resident Magistrate in May 2010 of buggery and indecent practices.[471]

My examination of jurisprudence on sodomy in Southern Africa (excluding South Africa) reveals that society's conservative outlook has diverted the judiciary in some quarters at least from taking cognisance of the dignity of the individual in its equality decisions where non-conforming sexual behaviour arises. A broader comparative analysis shows that a deeper less superficial approach to human dignity is essential in order to recognise the worth of each individual and to permit each life to flourish in a society where equality is the desired norm.[472] The South African structured use of dignity in equality jurisprudence with the context in which it is being used clearly defined in accordance with constitutional norms illustrates this truth.

At the conclusion of my review of the impact of human dignity on equality in South Africa, it is pertinent to remind ourselves of the dual place of

469 *Kanane v S* (Crim Trial No F94/1995) (Botswana High Court) 22 March 2002.

470 Quansah (n 357 above) 205, citing n 469 above, 21:

> [T]he law exists for the protection of society. It does not discharge its function by protecting the individual from injury, annoyance, corruption and exploitation; the law must protect also the institutions and the community of ideas, political and moral, without which people cannot live together. Society cannot ignore the morality of the individual any more than it can his loyalty; it flourishes on both and without either it dies.

471 *R v Soko* [2010] MWHC 2. See L Price 'The treatment of homosexuality in the Malawian justice system: *R v Steven Monjeza Soko and Tiwonge Chimbalanga Kachepa*' (2010) 10 *African Human Rights Law Journal* 524. The men were freed following a presidential pardon granted on humanitarian grounds: G Mapondera & D Smith 'Gay couple freed by Malawi presidential pardon return to home villages' *Guardian* (London 31 May 2010) 13.

472 Ackermann considered 'that dignity, and its relationship to equality, is ... an indispensable constituent in neutrally principled and correct adjudication on issues of unfair discrimination': n 329 above, 556.

dignity in the equality analysis under Section 9 of the Constitution: first, impairment of dignity is the test of unfairness; and, second, it is one of the values underpinning the assessment of reasonable limitation on equality in a democracy.[473]

473 The various steps to assess inequality under Section 9 can be summarised as:

(1) The threshold test under Section 9(1) is whether the challenged measure differentiates between people or groups of people, and, if so, whether there is a rational connection between the differentiation and a legitimate government purpose at which it is aimed. The lack of rationality is a fatal blow to the measure.
(2) If it passes the rationality examination, it may be justified as corrective action for past discrimination under Section 9(2).
(3) Even if rationally connected to the legislative aim, the measure may be unfair discrimination on one of the listed grounds in Section 9(3). There is a presumption of unfairness, if the differentiation is on one of the listed grounds (Sec 9(5)).
(4) Alternatively, it may be unfair discrimination on an unlisted ground (*Prinsloo* (n 304 above) [28]). No presumption of unfairness applies in this case.
(5) The impact on the victims is the test of unfairness. If the measure has the potential to impair dignity or an analogous effect, it is unfair.
(6) Equality may be limited in accordance with Section 36, to the extent that the restriction is reasonable in a society based on the democratic values of dignity, freedom and equality.

More than one ground can be taken into account when assessing whether there is unfair discrimination at step 3. This is evident from the wording of Section 9(3) and from Sachs J's judgment in the *Sodomy* case, where he pointed out that an approach based on context and impact acknowledges that grounds of unfair discrimination can intersect and allows evaluation of discriminatory impact on a combination of grounds 'globally and contextually, not separately and abstractly'; alternatively, he opined that 'a context rather than category-based approach might suggest that overlapping vulnerability is capable of producing overlapping discrimination': n 356 above, [113] (footnote omitted). The more complex multidimensional approach used in South Africa is very difficult within the US constitutional context: Wing (n 369 above) 79.

6

Economic and Social Rights

6.1 Interpretation of economic and social rights

Because there are specific provisions in the South African Constitution making socio-economic rights justiciable, Yacoob J in *Grootboom* could quickly dispose of any argument to the contrary, but the difficult issue, as he said, was 'how to enforce them in a given case'.[1] Each situation is considered separately in context.[2] He saw civil and political rights and socio-economic rights as being interlinked, each being necessary to enjoy the other, to advance equality and to develop the individual's personality.[3]

1 *Government of the Republic of South Africa v Grootboom* 2001 1 SA 46 (CC) [20]. See A Chaskalson 'Dignity and justice for all' (2009) 24 *Maryland Journal of International Law* 24 at 32. Even though there are explicit socio-economic rights in the South African Constitution, Heinz Klug considers that human dignity will remain an important underlying value underpinning this jurisprudence: H Klug 'The dignity clause of the Montana Constitution: May foreign jurisprudence lead the way to an expanded interpretation?' (2003) 64 *Montana Law Review* 133 at 154 - 155.

2 On the benefits of a court's contextual awareness, see D Brand 'Socio-economic rights and courts in South Africa: Justiciability on a sliding scale' in F Coomans (ed) *Justiciability of economic and social rights: Experiences from domestic systems* (2006) 236.

3 n 1 above, [23]:

> There can be no doubt that human dignity, freedom and equality, the foundational values of our society, are denied those who have no food, clothing or shelter. Affording socio-economic rights to all people therefore enables them to enjoy the other rights enshrined in Chapter 2. The realisation of these rights is also key to the advancement of race and gender equality and the evolution of a society in which men and women are equally able to achieve their full potential.

Yacoob J reiterated the link between poverty and the reduction of a person in their human dignity, which was separate from the physical discomfort of deprivation, in *Njongi v MEC, Department of Welfare, Eastern Cape* 2008 4 SA 237 (CC) [81].

As the provisions of the South African Constitution were modelled on those in the International Covenant on Economic Social and Cultural Rights (CESCR),[4] United Nations material is relevant and a valuable source of guidance for South African courts.[5] Yacoob J confirmed that the South African requirement of 'progressive realisation' of housing was taken from article 2.1 of CESCR and that it bore the same meaning in both documents.[6] In *Grootboom* there was a need to balance the right to human dignity with the available resources[7] of the state,[8] the 'available resources' term being common to CESCR and the Constitution. *Grootboom* is the seminal case not just on the right to housing and shelter, but also because of its impact on the interpretation of all socio-economic constitutional rights.[9]

4 International Covenant on Economic, Social and Cultural Rights (adopted 16 December 1966, entered into force 3 January 1976) 993 UNTS 3 (CESCR).

5 DL Carey Miller 'The great trek to human rights: The role of comparative law in the development of human rights in post-reform South Africa' in E Örücü (ed) *Judicial comparativism in human rights cases* (2003) 214 (footnote omitted).

6 n 1 above, [45]. However, he found the UN material of little help in ascertaining the extent of the housing provision, as there was a significant distinction between a *right to adequate housing* in article 11.1 of CESCR and the *right of access* to adequate housing in Section 26 of the South African Constitution; there was also a difference between the obligations on the state in both documents, CESCR requiring *appropriate steps* and the Constitution *reasonable* legislative and other measures: n 1 above, [28].

The UN Committee on Economic, Social and Cultural Rights (Committee on ESCR) requires that states take reasonable measures in light of their specific circumstances, the burden of proof resting on the states: MM Sepúlveda *The nature of the obligations under the International Covenant on Economic, Social and Cultural Rights* (2003) 337. Magdalena Sepúlveda's view was that the Committee needed to further elaborate the 'reasonableness' requirement and she thought it desirable if it took into account some relevant domestic jurisprudence, including *Grootboom*: as above.

7 The obligation on the state under CESCR is 'to take steps, individually and through international assistance and co-operation ... to the maximum of its available resources': CESCR (n 4 above), art 2(1). The Committee on ESCR has noted that the phrase 'to the maximum of its available resources' was intended to refer to both the resources existing within a state and those available from the international community: UN Committee on Economic, Social and Cultural Rights 'General Comment No 3' 5th Session (1990) in 'Compilation of General Comments and General Recommendations adopted by Human Rights Treaty Bodies' (29 July 1994) UN Doc HRI/GEN/1/Rev.1, 48 [13]. In view of this, it is clear that in assessing resources a court has jurisdiction to look beyond the available budget: J Ansah 'The right to development as applied in national law' in MA Baderin & R McCorquodale (eds) *Economic, social and cultural rights in action* (2007) 441 fn 150.

8 David Carey Miller regarded this as the most significant aspect of the final decision, with the Court pointing out the realisation of socio-economic rights would be progressive – the most urgent need being dealt with first: n 5 above, 215, citing *Grootboom* (n 1 above) [45].

9 In *Grootboom* the Constitutional Court began to develop more clearly a general test for adjudication of constitutional rights: K Lehmann 'In defense of the Constitutional Court: Litigating socio-economic rights and the myth of the minimum core' (2006) 22 *American University International Law Review* 163 at 169.

A review of the case-law seeking enforcement of socio-economic rights emphasises the Constitutional Court's understanding that the Constitution is to be read as a whole. The provisions for housing, healthcare, welfare and other socio-economic rights are not construed in isolation, but are informed by the foundational values. Human dignity comes to the fore constantly as the lodestar in all aspects of the Constitutional Court's deliberations, whether they be for the purpose of ascertaining the threshold right, its interpretation and application to particular situations, or the limitation assessment.[10] Albie Sachs confirmed that in *Grootboom* the Court was strongly influenced by the need to deal with rights in the Bill of Rights as interrelated and interdependent.[11] The Court was guided by respect for the foundational values (especially human dignity), which necessitated that the right of access to housing not be separated from the right to human dignity, resulting in the State being obliged to take account of the qualitative dimension and not to give just a quantitative response.[12]

10 To remove the difficulties caused by measuring dignity subjectively, Katharine Young advocates an objective notion of dignity and cites as an example South Africa's constitutional protection of equality, which prohibits harm to dignity experienced according to some society-wide standard: KG Young 'The minimum core of economic and social rights: A concept in search of content' (2008) 33 *Yale Journal of International Law* 113 at 136.

11 A Sachs *The strange alchemy of life and law* (2009) 179. The 'tripartite typology of interdependent duties' (first developed by Henry Shue and endorsed by some of the General Comments issued by the Committee on ESCR) is explicitly embraced by the South African Constitution in Section 7(2), which obliges the state to respect, protect, promote and fulfil the rights in the Bill of Rights: M Pieterse 'Possibilities and pitfalls in the domestic enforcement of social rights: Contemplating the South African experience' (2004) 26 *Human Rights Quarterly* 882 at 888 - 889. Pierre de Vos has substantiated the interdependence and indivisibility of all human rights in the South African Bill of Rights, and stated that all rights are aimed at guaranteeing each individual the freedom to live his or her life with dignity and respect: P de Vos 'Pious wishes or directly enforceable human rights? Social and economic rights in South Africa's 1996 Constitution' (1997) 13 *South African Journal on Human Rights* 67 at 70, fn 12.

12 Sachs (n 11 above) 179. Albie Sachs pointed out that in securing protection of the rights of particularly vulnerable people, courts are guided by the values of an open democratic society, which repudiates past 'forms of oppression, hardship, division and discrimination'; he continued, '[this society] acknowledges the foundational character of the principle of human dignity, and aspires to accept people for who they are': n 11 above, 214.

6.2 Enforceability of socio-economic rights

Socio-economic rights can impose positive duties on the state as well as negative obligations not to interfere to prevent or reverse progress.[13] It is more difficult for the courts to frame effective orders when positive duties are involved. In relation to socio-economic matters, there is the perennial problem of scarce resources and the fear of prejudicing other people's rights by prioritising those that seek a legal remedy.[14] The South African Constitutional Court has grappled with the constitutional obligation on the State to take reasonable legislative and other measures within its available resources to progressively realise socio-economic rights such as those to housing and healthcare.[15] It has not hesitated to intervene when the dignity of the litigant is threatened. The range of remedies available to the Court is wide.

13 A formerly widespread presumption (still prevailing in the United States) is that civil and political rights entailing negative obligations were justiciable, but that socio-economic rights imposing positive duties were not. Mark Kende sees two problems with the American constitutional tradition where the courts are reluctant to determine funding, which is regarded as preserve of the executive = first, it is an oversimplification since the South African Constitutional Court's experience is that protecting socio-economic rights sometimes requires the Court to negative government actions; second, enforcing negative rights also implicates budgetary matters: MS Kende 'The South African Constitutional Court's embrace of socio-economic rights: A comparative perspective' (2003) 6 *Chapman Law Review* 137 at 155 - 156. The US Supreme Court has not embraced President Franklin D Roosevelt's 'freedom from want' as a constitutional norm: Kende above, fn 9, citing FD Roosevelt 'The annual message to the Congress' (6 January 1941) in 9 *The public papers and addresses of Franklin D Roosevelt* (1969) 663 at 672 (1941).

14 Arthur Chaskalson concluded that the Constitutional Court foregrounded 'equal concern' in its decisions on claims for socio-economic rights and that this was consistent with Dworkin's regard for equal concern as the sovereign virtue: A Chaskalson 'From wickedness to equality: The moral transformation of South African Law' (2003) 1 *International Journal of Constitutional Law* 590 at 600 - 601, citing R Dworkin *Sovereign virtue: The theory and practice of equality* (2000) 1.

15 The South African case-law has evolved from the rejection of individual rights claims to recognition of collective rights to comprehensive government programmes to address urgent social needs: JM Woods 'Justiciable social rights as a critique of the liberal paradigm' (2003) 38 *Texas International Law Journal* 763 at 790. A remedy was granted to an individual when the state was ordered to reinstate a social grant and to pay arrears with interest to a poor vulnerable woman with 100% permanent disability, who was probably unaware of her entitlement to arrears, Yacoob J finding that the state had acted unconscionably in relying on prescription of her claim: *Njongi* (n 3 above) [80], [85], [92]. For a review and assessment of *Njongi*, see EC Christiansen 'Transformative constitutionalism in South Africa: Creative uses of Constitutional Court authority to advance substantive justice' (2010) 13 *Journal of Gender, Race & Justice* 575 at 604 - 607, 612.

6.3 Separation of powers

An argument regularly used against the enforcement by the courts of socio-economic rights is that under the separation of powers doctrine, these are matters of policy more properly left to the legislature and executive.[16] The separation of powers issue arose in the *TAC* case[17] over the right to healthcare, when Counsel for the State argued that the questions raised belonged to the sphere of government policy and were outside the judiciary's domain.[18] This argument, if accepted, would have curtailed somewhat the scope of the decision in *Grootboom*.[19] The judges did not retreat, as the Constitution itself had given them the task of enforcing constitutional rights and of considering whether the State had given effect to its corresponding obligations.[20] Although conceding that the judicial arm is ill-suited to adjudicate on socio-economic issues, the Court pointed out that the Constitution obligated the courts, first, to insist that measures be taken by the State as mandated by the Constitution and, second, to test those measures against the reasonableness standard.[21]

The right to basic education under Section 29(1)(a) of the Constitution is immediately realisable: *Governing Body of the Juma Musjid Primary School v Essay NO* [2011] ZACC 13, 2011 8 BCLR 761 (CC) [37].

16 It is said that democracy requires accountability from the elected legislature rather than intervention by an unelected judiciary without the competencies, knowledge or resources to decide on social priorities.

17 *Minister of Health v Treatment Action Campaign (No 2)* 2002 5 SA 721 (CC).

18 Sachs (n 11 above) 181.

19 As above.

20 n 17 above, [99]. The Court rebuffed any notion that it would be exceeding its remit if it found the State had failed to give effect to its constitutional obligations and in its judgment defended its position in strident terms, '[i]n so far as that constitutes an intrusion into the domain of the executive, that is an intrusion mandated by the Constitution itself.': as above.

21 n 17 above, [38]. The reasonableness test may not be adequate to translate social rights into tangible benefits for rights-holders as a group in accordance with international law provisions: Pieterse (n 11 above) 896. David Bilchitz also criticised the reasonableness test, because reasonableness cannot alone provide content to adjudicate cases based on socio-economic rights; it is context-dependent and lacks a principled basis on which to found decisions: D Bilchitz 'Towards a reasonable approach to the minimum core: Laying the foundations for future socio-economic rights jurisprudence' (2003) 19 *South African Journal on Human Rights* 1 at 9 - 10.

On the reasonableness review generally, see Brand (n 2 above) 221 - 223, 227 - 228; S Liebenberg 'South Africa: Adjudicating social rights under a transformative constitution' in M Langford (ed) *Social rights jurisprudence: Emerging trends in international and comparative law* (2008) 83 - 86, 89 - 91; M Wesson 'Disagreement and the constitutionalisation of social rights' (2012) 12 *Human Rights Law Review* 221 at 233 - 238; IT Winkler & C Mahler 'Interpreting the right to a dignified minimum existence: A new era in German socio-economic rights jurisprudence?' (2013) 13 *Human Rights Law Review* 388 at 395 - 397.

The South African Constitutional Court has frequently used a collaborative approach to resolve breaches of socio-economic rights.[22] Starting with *Grootboom*, it found that the State should include in its housing plan provision for shelter for those who were in desperate need.[23] The Court placed the dignity of human beings in a central position in assessing the reasonableness of state action in housing.[24] Consideration of dignity is invariably involved in assessment of a socio-economic right.[25] Instead of

22 In the early cases the Court began to develop a flexible conception of the separation of powers, which benefits all branches of government, as the courts have the power to make orders that affect government policies directly and it also permits the executive and legislative branches to have a role in interpreting the extent of their obligations under the Constitution: B Ray 'Policentrism, political mobilization, and the promise of socioeconomic rights' (2009) 45 *Stanford Journal of International Law* 151 at 175.

23 n 1 above. The extent of shelter to be provided was contextual depending on the exact circumstances of those who were homeless including factors such as the weather conditions. The plan should be balanced, flexible and cover emergency situations as well as providing for short, medium and long term needs: n 1 above, [43]. The Court ordered that the State should build into its housing plan provisions for those 'with no access to land, no roof over their heads, and who were living in intolerable conditions or crisis situations': n 1 above, [99].

24 n 1 above, [83]. Cf *City of Johannesburg Metropolitan Municipality v Blue Moonlight Properties 39 (Pty) Ltd* [2011] ZASCA 47. In that case the Supreme Court of Appeal found that the inflexible application of the City's policy of not providing temporary accommodation to those most in need who were evicted from privately-owned buildings subjected them to continued violation of their dignity as its effect was that they were rendered homeless on eviction and vulnerable to eviction wherever they went because they were unable to afford other accommodation: above, [66]-[67].

25 There are many juridical examples of how the norm of dignity has practically guided the interpretation of economic and social rights, including its use by the German Constitutional Court to give meaning to the 'existential minimum' of social welfare in the German Basic Law, by which society is obliged to provide everyone with the socio-economic conditions adequate for a dignified existence: Young (n 10 above) 134.

In refugee law a human rights approach has broadened the scope of application of socio-economic rights in New Zealand by focusing on human dignity rather than on the traditional criterion of economic proscription, which is an almost complete denial of the ability to earn a living: A Anderson 'On dignity and whether the Universal Declaration of Human Rights remains a place of refuge after 60 years' (2009) 25 *American University International Law Review* 115 at 136. In one example the New Zealand Refugee Status Appeals Authority granted refugee status to a Roma family from the Czech Republic who had experienced severe discrimination in employment, provision of healthcare and housing, and the education of their children, and would face the same upon return; the Authority acknowledged the dignity aspect of these types of claims and gave significant weight to the effect on the appellants of their 'long experience of involuntary abasement': Anderson above, 138, citing Refugee Appeal No 71193/98 (Sept 9, 1999) (NZ Refugee Status App Auth) 14 - 15, *available at* http://www.nzrefugeeappeals.govt.nz/PDFs/Ref_19990909_71193. pdf.

Jeanne Woods thinks human dignity may be too elusive a concept to provide a foundation on which to ground the full range of human rights, as the social, economic

coming to a decision on the extent of the right, the Court left it to the State to build the protection to be afforded to the destitute homeless into its plans.[26] It did not accept that the minimum core obligation formulated by the UN Committee on Economic, Social and Cultural Rights (Committee on ESCR) applied to socio-economic rights in the South African Constitution.[27] In any

and cultural pre-conditions of a dignified human life remain marginalised in the dominant rights discourse; she proposed human need as a more comprehensive framework for theorising social rights claims, which are indispensable to full development of the person represented by the concept of dignity: n 15 above, 763 - 764. Woods predicted that the demand for second- and third-generation rights will play a galvanising role in the ongoing struggle of the impoverished to realise fully the dream of human dignity: n 15 above, 793.

26 In assessing reasonableness, it would not 'enquire whether other more desirable or favourable measures could have been adopted, or whether public money could have been better spent': n 1 above, [41]. Eva Brems commented that this approach to progressive realisation – avoiding a court enquiry on whether more favourable measures could have been adopted – did not lead to maximisation of human rights protection: E Brems 'Human rights: Minimum and maximum perspectives' (2009) 9 *Human Rights Law Review* 349 at 357.

27 It rejected the minimum core approach as insufficiently flexible and dependent on a level of knowledge and expertise that the Court lacked: n 1 above, [33]. Yacoob J pointed out that the minimum core obligation in international law is determined generally by having regard to the needs of the most vulnerable group entitled to the protection of the right in question: n 1 above, [31]. Adoption of the minimum core would have established an objective minimum standard; failure to meet that standard by the government would have meant automatic violation of the right: Ray (n 22 above) 159.

The view of the Committee on ESCR is that there is incumbent on every state party 'a minimum core obligation to ensure the satisfaction of, at the very least, minimum essential levels of each of the rights' in CESCR; an assessment as to whether a state has discharged its minimum core obligation must take account of resource constraints applying within the country concerned; to succeed in attributing its failure to meet its minimum core obligations to a lack of available resources, a state 'must demonstrate that every effort has been made to use all resources that are at its disposition in an effort to satisfy, as a matter of priority, those minimum obligations': UN Committee on Economic, Social and Cultural Rights 'General Comment No 3' (n 7 above) [10].

By referring to 'minimum core obligation' rather than 'minimum core content' (often defined as the nature or essence of a right), the Comment has avoided the minimum content becoming the ceiling rather than the floor; instead of ranking the various components of a human right in some sort of hierarchy according to relative worth, the question changes to one of timing, so that a state that has ratified CESCR will ask what it must do immediately to realise the right: AR Chapman & S Russell 'Introduction' in AR Chapman & S Russell (eds) *Core obligations: Building a framework for economic, social and cultural rights* (2002) 9. The minimum core obligation formulation is a way to accommodate the reality that many economic, social and cultural rights (and often civil and political rights as well) require resources that are simply not available in poor countries; this approach affirms that even in highly straitened circumstances, a state has irreducible obligations that it is assumed to be able to meet: above, 10.

See J Church *et al*, *Human rights from a comparative and international law perspective* (2007) 289 - 290. For criticism of the Constitutional Court's rejection of the minimum core standard, see Pieterse (n 11 above) 897 - 898.

event, the Court built its decision around dignity and what was reasonable rather than on a minimum core or housing on demand for the most needy.[28] The contextual assessment of reasonableness was wide-ranging considering not solely the position of the needy, but also the social, economic and historical environments and the institutional capacity for implementation of the housing programme.[29]

28 It left open the possibility of invoking the minimum core in other cases to assist in determining whether the measures taken were reasonable, but to do that it would need to have enough information to assess what would be the appropriate level in the conditions pertaining in South Africa: n 1 above, [33].

For a defence of the Constitutional Court's refusal to adopt directly the minimum core, see Kende (n 13 above) 153; MS Kende 'The South African Constitutional Court's construction of socio-economic rights: A response to critics' (2004) 19 *Connecticut Journal of International Law* 617 at 622 - 624. John Bessler has urged the Constitutional Court to move towards minimum core entitlements for HIV/AIDS-affected children without familial support in order to protect orphans and the vulnerable consistent with children's constitutional rights and the overarching philosophy of *ubuntu*: JD Bessler 'In the spirit of *ubuntu*: Enforcing the rights of orphans and vulnerable children affected by HIV/AIDS in South Africa' (2008) 31 *Hastings International and Comparative Law Review* 33 at 111.

Young prefers the Court's use of reasonableness instead of enquiring into a minimum essential core of a right, as it is more normatively open and sociologically framed: n 10 above, 140. Karin Lehmann considers the reasonableness approach to be jurisprudentially sounder than the minimum core, which she views as inappropriate as a tool of judicial decision making, but she takes issue with the Court's insistence on not examining *how* the public purse is spent: n 9 above, 165.

As a precursor to the proportionality test, one of the requirements to justify a human rights restriction set out by the Canadian Supreme Court in *R v Oakes* [1986] 1 SCR 103 was a 'minimal impairment' test; but the Court was not able to apply the *Oakes* test strictly and consistently, so it reformulated it to a reasonable impairment test: Brems (n 26 above) 360, 365.

29 n 1 above, [43]. It would not be reasonable to exclude those existing in critical conditions. To take account of changing situations, the programme itself should be continuously reviewed and updated: as above. On the need for an adaptable housing plan, see also *President of the Republic of South Africa v Modderklip Boerdery (Pty) Ltd* 2005 5 SA 3 (CC) [49].

The extent of deference to the other branches of government can be gauged from the reticence of the Court to impose its own views, thereby emphasising the principal role of the other branches of government in developing appropriate policies to enforce socio-economic rights; the Court also noted that enforcement of these rights required considerable flexibility, as 'a wide range of possible measures could be adopted by the state to meet its obligations': Ray (n 22 above) 159 - 160, citing n 1 above, [41].

6.4 International Covenant on Economic, Social and Cultural Rights

To supplement the analysis of the South African cases, this section will look at the obligations under CESCR in more depth. It is clear that its roots are firmly based on a belief in the inherent dignity of all,[30] as the Preamble in a somewhat circuitous fashion asserts that rights derive from it,[31] and that it and rights are the foundation of freedom, justice and peace.[32] Part III recognises specific rights such as to an adequate standard of living including food, clothing and housing, with continuous improvement in living conditions,[33] to the highest attainable standard of physical and mental health,[34] and to education directed to 'the full development of the human personality and the sense of its dignity'.[35]

The general obligation of states in relation to rights recognised in CESCR set out in article 2.1 encompasses the following elements:

- an obligation to take steps to achieve the rights immediately on ratification of CESCR;
- a duty to avail of externally available aid to do so;
- a commitment to use resources to the fullest possible extent;
- the aim of continuous progress to the goal of comprehensive provision of the rights; and

30 Although CESCR is politically neutral (n either supporting nor condemning any particular socio-economic system), it is ideological to the extent that it synthesises portions of each of major political ideologies as they converge on principles of human dignity and economic, social and cultural rights: P Alston & G Quinn 'The nature and scope of states parties' obligations under the International Covenant on Economic, Social and Cultural Rights' (1987) 9 *Human Rights Quarterly* 156 at 219. The Committee on ESCR asserted CESCR's neutrality between political and economic systems, subject to the proviso that government be democratic, that all human rights be respected, and that those systems recognise the interdependence and indivisibility of the two sets of human rights: UN Committee on Economic, Social and Cultural Rights 'General Comment No 3' (n 7 above) [8].

31 CESCR (n 4 above) Preamble, 2nd para.

32 Preamble, 1st para.

33 Art 11.1.

34 Art 12.1.

35 Art 13.1.

- the use of whatever means are appropriate to achieve the aim in the context prevailing in relation to each right in the particular state in question with encouragement to enact legislation to do so.[36]

States are obligated to guarantee the exercise of the recognised rights without discrimination on stipulated grounds.[37]

Some illumination of the onus imposed by article 2.1 can be found in General Comment No 3 of the Committee on ESCR on the nature of states' obligations.[38] By ratifying CESCR, states undertake obligations of conduct and of result.[39] The unqualified phrase 'to take steps' requires 'deliberate, concrete and targeted' action within a reasonably short time towards the goal of full realisation of the rights to be achieved progressively.[40] While recognising that full realisation of all economic, social and cultural rights takes time and requires some flexibility, the principal obligation of result is

36 It reads:

> Each State Party to the present Covenant undertakes to take steps, individually and through international assistance and co-operation, especially economic and technical, to the maximum of its available resources, with a view to achieving progressively the full realization of the rights recognized in the present Covenant by all appropriate means, including particularly the adoption of legislative measures.

37 The stipulated grounds are race, colour, sex, language, religion, political or other opinion, national or social origin, property, birth or other status: art 2.2. Developing countries, 'with due regard to human rights and their national economy,' have the option to decline to extend the full benefit of economic rights to non-nationals: art 2.3.

38 UN Committee on Economic, Social and Cultural Rights 'General Comment No 3' (n 7 above). Some observers consider that the General Comments have developed an authoritativeness usually reserved for advisory opinions and enjoy a significant degree of acceptance by state parties: Young (n 10 above) 143.

39 UN Committee on Economic, Social and Cultural Rights 'General Comment No 3' (n 7 above) [1].

40 UN Committee on Economic, Social and Cultural Rights 'General Comment No 3' (n 7 above) [2]. The undertaking to take steps is an obligation of conduct distinguishable from and less demanding than a guarantee, but nonetheless represents a clear legal undertaking of immediate application: Alston & Quinn (n 30 above) 165 - 166.

Legislation is highly desirable and may even be indispensible in cases such as effective combating of discrimination: UN Committee on Economic, Social and Cultural Rights 'General Comment No 3' (n 7 above) [3]. 'All appropriate means' is not confined to legislation, which on its own may not be sufficient to achieve implementation of the rights; the initial decision on what is appropriate rests with the states, subject to the Committee's ultimate determination on whether all appropriate measures have been taken: UN Committee on Economic, Social and Cultural Rights 'General Comment No 3' (n 7 above) [4]. The Committee tentatively urged judicial remedies, being of opinion that a number of rights in CESCR should be capable of immediate application and therefore justiciable: UN Committee on Economic, Social and Cultural Rights 'General Comment No 3' (n 7 above) [5]. Other appropriate means may also be administrative, financial, educational and social: UN Committee on Economic, Social and Cultural Rights 'General Comment No 3' (n 7 above) [7].

their progressive realisation, which is a clear requirement that states 'move as expeditiously and effectively as possible towards that goal.'[41]

In the light of its experience of over 10 years, the Committee on ESCR concluded that the *raison d'être* of CESCR[42] demanded a minimum core obligation. The onus is on a state claiming inability to achieve the minimum core to show that the deficiency occurred notwithstanding every effort to use all available resources to satisfy the minimum requirement as a matter of priority.[43] There are varying views as to whether the minimum applies primarily to the individual enjoyment of a right or to society-wide levels of

41 UN Committee on Economic, Social and Cultural Rights 'General Comment No 3' (n 7 above) [9]. The principle of progressive realisation places a burden on states to show discernible progress towards the enjoyment by everyone of the rights established by CESCR: S Leckie 'Another step towards indivisibility: Identifying the key features of violations of economic, social and cultural rights' (1998) 20 *Human Rights Quarterly* 81 at 93.

The obligation to ensure progressive achievement exists independently of an increase in resources; regardless of constraints on resources, a state will have to demonstrate that it is taking steps to realise the rights progressively; in the absence of increased resources, what is required is at least the effective use of existing resources; progressive implementation can be effected by the development of the societal resources necessary for the realisation of the recognised rights for everyone: de Vos (n 11 above) 97.

Any deliberately retrogressive measures must be taken only after 'the most careful consideration', bearing in mind all the rights in CESCR and continuing to utilise fully 'the maximum available resources': UN Committee on Economic, Social and Cultural Rights 'General Comment No 3' (n 7 above) [9]. It would require to be justified under the limitations provisions in art 4 CESCR: Leckie above, 99.

Dennis Davis pointed out a significant difference between the Committee's approach and the concept of reasonableness developed by the Constitutional Court from international jurisprudence, *ie*, the former imposes on the state the obligation to implement elements of the right immediately, but the concept of reasonableness adopted in *Grootboom* provides far less clarity about the core content of the right: DM Davis 'Socioeconomic rights: Do they deliver the goods?' (2008) 6 *International Journal of Constitutional Law* 687 at 698 - 699.

Progressive realisation is mostly monitored through the use of indicators and benchmarks; indicators allow both comparisons and follow-up over time, yet, as Brems concluded, they are generally not suited for the evaluation of individual instances of rights restrictions: n 26 above, 356.

42 Its *raison d'être* is to establish clear state obligations: UN Committee on Economic, Social and Cultural Rights 'General Comment No 3' (n 7 above) [9]. CESCR is a treaty that gives rise to formal obligations and, as such, it must be interpreted in the light of the customary rules of treaty interpretation in international law with particular emphasis on the principle of good faith, which indicates that states ratifying a treaty undertake to give substantial effect to it: Alston & Quinn (n 30 above) 160.

43 UN Committee on Economic, Social and Cultural Rights 'General Comment No 3' (n 7 above) [10].

enjoyment.[44] Even in dire circumstances, states have to 'strive to ensure the widest possible enjoyment of the relevant rights'; neither is the need for monitoring and plans to promote the rights removed by lack of resources.[45] When there are severe financial constraints, such as in a recession, states must adopt relatively low-cost targeted programmes to protect the vulnerable.[46] The more affluent states have an obligation to assist those less fortunate.[47]

The minimum core concept inherits its structure from the German Basic Law, where the core or essential content of certain constitutional rights lies beyond the reach of permissible limitation.[48] The Committee on ESCR was the first international body to articulate the concept.[49] Katharine Young has identified three accomplishments anticipated by the concept: first, it initiates a common legal standard; second, it purports to advance a baseline of socio-economic protection across varied economic policies and different levels of available resources; third, its minimalist connotations signal an acceptable moderation.[50] The focus on the duties required to implement the rights, rather than the elements of the rights themselves, enables the analysis of realistic, institutionally informed strategies for rights protection; furthermore, the analysis of the duties that correlate to each right confronts the erroneous dichotomy of positive and negative rights.[51]

In contrast, Karin Lehmann believes that there are significant conceptual flaws with the minimum core, as it has inherent contradictions, and does not take into account 'the starkly utilitarian choices that inform the allocation of resources among the beneficiaries of socio-economic rights'.[52] She pointed out that the Committee and scholars are not always clear whether their conception of the minimum core is absolute or relative and neither are they specific on how competing interests should be ranked.[53]

44 Leckie (n 41 above) 101.

45 UN Committee on Economic, Social and Cultural Rights 'General Comment No 3' (n 7 above) [11].

46 UN Committee on Economic, Social and Cultural Rights 'General Comment No 3' (n 7 above) [12].

47 UN Committee on Economic, Social and Cultural Rights 'General Comment No 3' (n 7 above) [14].

48 Young (n 10 above) 124.

49 Young (n 10 above) 115.

50 n 10 above, 121 - 122.

51 Young (n 10 above) 151.

52 n 9 above, 182.

53 n 9 above, 183, 185.

Debate on the rights and obligations under CESCR has focused on whether legislation is necessary, justiciability,[54] progressivity, and the impact of retrograde steps. The General Comment provides answers to these questions, although academic scholars are sharply divided on some of them. While not clearly mandated by CESCR, legislation is advocated by the Committee and it will not be possible to achieve non-discriminatory exercise of the rights without it.[55]

6.4.1 Justiciability

Since some – at least – of the rights are immediately realisable, they are justiciable. The originally perceived division between negative civil and political rights, on the one hand, and positive socio-economic rights, on the other, is false.[56] Even the former impose some expenditure on the state. The South African experience demonstrates that socio-economic rights are justiciable, and that judicial decisions can respect the separation of powers in a democracy in the process of promoting their universal progressive realisation. The UN Justiciability Report recounts that Sandra Liebenberg advised that the South African Constitution encompassed a wide range of socio-economic rights on an equal footing with civil and political rights and

54 Justiciability refers to the ability of a court to adjudicate a dispute and order remedies for constitutional violations: Woods (n 15 above) fn 19.

Differences of opinion on the justiciability of socio-economic rights surfaced during the drafting of CESCR as early as 1951, when the French representative (René Cassin) considered that recourse to legal proceedings was envisaged in the event of deprivation of those rights, but he was contradicted by the US representative (Eleanor Roosevelt), who responded that they were not justiciable: Alston & Quinn (n 30 above) 170.

At international level there has been little judicial attention to socio-economic rights, which has given rise to the self-fulfilling perception that they are non-justiciable – despite challenges to this perception from 'a rich theoretical literature' and emerging case-law from domestic courts: D Marcus 'The normative development of socioeconomic rights through supranational adjudication' (2006) 42 *Stanford Journal of International Law* 53 at 58 - 59.

55 Where existing legislation is in violation of the obligations under CESCR, article 2.1 would require legislative action to be taken: Alston & Quinn (n 30 above) 167.

56 On the arguments concerning the nature of socio-economic rights and whether they are qualitatively different from civil and political rights, see Ray (n 22 above) 151 - 152. Jürgen Habermas considers that universal equal human dignity grounds the indivisibility of all categories of human rights, the classical civil rights (the liberal rights and the democratic rights of participation) only acquiring equal value when supplemented by social and cultural rights: J Habermas 'The concept of human dignity and the realistic utopia of human rights' (2010) 41 *Metaphilosophy* 464 at 468.

that the courts were moving towards improved protection of human rights.[57] She referred to *Grootboom* as establishing three important principles: first, the justiciability of economic, social and cultural rights could not be determined in the abstract; second, all rights were interdependent and interrelated; and, third, it developed the 'reasonableness' standard to determine whether the state was complying with its socio-economic obligations, the Court citing with approval the interpretation of progressive implementation in General Comment No 3.[58] Liebenberg's conclusion indicated that the Constitutional Court's approach showed respect for the other branches of government.[59] From her observations it is clear that socio-economic rights can be justiciable without infringing on the separation of powers.

57 UN Commission on Human Rights, 57th Session 'Report on the workshop on the justiciability of economic, social and cultural rights, with particular reference to the draft optional protocol to CESCR' (22 March 2001) UN Doc E/CN.4/2001/62/Add.2 (UN Justiciability Report) [8]. The Report issued following a workshop in 2001.

58 As above.

59 She stated (as above) that *Grootboom:*

> sought to strike an appropriate balance between the constitutional responsibility of the courts to enforce the duties imposed by socio-economic rights, and the role of the legislature and the executive in a democracy to make and implement laws and policies, thereby fostering a relationship of accountability, transparency and responsiveness between judiciary, legislature and executive.

There has been a trend towards the justiciability of socio-economic rights nationally[60] and internationally.[61] The duty not to discriminate is justiciable since it has immediate full application.[62]

60 The Canadian delegate at the workshop that gave rise to the UN Justiciability Report urged that the relationship between the courts and the legislature should be constructive rather than a power struggle, so that adjudicating socio-economic rights enhanced participatory democracy; he pointed out that even in a country without explicit domestic legal recognition of social and economic rights, and one in which there remained considerable caution about excessive judicial interference, there was a solid foundation on which social and economic rights could be claimed and adjudicated, and, furthermore, it was wrong to assume that adjudication of socio-economic rights was not relevant in an affluent country: UN Justiciability Report (n 57 above) [9]. For an assessment of justiciability of social and economic rights in Canada, see F Coomans 'Some introductory remarks on the justiciability of economic and social rights in a comparative constitutional context' in Coomans (n 2 above) 12; D Wiseman 'Methods of protection of social and economic rights in Canada' in Coomans (n 2 above) 173 - 205.

In India the judiciary invoked powers under the Constitution to interpret and press for implementation of social and economic rights, there having been a change of attitude in the 1950s by the Supreme Court, progressively deeming fundamental rights contained in the Constitution justiciable through the requirement that all State action was to conform to requirements of justice and reasonableness: UN Justiciability Report (n 57 above) [11]. On enforcement of social rights in India, see Coomans above, 13; S Muralidhar 'Judicial enforcement of economic and social rights: The Indian scenario' in Coomans (n 2 above) 237 - 267; S Muralidhar 'India: The expectations and challenges of judicial enforcement of social rights' in Langford (n 21 above) 102 - 123.

All the presentations on the national experiences at the UN workshop demonstrated the reasonableness requirement; the delegates emphasised that there were many ways to ensure the enjoyment of economic, social and cultural rights, and that both courts and treaty bodies tended to defer largely to states on how to implement rights: UN Justiciability Report (n 57 above) [12].

61 An analysis by David Marcus of the case-law of supranational tribunals by level of obligation confirmed that failures to *respect* socio-economic rights as defined in international law were in fact justiciable, but that these courts had issued virtually no decisions concerning obligations to *protect* or *fulfil*: n 54 above, 55 - 56.

At the international level, the European system confirmed the justiciability of economic and social rights as a common European heritage with positive obligations on states: UN Justiciability Report (n 57 above) [13]. The Inter-American structure had particular success in implementing rights to education, but also guaranteed trade union rights: UN Justiciability Report (n 57 above) [14].

62 UN Justiciability Report (n 57 above) [6], [16]. Other CESCR rights that are described with sufficient clarity and precision are also justiciable; in common with civil and political rights, there are some elements which need to be spelled out in more detail in national legislation, and tailored to the specific national context, needs and resources: UN Justiciability Report (n 57 above) [6]. Woods has counteracted the argument that the normative contents of social rights are too vague to be legally enforceable by pointing out that it overlooks the valuable work at international level to define these norms as well as the collective judicial expertise in constitutional construction: n 15 above, 771.

6.4.1.1 *Judicial enforcement in Europe*

This subsection will review the judicial enforcement of socio-economic rights nationally in a number of countries in Europe, where quite a few constitutions invoke the importance of the two ideals of human dignity and fundamental equality.[63] The explicit rights to work[64] and to social security[65] contained in the Constitution of Finland, which also guarantees the inviolability of human dignity,[66] have been implemented by the courts.[67] Invoking the constitutional guarantees by public authorities of adequate social, health and medical services and of support for families and others responsible for providing for children, the Helsinki Court of Appeals held in the *Child-Care Services* case that the city was responsible to a parent for the damage caused as a result of its delay in providing day care places.[68]

Positive socio-economic rights guaranteed by the Preamble to the French Constitution of 1946[69] are legally binding on all public authorities,[70] but their justiciability is understood differently when compared to civil and political rights.[71] In *Lefevre v Ville d'Amiens* the French Supreme Court

63 C Fabre 'Social rights in European constitutions' in G de Búrca *et al* (eds) *Social rights in Europe* (2005) 23. For an overview of the justiciability of social rights in Europe, see Fabre above, 21 - 23.

64 Constitution of Finland 1999, Sec 18.

65 Sec 19.

66 Sec 1.

67 See M Langford 'The justiciability of social rights: From practice to theory' in Langford (n 21 above) 22, fn 139.

68 Case No S 98/225 (*Child-Care Services* case) Helsinki Court of Appeals 28 October 1999. See summary in Centre on Housing Rights and Evictions, *Leading Cases on Economic, Social and Cultural Rights: Summaries* (Working Paper No 7, ESC Rights Litigation Programme, Geneva 2009) (COHRE Leading Cases) 45. In Finland all human rights are indivisible and interdependent, which demands that they all be given equal importance and treatment: UN Justiciability Report (n 57 above) [4].

69 Constitution of the French Republic 1946, Preamble, paras 5, 10 - 13. See L Pech 'France: Rethinking "*droits-créances*"' in Langford (n 21 above) 268.

70 Pech (n 69 above) 270. On the development of binding socio-economic constitutional principles in France, see Pech (n 69 above) 268 - 270.

71 Pech (n 69 above) 270. A French judge speaking extrajudicially stated that his role consisted primarily of the daily determination of the justiciability of economic, social and cultural rights, with much jurisprudence existing on rights such as those relating to work: UN Justiciability Report (n 57 above) [10].

confirmed that adequate accommodation (one of the constitutional objectives to protect human dignity) includes the provision of potable water.[72]

The German Constitutional Court has imposed socio-economic duties on the state from an expansion of the positive obligations that flow from civil and political rights and has been willing to intervene to ensure that the government has taken sufficient steps where rights are manifestly violated.[73] Although a considerable margin of discretion must be given to the German state in deciding how it ought to effect socio-economic rights, a court can evaluate the reasonableness of the measures applied.[74] The courts have translated the constitutional principles of the welfare state and the concept of human dignity into state obligations to provide an 'existential minimum' or 'vital minimum' giving those in need access to food, housing and social assistance.[75]

The Swiss Federal Court derived an implied constitutional right to basic necessities and, acknowledging its lack of competence to determine resource allocation, it said it would set aside legislation if the outcome failed to meet

72 Cour de Cassation, Troisième chambre civile, [Supreme Court, 3rd Civil Chamber], Arrêt No 1362, 15 December 2004. The Court ruled that a landlord is responsible for providing access to potable water to a tenant as part of the conditions to provide reasonable accommodation. See summary in COHRE Leading Cases (n 68 above) 45 - 46.

The guarantee of health, material security, rest and leisure, and the right of those incapable of working because of their age, physical or mental condition, or economic situation, contained in the 1946 Preamble (para 11) were the basis of a decision by the Court of Appeal of Riom to set aside a private body's implementation of a legislative measure excluding foreigners from the ambit of a welfare benefit aimed at disabled people: Pech (n 69 above) 274, citing CA Riom, 29 January 1996, *Droit social* (1996), 987.

73 M Langford 'Hungary: Social rights or market redivivus?' in Langford (n 21 above) 255. The Germans' constitutional right to choose their occupation and place of training and the equality clause in the Basic Law (Basic Law for the Federal Republic of Germany 1949, Arts 12(1) & 3 respectively) were the foundations for the Constitutional Court's placing the onus on the state to prove that the maximum possible number of places were provided in medical school to candidates selected fairly in accordance with objective criteria: *Numerus Clausus I* case (1972), 33 BverfGE 303 (German Constitutional Court). See summary in COHRE Leading Cases (n 68 above) 46; Langford (n 67 above) 6; Langford 'Hungary: Social rights or market redivivus?' above, 255; Marcus (n 54 above) 66.

74 H Choma 'Constitutional enforcement of socio-economic rights: South African case study' (2009) 6(6) *US-China Law Review* 41 at 44.

75 International Commission of Jurists, *Courts and the Legal Enforcement of Economic, Social and Cultural Rights: Comparative Experiences of Justiciability* (Report, Human Rights and Rule of Law Series No 2, Geneva 2008) (ICJ Justiciability Report) 23 - 25; Winkler & Mahler (n 21 above) 392.

the minimum claim required by constitutional rights.[76] In a case in 1995 brought by three non-nationals excluded from social welfare support on the basis of their illegal status in Switzerland, it held that such exclusion was a violation of an implied constitutional right to a basic minimum level of subsistence.[77] It derived this right from, first, the constitutional principle of human dignity guaranteeing every person what they can expect from the community because of their humanity; second, the right to life as a core content of personal freedom, which would no longer be guaranteed were the most minimum prerequisites for survival not guaranteed; third, personal freedom as a guarantee of all elementary aspects of personality development; and, fourth, the equality principle guaranteeing minimum material justice.[78] The right to subsistence in this case met the conditions of justiciability, as it was oriented to the minimum required as a fundamental right and what constitutes an indefeasible prerequisite for a humanly dignified life was clearly determinable in judicial proceedings.[79] The Court did not find a constitutional right to a guaranteed minimum income, but held that all that was constitutionally required was that which was essential for a humanly dignified existence and which had the ability to guard against an undignified existence as a beggar.

Social rights are not labelled specifically justiciable fundamental rights in the Spanish Constitution,[80] but merely as principles governing economic and social policy[81] that are excluded from judicial review.[82] Notwithstanding this, the courts have succeeded in giving some protection to socio-economic

76 Langford (n 67 above) 24, citing *V v Einwohnergemeinde X und Regierunsgrat des Kantons Bern* BGE/ATF 121 I 367 (Swiss Federal Court) 27 October 1995.

77 *V v Einwohnergemeinde X (n* 76 above), available at ESCR-Net http://www.escr-net.org/docs/i/401055. See also summary in COHRE Leading Cases (n 68 above) 71 - 72.

78 The right to a minimum level of subsistence was a condition for the exercise of these other written constitutional rights. The minimum core approach is particularly evident in jurisdictions where social interests are judicially protected through civil rights: Langford (n 67 above) 24.

79 The Court considered that entitlements to benefits are justiciable if, first, they can be adequately defined normatively and, second, they can be concretised and implemented by the judge utilising the procedures and means at the disposal of the court.

The fact that the claimants were non-nationals was not a disqualifying factor – the Court invoked previous Federal Court decisions stressing the human-rights component which indicated that it was both a precept of humanity and also a duty inherent in the purpose of the modern state to protect those on its territory where necessary against physically perishing.

80 Constitution of Spain 1978, Arts 15 - 29.

81 Arts 39 - 52.

82 Art 53(3). See Coomans (n 60 above) 11.

rights, either directly by determining a certain minimum content of a right that should be guaranteed under all circumstances, or by recognising social rights in connection with fundamental rights that are fully justiciable.[83]

In contrast with the situation in Spain, the Portuguese Constitution contains detailed justiciable rights in relation to healthcare.[84] The Portuguese Constitutional Court held in 2002 that a statute abolishing a guaranteed minimum income scheme for all those aged 18 years or over and replacing it with another scheme that omitted to guarantee a social integration income for those aged between 18 and 25 years violated the right to a decent minimum income inherent in the principle of respect for human dignity.[85]

The theme of human dignity has also guided the Hungarian Constitutional Court in its adjudication of the right to social security enshrined in its country's Constitution,[86] which contains many social rights justiciable at the behest of

83 Coomans (n 60 above) 11. Social rights and principles can act as *safeguard clauses* to prevent the legislature from arbitrarily restricting previously recognised social standards in two ways, first, through recognition of a minimum essential core of benefits or social institutions which must be preserved and, second, through the control of reasonableness and proportionality exercised on social policies: MJ Añón & G Pisarello 'The protection of social rights in the Spanish constitutional system' in Coomans (n 2 above) 79 - 80. In 1982 in a decision on *prima facie* retrogressive measures, on the grounds of the obligation of public authorities to promote conditions promoting real and effective equality (Constitution of Spain 1978, Art 9(2)) and on the basis of the principle of the social state, the Constitutional Court stated, 'the workers cannot be deprived *without sufficient reason* for it, from social achievements already obtained': Añón & Pisarello above, 80, citing Decision 81/1982 [3].

The right to health (Art 43) is not included in the explicitly justiciable fundamental rights, but it has been protected by connecting it with other fundamental rights, especially the right to information (Art 20(1)(d)), the right to privacy (Art 18), and environmental rights (Art 45). See Añón & Pisarello above, 91. In 2003, the Supreme Court stipulated that the information given to patients ought to be punctual, correct, true, confidential, extended over time, accurate and thorough, and placed the onus on the doctors to prove compliance with these requirements: Añón & Pisarello above, 91 - 92, citing Decision 29 May 2003.

84 Constitution of the Portuguese Republic 1976, Art 64. The Constitution lists many social rights, distinguishes between various categories of people who might need, and deserve, material assistance, and is unusual in suggesting a number of ways in which the state can meet its obligations to the needy: Fabre (n 63 above) 18.

The Portuguese Constitutional Tribunal ruled in 1984 that abrogation of the National Health Service violated a negative obligation to protect services already established in pursuance of a constitutional duty: Portuguese Constitutional Tribunal (*Tribunal Constitucional*), Decision (*Acórdão*) N° 39/84, 11 April 1984. Once a social service was created in fulfilment of a positive constitutional duty, the constitutional respect for the then existing right gave rise to a negative obligation not to abolish it. See ICJ Justiciability Report (n 75 above) 32 - 33.

85 Portuguese Constitutional Court, Ruling N° 509/02, 19 December 2002.

86 Constitution of the Republic of Hungary 1949, as amended, Art 70/E.

an individual.[87] The government's 1995 austerity plan, which involved shifting to a new system of benefits, was challenged in the courts. In the *Social Benefits* case, the Court stressed that the constitutional requirement of legal certainty – the most significant basis for the protection of acquired rights – necessitated a changeover period to allow those affected time to adjust to the amended provisions.[88] In 1998 in the *Welfare Act* case, the Court suspended proceedings challenging the level of unemployment benefit pending receipt of a study to allow an assessment of whether regular social aid due under the Act together with other benefits would secure the minimum livelihood necessary for the realisation of the right to human dignity[89] in line

87 Langford (n 73 above) 251 - 252. Although there are specific social welfare rights in the Constitution, the Court has been reluctant to interfere with the roles of the legislature and the executive in making political decisions on the levels of benefit that are to apply and in setting priorities in the Hungarian welfare system: Coomans (n 60 above) 11. The Court will not enquire into the effectiveness or reasonableness of measures adopted by the state except in very limited cases: Langford (n 73) 252. It remarked that it was only in a few exceptional cases that certain social rights in the Constitution have an element of subjective (justiciable) right: Langford (n 73 above) 252, citing Constitutional Court of Hungary, Decision 28/1994, 20 May 1994 (*Environmental Protection* case) [29(b)]. The Court has also demonstrated a marked reticence to base its decisions on the constitutional rights to welfare, and, where the choice existed, it has opted to derive welfare rights indirectly either from property rights (Art 13) or by affirming the right to a basic minimum level of survival from the right to life (Art 54(1)). Other tactics it has used to avoid directly relying on welfare rights have been to subject government actions to the test of arbitrariness or to use a proportionality analysis to balance the individual's interests against the public interest: Langford (n 73 above) 253. The doctrine of legitimate expectation has prevented the precipitous deprivation of existing benefits.

Ofari Atta J of Ghana also expanded the right to life and linked it closely with human dignity, when he stated in *Asare v Ga West District Assembly* (Suit No 36/2007) (Ghana High Court) 2 May 2008 at 6:

> [T]he right to life is not limited to deprivation of life *per se*. It encompasses all other rights that make the enjoyment of the right complete and meaningful. Any treatment that derogates from the living of a full life constitutes violation of it. ... [T]he right to life must be read in conjunction with other rights especially the right to human dignity...

See R Uitz & A Sajó 'A case for enforceable constitutional rights? Welfare rights in Hungarian constitutional jurisprudence' in Coomans (n 2 above) 99 - 104.

88 Constitutional Court of Hungary, Decision 43/1995, 30 June 1995. The Court evaluated the reduction or termination of social security benefits according to the criteria for the protection of property. It noted that social benefits may not be reduced below a minimal level required for the right to social security: Langford (n 73 above) 258.

See summary in COHRE Leading Cases (n 68 above) 47. For an assessment of this case and related decisions, see Langford (n 73 above) 256 - 259; Uitz & Sajó (n 87 above) 110 - 113.

89 Art 54(1).

with the constitutional requirement specified in the *Social Benefits* case.[90] In a majority decision in the *Housing* case in 2000, having found that the right to social security did not establish subjective rights and therefore a fundamental constitutional right to housing could not be derived from it, the Constitutional Court held that the basic right to human life and dignity together with the right to social security only obliged the state to provide accommodation for the homeless if human life was in imminent danger.[91]

The Latvian Constitutional Court held that the right to social security in the Constitution[92] was breached by a law depriving people of benefits when their employer failed to pay compulsory state social insurance premiums and the state did not do its duty to ensure collection of the payments.[93] There

90 Constitutional Court of Hungary, Decision 32/1998, 22 June 1998 (*Welfare Act* case). See Langford (n 73 above) 260; N Rao 'Three concepts of dignity in constitutional law' (2011) 86 *Notre Dame Law Review* 183 at 238; Uitz & Sajó (n 87 above) 113 - 114.

91 Constitutional Court of Hungary, Decision 42/2000, 8 November 2000 (*Housing* case). See Langford (n 73 above) 262 - 263; Uitz & Sajó (n 87 above) 114 - 115. The decision has been criticised because the Court did not delve into international jurisprudence to determine the content of social right and failed to note that an independent right to housing had been repeatedly recognised at international level; a second criticism was levelled at the decision because the Court failed to develop a more robust jurisprudence for evaluating whether the state was meeting its constitutional obligations by simply meeting the demand of the minimum level: Langford (n 73 above) 263.

92 Constitution of the Republic of Latvia 1922, as amended, Art 109.

93 Constitutional Court of Latvia, Case No 2000-08-0109, 13 March 2001. See summary in COHRE Leading Cases (n 68 above) 56 - 57. It was significant that – even though the objective of payments was to protect employees – the workers could not opt to pay the premiums direct to the state and could control neither their employer's actions nor the state's efforts to collect the monies due. The Court did not relax the obligations on the state on account of the economic hardships – its duty to collect the funds endured in financially difficult times. Efficient and effective implementation measures were required to comply with international obligations – legislation on its own did not suffice. The availability of social aid to those who were unable to provide for themselves was not a substitute for the constitutional right to social security in the form of social insurance, which the state was obliged to implement.

The international obligations arising under the Universal Declaration of Human Rights (adopted 10 December 1948) UNGA Res 217 A(III) (Universal Declaration) and CESCR influenced the Court's decision. It noted that viewpoints on the legal nature and binding force of these international instruments had advanced since they were introduced, citing the Limburg Principles as requiring the state to immediately undertake measures, employing all the necessary standards, to ensure implementation of CESCR rights at least on the minimum level: UN Commission on Human Rights, 43rd Session 'The Limburg Principles on the Implementation of CESCR' (8 January 1987) UN Doc E/CN.4/1987/17 (Limburg Principles). It also cited the stipulation in General Comments 3 (UN Committee on Economic, Social and Cultural Rights 'General Comment No 3' (n 7 above)) and 9 (UN Committee on Economic, Social and Cultural Rights 'General Comment No 9' 19th Session (3 December 1998) UN Doc E/C.12/1998/24) that measures should be implemented in a reasonably short

was a failure to observe the objective of social insurance, which served to implement social justice, social security and rights indispensable for the dignity of the person.

Because the United Kingdom does not have a written constitution, there has been less scope there for an expansive jurisprudence on socio-economic issues. However, the principles of administrative law have come to the aid of some litigants[94] and the European Convention on Human Rights (ECHR)[95] has been the basis of some decisions favourable to claimants – particularly since enactment of the Human Rights Act 1998.[96] The judges are generally reluctant to interfere with the political role of the legislature and the executive, but have done so when necessary.[97] The House of Lords held that a local education authority – faced with a reduction in government funding – was not entitled to take the availability of financial resources into account when it reduced the amount of home tuition for a child, who was unable to attend school because of illness.[98] It based its decision on a strict interpretation of the statute, which had imposed a duty (not a discretionary power) on the education authority to provide education for ill children.[99]

Lord Woolf in *R v North and East Devon Health Authority, ex p Coughlan* critically appraised a health authority's actions in closing a nursing home without providing a suitable alternative for its residents.[100] He held that the closure was an unjustified breach of a promise to Miss Coughlan that she would have a home for life in the facility, which gave rise to a legitimate expectation that the health authority would not resile from its promise unless

time after CESCR has taken effect in a state and that every state was obliged to secure implementation of the most essential liabilities at least on the basic level.

The Latvian Constitutional Court's enthusiasm for considering international law contrasts with the attitude of its Hungarian counterpart, which rarely does so: Langford (n 73 above) 252. See Marcus (n 54 above) 64, fn 63.

94 For a review of the protection of welfare rights in administrative law in the UK, see JA King 'United Kingdom: Asserting social rights in a multi-layered system' in Langford (n 21 above) 279 - 284.

95 Convention for the Protection of Human Rights and Fundamental Freedoms, 213 UNTS 222 (ECHR).

96 On Human Rights Act 1998 jurisprudence involving welfare interests, see King (n 94 above) 286 - 292.

97 See E Palmer 'The role of courts in the domestic protection of socio-economic rights: The unwritten constitution of the UK' in Coomans (n 2 above) 169 - 171.

98 *R v East Sussex County Council, ex p Tandy* [1998] AC 714 (HL). For a review and assessment of *Tandy*, see Palmer (n 97 above) 149 - 150.

99 n 98 above, 749.

100 [2001] QB 213 (CA). See King (n 94) 283.

there was an overreaching justification for doing so.[101] The expectation related to a substantive benefit. Even though the Human Rights Act was not in force at the time of his decision, Lord Woolf considered the impact of Article 8 of the ECHR, which was relevant since the case concerned the applicant's home.[102] Miss Coughlan viewed the possible loss of her accommodation in the nursing home as life-threatening; the Court understood why she took such a serious view of the situation and accepted that an enforced move of the kind intended would be 'emotionally devastating and seriously anti-therapeutic'.[103] It found that the decision to close the nursing home constituted unfairness amounting to an abuse of power by the health authority and would be a breach of Article 8.[104]

The enactment of the Human Rights Act ensured that the House of Lords rejected a planning authority's plea for an injunction to prevent gypsies from occupying land with their mobile homes and caravans following the refusal of planning permission.[105] Because Article 8 of the ECHR was engaged, the Court would have regard to all the circumstances and would only grant an injunction when it was just and proportionate to do so.[106] The Court respected the separation of powers and would not examine matters of planning policy and judgment within the purview of the planners, but the courts would not grant an injunction simply because a planning authority considered it necessary or expedient to restrain a planning breach.[107]

The House of Lords in a majority decision in *Ghaidan v Godin-Mendoza* found that there was a breach of Article 8 in combination with the anti-discrimination provision in Article 14 of the ECHR because of the less favourable treatment of a homosexual couple under the Rent Act 1977.[108] One of the reasons Baroness Hale gave in her judgment for finding that the guarantee of equal treatment was essential to democracy was that democracy

101 n 100 above, [89].

102 n 100 above, [90]-[93].

103 n 100 above, [92].

104 n 100 above, [117].

105 *South Bucks District Council v Porter* [2003] UKHL 26, [2003] 2 AC 558. See King (n 94 above) 290.

106 n 105 above, [18], [28], [58], [74], [87]-[89].

107 n 105 above, [28], [30], [70], [98].

108 [2004] UKHL 30, [2004] 2 AC 557. There was no rational or fair ground for the distinction in the Act, which confined rights of succession to the husband or wife of a deceased tenant. The Court interpreted the legislation in conformity with the ECHR and held that the survivor in a homosexual relationship was entitled to succeed to the statutory tenancy. See King (n 94 above) 290 - 291.

was founded on the principle that each individual has equal value and was breached by regarding others as inferior.[109] As she stated:[110]

> Treating some as automatically having less value than others not only causes pain and distress to that person but also violates his or her dignity as a human being. The essence of the Convention, as has often been said, is respect for human dignity and human freedom.

6.4.1.2 Judicial enforcement under the African Charter

Moving from Europe to another continent, the African Charter affirms explicitly some socio-economic rights,[111] *ie*, the right to work under equitable and satisfactory conditions and to receive equal pay for equal work,[112] the right to education,[113] and the right to enjoy the best attainable state of physical and mental health[114] with an obligation on the states 'to take the necessary

109 n 108 above, [132]. The other reasons she gave were that unequal treatment damaged society as a whole because of the waste of resources in making wrong assumptions about people and because of the damage to social cohesion by the creation of an under-class with a rational grievance; unequal treatment was the reverse of the rational behaviour now expected of government and of the state requiring that power not be exercised arbitrarily; and it was a purpose of all human rights instruments to secure the protection of the essential rights of members of minority groups (even when they were unpopular with the majority); she summarised, '[d]emocracy values everyone equally even if the majority does not.': as above.

110 n 108 above, [132], citing *Pretty v UK* (2002) 35 EHRR 1 at 37, [65].

111 See C Heyns 'The African regional human rights system: The African Charter' (2004) 108 *Penn State Law Review* 679 at 690 - 691; S Ibe 'Implementing economic, social and cultural rights in Nigeria: Challenges and opportunities' (2010) 10 *African Human Rights Law Journal* 197 at 199 - 200; CA Odinkalu 'Implementing economic, social and cultural rights under the African Charter on Human and Peoples' Rights' in MD Evans & R Murray (eds) *The African Charter on Human and Peoples' Rights: The system in practice, 1986 - 2000* (2002) 192.

112 African Charter on Human and Peoples' Rights (adopted 27 June 1981, entered into force 21 October 1986) (1982) 21 ILM 58 (African Charter) Art 15.

113 Art 17(1).

114 Art 16(1). In view of their condition and disabilities, mental health patients should be accorded special treatment to enable them not only attain but also sustain their optimum level of independence and performance: *Purohit v The Gambia* [2003] AHRLR 96 (ACHPR 2003) [81]. As fundamental rights are at stake, the African Commission does not give much leeway to the states in relation to mental healthcare, and considers that the mentally ill 'should never be denied their right to proper health care, which is crucial for their survival and their assimilation into and acceptance by the wider society': above, [85]. Their inherent human dignity (a basic right to which all human beings, regardless of their capabilities, are entitled) was not respected and they were dehumanised by being branded 'lunatics' and 'idiots' in the Gambia's Lunatics Detention Act: above, [57], [59]. The Act also infringed the patients' right to be heard prior to being detained and to their right to challenge the two medical certificates from general practitioners forming the basis of their detention: above, [71]-[72].

measures to protect the health of their people and to ensure that they receive medical attention when they are sick'.[115] The African Commission on Human and Peoples' Rights interpreted the Charter as containing unenumerated rights in *Social and Economic Rights Action Centre v Nigeria*,[116] when it held that the internationally recognised socio-economic rights which are not explicitly recognised in the Charter should be regarded as implicitly included.[117] It found that the right to food was 'inseparably linked to the dignity of human beings' and was therefore essential for the enjoyment and fulfilment of other rights such as health, education, work and political participation.[118]

The Preamble to the Charter leaves no doubt that all rights are interconnected and states, 'the satisfaction of economic, social and cultural rights is a guarantee for the enjoyment of civil and political rights'.[119] The specific embodiment in Article 5 of every individual's right to 'the respect of the dignity inherent in a human being'[120] has provided a basis on which the Commission has found violations of the Charter where economic and social issues have arisen in conjunction with alleged violations of civil and

115 Art 16(2). The Charter permits states to make complaints of Charter violations by other states to the African Commission on Human and Peoples' Rights, and empowers the Commission to consider, study and report on communications from individuals, groups and organisations in respect of human rights violations: Arts 48 - 49, 55 - 59. See UN Justiciability Report (n 57 above) [15].

116 *Social and Economic Rights Action Centre (SERAC) v Nigeria* [2001] AHRLR 60 (ACHPR 2001). See TS Bulto 'The utility of cross-cutting rights in enhancing justiciability of socio-economic rights in the African Charter on Human and Peoples' Rights' (2010) 29 *University of Tasmania Law Review* 142 at 144, 149 - 150, 156, 159, 168 - 169; ICJ Justiciability Report (n 75 above) 44 - 45, 46.

117 Heyns (n 111) 691. The Commission read in a right to shelter or housing deduced from the provisions on health, property and family life: n 116 above, [60], referring to African Charter (n 112 above) Arts 16, 14 and 18(1) respectively. The corollary of the combination of the provisions protecting the right to health, the right to property, and the protection accorded to the family forbade the wanton destruction of shelter because when housing was destroyed, property, health, and family life were adversely affected: n 116 above, [60].

118 n 116 above, [65].

119 African Charter (n 112 above) Preamble, 8th para. See Odinkalu (n 111 above) 188; UN Justiciability Report (n 57 above) [15].

120 The African Charter is unlike international Covenants and regional instruments in recognising respect for human dignity as a distinct right: Odinkalu (n 111 above) 214. Chidi Odinkalu considers that this achieves the radical consequence of breaking down artificial barriers imposed on the implementation of economic, social and cultural rights, for, as Odinkalu states, 'respect for human dignity is a primordial value incapable of being pigeon-holed into any artificial categories of rights': as above.

political rights. In the absence of an express guarantee of a right to housing, the Commission based protection for housing-related rights on the guarantee of human dignity, including the prohibition of torture and cruel, inhuman and degrading treatment also mentioned in Article 5.[121] The Commission found in *Modise v Botswana*[122] that the state had breached, *inter alia*, the right to dignity of a stateless man on whom it had enforced homelessness.[123] On similar lines the Commission ruled in *Amnesty International v Zambia* that by forcing two political opponents to live as stateless people under degrading conditions, Zambia had deprived them of their family and deprived their families of their support in violation of the dignity of a human being guaranteed in Article 5.[124]

6.4.2 Progressivity

Having completed my review of justiciability of socio-economic rights in Europe and under the African Charter, I am returning to CESCR to consider the progressivity element. In this, socio-economic rights differ from civil and political rights, which are all immediately enforceable.[125] But the variable economic conditions pertaining in each state mean that not every socio-economic benefit can be extended to the general populace instantaneously.[126] The continuous obligation to improve until all the rights have been fully

121 Odinkalu (n 111 above) 209 - 210.

122 [2000] AHRLR 30 (ACHPR 2000).

123 Odinkalu (n 111 above) 210. He had been forced to live for seven years in 'No Man's Land' between South Africa and Botswana, which the Commission stated exposed him to 'personal suffering and indignity' in violation of his right to freedom from cruel, inhuman or degrading treatment: n 122 above, [91].

124 [2000] AHRLR 325 (ACHPR 1999) [50]. See Odinakalu (n 111 above) 210.

125 Brems categorised the minimum core obligation as 'a bottom line', which is much lower than the borderline under civil and political rights; full realisation is 'a horizon line', which is not a maximum, but approaches good or best practice; in between the two lines, state behaviour may or may not conform to treaty obligations, depending amongst others on the availability of resources: n 26 above, 355.

126 The African Commission has adopted a realistic stance taking cognisance of the poverty in African countries. It has interpreted the right to health in Article 16 of the African Charter as imposing a progressive duty on the state, which is obliged 'to take concrete and targeted steps, while taking full advantage of its available resources, to ensure that the right to health is fully realised in all its aspects without discrimination of any kind': *Purohit (n* 114 above) [84].

Cf *Swaziland National Ex-Mine Workers Association v Minister of Education* [2010] SZSC 35 (SC of Swaziland) on the right to free primary education under the Constitution of the Kingdom of Swaziland 2005, Sec 29(6).

realised is a practical solution, which is flexible enough to cater for different situations and financial changes over time.[127]

When resources are so severely stretched as to require unavoidable cutbacks, states need to be very careful not to act precipitously or indiscriminately. Priority must be given to the vulnerable, international funds and aid tapped,[128] cost-effective measures pursued, monitoring of progress on implementation maintained, and strategies pursued to ultimate achievement of socio-economic goals. Any regressive measures should have the least impact on the marginalised in society.

6.5 Judicial enforcement in South Africa

Reverting to South Africa, the decision in *Grootboom* has been hailed worldwide as a laudable precedent for the judicial enforcement of socio-economic rights.[129] However, it has been criticised for failing to lead to an

127 The *travaux préparatoires* for CESCR show that supporters of the idea of progressive achievement defended it as a necessary accommodation to the vagaries of economic circumstances, while opponents held the opposite view and feared that it enabled lame excuses to be pleaded in justification of non-implementation: Alston & Quinn (n 30 above) 175.

128 There is a view that we are collectively charged with seeking a world in which each person has the possibility of a life of dignity and that this demands that each one contributes (or at the very least does not undermine) the processes of global governance aimed at securing human dignity: KA Appiah 'Dignity and global duty' (2010) 90 *Boston University Law Review* 661 at 671, 672, 674 - 675. Participation as citizens of nation-states in the creation of international institutions to achieve this aim and through other forms of collective action (such as supporting aid organisations) is urged on individuals by concern for the dignity of each human being: above, 671 - 672.

Habermas urged that in international relations moral obligations between states (and citizens) should be recognised as being grounded in the democratic status-bound idea of human dignity: n 56 above, 478 - 479.

129 It has been described as establishing a relationship of collaboration between the State and the judiciary whereby each branch of government brings its particular skills to bear on the problem of realising socio-economic rights: M Wesson '*Grootboom* and beyond: Reassessing the socio-economic jurisprudence of the South African Constitutional Court' (2004) 20 *South African Journal on Human Rights* 284 at 307. The Court's strategy in *Grootboom* and other socio-economic rights cases may have been to devise a review standard that allowed it greater flexibility to manage its relationship with the political branches: T Roux 'Principle and pragmatism on the Constitutional Court of South Africa' (2009) 7 *International Journal of Constitutional Law* 106 at 136.

effective remedy for Ms Grootboom and her unfortunate companions.[130] The Court did not utilise its supervisory jurisdiction to impose a time limit on revision of the housing plan to incorporate assistance for the destitute homeless.[131] Neither did it follow up to ensure that the dignity of Irene Grootboom was given the respect it deserved in the long run. This unfortunate and brave lady died in her forties eight years after the Constitutional Court ruled in her favour.[132] At the time of her death she was still living in a shack, homeless and penniless.[133] In theory the claimants could have reverted to the courts to take more strident action to have the State relieve their situation, but they did not have the financial resources to do so.

It is not the judgments *themselves* that are the problem, according to Murray Wesson, but the State's subsequent implementation of them.[134] The most effective means of remedying this difficulty would, Wesson submits, be for the Court to exercise supervisory jurisdiction thereby extending the relationship of collaboration with the executive.[135]

6.6 Housing

The *Grootboom* litigation arose after Ms Grootboom with 510 children and 390 other adults, who had been living in appalling conditions in an informal

130 The Constitutional Court developed its jurisprudence in later cases to provide more valuable relief, and even based its decision to award damages to a private property owner for the absence of an appropriate mechanism to give effect to an eviction order against unlawful occupiers on the failure of the state to provide an effective remedy as required by the rule of law and entrenched in Section 34 of the Constitution: *Modderklip* (*n* 29 above) [51].

131 See Davis (n 41 above) 701. In later cases the Court refined its approach and retained a supervisory role: see *Residents of Joe Slovo Community, Western Cape v Thubelisha Homes* 2010 3 SA 454 (CC) [7].

132 P Joubert 'Grootboom dies homeless and penniless' *Mail & Guardian Online* (Johannesburg 8 August 2008) http://www.mg.co.za/article/2008-08-08-grootboom-dies-homeless-and-penniless (accessed 24 September 2013).

133 As above. The fact that her family were not yet housed in reasonable accommodation showed how difficult it was to realise the socio-economic rights in the Constitution: Sachs (n 11 above) 274.

134 n 129 above, 306.

135 n 129 above, 307. See also Liebenberg (n 21 above) 100. The Constitutional Court has an increased understanding that more judicial oversight is critical and has utilised it to develop an effective enforcement mechanism: B Ray '*Residents of Joe Slovo Community v Thubelisha Homes and Others*: The two faces of engagement' (2010) 10 *Human Rights Law Review* 360 at 368.

squatter settlement in the Western Cape, decided to move out and illegally occupied someone else's land.[136] Having been evicted, they were left homeless and were living again in intolerable conditions while waiting in the queue for their turn to be allocated low-cost housing. Their legal challenge was based on claims that the government was obliged under Section 26 of the Constitution to provide them with adequate basic shelter (a minimum core) until they obtained permanent housing and that the children had an unqualified right to shelter under Section 28(1)(c) of the Constitution.[137]

Yacoob J amalgamated the right to access to adequate housing in Section 26(1) of the Constitution with the progressive realisation obligation on the State in Section 26(2), thereby eliminating a finding of the immediate right to a home.[138] There was at the very least, a negative obligation placed on the State and others 'to desist from preventing or impairing the right of access to adequate housing.'[139] He regarded the prohibition on arbitrary evictions in Section 26(3) as an elaboration on the negative right.[140] As Yacoob J described it, the manner in which the eviction took place did not respect the dignity of those being moved on and affected them in a fundamental way.[141] At the least, the State had breached its negative obligation in relation of housing, as it had not ensured that the evictions were executed humanely.[142]

136 n 1 above, [4]. See Chaskalson (n 14 above) 603 - 605; Choma (n 74 above) 43 - 46, 50 - 51; Davis (n 41 above) 692 - 694, 697; Kende (n 13 above) 142 - 145; MS Kende *Constitutional rights in two worlds: South Africa and the United States* (2009) 245 - 248; Pieterse (n 11 above) 892 - 894, 901 - 902; Rao (n 90 above) 237 - 238, 265; LA Williams 'The justiciability of water rights: *Mazibuko v. City of Johannesburg*' (2009) 36 *Forum for Development Studies* 5 at 14 - 16; Woods (n 15 above) at 783 - 786.

137 n 1 above, [18].

138 n 1 above, [34]. Daniel Erskine considered that the judicial gloss of reading the two subsections together as mutually supportive because of their textual proximity solved the inherent conflict between them, but diminished one right by subsuming the other within the primary right: DH Erskine 'Judgments of the United States Supreme Court and the South African Constitutional Court as a basis for a universal method to resolve conflicts between fundamental rights' (2008) 22 *St John's Journal of Legal Commentary* 595 at 621 - 622.

139 n 1 above, [34], citing *Certification of the Constitution of the Republic of South Africa, 1996* 1996 4 SA 744 (CC) [78].

140 n 1 above, [34].

141 '[T]he eviction was reminiscent of the past and inconsistent with the values of the Constitution. The respondents were evicted a day early and to make matters worse, their possessions and building materials were not merely removed, but destroyed and burnt.': n 1 above, [88]. The State had funded, and assisted in, the eviction of the claimants and had failed to engage in mediation aimed at reaching a settlement: as above.

142 As above. Section 26(3) specifically prohibits demolition of a person's home without a court order, as well as controlling evictions. The Western Cape High Court held that

The Court did not put the primary obligation under Section 28(1)(c) to provide shelter for children on the State, but instead placed this duty on the parents.[143] As the children implicated in *Grootboom* were not in care or abandoned, the State had no separate obligation to them under Section 28.[144] The Constitutional Court unanimously found that neither Section 26 nor 28 gave an entitlement to shelter or housing immediately upon demand, but that the housing programme in the Cape Metro (the supervisory tier of local government in the area) fell short of the obligations imposed upon the State in that it failed to provide for any form of relief to those desperately in need of access to housing.[145] The need to give central place to human dignity in assessing individual needs and state action came from the requirement that human beings 'be treated as human beings.'[146]

In formulating a solution, the Court emphasised the need to consider individual circumstances and not to rely on merely showing that its measures were capable of achieving a 'statistical advance' in the realisation of the right; according to Yacoob J, the Constitution required that everyone be treated with 'care and concern' and even statistically successful measures which 'fail to respond to the needs of those most desperate' might not pass the test.[147] In addition to the duty to respect socio-economic rights by requiring the state to refrain from law or conduct depriving people of access to their rights, the Court set out the criteria for judging whether it had fulfilled its positive duties to protect, promote and fulfil them – the state must take reasonable legislative and other measures within its available resources to achieve progressive realisation of each of the rights.[148]

Section 26(3) modified the common law by requiring a plaintiff, who seeks to evict a person from his or her home, to allege relevant circumstances which entitle the court to issue an eviction order: *Ross v South Peninsula Municipality* [2000] 4 All SA 85 (C).

143 n 1 above, [77]. If the parents failed, the State was obliged to intervene: as above. The Court sought to harmonise rights and solved the conflict between an adult's and a child's right to adequate housing by qualifying the child's right so that it is effectuated through the parents or family, or, in default, through governmental measures: Erskine (n 138 above) 622.

144 n 1 above, [79].

145 n 1 above, [95].

146 n 1 above, [83]. The need to treat people as human beings has been a recurrent theme in Yacoob J's judgments: see, *eg*, *Joe Slovo (n* 131 above) [65], [69], [76].

147 n 1 above, [44].

148 S Liebenberg 'The courts and socio-economic rights: Carving out a role' (2002) 3(1) *ESR Review: Economic and Social Rights in South Africa.*

The housing policy was unreasonable not only from the perspective of the class of person excluded, but also for the effect such exclusion could have on the national housing programme as a whole.[149] Lehmann described the Court's approach as utilitarian, since sacrificing the interests of those desperately in need of shelter would not have led to the actual realisation of medium- and long-term housing needs; the scale of the problem was such that there would have been continuing land invasions from the landless and homeless.[150] Jeanne Woods considers that *Grootboom* illustrates that because of the collective character of social rights the standards of minimum core obligations and progressive realisation in international human rights law do not necessarily impose limitations on rights, but can be stringent criteria by which a court can measure states' compliance.[151]

The South African Human Rights Commission was an *amicus* in *Grootboom* and the Court noted that it would monitor the efforts made by the State to comply with its Section 26 obligations in accordance with the Court's judgment.[152] The Commission's efficacy must be questioned in view of the State's failure to relieve Ms Grootboom's personal position before her demise.[153] While the Court's implementation of socio-economic rights in South Africa is significant, the Order it made in *Grootboom* was unsatisfactory. It relied on the Human Rights Commission to monitor implementation of the declaratory order. Although the Court found that the State had breached its constitutional obligations in not protecting the claimants during their eviction, it did not recognise this or provide redress for this lapse in its Order.[154]

149 Lehmann (n 9 above) 172.

150 n 9 above, 172.

151 n 15 above, 786.

152 n 1 above, [97]. The Commission has a constitutional duty to 'monitor and assess the observance of human rights': Constitution of the Republic of South Africa 1996, Sec 184(1)(c). It has power 'to investigate and to report on the observance of human rights' and 'to take steps to secure appropriate redress where human rights have been violated': Sec 184(2)(a) & (b).

The Court made it clear that mere legislation was not enough and that the state was obliged to act to achieve the intended result, with legislation being supported by policies reasonably conceived and reasonably implemented: n 1 above, [42]. As superficial compliance through development of a written programme is insufficient to meet the reasonableness standard, the deference to legislative judgments is not absolute: Ray (n 22 above) 160.

153 See K Pillay 'Implementing *Grootboom*: Supervision needed' (2002) 3(1) *ESR Review: Economic and Social Rights in South Africa*; Bilchitz (n 21 above) 25.

154 There was no specific right of return to Court, if the claimants' plight was not addressed adequately or at all within a stipulated or reasonable period. In contrast in *Joe Slovo*, the Court permitted the parties to approach the Court in the event of its

The Constitutional Court found a more precise and effective solution in *Jaftha v Schoeman*, the first case where the concept of adequate housing – briefly discussed in *Grootboom* – was considered at length and where the problem was perhaps less complicated with just one person aggrieved and a readily available remedy capable of effecting an immediate improvement.[155] The Order was framed as an answer to prevent interference rather than as a positive obligation requiring vast expenditure by the state.[156] Maggie Jaftha (unemployed and in ill-health) borrowed R250, which was to be repaid in instalments, but she failed to meet all of the repayments, was sued for the amount due and her house was sold to pay the debt.[157] The Court found that the Magistrates' Courts Act 1944, as a measure which permitted a person to be deprived of existing access to adequate housing, limited the rights protected in Section 26(1) of the Constitution.[158] It allowed execution against the homes of indigent debtors resulting in them losing their security of tenure and,

order not being complied with or if the order gave rise to unforeseen difficulties: n 131 above, [7].

In a dispute over the eviction of squatters in Ghana, the High Court pointed out that even in *Grootboom*, the court did not interfere with the executive's execution of its housing programme and did not reverse the eviction of the plaintiffs, which had already taken place; Appau J distinguished the situation in Ghana from the position in South Africa, where the Constitution made provision for adequate housing in order to redress the forcible appropriation of black people's land during the apartheid era: *Abass v Accra Metropolitan Assembly* (Misc 1203/2002) (Ghana High Court) 24 July 2002 (*Sodom and Gomorrah* case) 12. The Court found that the planned eviction was lawful and would not infringe the squatters' fundamental rights. Appau J referred to Yacoob J's condemnation of land invasions in *Grootboom* and his view that it might be reasonable for the state not to provide housing in response to repeated land invasions, as reasonableness must be determined on the facts of each case: above, 12 - 13, citing n 1 above, [92].

155 2005 2 SA 140 (CC). The decision was a significant development in the Court's approach to the review of the obligations imposed by social rights: S Liebenberg 'Needs, rights and transformation: Adjudicating social rights in South Africa' (2005) 6(4) *ESR Review: Economic and Social Rights in South Africa* 3 at 6. See also Brand (n 2 above) 217 - 218; Liebenberg (n 21 above) 93 - 94, 100.

156 The Constitutional Court (in contrast to the court below's view) found that there was a negative content to socio-economic rights: n 155 above, [33]. In 1997 Pierre de Vos correctly discerned the negative element in socio-economic rights, which placed a duty on the state to respect an individual's existing access to adequate housing; therefore the specific constitutional protection from eviction in Section 26(3) was unnecessary, but was useful in overcoming courts' reluctance to explore the full range of the negative obligations engendered by socio-economic rights: n 11 above, 80 - 81.

157 n 155 above, [4]. In her challenge to the validity of provisions in the Magistrates' Courts Act 1944 dealing with the sale in execution of property to satisfy a debt, Jaftha relied on her constitutional right to have access to adequate housing: n 155 above, [2]. An eviction would mean that she could not apply for state housing: n 155 above, [12].

158 n 155 above, [34].

even worse, losing the chance of being re-housed so that they could enjoy conditions in which their dignity could prosper again.[159] Judicial oversight of the execution process would be the most appropriate method of remedying the over-breadth of the legislation.[160] The Constitutional Court read in words to the Act so that a court would consider the circumstances before ordering a sale in execution of immovable property where insufficient movables had been found to satisfy the judgment debt.[161]

Mokgoro J, delivering the judgment in *Jaftha* on behalf of a unanimous Court, confirmed the view in *Grootboom* that any claim based on socio-economic rights 'must necessarily engage the right to dignity', which is 'invariably implicated.'[162] The lack of adequate food, housing and healthcare was 'a blight' on people's dignity.[163] The Committee on ESCR also viewed the right to dignity as inherently linked with socio-economic rights and had emphasised the need not to give the right to housing a restrictive interpretation, but to see it as 'the right to live somewhere in security, peace and dignity'.[164] The history of forced summary evictions in the apartheid days and the criminalisation of those bucking the system by remaining in occupation showed the extent to which access to adequate housing was linked to 'dignity and self-worth', as transgressors suffered 'double indignity – the loss of one's home and the stigma that attaches to criminal sanction.'[165] The importance to dignity of a home and the onslaught to a person's humanity by arbitrary deprivation of the opportunity to regain a home is evident.[166]

159 n 155 above, [39]. The legislation was not justifiable and could not be saved to the extent that it allowed executions where no countervailing considerations in favour of the creditor justified the sales in execution: n 155 above, [52].

160 n 155 above, [61].

161 n 155 above, [64].

162 n 155 above, [21], citing n 1 above, [83].

163 n 155 above, [21].

164 n 155 above, [24], citing *The Right to Adequate Housing (Art 11(1)) UNCESCR General Comment 4* (1991) 13 December 1991 E/1992/23 [7]. The UN Committee identified security of tenure as one factor in determining adequacy: n 155 above, [24], citing *General Comment 4* above, [8].

165 n 155 above, [27] (footnote omitted).

166 n 155 above, [39] (Mokgoro J):

> Relative to homelessness, to have a home one calls one's own, even under the most basic circumstances, can be a most empowering and dignifying human experience. The impugned provisions have the potential of undermining that experience. The provisions take indigent people who have already benefited from housing subsidies and, worse than placing them at the back of the queue to benefit again from such subsidies in the future, put them in a position where they might never again acquire

The Court found it unnecessary to decide whether the right of access to housing had horizontal application,[167] but focused on the constitutionality of the eviction process on account of the sale of property for a relatively trivial debt. It balanced the rights of the debtors against those of creditors and achieved a fair outcome. The remedy was satisfactory for the applicant and ensured that there would not be a recurrence. The Court was not prepared to simply declare the legislation invalid and leave it to the legislature to bring in new provisions. It steered a delicate course between two competing interests and reached an excellent decision.

The Constitutional Court favoured reconciliation of interests in preference to the triumph of one right over another when it tried to resolve a large-scale squatter issue that came before it in *Port Elizabeth Municipality*.[168] In response to a petition signed by 1,600 people living in the neighbourhood and the landowners, the Port Elizabeth Municipality sought eviction orders against 68 people, including 23 children, who occupied 29 shacks erected on privately-owned land, where some of the squatters had lived for up to eight years.[169]

> such assistance, without which they may be rendered homeless and never able to restore the conditions for human dignity.

Mokgoro J noted that poverty had converted a welfare issue to a property problem: n 155 above, [30].

167 There is a contrast between the duty of government to its citizens and the duty of one private person to another, as, first, private persons rarely have power over decisions of others remotely comparable to the power of government over its citizenry and, second, private individuals ordinarily have liberty to act for a wide variety of reasons: KW Simons 'Dworkin's two principles of dignity: An unsatisfactory nonconsequentialist account of interpersonal moral duties' (2010) 90 *Boston University Law Review* 715 at 732.

Habermas considers that the more deeply civil rights suffuse the legal system as a whole, the more often their influence permeates the horizontal relations among individuals and groups, collisions between competing rights in hard cases often being resolved by appealing to a violation of human dignity whose absolute validity grounds a claim to priority: n 56 above, 469.

On the horizontal application of the South African Bill of Rights, see Liebenberg (n 21 above) 78 - 79.

168 *Port Elizabeth Municipality v Various Occupiers* 2005 1 SA 217 (CC). The Court sought a solution that would best comport with dignity, as there were commensurate interests on both sides of the conflict; the use of the concept of human dignity allowed the Court to contextualise its decision in light of the history of apartheid: C McCrudden 'Human dignity and judicial interpretation of human rights' (2008) 19 *European Journal of International Law* 655 at 718, 719. See also Brand (n 2 above) 214, 228 - 229; Liebenberg (n 21 above) 92.

169 n 168 above, [1]-[2]. The squatters were willing to move provided they were given notice and were allocated suitable alternative land: n 168 above, [2]. The Municipality resisted their entreaties, as they would be queue-jumping by being given alternative accommodation over those on the housing list: n 168 above, [3].

It sought a ruling that it was entitled to evict unlawful occupiers without providing alternative accommodation or land.[170] The Court felt obliged to go beyond its normal remit and to enter the realm of judicial management to find a just and equitable solution balancing all the interests based on good neighbourliness and shared concern.[171] Sachs J,[172] delivering the Court's unanimous judgment, pointed out the indignity to society as well as to the poor caused by homelessness exacerbated by the State.[173] He encouraged the poor as autonomous beings not to abrogate responsibility for relieving their own plight and admonished the landowners not to stereotype the squatters by refusing to treat each one as a human being.[174] The reconciliation of the individual with the community was evident in the concept of *ubuntu*, which

170 n 168 above, [6]. Property rights under Section 25 and the housing provisions in Section 26 of the Constitution were in contention. In Ghana, Ofari Atta J rejected a somewhat similar claim from those whose occupation or activities were tainted by illegality, when he stated, '[e]ncroachers cannot have any right to compensation or alternative accommodation': *Asare (n* 87 above) 10.

171 n 168 above, [36]-[37]. The Municipality had not engaged properly with the squatters and the Court encouraged it to try to resolve the issue itself or to agree to the appointment of a skilled negotiator to reach a solution acceptable to the trespassers and to the landowners: n 168 above, [61]. When the Court decided that it would not uphold the eviction order, it justified its decision to limit the right of the landowners to be free from unlawful deprivation of their land as being the choice more congruent with dignity: McCrudden (n 168 above) 718. In contrast in *Joe Slovo*, the Court ordered the residents in an informal settlement to vacate to faciliate redevelopment plans, but required the state to provide them with temporary accommodation pending their being rehoused and also gave a substantive remedy by directing the state to provide 70% of the new houses in the redeveloped area to residents of the informal settlement: n 131 above, [7]. On the innovations in *Joe Slovo*, see Ray (n 135 above) 368 - 370. On *Joe Slovo*, see also A Pillay 'Economic and social rights adjudication: Developing principles of judicial restraint in South Africa and the United Kingdom' [2013] *Public Law* 599 at 611 - 613. Cf *Kariuki v Town Clerk, Nairobi City Council* [2011] eKLR (High Court of Kenya, 4 March 2011).

172 Sandra Liebenberg approved of Sachs J's careful analysis of the historical, socio-economic, political and legal factors that fuel occurrences such as the eviction of poor people from their homes: n 155 above, 5.

173 'It is not only the dignity of the poor that is assailed when homeless people are driven from pillar to post in a desperate quest for a place where they and their families can rest their heads. Our society as a whole is demeaned when state action intensifies rather than mitigates their marginalisation.': n 168 above, [18].

174 n 168 above, [41]:

> [T]hose seeking eviction should be encouraged not to rely on concepts of faceless and anonymous squatters automatically to be expelled as obnoxious social nuisances. Such a stereotypical approach has no place in the society envisaged by the Constitution; justice and equity require that everyone is to be treated as an individual bearer of rights entitled to respect for his or her dignity. At the same time those who find themselves compelled by poverty and landlessness to live in shacks on the land of others, should be discouraged from regarding themselves as helpless victims, lacking the possibilities of personal moral agency.

combines individual rights with a communitarian philosophy.[175] Mediation was compatible with *ubuntu*, as Sachs J considered that its use in the avoidance of 'polarising litigation' could promote respect for human dignity and underline the fact that we all live in a shared society.[176]

A similar reconciliatory attitude was adopted in *Occupiers of 51 Olivia Road* when the Court required the parties to co-operate together to find a solution.[177] The City of Johannesburg wanted to evict more than 400 occupiers of buildings in the inner city because they were unsafe and unhealthy.[178] The Court held unanimously that Section 26(2) of the Constitution obliged the municipality to engage meaningfully before ejecting people from their homes if they would become homeless after the eviction.[179] The legislation making it a crime for people to remain in buildings after an eviction notice by the City, but before any court order for eviction, was unconstitutional.[180]

The Constitutional Court gave an instant remedy and read in words to the legislation so that it included a proviso that criminalised only those people

175 n 168 above, [37]. African traditions more fully encompass the social dimensions of the person and human need, the concept of personhood having a normative content that expresses the relationship between social rights and duties: Woods (n 15 above) 778.

176 n 168 above, [42]. Sachs J adopted a Dworkinian attitude when he advocated the adoption by the judiciary of a practical route when balancing conflicting intrinsic interests, 'the courts must accordingly do as well as they can with the evidential and procedural resources at their disposal.': n 168 above, [38].

177 *Occupiers of 51 Olivia Road, Berea Township v City of Johannesburg* 2008 3 SA 208 (CC). See Christiansen (n 15 above) 601 - 603; Davis (n 41 above) 705 - 706, 709; Liebenberg (n 21 above) 95; A Pillay 'Toward effective social and economic rights adjudication: The role of meaningful engagement' (2012) 10 *International Journal of Constitutional Law* 732 at 732 - 734, 740 - 741; Ray (n 135 above) 361 - 362, 367, 368, 369.

178 n 177 above, [1]. At issue was whether the municipal authority had made reasonable provision for housing for those thousands of people who were said to be living in desperate conditions in the inner city and also whether eviction provisions were constitutional. The Court had made an interim order requiring the parties to engage meaningfully with each other with a view to addressing the possibilities of short term steps to improve current living conditions and of alternative accommodation for those who would be rendered homeless: n 177 above, [5]. The parties reached consensus that the City would not eject the occupiers, that it would upgrade the buildings and that it would provide temporary accommodation, and they agreed to meet to discuss permanent housing solutions: n 177 above, [24]-[26]. There was a conflict between the local authorities' duty to control unsafe buildings and their obligation to provide shelter for the homeless.

179 n 177 above, [18]. While the City has obligations to eliminate unsafe and unhealthy buildings, its constitutional duty to provide access to adequate housing meant that potential homelessness must be considered when it decides whether to evict people from buildings: n 177 above, [46].

180 n 177 above, [49].

who, after service upon them of an order of court for their eviction, continue to occupy the property.[181]

Yacoob J placed human dignity and respect for life as the priorities for the municipality in the balance between protecting property and the housing rights of city dwellers.[182] The Court reiterated that because dignity is a constitutional value, rights such as housing in Section 26 cannot be regarded in isolation, the requirement to bear dignity in mind involves treating people as human beings, and state action must be reasonable.[183] There must be engagement with the people affected to try to find a solution.[184] Sandra Fredman praised the collaborative way in which the Court dealt with the difficult task of enforcing socio-economic rights in this case, resulting in the Court's being enabled to issue a mandatory remedy without stepping on the toes of democratic decision-makers as well as incorporating those affected so they can monitor the remedy.[185]

181 n 177 above, [51], [54].

182 n 177 above, [16] (footnotes omitted):

> [The City] also has the obligation to fulfil the objectives mentioned in the preamble to the Constitution to '[i]mprove the quality of life of all citizens and free the potential of each person'. Most importantly it must respect, protect, promote and fulfil the rights in the Bill of Rights. The most important of these rights for present purposes is the right to human dignity and the right to life. In the light of these constitutional provisions a municipality that ejects people from their homes without first meaningfully engaging with them acts in a manner that is broadly at odds with the spirit and purpose of the constitutional obligations set out in this paragraph taken together.

183 n 177 above, [10], citing *Grootboom* (n 1 above) [82]-[83]. A holistic approach was required by local authorities when reaching decisions – they should not deal with issues of safety of buildings and housing of the evicted occupants separately: n 177 above, [44]. Bessler has called for a holistic, multi-faceted approach to protect children affected by HIV/AIDS: n 28 above, 94.

184 n 177 above, [11], citing *Grootboom* (n 1 above) [87]. The Court developed the engagement process further in *Joe Slovo*, where it set out detailed agendas for the content of the engagement with timelines: n 131 above, [7].

185 S Fredman *Human rights transformed: Positive rights and positive duties* (2008) 122. Fredman considers it possible to structure the adjudication of positive human rights duties in a way which strengthens rather than detracts from democracy: above, 123. There is scope for this in South Africa where the *locus standi* rules are wide permitting easy access to the courts for pursuing public interest litigation and where there is fertile ground for development because of the tradition of resistance to apartheid: above, 122. To develop the process she advocates that the courts resile from relying on the adversarial system to solve issues involving positive obligations on the state and pay more attention to alternatives aimed at securing the appropriate response: above, 123.

Brian Ray deduced from the judgment that the Court continues to prefer political over legal solutions, as it expressed optimism that future engagement would be meaningful and emphasised that both parties had a duty to continue to negotiate; the

On reviewing the housing litigation, it is clear that Section 26 of the Constitutional has been interpreted in the light of right to dignity in Section 10 and the constitutional value of respect for human dignity. The Prevention of Illegal Eviction from and Unlawful Occupation of Land Act 1998 protected the dignity of unlawful occupiers, while endeavouring to allow landowners recover their property. It emphasised the individual treatment of occupiers with particular attention being paid to the most vulnerable.[186] The consideration by the court of the availability of suitable alternative accommodation in evictions is based not just on the right to access to housing, but on the individual's right to be treated with dignity, as there is an obligation on the State to ensure that evictions are conducted humanely.[187] Enforcement of rights to housing is difficult for individuals and for government. The South African executive has not been vigilant to prevent illegal occupation of land and buildings. Neither has its housing programme kept pace with the demand.[188] Lilian Chenwi observed that the South African experience shows that having a myriad of progressive laws and policies on housing rights and evictions is not sufficient, as their actual enforcement is the most vital facet.[189]

The proliferation of informal settlements is a highly visible sign in South Africa of the shortage of housing. Provincial legislation – the KwaZulu-Natal Elimination and Prevention of Re-emergence of Slums Act 2007 – was enacted to address the elimination and upgrading of slums.[190] Abahlali baseMjondolo Movement of South Africa, an organisation representing thousands of shackdwellers, challenged the constitutionality of section 16

Court formalised the negotiation/mediation requirement it had begun to develop in earlier cases, adopting the term 'engagement' to describe this requirement and explaining at length the need for engagement among the government, affected citizens and civil society organisations to develop effective socio-economic policies: n 22 above, 194.

186 L Chenwi 'Putting flesh on the skeleton: South African judicial enforcement of the right to adequate housing of those subject to evictions' (2008) 8 *Human Rights Law Review* 105 at 117.

187 Chenwi (n 186 above) 128.

188 The virtually uncontrolled influx of refugees from neighbouring countries has exacerbated the problem, as has the attraction of comparatively rich South Africa for foreign drug peddlers.

189 n 186 above, 137. She continued, '[t]hough courts do have an important role in ensuring adequate enforcement of the rights to adequate housing and to protection from forced evictions, their impact is limited if their decisions are not enforced adequately.': as above.

190 If successful, it was expected to become a blueprint for similar legislation in other provinces: *Abahlali baseMjondolo Movement SA v Premier of the Province of Kwazulu-Natal* [2009] ZACC 31 [16], [126].

of the Slums Act, which would oblige the owner of property illegally occupied to take eviction proceedings against the occupiers and, in default, would compel the municipality to do so.[191] The plaintiffs failed in the High Court, so the matter came before the Constitutional Court, where the judges unanimously agreed on the competence of the provincial legislature to pass the legislation, as it related to housing – a concurrent national and provincial legislative competence.[192] The majority held that section 16 breached the right of access to housing in Section 26(2) of the Constitution and also contravened the rule of law.[193] The Court found that the legislation obliged the institution of eviction proceedings even if the owner or the municipality thought it would not be justified. Moseneke DCJ for the majority considered that this elimination of discretion eroded and considerably undermined the protections against the arbitrary institution of eviction proceedings.[194]

This decision reinforced the need to treat illegal occupiers humanely and to engage with them to try to find a solution before resorting to the courts for

191 The timeframe for complying with the obligation would be determined by notice issued by the provincial government, which had not yet acted to bring the section into operation: n 190 above, [49].

192 n 190 above, [40], [97].

193 n 190 above, [92], [125], [127]. On the resurrection of the rule of law in South Africa's new legal system, see P Langa 'Legal visions – South Africa in the 21st century' in A Anghie & G Sturgess (eds) *Legal visions of the 21st century: Essays in honour of Judge Christopher Weeramantry* (1998) 113. On the rule of law in Roman-Dutch law and its limitations as a principle to protect human rights in the apartheid era, see J Dugard *Human rights and the South African legal order* (1978) 38 - 49. On the rule of law generally, see W Binchy 'Constitutionality, the rule of law and socio-economic development' (Lecture at Southern African Chief Justices Forum in Botswana 2009) 2 http://www.venice.coe.int/SACJF/2009_08_BTW_Kasane/speeches/Binchy_constitutionality.pdf (accessed 24 September 2013); G Butler 'The essence of human rights: A religious critique' (2009) 43 *University of Richmond Law Review* 1255 at 1276 - 1278; G Quinn 'Human rights – themes and values: Establishing Irish foreign policy priorities' in G Quinn (ed) *Irish human rights yearbook 1995* (1995) 135 - 136; P Shivute 'The rule of law in sub-Saharan Africa – An overview' in N Horn & A Bösl (eds) *Human rights and the rule of law in Namibia* (2008) 213 - 216.

194 n 190 above, [112]. Eviction was not a last resort and meaningful engagement with the occupiers was not required by section 16: n 190 above, [113]-[115]. The legislation was overbroad, as it applied to all illegal occupiers, whether in slums or not: n 190 above, [116], [118].

Yacoob J, who dissented on the housing rights aspect, proposed an interpretation of section 16 in conformity with the Constitution, which effectively involved reading in six safeguards: n 190 above, [80]. This was a step too far for Moseneke DCJ, as it would have the effect of rewriting section 16 in a manner that was not apparent on its face and that was in conflict with the coercive design of section 16 to eliminate slums and informal settlements: n 190 above, [115]. He expanded on the implications of the legal uncertainty that would arise for vulnerable people and others concerned with implementing the legislation: n 190 above, [124].

an eviction order. Chenwi has assessed the effect of the Constitutional Court's ruling as requiring the government to focus more on providing adequate housing rather than on eliminating slums.[195]

6.7 Healthcare, water and social security

In *Soobramoney*, the first case to be brought seeking socio-economic rights, the Constitutional Court was reluctant to interfere with the executive's role in deciding priorities in healthcare and in fixing budgets.[196] Mr Soobramoney was an unemployed diabetic who suffered from heart disease and chronic irreversible renal failure.[197] He had been availing himself of private medical treatment, but was no longer able to afford it.[198] He asked to be admitted to the dialysis program of a state hospital, but did not qualify for admission.[199] His claim to receive renal dialysis treatment was based on the provision in Section 27(3) of the Constitution that no-one may be refused emergency medical treatment and on the right to life in Section 11.[200]

195 L Chenwi 'Slums Act unconstitutional' (2009) 10(4) *ESR Review: Economic and Social Rights in South Africa* 9 at 12. Contrast *Kimani v AG* [2010] eKLR (High Court of Kenya, 12 March 2010).

196 1998 1 SA 765 (CC) [29]. See Bessler (n 28 above) 62; Chaskalson (n 14 above) 602 - 603, 607; Choma (n 74 above) 41 - 44, 45, 50; EC Christiansen 'Using constitutional adjudication to remedy socio-economic injustice: Comparative lesson from South Africa' (2008) 13 *University of California at Los Angeles Journal of International Law and Foreign Affairs* 369 at 382 - 383; Davis (n 41 above) 692; DM Davis *et al* 'Social rights, social citizenship, and transformative constitutionalism: A comparative assessment' in J Conaghan *et al* (eds) *Labour law in an era of globalization: Transformative practices and possibilities* (2002) 522 - 524; L Forman 'Ensuring reasonable health: Health rights, the judiciary, and South African HIV/AIDS Policy' (2005) 33 *Journal of Law, Medicine & Ethics* 711 at 713 - 714, 715; G Hogan 'Directive principles, socio-economic rights and the Constitution' (2001) 36 *Irish Jurist* 174 at 192 - 193; Kende (n 13 above) 145 - 147; JC Mubangizi 'The constitutional protection of socio-economic rights in selected African countries: A comparative evaluation' (2006) 2 *African Journal of Legal Studies* 1 at 6; Pieterse (n 11 above) 891 - 892, 899 - 901; Pillay (n 171 above) 603, 609; C Scott & P Alston 'Adjudicating constitutional priorities in a transnational context: A comment on *Soobramoney's* legacy and *Grootboom's* promise' (2000) 16 *South African Journal on Human Rights* 206 at 233 - 256; Woods (n 15 above) 779 - 783.

197 n 196 above, [1].

198 n 196 above, [5].

199 The hospital had a shortage of dialysis machines and trained nursing staff: n 196 above, [2]. Because of limited resources it had adopted a policy of admitting only those patients who could be cured within a short period and those with chronic renal failure who were eligible for a kidney transplant.

200 n 196 above, [7].

The Court held that the right not to be refused emergency medical treatment meant that a person who suffers a sudden catastrophe which calls for immediate medical attention should not be denied ambulance or other emergency services which are available and should not be turned away from a hospital which is able to provide the necessary treatment, but Mr Soobramoney did not fall into this category.[201] Chaskalson P considered the Indian case of *Paschim*,[202] where the Supreme Court in the context of a welfare state had found that a government hospital had a duty to provide timely medical assistance to a person needing life-saving treatment.[203] However, he distinguished it because there was a different context in India where the treatment was available but denied.[204]

Having rejected consideration of Mr Soobramoney's claim under Section 27(3), the Court turned to Section 27(1) and (2) to determine his right to have access to healthcare services provided by the state within its available

201 n 196 above, [20]-[21]. The 'able and available' limitation read into Section 27(3) followed on from the Court's stating without analysis that the subsection creates a negative right only: Scott & Alston (n 196 above) 236.

202 *Paschim Banga Khet Mazdoorsamity v State of West Bengal* [1996] INSC 659, 1996 (4) SCC 37. For an analysis of *Paschim*, see V Sripati 'Constitutionalism in India and South Africa: A comparative study from a human rights perspective' (2007) 16 *Tulane Journal of International and Comparative Law* 49 at 102 - 103.

203 n 196 above, [18]. Chaskalson P highlighted the context of historical disadvantage in South Africa, where there were great disparities in wealth as a legacy of apartheid, necessitating the tranformation of society by improving living conditions – including access to adequate health services – in order to achieve the constitutional aim of a society where there would be 'human dignity, freedom and equality': n 196 above, [8]. See J Small & E Grant 'Dignity, discrimination, and context: New directions in South African and Canadian human rights law' (2005) 6(2) *Human Rights Review* 25 at 43 - 44. On the need to overcome the social problems that resulted from apartheid by establishing a society based on social justice, see *Modderklip (n* 29 above) [36].

204 n 196 above, [20]. Chaskalson P pointed out that the right to medical treatment was a discrete right in the South African Constitution and, as it was not dependent on being inferred from the right to life, it could not mean that the treatment of terminal illnesses had to be prioritised over other forms of medical care such as preventative healthcare: n 196 above, [19]. The right to emergency treatment in South Africa had to be interpreted in the context of the availability of health services generally.

Craig Scott and Philip Alston have criticised the Constitutional Court for not considering *Paschim* in greater depth, as far-reaching positive duties were imposed on the state: n 196 above, 245 - 247. They considered that had Section 27(3) been interpreted in light of the right to life and the general duties to fulfil rights in Section 7 so as to generate a positive claim on resources, it would have mandated a heightened constitutional priority for emergency medical services: n 196 above, 245. See also Sripati (n 202 above) 110 - 111.

resources.[205] It deferred to the executive, as its view was that responsibility for making the difficult decisions of fixing the health budget and deciding upon the priorities that needed to be met lay with political organs and the medical authorities; it would be slow to interfere, if the decisions were rational and taken in good faith.[206] Sachs J remarked on our interdependence in society, which required a sharing of resources rather than priority being given to the rights of the autonomous individual.[207] The threshold at which one may avail oneself of a right is fixed by adjudicating between equal claims and the balancing process is not to be regarded as limiting the right of the individual failing to qualify for the service.[208] The Court accepted the reality that socio-economic rights can only be provided by the State in accordance with the resources available. It was hampered in taking action because priority-setting was the role of the executive.[209] The importance of having a healthcare policy and implementing it was stressed. Here there was a plan which ranked entitlements to medical treatment.[210]

205 n 196 above, [22]. The Court did not analyse separately the nature of his rights under Section 27(1), but focused on the state's management of scarce resources to achieve the progressive realisation of the entitlement of everyone to have access to healthcare in Section 27(2).

206 n 196 above, [29]. See D Langwallner 'Separation of powers, judicial deference and the failure to protect the rights of the individual' in O Doyle & E Carolan (eds) *The Irish Constitution: Governance and values* (2008) 270 - 271.

207 n 196 above, [54]. Woods construed Sachs J's remarks as proposing a new framework for collective rights, which substituted interdependence for autonomy as its bedrock principle: n 15 above, 782. See also Bilchitz (n 21 above) 22.

208 Contrast Young's deduction that the decision in *Soobramoney* constituted a state limitation of the right that was deemed a justifiable infringement: n 10 above, 169.

209 Scott and Alston urged the courts not to defer unduly to the other branches of government when adjudicating on the socio-economic rights in the Constitution and to take the active role envisaged for them by promoting the values of dignity, freedom and equality to transform the living conditions of the poor: n 196 above, 268.

Dikgang Moseneke pointed out that the judiciary, being vested with substantive powers of review over the exercise of public or private power, was commanded by the Constitution to observe its transformative mission; his assessment was that – but for a few decisions – the Constitutional Court had crafted an impressive body of progressive constitutional jurisprudence true to the overarching constitutional enterprise of transforming society: D Moseneke 'Transformative adjudication' (2002) 18 *South African Journal on Human Rights* 309 at 319.

210 While Mr Soobramoney contended that the refusal by the renal unit to give him the dialysis treatment he required to stay alive was unreasonable, it was not suggested that the hospital *guidelines* were unreasonable or that they were not applied fairly and rationally when the hospital decided that he did not qualify for dialysis: n 196 above, [25], [44]. Madala J pointed out that constitutional rights are not absolute and may be limited by scarce resources, stating, 'the Constitution accepts that it cannot solve all of our society's woes overnight, but must go on trying to resolve these problems.': n 196 above, [43].

Daniel Erskine described the Court's purposive rational decision approach to the interpretation of conflicting rights in this case as pragmatic, acutely focusing on the exercise of rights within the reality presented, and concluded that the Court's interpretation allowed full effect to be given to Mr Soobramoney's rights while honouring them in relation to the overall constitutional text.[211] Mark Kende commented that the ruling illustrated that a court can take socio-economic rights seriously and yet still respect separation of powers concerns and legislative competence.[212] The Court supported the utilitarian choice by the political organs and the medical authorities; most scholars accept that Mr Soobramoney's interest in prolonging his life had to be sacrificed in the interest of the general welfare.[213]

However, Woods criticised the Court's adoption of a utilitarian perspective as 'extremely problematic' reasoning in a rights context, since the point of giving policy choices the priority status of fundamental rights is to avoid the utilitarianism inherent in majority decision making.[214] She has interpreted the decision as indicating that the Court would not consider the state's resources as a whole, but in effect limited the state's duty to whatever resources it had already allocated to healthcare in general, and dialysis in particular.[215] Brian Ray pointed out that the Court established a restrained approach to interpreting the right to healthcare in *Soobramoney*, as it deferred to the government's justification for the resource allocation policy by applying a basic rationality standard.[216] But the Court nonetheless signalled a willingness to look behind government justifications for particular socio-economic programmes where appropriate and required that the justifications also be taken in good faith, suggesting that the Court will not only test the government's policy decisions against an objective rationality standard but will consider subjective evidence that the government's objectively reasonable actions are designed to evade its constitutional obligations.[217]

Writing extrajudicially, Arthur Chaskalson indicated that where the lack of human or financial resources is put in issue by the state, more than a 'bald

211 n 138 above, 610 - 611.

212 n 13 above, 147.

213 Lehmann (n 9 above) 169. See also Brand (n 2 above) 215, 223, 227.

214 n 15 above, 782. See also Liebenberg (n 155 above) 5.

215 n 15 above, 780.

216 n 22 above, 157 - 158.

217 Ray (n 22 above) above, 158.

assertion' of resource constraints will be required.[218] He cited *Soobramoney* as an example of where the state had to give details of the character of the constraints to be assessed on the reasonableness standard, thereby conforming to the principles of accountability and effectiveness.[219] The Court concluded that 'available resources' has both a wide and narrow application; the wide application of the term resources means the national resources, including donor aid money, and the narrow application of resources refers to the executive's budgeted resources for a particular section/department; while the Court took the view that budget allocation should be primarily left to the executive, the Court, however, could examine the use of resources.[220]

In later cases where there was more scope for criticising the authorities' guidelines and their implementation, the Constitutional Court developed the reasonableness criterion – the seeds of which had been sown in *Soobramoney* – and showed that it was prepared to exercise its constitutional role in upholding individual rights against the state. As a consequence of the decision, Mr Soobramoney had to face death without further medical intervention, but it is difficult to put forward a cogent argument from a legal perspective that the Court's finding should have been different in circumstances where there were reasonable guidelines in place to deal with limited resources and where the guidelines had been applied rationally.[221] I disagree with Wesson's view that the approach in *Soobramoney* seems to have been largely abandoned and that instead *Grootboom* laid the foundation for the adjudication of socio-economic rights.[222] He does not support his allegation with any evidence or arguments.[223]

Access to healthcare under Section 27 was in issue again in the *TAC* case, which arose because the government restricted dissemination of an anti-

218 n 1 above, 33.

219 n 1 above, 33 - 34, fn 30.

220 Ansah (n 7 above) 441.

221 See Hogan (n 196 above) 193.

222 n 129 above, 285.

223 Other scholars have made reasoned criticism of the Court's methodology in *Soobramoney* on the grounds that it was utilitarian, employed a basic rationality standard, or failed to marshall far-reaching positive duties latent in the Constitution by a superficial analysis of comparative jurisprudence and by not giving full force to Section 27(1) independently of Section 27(2). But they have not seriously challenged the outcome. There have been yet more scholars who have praised the Court in *Soobramoney* for being pragmatic, respecting the separation of powers, and requiring details of the adoption and implementation of the guidelines.

HIV drug for pregnant mothers.[224] The Treatment Action Campaign (TAC) wanted the restrictions lifted. Not only did the Court make a declaratory order that Section 27(1) and (2) of the Constitution require the government to devise and implement within its available resources a comprehensive and co-ordinated programme to realise progressively the rights of pregnant women and their newborn children to have access to health services to combat mother-to-child-transmission of HIV, but it went further and made a mandatory order directing the government without delay to make the drug available and to take reasonable measures to extend the testing and counselling facilities at hospitals and clinics throughout the public health sector.[225] It reiterated the attitude it had taken to the minimum core in *Grootboom*, ruling out a self-standing right 'entitling everyone to demand that the minimum core be provided to them', although the minimum core

224 n 17 above. See Brand (n 2 above) 220, 223 - 224, 228, 229; Chaskalson (n 14 above) 605 - 607; Choma (n 74 above) 46 - 48; Davis (n 41 above) 694 - 697; Erskine (n 138 above) 632 - 634; Forman (n 196 above) 715, 717 - 718, 719; Kende (n 13 above) 147 - 150; Kende (n 136 above) 251 - 254; JC Mubangizi & BK Twinomugisha 'The right to health care in the specific context of access to HIV/AIDS medicines: What can South Africa and Uganda learn from each other?' (2010) 10 *African Human Rights Law Journal* 105 at 115 - 116, 118 - 119, 131 - 132; Pieterse (n 11 above) 894 - 895; Pillay (n 171 above) 604 - 605, 607; Woods (n 15 above) 786 - 790.

225 n 17 above, [135]. The Court recognised the government's role in developing policies when it acknowledged that the mandatory orders it made did not preclude the government from adapting its policy in a manner consistent with the Constitution if equally appropriate or better methods became available to it for the prevention of mother-to-child-transmission of HIV: as above. The Constitutional Court did not go as far as the High Court, which had granted a structural interdict requiring the State to submit its revised policy to the court to enable it to satisfy itself that it was consistent with the Constitution; it felt that was not necessary since the government had always respected and executed orders of the Constitutional Court and there was no reason to believe that it would not do so: n 17 above, [129].

In 2006 the High Court made a structural interdict (an order with a supervisory component) compelling the provision of anti-retroviral treatment to prisoners with HIV/AIDS: *EN v Government of RSA* [2006] AHRLR 326 (SAHC 2006) [32]-[33], [35]; it subsequently ordered that it be implemented forthwith: *EN v Government of RSA* 28 August 2006 (High Court, Durban and Coast Local Division). See K Roach & G Budlender 'Mandatory relief and supervisory jurisdiction: When is it appropriate, just and equitable?' (2005) 122 *South African Law Journal* 325 at 328 - 335.

Ray considered that the most significant aspect of the decision in *TAC* was the specific terms of the order, when the Court – in a marked departure from previous cases – required the government to take specific action to correct the constitutional defect, but later in the same order gave the government express permission to ignore that directive and determine for itself what specific action Section 27 required: n 22 above, 164.

Eric Christiansen pointed out that the order in *TAC* had a wide impact, as it not only resulted in a significant expansion of testing and counselling related to HIV

might be relevant in certain circumstances to the test of reasonableness under Section 27(2).[226]

TAC had argued that *Grootboom* did not go far enough, that the Bill of Rights was based on the notion of individual rights and therefore the courts should assist an individual whose circumstances fell short of achieving the minimum core of entitlements consistent with the maintenance of human dignity.[227] The Court rejected that argument and decided that the minimum core obligation could be satisfied through broad government programmes aimed at meeting minimum needs.[228] While Rosalind Dixon confirmed that the Court granted a stronger remedy than it had in *Grootboom* by making a mandatory order, she pointed out the weakness in the Court's decision by prescribing a purely declaratory remedy – without a deadline – with regard to the government's general obligation to develop and implement a plan for the full rollout of the drug.[229] There has been criticism of *TAC* for not embracing the minimum core.[230] David Bilchitz suggested that the Order in *TAC*

transmission, but also identified minimum standards that presumably apply in many related healthcare circumstances; furthermore, it highlighted the additional risk that the judiciary may require greater action than might have been taken by the executive or legislature had governmental discretion been exercised in an adequate timely manner: n 196 above, 401. See also Christiansen (n 15 above) 590; Langwallner (n 206 above) 271.

226 n 17 above, [34].

227 n 17 above, [28]; Sachs (n 11 above) 181.

228 Sachs (n 11 above) 182. Sachs, writing extrajudicially, considered that the Court's decision made the best use of scarce resources to realise socio-economic rights and that to concede to TAC's submission would have been to prioritise those who pursued their rights vigorously with the best lawyers: n 11 above, 181.

If social rights are understood as collective rights, individual remedies are not necessarily the most efficacious response; *TAC* illustrates that a court order enforcing a constitutional legislative command ultimately will benefit specific individuals: Woods (n 15 above) 790. As Christiansen concluded, even a holding affecting only a single person can force the government to rethink and reformulate its response to a diverse set of social welfare needs: n 196 above, 401, citing *Njongi* (n 3 above).

229 R Dixon 'Creating dialogue about socioeconomic rights: Strong-form versus weak-form judicial review revisited' (2007) 5 *International Journal of Constitutional Law* 391 at 398. Wesson considered that the crucial factor that separated *TAC* from *Grootboom* was not greater assertiveness on the part of the Court, but the fact that extending an entitlement to a drug – where medically indicated and where, if necessary, testing and counselling were available – had only limited cost-implications and did not involve issues requiring great expertise: n 129 above, 296. Lehmann also identified the negligible cost implications as a distinguishing feature in *TAC*: n 9 above, 175. Another distinction was that the interests of the individual HIV-positive pregnant women and their children were commensurate with the general public welfare that they receive treatment: n 9 above, 176.

230 Wesson (n 129 above) fn 6, citing Bilchitz (n 21 above).

could have been improved by the Court retaining supervisory jurisdiction, the absence of which shows undue deference to the other branches of government and an unwillingness to retain responsibility for the effectiveness of its orders.[231] Where a person's survival is at stake, the Court should adopt a robust approach to protect the most vulnerable.[232] *TAC* was not revolutionary and did not copper-fasten the right to a minimum core in all circumstances, but the Court found a more practical remedy that proved more effective than that in *Grootboom*.[233]

The issue of immigrants' entitlements to welfare was raised in *Khosa*.[234] Destitute Mozambicans with permanent residency in South Africa had been refused welfare assistance on the basis that they were not South African citizens.[235] The Court unanimously held that the provisions relating to children were unconstitutional, as they established grants for children whose parents were South African citizens but failed to provide for children who might be South African citizens and whose parents were not.[236] The Court was divided on the rights of adult immigrants. The majority held that the Constitution vests the right to social security in 'everyone' and that permanent residents are bearers of this right, so their exclusion from the welfare scheme was not a reasonable way to achieve the realisation of the right to social

231 n 21 above, 26.

232 As above. Bilchitz has proposed that there be progressive realisation of the recognition of animals as having worth in their own right, which would most likely mean that meat-eating would only be permissible where necessary for a human being's survival, as the animals' interest in life and to be free from suffering would outweigh the right of most humans to kill them for food: D Bilchitz 'Moving beyond arbitrariness: The legal personhood and dignity of non-human animals' (2009) 25 *South African Journal on Human Rights* 38 at 69.

233 Iain Currie and Johan de Waal comment that the Constitutional Court's treatment of the content of the right to healthcare is minimal, because its general approach to the positive dimensions of socio-economic rights is to avoid giving them content and to adjudicate instead of the reasonableness of the implementation measures: I Currie & J de Waal *The Bill of Rights handbook* (2005) 591.

234 *Khosa v Minister of Social Development* 2004 6 SA 505 (CC). See Brand (n 2 above) 215, 228; Choma (n 74 above) 49; Kende (n 136 above) 254 - 256; Liebenberg (n 21 above) 82 - 83, 87 - 89; S Liebenberg & B Goldblatt 'The interrelationship between equality and socio-economic rights under South Africa's transformative constitution' (2007) 23 *South African Journal on Human Rights* 335 at 344 - 345, 356 - 357, 358 - 359; KG Young 'A typology of economic and social rights adjudication: Exploring the catalytic function of judicial review' (2010) 8 *International Journal of Constitutional Law* 385 at 407 - 409, 415 - 417.

235 n 234 above, [2]-[3].

236 n 234 above, [78], [136].

security in Section 27.[237] The legislation also infringed the right to equality, as it was discriminatory and unfair, and not justified under the limitation clause.[238] The Court read in the words 'or permanent resident' after the word 'citizen' in each of the challenged provisions in the relevant legislation.[239]

Mokgoro J for the majority saw that the basic necessities were essential in a country where human dignity was valued.[240] She considered that the lack of funds to survive without seeking help from the community was likely to have a 'serious impact on the dignity' of the permanent residents who were 'cast in the role of supplicants.'[241] Notwithstanding their disagreement on the outcome, dignity was accepted by all the judges as a central con-

237 n 234 above, [85]. Context was all important when considering reasonableness and it was relevant to consider the purpose served by social security, the impact of the exclusion from it, the relevance of the citizenship requirement to that purpose and the impact on other intersecting rights – in this case equality rights: n 234 above, [49]. Wesson thought that *Khosa* sharpened the reasonableness standard to some extent and that the Court was certainly more willing than in *Grootboom* to impose far-reaching financial obligations on the state where it failed to meet the reasonableness standard: n 129 above, 297.

Unlike in *Soobramoney* and *Grootboom* where the Court specifically noted that the government policies were developed in good faith, the majority in *Khosa* found that the policy judgments in this case were the result of a flawed process as evidenced by the government's conduct throughout the litigation, when it failed to meet deadlines set by the Court and incurred a punitive wasted costs order, which the Court felt was warranted because of its wilful default in both the High and Constitutional Courts and its failure to comply with Court directions: Ray (n 22 above) 165 - 166.

238 n 234 above, [80]. The fact that the applicants were part of a vulnerable group in society was relevant and rendered them worthy of constitutional protection in circumstances where intentional, statutorily sanctioned unequal treatment stigmatised them in the community: n 234 above, [74]. A central constitutional principle is that the interests of the most vulnerable must be protected: Bilchitz (n 232 above) 39. Bilchitz gave *Khosa* as an example of a case where, in relation to equality, the vulnerability of a particular group was an important factor in determining whether or not unfair discrimination was present: n 232 above, fn 5, citing n 234 above, [71]-[74].

239 n 234 above, [89]. The minority thought that the exclusions were a reasonable limitation of the right of access to social security, and accepted the State's argument that there were insufficient resources to provide for everyone within the country's borders and it was entitled to prioritise its citizens: n 234 above, [120], [134].

240 n 234 above, [52] (footnote omitted):

> The right of access to social security, including social assistance, for those unable to support themselves and their dependants is entrenched because as a society we value human beings and want to ensure that people are afforded their basic needs. A society must seek to ensure that the basic necessities of life are accessible to all if it is to be a society in which human dignity, freedom and equality are foundational.

241 n 234 above, [76]. Liebenberg pointed out that Mokgoro J subverted the normal discourse around social assistance creating dependency on the state by highlighting its role in relieving the burden on poor communities and fostering the dignity of permanent residents; she used this to illustrate how the courts can contribute to transformation

stitutional value.[242] Dignity was a criterion to be applied in assessing other rights and in coming to a decision on whether a limitation on a right was justifiable.[243] The constitutional guarantee of social security was given concrete effect even though resources were limited.[244] Perhaps this is because the extension of welfare was achievable and affordable – unlike the granting of housing rights.

Mazibuko was the first case to raise the right of access to water.[245] Residents in Phiri, an area in Soweto, challenged arrangements for the supply of water because they considered that the free basic water allowance was insufficient and that the introduction of pre-paid meters was unlawful and discriminatory. They relied, *inter alia*, on the right of access to sufficient water in Section 27(1)(b), which led to consideration of the extent of the state's duty under Section 27(2) to progressively realise that right within available resources. The selection of Phiri for installation of pre-paid meters founded their claim of violation of the right to equality in Section 9(1) by differentiating without rational connection to a legitimate government purpose. The absence in Phiri of the choice of using credit meters, which were installed in households in the affluent white suburbs, was the basis of their allegation of unfair racial discrimination contrary to Section 9(3). The High Court[246] and the Supreme

by their rhetorical role in social rights judgments, which is important even where the courts feel constrained by institutional politics from making orders that will have an extensive impact on existing budgetary allocations: n 155 above, 7.

242 n 234 above, [52], [114].

243 Davis considers that the Court took the bold decision to extend social benefits to permanent residents by focusing on the concepts of dignity and equality rather than on the express wording of Section 27 – its approach apparently unfettered by the reasonableness standard that dominated the earlier cases: n 41 above, 703.

244 The majority imposed a higher standard on the South African State for the granting of welfare than on more affluent countries like the US, Canada and the UK, where citizenship was a qualifying criterion: n 234 above, [54], [124]. Davis concluded that *Khosa* and *Modderklip (n* 29 above) moved beyond the administrative law approach to socioeconomic rights adopted in the early cases: n 41 above, 704. On *Modderklip*, see Brand (n 2 above) 214; Davis (n 41 above) 704, 708; Kende (n 136 above) 258 - 259; Liebenberg (n 21 above) 92 - 93, 100; Ray (n 22 above) 188 - 191.

245 *Mazibuko v City of Johannesburg* [2009] ZACC 28. See T Humby & M Grandbois 'The human right to water in South Africa and the *Mazibuko* decisions' (2010) 51 *Les Cahiers de Droit* 521; Pillay (n 171 above) 613 - 616; M Wesson 'Reasonableness in retreat? The judgment of the South African Constitutional Court in *Mazibuko v City of Johannesburg*' (2011) 11 *Human Rights Law Review* 390 at 390 - 391, 394 - 405.

246 For reviews and assessments of the High Court decision, see Choma (n 74 above) 51 - 53; M Langford & A Russell '"Global precedent" or "reasonable no more"? The *Mazibuko* case' (2008) 19 *Journal of Water Law* 73; SC McCaffrey & KJ Neville 'Small capacity and big responsibilities: Financial and legal implications of a human

Court of Appeal[247] held in their favour against the City of Johannesburg, but the Constitutional Court unanimously overturned the lower courts' decisions and found that the state's measures were reasonable and not in breach of equality rights.

O'Regan J delivered the Court's judgment and analysed the considerable amount of evidence presented in great detail.[248] Consistently with its stance in *Grootboom* and *TAC*, the Court found that Section 27(1) did not grant a right to everyone on demand to sufficient water, but had to be read with the positive duty on the state in Section 27(2) to take reasonable measures within available resources to implement progressively the right of access to water.[249] O'Regan J deferred to the government's better institutional capacity to decide on the level of service to provide based on the resources available.[250]

One important limitation of *Grootboom* is that usually there is no obligation on the state to go beyond the national targeted minimum standard for those already receiving it until all have achieved the minimum.[251] On the equality aspect, the Constitutional Court found that the installation of pre-paid meters in Soweto was because the revenue generated from the water service there was much less proportionate to that received from other areas and, as the unaccounted for water was greatest there, the introduction of pre-

right to water for developing countries' (2009) 21 *Georgetown International Environmental Law Review* 679 at 686 - 693; LJ van Rensburg 'The right of access to adequate water [discussion of *Mazibuko v the City of Johannesburg* case no 13865/06]' (2008) 19 *Stellenbosch Law Review* 415; Williams (n 136 above) 22 - 35.

247 See Williams (n 136 above) 45 - 46.

248 The state was obliged to justify its water policy in Johannesburg meticulously. Every aspect was examined, such as the purpose of the measures, which was to address the serious problems of unaccounted for water loss and the high level of non-payment of water charges in Soweto. The City of Johannesburg accepted its constitutional obligation to progressively provide sufficient water to all. It had considered the advantages and disadvantages of the various options available before selecting the solution to be implemented in Phiri as a pilot project before being rolled out to other areas in Soweto. The policy catered for those who could not afford to pay by allowing them to come forward to be means-tested and registered as indigent; those on the register were obliged to accept pre-paid meters.

249 n 245 above, [50].

250 She felt it desirable that the democratically elected and accountable organ of state should have that role: n 245 above, [61].

251 n 245 above, [76] (O'Regan J) (footnote omitted):

> In most circumstances it will be reasonable for municipalities and provinces to strive first to achieve the prescribed (and, in the absence of a challenge, presumptively reasonable) minimum standard, before being required to go beyond that minimum standard for those to whom the minimum is already being supplied. This is consistent with this Court's jurisprudence in *Grootboom* where the Court held that a government policy may not ignore the needs of the most vulnerable.

paid meters was not irrational.[252] Therefore the differentiation between categories of people was rationally connected to a legitimate government purpose and passed muster under Section 9(1).

O'Regan J used the *Harksen*[253] criteria to determine whether the measures were unfair discrimination.[254] There was no racial discrimination, since other poor black areas did not have pre-paid meters.[255] According to O'Regan J's analysis, in any event, the difference between the pre-paid and credit meters was not disadvantageous to the residents in Phiri.[256] The fact that there was no choice to have a credit meter in Phiri was not discriminatory, because those in the white suburbs had effectively little option to have a pre-paid meter.[257] She pointed out the need for differential measures to redress poverty caused by past inequality, 'correcting the deep inequality which characterises our society, as a consequence of apartheid policies, will often require differential treatment.'[258]

Unlike the lower courts, the Constitutional Court, in line with previous decisions, refused to specify a minimum core or to give content to the concept of 'sufficient water'.[259] In answer to the residents' submission that it was pointless to litigate socio-economic rights if the courts were not going to specify the content of the rights, O'Regan J – conscious of the limitations on the judicial system to assess these matters – pointed out that the court's role was to hold the government to account for the reasonableness of its measures.[260] If the government failed to act at all, the courts would oblige it

252 n 245 above, [145]-[147].

253 *Harksen v Lane* 1998 1 SA 300 (CC).

254 n 245 above, [151].

255 n 245 above, [149].

256 n 245 above, [154]. Although they formed a vulnerable group, the purpose for which the pre-paid meters were installed was 'a laudable, indeed necessary, government objective, clearly tailored to its purpose': as above.

257 n 245 above, [155].

258 n 245 above, [156]. Where there is a wide wealth gap in society, the concentration of economic power at the upper end of the income distribution has tremendous effects on the distribution of power and benefits the wealthy: S Sreedhar & C Delmas 'State legitimacy and political obligation in *Justice for hedgehogs*: The radical potential of Dworkinian dignity' (2010) 90 *Boston University Law Review* 737 at 756.

259 n 245 above, [56]. What was a reasonable quantity amounting to sufficient water would vary depending on the contextual issues such as the geographical and temporal circumstances – the state's obligation, after all, was to progressively implement the right of access to water within available resources, both of which can change over time.

260 n 245 above, [161].

to do so.[261] It if had acted, it would assess its policy for reasonableness.[262] A policy could be unreasonable, as in *Grootboom*, because it omitted to provide for those in desperate need,[263] or, as in *TAC*, because its policy contained unreasonable limitations or exclusions.[264] There was also an obligation on the state to keep its policy under review,[265] and this the City had done in *Mazibuko* by making changes following monitoring, research and analysing surveys carried out to see how the policy was being implemented.[266] The constitutional obligation on the government did not require it 'to be held to an impossible standard of perfection' and the Constitution did not require courts 'to take over the tasks that in a democracy should properly be reserved for the democratic arms of government.'[267] Rather, through the medium of the courts, the government could 'be called upon to account to citizens for

261 n 245 above, [67].

262 As above.

263 As above. Jenny Wakely described O'Regan J's statement that a measure would be unreasonable only if it made *no* provision for those most desperately in need as an 'extremely low standard' for determining reasonableness (arguably no higher than the 'rationality' requirement in *Soobramoney*) and submitted that a higher standard would be constitutionally permissible without infringing on the separation of powers or on the State's democratic legitimacy particularly in light of the express protection for socio-economic rights in the Constitution: J Wakely 'Social and economic rights – A retreat by the South African Constitutional Court?' (2010) 28 *Irish Law Times* 153 at 155. However, Wakely does not seem to have taken into account that O'Regan J went on to confirm that limitations in the policy would also be assessed for reasonableness. The limitations to be examined would presumably include those applicable to the most needy.

264 n 245 above, [67].

265 As above.

266 Some changes had been made since the litigation started, which indicated that the City was pro-active. O'Regan J commented that if the litigation has prompted the changes, this was beneficial: n 245 above, [163]. It justified the considerable effort and cost of litigating. She outlined what litigation adds to a participative democracy, n 245 above, [160]:

> The purpose of litigation concerning the positive obligations imposed by social and economic rights should be to hold the democratic arms of government to account through litigation. In so doing, litigation of this sort fosters a form of participative democracy that holds government accountable and requires it to account between elections over specific aspects of government policy.

A participative democracy is a partnership between the people as a whole and government, and is distinct from a majoritarian, merely statistical conception of democracy, as it fuses democracy and state legitimacy: Sreedhar & Delmas (n 258 above) 749. In this passage the Constitutional Court re-emphasised that socio-economic rights play primarily a political role: Ray (n 135 above) 371.

267 n 245 above, [161].

its decisions' in compliance with the constitutional principles requiring government to be responsive, accountable and open.[268]

Some elements of O'Regan's reasoning are questionable. At times she strained the meaning of words and the text she was interpreting.[269] However, she did keep pressure on the state by requiring a continual review of policies and making it clear that the courts would insist that this be done and be shown to be done. She enhanced understanding of the role of the courts in conflicts over socio-economic demands by illustrating how litigation arising is part of the participative democratic system of holding government accountable. Her judgment showed considerable deference to the other organs of state.[270] It must be disheartening for some to find that there can be no hope of compelling the state to improve their conditions until all have achieved the same standard they have already reached.

268 As above. Davis pointed out that socio-economic jurisprudence is one important means to achieve the implementation of the critical principles of transparency, accountability and participation: n 41 above, 710. On the interests of all in transparency and responsiveness in a constitutional democracy, where 'dialogue and the right to have a voice on public affairs is constitutive of dignity', see Sachs J in *Minister of Health v New Clicks South Africa (Pty) Ltd* 2006 2 SA 311 (CC) [627]. Jonathan Lewis has criticised the latter case: J Lewis 'The Constitutional Court of South Africa' (2009) 125 *Law Quarterly Review* 440 at 444, 455 - 456, 465.

269 *Eg*, when she downplayed the significance of *TAC*: n 245 above, [64]. See P de Vos 'Water is life (but life is cheap)' (13 October 2009) http://constitutionallyspeaking.co.za/water-is-life-but-life-is-cheap/ (accessed 18 March 2010).

270 Wakely described the Court's approach as 'conservative' and found its decision surprising as it represented 'a significantly deferential attitude' in comparison with some of its earlier judgments: n 263 above, 154, 155.

7

Human Dignity and Human Rights in Irish

7.1 Historical development

The Irish courts have referred to dignity sporadically.[1] Initially it was solely in the context of using the Preamble to the Constitution as an interpretative tool.[2] One of the Constitution's goals is to assure the dignity and freedom of the individual. It is combined with the aim of attaining true social order.[3] As Irish society and law moved closer to Europe, the European socialist emphasis on dignity crept into Irish jurisprudence. Its significant place in the case-law on the European Convention on Human Rights (ECHR)[4] had an influence on the Irish outlook and with the incorporation of the ECHR into Irish law, European legal norms have binding force.

1 T John O'Dowd identified four themes in the use of human dignity by Irish judges, *ie*, first, it is a, if not *the*, fundamental constitutional value; second, it implies that each human being is entitled to be treated as being of equal worth and value in and for themselves; third, it relates to a conception of the essential attributes of human personality, which are typically realised through the development of natural human capacities; fourth, it is the basis for specific rights or entitlements and helps to determine their weight and content: TJ O'Dowd 'Dignity and personhood in Irish constitutional law' in G Quinn *et al* (eds) *Justice and legal theory in Ireland* (1995) 165 - 166.

2 See *State (Burke) v Lennon* [1940] IR 136 at 143 (HC, Gavan Duffy J), 178 (SC, Geoghegan J); *Buckley (Sinn Féin) v AG* [1950] IR 67 (SC) 80; *Re Philip Clarke* [1950] IR 235 (SC) 246, 248.

3 The other aims are to achieve national unity and establish harmonious international relationships.

4 Convention for the Protection of Human Rights and Fundamental Freedoms, 213 UNTS 222 (ECHR).

In contrast to the English tradition, Continental European culture and law has placed a high value on dignity.[5] In Europe dignity was associated with republicanism, 'dignities' in the sense of aristocratic privileges being extended to all citizens as a result of the French Revolution.[6] Based on the philosophy of Jean-Jacques Rousseau, it had a communitarian emphasis and was linked with fraternity rather than with liberty, which is more highly esteemed in North America.[7] The movement for social reform during the nineteenth century invoked the concept of dignity.[8] From the middle of that century the demand for humane conditions of existence became a prominent socialist slogan.[9] The 'dignity of labour' supported calls for egalitarianism and the provision of social welfare by the state.[10] The French Catholic philosopher, Jacques Maritain, was influential in bringing the concept of human dignity into practical international politics after World War II in reaction to the excesses of Nazism.[11] He viewed human rights as essential for promotion of the common good rather than as espousing radical ethical individualism.[12] Eschewing communism as well as liberal individualism, Maritain promoted a personalistic type of society, whose advocates he described as seeing the mark of human dignity in the power to make the 'goods of nature serve the common conquest of intrinsically human, moral, and spiritual goods and of man's freedom of autonomy.'[13]

In Ireland dignity as a value has informed other constitutional rights. In his seminal judgment in *Quinn's Supermarket v AG* in 1971, Walsh J

5 The tension between the two traditions manifested itself in Quebec, where the Francophones felt that the cultural dignity of the French was insufficiently respected by much of Anglo Canada: CA MacKinnon *Are women human? And other international dialogues* (2006) 77.

6 C McCrudden 'Human dignity and judicial interpretation of human rights' (2008) 19 *European Journal of International Law* 655 at 660.

7 As above. See also MA Glendon *A world made new: Eleanor Roosevelt and the Universal Declaration of Human Rights* (2001) xvii.

8 McCrudden (n 6 above) 660.

9 J Eckert 'Legal roots of human dignity in German law' in D Kretzmer & E Klein (eds) *The concept of human dignity in human rights discourse* (2002) 47.

10 McCrudden (n 6 above) 661.

11 McCrudden (n 6 above) 662. On Maritain's participation in the human rights project, see S Waltz 'Universalising human rights: The role of small states in the construction of the Universal Declaration of Human Rights' (2001) 23 *Human Rights Quarterly* 44 at 47.

12 McCrudden (n 6 above) 662.

13 J Maritain *Natural law: Reflections on theory and practice* (2001) 74.

pronounced the equality guarantee in Article 40.1 as relating to the dignity of human beings:[14]

> [T]his provision [Art 40.1] is not a guarantee of absolute equality for all citizens in all circumstances but it is a guarantee of equality as human persons and ... is a guarantee related to their dignity as human beings and a guarantee against any inequalities grounded upon an assumption, or indeed a belief, that some individual or individuals or classes of individuals, by reason of their human attributes or their ethnic or racial, social or religious background, are to be treated as the inferior or superior of other individuals in the community. This list does not pretend to be complete; but it is merely intended to illustrate the view that this guarantee refers to human persons for what they are in themselves rather than to any lawful activities, trades or disputes which they may engage in or follow.

Kenny J demonstrated an extraordinarily restrictive view of equality in *Murtagh Properties v Cleary*, where he completely emasculated Article 40.1 in his consideration of the objection by the barmen's union to the employment of women in pubs.[15] The guarantee in relation to personal rights under Article 40.3 has proven more useful in practice than the equality guarantee in Article 40.1.[16]

14 [1972] IR 1 (SC) 13. See W Binchy 'Dignity as a constitutional concept' in O Doyle & E Carolan (eds) *The Irish Constitution: Governance and values* (2008) 317, 320 - 321; O Doyle 'Article 44: Privileging the rights of the religious' in Doyle & Carolan above, 479 - 481; O Doyle 'The human personality doctrine in constitutional equality law' (2001) 9 *Irish Student Law Review* 101 at 103 - 106, 112; O Doyle *Constitutional equality law* (2004) 70 - 71, 82 - 83, 89, 111 - 112, 127 - 130, 136; O Doyle *Constitutional law: Text, cases and materials* (2008) [3-34]–[3-38], [3-42], [10-07]–[10-08], [10-23], [17-08].

15 [1972] IR 330 (HC). See Doyle 'The human personality doctrine in constitutional equality law' (n 14 above) 104; Doyle *Constitutional equality law* (n 14 above) 128, 160; Doyle *Constitutional law: Text, cases and materials* (n 14 above) [3-35], [5-34].

16 G Hogan & G Whyte *JM Kelly: The Irish Constitution* (2004) [7.2.05]. Some members of the Supreme Court relied on Article 40.1 in finding that the exclusion of non-ratepayers and women from juries was unconstitutional, while others considered that there was a breach of Article 38.5 because juries were not representative: *de Búrca v AG* [1976] IR 38 (SC). Article 40.1 was one of the constitutional provisions breached in: *King v AG* [1981] IR 233 (HC, SC) (the offence of loitering with intent); *CM v TM (No 2)* [1990] 2 IR 52 (HC) (wife's dependent domicile); *W v W* [1993] 2 IR 476 (SC) (approved of *CM v TM (No 2)*; *McKinley v Minister for Defence* [1992] 2 IR 333 (SC) (extension to wife of husband's common law right to sue for loss of *consortium* and *servitium*). It was also breached in: *O'G v AG* [1985] ILRM 61 (HC) (ineligibity of a childless widower to adopt a child already in his custody); *McMahon v Leahy* [1984] IR 525 (SC) (unequal treatment in extradition of an escaper); *SM v Ireland*

O'Hanlon J made extensive references to dignity and equality in Catholic tracts, the primary school curriculum and UN texts, when he made a declaration in the High Court in 1993 in *O'Donoghue v Minister for Health* that the State had failed to provide for free primary education of a profoundly handicapped boy contrary to Article 42.[17]

Because of excessive reverence for the separation of powers doctrine[18] and a fear of intruding on the territory of the legislature and executive, the Irish courts have failed to deliver socio-economic rights backed by effective remedies. There were some exceptional cases where mandatory orders were made in the 1990s in the High Court.[19] In 1988 Costello J in *O'Reilly v*

(No 2) [2007] IEHC 280, [2007] 4 IR 369 (difference in maximum sentence for indecent assault based on gender of victim). Article 40.1 'requires that people who appear before the Courts in essentially the same circumstances should be dealt with in essentially the same manner': *State (Keegan) v Stardust Victims' Compensation Tribunal* [1986] IR 642 (SC) 658; *Dunphy v DPP* [2005] IESC 75, [2005] 3 IR 585 [30].

There was no breach of Article 40.1 in: *Heaney v Minister for Finance* [1986] ILRM 164 (HC) (alleged inequality in the prize bond scheme); *Kerry Co-Operative Creameries Ltd v An Bord Bainne Co-Operative Ltd* [1990] ILRM 664 (HC) (allocation of shares based on a member's current trading); *Browne v AG* [1991] 2 IR 58 (HC) (taxation of company cars also used privately by sales representatives); *People (DPP) v Quilligan (No 3)* [1993] 2 IR 305 (SC) (no invidious discrimination in treatment of those arrested under Offences against the State Act 1939 and those arrested on other grounds); *Bloomer v Incorporated Law Society of Ireland* [1995] 3 IR 14 (HC) (value of an academic qualification); *McMenamin v Ireland* [1996] 3 IR 100 (HC, SC) (judges' qualification for full pension); *Molyneux v Ireland* [1997] 2 ILRM 241 (HC) (power of arrest without warrant for aggravated assault in Dublin only); *Riordan v An Taoiseach* [2000] 4 IR 537 (HC, SC) (government appointment without prior public advertisement); *Re Article 26 and ss. 5 and 10 of the Illegal Immigrants (Trafficking) Bill 1999* [2000] IESC 19, [2000] 2 IR 360 (non-nationals' access to courts); *Criminal Assets Bureau v PS* [2004] IEHC 351, [2009] 3 IR 9 (anonymity of CAB witnesses); *Gavrylyuk v Minister for Justice, Equality and Law Reform* [2008] IEHC 321 (immigrants who had not been informed of deportation order permitted to seek subsidiary protection); *JD v Residential Institutions Redress Review Committee* [2009] IESC 59, [2010] 1 IR 262 (exclusion on grounds of age from voluntary redress scheme).

17 [1993] IEHC 2, [1996] 2 IR 20 at 48, 52 - 56. On *O'Donoghue*, see Doyle *Constitutional law: Text, cases and materials* (n 14 above) [9-116]; G Shannon *Child law* (2010) [3-03], [3-197].

18 The separation of powers doctrine (a central feature of the Constitution) is dealt with in provisions relating to the legislature, executive and judiciary, *viz*, no law is to be made save by the Oireachtas (Art 15.2.1°), the executive power of the State in both domestic and foreign affairs is vested in the Government (Arts 28.2 & 29.4.1°), and only the courts may exercise the judicial function save in the case of limited functions in the non-criminal field (Arts 34.1 & 37.1): DG Morgan *A judgment too far? Judicial activism and the Constitution* (2001) 84. See also DG Morgan '"Judicial-o-centric" separation of powers on the wane?' (2004) 39 *Irish Jurist* 142.

19 *DB v Minister for Justice* [1999] 1 IR 29; *Sinnott v Minister for Education* [2001] 2 IR 545 (overturned on appeal). See G Whyte 'The role of the Supreme Court in our democracy: A response to Mr Justice Hardiman' (2006) 28 *Dublin University Law Journal* 1 at 9 - 10.

Limerick Corporation in the High Court opened the door to the possibility of judicial activism in this area when he accepted it was arguable that freedom and dignity required the provision of basic services for homeless and deprived young people.[20] However, he distinguished between commutative and distributive justice,[21] and concluded that the courts had no role in deciding the latter, stating:[22]

> I am sure that the concept of justice which is to be found in the Constitution embraces the concept that the nation's wealth should be justly distributed (that is the concept of distributative justice), but I am equally sure that a claim that this has not occurred should, to comply with the Constitution, be advanced in Leinster House rather than in the Four Courts.

A person's home is constitutionally inviolable because free and secure occupation of it is necessary for human dignity. When the Court of Criminal Appeal held in *Barnes* that an occupier can use retaliatory force to protect his dwellinghouse against a burglar, Hardiman J expanded on its intangible significance:[23]

> [A] dwellinghouse is at a higher level, legally and constitutionally, than other forms of property. The free and secure occupation of it is a value very deeply embedded in human kind and this free and secure occupation of a dwellinghouse, apart from being a physical necessity, is a necessity for the human dignity and development of the individual and the family.

In condemning the requirement to pay a deposit to become an election candidate as contrary to the equality guarantee, Herbert J in the High Court in *Redmond v Minister for the Environment* held that discrimination on the

20 [1989] ILRM 181 at 193.

21 n 20 above, 193 - 194.

22 n 20 above, 195. Despite these observations, there is some basis for claiming that the Constitution commits itself to a more substantive conception of democracy: Doyle *Constitutional law: Text, cases and materials* (n 14 above) [13-57]–[13-58]. See also Doyle *Constitutional equality law* (n 14 above) 42 - 46; G Whyte *Social inclusion and the legal system: Public interest law in Ireland* (2002) 13 - 14, 43 - 54, 360 - 362; Whyte (n 19 above) 3 - 8; G Whyte 'Rights and judicial activism' in B Fanning *et al* (eds) *Theorising Irish social policy* (2004); G Whyte 'A tale of two cases – Divergent approaches of the Irish Supreme Court to distributive justice' (2010) 32 *Dublin University Law Journal* 365.

23 *People (DPP) v Barnes* [2006] IECCA 165, [2007] 3 IR 130 [58]. On the extent of the right to use force to effect an arrest, compare *Ex p Minister of Safety and Security: Re S v Walters* 2002 4 SA 613 (CC).

grounds of wealth attacked the dignity of the poor.[24] This was a refreshing decision in which Herbert J was faithful to the idea of dignity enunciated by Walsh J in *Quinn's Supermarket*.[25] If applied in other areas, it could be the springboard for making a real difference to people's lives and in achieving social justice[26] for the underprivileged in our society.

Dignity is integral to the right to life. McCarthy J in *Murray v Ireland* considered the right to procreate children within marriage essential to the human condition and personal dignity.[27] The Supreme Court was confronted with a dispute over the status of frozen embryos in *Roche v Roche*.[28] As the human embryo was generally accepted as having moral qualities and a moral status, having present in it all the genetic material for the formation of life, being the first step in procreation and containing within it 'the potential, at least, for life', Murray CJ confirmed that its creation and use cannot 'be divorced from our concepts of human dignity'.[29]

There are different judicial opinions on whether a child has the right to realise its personality and dignity. They were included in the rights of the child listed by O'Higgins CJ in his dissent in *G v An Bord Uchtála*.[30] Hamilton CJ and Denham J in the Supreme Court in *DG v Eastern Health Board* agreed with his views.[31] However, there was disagreement over children's rights

24 [2001] IEHC 128, [2001] 4 IR 61 at 80. The Supreme Court overruled Herbert J's finding that the Oireachtas did not have power pursuant to Article 16.7 to regulate elections by establishing conditions (monetary or otherwise) for the nomination of candidates: *King v Minister for the Environment (No 2)* [2006] IESC 61, [2007] 1 IR 296 [53]. See R Byrne & W Binchy *Annual review of Irish law 2006* (2007) 190 - 191; Doyle *Constitutional law: Text, cases and materials* (n 14 above) [15-46]–[15-47]. The deposit payable to appeal against a planning decision did not breach the equality guarantee: *Finnegan v An Bord Pleanála* [1979] ILRM 134 (HC, SC).

25 n 14 above, 13.

26 For a critique of a social justice theory of human rights, see J Donnelly 'Human rights as natural rights' (1982) 4 *Human Rights Quarterly* 391 at 401 - 404.

27 [1991] ILRM 465 (SC) 476. The Supreme Court upheld Costello J's finding in the court below that the right to procreate was a personal right under Article 40 rather than one falling within the ambit of the rights of the family as an institution in Article 41: above, 469, 472 (Finlay CJ); above, 474, 476 (McCarthy J).

See W Binchy 'Constitutional remedies and the law of torts' in J O'Reilly (ed) *Human rights and constitutional law: Essays in honour of Brian Walsh* (1992) 203; Doyle *Constitutional law: Text, cases and materials* (n 14 above) [7-19]–[7-20], [9-08], [9-32].

28 [2009] IESC 82, [2010] 2 IR 321.

29 n 28 above, [44].

30 [1980] IR 32 (SC) 56. See Doyle *Constitutional law: Text, cases and materials* (n 14 above) [4-21]–[4-25], [4-29], [5-10]; Shannon (n 17 above) [1-11], [1-14], [12-05].

31 [1997] IESC 7, [1997] 3 IR 511 at 523, 537. See Shannon (n 17 above) [1-16], [11-127]–[11-128].

between the Supreme Court judges in *TD v Minister for Education*.[32]

In the Preamble to the Constitution, dignity is coupled with freedom as a constitutional aim. Rationality and free will are the *raison d'être* of dignity. So in the case-law, the values of freedom and dignity are intertwined. Henchy J referred to them in tandem in *McGee v AG*, which established the right to marital privacy.[33] Hamilton P in *Kennedy v Ireland* identified them as the basis of the right to privacy.[34] The Irish courts have consistently described the right to privacy in a way which emphasises its connection with dignitary values.[35]

A conflict can be perceived between the claims of the common good and the individual's freedom.[36] Three different concepts of the common good are operative in Irish constitutional law, *ie*, first, a utilitarian interpretation of the common good identified with what the majority believe to be in their own best interests in the disposition of specific 'goods'; second, an ideological ideal proposed for the community by those who consider themselves to be wiser than the electorate in matters of this nature (at the time when the Constitution was drafted, this reflected a rather homogeneous picture of Irish identity as Roman Catholic, rural, and republican); third, presupposing agreement among the members of the community that there are some individual rights which are so basic that they should never be compromised, and that other individual rights may only be compromised as an unavoidable means of guaranteeing other basic rights, this approach interprets the common

32 [2001] IESC 101, [2001] 4 IR 259 at 295, 318. See Doyle *Constitutional law: Text, cases and materials* (n 14 above) [4-53]; Shannon (n 17 above) [4-31]–[4-34], [4-67]–[4-69].

In a referendum held in 2012 on the amendment of the Constitution to incorporate the provisions on children's rights contained in the Thirty-first Amendment of the Constitution (Children) Bill 2012, the people approved the repeal of Article 42.5 and the insertion of Article 42A.

33 [1974] IR 284 (SC) 326. *McGee* has been described as the most important decision in Irish constitutional jurisprudence: W Binchy 'Autonomy, commitment and marriage' in O Doyle & W Binchy (eds) *Committed relationships and the law* (2007) 171.

On *McGee*, see H Delany *et al*, *The right to privacy: A doctrinal and comparative analysis* (2008) 34 - 35, 39; Doyle *Constitutional law: Text, cases and materials* (n 14 above) [4-11]–[4-12], [4-14], [4-18]–[4-19], [4-34]–[4-36], [5-07]–[5-09], [10-02], [17-16]; L Flynn 'Missing Mary McGee: The narration of woman in constitutional adjudication' in Quinn *et al* (n 1 above) 96 - 104; Morgan *A judgment too far? Judicial activism and the Constitution* (n 18 above) 23 - 24.

34 [1987] IR 587 (HC) 593.

35 Delany *et al* (n 33 above) 37.

36 On the tension between the 'good' and the 'right' within political thought, see G Quinn 'Human rights – themes and values: Establishing Irish foreign policy priorities' in G Quinn (ed) *Irish human rights yearbook 1995* (1995) 131 - 132.

good as a means to an end, or at least as a subsidiary end, and includes the whole complex of institutional and social arrangements which the community recognises as instrumental or necessary for living together in harmony.[37]

Henchy and McCarthy JJ (both dissenting) in *Norris v AG* were loath to allow the intolerant view of homosexual conduct triumph over the freedom of the individual to express a deeply personal choice in a central feature of his being.[38] Based on Costello J's understanding of the common good, reconciliation of individual rights with the moral aspect of society is the aim rather than one taking precedence over the other.[39] In an essay in 1987 Costello defined the common good as 'the whole ensemble of conditions which are brought about by collaboration in a political community for the benefit of each person in it.'[40] His definition was based on the sense in which it was used in the Preamble to ensure the 'dignity and freedom of the individual.' He thought it necessary 'to reconcile other aspects of the common good (for example the attainment of social justice) with the need to promote, as part of the common good, the exercise of fundamental rights.'[41]

The plaintiffs in *Zappone v Revenue Commissioners* invoked their dignity as human beings as the basis of a right to marry and argued that to prohibit same-sex marriage was discrimination on the grounds of gender and sexual orientation.[42] Dunne J rejected the challenge and stated that the right to

37 DM Clarke 'The concept of the common good in Irish constitutional law' (1979) 30 *Northern Ireland Legal Quarterly* 319 at 340 - 341.

38 [1984] IR 36 (SC) 78, 102. On *Norris*, see Binchy (n 33 above) 164 - 167; E Carolan 'Committed non-marital couples and the Irish Constitution' in Doyle & Binchy (n 33 above) 244 - 245; Delany *et al* (n 33 above) 35 - 36, 37 - 38, 40, 44, 58, 63, 230, 231; Doyle *Constitutional law: Text, cases and materials* (n 14 above) [3-31]–[3-32], [4-13]–[4-16], [5-35]; Morgan *A judgment too far? Judicial activism and the Constitution* (n 18 above) 28 - 29.

39 See DR Phelan *Revolt or revolution: The constitutional boundaries of the European Community* (1997) 307 - 310.

40 D Costello 'Natural law, the Constitution and the courts' in P Lynch & J Meenan (eds) *Essays in memory of Alexis Fitzgerald* (1987) 116.

41 As above.

42 [2006] IEHC 404, [2008] 2 IR 417 [117]. The plaintiffs also sought, but did not pursue, recognition of their Canadian marriage under private international law; because they were domiciled in Ireland, their capacity to marry was in issue: above, [1], [45], [139]. For reviews of *Zappone*, see Carolan (n 38 above) 263 - 266; Doyle *Constitutional law: Text, cases and materials* (n 14 above) [9-27]–[9-29]; A O'Sullivan 'Same-sex marriage and the Irish Constitution' (2009) 13 *International Journal of Human Rights* 477 at 482 - 483, 485 - 488. Contrast *Minister of Home Affairs v Fourie* 2006 1 SA 524 (CC).
The *lex domicilii* of the parties governs the capacity to marry, while the formalities must comply with the *lex loci celebrationis*. Even if the marriage complies with these requirements, recognition can be withheld on the grounds of public policy. On

marry implied in Article 41 had always been understood as opposite sex marriage.[43] She discerned little evidence of a consensus around the world to support a widespread move towards same-sex marriage.[44]

public policy, see J Fawcett & JM Carruthers *Cheshire, North & Fawcett: Private international law* (2008) 908 - 910. Ease of dissolution of a marriage does not affect its validity; a foreign marriage contracted in accordance with a local law allowing its dissolution by mutual consent or at the will of one of the parties, with merely formal conditions of official registration, was recognised on appeal: *Nachimson v Nachimson* [1930] P 217 (CA). This decision has received some criticism: W Binchy *Irish conflicts of law* (1988) 212.

On the moral arguments for recognition of same-sex partnerships, see O Doyle 'Moral argument and the recognition of same-sex partnerships' in Doyle & Binchy (n 33 above) 124 - 158. The crucial difference between non-sexual committed relationships and same-sex committed sexual relationships is not the presence of a sexual relationship but the willingness explicitly to assume exclusive and presumptively lifelong commitment: O Doyle 'Sisterly love: the importance of explicitly assumed commitment in the legal recognition of personal relationships' in S FitzGibbon *et al* (eds) *The jurisprudence of marriage and other intimate relationships* (2010) 324.

43 n 42 above, [241]. Dunne J also refused recognition to a polygamous marriage contracted in Lebanon by parties domiciled there, even though their capacity to marry was not in doubt: *H v A* [2010] IEHC 497. Her refusal was based on public policy grounds and on the traditional meaning of marriage in Ireland informed and guided by the status given to marriage in the Constitution, which she indicated involved a lifelong commitment (notwithstanding the introduction of divorce). The private international law issue deserved a deeper analysis than that given by Dunne J. She did not probe the effect of non-recognition on the parties to the polygamous marriage, which was in accordance with their religious beliefs and cultural background. The human rights aspect was not explored, in contrast to the approach in *Daniels v Campbell* 2004 5 SA 331 (CC). Neither did she consider invoking international norms to develop Irish law by embracing a broader notion of marriage to accommodate a pluralist and multi-cultural society; like heterosexual monogamous marriage, same-sex or polygamous marriage establishes a lifelong commitment respectful of the parties' autonomy and human dignity. Dunne J rightly discounted *Conlon v Mohamed* [1989] ILRM 523 (SC) as a relevant precedent. In that case a potentially polygamous Islamic religious marriage in South Africa was not recognised; however, one of the parties was not domiciled in South Africa and did not have the capacity to contract a polygamous marriage.

For the position on recognition of polygamous marriages in England, see AV Dicey *et al*, *Dicey, Morris and Collins on the conflict of laws* (2012) 964 - 986.

On the growth of international norms in private international law and its deepening pluralist orientation, see: PS Berman 'A pluralist approach to international law' (2007) 32 *Yale Journal of International Law* 301 at 311 - 312, 316 - 320, 322 - 329; A Mills 'The private history of international law' (2006) 55 *International and Comparative Law Quarterly* 1 at 3 - 4, 45, 47 - 49. For an analysis of the effect of globalisation on business and the potential for development of private international law norms, see: R Wai 'Transnational liftoff and juridical touchdown: The regulatory function of private international law in an era of globalization' (2002) 40 *Columbia Journal of Transnational Law* 209; R Wai 'The interlegality of transnational private law' (2008) 71 *Law and Contemporary Problems* 107.

44 n 42 above, [242]. Jeffrey Redding concluded that dignity is a much more complicated, contested and dynamic concept than same-sex marriage advocates and supportive courts acknowledge: JA Redding 'Dignity, legal pluralism, and same-sex marriage' (2010) 75 *Brooklyn Law Review* 791 at 832. The core of human dignity is the distinctive

Freedom of choice in *morality* and religion was above interference by the law according to McGovern J in *Roche v Roche*:[45]

> It is not for the Courts to weigh the views of one religion against another, or to choose between one moral view point and another. All are entitled to equal respect provided they are not subversive of the law, and provided there are no public policy reasons requiring the Courts to intervene. Moral responsibility exists even in the absence of law and arises out of the freedom of choice of the individual.

There was a significant development in *Re a Ward of Court (withholding medical treatment) (No 2)*, when Denham J declared that there was an unenumerated right[46] to dignity under Article 40.3.1°.[47] It was combined with the rights to self-determination and to refuse medical treatment.[48] The right to be treated with dignity was in addition to the right to privacy.[49] Since then, the self-standing right to dignity has been accepted by the Supreme Court in *Re Article 26 and the Health (Amendment) (No 2) Bill 2004*.[50] The Court discerned in the right to private ownership in Article 43.1.1° a moral quality 'intimately

capacities of human beings to reason, to relate to one another and to make and adhere to free choices: W Binchy 'Human dignity: Its implications for marriage, the family and society' in FitzGibbon *et al* (n 42 above) 5.

On the extent of recognition or rejection of same-sex marriage, see LD Wardle 'Gender neutrality and the jurisprudence of marriage' in FitzGibbon *et al* (n 42 above) 40 - 44, 62 - 65.

For the position taken by the European Court of Human Rights, see *Schalk v Austria* (App no 30141/04) (2011) 53 EHRR 20; L Hodson 'A marriage by any other name? *Schalk and Kopf v Austria*' (2011) 11 *Human Rights Law Review* 170.

45 [2006] IEHC 359, [2010] 2 IR 321 [39].

46 See *Ryan v AG* [1965] IR 294 at 313 (HC), 344 - 345 (SC); O Doyle 'Legal positivism, natural law and the Constitution' (2009) 31 *Dublin University Law Journal* 206 at 207 - 209; TA Finlay 'The Constitution of Ireland in a changing society' in D Curtin & D O'Keeffe (eds) *Constitutional adjudication in European Community and national law: Essays for the Hon. Mr. Justice T.F. O'Higgins* (1992) 140 - 141; N McCarthy 'Observations on the protection of fundamental rights in the Irish Constitution' in Curtin & O'Keeffe above, 182.

47 [1996] 2 IR 79 (SC) 163. See Binchy (n 33 above) 163 - 164; Carolan (n 38 above) 250; Delany *et al* (n 33 above) 13, 37, 40 - 41; Doyle *Constitutional equality law* (n 14 above) 196 - 197; Doyle *Constitutional law: Text, cases and materials* (n 14 above) [5-03]–[5-06], [5-38]–[5-40].

48 n 47 above, 126, 129, 132, 161.

49 n 47 above, 163. Charleton J also treated dignity and privacy as separate rights when considering the treatment of a mentally ill patient involuntarily detained: *Maria (ET) v Clinical Director of the Central Mental Hospital* [2010] IEHC 378 [24].

50 [2005] IESC 7, [2005] 1 IR 105 [28]. See Doyle *Constitutional law: Text, cases and materials* (n 14 above) [6-03]–[6-05], [6-14], [6-17], [6-55]–[6-56], [6-60]–[6-61], [6-67], [11-07]–[11-08], [11-24]–[11-27], [17-18].

related to the humanity of each individual', but since property owners must respect the rights of other members of society, Article 43.2.1° declared that their rights were regulated by the principles of social justice.[51] Therefore, Murray CJ deduced that the property interests of the less wealthy required to be especially defended, stating, '[t]he property of persons of modest means must necessarily, in accordance with those principles, be deserving of particular protection, since any abridgement of the rights of such persons will normally be proportionately more severe in its effects.'[52]

Charlton J dismissed wealth as a feature of the human personality in *Prendergast*, when he rejected an aspiring Irish medical student's claim to parity with fee-paying non-Europeans in entry to university and held that the government was entitled to set the educational training policy for medicine.[53] Individual wealth and the ability to pay fees did not trump the state aim to establish equality of opportunity in education. The disassociation of wealth from human dignity and the endorsement of equality of opportunity in this case could be the foundation for the courts to intervene when the other arms of government have failed to correct social deprivation.

The values of human dignity took centre stage in Hardiman J's decision in *North Western Health Board v HW*, when he refused to order compulsory medical tests and deferred to the views of the individual, albeit those views were held on non-medical and objectively irrational grounds.[54] In *People*

51 n 50 above, [120]. Cf *Re Article 26 and Part V of the Planning and Development Bill 1999* [2000] IESC 20, [2000] 2 IR 321.

52 n 50 above, [120]. In an exception to a deferential interpretation of the principles of social justice, the Supreme Court developed Article 43.1.1° in a manner unprecedented in modern property rights jurisprudence: R Walsh 'The Constitution, property rights and proportionality: A reappraisal' (2009) 31 *Dublin University Law Journal* 1 at 7, 20. It was the first suggestion in any Irish property rights judgment that there may be a link between the degree to which people are politically protected and the judges' willingness to intervene in defence of their property rights: above, 30. This approach could lead to a holistic assessment of the fairness of laws and counteract a tendency towards a means-end 'fit' in the proportionality analysis: above, 9.

Eoin O'Dell and Gerry Whyte considered that this sensitivity to the plight of vulnerable citizens may require fiscal legislation dealing with tax liability or imposing public charges to make provision for hardship cases as well as requiring heightened judicial scrutiny of legislation that primarily affects vulnerable persons of modest means: E O'Dell & G Whyte 'Is this a country for old men and women? – *In re Article 26 and the Health (Amendment) (No. 2) Bill 2004*' (2005) 27 *Dublin University Law Journal* 368 at 390.

53 *Prendergast v Higher Education Authority* [2008] IEHC 257, [2009] 1 ILRM 47 [74].

54 [2001] IESC 90, [2001] 3 IR 622 at 746 - 747. See Doyle *Constitutional law: Text, cases and materials* (n 14 above) [9-02]–[9-03], [9-87]–[9-97]; Shannon (n 17 above) [1-02], [1-18], [1-23], [1-37]–[1-38], [1-48], [2-02], [11-60], [12-33]–[12-38], [12-56], [16-11], [16-36]–[16-39], [16-49].

(DPP) v Davis he drew attention to 'the profound values, based fundamentally on respect for human rights and dignity, which underlie the need to ensure proper treatment for prisoners and other accused persons'.[55]

7.2 Philosophy

The depth of philosophical assessment by the judiciary of the meaning of dignity has been shallow with a handful of exceptions. Frequently the courts have avoided dealing with the dignity factor at all, particularly if there is another value, right or express constitutional provision giving an answer to the problem. This attitude has prevented a holistic view of the Constitution. The Constitution is perceived as being out of tune with twenty-first century Ireland in certain respects.[56] It has been overshadowed recently by the ECHR, which some think is a better fit for resolution of the conflicts and demands arising in modern Ireland. Apart from the direct benefits to the protection of rights from the ECHR, Colm O'Cinneide considers that its incorporation into Irish law may have the indirect effect of giving an impetus to Irish constitutional jurisprudence.[57] The emphasis on dignity in the European Court of Human Rights may give a fillip to dignity in the Irish courts and result in more attention being paid to this prime constitutional concept.[58]

While there are no obvious reference points for philosophical analysis in the Irish case-law, a trawl of judgments does bear some fruit. The uniqueness of the individual is acknowledged. Keane J (dissenting) in *IO'T v B* in 1997 highlighted the unique value of each person irrespective of parentage, when

55 [2001] 1 IR 146 (CCA) 154. The right to a fair trial is superior to the community's right to prosecute: *People (DPP) v Z* [1994] 2 IR 476 (HC, SC); *PO'C v DPP* [2000] 3 IR 87 (SC) 96 - 97.

56 I Bacik 'Future directions for the Constitution' in Doyle & Carolan (n 14 above) 135.

57 C O'Cinneide 'The European Convention on Human Rights and the Irish constitutional system of rights protection: Complementary or divergent?' in Doyle & Carolan (n 14 above) 529.

58 The concept of human rights is the result of a synthesis of morality and law, with human dignity playing a mediating function; human dignity served as a conceptual hinge in establishing the connection between the internalised, rationally justified morality anchored in the individual conscience and the coercive, positive, enacted law: J Habermas 'The concept of human dignity and the realistic utopia of human rights' (2010) 41 *Metaphilosophy* 464 at 470.

he ruled out the centrality to dignity and the personality of the right to know one's natural parents.[59]

The human personality doctrine has received judicial recognition.[60] McKechnie J in *Foy v An t-Ard Chlaraitheoir* articulated the right of everyone to human dignity and considered that each person should have the freedom to express their own personality.[61] The need to forge one's own identity and the rights to self-determination and autonomy are essential.

Dignity does not apply solely to a lonely figure. Relationships (familial and companionship) are important to the individual. Finlay CJ in *AG v X* had regard to the mother's relationships with her family and society where her activities occur.[62] O'Higgins J in *Equality Authority v Portmarnock Golf Club* said that friendships are based on delight in others' company, which cannot be analysed logically.[63] According to Hardiman J in an *obiter dictum* in the Court of Criminal Appeal, perception by others is important to the individual as well as subjective well being.[64] Denham J (dissenting) in *DPP v Redmond* referred to the fact that a person not guilty by reason of insanity has not the status of a convict and that this perception affected a person's dignity.[65]

The sanctity of life and death with dignity were examined extensively by the Supreme Court in the *Ward of Court* case.[66] Lynch J in the High Court had proceeded on the basis that the right to life was not absolute and that a person

59 [1998] 2 IR 321 (SC) 371. See Doyle *Constitutional law: Text, cases and materials* (n 14 above) [4-46]–[4-52], [4-55]; Shannon (n 17 above) [9-216]–[9-217].

60 See Doyle 'The human personality doctrine in constitutional equality law' (n 14 above).

61 [2002] IEHC 116 [135], [140], [163]; [2007] IEHC 470 [118]. See O'Sullivan (n 42 above) 481 - 482.

62 [1992] IESC 1, [1992] 1 IR 1 at 53. On the *X* case, see Doyle *Constitutional law: Text, cases and materials* (n 14 above) [5-13]–[5-20]; Morgan *A judgment too far? Judicial activism and the Constitution* (n 18 above) 25 - 28.

63 [2005] IEHC 235. See Doyle *Constitutional law: Text, cases and materials* (n 14 above) [8-39]–[8-41].

64 *Davis* (n 55 above) 153.

65 [2006] IESC 25, [2006] 3 IR 188 [36].

66 n 47 above, 123, 125, 131 - 132, 134, 161, 167, 169. For critical assessments of this case, see GF Whyte 'The right to die and the Irish Constitution' (1997) 3 *European Public Law* 235 at 236, 246 – 260; E Wicks 'The meaning of "life": Dignity and the right to life in international human rights treaties' (2012) 12 *Human Rights Law Review* 199 at 214 - 215.

The Supreme Court has found that there is no constitutional right to commit suicide or to arrange for the termination of one's life at a time of one's choosing: *Fleming v Ireland* [2013] IESC 19 [114], [137]. See J Mortimer 'Supreme Court dismisses assisted suicide appeal' (2013) 107(7) *Gazette of the Law Society of Ireland* 14.

had a right to die a natural death, to decline medical treatment.[67] He accepted that a person may elect not to enforce personal rights, having autonomy over her own life, subject to the common good and public order and morality.[68] On appeal, Hamilton CJ took the same approach and based the sanctity of human life 'on the nature of man'.[69] O'Flaherty J emphasised the right to be let alone (founded on bodily integrity and privacy) and focused on the ward's quality of life.[70] It was in her best interests that 'nature should take its course … without artificial means of preserving what technically is life, but life without purpose, meaning or dignity.'[71] In contrast, Egan J (dissenting) gave precedence to the right to life (the highest constitutional right), and therefore stated, '[i]n view of the constitutional guarantees it would require … a strong and cogent reason to justify the taking of a life.'[72]

Denham J associated dignity with privacy.[73] In her comprehensive judgment, she (unlike Hamilton CJ) recognised a conflict between the rights of the individual and the common good (the community interest in preserving life).[74] Her thorough analysis of the right to life distinguished between the absolute respect for life and the lower standard for the State to defend, vindicate and protect life.[75] She was correct in regarding the sanctity of life

67 'A person has a right to be allowed to die in accordance with nature and with all such palliative care as is necessary to ensure a peaceful and dignified death.': n 47 above, 94.

68 '[D]espite the fact that the right to life ranks first in the hierarchy of personal rights, it may nevertheless be subjected to the citizen's right of autonomy or self-determination or privacy or dignity': as above. Contrast *S v Makwanyane* 1995 6 BCLR 665 (CC) [214] (Kriegler J).

69 n 47 above, 123. The naturalistic fallacy he applied to conclude that the ward ought to be allowed to die has been described as 'a very dubious form of natural law reasoning': Doyle *Constitutional law: Text, cases and materials* (n 14 above) [5-04].

70 'The ward may be alive but she has no life at all. … she is not living a life in any meaningful sense.': n 47 above, 130, 131.

71 n 47 above, 134.

72 n 47 above, 136.

73 'A constituent of the right of privacy is the right to die naturally, with dignity and with minimum suffering.': n 47 above, 163. 'Decision-making in relation to medical treatment is an aspect of the right to privacy; however, a component in the decision may relate to personal dignity.': as above.

74 n 47 above, 162:

> The primary constitutional concept is to protect life within the community. The State has an interest in the moral aspect of society – for the common good. But, balanced against that is the person's right to life – which encompasses a right to die naturally and in the privacy of the family and with minimum suffering.

75 'The requirement to defend and vindicate the life is a requirement "as far as practicable", it is not an absolute. Life itself is not an absolute.': n 47 above, 160.

as not mandating preservation of life at all costs.[76] However, she took a restricted view of human dignity and did not see it as inherent.[77] Her interpretation of the constitutional equality right was expansive.[78]

Edwards J in the High Court stressed the importance of communication to the individual's dignity when he enquired into the lawfulness of the detention in hospital of a South African woman kept in isolation as a probable source of an infectious disease.[79] He posed the question, '[d]oes her right to human dignity not entitle her to be appraised of the full implications of her situation?'.[80]

Hardiman J used the Kantian terminology of the individual's sense of worth and the importance of not using people as a means to an end in *CC v Ireland*.[81] The social stigma attached to an employer labelled a criminal for an employee's acts done without the employer's knowledge or approval was a factor in the Supreme Court's finding that the knowledge and guilty intent necessary for criminal responsibility were missing from the attempt to impose vicarious liability in the Employment Equality Bill 1996.[82]

76 n 47 above, 161:

> In respecting a person's death we are also respecting their life – giving to it sanctity. That concept of sanctity is an inclusive view which recognises that in our society persons, whether members of a religion, or not, are all under the Constitution protected by respect for human life. A view that life must be preserved at all costs does not sanctify life. A person, and/or her family, who have a view as to the intrinsic sanctity of the life in question are, in fact, encompassed in the constitutional mandate to protect life for the common good – what is being protected (and not denied or ignored or overruled), is the sanctity of that person's life. To care for the dying, to love and cherish them, and to free them from suffering rather than simply to postpone death, is to have fundamental respect for the sanctity of life and its end.

77 'The medical treatment is invasive. This results in a loss of bodily integrity and dignity.': n 47 above, 158. See Binchy (n 14 above) 316 - 317.

78 '[A]ll citizens as human persons are equal before the law. This is not a restricted concept, it does not mean solely that legislation should not be discriminatory. It is a positive proposition.': n 47 above, 159.

79 *VTS v Health Service Executive* [2009] IEHC 106 at 63.

80 As above. He pointed out, as above:

> [N]o one has sat down to work out, or to plan, exactly what information the patient needs to have, how it is to be communicated, how issues of trust and confidence tending to undermine effective communication are to be addressed, what special skills may be necessary to ensure effective advocacy both with and on behalf of the patient, and who is to have responsibility for it.

81 [2006] IESC 33, [2006] 4 IR 1 [44]. See Binchy (n 14 above) 322; DM Clarke 'Interpreting the Constitution: Essentially contested concepts' in Doyle & Carolan (n 14 above) 107, 108.

82 *Re Article 26 and the Employment Equality Bill 1996* [1997] IESC 6, [1997] 2 IR 321. See Doyle *Constitutional law: Text, cases and materials* (n 14 above) [2-88]; Morgan *A judgment too far? Judicial activism and the Constitution* (n 18 above) 36 - 38.

As can be seen from the instances of judicial comments on the philosophical basis of dignity and the meaning of life, there is no discernible coherent thread running through the Irish case-law and, overall, there was no great debate on the meaning of life.[83] Doubtless, the human personality and the dignity of the individual are key. While personality has been mentioned in many cases, the analysis was scant.[84] There is a right and freedom to express one's unique personality, subject to harmonisation with the rights of others and the common good. Self-esteem is important, but relationships with others and others' perception of the individual are also central aspects of one's dignity.

The expansive interpretation of the Constitution backed by deeper analysis during the fertile era initiated by Walsh J in the 1960s waned and was succeeded by a constrained formalistic period of withdrawal marked by a naïve faith in the legislature and executive to uphold human rights and secure social justice. The judiciary has taken a restricted view of its role and, on the spurious grounds of policy, has been too ready to relinquish the obligations endowed on it by the Constitution. Unlike their South African counterparts, the Irish judges have not engaged in the deep analysis of legal philosophy that is desirable to yield a cohesive body of case-law charting the practical implications of constitutional rights to enlighten the populace on the meaning of the Constitution in daily life. Of course, this assessment is a generality and there have been judges who have attempted to break the mould. A brief appraisal of the performance of some of the more noteworthy figures will illustrate these views.

Many of the now well-established and frequently-cited principles of Irish law were enunciated originally by Walsh J.[85] With his courageous scrutiny of the Constitution, he identified its core values and the basis of its equality guarantee in human dignity linked to social justice.[86] However, not all of his judgments can survive criticism – beside his advances for equality[87] are instances where he gave less meritorious factors precedence, eschewing the equality guarantee or avoiding consideration of human dignity for alterna-

83 See W Binchy 'The Supreme Court of Ireland' in B Dickson (ed) *Judicial activism in common law supreme courts* (2007) 178, 214 - 215.

84 See S Mullally 'Substantive equality and positive duties in Ireland' (2007) 23 *South African Journal on Human Rights* 291 at 295 - 296.

85 *Eg, People (AG) v O'Brien* [1965] IR 142 (SC); *East Donegal Co-Operative Livestock Mart Ltd v AG* [1970] IR 317 (SC); *Glover v BLN Ltd* [1973] IR 388 (SC).

86 *Crotty v An Taoiseach* [1987] IESC 4, [1987] IR 713 at 776.

87 *de Búrca* (n 16 above).

tive options.[88] Although he regarded the child as having an independent personality,[89] he did not support the human dignity of unmarried fathers and his decision in *Nicolaou*[90] was rightly criticised by Barrington J three decades later.[91] Constitutional supremacy dominated his thinking.[92] He did not treat the judicial role as inferior to that of the other arms of state. His judicial legacy will be long-lasting, but the potential of the equality guarantee he outlined[93] has not been realised.

A significant, but less pervasive,[94] contribution to Irish jurisprudence was made by Barrington J. His classification test in *Brennan v AG*[95] was adopted by the Supreme Court.[96] He searched for norms on which to ground his decisions and was willing to act to compel the government to protect human rights.[97] In *Corway* he displayed frustration with the emphasis on religion in the Constitution.[98] Two other defenders of human rights were Henchy and McCarthy JJ, the dissentients in *Norris*.[99] The former's definition of the right to marital privacy as an unenumerated constitutional right in *McGee*[100] hastened the liberation of Irish society. He considered the meaning of human dignity,[101] and leveraged the equality guarantee.[102] Although he believed in a harmonious interpretation of the Constitution,[103] he shirked from reshaping the law of torts in *Hanrahan*.[104] McCarthy J's humane

88 *O'Brien v Stoutt* [1984] IR 316 (SC).

89 *G* (n 30 above).

90 *State (Nicolaou) v An Bord Uchtála* [1966] IR 567 (SC).

91 *WO'R v EH (Guardianship)* [1996] 2 IR 248 (SC) 278 - 280.

92 *Byrne v Ireland* [1972] IR 241 (SC); *Meskell v CIE* [1973] IR 121 (SC).

93 *Quinn's Supermarket* (n 14 above) 13.

94 *McDonnell v Ireland* [1998] 1 IR 134 (SC).

95 [1983] ILRM 449 (HC).

96 *Employment Equality Bill* (n 82 above).

97 *State (Richardson) v Governor of Mountjoy Prison* [1980] ILRM 82 (HC); *Hyland v Minister for Social Welfare* [1989] IR 624 (HC); *Blascaod Mór Teo v Commissioners of Public Works in Ireland (No 3)* [1999] IESC 4, [2000] 1 IR 6.

98 *Corway v Independent Newspapers (Ireland) Ltd* [1999] IESC 5, [1999] 4 IR 484.

99 n 38 above.

100 n 33 above, 325 - 326.

101 *Garvey v Ireland* [1981] IR 75 (SC) 99 - 101.

102 *King v AG* (n 16 above) (SC) 257; *State (DPP) v Walsh* [1981] IR 412 (SC) 449 - 450; *McMahon v Leahy* (n 16 above) 540 - 542; *People (DPP) v Quilligan (No 2)* [1989] IR 46 (SC) 56.

103 *Dillane v AG* [1980] ILRM 167 (SC).

104 *Hanrahan v Merck Sharp & Dohme (Ireland) Ltd* [1988] ILRM 629 (SC).

approach was evident in *JK v VW*, where he took greater cognisance than the majority of the position of the committed unmarried father, whom he considered should have natural rights.[105] His commitment to equality is evident in *McKinley*.[106] Unlike the current Supreme Court, he did not avoid philosophical analysis and, dissenting in *Cooke v Walsh*, he reserved for a future case with a full debate the issue of whether a plaintiff with no real appreciation of her plight should get only nominal damages.[107]

Kenny J will be remembered for his finding in *Ryan v AG* (upheld by the Supreme Court)[108] that there are unenumerated constitutional rights,[109] but his view that the equality guarantee did not apply to women in their work activity in *Murtagh Properties* is best forgotten – although he redeemed matters by finding that reference in Article 45 to all men and women having equal rights to an adequate means of livelihood[110] meant that all had a right to earn a livelihood under Article 40.3.[111]

Murray CJ had a repressed perception of the judiciary's function. In *Roche* he placed the onus firmly on the Oireachtas to make the initial policy determination to enable a legal definition to be made of when 'the life of the unborn' begins to enjoy constitutional protection.[112] However, he did not hesitate to address governmental lapses when social justice was endangered and the Supreme Court struck down the Health Amendment Bill in defence of the less wealthy,[113] or when a moral sanction was required to reflect the public indignation at executive action in *Shortt*.[114] He associated dignity with status in *PO'C v DPP*.[115]

Of the current judges, Denham CJ is notable for her finding of a right to dignity in the *Ward of Court* case, where her diligent judgment was most thorough.[116] Based on the concept of equality allied to the separation of

105 [1990] 2 IR 437 (SC) 449 - 450.

106 n 16 above.

107 [1984] ILRM 208 (SC).

108 n 46 above, 344 - 345.

109 n 46 above, 313.

110 Constitution of Ireland 1937, Art 45.2.i.

111 n 15 above, 335 - 336.

112 n 28 above, [54].

113 n 50 above, [120].

114 *Shortt v Commissioner of An Garda Síochána* [2007] IESC 9, [2007] 4 IR 587 [110].

115 n 55 above, 103.

116 n 47 above.

powers doctrine, she upheld the application of legislation to the executive in *Howard*.[117] She applies a harmonious interpretation[118] and can support her comprehensive judgments by well-researched arguments.[119] Similar to the South African style, she employs the tools of proportionality and reasonableness.[120] She is conscious of the importance of ensuring children's welfare[121] while respecting their rights to liberty, equality and to realise their personality and human dignity.[122] For her the separation of powers is not an inhibiting factor.[123] Hers was the lone voice to favour of the rights of the mother and parent in *Sinnott v Minister for Education*.[124] Denham CJ's record is one of support for human rights on sound legal grounds.

An intellectual capable of impressive legal reasoning, Hardiman J produces interesting judgments that uphold individual rights against state interference.[125] He has a rigid aversion to judges meddling in policy matters, which he regards as strictly the preserve of the legislature and executive.[126] For him, immigration decisions are administrative issues for the executive without much judicial oversight.[127] His perception of human dignity is of the adult viewed as a worthy[128] secure[129] member of society.[130] He upholds the principle of personal responsibility in criminal law,[131] but he has not recognised the presence of social justice in modern tort law.[132] He located the child's constitutional rights within the family protected by the state.[133] His

117 *Howard v Commissioners of Public Works in Ireland* [1994] 1 IR 101 (SC) 161.

118 *Roche* (n 28 above) [147].

119 *Eg, De Rossa v Independent Newspapers plc* [1999] IESC 63, [1999] 4 IR 432; *O'Brien v Mirror Group Newspapers Ltd* [2000] IESC 70, [2001] 1 IR 1; *Equality Authority v Portmarnock Golf Club* [2009] IESC 73, [2010] 1 ILRM 237.

120 *Meadows v Minister for Justice, Equality and Law Reform* [2010] IESC 3 [19], [40].

121 *McD v L* [2009] IESC 81 [50].

122 *DG* (n 31 above) 534 - 538. See also *TD* (n 32 above) 295; *North Western Health Board* (n 54 above) 719.

123 *TD* (n 32 above) 299, 311, 314 - 315.

124 n 19 above, (SC).

125 *North Western Health Board* (n 54 above); *Shortt* (n 114 above).

126 *TD* (n 32 above) 360 - 362.

127 *Meadows* (n 120 above).

128 *CC* (n 81 above) [44].

129 *Barnes* (n 23 above) [58], [62], [64].

130 *Davis* (n 55 above) 150 - 154.

131 *CC* (n 81 above).

132 *O'Keeffe v Hickey* [2008] IESC 72, [2009] 2 IR 302.

133 *North Western Health Board* (n 54 above) 755.

preference is for a harmonious interpretation[134] with a restricted role for proportionality.[135]

In *Shortt* the same stance as Murray CJ and Hardiman J was adopted by Fennelly J,[136] who has a broader view of equality[137] and the meaning of human dignity than some of his colleagues. He has articulated that the dignity of prisoners should be respected,[138] which has translated into the provision of a remedy for a prisoner assaulted in an unprovoked attack by a fellow inmate.[139] He did not sideline the humanity of the natural father in *McD v L*.[140]

There was a display of human empathy in McKechnie J's judgments in *Foy*, where he was constrained initially by the rights of the transsexual's family and by the terms of the Constitution from finding in favour of Dr Foy.[141] He expressed his personal views in *GT v KAO* that the unmarried father should have more rights recognised because of the constitutional values of prudence, justice, charity and dignity, but again these views were not legally sustainable because Article 41 has been interpreted in a narrow way to accord recognition only to the marital family.[142]

Of the current High Court judges, two of those with long service (Laffoy and Kelly JJ) deserve to be mentioned. Laffoy J held in *McCann v Judge of Monaghan District Court* that the provisions for imprisonment for debt infringed the liberty of the individual and violated the constitutional guarantee of fair procedures.[143] When faced with inequality and unfair treatment of the vulnerable and powerless, she has intervened to redress the wrong being caused.[144] She has not demurred from applying the equality guarantee.[145] Although her decision to order the release of the prisoner in *A v Governor of Arbour Hill Prison* was logical, it was overturned on appeal

134 *Roche* (n 28 above) [181], [183].
135 *Meadows* (n 120 above).
136 n 114 above, [274].
137 *Portmarnock Golf Club* (n 119 above).
138 *Creighton v Ireland* [2010] IESC 50 [4].
139 *Creighton v Ireland* 14 June 2013 (HC).
140 n 121 above, [78]-[79], [81].
141 n 61 above.
142 *GT v KAO (Child Abduction)* [2007] IEHC 326, [2008] 3 IR 567 [50]-[51].
143 [2009] IEHC 276.
144 *O'Donnell (a minor) v South Dublin County Council* [2007] IEHC 204.
145 *SM v Ireland (No 2)* (n 16 above).

because of the far reaching consequences.[146] Also overturned on appeal has been the fearless decision of Kelly J addressed to the state in defence of neglected children in *TD*.[147] In contrast, his decision to ensure the welfare of a homeless youth with a serious personality disorder by ordering his detention was upheld.[148]

To widen the analysis, the remainder of this Chapter will probe deeper into some areas where constitutional values have been examined in the Irish courts and will assess the range of application of constitutional rights. It will drill down to the rationale for some legal principles and will draw comparisons with South Africa.

7.3 Personal responsibility

Freedom to act brings with it accountability for one's actions. In law the principle of personal responsibility has translated into the need for *mens rea* in criminal law and has constrained vicarious liability in tort.

7.3.1 Criminal law

It was held in *CC* that *mens rea* is necessary for a serious criminal offence.[149] Justice required that the person's dignity be respected[150] and this was not observed in crimes of absolute liability.[151] Similarly, vicarious liability for crimes is repugnant and was the basis on which a provision in the Employment Equality Bill was found to be unconstitutional.[152] The detriment to the individual in the eyes of society was not balanced by the laudable aim

146 [2006] IEHC 169, [2006] IESC 45, [2006] 4 IR 88.

147 *TD v Minister for Education* [2000] 3 IR 62 (HC); n 32 above (SC). Cf *DB* (n 19 above).

148 *DG* (n 31 above).

149 n 81 above, [61]. Cf *S v Coetzee* 1997 3 SA 527 (CC).

150 O'Higgins CJ associated justice with dignity: *State (Healy) v Donoghue* [1976] IR 325 (SC) 348. See also *AG v DMK* [2004] IEHC 609 (Peart J).

151 n 81 above, [48]-[49], [68].

152 n 82 above.

of the legislature.[153] As indicated in *S v Coetzee*, *mens rea* is also a requirement in South Africa.[154]

Before analysing the nature and purpose of *mens rea* in criminal law, it would be helpful to define criminal law, but that is impossible since there is no universally accepted definition.[155] The characteristics generally found in criminal conduct are that it usually involves a public wrong and a moral wrong.[156] A guilty mind (*mens rea*) is the traditional *sine qua non* of a crime.[157] It contains the mental fault ingredient of a crime and signifies intention to cause harm, or recklessness (whether deliberate or indifferent) as to the consequences of an action, but it is now sometimes deployed to describe negligence in the sense of failure to comply with a standard of conduct.[158] The beginning of the modern concept of *mens rea* is probably found in Anglo-

153 n 82 above, 373 - 374 (Hamilton CJ):

> [W]hat is sought to be done by this provision is that an employer, devoid of any guilty intent, is liable ... to be tainted with guilt for offences which are far from being regulatory in character but are likely to attract a substantial measure of opprobrium. The social policy of making the Act more effective does not, in the opinion of this Court, justify the introduction of so radical a change to our criminal law. The change appears to the Court to be quite disproportionate to the mischief with which the section seeks to deal.

154 n 149 above.

155 D Ormerod *Smith and Hogan's criminal law* (2011) [1.3]. There is a need for a global substantive criminal law. Catherine MacKinnon has called for an extension of the definition of rape as a crime against humanity to cover situations where rape has become banal, such as in South Africa: n 5 above, 246.

156 Ormerod (n 155 above) [1.3]. The public element invariably means a degree of stigmatisation – even if the individual is diverted before trial and dealt with by way of caution; there is a marked public condemnation publicly communicated – the public has an important role in punishing wrongs that have a harmful effect on society and do not merely interfere with private rights: Ormerod (n 155 above) [1.3.1]. Morality and the criminal law are not co-extensive; many acts are now prohibited simply on the grounds of social expediency: Ormerod (n 155 above) [1.3.2.1]. For the most part, it is inappropriate for the law (particularly the criminal law) to intervene in people's intimate personal lives if no harm is caused to society: Ormerod (n 155 above) [1.3.2.2]. A difficult question is when intervention is justified where the harm is self-inflicted or the recipient consents.

157 Ancient criminal law tried to make people answer for all their intentional misdeeds; exceptions to this harsh attitude were recognised gradually leading to the emergence and development of the *mens rea* concept: RM Perkins 'A rationale of *mens rea*' (1939) 52 *Harvard Law Review* 905 at 905.

158 Ormerod (n 155 above) [5.1]. *Mens rea* has no single meaning – every crime has its own *mens rea* which can only be ascertained by looking at its statutory definition or the case-law: Ormerod (n 155 above) [5.3]. The true meaning of *mens rea* as a blameworthy state of mind at common law requires not only that the accused's conduct be a voluntary expression of his will (intentional, not accidental or done in a state of somnambulism or automatism), but also knowledge of the consequences of the action (guilty knowledge): JLJ Edwards Mens rea *in statutory offences* (1955) 249

Saxon law.[159] The idea of punishment for intentional wrong in secular law has parallels with penance for evil thoughts in religion.[160]

The reception of *mens rea* into Anglo-American law may be ascribed to some extent to the significance of the Irish Catholic Church, which was at one time the most influential church in Britain and Ireland,[161] but in any event there is no doubt that the Christian Church with its absorption of Hebrew thought had an impact on the legal concept.[162] In Hebrew law, a guilty mind – initially punished on a tribal basis – evolved over time into personal guilt.[163] It contained the seeds of personal responsibility.[164] Christian theology influenced Anglo-Saxon law by requiring a moral basis to punishment – a guilty mind attracted a punitive sanction.[165]

- 250. Negligence (blameful inadvertence) describes the state of mind of a person who ought to have known, and is not so reprehensible as the state of mind of a person who wilfully shuts his eyes to the obvious: Edwards above, 256. See also Perkins (n 157 above) 913 - 915; JWC Turner 'The mental element in crimes at common law' in L Radzinowicz & JWC Turner (eds) *The modern approach to criminal law: Collected essays* (1945) 200 - 211.

159 A Lévitt 'The origin of the doctrine of *mens rea*' (1922) 17 *Illinois Law Review* 117 at 120. The mental state of the criminal was not a significant feature in Roman law: above, 118. Although the Irish Brehon law did not set up crime as a species of liability distinct from civil wrong, it differentiated in the way the law enforced criminal and civil liability based on the moral nature of the act by which liability was incurred: L Ginnell *The Brehon laws: A legal handbook* (1894) 184 - 185. A wilful act was punished more severely, *eg*, the amount of the fine payable for separating body from soul by killing another (*eiric* or *eric*) was higher for an intentional killing than for an accidental one: Ginnell above, 188. In Irish law, morality and law intermingled.

160 Lévitt (n 159 above) 133, 136.

161 Lévitt (n 159 above) 119. As the church leaders who came into power in Britain with the Norman Conquest had access to the writings of the church fathers of the Irish Church, the insistence on the part of the Irish law that *mens rea* was to be considered in punishing homicide may have had some influence on the development of the Anglo-Saxon theory of *mens rea*: as above.

162 Lévitt (n 159 above) 128. By the end of the 12th century canon law was a powerful influence on English law: FB Sayre '*Mens rea*' (1932) 45 *Harvard Law Review* 974 at 982 - 983.

163 Lévitt (n 159 above) 127. 'Noxal surrender' and deodand whereby the chattel or person that caused harm was delivered for punishment to the victim (or at a later stage in history to the state) was derived from Hebrew law: Lévitt (n 159 above) 120, 128.

164 As Lévitt put it, '[a]ll the ills which follow [a man's] acts must be paid for.': Lévitt (n 159 above) 120.

165 Lévitt (n 159 above) 136. In criminal law, compensation was payable to the victim for the damage to the body, while the interests of the king and of God were met by inflicting punishment for the evil thought that accompanied it: Lévitt (n 159 above) 136 - 137. Early criminal law developed out of the blood feud and rested upon the desire for vengeance, which sought a blameworthy victim based on fault or evil design: Sayre (n 162 above) 975. In time, blood-vengeance was abolished and the state stepped in to replace the victim's family; later, the religious influence gradually

One of the conclusions Francis Sayre drew from his study of the development of the mental requisites of crime was that the strong tendency of the early days to link criminal liability with moral guilt made it necessary to free from punishment those who perhaps satisfied the requirements of specific intent for particular crimes but who, because of some personal mental defect or restraint, should not be convicted of any crime.[166] Many commentators consider that *mens rea* should continue as the normative base for crime.[167] Despite the requirement at common law for *mens rea* to be a

came to be ignored in theory, but remained in practice: Lévitt (n 159 above) 137. *Mens rea* from the middle of the 13th century smacked strongly of general moral blameworthiness: Sayre (n 162 above) 988. This was an exceedingly vague concept, which was refined by the judiciary on a case by case basis to delineate the mental requisites for felonies, each crime being analysed separately to take into account the different social and public interests that were relevant: Sayre (n 162 above) 994. The moral test in the law focused at first on moral guilt, asking whether the act was voluntary: Turner (n 158 above) 201. As the conception of moral guilt is necessarily grounded on a free mind voluntarily choosing evil rather than good, new general defences, such as insanity, infancy and compulsion also began to take shape based upon the lack of a guilty mind and thus negativing moral blameworthiness: Sayre (n 162 above) 1004. The focus on moral guilt gave way to a doctrine that looked at whether the accused had foresight of the act's consequences, but inadvertence did not ground liability at common law: Turner (n 158 above) 215 - 216. The expression *mens rea* was used to find out whether the action could be imputed to the accused (a voluntary act) and also to ascertain whether the accused realised its probable consequences: RM Jackson 'Absolute prohibition in statutory offences' in Radzinowicz & Turner (n 158 above) 270. For criticism of use of the phrase 'voluntary act', see Perkins (n 157 above) 912 - 913.

166 n 162 above, 1021. Sayre also concluded that whatever the early conception of *mens rea* may have been, as the law grew the requisite mental elements of the various felonies developed along different lines to meet exigencies and social needs which varied with each felony: n 162 above, 1019. The nature of the crime was central, criminal responsibility being more readily assigned to corporations irrespective of motive for breaches of laws protecting public health, regulating gambling and controlling the sale of liquor and food: HJ Laski 'The basis of vicarious liability' (1916) 26 *Yale Law Journal* 105 at 131 - 132. *Mens rea,* the mental factor necessary to prove criminality, has no fixed continuing meaning: Sayre (n 162 above) 1016. There remained a residuum of cases where criminality was absent by reason of the general lack of a law-breaking or criminal mind, and the lack of *mens rea* developed as a recognised defence – they included cases where the defendant acted under a reasonable mistake of fact, and cases where the defendant intended an act constituting only a trivial infraction of the law which without the defendant's negligence resulted in death or some serious unintended criminal consequence: Sayre (n 162 above) 1022.

167 Sayre, writing in 1933 concerning the growth of statutory offences punishable without any criminal intent, anticipated opposition from the community if a significant sanction were imposed, FB Sayre 'Public welfare offenses' (1933) 33 *Columbia Law Review* 55 at 55 - 56:

> Does the modern conception of criminality, which seems to be shifting from a basis of individual guilt to one of social danger, presage the abandonment of the classic requirement of a *mens rea* as an essential of criminality? ... Criminality is and always will be based upon a requisite state of mind as one of its prime factors. ... To inflict substantial punishment upon one who is morally entirely innocent, who

precursor for criminal responsibility, early tendencies towards strict responsibility were revived on a large scale in the later part of the nineteenth century through the literal construction of legislation on public welfare offences.[168] In *Woodrow*, strict liability was imposed on a tobacco retailer for possession of adulterated tobacco, although he was unaware that it was contaminated.[169] In effect the statute criminalised negligence. The rationale for dispensing with *mens rea* was the difficulty for the prosecution in proving knowledge of the content where public welfare was at stake.

Twenty years later in *R v Stephens*, the octogenarian owner of a quarry managed by his sons as his agents was convicted of public nuisance caused by rubbish falling into a river when a wall collapsed.[170] He sought a new trial, on the ground that the judge misdirected the jury by telling them that he would be liable for the acts of his workers in depositing the rubbish from the quarries so as to become a nuisance, though without his knowledge and against his orders.[171] The Queen's Bench Division unanimously upheld the trial judge's direction. Mellor J identified the object of the indictment as the prevention of the recurrence of the nuisance.[172] He described the proceedings as criminal in form, but civil in substance.[173] The same approach was adopted

caused injury through reasonable mistake or pure accident, would so outrage the feelings of the community as to nullify its own enforcement.

168 GL Williams *Criminal law: The general part* (1961) [75].

169 *R v Woodrow* (1846) 15 M & W 404, 153 ER 907. See Williams (n 168 above) [76], [78]. Pollock CB considered that it was reasonable for the legislation to require dealers to be responsible for the quality of the product supplied to the public and to be aware of its character, and regarded the legislature's policy decision imposing a duty to take care as justified on the basis of traders' responsibility for the 'goodness' of products 'whether they know it or not': *Woodrow* above, 415, 912. Parke B (construing the statute literally and satisfied that the authorities had discretion to relieve hardship) found that the public inconvenience of proving knowledge, which would seldom be achieved, warranted criminalisation for possession and outweighed the hardship caused by conviction of 'an innocent man' who had not taken a warranty: *Woodrow* above, 417, 913. Although Alderson B equated knowledge of possession with knowledge of the facts, he confined this to physical possession – not actual knowledge of the contents: *Woodrow* above, 418, 913. On the variable relation of knowledge to guilt, see Perkins (n 157 above) 917 - 921.

170 (1866) LR 1 QB 702 (QB).

171 n 170 above, 703.

172 n 170 above, 709.

173 n 170 above, 708. The prosecutor was unable to bring an action in tort – hence, the need to proceed by indictment; if it were strictly a criminal proceeding, the defence would rightly be entitled to object that there was no *mens rea*; the fact that the owner was responsible for and benefited from the carrying on of a continuous business activity was relevant, whereas his desire not to offend did not lessen his liability for the nuisance committed by his employees: n 170 above, 709.

by Blackburn J, who was keen not to erode the general rule that a principal is not criminally answerable for the act of an agent.[174] Both Mellor and Blackburn JJ attempted to remove the stigma of a crime where moral impropriety in the form of an intention to offend was absent and the protection of the public warranted a stringent deterrent to induce more care in the future by operators profiting from an economy growing increasingly more industrialised.

By 1909 the jettisoning of mens *rea* for a statutory offence[175] aimed at protecting the public had become accepted in England.[176] The pattern in the United Kingdom was paralleled in countries such as Canada, Australia and New Zealand, but some legal systems did not follow this path.[177] In the United States the movement towards public welfare offences commenced

174 He aligned the conviction with civil liability, n 170 above, 710:

> [W]here a person maintains works by his capital, and employs servants, and so carries on the works as in fact to cause a nuisance to a private right, for which an action would lie, if the same nuisance inflicts an injury upon a public right the remedy for which would be by indictment, the evidence which would maintain the action would also support the indictment.

175 In1895 Wright J had affirmed the presumption that *mens rea*, 'an evil intention, or a knowledge of the wrongfulness of the act,' was an essential ingredient in every offence, although that presumption was liable to be displaced by the words of the statute creating the offence or by the subject-matter: *Sherras v De Rutzen* [1895] 1 QB 918 (DC) 921. He identified three principal classes of exceptions to the norm, *ie*, first, a class of acts which were not criminal in any real sense, but were prohibited under a penalty in the public interest; second, some (and perhaps all) public nuisances; third, cases in which, although the proceeding was criminal in form, it was really only a summary mode of enforcing a civil right: above, 921 - 922. Remarkable exceptions – apart from these classes – were bigamy and abduction of a girl under 16 even though the abductor believed in good faith and on reasonable grounds that she was over that age: above, 921.
See Jackson (n 165 above) 268. On bigamy, see Sayre (n 167 above) 74 - 75.

176 In the prosecution of a motor cab company because an employee drove its cab without a rear light on its number plate, Lord Alderstone CJ asserted, *Provincial Motor Cab Co v Dunning* [1909] 2 KB 599 (DC) 602 - 603:

> A breach of that regulation is not to be regarded as a criminal offence in the full sense of the word; that is to say, there may be a breach of the regulation without a criminal intent or *mens rea*. ... The doctrine that there must be a criminal intent does not apply to criminal offences of that particular class which arise only from the breach of a statutory regulation.

Strict responsibility became commonplace for minor offences relating to public welfare: Williams (n 168 above) [76].

177 Williams (n 168 above) [76] fn 2. An example is Switzerland, where the only absolute prohibition was on Press libels: as above. It was long-established at common law that a master was responsible for criminal libels committed by a servant without the master's knowledge or consent; the rationale was not simply that entrepreneurs benefiting from the sale of books or newspapers should pay because they enjoyed the profits of the enterprise, but liability was attributed because publication could cause irreparable damage and the law should protect the interests of the personality as best it could: Laski (n 166 above) 132.

about the middle of the nineteenth century quite independently of the English development.[178] The Supreme Court in *Morissette v US* accepted that the legislature had power to dispense with *mens rea* in new statutory offences.[179] The rationale identified in *Morissette* for requiring blameworthiness as a precursor to a crime was the free will of the individual and the person's capacity to choose to do right or wrong. Its basis was human dignity, although Justice Jackson did not use this term explicitly when he explained the embedded nature of *mens rea* in the US legal system.[180] The high value placed on freedom of the individual in the US explains the attraction of the core belief that guilty intent is essential to constitute a crime at common law.

178 Sayre (n 167 above) 62, 83.

179 Justice Jackson distinguished new offences from ones merely adopting into federal statutory law a concept of crime already well defined in common law; when common law definitions were adopted In statutes, the judiciary would not take silence on intent in the legislation as implying that intent was not necessary when it was a feature of the offence at common law: 342 US 246 (1952) 262. Justice Jackson resisted the prosecution's argument for dropping the need for guilty intent in the crime of conversion, the purpose and effect of which would be 'to ease the prosecution's path to conviction, to strip the defendant of such benefit as he derived at common law from innocence of evil purpose, and to circumscribe the freedom heretofore allowed juries'; it was not the judiciary's function to extend '[s]uch a manifest impairment of the immunities of the individual' to common law crimes: above, 263. For reviews of *Morissette*, see HL Packer '*Mens rea* and the Supreme Court' [1962] *Supreme Court Review* 107 at 119 - 121; FJ Remington & OL Helstad 'The mental element in crime – A legislative problem' [1952] *Wisconsin Law Review* 644 at 644 - 647.

In 1933, Sayre had discerned two cardinal principles to assist in determining practically which offences did and which did not require *mens rea,* where the statute creating the offence was silent as to the requisite knowledge: n 167 above, 72. The first criterion was the character of the offence. He identified the dual purpose of criminalisation, as 'singling out wrongdoers for the purpose of punishment or correction and of regulating the social order' – where the former purpose was the primary aim, *mens rea* was commonly required, but where the latter purpose was more important, the offences, which were 'of a merely regulatory nature', were frequently enforceable irrespective of any guilty intent. The second criterion depended on the possible penalty – if it were serious and imprisonment was a possibility, the individual interest of the defendant weighed too heavily to allow conviction without proof of a guilty mind.

180 n 179 above, 250 - 252 (footnotes omitted):

> The contention that an injury can amount to a crime only when inflicted by intention is no provincial or transient notion. It is as universal and persistent in mature systems of law as belief in freedom of the human will and a consequent ability and duty of the normal individual to choose between good and evil. A relation between some mental element and punishment for a harmful act is almost as instinctive as the child's familiar exculpatory 'But I didn't mean to'...
>
> Crime, as a compound concept, generally constituted only from concurrence of an evil-meaning mind with an evil-doing hand, was congenial to an intense individualism and took deep and early root in American soil.

Jerome Hall did not approve of the change from proof of knowledge of the offence,[181] and supported 'the general thesis that moral culpability should remain the essence of criminal liability'.[182] Glanville Williams considered that strict liability was reprehensible, as it was 'an affront to the personality', it did not deter the unscrupulous real culprits, and it abused the moral sentiments of the community.[183] His view was that a practice of branding people as criminals who were without moral fault tended to weaken respect for the law and the social condemnation of those who break it.

A focus on dignity and equality in South Africa and Ireland has shaped the criminal law by restricting strict liability for offences and requiring *mens rea* before a finding of guilt for breaches that are not minor or regulatory matters.[184] Likewise vicarious liability is only imposed for less serious

181 '[P]enalization of persons who are both innocent and careful smacks of an indiscriminate terrorism that is foreign to the common law.': J Hall 'Interrelations of criminal law and torts: II' (1943) 43 *Columbia Law Review* 967 at 994. He identified four general characteristics of public welfare offences: first, many of them applied not to the general public but only to certain traders, particularly suppliers of food or drugs and vendors of alcoholic beverages, while others, which had more general application as to potential offenders, were restricted to very few activities, such as the driving of cars, safety of highways, and health measures; second, the regulations and the conditions of conforming to them presupposed regular inspection, licensing, and other administrative supervision of a continuous pattern of activity; third, the public welfare enactments were relatively new and represented adaptations to an intricate economy, an impersonal market, and modern invention; fourth, the modern public welfare offences were not strongly supported by the mores – their occurrence did not arouse the resentment that characterised attitudes to the perpetrators of traditional crimes: above, 992 - 993. In addition to public welfare, *mens rea* was abrogated for certain sexual offences, bigamy and possession of drugs: above, 995. Hall advocated re-examination of these exceptions to the basic principles of criminal law, and considered that criminalisation was not justified, as imposition of a penalty cast a stigma on those convicted: above, 996.

182 n 181 above, 996.

183 He set out the arguments for and against strict liability: n 168 above, [89]. A frequent justification was that it would be a waste of time to have to enquire into each case because of the large number of transgressions before the courts and the fact that usually the defendant was probably culpable, but proof of this was difficult. The creation of strict responsibility was thought to be a better way of ensuring compliance with the law than responsibility based on fault. Its proponents regarded the exclusion of an enquiry into *mens rea* as not being unjust where the penalty was small. Williams rebutted this by pointing out that the humiliation of the trial and the odium of a conviction were more pertinent. Furthermore, there was no record that the accused was morally innocent – on the contrary, a finding of guilt gave rise to a criminal record.

184 Strict liability is odious because those whom we punish should have had, when they acted, the normal capacities, physical and mental, for doing what the law requires and abstaining from what it forbids, and a fair opportunity to exercise these capacities: HLA Hart *Punishment and responsibility: Essays in the philosophy of law* (2008) 152. While early English law had no subtle analysis of the mental element in liability, it

transgressions. The criminal law tolerates some vicarious liability and strict liability on the grounds of public policy in order to protect the welfare of the community, to support social order,[185] and where it is more effective in ensuring compliance to abandon proof of intent because of the difficulty in securing sufficient evidence of *mens rea* in each case.

7.3.2 Vicarious liability in tort

In tort law, vicarious liability may be necessary to support dignity. In South Africa the principle of accountability in the context of the state's duty to ensure enjoyment of human rights has justified vicarious liability of the state for failures by the police.[186] The state has a special responsibility (different from that of private persons), as its *raison d'être* is to serve and protect the public.[187] In Ireland the Supreme Court by a majority in *O'Keeffe v Hickey* declined to find the State liable in tort for sexual abuse of a primary school student by a school principal, as he was employed by the Catholic Church authorities and worked under their management.[188] The State was not the

considered at least sub-consciously the individual's state of mind for acts or omissions in a given set of circumstances: PH Winfield 'The myth of absolute liability' (1926) 42 *Law Quarterly Review* 37 at 37.

185 Social order is for the benefit of each person and for the common good of all. As noted in Hogan & Whyte (n 16 above) [2.1.32], [2.1.42], the Supreme Court indicated in *Re Article 26 and the Offences against the State (Amendment) Bill 1940* [1940] IR 470 (SC) 478 that the maintenance of true social order was a pre-condition to assuring the dignity and freedom of the individual. Teresa Iglesias described one of the fundamental ethico-legal claims upheld in the fifth paragraph of the Preamble: '*The only purpose of our socio-legal living together as a people, as a civil society under law, is our common good.* This is the good of every one, and the good of all living together. These two goods, the individual and the social, are inseparable.': T Iglesias 'The dignity of the individual in the Irish Constitution – The importance of the Preamble' (2000) 89 *Studies* 19 at 26.

186 The state acts through people (its employees). The Constitutional Court found that the courts had a duty to develop the common law delictual duty to act having regard to the spirit, purport and objects of the Bill of Rights: *Carmichele v Minister of Safety and Security* 2001 4 SA 938. See also *Minister of Safety and Security v Van Duivenboden* [2002] 3 All SA 741 (SCA) [22]; *Van Eeden v Minister of Safety and Security* [2002] 4 All SA 346 (SCA) [4], [24]; *K v Minister of Safety and Security* 2005 6 SA 419 (CC). On the *K* case, see CJ Roederer 'The constitutionally inspired approach to vicarious liability in cases of intentional wrongful acts by the people: One small step in restoring the public's trust in the South African police services' (2005) 21 *South African Journal on Human Rights* 575 at 577 - 579, 581 - 606; C Roederer 'The transformation of South African private law after ten years of democracy: The role of torts (delict) in the consolidation of democracy' (2006) 37 *Columbia Human Rights Law Review* 447 at 511 fn 308, 516 - 520.

187 F du Bois 'State liability in South Africa: A constitutional remix' (2010) 25 *Tulane European and Civil Law Forum* 139 at 170.

188 n 132 above. See N Cox *et al*, *Employment law in Ireland* (2009) [3-25]–[3-26], [3-81]–[3-87], [10-20]; C O'Mahony 'State liability for abuse in primary schools:

employer and therefore was not vicariously liable to compensate the victim.

Vicarious liability in tort has traditionally been applied to wrongful conduct by an employee in the course of employment.[189] The Court in *O'Keeffe* did not decide whether to give the common law an extended interpretation of the acts of the employee that would attach to the employer by adopting a 'close connection' test as the Canadians had done.[190] Hardiman J was quite opposed to doing so, as he stated, 'it is wrong to impose the status of wrongdoer and the liability to pay compensation without fault for acts outside the scope of employment on the basis of *pour encourager les autres*.'[191] Declining to

Systemic failure and *O'Keeffe v. Hickey*' (2009) 28 *Irish Educational Studies* 315 at 319 - 321; Shannon (n 17 above) [14-144]–[14-149].

189 The course of employment test articulated by John Salmond (previously couched in language resonant of power and subservience) deemed a master responsible for a wrongful act of a servant if it was either (1) authorised by the master, or (2) a wrongful and unauthorised mode of doing some act authorised by the master: RFV Heuston *Salmond on the law of torts* (1977) 465. While the test has been attractive in the context of the tort of negligence, its limits have been acknowledged in relation to intentional torts: D Ryan 'Making connections: New approaches to vicarious liability in comparative perspective' (2008) 30 *Dublin University Law Journal* 41 at 43 - 44.

190 The Canadian Supreme Court put a gloss on the Salmond test for employees' unauthorised intentional wrongs and, in a case involving sexual abuse of a child in a residential care facility, it asked instead the broad policy question (based on the provision of a remedy and the deterrent effect) of whether the wrongful act was sufficiently related to authorised conduct to justify the imposition of vicarious liability, which would generally be appropriate where there was a significant connection between the creation or enhancement of a risk and the wrong that accruing from it: *Bazley v Curry* [1999] 2 SCR 534. The Court thought it fair that an employer engaged in a particular business should pay the generally foreseeable costs of that business: above, [41]. Factors that might be considered to determine the sufficiency of the connection between the employer's creation or enhancement of the risk might include the opportunity that the enterprise afforded the employee to abuse power, the extent to which the wrongful act might have furthered the employer's aims, the extent to which the wrongful act was related to friction, confrontation or intimacy inherent in the employer's enterprise, the extent of power conferred on the employee in relation to the victim, and the vulnerability of potential victims: as above. The Court adopted the pragmatic enterprise risk theory approach in *Bazley*. On the day the judgment in *Bazley* was delivered, the Court distinguished it by a narrow majority in a companion decision concerning the sexual abuse of children, who were members of a club providing recreational activities: *Jacobi v Griffiths* [1999] 2 SCR 570.

On vicarious liability in Canada, see E Keane 'The test for imposing vicarious liability: A debate in the Irish courts' (2007) 2(1) *Quarterly Review of Tort Law* 12 at 12 - 13; DR Wingfield 'Perish vicarious liability?' in JW Neyers *et al* (eds) *Emerging issues in tort law* (2007) 399 - 400; Ryan (n 189 above) 45 - 55; Shannon (n 17 above) [14-150]–[14-153]. The Canadian judiciary has also utilised equitable principles to widen the remedy for sexual abuse: Shannon (n 17 above) [14-158]–[14-159].

191 n 132 above, [121]. For an analysis of Hardiman J's judgment, see D Ryan 'Connections without consensus: Recent approaches to vicarious liability in the Irish Supreme Court' (2009) 31 *Dublin University Law Journal* 457 at 460 - 465.

follow the decision of the House of Lords in *Lister v Hesley Hall Ltd*,[192] where some of the judges – influenced by the Canadian jurisprudence – adopted the close connection test, Hardiman J was critical of its utilitarian bias.[193] Neither was he persuaded by the Australian High Court decision in *New South Wales v Lepore* concerning liability of the education authority for sexual assault by a teacher on a student,[194] where the judges displayed opposing viewpoints.[195] Hardiman J believed that the true position at common law and in fact was that espoused by Callinan J (dissenting in part), who considered that vicarious liability should not be imposed because the commission of a criminal act by a teacher would be so far removed from his duties as an employee.[196]

Four observations made by Hardiman J on tortious liability are quite revealing and indicate the values underlying his judgment: first, as a tortfeasor is branded a 'wrongdoer', stigmatisation of the paying party is legally and morally a precondition to compensate *for one's own act*; second, the possibility of tortious liability has a chilling effect and leads to defensiveness; third, unpredictable tortious liability has a social and economic impact by making it difficult to gauge insurance requirements and has a very damaging financial impact; fourth, vicarious liability can be 'immensely burdensome' and could only justly occur when the paying party 'has a real and actually exercisable power of control, in the relevant area of behaviour, over the person for whom it is said to be vicariously liable.'[197] There are two themes running

192 [2001] UKHL 22, [2002] 1 AC 215. On *Lister*, see P Giliker 'Comparative perspectives on vicarious liability: Defining the scope of employment' in Neyers *et al* (n 190 above) 423 - 427, 436, 437; P Giliker & S Beckwith *Tort* (2011) [7-030]; WVH Rogers *Winfield and Jolowicz on tort* (2010) [20-9], [20-14]; R Ryan & D Ryan 'Vicarious liability of employers – Emerging themes and trends and their potential implications for Irish law' (2007) 4 *Irish Employment Law Journal* 3 at 4 - 5; Ryan (n 189 above) 55 - 59; Lord Steyn 'Perspectives of corrective and distributive justice in tort law' (2002) 37 *Irish Jurist* 1 at 6; Wingfield (n 190 above) 400 - 401.

193 n 132 above, [95]:

> I have nonetheless concluded, with a number of English academic authorities, that the judgment seems guided by a perceived need to find for the plaintiffs rather than 'any discernible sense of direction'. Apart from the very marked degree of enthusiasm for the Canadian cases, there is no development of a coherent legal principle nor is there even a clear articulation, which is certainly a feature of the Canadian cases, of what are said to be the 'policy issues'.

194 [2003] HCA 4, [2003] 3 LRC 726. See Wingfield (n 190 above) 402 - 403; Ryan (n 189 above) 59 - 63.

195 n 132 above, [116]-[118].

196 n 132 above, [117].

197 n 132 above, [51]. Hardiman J's concentration on the control test is incorrect, as in modern conditions the notion that an employer has the right to control the manner of work of all employees is a fiction, *eg*, a professionally trained person such as a house

through these remarks – responsibility for one's own actions (and not for those of others) is key, and the practical impact of taking responsibility for the tort can have many negative effects on commerce that attempts should be made to avoid.

Hardiman J did not give equal consideration to the impact of the wrong on the victim nor to the effect on the victim of not recovering compensation for the wrong done to him or her. He regarded blame only from the perspective of individual responsibility, and did not contemplate faulting the system for creating the relationship between the victim and the employee.[198] Social justice might require that the State be liable for failing to protect the individual's personal rights.[199]

The conflict between the desire that an innocent victim should receive financial recompense and that the State should not be 'the insurer of last resort' is evident in the judgments in *O'Keeffe*. Arguments can be put forward to support the proponents of both viewpoints. From the State's perspective, it is not fair that it should be expected to pay without being blameworthy simply because it could raise the financial resources to do.[200] Unless system blame is taken into account, it is difficult to sustain the normative foundation

surgeon at a hospital is a servant for whose torts the employer is responsible and it is unrealistic to suppose that a theoretical right to control how a skilled worker does his job can have much substance: Rogers (n 192 above) [20-4]. Nowadays it is common to take a 'composite' approach in which the various elements of the relationship are considered as a whole: Rogers (n 192 above) [20-5].

198 See AJ Sebok 'The fall and rise of blame in American tort law' (2003) 68 *Brooklyn Law Review* 1031 at 1050 - 1051.

199 The special relationship between a housing authority and a tenant created an implied warranty that the flat let was fit for human habitation: *Siney v Dublin Corporation* [1980] IR 400 (SC). In that case there was a proximity of relationship creating a general duty on one side and a justifiable reliance by the other side on the observance of that duty: above, 422. Because of their relationship, a housing authority owed a duty to an indigent borrower to ensure by a proper valuation that the mortgaged house would be a good security for the loan: *Ward v McMaster* [1988] IR 337 (SC) 342, 351. See BME McMahon & W Binchy *Law of torts* (2013) [19.08]-[19.11], [19.19]-[19.31].

In contrast, the Supreme Court held that it was unreasonable to impose a duty of care on employers to guard against mere fear of a disease even if such fear might have led to a psychiatric condition; policy considerations that disputed the imposition of liability in 'fear of disease' cases included the undesirability of awarding damages to plaintiffs who had suffered no physical injury and whose psychiatric condition was solely attributable to an unfounded fear of contracting a particular disease and the implications for the healthcare field of a more relaxed rule as to recovery for psychiatric illness (threats of numerous large monetary awards coupled with the added cost of insuring against such liability): *Fletcher v Commissioners of Public Works* [2003] IESC 13, [2003] 1 IR 465 at 483 - 484, 518 - 519.

200 See n 132 above, [41]-[50] (Hardiman J).

for extending vicarious liability in the absence of either an employer-employee relationship between the State and the perpetrator, or direct control over the activities of the perpetrator without an intervening party in a position of responsibility. To reduce the question of liability simply to the ability to pay is a utilitarian concept that does not survive critical analysis.

In *O'Keeffe* the Supreme Court did not consider whether the State should be liable for failure to exercise adequate supervision to detect the abuse because of constitutional obligations to defend and vindicate personal rights.[201] The European Court of Human Rights held in *Z v UK* that liability could accrue to the State for its failure to protect people by not preventing ill-treatment of which it knew or *ought* to have had knowledge.[202] The duty of the State to provide for education in Article 42.4 of the Constitution could give rise to a positive obligation to monitor the schools financed by the State in order to detect wrongdoing and to preserve the integrity of the pupils whom the State rightly requires to be educated pursuant to Article 42.3.2°.[203] Similar to the constitutional position in South Africa and Germany, the Irish State has a specific social mission, which could require a distinct notion of governmental liability to reflect adequately the implications of this understanding of the State.[204]

The issue of vicarious liability was directly confronted by the Supreme Court in 2009 in *Reilly v Devereux*[205] just three months after its decision in *O'Keeffe*. In *Reilly* a gunner in the army alleged he was sexually abused over a number of years by his sergeant major. The Supreme Court unanimously held that the Defence Forces could not be vicariously liable for sexual abuse committed by its employees.[206] In his judgment for the Court, Kearns J examined the formal relationship in the army structure between the two State employees – the sergeant major exercised a supervisory and disciplinary role over the gunner, but he was not in the same position as a school teacher or boarding house warden in relation to a child.[207] Neither was the nature of the employment one which would have encouraged close personal contact

201 On liability for systemic failure, see O'Mahony (n 188 above) 321 - 324.

202 (App no 29392/95) (2002) 34 EHRR 3 [73]. See O'Mahony (n 188 above) 325.

203 O'Mahony (n 188 above) 327 - 328.

204 Du Bois (n 187 above) 175.

205 [2009] IESC 22, [2009] 3 IR 660.

206 The judgment of Kearns J on behalf of the Court has attracted considerable criticism: Cox *et al* (n 188 above) [3-88]–[3-95]; Ryan (n 191 above) 468 - 471.

207 n 205 above, [28].

where some inherent risks might exist, such as between a swimming instructor and young recruits.[208] There was no intimacy implicit in the relationship nor was there any quasi-parental role or responsibility for personal nurturing.[209] Kearns J read the Supreme Court's earlier judgment in *O'Keeffe* as taking a firm stand on ruling out the close connection test for vicarious liability,[210] but he did not take into account that the Court was divided and the comments on the test for vicarious liability were *obiter dicta* since the *ratio decidendi* in *O'Keeffe* was that the abuser was not an employee of the State. The judgment of Hardiman J in *O'Keeffe* influenced Kearns J, who noted the former's antipathy towards any extension of the doctrine of vicarious liability which would make the taxpayer liable for the criminal actions of the employees of State bodies in circumstances where the State was not at fault.[211] He also referred to Hardiman J's reluctance to make findings that would raise policy issues.[212]

In view of the confusing picture on liability of the State that has arisen in Irish law, it will be helpful to remind ourselves of the traditional and modern rationales for imposing vicarious liability.[213] At common law vicarious liability (a form of secondary liability) was imposed on a blameless employer for the acts of an employee while acting in the course of his employment.[214] This was contrary to common law principles where responsibility followed fault, the idea being that competent individuals, being free to choose their course of action, should accept the consequences of their decisions.[215] The

208 As above.

209 As above.

210 n 205 above, [29].

211 n 205 above, [31].

212 As above.

213 On the justifications for vicarious liability, see Cox *et al* (n 188 above) [3-56]–[3-59]; Laski (n 166 above) 126 - 130.

214 *Majrowski v Guy's and St Thomas's NHS Trust* [2006] UKHL 34, [2007] 1 AC 224 [7].

215 Lord Nicholls explained, *Majrowski* (n 214 above) [8]:

> This principle of vicarious liability is at odds with the general approach of the common law. Normally common law wrongs, or torts, comprise particular types of conduct regarded by the common law as blameworthy. In respect of these wrongs the common law imposes liability on the wrongdoer himself. The general approach is that a person is liable only for his own acts.

In *Majrowski*, which arose from an allegation of harassment in the form of bullying and intimidation of one employee (a clinical auditor co-ordinator) by another (his departmental manager), it was held that, unless a statute expressly or impliedly indicated otherwise, the principle of vicarious liability applied where an employee, acting in the course of his employment, committed a breach of a statutory obligation: n 214 above, [2], [17], [57], [73]-[74, [78], [81]. See Ryan & Ryan (n 192 above) 4, 6 - 7.

early development of vicarious liability was founded on utilitarian considerations based on the notion of a wealthy master reaping the rewards from controlling a servant.[216] The traditional rationale has changed over the years because of various factors affecting policy, such as the risks caused by those benefiting from trade, the financial disparity between entrepreneurs and those whom they engage to put their ideas into effect, loss distribution,[217] and deterrence of risky behaviour by punishing aberrations.[218]

While causation is the indispensable element of every species of tort liability, the law has to make a decision reflecting a moral calculation about where in the chain of events that leads to a harmful occurrence responsibility for the occurrence is to be attributed.[219] It restricts the ability of an injured person to seek compensation from another to those circumstances where the latter is morally bound to pay.[220] Efficient loss distribution is morally justified only on utilitarian principles: the party who is better placed to bear the burden

216 *Imperial Chemical Industries Ltd v Shatwell* [1965] AC 656 (HL) 685 (Lord Pearce):

> The doctrine of vicarious liability has not grown from any very clear, logical or legal principle but from social convenience and rough justice. The master having (presumably for his own benefit) employed the servant, and being (presumably) better able to make good any damage which may occasionally result from the arrangement, is answerable to the world at large for all the torts committed by his servant within the scope of it.

217 Two competing moral principles are reflected in modern tort law – the first (by far the strongest) is the principle of justice derived from the social contract, and the second theory is derived from utilitarianism, which lurks behind the ideas of efficient loss distribution and deterrence (by this yardstick the law must distribute the burdens or risk-creating behaviour causing harm in a manner that expands social welfare over all): Wingfield (n 190 above) 407 - 408, 410. Although the primary aim of tort law is the pursuit of corrective justice, which requires somebody who has harmed another without justification to indemnify the other, Lord Steyn observed that it also involves notions of distributive justice: n 192 above, 4 - 5.

218 Lord Nicholls elaborated, *Majrowski* (n 214 above) [9]:

> [T]hese factors are that all forms of economic activity carry a risk of harm to others, and fairness requires that those responsible for such activities should be liable to persons suffering loss from wrongs committed in the conduct of the enterprise. This is 'fair', because it means injured persons can look for recompense to a source better placed financially than individual wrongdoing employees. It means also that the financial loss arising from the wrongs can be spread more widely, by liability insurance and higher prices. In addition, and importantly, imposing strict liability on employers encourages them to maintain standards of 'good practice' by their employees. For these reasons employers are to be held liable for wrongs committed by their employees in the course of their employment.

See Ryan & Ryan (n 192 above) 3.

219 Wingfield (n 190 above) 406. See J Goudkamp 'The spurious relationship between moral blameworthiness and liability for negligence' (2004) 28 *Melbourne University Law Review* 343 at 357.

220 Wingfield (n 190 above) 406.

of an injury-produced activity does so.[221] Using this moral justification for vicarious liability, David Wingfield has narrowed down the pertinent question to whether society is better off by making the enterprise whose activities carry an inherent risk of harm, which it is unreasonable to impose on other members of society, bear the costs of any harm that materialises from this risk or whether society is better off by making the victim bear the harm.[222]

7.4 Prisoners' rights

There is consensus on the broad statement that prisoners do not lose all their rights and liberties when they are imprisoned. The treatment of detainees and prisoners is governed by a requirement that their dignity be respected notwithstanding justifiable reasons for their detention or the heinous nature of their crimes. However, the nature, extent and implementation of their residual rights are contested issues. Two of these at least – humane detention conditions and the exercise of the right to vote – have received limited support in Irish law.

7.4.1 Humane detention conditions

Respect for dignity has become a feature in complaints by prisoners of the conditions under which they are detained.[223] The courts have been opposed to releasing prisoners because of unsuitable facilities, but have been somewhat more sympathetic to granting them lesser relief – albeit circumscribed by the demands on the prison service to maintain order and discipline and by the *de facto* constraints on prisoners' liberty attributable to their incarceration as a result of their own criminal conduct. Barrington J in the High Court in *State (Richardson) v Governor of Mountjoy Prison* was unequivocal in his recognition of prisoners' rights of access to the courts, stating, '[t]here is no iron curtain between the Constitution and the prisons in this Republic'.[224] He accepted that the slopping out procedures in Mountjoy Prison breached the prisoner's unenumerated right to health, but dismissed her right to privacy

221 Wingfield (n 190 above) 411. Enterprise liability is a normative claim: Sebok (n 198 above) 1035.

222 n 190 above, 412 - 413.

223 See R Byrne *et al*, *Prisoners' rights: A study in Irish prison law* (1981) 77, 80 - 81.

224 n 97 above, 90. See Byrne *et al* (n 223 above) 42, 79; Hogan & Whyte (n 16 above) [7.3.75], [7.4.35]–[7.4.36], [7.4.41]; PA McDermott *Prison law* (2000) [8-07], [9-21].

argument.[225] He did not analyse her right to dignity at all, although she invoked it.[226] This can be contrasted with the South African courts' long-standing analysis of the effect of detention conditions on the dignity of prisoners going back as far as *Whittaker v Roos* in 1912.[227] In simply distinguishing between the existence and the exercise of a right, Barrington J's analysis is scant – it is virtually meaningless to possess a right that one cannot exercise. An intensive examination of the justification for curtailing rights in prison and of the extent of the inroads into the prisoner's rights coupled with application of the proportionality test would have been more apt.

Although slopping out has been acknowledged by the courts and the prison authorities as breaching prisoner's rights, it has not been eliminated in Irish prisons. The courts have not granted orders of *mandamus* to redress the situation, but have been tolerant of the delays in reforming the system.[228] In *Brennan v Governor of Portlaoise Prison*, an application for habeas corpus, Budd J found that the threshold of 'exceptional circumstances' required for making the conditional order absolute had not been reached.[229] An order of habeas corpus would only be justified where for instance there was an element of bad faith and the prisoner's constitutional rights were being consciously and deliberately violated or where the prisoner was being subjected to inhuman or degrading treatment seriously threatening the life or health of the prisoner and the authorities were unwilling or unable to rectify those conditions.[230] Budd J was satisfied to rely on the prison authorities to implement the ending of slopping out in a modernisation programme.[231]

225 n 97 above, 92 - 93. Barrington J considered that the appropriate relief would be an absolute order of *mandamus* and adjourned the case to see if recommendations for improvement were implemented without the necessity for an order: n 97 above, 93. When it was re-entered, the court was informed that the matters complained of were in the process of being remedied and so Barrington J made no actual order of *mandamus*: noted by Budd J in *Brennan v Governor of Portlaoise Prison* [1998] IEHC 140, [1999] 1 ILRM 190 at 202. On slopping out in Scotland, see *Napier v Scottish Ministers* 2005 SC 229 (Court of Session Outer House, Scotland).

226 n 97 above, 84.

227 1912 AD 92 (SC).

228 This forbearance accords with the courts' antipathy towards granting mandatory orders in the last decade: Hogan & Whyte (n 16 above) [7.4.43] fn 79.

229 n 225 above, 201, 206.

230 n 225 above, 205, 208.

231 n 225 above, 207. Despite repeated criticism by the courts over many years, he thought it 'remarkable' that the Prison Rules have not been revised, but he did not see the courts having any role in intervening to amend them or to require the other arms of government to do so: n 225 above, 209.

A prisoner spokesperson for the Real IRA complained in *Mulligan v Governor of Portlaoise Prison* that slopping out procedures violated his personal rights under Article 40.3.1° to bodily integrity, not to have his health placed at risk, and not to be subjected to torture, inhuman or degrading treatment or punishment.[232] Alternatively he claimed that the prison conditions amounted to inhuman and degrading treatment under Article 3 and violated his right to private life in Article 8 ECHR.[233] He sought a declaration that his detention breached his rights and a remedy in damages.[234] Because constitutional issues were raised, MacMenamin J confirmed that the established norms of tort law were not adequate fairly and justly to address the range of issues arising, and it was necessary to balance the positive against the negative aspects of the applicant's detention.[235] The attenuation of rights necessitated by imprisonment must be proportionate, the diminution not falling below 'the standards of reasonable human dignity and what is to be expected in a mature society.'[236] The obligation on a prison authority was to vindicate the individual rights and dignity of each prisoner insofar as practicable.[237]

MacMenamin J found that the ventilation, sanitation and hygiene regime at the prison fell significantly below the standard expected at the time.[238] The constitutional rights at issue were not absolute and the state's duty was to defend and vindicate them insofar as was practicable.[239] Absent evidence of overcrowding or 'doubling up' in cells, he was unable to find that the use of a chamber pot in the cell actually violated the prisoner's rights of privacy or human dignity to a degree to give rise to a cause of action.[240] There was no violation of the applicant's negative right to be protected against inhuman or degrading treatment, as no 'evil purpose' was shown.[241]

232 [2010] IEHC 269 [2], [5]-[6].

233 n 232 above, [7].

234 n 232 above, [5].

235 n 232 above, [105], [109].

236 n 232 above, [14].

237 As above.

238 n 232 above, [43].

239 n 232 above, [90], [93].

240 n 232 above, [117]. The applicant as a Real IRA prisoner was relatively privileged to have a cell to himself at all times: n 232 above, [14]. The conditions of detention did not seriously endanger the prisoner's life or health: n 232 above, [111].

241 n 232 above, [91]. Cf *State (C) v Frawley* [1976] IR 365 (HC) 374 (Finlay P). On *State (C) v Frawley*, see Byrne *et al* (n 223 above) 40 - 42, 77 - 78.

Based on a review of the jurisprudence of the European Court of Human Rights, the minimum level of severity required to establish breaches of the ECHR was not achieved in *Mulligan*.[242] The factors to be taken into account in measuring the minimum level of severity for a breach of Article 3 ECHR as set out by the European Court of Human Rights in *Bakhmutskiy v Russia* include the duration of detention and 'the duration of the treatment, its physical and mental effects and, in some cases, the sex, age and state of health of the victim'.[243] The state is obliged to ensure that a prisoner

> is detained in conditions which are compatible with respect for his human dignity, that the manner and method of the execution of the measure do not subject him to distress or hardship of an intensity exceeding the unavoidable level of suffering inherent in detention and that, given the practical demands of imprisonment, his health and well-being are adequately secured.[244]

A positive intention to humiliate or to debase the prisoner was not necessary in order to impinge on human dignity, which occurred when a prisoner's self-esteem was lowered by living in overcrowded conditions for an extended period.[245] The Court held that, in addition to a violation of Article 3 ECHR, there was a breach of Article 13 because of the lack of an effective accessible remedy for the prisoner to complain about the general conditions of his detention.[246] Significantly, it noted that a remedy must be effective in practice as well as in law.[247]

The dignity claim was given some weight in *Devoy v Governor of Portlaoise Prison* when Edwards J acknowledged that among the residual constitutional rights of a prisoner which were not abrogated or suspended was 'the right to

242 n 232 above, [161], [164].

243 (App no 36932/02) ECHR 25 June 2009 [88].

244 As above.

245 n 243 above, [96]:

> [T]he Court finds that the fact that the applicant was obliged to live, sleep and use the toilet in the same cell as so many other inmates for almost six years was itself sufficient to cause distress or hardship of an intensity exceeding the unavoidable level of suffering inherent in detention, and to arouse in him feelings of fear, anguish and inferiority capable of humiliating and debasing him.

On overcrowding, see also *Orchowski v Poland* (App No 17885/04) ECHR 22 October 2009.

246 n 243 above, [101].

247 n 243 above, [98].

be treated humanely and with human dignity.'[248] The individual is viewed not in isolation, but in contact with others in the community.[249] On the facts, the Court held that the prisoner had not been isolated and therefore he had not been treated inhumanely.[250] The state's duty under Article 40.3.2° of the Constitution extends to protection of 'the integrity of the human mind and personality' and requires that a prisoner be given the opportunity of 'meaningful interaction with his human faculties of sight, sound and speech'.[251]

There has been a series of claims by prisoners for damages for assault by other prisoners. In *Muldoon v Ireland* Hamilton P affirmed that prisoners have a right to freedom from harassment.[252] The prison authorities are required to take all reasonable steps and reasonable care not to expose any of the prisoners to a risk of damage or injury, but the law does not expect them to guarantee an injury-free term of imprisonment.[253] A balance has to be stuck between the need to respect the dignity of all prisoners by avoiding excessively intrusive or frequent body searches in the search for weapons in order to protect prisoners from each other and the demands on the prison service to provide a safe environment by supervision and reasonable security measures. Murphy J in *Bates v Minister for Justice* posed the dilemma for the authorities, '[n]o doubt prison management is a constant battle between the need to preserve security and safety on the one hand and, on the other hand, the obligation to recognise the constitutional rights of the prisoners and their dignity as human beings.'[254]

248 [2009] IEHC 288.

249 As above:

> Because man is a social animal the Court recognises that the humane treatment, and respect for the human dignity, of a prisoner requires that he or she should not be totally or substantially deprived of the society of fellow humans for anything other than relatively brief and clearly defined periods. To that extent a prisoner such as the applicant may be entitled to a degree of freedom of association as an aspect of his constitutional right to humane treatment and human dignity.

250 As the restriction on the prisoner was not in accordance with the Prison Rules, which could have been justifiably invoked, the Court made a declaration of unlawfulness but declined to order his release.

251 *Kinsella v Governor of Mountjoy Prison* [2011] IEHC 235 [8]-[9] (Hogan J).

252 [1988] ILRM 367 (HC) 369. See McDermott (n 224 above) [7-23]. On remedies for harassment of borrowers, see TC Homburger 'Harassment of borrowers by licensed lenders' (1965) 1 *Columbia Journal of Law and Social Problems* 39 at 48 - 55.

253 n 252 above, 369, approved by the Supreme Court in *Bates v Minister for Justice* [1998] 2 IR 81 at 84. Cf *Bolger v Governor of Mountjoy Prison* [1997] IEHC 172 [4].

254 n 253 above, 86. See McDermott (n 224 above) [7-27].

The same theme resonated in Fennelly J's judgment in *Creighton v Ireland.*[255] In that case a prisoner had been awarded damages in the High Court for injuries suffered in a knife attack by a fellow inmate in a confined area. As it was not satisfied that White J had given the case proper consideration in the court below, where he had based the award on inadequate supervision, the Supreme Court remitted it to the High Court for further consideration.[256] Following a re-hearing before O'Neill J, Mr Creighton was awarded €150 000 for the injuries sustained.[257]

In *Sage v Minister for Justice*, Irvine J dismissed the damages action against the state brought by a prisoner who had been viciously assaulted by two fellow inmates in Fort Mitchel Prison, Cork, in what he claimed was a revenge attack because he was believed to have informed the police about the role of another man in a murder for which he was subsequently convicted and sentenced.[258] Irvine J was satisfied the state had not breached its duty of care and pointed out that it was not expected to be an insurer of prisoners' safety.[259] She noted the difficulties in crafting a humane system of imprisonment that safeguards both the bodily integrity and dignity of all

255 n 138 above, [4]:

> Prisons may, as an inevitable consequence of the character of persons detained, be dangerous places. Prisoners are entitled to expect that the authorities will take reasonable care to protect them from attack by fellow prisoners. What is reasonable will, as always, depend on the circumstances. As the cases recognise, prison authorities may have to tread a delicate line between the achievement of the objective of protecting the safety of prisoners and the risks of adopting unduly repressive and inhumane measures. They must balance the protective function and possible demand for intrusive searches against the need to permit prisoners an appropriate degree of freedom of movement and human dignity.

256 n 138 above, [15], [18], [22]. White J had not probed the facts thoroughly and avoided coming to any conclusion on the nature of the knife used or the level of overcrowding before concluding that the 'prison authorities could not reasonably have been expected to have been in a position to prevent an attack on the plaintiff': n 138 above, [19]-[21]. On his own initiative White J had recalled one of the plaintiff's witnesses (a former British prison governor), who had agreed that the injuries would have been less extensive if there had been an additional supervising officer: n 138 above, [2].

257 n 139 above. See E Keane 'Jailhouse rock' (2013) 107(7) *Gazette of the Law Society of Ireland* 28 at 28 - 29.

258 [2011] IEHC 84 [2]-[3], [6], [36]. Following an arson incident when he was on remand in Limerick Prison, Sage had been afforded protective custody on request in Mountjoy Prison where he was taken after sentencing: above, [3]-[4]. On his transfer to Cork, he maintained he believed he would remain in protective custody, but he was attacked on his second day there: above, [5]-[6], [14]. Evidence was given that the prison authorities in Cork had not been informed that the prisoner had concerns for his safety: above, [9].

259 n 258 above, [29].

prisoners.[260] The evidence of the prison authorities was more persuasive that that of the plaintiff, who did not discharge the burden of proof that the authorities had notice of his concerns for his safety in Cork.[261] The yard where the assault occurred was supervised at the time and the emergency response was adequate and timely.[262] The existence in prison of the weapon used in the assault did not necessarily connote negligence on the part of the defendants.[263] Because of the conflict in evidence, Irvine J's dismissal of the claim was understandable. She took cognisance of the need to protect prisoners' dignity by avoiding over-intrusive body searches and restrictions on their movements. The authorities had reacted promptly when it became aware of concerns for Mr Sage's safety and had no reason to believe he would be at risk when transferred to Cork.

The focus in many assault cases has been the degree of knowledge the authorities had of the attacker's violent propensities – if a prisoner has attacked other inmates recently, the prison authorities could be negligent for permitting him to mix with other prisoners without close surveillance.[264] Failure to discipline an assailant properly for prior incidents may also indicate negligence.[265] Adequate screening can determine whether inmates are capable of living successfully with others without endangering them.[266] How the assailant obtained the weapon is a key issue – it would be negligent to allow prisoners with known violent propensities to have access to tools in prison workshops.[267] Monitoring of visitors can prevent smuggling of weapons into prison. Searches and supervision are subject to reasonable limits to avoid unnecessary intrusion into prisoners' lives.

260 n 258 above, [17]:

> It is undoubtedly the case that the task faced by prison authorities in seeking to balance the prisoner's rights to bodily integrity against their competing right to a model of confinement, which will protect their dignity, will generate the notion of citizenship and avoid unnecessary dehumanisation is very difficult.

Cf *Casey v Governor of Midlands Prison* [2009] IEHC 466 [12], [22], [34]. See Keane (n 257 above) 31.

261 n 258 above, [23], [36]. The prison service's obligation was to take reasonable care for his safety, but they were not obliged to transfer him to what they considered to be the safest prison: n 258 above, [22].

262 n 258 above, [24].

263 n 258 above, [34].

264 (n 224 above) [7-19].

265 McDermott (n 224 above) [7-21].

266 McDermott (n 224 above) [7-19].

267 McDermott (n 224 above) [7-20].

The dignity of prisoners is not respected fully by the state. Calls for reform of our prison system have gone unheeded. Overcrowding is rife in some jails and impedes the privacy and dignity of prisoners.[268] A proper balance needs to be struck between all prisoners, so that preservation of the dignity of one is not at the expense of another. We could follow the example in French law and strive to protect the dignity of the victim as well as that of the accused.[269] Undoubtedly the state has a difficult task to ensure security, while respecting the dignity of prisoners. The courts have been too indulgent of the state's neglect of prisons and of its failure to provide reasonable living conditions with adequate space for those detained, although Hogan J's decision in *Kinsella v Governor of Mountjoy Prison* is a refreshing change.[270] By constructive engagement with the executive, he achieved prompt improvement in a prisoner's detention conditions without breaching the separation of powers.[271]

The state has taken no effective measures to address the systemic causes of persistent overcrowding in prisons nor to provide sanitation facilities respectful of prisoners' dignity. As has happened in South Africa, intervention by the courts to improve poor prison conditions can be done in a way that is consistent with the separation of powers, but makes the prison authorities accountable.[272] Lack of resources is no excuse for failing to address repeatedly highlighted deficiencies. As illustrated by the cases reviewed, some judges[273] have expressly accepted that the human dignity of prisoners is entitled to protection. But recognition of the state's constitutional obligation to protect their rights has not usually produced positive outcomes for prisoners.[274] Finlay P and MacMenamin J resiled from giving them a remedy because of the absence of an evil purpose, although this is not a requirement under the

268 Contrast the favourable outcomes for prisoners following judicial analysis of constitutional values in *Strydom v Minister of Correctional Services* 1999 3 BCLR 342 (W) (SA High Court, Witwatersrand Local Division) and *Stanfield v Minister of Correctional Services* 2003 12 BCLR 1384 (C) (SA High Court, Cape of Good Hope Division) with *Richardson* (n 97 above), *Brennan* (n 225 above) and *Mulligan* (n 232 above).

269 See *Davis* (n 55 above) 151.

270 n 251 above. See R Byrne & W Binchy *Annual review of Irish law 2011* (2012) 202 - 203.

271 n 251 above, [15], [17].

272 See McDermott (n 224 above) [2-03]–[2-04].

273 Edwards, Fennelly, Irvine, MacMenamin and Murphy JJ.

274 Hogan J's decision in *Kinsella* is a notable exception.

ECHR[275] and has not been a barrier in African cases. Cases have been lost on account of findings of fact against prisoners. This is an inevitable hazard in litigation and is understandable to some extent. Failure has also ensued when the wrong order (*habeas corpus*) has been sought.

7.4.2 The franchise

The Supreme Court denied equality to prisoners in relation to a fundamental right and duty of citizens in a democracy when it made a petty distinction between a prisoner's right to vote and curtailment of the exercise of the franchise in *Breathnach v Ireland*.[276] This can be contrasted with the outcome to similar challenges in South Africa[277] and Canada,[278] and before the European Court of Human Rights,[279] although in all of these cases, which were decided by a majority, the matter was controversial. In *NICRO*[280] the South African legislation was found unconstitutional, as it breached the right to vote[281] and did not pass the rationality test for limitation of rights.[282] Ngcobo J (dissenting) considered that the restriction on voting rights was justified, since crime struck at the very core of the fabric of society by violating fundamental human rights such as the right to life, the right to freedom and security, the right to property and the right to dignity, and undermining the rule of law.[283]

The majority of the Supreme Court of Canada in *Sauvé v Canada* asserted the need for clear justification for infringement of fundamental rights by the

275 On the more robust approach taken by the European Court of Human Rights, see L Herrick 'Prisoners' rights' in U Kilkelly (ed) *ECHR and Irish law* (2009) [11.37].

276 [2001] IESC 59, [2001] 3 IR 230.

277 *Minister of Home Affairs v National Institute for Crime Prevention and the Re-Integration of Offenders* (*NICRO*) 2005 3 SA 280 (CC). Cf *Centre for Human Rights & Civil Liberties (CHURCIL) v AG* (Suit No J1/5/2008) (Supreme Court of Ghana) 23 March 2010; *Kanyua v AG* [2010] eKLR (Interim Independent Constitutional Dispute Resolution Court of Kenya, 23 June 2010). On *CHURCIL*, see JS Nelson 'Fair measure of the right to vote: A comparative perspective on voting rights enforcement in a maturing democracy' (2010) 18 *Cardozo Journal of International and Comparative Law* 425 at fn 18, fn 45, fn 176, fn 178, 442 - 443, 447 - 448, 452 - 453, 457, 461, 463, 475.

278 *Sauvé v Canada (Chief Electoral Officer)* 2002 SCC 68, [2002] 3 SCR 519 (SC of Canada).

279 *Hirst v UK (No 2)* (App no 74025/01) (2006) 42 EHRR 41.

280 n 277 above.

281 Constitution of the Republic of South Africa 1996, Sec 19(3).

282 Sec 36(1).

283 n 277 above, [144]. Cf *Boulle v Government of Seychelles* [2011] SCCC 5 (Constitutional Court of Seychelles).

legislature, and was not persuaded that the court should defer – even in the interests of dialogue with the legislature.[284] The Grand Chamber of the European Court of Human Rights in *Hirst v UK* referred to *Sauvé* and the South African case of *August*.[285] It found that the right to vote[286] was not a privilege any longer, but neither was it an absolute right.[287] Ireland was among the 13 countries listed in *Hirst* where all prisoners were barred from or unable to vote,[288] but legislation has since been passed permitting prisoners to apply for a postal vote.[289] The offender's capacity for autonomy and participation in democracy can be strengthened by having the ability to vote

284 n 278 above, [9], [17]. McLachlin CJ, delivering judgment on behalf of the majority, accepted that there can be no precise proof of philosophy, politics or society's interests, but insisted that there must be convincing reasonable justification based on a constitutionally valid reason for infringement – not just 'a simple majoritarian political preference for abolishing a right altogether' or vague and symbolic objectives: n 278 above, [18], [20], [22]. She felt strongly that refusing to allow the exercise of the franchise reneged on the pledge to respect each person, 'denying citizens the right to vote runs counter to our constitutional commitment to the inherent worth and dignity of every individual': n 278 above, [35], citing *August v Electoral Commission* 1999 3 SA 1 (CC) [17]. Gonthier J for the minority took issue with her view that temporary disenfranchisement of prisoners undermined their inherent worth and, on the contrary, he regarded deprivation of voting as part of the punishment of an autonomous individual who had made a free choice to commit a crime, and stated, n 278 above, [73]:

> [I]t could be said that the notion of punishment is predicated on the dignity of the individual: it recognizes serious criminals as rational, autonomous individuals who have made choices. When these citizens exercise their freedom in a criminal manner, society imposes a concomitant responsibility for that choice.

He considered that temporary disenfranchisement of serious criminal offenders reiterated society's commitment to basic moral values and was 'morally educative for both prisoners and society as a whole' – rather than undermining the dignity or worth of prisoners, the removal of their vote took seriously the notion that they were free actors and attached consequences to actions that violated core values: n 278 above, [75], [92].

See PW Hogg *Constitutional law of Canada Vol 2* (2007) 41 - 42.

285 n 279 above, [35]-[37] (*Sauvé*) and [38]-[39] (*August* (n 284 above).

286 ECHR Protocol No 1, Art 3.

287 The states were allowed a margin of appreciation to justify restrictions on voting by prisoners perhaps on the grounds of security or the prevention of crime and disorder: n 279 above, [59]-[60], [69]. The legislation had legitimate aims (the prevention of crime by sanctioning the conduct of convicted prisoners, and the enhancement of civic responsibility and respect for the rule of law), but it failed the proportionality test since there was no evidence that the legislature had sought to weigh competing interests or to assess the proportionality of a blanket ban, which was 'a blunt instrument' stripping indiscriminately a significant category of persons of their right to vote: n 279 above, [74]-[75], [79], [82], [85]. See S Tsakyrakis 'Proportionality: An assault on human rights?' (2009) 7 *International Journal of Constitutional Law* 468 at 486.

288 n 279 above, [33].

289 Electoral (Amendment) Act 2006 secs 2 & 3.

while in prison.[290] The ethics of human dignity and rights are especially relevant to the moral standing of criminals, as they normally have little social standing and are in a similar position to those who cannot be protected by any moral concept *other than* respect for humans as such.[291]

7.5 Family

The institution of marriage[292] has been designated specifically for protection in Article 41 of the Constitution.[293] In the absence of a similar provision in the South African Constitution, the safeguards for marriage and the family there are based on the foundational constitutional values and on human dignity.[294] The nexus between marriage and the family in the Irish document and the omission of a clause prohibiting discrimination on the grounds of marital status have meant that less protection has been afforded to extra-marital family units, which are not given recognition.[295]

Unmarried fathers have been the target of arbitrary differentiation and unreasonably denied the opportunity to express their identity through their relationship with their children and by participating in the lives of their offspring.[296] The Irish courts have not considered the constitutional rights of

290 MD Dubber 'Dignity in penal law and penal police' (2009) Working Paper http://ssrn.com/abstract=1530545 (accessed 28 September 2013) 4.

291 YM Barilan 'From *imago dei* in the Jewish-Christian traditions to human dignity in contemporary Jewish law' (2009) 19 *Kennedy Institute Ethics Journal* 231 at 232. Those who cannot be protected by any other moral concept include people with severe developmental disabilities, comatose persons, and cadavers: as above.

292 The right to marry is a personal right protected by Article 40.3.1, and can be regulated by the Oireachtas in accordance with the common good: *O'Shea v Ireland* [2006] IEHC 305, [2007] 2 IR 313.

293 Art 41.3.1°. See *Murphy v AG* [1982] IR 241 (HC, SC); *Muckley v Ireland* [1985] IR 472 (HC, SC); *Greene v Minister for Agriculture* [1990] 2 IR 17 (HC); *Hyland* (n 97 above) (HC, SC). Contrast *Madigan v AG* [1986] ILRM 136 (HC, SC).

294 *Certification of the Constitution of the Republic of South Africa, 1996* 1996 4 SA 744 (CC) (*First Certification* case) [100]. See also *Dawood v Minister of Home Affairs* 2000 3 SA 936 (CC) [28], [36]-[37]; *Booysen v Minister of Home Affairs* 2001 4 SA 485 (CC) [8], [10]; *Volks v Robinson* 2005 5 BCLR 446 (CC) (majority view).

295 See *O'Brien v Stoutt* (n 88 above) (HC, SC). The right to travel (but not the disparate treatment of marital and non-marital children) ensured a satisfactory outcome in *State (M) v Minister for Foreign Affairs* [1979] IR 73 (HC).

296 Only in the last 100 years have Western countries recognised the duties of fathers to their non-marital children: Barilan (n 291 above) 239. On the non-marital family in Irish law, see Binchy (n 83 above) 202 - 203. On unmarried fathers and guardianship,

unmarried fathers in the full light of the constitutional values of human dignity, equality and freedom. In *Nicolaou* the Supreme Court addressed the rights (or lack of rights, as it emerged) of the unmarried father of a child sent for adoption without his consent.[297] The father claimed that that he had rights that could be exercised when the mother abrogated her entitlements, and alleged unfair discrimination based on sex and paternity. While Walsh J in the Supreme Court was willing to accept that the mother had natural rights, he did not examine when her rights could be limited. He had no hesitation in condemning all unmarried fathers to be without rights in relation to their child, irrespective of the individual circumstances. He referred to children conceived as a result of rape and to fathers who might have no interest in their children, but he sacrificed the committed fathers with the uninvolved ones.[298] No distinction was made between responsible and irresponsible fathers. This was not the case in South Africa, when in *Fraser* the Constitutional Court found that legislation dispensing with the unmarried father's consent to adoption in all circumstances breached the constitutional rights to equality and was discriminatory.[299]

In *WO'R v EH* the Irish Supreme Court by a majority held that the concept of *de facto* family ties was not recognised under the Constitution, which defined the family as one founded on marriage.[300] The Court unanimously accepted Finlay CJ's recognition in *JK v VW* that the natural father could have extensive rights (but not based on the Constitution), where the child was born as a result of a stable and established relationship and was nurtured at the commencement of its life by a father and mother in a situation bearing nearly all of the characteristics of a constitutionally protected family.[301] Barrington J (dissenting) criticised Walsh J's judgment in *Nicolaou*, on the grounds that, although Walsh J referred to equality as human persons under Article 40.1, he went on to treat Mr Nicolaou (a caring parent) the same way as a natural father with no interest in his child, which amounted to unfair

see T Finegan 'An unmarried father's right to guardianship of his child and a child's right to the support of his/her father: A Hohfeldian view of the Irish Constitution' (2010) 32 *Dublin University Law Journal* 320. For the South African position, see CJ Davel & RA Jordaan *Law of persons* (2005) 124 - 127.

297 n 90 above.

298 n 90 above, 641.

299 *Fraser v Children's Court Pretoria North* [1997] ZACC 1, 1997 2 SA 218 (CC).

300 n 91 above.

301 n 105 above, 447. See Shannon (n 17 above) [9-125]–[9-127]. Note observations of McKechnie J: *GT v KAO* (n 142 above) [50]-[51].

discrimination by treating people in different situations equally.[302] Furthermore, the failure of the Adoption Board to inform Mr Nicolaou of the proposal to give his child for adoption, even though he had notified the Board he would oppose it, was extraordinary and Walsh J's description of its omission as 'impolitic' was too mild.[303] Barrington J considered that it was illogical to acknowledge the rights of the child and the mother under Article 40.3 and to deny that the concerned father also had rights under the same provision.[304]

In addition to the South African example, Canadian jurisprudence can be an indicator of how the Irish courts could address the fragile legal standing of fathers. Wilson J (dissenting) in *R v Jones* pointed out the significance to identity of familial bonds from the viewpoint of fulfilling obligations rather than of exercising rights.[305] The Supreme Court of Canada approved of this view in *Trociuk*, when Deschamps J delivering the Court's unanimous judgment based her analysis of the breach of the equality right on the impairment of dignity and stated, '[p]arents have a significant interest in meaningfully participating in the lives of their children.'[306]

7.6 Children's rights

The uncertainty over the nature of children's rights was epitomised by the divergence between the judges in *TD*.[307] The applicants in *TD* were disadvantaged children in need of accommodation and treatment in high support units. The responsible state authorities had been found to have failed

302 n 91 above, 278 - 280.

303 n 91 above, 280, citing n 90 above, 639.

304 n 91 above, 284.

305 'The relations of affection between an individual and his family and his assumption of duties and responsibilities towards them are central to the individual's sense of self and of his place in the world.': [1986] 2 SCR 284 (SC of Canada) [79].

306 *Trociuk v British Columbia (AG)* 2003 SCC 34, [2003] 1 SCR 835 [15]. In this case it was held that legislative provisions giving the mother absolute discretion to unacknowledge the biological father on the birth registration forms and not to include the father's surname in the child's surname violated the father's right to equality, as they discriminated on the grounds of sex (Canadian Charter of Rights and Freedoms 1982, Sec 15(1), and were not justified under the limitations clause since they did not impair the father's rights as little as reasonably possible (Sec 1). The absence of historical disadvantage against fathers as a group was not determinative: above, [20]. See Hogg (n 284 above) 664.

307 n 147 above (HC); n 32 above (SC).

in their obligations to vindicate the children's rights. As there were delays in implementing the policy formulated by the authorities to deal with the general problem of children with special needs, Kelly J in the High Court granted a mandatory injunction directing that the facilities be provided for them in accordance with the adopted policy.[308] The Supreme Court in a majority decision allowed the respondents' appeal. In the High Court, Kelly J referred to the High Court case of *FN v Minister for Education* decided some five years earlier when Geoghegan J made a declaration that a minor was entitled to treatment to ensure his welfare.[309] Kelly J approved of Geoghegan J's identification of needy children's rights to appropriate facilities and granted the injunction because of the delays.[310] In *FN* Geoghegan J had endorsed the rights of the child enunciated by O'Higgins CJ in *G v An Bord Uchtála* as 'a child having been born has the right to be fed and to live, to be reared and educated, and to have the opportunity of working and realising his or her full personality and dignity as a human being' and approved of his view that these rights must be protected and vindicated by the State.[311] Geoghegan J commented that Walsh[312] and Henchy JJ[313] had made similar observations.[314]

308 n 147 above.

309 n 147 above, 67 - 68, 82, 85, citing [1995] 1 IR 409.

310 n 147 above, 85.

311 n 309 above, 415, citing *G* (n 30 above) 56.

312 Walsh J expounded on the child's independent natural right to life as a person, stating, *G* (n 30 above) 69:

> The child's natural rights spring primarily from the natural right of every individual to life, to be reared and educated, to liberty, to work, to rest and recreation, to the practice of religion, and to follow his or her conscience. The right to life necessarily implies the right to be born, the right to preserve and defend (and to have preserved and defended) that life, and the right to maintain that life at a proper human standard in matters of food, clothing and habitation. It lies not in the power of the parent who has the primary natural rights and duties in respect of the child to exercise them in such a way as intentionally or by neglect to endanger the health or life of the child or to terminate its existence. The child's natural right to life and all that flows from that right are independent of any right of the parent as such.

313 Henchy J's view of the child's constitutional right was more circumscribed, his description of it being within the realms of education, *G* (n 30 above) 91:

> As to the constitutional right of the child, it arises under Article 40, s. 3, by analogy with Article 42, s. 1, and it amounts to a right to be accorded, with due regard to what the circumstances reasonably allow, an upbringing which will provide for the religious and moral, intellectual, physical and social education of the child. Whereas this right, as guaranteed by Article 42, s. 1, to legitimate children, is coupled with a correlative duty imposed on the parents – a duty which is related to their means – the analogous right of illegitimate children which is to be implied under Article 40, s. 3, cannot be necessarily exercisable in the context of a correlative duty imposed on the father or mother.

314 n 309 above, 415.

The South African Constitutional Court in *S v M* also took the view that the child has its own independent personality and dignity.[315]

To summarise the Supreme Court's attitude to children's rights in *TD*, one judge (Denham J in dissent) had a strong belief that they attached to the children in their own right;[316] another (Keane CJ) considered children had rights, but only on the assumption that *G v An Bord Uchtála* had been correctly decided;[317] Murphy J did not accept that the *ratio decidendi* in *G v An Bord Uchtála* was as extensive as Geoghegan J held in *FN*;[318] the remaining two judges (Hardiman[319] and Murray[320] JJ) reserved their position.

There were concerns in Ireland that because of the prime position occupied by the institution of the (marital) family under Articles 41 and 42, parental autonomy and control could take priority over the child's welfare and best interests.[321] The welfare of the child encompassed within the Constitution was focused on preventing serious impairment of the child's welfare interests rather than on actively promoting them.[322] Conflict existed between national law and Ireland's international obligations to protect children.[323] The general trend in international law is to regard children as individuals possessing rights independently of their parents.[324] The emphasis has switched from parental rights to parental responsibilities in South Africa,[325] where the courts have begun to recognise the interests of the child as occurring in communion with the interests of the parents and the common

315 2008 3 SA 232 (CC) [18]-[19].

316 n 32 above, 295 - 296.

317 n 32 above, 281 - 282.

318 n 32 above, 318.

319 n 32 above, 345.

320 n 32 above, 325.

321 Shannon (n 17 above) [1-05]–[1-07].

322 Shannon (n 17 above) [1-09]. Cf F Ryan '21st century families, 19th century values: Modern family law in the shadow of the Constitution' in Doyle & Carolan (n 14 above) 371 - 374. See *North Western Health Board* (n 54 above).

323 Shannon (n 17 above) [1-54], [1-56], [1-72]. On the domestic effect of international treaties in Ireland, see S Egan *The United Nations human rights treaty system: Law and procedure* (2011) [1.16].

324 S Pete 'To smack or not to smack? Should the law prohibit South African parents from imposing corporal punishment on their children?' (1998) 14 *South African Journal on Human Rights* 430 at 447; B Shmueli 'The influence of the United Nations Convention on the Rights of the Child on corporal punishment – A comparative study' (2008) 10 *Oregon Review of International Law* 189 at 197 - 198.

325 Shannon (n 17 above) [1-65]. See *Bannatyne v Bannatyne* [2002] ZACC 31, 2003 2 SA 363 (CC) [30].

good.[326] A comprehensive provision in the Irish Constitution similar to that in Section 28 of the South African Constitution setting out the rights of the child and stipulating that the child's best interests are paramount in every matter concerning the child would be appropriate.[327] In a referendum held in 2012 the people approved the amendment of the Irish Constitution to affirm each individual child's inherent rights and to provide that in stipulated circumstances the child's best interests should be paramount.[328]

7.6.1 Corporal punishment

Is there an obligation on the state to ban corporal punishment by a parent? If corporal punishment is bad for adults, then is it not bad for children, who are people too?[329] There is an inherent conflict between smacking, which is fundamentally violent and authoritarian, as a form of punishment and the ideals of peace, harmony and dignity contained in international human rights instruments.[330] As we have seen, some interpret the Convention on the Rights of the Child (CRC)[331] with the guidelines in the UN general comments[332] as outlawing all parental corporal punishment. Legalised violence against children is prohibited, but the definition of 'violence' is critical to resolving the issue. Parents may defend smacking on the grounds that it is not violence

326 Shannon (n 17 above) [1-71].

327 Law Society of Ireland Law Reform Committee 'Rights-based Child Law: The Case for Reform' (Report) (March 2006) Dublin at 8, 34, 61. On the child's best interests, see *Minister for Welfare and Population Development v Fitzpatrick* 2000 3 SA 422 (CC); *Du Toit v Minister of Welfare and Population Development* 2003 2 SA 198 (CC).

328 The amendment provided for the repeal of Article 42.5 and the insertion of Article 42A. But even without an amendment, there was scope for improving the protection given to children in the existing legal system. Under the guise of respecting the separation of powers, the Supreme Court as guardian of the Constitution had been remiss in not intervening to protect children by directing mandatory orders to the State where warranted: Law Society of Ireland Law Reform Committee (n 327 above) 8, 60; Shannon (n 17 above) [1-106]. Intervention by the courts is not a breach of the separation of powers, which has to bow to the supremacy of the Constitution: DG Morgan *The separation of powers in the Irish Constitution* (1997) 231 - 232.

329 Pete (n 324 above) 447.

330 As above.

331 Convention on the Rights of the Child (adopted 20 November 1989, entered into force 2 September 1990) 1577 UNTS 3.

332 In particular see UN Committee on the Rights of the Child 'General Comment No 8' (2 March 2007) UN Doc CRC/C/GC/8. On General Comment No 8, see MDA Freeman 'Upholding the dignity and best interests of children: International law and the corporal punishment of children' (2010) 73(2) *Law and Contemporary Problems* 211 at 220 - 224. The views of a UN Committee do not prevail over Irish law where the terms of a Covenant have not been enacted: *Kavanagh v Governor of Mountjoy Prison* [2002] IESC 13, [2002] 3 IR 97.

in retribution[333] for bad behaviour but is for educational purposes – they may even say (as maintained by the parents in *Christian Education*)[334] that it is warranted in service of the fundamental right to a proper education required by their duty to educate their children.[335] This is a subjective view that is not amenable to independent scrutiny. The perspective of society on the value of corporal punishment as an educational mechanism has changed – particularly in Ireland where we have seen widespread child abuse by those entrusted with the care of children or in positions where they had access to them.[336]

The supremacy of the Constitution may prevent Ireland from complying with the ECHR requirement that a state take positive steps to protect children from inhuman or degrading treatment or punishment. Following the European Court of Human Rights' decision in *A v UK* the imprecise common law defence of 'reasonable chastisement' should no longer be available to a parent

333 Retributivists argue that moral guilt requires punishment, whereas utilitarians claim that punishment is justified solely by its beneficial consequences to the public: H Morris (ed) *Freedom and responsibility: Readings in philosophy and law* (1961) 500. On retributivism and consequentialism, see D Dolinko 'Restorative justice and the justification of punishment' [2003] *Utah Law Review* 319 at 321; K Huigens 'Dignity and desert in punishment theory' (2003) 27 *Harvard Journal of Law and Public Policy* 33 at 40 - 41. Suffering is redeemed by its relationship to the wrong: J Gardner 'In-troduction' in Hart (n 184 above) xvi.

Some philosophers pushed the retributive theory to its boundary by asserting that the criminal has a *right* to be punished: H Morris *On guilt and innocence: Essays in legal philosophy and moral psychology* (1976) 32. On Herbert Morris' account of punishment, see LR Meyer 'Herbert Morris and punishment' (2003) 22 *Quinnipiac Law Review* 109 at 112.

The emphasis in punishment theories has shifted from retribution to deterrence, reparation to the victim, and reform of the perpetrator. The salient feature of English penal policy at the end of the 18th century has been described as 'a crude utilitarianism aiming at the reduction of crime through terror': L Radzinowicz & JWC Turner 'Punishment: Outline of developments since the 18th century' in Radzinowicz & Turner (n 158 above) 39.

334 *Christian Education South Africa v Minister of Education* 2000 4 SA 757 (CC).

335 Shmueli (n 324 above) 210.

336 Despite the express recognition of children in their own right in the constitutional amendment of 2012, the remaining emphasis in the Irish Constitution on parental autonomy may still be an obstacle to an outright ban on all corporal punishment and make it difficult to formulate an exemption for parental punishment based on an objectively reasonable standard.

Recognising the difficulties and noting the gradual development of the criminal law of assault, the Law Reform Commission had recommended waiting to abolish the common law chastisement exception until parents had been re-educated: Law Reform Commission 'Report on Non-Fatal Offences Against the Person' (LRC 45-1994) [9-212], [9-214]. See Shannon (n 17 above) [2-33]–[2-34].

as a defence to an assault charge.[337] I will now consider whether Irish law is in conformity with the ECHR requirements. Has any gap that existed in the common law been sealed by the Non-Fatal Offences against the Person Act 1997?

Corporal punishment in schools is a thing of the past insofar as Irish law is concerned.[338] There has not been as decisive a ban on parental corporal punishment.[339] Statutory exceptions and definitions leave room for a parent charged with assault to plead that the force applied to the child constituted reasonable chastisement as permitted at common law, that there was a lawful excuse for the attack, or that Irish society accepts that parents can hit their children. The law is imprecise and does not provide adequate protection for children against ill-treatment in the home. Despite its positive obligation to intervene to protect rights,[340] the Irish State continues to collude in the violation of a minor's dignity by standing on the sidelines and declining to criminalise unambiguously an assault by a parent on a child.[341] If children are regarded as possessing independent dignity,[342] the idea that they are the property of their parents so as to permit authoritarian control to be maintained

337 (App no 25599/94) (1999) 27 EHRR 611. See Freeman (n 332 above) 235. Although it appears to support a general prohibition on physical punishment, it could be argued that this decision does not have a direct connection to the legitimacy of moderate, measured, and reasonable corporal punishment because the beatings in this case – perpetrated using an implement – were severe and unreasonable: Shmueli (n 324 above) 216.

Reforms in the UK since that *A v UK* did not abolish the defence of reasonable chastisement entirely and the law there retains the concept that hitting children can be not only acceptable, but right: L Hoyano & C Keenan *Child abuse: Law and policy across boundaries* (2010) 187.

338 Shannon (n 17 above) [3-45]. The common law rule granting teachers immunity from criminal liability for punishing pupils has been abolished: Non-Fatal Offences against the Person Act 1997 sec 24.

339 Sec 22(1) of the 1997 Act stipulates that the Act has effect 'subject to any enactment or rule of law providing a defence, or providing lawful authority, justification or excuse for an act or omission.' Section 2 decriminalises assault if there is a 'lawful excuse': sec 2(1). Neither is an offence committed 'if the force or impact, not being intended or likely to cause injury, is in the circumstances such as is generally acceptable in the ordinary conduct of daily life and the defendant does not know or believe that it is in fact unacceptable to the other person': sec 2(3).

340 Shannon (n 17 above) [2-29]–[2-30].

341 See JA Scutt 'Sparing parents pain or spoiling the child by the rod: Human rights arguments against corporal punishment' (2009) 28 *University of Tasmania Law Review* 1 at 7.

342 Some Irish judges have referred to the child's dignity in his or her own right, including Geoghegan J in *FN* (n 309 above) 415; Denham J (dissenting) in *TD* (n 32 above) 295. Cf *S v M* (n 315 above) [18]; *DPP, Transvaal v Minister for Justice and Constitutional Development* [2009] ZACC 8, 2009 4 SA 222 (CC) [123] (Ngcobo J).

by violence is no longer tenable.[343] A clear ban outlawing parental corporal punishment is necessary to comply with our international obligations.[344]

Forbidding parental corporal punishment need not disturb the general defences that apply to all (including parents) charged with assault. In accordance with the parameters of the criminal law, parents may invoke the defence of necessity where there was a proportionately violent response to an extremely urgent situation with no reasonable alternative.[345] Self-defence could be pleaded when faced with an attack from a violent child. The use of reasonable force to protect people or property or to prevent crime is permitted by statute.[346] The law recognises the special relationship between parents and children, who need direction while they are growing, learning and developing into responsible adults.[347] Discipline is a part of the guidance of children, but that is different from violence and humiliation.[348]

I will now outline the duties imposed on parents, as the steps they take to fulfil those duties are relevant to the question of whether they may use corporal punishment as an educational tool. The primary duty to care for, protect, and raise the child rests on the parent,[349] who may have a liability in tort law for negligence for damage or injury caused by a child because of entrusting the child with dangerous articles, the child's dangerous propensities or failure to control the child properly.[350] Article 42.1 of the Constitution refers to the right and duty of parents to provide for 'the religious and moral,

343 Scutt (n 341 above) 22.

344 Freeman (n 332 above) 216.

345 H Stewart 'Parents, children, and the law of assault' (2009) 32 *Dalhousie Law Journal* 1 at 15.

346 Non-Fatal Offences against the Person Act 1997 sec 18. See D Glendenning 'School disci-pline: Balancing individual student rights and the common good' in D Glendenning & W Binchy (eds) *Litigation against schools: Implications for school management* (2006) 198 - 201.

347 Stewart (n 345 above) 33.

348 Freeman (n 332 above) 221.

349 Stewart (n 345 above) 33. See also CRC (n 331 above) art 18(1).

350 D Glendenning *Education and the law* (2012) [9.105]. The incident giving rise to the claim may be attributable to the parent's lack of success in supervising and controlling the child's activities, or, more broadly, to some deficiency in parenting: S Van Praagh '"*Sois sage*" – Responsibility for childishness in the law of civil wrongs' in Neyers *et al* (n 190 above) 76.

intellectual, physical and social education of their children.'[351] The extent of that duty and the leeway given to parents to decide the tactics to fulfil it change in accordance with societal views, which are influenced by the law (including international instruments).

As well as condemning clearly violence and the degrading treatment of children, the CRC acknowledges parents' rights and duties.[352] States have to assist parents in the performance of their child-rearing responsibilities,[353] which are underpinned by the best interests of the child.[354] Although recognising parents' rights and duties, the CRC places them in the context of the child's rights and best interests. Notwithstanding the fact that the latter is a vague principle open to various interpretations in different places and times, the CRC does not give any scope for parental discretion to use corporal punishment for educational or other purposes. The parents' rights are supplemental to those of the child.

The margin of appreciation allowed to states under the ECHR is not replicated in the CRC. Furthermore to constitute degrading treatment or punishment under Article 3 ECHR, a minimum level of severity must be

351 Parents have a dual role – they are expected to foster a child's sense of autonomy and self-fulfilment, and also to underline the child's sense of responsibility for self and others: Van Praagh (n 350 above) 64. The rights that parents have over their children flow partly from their interest in having a relationship with them, and partly from their need to have these rights to carry out their duties: Stewart (n 345 above) 22.

352 Article 5 obliges states to respect their 'responsibilities, rights and duties ... to provide, in a manner consistent with the evolving capacities of the child, appropriate direction and guidance in the exercise by the child of the rights recognized in the present Convention.' Article 14 asserts that parents can and must provide direction to the child in 'a manner consistent with the evolving capacities of the child' (art 14(1) in the exercise of his or her right to freedom of thought, conscience and religion (art 14(2).

Ayoola JSC in the Nigerian Supreme Court stated, '[t]he right to freedom of thought, conscience or religion implies a right not to be prevented, without lawful justification, from choosing the course of one's life, fashioned on what one believes in, and a right not to be coerced into acting contrary to religious belief': *Medical and Dental Practitioners Disciplinary Tribunal v Okonkwo* [2002] AHRLR 159 (NgSC 2001) [73].

353 CRC (n 331 above) art 18(2).

354 CRC (n 331 above) art 18(1). On the best interests of the child, see Freeman (n 332 above) 216 - 219. The amendment of the Irish Constitution approved by the people in 2012 would allow provision to be made by law (a) for adoption of a child when its best interests so require and (b) for the best interests of the child to be the paramount consideration when certain proceedings are being resolved: Art 42A.2.2°, 42A.4.1°.

The child has a right to education directed, *inter alia*, to development of the child's personality and respect for human rights, and to preparation of the child for responsible life in a free society in the spirit of peace and tolerance: CRC (n 331 above) arts 28(1) & 29(1)(a), (b) & (d).

reached.[355] In *A v UK* the European Court of Human Rights looked at the context.[356] The difficulty arises in framing a provision that would allow corporal punishment by a parent below the minimum threshold of severity. The attempt by the UK to do so has not been successful and has satisfied neither abolitionists, supporters, the police nor social workers.[357]

On one side of the fence stand paternalistic traditionalists who believe parents know best and place the authority of the family centre stage.[358] On the other side are those – fearful of inflicting injury – who support individual rights viewing the child as an independent entity.[359] Benjamin Shmueli has proposed an approach mid-way between these protagonists based on a relational worldview where the individual is connected to society and not isolated.[360] His model has educational and preventative elements.[361] He considers that an integrated approach which focuses mainly on the human rights of the child, but does not ignore parental rights, is best.[362] He maintains that this approach is in line with the CRC that sees the child as a human being with rights and not merely as a person who needs extensive protection by society and the law.[363]

355 On assessment of the minimum level of severity, see *A v Ireland* (App no 25579/05) (2011) 53 EHRR 13 [164].

356 'The assessment of this minimum is relative: it depends on all the circumstances of the case, such as the nature and context of the treatment, its duration, its physical and mental effects and, in some instances, the sex, age and state of health of the victim.': n 337 above, [20] (footnote omitted).

357 Freeman (n 332 above) 236. The Committee of Ministers of the Council of Europe continued to supervise execution of *A v UK* after legislation permitting a parent to hit a child was enacted following the judgment by the European Court of Human Rights: Freeman (n 332 above) 235. On corporal punishment in the UK, see B Shmueli 'Corporal punishment in the educational system versus corporal punishment by parents: A comparative view' (2010) 73(2) *Law and Contemporary Problems* 281 at 299.

358 B Shmueli 'Who's afraid of banning corporal punishment? A comparative view on current and desirable models' (2007) 26 *Penn State International Law Review* 57 at 62 - 63. They consider that the benefits of corporal punishment outweigh any damage caused: above, 62.

359 Shmueli (n 358 above) 62. They wish society to have uniform desirable norms that do not bend before different cultural viewpoints and are enforced in an egalitarian manner on the whole population: as above.

360 n 358 above, 64.

361 n 358 above, 137. The criteria Shmueli lists as justification for a criminal prosecution include, first, intentional or reckless parental conduct without good faith and not in the best interest of the child; second, a negative motive (not educational, which is *prima facie* positively motivated); and, third, deviation from reasonable, proportionate and moderate parental conduct: n 358 above, 132 - 134.

362 n 357 above, 320.

363 As above.

There is much merit in the state exerting its influence to sway public opinion towards a humane method of disciplining children that does not involve corporal punishment. Indeed, the CRC obliges states to take social and educational measures to protect children. But this does not absolve the legislature from addressing the issue. Although civil remedies may be appropriate in certain circumstances, a prohibition on parental corporal punishment in criminal law is still necessary. Ireland has already been found in breach of its obligation under the European Social Charter to protect children against violence[364] because it had the defence of 'reasonable chastisement' and therefore corporal punishment was not fully prohibited.[365] In 2006 the UN Committee on the Rights of the Child expressed concern at Ireland's continuing failure to prohibit corporal punishment within the family,[366] and urged that this be done.[367] It also pressed Ireland to educate parents and the general public about the unacceptability of corporal punishment, to promote positive non-violent forms of discipline as an alternative, and to take into account its General Comment No 8.[368]

7.6.2 Privacy and property interests

When students bring their personal property to school, it may lead to a conflict between the exercise of their rights of ownership and the school authorities' right (and duty) to provide a safe environment conducive to learning.[369] The contested property may be things like illicit drugs or weapons such or guns or knives that it may be illegal to possess, cigarettes that are a danger to health, mobile phones which, although not illegal, may be disruptive in class, or clothing accessories that are not part of the school uniform or that are forbidden by the school rules. They might be items of religious or cultural significance, which will implicate the child's identity and human dignity, as

364 European Social Charter (revised) ETS No 163 (ESCR) Art 17.

365 Freeman (n 332 above) 238 - 241.

366 UN Committee on the Rights of the Child 'Consideration of Reports Submitted by States Parties under Article 44 of the Convention on the Rights of the Child. Concluding Observations: Ireland' (29 September 2006) UN Doc CRC/C/IRL/CO/2 [39].

367 n 366 above, [40].

368 n 366 above, [40], citing UN Committee on the Rights of the Child 'General Comment No 8' (n 332 above).

369 On the duty to ensure a safe environment, see Glendenning (n 350 above) [6.114], [9.04], [10.21], [12.68]. The State may impinge on a child's property rights while protecting the common good: *Landers v AG* [1975] 109 ILTR 1 (HC) 5 - 6.

arose in the South African case of *Pillay*.[370] A balance is sought between the property and privacy rights of the students and their freedom of expression, religion and culture, on the one hand, and the school's authority to educate, on the other.

The US Supreme Court in *New Jersey v TLO* held that schoolchildren have legitimate expectations of privacy, which are not waived at the school gates.[371] However, an individual's expectation of privacy depends on the context and the locus. The Court viewed the school's need to maintain a proper learning environment as equally legitimate as the child's expectations of privacy.[372] In striking the balance between the two, it examined the reasonableness in all the circumstances of the search.[373] There was a two-step test in determining reasonableness – the search had to be justified as reasonable at its inception and also in the manner in which it was conducted.[374]

In the legal analysis on confiscation of a student's belongings, the student has a favourable start by having his or her interest defined within the property prism. The school is on the defensive and has the onus of justifying the forfeiture. Non-property interests are not given the same venerated stature. A better resolution could be achieved by aiming to harmonise the rights and duties of all the parties affected beginning with a level playing pitch where all students have equal rights to education and development in a safe environment and the school has the capacity to act to provide that environment. With due regard for the rights to privacy and bodily integrity, the school authorities have sufficient latitude to foster acceptable behaviour that does not threaten the well-being of students or teachers and is conducive to the growth of all students into responsible adults.

7.6.3 Non-traditional relationships

Scientific and medical advances combined with the acceptance of non-traditional personal relationships have given rise to contentious and difficult legal issues relating to the rights and duties to children and their welfare and best interests. The Supreme Court in *McD v L* adjudicated on the position of

370 *MEC for Education: KwaZulu-Natal v Pillay* 2008 1 SA 474 (CC).

371 469 US 325 (1985) 338. See CJ Russo *et al* 'Safety and student searches in schools in the USA, New Zealand and Australia' (2007) 8 *Education Law Journal* 26 at 29 - 30.

372 n 371 above, 340.

373 n 371 above, 341. In this case the search was of a 14 year-old girl found smoking cigarettes in a school lavatory contrary to a school rule: n 371 above, 328.

374 n 371 above, 341.

a sperm donor known to the natural mother of the child and her lesbian partner.[375] When the father's rights to access and guardianship of the child were disputed, the Court decided the matter on the basis of the child's best interests and remitted the action to the High Court to consider his access arrangements. The biological father had no constitutional rights of access or guardianship, but had a statutory right to apply to court for such orders. Fennelly J emphasised the relevance of the circumstances arising in each case, '[i]t is both right and natural to have particular regard to the context of conception, birth and subsequent family links.'[376] On a scale of interested parties, the sperm donor did not carry much weight, as Fennelly J reasoned, '[t]o the extent that Finlay CJ and Denham J postulated a scale for assessment of "rights of interests or concern," it seems likely that the sperm donor would be placed quite low, certainly by comparison with the natural father in a long-term relationship approximating to a family.'[377]

A consideration of the dignity of the various parties might assist in reaching a resolution of these modern-day dilemmas in accordance with constitutional norms. New technologies are challenging legal systems to solve novel disputes arising from their development and application. Established principles can be adapted and new and better ways devised to cope with the legal issues arising from the ever-increasing breakthroughs in science, medicine and information technology. These issues raise concerns over privacy, property, autonomy, dignity and equality, and involve analysis of contract, tort and constitutional law. Utilitarian goals and the adaption of cultures to enhance human flourishing can conflict with preservation of the *status quo*, which may inhibit scientific research and development. There is no simple answer in legal terms. A broad approach encompassing an assessment of the various interests of all the parties involved in the context of supporting innovative ways of advancing society with the aim of improving the quality of people's lives and facilitating the achievement of individuals' personal goals may be worthwhile.

375 n 121 above. See M Farrell 'Court rejects "*de facto* families" in lesbian couple case' (2010) 104(1) *Gazette of the Law Society of Ireland* 14; Shannon (n 17 above) [16-93]–[16-96].

376 n 121 above, [78].

377 n 121 above, [79].

7.7 The embryo, body parts and human tissue

The right to control one's own property is a well-established basic legal principle.[378] The question has arisen as to whether the interests arising in scientific development can be regarded as property and, if so, whether it is appropriate to decide the rights and obligations arising solely or partly from that viewpoint. There are conflicting views as to whether humans can or should have proprietary rights over their body or body parts.[379] Roger Brownsword identified two critical claims concerning, first, the right to control access to and use of a particular body or body part, and, second, the right to exploit commercially a particular body or body part.[380]

Let us begin by looking at the embryo. From a moral perspective, the status of the embryo depends on whether and to what extent it is thought to possess human dignity.[381] At one extreme, is the *full dignity* position granting the embryo full moral status worthy of the same level of protection as an adult.[382] At the other extreme, is the *no dignity* position, which views the embryo itself as having no intrinsic value or status.[383] Between these extremes comes the intermediate stance dubbed the *limited dignity* position by Deryck Beyleveld and Shaun Pattison.[384] The most popular limited stand is the *proportional dignity* position, which regards the moral status of the embryo as increasing with gestational development.[385]

378 See GT Laurie *Genetic privacy: A challenge to medico-legal norms* (2002) 316 - 317.

379 For an argument in favour of the existence of such rights, see D Beyleveld & R Brownsword 'My body, my body parts, my property?' (2000) 8 *Health Care Analysis* 87.

380 R Brownsword *Rights, regulation and the technological revolution* (2008) 63. He posed 'the burning question' whether an individual should have property claims of this kind in relation to that individual's own body or removed body parts: as above.

381 D Beyleveld & SD Pattinson 'Globalisation and human dignity: Some effects and implications for the creation and use of embyros' in R Brownsword (ed) *Global governance and the quest for justice. Vol IV: Human rights* (2004) 186. On the conception of human dignity as a shelter for the preservation of the value of all human beings, see G Duttge 'Research on embryos and human dignity' (2009) 42 *Israel Law Review* 398 at 402 - 407. On the status of the foetus, see A Alghrani & M Brazier 'What is it? Whose it? Re-positioning the fetus in the context of research?' (2011) 70 *Cambridge Law Journal* 51.

382 Beyleveld & Pattinson (n 381 above) 186.

383 As above.

384 As above.

385 As above. The fundamentally different viewpoints in Europe concerning the moral status and dignity of the embryo generated a patchwork of local regulatory positions

Having sketched the moral position, it is time to analyse the case-law on the embryo. In *Roche* Hardiman J did not regard the fertilised but unimplanted ovum as property, and considered that the applicant wife could not rely on her personal rights under Article 40.3.1° as an alternative to having the fate of the frozen embryo decided on the basis of whether it came within the definition of 'unborn' in Article 40.3.3°.[386] All the Supreme Court judges in that case resiled from analysing the meaning of life. According to Murray CJ, as it raised contentious moral, philosophical, theological and scientific issues, it was a matter for the legislature to decide based on policy choices or for a constitutional amendment.[387] He avoided deciding on whether frozen embryos constituted 'life of the unborn',[388] as it was not a justiciable issue and the appellant had not succeeded in establishing it.[389] Denham J was satisfied that the term 'unborn' does not refer to an unimplanted embryo.[390]

on the use of human embryos for research: R Brownsword 'Introduction: Global governance and human rights' in Brownsword (n 381 above) 5. In Ireland, the issue of when human life should begin to enjoy the benefit of legal protection is contentious, as was evident in the Report on Assisted Human Reproduction, when Gerry Whyte dissented strongly from recommendations envisaging the deliberate destruction of the embryo: Commission on Assisted Human Reproduction, *Report* (Dublin, April 2005) 73 - 76.

386 n 28 above, [184]. For reviews of *Roche*, see R Byrne & W Binchy *Annual review of Irish law 2009* (2010) 246 - 251, 313 - 319, 469 - 480; A Mulligan '*Roche v Roche*: Some guidance for frozen embryo disputes' (2010) 13 *Trinity College Law Review* 168. On the High Court decision (n 45 above), see Doyle *Constitutional law: Text, cases and materials* (n 14 above) [5-23]–[5-28].

387 n 28 above, [48], [50], [54]. See J Mortimer 'Judges call for legislation on assisted human reproduction' (2010) 104(2) *Gazette of the Law Society of Ireland* 12.

388 Art 40.3.3°.

389 n 28 above, [55]. The conclusion of all of the judges (except Murray CJ) was that the term 'unborn' did not refer to the frozen embryo. The underlying reason for their stance was their interpretation of the goal of the Eighth Amendment inserting Article 40.3.3° into the Constitution and its language. The aim of the Amendment was to prevent abortion being legalised in Ireland. Four of the judges confined the Amend-ment's reach to the child or foetus intra-womb. Murray CJ disagreed and considered that simply because the embryo existed outside the womb did not mean it was excluded from protection: n 28 above, [36].

390 n 28 above, [148]. She analysed the context in which the Eighth Amendment was passed and its wording: n 28 above, [126]-[144]. It was introduced 'to copper fasten the protection provided in the statutory regime, to render unconstitutional the procuring of a miscarriage': n 28 above, [130]. She was satisfied that the mischief to which it was addressed was that of 'the termination of pregnancy, the procuring of a miscarriage, an abortion': n 28 above, [134]. 'The capacity to be born, or birth' defined the right protected and arose after implantation: n 28 above, [144].

Hardiman J (with whose interpretation Geoghegan[391] and Fennelly[392] JJ agreed) concluded that the 'unborn' referred to 'the foetus *en ventre sa mere*, the embryo implanted in the womb of the mother.'[393]

Moving to the other side of the Atlantic, the US District Court of the Eastern District of Virginia treated frozen embryos as property in *York v Jones*.[394] Justice Daughtrey of the Supreme Court of Tennessee in *Davis v Davis* considered it was not helpful to ask whether pre-embryos were property in order to decide their legal status, since embryos had no intrinsic value to either party, their value lying in their potential to become *children*.[395] While

391 From the wording of the Eighth Amendment and its historical context, Geoghegan J took the view that 'the unborn' refers to a child in the womb not yet born and that the constitutional provision dealt exclusively with the baby in the mother's womb: n 28 above, [209], [217].

392 Fennelly J was satisfied that Article 40.3.3° did not extend to nor include frozen embryos which have not been implanted: n 28 above, [229].

393 n 28 above, [183]. Hardiman J adopted this position because of the context of the Eighth Amendment – those who promoted it thought it necessary to take active steps to prevent the legalisation of abortion whether by legislation or by judicial decision: n 28 above, [178]. The frozen embryo was not implanted and therefore did not fall within the ambit of the Amendment.

394 717 F.Supp 421 (1989). The Court held that a husband and wife were entitled to have a frozen embryo transferred from an institute for reproductive medicine in Virginia to California. A disposition agreement between the institute and the couple created a bailment relationship, which imposed an absolute obligation on the bailee to return the embryo to the bailor when the purpose of the bailment had terminated: above, 425. The plaintiffs' claims for breach of contract and detinue were well-founded. See NR Walz 'Abandoned frozen embryos and embryonic stem cell research: Should there be a connection?' (2007) 1 *University of St Thomas Journal of Law and Public Policy* 122 at 138.

395 842 SW 2d 588 (1992) 598. See Walz (n 394 above) 129 - 130.

The modern view of property and legal rights over it has also generated divergent views in the less controversial and deeply personal area of the use of domain names on the internet. Questions have arisen as to whether domain names are regarded as property and whether an action lies for conversion of intangible property. Conversion of intangible property varies significantly across jurisdictions in the US: CW Franks 'Analyzing the urge to merge: Conversion of intangible property and the merger doctrine in the wake of *Kremen v. Cohen*' (2005) 42 *Houston Law Review* 489 at 492. The US Court of Appeals held that in California the owner of a domain name could sustain an action for conversion: *Kremen v Cohen* 337 F.3d 1024 (2003) (US Court of Appeals 9th Circuit). It confirmed that a plaintiff must fulfil three requirements to establish the tort of conversion: first, ownership or right to possession of property; second, wrongful disposition of the property right; and, third, damages: above, 1029, citing *GS Rasmussen & Associates, Inc v Kalitta Flying Services, Inc* 958 F.2d 896 (1992) (US Court of Appeals 9th Circuit) 906. It affirmed that the concept of property is broad and includes 'every intangible benefit and prerogative susceptible of possession or disposition': above, 1030, citing *Downing v Municipal Court* 88 Cal App.2d 345 (1948) (Court of Appeals of California) 350.

On the historical development of conversion and its modern elements in the US, see Franks above, 494 - 502; E Kohm 'When "sex" sells: Expanding the tort of conversion to encompass domain names' (2003) 23 *Loyola of Los Angeles Entertainment Law*

they were neither persons nor property, they were deserving of more respect than other human tissue because of that potential.[396] He found that the couple who provided the gametes had decision-making rights.[397] The societal interest as expressed in public policy is a constraint on the individuals' freedom to decide the embryos' fate. In the absence of their wishes being ascertained or a prior agreement between them, the constitutional right to privacy grounded in the concept of liberty was determinative.[398]

In contrast, the New York Court of Appeals held in *Kass v Kass* that the disposal of embryos did not implicate a woman's right of privacy or bodily integrity in the area of reproductive choice.[399] As they were not 'persons', Kaye CJ dealt with the dispute over their use by treating the progenitors as holding a 'bundle of rights'[400] in relation to them that could be exercised

Review 443 at 448 - 452. For a description of a domain name, see Kohm above, 444 - 445. The domain name system is at the internet's core: R Balleste 'Persuasions and exhortations: Acknowledging internet governance and human dignity for all' (2011) 38 *Syracuse Journal of International Law and Commerce* Spring 227 at 228. Roy Balleste has advocated that we envision an internet that promotes a world public order of human dignity: above, 230. See also Balleste above, 231, 238 - 240, 248 - 249, 253 - 255.

The House of Lords in a majority decision in *OBG Ltd v Allan* held that strict liability for conversion applied only to an interest in chattels, and declined to expand it to choses in action: [2007] UKHL 21, [2008] 1 AC 1. See G Mitchell 'Should the tort of conversion apply to intangible property?' (2007) 157 *New Law Journal* 958.

396 n 395 above, 597.

397 As above:

> [P]reembryos are not, strictly speaking, either 'persons' or 'property,' but occupy an interim category that entitles them to special respect because of their potential for human life. It follows that any interest that Mary Sue Davis and Junior Davis have in the preembryos in this case is not a true property interest. However, they do have an interest in the nature of ownership, to the extent that they have decision-making authority concerning disposition of the preembryos, within the scope of policy set by law.

398 n 395 above, 598, 604. The right of procreational autonomy (composed of two rights of equal significance – the right to procreate and the right to avoid procreation) is a vital part of an individual's right to privacy: n 395 above, 600 - 601. In the event of a dispute over conflicting constitutional claims, the Court balanced the interests of the parties: n 395 above, 603 - 604. Under contract law, the Court would have been prepared to enforce a prior agreement between the couple on the disposal of unimplanted embryos: n 395 above, 597.

On federal privacy-related rights in the US, see SW Brenner 'Constitutional rights and new technologies in the United States' in RE Leenes *et al* (eds) *Constitutional rights and new technologies: A comparative study* (2008) 230 - 231.

399 91 NY 2d 554 (1998) 564.

400 Traditionally people regarded property as 'things', but lawyers moved from that integrated concept to speaking about property abstractly using metaphors like 'bundles of rights': SJ Eagle 'The really new property: A skeptical appraisal' (2010) 43 *Indiana Law Review* 1229 at 1248. It also carries now connotations of correlative obligations as incidents of ownership: above, 1249. The legal conception of property involves a constellation of Hohfeldian elements, correlatives and opposites: SR Munzer *A theory of property* (1990) 23.

through joint disposition agreements.[401] The Supreme Court of Massachusetts took a more restrained view of the enforceability of the parties' agreement on the use of embryos, when in *AZ v BZ* it was dubious that an agreement prepared by and for the assistance of the clinic represented the intent of the husband and the wife regarding disposition of the preembryos in the case of a dispute between them.[402] Moreover, even if the document had represented the couple's intentions, the Court would have declined to enforce it on the grounds of public policy upholding their privacy and liberty interests.[403] Another nuance was added by the Supreme Court of New Jersey in *JB v MB*, where it accepted that agreements on the use of embryos were enforceable, but public policy permitted either party to resile later.[404]

From these cases, it can be seen that the trend in the US has been to assess rights in relation to the embryo from the perspective of privacy tempered by public policy. The starting point has been that freedom to contract is upheld

JE Penner formulated two versions of the bundle of rights thesis – first, the 'substantial' version, where property is a bundle of rights in the sense that property is a naturally complex normative relation that should be regarded as an historically contingent association of various rights; and, second, the 'conceptual' version, which expresses the idea that 'property' is a concept that is not applied on the basis of some set of necessary and sufficient criteria, but that in a particular case the various incidents or indicia of property may add up in some way, or show sufficient resemblance to a paradigm, such that 'property' is correctly applied to describe it: JE Penner 'The "bundle of rights" picture of property' (1996) 43 *University of California at Los Angeles Law Review* 711 at 722 - 723.

Instead of defining the relationship between a person and 'his' things, property law discusses the relationships that arise *between people* with respect to things: BA Ackerman *Private property and the Constitution* (1977) 26. Justice Pitney in the US Supreme Court approached the issue of whether news was property by looking at the relationship between the parties rather than at the relationship between the agency and the news itself: *International News Service v Associated Press* 248 US 215 (1918) 236. For a critique of *International News Service*, see Penner above, 715 - 718, 722, 816 - 817.

401 n 399 above, 564. She summarised, '[t]he relevant inquiry thus becomes who has dispositional authority over them.': as above. This suggests a similarity to property law: Walz (n 394 above) 132 - 133.

402 431 Mass 150 (2000) 158. See Walz (n 394 above) 133 - 134.

403 n 402 above, 162 (Justice Cowin):

> We derive from existing State laws and judicial precedent a public policy in this Commonwealth that individuals shall not be compelled to enter into intimate family relationships, and that the law shall not be used as a mechanism for forcing such relationships when they are not desired. This policy is grounded in the notion that respect for liberty and privacy requires that individuals be accorded the freedom to decide whether to enter into a family relationship.

404 '[T]he better rule, and the one we adopt, is to enforce agreements entered into at the time in vitro fertilization is begun, subject to the right of either party to change his or her mind about disposition up to the point of use or destruction of any stored preembryos.': 783 A.2d 707 (2001) 719. See Walz (n 394 above) 134 - 135.

and agreements are enforceable when they are not in conflict with public policy to further research of benefit to society. Although not overtly expressed as such, the interests of the parties in relation to the embryo have been regarded as analogous to property rights. The embryo has generally not got the venerated status of a person or the inanimate rank of property, but its progenitors have decision-making rights over it which may be limited by public policy.

After this analysis of the position of the embryo, I will now review some decisions on rights over body parts and human tissue. Staying in the US, the case of *Moore v Regents of University of California* heard by the California Supreme Court illustrates well the divisive nature of the issues arising and the contrasting views on ways to resolve them.[405] Mr Moore's spleen had been removed and was used for research purposes without his knowledge. The majority held that he had a cause of action for breach of the physician's disclosure obligations, but not for conversion.[406] Justice Panelli dismissed the artificial attempt to construct a property-based claim – an unnecessary exercise since there were more appropriate avenues of redress that would protect privacy and dignity.[407] Justice Mosk (dissenting) gave a more con-

405 51 Cal.3d 120 (1990). See J Boyle *Shamans, software, and spleens: Law and the construction of the information society* (1996) 21 - 24, 98 - 107, 116; R Brownsword 'An interest in human dignity as the basis for genomic torts' (2003) 42 *Washburn Law Journal* 413 at 463 - 465; R Hakimian & D Korn 'Ownership and use of tissue specimens for research' (2004) 292 *Journal of the American Medical Association* 2500 at 2502; R Hardcastle *Law and the human body: Property rights, ownership and control* (2009) 65 - 71; Laurie (n 378 above) 314 - 315; D Madden *Medicine, ethics and the law* (2011) [10.16]-[10.21]; Penner (n 400 above) 718 - 723, 817; N Ram 'Assigning rights and protecting interests: Constructing ethical and efficient legal rights in human tissue research' (2009) 23 *Harvard Journal of Law and Technology* 119 at 121 - 122, 169, 170; R Vard 'Proprietary rights in human tissue' (2013) 12 *Hibernian Law Journal* 100 at 118 - 123; Walz (n 394 above) 136 - 138, 152.

406 Justice Panelli pointed out that Moore did not expect to retain possession of his cells following their removal, and therefore he was unable to sustain an action for their conversion, which required retention of an ownership interest in them: n 405 above, 136 - 137.

407 n 405 above, 140:

> [O]ne may earnestly wish to protect privacy and dignity without accepting the extremely problematic conclusion that interference with those interests amounts to a conversion of personal property. Nor is it necessary to force the round pegs of 'privacy' and 'dignity' into the square hole of 'property' in order to protect the patient, since the fiduciary-duty and informed-consent theories protect these interests directly by requiring full disclosure.

He gave three reasons why Moore's tissue should not be treated as property, which the plaintiff needed to establish in order to ground an action for conversion: first, a fair balancing of the relevant policy considerations counselled against extending the tort; second, problems in this area were better suited to legislative resolution; and,

sidered analysis of the nature of property, a variable concept subject to limitation, and found in effect that decision-making rights were property interests.[408] He deduced that protection of Moore's dignity pointed to the vesting in him of a right to profit from his own cells.[409]

Confronted with a dispute over the commercialisation of the results of research into Canavan disease based on tissue, blood samples and genetic information donated voluntarily by the plaintiffs in *Greenberg v Miami* Children's *Hospital Research Institute, Inc*, the US District Court of the Southern District of Florida followed Justice Panelli's reasoning in *Moore* and held that no action lay for conversion, as a donor retained no property interest after the donation was made.[410] With resonances of Justice Mosk's

third, the tort of conversion was not necessary to protect patients' rights: n 405 above, 142 - 143. Two policy considerations of overriding importance were, first, protection of a competent patient's right to make autonomous medical decisions, which was grounded in well-recognised and long-standing principles of fiduciary duty and informed consent; the second one was not to threaten with disabling civil liability innocent parties engaged in socially useful activities, such as researchers who have no reason to believe that their use of a particular cell sample was, or might be, against a donor's wishes: n 405 above, 143.

408 n 405 above, 165 - 166. Justice Mosk's argument as to why the judiciary should adju--dicate and develop tort law, even when the legislature has competence, was persuasive: n 405 above, 176.

409 n 405 above, 166. Contradictory policy considerations were in tension. Justice Mosk highlighted the ethical implications and also mentioned equity – particularly when the parties were not in an equal bargaining position – as a second policy determinant promoted by recognising that every individual has a legally protectible property interest in his own body and its products: n 405 above, 173 - 174. He stated, '[o]ur society values fundamental fairness in dealings between its members, and condemns the unjust enrichment of any member at the expense of another.': n 405 above, 174. Justice Arabian appreciated the problem outlined by Justice Mosk, but disagreed on the solution, being unwilling to decide the contentious moral, philosophical and religious issues arising simply at the level of tort law, n 405 above, 149:

> Does it uplift or degrade the 'unique human persona' to treat human tissue as a fungible article of commerce? Would it advance or impede the human condition, spiritually or scientifically, by delivering the majestic force of the law behind plaintiff's claim? I do not know the answers to these troubling questions, nor am I willing – like Justice Mosk – to treat them simply as issues of 'tort' law, susceptible of *judicial* resolution. ... The ramifications of recognizing and enforcing a property interest in body tissues are not known, but are greatly feared – the effect on human dignity of a marketplace in human body parts...

410 264 F.Supp 2d 1064 (2003) 1074. The Florida Court accepted the distinction made in *Moore* between the patented results of research and the excised material used in the research: above, 1074 - 1075. In the interests of encouraging research, the claim for an extension of the duty of informed consent to cover economic interests was dismissed decisively on the basis that the plaintiffs, being voluntary donors rather than objects of human experimentation, were to be treated differently: above, 1070 - 1071. Moreno J was wary of the consequences of requiring the sharing of information with the donors, as he stated, 'imposing a duty of the character that Plaintiffs seek would be

dissent in *Moore*, the plaintiffs' claim for unjust enrichment in *Greenberg* was successful.[411]

Stephen Munzer divided all body rights into *personal rights* and *property rights*, differentiating between them on the basis that the latter protected the choice to transfer, while the former protected interests or choices other than the choice to transfer.[412]

There have been several instruments adopted at international and regional level regulating scientific development and requiring protection of human rights and human dignity in the process.[413] This can be seen in the Universal Declaration on Bioethics and Human Rights adopted by UNESCO in 2005,[414] when it continued the same theme evident in the Universal Declaration on

unworkable and would chill medical research as it would mandate that researchers constantly evaluate whether a discloseable event has occurred.': above, 1070 (footnote omitted). If this additional requirement were imposed on researchers, it 'would give rise to a type of dead-hand control that research subjects could hold because they would be able to dictate how medical research progresses': above, 1071.

Also like *Moore*, the individual's expectations were relevant, Moreno J dismissing the conversion claim because 'these were donations to research without any contemporaneous expectations of return': above, 1076.

For an analysis of expectations and an explanation of the connection between property and expectations, see Munzer (n 400 above) 28 - 31. For reviews of *Greenberg*, see Brownsword (n 405 above) 476 - 477; Hakimian & Korn (n 405 above) 2502 - 2504; Hardcastle (n 405 above) 71 - 73; Laurie (n 378 above) 321 - 322; Ram (n 405 above) 157, 165 fn 224, 169, 170 fn 247; Vard (n 405 above) 123 - 125.

411 n 410 above, 1072. They were entitled to recompense for a continuing research collaboration, into which they had invested 'time and significant resources in the race to isolate the Canavan gene': n 410 above, 1072 - 1073.

412 n 400 above, 48 - 49. He arrayed those personal rights on two different but related spectra; the first spectrum ranged from rights that protect only interests, through rights that protect both interests and choices, to rights that protect only choices; the second ranged from non-waivable rights, through those that were waivable with qualifications, to rights waivable at the option of the right-holder; property rights in the body could be sub-divided into weak and strong varieties, a *weak property right* involving only a choice to transfer gratuitously and a *strong property right* involving a choice to transfer for value: n 400 above, 49.

413 On the linkage between human rights and new technologies, and on the bioethical triangle (human rights, a dignitarian ethic and a utilitarian ethic) in the emerging international regulatory framework, see: Brownsword (n 308 above) 35 - 41; R Brownsword 'Human dignity, ethical pluralism, and the regulation of modern bio-technologies' in T Murphy (ed) *New technologies and human rights* (2009) 21 - 26; T Murphy 'Repetition, revolution, and resonance: An introduction to new technologies and human rights' in Murphy above, 1 - 2. On the meaning of dignity in these instruments, see C Foster *Human dignity in bioethics and law* (2011) 92 - 95.

414 UNESCO 'Universal Declaration on Bioethics and Human Rights' (19 October 2005) Gen Conf 33 C/Res 36, Preamble, arts 2, 3, 10 - 12 & 28. See Brownsword (n 308 above) 32 - 35; IV Motoc 'The international law of genetic discrimination: The power of "never again"' in Murphy (n 413 above) 229, 242.

the Human Genome and Human Rights of 1997[415] and in the intervening International Declaration on Human Genetic Data.[416] Dignity in the context of scientific advances concerning our genetic make-up seems synonymous with individual uniqueness and worth.[417] The Council of Europe has stressed the imperative of protecting human dignity in instruments such as the Convention on Human Rights and Biomedicine,[418] and the several Additional Protocols to the latter on Cloning,[419] the Transplantation of Organs and Tissues of Human Origin,[420] and Biomedical Research.[421] Even though regulating ethical issues does not fall within the competence of the European Union, bioethics became a central part of the EU public debate and an integral component of governance because the European authorities deemed it necessary not to neglect moral debate in the face of rising competition on the internal market.[422] Unlike in the US, an increasing amount of European

415 UNESCO 'Universal Declaration on the Human Genome and Human Rights' (11 November 1997) Gen Conf 29 C/Res 16. See E Benda 'The protection of human dignity (Article 1 of the Basic Law)' (2000) 53 *Southern Methodist University Law Review* 443 at 452 - 453; H Boussard 'Individual human rights in genetic research: Blurring the line between collective and individual interests' in Murphy (n 413 above) 246 - 247; R Brownsword 'Freedom of contract, human rights and human dignity' in D Friedmann & D Barak-Erez (eds) *Human rights in private law* (2001) 196; Motoc (n 414 above) 223, 226 - 227.

416 UNESCO 'International Declaration on Human Genetic Data' (16 October 2003) Gen Conf 32 C/Res 22, Preamble, arts 1, 7, 26 & 27. See Motoc (n 414 above) 224, 228 - 229, 232 - 233.

417 A Clapham *Human rights obligations of non-state actors* (2006) 540.

418 Convention for the Protection of Human Rights and Dignity of the Human Being with regard to the Application of Biology and Medicine: Convention on Human Rights and Biomedicine (1997) ETS No 164, Preamble, Art 1. See Brownsword (n 415 above) 190, 194 - 196.

419 Additional Protocol to the Convention for the Protection of Human Rights and Dignity of the Human Being with regard to the Application of Biology and Medicine, on the Prohibition of Cloning Human Beings (1998) ETS No 168, Preamble.

420 Additional Protocol to the Convention on Human Rights and Biomedicine, on Transplantation of Organs and Tissues of Human Origin (2002) ETS No 186, Pre-amble, Art 1.

421 Additional Protocol to the Convention on Human Rights and Biomedicine, concerning Biomedical Research (2005) CETS No 195, Preamble, Arts 1 & 9. The European Court of Human Rights has made little reference to the Convention and its Additional Protocols: T Murphy & G Ó Cuinn 'Works in progress: New technologies and the European Court of Human Rights' (2010) 10 *Human Rights Law Review* 601 at 610 - 611. Neither has the Court made any substantial reference to human dignity in new technologies and human rights cases: above, 612.

422 N Lenoir 'Biotechnology, bioethics and law: Europe's 21st century challenge' (2006) 69 *Modern Law Review* 1 at 3. There has been criticism of EU governance of new

legislation dealing with the market includes ethical considerations and references to human dignity in legislation do not seem out of place.[423]

The European Court of Justice ruled in *Brüstle v Greenpeace* that the concept of 'human embryo' for the purpose of ascertaining the scope of the prohibition on patentability includes any human ovum, as soon as fertilised, if it is such as to commence the process of development of a human being.[424] It also encompasses any non-fertilised human ovum capable of commencing that process because of the technique used to obtain it.[425]

Francis Fukuyama has advocated the defence of human dignity by viable political institutions in the real world of politics and not just in philosophical tracts.[426] South Africa has legislated to control the use of human tissue and gametes and to regulate research in the National Health Act 2003. Consent of the donor is necessary[427] and payment to the donor is prohibited except for reimbursement of reasonable costs.[428] Irish legislation on these moral and ethical questions would assist in clarifying the legal implications and would give much-needed guidance to medical personnel and researchers.

technologies because it appears to have deployed citizen participation as a legitimating technique rather than as a substantive input into governance, thus failing to fully empower individuals to uphold human rights: ML Flear & A Vakulenko 'A human rights perspective on citizen participation in the EU's governance of new technologies' (2010) 10 *Human Rights Law Review* 661 at 664, 678, 681 - 682, 687.

423 Lenoir (n 422 above) 4.

424 Case C 34/10 *Brüstle v Greenpeace eV* (ECJ, 18 October 2011) [35].

425 n 424 above, [36]. The Advocate General had proposed that an invention should be excluded from patentability where the application of the technical process for which the patent was filed necessitated the prior destruction of human embryos or their use as base material: n 424 above, (ECJ, Opinion Adv G Bot, 10 March 2011) [8], [119]. He pointed out in his Opinion that human dignity is a principle that must be applied to the human body from fertilisation (the first stage in its development): above, [96]. See F Duffy 'Seed money' (2011) 105(4) *Gazette of the Law Society of Ireland* 38.

426 F Fukuyama *Our posthuman future: Consequences of the biotechnology revolution* (2002) 177; Brownsword (n 308 above) 314. On Fukuyama's conception of human dignity, see above, 171 - 174; R Brownsword 'What the world needs now: Techno-regulation, human rights and human dignity' in Brownsword (n 381 above) 217 - 218; Brownsword (n 308 above) 314 - 315.

427 Secs 55(a), 57(4)(b), 62(1)(a), 71(1)(b), 71(2)(d) & 71(3)(a)(iv).

428 Sec 60(4)(a).

7.8 Privacy

Legislation making contraceptives unavailable was found to be unconstitutional in *McGee*, as it breached the right to marital privacy.[429] Henchy J assessed the effect of the legislation denying access to contraceptives as being

> to condemn the plaintiff and her husband to a way of life which, at best, will be fraught with worry, tension and uncertainty that cannot but adversely affect their lives and, at worst, will result in an unwanted pregnancy causing death or serious illness with the obvious tragic consequences to the lives of her husband and young children. And this in the context of a Constitution which in its preamble proclaims as one of its aims the dignity and freedom of the individual ...[430]

In the context of the right to privacy, Hamilton P in *Kennedy* linked freedom and dignity to democracy, '[t]he nature of the right to privacy must be such as to ensure the dignity and freedom of an individual in the type of society envisaged by the Constitution, namely, a sovereign, independent and democratic society.'[431]

Getting the correct balance between the expression of the individual personality at the heart of the concept of the right to privacy[432] and the common good in the pluralist society defined by the Constitution does not warrant deterrence by attaching the stigma of a criminal offence to what a minority regard as essential to self-fulfilment, as Henchy J stated in dissent in *Norris*:[433]

> What are known as the seven deadly sins are anathematised as immoral by all the Christian Churches and it would have to be conceded that they are capable, in different degrees and in certain contexts, of undermining vital aspects of the common good. Yet it would be neither constitutionally permissible nor otherwise desirable to seek by criminal sanctions to legislate their commission out of existence in all possible circumstances. To do so would upset the necessary balance which the Constitution posits between the common good and the dignity and freedom of the individual. What is deemed necessary to his dignity and freedom by one

429 n 33 above.

430 n 33 above 326.

431 n 34 above, 593.

432 The right to privacy inevitably engages the rights of autonomy and dignity: Binchy (n 33 above) 166.

433 n 38 above, 78.

> man may be abhorred by another as an exercise in immorality. The pluralism necessary for the preservation of constitutional requirements in the Christian, democratic State envisaged by the Constitution means that the sanctions of the criminal law may be attached to immoral acts only when the common good requires their proscription as crimes.

Self-determination insists on the freedom to express one's individuality and to live one's life in the community by exercising rational choices. Where that choice conflicts with the norms of the majority, the latter must defer to allow the non-conforming identity flourish as an esteemed equal member of the group. This has implications for intimate personal relationships and control over one's body. As the South African Constitutional Court did subsequently in the *Sodomy* case,[434] in *Norris* the importance of dignity and freedom for the human personality was emphasised by the dissenting judges, Henchy and McCarthy JJ.[435] They recognised the breadth of the right to privacy and carried out a balancing exercise between it and the common good. McWilliam J in the High Court and the other judges in the Supreme Court did not even find that the right to privacy extended to homosexual activities. The toothlessness of the equality guarantee in practice is apparent from all the judgments, McCarthy J being the only judge who left it open that the equality right could protect Mr Norris.[436]

In *JF v DPP* the prosecutor refused to consent to the request of an accused facing sexual assault charges to have the complainant assessed by a psychological expert nominated by him in addition to the psychologist, who had reported to the DPP and was a witness in the prosecution.[437] The DPP alleged that a second examination would breach the complainant's rights to dignity, privacy and security.[438] As the complainant himself had not supported the argument that a second examination would be 'excessive, unduly intrusive or objectionable', Hardiman J rejected the DPP's stance on the facts, but left open the possibility that circumstances could arise where an examination could be refused because, in effect, it was oppressive.[439] He

434 *National Coalition for Gay and Lesbian Equality v Minister of Justice* 1998 12 BCLR 1517 (CC).

435 n 38 above, 71, 78, 95, 100.

436 n 38 above, 104. See Binchy (n 83 above) 189 - 190.

437 [2005] IESC 24, [2005] 2 IR 174.

438 n 437 above, [13].

439 n 437 above, [31].

pointed out that by instigating a prosecution the complainant forfeited the right to privacy to an extent.[440] The effect of a conviction on an accused would be significant, as he would be disgraced, lose his liberty and reputation, and be consigned to professional oblivion.[441] These high stakes merited intruding on the complainant's right to privacy.[442]

A contentious contemporary issue is whether compulsory testing for HIV is justified, and, if so, in what circumstances.[443] In *Diau v Botswana Building Society* the Botswana Industrial Court held that termination of a woman's employment for refusing to undergo a HIV test constituted inhuman and degrading treatment,[444] which conclusion was derived from 'the premise that the human body is inviolable and respect for it is a fundamental element of human dignity and freedom.'[445] Dingake J pinpointed the right to dignity as the key value underlying equality and other human rights.[446] An individual is free 'to resist any potential violation to his or her privacy or bodily integrity.'[447] Dismissal for refusing to undergo the test constituted an assault

440 n 437 above, [27].

441 As above.

442 Neither did the principle of equality of arms inherent in a fair trial, which required equal treatment between the parties, allow a superior status to be given to one side's expert: n 437 above, [16], [32]-[33]. See also *Mackie v Wilde* [1998] 2 IR 570 (HC); *Murphy v GM* [2001] IESC 82, [2001] 4 IR 113 at 155, aff'g [1999] IEHC 5.

443 Policies purportedly designed for prevention and control of HIV/AIDS can them-selves lead to human rights violations, either because they are poorly conceived or applied in an arbitrary and biased manner, *eg*, both quarantine and involuntary testing policies are counterproductive and/or harmful because they result in discrimination and excessive infringements on personal freedoms; that, in turn, drives people away from testing, eclipses the opportunity for treatment and care, and undermines prevention efforts: V Iacopino *et al* 'HIV/AIDS and human rights in Botswana and Swaziland: A matter of dignity and health' (2011) 34 *Hastings Inter-national and Comparative Law Review* 149 at 166.

The Namibian Labour Court set out the precise tests required as part of the compulsory medical examination for military service and held that no otherwise fit and healthy person may be excluded from enlistment solely on the basis of such person's HIV status: *Nanditume v Minister of Defence* [2002] AHRLR 119 (NaLC 2000) [40].

444 Constitution of the Republic of Botswana 1966, Sec 7(1).

445 2003 (2) BLR 409 (BwIC) 41. The same court had held in an earlier case that termination of the contract of employment of another employee because she tested HIV positive was unfair: *Jimson v Botswana Building Society* [2005] AHRLR 86 (BwIC 2003).

446 'In liberal moral philosophy human dignity is considered to be what gives a person their intrinsic worth as human beings, consequently every human being must be treated worthy of respect.': n 445 above, 38.

447 As above.

on the employee's *dignitas*, which Dingake J defined by reference to South African case-law as that 'valued and serene condition in her social or individual life which is violated when she is, either publicly or privately subjected by another to offensive and degrading treatment, or when she is exposed to ill-will, ridicule, disesteem or contempt'.[448] The Court in *Diau* also found that the termination of her employment infringed the employee's right to liberty,[449] to which Dingake J gave a broad meaning, going beyond 'mere freedom from physical constraint' to grant protection to 'a narrow sphere of personal autonomy wherein individuals may make inherently private choices free from irrational and unjustified interference by others.'[450]

A pre-requisite for voluntary testing is informed consent mandated by the individual's right to self-determination and freedom to choose.[451] Before consent is classified as 'informed', the person 'must be made to fully appreciate the consequences and implications of his or her consent.'[452] South African case-law has fleshed out the parameters of informed consent. In *C v Minister of Correctional Services* it was held that a prisoner could validly consent to a HIV test only if he or she understood the object and purpose of the test, understood what a positive result could entail, had time and place to reflect on the information received about the test, and had the freedom to refuse the test.[453] Pre-test counselling is the norm, as is post-test counselling when there is a positive test result.[454] Kirk-Cohen J found that failure to obtain a prisoner's informed consent could give rise to civil liability by way of an *actio injuriarum* for invasion of privacy.[455] Innes CJ in *Waring & Gillow Ltd v Sherborne*

448 n 445 above, 41, citing Gardiner AJA in *Minister of Posts and Telegraphs v Rasool* 1934 AD 167.

449 Sec 3(a).

450 n 445 above, 45. The autonomy protected encompassed 'only those matters that can properly be characterized as inherently personal, such that, by their very nature, they implicate basic choices going to the core of what it means to enjoy individual dignity and independence': as above.

451 n 445 above, 41 - 42.

452 As above.

453 1996 4 SA 292 (T) (High Court) 301. See E Cameron 'Legal and human rights responses to the HIV/AIDS epidemic' (2006) 17 *Stellenbosch Law Review* 47 at 73 - 74. In *C* it was held that the prisoner had not given informed consent: F Veriava 'Ought the notion of informed consent to be cast in stone? *VRM v The Health Professions Council of South Africa*' (2004) 20 *South African Journal on Human Rights* 309 at 314 - 315.

454 n 453 above, 301. See Cameron (n 453 above) 74.

455 n 453 above. See CM Fombad 'Children and informed consent to HIV/AIDS testing and treatment in Botswana' (2005) 2 *University of Botswana Law Journal* 33 at 46.

formulated the essential independent elements of consent as knowledge, appreciation and consent.[456] Since then the additional elements of voluntariness of consent, consent not *contra bonos mores* and the capacity to consent have been added.[457]

When compulsory testing against the individual's will is allowed, the concern is not usually solely the patient's health, but rather society's interest in protecting others.[458] The *Diau* decision was influenced by international guidelines, which encouraged voluntary testing and discouraged compulsory testing of employees because it was unnecessary and promoted stigmatisation.[459] The fact that the building society employer was not an arm of state did not prevent constitutional rights from having horizontal effect.[460] In line with foreign jurisprudence, a broad purposeful interpretation was given to the Constitution.[461]

Those who have tested positive for HIV are safeguarded from discrimination in various spheres in many countries including in the labour market in South Africa[462] and India,[463] and in prison in Botswana.[464] In Nigeria the state breached the prohibition on torture,[465] which comes under the umbrella of the right to dignity in the Nigerian Constitution,[466] and also failed to

456 Fombad (n 455 above) 49, citing 1904 TS 340 at 344.

457 Fombad (n 455 above) 49 (footnote omitted).

458 Fombad (n 455 above) 69. *Eg*, in *C*, the dispute arose because the defendant adopted a new policy which required prisoners who served in the kitchen to undergo an HIV test to ensure that those with the virus were not allowed to prepare or serve food and in this way, it was hoped, reduce any chances of transmitting the virus to others: n 453 above. See Fombad (n 455 above) 69.

459 n 445 above, 19.

460 n 445 above, 22, 31.

461 n 445 above, 28, 44.

462 *Hoffmann v South African Airways* 2001 1 SA 1 (CC).

463 *X v State Bank of India* (Writ Petition No 1856 of 2002) (Bombay High Court) 16 January 2004. See E Durojaye 'Discrimination based on HIV/AIDS status: A comparative analysis of the Nigerian court's decision in *Festus Odaife & Ors v Attorney General of the Federation & Ors* with other Commonwealth jurisdictions' (2007) 11(2) *Law, Democracy & Development* 133 at 149 - 150.

464 *Makuto v S* [2000] 2 BLR 130 (CA). See Durojaye (n 463 above) 149; EK Quansah 'Human rights and HIV/AIDS in Botswana: Current perspectives and future prospects' in E Quansah & W Binchy (eds) *The judicial protection of human rights in Botswana* (2009) 258 - 259, 261 - 262.

465 Constitution of the Federal Republic of Nigeria 1999, Sec 34(1)(a).

466 Sec 34(1).

provide healthcare as required by the African Charter[467] when prison authorities detained HIV infected prisoners without giving them medical treatment.[468]

As found by the South African Constitutional Court in *NM v Smith*, although the worth of an individual is not reduced by being HIV positive, because of her privacy rights and autonomy she has control over revelation of information about her condition, which affects a deeply personal feature touching her dignity.[469] Her consent before publication of her HIV status is essential. Patient care in the context of HIV and AIDS requires the application of strict protocols for the testing, treatment, and disclosure of a patient's HIV status to ensure that patients are effectively treated and that their rights *inter alia* to dignity, freedom and security of the person and privacy are protected.[470]

Edward Bloustein regarded privacy as 'a dignitary tort', since the injury was 'to our individuality, to our dignity as individuals'.[471] The right to privacy is not absolute and restrictions may be necessary because of society's interest in dignity and the fact that rights are reciprocal.[472] Ackermann J indicated in *Bernstein v Bester* that there are limitations on the right to privacy when an individual's activities acquire a social dimension by the person entering into relationships beyond the 'most intimate core of privacy'.[473] The development

467 African Charter on Human and Peoples' Rights (adopted 27 June 1981, entered into force 21 October 1986) (1982) 21 ILM 58 (African Charter), Art 16.

468 *Odafe v AG* [2004] AHRLR 205 (NgHC 2004). See Durojaye (n 463 above) 134 - 136. Ebenezer Durojaye has criticised the decision for failing to find that the denial of treatment to HIV positive prisoners amounted to discrimination and a violation of the right to life, and for not taking a critical look at international human rights jurisprudence on the link between right to health and other rights: n 463 above, 150.

469 2007 5 SA 250 (CC).

470 Veriava (n 453 above) 309.

471 EJ Bloustein 'Privacy as an aspect of human dignity: An answer to Dean Prosser' (1964) 39 *New York University Law Review* 962 at 1002 - 1003.

472 Delany *et al*, (n 33 above) 58. See also Steyn (n 192 above) 7 - 8. An infringement of the right to privacy may be justified on a paternalistic basis to protect the individual from harm and also to protect others: see *Maria* (n 49 above) [24].

473 1996 2 SA 751 (CC) [77]. Limitations on the right to privacy were justifiable in *Investigating Directorate: Serious Economic Offences v Hyundai Motor Distributors (Pty) Ltd* 2001 1 SA 545 (CC), *S v Jordan* 2002 6 SA 642 (CC) and *De Reuck v DPP (Witwatersrand Local Division)* 2004 1 SA 406 (CC), but not in *Case v Minister of Safety and Security* 1996 3 SA 617 (CC) nor *Magajane v Chairperson, North West Gambling Board* 2006 5 SA 250 (CC). As less restrictive means were available to protect privacy and dignity, restrictions on freedom of expression were not justified in *Johncom Media Investments Ltd v M* [2009] ZACC 5, 2009 4 SA 7 (CC).

of the common law to provide the defence of reasonable publication in defamation actions had its origins in many countries in dignity.[474] Justification for violation of privacy could be developed along similar lines.[475]

7.9 Socio-economic rights

Judicial timidity in social and economic disputes has been at the expense of enforcing constitutional values in circumstances where the State's protracted inaction was inexcusable. After *O'Reilly* in 1988, the trail ran cold and the judiciary did not advance down the road of judicial activism, preferring the safer highway of trusting the other organs of state to fulfil their primary role under the Constitution – a misplaced trust as shown in hindsight. While Costello J held he had no power to adjudicate on distributive justice nor to award damages for past breaches of the plaintiff's constitutional rights, he did grant a declaration that the defendant was obliged to review its building programme and to vary it if housing needs for which no proposals had been made arose subsequent to the programme's adoption.[476] In another case six years later, Costello J modified his views on the courts' powers, when he found that Travellers' constitutional right to bodily integrity was infringed by the appalling conditions unfit for human habitation under which they were living.[477] Construing the Housing Act 1988 in the light of the constitutional duty towards the plaintiffs and the factual position in which they found themselves, he concluded:[478]

474 See *National Media Ltd v Bogoshi* 1998 4 SA 1196 (SCA); *Khumalo v Holomisa* 2002 5 SA 401 (CC).

475 See HL MacQueen 'Delict, contract, and the Bill of Rights: A perspective from the United Kingdom' (2004) 121 *South African Law Journal* 359 at 391.

476 n 20 above, 181, 191. On *O'Reilly*, see G Whyte 'Travellers and the law' (1988) 10 *Dublin University Law Journal* 189.

477 *O'Brien v Wicklow Urban District Council* 10 June 1994 (HC) 2 - 4. Costello J stated, above 3 - 4:

> I don't think it is necessary to say whether I am now expressing a different view to the one which I expressed in the case of *O'Reilly and Ors. v. Limerick Corporation*. ... Even, however, if the view which I am now expressing represents a change of views on my part then I accept that my views have changed.

See Hogan & Whyte (n 16 above) [7.3.220]; E Keane 'Public interest litigation: Socio-economic rights and national law' (2008) 26 *Irish Law Times* 62 at 63; Whyte *Social inclusion and the legal system: Public interest law in Ireland* (n 22 above) 57, 241 - 242.

478 n 477 above, 4.

> If statutory powers are given to assist in the realisation of constitutionally protected rights by a Local Authority and if the powers are given to relieve from the effects of deprivation of such constitutionally protected rights and if there are no reasons why such statutory powers should not be exercised then I must interpret such powers as being mandatory.

Although he considered he could not order that serviced halting sites be provided for particular plaintiffs or in any particular order, he did grant a mandatory injunction addressed to the local authority to provide serviced sites at particular locations.[479] However, the Supreme Court has not qualified its opposition to enforcing socio-economic rights.

Respect for humanity permeates from the civil and political sphere into the socio-economic realm. Survival *simpliciter* is not enough – living conditions suitable for the maintenance of a lifestyle conducive to development of a person's full potential are vital components of a meaningful existence. This results in rights to education, work, housing, health, and welfare in an amenable environment. There is also a view that full participation in a democracy and enjoyment of civil and political rights is only possible when the necessities of life have been fulfilled. The differences in quality and justiciability between civil and political rights on the one hand and socio-economic rights on the other have been eroded in recent decades and they are no longer corralled as strictly as they used to be perceived.[480]

There are several ways in which the Irish Constitution could be interpreted to give proper effect to the underlying constitutional values. The references to dignity and freedom in the Preamble deserve to be emphasised more in judgments as indicators of these values which are to be reflected in outcomes.[481]

The equality guarantee in Article 40.1 has been under-estimated. The true reach and intent of Walsh J's views in *Quinn's Supermarket*[482] can be gleaned from his assessment in *Crotty v An Taoiseach* that the promotion of

479 n 477 above, 5 - 7.

480 See P de Vos 'Pious wishes or directly enforceable human rights? Social and economic rights in South Africa's 1996 Constitution' (1997) 13 *South African Journal on Human Rights* 67 at 68 - 71.

481 See Whyte *Social inclusion and the legal system: Public interest law in Ireland* (n 22 above) 45 - 52. The significance of the ideal of human dignity is not restricted to those constitutions that expressly refer to it: H Botha 'Human dignity in comparative perspective' (2009) 20 *Stellenbosch Law Review* 171 at 176.

482 n 14 above.

equality and social justice accorded with the constitutional goals of personal dignity and freedom.[483] Because Walsh J found that freedom, equality and social justice were compatible with the Constitution's aims of the dignity and freedom of the individual, it can be deduced that dignity embraces social justice as well as equality.[484]

The unenumerated rights in Article 40.3.1° which the State is enjoined to respect, defend and vindicate, and the obligation on the State in Article 40.3.2° to protect and vindicate the life, person, and property rights of every citizen are sources on which rights to decent living conditions can be based.[485] Traditionally there has been a bias towards upholding property rights. In post-colonial societies, when indigenous people wish to preserve their culture and to fulfil their development needs they focus on their affinity with a place and try to affirm their identity by claiming property rights. However, attempting to fit their desires within the contours of property may not express fully what they require to live a dignified life where their heritage and lifestyle preferences are respected.

The experience of the San people in Botswana illustrates the futility of establishing rights to land *simpliciter*.[486] They established their property and

483 n 86 above, 776:

> The preamble [to the Single European Act] goes on to state that the parties are determined 'to work together to promote democracy on the basis of the fundamental rights recognised in the constitutions and laws of the Member States, in the Convention for the Protection of Human Rights and Fundamental Freedoms and the European Social Charter, notably freedom, equality and social justice.' So far as the latter aspirations are concerned no objection could be taken to them having regard to the fact that the preamble of the Constitution of Ireland sets out that one of the aims of the Constitution is to safeguard the dignity and freedom of the individual and to assist in establishing concord with other nations.

484 See S Liebenberg & B Goldblatt 'The interrelationship between equality and socio-economic rights under South Africa's transformative constitution' (2007) 23 *South African Journal on Human Rights* 335 at 343 - 344.

485 See W Binchy 'Protecting economic, social and cultural rights in Ireland' (Irish Human Rights Commission & Law Society Annual Conference 2009) http://www.ihrc.ie/download/pdf/paper20091121_annconf_binchy.pdf (accessed accessed 24 September 2013) 7 - 11; A Nolan 'Ireland: The separation of powers doctrine vs. socio-economic rights?' in M Langford (ed) *Social rights jurisprudence: Emerging trends in international and comparative law* (2008) 296.

486 On the origins and location of the San, see A Cook & J Sarkin 'Who is indigenous?: Indigenous rights globally, in Africa, and among the San in Botswana' (2009) 18 *Tulane Journal of International and Comparative Law* 93 at 95 - 96; N Olmsted 'Indigenous rights in Botswana: Development, democracy and dispossession' (2004) 3 *Washington University Global Studies Law Review* 799 at 809 - 810. On Botswana government policy in relation to the San, see K Bojosi (with comments by A Mogwe incorporated), *Botswana: Constitutional, legislative and administrative provisions con-*

gaming rights in the High Court, when it was held in a majority decision that their native title to what became the Central Kalahari Game Reserve had not been extinguished and that the government had wrongfully deprived them of possession of their land, but the Court rejected their claim for restoration of water – the government having terminated their supplies of essential services when they removed them from the Reserve.[487] Subsequently residents in the Reserve brought proceedings, which were successful on appeal, for the right to sink boreholes themselves for water.[488] The Court held in favour of the applicants on statutory and on constitutional grounds. The constitutional prohibition on inhuman or degrading treatment was an absolute and unqualified right, which involved the Court making a value judgment, in the exercise of which it was entitled to have regard to international consensus on the importance of access to water.[489] On that basis, the Court referred to two documents – first, a UN Committee report of 2003 on the implementation of the International Covenant on Economic, Social and Cultural Rights which stated that the human right to water was indispensible for leading a life in human dignity; and, second, to the recognition by the UN General Assembly in July 2010 of the right to water, when it called on states to ensure full transparency of the planning and implementation process in the provision of safe drinking water and sanitation and the active, free and meaningful participation of local communities and stakeholders.[490]

cerning indigenous peoples (ILO & ACHPR Country Report on Botswana) (ILO, Geneva 2009) [8.2.3], [9]; S Saugestad '"Improving their lives." State policies and San resistance in Botswana' [2005] 4 article 1 *Before Farming*.

487 *Sesana v AG* [2006] BWHC 129, [2006] 2 BLR 633. See ILO & ACHPR, *Overview Report of the Research Project by the International Labour Organization and the African Commission on Human and Peoples' Rights on the constitutional and legislative protection of the rights of indigenous peoples in 24 African countries* (ILO, Geneva 2009) 99; ILO & ACHPR Country Report on Botswana (n 486 above) [8.2.3]; Cook & Sarkin (n 486 above) 121, fn 200, 129; RK Hitchcock *et al* 'What about our rights? Settlements, subsistence and livelihood security among Central Kalahari San and Bakgalagadi' (2011) 15 *International Journal of Human Rights* 62 at 62, 66, 80; S Saugestad 'Impact of international mechanisms on indigenous rights in Botswana' (2011) 15 *International Journal of Human Rights* 37 at 40 - 50; JJ Taylor 'Celebrating San victory too soon? Reflections on the outcome of the Central Kalahari Game Reserve case' (2007) 23(5) *Anthropology Today* 3.

488 *Mosetlhanyane v AG* (BwCA 27 January 2011).

489 n 488 above, [19], referring to Sec 7(1).

490 n 488 above, [19], citing International Covenant on Economic, Social and Cultural Rights (adopted 16 December 1966, entered into force 3 January 1976) 993 UNTS 3 (CESCR).

The social and economic benefits necessary to support a life going further than mere existence to the full flourishing of a human being cannot be obtained easily (or at all) through the property lens. The concerns of vulnerable and marginalised indigenous groups can be addressed best by a multi-pronged approach embracing socio-economic rights, cultural and ethnic identity, and property interests, while having due regard to their right to participate in determining their future.[491]

The right to fair procedures can ensure that benefits already granted cannot be removed without due notice. The prior right to be heard protects against arbitrary deprivation of existing entitlements.

Although the definition of the family in Article 41.1 has been interpreted to apply only to the marital grouping, it can – even within its restricted range – place positive obligations on the State to provide tangible benefits to enable family members to thrive. Economic support to facilitate women working outside the home as well as undertaking duties as a home-maker are warranted by Article 41.2. The State has a pledge to guard marriage under Article 41.3.1° and presumably this extends to tangible measures.

As education rights in Article 42 are clearly justiciable, one might expect that there would be no hesitation by the judiciary in enforcing individual claims in this area on the grounds of the separation of powers. Nevertheless, there is a reticence to grant mandatory orders directed to the State to fulfil its constitutional role.

Like in India, the directive principles of social policy in Article 45 can be used by the judiciary at the very least as an interpretative aid to ascertain the existence of an unenumerated right under Article 40.3.1°.[492] They could also be referenced to interpret statutory law.

491 See ILO & ACHPR, *Overview Report* (n 487 above) v, ix, 123.

492 See Binchy (n 83 above) 190 - 191; N Fennelly 'Judicial decisions and allocation of resources' (2010) 23(3) *Advocate (South Africa)* 48 at 50; G Hogan 'Directive principles, socio-economic rights and the Constitution' (2001) 36 *Irish Jurist* 174 at 179 - 181; Keane (n 477 above) 62 - 63; Nolan (n 485 above) 296 - 297.

Costello J held that the court might for certain purposes have regard to the principles of social policy set out in Article 45, notwithstanding the wording of the Preamble thereto: *AG v Paperlink Ltd* [1984] ILRM 373 (HC). Cf *Murtagh Properties* (n 15 above) 335 - 336; *Nova Media Services Ltd v Minister for Posts and Telegraphs* [1984] ILRM 161 (HC). The Supreme Court has queried whether the High Court was correct in having regard to the directive principles: *Planning and Development Bill* (n 51 above) 356.

The judiciary's fear of over-stepping the constitutional boundary and breaching the separation of powers is too cautious.[493] The South African Constitutional Court is an example of a court fulfilling its role of protecting and enforcing constitutional rights without usurping the functions of the legislature or the executive.[494] It has gradually become more confident in asserting itself as a defender of human rights, while simultaneously involving the other arms of government in matters properly within the ambit of political decision making. It has left the minutiae of welfare plans to the politicians and the administrative authorities, while encouraging engagement with the people affected and showing a preference for resolution between the parties by direct negotiation or a mediated settlement. The democratic principles of transparency and accountability[495] are applied to the executive, which the Court has called to justify its decisions and actions with evidence produced from proper records. Times and circumstances change, so flexibility in policies and plans is not only permitted, but is a necessary ingredient. Good faith is a pre-requisite for state involvement in the solution to conflicts arising – the Constitutional Court has not hesitated to grant mandatory orders and to exercise supervisory jurisdiction when it doubts the *bona fides* of the

493 G Hogan 'Judicial review and socio-economic rights' in J Sarkin & W Binchy (eds) *Human rights, the citizen and the state: South African and Irish approaches* (2001) 12. Brian Foley has argued that judicial deference is not defensible when constitutionality is presumed and hypothetical assumptions are made about legislative constitutional decision making; he proposed substituting instead what he termed 'due deference' to be extended only if the legislature justifies its answer to the constitutional question under examination, the state bearing the burden of laying this justification before the court: B Foley *Deference and the presumption of constitutionality* (2008) 356.

Tim Murphy concluded that the reason why economic rights are not afforded constitutional recognition in Ireland is because the state and its institutions (including the judiciary and virtually all political parties) are committed to a form of liberal-capitalist economic system which tacitly incorporates inequalities and poverty: T Murphy 'Economic inequality and the Constitution' in T Murphy & P Twomey (eds) *Ireland's evolving constitution, 1937 - 1997: Collected essays* (1998) 179.

On the legitimacy of judicial activism promoting social inclusion, see G Whyte 'Socio-economic rights and the Irish Constitution' in A Lavan (ed) *Social rights and social cohesion* (2003) 60 - 64.

494 See KG Young 'A typology of economic and social rights adjudication: Exploring the catalytic function of judicial review' (2010) 8 *International Journal of Constitutional Law* 385.

495 On the importance of establishing the state's legal (as opposed to ethical or political) accountability, see AE Yamin 'The future in the mirror: Incorporating strategies for the defense and promotion of economic, social, and cultural rights into the mainstream human rights agenda' (2005) 27 *Human Rights Quarterly* 1200 at 1212 - 1215.

government.[496] In this it is fulfilling its constitutional mandate. By doing less it would fail to carry out its proper function.

A similar argument applies to the Irish judiciary. The South African judiciary's development of a system of judicial review[497] applicable to social rights can be a model for the Irish judges,[498] as it takes into account the fears that the courts could exceed the constitutional mandate to respect the separation of powers by over-reaching into the political arena and usurping the roles of the other arms of government in a democracy.[499] There are sufficient constraints in place to ensure that the democratic boundaries are left in place, while the judiciary fulfils its proper role under the separation of powers. The reticence of the Irish judiciary to do so could be overcome by adopting a reasonableness standard in a context-sensitive review in relation to social rights. This approach would give the courts greater flexibility to manage their relationship with the political branches of government.[500] It would avoid laying down strict rules, which might jeopardise that relationship.

The South African example in applying constitutional principles to relationships between private parties could also be followed by the Irish courts. The seeds for finding that social and economic rights have horizontal

496 Even though the Constitutional Court accepted the government's *bona fides*, it ordered that a decision be taken on whether to upgrade an informal settlement within 14 months: *Nokotyana v Ekurhuleni Metropolitan Municipality* [2009] ZACC 33, 2010 4 BCLR 312.

497 Judicial review is the principal method of protecting constitutional rights when there may be scepticism about the capacity of ordinary politics (especially during stressful times) adequately to do so or when a margin of additional protection is considered desirable: MJ Perry *The Constitution in the courts: Law or politics?* (1994) 19 - 21, 209 fn 16.

498 The South African courts' role in taking seriously the adverse effects of policy on the poor is less dependent on specific clauses in the Constitution than on broader jurisprudential considerations that can alter existing legal concepts: DM Davis 'Socio-economic rights: Do they deliver the goods?' (2008) 6 *International Journal of Constitutional Law* 687 at 708. See also EC Christiansen 'Transformative constitutionalism in South Africa: Creative uses of Constitutional Court authority to advance substantive justice' (2010) 13 *Journal of Gender, Race & Justice* 575 at 577.

499 See EC Christiansen 'Exporting South Africa's social rights jurisprudence' (2007) 5 *Loyola University Chicago International Law Review* 29 at 30, 35 - 37, 40, 42; EC Christiansen 'Using constitutional adjudication to remedy socio-economic injustice: Comparative lesson from South Africa' (2008) 13 *University of California at Los Angeles Journal of International Law and Foreign Affairs* 369 at 387 - 389; Young (n 494 above) 418 - 420.

500 See D Brand 'Socio-economic rights and courts in South Africa: Justiciability on a sliding scale' in F Coomans (ed) *Justiciability of economic and social rights: Experiences from domestic systems* (2006) 226 - 227; T Roux 'Principle and pragmatism on the Con-stitutional Court of South Africa' (2009) 7 *International Journal of Constitutional Law* 106 at 136.

effect in tort law have already been sown and could be nurtured to vindicate constitutional rights.[501]

The plight of Travellers[502] has received sympathy in Ireland, but frequently it has simply been a nominal sympathy that has not been translated into concrete improvements in their living conditions or into the removal of prejudice against them. They fall into the category of a vulnerable minority group, which has been the object of historic discrimination. The incorporation of the ECHR into Irish law has had a favourable – albeit limited – impact on their situation. Laffoy J held in the High Court in *O'Donnell (a minor) v South Dublin County Council* that the right of a Traveller family with three severely disabled members to respect for their private and family life, and their home in Article 8 ECHR was breached by having to live with the knowledge of the local authority in severely overcrowded conditions in a mobile home.[503] However, the Irish Constitution could have produced the same result, if the personal rights enshrined in it had been given a purposive meaning. The Supreme Court's view in *TD*[504] that the courts had no role in interfering with the role of the Oireachtas on the allocation of resources and its admonition to exercise restraint in finding any more unenumerated rights (particularly of a socio-economic nature) in Article 40.3.1° constrained Laffoy J in *O'Donnell*.

The Traveller status of the family was not relevant in *O'Donnell*.[505] Laffoy J distinguished *Doherty v South Dublin County Council*, in which Charleton J held that an elderly homeless Traveller couple living in an unsuitable damp caravan without toilet facilities were not entitled to have a plumbed centrally

501 See Binchy (n 485 above) 11 - 13.

502 See Whyte *Social inclusion and the legal system: Public interest law in Ireland* (n 22 above) 218 - 219.

503 n 144 above. See F de Londras & C Kelly *European Convention on Human Rights Act: Operation, impact and analysis* (2010) [5-31]; P Kenna 'Land law, property, housing and environment law' in Kilkelly (n 275 above) [6.43]-[6.46]; D Langwallner 'Separation of powers, judicial deference and the failure to protect the rights of the individual' in Doyle & Carolan (n 14 above) 273 - 276.

504 n 32 above. See Doyle *Constitutional law: Text, cases and materials* (n 14 above) [4-53]–[4-54], [13-19]–[13-52]; Foley (n 493 above) 196 - 204; Mullally (n 84 above) 301 - 303; Whyte *Social inclusion and the legal system: Public interest law in Ireland* (n 22 above) 358 - 362. The conclusions of Denham J (in dissent) in *TD* imported a reasonableness criterion analogous to that in South Africa: Langwallner (n 503 above) 272.

505 Laffoy J was careful to make it clear that she was not finding that the State had a positive obligation to make provision for every Traveller family, but the case was about the particular circumstances of one family, which had three severely disabled members, who were acknowledged by the housing authority to have been living in unacceptable conditions for two years and whose plight was not going to be alleviated for more than another year.

heated mobile home with an electricity supply provided for them when they opted for halting site accommodation and refused a reasonable offer of standard housing in an apartment pending the provision of a permanent place for them in a new residential caravan park.[506] Charleton J accepted as authoritative Barron J's judgment in *University of Limerick v Ryan*[507] that the courts had a role to play in ensuring that the housing authority fulfilled its statutory duty, which involved not only an assessment of the housing needs of all (the Traveller and settled communities alike), but acting upon it.[508]

In *Doherty* Charleton J differentiated between positive and negative obligations under the Constitution – the state guarantee in Article 40.3 being 'a promise never to infringe a right' fell within the latter category.[509] When it came to positive action to defend and vindicate the personal rights of the citizen, the text of the Constitution limited the State's duty to doing as much as was practicable.[510] Charleton J concluded that the obligation to take into account the sensitivities of various communities, including Travellers, when interpreting administrative measures was not unlimited and, following the decision of the European Court of Human Rights in *Chapman v UK*, he held that a nomadic lifestyle did not give rise to an automatic duty on states to

506 *Doherty v South Dublin County Council (No 2)* [2007] IEHC 4, [2007] 2 IR 696. See de Londras & Kelly (n 503 above) [4-41], [5-31].

507 21 February 1991 (HC).

508 n 506 above, [29]. He cited two cases, where orders were made that serviced halting sites should be provided by housing authorities within twelve months: n 506 above, [29], citing *O'Brien* (n 477 above), *County Meath VEC v Joyce* [1997] 3 IR 402 (HC).

509 n 506 above, [36].

510 As above. In certain circumstances, the State might have an obligation to intercede consistent with its financial and administrative commitments; Charlton J observed that a similar problem arose in relation to the ECHR, as there was no positive requirement to act to uphold private and family life in Article 8: as above. Although he noted Costello J's remarks in *O'Brien* (n 477 above) that conditions which were 'totally unacceptable in a Christian community and which could be relieved if the statutory powers of a local authority were exercised and without any great expense' could give rise to an obligation to intervene, the present case did not pass that threshold: n 506 above, [39]. He stated, 'I would find it impossible to apply the tests of culpability and of inhuman treatment where a number of offers of housing have been made, and where the best form of halting site accommodation is to be made available to the applicants within eighteen months.': n 506 above, [40].

intervene in favour of preserving this way of life under the ECHR.[511] The European Court of Human Rights in *Chapman* was reluctant to become embroiled in policy matters which it adjudged were properly the preserve of the politicians.[512] The same reticence is evident in the Irish courts and can be seen in Charleton J's judgment, which sets a high bar to be overcome before judicial action is warranted.[513]

Three deficiencies in Charleton J's judgment are worth mentioning. First, although he rightly concluded that the Court in *Chapman* did not say that states had an *automatic* duty to intervene to preserve a nomadic lifestyle, he did not give sufficient weight to its finding that the vulnerable position of gypsies as a minority meant that 'some special consideration should be given to their needs and their different lifestyle … in arriving at … decisions in particular cases' and therefore Article 8 ECHR imposed on states a positive obligation (albeit limited) to facilitate the gypsy way of life.[514] Second, he did not refer to the subsequent decision of the European Court of Human

511 n 506 above, [43], citing (App no 27238/95) (2001) 33 EHRR 18 [96]-[99]. On *Chapman*, see R Sandland 'Developing a jurisprudence of difference: The protection of the human rights of travelling peoples by the European Court of Human Rights' (2008) 8 *Human Rights Law Review* 475 at 487 - 492.

512 n 511 above, [99]. The Court only went so far as to say it was 'clearly desirable' that every human being should have 'a place where he or she can live in dignity and which he or she can call home', but it recalled that Article 8 did not give a right to be provided with a home and neither did any of the jurisprudence of the Court acknowledge such a right: n 511 above, [99].

See S Fredman *Human rights transformed: Positive rights and positive duties* (2008) 204; Kenna (n 503 above) [6.34]; C O'Cinneide 'Equality, Irish law and the ECHR' in Kilkelly (n 275 above) [3.30].

513 n 506 above, [46]:

> I would add that the decisions to date show a reluctance to require state authorities to intervene with forms of welfare as an aid to the exercise of rights. Whether welfare is provided, and at what level, and in what particular circumstances, is essentially a matter of political decision. The discourse of politics in this area tends to move between the poles of urging self reliance and of offering cradle to grave support. Like a family, the resources of any nation are limited and it is a matter for political and executive decision as to what resources should be committed to what problems and with what priority. A breach of legislation prescribing such an allocation, as in housing, calls for judicial intervention. Where, however, a plea is made that the court should declare the absence of welfare support to be wrong in a particular situation of itself, the applicant should show a complete inability to exercise a human right for his or her own means and a serious situation that has set the right at nought with the prospect of serious long term harm. Any proposed intervention by the court should take into account that it is the responsibility of the legislature and executive to decide the allocation of resources and the priorities applied by them.

514 n 511 above, [96].

Rights in *Connors v UK* which repeated that this positive obligation existed and strengthened it by finding that the states' margin of appreciation will tend to be narrower where the right at stake is crucial to 'the individual's effective enjoyment of intimate or key rights.'[515] Third, he did not consider the fact that life in a caravan was part of the Travellers' identity and that what was in contention was more than their home, but an integral part of their way of being.[516]

The criminalisation of trespass in 2002[517] was directed at travellers. This has resonances of a similar provision in the apartheid era's Prevention of Illegal Squatting Act 1951.[518] Next I will look at the case-law in this area and compare the legal position in both jurisdictions.

In *McDonagh v Kilkenny County Council* members of the Travelling community refused to comply with notices served by the police directing them to leave lands owned by the Council and to remove their caravans.[519] They were charged then with the offence of failing to comply with the directions.[520] In addition to attacking the criminalisation provisions,[521] the Travellers sought to compel the housing authority to give them priority in the provision of accommodation and, in the meantime, to consent to them remaining on the land they were occupying. Their action failed *in toto*. O'Neill J held that Kilkenny County Council had considered their housing application, which it had rightly refused based on the material presented to it. Because it was uncontested that Kilkenny County Council owned the

515 (App no 66746/01) (2005) 40 EHRR 9 [82], [84]. The Court in *Connors* was of opinion that a serious interference with rights under Article 8 required 'particularly weighty reasons of public interest by way of justification and the margin of appreciation to be afforded to the national authorities must be regarded as correspondingly narrowed': above, [86]. On *Connors*, see Sandland (n 511 above) 493 - 496.

516 The European Court of Human Rights in *Chapman* categorised the applicant's occupation of her caravan as 'an integral part of her ethnic identity as a gypsy, reflecting the long tradition of that minority of following a travelling lifestyle': n 511 above, [73].

517 Housing (Miscellaneous Provisions) Act 2002 sec 24.

518 See *Jaftha v Schoeman* 2005 2 SA 140 (CC) [27]; *Port Elizabeth Municipality v Various Occupiers* 2005 1 SA 217 (CC) [8]-[10].

519 [2007] IEHC 350. See E Brown 'Article 6 and civil cases' in Kilkelly (n 275 above) [4.44]. The notices were served under section 19C Criminal Justice (Public Order) Act 1994, as amended by section 24 Housing (Miscellaneous Provisions) Act 2002, which criminalised trespass.

520 Criminal Justice (Public Order) Act 1994 sec 19D.

521 The Travellers challenged the validity of the statute on the basis that criminal trespass was a strict liability offence excluding the operation of defences like necessity or mistaken belief as to consent to enter. They maintained that the legislation was vague

property onto which the Travellers had moved with their caravans without the Council's consent, they were undoubtedly trespassers and in breach of the Council's rights.[522] Although O'Neill J referred to jurisprudence of the European Court of Human Rights, he did not use it to inform his decision. Neither did he review critically the stance of the housing authority to the Travellers' application for accommodation, which was rejected on procedural grounds. Their failure to obtain housing resulted in them being rendered illegal by trespassing because they had nowhere to go.[523] The nomadic lifestyle as a legitimate aspect of their identity central to their humanity and dignity was not recognised. The situation was akin to that found in *Connors*.[524]

In December 2008 Peart J also rejected the defence of necessity in *Dublin City Council v Gavin* when the plaintiff sought an injunction to remove Travellers who were trespassing with about 30 caravans on the Council's lands.[525] Even though he found against the Travellers, he adjourned the question of what order the Court should make until the Council had a site ready for occupation by the Gavins. He pointed out that common sense suggested that consultations should take place between the parties to try to resolve the issues in contention. Within a year the Council returned to Court

and reversed the presumption of innocence in Article 38.1 of the Constitution and Article 6(2) of the ECHR. They claimed that the orders violated their dwelling (their caravan homes) contrary to Article 40.5. Their rights to a fair trial under Article 6 ECHR and to private or family life under Article 8 were also in contention.

522 The constitutional right to protection for their dwelling did not permit them to invade land and establish their dwelling on it. Just because they were disgruntled with the outcome of their application for accommodation did not mean they could take the law into their own hands. Neither could they use the defence of necessity as justification for illegal entry.

523 There was a minimum residence requirement for inclusion in the Traveller Accom-modation Programme, but the problem these Travellers faced was that they had no place where they could reside legally in the area to qualify.

524 n 515 above, [94]:

> It would rather appear that the situation in England as it has developed, for which the authorities must take some responsibility, places considerable obstacles in the way of gypsies pursuing an actively nomadic lifestyle while at the same time excluding from procedural protection those who decide to take up a more settled lifestyle.

525 [2008] IEHC 444. Because they feared for their safety on account of bad relationships with other Travellers with whom they were in dispute, the extended Gavin family did not engage with the Council who had identified what it regarded as a site suitable for their accommodation needs. Necessity did not justify an 'uncontrolled and un-con-trollable regime' in which people could enter another's land and claim a right to remain until they were re-housed. The defence of necessity in emergency situations could only be invoked when the interests that were being protected were those of the property owner – not the interests of the trespasser.

to seek an injunction against the Gavins, as it had a site available for them. Despite the 'minimalist approach' taken by the Council to address the Gavins' legitimate concerns about safety at the site proposed for them, Peart J granted the injunction with a stay for three months and hoped again that meaningful discussions would take place.[526] The Council had complied with its duties to prepare a Traveller Accommodation Programme.

There are some common features in South Africa and Ireland – in both countries there is an obligation on the state to develop a housing plan and to keep it under review; in neither jurisdiction does an individual have an immediate right to a home.[527] However, the South African judiciary has developed a more innovative and effective approach to solving conflicts between the homeless and property owners (whether private or the state). It places responsibility on the state to act positively to reconcile interests and to achieve social cohesion. The courts consider the effect on human dignity of being homeless. Steps taken to address homelessness and to protect property-owners' rights are measured against human rights standards where dignity is to the fore.[528] Everyone has the right to be treated with respect for dignity. Property owners' rights are not given priority over other rights – unlike the position in Ireland.[529] The yardstick of reasonableness is used to balance rights. The most vulnerable are protected to a much greater extent. The courts have not been content simply to exhort the parties to consult[530] with each other in an effort to reach a mutually acceptable solution, but have exercised judicial management[531] in a dynamic fashion monitoring progress to relieve inhuman conditions, taking steps to ensure that meaningful engagement actually takes place[532] and requiring all involved to take

526 [2009] IEHC 477. He urged 'a fresh, imaginative and realistic approach' to dealing with an otherwise intractable enduring problem.

527 *Government of the Republic of South Africa v Grootboom* 2001 1 SA 46 (CC).

528 On the positive duties that ensue when human rights values are articulated in assessing the right to housing, see Fredman (n 512 above) 204 - 206.

529 See Mullally (n 84 above) 294, 295; *Blake v AG* [1982] IR 117 (HC, SC). However, property owners' rights ceded to the common good in *AG v Southern Industrial Trust Ltd* [1960] 94 ILTR 161 (HC, SC).

530 On the key elements necessary to have a consultative process that fosters participation and deliberative democracy, see Fredman (n 512 above) 210 - 211.

531 On the need for the court to engage in judicial management, see *Port Elizabeth Municipality* (n 518 above) [36].

532 See *Occupiers of 51 Olivia Road, Berea Township v City of Johannesburg* 2008 3 SA 208 (CC) [16]-[18]; *Residents of Joe Slovo Community, Western Cape v Thubelisha Homes* 2010 3 SA 454 (CC) [7].

responsibility to act so as to achieve a resolution that respects the rights of others and advances harmony in the community.

The principles in *ubuntu* of respect for dignity while living in a shared society have been influential in shaping the solutions reached. The effect of not protecting the human dignity of the vulnerable impacts on the dignity of all in society and not solely on the people directly involved. The South African judges have enhanced the democratic value of equality by holding the other branches of the state accountable for fulfilling their constitutional duties. They have engaged all parties in that process to work together to devise and implement housing programmes that satisfy the needs of the vulnerable and the demands of social solidarity insofar as is reasonably possible. The state is obliged to provide an effective remedy as required by the rule of law.[533]

The new constitutional order in South Africa prevents the branding of unlawful occupiers of buildings as criminals without a court order having first been obtained. In *Occupiers of 51 Olivia Road, Berea Township v City of Johannesburg,* the Constitutional Court ordered the reading into legislation of a proviso that a crime was only committed when those who had been served with a court order for eviction failed to obey it.[534] In Ireland the constitutional rights to fair procedures based on Articles 34 and 40.3.1° and to liberty in Article 40.4.1° could ground a challenge to the trespass crime.[535]

The international instruments having a bearing on socio-economic rights which have been ratified by Ireland are a ready and fertile source of guidance for the Irish courts when assessing claims for improvements in living conditions.[536] The Irish courts have not availed themselves of their assistance – unlike their South African counterparts.

533 *President of the Republic of South Africa v Modderklip Boerdery (Pty) Ltd* 2005 5 SA 3 (CC) [51]. On *Modderklip*, see Fredman (n 512 above) 210.

534 n 532 above, [51].

535 These provisions were the basis of Laffoy J's finding that legislation permitting imprisonment for debt was unconstitutional in *McCann* (n 143 above).

536 The fact that a country is a signatory to international or regional human rights treaty containing social rights may be a sufficient basis to ground judicial authority in those areas, given that asserting judicial authority may ultimately rely on individual and institutional judicial choices (rather than constitutional entrenchment): L Forman 'Ensuring reasonable health: Health rights, the judiciary, and South African HIV/AIDS Policy' (2005) 33 *Journal of Law, Medicine & Ethics* 711 at 720.

7.10 Equality

7.10.1 Substantive equality?

Walsh J's profound statement linking equality with human dignity in *Quinn's Supermarket*[537] was utilised in subsequent cases to restrict the ambit of the equality guarantee from applying to situations where the individual was involved in activities. It could have been interpreted in an expansive manner to deliver substantive equality.[538] In *Murtagh Properties* the trade union did not maintain that women were incapable of bar waitressing or inadequate as such, which gave Kenny J the latitude to hold that Article 40.1 did not apply, as it related to peoples' 'essential attributes as persons, those features which make them human beings' and had 'nothing to do with their trading activities or with the conditions on which they are employed'.[539] This viewpoint is wrong, as the antagonism towards women was based on their attributes as persons and not on their working capacity. Their female gender was innate and incapable of change. A positive aspect of the decision was Kenny J's reliance on the Directive Principles of Social Policy in Article 45 to aid his interpretation of Article 40.3.[540] The statement in the former that all men and women have equal rights to an adequate means of livelihood was key to his finding that all people (women as well as men) had a right to earn a livelihood under Article 40.3.[541]

537 n 14 above, 13.

538 Substantive inequality has been described as socially institutionalised subordination, which cumulatively and systematically shapes access to human dignity, respect, resources, physical security, credibility, membership in community, speech and power: CA MacKinnon 'Reflections on sex equality under law' (1991) 100 *Yale Law Journal* 1281 at 1298.

539 n 15 above, 334 - 335. On the scope for differentiating in legislation on the grounds of capacity and social function, or for abridging rights for the common good, see *East Donegal Co-Operative Livestock Mart* (n 85 above); *O'Brien v Manufacturing Engineering Co Ltd* [1973] IR 334 (HC, SC); *Moynihan v Greensmyth* [1977] IR 55 (SC); *Abbey Films Ltd v AG* [1981] IR 158 (SC); *Somjee v Minister for Justice* [1981] ILRM 324 (HC); *Dillane* (n 103 above); *MacMathúna v Ireland* [1989] IR 504 (HC), [1995] 1 IR 484 (SC); *DPP (Stratford) v O'Neill* [1998] 2 IR 383 (HC); *Lowth v Minister for Social Welfare* [1998] 4 IR 321 (HC, SC); *Liddy v Minister for Public Enterprise* [2004] 1 ILRM 9 (HC). On the High Court decision in *MacMathúna*, see G Whyte 'Constitutional protection for the married family' (1989) 7 *Irish Law Times* 115.

540 n 15 above, 335 - 336. See AS Butler 'Private litigation and constitutional rights under sections 8 and 9 of the 1996 Constitution – Assistance from Ireland' (1999) 116 *South African Law Journal* 77 at 92.

541 n 15 above, 336.

Gerard Hogan and Gerry Whyte consider that the judiciary has not fleshed out the constitutional guarantee of equality.[542] They saw signs of judicial re-appraisal of the restrictive version of the human personality doctrine, but speculated that the constitutional guarantee could be bypassed in favour of domestic and European legislation on equality.[543]

The scope for substantive rather than formal equality is greatly enhanced by aligning it with dignity. Human dignity evolves in meaning with a social process concerned with dynamic patterns of human expectation and interaction.[544] Substantive equality operating by equal worth, as in South Africa, may demand different treatment to respect specific needs.[545] This requires a contextual enquiry supported by a structure – not simply an outcome based on the subjective opinion of a judge.[546] The methodology of human rights litigation in South Africa and in Canada supports dialogue between the courts and the legislature, which can lead to the latter responding by promoting concepts of human dignity and equality developed by the judiciary.[547]

Anti-discrimination laws provide effective redress leading to structural change when they are interpreted in the light of their effect on human dignity. There are circumstances when the constitutional equality guarantee and the precept to respect human dignity have horizontal application, thereby affecting relationships between private individuals. Non-discrimination against vulnerable groups such as Travellers, homosexuals, migrants and asylum seekers could be addressed in a deeper way in Ireland by a focus on

542 n 16 above, [7.2.05] (footnotes omitted):

> In contrast to comparative and international jurisprudence, jurisprudence on the guarantee of equality in the Irish Constitution is remarkably underdeveloped. To date, the debate about the differing conceptions of equality has, to a large extent, passed Article 40.1 by; Irish judges have also yet to consider whether that provision embraces the concept of indirect discrimination. ... during much of its history, Article 40.1 was effectively sidelined by a restrictive judicial interpretation of the human personality doctrine and during the heyday of judicial activism that commenced in the 1960s, the judiciary showed a marked preference for other constitutional provisions, notably Article 40.3, over Article 40.1 as a basis for their decisions.

543 n 16 above, [7.2.06].

544 JJ Paust 'Human dignity as a constitutional right: A jurisprudentially based inquiry into criteria and content' (1984) 27 *Howard Law Journal* 145 at 147.

545 J Small & E Grant 'Dignity, discrimination, and context: New directions in South African and Canadian human rights law' (2005) 6(2) *Human Rights Review* 25 at 52.

546 Small & Grant (n 545 above) 51.

547 Small & Grant (n 545 above) 54 - 55.

dignity and the real import of Article 40.1 of the Constitution. In Ireland the equality guarantee in the Constitution has been sidelined for too long[548] and is ripe for development.

7.10.2 Public recognition

Freedom to associate with friends or colleagues of one's choice is a critical part of identity. It is undesirable, even if it were possible, to force men to allow women to become full members of all private clubs. Nevertheless, the common good demands that any public benefit or recognition be denied clubs restricted to men – the traditionally dominant sex. Therefore all clubs where alcohol is licensed to be sold should be open to both sexes – and, indeed, to members of all minority groups.

What are the contours of the concept of public benefit and recognition of clubs? The most widely known advantage of registered clubs[549] is the entitlement to sell alcoholic drinks.[550] In an exception to the norm, only a registered club devoted primarily to athletics can admit persons under 18 as members.[551] A registered club may hold functions for its own benefit,[552] and public functions for community, charitable or benevolent purposes.[553] If it wishes to hold a lottery for members, a club does not need to seek a permit.[554] Exemption from income tax is a benefit that a club established to promote athletics or amateur games or sports may claim.[555] From the foregoing listing,

548 See Butler, (n 540 above) 92.

549 Registration takes place following a successful court application pursuant to the Registration of Clubs Acts 1904 - 2004: D McNamara *A legal guide for clubs and associations* (2005) 25.

550 Sales are generally restricted to members and their guests on the club premises: McNamara (n 549 above) 25. See also McNamara (n 549 above) 39 - 40. Although not usually utilised by clubs, they may also operate an 'off-licence' for members only: McNamara (n 549 above) 40 - 41. Subject to complying with the licensing laws, they can avail themselves of other privileges such as obtaining a permit to have a club extension when alcohol may be sold to members after the hours normally permitted: McNamara (n 549 above) 41. A sports club may be allowed to serve alcohol once a year to the general public attending a special event in its premises or grounds: Intoxicating Liquor Act 1962 sec 14. See C Cassidy *Cassidy on the Licensing Acts* (2010) [14-36]; McNamara (n 549 above) 42 - 43.

551 Registration of Clubs (Ireland) Act 1904 sec 4, as amended by Intoxicating Liquor Act 1988 sec 42.

552 Intoxicating Liquor Act 2000 sec 29(1).

553 Sec 29(2)(a). A registered club can organise weddings or other functions for a member or a member's family: sec 29(2)(b). See McNamara (n 549 above) 43.

554 Gaming and Lotteries Act 1956 sec 23. See McNamara (n 549 above) 60.

555 Taxes Consolidation Act 1997 sec 235.

it is clear that there are many advantages that accrue to clubs. In addition to prohibiting the sale of alcohol by discriminating clubs, there is scope for further restrictions to be applied to them. However, given the difficult task of achieving a harmonious interpretation of the constitutional rights to freedom of association[556] and to equality in these circumstances, a balance between them is required taking into account the common good and the freedom of the individual. The Constitution allows the regulation and control in the public interest of the exercise of the right to associate.[557] Respect for human dignity and the aim of encouraging all to achieve their full potential should tilt the balance in favour of the restrictions.

The limitations proposed would be a significant sanction on a club. An objection might be made that it would be unfair to impose a penalty solely on the grounds of discrimination in the absence of a breach of the licensing or criminal laws, as was canvassed in the Supreme Court in *Portmarnock Golf Club*.[558] The decision in that case was based on an interpretation of the statute, so it did not resolve the constitutional issue. In his comments, which we can regard therefore as *obiter dicta*, Hardiman J criticised the penalisation of a discriminating club by targeting a legitimate activity.[559] In view of the

556 Art 40.6.1°(iii).

557 As above.

558 n 119 above. For reviews of this case, see Cassidy (n 550 above) [35-15]; C Marry 'Portmarnock Golf Club decision: A step backwards for equality law?' (2010) 15 *Bar Review* 39.

559 n 119 above, 269:

> The first oddity about this particular sanction is that it is imposed without any necessity to establish a breach of rule or law and indeed none is alleged. An ordinary licence to sell alcoholic drink can be lost for repeated breaches of the licensing law or on objection on the grounds of bad character. Nothing of the sort is alleged here nor is any irregularity whatsoever concerning the club's making alcoholic drinks available.

He went on to find fault with the wording of the particular statute in dispute, stating, 'there is a rule of law, and a canon of statutory interpretation, prohibiting doubtful penalisation *i.e.* the imposition of a penalty by language which is less than clear.': as above. Geoghegan J was forthright in his condemnation of the method adopted by the legislature in the Equal Status Act 2000, n 119 above, 280:

> The method by which the Oireachtas has chosen to encourage (and in reality to force) 'discriminating clubs' to abandon the 'discrimination' is not merely unusual but quite extraordinary. The sanction is the future prohibition on the sale of intoxicating liquor even though that trade had nothing whatsoever to do with any alleged 'discrimination'. Furthermore, the effect of the provision is that … the 'discriminating' club may continue forever 'discriminating' if it is satisfied to lose its club registration and, therefore, the authority to sell liquor. … [T]he Act provides for the unusual indirect means of enforcement in relation to 'discrimination' within the internal arrangements of a club.

attenuation of the scope for achieving equality, a legislative amendment is desirable to preclude the narrow interpretation of the exemption for discriminating clubs in the Equal Status Act[560] adopted by O'Higgins J in the High Court[561] and by the majority in the Supreme Court. The minority interpretation by Denham and Fennelly JJ is to be preferred.

In South Africa a stronger positive stance has been taken in the Promotion of Equality and Prevention of Unfair Discrimination Act 2000. There is a 'duty and responsibility' on 'all persons' (not just on the State) to promote equality.[562] Ministerial regulations are mandated to require, *inter alia*, clubs and sports organisations to prepare equality plans, abide by prescribed codes of practice, or report on measures to promote equality.[563] Race, gender and disability are singled out as particular targets for the promotion of equality.[564] Clubs and sports associations are among the sectors included in an illustrative list where widespread unfair practices need to be addressed.[565]

7.10.3 Contractual freedom

Autonomy as an aspect of human dignity is the foundation of the basic principle of freedom of contract.[566] Individuals can reason and choose their route in life. They are viewed as having the capacity to take responsibility to judge and evaluate their ends and needs in the light of what is reasonable and fair in their own circumstances, and to act on this assessment.[567] Another principle is that the parties to a contract are equals and can bargain with each other in good faith to reach a mutually acceptable agreement on terms. The dignity that is inherent in every person is also at the root of equality.[568] Mutual respect is the associative side of dignity.[569] A third feature is the

560 Equal Status Act 2000 sec 9(1)(a). On the definition of a 'discriminating club' and the legal consequences of being determined as such, see Cassidy (n 550 above) [14-24], [35-12]–[35-14].

561 n 63 above. See E Song 'No women (and dogs) allowed: A comparative analysis of discriminating private golf clubs in the United States, Ireland, and England' (2007) 6 *Washington University Global Studies Law Review* 181 at 181, 184, 194 - 195.

562 Secs 24(2), 27(1) & 28(3)(a).

563 Sec 27(2).

564 Sec 28.

565 Sec 29.

566 Brownsword (n 415 above) 183.

567 P Benson 'Equality of opportunity and private law' in Friedmann & Barak-Erez (n 415 above) 219.

568 Brownsword (n 415 above) 188.

569 See *Barkhuizen v Napier* 2007 5 SA 323 (CC) [140] (Sachs J in dissent).

public interest in certainty, which inspires confidence in the market place and supports the sanctity of contract.[570]

But where deeply personal issues are concerned, contractual freedom may have to cede to society's interest in protecting the dignity of humanity. Profound moral questions are raised when an individual wishes to treat their body as a marketable commodity. Only things – not people – can be bought and sold. The Kantian command inhibiting the treatment of a person as an object prevents the marketing of body parts.[571] It has also stopped dwarf-throwing contests and is relevant to contracts concerning the use of embryos, surrogacy and body parts.[572] The responsibility to recognise the equal standing of others should avoid a contract to discriminate against others or imposing such an obligation on another.[573] In *Horwood v Millar's Timber and Trading Co Ltd* all three judges were united in their outright opposition to the constraints placed on a borrower in a contract under which he assigned to the lender all his earnings and covenanted that he would not leave his employment without the latter's consent.[574]

Sometimes autonomy and equality are absent or diminished by the imbalance of power between the bargaining sides. The apparent freedom to choose may be illusory. An assessment of the effects of the contract on the

570 D Moseneke 'Transformative constitutionalism: Its implications for the law of contract' (2009) 20 *Stellenbosch Law Review* 3 at 9.

571 Brownsword (n 415 above) 192.

572 Brownsword (n 415 above) 192 - 193. Aurelia Colombi Ciacchi concluded that without addressing the issue of dignity, public policy cannot open itself satisfactorily to a consideration and balancing of the conflicting interests arising: AC Ciacchi 'Social rights, human dignity and European contract law' in S Grundmann (ed) *Constitutional values and European contract law* (2008) 160.

573 Benson (n 567 above) 224 - 225. A contract of self-enslavement or one that severely limits a person's ability to participate in economic and social life or to fulfil familial or political responsibilities is void *ab initio* by policy: Benson (n 567 above) 224.

574 [1917] 1 KB 305 (CA). The Court held that the contract was bad as being contrary to public policy, since it unduly and improperly fettered the borrower's liberty of action. Lord Cozens-Hardy MR equated the situation to slavery, above, 312:

> [I]t certainly seems to me to savour of serfdom to say 'You shall not leave the house in which you are living without my consent; you shall not dispose of a chair or a table in your house on which I have no charge without my consent, and if you do the whole amount of principal and interest will immediately become payable instead of being payable by instalments.'

Warrington LJ stated, '[t]he man has put himself ... almost body and soul in the power of this money-lender.': above, 314. Scrutton LJ was not using 'overstrained or poetical language' by depicting the unfortunate man as 'the slave of the money-lender': above, 317. The terms of the contract went far further than was reasonably necessary to protect the moneylender and were dangerous to the interests of the public: above, 318.

dignity and equality of the parties to it might show that one party had no real choice whether to enter into the agreement in the first place or to negotiate the terms. Unfair conditions may be oppressive. Even though there is a reluctance to interfere with contracts, they have been eroded in some circumstances when they have been deemed unreasonable. In her comparative study of fundamental rights application in contract cases, Chantal Mak found a preoccupation with the equilibrium of contractual relationships.[575] Despite the fact that systemic bias and the effects of systemic exclusion prevail in social relations, recognition of the other as equal informs the contract, and the law's task is to ensure that inequalities do not translate into legal realities.[576]

In Germany this has resulted in the judicial scrutiny of contracts between banks and individuals.[577] The courts there have paid particular attention to contracts of suretyship entered into by close relatives of the main debtor.[578] Children have a right not to be subjected to a loan guarantee that was part of a contract between a bank and their parents, if it was given simply to comply with the bank's policy to gain as much loan security as possible, even from people who neither profit from the loan nor know whether they will ever be able to guarantee it, and where it is most likely that the parent–child hierarchy

575 C Mak *Fundamental rights in European contract law: A comparison of the impact of fundamental rights on contractual relationships in Germany, the Netherlands, Italy and England* (2008) 301.

576 S Baer 'Dignity, liberty, equality: A fundamental rights triangle of constitutionalism' (2009) 59 *University of Toronto Law Journal* 417 at 450.

577 Baer (n 576 above), citing FCC (*Loan guarantee*), 1 BvR 567, 1044/89, BVerfGE 89, 214 (19 October 1993). On this case, see also M Habersack & R Zimmermann 'Legal change in a codified system: Recent developments in Germany suretyship law' (1999) 3 *Edinburgh Law Review* 272 at 276 - 277; K Heine & R Janal 'Suretyships and consumer protection in the European Union through the glasses of law and economics' in AC Ciacchi & S Weatherill (eds) *Regulating unfair banking practices in Europe: The case of personal suretyships* (2010) [4.2.1]-[4.2.2]; MacQueen (n 475 above) 376; P Rott 'Germany' in Ciacchi & Weatherill above, 257 - 258, 260 - 261.

578 If there is a striking discrepancy between the obligation incurred and the surety's financial potential, the courts examine closely the surety's motivation and the circumstances in which the contract was concluded; the aim is to protect the surety from a lifelong liability if the guarantee was not given as a result of an act of free self-determination: Habersack & Zimmermann (n 577 above) 281. For the agreement to be set aside, an intolerable imbalance must have been created between the contracting parties because of the impairment of the surety's ability to reach a free and responsible decision: Habersack & Zimmermann (n 577 above) 282.

was influential.[579] Social inequality as well as respect for and recognition of the individual inform an assessment of liberty.[580]

The Irish courts may set aside a contract entered into under duress[581] or undue influence.[582] They also have equitable jurisdiction to intervene in unconscionable bargains.[583] This power has been exercised sparingly and the criteria for intervention have not been considered by the Supreme Court. The concern is with procedural justice.[584] One of the elements to the transaction that the party seeking relief must show in order to succeed is that the weaker party was under a bargaining impairment, as the parties did not meet on equal terms, and was therefore placed at a serious disadvantage.[585] In a commercial loan or when a bank deals with a surety, the abuse of the imbalance in power between the parties where the lender is aware of the vulnerability of the customer is a critical issue. To insist on people taking responsibility for the consequences of their freely-made decisions (even though they may be foolhardy choices) respects their dignity.

The South African courts have accepted the principle that unconscionable, unduly harsh or oppressive contractual provisions could be struck down for

579 Baer (n 576 above) 450. An unintended result of section 8 of the Married Women's Status Act 1957, which was enacted in recognition of the family solidarity, is that the beneficiary of a contract where threats or pressure were involved may not have engaged in the intimidation, and, indeed, might not even be aware of it. This is because section 8 of the Act provides that when a contract expressly benefits a third party, who is the spouse or child of one of the contracting parties, the third party can enforce it.

580 Baer (n 576 above) 450.

581 *Smelter Corporation of Ireland Ltd v O'Driscoll* [1977] IESC 1, [1977] IR 305. See R Clark *Contract law in Ireland* (2008) 362.

582 *O'Flanagan v Ray-Ger Ltd* [1983] IEHC 83. See Clark (n 581 above) 387. The equitable rule of undue influence is part of a broader general principle of public policy to save people from being victimised by other people: PA McDermott *Contract law* (2001) [14.45].

583 *Grealish v Murphy* [1946] IR 35 (HC). See Clark (n 581 above) 385, 391, 393, 505. Unconscionable bargain is concerned with contracts where the stronger party knows that the weaker party labours under a special disadvantage: McDermott (n 582 above) [14.148].

584 M Enright *Principles of Irish contract law* (2007) [18-87].

585 Enright (n 584 above) [18-86]. The other elements to be shown appear to be that the other party took advantage of that weakness by exploitative conduct, that the transaction was manifestly improvident, and that she did not obtain adequate advice: as above. Murphy J stated that the availability of 'appropriate independent legal advice' would afford a bank a defence, see *Bank of Nova Scotia v Hogan* [1996] IESC 2, [1996] 3 IR 239 at 249. O'Donovan J considered that in the absence of any actual or constructive knowledge that a co-guarantor was not a free agent, a bank was not under any obligation to ensure she obtained independent legal advice: *Ulster Bank Ireland Ltd v Fitzgerald* [2001] IEHC 159 [10]; see P O'Callaghan & A O'Donoghue 'Ireland' in Ciacchi & Weatherill (n 577 above) 344 - 345.

being against public policy,[586] but have been slow to allow fundamental rights or values to influence the law of contract in practice.[587]

Anti-discrimination laws interfere with the prerogative not to sell goods or services to the public. They also prevent differentiation in the recruitment and treatment of employees on specified grounds, thereby encroaching on the contract of employment. There is statutory protection for recognised categories of inequality, most notably consumers and employees, and this section will analyse these areas next.

7.10.4 Consumers

It is a myth that the parties in business to consumer commerce are equal. In modern life everyday purchases are made in stores or online where there is no question of the customer negotiating the terms. Consumers have the freedom not to buy and to shop around, but they will not be able to find an alternative vendor who will treat them as equals and negotiate every term individually with them. The development of mass consumer markets, standard form dealing and carefully crafted exclusion clauses have resulted in the erosion of freedom of contract.[588] To augment the autonomy of the customer, modern law regulates the bargaining process without directly regulating the bargain itself.[589] Where the parties dealt on an informed consent basis and entered freely into the agreement, the sanctity of the contract will be upheld.[590] Accordingly there is much legislation to protect consumers of goods and services by having an obligatory 'cooling-off' period, bringing terms to their notice to make them aware of the consequences and prohibiting unfair conditions. Although some exclusionary provisions are declared void, the preference is to subject questionable provisions to a test of reasonableness, which is a check on the integrity of the particular bargaining situation.[591] There is a limit to paternalist intervention to protect parties from the

586 PJ Sutherland 'Ensuring contractual fairness in consumer contracts after *Barkhuizen v Napier* 2007 5 SA 323 (CC) – Part 1' (2008) 19 *Stellenbosch Law Review* 390 at 411. See also L Hawthorne 'Constitution and contract: Human dignity, the theory of capabilities and *Existenzgrundlage* in South Africa' [2011] (2) *Studia Universitatis Babeº-Bolyai Iurisprudentia* 27 at 29 - 30, 33 - 34, 37 - 39.

587 Moseneke (n 570 above) 10. See also H Corder 'Judicial activism of a special type: South Africa's top courts since 1994' in Dickson (n 83 above) 358 - 359.

588 Brownsword (n 415 above) 184. See also Brownsword (n 405 above) 481.

589 Brownsword (n 415 above) 186.

590 As above.

591 As above.

consequences of their own decisions. Dignity can empower people to choose, but it can also be a constraint warranting an examination of the circumstances to see if the parties chose with full knowledge of what they were doing.

Term freedom is modified, first, by regulating contracts that compromise the contractor's own dignity, and, second, when contracts compromise the community's vision of respect for human dignity.[592] By adding respect for human dignity to public policy, the community takes control of what is good for contractors and society at large.[593] Partner freedom is constrained by equality laws.[594] The European notion of dignity as having a relational character is closely connected with solidarity and can require private actors performing vital services to take into account the needs of all citizens.[595] Clauses in contracts can be avoided because they fail to align with the right to material conditions that make life worthwhile.[596] Health insurance[597] and the provision of services of general interest like telecommunications, electricity and gas[598] in the era of privatisation might be affected. Non-discriminatory access to credit with fair contractual terms and suitable remedies against over-indebtedness are required to remove barriers to self-development.[599]

The reticence of the South African courts to interfere with consumer contracts is evident from the Supreme Court of Appeal's decision in *Afrox*

592 Brownsword (n 415 above) 195.

593 As above. Public policy cannot be used to dismantle autonomy or human dignity in the name of the community of moral agents: A Reichman 'Property rights, public policy and the limits of the power to discriminate' in Friedmann & Barak-Erez (n 415 above) 272.

594 Brownsword (n 415 above) 197.

595 MR Marella 'Human dignity in a different light: European contract law, social dignity and the retreat of the welfare state' in Grundmann (n 572 above) 132, 135, 140.

596 Marella (n 595 above) 140. This could happen when limits are placed on a tenant's right to have her family live with her, as happened in a French case: Marella (n 595 above) 141 - 142, citing Cour de Cassation, 3e Civ, 6 March 1996, *Dalloz* 1996, 167, annotated by Lamy.

597 Marella (n 595 above) 142 - 143.

598 Marella (n 595 above) 144 - 145. Procedural fairness before disconnection of an electricity supply is required: *Joseph v City of Johannesburg* [2009] ZACC 30, 2010 4 SA 55 (CC).

599 Marella (n 595 above) 145.

Healthcare, when it would not set aside an exemption clause in a standard form contract for patients in a private hospital.[600]

7.10.5 Employees

From one perspective, a contract of employment could be looked at as the commodification of a person – the sale and objectification of people has long been condemned as contrary to the most basic human right not to be a slave.[601] Therefore, the labour market is subject to stricter scrutiny.[602] An alternative view is that the employment relationship empowers people to realise their goals and to earn money to enable them to thrive in life. If an individual freely chooses to work in return for payment without duress or coercion, in the modern market economy there is no normative basis for objecting to it in principle.[603] Concern for human dignity[604] can ground intervention to nullify contracts of an exploitative nature, such as human

600 *Afrox Healthcare Bpk v Strydom* 2002 6 SA 21 (SCA). See Corder (n 587 above) 358; MacQueen (n 475 above) 379.

The Supreme Court of Appeal also declined to develop the common law by imposing strict liability on a manufacturer in delict for unintended harm caused by defective manufacture of a product (in this case a local anaesthetic called Regibloc Injection): *Wagener v Pharmacare Ltd* [2003] ZASCA 30, [2003] 2 All SA 167 (SCA). The plaintiff alleged that the common law remedy (the Aquilian action for damages) to protect and enforce her right to bodily integrity under Section 12(2) of the Constitution was inadequate: above, [9]. The Court found that the Aquilian action was adequate to protect her right to bodily integrity, given that there was scope for incremental development of the approach to *res ipsa loquitur* and to the incidence of the onus of proof: above, [38]. Legislation was enacted subsequently providing for strict liability for damage caused by defective goods: Consumer Protection Act 2008 sec 61.

601 TD Rakoff 'Enforcement of employment contracts and the anti-slavery norm' in Friedmann & Barak-Erez (n 415 above) 283 - 285.

602 The Supreme Court of Namibia put it: 'unlike a commodity, it [labour] may not be bought or sold on the market without regard to the inseparable connection it has to the rights and human character of the individual who produces it.': *Africa Personnel Services (Pty) Ltd v Government of Republic of Namibia* [2009] NASC 17 [70], [100]. The African Commission deemed that Mauritania had failed to take effective measures to eradicate the practice of slavery, which it had officially abolished, and found that practices analogous to slavery violated the African Charter: *Malawi African Association v Mauritania* [2000] AHRLR 149 (ACHPR 2000) [134]-[135]. It emphasised that unremunerated work was 'tantamount to a violation of the right to respect for the dignity inherent in the human being': above, [135].

603 Control in the workplace takes place as a matter of institutional organisation rather than personal domination: Rakoff (n 601 above) 292.

604 On the relevance of dignity to modern employment law, see DC Yamada 'Human dignity and American employment law' (2009) 43 *University of Richmond Law Review* 523 at 546 - 552.

trafficking and prostitution, as well as employment in inhumane conditions for low pay below subsistence level.[605]

The freedom to select employees is curtailed by anti-discrimination laws.[606] The requirement to respect the dignity of the individual in the way workers are treated is evident in anti-bullying and harassment policies, and is recognised in law.[607] Newman J made this clear in *Horkulak v Cantor Fitzgerald International* when he pointed out, '[t]he law has developed so as to recognise an employment contract as engaging obligations in connection with the self esteem and dignity of the employee.'[608]

Participation in negotiating working conditions is mandated in some circumstances and gives workers a measure of control over their daily activities by eroding somewhat a hierarchical structure.[609] As the worker is free to quit, work ceases to be 'involuntary servitude'.[610] Contracts that restrict former employees from setting up in competition or working for other employers are examined for compliance with competition rules and could also be challenged on the basis of dignity. On the latter argument, quitting work is regarded as a positive act encapsulating a human power to start life afresh.[611] The denial of the opportunity to do so may be tested for reasonableness taking into account the individual circumstances.

In the *Handelsvertreter* case, a commercial agent employed by a wine company succeeded in his appeal to the German Federal Constitutional Court against an injunction obtained by his former employers based on a non-compete clause in his contract of employment, which stipulated that he would be entitled to no compensation in certain circumstances provided for in the German

605 Human dignity has been described as 'a flexible valve for broad public intervention': G Mundlak 'Human rights and the employment relationship: A look through the prism of juridification' in Friedmann & Barak-Erez (n 415 above) 311.

606 See *Bel Porto School Governing Body v Premier of the Western Cape Province* [2002] ZACC 2, 2002 3 SA 265 (CC).

607 On workplace bullying, see Yamada (n 604 above) 562 - 565.

608 [2003] EWHC 1918 (QB), [2004] ICR 697 [17]. See G Moon & R Allen 'Dignity discourse in discrimination law: a better route to equality?' [2006] *European Human Rights Law Review* 610 at 629 - 630.

609 In *RWDSU v Saskatchewan*, Wilson J (dissenting) pointed out that free negotiation was valued because it enabled workers to participate in establishing their own working conditions, and, she continued, '[i]t is an exercise in self-government and enhances the dignity of the worker as a person.': *Retail, Wholesale and Department Store Union, Locals 544, 496, 635 and 955 v Saskatchewan* [1987] 1 SCR 460 (SC of Canada) [54].

610 Rakoff (n 601 above) 292.

611 Rakoff (n 601 above) 293.

Commercial Code.[612] The legislator's rules did not sufficiently protect the agent's economic basis of existence. The Court alluded to the basic precondition of freedom of contract – there can only be fair and just results if there is an 'approximate equilibrium of bargaining power' between the parties.[613]

The South African Constitutional Court acknowledged the disparity in power between workers and employers in the *First Certification* case, when it discerned that collective bargaining was based on 'the recognition of the fact that employers enjoy greater social and economic power than individual workers' and workers therefore needed 'to act in concert to provide them collectively with sufficient power to bargain effectively with employers'.[614]

The working relationship is subject to other constraints that may not be spelled out in the contract of employment.[615] It was held in *Halford v UK* that, in the absence of a warning that calls were liable to interception, an employee could have a reasonable expectation of privacy for telephone calls.[616] There is probably a similar expectation that other forms of secret monitoring will not take place.[617]

612 Mak (n 575 above) [2.2.2.1], citing BVerfG 7 February 1990, BVerfGE 81, 242. The Court found that the clause was formulated so broadly that it would effective prevent him from working in his line of business for two years: Mak (n 575 above) 72. The agent might have to change professions, but compensation for the inherent disadvantages had been generally excluded. Even though he had agreed to the non-competition clause, the Court considered that the contract gave the employer too much power to restrict his autonomy. See also O Cherednychenko 'Fundamental rights and contract law' (2006) 2 *European Review of Contract Law* 489 at 492; OO Cherednychenko 'Fundamental rights and private law: A relationship of subordination or complementarity?' (2007) 3(2) *Utrecht Law Review* 1 at 6 - 7; R Ellger 'The European Convention of Human Rights and Fundamental Freedoms and German private law' in Friedmann & Barak-Erez (n 415 above) 177.

613 Ellger (n 612 above) 177, citing BVerfG 7 February 1990 [1990] JZ 691 at 692.

614 n 294 above, [66].

615 Legislation concerning dismissal should be interpreted in a manner compatible with the values of reasonableness and fair dealing in an open and democratic society and should not be confined to review on 'the very narrow grounds of procedural misconduct': *Sidumo v Rustenburg Platinum Mines Ltd* [2007] ZACC 22, 2008 2 SA 24 (CC) [158] (Sachs J).

616 (App no 20605/92) (1997) 24 EHRR 523 [45].

617 H Beale & N Pittam 'The impact of the Human Rights Act 1998 on English tort and contract law' in Friedmann & Barak-Erez (n 415 above) 156.

7.11 Blasphemy

The prohibition on blasphemy in Article 40.6.1°(i) of the Constitution has become controversial. The right of believers to enjoy freedom of religion does not trump the right of others to be free from religion and to express their beliefs on matters of public importance.[618] Since dignity is a public value, claims about its meaning cannot be grounded in private beliefs.[619] A referendum to remove the blasphemy provision is warranted.[620]

Accepting that the criminalisation of blasphemy is at present enshrined in the Constitution and was given legislative effect eventually in the Defamation Act 2009,[621] every effort should be made to interpret it in harmony with the rights of all in society. The constitutional rights in contention include the freedom to express convictions and opinions,[622] freedom of conscience and of religion,[623] equality before the law,[624] the parental right and duty to provide for their children's religious, moral, intellectual and social education,[625] and the personal rights to dignity and privacy.[626] These should be construed in the light of the constitutional values of the dignity and freedom of the individual, while at the same time maintaining social cohesion and promoting democratic participation in a changing society.[627]

618 J Weinrib 'What is the purpose of freedom of expression?' (2009) 67 *University of Toronto Faculty of Law Review* 165 at 185. On the principle of using religious norms to interpret the Constitution, see GF Whyte 'Some reflections on the role of religion in the constitutional order' in Murphy & Twomey (n 493 above) 54 - 60.

619 Weinrib (n 618 above) 185.

620 The Law Reform Commission recommended that it be deleted in any revision of the Constitution: Law Reform Commission 'Report on the Crime of Libel' (LRC 41-1991) 12, 15. This recommendation was endorsed by an advisory group established by the Minister for Justice, Equality and Law Reform: Legal Advisory Group on Defamation, *Report* (Dublin, March 2003) [59].

621 Secs 36 & 37. There was vehement opposition to the new statutory offence: TJ O'Dowd 'Ireland's new Defamation Act' (2009) 1 *Journal of Media Law* 173 at 173.

622 Art 40.6.1°(i).

623 Art 44.2.1°.

624 Art 40.1.

625 Art 42.1.

626 Unenumerated personal rights: Art 40.3.1°.

627 Relevant also are the ECHR provisions relating to respect for private and family life (Art 8), freedom of thought, conscience and religion (Art 9), and freedom of expression (Art 10): ECHR (n 4 above). Any restriction of these ECHR rights that are necessary in a democratic society must be prescribed by law and proportionate to a legitimate aim. Their exercise is to be secured without discrimination on the grounds of religion, political or other opinion, minority association or other status: Art 14.

As freedom of speech benefits democratic government, enhances the quest for truth and promotes individual self-fulfilment,[628] its limitation is not permitted lightly.[629] The constitutional guarantee relating to it is subject to public order and morality,[630] as is the guarantee concerning freedom of conscience and religion.[631] Although the preservation of public order is essential to enable all members of society live in peace free from fear and violence with their equal status and dignity in society recognised by the rest of the community,[632] the rare threat to it is no longer a credible justification for criminalising blasphemy.[633] There are other means available to provide a non-threatening supportive environment where all may strive to realise their full potential and life ambitions, and where human flourishing and respect for dignity in its broadest meaning can take place.[634] The strongest argument for prohibiting blasphemy is that it causes injury to feelings in the special

628 See T Daly 'Strengthening Irish democracy: A proposal to restore free speech to Article 40.6.1°(I) of the Constitution' (2009) 31 *Dublin University Law Journal* 228 at 231.

629 Contrary to the liberal emphasis on freedom of speech, in Islamic law a different normative understanding of the public sphere justifies the suppression of blasphemy: PG Danchin 'Defaming Muhammad: Dignity, harm, and incitement to religious hatred' (2010) 2 *Duke Forum for Law & Social Change* 5 at 21.

630 Art 40.6.1°.

631 Art 44.2.1°.

632 Public order has two dimensions – the narrow one of *keeping the peace* by preventing fighting or violence from breaking out, and the broader one of society's interest in maintaining among us a proper sense of one another's social or legal *status*: J Waldron 'Dignity and defamation: The visibility of hate' (2010) 123 *Harvard Law Review* 1596 at 1604.

633 See Law Reform Commission 'Consultation Paper on the Crime of Libel' (August 1991) [231]; KA O'Brien 'Ireland's secular revolution: The waning influence of the Catholic Church and the future of Ireland's blasphemy law' (2002) 18 *Connecticut Journal of International Law* 395 at 429.

634 The publication of material and speech likely to stir up hatred against a group on account of listed characteristics (including religion) is an offence: Prohibition of Incitement to Hatred Act 1989 secs 1 & 2.

sphere of deeply personal religious beliefs.[635] The concern is for the effect on the targets – not with the right to express moral disapproval of their beliefs.[636]

I propose to consider whether it is possible to frame a blasphemy offence with a defence that does not compromise dignity. But before doing that, I will outline the legislation brought in to remedy the lacuna in the law that was identified in *Corway*.[637] In the absence of a legislative definition, the Court found it impossible to say of what the offence of blasphemy consisted.[638] By section 36 of the Defamation Act 2009, a fine of up €25 000 can be imposed for the offence of publishing or uttering 'blasphemous matter'[639] defined as that which is 'grossly abusive or insulting in relation to matters held sacred by any religion, thereby causing outrage among a substantial number of the adherents of that religion'.[640] *Mens rea* is a requirement, as

635 LRC Consultation Paper (n 633 above) [231]. In 1917 the House of Lords held that a denial of Christianity, apart from scurrility or profanity, did not constitute the offence of blasphemy: *Bowman v Secular Society* [1917] AC 406. Lord Finlay stated, 'the crime of blasphemy is not constituted by a temperate attack on religion in which the decencies of controversy are maintained': above, 423. By then the purpose of blasphemy law had shifted from protecting religion *per se*, to preventing religious offence: S Ranalow 'Bearing a constitutional cross: Examining blasphemy and the judicial role in *Corway v. Independent Newspapers*' (2000) 3 *Trinity College Law Review* 95 at 98. Later in English law the rationale of the offence moved from the public (the tendency to corrupt public order) to the private (the hurt caused to the feelings of individual citizens): LRC Consulatation Paper (n 633 above) [121]. On *Bowman*, see O'Brien (n 633 above) 421.

Some commentators dismiss arguments about offended religious feelings as sentimental claims and consider that in a democracy there should be no protection against insult to feelings (even those related to values held sacred): M Pinto 'What are offences to feelings really about? A new regulative principle for the multicultural era' (2010) 30 *Oxford Journal of Legal Studies* 695 at 696 - 697. Meital Pinto has proposed that the claims of offence to feelings be reconceptualised as claims of offence to integrity of cultural identity and has argued that vulnerable cultural identies ought to be protected: above, 697, 722 - 723.

636 SJ Brison 'The autonomy defense of free speech' (1998) 108 *Ethics* 312 at 325.

637 The Supreme Court held that the common law crime of blasphemy related to an established church that pre-dated the enactment of the Constitution and could not have survived it: n 98 above, 501. See N Cox *Blasphemy and the law in Ireland* (2000) 53 - 59; N Cox *Defamation law* (2007) [1.4.3]; M Kealey 'Publish and be damned' (2006) 100(3) *Gazette of the Law Society of Ireland* 20; O'Brien (n 633 above) 396, 425 - 427, 429; Ranalow (n 635 above) 96, 101.

638 n 98 above, 502. The Supreme Court's decision suggests an impatience with the religious character of the Constitution and a reluctance to seek to rehabilitate its language in the light of other contemporary constitutional values: Binchy (n 83 above) 196. See also Daly (n 628 above) 249 - 250; Ranalow (n 635 above) 104, 107 - 110.

639 Sec 36(1).

640 Sec 36(2)(a).

there must be an intention to cause outrage.[641] Excluded from protection are profit-making organisations or cults and those that employ 'oppressive psychological manipulation'.[642]

Should any prosecutions ensue, there are several avenues of attack that could be launched on the legislation. First, 'religion' is not defined, so the boundaries of the curtailment of free speech are neither certain nor readily ascertainable and the offence could be challenged on the grounds of vagueness.[643] It would appear from the reference to 'any' religion that Christian[644] and non-Christian faiths are protected. But does the protection extend to polytheistic creeds or to religions which deny the existence of personal deities?[645] The human dignity of those with such beliefs merits protection on an equal basis with adherents to more widely practiced theologies. Second, an offence could be committed by a vigorous challenge to a religious activity such as human sacrifice that denigrates human dignity and is a crime.[646] The legislation has not been qualified by the exclusion of criminal offences from matters held sacred. Third, robust criticism of a religion's treatment of one gender (normally women) as inferior and of unequal status could lead to the critic being prosecuted. Fourth, an accused could attempt to show that virtually all religions employ oppressive psychological manipulation and curtail free thinking thereby inhibiting the exercise of freedom of conscience. This argument would fail, as the legislation would be given a purposive interpretation precluding the extension of the exclusion to established religions not generally regarded as organisations or cults.

Reverting to the question posed earlier concerning the possibility of designing a dignity-respecting blasphemy defence and taking the current Irish legislation as the base line, some of the defects in it that have been mentioned might be remedied by amending the 2009 Act. With regard to the first flaw, 'religion' could be defined as extending beyond the Judaeo-

641 Sec 36(2)(b). There is an exemption for matter having 'genuine literary, artistic, political, scientific, or academic value' in the eyes of a reasonable person: sec 36(3).

642 Sec 36(4).

643 The ECHR requires that a law restricting freedom of expression be formulated with sufficient precision to enable a citizen to regulate his or her conduct: LRC Report (n 620 above) 12.

644 On the Christian character of the Constitution, see D Costello 'The natural law and the Irish Constitution' (1956) 45 *Studies* 403 at 405, 414; *Re Tilson* [1951] IR 1 (HC) 13 - 15.

645 See LRC Consultation Paper (n 633 above) [107].

646 See LRC Consultation Paper (n 633 above) [237].

Christian tradition to all religions – monotheistic and polytheistic, and those that deny the existence of personal deities. However, this inclusive treatment of religion might be deemed contrary to the text of the Constitution, as Article 44.1 sets the freedom of religion provisions in the context of there being one God – not multiple gods or no god at all. To exclude some from the protection against insult extended to other believers would be to fail to respect the dignity of the former and to afford them unequal treatment.

The second flaw is easily remedied by an amendment excluding criminal activities from the definition of 'sacred'. A similar solution could be adopted to address the third flaw, which allows inequality to become embedded and accepted even by those whose equal dignity is denied. An amendment to permit strident critiques of inequalities in religion would correct the position. Fervent believers in the inferiority of women would not prevail by claiming a right to give expression to their deeply held tenets of male supremacy, as to do so would from an objective standpoint deny the dignity of women and humanity in general.

However, there is an overarching objection to criminalising blasphemy that falls foul of the ECHR – it is not necessary to do so in a democratic society. Maintenance of public safety or protection of the rights of others does not demand it. To categorise it as a crime is a disproportionate reaction. It has been invoked so rarely that it has been described as 'a constitutional oddity'.[647]

In its analysis of restrictions on freedom of expression, the European Court of Human Rights has been prepared to undertake an exacting appraisal of national decisions by emphasising pluralism, tolerance and broad-mindedness.[648] The case-law shows an evolution from a timid and over-cautious stance to a more robust review, where the Court analyses the allegedly offensive nature of the contested statements in the light of more objective public sentiments, rather than the subjective feelings of specific individuals.[649] It has required all exercising the freedom to manifest their religion (irrespective of whether they do so as members of a religious majority or a minority) to 'tolerate and accept the denial by others of their religious beliefs and even the propagation by others of doctrines hostile to their

647 Ranalow (n 635 above) 95.

648 D Harris *et al*, *Harris, O'Boyle & Warbrick: Law of the European Convention on Human Rights* (2009) 483.

649 Harris *et al* (n 648 above) 482.

faith'.[650] In *Klein v Slovakia* the Court held that the right to freedom of expression had been breached when a journalist was convicted of 'defamation of nation, race and belief' for defaming the highest representative of the Roman Catholic Church in Slovakia and thereby offending its members.[651]

The conclusion is that it is possible to craft a dignity-respecting blasphemy defence, but it would have considerable hurdles to overcome because of the Constitution's Christian foundation and the ECHR's requirements of precision in law, necessity and proportionality.

In South Africa there are doubts that the crime of blasphemy would survive constitutional challenge, as it applies only to the Christian God.[652] The constitutional exclusion of hate speech based on religion or on race, ethnicity or gender that incites people to cause harm from the protection afforded to freedom of expression is an alternative model that Ireland could consider.[653] The harm targeted might be confined to the narrow range of physical harm, but it would be more in conformity with constitutional values to adhere to a broader definition of harm to dignity interests.[654] Supplementary legislation would be necessary to prohibit hate speech and to provide for remedies for breach that could include criminal sanctions.[655] As it would not be appropriate or proportionate to criminalise comments intended to be hurtful (as opposed to harmful), the ambit of criminal activity should be confined within narrow clearly defined parameters.

650 *İA v Turkey* (App no 42571/98) (2007) 45 EHRR 30 [43]. They 'cannot reasonably expect to be exempt from all criticism': as above. On *A*, see Tsakyrakis (n 287 above) 484 - 485.

651 (App no 72208/01) (2010) 50 EHRR 15 [50], [55]. The journalist had sharply criticised the prelate for calling for the withdrawal of the film 'The People vs. Larry Flynt' and the accompanying poster, and he wondered why Catholics did not leave the Church as it was headed by such an 'ogre': above, [10]-[12], [51]. The Court was unanimously of the view that the 'strongly worded pejorative opinion' related ex-clusively to the archbishop personally and disagreed with the domestic courts' findings that the journalist discredited and disparaged a sector of the population on account of their Catholic faith: above, [51]. See Harris *et al* (n 648 above) 484.

652 *Du Plessis v De Klerk* 1996 3 SA 850 (CC) [19], [50], [54]; *S v Lawrence* 1997 4 SA 1176 (CC) [149]; I Currie & J de Waal *The Bill of Rights handbook* (2005) 394.

653 Sec 16(2)(c).

654 See Currie & de Waal (n 652 above) 377.

655 In South Africa legislation has widened the constitutional conception of hate speech to encompass discriminatory speech that undermines human dignity, where the intention is to be hurtful: Promotion of Equality and Prevention of Unfair Discrimination Act 2000 secs 1(1)(xxii)(b)(ii) & 10(1). See Currie & de Waal (n 652 above) 377 - 379.

8

Rights to Constitutional Remedies and Restrictions on Fundamental Rights

Having reviewed fundamental rights in substantive law in Ireland, this Chapter will consider remedies and the scope of fundamental rights in Irish law.

8.1 Remedies

8.1.1 Damages

Consideration of human dignity could affect the question of whether or not damages should be awarded and, if so, the quantum warranted. Should there be specific damages for breach of constitutional rights? Where there is no remedy in tort or contract, a strong case can be made for compensation being paid for violation of fundamental rights.

8.1.1.1 Defamation

There have been wild excesses to what is adjudged fair compensation in defamation actions. I will now look at the Irish case-law. In *De Rossa v Independent Newspapers* the Supreme Court by a majority of four to one upheld an award of £300 000 to a politician for libel in a newspaper article alleging that he had been involved in serious crime.[1] Hamilton CJ found that Irish law complied with the requirements of the Constitution and of the European

1 *De Rossa v Independent Newspapers plc* [1999] IESC 63, [1999] 4 IR 432. See N Cox *Defamation law* (2007) [11.2.1.2.1].

Convention on Human Rights (ECHR),[2] as it provided 'that the award must always be reasonable and fair and bear a due correspondence with the injury suffered' and there was a requirement to set aside a disproportionately high award.[3] He placed a high value on the emotional impact, stating, '[o]ne of the most important factors in the assessment of damages is the effect of the libel on the plaintiff's feelings.'[4] The concern was not solely with reputation and loss of good name in the eyes of the public, but with the impingement of a hurtful and humiliating attack on the individual's core personality. Denham J (dissenting) favoured guidelines being given to the jury on quantum[5] and more searching scrutiny on appeal based on the criteria of reasonableness and proportionality.[6] She considered large awards ineffective as a compensation mechanism.[7]

The criterion of proportionality to determine whether or not an award is excessive also applies in South Africa, but the threshold to be reached before it will be upset is higher. Mokgoro J pointed out in the Constitutional Court in *Dikoko v Mokhatla*, that an appellate court would only interfere 'if ... the award ... was palpably excessive, clearly disproportionate in the circumstances of the case, grossly extravagant or unreasonable or so high as to be manifestly unreasonable.'[8] According to Moseneke DCJ, special circumstances justifying encroachment were found when the trial court awarded high or low damages on the wrong principle or when the award was 'so

2 Convention for the Protection of Human Rights and Fundamental Freedoms, 213 UNTS 222 (ECHR). In a complaint by the newspaper against Ireland, the European Court of Human Rights agreed with the parties that the award interfered with the newspaper's freedom of expression, that it was prescribed by law and that it pursued the legitimate aim of protecting the reputation and rights of others: *Independent News and Media plc v Ireland* (App no 55120/00) (2006) 42 EHRR 46 [109]; to be necessary in a democratic society, an award of damages following a finding of libel had to bear a reasonable relationship of proportionality to the injury to reputation suffered: above, [110]; in view of the measure of appellate control and the margin of appreciation, the Court did not find that the safeguards against a disproportionate award were ineffective or inadequate: above, [132]. See Cox (n 1 above) [13.3.2.2].

3 n 1 above, 458.

4 n 1 above, 464.

5 n 1 above, 483.

6 n 1 above, 481.

7 n 1 above, 478:

> The jury should be able to compare the value of what courts usually award to people in personal injury actions. Compensation is a notional remedy in both instances. The lame do not walk after an award of compensation. The defamed do not cease to have been defamed after an award of damages. An order of damages is an artificial form by which a court gives a remedy to an injured person.

8 2006 6 SA 235 (CC) [58] (footnotes omitted).

unreasonable as to be grossly out of proportion to the injury inflicted.'[9] Unlike Ireland, damages for defamation in South Africa are determined by the judge – there is no jury. This difference may influence the greater reliance placed on the assessment by the judge at first instance in South Africa. *De Rossa* and *Dikoko*, where a public official successfully sued a politician for defamation, followed somewhat similar paths and had the same outcome – notwithstanding the apparent difference between the two countries in the leeway allowed to the lower court. The majority in both cases upheld the awards and there were dissenting views in both cases that high awards should be curtailed. However, in South Africa the two judges who dissented on quantum (Sachs and Mokgoro JJ) considered the effect on the dignity of the target of the defamatory remarks and favoured a smaller award coupled with an apology and restoration of the relationship between the parties. The dignity of the parties was not mentioned in Ireland.

The Supreme Court of Namibia followed the *Dikoko* test in *Trustco v Shikongo*.[10] O'Regan AJA noted that although money was not sufficient to restore the individual's reputation,[11] in a commercialised world it could not be discounted as it carried symbolic weight and was a deterrent.[12] She went on to compare awards in other defamation actions and, having found that the damages in *Trustco* were 'considerably in excess of the awards generally made for defamation', she reduced them significantly.[13] The allegations in *Trustco* concerned abuse of public office by an elected mayor in a land deal, but – unlike *De Rossa* – there was no implication of involvement in serious crimes like armed robbery, forgery, drug-dealing, prostitution and protection rackets.[14] If financial recompense were felt to be the appropriate remedy, the gravity of the crimes imputed to *De Rossa* warranted a high award. However, there was no consideration of other ways of repairing the damage to De Rossa's dignity or of restoring relationships with the journalist who wrote the offensive article.

9 n 8 above, [95] (footnote omitted). The standard at issue was whether there was 'a glaring disproportionality between the amount awarded and the injury to be assuaged', the ultimate test being whether in all the circumstances of the case the compensation was 'a reasonable and just measure of the harm': n 8 above, [95].

10 O'Regan AJA asked the primary question whether the award was 'grossly disproportionate to the injury suffered as a result of the defamation' and acknowledged that one of the difficulties in applying the test was how to quantify harm to reputation in monetary terms: *Trustco Group International Ltd v Shikongo* [2010] NASC 6 [90].

11 As above, citing *Dikoko* (n 8 above) [110] (Sachs J).

12 n 10 above, [91], citing *Dikoko* (n 8 above) [120] (Sachs J).

13 n 10 above, [96].

14 n 1 above, 437 - 438.

The year following the *De Rossa* decision, Denham J dissented in part again when the same issues arose in *O'Brien v Mirror Newspapers* in an appeal against an award of £250 000 for libel in an article alleging bribery of a politician in order to secure radio and mobile phone licences.[15] The standing in the community of the person libelled was a relevant factor.[16] By a majority the Supreme Court held that the award was disproportionately high and remitted the matter to the High Court for a new trial on the issue of damages only. When the case was re-heard some six years later, the jury more than doubled the award to €750 000.[17]

In the libel action brought by Monica Leech, a public relations consultant, against Independent Newspapers following allegations that she had obtained public contracts from a government minister because she was having an extra-marital affair with him, an issue arose over whether the defendant should be entitled to third-party discovery of documents submitted to an inquiry into the allegations ordered by the Dáil.[18] Public interest straddled both sides of the equation – on the one hand, in ensuring the viability of *ad hoc* inquiries by fulfilling the obligation of confidentiality to the participants, and, on the other, in full disclosure and the administration of justice.[19] O'Neill J, refusing to order discovery,[20] held that there were cases where confidentiality was itself in the public interest. The jury awarded her €1 872 000 – a

15 *O'Brien v Mirror Group Newspapers Ltd* [2000] IESC 70, [2001] 1 IR 1. See Cox (n 1 above) [11.2.1.2.2].

16 n 15 above, 37. Denham J adhered to her view that instructions to juries on *quantum* should be altered so as to give them greater guidance and that there should be more searching scrutiny on appeal to maintain the appropriate balance between the rights of the individual and of freedom of expression: n 15 above, 37. Information on the compensation granted in other libel and personal injuries actions might help to maintain a proper monetary balance, n 15 above, 35:

> At the least, reference could be made to the level of damages in previous libel cases decided by the Supreme Court and to the level of awards in serious personal injury cases, as has been introduced in other common law countries. Such judicial guidelines may be a safeguard against a disproportionate award. In the absence of such guidelines, merely to require the award to be proportionate is an inadequate protection against a disproportionate award.

17 *O'Brien v Mirror Group Newspapers Ltd* 23 November 2006 (HC). See 'O'Brien happy to have been "vindicated"' *Irish Times* (Dublin, 24 November 2006) 4.

18 *Leech v Independent Newspapers (Ireland) Ltd* [2009] IEHC 259, [2009] 3 IR 766.

19 n 18 above, [12].

20 The parties had considerable other resources available to them, including the report from the inquiry: n 18 above, [15].

record for a libel action.[21] That record was broken in November 2010 in *Kinsella v Kenmare Resources* when a businessman was awarded €10m damages (€9m compensatory and €1 aggravated damages)[22] for a libellous press release issued by his employers after he went naked into the company secretary's hotel bedroom in Mozambique where they were attending a board meeting.[23]

The size of these awards reflects the very high value the general public (as articulated by the jury) places on the individual's dignity. False allegations of deliberate wrong-doing involving crime and corruption, and – even more so – sexual impropriety, strike at the core of a person's being, since they concern the exercise of free will for an odious purpose affecting the person's standing in the community. They wound their feelings and humiliate them. A good reputation in society is guarded zealously and is essential for self-esteem. The significance of these rights is underlined in Article 40.3.2° of the Constitution, where the 'good name' of the citizen is one of four aspects of the citizen singled out for particular state protection and vindication. Given the undoubted worth of the rights protected by defamation actions, the question must be posed as to what is the most appropriate remedy. Is society's disapproval to be marked by the size of the award and, if so, is an extremely generous sum appropriate? Perhaps the finding that the individual has been defamed should go a considerable distance towards relieving the public opprobrium and vindicating the plaintiff. Maybe the damage caused could be redressed by other measures such as publicising the court's findings widely and a public acknowledgment by the defendant of the falseness of the libellous remarks.

Apart from the conflict between freedom of expression and the individual's right to a good name, there are two competing interests in play in the assessment of damages for defamation – on the one hand, the individual's

21 *Leech v Independent Newspapers (Ireland) Ltd* 24 June 2009 (HC). See: M Carolan 'Newspaper to appeal record €1.87m libel award: Jury decides "Herald" articles alleged Leech had affair' *Irish Times* (Dublin, 25 June 2009) 4; M Minihan 'Leech "absolutely vindicated" by record €1.87m libel award' *Irish Times* (Dublin, 25 June 2009) 1.

22 On compensatory and aggravated damages, see P Giliker & S Beckwith *Tort* (2011) [17-004]–[17-005], [17-008].

23 *Kinsella v Kenmare Resources plc* 17 November 2010 (HC). Mr Kinsella was prone to sleep-walking and an investigation by an independent solicitor on behalf of the company found there was no conscious attempt on his part to enter her room and that he had no improper motive. The press release said he was being asked to resign from the company's audit committee. See C Coulter 'Businessman wins €10m libel award against ex-employers' *Irish Times* (Dublin, 18 November 2010) 1; E Keane 'Defame game' (2011) 105(1) *Gazette of the Law Society of Ireland* 36 at 37. The case is under appeal to the Supreme Court.

reputation which can be repaired to a large extent by an apology accompanied by publicity and is not dependent entirely on money for restoration, and, on the other, the deterrent effect to protect the individual and the community generally from a culture of malicious or careless commentary.[24] Steps have been taken in Ireland to reform the law in this area. The Defamation Act 2009 permits the parties to an action to make submissions on damages to the court[25] and the judge is obliged to give directions to the jury on damages[26] where the cause of action accrued after the commencement of the Act.[27] Previously when no guidelines were given to jurors on quantum, it was unsurprising that juries had unrealistic ideas about what was the appropriate financial recompense for a damaged reputation. As favoured by the minority in *Dikoko*[28] there is a school of thought that money is inappropriate reparation for hurt to one's name and that a modest sum coupled with a public apology is more compatible with restoring respect for the dignity of the injured party. The Defamation Act provides the defendant wishing to make amends with the facility to offer to do so.[29] As occurs in Britain,[30] such an offer may lead to a discount in compensation, since damages are to be assessed having regard to all of the circumstances of the case,[31] including the making of an offer to make amends,[32] and the offering or making of an apology,[33] correction or retraction.[34]

24 See A Kenyon 'Problems with defamation damages?' (1998) 24 *Monash University Law Review* 70 at 76 - 77, 90 - 91.

25 Sec 31(1).

26 Sec 31(2). On submissions and directions on damages, see HI Mohan & MW Murphy 'Defamation reform and the 2009 Act: Part II' (2010) 15 *Bar Review* 50 at 52 - 53; TJ O'Dowd 'Ireland's new Defamation Act' (2009) 1 *Journal of Media Law* 173 at 185. On the policy background, see O'Dowd above, 174 - 175, 177.

27 Sec 3(1).

28 n 8 above.

29 Sec 22. See Mohan & Murphy (n 26 above) 51 - 52.

30 M Kealey 'Defame and fortune' (2010) 104(1) *Gazette of the Law Society of Ireland* 20 at 23.

31 Sec 31(3).

32 Sec 31(4)(e).

33 A defendant may give evidence in mitigation of damages of the making or offering of an apology: sec 24. See Mohan & Murphy (n 26 above) 52.

34 Sec 31(4)(d).

8.1.1.2 Catastrophic injuries

A somewhat similar analysis could apply to damages for catastrophic injuries. If the injured party is so badly impaired as not to appreciate the extent of the impairment, should damages be reduced? Some would say yes – the non-pecuniary loss is not redressed by high damages. In fact, it is more likely that the injured party's relatives will benefit rather than the injured person herself. There is a middle ground – instead of denying any general damages to a badly impaired individual, compensation could be awarded for infringement of the person's dignity at a modest level.

In *Cooke v Walsh* the majority in the Supreme Court considered that compensation should be moderate where the plaintiff had 'only a mild awareness or appreciation of his condition due to the severe brain damage he sustained in the accident' and therefore he had 'been spared the considerable mental suffering which would follow from knowledge or appreciation of the virtual destruction of his life.'[35] McCarthy J (dissenting) had reservations about that approach and pointed out that the trial judge did not consider the significance of the injury itself in measuring damages, but only the plaintiff's appreciation of it.[36]

The Supreme Court in *Sinnott v Quinnsworth Ltd* held that in assessing general damages 'the objective must be to determine a figure which is fair and reasonable', having regard, *inter alia*, 'to the ordinary living standards in the country, to the general level of incomes, and to the things upon which the plaintiff might reasonably be expected to spend money.'[37] The factors considered by the Supreme Court in *Dunne v National Maternity* Hospital included the extent to which the plaintiff had 'any appreciation or awareness of his condition and of the amenities of living' which he had lost.[38] The Court raised – but did not decide – the issue of whether a plaintiff who has no awareness of his condition as a result of injuries tortiously inflicted should be entitled to nil or nominal general damages only.[39] In *Lindsay v Mid-Western Health Board*, Morris J in the High Court held that where the plaintiff had little or no awareness of his or her condition, there was no rule of law either

35 [1984] ILRM 208 at 219.

36 n 35 above, 223. As the issue had not been fully debated, he preferred to await a suitable case on 'the question as to whether or not an individual who has no real appreciation of his plight should be awarded other than a relatively nominal sum for general damages': n 35 above, 223.

37 [1984] ILRM 523 at 532.

38 [1989] IR 91 at 118 - 119.

39 n 38 above, 119.

limiting the general damages to be awarded to a nominal figure or precluding the awarding of such damages altogether.[40] In contrast to this view are *obiter* comments by Quirke J in *Yun v Motor Insurers Bureau of Ireland* when he countenanced no general damages at all for an unconscious plaintiff.[41]

The House of Lords took a different stance in *H West & Son Ltd v Shephard* when in a majority decision it confirmed that general damages should be assessed objectively and therefore a permanently unconscious claimant should receive damages for loss of amenity at the top end of the scale of compensation.[42] The majority of consultees in a study by the English Law Commission on damages for non-pecuniary loss felt that to apply a subjective test based on the victim's awareness – thereby awarding lower compensation for catastrophic injuries than for less serious ones – would be unjust and would have an anti-deterrent effect; it was considered that although permanently unconscious victims do not go through pain and suffering, substantial damages were justified by the unconscious victim's complete loss of amenity, and that failure to recognise this would be to undervalue victims and to trivialise their experiences.[43]

Dickson J in the Supreme Court of Canada in *Andrews v Grand & Toy Alberta Ltd* – rather than attempting to set a value on lost happiness – was attracted to the functional approach, which assessed the compensation required to provide the injured person 'with reasonable solace for his misfortune', solace in this sense being taken to mean 'physical arrangements which can make his life more endurable rather than "solace" in the sense of sympathy.'[44] A similar focus on solace is apparent in the High Court of

40 [1993] 2 IR 147. The case was brought on behalf of a plaintiff who had suffered irreversible brain damage and had been in a deep coma for 18 years at the time of trial.

41 [2009] IEHC 318, [2009] 7 JIC 1701 at 22 - 23. Quirke J indicated that general damages in tort may be reduced, or even eliminated altogether, where there is a lack of insight into one's own condition: above, 22. In catastrophic injuries cases 'a modest or no award for general damages may be made where general damages will have little or no compensatory consequence for the injured person': above, 23.

42 [1964] AC 326 (HL). See Law Commission 'Damages for Personal Injury: Non-Pecuniary Loss' (Law Com No 257, 1999) [2.9].

43 n 42 above, [2.13]. The Law Commission did not recommend any change in the rules for general damages for permanently unconscious claimants nor for conscious, but severely brain-damaged, victims: n 42 above, [2.19], [2.24]. It also rejected moving from the traditional 'diminution of value' approach – where damages put a value on what the claimant has lost, irrespective of how the sum awarded will be spent – to the Canadian 'functional' approach where damages are meant to provide comfort and solace to the claimant, by enabling him or her to obtain other means of satisfaction to replace what has been lost: n 42 above, [2.4], [2.7].

44 [1978] 2 SCR 229 at 261 - 262.

Australia's decision in *Skelton v Collins*, when it adopted a subjective approach and favoured the dissents of Lord Devlin and Lord Reid in *H West & Son Ltd*.[45]

In Ireland there are constitutional obligations for laws to defend and *vindicate* life[46] and personal rights.[47] When a serious injury has been caused, it will be necessary to vindicate the person's life, bodily integrity and human dignity even (or perhaps more so) when the injury is so severe as to cause loss of consciousness and to shorten the normal lifespan. An admission of liability by a defendant is an acceptance of blame for wrongfully causing the injury and, if coupled with an apology, would go some way towards vindication. If liability is in issue, vindication requires a judicial determination on this point. We can apply to situations of catastrophic injury the Supreme Court's view in *Grant v Roche Products (Ireland) Ltd* that compensation alone payable by a drug company whose product was alleged to have caused a young man to commit suicide was insufficient vindication for his life without a judicial finding on responsibility for that drastic step.[48]

The question is whether compensation defends against encroachment or exonerates blame in the case of serious injury. A finding on liability fulfils the need to establish blame for a catastrophic injury. Damages will be a deterrent for the minority who have more regard for material goods than for human life or dignity. However, to take the view that no compensation for non-pecuniary losses is appropriate and to rely on an admission or finding of liability alone to vindicate life and dignity would be wrong. Ackermann J in the *Sodomy* case explained that the minimum the protection of dignity required was an acknowledgment of 'the value and worth of all individuals as members of our society.'[49] The constitutional value of dignity was considered by O'Regan J in *Dawood* 'to inform the future, to invest in our democracy respect for the intrinsic worth of all human beings.'[50]

45 (1966) 115 CLR 94. See JG Fleming *The law of torts* (1998) 269.

46 Constitution of Ireland 1937, Art 40.3.2°.

47 Art 40.3.1°.

48 [2008] IESC 35, [2008] 4 IR 679. Hardiman J considered that the best rendition of 'vindicate' combined the definitions 'defend against encroachment or interference' and 'clear of blame, justify by evidence or argument': above, [75].

49 *National Coalition for Gay and Lesbian Equality v Minister of Justice* 1998 12 BCLR 1517 (CC) [28].

50 *Dawood v Minister of Home Affairs* 2000 3 SA 936 (CC) [35]. As David Bilchitz put it, '"dignity" is essentially about the recognition of worth and the consequent treatment that must be accorded to individuals who have such worth': D Bilchitz 'Moving beyond arbitrariness: The legal personhood and dignity of non-human animals' (2009) 25 *South*

By considering the implications for the human dignity of the victim and bearing in mind society's values, a modest sum in compensation for injuries to the unaware plaintiff could be sufficient. Too high a figure runs the risk of appearing to value life and dignity only as commodities and not for their intrinsic value, whereas too low an amount would be regarded as demeaning. The same rationale can be adapted to apply to injuries caused to those who are what David Bilchitz described as 'moral patients' (infants, young children, the senile and those with severe mental impairments) as opposed to 'moral agents' (all adult, rational human beings).[51] Though unable to act out of a sense of duty, moral patients have certain rights that moral agents must respect.[52]

Compensation for future pecuniary losses poses separate problems that could be solved by the introduction of structured settlements with periodic payments, which would give financial security to the plaintiff while avoiding the risk of unjust enrichment of the next-of-kin in the event of an early demise.[53] A report undertaken for the High Court recommending periodic payments justified the change by invoking the values of justice and fairness, as well as taking into account the best interests of those injured.[54] In the United Kingdom the government has encouraged the use of periodic payments ostensibly simply because it is a fairer system, but in reality there are political reasons for the reform.[55]

African Journal on Human Rights 38 at 51. He proposed that value in an individual life be understood in terms of functionings and capabilities determined 'according to what enables individual creatures to flourish as the kind of being that it is': above, 62 - 63.

51 n 50 above, 42.

52 As above.

53 A report commissioned by the President of the High Court recommended that legislation be enacted to empower the courts to order periodic payments for future pecuniary losses: Working Group on Medical Negligence and Periodic Payments 'Report on periodic payments (Module 1)' (29 October 2010) http://www.courts.ie/courts.ie/library3.nsf/%28WebFiles%29/5CEEA19C4A5959BC802577DC0055C 9F4/$file/Medical%20Negligence%201.pdf (accessed 24 September 2013) 7, 23, 26.

54 n 53 above, 7, 12 - 15, 21, 26 - 27, 33. The report discounted a contrary argument that the change would deprive the plaintiff of the freedom to choose to dispose of the full capital value of the compensation as he or she wished: n 53 above, 15, 22. Lump sum awards contained risks for the state as well as for the plaintiff and defendant, because if the return on investment were insufficient to meet the plaintiff's needs, the state would probably be required to fund provision for them: n 53 above, 13 - 14.

55 R Lewis 'Tort law in practice: Appearance and reality in reforming periodical payments of damages' in JW Neyers *et al* (eds) *Emerging issues in tort law* (2007) 501 - 503, 507. The reform has been driven by government concern about the impact of lump sum awards on the National Health Service budgets in clinical negligence cases: above, 488. On periodic payments in the UK, see Giliker & Beckwith (n 22 above) [17-042]-[17.043].

Applying a dignity analysis, the plaintiff is better served by periodic payments for future pecuniary losses, as they would provide the resources to live independently without having to resort to the state for support and without the fear that a lump sum would turn out not to be sufficient. The countervailing argument that the plaintiff should have immediate control over a capitalised sum is unsound – the purpose of damages for future outlays is to restore the plaintiff to the original position and this is more likely to be done by periodic payments than by the lump sum lottery. The aim is not to put the plaintiff in a better position than before the accident by having ready access to a fund provided for future outlays over an indefinite period, but to relieve any worries about inability to meet expenses.

8.1.2 Detention of mentally ill patients

A parallel area where rights to freedom and personal autonomy may not be adequately protected is that of detention of compliant non-competent mentally ill people. Legislation provides that in making a decision on a person's care and treatment, that person's right to 'dignity, bodily integrity, privacy and autonomy' is to be respected.[56] However, the statutory definition of 'voluntary patient' is not aimed at ascertaining whether the individual truly consented to being admitted.[57] The Supreme Court held in *EH v Clinical Director of St Vincent's Hospital* that it was not framed in terms of a person who freely and voluntarily gave consent to an admission order but rather someone who was not the subject of an admission or renewal order.[58] Adopting a paternalistic rather than a rights-based view, the Court dismissed non-compliance with the formalities required for detention where there was no gross abuse of power as a mere technicality that did not require a remedy provided the detention was in the best interests of the patient.[59]

A voluntary patient is not free to leave, as he or she may be detained for 24 hours, during which period a psychiatrist may certify that the patient suffers from a mental disorder and should be detained.[60] In *McN v Health Service Executive* Peart J justified the detention of vulnerable patients with dementia

56 Mental Health Act 2001 sec 4(3). See D Whelan *Mental health law and practice: Civil and criminal aspects* (2009) [5-10]–[5-22], [5-31].

57 Mental Health Act 2001 sec 2(1).

58 [2009] IESC 46, [2009] 3 IR 774 [41]. See Whelan (n 56 above) [5-32]–[5-37].

59 n 58 above, [50].

60 Mental Health Act 2001 secs 23 & 24.

initially admitted as involuntary patients, but whose status was changed to voluntary even though they lacked sufficient mental capacity to choose to consent to remain.[61] They could leave if they were in a position to do so accompanied by a responsible family member. Their continuing presence at the hospital was permissible on the basis that it was in their best interests, there was a duty of care to them and it would be grossly negligent to release them immediately simply because there was no legal basis for keeping them.

McMahon J in *SM v Mental Health Commission*, while acknowledging the paternal nature of the legislation, gave effect to the rights and protections specifically included in the Mental Health Act 2001, when he found that a renewal order relating to an involuntary patient which did not specify a particular period of time, but merely provided that it was 'for a period not exceeding 12 months' was void for uncertainty and did not provide a legal basis for detention.[62] His finding of a violation of the patient's right to liberty (albeit it did not result in immediate release of the patient, as his order was with a stay of four weeks) was a vindication of her rights and would have been 'just satisfaction' for violations of a procedural nature as required by Article 41 ECHR.[63]

In *Bournewood* in the UK it was held that the informal admission of compliant patients without capacity to consent was justified by the common law doctrine of necessity.[64] In that case the tort of false imprisonment had not been committed, since the actions taken were in accordance with the duty of care to the patient in his best interests. Lord Steyn thought it was an unfortunate result of the decision that compliant incapacitated patients did not have statutory protections and considered that '[t]heir moral right to be treated with dignity' required nothing less.[65] The key factor according to the

61 [2009] IEHC 236. See Whelan (n 56 above) [5-38]–[5-40].

62 [2008] IEHC 441, [2009] 3 IR 188. See C Murray 'Reinforcing paternalism within Irish mental health law – Contrasting the decisions in *EH v St. Vincent's Hospital and Others* and *SM v The Mental Health Commission and Others*' (2010) 32 *Dublin University Law Journal* 273.

63 See *HL v UK* (App no 45508/99) (2005) 40 EHRR 32 [148]-[150].

64 *R v Bournewood Community and Mental Health NHS Trust, Ex p L* [1998] UKHL 24, [1999] 1 AC 458. On *Bournewood*, see LO Gostin & L Gable 'The human rights of persons with mental disabilities: A global perspective on the application of human rights principles to mental health' (2004) 63 *Maryland Law Review* 20 at 60, 61, fn 303; AM O'Neill *Irish mental health law* (2005) 94; Whelan (n 56 above) [5-26]–[5-30]. The absence of legal safeguards for the compliant non-competent has been described as 'the *Bournewood* gap'.

65 n 64 above, 497.

European Court of Human Rights was that healthcare professionals had exercised complete and effective control over the patient's care and movements.[66] It found a breach of his right to liberty and security under Article 5(1) ECHR, as the common law doctrine of necessity at the time was underdeveloped and his detention was unlawful because of the absence of fixed procedural safeguards to avoid arbitrariness.[67] The right to judicial review of the lawfulness of his detention in Article 5(4) ECHR was also breached, since *habeas corpus* or judicial review proceedings were not wide enough to bear on the essential conditions for the lawful detention of a person on the ground of unsoundness of mind.[68]

8.1.3 Mediation

Engagement and mediation are dignity-respecting methods of avoiding or resolving disagreements.[69] There are benefits to exploring them in a co-operative spirit before there is resort to litigation. In addition to allowing the parties involved the opportunity to work out their differences themselves by reaching a mutually acceptable settlement, there could be a considerable saving in costs, resources and court time.

A community shaped by the value of harmony will put significant value in mediated solutions.[70] Mediation is now encouraged in Ireland as an alternative dispute mechanism.[71] The South African courts have formalised

66 *HL* (n 63 above) [91].

67 *HL* (n 63 above) [118]-[120], [124].

68 *HL* (n 63 above) [135], [140], [142].

69 Self-determination is the intrinsic value of mediation: J Nolan-Haley 'Self-determination in international mediation: Some preliminary reflections' (2006) 7 *Cardozo Journal of Conflict Resolution* 277 at 278 - 279. It is connected to self-governance and individual autonomy, and offers procedural justice protections, providing parties with fairness and dignity: above, 278. By actively participating in the mediation process and voluntarily consenting to an outcome that is free of any coercive influences, respect for human dignity is promoted and parties' perceptions of procedural justice are enhanced: above, 278 - 279. See also Law Reform Commission 'Consultation Paper on Alternative Dispute Resolution' (LRC CP50-2008) [3.140]-[3.145], [3.150]; Law Reform Commission 'Report on Alternative Dispute Resolution: Conciliation and Mediation' (LRC 98-2010) [3.74], [3.76].

70 SC Angle 'Human rights and harmony' (2008) 30 *Human Rights Quarterly* 76 at 88.

71 In 2010 the Law Reform Commission recommended that there should be a statutory framework for mediation and conciliation: LRC Report (n 69 above) [2.15], [2.47], [2.51], [3.04], [12.01], [12.09]-[12.10], [12.15], app (draft Mediation and Conciliation Bill 2010).

the mediation process, which promotes human dignity in recognition of the fact that we live in a shared society.[72]

8.2 Scope of fundamental rights

Using the Hohfeldian model[73] to translate constitutional values, rights and obligations into tangible legal concepts, it is essential to have clarity on who has rights and obligations, to give coherent answers to what those rights and obligations are in varying circumstances, to define the types of obligations owed by different actors, to specify whether the obligations are actual or potential, and to identify their triggers. Solutions develop over time as different situations affecting relationships emerge. The nature of the obligations will vary. Do they apply only to the relationship between the individual and the state or have they horizontal application? Are they negative or positive? Is there a time constraint on claiming constitutional rights?

8.2.1 Who has obligations?

Historically a constitution was regarded as necessary to protect the individual from intrusion by the state. With the development of human rights law, its reach has expanded to cover the activities of non-state actors – at least in some spheres. As human rights are now regarded as indivisible, a cogent case can be made to apply the principles of equality, non-discrimination and other fundamental rights between private citizens.[74] Full protection for human dignity cannot be achieved by confining constitutional rights to the vertical relationship between the citizen and the state.

72 *Port Elizabeth Municipality v Various Occupiers* 2005 1 SA 217 (CC) [42]. See also *S v Williams* 1995 3 SA 632 (CC) [75]; *Du Plessis v De Klerk* 1996 3 SA 850 (CC) [186]; *Government of the Republic of South Africa v Grootboom* 2001 1 SA 46 (CC) [88]; *Sidumo v Rustenburg Platinum Mines Ltd* [2007] ZACC 22, 2008 2 SA 24 (CC) [94]; *Occupiers of 51 Olivia Road, Berea Township v City of Johannesburg* 2008 3 SA 208 (CC); *Residents of Joe Slovo Community, Western Cape v Thubelisha Homes* 2010 3 SA 454 (CC) [166], [337].

73 See MK Addo 'Does Hohfeld still matter?' (1997) 29 *Bracton Law Journal* 7; LH LaRue 'Hohfeldian rights and fundamental rights' (1985) 35 *University of Toronto Law Journal* 86; H Ross 'Social power and the Hohfeldian jural relation' (2001) 10(1) *Nottingham Law Journal* 47 at 49 - 51; NE Simmonds *Central issues in jurisprudence: Justice, law and rights* (2008) 289 - 290, 295 - 300, 303 - 308, 326; E Smartt 'The right to associate: Hohfeld revisited' (1993) 3 *Irish Student Law Review* 116 at 116 - 117.

74 See J Habermas 'The concept of human dignity and the realistic utopia of human rights' (2010) 41 *Metaphilosophy* 464 at 468 - 469.

8.2.1.1 The state and public enterprises

It is uncontroversial now that rights enforceable against the state can be enforced against state-owned enterprises. Depending on the context and the purpose of the right, they may also be invoked in relation to private parties. In Botswana in *Diau* a building society, which was not an organ of state but which operated in the public domain, was bound to obey the constitutional strictures respecting the liberty and privacy of its employees and forbidding discrimination and inhuman and degrading treatment.[75] There is an analogy between the power of the state – the original rationale for introducing constitutional rights aimed at restricting government interference with citizens – and that wielded by the modern corporation (frequently operating on a global basis). In both situations there is gross inequality between the strength and influence of the powerful body, on the one hand, and the weak bargaining power residing in citizens, employees, consumers and members of the public affected by corporation's activities, on the other.[76] Dingake J saw no reason to differentiate between state and private conduct when considering the scope of the right to liberty, equality before the law and human dignity, because, as he put it, 'to draw such differentiation may authorize constitutional violations by private persons, that properly ought not be permitted.'[77]

To ensure certainty in the law and to avoid a haphazard approach to constitutional interpretation, some guidelines are necessary on when and in what situations the horizontal application of rights is required. A good starting point is the principle enunciated by Friedman JP in South Africa in *Baloro v University of Bophuthatswana* that any activity, operation, undertaking or enterprise operating in the community and open to the public, is subject to the horizontal application of fundamental rights.[78]

75 *Diau v Botswana Building Society* 2003 (2) BLR 409 (BwIC) (Botswana Industrial Court).

76 See n 75 above, 30.

77 n 75 above, 31.

78 1995 4 SA 197 (B), cited in *Diau* (n 75 above) 30. Application of this principle means that rights would be enforceable against entities such as, first, corporations, multinational and local companies that engage in trade, commerce and business with the public, have employees and are involved in numerous undertakings; second, commercial and professional firms which rely on the public for their custom or support; and, third, hotels, restaurants and the like: as above.

8.2.1.2 Transnational corporations

In the past decade attempts have been made to render transnational corporations (TNCs) accountable in law for their actions, which may breach human rights. With the extraordinary growth of businesses that span multiple jurisdictions and have more wealth than many countries,[79] they have been able to evade responsibility despite having the capacity to infringe human dignity on a wide scale by their activities. The general public and the environment have been affected as well as TNCs' employees, suppliers, consumers and others in direct relationships with them. There is widespread acceptance that businesses should not infringe human rights, but there was a view (resisted by many enterprises and states) that they also had positive obligations to protect human dignity.[80] I will now look at the efforts made to control TNCs and to hold them to account and will probe the underlying rationales for doing so.

As concern grew at the capacity of TNCs to endanger human rights, in 2000 the UN initiated the Global Compact, which is a voluntary network for businesses and other stakeholders that encourages corporate social responsibility[81] by adhering to ten principles.[82] The latter are derived from

79 See P Alston 'The "not-a-cat" syndrome: Can the international human rights regime accommodate non-state actors?' in P Alston (ed) *Non-state actors and human rights* (2005) 17; A de Jonge 'Transnational corporations and international law: Bringing TNCs out of the accountability vacuum' (2011) 7 *Critical Perspectives on International Business* 66 at 66; NMCP Jägers *Corporate human rights obligations: In search of accountability* (2002) 5 - 6; JG Ruggie 'Business and human rights: The evolving international agenda' (2007) 101 *American Journal of International Law* 819 at 823; D Weissbrodt 'Business and human rights' (2005) 74 *University of Cincinnati Law Review* 55 at 58 - 59; C Wells & J Elias 'Catching the conscience of the King: Corporate players on the international stage' in Alston above, 147 - 148.

80 Globalisation and privatisation of hitherto publicly provided services have extended the reach of TNCs giving them power frequently exceeding that of individual states. The respective roles and responsibilities in the human rights matrix of states and TNCs are in contention. By imposing duties to protect human rights on TNCs, some feared that this would relieve states of their well-recognised obligation to do so and might foster a *laissez-faire* attitude towards human rights among governments. TNCs doing business with corrupt states were accused of being complicit in human rights abuses. On corporations as complicit with governments, see SR Ratner 'Corporations and human rights: A theory of legal responsibility' (2001) 111 *Yale Law Journal* 443 at 500 - 504.

81 On corporate social responsibility, see JG Ruggie 'Taking embedded liberalism global: The corporate connection' in JG Ruggie (ed) *Embedding global markets: An enduring challenge* (2008) 243 - 244.

82 UN 'Global Compact' http://www.unglobalcompact.org/AboutTheGC/TheTen Principles/index.html (accessed 24 September 2013). It is *not* a code of conduct, but is a partnership between the UN, business, international labour and major transnational civil society organisations: G Kell & JG Ruggie 'Global markets and social legitimacy: The case for the "Global Compact"' (1999) 8(3) *Transnational Corporations* 101 at 104.

the Universal Declaration of Human Rights (Universal Declaration)[83] and other United Nations instruments in the areas of human rights, labour, the environment and anti-corruption.[84]

The UN Sub-Commission on the Promotion and Protection of Human Rights adopted draft Norms on the Responsibilities of TNCs for Human Rights in August 2003.[85] While confirming the primary responsibility of states for promoting and respecting human rights,[86] the draft Norms pointed out that TNCs, their officers and employees had human rights responsibilities, being obliged to respect norms in UN treaties.[87] They

See DG Arnold 'Transnational corporations and the duty to respect basic human rights' (2010) 20 *Business Ethics Quarterly* 371 at 372 - 373; A Clapham *Human rights obligations of non-state actors* (2006) 218 - 225; de Jonge (n 79 above) 72; O De Schutter 'The challenge of imposing human rights norms on corporate actors' in O De Schutter (ed) *Transnational corporations and human rights* (2006) 10 - 11; I Halpern 'Tracing the contours of transnational corporations' human rights obligations in the twenty-first century' (2008) 14 *Buffalo Human Rights Law Review* 129 at 174 - 175; Jägers (n 79 above) 128 - 130; S Jerbi 'Business and human rights at the UN: What might happen next?' (2009) 31 *Human Rights Quarterly* 299 at 304; A Rasche '"A *necessary* supplement" – What the United Nations Global Compact is (and is not)' in K Buhmann *et al* (eds) *Corporate social and human rights responsibilities: Global, legal, and management perspectives* (2011) 75; Ruggie (n 81 above) 246 - 250; RG Steinhardt 'Corporate responsibility and the international law of human rights: The new *lex mercatoria*' in Alston (n 79 above) 206 - 207; Weissbrodt (n 79 above) 63.

83 Universal Declaration of Human Rights (adopted 10 December 1948) UNGA Res 217 A(III).

84 The exhortatory nature of the principles is evident as companies are simply asked to 'embrace, support and enact, within their sphere of influence, a set of core values'. Businesses are told that they 'should' support and respect the protection of internationally proclaimed human rights: principle 1. A stronger warning is given against assisting others to breach human rights, as they should 'make sure' they are not complicit in human rights abuses: principle 2.

85 UN Commission on Human Rights (Sub-Commission) 'Norms on the Responsibilities of Transnational Corporations and Other Business Enterprises with Regard to Human Rights' (13 August 2003) UN Doc E/CN.4/Sub.2/2003/12/Rev.2 (UN draft Norms). See Clapham (n 82 above) 226 - 237; de Jonge (n 79 above) 74 - 75; P Feeney 'Business and human rights: The struggle for accountability in the UN and the future direction of the advocacy agenda' (2009) 11 *SUR - International Journal on Human Rights* 161 at 165 - 166; J Gelfand 'The lack of enforcement in the United Nations draft Norms: Benefit or disadvantage?' in De Schutter (n 82 above) 313 - 333; Halpern (n 82 above) 175 - 176; Jerbi (n 82 above) at 305 - 306; D Kinley & R Chambers 'The UN human rights norms for corporations: The private implications of public international law' (2006) 6 *Human Rights Law Review* 447; Ruggie (n 79 above) 820 - 821, 824 - 825, 827, 832; D Weissbrodt & M Kruger 'Human rights responsibilities of businesses as non-state actors' in Alston (n 79 above) 322 - 328, 338 - 350.

86 Preamble, paras 1 & 19.

87 Preamble. Having acknowledged the Global Compact, the Sub-Commission felt that more than a voluntary initiative was warranted and was motivated to set standards by the increasing influence of TNCs on account of globalisation combined with their

imposed a widespread onus on TNCs to 'promote, secure the fulfilment of, respect, and ensure respect of and protect human rights' within their 'spheres of activity and influence'.[88] The UN Commission on Human Rights was not impressed with the draft Norms and did not approve them.[89] Instead in 2005 the UN Secretary-General appointed John Ruggie as a Special Representative on human rights and business.[90] Ruggie criticised the Norms stridently in his report in 2006 for inventing a new avenue of international law that spoke directly to TNCs and for failing to define properly the obligations falling on states and TNCs.[91] His report in 2008 presented a three part policy framework

capacity to do good ('to foster economic well-being, development, technological improvement and wealth') and to do harm affecting the lives of individuals through their business and employment practices and their interactions with governments; a justification given for UN intervention was the universality of human rights: as above. The draft Norms proposed to impose direct responsibilities on TNCs and to make them accountable to the UN: paras 15 - 16. States were to be responsible for implementation by TNCs of the Norms and 'other relevant national and international laws' backed by criminal sanctions: paras 17 - 18. A civil remedy was also envisaged with TNCs being liable to pay compensation to those affected by failure to comply with the Norms: para 18.

88 Specifically included were the human rights of 'indigenous peoples and other vulnerable groups': para 1. The draft Norms proposed substantive obligations for TNCs in the areas of equality of opportunity and non-discrimination (para 2), security of persons forbidding war crimes and other international crimes (para 3) and requiring security arrangements for TNCs to observe international and national standards (para 4), workers rights (paras 5 - 9), and consumer (para 13) and environmental protection (para 14). Recognising the necessity to give workers a just wage to live a life where their dignity was respected, they required TNCs to 'provide workers with remuneration that ensures an adequate standard of living for them and their families' and that takes 'due account of their needs for adequate living conditions with a view towards progressive improvement': para 8. They targeted bribery and corruption: para 11. In addition to prohibiting infringements, TNCs were to have positive obligations to promote human rights (socio-economic and cultural rights as well as civil and political ones) by contributing to their realisation: para 12.

89 See Ruggie (n 79 above) 821. For a critical appraisal of the draft Norms, see Arnold (n 82 above) 373 - 376.

90 The Special Representative's mandate was, *inter alia*, to identify and clarify standards of corporate responsibility and accountability, and to compile a compendium of best practices of states and TNCs: Arnold (n 82 above) 376. On John Ruggie in his role as Special Representative, see C Broecker '"Better the devil you know": Home state approaches to transnational corporate accountability' (2008) 41 *New York University Journal of International Law and Politics* 159 at 176 - 177; Feeney (n 85 above) 166 - 168; G Mantilla 'Emerging international human rights norms for transnational corporations' (2009) 15 *Global Governance* 279 at 289 - 293; JG Ruggie 'The construction of the UN "protect, respect and remedy" framework for business and human rights: the true confessions of a principled pragmatist' [2011] *European Human Rights Law Review* 127.

91 UNCHR 'Interim Report of the Special Representative of the Secretary-General on the Issue of Human Rights and Transnational Corporations and Other Business Enterprises' (22 February 2006) UN Doc E/CN.4/2006/97 [59]-[69]. See de Jonge (n 79 above) 74.

involving the state obligation to *protect* against human rights abuses, corporate responsibility to *respect* all human rights, and the need for *remedies* to address breaches of human rights standards.[92]

Ruggie continued his work by developing Guiding Principles to make the 'Protect, Respect and Remedy' framework operational.[93] Following an extensive consultation process, they were endorsed by the UN Human Rights Council in June 2011.[94] They start with the state's unequivocal duty to *protect* human rights – grounded in international human rights law – by taking appropriate steps to prevent, investigate, punish and redress human rights

In his second report in 2007, Ruggie saw potential for consensus on state duties to address corporate involvement in human rights abuses: UN Human Rights Council 'Report of the Special Representative of the Secretary-General on the Issue of Human Rights and Transnational Corporations and Other Business Enterprises, Business and Human Rights: Mapping International Standards of Responsibility and Accountability for Corporate Acts' (19 February 2007) UN Doc A/HRC/4/35 [10]. Ruggie reflected on the strengths and weaknesses of soft law mechanisms and self-regulation and referred to developments in international criminal law and rules governing extraterritorial jurisdiction: above, [19]-[32], [45]-[81]. See Jerbi (n 82 above) 307 - 309.

92 UNHRC 'Protect, Respect and Remedy: A Framework for Business and Human Rights, Report of the Special Representative of the Secretary-General on the Issue of Human Rights and Transnational Corporations and Other Business Enterprises' (7 April 2008) UN Doc A/HRC/8/5. See Arnold (n 82 above) 377 - 378; D Bilchitz 'The Ruggie framework: An adequate rubric for corporate human rights obligations?' (2010) 12 *SUR - International Journal on Human Rights* 199 at 203 - 207; Jerbi (n 82 above) 310 - 311.

93 UNHRC 'Report of the Special Representative of the Secretary-General on the Issue of Human Rights and Transnational Corporations and Other Business Enterprises – Guiding Principles on Business and Human Rights: Implementing the UN "Protect, Respect and Remedy" Framework' (21 March 2011) UN Doc A/HRC/17/31 (UN Guiding Principles). See also UNHRC 'Business and Human Rights: Towards Operationalizing the "Protect, Respect and Remedy" Framework, Report of the Special Representative of the Secretary-General on the Issue of Human Rights and Transnational Corporations and Other Business Enterprises' (22 April 2009) UN Doc A/HRC/11/13; UNHRC 'Report of the Special Representative of the Secretary-General on the Issue of Human Rights and Transnational Corporations and Other Business Enterprises, Business and Human Rights: Further Steps toward the Operationalization of the "Protect, Respect and Remedy" Framework' (9 April 2010) UN Doc A/HRC/14/27.

94 Draft Guiding Principles were issued for public comment in November 2010: UNGA 'Draft report of the Special Representative of the Secretary-General on the issue of human rights and transnational corporations and other business enterprises: Guiding Principles for the implementation of the UN "Protect, Respect and Remedy" Framework' http://www.reports-and-materials.org/Ruggie-UN-draft-Guiding-Principles-22-Nov-2010.pdf (accessed 24 September 2013).

The principles articulate a new due diligence standard for shared responsibility of corporations, the state, and their respective legal counsel, to adhere to national laws and international frameworks of human rights: S Ferrey 'The Ruggie United Nations principles framing international indigenous human rights' (2010) 33 *Suffolk Transnational Law Review* 409 at 409.

abuse through 'effective policies, legislation, regulation, and adjudication.'[95] The provisions on corporate responsibility to *respect* human rights place the onus to avoid infringing internationally-recognised human rights, to address adverse human rights impacts with which they are involved in their own activities, and to try to prevent or mitigate those to which they are directly linked by their relationships, on *all* enterprises irrespective of 'their size, sector, operational context, ownership and structure.'[96] This has horizontal application and does not depend on state-involvement. The final part of the trilogy is the provision of an effective *remedy* as part of the state's duty to protect human rights with the Guiding Principles envisaging a range of measures not confined to judicial, administrative and legislative means.[97]

The normative base for the protection of human rights in the globalised business world has its roots firmly in human dignity, which is inherent in

95 n 93 above, principle 1 & commentary. Less dogmatic is the requirement that states 'set out clearly the expectation' that TNCs respect human rights, but significantly its reach extends throughout their operations: principle 2. Policy coherence is to be achieved by states ensuring that government departments, agencies and state institutions are aware of and observe the state's human rights obligations in fulfilling their mandates: principle 8. That coherence is to be maintained when states conclude international agreements or contracts – they should retain adequate policy and regulatory ability to protect human rights while providing the necessary protection for investors: principle 9 & commentary. More muted is the stipulation to 'promote respect for human rights' in public procurement: principle 6 & commentary. When involved in multilateral institutions, states are encouraged to spread respect for human rights and to promote the Guiding Principles: principle 10 & commentary. The state should foster respect for human rights in the business community by enforcing human rights-friendly laws, giving guidance and encouraging (sometimes requiring) enterprises to communicate their human rights performance: principle 3. It has stricter obligations to ensure respect for human rights by businesses with which it has closer connections, *ie*, those that are state-owned or controlled, receive state support and services, or provide outsourced services: principles 4 - 5.

As the 'host' state in conflict-affected areas may be unable to protect human rights adequately because it lacks effective control, the 'home' state has a role to play to assist in ensuring that businesses are not involved with human rights abuse: principle 7 & commentary. A state should deny access to public support and services for a business that refuses to co-operate in addressing its involvement in gross human rights abuses: principle 7(c). State policies, legislation, regulation and enforcement measures must be effective in addressing the risk of business involvement in gross human rights abuses: principle 7(d). See SL Seck 'Conceptualizing the home state duty to protect human rights' in Buhmann *et al* (n 82 above) 50 - 51.

96 n 93 above, principles 11 - 14. Policies (based on a policy statement to which enterprises express commitment thereby embedding their responsibility to respect human rights) and processes should be in place to identify human rights risks, remediate adverse impacts that occur and to ensure accountability: principles 15 - 16. A reduction in the risks of claims is a collateral benefit of continual due diligence to rule out complicity: principle 17 & commentary. Remediation is obligatory in the event of a lapse with priority being given to the most severe or urgent impacts: principles 22, 24.

97 n 93 above, principles 25 - 31.

every person and is the rationale for human rights and obligations. The autonomy and consciousness of those subject to humiliation generates human rights.[98] The concept of dignity is concerned not just with the absence of indignities, but also with ensuring access to basic amenities to allow for the full development of the human personality.[99]

Human rights are universal and are not contingent on being granted by the international order or the state. Their compass is not confined within narrow parameters.[100] As Ruggie put it in his draft report submitting the Guiding Principles, '[t]he idea of human rights is as simple as it is powerful: treating people with dignity.'[101] Since human rights are considered to be fundamental for the dignity of the individual, the individual should be protected against all violations of human rights, and not only when the violator can be directly identified as an agent of the state.[102] Because dignity is vested in the individual and emanates outwards from their person, all those who come into contact and have the power to affect it bear obligations proportional to their capacity to do harm or help.[103]

The question can be posed as to whether TNCs are participants in society with mutual rights and duties. For Denis Arnold, the answer is 'yes' on two alternative grounds: first, corporations are properly understood as agents capable of intentional action and can be duty bearers that are morally responsible for their actions; second, all corporations are populated by

98 Clapham (n 82 above) 536.

99 Clapham (n 82 above) 546. This intrinsic view deriving rights from human agency also has an instrumental aspect, since people have a fundamental interest in having the freedom to pursue the goals they have identified as making their lives worthwhile and in a minimal provision of health, physical welfare, and education necessary to pursue those goals: Arnold (n 82 above) 385.

Four secure moral claims (to have a life, to lead one's life, to freedom from cruel degrading treatment and against severe unfairness) can all be thought of as requirements of human dignity and are the grounds of human rights: JW Nickel *Making sense of human rights* (2007) 66, 69.

100 Andrew Clapham reasoned that non-state actors must have obligations to protect human rights and to allow for the full realisation of the human potential: n 82 above, 546.

101 n 94 above, [3]. The Global Compact's principles are derived from the Universal Declaration, whose *raison d'être* is human dignity and equality.

102 Jägers (n 79 above) 39. The object and purpose of the provisions in the core human rights documents increasingly require that the obligations apply at the horizontal level to private entities: Jägers (n 79 above) 70.

103 Halpern (n 82 above) 139. 'All participants in society interact with an individual's dignity and thus have human rights obligations; dignity does not spring from the relationship between an individual and the state, but between an individual and all others.': Halpern (n 82 above) 139 - 140. The placing of the individual in a community and in relationships implicates others who have mutual rights and duties: Arnold (n 82 above) 385.

individual employees who are agents and, as such, are duty bearers.[104] Yet another justification for regarding TNCs as bearing duties is that they frequently assert their own legal rights in society and have the resources to pursue them. Therefore justice and equality require that they carry reciprocal duties.[105]

The more difficult task is to identify what precise duties TNCs have and in what circumstances. The tripartite typology of duties developed by Henry Shue is a useful tool in this endeavour.[106] Negative obligations to respect human rights by not interfering with them can clearly be attributed to TNCs where they have a special relationship with the rights holders, such as employees, consumers and the wider community affected by their activities.[107] Where TNCs operate in partnership with others violating human rights or when they enter into contracts with abusive states, they may be complicit in breaching people's rights and have a duty not to co-operate or to disengage.[108]

Even when they are not embroiled in situations of abuse, TNCs may have an opportunity to take positive action to fulfil human rights by aiding the deprived.[109] Ethical claims of imperfect obligation cannot be transcribed

104 n 82 above, 387 - 388.

105 See A Reinisch 'The changing international legal framework for dealing with non-state actors' in Alston (n 79 above) 85. This is what Arnold calls the moral principle of 'fair play': n 82 above, 389.

106 H Shue *Basic rights: Subsistence, affluence, and US foreign policy* (1996) 52. Shue distinguished between duties to *avoid* depriving, to *protect* from deprivation and to *aid* the deprived: above, 52. He elaborated his typology, first, by requiring (as part of protection from deprivation) enforcement of duty and the designing of institutions that avoid the creation of strong incentives to violate duty and, second, by setting out the categories of deprived to whom the duty to aid arises (those who are one's special responsibility, who are victims of social failures in the performance of duties, and who are victims of natural disasters): above, 60. See Jägers (n 79 above) 76.

107 Jägers (n 79 above) 79 - 80.

108 Jägers (n 79 above) 80 - 83.

109 From an ethical perspective, Amartya Sen deduced that we should not proceed on the assumption that we owe nothing to others, unless we have actually harmed them, as we have a basic general obligation to be willing to *consider* seriously what we should reasonably do: A Sen 'Elements of a theory of human rights' (2004) 32 *Philosophy & Public Affairs* 315 at 340. See also A Sen *The idea of justice* (2009) 372 - 373.

Arnold considers that the world's affluent populations may hold a common obligation to ensure that global institutions that have a direct impact on poverty and economic development, such as the World Bank, the UN and the International Monetary Fund, operate within the bounds of justice and respect human rights: n 82 above, 387. On the IMF, see F Gianviti 'Economic, social, and cultural human rights and the International Monetary Fund' in Alston (n 79 above) 113 - 138; Reinisch (n 105 above) 63.

readily into precise legal rights.[110] Where a TNC operates an essential service or one normally provided by the state, a credible case can be made for finding it has inherited obligations to protect human rights. This is relevant when public services and utilities are privatised, and monopolies are dismantled to make way for competition in the market.

Public acceptance of the content of human rights and of their enforceability can ensure that they become a reality in law – open debate advances this process.[111] Voluntary codes of conduct or exhortations by the UN can help. However, sometimes TNCs can profess to adhere to certain standards in order to improve their public image, while at the same time ignoring them in practice. Recently there has been depressingly stark evidence in the financial markets of the mayhem that can follow when reliance is placed on 'light touch regulation'. Therefore it is worthwhile identifying those human rights that engender correlative obligations on TNCs and enshrining them as legal obligations in an international instrument. The UN draft Norms attempted to do that, but they failed to provide a normative publicly acceptable base for their proposals and were much too ambitious in equating the obligations on TNCs with the duties on states. Ruggie's approach of requiring compliance with clear obligations and encouraging adherence to those that are still not widely accepted will be more successful.

The mechanisms for enforcing human rights against TNCs could be developed. The International Criminal Court might be given a remit to try TNCs for international crimes. Whether or not this happens depends on the political will to do so by a significant number of players. In the meantime, TNCs can be held to account before national courts. Because of the transnational nature of TNCs' operations, this situation is not ideal. Jurisdiction

110 In the laws of some countries there is a legal demand to provide reasonable help to third parties: Sen *The idea of justice* (n 109 above) 375. See also Sen 'Elements of a theory of human rights' (n 109 above) 342.

It is not easy to imply a legal obligation on TNCs to use the opportunities presented, except where the TNC acts *de facto* in place of a 'failed state' and, even then, its responsibility will be mostly confined to ensuring that an individual has access to resources needed for survival: Jägers (n 79 above) 84 - 85. The size and resources of a corporation will govern the extent of the obligation: Jägers (n 79 above) 85.

111 As Sen indicated, 'the understanding and viability of human rights are ... intimately linked with the reach of public discussion, between persons and across borders. The viability and universality of human rights are dependent on their ability to survive open critical scrutiny in public reasoning.': 'Elements of a theory of human rights' (n 109 above) 356. Apart from being legally enforceable, there are other ways, such as recognition, monitoring and agitation, which can be effective in advancing the cause of human rights: 'Elements of a theory of human rights' (n 109 above) 343. See also Reinisch (n 105 above) 69.

may be contested or individual states may not have the capacity or resources to deal with the complexity of the legal and evidentiary issues arising.

8.2.1.3 Private relationships

Examples of countries where constitutional rights are applied horizontally are Brazil,[112] India,[113] Malawi,[114] Namibia,[115] Sri Lanka,[116] South Africa,[117] and Zambia.[118] In contrast, the Canadian Supreme Court found in *RWDSU v Dolphin Delivery* that the Canadian Charter did not apply to private litigation completely divorced from any connection with government.[119]

There are several reasons why constitutional rights in Ireland apply to private relationships where there is no public element. To ascertain whether they have horizontal application, the purpose of the right as well as the text and spirit of the Constitution will be relevant. Support for the proposition that rights have horizontal application can be drawn from the fact that the Constitution is binding on the judiciary as an arm of the State.[120] Therefore, the courts are obliged to play their part in respecting, defending and vindicating personal rights under Article 40.3.1° and in the State's protection

112 AS Butler 'Private litigation and constitutional rights under sections 8 and 9 of the 1996 Constitution – Assistance from Ireland' (1999) 116 *South African Law Journal* 77 at 78, fn 8.

113 See *Diau* (n 75 above) 26. On the application of fundamental rights in India to private action, see MP Singh 'Protection of human rights against state and non-state action' in D Oliver & J Fedtke (eds) *Human rights and the private sphere: A comparative study* (2007) 197 - 212.

114 Butler (n 112 above) 78.

115 See *Diau* (n 75 above) 26.

116 See *Diau* (n 75 above) 27.

117 See *Diau* (n 75 above) 27 - 28.

118 Butler (n 112 above) 78, fn 8.

119 *Retail, Wholesale and Department Store Union, Local 580 v Dolphin Delivery Ltd* [1986] 2 SCR 573. See L Ackermann *Human dignity: Lodestar for equality in South Africa* (2012) 330 - 331, 333; A Barak 'Constitutional human rights and private law' in D Friedmann & D Barak-Erez (eds) *Human rights in private law* (2001) 19; E Barendt 'The United States and Canada: State action, constitutional rights and private actors' in Oliver & Fedtke (n 113 above) 416 - 418; S Gardbaum 'The "horizontal effect" of constitutional rights' (2003) 102 *Michigan Law Review* 387 at 398 - 400, 444; PW Hogg *Constitutional law of Canada Vol 2* (2007) 95 - 98, 101 fn 141, 290 - 291; C O'Cinneide 'Taking horizontal effect seriously: Private law, constitutional rights and the European Convention on Human Rights' (2003) 4 *Hibernian Law Journal* 77 at 95, 97; LE Weinrib & EJ Weinrib 'Constitutional values and private law in Canada' in Friedmann & Barak-Erez above, 43 - 45.

This decision has been severely criticised for being contrary to the spirit of the Charter: *Diau* (n 75 above) 25 - 26.

120 Butler (n 112 above) 81.

and vindication duties in Article 40.3.2°.[121] As judicial acts must conform to the Constitution, the common law whether invoked in private litigation or in cases where there is a public element is subject to constitutional scrutiny. If the Constitution provides a comprehensive normative system for all law within the State, harmony with that value system throughout the legal system is desirable – particularly when the people is sovereign under the Constitution.[122] True concern with protection of individuals' rights from private persons requires the Constitution to apply horizontal relations when the existing private common law is inadequate.[123]

8.2.1.3.1 Irish case-law

Walsh J affirmed the doctrine of constitutional supremacy in *Meskell v CIE* when he stated, 'the Constitution ... is superior to the common law and ... must prevail if there is a conflict between the two.'[124] He reiterated that the courts are obliged to develop a remedy for breach of a constitutional right where none currently exists.[125] This principle has given rise to a theory of 'constitutional torts'.[126] It is the courts' role to define when and which constitutional rights are enforceable between private citizens.[127] The judiciary has been content to rely on tort law to fulfil a role for which it was not

121 Butler (n 112 above) 81 - 82.

122 CJ Roederer 'Working the common law pure: Developing the law of delict (torts) in light of the spirit, purport and objects of South Africa's Bill of Rights' (2009) 26 *Arizona Journal of International and Comparative Law* 427 at 459; Constitution of Ireland 1937, Art 6.1.

123 Roederer (n 122 above) 459 - 460.

124 [1973] IR 121 (SC) 135. See DG Morgan & G Hogan *Administrative law in Ireland* (2010) [18-69]–[18-70]; C O'Cinneide 'Irish constitutional law and direct horizontal effect – A successful experiment?' in Oliver & Fedtke (n 113 above) 219 - 225.

125 n 124 above, 132 - 133:

> [A] right guaranteed by the Constitution or granted by the Constitution can be protected by action or enforced by action even though such action may not fit into any of the ordinary forms of action in either common law or equity and ... the constitutional right carries within it its own right to a remedy or for the enforcement of it.

See Gardbaum (n 119 above) 396; B Walsh "The judicial power, justice and the Constitution of Ireland' in D Curtin & D O'Keeffe (eds) *Constitutional adjudication in European Community and national law: Essays for the Hon. Mr. Justice T.F. O'Higgins* (1992) 150.

126 Butler (n 112 above) 81 - 82, fn 24.

127 There are important distinctions between enforceability of a constitutional right against the State and against an individual, as the relationship between the citizen and the State is not the same as that between citizens: W Binchy 'Constitutional remedies and the law of torts' in J O'Reilly (ed) *Human rights and constitutional law: Essays in honour of Brian Walsh* (1992) 201 - 202. The political ties between the citizen and the State are based on normative premises which differ from the ties between citizens as members of society: above, 202. Although a constitutional right may be enforceable against the

designed.[128] Henchy J's reluctance in *Hanrahan v Merck Sharp & Dohme (Ireland) Ltd* to re-shape the contours of tort to align with constitutional norms is evident from the excuse he offered for not doing so, 'the constitutional provisions relied on have never been used in the courts to shape the form of any existing tort or to change the normal onus of proof.'[129] He conceded that judicial intervention *might* be justified if it could be shown that the tort in question was 'basically ineffective' to protect a constitutional right.[130]

Because the Irish Constitution confers subjective rights on individuals against the state and also generates objective norms that determine the validity of all other forms of law, litigants are able to challenge the constitutionality of legislation or the common law in private law actions, even when no state action is directly involved.[131] In *McDonnell v Ireland*, Barrington J asserted that constitutional rights did not need recognition by the legislature or by the common law to be effective – the courts would define them if necessary and 'fashion a remedy for their breach.'[132] He sounded a note of caution when he said, 'constitutional rights should not be regarded as wild cards which can be played at any time to defeat all existing rules.'[133] Constitutional rights were applied directly to regulate the internal affairs of a private body in *Glover v BLN Ltd*.[134] McCracken J distinguished *Glover* in *Carna Foods Ltd v Eagle Star Insurance Co (Ireland) Ltd*, when he held that there was no requirement for an

State and against another citizen, this does not necessarily mean that the conditions for eligibility for an award of compensation against both are identical: as above.

128 Binchy (n 127 above) 207; O'Cinneide (n 124 above) 245 - 246.

129 [1988] ILRM 629 (SC) 636. See O'Cinneide (n 124 above) 236 - 238.

130 n 129 above, 636.

131 O'Cinneide (n 124 above) 217. Colm O'Cinneide explained it thus, 'a private litigant in the private law case can assert that the law being challenged is not a binding legal norm, on the basis that it is incompatible with the Constitution, and therefore should not be applied in the case, or alternatively should be applied in a manner compatible with the Constitution.': as above.

132 [1998] 1 IR 134 (SC) 148. See O'Cinneide (n 124 above) 239.

133 n 132 above, 148.

134 [1973] IR 388 (SC). Walsh J stated, 'public policy and the dictates of constitutional justice require that statutes, regulations or agreements setting up machinery for taking decisions which may affect rights or impose liabilities should be construed as providing for fair procedures.': above, 425.

A company director's contract had been terminated for serious misconduct and neglect without giving him prior notice of any complaints. See O'Cinneide (n 124 above) 220 - 221. The right to fair procedures under Article 40.3 of the Constitution applies to the Government's exercise of the power of removal: *Garvey v Ireland* [1981] IR 75 (SC).

insurance company to give reasons for cancelling or refusing to renew a policy.[135] He did not consider that any principle of natural justice or constitutional justice applied to that decision.[136]

The High Court applied the constitutional right to a livelihood (but not the right to equality) to the private relationship between a publican and a trade union representing the former's employees in *Murtagh Properties v Cleary*.[137] The courts' reluctance to intrude on the individual's autonomy in private relationships on the grounds of equality (even when discrimination occurs on the basis of gender, an innate immutable characteristic) exceeded the realms of what is constitutionally tolerable in *Equality Authority v Portmarnock Golf Club*, where state endorsement of discrimination against women in clubs was upheld by allowing those clubs to obtain official recognition and to hold licences granted by the state.[138] In the High Court, O'Higgins J confirmed that as interpreted by the courts Article 40.1 of the Constitution guaranteed 'process equality' and did not impose obligations on citizens in their private relations.[139] However, neither he nor the Supreme Court considered whether the state had failed in its constitutional remit by supporting the club's discriminatory conduct in licensing it to sell alcohol and exempting it from tax.

The relationship between a union and its members is subject to its members having the democratic right to participate in its processes as a corollary to the constitutional right to join it.[140] The special position of a teachers' union towards pupils warranted an award of exemplary damages for its intentional breach of a child's right to free primary education.[141] A road transport operator obtained an injunction against a competitor carrying on an unlicensed service to stop a breach of his constitutional right to earn a livelihood, as the maximum fine possible was derisory and did not protect him.[142]

135 [1995] 1 IR 526 (HC).

136 He expressed concern at the effect of imposing constitutional rights directly in the context of purely commercial relationships between private parties, as it 'would be a serious interference in the contractual position of parties in a commercial contract and with very wide-ranging consequences': n 135 above, 531. See O'Cinneide (n 124 above) 236.

137 [1972] IR 330 (HC).

138 [2005] IEHC 235; [2009] IESC 73, [2010] 1 ILRM 237.

139 As above.

140 *Rodgers v ITGWU* [1978] ILRM 51 (HC). See O'Cinneide (n 124 above) 221.

141 *Conway v Irish National Teachers Organisation* [1991] 2 IR 305 (HC, SC). See O'Cinneide (n 124 above) 225.

142 *Lovett v Gogan* [1995] 3 IR 132 (SC). See O'Cinneide (n 124 above) 226. Cf *Parsons v Kavanagh* [1990] ILRM 560 (HC). In the latter case, it was held that the right to

The children of a man who suffered brain damage necessitating permanent hospitalisation in an industrial accident claimed damages from his employer for the non-pecuniary benefits deriving from the parent-child relationship in *Hosford v John Murphy and Sons Ltd.*[143] They invoked their constitutional rights as a family under Article 41 as well as a right that their father should not be prevented by injury from fulfilling his right and duty to educate them under Article 42. Costello J thought that damages would in principle be recoverable if the employer's careless act amounted to a constitutional wrong which inflicted harm on them, as 'otherwise, the protective provisions of the Constitution would be vacuous and valueless.'[144] His analysis of the nature of the rights granted showed that Article 41.1 gave a right to protection from legislation or *deliberate* acts of *state* officials attacking or impairing the constitution or the authority of the family.[145] The Constitution targeted arbitrary state action – not negligence.[146] It followed that the employer's *negligent* action had not infringed any constitutional right enjoyed by members of the affected family.[147]

When a breach of constitutional rights by the state has been established, damages are not necessarily awarded. In the *Blascaod Mór* case, where legislation was declared invalid because it used pedigree as a basis of classification, Budd J refused to award damages.[148] For public policy reasons he felt that there must be considerable tolerance of the legislature.[149] In any event, the plaintiffs had 'largely been vindicated' by the declaration of

earn one's livelihood by any lawful means carried with it the entitlement to be protected against any unlawful activity on the part of another which materially impaired or infringed that right; the plaintiff had made out a case for the granting of an injunction. There is potential for damages to be granted for breach of a constitutional right by criminal activity that is subject only to a minor sanction. The application of this principle could extend beyond the right to earn a livelihood to other constitutional rights. The courts have not limited liability to cases where there is intention to damage or to infringe a constitutional right; neither is foreseeability a requirement.

143 [1988] ILRM 300 (HC).

144 n 143 above, 303.

145 n 143 above, 305.

146 As above.

147 As above.

148 *Blascaod Mór Teo v Commissioners of Public Works in Ireland (No 4)* [2000] IEHC 130, [2000] 3 IR 565 at 590.

149 Tolerance was required because of the balance the legislature had to strike between individual rights and the common good, and therefore there was 'little justification for a regime of strict liability for infringement of a constitutional right': n 148 above, 581, 590.

invalidity of the legislation.[150] Budd J's explanation for his thinking this shows that how one is viewed by others is important.[151] Restoring a person's standing in the community can be more supportive of dignity than monetary compensation.

On the other hand, damages may not be sufficient to vindicate a personal right and a judicial determination may be necessary. The Supreme Court refused to strike out as an abuse of process the action *Grant v Roche Products* brought by the father of a man who committed suicide following the taking of a prescribed drug.[152] The drug company offered to settle for the full value of the claim, but the father refused to accept it. Hardiman J confirmed that the only way the deceased's right to life could be vindicated was by a judicial hearing into the claim that his death was caused by the defendant's wrongdoing followed by a determination of liability.[153]

Laffoy J grappled with the issue of whether damages should be awarded in the problematic long-running Blehein litigation,[154] in which it had been held that a statutory restriction on issuing proceedings to challenge treatment while involuntarily detained in a mental hospital infringed the constitutional right to access to the court.[155] The context was important – here the fundamental right to liberty had been restricted, a serious infringement 'on any consideration of the hierarchical framework of constitutional rights'.[156] The difficulty in ascertaining the measure of damages had to be distinguished

150 n 148 above, 590.

151 'The informed public is aware of their [the plaintiffs'] stance and their vindication by the pronouncements of the Supreme Court as to the unjustified discrimination against them and the infringement of their property rights.': as above.

152 n 48 above.

153 n 48 above, [70], [75]. He held that a finding of wrongful death, might, in certain circumstances, confer a tangible benefit on the relatives of the deceased person: n 48 above, [68], [82].

154 *Blehein v Minister for Health and Children* [2010] IEHC 329, [2013] IEHC 319.

155 *Blehein v Minister for Health and Children* [2004] IEHC 374, [2004] 3 IR 610. On the right of access to court, see *Macauley v Minister for Posts and Telegraphs* [1966] IR 345 (HC). On the right to litigate, see *O'Brien v Keogh* [1972] IR 144 (SC).

156 [2010] IEHC 329 [12.9]. Another factor to be taken into account was the nature and extent of the adverse impact on the plaintiff resulting from such civil wrong as he would have been in a position to establish in the litigation which he was precluded from prosecuting; a significant countervailing factor was the status of the impugned legislation (in *Blehein* the Act had survived for almost 60 years after its enactment, benefited from the presumption that it was constitutionally valid and had been applied consistently in the courts): as above.

from the impracticability or impossibility of providing redress.[157] Public policy and the common good justified the Supreme Court's demurral from awarding damages for the *ultra vires* exercise of statutory power in *Pine Valley Developments Ltd v Minister for the Environment*[158] and *Glencar Explorations plc v Mayo County Council (No 2)*.[159]

8.2.1.3.2 Analysis of Irish approach

The case-law shows that the use of the direct horizontal effect approach of the constitutional tort endorsed in *Meskell* and *Glover* is uncommon, occurring only when the existing statutory or common law has not addressed the wrong in question.[160] If a remedy for the constitutional breach can be found in tort, the courts have accepted the law 'warts and all'. They have not attempted to develop it to bring it into conformity with constitutional norms. The scope and extent of the *Meskell* doctrine is uncertain.[161] It is unclear whether the constitutional tort is actionable *per se* or only on proof of damage, whether liability is strict, whether all constitutional rights are actionable in the private sphere, and how the balancing process works in the resolution of private disputes where conflicting rights and interests are at stake.[162]

The uncertainty has its foundation in the Supreme Court's failure to establish an overarching test to determine whether a constitutional right will be given horizontal effect, and, if so, to what degree and extent.[163] The absence

157 [2010] IEHC 329 [12.7]. Laffoy J decided to deal with the issue of whether the claim was statute-barred first, considering it undesirable (unless necessary to do so) to embark on the determination of a fundamental issue as to whether transcendent considerations existed which rendered it undesirable that the plaintiff be awarded damages: [2010] IEHC 329) [12.10]. In 2013 she found that the plaintiff's personal constitutional rights were subject to limitation by statute, that they were vindicated by the declaration of invalidity of the statutory restriction on issuing proceedings, but that he did not have an entitlement to damages: [2013] IEHC 319 [60], [65]-[66].

158 [1987] IR 23 (SC) 38, 40.

159 [2001] IESC 64, [2002] 1 IR 84 at 128.

160 The courts have not analysed the legitimacy of the direct horizontal effect approach, as contrasted with the vertical 'state action' or indirect horizontal effects doctrines: O'Cinneide (n 124 above) 223. The ambiguity in the key precedents has led to questioning of whether the direct horizontal approach has actually been established as a fixed constitutional doctrine in Irish constitutional law: O'Cinneide (n 124 above) 224.

161 O'Cinneide (n 124 above) 223. See also C O'Cinneide 'The European Convention on Human Rights and the Irish constitutional system of rights protection: Complementary or divergent?' in O Doyle & E Carolan (eds) *The Irish Constitution: Governance and values* (2008) 522.

162 D Oliver & J Fedtke 'Comparative analysis' in Oliver & Fedtke (n 113 above) 480.

163 O'Cinneide (n 124 above) 229.

of guidance on horizontal effect could impact on personal autonomy, as private individuals and bodies may be unsure or unaware of the constitutional obligations that may be imposed on them.[164] Timidity about applying the equality guarantee in Article 40.1 in private relations will ensure that entrenched views rooted in prejudice and stereotyping will continue unchallenged and that a powerful elite will remain in the ascendant.[165] In contrast to its attitude to equality, the Supreme Court imposed constitutional norms directly to restrain private clinics, advice centres[166] and student unions[167] from giving information on abortion, despite the fact that they had not acted contrary to any specific common law or legislative rules.[168]

Because of the greater caution exhibited since the early 1990s, the Irish courts develop existing law which regulates a matter within the scope of constitutional rights only where the scope of the tort is 'basically ineffective' or 'plainly inadequate' to vindicate the constitutional rights at issue.[169] Costello P in *W v Ireland (No 2)* ruled out adjusting the existing law of torts where it addressed the constitutional right invoked.[170] He accepted the *Meskell* doctrine that the Constitution was to be construed as providing a discrete cause of action for damages for infringement of a constitutional right which was not protected by common law or by statute law, and that an injunction

164 O'Cinneide (n 124 above) 230.

165 On the doubt that exists as to whether Article 40.1 applies as between private individuals, see O'Cinneide (n 124 above) 230 - 232.

166 *AG (Society for the Protection of Unborn Children Ireland Ltd) v Open Door Counselling Ltd* [1988] IR 593 (SC). See O Doyle *Constitutional law: Text, cases and materials* (2008) [5-12].

167 *Society for the Protection of Unborn Children (Ireland) Ltd v Grogan* [1989] IR 753 (SC). See M Cahill 'Constitutional exclusion clauses, Article 29.4.6° and the constitutional reception of European law' (2011) 34 *Dublin University Law Journal* 74 at 93 - 96.

168 O'Cinneide (n 124 above) 233 - 234. This severely infringed the freedom of action and communication of the defendants, who prior to being injuncted could not have known that they were necessarily acting contrary to Irish law: O'Cinneide (n 124 above) 234. It transpired ultimately that the State's actions were not justified, as the European Court of Human Rights found a breach of Article 10 ECHR because the restraint imposed on receiving or imparting information was disproportionate to the aims pursued: *Open Door Counselling v Ireland* (App no 14234/88) (1993) 15 EHRR 244. See F de Londras & C Kelly *European Convention on Human Rights Act: Operation, impact and analysis* (2010) [6-32].

169 O'Cinneide (n 124 above) 237.

170 [1997] IEHC 212, [1997] 2 IR 141. The victim of sexual offences by a priest subsequently convicted in Northern Ireland of sexual abuse was not entitled to damages for the delay in prosecuting him attributable to the failure of the Attorney General to endorse extradition warrants. The High Court held that the Attorney

could be granted to prohibit an infringement.[171] He construed the State's duty to respect, defend and vindicate the personal rights of the citizens in Article 40.3.1° of the Constitution as being implemented by the 'existence of laws (common law and statutory) which confer a right of action for damages (or a power to grant injunctive relief) in relation to acts or omissions which may constitute an infringement of guaranteed rights'.[172] However, he also accepted that if a provision of the law to be applied did not adequately protect the guaranteed right in a particular case, then the law would be applied without the provision, which would be rendered invalid by the Constitution.[173] There is a contradiction within Costello P's judgment, as he simultaneously ruled out shaping the existing law which deals with a constitutional right, and at the same time agreed that an inadequate provision in that law could be annulled.

From this review of the application of constitutional rights in private relations, some questions arise: first, when is a tort basically ineffective so as to trigger a constitutional tort?[174] Second, what rights are enforceable between private parties? Third, what kinds of infringement give a right of redress? Fourth, what remedy is appropriate? I will address each of these in turn. Ineffectiveness is not necessarily identified with unconstitutionality – the

General did not owe a duty of care to the victim because there was no relationship between him and her: above, 163. Even if he did have a sufficiently proximate relationship with her, it would be contrary to public policy to impose a duty of care on him: above, 164. His role in the extradition process was to ensure proper compliance with the State's international obligations: above, 160. See Morgan & Hogan (n 124 above) [18-32], [18-40], [18-83]–[18-84]; O'Cinneide (n 124 above) 238.

Neither do the gardaí owe a duty of care such as would create an entitlement to damages arising from the manner in which they conduct an investigation: *Lockwood v Ireland* [2010] IEHC 430.

171 n 170 above, 166. Costello P considered that constitutionally protected rights which are regulated and protected by existing common and/or statutory law comprise 'all those fundamental rights which the Constitution recognises that man has by virtue of his rational being antecedent to positive law and are rights which are regulated and protected by law in every State which values human rights': n 170 above, 164. His distinction between these fundamental rights and other secondary constitutional rights is unsound, as it not necessarily true that all fundamental rights are protected by the existing law; neither is it inevitable that constitutionally protected minor rights are not already regulated.

172 n 170 above, 166 - 167.

173 n 170 above, 167. As an example of a provision that would be rendered invalid, Costello P mentioned a limitation period which in the particular circumstance 'trenched unfairly on a guaranteed right' and deprived the plaintiff of a right to compensation: as above.

174 See C Donnelly 'The privatisation of governmental functions' in Doyle & Carolan (n 161 above) 253.

courts should try to fill the gap.[175] The inefficacy may be regarded as generic or contextual.[176] Costello P took the former view in *W v Ireland (No 2)*. The private law framework provided protection *in general* for bodily integrity, so he accepted the existing restrictions without interrogating their adequacy in the particular circumstances.[177] A very narrow interpretation of the Constitution could mean that the courts would give effect to constitutional norms in private law only when the *legislature*, as distinct from the private parties involved, had failed in its constitutional duty to uphold fundamental rights.[178] The current law, in the absence of 'plain inadequacy', is considered to be entirely in conformity with the Constitution and immune from alteration.[179] The law will be scrutinised not just in relation to the plaintiff's rights, but also as to whether it protects the defendant's constitutional rights.[180]

The answer to the second question as to which rights are enforceable will depend on the nature and extent of the particular right taking into account the text of the Constitution and its underlying values. The wording might show a clear intention that the onus of compliance rests solely on the state. Not all of the provisions in Articles 40 - 44, which are fundamental rights primarily for the protection of individuals, could create rights of action for breach of constitutional duty.[181] From the cases mentioned so far, it can be seen that an individual can rely in litigation against another private actor on the rights to bodily integrity, to a livelihood, and to fair procedures under Article 40.3, and on the right of association and non-association in Article 40.6.1°.[182] Children may obtain damages for unlawful interference with their

175 Binchy (n 127 above) 208.

176 As above.

177 O'Cinneide (n 124 above) 240.

178 O'Cinneide (n 124 above) 241; Binchy (n 127 above) 202.

179 O'Cinneide (n 124 above) 241.

180 Binchy (n 127 above) 209.

181 J Temple Lang 'Private law aspects of the Irish Constitution' (1971) 6 *Irish Jurist* 237 at 246.

182 See Binchy (n 127 above) 202 - 203. The *Meskell* doctrine could give horizontal protection to socio-economic rights as well as to civil and political rights. Walsh J stated, '[t]o infringe another's constitutional rights or to coerce him into abandoning them or waiving them (in so far as that may be possible) is unlawful as constituting a violation of the fundamental law of the State': *Meskell* (n 124 above) 134. He did not qualify his remarks by confining them to civil and political rights. In *Meskell* the rights of association and dissociation in contention were raised in the context of the right to earn a livelihood, which is an economic right. Tort law involves notions of distributive justice (in addition to corrective justice) and constitutional rights have a social justice element.

right to free primary education in Article 42.4.[183] The rights in Article 41 apply to the family and to marriage as institutions, so an individual has difficulties (to say the least) in trying to invoke it. The wording of Article 44.2.1° suggests that individuals have a civil right of action against those interfering with religious activities.[184]

The potential of the equality guarantee in Article 40.1 to be utilised in private relationships has been curbed by the countervailing right to autonomy,[185] as well as by concerns over its impact on legal certainty and the separation of powers.[186] Violations of human dignity, a constitutional value and recognised as an unenumerated right under Article 40.3, should, in theory, give a right of redress against private actors.[187] Torts such as defamation and assault already give a remedy for infringements of dignity. Extension of respect for dignity beyond what is already enshrined in statute or well-established in common law will require judicial analysis and elucidation of the circumstances in which this is appropriate. Since it is the foundation for the equal worth of all human beings, human dignity as well as equality should receive consideration commensurate with that accorded liberty in the harmonisation or balancing of rights.[188] As a right might be enforceable in one circumstance but not in another, the context will also impact on whether a particular right can be pursued.

The third issue of the type of infringement that gives a right to redress has several possible answers ranging from strict liability through responsibility based on negligence or intent, to culpability only for intentional actions. Writing in 1971, John Temple Lang thought it would be odd if negligence were the basis of civil liability, as it was irrelevant to the state's obligation to respect constitutional rights; therefore, superficially, reasonable care should not be a valid defence, leaving absolute liability as the logical choice.[189] But *Hosford* took a different route, and leaned towards imposing liability only for intentional or irrational actions. Because of the difficulties (and perhaps impossibility) of framing an overarching general rule to apply in all circumstances, an alternative

183 Binchy (n 127 above) 203.

184 Temple Lang (n 181 above) 247.

185 On the potential of Article 40.1, see G Hogan & G Whyte *JM Kelly: The Irish Constitution* (2004) [7.2.24]; Temple Lang (n 181 above) 248 - 249.

186 O'Cinneide (n 124 above) 232.

187 W Binchy 'Dignity as a constitutional concept' in Doyle & Carolan (n 161 above) 324.

188 See Binchy (n 187 above) 325.

189 n 181 above, 247.

contextual approach addressing issues of intention and negligence in precise factual situations would be more appropriate.[190]

The judiciary has focused on tort law for the answer to the final question of the appropriate remedy. Damages or an injunction are accepted options.[191] However, the nature of constitutional rights varies enormously and the severity of the interference with them can fluctuate widely. Sometimes it might be more satisfactory to apply the contract model rather than tort.[192] Divergence from compensatory damages for violation of constitutional rights can range from nominal damages for trivial infringements to punitive damages. The latter should be awarded for a serious breach of a constitutional right irrespective of whether the right itself is categorised as important.[193] Occasionally no compensation at all may be appropriate, as the court's finding that a person's rights have been breached is sufficient vindication – restoration in the eyes of the community is enough in the circumstances. But in our consumerist society, which places an inordinate value on money, there is a danger that the failure to be recompensed in tangible terms may undermine the value of a simple court verdict in one's favour.

8.2.1.4 Alternative models

Before considering how the Irish system for the enforcement of fundamental rights in private law might be improved, this subsection will compare briefly how some other jurisdictions (namely the United States and Germany) have dealt with this aspect of constitutional law.

190 Binchy (n 127 above) 207.

191 Because of the courts' reluctance to breach the separation of powers, they may not intervene to *prevent* infringements of constitutional rights involving policy decisions on the application of state resources. However, *Meskell* and tort law may provide a remedy in damages for *actual* infringements. The Supreme Court was opposed to granting mandatory relief in relation to the state's constitutional obligation to provide for free primary education under Article 42.4 of the Constitution, but the High Court award of damages for breaching that right was not appealed: *Sinnott v Minister for Education* [2001] 2 IR 545 at 631, 640, 656, 668, 669, 697 - 712, 715, 723 - 724. While the majority in the Supreme Court did not countenance granting a mandatory injunction obliging the state to implement its policy in relation to disadvantaged children forthwith, it did not seek to prevent an award of damages if a breach had actually occurred: *TD v Minister for Education* [2001] IESC 101, [2001] 4 IR 259 at 285 - 288, 316, 334 - 337, 372. The courts declined to grant a health board an order permitting it to carry out a screening test on an infant whose parents had refused to consent, but it can be deduced from the judgment of Denham J in the Supreme Court that the parents would be liable to the child if disease developed: *North Western Health Board v HW* [2001] IESC 90, [2001] 3 IR 622 at 723, 726 - 728.

192 Binchy (n 127 above) 217.

193 Binchy (n 127 above) 218.

In contrast to the assumption in Ireland that the Constitution of 1937 altered private law, the US Supreme Court confined its protection of citizens to vertical state action because of the more restricted wording of the Fourteenth Amendment.[194] This apparently firm approach has been softened by regarding the courts as part of the state and therefore restricted from enforcing unconstitutional activities in the private sphere. In *Shelley v Kraemer* the Court found that a private agreement containing a restrictive covenant preventing occupation of land by non-white people did not violate the Fourteenth Amendment, but enforcement of the racially-discriminating agreement by the courts constituted state action denying equal protection of the laws.[195] The Court substantially modified the common law of defamation to ensure it conformed to the First Amendment guarantee of free speech in *New York Times v Sullivan*, a civil lawsuit between private parties.[196]

The Federal Constitutional Court in Germany in the *Lüth* decision in 1958 developed the doctrine known as *Drittwirkung* (third-party effect of constitutional rights), which states that, although constitutional rights bind only governmental organs, they apply directly to all private law and so have indirect effect on private actors whose legal relationships are regulated by that law.[197] According to the Court, constitutional rights form 'an objective order of values', where the value system 'centers upon human dignity and

194 Temple Lang (n 181 above) 243. Unlike in the US, the Irish Constitution's conferral of a right of action for breach of constitutional rights provides a mechanism for increasing accountability of private actors engaged in the performance of governmental functions: Donnelly (n 174 above) 252.

195 334 US 1 (1948). Positive action by the state courts supported discrimination, above, 19 (Chief Justice Vinson):

> These are not cases ... in which the States have merely abstained from action, leaving private individuals free to impose such discriminations as they see fit. Rather, these are cases in which the States have made available to such individuals the full coercive power of government to deny to petitioners, on the grounds of race or color, the enjoyment of property rights in premises which petitioners are willing and financially able to acquire and which the grantors are willing to sell.

See Gardbaum (n 119 above) 389, 414; O'Cinneide (n 119 above) 95 - 96; Temple Lang (n 181 above) 243 - 244.

196 376 US 254 (1964). Justice Brennan, delivering the Opinion of the Court, precluded the courts from applying a state rule of law that would have imposed invalid restrictions on the newspaper's constitutional freedoms: above, 265. See Gardbaum (n 119 above) 389, 428 - 429, 432, 440; O'Cinneide (n 119 above) 96.

197 Gardbaum (n 119 above) 403, citing BVerfGE 7, 198 (1958). See also Ackermann (n 119 above) 317 - 318, 320 - 321; OO Cherednychenko 'Fundamental rights and private law: A relationship of subordination or complementarity?' (2007) 3(2) *Utrecht Law Review* 1 at 4 - 5; DM Chirwa 'In search of philosophical justifications and suitable models for the horizontal application of human rights' (2008) 8 *African Human Rights Law Journal* 294 at 307 - 308; J Church *et al*, *Human rights from a*

the free unfolding of personality within the social community' and is 'a fundamental constitutional decision affecting the entire legal system.'[198] It influences private law, so that 'no rule of private law may conflict with it, and all such rules must be construed in accordance with its spirit.'[199]

The American modification of the vertical state action doctrine by regarding the judiciary as part of the state and therefore precluded from enforcing activities contrary to constitutional norms in the private sphere contrasts with the position in Ireland, as does the German indirect horizontal application of constitutional norms emphasising human dignity and the place of the person in the community.

8.2.1.5 The way forward in Ireland

The direct horizontal approach is essentially sound and should be continued.[200] Like what happened in the US in the vertical state action model, the courts can be regarded as part of the state, so that they cannot enforce measures contrary to constitutional norms in the private sector. The indirect horizontal effect doctrine could also be adopted as in South Africa. If the existing law cannot be remodelled, the constitutional tort is a last resort.[201] An analysis of the scope and nature of the right in question and the extent to which it is capable and appropriate to use it to alter the legal rights and obligations of individuals is an indispensable first step.[202] The second step is full consideration of all the constitutional norms (particularly human dignity and equality), which have been overlooked in Irish jurisprudence. The third step, following the German example, is application of those norms as an objective order of values suited to a more complex diverse society in the context of the emerging liberal democratic theory in Ireland.[203] To conform

comparative and international law perspective (2007) 109 - 110, 153 - 154; M Kumm 'Who is afraid of the total constitution? Constitutional rights as principles and the constitutionalization of private law' (2006) 7 *German Law Journal* 341 at 350; O'Cinneide (n 119 above) 98 - 99.

198 Gardbaum (n 119 above) 403 - 404, citing *Lüth* (n 197 above) 205.

199 Gardbaum (n 119 above) 404, citing *Lüth* (n 197 above) 205.

200 O'Cinneide (n 124 above) 247.

201 See O'Cinneide (n 124 above) 249.

202 As above.

203 See A Coughlan 'The Constitution and social policy' in F Litton (ed) *The Constitution of Ireland 1937 - 1987* (1988) 143 - 144; D Keogh 'The Irish constitutional revolution: An analysis of the making of the Constitution' in Litton above, 5; D Keogh & AJ McCarthy *The making of the Irish Constitution 1937: Bunreacht na hÉireann* (2007) 16; E McDonagh 'Philosophical-theological reflections on the Constitution' in Litton above, 199 - 201; O'Cinneide (n 124 above) 248 - 249.

with the constitutional vision of promoting the common good to assure the dignity and freedom of the individual, the person is seen as a member of the social community.

It is clear from the wording of Articles 41 - 43 that the norms enshrined in the Constitution are derived from natural law and not from the state.[204] The family is identified as 'a moral institution possessing inalienable and imprescriptible rights, antecedent and superior to all positive law.'[205] Parents have 'the inalienable right and duty' to provide for their children's education.[206] It is acknowledged 'that man, in virtue of his rational being, has the natural right, antecedent to positive law,' to private ownership of property.[207] Since constitutional rights do not depend for their existence on the state, they are enforceable against all comers insofar as they are capable of being so applied. The Constitution delineates when it is proper for the State to intervene to protect and vindicate these inherent rights.

Unlike in the US, the Irish Constitution is not inhibitory – its primary aim is not to guard against state intervention. The courts' role is to delve into the normative issues, to interpret them and apply them in particular situations, so that people can understand how those norms should operate in

204 The ethos of the Constitution is Christian, as is evident from the Preamble and the acknowledgment in Article 44.1 that 'the homage of public worship is due to Almighty God'. On the Christian influence on the drafting of the Constitution, see G Hogan *The origins of the Irish Constitution: 1928-1941* (2012) 156, 210 - 218, 223 - 224, 226; Keogh (n 203 above) 19 - 25, 27 - 56, 69; Keogh & McCarthy (n 203 above) 109 - 122, 153 - 173. The prevailing superior natural law recognised in the Constitution has its foundations in the human body and soul created in God's image giving individuals the power of reason and the obligation of conscience, which inherent characteristics demand respect and reverence from fellow citizens and the state: D Costello 'Natural law, the Constitution and the courts' in P Lynch & J Meenan (eds) *Essays in memory of Alexis Fitzgerald* (1987) 108. See also Binchy (n 187 above) 311; D Costello 'The Irish judge as law-maker' in Curtin & O'Keeffe (n 125 above) 162, 164; G Hogan 'Constitutional interpretation' in Litton (n 203 above) 177 - 181; G Quinn 'Legal change, natural law and the authority of courts' in B Treacy & G Whyte (eds) *Religion, morality and public policy* (1995) 105 - 106; B Walsh 'The Constitution and constitutional rights' in Litton (n 203 above) 89 - 91, 104; Walsh (n 125 above) 149; G Whyte 'Introduction' in Treacy & Whyte above, 14 - 15; GF Whyte 'Natural law and the Constitution' (1996) 14 *Irish Law Times* 8.

Natural law has been defined as 'the set of principles of practical reasonableness in ordering human life and human community': J Finnis *Natural law and natural rights* (2011) 280. Natural law is a philosophy of rights affirming the reality of individual responsibility within the determinate natural order: LL Weinrib 'Natural law and rights' in RP George (ed) *Natural law theory: Contemporary essays* (1992) 298.

205 Art 41.1.1°.

206 Art 42.1.

207 Art 43.1.1°.

legal harmony.[208] Interpretation is necessary because it does not automatically follow that there is a right to sue on foot of a constitutional right – the defendant may not have a correlative obligation.[209] The courts should make the connection between the moral framework of the Constitution and the implemented moral right.[210] Their task is to create the legal network to deliver a constitutional vision.

The South African courts have demonstrated how the common law can be moulded to reflect constitutional norms. The Supreme Court of Appeal developed the defence of reasonable publication to defamation in *National Media Ltd v Bogoshi*,[211] which was approved by the Constitutional Court in *Khumalo v Holomisa* as it struck an appropriate balance between the protection of freedom of expression and the constitutional value of human dignity.[212]

208 Jürgen Habermas explained that law has a more complex structure than morality because, first, it simultaneously 'unleashes and normatively limits individual freedom of action (with its orientation toward each individual's own values and interests)' and, second, it incorporates 'collective goal setting, so that its regulations are too concrete to be justifiable by moral considerations alone': J Habermas *Between facts and norms: Contributions to a discourse theory of law and democracy* trans W Rehg (1998) 452. Actionable positive law can be viewed as a functional complement to morality: as above.

209 The term 'rights' tends to be used indiscriminately to cover what may in a given case be a privilege, power or an immunity rather than a right in the strictest sense: WN Hohfeld 'Some fundamental legal conceptions as applied in judicial reasoning' (1913) *23 Yale Law Journal* 16 at 30. 'Duty' is the correlative of 'right': above, 31 - 32; WN Hohfeld 'Fundamental legal conceptions as applied in judicial reasoning' (1917) 26 *Yale Law Journal* 710 at 710, 717. Instead of there being a single right with a single correlative duty resting on all the persons against whom the right avails, there are many separate and distinct rights, actual and potential, each one of which has a correlative duty resting upon some one person: Hohfeld 'Fundamental legal conceptions as applied in judicial reasoning' above, 742.

A *correlative* duty differs from a *corresponding* duty: HN Morse 'Applying the Hohfeld system to constitutional analysis' (1988) 9 *Whittier Law Review* 639 at 647.

For assessments of Wesley Hohfeld's analysis of legal relations and conceptions, see WW Cook 'Hohfeld's contributions to the science of law' (1919) 28 *Yale Law Journal* 721 at 723 - 737; C Nyquist 'Teaching Wesley Hohfeld's theory of legal relations' (2002) 52 *Journal of Legal Education* 238 at 239 - 241, 255 - 256; JW Singer 'The legal rights debate in analytical jurisprudence from Bentham to Hohfeld' [1982] *Wisconsin Law Review* 975 at 978 - 979, 986 - 994, 1049 - 1050, 1056 - 1059.

For criticism of Hohfeld's classification of jural conceptions, see I Husik 'Hohfeld's jurisprudence' (1924) 72 *University of Pennsylvania Law Review* 263 at 264 - 268; M Radin 'A restatement of Hohfeld' (1938) 51 *Harvard Law Review* 1141 at 1147 - 1151, 1157 - 1158, 1163.

210 The Constitution has been viewed as a philosophical and theological document: Keogh & McCarthy (n 203 above) 108. From that perspective, its legal import needs to be articulated.

211 1998 4 SA 1196.

212 2002 5 SA 401.

In contrast, the Irish courts have not produced coherent and analytically persuasive explanations of horizontality from conceptual, juridical and jurisdictional perspectives.[213]

8.2.2 Positive obligations on the state

The extent of the state's obligations to protect dignity can require it to take positive steps to prevent infringements not only by state actors, but also by private individuals. This may mean criminalisation of certain activities and follow up to prosecute, punish and rehabilitate offenders.[214] It can also necessitate state action to ensure that the law provides an effective remedy for civil wrongs extending to judicial intervention to secure redress for individuals in addition to legislative and administrative measures.

The judiciary is an arm of the state entrusted with a particular obligation to uphold the Constitution where the other branches of government have failed to do so.[215] Its role in fulfilling that duty is to provide a proper enforcement mechanism to deliver a remedy to those aggrieved. In Ireland a

213 S Banda 'Taking indirect horizontality seriously in Ireland: A time to magnify the nuance' (2009) 31 *Dublin University Law Journal* 263 at 295.

214 International human rights law based on human dignity has eroded the formerly sacrosanct principle of state sovereignty. From the time of the Nuremberg Tribunal, a crime by a head of state or a government official has not relieved the individual from responsibility under international law: SRS Bedi *The development of human rights law by the judges of the International Court of Justice* (2007) 244; A Seibert-Fohr (2009) *Prosecuting serious human rights violations* 289. See *Arrest Warrant of 11 April 2000 (Democratic Republic of the Congo v Belgium)* (Merits) [2002] ICJ Rep 3; C de Than & E Shorts *International criminal law and human rights* (2003) [3-016]; P Alston & R Goodman *International human rights: the successor to international human rights in context: law, politics and morals* (2013) 1130 - 1137.

International criminal tribunals were established at the end of the 20th century to hold individuals accountable for their part in atrocities. See, *eg*, *Prosecutor v Akayesu* (Judgment) ICTR-96-4-T, T Ch I (2 September 1998); I Bantekas *International criminal law* (2010) [2.6], [7.3.2], [8.3], [9.3], [9.4], [9.7], [21.11.5]; H Charlesworth & C Chinkin *The boundaries of international law: A feminist analysis* (2000) 237, 312, 318 - 319, 323; CA MacKinnon *Are women human? And other international dialogues* (2006) 238 - 239, 245.

On the development of an exception to state official immunity for core international crimes, see MA Summers 'Immunity or impunity – The potential effect of prosecutions of state officials for core international crimes in states like the United States that are not parties to the Statute of the International Criminal Court' (2006) 31 *Brooklyn Journal of International Law* 463 at 482 - 486.

215 The Community Court of Justice of the Economic Community of West African States held that the state was to be blamed for the inaction of its judicial and administrative authorities in not protecting a woman from violation of her human rights by a tribal practice of slavery: *Koraou v Niger* [2008] AHRLR 182 (ECOWAS 2008). State liability arose as a result of 'the tolerance, passiveness, inaction, and abstention' of the judiciary in Niger *vis-à-vis* the practice: above, [85].

re-evaluation of the unnecessary excessive deference to the legislature and executive because of the separation of powers would be timely. If it were jettisoned, that would remove an obstacle to performance of the courts' legitimate function.[216] A context-sensitive review allows flexibility in the judiciary's relationship with the executive.[217]

The police as representatives of the state have an obligation to protect human rights. Yet the Irish courts have shielded the state from the natural legal consequences of failing to fulfil this duty. In *Lockwood v Ireland* a rape victim claimed damages for the acquittal of her alleged rapist because his arrest was wrongful and therefore his confession was inadmissible.[218] In her action against the state she based her case on negligence and breach of duty on the part of the police in invoking an invalid power of arrest. She asserted that there had been a failure to vindicate her constitutional right to bodily integrity and to ensure that justice was achieved in her case. Kearns P dismissed her claim and held that a duty of care creating an entitlement to damages from the manner in which the gardaí conduct an investigation does not arise in the absence of *mala fides*.[219]

Hedigan J in *G v Minister for Justice Equality and Law Reform* applied the 'now well established law' arising from public policy that the gardaí owe no duty of care in respect of actions taken in the course of their duty to investigate and prosecute crime.[220] Here the gardaí brought the husband of a woman

216 In the Supreme Court, the majority (including Hardiman J) has regarded the separation of powers as rigid, whereas Denham CJ has a functional conception of it which allows greater innovation on the part of the courts: Doyle (n 166) [13-21], [13-32]–[13-33], citing *TD* (n 191 above) 367 - 371, 298 - 299. See also J Wakely 'Social and economic rights – A retreat by the South African Constitutional Court?' (2010) 28 *Irish Law Times* 153 at 154.

Irish judges have given the doctrine of the separation of powers a more stringent application than it has received in other jurisdictions such as the US or Australia, where it also occupies a central constitutional position: DG Morgan *A judgment too far? Judicial activism and the Constitution* (2001) 84.

217 Binchy (n 127 above) 220.

218 n 170 above. Hedigan J followed *Lockwood* when he found that a rape victim had no cause of action when she was traumatised following the collapse of the trial of the man accused of raping her because of a bungled prosecution: *M v Commissioner of an Garda Síochána* [2011] IEHC 14 [6.7]. See R Byrne & W Binchy *Annual review of Irish law 2011* (2012) 600 - 601.

219 The policy grounds Kearns P relied on were, first, fear of the floodgates opening by extending the ambit of those to whom a duty of care was owed to a witness in the trial or to the event, or to the family of the victim, and, second, the inhibitory effect of the duty, which could cripple the capacity of the gardaí to investigate and prosecute crime effectively and promptly.

220 [2011] IEHC 65 [6.2], [6.4].

murdered in their home from the crime scene to G's house, where he stayed and raped her. He had a history of violence and rape. The Court found that bringing the husband to G's house after removing him from his home in order to preserve the scene of the crime was part of the gardaí's investigatory functions and therefore no duty of care was owed to G.[221] This was a premature conclusion based on the general rule without any considered analysis of the particular context. Hedigan J dealt with the case solely as a negligence claim and made no reference to the state's constitutional obligations – even though the plaintiff invoked her constitutional rights.[222] The decision is in stark contrast to the South African court's *modus operandi* in *Carmichele*.[223]

The UK has taken a somewhat similar approach to that in Ireland and the police there owe a duty of care in their investigative role only in exceptional circumstances.[224] The Court of Appeal in *Desmond v Chief Constable of Nottinghamshire Police* set out the current core principle – based on public policy – that the police do not generally owe individuals a duty of care.[225] But the police do not have (and cannot be given) a blanket immunity.[226] In establishing whether or not a duty of care exists, it is relevant to see if the aggrieved person has other remedies, such as those available under statute,

221 n 220 above, [6.4]. Hedigan J indicated that even if a duty did exist, he would have found on the evidence that what happened was not reasonably foreseeable: n 220 above, [6.5].

222 n 220 above, [1].

223 *Carmichele v Minister of Safety and Security* 2001 4 SA 938 (CC).

224 See *Van Colle v Chief Constable of the Hertfordshire Police* [2008] UKHL 50, [2009] 1 AC 225; F du Bois 'State liability in South Africa: A constitutional remix' (2010) 25 *Tulane European and Civil Law Forum* 139 at 143 - 145, 154, 156.

225 [2011] EWCA Civ 3, [2011] All ER (D) 37 [31]:

> [I]n the absence of special circumstances, the police and the Crown Prosecution Service do not generally in the interests of the whole community owe individual members of the public, be they victims, witnesses or those who are prosecuted, a common law duty of care in undertaking and performing their operational duties of investigating, detecting, suppressing and prosecuting crime. The principle is one of public policy which has regard to the practical needs of law enforcement; the need not to inhibit the police from taking difficult operational decisions and so as to avoid defensive policing; and the undesirability that judgments of policy and discretion in the most advantageous deployment of resources and so forth should be elaborately and expensively investigated in litigation or otherwise with consequent diversion of police or CPS resources.

Although the core principle might lead to hardship in some individual cases, the greater public good outweighed individual hardship: as above.

226 n 225 above, [41], [52]. State immunity in Ireland was held to be unconstitutional: *Byrne v Ireland* [1972] IR 241 (SC). See Walsh (n 125 above) 152. There is no presumption that a general statute does not apply to the State; the courts' task is to ascertain the legislature's intention primarily from the statute's words: *Howard v Commissioners of Public Works in Ireland* [1994] 1 IR 101 (SC).

judicial review, for misfeasance in public office, for maladministration to an ombudsman,[227] or under the Police Conduct Complaints Procedure.[228] Other relevant factors are whether the claimant relied on the police in the event of economic rather than physical loss, and if the police assumed responsibility to the claimant to guard against the damage for which compensation is claimed.[229] It is an established requirement in the UK that the courts consider carefully the individual circumstances in each case before coming to a decision on whether the police owe a duty of care.[230]

The House of Lords in *Van Colle v Chief Constable of the Hertfordshire Police* was divided on the issue of whether the common law should be developed to provide a remedy in damages against the state for an individual injured by another after the police were aware of the threat.[231] The majority upheld the core principle enunciated in *Hill v Chief Constable of West Yorkshire*[232] that in the absence of special circumstances the police owe no common law duty of care to protect individuals against harm caused by criminals.[233] They disagreed with Lord Bingham's proposed 'liability principle' that if a member of the public furnishes a police officer with apparently credible evidence that an identified third party presents a specific and imminent threat to his life or physical safety, the officer owes a duty to

227 On the role of the ombudsman in Ireland, see DG Morgan 'Ireland's ombudsman' in J Sarkin & W Binchy (eds) *Human rights, the citizen and the state: South African and Irish approaches* (2001) 94 - 109.

228 n 225 above, [51].

229 n 225 above, [32], [35].

230 There have been some exceptions to the general rule, *eg*, it was held that the police owed an informant a duty to take reasonable care to avoid unnecessary disclosure to the general public of information given to the police in confidence: *Swinney v Chief Constable of Northumbria Police (No 2)* 25 May 1999 Times Law Reports (QB). The case was dismissed on the merits because the police were not in breach of that duty. The Court of Appeal had refused to strike out the claim on the grounds that it disclosed no reasonable cause of action and held that the immunity generally conferred on police officers from actions in negligence in relation to the investigation or suppression of crime had to be weighed against the need to protect the confidentiality of informants and to encourage them to come forward without fear of disclosure of their identity; it is necessary to make a balanced assessment of all the public policy considerations in order to determine the question of immunity: *Swinney v Chief Constable of Northumbria Police Force* [1997] QB 464 (CA). See H Beale & N Pittam 'The impact of the Human Rights Act 1998 on English tort and contract law' in Friedmann & Barak-Erez (n 119) 144; E McKendrick 'Negligence and human rights: Re-considering *Osman*' in Friedmann & Barak-Erez (n 119) 343 - 344.

231 n 224 above.

232 [1989] AC 53 (HL).

233 n 224 above, [97].

take reasonable steps to assess the threat and, if appropriate, to take reasonable steps to prevent it being executed.[234] Their rationale was based on public policy favouring the interests of the community as a whole, since the proposed duty would encourage defensive policing and divert manpower and resources from their primary function of suppressing crime and apprehending criminals. They also rejected Lord Bingham's view that the common law should be developed in harmony with ECHR rights.[235] Lord Brown considered that common law claims had different objectives from those under the ECHR – the former were designed to compensate claimants, whereas the latter were intended to uphold minimum human rights standards and to vindicate those rights.[236]

Under the ECHR there is an obligation in applying the law of negligence not to grant a blanket immunity to the police and to include the fair, just and reasonable criterion as an intrinsic element of the duty of care when considering the particular circumstances.[237] The European Court of Human Rights in *Z v UK* concluded that the inability to sue a local authority flowed not from an immunity but from the applicable principles governing the substantive right of action in domestic law.[238] The right of access to the

234 n 224 above, [44].

235 n 224 above, [58].

236 n 224 above, [138]. The situation in Ireland is different because constitutional values are supreme. The Supreme Court has held that the vindication of personal rights can be enforced through the law of tort, and not only through criminal or regulatory law: *Grant v Roche Products* (n 48 above). Hardiman J stated, n 48 above, [79]:

> There is thus authority, both judicial and academic, for the proposition that the law of tort is, at least in certain circumstances, an important tool for the vindication of constitutional rights, and no authority whatever for the proposition that it is concerned exclusively for the allocation of damages and with nothing else whatsoever.

Fundamental legal norms and constitutional rights take precedence over established common law norms: O'Cinneide (n 119) 84. The common law should be developed if possible to vindicate constitutional rights. *Eg*, in a conflict between reputation and freedom of expression, Ó Caoimh J was satisfied that he must consider whether the law of defamation as traditionally understood represented a violation of the constitutional right to freedom of expression and whether it should result in a fundamental re-statement of that law or a tempering of same: *Hunter v Gerald Duckworth & Co Ltd* [2003] IEHC 81 at 47. He favoured incremental development of the common law having regard to the requirements of the Constitution and the ECHR: above, 59.

On development of the common law and the constitutional tort, see: *Meskell* (n 124); *Glover* (n 134).

237 *Z v UK* (App no 29392/95) (2002) 34 EHRR 3 [100].

238 As above. The action was for the local authority's alleged failure to take adequate protective measures in respect of the severe neglect and abuse which children were known to be suffering because of ill-treatment by their parents.

courts under Article 6 ECHR had been affirmed in *Osman v UK*, where the early striking out of a tort claim against the police breached that right.[239] There the victims of a shooting incident were entitled to have the police account for their actions and omissions in adversarial proceedings.[240] The House of Lords in *Van Colle* (applying the decision in *Osman*) held that to comprise a violation of the state's positive obligation to protect life under Article 2 ECHR by taking preventative measures to protect an individual whose life is at risk from the criminal acts of another, it had to be shown that a public authority had, or ought to have, known at the time of the existence of a real and immediate risk to the life of an identified individual from the criminal acts of a third party and that it had failed to take reasonable measures to avoid that risk.[241] In *MC v Bulgaria*, the Court noted that the police investigation was handled with significant delays and found that the effectiveness of the investigation of an allegation of rape in that case fell short of the requirements inherent in the positive obligations 'to establish and apply effectively a criminal-law system punishing all forms of rape and sexual abuse.'[242] An effective remedy for rape requires criminal sanctions – a civil action for damages is insufficient.

The decisions in *Lockwood* and *G* were defective in that no consideration was given to whether a duty of care arose in the precise circumstances by application of the 'fair, just and reasonable' criteria. The judges in those cases operated on the basis that a virtual blanket immunity existed in relation to the police investigation. They only countenanced an action against the police for misfeasance. Neither was any analysis done of whether the victims' right to bodily integrity or entitlement to an effective remedy had been vindicated by an alternative form of redress. In *Lockwood* the state had

239 (App no 23452/94) (2000) 29 EHRR 245 [154]. On *Osman*, see McKendrick (n 230 above) 332 - 337.

240 n 239 above, [153].

241 n 224 above, [28]-[29], citing n 239 above, [115]-[116].

242 (App No 39272/98) (2005) 40 EHRR 20 [184]-[185]. The Bulgarian authorities had not investigated thoroughly a girl's rape allegation when the perpetrators maintained she had consented to sexual intercourse and there was no direct proof of rape: above, [181]-[182]. As rape is an exercise of power, consent is irrelevant when the victim is not treated as an equal and hence is unable to protest because of her situation: CA MacKinnon *Women's lives, men's laws* (2005) 182.

The refusal to investigate the assassination of the President of Burkina Faso constituted inhuman treatment of his widow and sons: *Sankara v Burkina Faso* UNHR Committee (11 April 2006) 86th Session UN Doc CCPR/C/86/D/1159/2003 [12.2], citing International Covenant on Civil and Political Rights (adopted 16 December 1966, entered into force 23 March 1976) 999 UNTS 171 (ICCPR) art 7.

submitted that she had a remedy in law to sue the accused directly for damages in a civil case, but Kearns P did not address this in his decision. Vindication of the plaintiff's position was not necessarily grounded solely in damages – she could have wanted to hold the police accountable and to have the court assess whether they had protected her right to bodily integrity by carrying out an effective investigation.

The state's obligation to protect the life, person, good name, and property rights of individuals under Article 40.3.2° of the Constitution requires positive action to *prevent* an infringement and this obligation is not satisfied by the possible existence of a common law remedy where a personal right *has actually been* infringed.[243] The ECHR also imposes positive obligations on the state to protect and ensure respect for rights.[244] These duties cannot be fulfilled simply by relying on the existing law of torts after the event.

In South Africa it was held in *Minister of Safety and Security v Van Duivenboden* that police officers are under an actionable duty to members of the public to take reasonable steps to act on information reflecting on the fitness of a person to possess firearms in order to avoid harm occurring.[245] Nugent JA explained that what was ultimately required was an assessment, in accordance with prevailing norms, of the circumstances in which it should be unlawful to culpably cause loss.[246] Accountability had an important role in determining whether a legal duty ought to be recognised, although accountability could sometimes be secured without damages through the political process or through another judicial remedy.[247]

As in South Africa (and unlike the UK, which does not have a distinct concept of state liability), the positive constitutional obligations imposed on the state in Ireland have broken down the rigid distinction between private and public law.[248] The power of judicial review of laws for conformity with

243 Hogan & Whyte (n 185 above) [7.1.112].

244 See *Airey v Ireland* (App no 6289/73) (1979-80) 2 EHRR 305 (Arts 6(1) & 8 ECHR); *X v Netherlands* (App no 8978/80) (1986) 8 EHRR 235 (Art 8 ECHR); *Osman* (n 239 above) (Art 2 ECHR); *MC v Bulgaria* (n 242 above) (Arts 3 & 8 ECHR). On *Airey*, see G Whyte 'And justice for some' (1984) 6 *Dublin University Law Journal* 88 at 89 - 92.

245 [2002] 3 All SA 741 (SCA) [22]. A year later the Supreme Court of Appeal held that the police had a legal duty to exercise reasonable care in relation to the grant of firearm licences and that breach of this duty gave rise to an action for damages: *Minister of Safety and Security v Hamilton* [2003] 4 All SA 117 (SCA).

246 n 245 above, [16].

247 n 245 above, [21].

248 See du Bois (n 224 above) 148, 170 - 172.

the Constitution is vested in the higher courts.[249] The Constitution with its normative base imposes additional responsibilities on the state that do not apply to private individuals and therefore facilitates the alignment of tort law with the Constitution. The Irish courts have not shown the required diligence in weighing up the duty of care owed by the police against public policy. Only intentional transgressions by the police give rise to liability. When a right that is integral to human dignity, such as life, bodily integrity or access to justice, is put in the balance, the constitutional values of dignity and freedom should be to the fore in the judicial analysis.

8.2.3 Limitation of actions

The time limitation imposed on commencing a tort action was held to apply to a constitutional tort in *McDonnell*.[250] The Supreme Court decreed that it was subject to the same limitation period that applied in general law and therefore the claim was statute-barred. Keane J trivialised breaches of all constitutional rights (irrespective of their serious nature) with this remark:[251]

> I can see no reason why an actress sunbathing in her back garden whose privacy is intruded upon by a long-range camera should defer proceedings until her old age to provide herself with a nest egg, while a young man or woman rendered a paraplegic by a drunken motorist must be cut off from suing after three years.

249 Art 34.3.2°.

250 n 132 above. See Morgan and Hogan (n 124 above) [18-84].
McDonnell is inconsistent with the Supreme Court's later finding that intentional trespass to the person did not constitute 'breach of duty' in section 3(1) of the Statute of Limitations (Amendment) Act 1991, and therefore did not attract the shorter limitation period applying to personal injuries claims based on negligence and nuisance: *Devlin v Roche* [2002] IESC 34, [2002] 2 IR 360. For an analysis of *Devlin*, see R Byrne & W Binchy *Annual review of Irish law 2001* (Thomson Round Hall, Dublin 2002) 435 - 442.
McDonnell is also inconsistent with Carroll J's finding in the High Court that a claim for damages for unlawful interference with a constitutional right was not an action based on tort: *Hayes v Ireland* [1987] ILRM 651 (HC).

251 n 132 above, 160. Keane J was aware that 'significant differences' might arise in some contexts when general tort law was applied to constitutional rights, but it was 'unnecessary to embark on those uncharted seas': n 132 above, 159. He found that the same policy considerations (protection of the defendant against stale claims, expeditious trials and legal certainty) applied in an action for breach of a constitutional right, and dismissed as 'a classically circular argument' the proposition that an action for breach of a constitutional right with 'all the indicia of an action in tort should have a different limitation period from that applicable to actions in tort generally, or indeed no limitation period at all, other than its origin in the Constitution itself': n 132 above, 159 - 160, citing *Tuohy v Courtney* [1994] 3 IR 1 (SC) 48.

No consideration was given to the fact that the constitutional right infringed in *McDonnell* was the right to a livelihood and that it was violated in a serious manner by the loss of a person's job on grounds subsequently found unconstitutional.[252] Furthermore, the first case in which damages for breach of constitutional rights were expressly awarded was not decided until 15 years after enactment of the Statute of Limitations 1957,[253] so it could not be said that the legislature intended that the same limitations should apply to constitutional torts. The Court also noted that no blame could be attributed to the plaintiff for presuming that the legislation under which he lost was job did not violate the Constitution.[254]

If it had wished to do so, the Supreme Court in *McDonnell* could have devised a new rule to apply to constitutional torts. A suitable solution would be for the cause of action for breach of the right to a livelihood to accrue from the date of knowledge of unconstitutionality, which in the case of a constitutional tort based on a statute declared unconstitutional should be the date of declaration of invalidity.[255] The policy reasons for the limitation of the constitutional right to a livelihood could have been examined in more depth. The Court did not analyse fully the implications of that right nor attempt to test the limitation on the grant of a remedy for its breach against policy objectives. In *Tuohy v Courtney*, Finlay CJ set the parameters of the Court's role in assessing the impact of the statutory limitation in the light of policy around the degree of hardship caused.[256] If the Court in *McDonnell* had applied these parameters, the extent of the hardship imposed on the plaintiff by restricting the time within which he could sue to a period that expired before the statute under which he forfeited his job was declared

252 See *Cox v Ireland* [1992] 2 IR 503 (SC). Ngcobo J associated dignity with the right to choose one's livelihood, when he stated, '[f]reedom to choose a vocation is intrinsic to the nature of a society based on human dignity': *Affordable Medicines Trust v Minister of Health* 2006 3 SA 247 (CC) [59].

253 n 132 above, 147, citing *Meskell* (n 124).

254 n 132 above, 146.

255 O'Flaherty J acknowledged that the consequences of striking down legislation 'can only crystallise in respect of the immediate litigation which gave rise to the declaration of invalidity': n 132 above, 144.

256 n 251 above, 48:

> The counter-balance to these objectives is the necessity as far as is practicable, or as best it may, for the State to ensure that such time limits do not unreasonably or unjustly impose hardship. Any time limit statutorily imposed upon the bringing of actions is potentially going to impose some hardship on some individual. What this Court must do is to ascertain whether the extent and nature of such hardship is so undue and so unreasonable having regard to the proper objectives of the legislation as to make it constitutionally flawed.

unconstitutional would surely have been seen to be unreasonable and unjust.

There are major exceptions to the general rule that an invalid statute, which is void *ab initio*, has no legal consequences.[257] If the natural consequences of a ruling that a statute is invalid always ensued, the policy aims of legal certainty required by application of the rule of law and the attainment of social order in an organised society would be shaken. To avoid a chaotic legal system, the courts have taken a pragmatic approach and have devised methods to curtail the reach of a finding of invalidity.

The Supreme Court in *A v Governor of Arbour Hill Prison*[258] dealt with the consequences of the findings in *CC v Ireland* that a provision in the Criminal Law (Amendment) Act 1935 was inconsistent with the Constitution.[259] Prior to the latter finding, A had pleaded guilty to an offence under the invalid statutory provision and was serving a prison sentence for it. He sought his release, which Laffoy J ordered in the High Court because the pre-1937 statute had ceased to have legislative existence on the enactment of the Constitution – therefore the conviction was a nullity and his detention lacked due process.[260] The Supreme Court overruled her decision and held that there was neither an express nor an implied principle of retrospective application of unconstitutionality in the Constitution.[261] The approach to be taken to the application of retrospectivity was to assess whether the compulsion of public order and the common good would allow the application to succeed.[262] The element of good faith on the part of the state in relying on the statute disposed the Court to hold that the conviction should be deemed to be and remain lawful. While the declaration that a law was unconstitutional applied to the parties to the litigation in which the issue arose, the principle of prospective overruling applied to others.[263]

257 Morgan & Hogan (n 124 above) [11-84].

258 [2006] IESC 45, [2006] 4 IR 88. See A O'Neill 'Invalidity and retrospectivity under the Irish and Canadian constitutions' (2006) 15 *Constitutional Forum* 147 at 150 - 152; A O'Neill 'The effect of a finding that legislation is unconstitutional: The approach of the Irish Supreme Court' (2007) 36 *Common Law World Review* 220 at 223 - 230.

259 [2006] IESC 33, [2006] 4 IR 1.

260 [2006] IEHC 169, [2006] 4 IR 88.

261 Cases that had been finally decided and determined on foot of a statute which was later found to be unconstitutional were deemed valid once the parties had exhausted their actual or potential remedies.

262 A harmonious interpretation of the Constitution necessitated looking at the document as a whole.

263 Although there was no general retrospective application, the Court left open the possibility that an exception might arise in wholly exceptional circumstances in the interests of justice. In this case A's guilty plea indicated that he accepted the validity

The courts could bear in mind the requirement for an effective remedy while they are developing the broad notion of dealing intelligently with invalid statutes. Judicial review followed merely by a declaration of invalidity under section 5 of the European Convention on Human Rights Act 2003 is not an effective remedy. In *Carmody v Minister for Justice, Equality and Law Reform* Murray CJ described a declaration of incompatibility as a 'remedy, such as it is, … both limited and *sui generis*' and confirmed that it did not accord to a plaintiff any direct or enforceable judicial remedy.[264] The courts have a duty to deliver an effective remedy to litigants and could test the consequences of a finding of invalidity for compatibility with the principles of justice. The adjudication as to what are exceptional cases requiring the invalidity to have retrospective effect should involve consideration of the impact on the dignity of the individuals concerned.

The South African Constitutional Court refused to allow the state to rely on a limitation period to preclude Mrs Njongi, a poor uneducated woman, from recovering arrears of disability grant, which it had unlawfully decided to stop paying.[265] The state had acted unconscionably in deciding to oppose her claim and in the way it conducted the case.[266] In *Barkhuizen v Napier*, a challenge to a time limit on suing for damage to a car in a motor insurance contract, the courts accepted that the correct way of evaluating the validity of the clause was by determining whether it offended public policy as evidenced by constitutional values.[267] Dignity was used to assess the weight

of the charge against him at the time. He had not been able to allege any departure from natural justice in the way he had been treated but acknowledged his guilt and that his claimed release would be a windfall: n 258 above, [169], [211], [256], [260].

264 [2009] IESC 71, [2010] 1 ILRM 157 at 168. In *Carmody* the Supreme Court held that where a claim is made that a statute is invalid under the Constitution and a declaration of incompatibility with the ECHR is also sought, the constitutional issue should be decided first. See de Londras & Kelly (n 168 above) [2-36]–[2-38], [7-20].

265 *Njongi v MEC, Department of Welfare, Eastern Cape* 2008 4 SA 237. The Court held that the state had not disavowed the unlawful decision, so the time had not started to run against her: above, [58]. In the absence of a full disavowal or full reinstatement, she would not have known that the statutory claim period had commenced: EC Christiansen 'Transformative constitutionalism in South Africa: Creative uses of Constitutional Court authority to advance substantive justice' (2010) 13 *Journal of Gender, Race & Justice* 575 at 605.

266 n 265 above, [85].

267 2007 5 SA 323 (CC) [11]. For analyses of *Barkhuizen*, see Ackermann (n 119) 290 - 295; PJ Sutherland 'Ensuring contractual fairness in consumer contracts after *Barkhuizen v Napier* 2007 5 SA 323 (CC) – Part 1' (2008) 19 *Stellenbosch Law Review* 390.

on both sides of the scales – the dignity of autonomy and freedom to contract on the one hand and oppression of dignity by unfair terms on the other.[268]

As the values of dignity, freedom and equality are also enshrined in the Irish Constitution, the Irish courts could employ them as yardsticks to adjudge whether a time limit sought to be imposed on bringing a claim for a breach of a constitutional right can be allowed to stand.

268 Sachs J (in dissent) felt that a strong case could be made that terms that were unreasonable, oppressive or unconscionable in a standard form contract were inconsistent with the values of an open and democratic society that promotes human dignity, equality and freedom: n 267 above, [140].

9

Conclusion

After my study of the provisions in the South African and Irish Constitutions affecting fundamental rights and their interpretation by the judiciary, and my analysis of the philosophical and historical origins of the values of human dignity and equality, it is time to draw some conclusions. The propositions throughout this work have been supported with illustrations from various jurisdictions demonstrating that the South African approach is not idiosyncratic on account of the apartheid legacy of oppression and profound inequalities, but is suitable for application in other countries.

9.1 Normative framework

As there was a gap of more than half a century between the dates of adoption of the Constitutions in Ireland and South Africa, they are products of different eras and historical backgrounds. However, they are both values-based and therefore each jurisdiction can learn from the other.[1] A reader of the South African document could be left in no doubt that it places enormous emphasis on the fundamental values of human dignity, equality and freedom. The scholar of the Irish fundamental law has to look a little more closely to discern that it has a similar normative spirit.

1 AS Butler 'Private litigation and constitutional rights under sections 8 and 9 of the 1996 Constitution – Assistance from Ireland' (1999) 116 *South African Law Journal* 77 at 99.

The meaningful outcomes evident in the South African cases are products of a transformative Constitution urgently required after a turbulent history produced a dysfunctional society based on fundamentally perverse values. The judiciary in the post-apartheid era had clear signposts based on newly-adopted norms democratically chosen and supported. Even though the Irish Constitution was adopted in 1937 in different circumstances, it is set in a comparable normative framework founded on human dignity and demanding mutual respect in relationships. It is obvious even from the text that religion had a strong influence on the drafting of the Constitution.[2] Its philosophy is founded on the fact that human beings, by virtue of their humanity, have rights and obligations.[3] In this, it anticipated the Universal Declaration of Human Rights[4] by a decade. Individuals have inherent rights. While religion and conscience are deeply personal matters, they should prompt responsibility for a just and equal society.[5] Social justice is a community aspiration.[6]

Ronald Dworkin pointed out that fidelity to a constitutional tradition requires an appeal to the theory or principles that are either explicit or implicit in a constitution itself.[7] In order to maintain ethical relevance, a constitution ought to be interpreted in the light of the changing social context.[8]

2 I Bacik 'Future directions for the Constitution' in O Doyle & E Carolan (eds) *The Irish Constitution: Governance and values* (2008) 139 - 140; DM Clarke 'The concept of the common good in Irish constitutional law' (1979) 30 *Northern Ireland Legal Quarterly* 319 at 341; O Doyle 'Article 44: Privileging the rights of the religious' in Doyle & Carolan above, 488; P Hannon 'In God's name, what next? Religion, the Constitution and the new Ireland' in Doyle & Carolan above, 462 - 463; B Sullivan 'The Irish Constitution: Some reflections from abroad' in Doyle & Carolan above, 8 - 11; KC Wheare *Modern constitutions* (1966) 70.

3 W Binchy 'Dignity as a constitutional concept' in Doyle & Carolan (n 2 above) 311.

4 Universal Declaration of Human Rights (adopted 10 December 1948) UNGA Res 217 A(III).

5 K Zappone 'Article 18' in D O'Connell (ed) *Sixty years, thirty perspectives: Ireland and the Universal Declaration of Human Rights* (2009) 117. Cf L Sossin 'The "supremacy of God", human dignity and the *Charter of Rights and Freedoms*' (2003) 52 *University of New Brunswick Law Journal* 227 at 237 - 238.

6 See Constitution of Ireland 1937, Art 43.2.1°. On the balance between private ownership and social justice in the Constitution, see R Walsh 'Private property rights in the drafting of the Irish Constitution: A communitarian compromise' (2011) 33 *Dublin University Law Journal* 86.

7 R Dworkin *Justice in robes* (2006) 117 - 118, 122 - 123, 138 - 139, 141, 183 - 184, 252. See DM Clarke 'Interpreting the Constitution: Essentially contested concepts' in Doyle & Carolan (n 2 above) 105.

8 Zappone (n 5 above) 117.

9.2 Philosophical understandings of dignity in South Africa and Ireland

The text of the reference to dignity in the Preamble of the Irish Constitution contains similar concepts to the judicial interpretation of the fundamental constitutional values in South Africa – the individual's freedom and dignity is set in the context of the common good prescribing social justice. It is surprising therefore that there is a notable difference in the philosophical understanding of dignity as expressed in the case-law in Ireland.[9] *Ubuntu*, which places the individual firmly within the community, has reinforced the South African courts' endorsement of a communitarian perception of dignity that harmonises the rights of the individual with the reciprocal rights and duties of others in society.[10] The constitutional values of human dignity, equality and freedom require the government to support the individual in the community with socio-economic benefits when necessary.[11] It contrasts with the American association of dignity primarily with individual rights described by Neomi Rao as 'a classical liberal understanding of freedom from interference.'[12]

The South Africans have adopted the amalgamated notion of human dignity derived from the nature and spirituality of the social human being with the capacity to reason and free will.[13] In the case-law there have been references resounding of Immanuel Kant's imperative not to treat people as objects because of their dignity stemming from these characteristics.[14] Dworkin's view of the sanctity of life was endorsed,[15] as was his stress on the

9 There is little evidence that the judicial use of the concept of human dignity has been directly affected by recent philosophical analysis: C McCrudden 'Human dignity and judicial interpretation of human rights' (2008) 19 *European Journal of International Law* 655 at 663.

10 *S v Makwanyane* 1995 6 BCLR 665 (CC) [224] (Langa J), [263] (Mahomed J) (see text to n397 and n399 in Ch III). See also n415-n416 and text thereto in Ch III.

11 N Rao 'American dignity and healthcare reform' (2012) 35 *Harvard Journal of Law and Public Policy* 171 at 173. See 6.5 - 6.7 in Ch VI.

12 n 11 above, 174.

13 *Bernstein v Bester* 1996 2 SA 751 (CC) [150] (O'Regan J) (see n395 and text thereto in Ch III).

14 *Makwanyane* (n 10 above) [26] (Chaskalson P) (see text to n389 in Ch III); *Prinsloo v Van der Linde* 1997 3 SA 1012 (CC) [31]; *S v Dodo* 2001 3 SA 382 (CC) [38] (Ackermann J) (see n 95 and text thereto in Ch IV); *Mohunram v National DPP* 2007 4 SA 222 (CC) [146] (Sachs J) (see n413 in Ch III).

15 *Soobramoney v Minister of Health (Kwazulu-Natal)* 1998 1 SA 765 (CC) [55] (see n387 and text thereto in Ch III). Dworkin's views on the sanctity of life also influenced the House of Lords: *Airedale NHS Trust v Bland* [1993] AC 789 (HL) 826 (Hoffmann LJ).

importance of dignity in democracies[16] and his interpretation of the right to equality as being the right to be treated as equals.[17] Mokgoro J, dissenting in *Case v Minister of Safety and Security*, referred to his insistence that pornography is guaranteed by freedom of expression because of the latter's egalitarian role.[18]

Perhaps because of a fear in recent decades of bringing religious beliefs into the public domain and a reluctance to analyse the various roots of natural law, the Irish courts have not taken the same path as South Africa and have not communicated a lucid reasoned philosophical base for human dignity.[19] The Constitution's Christian ethos is undeniable.[20] Clearly it is a normative instrument acknowledging that rights are derived from natural law or some form of higher order than the State or the Constitution itself.[21] Henchy J construed Article 40.3 of the Constitution in *Norris* in a non-religious fashion and voiced a secular version of that higher order.[22] Kant's dictum not to use people solely as a means to an end has been employed by Hardiman J.[23] There is a liberal democratic thread in the Constitution in addition to its Christian democratic character.[24] As it balances the rights of the individual and the interests of society, the Constitution has the potential to promote the communitarian goal of social inclusion.[25]

The lack of philosophical analysis leaves a void with litigants and the public free to wander directionless in a legal wilderness. The strong Irish value system has been ignored by the majority of the judges who avoid considering norms. As a result they have not expressed the coherent moral thread underpinning human dignity. The sparse legal application of the

16 *Makwanyane* (n 10 above) [330] (O'Regan J).

17 *Prinsloo* (n 14 above) [32] (see text to n310 in Ch V); *City Council of Pretoria v Walker* 1998 2 SA 363 (CC) [126], [128] (Sachs J).

18 1996 3 SA 617 (CC) [23] fn 34, [45] fn 76. See also above, [26] fn 37.

19 Dignity's connection with religion has been noted: *O'Donoghue v Minister for Health* [1993] IEHC 2, [1996] 2 IR 20 at 52 - 54 (O'Hanlon J).

20 See n 204 and text thereto in Ch VIII.

21 See text to n205-n207 in Ch VIII.

22 *Norris v AG* [1984] IR 36 (SC) (see text to n433 and n435 in Ch VII); G Hogan 'Constitutional interpretation' in F Litton (ed) *The Constitution of Ireland 1937 - 1987* (1988) 180 - 181.

23 *CC v Ireland* [2006] IESC 33, [2006] 4 IR 1 [44] (see text to n 81 in Ch VII).

24 GF Whyte 'Discerning the philosophical premises of the Report of the Constitution Review Group: An analysis of the recommendations on fundamental rights' (1998) *Contemporary Issues in Irish Law and Politics* 216 at 222, 223. See also n203 in Ch VIII.

25 Whyte (n 24 above) 224.

concept has not unearthed the full breadth of reciprocal respect for the inherent worth of the person as part of the community, but has been confined for the most part to individual dignity based only on random remarks.[26]

Court decisions where the right to respect for dignity has been upheld have been based on the liberal view of preventing interference with the individual.[27] They have not required active measures by the State to assist and protect the person living in the community as envisaged by the Constitution;[28] hence the leeway given to the police when it comes to protecting the public against infringements of dignity by private individuals,[29] as well as the refusal to recognise unenumerated socio-economic rights and to grant effective remedies even when the State's abject continuous failure to uphold those express socio-economic rights that do exist in the Constitution is apparent.[30] The State's duty not to lend its support to the continuation of discrimination between private individuals has been ignored by the courts, which have not appreciated the attack on the status of a person in the community by being regarded as inferior on the basis of a human attribute or one's background.[31]

9.3 Substantive rights

The fundamental constitutional values could be the basis for advancements in many areas, particularly in producing a more stringent ban on parental corporal punishment, striving towards substantial equality, recognition of the ethnic identity of Travellers, and reduction of overcrowding in prisons. Enforcement of socio-economic rights could have a powerful impact. When deciding on how to enforce social and economic rights in South Africa, the Constitutional Court invoked the principles of proportionality, fairness and

26 See 7.2 in Ch VII.

27 *North Western Health Board v HW* [2001] IESC 90, [2001] 3 IR 622; *Shortt v Commissioner of An Garda Síochána* [2007] IESC 9, [2007] 4 IR 587.

28 *O'Keeffe v Hickey* [2008] IESC 72, [2009] 2 IR 302; *Reilly v Devereux* [2009] IESC 22, [2009] 3 IR 660.

29 See 8.2.2 in Ch VIII.

30 *TD v Minister for Education* [2001] IESC 101, [2001] 4 IR 259. Going against the pattern, social justice required the property rights of the less wealthy to be especially defended (in this case against erosion by the State): *Re Article 26 and the Health (Amendment) (No 2) Bill 2004* [2005] IESC 7, [2005] 1 IR 105.

31 See 7.10.1 - 7.10.2 in Ch VII.

reasonableness to assist it in making value judgments on issues of major social and moral importance in a principled way that was true to the letter and spirit of the Constitution.[32] A textual analysis and logic were no longer sufficient.[33]

Values could also be applied to develop contract law to provide further protection for consumers and for others in an unequal bargaining position with powerful institutions and corporate entities in the marketplace. In tort there is room for improvements in negligence, nuisance and trespass as causes of action to redress civil wrongs. As has been hinted at in South Africa, the law of privacy might be scoped by the engagement of values to develop the common law.

A deeper meaning could be given to human dignity by seeing it in a relational context, rather than accepting simply the restricted individualistic view taken of it in the *Ward of Court* case.[34] If its import had been examined in *Norris*,[35] the same ultimate outcome could have been achieved by reference to the Irish Constitution instead of having to resort to the European Court of Human Rights in reliance on the European Convention on Human Rights (ECHR).[36]

9.4 Scope

The horizontal application of constitutional rights between non-state parties in Irish law is required to ensure the observance of constitutional personal rights in private legal relations.[37] However, the judges do not discharge this

32 A Sachs *The strange alchemy of life and law* (2009) 211.

33 As above.

34 *Re a Ward of Court (withholding medical treatment) (No 2)* [1996] 2 IR 79 (SC).

35 n 22 above.

36 Convention for the Protection of Human Rights and Fundamental Freedoms, 213 UNTS 222 (ECHR). On the relationship between Irish constitutional law and the ECHR, see M Cahill '*McD v L* and the incorporation of the European Convention on Human Rights' (2010) 45 *Irish Jurist* 221; O Doyle & D Ryan 'Judicial interpretation of the European Convention on Human Rights Act 2003: Reflections and analysis' (2011) 33 *Dublin University Law Journal* 369.

37 See DR Phelan *Revolt or revolution: The constitutional boundaries of the European Community* (1997) 317 - 319.

Waiver of constitutional rights is another potential area for development by analogy with South African constitutional jurisprudence: Butler (n 1 above) 94, 99. See W Binchy 'Autonomy, commitment and marriage' in O Doyle & W Binchy (eds) *Committed relationships and the law* (2007) 177.

precept consistently or regularly. There is a firm constitutional base for not only allowing, but mandating, the courts to enforce rights where the state is not a direct protagonist. In his review of Irish case-law, Sibo Banda found three common features supporting this conclusion: first, there is a clear constitutional duty on the state to ensure, and an individual has a corresponding right to seek, the protection and enforcement of a constitutional right; second, the satisfaction of obligations and the exercise of individual rights is not confined to the vertical relationship an individual has with the state but will also arise out of the horizontal relationship private individuals have with each other; third, the term 'State' under the Constitution includes the judiciary and so it is also expected to vindicate constitutional rights.[38] The Hohfeldian view of jural relations can be commended, as it casts light on important distinctions within legal reasoning and avoids any commitment to a highly contestable view of justice and policy.[39]

The positive obligations on the State to implement human rights are wider than have been recognised by the courts in Ireland. The key place played by accountability in a democracy has been emphasised by the South African judiciary, but as of yet the Irish prosecuting and enforcement authorities have been slow to change the culture of forgiving what at its mildest has been gross mismanagement of the financial sector without demanding even a plausible public explanation. Individuals are answerable for their actions to the people through the courts.

9.5 Remedies

The range of remedies utilised by the Irish courts could be expanded in line with those used in South Africa and Canada. If a court finds that the existing law does not uphold constitutional rights, but that there are policy choices to be made in arriving at a solution, it would enhance democracy if it made a declaration of constitutional incompatibility and allowed the legislature

38 S Banda 'Taking indirect horizontality seriously in Ireland: A time to magnify the nuance' (2009) 31 *Dublin University Law Journal* 263 at 276.

39 NE Simmonds *Central issues in jurisprudence: Justice, law and rights* (2008) 308. See G Hogan & G Whyte *JM Kelly: The Irish Constitution* (2004) [7.1.109]-[7.1.111].

time to debate and enact legislation to address the lacuna in the law.[40] In South Africa words can be read into legislation to make it compatible with the Constitution.[41] The approach that emerged in Ireland in 2011 in *G v District Judge Murphy* of giving an effective remedy by looking at 'the heart of the objective' of the constitutional provision[42] should be replicated by more judges and they could also embrace some of the remedies employed in South Africa.

As suggested in the South African jurisprudence, a more coherent values-driven structure could be created for ascertaining the appropriate level of damages for defamation and catastrophic injuries. Alternative reconciliatory remedies for defamation could also be considered. The attempts to encourage mediation to reach mutually acceptable solutions should be continued.

40 *Eg*, the Canadian Supreme Court suspended a declaration of invalidity of offending legislation for 12 months: *Trociuk v British Columbia (AG)* 2003 SCC 34, [2003] 1 SCR 835 [46]. The South African Constitutional Court took a similar stance to allow parliament to correct the defect in the common law definition of marriage to the extent that it did not permit same-sex couples to enjoy the status and the benefits coupled with responsibilities accorded to heterosexual couples: *Minister of Home Affairs v Fourie* 2006 1 SA 524 [162]. Where provisions in road accident legislation were unconstitutional, the Court made a declaration of invalidity, but suspended it for 18 months to allow Parliament to cure the defect; if Parliament failed to do so, the declaration would not apply retrospectively to claims finally settled or adjudicated before the date of judgment: *Mvumvu v Minister of Transport* [2011] ZACC 1, 2011 2 SA 473 (CC) [53]-[54], [57].

41 *Eg*, the Constitutional Court re-phrased the statute to correct an invalid reverse onus of proof, which was not justified under the limitations clause as the intrusion on the presumption of innocence of a person accused of receiving stolen goods was too sweeping: *S v Manamela* 2000 3 SA 1 (CC) [59].

42 [2011] IEHC 445 [36]-[37]. More than 20 years earlier, Keane J had thought that where the constitutional validity of an Act was questioned, the High Court was confined to declaring the Act or the offending provision invalid in its entirely and he did not accept that he could declare that rights had not been vindicated by the Oireachtas in the expectation that the Oireachtas would take the necessary steps to ensure that those rights were in fact protected: *Somjee v Minister for Justice* [1981] ILRM 324 (HC) 327. Hogan J in *G v District Judge Murphy* disagreed with this view, as it could compromise the capacity of the courts to provide an effective remedy where the Oireachtas had breached Article 40.1 by unjustly conferring a privilege or benefit on one select group of society: above, [36]. On the contrary, he noted that by requiring the problems created by unconstitutional omissions to be either judicially resolved or legislatively addressed, the courts contributed to 'the proper and effective functioning of the political process in the manner envisaged by the Constitution': above, [38]. He proposed a form of declaration regarding the scope of application of the legislation thereby remedying a legislative omission that would confine the invalidity to the plaintiffs' circumstances: above, [40], [45]. This would be 'a healthy feature of the separation of powers' and 'advance the dialogue between the three branches of government': above, [39]. The Oireachtas could amend the legislation in future to deal with the gap exposed in the case under review and any other gaps that might become apparent: above, [45].

9.6 Constitutional imperatives

To allow the Constitution reach its full potential, some legal principles, such as the interpretative techniques employed by the courts, proportionality and accountability, can be developed further. The refashioning of torts would also be beneficial. This section will consider each of these in turn.

9.6.1 Interpretation of the Constitution

A broad purposeful interpretation is necessary to give full effect to the spirit of a constitution and to its underlying values. The literal or historical views are inappropriate.[43] The courts in South Africa and other democracies have demonstrated the effectiveness of a wider ambit in having a significant impact on society while upholding individual rights.

Dingake J, with the support of jurisprudence from the US, captured the need to adapt to change and to make fundamental values meaningful by a wide understanding of a constitution in this passage from *Diau*:[44]

> The provisions of our Bill of Rights are not time-worn adages. We (judiciary) must implement those provisions in a dynamic and purposeful manner that does not lag behind societal developments. If we don't, the words of the constitution will be beholden to the values of the past, not the present.

A harmonious interpretation of rights can give the best effect possible to all of them, taking into account the interests of all parties and of society. This approach is preferable to a rigid hierarchy of rights, where rights conflict with each other and one gives way to the other. The African concept of *ubuntu* is a useful guide, as the individual is seen as a member of the community – but not at the expense of a sphere of autonomous personal

43 See D Costello 'The Irish judge as law-maker' in D Curtin & D O'Keeffe (eds) *Constitutional adjudication in European Community and national law: Essays for the Hon. Mr. Justice T.F. O'Higgins* (1992) 163 - 165; Hogan (n 22 above) 174 - 176.

44 *Diau v Botswana Building Society* 2003 (2) BLR 409 (BwIC) (Botswana Industrial Court) 44.

intimacy honed by a rational mind. Harmony involves a balanced mutual connectedness, but is not uniformity.[45]

In *Roche v Roche* Denham J favoured a harmonious interpretation of the Constitution[46] that would avoid a conflict between different provisions in it.[47] Hardiman J in the same case adopted a similar type of construction and was satisfied that two different analyses (a linguistic one and one based on the authorities) of Article 40.3.3° led harmoniously to the same conclusion.

Unfortunately the ultimate aim of harmonising rights is not always achievable.[48] Having analysed case-law in the US and South Africa, Daniel Erskine presented a universal method to resolve conflicting rights.[49] There are five steps involved in this process – first, define the issues by identifying the specific fundamental rights in conflict; second, classify them by evaluating each fundamental right against the background of the legal text containing the right; third, discern the policy and function of each right by establishing its aim and whether that aim is achieved under the factual scenario presented; fourth, see if equal respect for the fundamental rights in issue can be achieved by looking to whether both rights may harmoniously coexist through equal enforcement; finally, if harmonisation is not possible and the rights cannot coexist, resolve the conflict by applying the most rational and pragmatic construction of the rights to establish an amalgamated solitary right employing the most significant ends of the two conflicting rights.[50]

A systematic interpretation using a holistic understanding of fundamental rights where dignity, equality and liberty are seen as a triangle as in South

45 SC Angle 'Human rights and harmony' (2008) 30 *Human Rights Quarterly* 76 at 79. Harmony recognises an interconnectedness based in our complementary differences rather than seeing all as equivalent in value: as above. The value of harmony is in its ability to preserve and respect differences: above, 80. It demands a situationally appropriate reaction to ever-changing circumstances where continual growth occurs, requiring that it be seen as multidimensional and dynamic, and looks to the longer-term impact of short-term solutions: above, 87, 89 - 90.

46 [2009] IESC 82, [2010] 2 IR 321 [147], citing *Tormey v Ireland* [1985] IR 289 (SC) 296 (Henchy J).

47 n 46 above, [147], citing *State (DPP) v Walsh* [1981] IR 412 (SC) 425 (O'Higgins CJ).

48 Constitutional rights to a fair trial took priority over the constitutional duty to promote an accused child's welfare rights: *DPP (Murphy) v PT* [1999] 3 IR 254 (HC) 270 - 271.

49 DH Erskine 'Judgments of the United States Supreme Court and the South African Constitutional Court as a basis for a universal method to resolve conflicts between fundamental rights' (2008) 22 *St John's Journal of Legal Commentary* 595 at 596.

50 n 49 above, 639 - 640.

Africa is recommended by Susanne Baer.[51] Confusion may arise by dignity being regarded as a status, which some have and others do not, rather than being inherent and incapable of being waived.[52] Hence it is all-important that judges clarify the sense in which they are using the concept of dignity and give content to the concept.[53] The holistic understanding where human dignity draws rights together is a reminder of their indivisibility.[54] The involvement of human dignity, which is multi-dimensional, facilitates adapting to changing times, whether that is growth of society in general or working through different phases or experiences in people's lives.[55]

The Irish courts have not developed a coherent approach to constitutional interpretation. Oran Doyle concluded that in Irish constitutional law, 'methods of interpretation function as *ex post facto* justifications for intuitively reached conclusions rather than as fetters on judicial power.'[56] It is important to have a strong judiciary respected by the public and the politicians.[57] As David Gwynn Morgan stated, continuation of that respect is conditional on the judges' decisions being perceived as derived from some clearly articulated,

51 S Baer 'Dignity, liberty, equality: A fundamental rights triangle of constitutionalism' (2009) 59 *University of Toronto Law Journal* 417 at 418, 420, 446. This contrasts with imagining them as a pyramid where dignity is foundational and equality and liberty are elaborations of dignity: above, 447. It is also preferable to seeing equality and liberty as competing items to be balanced on a scale where one trumps the other and dignity is absent: above, 448. Baer's model is beyond isolated rights: above, 418 - 419. While the pyramid founded on human dignity is a good starting point for ethical considerations, it is removed from daily injustices and may fail to protect less severe cases of inhumane treatment: above, 447. Liberty is limited by the presence of others and is only sensible when connected with equality and based on recognition of dignity as self-determination: above, 449. Dignity can sometimes be too abstract and foster paternalism by imposing the majority view of moral conduct on all: above, 457. The benefits of the triangle approach are explained by Baer, '[f]undamental rights, if seen in light of one another, serve as reciprocal warnings against the isolated use of any one of them, or of any right merely to trump another. Each fundamental right has distinct meaning; yet they are not alone but are better understood as relating to one another, like a triangle.': above, 468.

52 n 51 above, 457 - 458.

53 S Cowen 'Can "dignity" guide South Africa's equality jurisprudence?' (2001) 17 *South African Journal on Human Rights* 34 at 54.

54 C Dupré 'Unlocking human dignity: towards a theory for the 21st century' [2009] *European Human Rights Law Review* 190 at 202.

55 Dupré (n 54 above) 198 - 201. A more time-sensitive approach to rights is often signalled by references to the importance of human dignity: Dupré (n 54 above) 199.

56 O Doyle *Constitutional law: Text, cases and materials* (2008) [17-32].

57 DG Morgan 'Judicial activism – Too much of a good thing' in T Murphy & P Twomey (eds) *Ireland's evolving constitution, 1937 - 1997: Collected essays* (1998) 119.

consistently followed and rationally grounded principles.[58] By devising and implementing guidelines for the interpretation and enforcement of fundamental rights – starting as outlined here – the courts could secure an esteemed position as powerful defenders of constitutional values. The judiciary might regenerate life in many long-dormant provisions of the Constitution and nurture them so that they realise their potential to transform our economy into a more equal and just society.

9.6.2 Proportionality

Since human dignity is an inherent trait, it is not always appropriate to lessen its protection by balancing it against other rights.[59] A harmonious interpretation of rights is the ideal aim. But in less extreme situations a properly applied proportionality test is a principled systematic way of resolving conflicts.[60] The South African[61] and Canadian courts have employed a proportionality analysis which takes into account the context and is adaptable to different situations. Although rigid fixed rules are not appropriate when making value judgments, the methodology has to be objective and not left to the discretion of the individual judge.[62] Human

58 As above. See Costello (n 43 above) 161; N McCarthy 'Observations on the protection of fundamental rights in the Irish Constitution' in Curtin & O'Keeffe (n 43 above) 181.

59 *Eg*, torture, which is an extreme invasion of dignity, is not conducive to balancing and does not meet the standard of proportionality commonly applied in liberty cases: Baer (n 51 above) 467.

60 See DG Morgan *A judgment too far? Judicial activism and the Constitution* (2001) 101 - 102.

61 The Constitutional Court endorsed its adoption of proportionality, when it set the standard to be met by the limitations provision in the new Constitution as 'the conceptual requirement established by international norms relative to proportionality or balancing': *Certification of the Constitution of the Republic of South Africa, 1996* 1996 4 SA 744 [90]. Chaskalson P had outlined the process in *Makwanyane* (n 10 above) [104] (footnote omitted):

> The limitation of constitutional rights for a purpose that is reasonable and necessary in a democratic society involves the weighing up of competing values, and ultimately an assessment based on proportionality. ... The fact that different rights have different implications for democracy... means that there is no absolute standard which can be laid down for determining reasonableness and necessity. Principles can be established, but the application of those principles to particular circumstances can only be done on a case by case basis. This is inherent in the requirement of proportionality, which calls for the balancing of different interests.

On application of the proportionality principle in the Constitutional Court, see Sachs (n 32 above) 208 - 209, 211.

62 Albie Sachs (writing extrajudicially) stated that the South African Constitutional Court's role in reconciling the diverse interests in an open democratic society led to

dignity is an invaluable and essential yardstick in the proportionality exercise, as it embodies and encodes elements of balancing.[63]

Irish judges have tended to apply the proportionality principle with deference to the legislature on the objective and the means. They have ignored the impact of the measures, although there have been some exceptions.[64] Proportionality should be applied systematically as a standard, not a rule.[65] The South African or Canadian models could be adapted in Ireland to provide a robust framework.[66]

There are signs of a change to a more stringent analysis of executive decisions in the Supreme Court. In *Meadows v Minister for Justice, Equality and Law Reform*, Murray CJ, endorsing use of the proportionality principle in association with a reasonableness standard, stated, '[a]pplication of the principle of proportionality is in my view a means of examining whether the decision meets the test of reasonableness.'[67] A similar stance was taken by Denham J, who said, '[a] decision which interferes with constitutional rights, if it is to be considered reasonable, should be proportionate.'[68] However, the Court was sharply divided with Hardiman J in dissent objecting to the effective introduction of the substance of an anxious scrutiny formula into Irish law. Kearns J (also dissenting) asserted that the proportionality test

abstract legal reasoning giving way to a form of adjudication in which purpose, context, impact and values took centre-stage, but '[t]his did not mean that principled legal argument and ... legal coherence gave way to vague and subjective notions of the good and the desirable': n 32 above, 202 - 203. He continued, '[i]t became more necessary than ever to spell out the objective principles and factual material on which the judgment relied': n 32 above, 203.

63 Sachs (n 32 above) 203.

64 See R Walsh 'The Constitution, property rights and proportionality: A reappraisal' (2009) 31 *Dublin University Law Journal* 1 at 28 - 29.

65 Walsh (n 64 above) 33.

66 See *Enright v Ireland* [2003] 2 IR 321 (HC) 342.

67 [2010] IESC 3. He indicated that a purely formulaic decision of the executive may not be a sufficient statement of the rationale or reasons underlying a decision and that an administrative decision affecting rights and obligations should at least disclose the essential rationale on foot of which the decision was taken. The Court in *Meadows* raised the standard of scrutiny in judicial review decisions affecting fundamental rights: J Mortimer 'Standard of scrutiny raised in judicial review decisions' (2010) 104(3) *Gazette of the Law Society of Ireland* 10 at 13.

The South African Constitutional Court, reiterating its commitment to proportionality, stated, '[t]here can be no absolute standard for determining reasonableness': *Manamela* (n 41 above) [33].

had no role to play in determining whether a court should intervene to quash the kind of administrative decision in issue.[69]

A contentious issue which could very well be subject to litigation in the future is the vetting procedure for people operating in roles where they have contact with children and the vulnerable.[70] A proportionality analysis will be relevant to ascertain if the information used breaches the rights of teachers, social workers and volunteers to their good name, to earn a living and to privacy,[71] as well as a fair trial and the presumption of innocence.[72]

9.6.3 The democratic mandate for accountability

The requirement for accountability stems from acceptance of personal responsibility for the consequences of decisions made.[73] Democracy necessitates respect for the dignity of individuals by enabling the participation of all in society, listening to their views, making decisions taking their opinions into account, and informing them of the reasons for the conclusions.[74]

68 n 67 above, [40].

69 He described it as 'a decision on an *ad misericordiam* plea made after two merit-based hearings which were not themselves challenged.' In his view, the proportionality test was more appropriate to determine if a statutory provision was compatible with the Constitution or to consider if it invaded a constitutional right more than is necessary.

70 See F Mawe 'Innocent until proven guilty – or not?' (2010) 104(4) *Gazette of the Law Society of Ireland* 20. Vetting has become widespread and extends beyond employers, voluntary organisations and church groups to universities, where it is applied to students in some courses: above, 21.

71 In assessing the state's obligations concerning respect for private life under the ECHR, regard must be had to the fair balance that has to be struck between the competing interests of the individual and of the community as a whole, the aims of the restrictions in the ECHR being relevant: *A v Ireland* (App no 25579/05) (2011) 53 EHRR 13 [247], citing ECHR (n 36 above) Art 8(2).

72 Mawe (n 70 above) 20. The Irish courts held that a statutory restriction on the right to silence was justified because there was a proper proportionality between the restriction and the entitlement of the State to protect itself: *Heaney v Ireland* [1996] 1 IR 580 (SC) 590, aff'g [1994] 3 IR 593 (HC) 610. This was not accepted by the European Court of Human Rights, which found that the provision extinguished the very essence of the rights to silence and against self-incrimination: *Heaney v Ireland* (App no 34720/97) (2001) 33 EHRR 12 [55], [58].

73 In organisational terms, the principle that social power should be blocked from directly seizing administrative power finds expression in the principle of democratic accountability that occupants of political offices have vis-à-vis voters and parliaments: J Habermas *Between facts and norms: Contributions to a discourse theory of law and democracy* trans W Rehg (1998) 175.

74 Privileged access to the sources of knowledge used in policymaking and administration makes possible an inconspicuous domination over the colonised public of citizens cut off from these sources and placated with symbolic politics: Habermas (n 73 above) 317.

When things go wrong, there is a call for identifying the wrongdoers in order to hold them accountable.[75] In a democratic society, those responsible are answerable to the populace for the consequences of their lapse and, in the interests of the common good, should make reparation for the harm they have caused. Autonomy, which is a feature of dignity, endows an individual with the right to act in accordance with rational choices, subject to respecting a similar right in other members of society. There is an accompanying duty on individuals to accept responsibility for the results of their actions. They are accountable and ought to accept the obligation to make good the injury caused by their failings. If they do not do so and are not pursued by the state until they have made amends, their dignity as human beings is not being respected and they are being treated as less than equal adults.[76]

The principle of accountability is apposite in recessionary Ireland. Whatever solution is reached by the government as representatives of the Irish people in the global marketplace for solving the complicated economic, financial and human issues attributable to reckless lending and what was in retrospect foolish borrowing, society is entitled to have the causes of the problem investigated and those responsible held to account. Where there is sufficient evidence of breaches of the criminal law, charges must be brought. In civil law, the culprits are liable to pay compensation, which democratic principles require that they do to the extent that they are able. To salvage some degree of self-respect and respect for the rest of the community, they could utilise their skills to the utmost to assist in resolving the ills they have caused to others and to society in general, which has been burdened with a financial millstone for at least a decade.

There is no outward sign of the principle of accountability having been put into practice yet. Democracy and dignity suffers because of this undue forbearance.

75 See DG Morgan 'Enforcing public accountability: A *tour d'horizon*' (2009) 27 *Irish Law Times* 71.

76 On the right to equal treatment in the political process, see *O'Donovan v AG* [1961] IR 114 (HC) 137; *McKenna v An Taoiseach (No 2)* [1995] 2 IR 10 (SC) 52 - 53; *Coughlan v Broadcasting Complaints Commission* [2000] 3 IR 1 (HC, SC); *Kelly v Minister for the Environment* [2002] IEHC 38, [2002] IESC 73, [2002] 4 IR 191; *Green Party v Radio Telefís Éireann* [2003] 1 IR 558 (HC); *Ring v AG* [2004] IEHC 14, [2004] 1 IR 185; *King v Minister for the Environment (No 2)* [2006] IESC 61, [2007] 1 IR 296.

9.6.4 Refashion torts

Drawing on the experience of the South African courts, it is clear that the law of torts could be refashioned. The Constitutional Court has explored the circumstances in which the common law should advance incrementally with the courts effecting the required change in tune with the spirit of the Constitution.[77] In *S v Thebus*, Moseneke J described two instances where the need to develop the common law arises: first, when a rule of the common law is inconsistent with a constitutional provision, its repugnancy would compel an adaptation of the common law to resolve the inconsistency; second, when a rule of the common law is not inconsistent with a specific constitutional provision but falls short of its spirit, purport and objects, the common law must be adapted so that it grows in harmony with the constitution's 'objective normative value system'.[78] Not every development of the common law means a complete change of the rule or the introduction of a new rule.[79] O'Regan J in *K v Minister of Safety and Security* explained what happens in cases that fall beyond the scope of an existing rule:[80]

> A court faced with a new set of facts, not on all fours with any set of facts previously adjudicated, must decide whether a common-law rule applies to this new factual situation or not. If it holds that the new set of facts falls within the rule, the ambit of the rule is extended. If it holds that it does not, the ambit of the rule is restricted, not extended.

She emphasised the constitutional imperative to infuse the common law with constitutional values requiring the courts 'to be alert to the normative framework of the Constitution not only when some startling new development of the common law is in issue, but in all cases where the incremental development of the rule is in issue.'[81]

77 See SA Dersso 'The role of courts in the development of the common law under s 39(2): *Masiya v. Director of Public Prosecutions Pretoria (The State) and Another* CCT case 54/06 (10 May 2007)' (2007) 23 *South African Journal on Human Rights* 373.

78 2003 6 SA 505 [28]. The common law's incremental development results from the rules of precedent, which derives from a fundamental principle of justice that like cases be determined alike: *K v Minister of Safety and Security* 2005 6 SA 419 (CC) [16].

79 *K* (n 78 above) [16]. Straightforward cases are decided within the framework of an existing rule which the court applies to the set of facts presented: as above.

80 As above. See Banda (n 38 above) 274, 292.

81 n 78 above, [17].

But the Irish courts have been reluctant to apply the Constitution in a positive manner to ensure that the common law promotes constitutional values.[82] In *Hanrahan v Merck Sharp & Dohme (Ireland) Ltd*, the plaintiffs in a nuisance action had an uphill struggle to secure evidence that the cause of ill-health in their farm animals and in themselves as occupiers of the farm resulted from the activities of a nearly factory manufacturing pharmaceuticals.[83] Henchy J felt constrained from shifting the onus of proof to the defendant because Article 40.3 of the Constitution, which placed a duty on the State to defend personal rights, had never been used in the courts to shape the form of any existing tort nor to change the normal onus of proof.[84] He regarded 'the State' as excluding the judiciary and confined the courts' authority to intervene only in the case of inaction by the other arms of government or when the action taken was blatantly inadequate.[85] If a plaintiff sues on the basis of an existing tort, the limitations of that tort normally apply.[86]

Although Henchy J acknowledged in *Hanrahan* that in the absence of a common law or statutory cause of action, a plaintiff could sue directly for breach of a constitutional right,[87] the courts have not devised sufficient alternative remedies based directly on the Constitution. There is scope for more to be done by the articulation of constitutional torts, development of the common law, and a principled-based resumption of declaring unenumerated personal rights under Article 40.3.[88]

82 On the relationship between the Constitution and tort law, see W Binchy '*Meskell*, the Constitution and tort law' (2011) 33 *Dublin University Law Journal* 339.

83 [1988] ILRM 629 (SC). On *Hanrahan*, see Banda (n 38 above) 272 - 276.

84 n 83 above, 636. See W Binchy 'Constitutional remedies and the law of torts' in J O'Reilly (ed) *Human rights and constitutional law: Essays in honour of Brian Walsh* (1992) 204 - 205.

85 '[T]he courts are entitled to intervene only when there has been a failure to implement or, where the implementation relied on is plainly inadequate, to effectuate the constitutional guarantee in question.': n 83 above, 636.

86 As above.

87 n 83 above, 636, citing *Meskell v CIE* [1973] IR 121 (SC).

88 In recent years the courts have shown an antipathy towards declaring any further unenumerated rights. On the debate over the legitimacy of judicial activism in this way and the basis for the recognition of unenumerated rights under Article 40.3.1°, see T Murphy 'Economic inequality and the Constitution' in Murphy & Twomey (n 57 above) 173 - 179.

9.7 Lessons from the comparative study

The courts in Ireland could learn much from the South African courts' thorough examination of the communitarian understanding of dignity. The Irish Constitution contains similar (though less prominent) norms with the person placed in society where participants have reciprocal rights and duties. The lessons from South Africa could be applied in many areas, the most pertinent of which will be summarised in this section.

The equality guarantee in Article 40.1 of the Constitution if aligned with dignity could be rescued from its continuous subordination to other constitutional rights such as freedom of association.[89] South Africa enforces substantive equality which is transformative – it is not just the process equality that applies in Ireland.[90] The circumstances when equality rights have horizontal application affecting private individuals might be explored in a contextual objective enquiry to yield a structured body of jurisprudence for future guidance.[91] Discrimination against women and vulnerable groups – particularly Travellers, homosexuals, migrants and asylum seekers – requires to be addressed.[92] Contrast the outcome in *Norris*[93] with that in the South African *Sodomy* case[94] – dignity did not feature in the judgment of the majority in *Norris*.[95]

As has occurred in South Africa and as is mandated by the constitutional obligation on the judiciary to intervene to ensure vindication of constitutionally protected rights and values, equality read in the context of

89 *Eg, Equality Authority v Portmarnock Golf Club* [2005] IEHC 235; [2009] IESC 73, [2010] 1 ILRM 237.

90 *Portmarnock Golf Club* (HC) (n 89 above) (see text to n 139 in Ch VIII).

91 Hamilton CJ left this avenue open for development: *Re Article 26 and the Employment Equality Bill 1996* [1997] IESC 6, [1997] 2 IR 321 at 346. See G Whyte 'A comment on the Constitution Review Group's proposals on equality' in R Byrne & W Duncan (eds) *Developments in discrimination law in Ireland and Europe* (1997) 103 - 105.

92 Legislation obliging clubs to adopt and implement equality plans in targeted sectors such as gender, disability, race and cultural background – certainly where clubs receive public benefits – modelled on the South African Promotion of Equality and Prevention of Unfair Discrimination Act 2000 would be a move in the right direction: see 7.10.2 in Ch VII.

93 n 22 above, (see text to n434-n436 in Ch VII).

94 *National Coalition for Gay and Lesbian Equality v Minister of Justice* 1998 12 BCLR 1517 (CC) (see text to n8-n11 in Ch IV and to n357 in Ch V).

95 W Binchy 'The Supreme Court of Ireland' in B Dickson (ed) *Judicial activism in common law supreme courts* (2007) 189 - 190; Binchy (n 3 above) 321 - 322.

the constitutional commitments to social justice, dignity and freedom could lead to the Irish courts consistently upholding socio-economic rights where the State failed to do so.[96] Charlton J's distinction between the State's positive and negative obligations in *Doherty* and his omission to consider the Travellers' identity[97] is in sorry contrast to the Constitutional Court's decision in *Grootboom* where it regarded rights as interrelated and it required the reasonableness of state action concerning the homeless to be assessed in the light of the constitutional value of human dignity.[98] The High Court's lack of consideration for the fate of evicted Travellers in *McDonagh*[99] compares poorly with the Constitutional Court's narrow application of legislation on management of disasters in *Pheko v Ekurhuleni Metropolitan Municipality* where it insisted that the municipal authority resettle those unlawfully evicted in comparable conditions within a stipulated timeframe to be monitored by the Court.[100]

The stereotyping and the denial of constitutional rights on the grounds of civil status to all unmarried fathers (the committed ones as well as the uninvolved) by unreservedly allowing adoption without their consent in *Nicolaou*[101] was not replicated by the Constitutional Court in *Fraser*.[102] Having found that the legislation was discriminatory, the Court ensured the co-operation of the democratic Parliament by giving it time to devise a solution.[103]

96 See Binchy (n 3 above) 318 - 319.

97 *Doherty v South Dublin County Council (No 2)* [2007] IEHC 4, [2007] 2 IR 696 (see text to n506-n516 in Ch VII).

98 *Government of the Republic of South Africa v Grootboom* 2001 1 SA 46 (CC) (see text to n1-n9, n11-n12, n23-n29, n129-n133 and n136-n154 in Ch VI). The concept of reasonableness was central when the Constitutional Court assessed the City's housing policy and found it unconstitutional to the extent that it excluded those evicted by private property owners from consideration for temporary accommodation in emergency situations: *City of Johannesburg Metropolitan Municipality v Blue Moonlight Properties 39 (Pty) Ltd* [2011] ZACC 33 [87].

99 *McDonagh v Kilkenny County Council* [2007] IEHC 350 (see text to n519-n524 in Ch VII).

100 [2011] ZACC 34 (CC) [53].

101 *State (Nicolaou) v An Bord Uchtála* [1966] IR 567 (SC).

102 *Fraser v Children's Court Pretoria North* [1997] ZACC 1, 1997 2 SA 218 (CC) (see text to n297-n299 in Ch VII). Notwithstanding the growth in cohabitation, the distinction in Irish law between the constitutional recognition given to the natural mothers' personal right to custody of their children and the very limited right vested in natural fathers continues: *JMcB v LE* [2010] IEHC 123, [2010] 4 IR 433 [100], [105].

103 n 102 above, [52].

Makwanyane established decisively that the prohibition of cruel and unusual punishment based on 'the dignity of man' meant that people should not be humiliated physically or mentally.[104] If tolerated by the state (even when it occurs without any direct state involvement), the failure to insist on civilised standards offends all in society. Whether corporal punishment should be forbidden in the home is a contentious topic in many countries (South Africa and Ireland included).[105] There has been much international condemnation of Ireland for not prohibiting corporal punishment within the family. It is time that Ireland banned all chastisement in the home in response to the international denunciation and the many calls for change. Combined with an educational campaign and the promotion of alternative forms of discipline, a legal prohibition could headline a change in attitudes.

Similarly, the government has procrastinated for too long in heeding the denouncements of overcrowding and bad conditions in prison.[106] The Irish courts must stop their naïve indulgence of the executive by relying on it to address the State's failure to respect prisoners' dignity – at this stage there is no justification for the toleration of humiliating practices like slopping out and the deterioration of overcrowded conditions to such an extent that assaults on fellow prisoners are more likely to occur.[107] The South African courts' century-old tradition of recognising the residual rights of prisoners (expressed so well by Innes J in *Whittaker v Roos*)[108] and the judiciary's post-apartheid practice of engaging with the executive to ensure that infringements of human dignity do not continue provide a good template for Ireland.[109] As

104 n 10 above, (see text to n412 in Ch III).

105 See 4.2.1 in Ch IV and 7.6.1 in Ch VII. The Court did not deal with this aspect in *Christian Education South Africa v Minister of Education* 2000 4 SA 757 (CC). The tension between protection of the child and state intrusion in family life was evident in the Constitutional Court when the majority held that the lack of automatic review on taking a child into temporary care was unconstitutional: *C v Department of Health and Social Development, Gauteng* [2012] ZACC 1 (CC).

106 See 7.4.1 in Ch VII. The United States Supreme Court in a majority decision affirmed a lower court order to the State of California to reduce its prison population to 137.5% of design capacity within two years and to submit a compliance plan for court approval: *Brown v Plata* 131 S Ct 1910 (2011) 1923, 1928, 1947.

107 MacMenamin J's narrow view that prisoners only had a negative right to be protected against state intervention, which required that *mala fides* be demonstrated to prove a breach of duty, fails to take into account the State's positive obligation to vindicate personal rights – an 'evil purpose' is not a prerequisite for a violation: *Mulligan v Governor of Portlaoise Prison* [2010] IEHC 269.

108 1912 AD 92 (SC).

109 See 5.2.2 in Ch V.

prisoners lose the freedom to regulate their own situation when incarcerated, there is a particular duty on the State to protect them while they are in its custody. Happily there are signs that change may be on the way, as seen in Hogan J's handling of *Kinsella*.[110]

But no such change of direction can be observed in the case-law concerning the civil liability of the State for the failure of the police to protect human rights.[111] Instead of requiring *mala fides* to establish an actionable failure and granting virtual blanket immunity from liability for botched police investigations as in *G v Minister for Justice Equality and Law Reform*,[112] the Irish courts should apply the fair, just and reasonable criterion as an element of the duty of care and could follow the path taken in *Carmichele*.[113] At least the courts should ensure that the police are answerable for their actions – accountability is a feature of a democratic society. Vindication of personal rights requires more than simply resorting to the established rules of tort without even considering whether the victim has an alternative remedy or can establish accountability before another forum. A remedy only for an intentional breach is insufficient.

If the police or other state employees deviate from the normal performance of their duties and abuse the public, the South African courts' decisions in *K v Minister of Safety and Security*[114] and *F v Minister of Safety and Security*,[115] where they developed the common law on vicarious liability, are exemplars of best practice. When the obligation to protect rights is in issue, the existing boundaries of tort may be inadequate to accommodate the constitutional and statutory duties of the state and of the police; it will also be relevant to consider the context – perhaps the victim was vulnerable, she may have relied on the police for protection and the police may have accepted

110 *Kinsella v Governor of Mountjoy Prison* [2011] IEHC 235.

111 See 8.2.2 in Ch VIII.

112 [2011] IEHC 65.

113 *Carmichele v Minister of Safety and Security* 2001 4 SA 938 (CC) (see text to n236-n243 in Ch IV).

114 n 78 above (see text to n249-n261 in Ch IV).

115 [2011] ZACC 37. The Constitutional Court in a majority decision extended the vicarious liability of the state to cover the wrongful act of a policeman on standby duty because there was a sufficiently close connection between the wrongful conduct and his employment assessed by giving explicit recognition to the norms involved: above, [50], [76], [81]-[82], [88].

that role. This model could be adapted to adjudicate on state liability for abuse where the perpetrator is not a state employee.[116]

The law of privacy is evolving in Ireland. It is desirable to have clear identification of the circumstances when the media can be restricted from publishing private information.[117] The law might be developed along the lines suggested in *NM v Smith* to allow publication of such information where it was reasonable to conclude that consent had been given.[118]

In a different context, the parameters of informed consent established in South Africa in *C v Minister of Correctional Services* could be applied if a prisoner challenged the voluntariness of consent to a HIV test.[119] Legislation regulating research and controlling the use of human tissue modelled on the South African National Health Act 2003 would bring legal certainty in a potentially contentious sphere in Ireland.[120] The new legislation could also regulate artificial insemination and *in vitro* fertilisation to deal in an orderly manner with the rights and duties of donors and to avoid disputes over access and guardianship.[121] The European Court of Human Rights upheld a prohibition of *in vitro* fertilisation using donor sperm or ova in *SH v Austria*, but it alerted states to keep the law under review in this continuously evolving area which is subject to dynamic scientific and legal developments.[122]

If a referendum is held to remove the blasphemy provision from the Irish Constitution, it could be replaced by a provision modelled on that in the South African Constitution which excludes hate speech from the protection

116 The factors considered by the Supreme Court in *O'Keeffe* (n 28 above) and in *Reilly* (n 28 above) were too limited – social justice was ignored: see 7.3.2 in Ch VII. Additional elements here should be the responsibility of the state for the *system* that created the relationship between the victim and the perpetrator as well as the role of efficient loss distribution in tort liability.

117 The High Court indicated that, even though the media is free to publish information regardless of public interest, freedom of expression can be curtailed to stop widespread offensive publicity of very personal or private information which could be humiliating, violate dignity or injure the claimant's feelings to a significant extent: *Hickey v Sunday Newspapers Ltd* [2010] IEHC 349, citing *Hosking v Runting* [2004] NZCA 34, [2005] 1 NZLR 1 [125]-[127]. For the right to privacy to prevail, there must be a legitimate expectation of privacy and publication must not be justified by legitimate public concern: as above.

118 2007 5 SA 250 (CC) (see text to n174-n185 in Ch V).

119 1996 4 SA 292 (T) (High Court) (see text to n453-n457 in Ch VII).

120 See text to n427-n428 in Ch VII.

121 See 7.6.3 in Ch VII.

122 (App no 57813/00) ECHR 3 November 2011 [118].

afforded to freedom of expression.[123] The diverse character of an increasingly multi-cultural society demands more tolerance for the expression of dissenting views than in the past.[124] After more than two decades in operation, it is time to review the Irish legislation prohibiting incitement to hatred,[125] which has proven to be inadequate to deal with changes in technology and the advent of social networking since then.[126] As was done in South Africa in 2000, consideration could be given to widening the concept of hate speech to cover discriminatory speech undermining human dignity where the intention is to be hurtful.[127]

The Constitutional Court unanimously developed the law of defamation in *Le Roux v Dey* to allow the court to order an apology where there has been an impairment of actionable dignity in personal relationships,[128] but this development has not extended yet to media defendants.[129] Irish law could be expanded on the same basis, although the issue of whether the media should be ordered to apologise will need more thorough examination. Even if the bold step of a court-ordered apology is not taken, quantum should be reduced where an apology has been made or offered.[130] Similarly in cases of catastrophic injuries the unaware plaintiff could receive a smaller award than a fully-conscious person.[131]

The law of contract might be refined by applying constitutional values to re-assess the unequal bargaining position of the ordinary citizen with banks and other powerful institutions.[132] However, as in South Africa, courts generally are reluctant to interfere with a *free, equal* and *informed* bargaining

123 See text to n652-n655 in Ch VII.

124 The margin of appreciation given by the European Court of Human Rights has narrowed from its decisions in *Otto-Preminger Institute v Austria* (App no 13470/87) (1995) 19 EHRR 34 and *Wingrove v UK* (App no 17419/90) (1997) 24 EHRR 1: see text to n648-n651 in Ch VII.

125 See n634 in Ch VII.

126 S Cummiskey '"Face-booked": Anti-social networking and the law' (2011) 105(9) *Gazette of the Law Society of Ireland* 16.

127 See n655 in Ch VII.

128 [2011] ZACC 4, 2011 3 SA 274 (CC) [10], [195]-[203]. The Court reduced the amount of damages and ordered an apology.

129 In *The Citizen 1978 (Pty) Ltd v McBride* the Court did not order a newspaper to apologise and left open the question of whether it was appropriate to do so where a media defendant has defamed: [2011] ZACC 11, 2011 4 SA 191 (CC) [134].

130 See text to n176-n179 in Ch IV and to n28-n34 in Ch VIII.

131 See 8.1.1.2 in Ch VIII.

132 See 7.10.3 - 7.10.4 in Ch VII.

process. In *Everfresh Market Virginia (Pty) Ltd v Shoprite Checkers (Pty) Ltd* all the judges agreed in principal that constitutional values should infuse contract law to ensure that justice is done – particularly when poor vulnerable people are involved in negotiations with powerful companies.[133]

Extension of the range of remedies[134] and the remoulding of tort as pioneered in South Africa would be a welcome improvement.[135] The Irish courts could play a more active role in holding the State accountable as is essential in a well-functioning democracy.[136] The State should ensure that corporations and individuals are held to account civilly and (where appropriate) criminally before the courts.[137] The establishment and resourcing of independent bodies to investigate white-collar crime and corruption would improve the democratic process.[138]

If the Irish courts embraced the values enshrined in the Constitution in as enthusiastic a fashion as the judiciary in South Africa, the effect on the community and on the individuals in it could be quite dramatic. It would lead to a more open society embracing wholeheartedly minority viewpoints and cultures. There is much potential for the Irish judiciary to develop the case-law on the Constitution to give effect to its underlying values.[139] It is the role of all three branches of government to uphold the principles supporting a society of equals in a representative democracy.[140] While it is the duty of

133 [2011] ZACC 30, 2012 1 SA 256 (CC) [23]-[24], [48], [71]-[72]. The majority held that this was not a suitable case in which to decide the issue of whether constitutional values required that the common law must be adapted to impose a duty on a lessor and a lessee to negotiate renewal of a lease and a rent review in good faith in compliance with a clause in the lease.

134 See text to n40-n42 above.

135 See 9.6.4 above.

136 *Eg, Rail Commuters Action Group v Transnet Ltd t/a Metrorail* 2005 2 SA 359 (CC) (see text to n 73 in Ch V), *Mazibuko v City of Johannesburg* [2009] ZACC 28 (CC) (see text to n245-n270 in Ch VI).

137 See 9.6.3 above.

138 On the requirement for independence (of an anti-corruption unit in this case), see *Glenister v President of the Republic of South Africa* [2011] ZACC 6, 2011 3 SA 347 (CC).

139 The task of the framers of constitutions is to discover and express the fundamental jural presuppositions of the accommodation that people living together have made and continue to make, while the task of the courts, apart from applying statutes and explicit constitutional provisions, is to discern and express that constitutional accommodation, and the legislators' task is to discover in it the contours of what is just in daily living: G Barden 'Discovering a constitution' in Murphy & Twomey (n 57 above) 9.

140 C Gearty 'Civil liberties and human rights' in N Bamforth & P Leyland (eds) *Public law in a multi-layered constitution* (2003) 389 - 390.

every institution exercising constitutional powers to keep within the limits of those powers, it is the duty of the courts to say what these limits are.[141] Judges are obliged to defend the constitution when required, and it is a breach of their constitutional duties if they do not act decisively to defend the human dignity, equality and liberty of the vulnerable. A mutually supportive relationship could develop between the judiciary and the executive, as the courts are relatively immune from public opinion and in a position to enforce or declare fundamental rights that may perhaps be unpopular with the majority of society, while politicians could point to the judiciary as the *raison d'être* for the change.

A body of jurisprudence developed incrementally and grounded on lucid consistent rationales would fulfil the judiciary's obligation to ensure that the Constitution's reach is not unduly confined and that it achieves its transformative potential in private relationships. In a well-functioning legal system, the case-law will be refined and adapted to cope with the intricate dilemmas that can occur in a modern technology-driven society. Following the South African model,[142] human dignity viewed in association with equality and liberty would be an excellent guide in this judicial journey.[143]

141 Wheare (n 2 above) 101.

142 The South African, Irish and Australian judiciary have much in common (a culture of judicial independence, conflicts with electorally legitimated actors, a broadly common law tradition, and the privilege of finality): B Flanagan & S Ahern 'Judicial decision-making and transnational law: A survey of common law Supreme Court judges' (2011) 60 *International and Comparative Law Quarterly* 1 at 10.

143 Sibo Banda suggested adding the ideal of justice as personal dignity to the aims of private law in addition to it being seen as corrective justice or the promotion of economic efficiency: n 38 above, 296.

Bibliography

Books

(1991) *Concise Oxford dictionary of current English, The* 8th edn Oxford University Press: Oxford

Ackerman, BA (1977) *Private property and the Constitution* Yale University Press: New Haven

Ackermann, L (2012) *Human dignity: Lodestar for equality in South Africa* Juta: Cape Town

Alston, P & Goodman, R (2013) *International human rights: the successor to international human rights in context: law, politics and morals* Oxford University Press: Oxford

Bantekas, I (2010) *International criminal law* 4th edn Hart: Oxford

Barendt, EM (2005) *Freedom of speech* 2nd edn Oxford University Press: Oxford

Beatty, DM (2004) *The ultimate rule of law* Oxford University Press: Oxford

Bedi, SRS (2007) *The development of human rights law by the judges of the International Court of Justice* Studies in International Law, Hart: Oxford

Beyleveld, D & Brownsword, R (2001) *Human dignity in bioethics and biolaw* Oxford University Press: Oxford

Binchy, W (1988) *Irish conflicts of law* Butterworths: Dublin

Boyle, J (1996) *Shamans, software, and spleens: Law and the construction of the information society* Harvard University Press: Cambridge, Mass

Brain, JB (1983) *Christian Indians in Natal 1860 - 1911: An historical and statistical study* Human Sciences Research Council Publication Series, Oxford University Press: Cape Town

Brownsword, R (2008) *Rights, regulation and the technological revolution* Oxford University Press: Oxford

Burchell, JM (1998) *Personality rights and freedom of expression: The modern actio injuriarum* Juta: Kenwyn

Byrne, R & Binchy, W (2002) *Annual review of Irish law 2001* Thomson Round Hall: Dublin

Byrne, R & Binchy, W (2007) *Annual review of Irish law 2006* Thomson Round Hall: Dublin
Byrne, R & Binchy, W (2010) *Annual review of Irish law 2009* Round Hall/Thomson Reuters: Dublin
Byrne, R & Binchy, W (2012) *Annual review of Irish law 2011* Round Hall/Thomson Reuters: Dublin
Byrne, R; Hogan, G & McDermott, P (1981) *Prisoners' rights: A study in Irish prison law* Co-Op Books: Dublin
Byrne, R & McCutcheon, JP (2009) *The Irish legal system* 5th edn Bloomsbury Professional: Haywards Heath, West Sussex
Capps, P (2009) *Human dignity and the foundations of international law* Hart: Oxford
Cassidy, C (2010) *Cassidy on the Licensing Acts* 3rd edn Clarus Press: Dublin
Catholic Church (1999) *Catechism of the Catholic Church* Rev edn Geoffrey Chapman: London
Chandra, B (1989) *India's struggle for independence 1857 - 1947* Penguin Books: New Delhi
Charlesworth, H & Chinkin, C (2000) *The boundaries of international law: A feminist analysis* Melland Schill Studies in International Law, Manchester University Press: Manchester
Church, J; Schulze, C & Strydom, H (2007) *Human rights from a comparative and international law perspective* Unisa Press: Pretoria
Clapham, A (2006) *Human rights obligations of non-state actors* Oxford University Press: Oxford
Clark, R (2008) *Contract law in Ireland* 6th edn Thomson Round Hall: Dublin
Cooley, TM (1880) *A treatise on the law of torts* Callaghan & Co: Chicago
Cox, N (2000) *Blasphemy and the law in Ireland* Edwin Mellen Press: Lewiston, NY
Cox, N (2007) *Defamation law* First Law: Dublin
Cox, N; Corbett, V & Ryan, D (2009) *Employment law in Ireland* Clarus Press: Dublin
Craig, P & de Búrca, G (2011) *EU law: Text, cases, and materials* 5th edn Oxford University Press: Oxford
Currie, I & de Waal, J (2005) *The Bill of Rights handbook* 5th edn Juta: Cape Town

Davel, CJ & Jordaan, RA (2005) *Law of persons* 4th edn Juta: Cape Town
Davenport, TRH & Saunders, C (2000) *South Africa: A modern history* 5th edn Macmillan: Basingstoke
Delany, H; Carolan, E & Murphy, C (2008) *The right to privacy: A doctrinal and comparative analysis* Thomson Round Hall: Dublin
de Londras, F & Kelly, C (2010) *European Convention on Human Rights Act: Operation, impact and analysis* Round Hall/Thomson Reuters: Dublin
Dembour, MB (2006) *Who believes in human rights? Reflections on the European Convention* Cambridge University Press: Cambridge
de Than, C & Shorts, E (2003) *International criminal law and human rights* Sweet & Maxwell: London
Devenish, G (1999) *A commentary on the South African Bill of Rights* Butterworths: Durban
Dicey, AV (1915) *Introduction to the study of the law of the constitution* 8th edn Macmillan: London

Dicey, AV; Morris, JHC & Collins, L (2012) *Dicey, Morris and Collins on the conflict of laws* Lord Collins (ed) 15th edn Sweet & Maxwell: London
Donnelly, J (2003) *Universal human rights in theory and practice* 2nd edn Cornell University Press: Ithaca
Doyle, O (2004) *Constitutional equality law* Thomson Round Hall: Dublin
Doyle, O (2008) *Constitutional law: Text, cases and materials* Clarus Press: Dublin
Dugard, J (1978) *Human rights and the South African legal order* Princeton University Press: Princeton
Dworkin, R (1977) *Taking rights seriously* Harvard University Press: Cambridge, Mass; (1978) New Impression with a Reply to Critics edn Duckworth: London
Dworkin, R (1993) *Life's dominion: An argument about abortion and euthanasia* Harper Collins: London
Dworkin, R (1996) *Freedom's law: The moral reading of the American Constitution* Oxford University Press: Oxford
Dworkin, R (2000) *Sovereign virtue: The theory and practice of equality* Harvard University Press: Cambridge, Mass
Dworkin, R (2006) *Justice in robes* Belknap Press of Harvard University Press: Cambridge, Mass

Ebrahim, H (1998) *The soul of a nation: Constitution-making in South Africa* Oxford University Press: Cape Town
Edwards, JLJ (1955) Mens rea *in statutory offences* English Studies in Criminal Science, Macmillan: London
Egan, S (2011) *The United Nations human rights treaty system: Law and procedure* Bloomsbury Professional: Haywards Heath, West Sussex
Enright, M (2007) *Principles of Irish contract law* Clarus Press: Dublin

Falk, RA (1995) *On humane governance: Toward a new global politics* Polity: Cambridge
Fawcett, J & Carruthers, JM (2008) *Cheshire, North & Fawcett: Private international law* P North (ed) 14th edn Oxford University Press: Oxford
Feldman, D (2002) *Civil liberties and human rights in England and Wales* 2nd edn Oxford University Press: Oxford
Finnis, J (2011) *Natural law and natural rights* 2nd edn Clarendon Law Series, Oxford University Press: Oxford
Fleming, JG (1998) *The law of torts* 9th edn LBC Information Services: Sydney
Foley, B (2008) *Deference and the presumption of constitutionality* Institute of Public Administration: Dublin
Foster, C (2011) *Human dignity in bioethics and law* Hart: Oxford
Fredman, S (2008) *Human rights transformed: Positive rights and positive duties* Oxford University Press: Oxford
Fukuyama, F (2002) *Our posthuman future: Consequences of the biotechnology revolution* Profile Books: London

Giliker, P & Beckwith, S (2011) *Tort* 4th edn Sweet & Maxwell's Textbook Series, Sweet & Maxwell: London
Ginnell, L (1894) *The Brehon laws: A legal handbook* TF Unwin: London
Glendenning, D (2012) *Education and the law* 2nd edn Bloomsbury Professional: Haywards Heath, West Sussex

Glendon, MA (1991) *Rights talk: The impoverishment of political discourse* Free Press: New York
Glendon, MA (2001) *A world made new: Eleanor Roosevelt and the Universal Declaration of Human Rights* Random House: New York
Glover, J (2012) *Humanity: A moral history of the twentieth century* 2nd edn Yale University Press: New Haven

Habermas, J (1998) *Between facts and norms: Contributions to a discourse theory of law and democracy* trans W Rehg, Studies in Contemporary German Social Thought, MIT Press: Cambridge, Mass
Hardcastle, R (2009) *Law and the human body: Property rights, ownership and control* Hart: Oxford
Harris, D; O'Boyle, M; Bates, E & Buckley, C (2009) *Harris, O'Boyle & Warbrick: Law of the European Convention on Human Rights* 2nd edn Oxford University Press: Oxford
Hart, HLA (2008) *Punishment and responsibility: Essays in the philosophy of law* 2nd edn Oxford University Press: Oxford
Hepple, A (1966) *South Africa: A political and economic history* Pall Mall Press: London
Heuston, RFV (1977) *Salmond on the law of torts* 17th edn Sweet & Maxwell: London
Heyman, SJ (2008) *Free speech and human dignity* Yale University Press: New Haven
Hicks, D (2011) *Dignity: The essential role it plays in resolving conflict* Yale University Press: New Haven
Hill, TE, Jr (1991) *Autonomy and self-respect* Cambridge University Press: New York
Hill, TE, Jr (1992) *Dignity and practical reason in Kant's moral theory* Cornell University Press: Ithaca
Hogan, G (2012) *The origins of the Irish Constitution: 1928-1941* Royal Irish Academy: Dublin
Hogan, G & Whyte, G (2004) *JM Kelly: The Irish Constitution* 4th edn Tottel Publishing: Dublin
Hogg, PW (2007) *Constitutional law of Canada Vols 1 & 2*, 5th edn Thomson Carswell: Scarborough, Ont
Honoré, T (1999) *Responsibility and fault* Hart: Oxford
Hoyano, L & Keenan, C (2010) *Child abuse: Law and policy across boundaries* Oxford University Press: Oxford
Humphrey, JP (1984) *Human rights and the United Nations: A great adventure* Bowker: Epping
Huttenback, RA (1971) *Gandhi in South Africa: British imperialism and the Indian question, 1860 - 1914* Cornell University Press: Ithaca

Jägers, NMCP (2002) *Corporate human rights obligations: In search of accountability* School of Human Rights Research Series, Intersentia: Antwerpen

Kamali, MH (2002) *The dignity of man: An Islamic perspective* Islamic Texts Society: Cambridge
Kant, I (1985) *The metaphysical elements of justice* trans J Ladd, Macmillan: New York

Kant, I (2005) *The moral law: Groundwork of the metaphysic of morals* trans HJ Paton, Routledge: London

Kateb, G (2011) *Human dignity* Belknap Press of Harvard University Press: Cambridge, Mass

Kaur, G (2006) *Fundamental rights* Shree Publishers & Distributors: New Delhi

Keeton, WP (ed) & Prosser, WL (1984) *Prosser and Keeton on the law of torts* 5th edn Hornbook Series, West Publishing: St Paul, Minn

Kelly, JM (1992) *A short history of Western legal theory* Clarendon Press: Oxford

Kende, MS (2009) *Constitutional rights in two worlds: South Africa and the United States* Cambridge University Press: Cambridge

Keogh, D & McCarthy, AJ (2007) *The making of the Irish Constitution 1937: Bunreacht na hÉireann* Mercier Press: Cork

Klug, H (2010) *The Constitution of South Africa: A contextual analysis* Hart: Oxford

Laurie, GT (2002) *Genetic privacy: A challenge to medico-legal norms* Cambridge University Press: Cambridge

Livingstone, S; Owen, T & Macdonald, A (2008) *Prison law* 4th edn Oxford University Press: Oxford

Loveland, I (1999) *By due process of law? Racial discrimination and the right to vote in South Africa, 1855 - 1960* Hart: Oxford

McDermott, PA (2000) *Prison law* Round Hall Sweet & Maxwell: Dublin

McDermott, PA (2001) *Contract law* Butterworths: Dublin

MacKinnon, CA (2005) *Women's lives, men's laws* Belknap Press of Harvard University Press: Cambridge, Mass

MacKinnon, CA (2006) *Are women human? And other international dialogues* Belknap Press of Harvard University Press: Cambridge, Mass

McMahon, BME & Binchy, W (2013) *Law of torts* 4th edn Bloomsbury Professional: Haywards Heath, West Sussex

McNamara, D (2005) *A legal guide for clubs and associations* First Law: Dublin

Madden, D (2011) *Medicine, ethics and the law* 2nd edn Bloomsbury Professional: Haywards Heath, West Sussex

Mak, C (2008) *Fundamental rights in European contract law: A comparison of the impact of fundamental rights on contractual relationships in Germany, the Netherlands, Italy and England* Private Law in European Context Series, Kluwer Law International: Alphen aan den Rijn

Manning, HE (1934) *The dignity and rights of labour, and other writings on social questions* Burns, Oates & Washbourne: London

Marcus, G (1998) *Incitement to hatred: A Southern African perspective* Media Law & Practice in Southern Africa, Article 19: London

Maritain, J (2001) *Natural law: Reflections on theory and practice* W Sweet (ed) St Augustine's Press: South Bend, Ind

Marks, S (2000) *The riddle of all constitutions: International law, democracy and the critique of ideology* Oxford University Press: Oxford

Meer, F (1975) *The ghetto people: a study of the effects of uprooting the Indian people of South Africa* Studies in the Mass Removal of Population in South Africa No 6, Africa Publications Trust: London

Mehra, S (2006) *Human rights: A Gandhian perspective* Sarup & Sons: New Delhi

Meron, T (1989) *Human rights and humanitarian norms as customary law* Clarendon Press: Oxford

Morgan, DG (1997) *The separation of powers in the Irish Constitution* Round Hall Sweet & Maxwell: Dublin

Morgan, DG (2001) *A judgment too far? Judicial activism and the Constitution* Undercurrents, Cork University Press: Cork

Morgan, DG & Hogan, G (2010) *Administrative law in Ireland* 4th edn Round Hall/Thomson Reuters: Dublin

Morris, H (ed) (1961) *Freedom and responsibility: Readings in philosophy and law* Stanford University Press: Stanford, Calif

Morris, H (1976) *On guilt and innocence: Essays in legal philosophy and moral psychology* University of California Press: Berkeley

Morsink, J (1999) *The Universal Declaration of Human Rights: Origins, drafting, and intent* Pennsylvania Studies in Human Rights, University of Pennsylvania Press: Philadelphia

Motala, Z & Ramaphosa, C (2002) *Constitutional law: Analysis and cases* Oxford University Press: Cape Town

Mubangizi, JC (2004) *The protection of human rights in South Africa: A legal and practical guide* Juta: Lansdowne

Munzer, SR (1990) *A theory of property* Cambridge Studies in Philosophy & Law, Cambridge University Press: Cambridge

Muzaffar, C (2002) *Rights, religion and reform: Enhancing human dignity through spiritual and moral transformation* RoutledgeCurzon: London

Naldi, GJ (1995) *Constitutional rights in Namibia: A comparative analysis with international human rights* Juta: Kenwyn

Nickel, JW (2007) *Making sense of human rights* 2nd edn Blackwell Publishing: Malden, Mass

Okafor, OC (2007) *The African human rights system, activist forces and international institutions* Cambridge University Press: Cambridge

O'Neill, AM (2005) *Irish mental health law* First Law: Dublin

Ormerod, D (2011) *Smith and Hogan's criminal law* 13th edn Oxford University Press: Oxford

Paine, T (1996) *The writings of Thomas Paine Vol III* MD Conway (ed) Routledge/ Thoemmes Press: London

Pandey, JN (2008) *The constitutional law of India* 45th edn Central Law Agency: Allahabad

Peirce, G (2010) *Dispatches from the dark side: On torture and the death of justice* Verso: London

Perry, MJ (1994) *The Constitution in the courts: Law or politics?* Oxford University Press: New York

Perry, MJ (2007) *Toward a theory of human rights: Religion, law, courts* Cambridge University Press: Cambridge

Phelan, DR (1997) *Revolt or revolution: The constitutional boundaries of the European Community* Round Hall Sweet & Maxwell: Dublin

Raju, CB (2007) *Social justice and the Constitution of India: With reference to SC's/ST's* Serials Publications: New Delhi

Rautenbach, IM (2012) *Rautenbach-Malherbe constitutional law* 6th edn LexisNexis: Durban

Regan, E (2010) *Theology and the boundary discourse of human rights* Georgetown University Press: Washington, DC

Rehman, J (2010) *International human rights law* 2nd edn Longman: Harlow

Ricoeur, P (1967) *Symbolism of evil* trans E Buchanan: Boston

Rogers, WVH (2010) *Winfield and Jolowicz on tort* 18th edn Sweet & Maxwell: London

Roosevelt, FD (1969) *The public papers and addresses of Franklin D Roosevelt* SI Rosenman (ed) Russell & Russell: New York

Rosen, M (2012) *Dignity: Its history and meaning* Harvard University Press: Cambridge, Mass

Sachs, A (2009) *The strange alchemy of life and law* Oxford University Press: Oxford

Seibert-Fohr, A (2009) *Prosecuting serious human rights violations* Oxford University Press: Oxford

Sen, A (2009) *The idea of justice* Allen Lane: London

Sepúlveda, MM (2003) *The nature of the obligations under the International Covenant on Economic, Social and Cultural Rights* School of Human Rights Research Series, Intersentia: Antwerpen

Shannon, G (2010) *Child law* 2nd edn Round Hall/Thomson Reuters: Dublin

Sharma, P (2005) *Welfare state, right to life and capital punishment in India* Sampark: Calcutta

Sharpe, RJ & Roach, K (2005) *The Charter of Rights and Freedoms* 3rd edn Essentials of Canadian Law, Irwin Law: Toronto

Shue, H (1996) *Basic rights: Subsistence, affluence, and US foreign policy* 2nd edn Princeton University Press: Princeton

Sieghart, P (1983) *The international law of human rights* Oxford University Press: Oxford

Simmonds, NE (2008) *Central issues in jurisprudence: Justice, law and rights* 3rd edn Sweet & Maxwell: London

Smith, RKM (2012) *Textbook on international human rights* 5th edn Oxford University Press: Oxford

Sparks, A (2003) *Beyond the miracle: Inside the new South Africa* Profile Books: London

Tedford, TL & Herbeck, DA (2005) *Freedom of speech in the United States* 5th edn Strata Publishing: State College, Pa

Thompson, L (2001) *A history of South Africa* 3rd edn Yale University Press: New Haven

Tinker, H (1993) *A new system of slavery: The export of Indian labour overseas 1830 - 1920* 2nd edn Hansib: London

Tribe, LH (1988) *American constitutional law* 2nd edn Foundation Press: New York

UN Secretariat (1949) *Our rights as human beings: A discussion guide on the Universal Declaration of Human Rights* UN: New York

UNESCO (ed) (1949) *Human rights: Comments and interpretations: A symposium* Allan Wingate: London

Vincent, A (2010) *The politics of human rights* Oxford University Press: Oxford

Waldron, J (2012) *Dignity, rank, and rights* M Dan-Cohen (ed) Oxford University Press: Oxford

Wheare, KC (1966) *Modern constitutions* 2nd edn Oxford University Press: Oxford

Whelan, D (2009) *Mental health law and practice: Civil and criminal aspects* Round Hall/Thomson Reuters: Dublin

Whyte, G (2002) *Social inclusion and the legal system: Public interest law in Ireland* Institute of Public Administration: Dublin

Williams, GL (1961) *Criminal law: The general part* 2nd edn Stevens: London

Contributions to Books

Albertyn, C 'Equality' in Cheadle, H; Davis, D & Haysom, N (eds) (2002) *South African constitutional law: The Bill of Rights* Butterworths: Durban

Alston, P 'The "not-a-cat" syndrome: Can the international human rights regime accommodate non-state actors?' in Alston, P (ed) (2005) *Non-state actors and human rights* Collected Courses of the Academy of European Law, Oxford University Press: Oxford

Amien, W 'Recent developments in the area of women's rights in South Africa: Focusing on domestic violence and femicide' in Sarkin, J & Binchy, W (eds) (2001) *Human rights, the citizen and the state: South African and Irish approaches* Round Hall Sweet & Maxwell: Dublin

Amoo, SK 'The constitutional jurisprudential development in Namibia since 1985' in Horn, N & Bösl, A (eds) (2008) *Human rights and the rule of law in Namibia* Macmillan: Namibia, Windhoek

Anand, Justice AS 'The constitutional model of equality and fraternity: The Indian experience' in Shabbir, M (ed) (2005) *Quest for human rights* Rawat Publications: Jaipur

Añón, MJ & Pisarello, G 'The protection of social rights in the Spanish constitutional system' in Coomans, F (ed) (2006) *Justiciability of economic and social rights: Experiences from domestic systems* Intersentia: Antwerp

Ansah, J 'The right to development as applied in national law' in Baderin, MA & McCorquodale, R (eds) (2007) *Economic, social and cultural rights in action* Oxford University Press: Oxford

Bacik, I 'Future directions for the Constitution' in Doyle, O & Carolan, E (eds) (2008) *The Irish Constitution: Governance and values* Thompson Round Hall: Dublin

Bailey, SD 'The Security Council' in Alston, P (ed) (1992) *The United Nations and human rights: A critical appraisal* Clarendon Press: Oxford

Barak, A 'Constitutional human rights and private law' in Friedmann, D & Barak-Erez, D (eds) (2001) *Human rights in private law* Hart: Oxford

Barden, G 'Discovering a constitution' in Murphy T & Twomey P (eds) (1998) *Ireland's evolving constitution, 1937 - 1997: Collected essays* Hart: Oxford

Barendt, E 'The United States and Canada: State action, constitutional rights and private actors' in Oliver, D & Fedtke, J (eds) (2007) *Human rights and the private sphere: A comparative study* University of Texas at Austin Studies in Foreign & Transnational Law, Routledge-Cavendish: Abingdon

Beale, H & Pittam, N 'The impact of the Human Rights Act 1998 on English tort and contract law' in Friedmann, D & Barak-Erez, D (eds) (2001) *Human rights in private law* Hart: Oxford

Bekink, B & Brand, D 'Constitutional protection of children' in Davel, CJ (ed) (2000) *Introduction to child law in South Africa* Juta Law: Lansdowne

Benson, P 'Equality of opportunity and private law' in Friedmann, D & Barak-Erez, D (eds) (2001) *Human rights in private law* Hart: Oxford

Beyleveld, D & Pattinson, SD 'Globalisation and human dignity: Some effects and implications for the creation and use of embyros' in Brownsword, R (ed) (2004) *Global governance and the quest for justice. Vol IV: Human rights* Hart: Oxford

Binchy, W 'Constitutional remedies and the law of torts' in O'Reilly, J (ed) (1992) *Human rights and constitutional law: Essays in honour of Brian Walsh* Round Hall Press: Dublin

Binchy, W 'Some unanswered questions in Irish defamation law' in Sarkin, J & Binchy, W (eds) (2001) *Human rights, the citizen and the state: South African and Irish approaches* Round Hall Sweet & Maxwell: Dublin

Binchy, W 'Autonomy, commitment and marriage' in Doyle, O & Binchy, W (eds) (2007) *Committed relationships and the law* Four Courts Press: Dublin

Binchy, W 'The Supreme Court of Ireland' in Dickson, B (ed) (2007) *Judicial activism in common law supreme courts* Oxford University Press: Oxford

Binchy, W 'Dignity as a constitutional concept' in Doyle, O & Carolan, E (eds) (2008) *The Irish Constitution: Governance and values* Thompson Round Hall: Dublin

Binchy, W 'Dignity as a core constitutional concept' in Quansah, E & Binchy, W (eds) (2009) *The judicial protection of human rights in Botswana* Clarus Press: Dublin

Binchy, W 'Human dignity: Its implications for marriage, the family and society' in FitzGibbon, S; Wardle, LD & Loveless, AS (eds) (2010) *The jurisprudence of marriage and other intimate relationships* William S Hein & Co: Buffalo, NY

Boshoff, C, (IV) & Boshoff, C 'The sociopolitical conditions for democratic nation-building: an Afrikaner point of view' in Rhoodie, N & Liebenberg, I (eds) (1994) *Democratic nation-building in South Africa* Human Sciences Research Council: Pretoria

Boussard, H 'Individual human rights in genetic research: Blurring the line between collective and individual interests' in Murphy, T (ed) (2009) *New technologies and human rights* The Collected Courses of the Academy of European Law, Oxford University Press: Oxford

Brand, D 'Socio-economic rights and courts in South Africa: Justiciability on a sliding scale' in Coomans, F (ed) (2006) *Justiciability of economic and social rights: Experiences from domestic systems* Intersentia: Antwerp

Brenner, SW 'Constitutional rights and new technologies in the United States' in Leenes, RE; Koops, BJ & De Hert, P (eds) (2008) *Constitutional rights and new technologies: A comparative study* Information Technology & Law Series, TMC Asser Press: The Hague

Brown, E 'Article 6 and civil cases' in Kilkelly, U (ed) (2009) *ECHR and Irish law* 2nd edn Jordans: Bristol

Brownsword, R 'Freedom of contract, human rights and human dignity' in Friedmann, D & Barak-Erez, D (eds) (2001) *Human rights in private law* Hart: Oxford

Brownsword, R 'Introduction: Global governance and human rights' in Brownsword, R (ed) (2004) *Global governance and the quest for justice. Vol IV: Human rights* Hart: Oxford

Brownsword, R 'What the world needs now: Techno-regulation, human rights and human dignity' in Brownsword, R (ed) (2004) *Global governance and the quest for justice. Vol IV: Human rights* Hart: Oxford

Brownsword, R 'Human dignity, ethical pluralism, and the regulation of modern biotechnologies' in Murphy, T (ed) (2009) *New technologies and human rights* The Collected Courses of the Academy of European Law, Oxford University Press: Oxford

Burchell, JM 'The protection of personality rights' in Zimmermann, R & Visser, D (eds) (1996) *Southern cross: Civil law and common law in South Africa* Clarendon Press: Oxford

Cancik, H '"Dignity of man" and "*persona*" in Stoic anthropology: Some remarks on Cicero, *De officiis I* 105-107' in Kretzmer, D & Klein, E (eds) (2002) *The concept of human dignity in human rights discourse* Kluwer Law International: The Hague

Carey Miller, DL 'The great trek to human rights: The role of comparative law in the development of human rights in post-reform South Africa' in Örücü, E (ed) (2003) *Judicial comparativism in human rights cases* UK National Committee of Comparative Law: London

Carolan, E 'Committed non-marital couples and the Irish Constitution' in Doyle, O & Binchy, W (eds) (2007) *Committed relationships and the law* Four Courts Press: Dublin

Chapman, AR & Russell, S 'Introduction' in Chapman, AR & Russell, S (eds) (2002) *Core obligations: Building a framework for economic, social and cultural rights* Intersentia: Antwerp

Chaskalson, A 'Human dignity as a constitutional value' in Kretzmer, D & Klein, E (eds) (2002) *The concept of human dignity in human rights discourse* Kluwer Law International: The Hague

Cheadle, H & Davis, D 'Equality' in Davis, D; Cheadle, H & Haysom N (eds) (1997) *Fundamental rights in the Constitution* Centre for Applied Legal Studies: Witwatersrand

Ciacchi, AC 'Social rights, human dignity and European contract law' in Grundmann, S (ed) (2008) *Constitutional values and European contract law* Private Law in European Context Series, Kluwer Law International: Alphen aan den Rijn

Clarke, DM 'Interpreting the Constitution: Essentially contested concepts' in Doyle, O & Carolan, E (eds) (2008) *The Irish Constitution: Governance and values* Thompson Round Hall: Dublin

Combrinck, H 'The right to freedom from violence and the reform of sexual assault law in South Africa' in Sarkin, J & Binchy, W (eds) (2001) *Human rights, the citizen and the state: South African and Irish approaches* Round Hall Sweet & Maxwell: Dublin

Coomans, F 'Some introductory remarks on the justiciability of economic and social rights in a comparative constitutional context' in Coomans, F (ed) (2006) *Justiciability of economic and social rights: Experiences from domestic systems* Intersentia: Antwerp

Corder, H 'Judicial activism of a special type: South Africa's top courts since 1994' in Dickson, B (ed) (2007) *Judicial activism in common law supreme courts* Oxford University Press: Oxford

Corder, H 'The Republic of South Africa' in Oliver, D & Fusaro, C (eds) (2011) *How constitutions change: A comparative study* Hart: Oxford

Costello, D 'Natural law, the Constitution and the courts' in Lynch, P & Meenan, J (eds) (1987) *Essays in memory of Alexis Fitzgerald* Incorporated Law Society of Ireland: Dublin

Costello, D 'The Irish judge as law-maker' in Curtin, D & O'Keeffe, D (eds) (1992) *Constitutional adjudication in European Community and national law: Essays for the Hon. Mr. Justice T.F. O'Higgins* Butterworth: Dublin

Coughlan, A 'The Constitution and social policy' in Litton, F (ed) (1988) *The Constitution of Ireland 1937 - 1987* Institute of Public Administration: Dublin

Davis, DM; Macklem, P & Mundlak, G 'Social rights, social citizenship, and transformative constitutionalism: A comparative assessment' in Conaghan, J; Fischl RM & Klare K (eds) (2002) *Labour law in an era of globalization: Transformative practices and possibilities* Oxford University Press: Oxford

De Schutter, O 'The challenge of imposing human rights norms on corporate actors' in De Schutter, O (ed) (2006) *Transnational corporations and human rights* Studies in International Law, Hart: Oxford

Devenish, G 'The evolution and development of a value-based and teleological interpretation of statute and common law in South Africa as a result of the 1996 Constitution' in Quansah, E & Binchy, W (eds) (2009) *The judicial protection of human rights in Botswana* Clarus Press: Dublin

de Vos, W 'Roman-Dutch law in South Africa at the end of the century – and thereafter' in Anghie, A & Sturgess, G (eds) (1998) *Legal visions of the 21st century: Essays in honour of Judge Christopher Weeramantry* Kluwer Law: The Hague

Dingake, Hon Justice K 'Expanding the frontiers of fundamental human rights: Judicial protection of human rights in Botswana' in Quansah, E & Binchy, W (eds) (2009) *The judicial protection of human rights in Botswana* Clarus Press: Dublin

Donnelly, C 'The privatisation of governmental functions' in Doyle, O & Carolan, E (eds) (2008) *The Irish Constitution: Governance and values* Thompson Round Hall: Dublin

Doyle, O 'Moral argument and the recognition of same-sex partnerships' in Doyle, O & Binchy, W (eds) (2007) *Committed relationships and the law* Four Courts Press: Dublin

Doyle, O 'Article 44: Privileging the rights of the religious' in Doyle, O & Carolan, E (eds) (2008) *The Irish Constitution: Governance and values* Thompson Round Hall: Dublin

Doyle, O 'Sisterly love: the importance of explicitly assumed commitment in the legal recognition of personal relationships' in FitzGibbon, S; Wardle, LD & Loveless, AS (eds) (2010) *The jurisprudence of marriage and other intimate relationships* William S Hein & Co: Buffalo, NY

Eckert, J 'Legal roots of human dignity in German law' in Kretzmer, D & Klein, E (eds) (2002) *The concept of human dignity in human rights discourse* Kluwer Law International: The Hague

Ellger, R 'The European Convention of Human Rights and Fundamental Freedoms and German private law' in Friedmann, D & Barak-Erez, D (eds) (2001) *Human rights in private law* Hart: Oxford

Fabre, C 'Social rights in European constitutions' in de Búrca, G; de Witte, B & Ogertschnig, L (eds) (2005) *Social rights in Europe* Oxford University Press: Oxford

Fedtke, J 'From indirect to direct effect in South Africa: A system in transition' in Oliver, D & Fedtke, J (eds) (2007) *Human rights and the private sphere: A comparative study* University of Texas at Austin Studies in Foreign & Transnational Law, Routledge-Cavendish: Abingdon

Finlay, TA 'The Constitution of Ireland in a changing society' in Curtin, D & O'Keeffe, D (eds) (1992) *Constitutional adjudication in European Community and national law: Essays for the Hon. Mr. Justice T.F. O'Higgins* Butterworth: Dublin

Flynn, L 'Missing Mary McGee: The narration of woman in constitutional adjudication' in Quinn, G; Ingram, A & Livingstone, S (eds) (1995) *Justice and legal theory in Ireland* Oak Tree Press: Dublin

Frowein, JA 'Human dignity in international law' in Kretzmer, D & Klein, E (eds) (2002) *The concept of human dignity in human rights discourse* Kluwer Law International: The Hague

Gardner, J 'Introduction' in Hart, HLA (2008) *Punishment and responsibility: Essays in the philosophy of law* 2nd edn Oxford University Press: Oxford

Gearty, C 'Civil liberties and human rights' in Bamforth, N & Leyland, P (eds) (2003) *Public law in a multi-layered constitution* Hart: Oxford

Gelfand, J 'The lack of enforcement in the United Nations draft Norms: Benefit or disadvantage?' in De Schutter, O (ed) (2006) *Transnational corporations and human rights* Studies in International Law, Hart: Oxford

Gianviti, F 'Economic, social, and cultural human rights and the International Monetary Fund' in Alston, P (ed) (2005) *Non-state actors and human rights* Collected Courses of the Academy of European Law, Oxford University Press: Oxford

Giliker, P 'Comparative perspectives on vicarious liability: Defining the scope of employment' in Neyers, JW; Chamberlain, E & Pitel, SGA (eds) (2007) *Emerging issues in tort law* Hart: Oxford

Glendenning, D 'School discipline: Balancing individual student rights and the common good' in Glendenning, D & Binchy, W (eds) (2006) *Litigation against schools: Implications for school management* First Law: Dublin

Govender, V 'Economic, social and cultural rights in South Africa: Entitlements, not mere policy options' in Klein Goldewijk, B; Contreras Baspineiro, A & Carbonari, PC (eds) (2002) *Dignity and human rights: The implementation of economic, social and cultural rights* Intersentia: Antwerp

Grewe, WG & Khan, DE 'Drafting history' in Simma, B (ed) (2002) *The Charter of the United Nations: A commentary Vol 1* 2nd edn Oxford University Press: Oxford

Hannon, P 'In God's name, what next? Religion, the Constitution and the new Ireland' in Doyle, O & Carolan, E (eds) (2008) *The Irish Constitution: Governance and values* Thompson Round Hall: Dublin

Heine, K & Janal, R 'Suretyships and consumer protection in the European Union through the glasses of law and economics' in Ciacchi, AC & Weatherill, S (eds) (2010) *Regulating unfair banking practices in Europe: The case of personal suretyships* Oxford University Press: Oxford

Herrick, L 'Prisoners' rights' in Kilkelly, U (ed) (2009) *ECHR and Irish law* 2nd edn Jordans: Bristol

Heyns, CH & Viljoen, F 'Country study – South Africa' in Heyns, CH & Viljoen, F (eds) (2002) *The impact of the United Nations human rights treaties on the domestic level* Kluwer Law International: The Hague

Heyns, CH & Viljoen, F 'Overview of study results' in Heyns, CH & Viljoen, F (eds) (2002) *The impact of the United Nations human rights treaties on the domestic level* Kluwer Law International: The Hague

Hogan, G 'Constitutional interpretation' in Litton, F (ed) (1988) *The Constitution of Ireland 1937 - 1987* Institute of Public Administration: Dublin

Hogan, G 'Judicial review and socio-economic rights' in Sarkin, J & Binchy, W (eds) (2001) *Human rights, the citizen and the state: South African and Irish approaches* Round Hall Sweet & Maxwell: Dublin

Hogan, L & D'Arcy May, J 'Constructing the human: Dignity in interreligious dialogue' in Ammicht-Quinn, R; Junker-Kenny, M & Tamez, E (eds) (2003) *The discourse of human dignity* Concilium, SCM Press: London

Horwitz, MJ 'Natural law and natural rights' in Sarat, A & Kearns, TR (eds) (1997) *Legal rights: Historical and philosophical perspectives* University of Michigan Press: Ann Arbor, Mich

Iyer, V 'The Supreme Court of India' in Dickson, B (ed) (2007) *Judicial activism in common law supreme courts* Oxford University Press: Oxford

Jackson, RM 'Absolute prohibition in statutory offences' in Radzinowicz, L & Turner, JWC (eds) (1945) *The modern approach to criminal law: Collected essays* English Studies in Criminal Science, Macmillan: London

Kelly, J 'The Constitution: Law and manifesto' in Litton, F (ed) (1988) *The Constitution of Ireland 1937 - 1987* Institute of Public Administration: Dublin

Kenna, P 'Land law, property, housing and environment law' in Kilkelly, U (ed) (2009) *ECHR and Irish law* 2nd edn Jordans: Bristol

Keogh, D 'The Irish constitutional revolution: An analysis of the making of the Constitution' in Litton, F (ed) (1988) *The Constitution of Ireland 1937 - 1987* Institute of Public Administration: Dublin

Khan, ZA 'Equality through legislative measures: The law in book versus the law in action' in Shabbir, M (ed) (2005) *Quest for human rights* Rawat Publications: Jaipur

King, JA 'United Kingdom: Asserting social rights in a multi-layered system' in Langford, M (ed) (2008) *Social rights jurisprudence: Emerging trends in international and comparative law* Cambridge University Press: Cambridge

Klein, E 'Human dignity in German law' in Kretzmer, D & Klein, E (eds) (2002) *The concept of human dignity in human rights discourse* Kluwer Law International: The Hague

Langa, P 'Legal visions – South Africa in the 21st century' in Anghie, A & Sturgess, G (eds) (1998) *Legal visions of the 21st century: Essays in honour of Judge Christopher Weeramantry* Kluwer Law: The Hague

Langford, M 'Hungary: Social rights or market redivivus?' in Langford, M (ed) (2008) *Social rights jurisprudence: Emerging trends in international and comparative law* Cambridge University Press: Cambridge

Langford, M 'The justiciability of social rights: From practice to theory' in Langford, M (ed) (2008) *Social rights jurisprudence: Emerging trends in international and comparative law* Cambridge University Press: Cambridge

Langwallner, D 'Separation of powers, judicial deference and the failure to protect the rights of the individual' in Doyle, O & Carolan, E (eds) (2008) *The Irish Constitution: Governance and values* Thompson Round Hall: Dublin

Levinson, S 'Do constitutions have a point? Reflections on "parchment barriers" and Preambles' in Paul, EF; Miller, FD, Jr & Paul, J (eds) (2011) *What should constitutions do?* Cambridge University Press: Cambridge

Lewis, R 'Tort law in practice: Appearance and reality in reforming periodical payments of damages' in Neyers, JW; Chamberlain, E & Pitel, SGA (eds) (2007) *Emerging issues in tort law* Hart: Oxford

Liebenberg, S 'South Africa: Adjudicating social rights under a transformative constitution' in Langford, M (ed) (2008) *Social rights jurisprudence: Emerging trends in international and comparative law* Cambridge University Press: Cambridge

Lindholm, T 'Article 1: A new beginning' in Eide, A; Alfredsson, G; Melander, G; Rehof, LA & Rosas, A (eds) (1992) *The Universal Declaration of Human Rights: A commentary* Scandinavian University Press: Oslo

Lorberbaum, Y 'Blood and the image of God: On the sanctity of life in biblical and early rabbinic law, myth, and ritual' in Kretzmer, D & Klein, E (eds) (2002) *The concept of human dignity in human rights discourse* Kluwer Law International: The Hague

McCarthy, N 'Observations on the protection of fundamental rights in the Irish Constitution' in Curtin, D & O'Keeffe, D (eds) (1992) *Constitutional adjudication in European Community and national law: Essays for the Hon. Mr. Justice T.F. O'Higgins* Butterworth: Dublin

McCrudden, C 'Human rights and judicial use of comparative law' in Örücü, E (ed) (2003) *Judicial comparativism in human rights cases* UK National Committee of Comparative Law: London

McCrudden, C 'Judicial comparativism and human rights' in Örücü, E & Nelken, D (eds) (2007) *Comparative law: A handbook* Hart: Oxford

McDonagh, E 'Philosophical-theological reflections on the Constitution' in Litton, F (ed) (1988) *The Constitution of Ireland 1937 - 1987* Institute of Public Administration: Dublin

McKendrick, E 'Negligence and human rights: Re-considering *Osman*' in Friedmann, D & Barak-Erez, D (eds) (2001) *Human rights in private law* Hart: Oxford

Marella, MR 'Human dignity in a different light: European contract law, social dignity and the retreat of the welfare state' in Grundmann, S (ed) (2008) *Constitutional values and European contract law* Private Law in European Context Series, Kluwer Law International: Alphen aan den Rijn

Maritain, J 'Introduction' in UNESCO (ed) (1949) *Human rights: Comments and interpretations: A symposium* Allan Wingate: London

Meyer, MJ 'Dignity as a (modern) virtue' in Kretzmer, D & Klein, E (eds) (2002) *The concept of human dignity in human rights discourse* Kluwer Law International: The Hague

Morgan, DG 'Judicial activism – Too much of a good thing' in Murphy T & Twomey P (eds) (1998) *Ireland's evolving constitution, 1937 - 1997: Collected essays* Hart: Oxford

Morgan, DG 'Ireland's ombudsman' in Sarkin, J & Binchy, W (eds) (2001) *Human rights, the citizen and the state: South African and Irish approaches* Round Hall Sweet & Maxwell: Dublin

Motoc, IV 'The international law of genetic discrimination: The power of "never again"' in Murphy, T (ed) (2009) *New technologies and human rights* The Collected Courses of the Academy of European Law, Oxford University Press: Oxford

Mundlak, G 'Human rights and the employment relationship: A look through the prism of juridification' in Friedmann, D & Barak-Erez, D (eds) (2001) *Human rights in private law* Hart: Oxford

Muralidhar, S 'Judicial enforcement of economic and social rights: The Indian scenario' in Coomans, F (ed) (2006) *Justiciability of economic and social rights: Experiences from domestic systems* Intersentia: Antwerp

Muralidhar, S 'India: The expectations and challenges of judicial enforcement of social rights' in Langford, M (ed) (2008) *Social rights jurisprudence: Emerging trends in international and comparative law* Cambridge University Press: Cambridge

Murphy, T 'Repetition, revolution, and resonance: An introduction to new technologies and human rights' in Murphy, T (ed) (2009) *New technologies and human rights* The Collected Courses of the Academy of European Law, Oxford University Press: Oxford

Murphy, T 'Economic inequality and the Constitution' in Murphy T & Twomey P (eds) (1998) *Ireland's evolving constitution, 1937 - 1997: Collected essays* Hart: Oxford

Murphy, T 'The cat amongst the pigeons: Garrett Barden and Irish natural law jurisprudence' in Doyle, O & Carolan, E (eds) (2008) *The Irish Constitution: Governance and values* Thompson Round Hall: Dublin

Nolan, A 'Ireland: The separation of powers doctrine vs. socio-economic rights?' in Langford, M (ed) (2008) *Social rights jurisprudence: Emerging trends in international and comparative law* Cambridge University Press: Cambridge

O'Callaghan, P & O'Donoghue, A 'Ireland' in Ciacchi, AC & Weatherill, S (eds) (2010) *Regulating unfair banking practices in Europe: The case of personal suretyships* Oxford University Press: Oxford

O'Cinneide, C 'Irish constitutional law and direct horizontal effect – A successful experiment?' in Oliver, D & Fedtke, J (eds) (2007) *Human rights and the private sphere: A comparative study* University of Texas at Austin Studies in Foreign & Transnational Law, Routledge-Cavendish: Abingdon

O'Cinneide, C 'The European Convention on Human Rights and the Irish constitutional system of rights protection: Complementary or divergent?' in Doyle, O & Carolan, E (eds) (2008) *The Irish Constitution: Governance and values* Thompson Round Hall: Dublin

O'Cinneide, C 'Equality, Irish law and the ECHR' in Kilkelly, U (ed) (2009) *ECHR and Irish law* 2nd edn Jordans: Bristol

Odinkalu, CA 'Implementing economic, social and cultural rights under the African Charter on Human and Peoples' Rights' in Evans, MD & Murray, R (eds) (2002) *The African Charter on Human and Peoples' Rights: The system in practice, 1986 - 2000* Cambridge University Press: Cambridge

O'Dowd, TJ 'Dignity and personhood in Irish constitutional law' in Quinn, G; Ingram, A & Livingstone, S (eds) (1995) *Justice and legal theory in Ireland* Oak Tree Press: Dublin

Oliver, D & Fedtke, J 'Comparative analysis' in Oliver, D & Fedtke, J (eds) (2007) *Human rights and the private sphere: A comparative study* University of Texas at Austin Studies in Foreign & Transnational Law, Routledge-Cavendish: Abingdon

Örücü, E 'Comparative law in practice: The courts and the legislator' in Örücü, E & Nelken, D (eds) (2007) *Comparative law: A handbook* Hart: Oxford

Osiatynski, W 'On the universality of the Universal Declaration of Human Rights' in Sajó, A (ed) (2004) *Human rights with modesty: The problem of universalism* Martinus Nijhoff Publishers: Leiden

Palmer, E 'The role of courts in the domestic protection of socio-economic rights: The unwritten constitution of the UK' in Coomans, F (ed) (2006) *Justiciability of economic and social rights: Experiences from domestic systems* Intersentia: Antwerp

Pech, L 'France: Rethinking "*droits-créances*"' in Langford, M (ed) (2008) *Social rights jurisprudence: Emerging trends in international and comparative law* Cambridge University Press: Cambridge

Perry, MJ 'Is the idea of human rights ineliminably religious?' in Sarat, A & Kearns, TR (eds) (1997) *Legal rights: Historical and philosophical perspectives* University of Michigan Press: Ann Arbor, Mich

Petersen, N 'Human dignity, international protection' in Wolfrum, R (ed) (2008) *The Max Planck encyclopedia of public international law* online edn Oxford University Press http://www.mpepil.com (accessed 10 October 2008)

Quansah, EK 'Human rights and HIV/AIDS in Botswana: Current perspectives and future prospects' in Quansah, E & Binchy, W (eds) (2009) *The judicial protection of human rights in Botswana* Clarus Press: Dublin

Quinn, G 'Human rights – themes and values: Establishing Irish foreign policy priorities' in Quinn, G (ed) (1995) *Irish human rights yearbook 1995* Round Hall Sweet & Maxwell: Dublin

Quinn, G 'Legal change, natural law and the authority of courts' in Treacy, B & Whyte, G (eds) (1995) *Religion, morality and public policy* Dominican: Dublin

Radzinowicz, L & Turner, JWC 'Punishment: Outline of developments since the 18th century' in Radzinowicz, L & Turner, JWC (eds) (1945) *The modern approach to criminal law: Collected essays* English Studies in Criminal Science, Macmillan: London

Rakoff, TD 'Enforcement of employment contracts and the anti-slavery norm' in Friedmann, D & Barak-Erez, D (eds) (2001) *Human rights in private law* Hart: Oxford

Rasche, A '"A *necessary* supplement" – What the United Nations Global Compact is (and is not)' in Buhmann, K; Roseberry, LM & Morsing M (eds) (2011) *Corporate social and human rights responsibilities: Global, legal, and management perspectives* Palgrave Macmillan: Basingstoke

Reichman, A 'Property rights, public policy and the limits of the power to discriminate' in Friedmann, D & Barak-Erez, D (eds) (2001) *Human rights in private law* Hart: Oxford

Reinisch, A 'The changing international legal framework for dealing with non-state actors' in Alston, P (ed) (2005) *Non-state actors and human rights* Collected Courses of the Academy of European Law, Oxford University Press: Oxford

Ritschl, D 'Can ethical maxims be derived from theological concepts of human dignity?' in Kretzmer, D & Klein, E (eds) (2002) *The concept of human dignity in human rights discourse* Kluwer Law International: The Hague

Rockefeller, SC 'Comment' in Taylor, C *et al* (1994) *Multiculturalism: Examining the politics of recognition* Gutmann, A (ed) Princeton University Press: Princeton

Roederer, C 'Founding provisions' in Woolman, S; Roux, T & Bishop, M (eds) (2006) *Constitutional law of South Africa* 2nd edn Juta: Cape Town

Rott, P 'Germany' in Ciacchi, AC & Weatherill, S (eds) (2010) *Regulating unfair banking practices in Europe: The case of personal suretyships* Oxford University Press: Oxford

Roux, T 'Democracy' in Woolman, S; Roux, T & Bishop, M (eds) (2006) *Constitutional law of South Africa* 2nd edn Juta: Cape Town

Ruggie, JG 'Taking embedded liberalism global: The corporate connection' in Ruggie, JG (ed) (2008) *Embedding global markets: An enduring challenge* Ashgate: Aldershot

Ryan, F '21st century families, 19th century values: Modern family law in the shadow of the Constitution' in Doyle, O & Carolan, E (eds) (2008) *The Irish Constitution: Governance and values* Thompson Round Hall: Dublin

Safrai, C 'Human dignity in a rabbinical perspective' in Kretzmer, D & Klein, E (eds) (2002) *The concept of human dignity in human rights discourse* Kluwer Law International: The Hague

Sarkin, J 'The role of national human rights institutions in post-apartheid South Africa' in Sarkin, J & Binchy, W (eds) (2001) *Human rights, the citizen and the state: South African and Irish approaches* Round Hall Sweet & Maxwell: Dublin

Seck, SL 'Conceptualizing the home state duty to protect human rights' in Buhmann, K; Roseberry, LM & Morsing M (eds) (2011) *Corporate social and human rights responsibilities: Global, legal, and management perspectives* Palgrave Macmillan: Basingstoke

Shivute, P 'The rule of law in sub-Saharan Africa – An overview' in Horn, N & Bösl, A (eds) (2008) *Human rights and the rule of law in Namibia* Macmillan: Namibia, Windhoek

Sibal, K 'Law, the Constitution, weaker sections, women, minorities, scheduled castes and their development' in Shabbir, M (ed) (2005) *Quest for human rights* Rawat Publications: Jaipur

Singh, MP 'Protection of human rights against state and non-state action' in Oliver, D & Fedtke, J (eds) (2007) *Human rights and the private sphere: A comparative study* University of Texas at Austin Studies in Foreign & Transnational Law, Routledge-Cavendish: Abingdon

Starck, C 'The religious and philosophical background of human dignity and its place in modern constitutions' in Kretzmer, D & Klein, E (eds) (2002) *The concept of human dignity in human rights discourse* Kluwer Law International: The Hague

Steinhardt, RG 'Corporate responsibility and the international law of human rights: The new *lex mercatoria*' in Alston, P (ed) (2005) *Non-state actors and human rights* Collected Courses of the Academy of European Law, Oxford University Press: Oxford

Sullivan, B 'The Irish Constitution: Some reflections from abroad' in Doyle, O & Carolan, E (eds) (2008) *The Irish Constitution: Governance and values* Thompson Round Hall: Dublin

Taylor, C 'The politics of recognition' in Taylor, C *et al* (1994) *Multiculturalism: Examining the politics of recognition* Gutmann, A (ed) Princeton University Press: Princeton

Thompson, L 'Co-operation and conflict: The Zulu Kingdom and Natal' in Wilson, M & Thompson, L (eds) (1969) *The Oxford history of South Africa* Clarendon Press: Oxford

Tshosa, Hon Justice O 'Judicial protection of human rights in Botswana and the role of international human rights law' in Quansah, E & Binchy, W (eds) (2009) *The judicial protection of human rights in Botswana* Clarus Press: Dublin

Turner, JWC 'The mental element in crimes at common law' in Radzinowicz, L & Turner, JWC (eds) (1945) *The modern approach to criminal law: Collected essays* English Studies in Criminal Science, Macmillan: London

Uitz, R & Sajó, A 'A case for enforceable constitutional rights? Welfare rights in Hungarian constitutional jurisprudence' in Coomans, F (ed) (2006) *Justiciability of economic and social rights: Experiences from domestic systems* Intersentia: Antwerp

Van Praagh, S '"*Sois sage*" – Responsibility for childishness in the law of civil wrongs' in Neyers, JW; Chamberlain, E & Pitel, SGA (eds) (2007) *Emerging issues in tort law* Hart: Oxford

Walsh, B 'The Constitution and constitutional rights' in Litton, F (ed) (1988) *The Constitution of Ireland 1937 - 1987* Institute of Public Administration: Dublin

Walsh, B 'The judicial power, justice and the Constitution of Ireland' in Curtin, D & O'Keeffe, D (eds) (1992) *Constitutional adjudication in European Community and national law: Essays for the Hon. Mr. Justice T.F. O'Higgins* Butterworth: Dublin

Wardle, LD 'Gender neutrality and the jurisprudence of marriage' in FitzGibbon, S; Wardle, LD & Loveless, AS (eds) (2010) *The jurisprudence of marriage and other intimate relationships* William S Hein & Co: Buffalo, NY

Weinrib, LL 'Natural law and rights' in George, RP (ed) (1992) *Natural law theory: Contemporary essays* Clarendon Press: Oxford

Weinrib, LE & Weinrib, EJ 'Constitutional values and private law in Canada' in Friedmann, D & Barak-Erez, D (eds) (2001) *Human rights in private law* Hart: Oxford

Weissbrodt, D & Kruger, M 'Human rights responsibilities of businesses as non-state actors' in Alston, P (ed) (2005) *Non-state actors and human rights* Collected Courses of the Academy of European Law, Oxford University Press: Oxford

Weisstub, DN 'Honor, dignity, and the framing of multiculturalist values' in Kretzmer, D & Klein, E (eds) (2002) *The concept of human dignity in human rights discourse* Kluwer Law International: The Hague

Wells, C & Elias, J 'Catching the conscience of the King: Corporate players on the international stage' in Alston, P (ed) (2005) *Non-state actors and human rights* Collected Courses of the Academy of European Law, Oxford University Press: Oxford

Whyte, G 'Introduction' in Treacy, B & Whyte, G (eds) (1995) *Religion, morality and public policy* Dominican: Dublin

Whyte, G 'A comment on the Constitution Review Group's proposals on equality' in Byrne, R & Duncan, W eds (1997) *Developments in discrimination law in Ireland and Europe* Irish Centre for European Law: Dublin

Whyte, GF 'Some reflections on the role of religion in the constitutional order' in Murphy T & Twomey P (eds) (1998) *Ireland's evolving constitution, 1937 - 1997: Collected essays* Hart: Oxford

Whyte, G 'Socio-economic rights and the Irish Constitution' in Lavan, A (ed) (2003) *Social rights and social cohesion* Department of Social and Family Affairs: Dublin

Whyte, G 'Rights and judicial activism' in Fanning, B; Kennedy, P; Kiely, G & Quin, S (eds) (2004) *Theorising Irish social policy* University College Dublin Press: Dublin

Wingfield, DR 'Perish vicarious liability?' in Neyers, JW; Chamberlain, E & Pitel, SGA (eds) (2007) *Emerging issues in tort law* Hart: Oxford

Wiseman, D 'Methods of protection of social and economic rights in Canada' in Coomans, F (ed) (2006) *Justiciability of economic and social rights: Experiences from domestic systems* Intersentia: Antwerp

Woolman, S 'Dignity' in Woolman, S; Roux, T & Bishop, M (eds) (2006) *Constitutional law of South Africa* 2nd edn Juta: Cape Town

Zappone, K 'Article 18' in O'Connell, D (ed) (2009) *Sixty years, thirty perspectives: Ireland and the Universal Declaration of Human Rights* New Island: Dublin

Articles

Ackermann, LWH 'Equality and the South African Constitution: The role of dignity' (2000) 60 *Heidelberg Journal of International Law* 537

Ackermann, LWH 'The legal nature of the South African constitutional revolution' [2004] *New Zealand Law Review* 633

Addo, MK 'Does Hohfeld still matter?' (1997) 29 *Bracton Law Journal* 7

al-Ahsan, A 'Law, religion and human dignity in the Muslim world today: An examination of OIC's Cairo Declaration of Human Rights' 24 (2008 - 2009) *Journal of Law and Religion* 569

Albertyn, C & Goldblatt, B 'Facing the challenge of transformation: Difficulties in the development of an indigenous jurisprudence of equality' (1998) 14 *South African Journal on Human Rights* 248

Alghrani, A & Brazier, M 'What is it? Whose it? Re-positioning the fetus in the context of research?' (2011) 70 *Cambridge Law Journal* 51

Alston, P & Quinn, G 'The nature and scope of states parties' obligations under the International Covenant on Economic, Social and Cultural Rights' (1987) 9 *Human Rights Quarterly* 156

Amoah, J & Bennett, T 'The freedoms of religion and culture under the South African Constitution: Do traditional African religions enjoy equal treatment?' (2008) 8 *African Human Rights Law Journal* 357

Anderson, A 'On dignity and whether the Universal Declaration of Human Rights remains a place of refuge after 60 years' (2009) 25 *American University International Law Review* 115

Angle, SC 'Human rights and harmony' (2008) 30 *Human Rights Quarterly* 76

Appiah, KA 'Dignity and global duty' (2010) 90 *Boston University Law Review* 661

Arnold, DG 'Transnational corporations and the duty to respect basic human rights' (2010) 20 *Business Ethics Quarterly* 371

Baer, S 'Dignity, liberty, equality: A fundamental rights triangle of constitutionalism' (2009) 59 *University of Toronto Law Journal* 417

Balleste, R 'Persuasions and exhortations: Acknowledging internet governance and human dignity for all' (2011) 38 *Syracuse Journal of International Law and Commerce* Spring 227

Banda, S 'Taking indirect horizontality seriously in Ireland: A time to magnify the nuance' (2009) 31 *Dublin University Law Journal* 263

Barilan, YM 'From *imago dei* in the Jewish-Christian traditions to human dignity in contemporary Jewish law' (2009) 19 *Kennedy Institute Ethics Journal* 231

Barrie, GN '*Ubuntu ungamntu ngabanye abantu*: The recognition of minority rights in the South African Constitution' [2000] *Journal of South African Law* 271

Baruah, P 'Logic and coherence in *Naz Foundation*: The arguments of non-discrimination, privacy, and dignity' (2009) 2 *National University of Juridical Sciences Law Review* 505

Bates, J 'Human dignity – an empty phrase in search of meaning?' (2005) 10 *Judicial Review* 165

Beattie, K 'New life for the Reynolds "public interest defence"? Jameel v Wall Street Journal Europe' [2007] European Human Rights Law Review 81

Beck, JM 'The Preamble of the Constitution' (1926) 14 *Georgetown Law Journal* 217

Benda, E 'The protection of human dignity (Article 1 of the Basic Law)' (2000) 53 *Southern Methodist University Law Review* 443

Bergelson, V 'Autonomy, dignity, and consent to harm' (2008) 60 *Rutgers Law Review* 723

Berman, PS 'A pluralist approach to international law' (2007) 32 *Yale Journal of International Law* 301

Bessler, JD 'In the spirit of *ubuntu*: Enforcing the rights of orphans and vulnerable children affected by HIV/AIDS in South Africa' (2008) 31 *Hastings International and Comparative Law Review* 33

Beyleveld, D & Brownsword, R 'My body, my body parts, my property?' (2000) 8 *Health Care Analysis* 87

Beytagh, FX, Jr 'Privacy in perspective: The experience under foreign constitutions' (1984) 15 *University of Toledo Law Review* 449

Biegon, J & Killander, M 'Human rights developments in the African Union during 2009' (2010) 10 *African Human Rights Law Journal* 212

Bilchitz, D 'Towards a reasonable approach to the minimum core: Laying the foundations for future socio-economic rights jurisprudence' (2003) 19 *South African Journal on Human Rights* 1

Bilchitz, D 'Moving beyond arbitrariness: The legal personhood and dignity of non-human animals' (2009) 25 *South African Journal on Human Rights* 38

Bilchitz, D 'The Ruggie framework: An adequate rubric for corporate human rights obligations?' (2010) 12 *SUR - International Journal on Human Rights* 199

Binchy, W 'Constitutionality, the rule of law and socio-economic development' (Lecture at Southern African Chief Justices Forum in Botswana 2009) http://www.venice.coe.int/SACJF/2009_08_BTW_Kasane/speeches/Binchy_constitutionality.pdf (accessed 24 September 2013)

Binchy, W 'Protecting economic, social and cultural rights in Ireland' (Irish Human Rights Commission & Law Society Annual Conference 2009) http://www.ihrc.ie/download/pdf/paper20091121_annconf_binchy.pdf (accessed 24 September 2013)

Binchy, W 'The role of comparative and public international law in domestic legal systems' (2010) 23(3) *Advocate (South Africa)* 58

Binchy, W '*Meskell*, the Constitution and tort law' (2011) 33 *Dublin University Law Journal* 339

Birks, P 'Harassment and hubris: The right to an equality of respect' (1997) 32 *Irish Jurist* 1

Bloustein, EJ 'Privacy as an aspect of human dignity: An answer to Dean Prosser' (1964) 39 *New York University Law Review* 962

Bojosi, KN 'An opportunity missed for gay rights in Botswana: *Utjiwa Kanane v The State*' (2004) 20 *South African Journal on Human Rights* 466

Botha, H 'Human dignity in comparative perspective' (2009) 20 *Stellenbosch Law Review* 171

Brems, E 'Human rights: Minimum and maximum perspectives' (2009) 9 *Human Rights Law Review* 349

Brennan, WJ, Jr 'The Constitution of the United States: Contemporary ratification' (1986) 27 *South Texas Law Review* 433

Brison, SJ 'The autonomy defense of free speech' (1998) 108 *Ethics* 312

Broecker, C '"Better the devil you know": Home state approaches to transnational corporate accountability' (2008) 41 *New York University Journal of International Law and Politics* 159

Brownsword, R 'An interest in human dignity as the basis for genomic torts' (2003) 42 *Washburn Law Journal* 413

Bulto, TS 'The utility of cross-cutting rights in enhancing justiciability of socio-economic rights in the African Charter on Human and Peoples' Rights' (2010) 29 *University of Tasmania Law Review* 142

Burnham, MA 'Cultivating a seedling charter: South Africa's Court grows its Constitution' (1997) 3 *Michigan Journal of Race & Law* 29

Buss, A 'Dual legal systems and the basic structure doctrine of constitutions: The case of India' (2004) 19(2) *Canadian Journal of Law and Society* 23

Butler, AS 'Private litigation and constitutional rights under sections 8 and 9 of the 1996 Constitution – Assistance from Ireland' (1999) 116 *South African Law Journal* 77

Butler, G 'The essence of human rights: A religious critique' (2009) 43 *University of Richmond Law Review* 1255

Cahill, M '*McD v L* and the incorporation of the European Convention on Human Rights' (2010) 45 *Irish Jurist* 221

Cahill, M 'Constitutional exclusion clauses, Article 29.4.6° and the constitutional reception of European law' (2011) 34 *Dublin University Law Journal* 74

Caley, SB & Caley, SD 'The *Olmstead* decision: The road to dignity and freedom' (2010) 26 *Georgia State University Law Review* 651

Cameron, E 'Legal and human rights responses to the HIV/AIDS epidemic' (2006) 17 *Stellenbosch Law Review* 47

Campbell, J 'Litigating human dignity: the Roman-Dutch common law' [2011] *European Human Rights Law Review* 375

Cannon, R 'Matters of Irish Constitutional debate: Originalism, democracy and natural law' (1995) 5 *Irish Student Law Review* 22

Carmi, GE 'Dignity versus liberty: The two western cultures of free speech' (2008) 26 *Boston University International Law Journal* 277

Carozza, PG 'My friend is a stranger: The death penalty and the global *ius commune* of human rights' (2003) 81 *Texas Law Review* 1031

Carozza, PG 'Human dignity and judicial interpretation of human rights: A reply' (2008) 19 *European Journal of International Law* 931

Carrasco, GP & Rodino, PW, Jr '"Unalienable rights," the Preamble, and the Ninth Amendment: The spirit of the Constitution' (1990) 20 *Seton Hall Law Review* 498

Cassese, A tr 'Respect for human dignity in today's Germany: Regional Court (*Landgericht*) of Frankfurt am Main, decision of 20 December 2004, *Daschner Wolfgang and E.* case' (2006) 4 *Journal of International Criminal Justice* 862

Chaskalson, A 'Human dignity as a foundational value of our constitutional order' (2000) 16 *South African Journal on Human Rights* 193

Chaskalson, A 'From wickedness to equality: The moral transformation of South African Law' (2003) 1 *International Journal of Constitutional Law* 590

Chaskalson, A 'Dignity and justice for all' (2009) 24 *Maryland Journal of International Law* 24

Chaskalson, A 'Dignity as a constitutional value: A South African perspective' (2011) 26 *American University International Law Review* 1377

Chenwi, L 'Putting flesh on the skeleton: South African judicial enforcement of the right to adequate housing of those subject to evictions' (2008) 8 *Human Rights Law Review* 105

Chenwi, L 'Slums Act unconstitutional' (2009) 10(4) *ESR Review: Economic and Social Rights in South Africa* 9

Cherednychenko, O 'Fundamental rights and contract law' (2006) 2 *European Review of Contract Law* 489

Cherednychenko, OO 'Fundamental rights and private law: A relationship of subordination or complementarity?' (2007) 3(2) *Utrecht Law Review* 1

Chirwa, DM 'In search of philosophical justifications and suitable models for the horizontal application of human rights' (2008) 8 *African Human Rights Law Journal* 294

Choma, H 'Constitutional enforcement of socio-economic rights: South African case study' (2009) 6(6) *US-China Law Review* 41

Christiansen, EC 'Exporting South Africa's social rights jurisprudence' (2007) 5 *Loyola University Chicago International Law Review* 29

Christiansen, EC 'Using constitutional adjudication to remedy socio-economic injustice: Comparative lesson from South Africa' (2008) 13 *University of California at Los Angeles Journal of International Law and Foreign Affairs* 369

Christiansen, EC 'Transformative constitutionalism in South Africa: Creative uses of Constitutional Court authority to advance substantive justice' (2010) 13 *Journal of Gender, Race & Justice* 575

Church, LM 'Mandating dignity: The United States Supreme Court's extreme departure from precedent regarding the Eighth Amendment and the death penalty [*Atkins v. Virginia*, 122 S. Court. 2242 (2002)]' (2003) 42 *Washburn Law Journal* 305

Clarke, DM 'The concept of the common good in Irish constitutional law' (1979) 30 *Northern Ireland Legal Quarterly* 319

Coetzee, S 'Discipline in Nigerian schools within a human rights framework' (2010) 10 *African Human Rights Law Journal* 478

Cohen, DS 'False imprisonment: A reexamination of the necessity for awareness of confinement' (1975) 43 *Tennessee Law Review* 109

Cook, A & Sarkin, J 'Who is indigenous?: Indigenous rights globally, in Africa, and among the San in Botswana' (2009) 18 *Tulane Journal of International and Comparative Law* 93

Cook, WW 'Hohfeld's contributions to the science of law' (1919) 28 *Yale Law Journal* 721

Corder, H & Davis, D 'The constitutional guidelines of the African National Congress: A preliminary assessment' (1989) 106 *South African Law Journal* 633

Costello, D 'The natural law and the Irish Constitution' (1956) 45 *Studies* 403

Coughlin, JJ 'Pope John Paul II and the dignity of the human being' (2003) 27 *Harvard Journal of Law and Public Policy* 65

Coundouriotis, E 'The dignity of the "unfittest": Victims' stories in South Africa' (2006) 28 *Human Rights Quarterly* 842

Cowen, S 'Can "dignity" guide South Africa's equality jurisprudence?' (2001) 17 *South African Journal on Human Rights* 34

Crooms, LA 'A stone's throw to justice: Liberty, equality, and women's rights in the Supreme Court opinions of Justice Thurgood Marshall' (2009) 52 *Howard Law Journal* 559

Cummiskey, S '"Face-booked": Anti-social networking and the law' (2011) 105(9) *Gazette of the Law Society of Ireland* 16

Dalal, M 'India's new constitutionalism: Two cases that have reshaped Indian law' (2008) 31 *Boston College International and Comparative Law Review* 257

Daly, E 'Constitutional dignity: Lessons from home and abroad' Widener Law School Legal Studies Research Paper Series no 08-07 http://ssrn.com/abstract=991608 (accessed 16 January 2009)

Daly, E 'Human dignity in the Roberts Court: A story of inchoate institutions, autonomous individuals, and the reluctant recognition of a right' (2011) 37 *Ohio Northern University Law Review* 381

Daly, T 'Strengthening Irish democracy: A proposal to restore free speech to Article 40.6.1°(I) of the Constitution' (2009) 31 *Dublin University Law Journal* 228

Danchin, PG 'Defaming Muhammad: Dignity, harm, and incitement to religious hatred' (2010) 2 *Duke Forum for Law & Social Change* 5

Dan-Cohen, M 'A concept of dignity' (2011) 44 *Israel Law Review* 9

D'Arcy May, J 'Human rights as land rights in the Pacific' (1993) 6 *Pacifica* 61

Davidson, J 'The history of judicial oversight of legislative and executive action in South Africa' (1985) 8 *Harvard Journal of Law and Public Policy* 687

Davis, DM 'Socioeconomic rights: Do they deliver the goods?' (2008) 6 *International Journal of Constitutional Law* 687

Davis, PC 'Responsive constitutionalism and the idea of dignity' (2009) 11 *University of Pennsylvania Journal of Constitutional Law* 1373

de Jonge, A 'Transnational corporations and international law: Bringing TNCs out of the accountability vacuum' (2011) 7 *Critical Perspectives on International Business* 66

Dersso, SA 'The role of courts in the development of the common law under s 39(2): *Masiya v. Director of Public Prosecutions Pretoria (The State) and Another* CCT case 54/06 (10 May 2007)' (2007) 23 *South African Journal on Human Rights* 373

de Vos, P 'Pious wishes or directly enforceable human rights? Social and economic rights in South Africa's 1996 Constitution' (1997) 13 *South African Journal on Human Rights* 67

de Vos, W le R 'Civil imprisonment: The impact of the new Constitution' (1994) 5 *Stellenbosch Law Review* 133

Dixon, R 'Creating dialogue about socioeconomic rights: Strong-form versus weak-form judicial review revisited' (2007) 5 *International Journal of Constitutional Law* 391

Dolinko, D 'Restorative justice and the justification of punishment' [2003] *Utah Law Review* 319

Dolovich, S 'Cruelty, prison conditions, and the Eighth Amendment' (2009) 84 *New York University Law Review* 881

Donnelly, J 'Human rights and human dignity: An analytic critique of non-Western conceptions of human rights' (1982) 76 *American Political Science Review* 303

Donnelly, J 'Human rights as natural rights' (1982) 4 *Human Rights Quarterly* 391

Doyle, O 'The human personality doctrine in constitutional equality law' (2001) 9 *Irish Student Law Review* 101

Doyle, O 'Legal positivism, natural law and the Constitution' (2009) 31 *Dublin University Law Journal* 206

Doyle, O & Ryan, D 'Judicial interpretation of the European Convention on Human Rights Act 2003: Reflections and analysis' (2011) 33 *Dublin University Law Journal* 369

Dubber, MD 'Dignity in penal law and penal police' (2009) Working Paper http://ssrn.com/abstract=1530545 (accessed 28 September 2013)

du Bois, F 'The past and present of South African law' (2004) 32 *International Journal of Legal Information* 217

du Bois, F 'State liability in South Africa: A constitutional remix' (2010) 25 *Tulane European and Civil Law Forum* 139

Duffy, DP 'Intentional infliction of emotional distress and employment at will: The case against tortification of labor and employment law' (1994) 74 *Boston University Law Review* 387

Duffy, F 'Seed money' (2011) 105(4) *Gazette of the Law Society of Ireland* 38

Dugard, J 'Should judges resign – A reply to Professor Wacks' (1984) 101 *South African Law Journal* 286

Du Plessis, LM 'The evolution of constitutionalism and the emergence of a constitutional jurisprudence in South Africa: An evaluation of the South African Constitutional Court's approach to constitutional interpretation' (1999) 62 *Saskatchewan Law Review* 299

Du Plessis, L 'Affirmation and celebration of the "religious Other" in South Africa's constitutional jurisprudence on religious and related rights: Memorial constitutionalism in action?' (2008) 8 *African Human Rights Law Journal* 376

Du Plessis, W & Britz, L 'The filling station saga: Environmental or economic concerns?' [2007] *Journal of South African Law* 263

Dupré, C 'Human dignity and the withdrawal of medical treatment: a missed opportunity?' [2006] *European Human Rights Law Review* 678

Dupré, C 'Unlocking human dignity: towards a theory for the 21st century' [2009] *European Human Rights Law Review* 190

Dupré, C 'Human dignity in Europe: A foundational constitutional principle' (2013) 19 *European Public Law* 319

Durojaye, E 'Discrimination based on HIV/AIDS status: A comparative analysis of the Nigerian court's decision in *Festus Odaife & Ors v Attorney General of the Federation & Ors* with other Commonwealth jurisdictions' (2007) 11(2) *Law, Democracy & Development* 133

Duttge, G 'Research on embryos and human dignity' (2009) 42 *Israel Law Review* 398

Eagle, SJ 'The really new property: A skeptical appraisal' (2010) 43 *Indiana Law Review* 1229

Eichner, M 'Families, human dignity, and state support for caretaking: Why the United States' failure to ameliorate the work-family conflict is a dereliction of the government's basic responsibilities' (2010) 88 *North Carolina Law Review* 1593

Elshtain, JB 'The dignity of the human person and The idea of human rights: Four inquiries' (1999) 14 Journal of Law and Religion 53

Englard, I 'Human dignity: From antiquity to modern Israel's constitutional framework' (2000) 21 *Cardozo Law Review* 1903

Erskine, DH 'Judgments of the United States Supreme Court and the South African Constitutional Court as a basis for a universal method to resolve conflicts between fundamental rights' (2008) 22 *St John's Journal of Legal Commentary* 595

Farrell, M 'Court rejects "*de facto* families" in lesbian couple case' (2010) 104(1) *Gazette of the Law Society of Ireland* 14

Feeney, P 'Business and human rights: The struggle for accountability in the UN and the future direction of the advocacy agenda' (2009) 11 *SUR - International Journal on Human Rights* 161

Feldman, D 'Human dignity as a legal value' Part 1 *Public Law* [1999] 682, Part 2 *Public Law* [2000] 61

Fennelly, N 'Judicial decisions and allocation of resources' (2010) 23(3) *Advocate (South Africa)* 48

Ferrey, S 'The Ruggie United Nations principles framing international indigenous human rights' (2010) 33 *Suffolk Transnational Law Review* 409

Finegan, T 'An unmarried father's right to guardianship of his child and a child's right to the support of his/her father: A Hohfeldian view of the Irish Constitution' (2010) 32 *Dublin University Law Journal* 320

Finnis, J 'Public reason, abortion and cloning' (1998) 32 *Valparaiso University Law Review* 361

Flanagan, B & Ahern, S 'Judicial decision-making and transnational law: A survey of common law Supreme Court judges' (2011) 60 *International and Comparative Law Quarterly* 1

Flear, ML & Vakulenko, A 'A human rights perspective on citizen participation in the EU's governance of new technologies' (2010) 10 *Human Rights Law Review* 661

Fletcher, GP 'In God's image: The religious imperative of equality under law' (1999) 99 *Columbia Law Review* 1608

Fombad, CM 'The constitutional protection against discrimination in Botswana' (2004) 53 *International and Comparative Law Quarterly* 139

Fombad, CM 'Children and informed consent to HIV/AIDS testing and treatment in Botswana' (2005) 2 *University of Botswana Law Journal* 33

Forman, L 'Ensuring reasonable health: Health rights, the judiciary, and South African HIV/AIDS Policy' (2005) 33 *Journal of Law, Medicine & Ethics* 711

Forst, R 'How not to speak about identity: the concept of the person in a theory of justice' (1992) 18 *Philosophy & Social Criticism* 293

Foster, A 'The role of dignity in Canadian and South African gender equality jurisprudence' (2008) 17 *Dalhousie Journal of Legal Studies* 73

Foster, S 'Prison conditions, human rights and article 3 ECHR' [2005] *Public Law* 35

Franks, CW 'Analyzing the urge to merge: Conversion of intangible property and the merger doctrine in the wake of *Kremen v. Cohen*' (2005) 42 *Houston Law Review* 489

Freeman, M 'The problem of secularism in human rights theory' (2004) 26 *Human Rights Quarterly* 375

Freeman, MDA 'Upholding the dignity and best interests of children: International law and the corporal punishment of children' (2010) 73(2) *Law and Contemporary Problems* 211

Fuller, JM 'The science and statistics behind spanking suggest that laws allowing corporal punishment are in the best interests of the child' (2009) 42 *Akron Law Review* 243

Fyfe, RJ 'Dignity as theory: Competing conceptions of human dignity at the Supreme Court of Canada' (2007) 70 *Saskatchewan Law Review* 1

Gaitan, A & Kuschnik, B 'Tanzania's death penalty debate: An epilogue on *Republic v Mbushuu*' (2009) 9 *African Human Rights Law Journal* 459

Gardbaum, S 'The "horizontal effect" of constitutional rights' (2003) 102 *Michigan Law Review* 387

Gardner, JA 'The dignity of voters – A dissent' (2010) 64 *University of Miami Law Review* 435

Garvey, SP 'Restorative justice, punishment, and atonement' [2003] *Utah Law Review* 303

Gertz, E 'Hortatory language in the Preamble and Bill of Rights of the 1970 Constitution' (1973) 6 *John Marshall Journal of Practice and Procedure* 217

Givelber, D 'The right to minimum social decency and the limits of evenhandedness: Intentional infliction of emotional distress by outrageous conduct' (1982) 82 *Columbia Law Review* 42

Glazewski, J & Witbooi, E 'Environmental law' [2004] *Annual Survey of South African Law* 397

Goehring, J 'Lawrence v. Texas: Dignity, a new standard for substantive rational basis review?' (2004) 13 Tulane Journal of Law & Sexuality: A Review of Lesbian, Gay, Bisexual and Transgender Legal Issues 727

Goldsworthy, J 'The Preamble, judicial independence and judicial integrity' (2000) 11 *Constitutional Forum* 60

Goodman, MD 'Human dignity in Supreme Court constitutional jurisprudence' (2006) 84 *Nebraska Law Review* 740

Goolam, NMI 'Human dignity – Our supreme constitutional value' (2001) 4 *Potchefstroom Electronic Law Journal* 1

Gostin, LO & Gable, L 'The human rights of persons with mental disabilities: A global perspective on the application of human rights principles to mental health' (2004) 63 *Maryland Law Review* 20

Goudkamp, J 'The spurious relationship between moral blameworthiness and liability for negligence' (2004) 28 *Melbourne University Law Review* 343

Grant, E 'Dignity and equality' (2007) 7 *Human Rights Law Review* 299

Grover, S 'A response to Bagaric and Allan's "The vacuous concept of dignity"' (2009) 13 *International Journal of Human Rights* 615

Gubbay, AR 'The protection and enforcement of fundamental human rights: The Zimbabwean experience' (1997) 19 *Human Rights Quarterly* 227

Habermas, J 'The concept of human dignity and the realistic utopia of human rights' (2010) 41 *Metaphilosophy* 464

Habersack, M & Zimmermann, R 'Legal change in a codified system: Recent developments in Germany suretyship law' (1999) 3 *Edinburgh Law Review* 272

Haigh, RF 'South Africa's criminalization of "hurtful" comments: When the protection of human dignity and equality transforms into the destruction of freedom of expression' (2006) 5 *Washington University Global Studies Law Review* 187

Hakimian, R & Korn, D 'Ownership and use of tissue specimens for research' (2004) 292 *Journal of the American Medical Association* 2500

Hall, J 'Interrelations of criminal law and torts: II' (1943) 43 *Columbia Law Review* 967

Halpern, I 'Tracing the contours of transnational corporations' human rights obligations in the twenty-first century' (2008) 14 *Buffalo Human Rights Law Review* 129

Handler, M; Leiter, B & Handler, CE 'A reconsideration of the relevance and materiality of the Preamble in constitutional interpretation' (1990) 12 *Cardozo Law Review* 117

Harrington, H 'Alabama Supreme Court recognizes intentional infliction of severe emotional distress as an independent cause of action: *American Road Service Co v Inmon*, 394 So. 2d 361 (Ala. 1980)' (1982) 12 *Cumberland Law Review* 525

Hasson, KJ 'Religious liberty and human dignity: A tale of two declarations' (2003) 27 *Harvard Journal of Law and Public Policy* 81

Hawthorne, L 'Constitution and contract: Human dignity, the theory of capabilities and *Existenzgrundlage* in South Africa' [2011] (2) *Studia Universitatis Babe°-Bolyai Iurisprudentia* 27

Henchy, S 'Precedent in the Irish Supreme Court' (1962) 25 *Modern Law Review* 544

Hennette-Vauchez, S 'A human *dignitas*? Remnants of the ancient legal concept in contemporary dignity jurisprudence' (2011) 9 *International Journal of Constitutional Law* 32

Henry, LM 'The jurisprudence of dignity' (2011) 160 *University of Pennsylvania Law Review* 169

Heyns, C 'The African regional human rights system: The African Charter' (2004) 108 *Penn State Law Review* 679

Himmelfarb, D 'The Preamble in constitutional interpretation' (1991) 2 *Seton Hall Constitutional Law Journal* 127

Hitchcock, RK; Sapignoli, M & Babchuk, WA 'What about our rights? Settlements, subsistence and livelihood security among Central Kalahari San and Bakgalagadi' (2011) 15 *International Journal of Human Rights* 62

Hoctor, S 'Dignity, criminal law, and the Bill of Rights' (2004) 121 *South African Law Journal* 304

Hodson, L 'A marriage by any other name? *Schalk and Kopf v Austria*' (2011) 11 *Human Rights Law Review* 170

Hoel, A 'What rights do you take to prison? *Habeas corpus* and prison conditions' (2009) 83 *Australian Law Journal* 395

Hogan, G 'Directive principles, socio-economic rights and the Constitution' (2001) 36 *Irish Jurist* 174

Hohfeld, WN 'Some fundamental legal conceptions as applied in judicial reasoning' (1913) *23 Yale Law Journal* 16

Hohfeld, WN 'Fundamental legal conceptions as applied in judicial reasoning' (1917) 26 *Yale Law Journal* 710

Homburger, TC 'Harassment of borrowers by licensed lenders' (1965) 1 *Columbia Journal of Law and Social Problems* 39

Hughes, G 'The concept of dignity in the Universal Declaration of Human Rights' (2011) 39 *Journal of Religious Ethics* 1

Huigens, K 'Dignity and desert in punishment theory' (2003) 27 *Harvard Journal of Law and Public Policy* 33

Humby, T & Grandbois, M 'The human right to water in South Africa and the *Mazibuko* decisions' (2010) 51 *Les Cahiers de Droit* 521
Hunt, M 'The "horizontal effect" of the Human Rights Act' [1998] *Public Law* 423
Husik, I 'Hohfeld's jurisprudence' (1924) 72 *University of Pennsylvania Law Review* 263

Iacopino, V; Weiser, SD; Dandu, M & Tuller, D 'HIV/AIDS and human rights in Botswana and Swaziland: A matter of dignity and health' (2011) 34 *Hastings International and Comparative Law Review* 149
Ibe, S 'Implementing economic, social and cultural rights in Nigeria: Challenges and opportunities' (2010) 10 *African Human Rights Law Journal* 197
Iglesias, T 'The dignity of the individual in the Irish Constitution – The importance of the Preamble' (2000) 89 *Studies* 19

Jackson, VC 'Constitutional dialogue and human dignity: States and transnational constitutional discourse' (2004) 65 *Montana Law Review* 15
Jacobsohn, GJ 'An unconstitutional constitution? A comparative perspective' (2006) 4 *International Journal of Constitutional Law* 460
Jerbi, S 'Business and human rights at the UN: What might happen next?' (2009) 31 *Human Rights Quarterly* 299
Jessberger, F 'Bad torture – good torture? What international criminal lawyers may learn from the recent trial of police officers in Germany' (2005) 3 *Journal of International Criminal Justice* 1059

Kamei, SA 'Partitioning paternity: The German approach to a disjuncture between genetic and legal paternity with implications for American courts' (2010) 11 *San Diego International Law Journal* 509
Kealey, M 'Publish and be damned' (2006) 100(3) *Gazette of the Law Society of Ireland* 20
Kealey, M 'Defame and fortune' (2010) 104(1) *Gazette of the Law Society of Ireland* 20
Keane, E 'The test for imposing vicarious liability: A debate in the Irish courts' (2007) 2(1) *Quarterly Review of Tort Law* 12
Keane, E 'Public interest litigation: Socio-economic rights and national law' (2008) 26 *Irish Law Times* 62
Keane, E 'Defame game' (2011) 105(1) *Gazette of the Law Society of Ireland* 36
Keane, E 'Jailhouse rock' (2013) 107(7) *Gazette of the Law Society of Ireland* 28
Keane, R 'Judges as lawmakers: The Irish experience' (2004) 4(2) *Judicial Studies Institute Journal* 1
Kell, G & Ruggie, JG 'Global markets and social legitimacy: The case for the "Global Compact"' (1999) 8(3) *Transnational Corporations* 101
Kende, MS 'The South African Constitutional Court's embrace of socio-economic rights: A comparative perspective' (2003) 6 *Chapman Law Review* 137
Kende, MS 'The South African Constitutional Court's construction of socio-economic rights: A response to critics' (2004) 19 *Connecticut Journal of International Law* 617
Kenyon, A 'Problems with defamation damages?' (1998) 24 *Monash University Law Review* 70

Kenyon, AT '*Lange* and *Reynolds* qualified privilege: Australian and English defamation law and practice' (2004) 28 *Melbourne University Law Review* 406

Khaitan, T 'Dignity as an expressive norm: Neither vacuous nor a panacea' (2012) 32 *Oxford Journal of Legal Studies* 1

Kidd, M 'Greening the judiciary' (2006) 9 *Potchefstroom Electronic Law Journal* 1

Kinley, D & Chambers, R 'The UN human rights norms for corporations: The private implications of public international law' (2006) 6 *Human Rights Law Review* 447

Klare, KE 'Legal culture and transformative constitutionalism' (1998) 14 *South African Journal on Human Rights* 146

Klug, H 'The dignity clause of the Montana Constitution: May foreign jurisprudence lead the way to an expanded interpretation?' (2003) 64 *Montana Law Review* 133

Knowles, HJ 'A dialogue on death penalty dignity' (2011) 11 *Criminology and Criminal Justice* 115

Kohm, E 'When "sex" sells: Expanding the tort of conversion to encompass domain names' (2003) 23 *Loyola of Los Angeles Entertainment Law Review* 443

Kotzé, LJ 'A critical survey of domestic constitutional provisions relating to environmental protection in South Africa' (2008) 14 *Tilburg Law Review* 298

Kriel, RR 'On how to deal with textual ambiguity, Ex parte Gauteng Provincial Legislature: In re dispute concerning the constitutionality of certain provisions of the Gauteng School Education Bill of 1995' (1997) 13 South African Journal on Human Rights 311

Krishnan, S 'What's the consensus? The Grand Chamber's decision on abortion in *A, B and C v Ireland*' [2011] *European Human Rights Law Review* 200

Kroeze, IJ 'Human dignity in constitutional law in South Africa' in European Commission for Democracy through Law, *The principle of respect for human dignity* (Proceedings of the UniDem Seminar, Montpellier, 2 - 6 July 1998) http://www.venice.coe.int/webforms/documents/CDL-STD%281998%29026-e.aspx#P1070_198886 (accessed 24 September 2013)

Kumm, M 'Who is afraid of the total constitution? Constitutional rights as principles and the constitutionalization of private law' (2006) 7 *German Law Journal* 341

Kwall, RR 'A perspective on human dignity, the First Amendment, and the right of publicity' (2009) 50 *Boston College Law Review* 1345

Lagodny, O 'Human dignity and its impact on German substantive criminal law and criminal procedure' (1999) 33 *Israel Law Review* 575

Langa, P 'Transformative constitutionalism' (2006) 17 *Stellenbosch Law Review* 351

Langa CJ 'A reply to Professor William Binchy on "Constitutionality, the rule of law and socio-economic development"' (Lecture at Southern African Chief Justices Forum in Botswana 2009) http://www.venice.coe.int//SACJF/2009_08_BTW_Kasane/default.htm (accessed 24 September 2013)

Langford, M & Russell, A '"Global precedent" or "reasonable no more"? The *Mazibuko* case' (2008) 19 *Journal of Water Law* 73

LaRue, LH 'Hohfeldian rights and fundamental rights' (1985) 35 *University of Toronto Law Journal* 86

Laski, HJ 'The basis of vicarious liability' (1916) 26 *Yale Law Journal* 105

Lebech, M 'What is human dignity?' (2004) *2 Maynooth Philosophical Papers* 59

Lebech, M 'On the problem of human dignity' (2010) 21(4) *Bioethics Outlook* 3

Leckie, S 'Another step towards indivisibility: Identifying the key features of violations of economic, social and cultural rights' (1998) 20 *Human Rights Quarterly* 81

Lee, MYK 'Universal human dignity: Some reflections in the Asian context' (2008) 3(1) *Asian Journal of Comparative Law* http://www.bepress.com/asjcl/vol3/iss1/art10/ (accessed 13 April 2010)

Lehmann, K 'In defense of the Constitutional Court: Litigating socio-economic rights and the myth of the minimum core' (2006) 22 *American University International Law Review* 163

Lenoir, N 'Biotechnology, bioethics and law: Europe's 21st century challenge' (2006) 69 *Modern Law Review* 1

Levit, N 'Theorizing and litigating the rights of sexual minorities' (2010) 19 *Columbia Journal of Gender and Law* 21

Lévitt, A 'The origin of the doctrine of *mens rea*' (1922) 17 *Illinois Law Review* 117

Lewis, J 'The Constitutional Court of South Africa' (2009) 125 *Law Quarterly Review* 440

Liebenberg, S 'The courts and socio-economic rights: Carving out a role' (2002) 3(1) *ESR Review: Economic and Social Rights in South Africa*

Liebenberg, S 'Needs rights and transformation: Adjudicating social rights in South Africa' (2005) 6(4) *ESR Review: Economic and Social Rights in South Africa* 3

Liebenberg, S & Goldblatt, B 'The interrelationship between equality and socio-economic rights under South Africa's transformative constitution' (2007) 23 *South African Journal on Human Rights* 335

Lockwood, BB, Jr; Finn, J & Jubinsky, G 'Working paper for the Committee of Experts on limitation provisions' (1985) 7 *Human Rights Quarterly* 35

Luban, D 'Lawyers as upholders of human dignity (when they aren't busy assaulting it)' [2005] *University of Illinois Law Review* 815

McCaffrey, SC & Neville, KJ 'Small capacity and big responsibilities: Financial and legal implications of a human right to water for developing countries' (2009) 21 *Georgetown International Environmental Law Review* 679

McCrudden, C 'Human dignity and judicial interpretation of human rights' (2008) 19 *European Journal of International Law* 655

McCrudden, C 'Multiculturalism, freedom of religion, equality, and the British constitution: The *JFS* case considered' (2011) 9 *International Journal of Constitutional Law* 200

McGinnis, JO 'The limits of international law in protecting dignity' (2003) 27 *Harvard Journal of Law and Public Policy* 137

McHugh, C 'Socio-economic rights in Ireland: Lessons to be learned from South Africa and India' (2003) 4 *Hibernian Law Journal* 109

McKenna, M; Simpson, A & Williams, G 'First words: The Preamble to the *Australian Constitution*' (2001) 24 *University of New South Wales Law Journal* 382

MacKinnon, CA 'Reflections on sex equality under law' (1991) 100 *Yale Law Journal* 1281

MacKinnon, CA 'The road not taken: Sex equality in *Lawrence v. Texas*' (2004) 65 *Ohio State Law Journal* 1081

MacKinnon, CA 'Sex equality under the Constitution of India: Problems, prospects, and "personal laws"' (2006) 4 *International Journal of Constitutional Law* 181
MacKinnon, CA 'Gender – The future' (2010) 17 *Constellations* 504
MacQueen, HL 'Delict, contract, and the Bill of Rights: A perspective from the United Kingdom' (2004) 121 *South African Law Journal* 359
McQuoid-Mason, D 'Pacemakers and "living wills": Does turning down a pacemaker to allow death with dignity constitute murder?' (2005) 18 *South African Journal of Criminal Justice* 24
Madala, TH 'The principle of respect for human dignity' in European Commission for Democracy through Law, *The principle of respect for human dignity* (Proceedings of the UniDem Seminar, Montpellier, 2 - 6 July 1998) http://www.venice.coe.int/webforms/documents/CDL-STD%281998%29026-e.aspx#P927_185139 (accessed 24 September 2013)
Mantilla, G 'Emerging international human rights norms for transnational corporations' (2009) 15 *Global Governance* 279
Marcus, D 'The normative development of socioeconomic rights through supranational adjudication' (2006) 42 *Stanford Journal of International Law* 53
Marry, C 'Portmarnock Golf Club decision: A step backwards for equality law?' (2010) 15 *Bar Review* 39
Mawe, F 'Innocent until proven guilty – or not?' (2010) 104(4) *Gazette of the Law Society of Ireland* 20
Metz, T 'Human dignity, capital punishment, and an African moral theory: Toward a new philosophy of human rights' (2010) 9 *Journal of Human Rights* 81
Metz, T 'African conceptions of human dignity: Vitality and community as the ground of human rights' (2012) 13 *Human Rights Review* 19
Meyer, LR 'Herbert Morris and punishment' (2003) 22 *Quinnipiac Law Review* 109
Michelman, FI 'A constitutional conversation with Professor Frank Michelman' (1995) 11 *South African Journal on Human Rights* 477
Miller, JM 'Dignity as a new framework, replacing the right to privacy' (2007) 30 *Thomas Jefferson Law Review* 1
Mills, A 'The private history of international law' (2006) 55 *International and Comparative Law Quarterly* 1
Mitchell, G 'Should the tort of conversion apply to intangible property?' (2007) 157 *New Law Journal* 958
Mohan, HI & Murphy, MW 'Defamation reform and the 2009 Act: Part II' (2010) 15 *Bar Review* 50
Möller, K 'Two conceptions of positive liberty: Towards an autonomy-based theory of constitutional rights' (2009) 29 *Oxford Journal of Legal Studies* 757
Monsalve, VB & Román, JA 'Tensions of human dignity: Conceptualization and application to international human rights law' (2009) 11 *SUR - International Journal on Human Rights* 39
Moon, G & Allen, R 'Dignity discourse in discrimination law: a better route to equality?' [2006] *European Human Rights Law Review* 610
Moore, LC & Wyatt Cummings, T 'Justice Thurgood Marshall and his legacy: A living legend's unceasing commitment to justice and equality' (1991) 35 *Howard Law Journal* 37
Morgan, DG '"Judicial-o-centric" separation of powers on the wane?' (2004) 39 *Irish Jurist* 142

Morgan, DG 'Enforcing public accountability: A *tour d'horizon*' (2009) 27 *Irish Law Times* 71

Morse, HN 'Applying the Hohfeld system to constitutional analysis' (1988) 9 *Whittier Law Review* 639

Morsink, J 'The philosophy of the Universal Declaration' (1984) 6 *Human Rights Quarterly* 309

Mortimer, J 'Judges call for legislation on assisted human reproduction' (2010) 104(2) *Gazette of the Law Society of Ireland* 12

Mortimer, J 'Standard of scrutiny raised in judicial review decisions' (2010) 104(3) *Gazette of the Law Society of Ireland* 10

Mortimer, J 'Failing to legislate for lawful abortion – The impact of *C*' (2011) 105(2) *Gazette of the Law Society of Ireland* 16

Mortimer, J 'Supreme Court dismisses assisted suicide appeal' (2013) 107(7) *Gazette of the Law Society of Ireland* 14

Moseneke, D 'Transformative adjudication' (2002) 18 *South African Journal on Human Rights* 309

Moseneke, D 'Transformative constitutionalism: Its implications for the law of contract' (2009) 20 *Stellenbosch Law Review* 3

Moseneke, D 'The role of comparative and public international law in domestic legal systems: A South African perspective' (2010) 23(3) *Advocate (South Africa)* 63

Mubangizi, JC 'The constitutional protection of socio-economic rights in selected African countries: A comparative evaluation' (2006) 2 *African Journal of Legal Studies* 1

Mubangizi, JC & Twinomugisha, BK 'The right to health care in the specific context of access to HIV/AIDS medicines: What can South Africa and Uganda learn from each other?' (2010) 10 *African Human Rights Law Journal* 105

Mujuzi, JD 'Why the Supreme Court of Uganda should reject the Constitutional Court's understanding of imprisonment for life' (2008) 8 *African Human Rights Law Journal* 163

Mujuzi, JD 'International human rights law and foreign case law in interpreting constitutional rights: The Supreme Court of Uganda and the death penalty question' (2009) 9 *African Human Rights Law Journal* 576

Mullally, S 'Substantive equality and positive duties in Ireland' (2007) 23 *South African Journal on Human Rights* 291

Mulligan, A '*Roche v Roche*: Some guidance for frozen embryo disputes' (2010) 13 *Trinity College Law Review* 168

Mureinik, E 'Administrative law in South Africa' (1986) 103 *South African Law Journal* 615

Murombo, T 'From crude environmentalism to sustainable development: *Fuel Retailers*' (2008) 125 *South African Law Journal* 488

Murphy, T & Ó Cuinn, G 'Works in progress: New technologies and the European Court of Human Rights' (2010) 10 *Human Rights Law Review* 601

Murray, C 'Reinforcing paternalism within Irish mental health law – Contrasting the decisions in *EH v St. Vincent's Hospital and Others* and *SM v The Mental Health Commission and Others*' (2010) 32 *Dublin University Law Journal* 273

Muzaffar, C 'From human rights to human dignity' (1995) 29(4) *Bulletin of Concerned Asian Scholars* 6

Nagarajan, K 'Compensatory discrimination in India sixty years after independence: A vehicle of progress or a tool of partisan politics' (2009) 15 *Washington and Lee Journal of Civil Rights and Social Justice* 483

Nahmod, SH 'Awareness of confinement for false imprisonment: A brief critical comment' (1976) 15 *Duquesne Law Review* 31

Narula, S 'Equal by law, unequal by caste: The "untouchable" condition in critical race perspective' (2008) 26 *Wisconsin International Law Journal* 255

Neff, SC 'Human rights in Africa: Thoughts on the African Charter on Human and Peoples' Rights in the light of case law from Botswana, Lesotho and Swaziland' (1984) 33 *International and Comparative Law Quarterly* 331

Nelson, JS 'Fair measure of the right to vote: A comparative perspective on voting rights enforcement in a maturing democracy' (2010) 18 *Cardozo Journal of International and Comparative Law* 425

Neuborne, B 'The Supreme Court of India' (2003) 1 *International Journal of Constitutional Law* 476

Nolan-Haley, J 'Self-determination in international mediation: Some preliminary reflections' (2006) 7 *Cardozo Journal of Conflict Resolution* 277

Novak, A 'The decline of the mandatory death penalty in common law Africa: Constitutional challenges and comparative jurisprudence in Malawi and Uganda' (2009) 11 *Loyola Journal of Public Interest Law* 19

Nussbaum, MC 'Skepticism about practical reason in literature and the law' (1994) 107 *Harvard Law Review* 714

Nussbaum, MC 'Compassion: The basic social emotion' (1996) 13(1) *Social Philosophy and Policy* 27

Nussbaum, MC 'Constitutions and capabilities: "Perception" against lofty formalism' (2007) 121 *Harvard Law Review* 4

Nyquist, C 'Teaching Wesley Hohfeld's theory of legal relations' (2002) 52 *Journal of Legal Education* 238

O'Brien, KA 'Ireland's secular revolution: The waning influence of the Catholic Church and the future of Ireland's blasphemy law' (2002) 18 *Connecticut Journal of International Law* 395

O'Cinneide, C 'Taking horizontal effect seriously: Private law, constitutional rights and the European Convention on Human Rights' (2003) 4 *Hibernian Law Journal* 77

O'Connell, R 'Guardians of the constitution: Unconstitutional constitutional norms' (1999) 4 *Journal of Civil Liberties* 48

O'Connell, R 'The role of dignity in equality law: Lessons from Canada and South Africa' (2008) 6 *International Journal of Constitutional Law* 267

O'Dell, E & Whyte, G 'Is this a country for old men and women? – In re Article 26 and the Health (Amendment) (No. 2) Bill 2004' (2005) 27 Dublin University Law Journal 368

O'Dowd, TJ 'Ireland's new Defamation Act' (2009) 1 *Journal of Media Law* 173

O'Hanlon, RJ 'Natural rights and the Irish Constitution' (1993) 11 *Irish Law Times* 8

Okeke, CN 'African law in comparative law: Does comparativism have worth?' (2011) 16 *Roger Williams University Law Review* 1

Olmsted, N 'Indigenous rights in Botswana: Development, democracy and dispossession' (2004) 3 *Washington University Global Studies Law Review* 799

O'Mahony, C 'State liability for abuse in primary schools: Systemic failure and *O'Keeffe v. Hickey*' (2009) 28 *Irish Educational Studies* 315

O'Neal, N 'Corporal punishment in public schools: A call for legal reform' (2008) 8 *African Human Rights Law Journal* 60

O'Neill, A 'Invalidity and retrospectivity under the Irish and Canadian constitutions' (2006) 15 *Constitutional Forum* 147

O'Neill, A 'The effect of a finding that legislation is unconstitutional: The approach of the Irish Supreme Court' (2007) 36 *Common Law World Review* 220

Orgad, L 'The preamble in constitutional interpretation' (2010) 8 *International Journal of Constitutional Law* 714

O'Sullivan, A 'Same-sex marriage and the Irish Constitution' (2009) 13 *International Journal of Human Rights* 477

O'Sullivan, A & Chan, PCW 'Judicial review in Ireland and the relationship between the Irish Constitution and natural law' (2006) 15(2) *Nottingham Law Journal* 18

Packer, HL '*Mens rea* and the Supreme Court' [1962] *Supreme Court Review* 107

Pagán, LAA 'Human dignity, privacy and personality rights in the constitutional jurisprudence of Germany, the United States and the Commonwealth of Puerto Rico' (1998) 67 *Revista Juridica de la Universidad de Puerto Rico* 343

Pasqualucci, JM 'The evolution of international indigenous rights in the Inter-American human rights system' (2006) 6 *Human Rights Law Review* 281

Paust, JJ 'Human dignity as a constitutional right: A jurisprudentially based inquiry into criteria and content' (1984) 27 *Howard Law Journal* 145

Penner, JE 'The "bundle of rights" picture of property' (1996) 43 *University of California at Los Angeles Law Review* 711

Penney, JW & Danay, RJ 'The embarrassing Preamble? Understanding the 'supremacy of God' and the *Charter*' (2006) 39 *University of British Columbia Law Review* 287

Perkins, RM 'A rationale of *mens rea*' (1939) 52 *Harvard Law Review* 905

Perry, MJ 'What do the free exercise and nonestablishment norms forbid? Reflections on the constitutional law of religious freedom' (2003) 1 *University of St Thomas Law Journal* 549

Perry, MJ 'A right to religious freedom? The universality of human rights, the relativity of culture' (2005) 10 *Roger Williams University Law Review* 385

Perry, MJ 'The morality of human rights: A nonreligious ground?' (2005) 54 *Emory Law Journal* 97

Pete, S 'To smack or not to smack? Should the law prohibit South African parents from imposing corporal punishment on their children?' (1998) 14 *South African Journal on Human Rights* 430

Pieterse, M 'Possibilities and pitfalls in the domestic enforcement of social rights: Contemplating the South African experience' (2004) 26 *Human Rights Quarterly* 882

Pieterse, M 'The potential of socio-economic rights litigation for the achievement of social justice: Considering the example of access to medical care in South African Prisons' (2006) 50 *Journal of African Law* 118

Pillay, A 'Toward effective social and economic rights adjudication: The role of meaningful engagement' (2012) 10 *International Journal of Constitutional Law* 732

Pillay, A 'Economic and social rights adjudication: Developing principles of judicial restraint in South Africa and the United Kingdom' [2013] *Public Law* 599

Pillay, K 'Implementing Grootboom: Supervision needed' (2002) 3(1) ESR Review: Economic and Social Rights in South Africa

Pinto, M 'What are offences to feelings really about? A new regulative principle for the multicultural era' (2010) 30 *Oxford Journal of Legal Studies* 695

Potts, LW 'Law as a tool of social engineering: The case of the Republic of South Africa' (1982) 5 *Boston College International and Comparative Law Review* 1

Price, L 'The treatment of homosexuality in the Malawian justice system: *R v Steven Monjeza Soko and Tiwonge Chimbalanga Kachepa*' (2010) 10 *African Human Rights Law Journal* 524

Prosser, WL 'False imprisonment: Consciousness of confinement' (1955) 55 *Columbia Law Review* 847

Quansah, EK 'Same-sex relationships in Botswana: Current perspectives and future prospects' (2004) 4 *African Human Rights Law Journal* 201

Radin, M 'A restatement of Hohfeld' (1938) 51 *Harvard Law Review* 1141

Ram, N 'Assigning rights and protecting interests: Constructing ethical and efficient legal rights in human tissue research' (2009) 23 *Harvard Journal of Law and Technology* 119

Ranalow, S 'Bearing a constitutional cross: Examining blasphemy and the judicial role in *Corway v. Independent Newspapers*' (2000) 3 *Trinity College Law Review* 95

Rao, N 'On the use and abuse of dignity in constitutional law' (2008) 14 *Columbia Journal of European Law* 201

Rao, N 'Gender, race, and individual dignity: Evaluating Justice Ginsburg's equality jurisprudence' (2009) 70 *Ohio State Law Journal* 1053

Rao, N 'Three concepts of dignity in constitutional law' (2011) 86 *Notre Dame Law Review* 183

Rao, N 'American dignity and healthcare reform' (2012) 35 *Harvard Journal of Law and Public Policy* 171

Ratner, SR 'Corporations and human rights: A theory of legal responsibility' (2001) 111 *Yale Law Journal* 443

Ray, B 'Policentrism, political mobilization, and the promise of socioeconomic rights' (2009) 45 *Stanford Journal of International Law* 151

Ray, B 'Residents of Joe Slovo Community v Thubelisha Homes and Others: The two faces of engagement' (2010) 10 Human Rights Law Review 360

Réaume, DG 'Indignities: Making a place for dignity in modern legal thought' (2002) 28 *Queen's Law Journal* 61

Redding, JA 'Dignity, legal pluralism, and same-sex marriage' (2010) 75 *Brooklyn Law Review* 791

Reed, S 'Is knowledge of the fact of imprisonment by the plaintiff a necessary element in false imprisonment?' (1944) 32 *Kentucky Law Journal* 212

Reinbold, J 'Political myth and the sacred center of human rights: The Universal Declaration and the narrative of "inherent human dignity"' (2011) 12 *Human Rights Review* 147

Remington, FJ & Helstad, OL 'The mental element in crime – A legislative problem' [1952] *Wisconsin Law Review* 644

Roach, K & Budlender, G 'Mandatory relief and supervisory jurisdiction: When is it appropriate, just and equitable?' (2005) 122 *South African Law Journal* 325

Roederer, CJ 'The constitutionally inspired approach to vicarious liability in cases of intentional wrongful acts by the people: One small step in restoring the public's trust in the South African police services' (2005) 21 *South African Journal on Human Rights* 575

Roederer, C 'The transformation of South African private law after ten years of democracy: The role of torts (delict) in the consolidation of democracy' (2006) 37 *Columbia Human Rights Law Review* 447

Roederer, CJ 'Working the common law pure: Developing the law of delict (torts) in light of the spirit, purport and objects of South Africa's Bill of Rights' (2009) 26 *Arizona Journal of International and Comparative Law* 427

Ross, H 'Social power and the Hohfeldian jural relation' (2001) 10(1) *Nottingham Law Journal* 47

Roux, T 'Principle and pragmatism on the Constitutional Court of South Africa' (2009) 7 *International Journal of Constitutional Law* 106

Ruggie, JG 'Business and human rights: The evolving international agenda' (2007) 101 *American Journal of International Law* 819

Ruggie, JG 'The construction of the UN "protect, respect and remedy" framework for business and human rights: the true confessions of a principled pragmatist' [2011] *European Human Rights Law Review* 127

Russo, CJ; Varnham, S & Squelch, J 'Safety and student searches in schools in the USA, New Zealand and Australia' (2007) 8 *Education Law Journal* 26

Ryan, D 'Making connections: New approaches to vicarious liability in comparative perspective' (2008) 30 *Dublin University Law Journal* 41

Ryan, D 'Connections without consensus: Recent approaches to vicarious liability in the Irish Supreme Court' (2009) 31 *Dublin University Law Journal* 457

Ryan, R & Ryan, D 'Vicarious liability of employers – Emerging themes and trends and their potential implications for Irish law' (2007) 4 *Irish Employment Law Journal* 3

Saastamoinen, K 'Pufendorf on natural equality, human dignity, and self-esteem' (2010) 71 *Journal of the History of Ideas* 39

Sandland, R 'Developing a jurisprudence of difference: The protection of the human rights of travelling peoples by the European Court of Human Rights' (2008) 8 *Human Rights Law Review* 475

Sarkin, J 'The political role of the South African Constitutional Court' (1997) 114 *South African Law Journal* 134

Sarkin, J 'Prisons in Africa: An evaluation from a human rights perspective' (2008) 9 *SUR - International Journal on Human Rights* 23

Saugestad, S '"Improving their lives." State policies and San resistance in Botswana' [2005] 4 article 1 *Before Farming*

Saugestad, S 'Impact of international mechanisms on indigenous rights in Botswana' (2011) 15 *International Journal of Human Rights* 37

Sayre, FB '*Mens rea*' (1932) 45 *Harvard Law Review* 974

Sayre, FB 'Public welfare offenses' (1933) 33 *Columbia Law Review* 55

Schachter, O 'Human dignity as a normative concept' (1983) 77 *American Journal of International Law* 848

Scott, C & Alston, P 'Adjudicating constitutional priorities in a transnational context: A comment on *Soobramoney's* legacy and *Grootboom's* promise' (2000) 16 *South African Journal on Human Rights* 206

Scutt, JA 'Sparing parents pain or spoiling the child by the rod: Human rights arguments against corporal punishment' (2009) 28 *University of Tasmania Law Review* 1

Sebok, AJ 'The fall and rise of blame in American tort law' (2003) 68 *Brooklyn Law Review* 1031

Sen, A 'Elements of a theory of human rights' (2004) 32 *Philosophy & Public Affairs* 315

Shadowen, SD 'Personal dignity, equal opportunity, and the elimination of legacy preferences' (2010) 21 *George Mason University Civil Rights Law Journal* 31

Shmueli, B 'Who's afraid of banning corporal punishment? A comparative view on current and desirable models' (2007) 26 *Penn State International Law Review* 57

Shmueli, B 'The influence of the United Nations Convention on the Rights of the Child on corporal punishment – A comparative study' (2008) 10 *Oregon Review of International Law* 189

Shmueli, B 'Corporal punishment in the educational system versus corporal punishment by parents: A comparative view' (2010) 73(2) *Law and Contemporary Problems* 281

Siegel, RB 'Dignity and the politics of protection: Abortion restrictions under *Casey/Carhart*' (2008) 117 *Yale Law Journal* 1694

Simons, KW 'Dworkin's two principles of dignity: An unsatisfactory nonconsequentialist account of interpersonal moral duties' (2010) 90 *Boston University Law Review* 715

Singer, JW 'The legal rights debate in analytical jurisprudence from Bentham to Hohfeld' [1982] *Wisconsin Law Review* 975

Singh, MP '*Ashoka Thakur v Union of India*: A divided verdict on an undivided social justice measure' (2008) 1 *National University of Juridical Sciences Law Review* 193

Slane, A 'From scanning to sexting: The scope of protection of dignity-based privacy in Canadian child pornography law' (2010) 48 *Osgoode Hall Law Journal* 543

Small, J & Grant, E 'Dignity, discrimination, and context: New directions in South African and Canadian human rights law' (2005) 6(2) *Human Rights Review* 25

Smartt, E 'The right to associate: Hohfeld revisited' (1993) 3 *Irish Student Law Review* 116

Smith, PJ 'A method for the madness: Restorative justice as a valid mode of punishment and an advancement of Catholic social thought' (2005) 44 *Journal of Catholic Legal Studies* 433

Song, E 'No women (and dogs) allowed: A comparative analysis of discriminating private golf clubs in the United States, Ireland, and England' (2007) 6 *Washington University Global Studies Law Review* 181

Sossin, L 'The "supremacy of God", human dignity and the *Charter of Rights and Freedoms*' (2003) 52 *University of New Brunswick Law Journal* 227

Sreedhar, S & Delmas, C 'State legitimacy and political obligation in *Justice for hedgehogs*: The radical potential of Dworkinian dignity' (2010) 90 *Boston University Law Review* 737

Sripati, V 'Constitutionalism in India and South Africa: A comparative study from a human rights perspective' (2007) 16 *Tulane Journal of International and Comparative Law* 49
Sripati, V & Thiruvengadam, AK 'India: Constitutional amendment making the right to education a Fundamental Right' (2004) 2 *International Journal of Constitutional Law* 148
Stewart, H 'Parents, children, and the law of assault' (2009) 32 *Dalhousie Law Journal* 1
Steyn, Lord 'Perspectives of corrective and distributive justice in tort law' (2002) 37 *Irish Jurist* 1
Stith, R 'The priority of respect: How our common humanity can ground our individual dignity' (2004) 44 *International Philosophical Quarterly* 165
Stone, A & Williams, G 'Freedom of speech and defamation: Developments in the common law world' (2000) 26 *Monash University Law Review* 362
Stone Sweet, A & Mathews, J 'Proportionality balancing and global constitutionalism' (2008) 47 *Columbia Journal of Transnational Law* 72
Summers, MA 'Immunity or impunity – The potential effect of prosecutions of state officials for core international crimes in states like the United States that are not parties to the Statute of the International Criminal Court' (2006) 31 *Brooklyn Journal of International Law* 463
Sutherland, PJ 'Ensuring contractual fairness in consumer contracts after *Barkhuizen v Napier* 2007 5 SA 323 (CC) – Part 1' (2008) 19 *Stellenbosch Law Review* 390

Taylor, JJ 'Celebrating San victory too soon? Reflections on the outcome of the Central Kalahari Game Reserve case' (2007) 23(5) *Anthropology Today* 3
Temple Lang, J 'Private law aspects of the Irish Constitution' (1971) 6 *Irish Jurist* 237
Tsakyrakis, S 'Proportionality: An assault on human rights?' (2009) 7 *International Journal of Constitutional Law* 468
Tsesis, A 'Dignity and speech: The regulation of hate speech in a democracy' (2009) 44 *Wake Forest Law Review* 497
Twomey, AF 'The death of the natural law?' (1995) 13 *Irish Law Times* 270

Udombana, NJ 'Life, dignity, and the pursuit of happiness: Human rights and living standards in Africa' (2008) 27 *University of Tasmania Law Review* 47

van Aggelen, J 'The Preamble of the United Nations Declaration of Human Rights' (2000) 28 *Denver Journal of International Law and Policy* 129
van der Vyver, JD 'Depriving Westminster of its moral constraints: A survey of constitutional development in South Africa' (1985) 20 *Harvard Civil Rights-Civil Liberties Law Review* 291
van Rensburg, LJ 'The right of access to adequate water [discussion of *Mazibuko v the City of Johannesburg* case no 13865/06]' (2008) 19 *Stellenbosch Law Review* 415
Vard, R 'Proprietary rights in human tissue' (2013) 12 *Hibernian Law Journal* 100
Venckiene, E 'The importance of historical discourse for the legal protection of human dignity at present' (2010) 119 *Jurisprudence* 147

Veriava, F 'Ought the notion of informed consent to be cast in stone? VRM v The Health Professions Council of South Africa' (2004) 20 South African Journal on Human Rights 309

Vold, L 'The legal allocation of risk in assault, battery, and imprisonment – The *prima facie* case' (1938) 17 *Nebraska Law Bulletin* 149

von der Pfordten, D 'On the dignity of man in Kant' (2009) 84 *Philosophy* 371

Wacks, R 'Judges and injustice' (1984) 101 *South African Law Journal* 266

Wacks, R 'Judging judges: A brief rejoinder to Professor Dugard' (1984) 101 *South African Law Journal* 295

Wade, W 'Horizons of horizontality' (2000) 116 *Law Quarterly Review* 217

Wagner, WJ 'Universal human rights, the United Nations, and the *telos* of human dignity' (2005) 3 *Ave Maria Law Review* 197

Wai, R 'Transnational liftoff and juridical touchdown: The regulatory function of private international law in an era of globalization' (2002) 40 *Columbia Journal of Transnational Law* 209

Wai, R 'The interlegality of transnational private law' (2008) 71 *Law and Contemporary Problems* 107

Wakely, J 'Social and economic rights – A retreat by the South African Constitutional Court?' (2010) 28 *Irish Law Times* 153

Waldron, J 'The dignity of groups' (2008) New York University School of Law Public Law Research Paper No 08-53 http://ssrn.com/abstract=1287174 (accessed 26 September 2013)

Waldron, J 'Dignity and defamation: The visibility of hate' (2010) 123 *Harvard Law Review* 1596

Waldron, J 'Dignity, rights, and responsibilities' (2011) 43 *Arizona State Law Journal* 1107

Walsh, B '200 years of American constitutionalism – A foreign perspective' (1987) 48 *Ohio State Law Journal* 757

Walsh, B 'Constitutional adjudication' (1995 - 1996) 17 *Holdsworth Law Review* 153

Walsh, R 'The Constitution, property rights and proportionality: A reappraisal' (2009) 31 *Dublin University Law Journal* 1

Walsh, R 'Private property rights in the drafting of the Irish Constitution: A communitarian compromise' (2011) 33 *Dublin University Law Journal* 86

Waltz, S 'Universalising human rights: The role of small states in the construction of the Universal Declaration of Human Rights' (2001) 23 *Human Rights Quarterly* 44

Walz, NR 'Abandoned frozen embryos and embryonic stem cell research: Should there be a connection?' (2007) 1 *University of St Thomas Journal of Law and Public Policy* 122

Weinrib, J 'What is the purpose of freedom of expression?' (2009) 67 *University of Toronto Faculty of Law Review* 165

Weissbrodt, D 'Business and human rights' (2005) 74 *University of Cincinnati Law Review* 55

Wermiel, SJ 'Law and human dignity: The judicial soul of Justice Brennan' (1998) 7 *William and Mary Bill of Rights Journal* 223

Wesson, M '*Grootboom* and beyond: Reassessing the socio-economic jurisprudence of the South African Constitutional Court' (2004) 20 *South African Journal on Human Rights* 284

Wesson, M 'Reasonableness in retreat? The judgment of the South African Constitutional Court in *Mazibuko v City of Johannesburg*' (2011) 11 *Human Rights Law Review* 390

Wesson, M 'Disagreement and the constitutionalisation of social rights' (2012) 12 *Human Rights Law Review* 221

Whitman, JQ 'Human dignity in Europe and the United States: The social foundations' (2004) 25 *Human Rights Law Journal* 17

Whitman, JQ 'The two Western cultures of privacy: Dignity versus liberty' (2004) 113 *Yale Law Journal* 1151

Whyte, G 'And justice for some' (1984) 6 *Dublin University Law Journal* 88

Whyte, G 'Travellers and the law' (1988) 10 *Dublin University Law Journal* 189

Whyte, G 'Constitutional protection for the married family' (1989) 7 *Irish Law Times* 115

Whyte, GF 'Natural law and the Constitution' (1996) 14 *Irish Law Times* 8

Whyte, G 'Religion and the Irish Constitution' (1997) 30 *John Marshall Law Review* 725

Whyte, GF 'The right to die and the Irish Constitution' (1997) 3 *European Public Law* 235

Whyte, GF 'Discerning the philosophical premises of the Report of the Constitution Review Group: An analysis of the recommendations on fundamental rights' (1998) *Contemporary Issues in Irish Law and Politics* 216

Whyte, G 'The role of the Supreme Court in our democracy: A response to Mr Justice Hardiman' (2006) 28 *Dublin University Law Journal* 1

Whyte, G 'A tale of two cases – Divergent approaches of the Irish Supreme Court to distributive justice' (2010) 32 *Dublin University Law Journal* 365

Wicks, E '*A, B, C v Ireland*: Abortion law under the European Convention on Human Rights' (2011) 11 *Human Rights Law Review* 556

Wicks, E 'The meaning of "life": Dignity and the right to life in international human rights treaties' (2012) 12 *Human Rights Law Review* 199

Williams, LA 'The justiciability of water rights: *Mazibuko v. City of Johannesburg*' (2009) 36 *Forum for Development Studies* 5

Willis, KL 'Willis v State: Condoning child abuse as discipline' (2010) 14 University of California Davis Journal of Juvenile Law and Policy 59

Winckel, A 'A 21st century constitutional Preamble – An opportunity for unity rather than partisan politics' (2001) 24 *University of New South Wales Law Journal* 636

Winfield, PH 'The myth of absolute liability' (1926) 42 *Law Quarterly Review* 37

Wing, AK 'The South African Constitution as a role model for the United States' (2008) 24 *Harvard BlackLetter Law Journal* 73

Winkler, IT & Mahler, C 'Interpreting the right to a dignified minimum existence: A new era in German socio-economic rights jurisprudence?' (2013) 13 *Human Rights Law Review* 388

Woods, JM 'Justiciable social rights as a critique of the liberal paradigm' (2003) 38 *Texas International Law Journal* 763

Yamada, DC 'Human dignity and American employment law' (2009) 43 *University of Richmond Law Review* 523

Yamin, AE 'The future in the mirror: Incorporating strategies for the defense and promotion of economic, social, and cultural rights into the mainstream human rights agenda' (2005) 27 *Human Rights Quarterly* 1200

Young, KG 'The minimum core of economic and social rights: A concept in search of content' (2008) 33 *Yale Journal of International Law* 113

Young, KG 'A typology of economic and social rights adjudication: Exploring the catalytic function of judicial review' (2010) 8 *International Journal of Constitutional Law* 385

Newspaper and Internet Publications

'O'Brien happy to have been "vindicated"' *Irish Times* (Dublin, 24 November 2006) 4

Carolan, M 'Newspaper to appeal record €1.87m libel award: Jury decides "Herald" articles alleged Leech had affair' *Irish Times* (Dublin, 25 June 2009) 4

Coulter, C 'Businessman wins €10m libel award against ex-employers' *Irish Times* (Dublin, 18 November 2010) 1

de Vos, P 'Water is life (but life is cheap)' (13 October 2009) http://constitutionallyspeaking.co.za/water-is-life-but-life-is-cheap/ (accessed 18 March 2010)

Joubert, P 'Grootboom dies homeless and penniless' *Mail & Guardian Online* (Johannesburg 8 August 2008) http://www.mg.co.za/article/2008-08-08-grootboom-dies-homeless-and-penniless (accessed 24 September 2013)

Mapondera, G & Smith, D 'Gay couple freed by Malawi presidential pardon return to home villages' *Guardian* (London 31 May 2010) 13

Minihan, M 'Leech "absolutely vindicated" by record €1.87m libel award' *Irish Times* (Dublin, 25 June 2009) 1

Permissions

All chapters in this book were first published in HDFRSAI, by Pretoria University Law Press (PULP) by Anne Hughes; hereby published with permission under the Creative Commons Attribution License or equivalent. Every chapter published in this book has been scrutinized by our experts. Their significance has been extensively debated. The topics covered herein carry significant information for a comprehensive understanding. They may even be implemented as practical applications or may be referred to as a beginning point for further studies.

We would like to thank the editorial team for lending their expertise to make the book truly unique. They have played a crucial role in the development of this book. Without their invaluable contributions this book wouldn't have been possible. They have made vital efforts to compile up to date information on the varied aspects of this subject to make this book a valuable addition to the collection of many professionals and students.

This book was conceptualized with the vision of imparting up-to-date and integrated information in this field. To ensure the same, a matchless editorial board was set up. Every individual on the board went through rigorous rounds of assessment to prove their worth. After which they invested a large part of their time researching and compiling the most relevant data for our readers.

The editorial board has been involved in producing this book since its inception. They have spent rigorous hours researching and exploring the diverse topics which have resulted in the successful publishing of this book. They have passed on their knowledge of decades through this book. To expedite this challenging task, the publisher supported the team at every step. A small team of assistant editors was also appointed to further simplify the editing procedure and attain best results for the readers.

Apart from the editorial board, the designing team has also invested a significant amount of their time in understanding the subject and creating the most relevant covers. They scrutinized every image to scout for the most suitable representation of the subject and create an appropriate cover for the book.

The publishing team has been an ardent support to the editorial, designing and production team. Their endless efforts to recruit the best for this project, has resulted in the accomplishment of this book. They are a veteran in the field of academics and their pool of knowledge is as vast as their experience in printing. Their expertise and guidance has proved useful at every step. Their uncompromising quality standards have made this book an exceptional effort. Their encouragement from time to time has been an inspiration for everyone.

The publisher and the editorial board hope that this book will prove to be a valuable piece of knowledge for students, practitioners and scholars across the globe.

Index

J

L

M

P

R

S

U

V

www.ingramcontent.com/pod-product-compliance
Lightning Source LLC
LaVergne TN
LVHW020629300926
849161LV00004B/646